ABOUT THE AUTHORS

BILL FLEISCHMAN

Bill Fleischman has been a member of the *Philadelphia Daily News* sports staff for more than 28 years. During the 1970s he covered the Philadelphia Flyers (authoring a book on Flyers' goaltender Bernie Parent called *Bernie, Bernie*), and since then he has served as an assistant sports editor, covering auto racing, tennis, and hockey. He is past president of the Philadelphia Sports Writers Association and the Professional Hockey Writers Association. Since, 1981, he has served as an adjunct professor of journalism at the University of Delaware. He has also written for *Inside Sports* and *PhillySports* magazines. He also has the best answering machine messages in the business.

AL PEARCE

Al Pearce saw his first NASCAR race in 1966 when he attended the Daytona 500. He has been a sportswriter since 1969 and has covered NASCAR for nearly as long for the *Newport News (VA) Daily Press*. He has traveled to France, Japan, and Australia to cover the Winston Cup cars and can tell you a story about every track and every driver on the circuit. He has contributed to a number of other books on NASCAR and has been the NASCAR correspondent for leading car magazine *Autoweek* for more than 25 years. In his travels while covering races, Al has been in every state in the continental United States except Wyoming.

INSIDE SPORTS
MAGAZINE

NASCAR RACING

INSIDE
SPORTS MAGAZINE
NASCAR RACING

Bill Fleischman and Al Pearce
Foreword by Bobby Allison

VISIBLE INK PRESS

Detroit • New York • Toronto • London

INSIDE SPORTS NASCAR RACING

Copyright © 1998 by Visible Ink Press™

Published by **Visible Ink Press™**
A division of Gale Research
835 Penobscot Building
Detroit, MI 48226-4094

Visible Ink Press™ is a trademark of Gale Research
Inside Sports Magazine ©1998 is a registered trademark of Inside Sports Inc.

Most Visible Ink Press™ books are available at quantity discounts when purchased in bulk by corporations, organizations, or groups. Customized printings, special imprints, messages, and excerpts can be produced to meet your needs. For more information, contact Special Markets Manager, Gale Research Inc., 835 Penobscot Building, Detroit, MI 48226. Or call 1-800-877-4253.

Art Director: Michelle DiMercurio
Front cover photograph of Daytona 500: W. Dennis Winn
Back cover photograph of Jeff Gordon and team: David Durochik, *Inside Sports Magazine*

Library of Congress Cataloging-in-Publication Data has been applied for.

ISBN 1-57859-033-7

Printed in the United States of America
All rights reserved
10 9 8 7 6 5 4 3 2 1

CONTENTS

FOREWORD

by Bobby Allison

There aren't many people who've been as blessed as I've been through my involvement with stock car racing. On the other hand, there aren't many who've been as beaten and battered around as I've been in the past 10 years. I can't go back and change what's happened, so I'm trying to move on the best way I know how—which is to stay busy. I don't have to like some of the things that have happened to me, but I have to accept it.

NASCAR racing has grown incredibly since I got into it about 40 years ago. Everything is so much bigger and better, but racing's still racing and competition is still competition. And, best of all, having fun doing what you love is still as much fun as it ever was. The speedways, the cars, the sponsorship opportunities, the purses, the media attention, the number of fans, and the technology have gone beyond what anybody might have imagined even 25 years ago. This *Ultimate Fan Guide* is another example of how racing has grown—just 10 or 12 years ago hardly anybody cared enough about it to sit down and write something like this.

But the biggest difference is that we used to race for one hundred dollars and now they're racing for more than one hundred thousand dollars. Everybody says racing has become such a big business that nobody can have any fun anymore. Well, I don't know about that. Don't you think that little kid in the 24 car is having a ball right about now? Sure, racing's changed from what it used to be, but the whole world has changed. The thing is, men still get in those race cars every weekend and try to win, just like we did all through the '50s, '60s, '70s, and '80s.

I've been there for most of it, starting in 1955 when I ran my first race at Hialeah Speedway near Miami. I worked my way up to NASCAR's Modified series, then into Winston Cup in the early 1960s. From then until I got hurt in the summer of 1988, I raced just about anything NASCAR or anyone else had to offer—Modified, Busch Grand National, Winston Cup, IROC, USAC Indianapolis-type cars, NASCAR Grand American, Grand National East, and Late Models. I spent most of my career running at least one race a weekend, flying from one end of the country to another. The three things I loved most were all right together: my family, racing, and flying my own planes.

There were plenty of great times and there have been some incredibly bad times, but I guess that's the way it is in life. I was fortunate enough to drive for some wonderful owners, men who knew what it took to win. We didn't always get along, mainly because highly competitive people sometimes think theirs is the only way something should be done. But I can say this without reservation: I always gave my best every time I crawled into a race car and started the engine. No matter what had happened up to then or what was probably going to happen later, I drove as hard as I could every lap I was out there. Nobody can ever say Bobby Allison didn't drive as hard as he could.

Racing and I go back a long way. I fell in love with it after my grandfather took me to a dirt track near Miami in the late-'40s. I was seven or eight, and right then I started figuring out how I could see more racing. Ten years later, in the winter of my senior year in high school, I took my '38 Chevrolet street car to Hialeah, painted 41 on the door and ran in the Amateur class. It took me three races before I won, and I got all of $8 for it. That was decent money back then, but it wasn't the money that excited me, it was winning. It's always been that way for me—winning was more important than what I got for winning.

My parents wanted me to go to college and become a doctor or a lawyer or something like that. I kept telling my mother that racing was going to catch on and get really, really good, but she didn't want to hear anything about it. She thought all racers were bums with dirt and grease under their fingernails, and she didn't want me doing it. I raced under an assumed name for a while before my father told me that if I was going to race, then do the best I could and use my own name. That was some of the best advice anybody ever gave me. With a lot of help from a lot of good people, I won some races and began working my way up. I was fortunate enough to be runner-up in the 1960 Modified national standings, the national champion in 1964 and 1965, and its most popular driver in 1965. That really got me going toward Winston Cup.

All in all, it was a great career, much of it detailed right here in the pages of *Inside Sports NASCAR Racing*. I won some poles (57, fifth on the all-time list), some races (84, tied for third on the all-time list), and was fortunate enough to win the 1983 Winston Cup championship. That was a great thrill, especially after having been runner-up five times and finishing top-five in points 10 other times. And I take a lot of pride in being named most popular driver seven times in Winston Cup, and once each in Modified and Busch Grand National. Through the good and bad times, my fans have always been a source of joy and inspiration.

It hurt terribly—more than anybody can possibly know—to lose my two sons at race tracks. Clifford was killed practicing for a Busch Series race in Michigan in August of 1992 and Davey died the day after his helicopter crashed at Talladega in July of 1993. People sometimes ask if I'm bitter because racing forced me to retire, then took my boys. No, I'm not bitter because that's what we chose to do and we knew what could happen. Sure, we had some bad times, but plenty of people have had bad times without enjoying any good times.

When you look at it that way, I guess I'm ahead of the game.

INTRODUCTION

by Bill Fleischman

With NASCAR celebrating its 50th anniversary this year, it's the ideal time to pick up *Inside Sports NASCAR Racing: The Ultimate Fan Guide*. NASCAR's Winston Cup, Busch Grand National, and Craftsman Truck series are enjoying unprecedented popularity, as are NASCAR's other sanctioned series nationwide.

The Ultimate Fan Guide covers all facets of stock car and truck racing. For the first time, fans have a comprehensive book about a true American sport. Included in the book are profiles of drivers, team owners, and NASCAR executives; year-by-year race results and driver standings; plus the colorful history of the sport and an inside look at sponsorships and corporate involvement.

The book traces the unique progress of NASCAR (the National Association of Stock Car Automobile Racing), from its beginnings on the wide sandy beaches of Daytona to the superspeedways of today. You'll read about the vision of NASCAR founder Bill France and his son, Bill Jr. "Big Bill" kept his goals in sight as he steered NASCAR toward its current status and built superspeedways in Daytona Beach and Talladega, Alabama. After succeeding his father in 1972, Bill Jr. began expanding NASCAR's horizons and brought in nonautomotive companies as sponsors.

Here you'll learn how NASCAR's original superspeedway, Darlington Raceway—"The Track Too Tough to Tame"—was built in South Carolina in 1950. You'll also find stories about NASCAR's renowned short tracks in Martinsville, Virginia; Bristol, Tennessee; and North Wilkesboro, North Carolina. *The Ultimate Fan Guide*'s up-to-the-minute coverage also provides a recap of the 1997 season and describes major events from recent seasons, such as how the fabled Indianapolis Motor Speedway, for decades strictly home for high-speed Indy-car racing, began hosting Winston Cup races.

The book is intended to be useful both for the longtime fan and for those who have just discovered how fascinating major league stock car racing is. Scattered throughout the book are compelling anecdotes about NASCAR's past and its people. The successful track owners who helped build NASCAR are chronicled—people such as Martinsville's Clay Earles, Richmond's Paul Sawyer, multi-track owner Bruton Smith, and North Wilkesboro's Enoch Staley. Learn more about H. A. "Humpy" Wheeler, president of Charlotte

Motor Speedway, who is one of the best promoters in any sport.

NASCAR TAKES OFF

NASCAR Winston Cup and Busch Grand National racing have grown from a regional attraction, followed by fans in the Southeast, to a national road show. NASCAR has an office on Park Avenue in New York City to handle its marketing and sponsorship sales. The Winston Cup season culminates with an annual black-tie awards dinner at the Waldorf-Astoria Hotel. In its formative years, NASCAR was more comfortable on Main Street than on Manhattan's Park Avenue. In the 1990s, however, NASCAR is big business and has ties to dozens of major corporations, many of which are based in New York City.

In *The Ultimate Fan Guide*, readers will learn about the racing exploits of NASCAR's great drivers. The talented Jeff Gordon, with two championships in three years, has brought considerable attention to NASCAR in recent years. But he is just the latest in NASCAR's parade of star drivers. Pioneers such as Lee Petty, Curtis Turner, "Fireball" Roberts, Ned Jarrett, Buck Baker, Junior Johnson, the Flock brothers (Tim, Bob, and Fonty), Red Byron, Marvin Panch, and Joe Weatherly paved the way. The next generation included such stars as Richard Petty, Bobby Allison, David Pearson, Cale Yarborough, Benny Parsons, Fred Lorenzen, and Bobby Isaac. They were succeeded by Dale Earnhardt, Darrell Waltrip, Buddy Baker, Bill Elliott, Terry Labonte, Harry Gant, Mark Martin, Rusty Wallace, Ricky Rudd, Ernie Irvan, Ken Schrader, Geoff Bodine, Davey Allison, Neil Bonnett, Tim Richmond, and Alan Kulwicki. Sadly, the latter four are deceased, gone too soon from a sport they brightened. As NASCAR marks its 50th year, Gordon, Dale Jarrett, Bobby Labonte, and Jeff Burton are leading the new wave of star-quality drivers.

The Ultimate Fan Guide includes a chapter on the loyal fans whose support has made NASCAR racing popular. There are chapters on car safety and the action in the pits during races, as well as team and fan club directories, making it easy for fans to keep in touch with their favorite drivers. And there's a section on the race tracks themselves, including how to get there and who to contact.

NASCAR is perhaps the most colorful and visually appealing of all the major sports, so inside you'll also find nearly 200 photos, 41 of them in full-color to capture the excitement of race day at the track. The photos cover NASCAR from it's earliest days on the beach course at Daytona to the exciting 1997 season, which featured the closest three-man race in Winston Cup history.

This year will be an exciting time for NASCAR and all those involved in the sport. NASCAR deserves to celebrate its accomplishments as the most successful racing organization in North America. The Gordons, Jarretts, Labontes, Martins, and Burtons are worthy successors to NASCAR's original stars. However, NASCAR must be concerned about the prevalence of multi-car teams squeezing out the dedicated single-car owners. And, as major sponsors and big corporations assume greater roles in the sport, NASCAR shouldn't abandon the grass-roots fan base that built the foundation for the sport's recent success. Fans still want their drivers to be genuine people who are accessible: this has been one of NASCAR's strengths.

LATE-BREAKING NEWS

As with many sports, the offseason in NASCAR is often busier than the regular season, at least when it comes to team news and personnel changes. As this book was going to press, an exciting new team was announced for the 1998 season. Veteran driver Bill Elliott and future Hall of Fame quarterback Dan Marino of the Miami Dolphins announced the creation of a team that will run a Ford Taurus as the No. 13 car with driver Jerry Nadeau and sponsor FirstPlus Financial. Marino is the third NFL personality to take the plunge into Winston Cup racing, joining former Washington

Redskins coach Joe Gibbs and veteran quarterback Mark Rypien, who both co-own NASCAR teams.

ACKNOWLEDGMENTS

There are too many thanks to go around, but I'll try. If miss anyone, may I be forced to cover a Winston Cup race from the pits at Talladega without ear plugs.

- Co-author Al Pearce and photographer Dennis Winn for their hard work.

- Brad Morgan, senior editor at Visible Ink Press, who saw the big picture for this book. Brad encouraged and gently guided co-author Al Pearce and me. I'd also like to thank the rest of the folks at Visible Ink, including Martin Connors, Terri Schell, Dean Dauphinais, Jeff Hermann, Jim Craddock, Christa Brelin, Michelle Banks, Judy Galens, Michelle DiMercurio, Marilou Carlin, Roger Janecke, Barbara Eschner, Randy Bassett, Pam Reed, Barbara Yarrow, Cynthia Morgan, the excellent data entry staff and the crew working on permissions, and anyone else whose hard work I've left out.

- NASCAR's Kevin Triplett; Chris Powell, manager of media relations for Sports Marketing Enterprises, the racing branch of RJ Reynolds Tobacco Co.; and NASCAR historian Bob Latford: they were always helpful when we needed information.

- The public relations directors at the racetracks on the Winston Cup and Busch Grand National circuits and many team publicists for their assistance. Al Robinson, of Dover Downs International Speedway in Delaware, was particularly helpful.

- Anne Johnson, the author of several books for Visible Ink, for recommending me to Brad Morgan for this challenging assignment and for finishing the index in record time while still finishing her Christmas shopping.

- Executive Sports Editor Mike Rathet and Sports Editor Pat McLoone of the *Philadelphia Daily News* who, while not racing enthusiasts, have recognized the growing interest in NASCAR.

- Greg Fielden's *Stock Car Racing Encyclopedia* was a valuable resource for some of NASCAR's history.

- Last, but hardly least, my family. My wife, Barbara, for being patient while I devoted time to the book; our daughter, Jill, and her husband, Roger Herr, for their support and enthusiasm about the book; and our late daughter, Heather, whose spirit is always with us. Heather was a racing fan: I'm sure she would be proud of this book.

My co-author, Al Pearce, echoes my words of thanks and would like to thank a few additional people who helped out along the way:

- Tom Cotter and his staff at Cotter Communications, Paul Sawyer of Richmond International Raceway, and Dick Thompson at Martinsville Speedway.

- Special thanks to my wife, Francie, for gently restarting me when I ran down, and extra-special thanks to Annie, already wise enough at age eight to know when Daddy had work to do.

1

THE BIRTH OF NASCAR

Bill France had had it up to here. In fact, up to and above his towering six-foot, six-inch frame that didn't take any guff from anyone.

He was sick and tired of shyster promoters who talked a good game and delivered less than a fraction of what they promised. He was fed up with rules that applied to one team and not another, or rules that changed from weekend to weekend, often without notice. And he'd had a belly full of rough and rutty old speedways that were supposed to be "major league." In truth, most of them didn't have even a casual acquaintance with the term.

But mostly, William Henry Getty France of Daytona Beach, Florida, by way of Washington, D.C. had had it with the uncertainty that generally accompanies unanswered questions central to one's life and times. For example:

Would the 100-mile race scheduled for next month near Atlanta be run as scheduled? Would the speedway promoter down in Tampa keep his promise and fix the wooden guard rail that clearly was unsafe not only for drivers, but fans as well? Would the newspaper in North Carolina run the national point standings this week, and would it get them right if it did? And speaking of which, would

somebody please finally figure out a way to recognize a single, undisputed, national stock car champion? And what about the rules? How come they kept changing from weekend to weekend, from track to track? It didn't happen in baseball so, by God, it shouldn't happen in stock car racing, either.

It's hard to say which of those questions most gnawed at "Big Bill" France in the years surrounding World War II. A man of considerable stature in the ever-changing world of stock car racing, he'd been there and done that, and he didn't especially like what he'd seen. He'd been a racer, a mechanic, a team owner, and a sponsor. He'd helped promote races at a time when hardly anyone had the stomach for the job. In his mind—and in truth, he was right about this—his dozen or so years as a serious racer gave him the right to ask tough questions about the future of stock car racing as the 1940s headed for the 1950s.

He had seen (as they would say years later) up close and personal the potential of the sport. He had noticed the way it was embraced in the South, a largely rural, blue-collar, poor region still decades away from its first major-league professional sports franchises. There was an unmistakable fervor for the sport, a passion for the daring young men in their souped-up street-appearing cars. At a time when World War II remained a painful memory for hundreds of thousands of Southerners, here was something they could watch and enjoy as their own. If only for a few hours on occasional Sunday afternoons, it offered a welcomed respite from the hardscrabble lives most of them lived.

THE EARLY YEARS

Bill France was not a true son of the South. He was born in Washington, D.C. and lived there until his mid-20s. That's when the promise of a better life in better weather lured him to Florida. His father was a teller at Park Savings Bank in Washington, and his only son might have followed in those footsteps if not for his fascination with the new-fangled automobile and its level of performance.

As a teenager, Bill Jr. (he wasn't really a junior, but that's another story) would often skip school and go make some hot laps in the family's Model-T Ford. He would sneak off to the high-banked, 1 1/8-mile, wooden speedway between near Laurel, Maryland, where he would run laps until there was just enough time to beat his father home. He worked at several hands-on jobs before eventually owning and operating his own service station at a time when "service" meant just that. He made a name for himself and built his customer base by rising before dawn in the dead of winter to help white-collar bureaucrats crank their cars. It was steady work that paid relatively well—these were the Depression years, mind you; hardly anyone was getting rich—but France wanted something better for his wife, Anne, and their infant son, William Clay France.

Whether it was simply the pursuit of bigger and better things or (as others have said) their hatred of winter weather, the Frances headed for the South. With a total of $25, they loaded all they could in their Hupmobile, gathered up Little Bill, and left Washington in the fall of 1934. Where they were headed has never been clearly established.

Some say Tampa, others say the Miami Beach area. In either case, the weather would be better and the cost of living more agreeable. Two days later, they arrived in Daytona Beach, 90 miles south of Jacksonville, 300 miles north of Miami, and 200 miles northeast of Tampa.

Here, myth and rumor again come into play. Did the Frances stay there (for all time, as it turned out) because they were broke as one story suggests? Did Anne lobby to briefly stay there because she had a sister in nearby New Smyrna Beach she wanted to visit? Or did the Hupmobile break down and leave them stranded until Bill could scrape up enough money to fix it?

Years later, as he ruled the multimillion dollar motorsports and speedway empire his parents had created almost 50 years before, William Clay France ("Bill, Jr." to almost everybody in racing) tried to set the record straight once and for all. No, he said emphatically, there had been no sister in New Smyrna Beach to urge Bill and Anne to settle in the area. He'd never fully known if his parents had been out of money and too impoverished to keep going, but he knew this much was fact: there was no way a broken-down car would have forced them to stay in Daytona Beach if they'd truly wanted to keep going to either Tampa or Miami Beach. Big Bill was an experienced mechanic with his own toolbox, and he could have fixed the car if it had needed fixing.

It's been suggested that nothing more unusual than pure happenstance was a factor. The Frances, as the story goes, arrived in Daytona Beach on a day when the coastal weather was ideal. After years in Washington, where November brought chilly winds, Bill and Anne France were immediately enamored with Florida's balmy temperature and soft breezes. Daytona Beach was a small, relatively undeveloped city at the time, and the pace of life suited them. It wasn't paradise—not then and certainly not now—but it was the closest they'd come in their years together. Clearly, it would have been hard to have done any better by pushing farther southward.

DAYTONA AND SPEED WENT HAND-IN-HAND

Then there's another reason they may have stayed put. His name was Sir Malcolm Campbell, and at the time, he was the fastest man on four wheels.

For years, the hard-packed sand between Daytona Beach and its northern neighbor, Ormond Beach, was the site of world-record automotive speed trials. They began with motoring pioneers Ransom Olds and Alexander Winton in 1902, picked up speed (literally and otherwise) in the years immediately before and after World War I, then reached their zenith in the 1930s. By then, speeds were approaching 300 miles per hour along the firm and smooth and inviting sand. The 20-mile stretch was ideal for speed, made such by the relentless pounding of the Atlantic surf since time began.

Campbell, it was widely rumored, planned to return to Daytona Beach in the spring of 1935. He would bring his legendary Bluebird rocket car in hopes of running an unprecedented 300 miles an hour for yet another land-speed record. France was a racer at heart, so it's altogether possible he and his wife added Campbell's visit to their list of reasons to stay. (In case you've lost count, here they are: they loved the weather; the city was far more hospitable and affordable than Washington ever hoped to be; Bill quickly found work painting houses and then a job at a local car dealership; and

Early cars like this one challenged the land-speed record at Daytona in the years before NASCAR.

the speed trials were coming up right on the beach near where they'd found a small apartment.)

Alas, Campbell didn't reach 300 mph on what turned out to be the last round of speed trials in Florida. He reached "only" 276.82 mph on March 7, 1935, then stunned everyone by announcing that future record runs would not be on the sand in Florida, but on the near-limitless expanse of the salt of the Bonneville Salt Flats in Utah. In a way, the hard-packed sand that had seen so many records was victimized by its success. Technology had become so precise that shifting winds and changing tides made it difficult for Campbell or anyone else to reach 300 on the beach. And the sand itself was becoming rough and rutted from the years of hard use.

Just like that, then, sleepy little Daytona Beach and still-sleepier Ormond Beach lost their only real claims to fame. And despite complaints from the chambers of commerce and tourism commissions, Campbell was right in leaving. He proved it later in 1935: he fulfilled his goal by easily running more than 300 mph at Bonneville.

It was quite by accident that France got into race promotions. In 1935, after Campbell and others speed-seekers left Daytona Beach for the wide-open spaces of Utah, area officials were determined to continue bringing in speed-related events. Such events had helped establish the area's identity and been a source of mid-winter income for hotels and restaurants for more than three decades. Then, just as now, speed, the men who chased it, and those who watched them were worth trying to keep on the beach.

City officials asked former championship dirt-track racer and local resident Sig Haugdahl to organize and promote an automobile race along a 3.2-mile course. It would included Highway A1A southbound from downtown Daytona Beach and the same beach that had been the sight of land-speed record runs for years. The 78-lap, 250-mile event for street-legal family sedans was sanctioned by the American Automobile Association for cars built in 1935 and 1936. Daytona Beach posted a $5,000 purse, with $1,700 for the winner.

Things couldn't have gone worse. Revenue was lost when some ticket-takers arrived for work after thousands of fans had wandered in and made themselves at home. The sandy turns at each end of the course became virtually impassable, leading to stalled or stuck cars, and a rash of scoring disputes and technical protests. Mercifully, the race was stopped after 75 laps with Milt Marion declared the winner. Not surprisingly, second-place Ben Shaw and third-place Tommy Elmore protested, but their appeals were squashed. AAA officials had seen enough to know they'd better get out of town ASAP. (France, by the way, finished fifth behind Marion, Shaw, Elmore, and Sam Purvis).

That was the first and last race the City of Daytona Beach ever promoted. Little wonder—it lost a reported $22,000 and its citizens, most of whom had just survived the Depression and were on modest fixed incomes, weren't about to stand for that again.

But Haugdahl didn't give up that easily. He and France had become fast friends, and together they talked the Daytona Beach Elks Club into helping promote a race over Labor Day weekend of 1937. Despite a paltry $100 purse and improved management, promotion, and track conditions, the Elks lost money, too. And like the city, they'd had their fill of motorsports promotion.

Haugdahl chose to quit promoting races, leaving France the last real hope to keep racing alive in the Daytona Beach area. More than anyone else in the area, he saw a bright future for stock car racing. He knew the drivers well enough to understand what they wanted, but he was a struggling filling-station operator who didn't have enough cash to pay the purse, advertise and promote the race, then pay the city to set up the course. When wealthy hotel owner Ralph Hankinson refused to come aboard in July of 1938, France turned to local restaurateur Charlie Reese. Rich, well-known, and popular, Reese agreed to post a $1,000 purse and let France recruit drivers and spread the word. Danny Murphy beat France in the 150-miler that generated just enough profit to convince the co-promoters to do it again.

They managed another successful stock car promotion on Labor Day weekend of 1938 (France beat Lloyd Moody and Pig Ridings), then organized and promoted three more races (in March, July, and September) in 1939. They did it again in 1940—a stock car race in March, when the old Speed Trials had been run years earlier; another around July 4; and a third around Labor Day weekend. France continued to show his meddle, finishing fourth in March, first in July, and sixth in September. The 1941 schedule showed two races in March, and one each in late July and early August.

France and Reese were busy planning their 1942 schedule when the Japanese attacked Pearl Harbor on Dec. 7, 1941. That brought a virtual halt to all motorsports in the United States, including the highly-successful and popular beach/highway races. France spent the war years in the Daytona Boat Works (his wife, Anne, ran the family filling station), but never quit thinking about ways to make racing better. He found himself leaning more and more toward the promotion and organization part of stock car racing and less and less toward the driving side.

TRYING TO BRING ORDER TO RACING

France quit the boat works shortly after peace was declared and the United States began returning to normal. By now, he was almost obsessed with the idea that a single, firmly governed sanctioning body was necessary if stock car racing was to succeed. As a driver first and a driver/promoter later, he'd seen enough of minor-league sanctioning bodies that reeked of inconsistency. He wanted an organization that not only would sanction and promote races, but also bring uniformity to race procedures and technical rules. He envisioned an association that would oversee a membership benefit and insurance fund, one that would keep its word about paying postseason awards, and, most of all, an association that would crown a single national champion through a clearly-defined points system.

At the time, several organizations claimed to sanction national championship races. The Ameri-

THE FIRST ROAD RACE

The first of what has turned out to be several dozen Winston Cup road races was full of surprises. For one, it was staged in New Jersey, hardly a hot-bed of stock car excitement in 1954. For another, it was on a temporary circuit at the Linden Airport. And for a third, it was won by a man driving a Jaguar sponsored by a popular American band leader.

Al Keller got his second and last NASCAR victory in the 50-lap road race around the 2-mile course on June 13. He started seventh in a Jaguar sponsored by Paul Whiteman and led the final 28 laps in winning ahead of Joe Eubanks and pole-sitter Buck Baker, and fellow Jaguar drivers Bob Grossman and Harry LaVois.

Almost half the 43 starters were in foreign cars, the first time NASCAR had permitted anything other than America-built products. There were 13 Jaguars and five MGs, and one each Austin-Healy, Porsche and Morgan. After the race, Keller announced that he was leaving NASCAR in hopes of working his way to the Indianapolis 500.

But not before his name was safely etched in the NASCAR record book.

can Automobile Association was among them, but it was more concerned with open-wheel, open-cockpit, champ-car racing that grew into the USAC/CART Indy-car racing. Three other groups were the United Stock Car Racing Association, the National Auto Racing League, and the American Stock Car Racing Association. The Georgia-based National Stock Car Racing Association dealt mostly with issues in that state, so it didn't claim to crown the national champion. And, naturally, the Daytona Beach Racing Association that promoted only within the city made no such claim, either.

In fact, not even France's own Florida-based National Championship Stock Car Circuit claimed to crown a national champion. That's why, in June of 1947, he finally retired from racing and turned his attention to organizing a body that would. He left an impressive driving resume: two victories and six other top-fives in 16 beach/highway races, plus several other major victories throughout the

Southeast, Midwest, and Northeast. He was declared the "unofficial" national champion in 1940, well before any sort of points system came into play.

NASCAR IS BORN

He began his quest with a "summit meeting" in December of 1947 in an upper-floor suite of the Streamline Hotel in Daytona Beach. It attracted about three dozen men, representing all aspects of stock car racing: team owners, track operators, drivers, technical inspectors, mechanics, businessmen, lawyers and of course, France himself. No question, he was in charge, a role he played to the hilt from then until the day he died. It took three days for France to cobble together what everyone agreed would be called the National Association of Stock Car Auto Racing.

Its stated goals were everything France had been working for: uniform rules at all member-tracks; a point fund with post-season bonuses based on final standings; a driver's insurance and benevolent fund (it wasn't a retirement fund because France ruled that drivers were self-employed independent contractors); a points system to crown a true national champion; and an increase in fan awareness through stronger promotions and attention from the media.

He was elected president (you were expecting maybe somebody else?), Cannonball Baker was elected national commissioner, Eddie Bland vice president, Bill Tuthill treasurer, and Marshall Teague secretary. The new organization sanctioned its first race on the Daytona Beach road/beach course in February of 1948, several days before it was legally incorporated. More than 14,000 fans watched that first event, a 150-miler that Red Byron won ahead of Teague, Raymond Parks, Buddy Shuman, and Swayne Pritchett.

France's original plan was for NASCAR to oversee three separate and distinct classes of cars: Strictly Stock, Modified, and Roadsters. Perhaps surprisingly, the Modified and Roaster classes were seen as more attractive to fans than Strictly

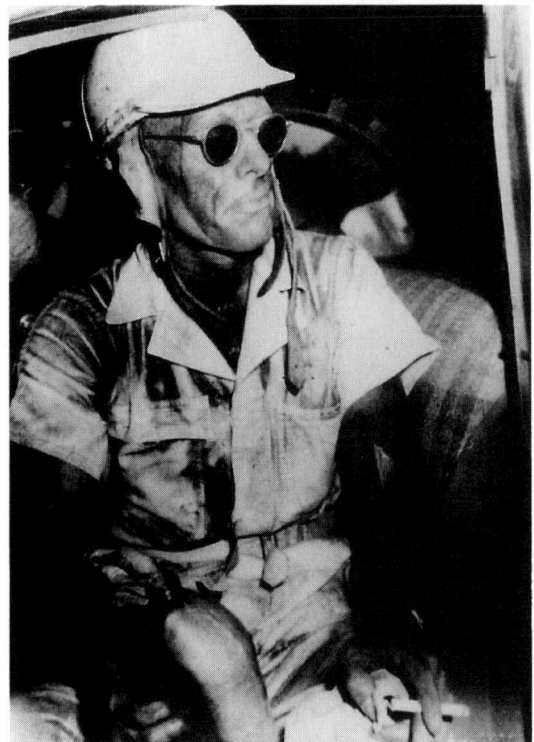

Red Byron, winner of the first NASCAR sanctioned race at Daytona.

Stock. As things turned out, though, the audience NASCAR attracted wanted nothing to do with Roadsters, a "Yankee" series more popular in the Midwest and Northeast. It didn't take long for France to recognize that he didn't need them.

And the Strictly Stock division quickly was put on hold. Since the end of World War II, Detroit automakers had been frantically converting their assembly lines from tank and jeep production to building family sedans. Demand far outstripped supply, and France didn't want NASCAR fans to see new models racing when they couldn't get the same model from their favorite dealer. So the heart and soul of NASCAR in 1948 were pre-1940s Fords and Chevrolets (plus a handful of new Buicks) that France and his staff agreed could race with major engine and bodywork changes. The 1948 schedule showed 52 dirt-track races for Modifieds, with Red Byron the national champion.

Things changed dramatically in 1949. In February, France staged a 20-mile exhibition race near Miami for his Strictly Stock division. In June, realizing he'd better stage a Strictly Stock points race or risk losing control of the series to a promoter in North Carolina, he scheduled a 200-lap, 150-mile race around a 3/4-mile dirt track in Charlotte, North Carolina. It carried a purse of $5,000 for the 33 street-legal family sedans that had been built since 1946. Pole-sitter Bob Flock led the first five laps in a 1946 Hudson, Bill Blair led laps 6-150 in a 1949 Lincoln, then Glenn Dunnaway led the rest of the way in his 1947 Ford.

But Dunnaway's car didn't survive the tough post-race tech inspection. Officials discovered altered rear springs and promptly moved him from first to dead-last 33rd (worth no money) on the rundown sheet. That elevated Roper to victory lane and moved Fonty Flock, Byron, Sam Rice, and Tim Flock into the top five. Even though his crew had been caught red-handed with "spread springs," team owner Hubert Westmoreland sued the new sanctioning body for $10,000. A North Carolina judge dismissed it, saying race officials had the right to make and enforce their rules without outside interference.

The mid-summer race drew a crowd of 13,000-plus, far more than France or anyone else in his organization would have imagined. NASCAR promoted six more Strictly Stock races that year: two each in North Carolina and Pennsylvania, and one each in Florida, New York, and Virginia. Just as he'd done the previous year in the Modified class, Byron won what later would become known as Grand National, then Winston Cup. Lee Petty was second in points, followed by Bob Flock, Curtis Turner, and Jack Smith. Fifty drivers ran at least one race and between 16 and 45 cars showed up for each one.

BRASINGTON'S FOLLY

But what NASCAR and its wildly popular new Strictly Stock division needed was a single blockbuster event to capture the nation's imagination. The USCA champ car circuit had the Indianapolis 500 and NASCAR's Modified and Sportsman divisions had their annual beach/road races in February in Daytona Beach. Alas, Strictly Stock didn't have such a showcase event. That changed in 1950 when South Carolina native Harold Brasington built a 1 1/4-mile, high-banked, egg-shaped speedway just west of his hometown of Darlington. He stunned everyone in racing by paving it and saying he wanted it to someday host a 500-mile stock car race.

Brasington was a retired racer. He'd gotten to know and respect France during beach/road races in Daytona Beach and at dirt tracks throughout the Southeast and Midwest. He'd quit driving in the late 40s to tend his farm and construction business, but still followed racing. He knew France's new organization was anxious to expand its image and he figured a 500-mile race would do the trick. He began planning his speedway after attending the 1948 Indy 500 and seeing the enormity of its crowd. "If Tony Hulman can do it here," Harold Brasington thought, "I can do it back home."

In the fall of 1949, after buying 70 acres from gentleman farmer Sherman Ramsey, he began carving a superspeedway out of what had been a cotton and peanut field. Instead of a true oval, he was forced to create an egg-shaped facility with one end tighter, more steeply-banked, and narrower than the other. It was that way because he'd promised Ramsey the new track wouldn't disturb Ramsey's beloved minnow pond on the property's western fringe. So while Brasington could make the eastern end as wide, sweeping, and flat as he wanted, his plans for the western end had to be just the opposite.

It took almost a year to build and pave the new track. In the summer of 1950, even as Sam Nunis spoke about promoting a 500-mile NASCAR race at Lakewood Speedway in Atlanta, Brasington and France struck a deal to run a 500-miler at Darlington on Labor Day. The inaugural Southern 500 carried a stock car-record $25,000 purse and was co-sanctioned by NASCAR and the rival Central States Racing Association. More than 80 cars showed up and qualifying took two weeks—similar to Indy 500 qualifying of the day. And much like the Indy 500 that had so inspired Brasington, the 75-car field was aligned in 25 rows, with three cars on each row.

All 9,000 seats were quickly filled and 6,000 other fans were allowed into the infield. Johnny Mantz needed more than six hours to cover the full 500 miles. He drove a 1950 Plymouth owned by France, Westmoreland (whose car had been DSQ'ed from the inaugural Strictly Stock race in Charlotte the previous year), driver Curtis Turner, and Alvin Hawkins. Fireball Roberts finished second, Red Byron third, Bill Rexford fourth, and Chuck Mahoney fifth. Despite repeated complaints from several also-rans about the winning engine—the complainers each paid a $500 protest fee—the car nevertheless passed tech inspection. (If France thought it odd to own a car in a race he promoted—or to associate with someone like Westmoreland, who'd already been caught cheating—he didn't let on).

With few exceptions, the NASCAR of the 1950s featured short races on dirt tracks. There was hardly any recognition from the mainstream media, which still considered NASCAR and its renamed Grand National division little more than junk cars racing around decrepit cow pasture tracks for the entertainment of Southern rednecks with nothing better to do on Sunday afternoons following church. The Southern 500 was NASCAR's only paved-track event in 1950 and there were only four (two at Dayton, Ohio and one each at Darlington and Thompson, Connecticut) in 1951.

Paved tracks didn't begin to gain widespread acceptance until the latter part of the '50s. Darlington and the half-miler at Dayton each had two races in 1952, and Darlington and the new 1-mile asphalt track at Raleigh, North Carolina each had a Grand National race in 1953. Darlington, Raleigh, and the paved road course at the Linden, New Jersey airport got races in 1954, then the half-mile at Martinsville, Virginia, joined Darlington (one race) and Raleigh (two) in 1955.

The future began coming into focus in 1956. NASCAR sanctioned 11 paved-track races among its 56 events that year. It sanctioned 14 paved-track races out of 53 in 1957 and 24 of 51 races in 1958. And instead of oval tracks, France was scheduling races on road courses at Watkins Glen, New York, Elkhart Lake, Wisconsin, and Bridgehampton, New York. Even more importantly, the sport was moving into almost every corner of the country. Suddenly, almost overnight, it seemed, NASCAR racing was becoming a national series rather than one with simply regional ties.

2

1949–1958: THE WILD BUNCH

1949

AT A GLANCE:

Strictly Stock Champion: Red Byron

Notable Events: A Greensboro, N.C. judge refused to intervene when team owner Hubert Westmoreland sued NASCAR over a rules interpretation. The ruling set a precedent (recognized to this day) that allows NASCAR to make its rules and enforce them, generally without outside interference.

NASCAR's first Strictly Stock points race (there had been an exhibition early in the year near Miami) went for 200 laps around a 3/4-mile dirt track in Charlotte, North Carolina. NASCAR president Bill France posted a $5,000 purse for 33 street-legal sedans, all of them built after World War II. Glenn Dunnaway led the final 49 laps in a 1947 Ford that failed post-race inspection because it had illegal rear springs. When Jim Roper inherited the victory, it gave birth to NASCAR's first great trivia question: Why was the winner of the very first Winston Cup race (even though it wasn't called that at the time) disqualified?

The event drew 13,000-plus on a Sunday afternoon, far more than France or any of his lieu-

tenants would have dared predict. Buoyed by that unexpected success, NASCAR scheduled seven more races the rest of that summer: two each in North Carolina and Pennsylvania, and one each in Florida, New York, and Virginia. Red Byron and Bob Flock each won two, and Lee Petty, Curtis Turner, and Jack White divided the other three. Byron was NASCAR's first champion by 117.5 points over Petty, with Bob Flock ranked third.

GRAND NATIONAL STANDINGS

	DRIVER	STARTS	WINS	POINTS	MONEY
1.	Red Byron	6	2	842.5	5,800
2.	Lee Petty	6	1	725	3,855
3.	Bob Flock	6	2	704	4,870
4.	Bill Blair	6	0	567.5	1,280
5.	Fonty Flock	6	0	554.5	2,015
6.	Curtis Turner	6	1	430	2,675
7.	Ray Erickson	4	0	422	1,460
8.	Tim Flock	5	0	421	1,510
9.	Glenn Dunnaway	6	0	384	810
10.	Frank Mundy	4	0	370	1,160
11.	Bill Snowden	4	0	315	660
12.	Bill Rexford	3	0	286	785
13.	Sara Christian	6	0	282	760
14.	Clyde Minter	0	0	280	760
15.	Gober Sosebee	3	0	265	1,305
16.	Jim Raper	2	1	253	2,130
17.	Sam Rice	2	0	231	680
18.	Jack White	1	1	200	1,580
19.	Dick Linder	3	0	180.5	1,305
20.	Billy Rafter	1	0	160	480
21.	Archie Smith	2	0	145	225
22.	Joe Littlejohn	1	0	140	300
23.	Jack Russell	3	0	140	175
24.	Mike Eagan	1	0	140	300

25.	Herb Thomas	4	0	132	225
26.	Sterling Long	2	0	100	150
27.	Frank Christian	1	0	100	175
28.	Frankie Schneider	1	0	100	150
29.	Lloyd Moore	1	0	100	150
30.	Roy Hall	1	0	100	150
31.	Slick Smith	4	0	99	275
32.	Al Keller	1	0	90	200
33.	John Wright	1	0	80	100
34.	Al Bonnell	2	0	80	150
35.	Otis Martin	4	0	69.5	200
36.	Jimmy Thompson	2	0	65	175
37.	Charles Muscatel	1	0	60	75
38.	Raymond Lewis	1	0	60	75
39.	Al Wagoner	1	0	60	75
40.	George Lewis	1	0	40	50
41.	Lou Volk	1	0	30	125
42.	Buddy Helms	1	0	27.5	75
43.	Bob Apperson	3	0	25	150
44.	Bill Bennett	1	0	24	100
45.	Ted Chamberlain	2	0	24	100
46.	Buck Baker	2	0	20	50
47.	Jack Etheridge	1	0	20	75
48.	Ellis Pearce	1	0	20	50
49.	Bobby Greene	2	0	19.5	50
50.	Ken Wagner	3	0	19	100

1950

AT A GLANCE:

Grand National Champion: Bill Rexford

Notable Events: After realizing that "Strictly Stock" sounded more like a rule than a professional series, France renamed his ever-growing stock car series "Grand National." He liked the sophistication of the term, particularly the image it portrayed as a quality product. It remained Grand National until the early 70s, when NASCAR re-named it Winston Cup in recognition of its new patron.

The popularity of stock car racing took a quantum leap when ex-racer Harold Brasington mounted a bulldozer and carved a 1 1/4-mile, high-banked, egg-shaped speedway near his backwater hometown of Darlington, South Carolina. Brasington stunned almost everyone in racing by paving it, then stunned them even more by saying his track would host the country's first 500-mile race for street-legal family sedans. He and France agreed in the summer that just such an event over Labor Day weekend would generate enormous attention for the series and Darlington.

The inaugural Southern 500 boasted a NASCAR-record $25,000 purse and an unprecedented 75-car field. Brasington aligned them three-wide on 25 rows, similar to how the Indi-

anapolis 500 set its grid. All 9,000 seats were quickly filled, leaving 6,000 late-comers to jam themselves into the track's vast infield. Johnny Mantz needed more than six hours to cover the distance in a 1950 Plymouth that was owned by France, Westmoreland (the self-same owner who'd been DQ'ed at Charlotte), driver Curtis Turner, and Alvin Hawkins. Fireball Roberts finished second, Red Byron third, Bill Rexford fourth, and Chuck Mahoney fifth. Despite suspicions by many of the losers that Mantz's car was blatantly illegal, it passed a cursory technical inspection and the victory stood.

There were 18 other races that year, but none came close to attracting the national attention generated by Darlington in one afternoon. Not only was it America's first 500-mile stock car race, but it drew a capacity crowd and was run to its conclusion with few serious incidents. The other 18 race were on dirt tracks, most of them measuring less than a mile. Thirteen drivers won races, including multiple winners Turner (four victories) and Dick Linder (three). Rexford won only one race in 17 starts, but was consistent enough (five top-5s and 11 top-10s) to beat Fireball Roberts and Lee Petty for the championship.

GRAND NATIONAL STANDINGS

	DRIVER	STARTS	WINS	POINTS	MONEY
1.	Bill Rexford	17	1	1,959	5,750
2.	Fireball Roberts	9	1	1,848.5	6,800
3.	Lee Petty	17	1	1,590	7,120
4.	Lloyd Moore	16	1	1,398	5,235
5.	Curtis Turner	16	4	1,375.5	8,080
6.	Johnny Mantz	3	1	1,282	10,810
7.	Chuck Mahoney	11	0	1,217.5	2,250
8.	Dick Linder	13	3	1,121	5,695
9.	Jimmy Florian	10	1	801	2,730
10.	Bill Blair	16	1	766	4,400
11.	Herb Thomas	13	1	590.5	2,645
12.	Buck Baker	9	0	531.5	2,145
13.	Cotton Owens	3	0	500	1,100
14.	Fonty Flock	7	1	458.5	2,195
15.	Weldon Adams	4	0	440	1,205
16.	Tim Flock	12	1	437.5	3,980
17.	Clyde Minter	8	0	427	1,155
18.	Dick Burns	8	0	341.5	780
19.	Art Laney	4	0	320	655
20.	Bob Flock	4	0	314	1,155
21.	George Hartley	8	0	298	875
22.	Gayle Warren	10	0	287	550
23.	Frank Mundy	8	0	275.5	550
24.	Jim Paschal	6	0	220.5	850
25.	Jack White	7	0	211.5	525
26.	Pappy Hough	5	0	207.5	325
27.	Ray Duhigg	5	0	202.5	450

Bill Rexford (car #60) and Tim Flock (car #91) battle it out in a 1950 race.

28.	Leon Sales	2	0	200	1,000
29.	Jimmy Thompson	4	0	200	525
30.	Harold Kite	3	1	187	1,550
31.	Neil Cole	2	0	183.5	300
32.	Jack Smith	3	0	180	775
33.	Bucky Sager	2	0	180	750
34.	Red Harvey	1	0	180	750
35.	Ted Swaim	1	0	180	750
36.	Buck Barr	2	0	180	575
37.	Pepper Cunningham	2	0	177.5	300
38.	Ewell Weddle	3	0	173.5	600
39.	Donald Thomas	2	0	164	300
40.	Bill Snowden	4	0	163	325
41.	Jimmie Lewallen	3	0	140	400
42.	Chuck James	1	0	140	400
43.	Dick Clothier	5	0	133.5	350
44.	Paul Parks	6	0	124.5	375
45.	Al Gross	3	0	124	550
46.	Jack Reynolds	2	0	120	300
47.	Jim Delaney	2	0	114	175
48.	Carl Renner	2	0	108	250
49.	Jack Holloway	2	0	107.5	225
50.	Bob Dickson	6	0	105	275
51.	J. C. Van Landingham	1	0	105	450

1951

AT A GLANCE:

Grand National Champion: Herb Thomas

Notable Events: To debunk the perception that NASCAR was a Southern and Eastern pastime, France scheduled five races in California and another in Arizona; 15 more were held above the Mason-Dixon line. Perhaps the year's most important event was a 250-miler in Detroit, home of the Big Three automakers, as part of that city's 250th anniversary. It was the first time automotive executives had seen close-up what this new-fangled sport was all about.

If it was the birth of a trend, hardly anyone noticed. After visiting only one paved track in its first two seasons, the Grand National schedule went to more in 1951. Four paved-track races didn't make a dent in the schedule, but it was a glimpse of where the sport was headed. Two of them were at the half-mile track in Dayton, Ohio, another on the half-miler at Thompson, Connecticut, and the other at Darlington Raceway. The series continued to expand, going into eight states for the first time, six of them outside the Southeast. The number of races also expanded dramatically, more than doubling to 41.

Herb Thomas (seven victories and 19 top-10 finishes) entered 33 of the 41 races and won the championship over eight-time winner Fonty Flock and seven-time winner Lee Petty. Through a quirk of scheduling (and in an effort to promote as many races as possible), France often scheduled conflicting events. On April 8, for example, he sanctioned Grand National races in Alabama and California. He did it again on April 29 and September 23, scheduled three conflicting races on October 14, and two on November 11. There were few complaints since nobody was planning to run them all, anyway, and everyone agreed the series needed all the national exposure it could get.

GRAND NATIONAL STANDINGS

	DRIVER	STARTS	WINS	POINTS	MONEY
1.	Herb Thomas	35	7	14,208.45	20,850 2.
	Fonty Flock	34	8	4,062.25	15,200
3.	Tim Flock	0	7	3,722.5	14,545
4.	Lee Petty	32	1	2,392.25	7,340
5.	Frank Mundy	27	3	1,963.5	7,085
6.	Buddy Shuman	7	0	1,368.75	2,830
7.	Jesse James Taylor	10	0	1,214	3,750
8.	Dick Rathmann	15	0	1,040	3,225
9.	Bill Snowden	12	0	1,009.25	2,640
10.	Joe Eubanks	12	0	1,005.5	3,415
11.	Lloyd Moore	22	0	996.5	2,600
12.	Fireball Roberts	9	0	930	1,190
13.	Jimmie Lewallen	12	0	874.25	2,430
14.	Bob Flock	17	1	869	3,680
15.	Jim Paschal	16	0	858.5	2,450
16.	Bill Blair	18	0	840	2,710
17.	Gober Sosebee	10	0	784	2,710
18.	Erick Erickson	12	0	723.5	2,435
19.	Tommy Thompson	5	1	755	5,510
20.	Donald Thomas	17	0	743.5	2,060
21.	Johnny Mantz	6	0	725	2,025
22.	Lou Figaro	13	1	684.2	2,135
23.	Buck Baker	11	0	644.5	1,650
24.	Dick Meyer	6	0	626.5	1,650
25.	Harold Kite	2	0	625	800
26.	Billy Carden	11	0	509.75	1,460
27.	Jimmy Florian	9	0	462.5	1,100
28.	Jim Fiebelkorn	17	0	455	1,355
29.	Ronnie Kohler	5	0	432	1,100
30.	Danny Weinberg	6	1	423.5	1,470
31.	Pappy Hugh	9	1	423	760
32.	Woody Brown	3	0	421	1,125
33.	Neil Cole	5	1	382	2,050
34.	Paul Newkirk	0	0	375	500
35.	John McGinley	6	0	372.5	1,300
36.	Marvin Panch	3	0	371.5	1,075
37.	Oda Greene	6	0	366.5	825
38.	Jack Goodwin	3	0	362.5	725
39.	Jack Smith	7	0	360.5	1,275
40.	Robert Caswell	3	0	350	1,325
41.	Lloyd Dane	7	0	323.5	975
42.	Cotton Owens	5	0	312.5	225
43.	Fred Steinbroner	6	0	306.5	700
44.	Ewell Weddle	7	0	293.5	435
45.	George Seeger	9	0	278	910
46.	Sam Hawks	3	0	262.5	650
47.	Don Bailey	10	0	239.5	625
48.	Bud Farrell	5	0	227.5	700
49.	Harvey Riley	8	0	262.5	475
50.	Fred Lee	6	0	224	450

1952

AT A GLANCE:

Grand National Champion: Tim Flock

Notable Events: Until now, many automotive-related companies had taken a "wait-and-see" attitude about NASCAR racing. But in 1952, for the first time, companies like Pure Oil Co. (later, Union 76 and Unocal) and Champion Spark Plug Inc. began paying contingency awards in exchange for publicity generated by drivers using their products.

In a startling turnabout, France and his staff moved away from scheduling conflicting events. Except for June 1—when NASCAR sent cars to points races at Toledo, Ohio and Augusta, Georgia—drivers found the Grand National schedule easier to take. The 34 races were spread among 33 dates, giving eight-time winner and champion Tim Flock the flexibility to make 33 starts. Herb Thomas, also an eight-time winner, started 32 races, as did three-time winner Lee Petty. Rounding out the top-five in points were Fonty Flock (two victories in 27 starts) and Dick Rathmann (five victories in 27 starts). As usual, all but four of the races—two each at Dayton and Darlington— were on dirt.

From the beginning, France's goal had been to create an organization to crown a single national champion. His plan to have the best stock car drivers facing each other on a regular basis had been undermined by the conflicting scheduling of 1952. Granted, a driver in Georgia wouldn't tow to California if there was a race closer to home, but the perception was that NASCAR sometimes didn't present the best fields it could. It was a situation that convinced France to move toward single-date scheduling.

GRAND NATIONAL STANDINGS

DRIVER	STARTS	WINS	POINTS	MONEY
1. Tim Flock	8	5	6,858.5	22,890
2. Herb Thomas	32	8	6,752.5	18,965
3. Lee Petty	32	3	6,498.5	16,876
4. Fonty Flock	29	2	5,183.5	19,112
5. Dick Rathmann	27	5	3,952.5	11,248
6. Bill Blair	19	1	3,449	7,899
7. Joe Eubanks	19	0	3,090.5	3,630
8. Ray Duhigg	18	0	2,986.5	3,811
9. Donald Thomas	21	1	2,574	4,477
10. Buddy Shuman	15	1	2,483	4,587
11. Ted Chamberlain	18	0	2,208	1,277
12. Buck Baker	14	1	2,159	3,187
13. Perk Brown	19	0	2,151.5	2,187
14. Jimmie Lewallen	20	0	2,033	2,052
15. Bub King	10	0	1,993	2,737
16. Herschel Buchanan	0	0	1,868	2,468
17. Johnny Patterson	5	0	1,708	3,618
18. Jim Paschal	15	0	1,694	1,483
19. Neil Cole	11	0	1,618	1,793
20. Lloyd Moore	8	0	1,513.5	2,193
21. Gene Comstock	8	0	1,339	785
22. Banjo Matthews	3	0	1,240	1,000
23. Ralph Ligouri	12	0	1,230	920
24. Jack Reynolds	10	0	1,177.5	1,450
25. Dick Passwater	6	0	1,148	945
26. Bucky Sager	10	0	1,119.5	710
27. Frankie Schneider	6	0	931	1,350
28. Otis Martin	5	0	873.5	275
29. Coleman Lawrence	8	0	846	375
30. Ed Samples	8	0	827	1,535
31. Fred Dove	0	0	780	390
32. Slick Smith	5	0	746	725
33. Iggy Katona	5	0	742	525
34. Jack Smith	8	0	729	820
35. Tommy Moon	6	0	726	1,145
36. Rollin Smith	1	0	700	350
37. Speedy Thompson	2	0	656	305
38. Jimmy Thompson	0	0	650	300
39. Bud Farrell	6	0	648	325
40. Weldon Adams	6	0	634	275
41. Clyde Minter	5	0	632	375
42. Elton Hildreth	6	0	614	375
43. Dave Terrell	5	0	612	475
44. Tommy Thompson	5	0	602.5	525
45. Bob Moore (OH)	5	0	579.5	575
46. Jim Reed	7	0	567	475
47. E. C. Ramsey	7	0	560	260
48. Jimmy Florian	6	0	551	175
49. Ed Benedict	5	0	526	360
50. Curtis Turner	7	0	505	265

1953

The much-heralded "Fabulous Hudson Hornet" lived up to its reputation in 1953. Series champion Herb Thomas used one to run all 37 races (the

first time anyone ran the full schedule), won a dozen, and had 31 top-10 finishes. Second-ranked Lee Petty won five races in 36 starts and third-ranked Dick Rathmann won five in 35 starts. All told, Hudsons won 22 races, including a run of 16-for-20 during the heart of the season. The Hudson lineup included Thomas, Rathmann, and Tim and Fonty Flock, and the success of racing Hudsons spurred sales of their street-legal cousins.

As part of NASCAR's ever-growing scope, many of the teams went on a three-race swing into South Dakota, Nebraska, and Iowa in late June and early August. Thomas won in South Dakota and Iowa, and Rathmann in Nebraska. A week later they were back home, racing again in the Southeast. As if anyone ever had any doubts, NASCAR racing was moving from infancy to a healthy, precocious childhood.

GRAND NATIONAL STANDINGS

DRIVER	STARTS	WINS	POINTS	MONEY
1. Herb Thomas	37	12	8,460	28,910
2. Lee Petty	36	5	7,814	18,447
3. Dick Rathmann	34	5	7,362	20,245
4. Buck Baker	33	4	6,713	18,167
5. Fonty Flock	33	4	6,174	17,756
6. Tim Flock	1	1	5,011	8,282
7. Jim Paschal	24	1	4,211	5,571
8. Joe Eubanks	24	0	3,603	5,254
9. Jimmie Lweallen	22	0	3,508	4,222
10. Curtis Turner	19	1	3,373	4,347
11. Speedy Thompson	7	2	2,958	6,547
12. Slick Smith	23	0	2,670	2,302
13. Elton Hildreth	25	0	2,625	1,997
14. Gober Sosebee	17	0	2,525	2,722
15. Bill Blair	21	1	2,457	4,535
16. Fred Dove	0	0	1,997	1,240
17. Bub King	14	0	1,624	1,036
18. Gene Comstock	13	0	1,519	990
19. Donald Thomas	17	0	1,408	1,765
20. Ralph Liguori	12	0	1,336	1,098
21. Pop Mcginnis	13	0	1,113	975
22. Otis Martin	8	0	1,068	610
23. Andy Winfree	7	0	954	300
24. Bob Welborn	11	0	761	1,160
25. Johnny Patterson	11	0	753	645
26. Ted Chamberlain	9	0	738	500
27. Neil Roberts	2	0	738	400
28. Buddy Shuman	5	0	713	395
29. Arden Mounts	10	0	644	395

(left to right) Tim Flock, Buckshot Morris, and Fonty Flock show off their cars. Notice the taped over headlights and the windshield wipers—strictly stock meant what it said.

30. Bobby Myers	2	0	644	390
31. Clyde Minter	8	0	636	405
32. George Osborne	2	0	612	300
33. Jim Reed	3	0	590	635
34. Gordon Bracken	6	0	538	215
35. Don Oldenberg	4	0	527	375
36. C. H. Dingler	5	0	520	250
37. Elbert Allen	4	0	488	250
38. Mike Magill	3	0	486	235
39. Lloyd Hulette	1	0	486	250
40. Bill Harrison	3	0	480	450
41. Tommy Thompson	3	0	463	865
42. Coleman Lawrence	8	0	446	250
43. Dub Livingston	6	0	435	225
44. Buck Smith	5	0	400	175
45. Jimmy Ayers	4	0	384	150
46. Bob Walden	4	0	356	250
47. Eddie Skinner	4	0	352	200
48. Bill Adams	2	0	346	250
49. Mel Krueger	3	0	336	175
50. Johnny Beauchamp	3	0	328	150

1954

AT A GLANCE:

Grand National Champion: Lee Petty

Notable Events: After running only oval-track races since 1949, NASCAR hosted its first road race on June 13. It was on a 2-mile course on the airport at Linden, New Jersey. Al Keller got his second and final Grand National victory in, perhaps appropriately in light of the type of course, a Jaguar.

After being one of NASCAR's most popular and successful drivers since its inception, Lee Petty finally won the first of his two Grand National championships. He won "only" seven of 34 races, but was consistent enough to have 32 top-10 finishes. Herb Thomas won 12 races in 34 starts, but had seven fewer top-10s and lost the title by 283 points. Buck Baker, destined to become one of NASCAR's all-time greats, won four races and was third in points. After being 12th in the 1952 standings and fourth in 1953, the former milkman from Charlotte was steadily moving toward the top.

If nothing else, 1954 proved what later came to be common knowledge: the sport was bigger than any of its stars. Early in the season, after being disqualified after apparently winning in Daytona Beach, Tim Flock quit the circuit. Later that spring, Fonty Flock quit NASCAR, as did Al Keller in the summer and Hershel McGriff in the fall. But the season-long scrap between Petty and Thomas—as well as the presence of Baker and Rathmann—kept Grand National racing alive and well. Indeed, even thriving.

GRAND NATIONAL STANDINGS

	DRIVER	STARTS	WINS	POINTS	MONEY
1.	Lee Petty	34	7	8,649	21,127
2.	Herb Thomas	34	12	8,366	30,975
3.	Buck Baker	34	4	6,893	19,368
4.	Dick Rathmann	32	3	6,760	16,264
5.	Joe Eubanks	33	0	5,467	8,559
6.	Hershel McGriff	24	4	5,137	13,250
7.	Jim Paschal	27	1	3,903	5,451
8.	Jimmie Lewallen	22	0	3,233	4,694
9.	Curtis Turner	10	1	2,994	10,120
10.	Ralph Liguari	23	0	2,905	3,495
11.	Blackie Pitt	27	0	2,661	1,925
12.	Dave Terrell	30	0	2,645	2,225
13.	Bill Blair	19	0	2,362	2,650
14.	Laird Bruner	24	0	2,243	2,080
15.	Gober Sosebee	18	1	2,114	3,150
16.	John Soares	9	1	2,072	3,262
17.	Marvin Panch	10	0	1,925	4,747
18.	Eddie Skinner	15	0	1,794	1,017
19.	Joel Million	9	0	1,779	1,092
20.	Elton Hildreth	14	0	1,710	1,152
21.	Arden Mounts	12	0	1,705	875
22.	Fireball Roberts	5	0	1,648	1,080
23.	Speedy Thompson	7	0	1,480	1,165
24.	Johnny Patterson	4	0	1,417	1,240
25.	Erick Erickson	6	0	1,337	1,365
26.	Ray Duhigg	12	0	1,245	1,375
27.	Slick Smith	6	0	1,122	950
28.	Clyde Minter	12	0	1,116	900
29.	Gwyn Staley	2	0	1,088	670
30.	Lloyd Dane	4	0	984	1,600
31.	Donald Thomas	9	0	980	1,675
32.	Ted Chamberlain	10	0	920	475
33.	Danny Letter	4	1	915	1,975
34.	Elmo Langley	2	0	864	450
35.	Tim Flock	5	0	860	1,050
36.	Fred Dove	0	0	832	525
37.	Bill Widenhouse	6	0	805	425
38.	Gene Comstock	1	0	780	400
39.	Walt Flinchum	8	0	756	425
40.	Charlie Cregar	5	0	716	405
41.	Bill Amick	6	0	700	250
42.	Harvey Eakin	7	0	698	425
43.	Lou Figaro	3	0	690	425
44.	Ken Fisher	5	0	668	400
45.	Jim Reed	9	0	631	965
46.	Russ Hepler	6	0	624	525
47.	Allen Adkins	2	0	624	1,150
48.	Van Van Wey	3	0	602	495
49.	Tony Nelson	3	0	568	325
50.	John Dodd Jr.	1	0	552	150

1955

AT A GLANCE:

Grand National Champion: Tim Flock

Notable Events: The phrase "Win On Sunday, Sell on Monday" began making the rounds as executives at Ford and Chevrolet took tentative steps toward factory backing of teams. But in one of the sport's most ironic twists, Chrysler products won 27 races—even though the company did nothing to back racers who drove Chryslers.

Tim Flock and NASCAR had settled their differences late in the 1954 season, and Flock was ready when the Grand National tour reached Daytona Beach in February. He returned with a flourish, winning 18 races in 38 starts, easily the most dominating performance in Grand National history to that point. He backed the 18 victories with 14 other top-fives and another top-10, and beat three-race winner Buck Baker by 508 points. Even though Lee Petty won six races and was third in the final standings, he was an astonishing 2,402 points behind Flock.

The champion drove Chrysler 300s for Carl Kiekhaefer, a wealthy Wisconsin businessman who stormed into NASCAR bent on outspending and outpreparing everyone to win the championship. In addition to Tim Flock, his Mercury Marine-sponsored stable also included Fonty Flock, Speedy Thompson, and Norm Nelson. The no-nonsense owner was so obsessed with the championship chase that he owned outright or sponsored seven cars in a late-season race in Arkansas. He hoped Tim Flock would lead, separated from his nearest title challenger by a squadron of Kiekhaefer-owned cars.

It worked — well, slightly, anyway. Flock finished fourth, his teammate and brother Bob finished fifth, and Buck Baker was sixth in a self-owned Ford that Kiekhaefer was sponsoring. All told, Kiekhaefer had the winning driver (Thompson), Tim and Bob Flock, and Baker in the top 10. Banks, Simpson, Nelson, and Fonty Flock were also in the field and associated with Kiekhaefer in one way or another.

GRAND NATIONAL STANDINGS

	DRIVER	STARTS	WINS	POINTS	MONEY
1.	Tim Flock	18	5	9,596	37,780
2.	Buck Baker	32	3	8,088	19,771
3.	Lee Petty	42	6	7,194	18,920
4.	Bob Welborn	32	0	5,460	10,147
5.	Herb Thomas	23	3	5,186	18,024
6.	Junior Johnson	36	5	4,810	13,803
7.	Eddie Skinner	38	0	4,652	4,737
8.	Jim Paschal	36	5	4,572	10,586
9.	Jimmie Lewallen	33	0	4,526	6,440
10.	Gwyn Staley	24	0	4,360	6,547
11.	Fonty Flock	31	3	4,266	13,100
12.	Dave Terrell	25	0	3,170	3,655
13.	Jimmy Massey	11	0	2,924	3,510
14.	Marvin Panch	10	0	2,812	4,385
15.	Speedy Thompson	15	2	2,452	7,090
16.	Jim Reed	14	0	2,416	2,703
17.	Gene Simpson	22	0	2,388	2,158
18.	Dick Rathmann	20	0	2,298	4,368
19.	Ralph Liguori	12	0	2,124	1,973
20.	Joe Eubanks	14	0	2,028	2,008
21.	Blackie Pitt	20	0	1,992	1,785
22.	Harvey Henderson	17	0	1,930	1,810
23.	Banks Simpson	7	0	1,852	870
24.	Dink Widenhouse	0	0	1,752	1,660
25.	John Dodd Jr.	13	0	1,496	1,695
26.	Bill Widenhouse	5	0	1,444	1,065
27.	Lou Spears	3	0	1,272	810
28.	Larry Flynn	1	0	1,260	1,175
29.	Cotton Owens	2	0	1,248	900
30.	Gordon Smith	15	0	1,212	975
31.	Billy Carden	13	0	1,172	1,340
32.	Arden Mounts	12	0	1,170	1,025
33.	Joel Milton	8	0	1,136	1,685
34.	Curtis Turner	9	0	1,120	2,605
35.	John Lindsay	6	0	1,052	575
36.	Nace Mattingly	3	0	992	700
37.	Bill Blair	12	0	974	440
38.	Donald Thomas	10	0	932	1,240
39.	Ed Cole Jr.	13	0	924	645
40.	Mack Hanbury	8	0	900	575
41.	Danny Letter	4	1	892	1,780
42.	George Parrish	12	0	880	750
43.	Banjo Matthews	3	0	860	745
44.	Carl Krueger	7	0	748	585
45.	Ted Cannady	9	0	744	450
46.	Allen Adkins	4	0	740	1,160
47.	Joe Weatherly	6	0	724	2,575
48.	John McVitty	7	0	684	550
49.	Lloyd Dane	5	0	674	780
50.	Fred Dove	0	0	668	750

1956

It shouldn't have surprised anyone when Buck Baker won the 1956 Grand National title. After all, he had been steadily climbing in the points: fourth in 1953, third in 1954, then second to Tim Flock in

AT A GLANCE:

Grand National Champion: Buck Baker

Notable Events: As if going 22-of-40 in 1955 wasn't enough of a thrill, Kiekhaefer assembled an even more formidable Grand National stable for 1956. Even so, he found that success didn't always bring happiness. After winning the 1955 and 1956 titles, he abruptly left the sport he had ruled for two years.

1955. He was almost assured the 1956 championship when Kiekhaefer hired him to join Tim Flock and Speedy Thompson as part of the Kiekhaefer stable. The powerful organization—it's been compared to Rick Hendrick Motorsports of the '80s and '90s—won 30 of the year's 56 races, including 21 of the first 25 and 16 straight during the middle of the season.

But all was not well. Feeling poorly and blaming it on unrelenting pressure to excel, Flock quit in April and moved into Mercurys owned by Bill Stroppe. He was replaced on Kiekhaefer's team by Herb Thomas, who soon tired of his owner's stern and demanding manner. He quit in July and began preparing and driving for himself, and it looked briefly like he might upstage his former boss by beating Baker for the Grand National championship.

Thomas led by 246 points entering a late-season race in Shelby, North Carolina, an "add-on" date that Kiekhaefer convinced NASCAR to schedule. Thomas' season and title hopes ended when he was critically injured in a controversial incident with Thompson. Even though Baker won the title by 586 points, he and Kiekhaefer were vilified by fans who thought Thompson wrecked Thomas to ensure that Baker won the championship. There's nothing to indicate that was the case at all, but the criticism stung Kiekhaefer deeply. He closed down his NASCAR stable and left stock car racing as quickly as he had come.

GRAND NATIONAL STANDINGS

	DRIVER	STARTS	WINS	POINTS	MONEY
1.	Buck Baker	48	14	9,252	34,077
2.	Speedy Thompson	42	8	8,788	27,169
3.	Herb Thomas	48	5	8,710	19,352
4.	Lee Petty	47	2	8,324	15,338

5.	Jim Paschal	42	1	7,878	17,204	28.	Al Watkins	14	0	1,710	1,185
6.	Billy Myers	42	2	6,976	15,830	29.	Chuck Meekins	7	0	1,656	2,815
7.	Fireball Roberts	33	5	5,794	14,742	30.	Harvey Henderson	18	0	1,634	1,310
8.	Ralph Moody	35	4	5,528	15,493	31.	Bill Champion	14	0	1,632	1,570
9.	Tim Flock	4	1	5,062	15,769	32.	Eddie Pagan	8	1	1,598	4,095
10.	Marvin Panch	20	1	4,680	11,520	33.	Pat Kirkwood	3	0	1,540	2,025
11.	Rex White	24	0	4,642	5,334	34.	Clyde Palmer	11	0	1,516	2,755
12.	Johnny Allen	32	0	4,024	4,559	35.	John Kieper	8	1	1,506	3,250
13.	Paul Goldsmith	9	1	3,788	8,569	36.	Johnny Dodson	11	0	1,488	1,450
14.	Gwyn Staley	22	0	3,550	5,159	37.	Bill Blair	9	0	1,284	1,005
15.	Joe Eubanks	26	0	3,284	5,584	38.	Junior Johnson	13	0	1,272	1,350
16.	Joe Weatherly	17	0	3,084	5,251	39.	Ed Cole	12	0	1,200	950
17.	Bill Amick	13	0	3,048	5,381	40.	Brownie King	15	0	1,140	925
18.	Jim Reed	11	0	2,890	5,077	41.	Scotty Cain	4	0	1,124	1,235
19.	Tiny Lund	0	0	2,754	2,811	42.	Allen Adkins	6	0	1,104	1,465
20.	Curtis Turner	13	1	2,580	14,541	43.	Bobby Keck	15	0	1,076	950
21.	Jack Smith	15	1	2,320	3,825	44.	Gordon Haines	7	0	1,066	1,500
22.	Billy Carden	23	0	2,108	2,175	45.	Bob Keefe	7	0	1,066	1,040
23.	Lloyd Dane	10	2	2,106	4,370	46.	Dick Beaty	15	0	1,036	910
24.	Frank Mundy	9	0	1,836	3,585	47.	Jim Blomgren	6	0	992	475
25.	Bobby Johns	9	0	1,832	1,450	48.	Ed Negre	5	0	952	1,255
26.	Blackie Pitt	27	0	1,760	1,545	49.	Jimmy Massey	7	0	950	1,545
27.	Harold Hardesty	9	0	1,724	2,380	50.	Fonty Flock	7	1	946	1,780

The beach at Daytona was a popular place in the 1950s.

1957

AT A GLANCE:

Grand National Champion: Buck Baker

Notable Events: The Automobile Manufacturers Association decided early in 1957 that its members should distance themselves from motorsports. After formerly providing financial and administrative support for Ford, GM and Chrysler teams, the factories got skittish and left racing after a car went in the stands at Martinsville, Virginia, and hurt five spectators, including a small boy.

Buck Baker won his second consecutive Grand National title, a title that wasn't the least bit tainted. Not that his 1956 championship was, but some fans and drivers recalled that Speedy Thompson, Baker's teammate, had caused the wreck that had sidelined runner-up Herb Thomas the year before. This time, preparing and driving self-owned Chevrolets, Baker raced in 40 of the series' 53 races and won 10 of them. He backed that with 28 other top-10 finishes and won the championship by 760 points. Second-ranked Marvin Panch won 6 of 42 races and third-ranked Thompson won twice in 38 starts.

The schedule featured a diverse lineup of venues. There were 14 paved-track races, the most in Grand National history. Darlington had always been paved, but it seemed that more dirt tracks were converting to asphalt. The popular half-milers at Martinsville, North Wilkesboro, and Weaverville, North Carolina, were among the first to make the switch. The '57 schedule also featured NASCAR's first trip to the famous Watkins Glen, New York, road course. Additional road courses included a 2-mile paved road course at Willow Springs, California, a 1.6-mile road course at Titusville, Florida, and a 1-mile paved track at Raleigh, North Carolina.

GRAND NATIONAL STANDINGS

	DRIVER	STARTS	WINS	POINTS	MONEY
1.	Buck Baker	40	10	10,716	30,764
2.	Marvin Panch	42	6	9,956	24,307
3.	Speedy Thompson	38	2	8,560	26,841
4.	Lee Petty	41	4	8,528	18,326
5.	Jack Smith	39	4	8,464	14,562
6.	Fireball Roberts	42	8	8,268	19,829
7.	Johnny Allen	42	0	7,068	9,815
8.	L. D. Austin	40	0	6,532	6,485
9.	Brownie King	36	0	5,740	5,589
10.	Jim Paschal	35	0	5,124	7,079
11.	Tiny Lund	32	0	4,848	6,424
12.	Billy Myers	28	0	4,640	6,566
13.	Paul Goldsmith	25	4	4,188	12,734
14.	Cotton Owens	17	1	4,032	12,784
15.	Eddie Pagan	15	3	3,612	7,274
16.	Bill Amick	21	1	3,512	8,073
17.	Dick Beaty	20	0	3,220	3,648
18.	Jim Reed	6	0	2,836	3,408
19.	Clarence DeZalia	25	0	2,828	3,308
20.	Frankie Schneider	10	0	2,516	4,588
21.	Rex White	9	0	2,508	3,870
22.	Curtis Turner	10	0	2,356	4,830
23.	George Green	17	0	2,216	2,240
24.	Whitey Norman	13	0	1,920	3,390
25.	Lloyd Dane	10	1	1,852	4,985
26.	Jimmie Lewallen	7	0	1,796	1,030
27.	Johnny Mackinson	5	0	1,764	1,330
28.	Bobby Keck	16	0	1,740	1,525
29.	Billy Carden	3	0	1,600	1,675
30.	Bill Benson	11	0	1,592	1,090
31.	Dick Getty	10	0	1,504	1,890
32.	Scotty Cain	11	0	1,492	1,165
33.	Roy Tyner	10	0	1,468	1,020
34.	T. A. Toomes	11	0	1,404	1,450
35.	Possum Jones	6	0	1,360	2,375
36.	Huck Spaulding	8	0	1,240	1,120
37.	Ralph Earnhardt	9	0	1,180	1,150
38.	George Seeger	6	0	1,108	2,740
39.	Ken Rush	16	0	1,104	2,045
40.	Peck Peckham	10	0	1,064	950
41.	Bill Champion	10	0	956	1,125
42.	Chuck Hansen	7	0	900	510
43.	Danny Graves	7	1	880	1,895
44.	Marvin Porter	6	1	872	1,770
45.	Eddie Skinner	4	0	848	605
46.	Jimmy Thompson	2	0	816	325
47.	Parnelli Jones	10	1	812	1,625
48.	Bobby Johns	1	0	800	225
49.	Don Porter	6	0	784	810
50.	Joe Weatherly	14	0	776	5,240

1958

AT A GLANCE:

Grand National Champion: Lee Petty

Notable Events: On July 19, at the .333-mile paved oval at Exposition Speedway in Toronto, the 21-year-old son of a two-time NASCAR champion made his debut. Richard Petty started seventh, crashed near the halfway point and finished 17th in the 19-car field. Needless to say, it was not a sign of things to come for the all-time winningest driver in NASCAR history.

You have to wonder how the final standings would have looked if Junior Johnson or Fireball Roberts had run the full 51-race schedule. Johnson won 6 races in 27 starts and finished eighth in points. Roberts was even more efficient: 6 wins in 10 starts, but that put him no better than a distant 11th in points. That compared to 1958 champion

Lee Petty, who won seven of 50 races and had 37 other top-10 finishes. He beat Buck Baker (3 victories in 44 starts, with 32 other top-10s) by 644 points. Speedy Thompson, who won 4 races in 36 starts, was third in points, well behind the front two. As for that young Petty kid: he ran nine races, had one top-10 finish, was 36th in points, and earned $760.

GRAND NATIONAL STANDINGS

	DRIVER	STARTS	WINS	POINTS	MONEY
1.	Lee Petty	50	7	12,232	26,565
2.	Buck Baker	44	3	11,588	25,841
3.	Speedy Thompson	37	4	8,792	17,295
4.	Shorty Rollins	29	1	8,124	13,399
5.	Jack Smith	39	2	7,666	12,634
6.	L. D. Austin	46	0	6,972	6,246
7.	Rex White	22	2	6,552	12,233
8.	Junior Johnson	27	6	6,380	13,809
9.	Eddie Pagan	27	0	4,910	7,472
10.	Jim Reed	17	4	4,762	9,644
11.	Fireball Roberts	10	6	4,420	32,219
12.	Bobby Keck	30	0	4,240	3,459
13.	Herman Beam	20	0	4,224	2,599
14.	Herb Estes	11	0	4,048	2,509
15.	Clarence DeZalia	27	0	3,448	3,004
16.	Doug Cox	14	0	3,736	3,404
17.	Cotton Owens	29	1	3,716	6,579
18.	Marvin Panch	11	0	3,424	4,114
19.	Billy Rafter	19	0	2,916	2,799
20.	Curtis Turner	17	3	2,856	10,029
21.	Lloyd Dane	5	0	2,844	2,490
22.	Bob Duell	7	0	2,740	2,415
23.	Jimmy Thompson	8	0	2,540	3,275
24.	Fred Harb	25	0	2,484	3,320
25.	Tiny Lund	22	0	2,436	3,155
26.	Bill Poor	24	0	2,292	3,115
27.	Gene White	9	0	2,040	1,400
28.	Joe Weatherly	15	1	2,032	6,330
29.	Johnny Mackison	11	0	1,680	1,255
30.	Jim Parsley	10	0	1,488	1,135
31.	Al White	9	0	1,464	920
32.	Jimmy Massey	9	0	1,300	1,625
33.	Parnelli Jones	3	1	1,140	1,010
34.	Joe Eubanks	7	1	1,120	2,070
35.	Brownie King	24	0	1,116	3,045
36.	G. C. Spencer	1	0	1,040	315
37.	Richard Petty	9	0	1,016	760
38.	Billy Carden	13	0	1,012	815
39.	Elmo Langley	9	0	980	1,090
40.	Buzz Woodward	9	0	964	1,195
41.	Possum Jones	11	0	960	1,790
42.	Jim Paschal	6	1	928	1,670
43.	Chuck Hansen	7	0	916	580
44.	Eddie Gray	3	1	910	3,375
45.	Peck Peckham	11	0	868	835
46.	Lennie Page	8	0	836	760
47.	Bob Keefe	2	0	782	925
48.	R. L. Combs	9	0	760	805
49.	Volney Shultze	7	0	680	490
50.	Dean Layfield	7	0	664	370

3

THE RISE OF THE SUPERSPEEDWAY:
THE 1960s AND BEYOND

Big-time stock car racing was slow to find its balance and stand with confidence. Like any infant born into a new and hostile culture, racing didn't always know quite how to control and coordinate its various parts and pieces. Sometimes they got in the way of each other and all hell broke loose. At other times, they worked in perfect harmony, as precisely as if an unseen hand from above was pulling strings at just the right moments.

There was no shortage of men and women willing to climb into almost any manner of souped-up family sedan and make left-hand turns around almost any kind of facility. Some were simply foolish thrill-seekers, veterans from World War II or Korea, bored with the slow pace and discouraged by the hard times of the South. Their beloved homeland had embraced this new-fangled stock car racing to the virtual exclusion of everything except college football and (some would argue) hunting and fishing.

But college football in the South during the early '50s only seemed to be Everyman's game. Even though Everyman hadn't actually gone to college and earned the right to live and die with his school's Saturday afternoon fortunes, he still loved

the sport with a passion. However, Everyman wasn't terribly interested in going to college, and he probably didn't have the money if he'd been so inclined. So while it was perfectly acceptable to cheer for Carolina or Georgia Tech or whoever Bear Bryant was coaching at the time, it was understood that college football truly belonged only to those fortunate enough to have attended. In this case, Everyman was little more than a red-headed stepchild at the family reunion.

As for hunting and fishing—well hell's bells, man. That was as much a part of a Southerners' birthright as breathing, making moonshine, and raising Cain on Saturday nights. To this day, almost every major NASCAR driver—especially those born and reared in the South—is a sportsman. Dale Earnhardt often spends hours in splendid solitude atop a deer stand. The late Neil Bonnett and Davey Allison often hunted with Earnhardt, sometimes for deer and at other times for bighorn sheep and elk in the Rockies. Team owner Richard Childress thinks nothing of jetting to Alaska to hunt grizzlies and Wally Dallenbach is an expert big-game hunter.

You must realize that the South of the '50s had no major-league sports franchises to bond the region's loyalties. The Braves didn't move from Milwaukee to Atlanta until 1966, the same year the NFL's Falcons arrived in town. The Atlanta Hawks became the South's first pro basketball team when it moved from St. Louis in 1968. So from the time NASCAR was created in 1948 until Atlanta got the Braves and Falcons, the South's only professional sports were stock car racing and minor-league baseball.

GOD, COUNTRY, AND NASCAR

Bill France saw this, and was quick to act. He knew full well that Southerners loved their cars only somewhat less than they loved their God, their country, and their family. And France knew that given the opportunity— an opportunity he planned to offer Everyman—almost every red-blooded Southerner would try racing at least once before he thought better of it. After all, that car he was taking to the local dirt track was the same street-legal, licensed and registered car he drove to work, to the woods for hunting, and to church on Sunday.

Even so, finding people to race proved no real problem. Likewise, finding them a time and a place to race was no problem, either. Almost every county in every Southern state had a public fairgrounds, and most of them had a rough and rutted dirt oval somewhere on the property. First used during the '30s and '40s when minor-league horse racing was popular, the tracks were tidied up by promoters who took over the ovals and staged stock car races in almost every town south of Washington. Name an area and it had a NASCAR race in the '50s and early '60s.

Southeastern Virginia had dirt tracks in Hampton, Newport News, Norfolk, and Virginia Beach. There were three tracks in the Richmond area, another near Washington, and dirt tracks in Roanoke, South Boston, Danville, and Martinsville.

There were more than two dozen tracks in the Carolinas alone. They stretched from Moyock, North Carolina, and Myrtle Beach, South Carolina, on the Atlantic Coast to Asheville-Weaverville, North Carolina, and Greenville-Pickens, South Carolina, near the Appalachian Mountains. There

A NEAR RIOT

Race fans are among sport's most intense. Perhaps not as wildly raucous as soccer fans (football in most of the world), but pretty intense just the same. You need only look at Aug. 13, 1961 at Weaverville, North Carolina, to see that for yourself.

The Western Carolina 500 at the half-mile paved Asheville-Weaverville Speedway was stopped shortly after halfway because its asphalt surface was tearing up. Drivers were told during a red-flag stop at lap 208 that the 500 would go only 50 more laps since conditions were awful. When it was stopped for good, Junior Johnson was ahead of Joe Weatherly, Rex White, Ned Jarrett, and Emanuel Zervakis.

While officials apparently did the right thing, a few of the fans didn't see it like that. Some of the more unruly among them blocked the team in the pits and kept them there for several hours. After a brief scuffle between a would-be peacemaker and a crowd leader, the drivers and crews finally were allowed to leave.

And where were the NASCAR officials all this time? Perhaps wisely, they'd slipped off their black-and-white shirts, melted into the crowd and quietly left before anyone in the crowd figured out what had happened.

were tracks in Concord, Fayetteville, Raleigh, Greensboro, North Wilkesboro, Charlotte, Gastonia, Spring Lake, Wilson, Hillsborough, Jacksonville, Shelby, Winston-Salem, High Point, and Randleman in North Carolina.

South Carolina tried, but it couldn't keep up with its northern neighbor. It "only" had tracks at Darlington, Newberry, Columbia, Spartanburg, Lancaster, Sumter, and Hartsville. There were tracks in Augusta, Macon, Savannah, and Atlanta in Georgia, and Birmingham, Huntsville, and Montgomery in Alabama. Among the more hospitable tracks in Tennessee: Nashville, Bristol, Newport, and Chattanooga. And Florida had Jacksonville, West Palm Beach, Pensacola, Titusville, and the famous 4.1-mile beach/highway course at Daytona Beach.

A SHOWPLACE IS BORN

Of all those tracks—and there may have been 100 different venues with NASCAR races in the '50s and early '60s—the new sanctioning body didn't have a showplace facility. Darlington was the longest, fastest, and most famous of NASCAR's paved tracks, but it was still in yesterday at a time when tomorrow was lurking around the next corner.

No sooner was the first Southern 500 in the books than NASCAR president Bill France began looking around for a place to build a superspeedway the likes of which the South had never seen. Not surprisingly, he looked first, last, and all times in between at his adopted hometown of Daytona Beach.

As history shows, Bill France was a man of uncommon foresight. He could see clearly what others could barely imagine. And while so many others involved in stock car racing were mired in day-to-day problem-solving, he had already moved beyond them and turned his attention to what racing would resemble decades down the road. What he saw was truly amazing.

Despite a legendary persistence and powers of persuasion, it took France more than seven years to cobble together the people, the finances, and the municipal support for the Daytona International Speedway. It had become evident in the early '50s that Daytona Beach's famous highway/beach course just south of town had seen its best days.

Nobody had to remind him to do something quickly or the area finally would lose racing as a tourist and economic attraction once and for all. He and Charlie Reese had kept stock car racing alive in the area in the '30s and early '40s, but now France risked losing what he had fought so hard to gain. He was not accustomed to losing, and that confidence would prove well-founded in several years.

He first approached city officials in 1953 with talk of building a 2.5-mile, high-banked, D-shaped, paved speedway on the west side of the Halifax River. Without such a permanent facility with 10,000 seats, he warned officials, it was doubtful the lucrative mid-winter Speed Week program would

return to the beach in 1954. When nothing came of that meeting, France promoted his inaugural "final" highway/beach races in February of 1954.

No progress meant another threat and another "final" highway/beach race in 1955. Likewise, France said the 1956 program would be his last, then repeated that dire prediction in 1957. But like the boy who cried wolf, he knew full well that someday the "last highway/beach race" would indeed be just that. As optimistic as he was, he simply couldn't continue promoting stock car races along an increasingly-busy public highway and an increasingly-crowded beach.

Frustrated and ready to act—even if it meant going out on a limb—France approached the Daytona Beach Racing and Recreation Facilities Authority in the fall of 1957. He presented a check for $27,000 from the new Daytona Beach International Speedway Corporation. That down payment got his new publicly-traded corporation a 50-year lease on 450 acres of gooey bottom land near the local airport.

He broke ground in November of 1957 and promised that by February of 1959 the world would see stock car racing like it had never seen before. Finally, the man who would cry wolf was right. The 1958 Speed Week program was, indeed, the final major race on the highway/beach course that had served stock car racing so well for so long.

It's almost impossible to underestimate the impact of Daytona International Speedway (DIS) on the growth of American stock car racing. Finally, at the start of the sport's 11th year, it had that era's version of a glittering, glamorous, showplace facility. But truth be told, the new track was only marginally less Spartan than any number of older tracks. But its length and massive turns more than made up for what it lacked in creature comforts. It had an outdoor press box and concession stands, and a thoroughly inadequate steel railing atop its high-banked turns.

It would be years before DIS reached the point where it might rightfully call itself (as it now does) "The World Center of Racing." But after a steady diet of half-mile and shorter dirt tracks—with only

BREAKING THE BARRIERS

This was the early 1960s in the Old South, and most of its citizens weren't ready for a man of color to succeed in any sport generally understood to be the white man's game. Which, of course, included stock car racing.

So imagine the uproar when a 43-year-old Virginia driver named Wendell Scott argued quietly yet forcefully that he had won a 100-mile race at the half-mile Jacksonville (Florida) Speedway Park in December of 1963.

Scott was a black man, a former moonshine runner who'd been recruited into legalized racing by the promoter of a short dirt track near his hometown of Danville, Virginia. It was partly out of curiosity and partly out of sympathy for his plight that fans came to watch him race. What they didn't realize was that beneath his quiet and respectful demeanor there beat a fiercely competitive heart and a prideful soul determined to reflect well on his race and his loving and supportive family.

So it should have come as no surprise when he refused to accept the scoring that had him third behind Buck Baker and apparent runner-up Jack Smith in the dirt-track race at Jacksonville. After starting 15th in his self-owned and underfinanced Chevrolet, Scott had come toward the front and clearly passed Baker and Smith several times.

It took hours for race officials to unscrambled the botched scoring. When all was said and done, Scott was rightfully credited with taking the lead with 25 laps remaining, then actually running two laps more than were needed. Baker was scored second, Smith third, Ed Livingston fourth, and Richard Petty fifth.

It's been said that race officials had hoped Scott would take his third-place that afternoon and be happy with it. They didn't want to think of what might happen if fans suddenly realized they were watching a black man win a stock car race. After all, the beauty queen waiting to greet and kiss the winner was white, and that posed a very obvious problem that neither NASCAR nor speedway operators wanted to face. So they flagged Baker and Smith 1-2 and hoped for the best. It took a four-hour review of the scoring before Scott was told he was the winner—a fact he knew all along.

a handful of paved tracks on the schedule—Daytona International Speedway literally took away the breath of the men and women who tried to tame it.

Charles Moneypenny, the track's designer, drew it at 2.5 miles, identical to the Indianapolis Motor Speedway. He banked the east and west turns an unprecedented 31 degrees, far more than the more-famous speedway in Indianapolis. The frontstretch apex was bowed towards the stands, giving fans in the best seats an unobstructed view of cars coming toward them and going away. The 4,000-foot backstretch was almost flat and the transitions from the flat to the banking was almost geometrically perfect.

Speeds for race-ready Grand National cars approached 145 mph when the track opened for the February, 1959 Speed Week program. By comparison, the fastest qualifier for the previous year's Southern 500 at Darlington Raceway had ran a mere 118 mph. Bob Welborn won the speedway's first race, a 100-mile Grand National qualifier. Shorty Rollins won 100-mile race for Convertibles, Banjo Matthews a 200-mile race for Modified/Sportsman cars, and Jack Smith won the 25-mile Grand National consolation race.

A RACE FOR THE AGES

The inaugural Daytona 500 was one for the ages. It was run without a caution, and Lee Petty's margin of victory over Johnny Beauchamp was a mere two feet. We know that because NASCAR (in the person of France himself) spent the better part of three days trying to figure out whether Petty had beaten Beauchamp or vice versa. The lapped car of Joe Weatherly was side-by-side with them under the flag, thus muddling the debate even more.

Seconds after the three cars took the checkered flag, Beauchamp was declared the winner. He went to Victory Lane to enjoy the sweet benefits of winning. He posed with Miss Daytona 500, had his picture taken with France and the huge winner's trophy, and generally had himself a high time. But Petty begged to differ with France's call, and his impassioned appeal was supported by reporters who'd seen the photo-finish from directly above the start/finish line. When they agreed that Petty had won by perhaps a yard, France had little choice but to reconsider.

Less than an hour after the race, he declared the result unofficial pending further review. The next morning, even as news accounts painted glowing pictures of the track and the race itself, France was appealing to the media and public to come forward with any solid evidence that clearly showed either Petty or Beauchamp the undisputed winner. As stills and motion picture footage arrived, he hunkered down and studied them for three days.

There was no doubt about it, his earlier call was wrong. Petty finally got his rightfully-won trophy and place in NASCAR history, and the speedway that would showcase big-time stock car racing and escort it into the future finally was up and running.

BEYOND DAYTONA

Consider this startling fact about speedways that ran major NASCAR races throughout the '50s: Only four of them—Martinsville Speedway, Darlington Raceway, Richmond International Raceway, and Daytona International Speedway— still have Winston Cup dates. The other 96 or so tracks that once hosted major events were left behind when NASCAR racing began moving into the '60s and '70s, and beyond.

The popular and picturesque half-mile Martinsville Speedway was a dirt track when it staged its first race in 1949. It was favored with races largely because France was a long-time friend and business partner of speedway builder and owner Clay Earles. They promoted 150- and 200-lap

races until 1956, when Earles gambled—successfully, as it turned out—on a 500-lapper.

The track has run 500s ever since, one in the spring, the other in the fall. With 60,000 seats and 43 cars leaning on each other for 500 laps, little wonder Martinsville tickets are among the tour's most cherished. If you go, heed these words of advice: feed the ducks at your own risk. You might end up with friends for life.

Darlington Raceway has been a NASCAR staple since its Labor Day weekend opening in 1950. It began with the Southern 500, then added a 300-miler in the spring of 1957. That event eventually grew to 400 miles and to 500 before dropping back to its current 400.

In 1997, in the name of corporate progress, the 1.366-mile track underwent a major face lift. Its start/finish line was moved to the opposite side of the track, meaning the turns would be renumbered. The change came to accommodate expansion along the southern straightaway that wasn't possible along the north straight. In this case, at least, tradition be damned.

The half-mile (when it was built) State Fairgrounds Raceway in Richmond, Virginia, opened in 1958 with 200- and 250-lap races. The 200 went to 250 laps and the 250 went to 300 laps the very next year. They both went to 500 laps in 1970, then back to 400 laps in 1976.

The quaint little facility was expanded from a half-mile to three-quarter mile between the spring and fall of 1988. Capacity has grown from 35,000 seats to almost 100,000 in less than 10 years, and both 1998 races are scheduled for prime-time TV on Saturday nights. It's been rumored that track founder Paul Sawyer (he's still active at age 80) plans to have his remains buried in the outside retaining wall beneath the flagstand. After 50 years on the job, what's another lifetime?

Daytona International Speedway has been thriving since that historic and memorable 500-mile opener in February of 1959. It hosted a 250-mile race in July of that year, a mid-summer race that reached its current 400-mile distance in 1963.

This summer's 400-miler will run at night, the first time any 2.5-mile speedway in the world has dared run a major full-distance race after dark. The hotel/motel people are delighted at the extra night's lodging they'll squeeze out of the fans. It doesn't matter to the drivers: they can jet home at midnight as easily as they used to at four in the afternoon.

Eight other tracks that helped shape and nurture stock car racing were built or came into prominence in the '60s:

The Atlanta International Raceway (renamed Atlanta Motor Speedway when it changed hands in the '90s) and the Charlotte Motor Speedway opened for business in 1960. Each was approximately 1.5 miles long, each suffered through several years of financial and managerial woes, and each is now owned by Bruton Smith and his ever-expanding Speedway Motorsports Inc.

Atlanta opened with 300- and 500-mile Grand National races, bumped its "secondary race" to 400 miles in 1961, then made it a 500-miler in 1967. Charlotte opened with 400- and 600-mile races and lengthened its fall race to 500 miles in 1966. Few will argue that Charlotte's powerful management team of Smith and promoter Humpy Wheeler have set the standard by which all other tracks are measured.

For example, it was the first superspeedway with lights, the first with elaborate and costly pre- and post-race entertainment, the first with corporate and VIP suites, the first with an on-site restaurant and night club, and the first with high-rise condominiums overlooking the track. Charlotte initiated (and still hosts) a pre-season media tour that visits the NASCAR team garages and meets with drivers each January. It is, in every sense of the word, the Madison Square Garden, Yankee Stadium, Rose Bowl, and Radio City Music Hall of stock car racing.

One of NASCAR's most popular short tracks began running major events in 1961. The track at Bristol, Tennessee, was born as Bristol Speedway, was renamed Bristol International Raceway in the '70s, then renamed Bristol Motor Speedway when Smith took over in the early '90s. What began as a modest, low-banked, half-mile with a few seats is now a spectacular, high-banked, half-mile with lights, dozens of VIP and corporate suites, 125,000 seats, and near-capacity crowds for its 500-lap races.

The 1-mile North Carolina Motor Speedway was built in 1965. Near the golfing hotbed of Pinehurst and Southern Pines in the Sandhills, it has grown slower than other NASCAR superspeedways. Its facilities are modest when compared to Charlotte (truth be told, most facilities are), but the recent purchase by Roger Penske will almost certainly change that.

Three more superspeedways came aboard in 1969. The 2-mile Michigan International Speedway (the "International" was dropped in 1996) opened with a 500-miler in June and a 600-miler in August of that year. The 1-mile Dover (Delaware) Downs International Speedway opened with a 300-mile race in July, then the 2.66-mile Alabama International Motor Speedway (mercifully shortened several years ago to Talladega Superspeedway) opened with a controversial 500-miler in September.

It didn't take long for NASCAR to "convince" Michigan to trim both of its races to their current 400-mile lengths. Dover ran 300s in '69 and '70, went to 500 miles with two races in 1971, and currently runs 400-mile events that attracts fans from throughout the Mid-Atlantic area. Talladega's opener was marred by a boycott by drivers who claimed the track was too fast for the tires coming from Firestone and Goodyear. It got a second 500-mile date the next year and has become known as NASCAR's fastest and most competitive track.

UNBELIEVABLE GROWTH

The growth NASCAR demonstrated in the '60s and the increase in the number of superspeedways was a sign of things to come. NASCAR's expansion continued almost unchecked into the '70s and '80s. Inroads into the lucrative Northeastern market didn't stop with Dover Downs. In 1974, NASCAR gave a 500-mile Winston Cup race to the new, 2.5-mile, triangular-shaped track near Mt. Pocono, Pa. The facility, built atop a spinach field by a Philadelphia dentist, got one race annually until 1982, when it got a second 500-miler. Despite its somewhat-remote locale and the area's inadequate road system, Pocono continues to draw huge crowds for its June and July events.

Three more tracks were added in the '80s. Significantly, their geographic diversity spoke volumes about the ever-growing popularity of stock car racing. After a 31-year hiatus, NASCAR returned to the famed Watkins Glen (New York) road course in the summer of 1986. Two years later, in the fall of 1988, it sanctioned a Winston Cup race at the 1-mile track near Phoenix, Arizona. A year after that, in

June, it sent its Winston Cup cars to the Sears Point Raceway road course near Sonoma, California.

Some will argue that the '90s have been a period of crucial growth for several reasons. In July of 1993, when Winston Cup cars made their first trip to 1-mile New Hampshire International Speedway at Loudon, it opened the New England market to NASCAR's sponsors and advertisers. Dover Downs had unlocked the door 24 years earlier, Pocono had nudged it open in the '70s, and Watkins Glen had pushed it further open in the '80s. But NHIS—located less than 90 minutes from downtown Boston—brought major league racing to an area starved for the sport that had ignored it for so long.

Bobby Allison, spinning out at Martisnville Speedway here, reached the level of racing superstar in the 1960s and continued to race well into the 1980s.

And then came Indy, and mainstream American finally woke up to what was going on. Not since the first Daytona 500 in 1959 had any new event quickened the pulse of NASCAR race fans like the inaugural Brickyard 400 in August of 1994 at the Indianapolis Motor Speedway. It had been a long time fermenting, this multimillion dollar union of American's most popular series (of that, there was no doubt) and the world's most famous venue (likewise, none could deny that).

NASCAR president Bill France Jr. and speedway president Tony George made the long-rumored announcement in April of 1993, fully 16 months before the race. More than 250,000 tickets were sold within days after going on sale several weeks after the Indianapolis 500. In every way imaginable, the race became a happening. Much like Woodstock was much more than a concert, the first Brickyard 400 was much more than just another race.

NASCAR being invited to Indy was almost as significant as the first Daytona 500. To millions of Americans, the Indianapolis Motor Speedway is nothing less than a sacred shrine to the men and women of open-wheel, open-cockpit, Indy-car racing. Stock cars at Indy? Blasphemy! Dale Earnhardt and Rusty Wallace in the same garages as A.J. Foyt and the Unsers? Unforgivable! Bill France Jr. walking the same grounds as the late Tony Hulman? Infidel!

But it happened because Bill France Sr.'s son and Tony Hulman's grandson knew a nationally-televised race before a sold-out house (with ticket revenue in the bank for more than a year) would line everyone's pocket. For NASCAR, taking its premier series to Indy meant instant acceptance by many who looked down their nose at "taxi cab racing." Millions of Americans who cared only for the Indy 500 took note that stock (by God!) cars were going to the speedway. To them, it was like the patient understudy finally getting the call—and at Carnegie Hall, no less.

To the speedway, it meant another sellout crowd just two months after its Indy 500. Much of Middle America was already bonkers over stock car racing, a fact not lost on George and his

accountants. No other series could have brought nearly as much publicity— and bottom-line profits—as NASCAR's Winston Cup division.

Some have foolishly argued that the inaugural Brickyard 400 and the three subsequent ones have helped NASCAR bore into the national motorsports consciousness. Quite the contrary: stock car racing was doing just fine, thank you, before August of 1994. And, of course, the Indianapolis Motor Speedway was doing just fine, too. All of which leads to this conclusion: each was equally good for the other. Why does it have to be a competition? Let it go at that.

Neither of the venues that opened in 1997 had nearly the impact of Darlington, Daytona Beach, or Indianapolis. The 1.5-mile Texas Motor Speedway (another of Smith's projects) opened between Denton and Fort Worth in April. Not even persistent rain, massive traffic jams, or complaints about the speedway's design could dampen the enthusiasm of 200,000 fans, many of whom had never seen a race in person.

There were no such problems at Penske's latest showplace, the 2-mile California Speedway at Fontana. Some 50 miles east of Los Angeles, it was built as a virtual clone of his Michigan Speedway. Its importance is in reopening the lucrative (perhaps ultra-lucrative is more appropriate) Southern California market to NASCAR's corps of sponsors and advertisers.

The car-crazy and sports-minded L.A. basin hadn't hosted a Winston Cup race since the road course at Riverside finally went under in 1988. Ironically, the California Speedway is four miles from the site of the financially-plagued Ontario Motor Speedway, a 2.5-mile track that hosted Cup races from 1971 through 1980. A shopping center now stands atop the site where legends of both Indy-car and NASCAR used to race, before a huge debt service and creeping commercialism brought it down. Perhaps fittingly, though, the sounds from Penske's new track still carry over to the site of the old. And what sweet sounds they are.

4

159–1971: ON TRACK FOR GROWTH

1959

AT A GLANCE:

Grand National Champion: Lee Petty

Notable Events: One of racing's most unusual stats is that neither of the first two races at the new Daytona International Speedway was slowed by caution. The Daytona 500 was run on Feb. 22 and the Firecracker 250 on July 4, and no other track has ever had two caution-free races the same season.

Top Newcomers: Richard Petty was 0-for-21, but he had six top-5 finishes and eight top-10s. Rookie of the Year was the first of dozens of honors he'd receive throughout his NASCAR career.

Lee Petty dominated the season, winning 11 times in 42 starts (their were 44 races in total) and finishing among the top-10 two dozen other times. Among his biggest victories: the inaugural Daytona 500 in February and a 150-miler in June on a 1-mile track in Atlanta. That's where Richard, his 21-year-old son, was flagged the winner, only to have Lee protest the scoring. He was proved right when a careful recheck of the cards showed Lee winning and Richard finishing second. Lee Petty also won twice at North Wilkesboro, North Carolina, and Columbia, South Carolina, and once each at Martinsville, Virginia and numerous tracks in North Carolina, including Weaverville, Char-

lotte, Hickory, and Hillsborough. After being steady but unspectacular throughout the season, he won four of the last eight races, including two of the last three to clinch his third championship.

A dozen drivers won at least once, but nobody came close to Lee Petty's 11 victories. Rex White and Junior Johnson each won five, but didn't run nearly enough to contend for the title. One-time winner Cotton Owens finished second in points, 1,830 behind Lee Petty. Third-place Speedy Thompson and fourth-place Herman Beam also were winless, with fifth-place Buck Baker winning just once.

GRAND NATIONAL STANDINGS

	DRIVER	STARTS	WINS	POINTS	MONEY
1.	Lee Petty	42	11	11,792	49,220
2.	Cotton Owens	37	1	9,962	14,640
3.	Speedy Thompson	29	0	7,684	6,816
4.	Herman Beam	30	0	7,396	6,380
5.	Buck Baker	35	1	7,170	11,061
6.	Tom Pistone	22	2	7,050	12,725
7.	L. D. Austin	35	0	6,519	4,671
8.	Jack Smith	21	4	6,150	13,290
9.	Jim Reed	14	3	5,744	23,534
10.	Rex White	23	5	5,526	12,360
11.	Junior Johnson	28	5	4,864	9,675
12.	Shep Langdon	21	0	4,768	3,526
13.	G. C. Spencer	28	0	4,260	3,701
14.	Tommy Irwin	25	0	3,876	9,190
15.	Richard Petty	21	0	3,694	8,111
16.	Fireball Roberts	8	1	3,676	10,661

Lee Petty (left) won his third Grand National championship, and second in a row, the same season that Richard (right) was the top NASCAR newcomer.

17. Bob Welborn	29	3	3,588	6,491
18. Joe Weatherly	17	0	3,404	9,816
19. Bobby Jones	1	0	2,732	5,951
20. Tiny Lund	27	0	2,634	4,941
21. Bob Burdick	6	0	2,392	10,050
22. Larry Frank	15	0	2,256	5,993
23. Bobby Keck	18	0	2,186	1,270
24. Curtis Turner	10	2	2,088	3,845
25. Jim Paschal	6	0	1,792	2,980
26. Buddy Baker	12	0	1,692	1,705
27. Shorty Rollins	10	0	1,600	1,500
28. Elmo Langley	13	0	1,568	2,286
29. Jimmy Thompson	5	0	1,528	1,580
30. Brownie King	18	0	1,480	1,875
31. Tim Flock	2	0	1,464	850
32. Joe Eubanks	13	0	1,432	2,000
33. Roy Tyner	28	0	1,416	5,425
34. Charlie Cregar	3	0	1,408	550
35. Dick Freeman	3	0	1,352	475
36. Raul Cilloniz	2	0	1,272	550
37. Ned Jarrett	17	2	1,248	3,860
38. Dave White	5	0	1,228	660
39. Dick Joslin	4	0	1,224	485
40. Tommy Thompson	3	0	1,168	510
41. Harvey Hege	10	0	1,152	955
42. Eduardo Dibos	3	0	1,128	1,050
43. Bill Champion	1	0	1,120	500

44. Joe Caspolich	1	0	1,040	470
45. Jim Austin	5	0	1,016	440
46. Marvin Porter	7	0	984	1,940
47. Jim McGuirk	4	0	928	325
48. Harlan Richardson	10	0	924	1,120
49. Al White	5	0	872	575
50. Richard Riley	10	0	760	910

1960

AT A GLANCE:

Grand National Champion: Rex White

Notable Events: NASCAR was moving away from short dirt ovals and to more paved superspeedways that were faster, more dangerous, and attracted far more fans and sponsors. By 1960, paved superspeedways were all the rage in Daytona Beach, Darlington, Hanford, California, and near Charlotte and Atlanta. The 44-race schedule included a record 23 races on pavement.

Top Newcomers: Rookie of the Year David Pearson emerged from the Saturday night bullrings in the Carolinas to run 22 Grand National races in 1959 Chevrolets. He was runner-up at Sumter, South Carolina, fourth at Hickory,. N.C., and fifth in his hometown of Spartanburg, S.C. He also had four other finishes between sixth and 10th, and was 23rd in points.

Unlike the previous season when Lee Petty dominated, there was more parity in the first decade of the '60s. Rex White won his first and only championship with six victories, 25 top-5 finishes, and 35 top-10s in 40 starts. He won the title by 3,936 points over three-race winner Richard Petty, with one-time winner Bobby Johns third in points and two-time winner Buck Baker fourth. Even though Ned Jarrett and Lee Petty each won five times, they finished fifth and sixth because they weren't as consistent as the front four.

Richard Petty got the first three of his record-setting 200 victories: in February at Charlotte, in April at Martinsville, and in September at Hillsborough. Buddy Baker, another second-generation driver, was winless in 15 starts, and a Chicago native named Fred Lorenzen managed three top-5s and five top-10s in the first 10 starts of what would turn into a sparkling career.

GRAND NATIONAL STANDINGS

	DRIVER	STARTS	WINS	POINTS	MONEY
1.	Rex White	40	6	21,164	57,525
2.	Richard Petty	40	3	17,228	41,873
3.	Bobby Johns	19	1	14,964	46,115
4.	Buck Baker	37	2	14,674	38,399
5.	Ned Jarrett	40	5	14,660	25,438
6.	Lee Petty	39	5	14,510	31,283
7.	Junior Johnson	34	3	9,932	38,990
8.	Emanuel Zervakis	14	0	9,720	12,124
9.	Jim Paschal	10	0	8,968	15,096
10.	Banjo Matthews	12	0	8,458	15,617
11.	Johnny Beauchamp	11	1	8,306	17,374
12.	Herman Beam	26	0	7,776	5,916
13.	Joe Lee Johnson	22	1	7,352	34,519
14.	Jack Smith	13	3	6,944	24,721
15.	Fred Lorenzen	10	0	6,764	9,136
16.	Bob Welborn	15	0	6,732	6,194
17.	Jimmy Pardue	32	0	6,682	5,610
18.	Tom Pistone	21	0	6,572	6,714
19.	Johnny Allen	10	0	6,506	14,789
20.	Joe Weatherly	24	3	6,380	20,124
21.	Doug Yates	24	0	6,374	5,205
22.	L. D. Austin	27	0	6,180	4,785
23.	David Pearson	22	0	5,956	5,030
24.	Gerald Duke	11	0	5,950	5,930
25.	Speedy Thompson	9	2	5,658	18,035
26.	Marvin Panch	11	0	5,268	3,225
27.	Paul Lewis	22	0	5,212	3,535
28.	Curtis Crider	24	0	4,720	3,645
29.	Fireball Roberts	9	2	4,700	19,895
30.	Shorty Rollins	4	0	4,374	2,120
31.	Possum Jones	13	0	4,270	6,330
32.	Tiny Lund	8	0	4,124	2,440
33.	G. C. Spencer	26	0	3,986	3,910
34.	Larry Frank	10	0	3,634	2,440
35.	Herb Tillman	9	0	3,504	2,605
36.	Curtis Turner	9	0	3,300	3,220
37.	Bunkie Blackburn	20	0	3,252	3,400
38.	Buddy Baker	15	0	3,070	1,745
39.	Cotton Owens	14	1	3,050	14,065
40.	Charley Griffith	5	0	2,684	1,300
41.	Wilbur Rakestraw	12	0	2,676	2,695
42.	Jimmy Massey	6	0	2,662	3,310
43.	Jimmy Thompson	9	0	2,472	1,940
44.	Jim Reed	8	0	2,340	2,240
45.	Jim Cook	3	1	2,178	1,600
46.	Ernie Gahan	2	0	2,080	625
47.	Elmo Henderson	6	0	2,072	1,425
48.	Bob Burdick	2	0	1,970	850
49.	Roz Howard	3	0	1,810	1,490
50.	Bob Potter	3	0	1,800	640

1961

AT A GLANCE:

Grand National Champion: Ned Jarrett

Notable Events: If there was ever any doubt, Bill France proved for all time that he alone controlled Southern-style stock car racing. When the Teamsters Union tried to organize the drivers (and perhaps bring parimutuel betting to the sport) France suspended maverick drivers and threatened to disband the series. He quickly reinstated several drivers who'd leaned toward the union, but waited five years before reinstating Curtis Turner, the union's primary loyalist.

Top Newcomers: Woody Wilson had a short and not-to-sweet career. He ran only five races in 1961 (one top-10 finish) and was 41st in the standings, then never raced Grand National again.

Ned Jarrett proved that consistency and determination were as valuable as speed and handling. He started 46 of the season's 52 races, won only one (at Birmingham, Alabama, in June), but finished in the top-10 of 33 others. That was enough to win the championship and finish 830 points ahead of seven-time winner Rex White. Emanuel ("The Golden Greek") Zervakis won twice in 38 starts and stood third in points at year's end. Joe Weatherly (nine victories in 25 starts) and Fireball Roberts (two victories in 21 races) were fourth and fifth in points.

Most of the racing world's attention continued to be focused on the high-speed races at superspeedways. While short tracks and sprint races made up the bulk of the schedule, it was the long-distance events at Daytona Beach, Darlington, Charlotte, and Atlanta that caught the nation's fancy. Marvin Panch and David Pearson won on the 2½-mile track at Daytona Beach; Bob Burdick, Fred Lorenzen, and Pearson won on the 1½-mile track near Atlanta; Lorenzen and Nelson Stacy won at the venerable 1¼-mile track at Darlington; and Pearson and Joe Weatherly won on a 1½-mile track near Charlotte.

In one of NASCAR's most spectacularly ironic moments, Lee Petty and Johnny Beauchamp were injured during a Daytona 500 qualifying race when they sailed over the wall on Turn 4 and tumbled down the back side of the high-banked curve. The accident ended Petty's career at 54 victories and Beauchamp's at two. The men will be forever linked by the bizarre finish of the inaugural Daytona 500 in 1959. In that race, Beauchamp was flagged the winner in a photo finish, but Petty declared the winner four days later. Petty, by the way, says he never got the trophy. "He carried it with him to wherever he went when he died," Petty once said. "I won the race, but he got the trophy."

GRAND NATIONAL STANDINGS

	DRIVER	STARTS	WINS	POINTS	MONEY
1.	Ned Jarrett	46	1	27,272	41,056
2.	Rex White	47	7	26,442	56,395
3.	Emanuel Zervokis	38	2	22,312	27,281
4.	Joe Weatherly	25	9	17,894	47,079
5.	Fireball Roberts	22	2	17,600	50,267
6.	Junior Johnson	41	7	17,178	28,541
7.	Jack Smith	25	2	15,186	21,410
8.	Richard Petty	42	2	14,984	25,239
9.	Jim Paschal	23	2	13,922	18,100
10.	Buck Baker	42	1	13,746	13,697
11.	Jimmy Pardue	44	0	13,408	10,562
12.	Johnny Allen	22	0	13,114	13,127
13.	David Pearson	19	3	13,088	51,911
14.	Bob Welborn	14	0	12,570	13,487
15.	Herman Beam	41	0	11,382	9,392
16.	Nelson Stacy	15	1	10,436	27,608
17.	Ralph Earnhardt	8	0	10,182	11,473
18.	Marvin Panch	9	1	9,392	30,478
19.	Fred Lorenzen	15	3	9,316	30,395
20.	G. C. Spencer	31	0	9,128	7,363
21.	Curtis Crider	41	0	8,414	7,420
22.	Cotton Owens	17	4	8,032	11,890
23.	Tiny Lund	10	0	7,740	5,545
24.	Bobby Johns	14	0	7,590	5,010
25.	L. D. Austin	20	0	7,306	4,530
26.	Tommy Irwin	26	0	7,300	7,170
27.	Doug Yates	32	0	5,878	1,090
28.	Paul Lewis	21	0	5,712	4,095
29.	Bob Barron	31	0	5,412	3,725
30.	Elmo Langley	15	0	5,376	3,530
31.	Banjo Matthews	14	0	4,924	5,560
32.	Wendell Scott	23	0	4,726	3,240
33.	Jim Reed	8	0	4,705	3,350
34.	Fred Harb	27	0	4,526	3,460
35.	Darel Dieringer	7	0	4,416	3,150
36.	Bob Burdick	5	1	4,382	18,750
37.	Lee Reitzel	17	0	4,380	2,910
38.	Tom Pistone	4	0	3,766	2,050
39.	Buddy Baker	14	0	3,668	4,965
40.	Roscoe Thompson	6	0	3,602	2,535
41.	Woodie Wilson	5	0	3,580	2,625
42.	Larry Frank	8	0	3,162	2,380
43.	Larry Thomas	14	0	3,140	2,015
44.	Harry Leake	15	0	3,092	2,000
45.	Paul Goldsmith	2	0	2,930	6,050
46.	Joe Lee Johnson	9	0	2,700	2,615
47.	Bill Morgan	5	0	2,430	1,900
48.	Theodore Hunt	7	0	2,430	2,750
49.	Marvin Porter	8	0	2,326	2,070
50.	Joe Eubanks	2	0	2,320	1,475

1962

AT A GLANCE:

Grand National Champion: Joe Weatherly

Notable Events: After turning a blind eye to motorsports for several years, Ford Motor Co. and Chrysler Corp. began offering "engineering assistance" to selected NASCAR teams. Little wonder: Pontiacs (12) and Chevrolets (6) had won 18 of the season's first 20 races. Only Richard Petty's twice-winning Plymouth could break GM's stranglehold. Things changed, though: Fords and Plymouths won 15 of the final 33 races after their factories took a renewed interest in NASCAR.

Top Newcomers: Tom Cox was 0-for-42 and finished 18th in points, which may not look impressive. But he was among the top-10 in 20 of his starts, and only the six drivers who finished ahead of him in points (all of them race winners and established stars) had more top-10s.

Finally, a championship battle in which five drivers—not just one or two or even three—were big winners and front-runners. Joe Weatherly, an ex-motorcycle racer and self-styled "Clown Prince of Racing," won nine races in 52 starts and had 45 top-10 finishes. He won the title by 2,396 points over eight-time winner Richard Petty, with six-time winner Ned Jarrett ranked third. Five-time winner Jack Smith was fourth and eight-time winner Rex White was fifth. The season lasted for 53 races.

Combined, the top five drivers won 34 of the season's 53 races. The other 19 were spread among Jim Paschal, Fred Lorenzen, Fireball Roberts, Larry Frank, Jimmy Pardue, Junior Johnson, Nelson Stacy, Johnny Allen, Bobby Johns, and Cotton Owens. Among the newcomers destined to make a name for themselves: Cale Yarborough and LeeRoy Yarbrough. And while Ralph Earnhardt never won a Grand National race, he fathered a kid who later would win a few.

Roberts won both the 500- and 250-milers in Daytona Beach, Stacy won near Charlotte and at Darlington, Johnson won near Charlotte, and White and Lorenzen at the track near Atlanta. And Frank won the Southern 500 after an extensive scoring recheck moved him from fourth to first. Johnson had been scored the winner, but Lee Petty (claiming Richard had finished higher than sixth), asked for a recheck. Eight hours later, Frank was declared the winner over Johnson, Marvin Panch, David Pearson, and Richard Petty.

GRAND NATIONAL STANDINGS

	DRIVER	STARTS	WINS	POINTS	MONEY
1.	Joe Weatherly	52	9	30,836	70,743
2.	Richard Petty	52	8	28,440	60,764
3.	Ned Jarrett	52	6	25,336	43,444
4.	Jack Smith	51	5	22,870	34,748
5.	Rex White	37	8	19,424	36,246
6.	Jim Paschal	39	4	18,128	27,348
7.	Fred Lorenzen	19	2	17,554	46,100
8.	Fireball Roberts	19	3	16,380	66,152
9.	Marvin Panch	17	0	15,138	26,746
10.	David Pearson	12	0	14,404	19,032
11.	Herman Beam	51	0	13,650	12,571
12.	Curtis Crider	52	0	13,050	12,016
13.	Buck Baker	37	0	12,838	12,787
14.	Larry Frank	19	1	12,814	32,987
15.	Bob Welburn	25	0	12,368	10,347
16.	George Green	46	0	12,132	9,221
17.	Larry Thomas	37	0	11,946	9,486
18.	Thomas Cox	42	0	11,688	10,181
19.	Jimmy Pardue	29	1	11,414	12,066
20.	Junior Johnson	23	1	11,140	34,841
21.	Nelson Stacy	15	3	10,934	43,080
22.	Wendell Scott	41	0	9,906	7,133
23.	Buddy Baker	31	0	9,828	7,578
24.	G. C. Spencer	42	0	9,788	7,995
25.	Bunkie Blackburn	10	0	8,016	5,890
26.	Johnny Allen	20	1	7,602	7,230
27.	Emanuel Zervakis	11	0	6,406	4,545
28.	Bobby Johns	13	1	5,670	15,863
29.	Ralph Earnhardt	17	0	5,472	4,545
30.	Cotton Owens	16	0	4,984	5,905
31.	Banjo Matthews	5	0	4,956	11,375
32.	Sherman Thompson	12	0	4,896	3,580
33.	Darel Dieringer	14	0	4,548	4,880
34.	Tiny Lund	10	0	4,384	2,880
35.	Stick Elliott	21	0	4,254	3,928
36.	LeeRoy Yarbrough	12	0	4,240	3,285
37.	Tommy Irwin	20	0	3,980	3,305
38.	Ed Livingston	13	0	3,604	2,940
39.	Fred Harb	21	0	3,430	2,220
40.	Elmo Langley	6	0	2,556	1,795
41.	Bill Morton	5	0	2,522	1,350
42.	Speedy Thompson	3	0	2,522	1,400
43.	Jimmy Thompson	3	0	2,346	1,650
44.	Red Foote	4	0	2,274	1,600
45.	Ernie Gahan	3	0	2,092	725
46.	Billy Wade	4	0	2,008	1,350
47.	Jim Cushman	4	0	1,954	850
48.	Bill Wimble	2	0	1,944	675
49.	Troy Ruttman	1	0	1,890	1,750
50.	Cale Yarborough	8	0	1,884	2,725

AT A GLANCE:

Grand National Champion: Joe Weatherly

Notable Events: Given the biggest opportunity of his life, Tiny Lund didn't blow it. The Iowa native was tapped for the Wood brothers' Ford in the Daytona 500 after pulling Marvin Panch from his burning sports car 10 days before the race. Lund made one fewer pit stop, didn't change tires, and led the final eight laps to beat fellow Ford drivers Fred Lorenzen and Ned Jarrett.

Top Newcomers: Billy Wade came out of Texas to run 31 of the year's 55 races. And although he didn't win, he had five top-5 finishes and 15 top-10s.

Seldom has any champion done more with less than Joe Weatherly in 1964. He opened the season lacking a full-time ride, but managed to beg, borrow (and, indeed, steal?) enough to run 53 races. He did most of them in Bud Moore-owned Pontiacs and Mercurys, but also raced twice in Dodges and once each in a Plymouth and Chrysler. Weatherly won only three times (at Richmond, Darlington, and Hillsborough), but had 20 top-5 finishes and 35 top-10s. That paled beside Richard Petty's 14 victories, 30 top-5s and 34 top-10s, but Weatherly's top-fives and top-10s were better than Petty's top-fives and top-10s.

Without question, the real star of the season was Fred Lorenzen. Granted, he ran only 29 races and finished a distant third in points, but he won long-distance superspeedway races near Atlanta and Charlotte, as well as short-tracks races at Martinsville, Huntington, North Wilkesboro, and Weaverville. The so-called "Golden Boy" had 21 top-5s and top-10s, and won a then-record $122,587.28. It was the first time a stock car racer had reached six figures in a season, another sign that the sport was growing up.

In addition to Lorenzen wins in Atlanta and Charlotte and Lund's Daytona triumph, the other superspeedway victories went to Weatherly at Darlington, Johnson near Atlanta and Charlotte, and Roberts at Daytona Beach and Darlington. And Dan Gurney and Darel Dieringer won 500- and 400-mile races, respectively, at the Riverside, California, road course. Gurney's victory in January

wasn't an upset since he was driving a Ford prepared by the potent Holman-Moody team of Charlotte. In the November race, the United States Auto
Club threatened to suspend any of its drivers who
raced in the NASCAR event. After entering and
qualifying, the likelihood of missing the 1964 Indy
500 caused Gurney, A.J. Foyt, Parnelli Jones, and
Rodger Ward to withdraw.

GRAND NATIONAL STANDINGS

	DRIVER	STARTS	WINS	POINTS	MONEY
1.	Joe Weatherly	53	3	33,398	74,624
2.	Richard Petty	54	14	31,170	55,964
3.	Fred Lorenzen	29	6	29,684	122,588
4.	Ned Jarrett	53	8	27,214	45,844
5.	Fireball Roberts	20	4	22,642	73,060
6.	Jimmy Purdue	52	1	22,228	20,359
7.	Darel Dieringer	20	1	21,418	29,725
8.	David Pearson	41	0	21,156	24,986
9.	Rex White	25	0	20,976	27,241
10.	Tiny Lund	22	1	19,624	49,397
11.	Buck Baker	47	1	18,114	18,616
12.	Junior Johnson	33	7	17,720	67,351
13.	Marin Panch	12	1	17,156	39,102
14.	Nelson Stacy	12	0	14,794	18,266
15.	Wendell Scott	47	0	14,814	10,966
16.	Billy Wade	31	0	14,646	15,204
17.	Curtis Crider	49	0	13,996	11,644
18.	G. C. Spencer	31	0	13,744	13,514
19.	Jim Paschal	32	5	13,456	20,979
20.	Bobby Isaac	27	0	12,858	9,529
21.	Bobby Johns	12	0	12,652	15,915
22.	Larry Thomas	32	0	11,010	8,945
23.	Stick Elliott	28	0	9,582	6,235
24.	Jack Smith	29	0	8,218	8,645
25.	Cale Yarborough	18	0	8,062	5,550
26.	LeeRoy Yarbrough	14	0	7,872	6,680
27.	Herman Beam	25	0	7,742	5,255
28.	Larry Frank	11	0	7,582	5,450
29.	Larry Manning	23	0	6,952	5,405
30.	Ed Livingston	20	0	6,818	4,930
31.	Neil Castles	28	0	5,928	5,165
32.	Tommy Irwin	7	0	5,176	2,655
33.	Reb Wickersham	14	0	4,812	3,800
34.	Worth McMillion	15	0	4,614	3,145
35.	Bob James	10	0	4,316	3,375
36.	Roy Mayne	20	0	4,188	3,490
37.	Bob Cooper	9	0	4,164	3,115
38.	Jimmy Massey	15	0	4,016	2,870
39.	Elmo Langley	11	0	3,982	2,170
40.	Bob Welborn	11	0	3,484	4,830
41.	Fred Harb	16	0	3,286	2,720
42.	Dave MacDonald	2	0	2,944	5,330
43.	Major Melton	17	0	2,806	1,910
44.	Sal Tavella	3	0	2,570	1,300
45.	Ron Hornaday	2	0	2,520	1,600
46.	J. D. McDuffie	12	0	2,498	1,620
47.	Bob Perry	5	0	2,478	1,550
48.	Bunkie Blackburn	7	0	2,454	2,525
49.	Bill Foster	10	0	2,168	1,410
50.	Bud Harless	5	0	2,156	1,550

1964

Richard Petty got the first of his record seven
championships with a performance that was more

workman-like than spectacular. He was 9-of-61,
had 37 top-5s, 43 top-10s, and earned $114,771,
only the second NASCAR driver to top $100,000
in a season. Ned Jarrett had a better season than
Petty—15 victories, 40 top-5s, and 45 top-10s in
59 starts—but wasn't nearly as consistent. Third-
ranked David Pearson won eight races in 61 starts,
second-year driver Billy Wade was fourth in
points, and Pardue was fifth, even though he was
killed 50 races into the season.

The sport reeled when Weatherly was killed,
staggered when Roberts finally died of his injuries,
and went to its knees when Pardue died. Weatherly's head and left shoulder apparently came out
the driver's side window and hit the wall when he
crashed at Riverside. Roberts survived his fiery
crash at Charlotte in May, but died of pneumonia
and burn-related infections six weeks later. And
Pardue was helping develop new and safer tires
when a tire failure sent his Plymouth over the Turn
3 wall and tumbling outside the Charlotte speedway grounds at almost 150 miles per hour.

GRAND NATIONAL STANDINGS

	DRIVER	STARTS	WINS	POINTS	MONEY
1.	Richard Petty	61	9	40,252	114,772
2.	Ned Jarrett	59	15	34,950	71,925
3.	David Pearson	61	8	32,146	45,542
4.	Billy Wade	35	4	28,474	36,095
5.	Jimmy Pardue	50	0	26,570	41,598
6.	Curtis Crider	59	0	25,606	22,171
7.	Jim Paschal	22	1	25,450	60,116
8.	Larry Thomas	43	0	22,950	21,226
9.	Buck Baker	34	2	22,366	43,781
10.	Marvin Panch	31	3	21,480	34,836
11.	Darel Dieringer	27	1	19,972	20,685
12.	Wendell Scott	56	1	19,574	16,495
13.	Fred Lorenzen	16	8	18,098	73,860
14.	Junior Johnson	29	3	17,066	26,975

15. LeeRoy Yarbrough	34	2	16,172	16,630
16. Roy Tyner	46	0	13,922	11,488
17. Neil Castles	58	0	13,372	14,318
18. Bobby Isaac	19	1	13,252	26,733
19. Cale Yarborough	24	0	12,618	10,378
20. Tiny Lund	22	0	12,598	9,913
21. Doug Cooper	39	0	11,942	10,445
22. Paul Goldsmith	14	0	11,700	20,835
23. J. T. Putney	17	0	10,744	7,295
24. Larry Frank	12	0	10,314	7,830
25. Jack Anderson	31	0	10,040	8,510
26. G. C. Spencer	20	0	10,012	9,490
27. Fireball Roberts	9	1	9,900	28,345
28. Rex White	6	0	8,222	12,310
29. Dave MacDonald	5	0	7,650	9,195
30. Worth McMillion	18	0	7,586	4,700
31. Buddy Baker	33	0	7,314	8,460
32. Bunkie Blackburn	14	0	7,264	6,630
33. Biill McMahan	20	0	7,240	7,205
34. Buddy Arrington	27	0	6,364	4,715
35. Earl Balmer	10	0	6,170	5,795
36. Bob Derrington	18	0	5,896	2,755
37. Bobby Johns	12	0	5,436	5,700
38. E. J. Trivette	26	0	5,118	5,495
39. Doug Moore	24	0	4,970	5,175
40. Ken Spikes	6	0	4,934	3,100
41. Earl Brooks	28	0	4,820	3,925
42. Elmo Langley	14	0	4,400	3,905
43. Roy Mayne	14	0	4,278	4,705
44. Gene Hobby	18	0	4,054	2,795
45. Doug Yates	15	0	3,778	3,290
46. Ralph Earnhardt	11	0	3,720	3,290
47. Bob Cooper	13	0	3,602	3,360
48. Joe Weatherly	5	0	3,132	5,290
49. Sam McQuagg	5	0	2,928	1,700
50. Bobby Keck	10	0	2,754	2,850

1965

AT A GLANCE:

Grand National Champion: Ned Jarrett

Notable Events: Another new superspeedway sprang up in 1965, this one near Rockingham, North Carolina. Not only was its opening a big deal in its own right, but it featured the return of fan favorite Curtis Turner. He'd been suspended from NASCAR since 1961, when Bill France banned him for trying to help the Teamsters Union organize the drivers. Turner came back in style, winning the 500-mile race in a Ford.

Top Newcomers: Sam McQuagg, a Georgia native, ran only 15 of the year's 55 races, but he had a pair of top-5 finishes and five top-10s, winning just $10,555. He got his only career victory the following year in the Firecracker 400 at Daytona Beach.

Three Ford drivers dominated the 55-race season while many teams with Chrysler equipment boycotted NASCAR because of a rules dispute. When Bill France banned Mopar's powerful Hemi engine, Richard Petty and David Pearson (among others) sat out rather than lose to Ford- and Mercury-drivers Ned Jarrett, Fred Lorenzen, Junior Johnson, Marvin Panch, Dick Hutcherson, Cale Yarborough, and A.J.

Foyt. By the time Bill France adjusted the rules to bring Chrysler teams back to the sport, Ford Motor Co. had won 34 races and Jarrett had a near-insurmountable points leads. Petty won four of the last 21 races and Pearson two, good for 38th and 39th, respectively, in the final standings.

Jarrett won 13 races, had 42 top-5s and 45 top-10s, but still didn't reach $100,000 in winnings. Hutcherson won nine races, third-ranked Darel Dieringer one, fourth-ranked G.C. Spencer was winless, and fifth-ranked Panch won four times. Johnson also won 13, but ran only 36 races and finished a distant 12th in points. Cale Yarborough, destined to become one of the sport's all-time winners, got his first victory in late-June at Valdosta, Georgia

GRAND NATIONAL STANDINGS

DRIVER	STARTS	WINS	POINTS	MONEY
1. Ned Jarrett	54	13	38,824	93,625
2. Dick Hutcherson	52	9	35,790	57,851
3. Darel Dieringer	35	1	24,696	52,214
4. G. C. Spencer	47	0	24,314	29,775
5. Marvin Panch	20	4	22,798	64,027
6. Bob Derrington	51	0	21,394	20,120
7. J. T. Putney	40	0	20,928	22,329
8. Neil Cates	51	0	20,848	22,329
9. Buddy Baker	42	0	20,672	26,837
10. Cale Yarborough	46	1	20,192	26,587
11. Wendell Scott	52	0	19,902	18,639
12. Junior Johnson	36	13	18,486	60,216
13. Fred Lorenzen	17	4	18,448	80,615
14. Paul Lewis	24	0	18,118	13,247
15. E. J. Trivette	39	0	13,450	13,248
16. Larry Hess	10	0	13,148	9,260
17. Buck Baker	31	0	13,136	21,580
18. Jimmy Helms	30	0	12,996	12,050
19. Doug Cooper	30	0	12,920	12,380
20. Bobby Johns	13	0	12,842	24,930
21. Tiny Lund	30	1	12,820	11,750
22. Buddy Arrington	31	0	11,744	11,600
23. Earl Balmer	9	0	11,636	19,045
24. Sam McQuagg	14	0	11,460	10,555
25. Elmo Langley	34	0	10,982	10,555
26. Henley Gray	38	0	9,552	8,320
27. Roy Mayne	14	0	8,838	9,060
28. Junior Spencer	21	0	8,436	9,345
29. H. B. Bailey	5	0	7,340	5,000
30. Wayne Smith	25	0	7,326	6,790
31. Donaldd Tucker	9	0	7,118	5,680
32. Tom Pistone	33	0	6,598	10,050
33. Bub Strickler	9	0	6,540	5,275
34. Bobby Allison	8	0	6,152	4,780
35. Jim Paschal	10	0	6,046	7,805
36. Roy Tyner	28	0	5,882	6,505
37. LeeRay Yarbrough	14	0	5,852	5,905
38. Richard Petty	14	4	5,638	16,450
39. Curtis Turner	7	1	5,542	17,440
40. David Pearson	14	2	5,464	8,925
41. Clyde Lynn	24	0	5,414	4,545
42. Gene Block	18	0	4,970	6,080
43. Ned Setzer	8	0	4,828	4,805
44. Stick Elliott	15	0	4,332	4,985
45. Reb Wickersham	7	0	3,322	4,410
46. Frank Warren	4	0	3,814	2,880
47. Worth McMillion	10	0	3,794	2,590
48. Lionel Johnson	8	0	3,510	3,105
49. Bud Moore	14	0	3,216	3,434
50. Sonny Hutchins	10	0	3,118	3,780

1966

AT A GLANCE:

Grand National Champion:
David Pearson

Notable Events: That'll show 'em. After winning only six times in 1965, Chrysler automobiles combined for 34 victories in 49 races in 1966. David Pearson won 15 races in Dodges, Richard Petty 8 in Plymouths, Paul Goldsmith 3 in Plymouths, Jim Paschal 2 in Plymouths, and Earl Balmer, Sam McQuagg, and LeeRoy Yarbrough 1 each in Dodges. Jim Hurtabise, Marvin Panch, and Paul Lewis each won once in Plymouths.

Top Newcomers: South Carolina native James Hylton proved that championship-caliber drivers and winners could be mutually exclusive. He was winless in 41 starts, but his 20 top-5 finishes and 32 top-10s pushed him to second in the points race, finishing just behind 15-time winner David Pearson. As if to prove it wasn't a fluke, he was 0-for-46 and finished second the following year, also.

David Pearson got the first of his three Grand National titles with one of the best seasons in NASCAR history. At the time, his 15 victories in one season was second only to the 18 of Tim Flock when he won the 1955 championship. Pearson had 26 total top-5 finishes and 33 top-10s, and beat Hylton by 1,950 points. Nobody else reached double-figures in victories: Petty won eight races; Paul Goldsmith, Dick Hutcherson, breakthrough winner Bobby Allison, and Darel Dieringer three each; and Elmo Langley, Fred Lorenzen, and Jim Paschal two wins apiece. Single victories went to Marvin Panch, Paul Lewis, Sam McQuagg, Tiny Lund, LeeRoy Yarbrough, and Earl Balmer.

David Pearson was one of the most dominating drivers of the 1960s and '70s.

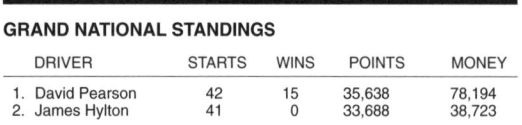

GRAND NATIONAL STANDINGS

	DRIVER	STARTS	WINS	POINTS	MONEY
1.	David Pearson	42	15	35,638	78,194
2.	James Hylton	41	0	33,688	38,723
3.	Richard Petty	39	8	22,952	94,666
4.	Henley Gray	45	0	22,468	21,901
5.	Paul Goldsmith	21	3	22,078	54,609
6.	Wendell Scott	45	0	21,702	23,052
7.	John Sears	46	0	21,432	25,192
8.	J. T. Putney	39	0	21,208	18,653
9.	Neil Castles	41	0	20,446	19,035
10.	Bobby Allison	33	3	19,910	23,420
11.	Elmo Langley	47	2	19,116	22,455
12.	Darel Dieringer	25	3	18,214	52,530
13.	Ned Jarrett	21	0	17,616	23,255
14.	Jim Paschal	18	2	16,404	30,985
15.	Sam Mcquagg	16	1	16,000	29,530
16.	Paul Lewis	21	1	15,352	17,827
17.	Marvin Panch	14	1	15,308	38,432
18.	Cale Yarborough	14	0	15,188	24,077
19.	G. C. Spencer	20	0	15,028	26,722
20.	Clyde Lynn	40	0	14,856	13,222
21.	Buck Baker	36	0	14,504	13,860
22.	Buddy Baker	41	0	14,302	21,325
23.	Fred Lorenzen	11	2	12,454	36,310

24. Curtis Turner	21	0	12,266	16,890
25. Roy Mayne	18	0	11,074	9,940
26. LeeRoy Yarbrough	9	1	10,528	23,925
27. J. D. McDuffie	36	0	9,572	8,545
28. Dick Hutcherson	14	3	9,392	22,985
29. Tiny Lund	31	1	9,332	11,880
30. Blackie Watt	20	0	8,518	7,000
31. Frank Warren	11	0	8,334	6,740
32. Buddy Arrington	25	0	7,636	8,510
33. Jimmy Helms	29	0	7,442	9,835
34. Jimmy Helms	29	0	6,530	5,815
35. Stick Elliott	19	0	6,358	7,335
36. Earl Balmer	9	1	5,794	7,935
37. Tom Pistone	28	0	5,788	7,765
38. Johnny Wynn	21	0	5,644	4,650
39. Larry Manning	13	0	4,964	3,920
40. Larry Hess	13	0	4,928	5,290
41. Roy Tyner	26	0	4,248	4,435
42. Bill Seifert	15	0	4,128	3,830
43. Bob Derrington	11	0	4,122	2,730
44. Joel Davis	21	0	4,066	4,685
45. Paul Connors	3	0	3,986	2,820
46. Jabe Thomas	13	0	3,820	3,580
47. Doug Cooper	21	0	3,808	5,185
48. Junior Johnson	7	0	3,750	3,610
49. Larry Frank	2	0	3,738	1,575

1967

AT A GLANCE:

Grand National Champion: Richard Petty

Notable Events: Mario Andretti, later known for his Indy-car and Grand Prix successes, did pretty well in his first stock car race. Given a shot with the potent Holman-Moody team, he promptly used every bit of asphalt in winning the Daytona 500 in a Ford. Thirty years later his nephew, John, got his first NASCAR victory in the mid-summer Pepsi 400 on the same track.

Top Newcomers: Donnie Allison became the latest in a series of brothers to run the tour, joining his brother, Bobby, as a full-timer. Donnie ran 20 races, had four top-5s and seven top-10s.

It takes only two words to describe the 49-race 1967 season: Richard Petty. He got his second Grand National title on the strength of 27 victories in 48 starts, including 10 straight between late August and early October. As if that wasn't enough, he added 11 more top-5 finishes and two more in the top-10, and beat winless James Hylton by 6,028 points. Two-time winner Dick Hutcherson was third, six-time winner Bobby Allison was fourth, and winless John Sears was fifth.

There was no secret to Petty's success—he and his blue No. 43 Plymouth were simply better than everyone else. They won 16 races on asphalt and 11 on dirt. They won four superspeedway races (two at Darlington, and one each at Rockingham and Trenton, New Jersey) and won on tracks as short as 1/5-mile (Islip, New York). Their 10-race winning streak began Aug. 12 at Winston-Salem, and continued in Columbia, Savannah, Darlington, Hickory, Richmond, North Wilkesboro, Hillsborough, Martinsville, and Beltsville, Maryland.

Cale Yarborough began making a name for himself by winning the spring 500-miler near Atlanta and the mid-summer race in Daytona Beach. Veteran Jim Paschal won four races, David Pearson two, and Parnelli Jones, LeeRoy Yarbrough, Fred Lorenzen, and Darel Dieringer one each. And another second-generation driver finally broke through: Buddy Baker, son of two-time champion and 44-time winner Buck Baker, won the late-season race near Charlotte.

GRAND NATIONAL STANDINGS

	DRIVER	STARTS	WINS	POINTS	MONEY
1.	Richard Petty	48	27	42,472	150,197
2.	James Hylton	46	0	36,444	49,732
3.	Dick Hutcherson	33	2	33,658	85,160
4.	Bobby Allison	45	6	30,812	58,250
5.	John Sears	41	0	29,078	28,937
6.	Jim Paschal	45	4	27,624	60,123
7.	David Pearson	22	2	26,302	72,651
8.	Neil Castles	36	0	23,218	20,683
9.	Elmo Langley	45	0	22,286	23,998
10.	Wendell Scott	45	0	20,700	19,510
11.	Paul Goldsmith	21	0	20,402	38,732
12.	Darel Dieringer	19	1	19,698	34,710
13.	Clyde Lynn	44	0	18,600	19,520
14.	Bobby Isaac	12	0	18,298	24,475
15.	Buddy Baker	20	1	17,502	46,950
16.	Donnie Allison	20	0	16,752	17,614
17.	Henley Gray	43	0	16,292	15,987
18.	J. T. Putney	29	0	16,228	15,687
19.	Tiny Lund	19	0	15,240	17,332
20.	Cale Yarborough	16	2	14,676	57,912
21.	G. C. Spencer	29	0	11,444	20,225
22.	Bill Seifert	41	0	9,992	11,905
23.	Charlie Glotzbach	9	0	9,952	14,790
24.	Frank Warren	12	0	9,768	9,185
25.	Earl Brooks	34	0	9,450	8,610
26.	Buddy Arrington	15	0	9,372	7,720
27.	Buck Baker	21	0	9,268	7,560
28.	Wayne Smith	27	0	9,262	10,225
29.	Fred Lorenzen	5	1	9,078	17,875
30.	Roy Mayne	14	0	8,820	8,830
31.	Bobby Wawak	14	0	8,492	8,070
32.	Friday Hassler	21	0	8,448	10,265
33.	Paul Lewis	14	0	7,812	8,620
34.	Sonny Hutchins	7	0	7,400	6,385
35.	Bud Moore	6	0	7,012	7,200
36.	Sam McQuagg	15	0	5,850	9,845
37.	LeeRoy Yarbrough	15	1	5,676	15,325
38.	Don Biederman	22	0	5,434	5,935
39.	Ramo Stott	3	0	5,254	3,335
40.	George Davis	21	0	5,006	4,400
41.	Jack Harden	10	0	4,936	4,450
42.	Paul Dean Holt	24	0	4,040	4,220
43.	Roy Tyner	27	0	3,954	8,170
44.	Bill Champion	11	0	3,780	6,205
45.	Dick Johnson	23	0	3,730	5,070
46.	George Poulos	23	0	3,780	3,040
47.	Bill Denniis	3	0	3,730	2,335
48.	Doug Cooper	21	0	3,666	5,665
49.	Ed Negre	14	0	3,578	3,805
50.	H. B. Bailey	3	0	3,482	3,850

Richard Petty enjoying a victory at Martinsville.

1968

AT A GLANCE:

Grand National Champion: David Pearson

Notable Events: Cale Yarborough began the season with three career victories and ended it with three times that many. He burst into the spotlight by winning both races at Daytona Beach, one each on the superspeedways near Atlanta and at Darlington, and one each on short tracks in Martinsville and Jefferson, Georgia.

Top Newcomers: Pete Hamilton was one of the first college graduates to come into big-time stock car racing. The University of Massachusetts grad headed south from Dedham, Massachusetts. and went into Grand National after making his mark in NASCAR's Sportsman division.

Two future Hall of Fame drivers made the season their personal playground. David Pearson and Richard Petty each won 16 of the season's 49 races (more than everyone else combined) and finished first (Pearson) and third (Petty) in the standings. And even though he won only three times and didn't have as many top-5s and top-10s, Bobby Isaac finished second in points. Winless drivers Clyde Lynn and John Sears were fourth and fifth in points. In fact, other than Pearson, Isaac, and Petty, nobody else in the top-10 won a race. Cale Yarborough won six, LeeRoy Yarbrough and Bobby Allison two each, and Donnie Allison, Buddy Baker, and Charlie Glotzbach one each.

By now, the trend toward paved tracks had gained momentum. Indeed, only 5 of the season's 49 races were on dirt: two each at Greensville and Columbia, and the spring race at Richmond. By the time the tour returned to Richmond in the fall, it had been paved, too. But while dirt was being replaced by asphalt, most of the NASCAR tracks were less than a mile long. Only 7 of the 24 facilities that hosted races were considered superspeedways. In fact, it was commonplace for teams to race on a 1/2-mile or shorter track at mid-week, then be at a superspeedway three days later.

GRAND NATIONAL STANDINGS

	DRIVER	STARTS	WINS	POINTS	MONEY
1.	David Pearson	48	16	3,499	133,065
2.	Bobby Isaac	49	3	3,373	60,342
3.	Richard Petty	49	16	3,123	99,535
4.	Clyde Lynn	49	0	3,041	29,226
5.	John Sears	49	0	3,017	29,179
6.	Elmo Langley	48	0	2,823	25,832
7.	James Hylton	41	0	2,719	32,608
8.	Jabe Thomas	48	0	2,687	21,166
9.	Wendell Scott	48	0	2,685	20,498
10.	Roy Tyner	8	0	2,504	20,247
11.	Bobby Allison	37	2	2,454	52,288
12.	Neil Castles	44	0	2,330	19,507
13.	Buddy Baker	38	1	2,310	56,023
14.	Bill Seifert	44	0	2,175	18,403
15.	Earl Brooks	40	0	1,957	14,233
16.	LeeRoy Yarbrough	26	2	1,894	87,920
17.	Cale Yarborough	21	6	1,804	138,052
18.	Paul Dean Holt	40	0	1,723	8,986
19.	Charlie Glotzbach	22	1	1,693	43,101
20.	Henley Gray	30	0	1,559	12,566
21.	Darel Dieringer	18	0	1,525	28,215
22.	Tiny Lund	7	0	1,443	17,775
23.	G. C. Spencer	26	0	1,401	10,120
24.	J. D. McDuffie	32	0	1,370	8,335
25.	Donnie Allison	13	1	1,307	50,815
26.	Stan Meserve	31	0	1,274	7,475
27.	Friday Hassler	20	0	1,224	12,000
28.	Bill Champion	18	0	1,155	10,170
29.	Bud Moore	16	0	1,086	12,325
30.	Paul Goldsmith	15	0	1,020	24,365
31.	Ed Negre	24	0	928	4,985
32.	Pete Hamilton	16	0	919	7,920
33.	Wayne Smith	18	0	901	7,235
34.	Dave Marcis	10	0	851	7,099
35.	Don Tarr	12	0	827	7,510
36.	E. J. Trivette	13	0	821	8,295
37.	Dick Johnson	11	0	735	5,920
38.	Bob Cooper	14	0	668	4,485
39.	Buck Baker	17	0	650	3,580
40.	Walson Gardner	14	0	640	4,275
41.	Larry Manning	12	0	640	6,995
42.	Frank Warren	10	0	611	5,365
43.	Jerry Grant	7	0	559	5,665
44.	Frog Fagan	12	0	531	3,680
45.	Richard Brickhouse	7	0	514	7,190
46.	Jim Hurtubise	6	0	504	4,490
47.	Curtis Turner	6	0	456	5,850
48.	Bobby Johns	7	0	453	5,010
49.	Eddie Yarboro	6	0	447	2,255
50.	Red Farmer	7	0	407	4,810

1969

AT A GLANCE:

Grand National Champion: David Pearson

Notable Events: The only organized driver boycott in NASCAR history marred the opening of the 2.66-mile superspeedway at Talladega, Alabama. Many of NASCAR's top stars left early rather than risk running laps in excess of 200 miles per hour on tires they considered dangerously inadequate. But the show went on, and unheralded Richard Brickhouse got his only victory in a winged Dodge Daytona.

Top Newcomers: Dick Brooks came from the mountains around Porterville, California, with nothing but dreams and determination. He fielded his own cars when he could and found enough other rides to start 28 races. He had three top-5 runs and 12 top-10s.

David Pearson won his third and final championship, but that was only half the story. New superspeedways popped up across America, and NASCAR moved to gain a foothold in areas once thought off-limits. Bill France opened the 2.66-mile track at Talladega, and a new 1-mile track opened in Dover, Deleware. NASCAR teams made their first trip to a year-old, 2-mile speedway just west of Detroit, Michigan, and to a similar 2-mile track near College Station, Texas. Again, only five dirt-track races were on the 54-race schedule: two each at Greensville and Columbia in South Carolina, and one at Raleigh, North Carolina.

Pearson won 11 races in 51 starts, had 42 top-5s, 44 top-10s, and won a then-record $229,760. Petty won 10 times in 50 starts, third-ranked James Hylton was 0-for-52, fourth-ranked Neil Castles was 0-for-53, and fifth-ranked Elmo Langley was 0-for-54. The most successful driver of the season was sixth-ranked Bobby Isaac, who won 17 races, had 29 top-5 finishes and 33 top-10s in 50 starts. LeeRoy Yarbrough won seven races, Bobby Allison five, Cale Yarborough two, and Donnie Allison and Richard Brickhouse one each.

Brickhouse's was perhaps the most unusual victory of them all. A journeyman with few prospects for stardom, he got to drive the potent Ray Nichels-owned Dodge Daytona when most of NASCAR's stars boycotted the opening race at

Talladega. Their concern was that Firestone and Goodyear hadn't spent enough time developing tires for the 200-mph-plus speeds. They didn't want NASCAR to cancel the race, simply delay it several weeks so the tire companies could upgrade their product. France refused, then invited drivers from the Grand American series to fill in when the Grand National teams left.

The race was run without serious incident — mainly because NASCAR ordered caution flags every 20 to 25 laps so teams could change tires before they failed. The last caution was timed so the final 25 laps could be run wide-open, and Brickhouse—in one of the few good cars on the track—beat Jim Vandiver and Ramo Stott (on the lead lap), Bobby Isaac (one down) and Dick Brooks, a whopping eight laps behind. Once again, France had proved who was boss.

GRAND NATIONAL STANDINGS

	DRIVER	STARTS	WINS	POINTS	MONEY
1.	David Pearson	51	11	4,170	229,760
2.	Richard Petty	50	10	3,813	129,906
3.	James Hylton	52	0	3,750	114,416
4.	Neil Castles	51	0	3,530	54,367
5.	Elmo Langley	52	0	3,383	73,092
6.	Bobby Isaac	50	17	3,301	92,074
7.	John Sears	52	0	3,166	52,281
8.	Jabe Thomas	51	0	3,103	44,989
9.	Wendell Scott	51	0	3,015	47,451
10.	Cecil Gordon	51	0	3,002	39,679
11.	E. J. Trivette	49	0	2,988	35,896
12.	Bill Champion	49	0	2,813	33,656
13.	Bill Seifert	50	0	2,765	44,361
14.	J. D. McDuffie	50	0	2,741	30,861
15.	Ben Arnold	48	0	2,736	33,256
16.	LeeRoy Yarborough	30	7	2,712	193,211
17.	Henley Gray	48	0	2,517	29,335
18.	Earl Brooks	49	0	2,454	34,793
19.	Dave Marcis	37	0	2,348	32,383
20.	Bobby Allison	27	5	2,055	69,483
21.	Dick Brooks	28	0	1,780	28,187
22.	Buddy Baker	18	0	1,769	62,928
23.	Cale Yarborough	19	2	1,715	74,240
24.	Donnie Allison	16	1	1,662	78,055
25.	Richard Brickhouse	24	1	1,660	45,637
26.	G. C. Spencer	26	0	1,562	21,660
27.	Ed Negre	31	0	1,465	15,160
28.	Friday Hassler	18	0	1,421	17,690
29.	Frank Warren	23	0	1,299	15,677
30.	Hass Ellington	15	0	1,210	16,552
31.	Roy Tyner	21	0	1,191	12,302
32.	Ed Hessert	16	0	1,113	17,690
33.	Buddy Arrington	16	0	1,099	12,975
34.	Dick Johnson	22	0	1,055	11,182
35.	Buddy Young	21	0	981	15,542
36.	Dub Simpson	20	0	959	12,915
37.	Charlie Glotzbach	12	0	944	36,090
38.	Roy Mayne	13	0	922	10,340
39.	Wayne Smith	16	0	922	10,610
40.	Paul Goldsmith	11	0	892	22,305
41.	Don Tarr	12	0	855	13,720
42.	Ken Meisenhelder	16	0	627	5,630
43.	Pete Hazelwood	16	0	598	4,160
44.	Sonny Hutchins	8	0	535	9,552
45.	Wayne Gillette	16	0	509	5,827
46.	Paul Dean Holt	14	0	485	4,442
47.	Johnny Holford	8	0	465	4,200
48.	Ray Elder	4	0	433	7,200
49.	John Kennedy	9	0	417	6,462
50.	Dick Poling	12	0	408	5,467

1970

AT A GLANCE:

Grand National Champion: Bobby Isaac

Notable Events: Richard Petty (who else, right?) made history on September 30 with his 117th career victory, this one at the 1/2-mile State Fairgrounds Speedway in Raleigh. The "Home State 200" was the third dirt-track race of the season and the last in Grand National history.

Top Newcomers: Bill Dennis graduated from weekend races on Virginia's short tracks and made 25 starts in his cars and those of several owners. He didn't win or get any top-5s, but had five top-10s. He was seen by many at NASCAR as more media-presentable than Minnesota native Joe Frasson (22 starts and two top-10s), his rival for rookie of the year.

After being second in the 1968 standings and sixth the next season, Bobby Isaac, crew chief Harry Hyde, and team owner Nord Krauskopf teamed up for a storybook season. Driving the No. 71 Dodge, they won 11 races in 47 starts and backed that with 32 top-5s and 38 top-10s. Three-time winner Bobby Allison was a closer-than-expected second, falling only 51 points short despite running one race less. James Hylton, who finally got his first Grand National victory at Richmond in the spring and had 38 other top-10 finishes, was third. Eighteen-time winner Richard Petty was fourth (he missed six races due to injuries and sat out two more) and winless Neil Castles was fifth.

GRAND NATIONAL STANDINGS

	DRIVER	STARTS	WINS	POINTS	MONEY
1.	Bobby Isaac	47	11	3,911	199,600
2.	Bobby Allison	46	3	3,860	149,745
3.	James Hylton	47	1	3,788	78,201
4.	Richard Petty	40	18	3,447	151,124
5.	Neil Castles	47	0	3,158	49,746
6.	Elmo Langley	47	0	3,154	45,193
7.	Jabe Thomas	46	0	3,120	42,958
8.	Benny Parsons	45	0	2,993	59,402
9.	Dave Marcis	47	0	2,820	41,111
10.	Frank Warren	46	0	2,697	35,161

11. Cecil Gordon	44	0	2,514	32,713
12. John Sears	40	0	2,465	32,675
13. Dick Brooks	34	0	2,460	53,754
14. Wendell Scott	41	0	2,425	28,518
15. Bill Champion	38	0	2,350	30,943
16. J. D. McDuffie	36	0	2,079	24,905
17. Ben Arnold	29	0	1,997	25,805
18. Bill Seifert	39	0	1,962	25,647
19. Henley Gray	34	0	1,871	23,130
20. Friday Hassler	26	0	1,831	27,535
21. Pete Hamilton	16	3	1,819	131,406
22. Joe Frasson	21	0	1,723	20,172
23. David Pearson	19	1	1,716	87,118
24. Buddy Baker	18	1	1,555	63,510
25. Bill Dennis	25	0	1,432	15,630
26. Ed Negre	31	0	1,413	14,580
27. G. C. Spencer	20	0	1,410	17,915
28. Charlie Glotzbach	19	2	1,358	50,649
29. Roy Mayne	16	0	1,333	16,910
30. Bill Shirley	29	0	1,244	12,215
31. Raymond Williams	21	0	1,204	12,535
32. Larry Baumel	23	0	1,138	16,645
33. Buddy Arrington	19	0	1,087	16,845
34. Cale Yarborough	19	3	1,016	115,875
35. Don Tarr	17	0	995	16,592
36. Johnny Halford	25	0	975	15,645
37. Earl Brooks	21	0	884	10,340
38. Coo Coo Marlin	13	0	876	14,799
39. Ron Keselowski	17	0	855	11,985
40. Donnie Allison	19	3	841	96,081
41. Ken Meisenhelder	19	0	812	7,020
42. Roy Tyner	14	0	631	5,565
43. LeeRoy Yarbrough	19	1	625	61,930
44. Dick May	16	0	551	4,510
45. Jim Vandiver	14	0	519	16,080
46. John Kenney	11	0	457	4,115
47. Dub Simpson	6	0	367	4,510
48. Lee Roy Carrigg	9	0	355	4,130
49. Joe Phipps	7	0	325	4,090
50. Wayne Smith	8	0	300	4,505

1971

AT A GLANCE:

Grand National Champion: Richard Petty

Notable Events: That sigh of relief was from drivers, crewmen, and fans exhaling after years of 40-, 50- and 60-race seasons. Finally, after being obsessed with presenting its product as often and in as many areas as possible, NASCAR (with prodding from its new sponsor, the R.J. Reynolds Tobacco Co.) chose to make 1971 the last of its "long seasons." No more midweek races on backwater short tracks and no more multirace weeks. Finally, a national series that made sense.

Top Newcomers: Walter Ballard was the latest in a long line of Texans (Shorty Rollins and Billy Wade preceded him) to come to the Southeast to race. He started 41 of the year's 48 races, had 3 top-5s, and 11 top-10s. He was NASCAR's second rookie (behind James Hylton) to finish among the top-10 in points.

Richard Petty and Bobby Allison dominated the season, combining to win 32 of the year's 48 races. The other 16 were divided among Bobby Isaac (four); two-time winners David Pearson, A.J. Foyt, and Tiny Lund; and one-time winners Pete Hamilton, Buddy Baker, Benny Parsons, Donnie Allison, Charlie Glotzbach, and Ray Elder. And just how dominant were Petty and Allison? They combined to win 17 of 20 races during one stretch of the season and ended the season winning seven of eight. Petty won the championship as Allison missed 14 races and finished a distant fourth. Winless James Hylton and Cecil Gordon were second and third, and winless Elmo Langley was fifth.

At the end of the season, 13 short tracks were lopped off the schedule. It had been a good run, but NASCAR had to move ahead. It needed new venues with tens of thousands of seats and better facilities for the print media and, perhaps most importantly, better ability to accommodate the increasingly important presence of television. And it was clear by the early '70s that while long-distance superspeedway racing might not be as exciting as 30 cars on a 1/3-mile track, it was the future of the sport.

So the short tracks were axed, some of them loyal NASCAR hosts since the early 1950s. The tracks that lost their race dates were Hickory, Asheville, and Winston-Salem, North Carolina; Columbia and Greenville, South Carolina; Maryville and Kingsport, Tennessee; South Boston, Virginia; Houston, Texas; Ona, West Virginia; Macon, Georgia; and Malta and Islip, New York. Here's what remained: 1 road course, 11 superspeedways ranging from 1 to 2.66 miles, and 5 tracks stretching approximately 1/2 mile.

And in Daytona Beach, they called it progress.

GRAND NATIONAL STANDINGS

	DRIVER	STARTS	WINS	POINTS	MONEY
1.	Richard Petty	46	21	4,435	351,071
2.	James Hylton	46	0	4,071	90,282
3.	Cecil Gordon	46	0	3,677	69,080
4.	Bobby Allison	42	11	3,636	254,316
5.	Elmo Langley	46	0	3,356	57,037
6.	Jabe Thomas	43	0	3,200	48,241
7.	Bill Champion	45	0	3,058	43,769
8.	Frank Warren	47	0	2,886	40,072
9.	J. D. McDuffie	43	0	2,862	35,578
10.	Walter Ballard	41	0	2,633	30,974
11.	Benny Parsons	35	1	2,611	55,896
12.	Ed Negre	43	0	2,528	29,738
13.	Bill Seifert	37	0	2,403	33,220
14.	Henley Gray	39	0	2,392	31,789
15.	Buddy Baker	19	1	2,358	115,150
16.	Friday Hassler	29	0	2,277	37,305
17.	Earl Brooks	35	0	2,205	25,360
18.	Bill Dennis	28	0	2,181	29,420

19.	Wendell Scott	37	0	2,180	21,701
20.	John Sears	37	0	2,167	26,735
21.	Dave Marcis	29	0	2,049	37,582
22.	Neil Castles	38	0	2,036	22,939
23.	Bobby Isaac	25	4	1,819	106,526
24.	Pete Hamilton	22	1	1,739	60,440
25.	Joe Frasson	17	0	1,619	20,975
26.	Ben Arnold	18	0	1,618	18,491
27.	Ron Keselowski	20	0	1,446	17,680
28.	Bill Shirley	27	0	1,303	9,160
29.	Donnie Allison	13	1	1,280	69,995
30.	Dean Dalton	19	0	1,276	13,910
31.	Raymond Williams	20	0	1,270	14,585
32.	Dick May	22	0	1,090	9,225
33.	Charlie Roberts	19	0	1,053	12,470
34.	G. C. Spencer	17	0	1,008	11,470
35.	Richard Brown	13	0	967	11,940
36.	Dick Brooks	20	0	939	32,921
37.	Larry Baumel	16	0	904	10,910
38.	Maynard Troyer	13	0	879	13,115
39.	Roy Mayne	11	0	852	10,330
40.	Ken Meisenhelder	15	0	797	5,405
41.	Tommy Gade	9	0	729	8,800
42.	Charlie Glotzbach	20	1	699	38,605
43.	Bill Hollar	11	0	644	4,275
44.	Marv Acton	11	0	627	8,620
45.	Fred Lorenzen	14	0	611	45,100
46.	Richard Childress	12	0	601	3,855
47.	Paul Tyler	10	0	561	6,360
48.	Jim Vandiver	7	0	553	13,575
49.	Coo Coo Marlin	12	0	527	9,085
50.	Eddie Yarboro	7	0	497	3,685

5

A DECADE OF CHANGE: RJR AND NASCAR JOIN FORCES

In retrospect and infused with the self-confidence brought on by 20/20 hindsight, it seems fairly safe to say that the face and nature of NASCAR Winston Cup racing changed more dramatically during the decade of the 70s than at any other time in the sport's 20 previous years. Indeed, the period between 1970 and 1979 may well have been the most important in stock car racing history.

There were major advances in almost every area of NASCAR. Many of them were on the track, where competition was more spirited than ever and where more well-sponsored teams were coming aboard to run the full schedule in pursuit of the national championship. Qualifying and race speeds were inching ever-upward as team owners got serious about testing and research and development. For the first time, drivers and crew chiefs were following aviation's lead and taking their cars to massive wind tunnels. Their goal was to find another one-tenth of a second by tucking the sheet metal here or rounding it there. Aerodynamics, once dismissed as relatively unimportant, suddenly became every bit as crucial to success as strong engines and transmissions.

But many of the on-track advancements were overshadowed by decisions being made in corporate boardrooms. These decisions and policy changes came in the areas of sponsorship and promotion. They resulted in increased attention by the media, in a radical departure from the schedule most teams were accustomed to running, and in the very way the championship was awarded. From the early '70s onward, neither NASCAR nor major-league stock car would ever be the same.

The most important of these changes came in 1971, when the Florida-based series received a significant financial and publicity boost from the beleaguered R. J. Reynolds Tobacco Co. With the medical community leaning on the government to do something about the dangers of smoking, Congress took steps in the late '60s to ban all cigarette advertising on television. Later, the Federal Drug Administration would see to it that the ban was extended outward toward print and billboard advertising as well.

With millions upon millions of budgeted advertising dollars suddenly available—and with the demographics of motorsports fans falling almost perfectly within its marketing and advertising strategy—executives at RJR headquarters in Winston-Salem, North Carolina, came up with a

Petty could win anywhere, including on the road courses.

plan. The year before, with rumors of a possible advertising ban already in the air, racer-turned-owner Junior Johnson had driven over from his shop in Wilkes County to pitch RJR on the idea of sponsoring his team. But the company was aiming significantly higher than just that. Thus came the startling announcement late in 1970 that RJR would become the primary sponsor of what was then known as NASCAR Grand National racing.

SMALL TRACKS DISAPPEAR

To be sure, the multibillion dollar corporation didn't come in empty-handed. Its new department for motorsports promotions looked at NASCAR's unwieldy schedule and suggested somewhat diplomatically that it be trimmed almost in half. The company then suggested that NASCAR make each of the remaining events count equally toward the series championship. Instead of running upward of 50 races a year—often two and sometimes three times a week—the schedule would be trimmed down to about 30 events, and limited to no more than one a week. In line with its imagine of a new and more professional stock car circuit, NASCAR abandoned most of the small backwater tracks that had been so important to the growth of racing for the previous 20 years.

Just like that, traditional venues like Columbia, Asheville, Macon, Hampton, Greenville, Hickory, and Winston-Salem were gone, left to the weekly racers who were trying to work their way to Grand National. It was, as some old-timers said, like seeing the beloved old neighborhood razed to make room for yet another shopping mall. Sure, the new mall would produce new jobs and generate income for the neighborhood, but it just wouldn't be the same without the corner grocery and the Mom 'n' Pop cafe where the food was average but the conversation was lively.

So 1971 was NASCAR's last long season. It included 47 races: two on road courses, 21 on short tracks, and 24 on superspeedways. The venues ranged in length from one-fifth of a mile at Islip, New York, to 2.66 miles at Talladega, Alabama. The shortest race was a mere 46 miles at Islip, and the longest covered 600 miles at Charlotte Motor Speedway. Richard Petty won 21 times, had 38 top-5 finishes and 41 top-10s in the 46 races he contested. He won slightly less than $300,000, a record at the time.

As if the precipitous drop in the number of races wasn't dramatic enough, there was the not-so-minor matter of the name change.

When Bill France, Sr. created his stock car racing sanctioning body in December of 1947, he designated its premier division Strictly Stock—which is exactly what his cars were at the time. But France thought "Strictly Stock" sounded too much like a rules interpretation, so he renamed his top division Grand National for the 1950 season. He and his staff agreed it more properly reflected the ever-increasing sophistication of the series. So, after millions of fans had grown up in the '50s and '60s watching Grand National racing, they were introduced in the early '70s to the Winston Cup Series, the name changed to acknowledge and publicize R. J. Reynolds' flagship brand of cigarettes.

Old-timers who bemoaned the loss of tradition soothed themselves with the startling news that RJR was going to pump $100,000 into NASCAR's 1971 post-season point fund. The first-ever Winston Cup champion would get $40,000 of that, more than twice as much as the sanctioning body was contributing into its own point fund. And $40,000 was almost as much as anyone could win at any single race. (Indeed, Petty, the 1971 champion, got $40,000 from R. J. Reynolds Inc. and $45,500 for winning that season's Daytona 500.) So much for traditionalists.

BILL FRANCE, SR. STEPS DOWN

Another major change came in January of 1972 when NASCAR founder and long-time president Bill France, Sr. retired to assume greater control of his burgeoning International Speedway Corporation. To the surprise of absolutely nobody, William Clay France was named to succeed his father as president of the sanctioning body. His younger brother, Jimmy, became vice-president and secretary, a low-key and low-profile role he has played well in the ensuing years.

Although he is neither, Bill France is spoken of universally as "Little Bill" or "Bill Jr." The original Bill France—often called "Big Bill" or "The Old Man"—was born William Henry Getty France. His first son isn't a junior, although that misconception has long been part of his identity. And even though he is neither as tall as his father was nor does he command the same presence, Bill France, Jr. (see, everybody does it) is every bit as tough and demanding. He remains a formidable adversary when it comes time to remove the gloves and settle delicate matters by indelicate means.

Several new speedways came along in the '70s as NASCAR expanded its scope and broke free of the perception that it was simply a quaint little Southern dalliance. The star-crossed 2.5-mile track at Ontario, California, hosted its first stock car race in 1971. Perhaps appropriately (since, after all, Ontario had been designed to resemble the Indianapolis Motor Speedway), A. J. Foyt won in a Jack Bowsher-owned Mercury. Even though Ontario didn't fare well in the long run, its presence helped keep motorsports alive in the car-crazy (and advertiser-friendly) Southern California market.

A 2½-mile, triangular superspeedway at Pocono, Pennsylvania, opened for a 500-mile Win-

Bill France, Jr., shown here in 1997, took over the reigns from his father in 1972.

ston Cup race in 1974. With the venerable Trenton Speedway finally gone, Pocono International Raceway arose from an spinach patch to deliver NASCAR superspeedway racing to the huge metropolitan area stretching from New York City, through Philadelphia and Baltimore, and into Washington, D.C. While series officials often wondered if anyone living along that corridor was paying attention, it was a market the sanctioning body simply couldn't afford to ignore.

TELEVISION TURNS ITS CAMERAS TO NASCAR

All of which leads directly to perhaps the most important change in NASCAR racing—either before or after the '70s.

Television had long been aware of the popularity of southern-style stock car racing. In fact, television and newsreel footage had been used to help Bill France figure out who had won the photo-finish battle between Lee Petty and Johnny Beauchamp in the 1959 Daytona 500. From time to time local TV stations in the East and Southeast would host 30-minute programs about motor-

sports, complete with talking heads, footage of races, and interviews with drivers. ABC's revered "Wide World of Sports" sometimes aired live snippets from races in progress. At other times it would televise the start and the first few laps before cutting away for God-knows-what (wrist-wrestling?) in who-knows-where (Petaluma?) before returning live for the final few laps.

It took the 1976 Daytona 500 for the suits in TV-land to acknowledge that maybe this Southern thing known as stock car racing might be something they should look into after all.

At the time, the 1976 season-opener from the Daytona International Speedway was the most talked-about race in NASCAR history. It starred respected rivals and fan favorites Richard Petty in a Dodge and David Pearson in a Mercury in a last-lap shoot-out for the Winston Cup series' most coveted prize. Petty already had five Daytona 500 trophies among his bulging collection. And despite being recognized among the sport's all-time best drivers, Pearson had only a 1970 second-place finish behind Pete Hamilton to show on his Daytona 500 resume.

The stage was set and the tension palpable as Petty and Pearson were bumper-to-bumper as they took the white flag for the 200th and last lap on Feb. 15, 1976. Petty passed Pearson going into Turn 3, but drove in too deep and drifted up the high-banking just a touch. Pearson shot by on the inside, but slipped a bit in Turn 4, allowing Petty to pull to the inside and get door-to-door as they exited Turn 4. They could almost see the checkered flag, waiting just beyond the short chute that led to the bend of the frontstretch trioval.

Petty inched ahead of Pearson and seemed to have the race won when he moved right to get fully ahead. But when he misjudged the clearance, the right-rear of his No. 43 Dodge nicked the left-front of Pearson's No. 21 Mercury. The contact made both cars fishtail and skitter, and eventually slam almost head-on into the outside wall. Both cars came off the wall and careened into the grassy apron separating the pit road from the frontstretch.

Darrell Waltrip (Gatorade car) wins the 1979 Talladega 500.

so, he still finished second to Pearson, the only driver to officially run all 200 laps.

CBS-TV was there to tape highlights for replay later in the afternoon. The footage of the last lap and interviews with the drivers (neither, by the way, held hard feelings against the other) went all over the world in some form or fashion. Given the extraordinary attention paid by the mainstream national and international media, it wasn't difficult to convince network executives to consider doing a major race live, from start to finish. When it finally happened three years later at Daytona Beach, it was the single most important event in the history of NASCAR racing.

There may have never been a race with greater theater than the 1979 Daytona 500. It had everything a race fan (or a ratings-conscious TV executive or Madison Avenue shill) could possibly want: safe and competitive racing throughout, a controversial and spectacular late-race incident involving two of the sport's biggest names, a last-lap victory by a bona fide Southern icon, plus a short and mostly-harmless post-race fight. And it was played out before a huge TV audience, much of which was held hostage indoors by a mid-winter storm that had paralyzed the Northeast and Middle Atlantic regions.

It happened like this:

Two-time (1968 and 1977) Daytona 500 winner Cale Yarborough and Donnie Allison began the last lap of the '79 race similar to how Petty and Pearson had begun their last lap in '76. The major

Pearson had had the presence of mind to engage the clutch and thus kept his car's engine alive. Petty's, on the other hand, had stalled and didn't care to restart. Given that reprieve, Pearson inched the final few hundred yards at maybe 20 miles an hour. He took the checkered flag on the apron of the track before heading directly for victory lane, the nose of his car pushed almost back to the front wheels. When Petty's car would go no farther, his crew rushed across pit road and pushed him across the finish line. (Alas, NASCAR docked him that lap for getting "outside assistance.") Even

difference was that Yarborough and Allison didn't wait until Turn 4 and the short chute to start wrecking each other. Indeed, they began over in Turn 2, then kept wrecking all the way down the 4,000-foot backstretch and into Turn 3.

When all was said and done, they ended up with two demolished race cars spewing smoke and steam on the grassy apron near the infield fence in Turn 3. Who first did what to whom remains in debate, and likely always will. To this day, each blames the other, and it's unlikely they'll ever truly forgive each other. The only thing not in dispute is that their bamming and framming opened the door for Petty to win the sixth of his record seven Daytona 500s. The thoroughly improbable victory

kick-started what turned out to be his seventh and final championship season.

He was running a distant third, hopelessly out of contention, when Allison and Yarborough began wrecking. By the time Petty, fourth-running Darrell Waltrip, and fifth-running A. J. Foyt cleared Turn 2 and started down the backstretch, they knew something major was going on somewhere. The caution lights were blinking, but since they'd already taken the white "one-to-go" flag, they were within their rights to race hard back to the checkered flag. Petty got there first, but not before blocking from right to left and from left to right to keep Waltrip at bay the final quarter-mile. Foyt was scored third, with Allison and Yarborough

Cale Yarborough's crew in motion at the 1974 Wilkes 400 at North Wilkesboro.

GENTLEMEN, START YOUR ENGINES

Ray Melton was one of NASCAR's most faithful salesmen throughout the '50s, '60s, and into the '70s. Huge of stature and possessing a deep and gravelly voice, he was the public address announcer at several tracks, including Darlington Raceway and the State Fairgrounds Raceway at Richmond, Virginia.

It was at the latter venue where Melton, a resident of Norfolk, Virginia, gave one of his most stirring performances. In his mind, at least.

Melton, you see, was convinced that a fair number of people at any race came to hear what he called The Command. His "Gentlemen, start your engines" was the highlight of his life, and God help anyone who didn't appreciate his performance. And that's why he was so incensed when Cecil Gordon started his engine—which led to a wholesale start up and down the grid—at Richmond toward the latter part of the '70s.

By the time the field had pulled off the grid and taken its pace laps, Melton was steaming. The Command, he told his PA sidekick; the people hadn't heard The Command. How can they have a race at Richmond without The Command?

So as the cars came off Turn 4 for the start, Melton improvised and shouted out, "Gentleman, REV your engines." After the race—as the winner did his post-race interview and the fans headed out—Melton gave them what he figured they'd come to hear. In the relative quiet of the rapidly emptying little half-mile paved track, he bellowed as only he could "GENTLEMEN, START YOUR ENGINES."

He put down his microphone and headed for home, his big day finally complete.

---

fourth and fifth. Each was scored a lap down since they never made it back around for the 200th lap.

If it had called a meeting and discussed it for a weekend, NASCAR couldn't have come up with a better finish. It was the most talked-about sports event of the weekend, attracting comment and analysis from members of the button-down media who possessed only a nodding acquaintance with motorsports. The result was altogether predictable: America's interest in Winston Cup racing soared, forcing the media to pay closer attention. That led to an increase in corporate sponsorship, which inevitably led NASCAR racing—once perceived as the domain of hooligans with dirty fingernails—to take on semblance of respectability.

NEW STARS EMERGE

A number of bright, new star drivers emerged during the '70s. Many had toiled for years in the minor leagues, and worked their way up through the Modified or Late Model Sportsman ranks. They were determined to make an impact on Winston Cup racing, and many of them did. In some cases, they did it by displaying not only nerve and talent, but refreshing and oft-time unorthodox views of the sport. It was clear that a new day was coming, and people like Waltrip, Ricky Rudd, Neil Bonnett, and Benny Parsons were going to play major roles.

To be sure, the old standbys were still as good as ever. Bobby Isaac won the 1970 Grand National championship in No. 71 Dodges prepared by Harry Hyde and owned by insurance magnate Nord Krasukopf. It was a bittersweet season for Isaac, who won 11 of 47 races, but only three of them—Martinsville, Nashville, and North Wilkesboro—were considered major events. Even so, he won the title by 51 points over three-time winner Bobby Allison.

Petty won the next two championships—by 364 points over winless James Hylton in '71 and by 128 points over 10-time winner Allison in '72. Petty's domination of those seasons is reflected in these stats: he was 21 of 46 in 1971, and 8 of 31 in the trimmed-down season of 1972. (That makes him the answer to yet another NASCAR trivia question: Who won the last "long-schedule" title and the first contested on the "short schedule?")

Benny Parsons, a polite and well-spoken ex-Detroit cabbie, won the '73 championship in a major upset. A one-time winner that season, he went into the finale at Rockingham needing only a decent finish to out-point four-time winner Cale Yarborough. A serious crash put Parsons' lead in jeopardy until crewmen from other teams offered spare parts and pieces, then helped Parsons' crew cobble his car together so he could finish the race. Despite running off the pace and finishing well behind, Parsons had his Winston Cup trophy by 76 points.

The '74 and '75 seasons were more of the same for Petty and his family-run team. He won 10 races and the '74 title by 567 points over Yarborough, then won 13 more races and beat one-time winner Dave Marcis by 722 points for the '75 championship. It was the first contested under the current system that rewards teams for running the full schedule and being consistent top-10 finishers. The system offered five bonus points for leading a lap and 10 bonus points for leading the most laps.

Yarborough, who never needed any additional incentive to run hard, dominated the latter half of the decade. The burly little no-neck South Carolinian won a combined 13 poles and 28 races in taking the '76, '77, and '78 titles. It remains the only time a driver has ever won three consecutive championships. He beat Petty by 196 and 385 points, then beat Allison by 474.

Petty closed out the '70s with five victories and his seventh and final NASCAR title. He secured it

Darrell Waltrip's Gatorade car in 1978.

with a fifth-place finish in the 500-mile season finale at Ontario (Calif.) Motor Speedway in November of '79. And the driver he beat by 11 points wasn't another good ol' veteran who'd been around forever and had paid his dues. Rather, it was Waltrip, whom Petty had beaten in the final moments of the early-season Daytona 500 after Yarborough and Donnie Allison had wrecked on the last lap.

Waltrip won 22 races between '75 and '79, all but one of them with the potent DiGard/Gatorade team owned by New England businessmen Bill Gardner and Mike DeProsperio. Waltrip had been top 10 in points each of those years and started the '79 campaign fully expecting to win the Winston Cup. He came close, leading by 53 points with four races remaining. But he finished 13th, 6th, 5th, and 8th while Petty was finishing 3rd, 1st, 6th, and 5th. In the end, Petty went from 53 points behind to 11 ahead at North Wilkesboro, Rockingham, Atlanta, and Ontario.

Waltrip had come along as a brash, outspoken, enormously talented, take-no-prisoners rookie in 1973. He dressed better than most of the old-timers, always had his wife on his arm, didn't run from controversy or intimidation, and usually delivered on most of his boasts. But he had a bad habit (as most youngsters do) of speaking his mind when it might have been more prudent to hold his tongue. Many feel just such an emotional outburst over the qualifying system at Riverside, Calif., in June of '73 probably hurt him when officials met after the '73 season to select their rookie of the year.

In the end, though, Waltrip had the last laugh. While Lennie Pond's career featured only one victory—at Talladega in the summer of 1978—Waltrip won three championships with owner Junior Johnson. As 1997 turned into 1998, Waltrip stood tied with Bobby Allison for third on NASCAR's all-time victory list. They trailed only Petty's 200 victories and Pearson's 105, and Waltrip is one of only six men with three or more titles.

Pearson, another of those three-time champions, was arguably the NASCAR driver of the decade—if they'd had such an award. Even though he never ran the full schedule during the '70s, the Spartanburg, South Carolina, driver won 46 races, most of them on superspeedways with the Wood brothers. Among his more notable successes in the '70s were the nine victories at Darlington, eight at Michigan, five each at Daytona Beach and Dover, four at Rockingham, three each at Atlanta, Charlotte, and Talladega, two each at Pocono and Riverside, and one victory each at Ontario and on the half-mile track at Martinsville, about 40 minutes from the Wood brothers' shop in Stuart, Virginia.

Alas, all good things must come to an end. Pearson and the Wood brothers split up in March of 1979 after an uncharacteristically sloppy pit stop during the spring 400-miler at Darlington Raceway. The crew had summoned him for a four-tire pit stop, but Pearson thought it was scheduled as a rights-and-gas stop. Even though crewmen were loosening the left-side lug nuts just a few feet from the driver-side window, Pearson left the pits the instant the jack was dropped, signaling the right-side tires had been changed.

Pearson got perhaps 100 yards before the left-side wheels came off and the Mercury floundered to a stop just shy of the racing surface in Turn 1. The spectacular mistake that left Pearson stranded at the end of pit road signaled an end to one of the most successful pairings in superspeedway history. The Woods hired Bonnett to finish out the season, and he responded for them by winning at Dover, Daytona Beach, and Atlanta.

As for Pearson, well, he went back to Darlington Raceway over the Labor Day weekend of 1979 and proved he was still as good as ever. Subbing for Dale Earnhardt, Pearson drove the Osterlund-owned No. 2 Chevrolet to victory ahead of Bill Elliott, Terry Labonte, Buddy Baker, and Benny Parsons. All told, the three-time champion proved to be a pretty decent pinch-hitter. In four races with Osterlund and crew chief Jake Elder, Pearson had two front-row starts, a win, a second, a fourth and a sixth. For many drivers, that's almost a career. To Pearson, it was just something to keep him busy.

The man who many feel eventually will win more Cups than anyone began his career in the '70s.

Dale Earnhardt had done a handful of races with mediocre teams in the mid-70s before California businessman Rod Osterlund recruited him to run the full Winston Cup schedule. At the time, the resume of the man who would become known as the "The Intimidator" was rather thin. He'd had some good runs in the minor-league Late Model Sportsman circuit, but his nine previous Winston Cup starts had been in suspect equipment, a no-win situation which had done nothing to showcase his talent.

Still, Osterlund took a chance that paid off. With veteran mechanic Jake Elder calling the shots, Earnhardt won four poles and a 500-lap race at Bristol. He beat Terry Labonte, Harry Gant, and Joe Millikan for rookie of the year, and was seventh in points. Just behind him was a journeyman driver named Richard Childress.

And, as the '80s and '90s would show us, that wasn't the only time their names would be linked in Winston Cup racing.

6

1972–1979: GOODBYE GRAND NATIONAL, HELLO WINSTON CUP

1972

AT A GLANCE

Winston Cup Champion: Richard Petty

Notable Events: First year for the Winston Cup points system.

Top Newcomers: Rookie of the Year Larry Smith, from Lenoir, North Carolina (seven top-10 finishes)

A milestone year for NASCAR: Bill France Sr., 62, stepped down in January, turning over control of the organization that he founded to his 28-year-old son, Bill Jr. Bill Sr. continued as board chairman of the International Speedway Corp., which operates Daytona International Speedway and Alabama International Motor Speedway, in Talladega, Alabama.

The R.J. Reynolds Tobacco Co. is in its first year of sponsoring the entire schedule, then called the Grand National series. RJR established a $100,000 points fund that would be distributed based on a driver's point total for the entire season. The race schedule was reduced to 31 "major" events, all 250 miles or more.

One week after Bill France Jr. succeeded his father, Andy Granatelli, the president of the STP

Corp., announced that STP would sponsor Richard Petty's car. The longest continuing sponsoring in NASCAR remains in place today with the Petty-owned No. 43 car driven by John Andretti.

On the track, the Petty-Bobby Allison feud heated up. The two rivals were clearly one level above their competitors. Allison, driving a Richard Howard-owned Chevrolet sponsored by Coca-Cola, and Petty, in the STP Plymouth, frequently dented each other's cars in races. At Richmond, Virginia, in September, Petty's car was tapped in the rear by Allison, causing it to careen toward the grandstand and slide along the steel guard rail. Somehow, Petty saved the car, remained in the lead, and won the race. Allison was second.

Two weeks later, at Martinsville, Virginia, Petty and Allison were at it again. Attempting to pass Allison on the inside, Petty's car scraped Allison's and knocked the fuel cap loose on the Chevrolet. Allison ignored the black flag from NASCAR officials and raced on until a caution flag enabled him to make a pit stop and fix the fuel cap. Petty beat Allison by six seconds. NASCAR fined Allison $500 for not responding to the black flag.

The race the following week at North Wilkesboro, North Carolina, was one of the most exciting short-track events in NASCAR history. Allison and Petty traded the lead 10 times in the final 39 laps. As the last lap began, Allison held a three-car-length lead. But with his right wheels rubbing against the car's sheet metal, the driver's compartment was filled with smoke. When Allison drove high on the track to avoid debris from Petty's car, the "King" raced under Allison to win by two car lengths. Afterward, the two were fuming. Said Petty: "There's not going to be any trouble until he hurts me. He's playing with my life out there. If I had films of this, I could sue him for assault with intent to kill, or something close to that." Replied Allison: "He hit me so hard that it bent my fender in. When he did that, I just ran back into him." Advised by NASCAR officials to knock it off, Allison and Petty shook hands before the Charlotte race, and there were no more incidents.

Allison won the 500-mile Charlotte race in early October, finishing ahead of Buddy Baker. Allison also took the next race, at North Carolina Motor Speedway in Rockingham, with Petty placing second. Baker won the season finale, the Texas 500. A.J. Foyt was second, Petty third, and Allison fourth. Allison won the most races for the year, 10, but Petty gained his fourth driving championship, 127.9 points ahead of Allison. Petty collected $40,000 of the $100,000 bonus fund as the first champion under RJR's sponsorship.

In other top races: Bobby Isaac, David Pearson, and Baker were racing for the checkered flag in the Winston 500 at Talladega when Jimmy Crawford spun and made contact with Isaac. Pearson won the race . . . A.J. Foyt, driving the Wood Brothers Mercury, won the Daytona 500 . . . At Talladega in August, James Hylton, in a Mercury, held off Ramo Stott to gain his second career Grand National victory and his first on a superspeedway.

WINSTON CUP STANDINGS

	DRIVER	STARTS	WINS	POINTS	MONEY
1.	Richard Petty	31	8	8,701	339,405
2.	Bobby Allison	31	10	8,573	348,939
3.	James Hylton	31	1	8,158	126,705
4.	Cecil Gordon	31	0	7,326	73,126
5.	Benny Parsons	31	0	6,844	102,043

6.	Walter Ballard	31	0	6,781	59,745
7.	Elmo Langley	30	0	6,656	59,644
8.	John Sears	28	0	6,298	51,314
9.	Dean Dalton	29	0	6,295	42,299
10.	Ben Arnold	26	0	6,179	44,547
11.	Frank Warren	30	0	5,788	45,048
12.	Jabe Thomas	28	0	5,772	43,438
13.	Bill Champion	29	0	5,740	42,242
14.	Raymond Williams	28	0	5,712	37,000
15.	Dave Marcis	27	0	5,459	45,012
16.	Charlie Roberts	26	0	5,354	32,488
17.	Henley Gray	28	0	5,093	38,461
18.	J. D. McDuffie	27	0	5,075	36,883
19.	Bobby Isaac	27	1	5,050	133,257
20.	David Pearson	17	6	4,718	142,440
21.	Ed Negre	26	0	4,696	30,538
22.	Buddy Arrington	20	0	4,555	28,700
23.	Larry Smith	23	0	4,173	24,215
24.	Buddy Baker	17	2	3,936	102,540
25.	Coo Coo Marlin	20	0	3,852	28,124
26.	David Ray Boggs	24	0	3,739	19,489
27.	Ron Keselowski	22	0	3,475	21,905
28.	Joe Frasson	16	0	3,152	21,570
29.	Richard Brown	16	0	2,939	19,283
30.	Neil Castles	21	0	2,789	18,760
31.	Jim Vandiver	16	0	2,514	27,983
32.	Clarence Lovell	12	0	2,360	10,770
33.	David Sisco	12	0	2,310	13,700
34.	LeeRoy Yarborough	18	0	2,157	40,705
35.	George Althiede	11	0	1,916	10,405
36.	Donnie Allison	10	0	1,849	16,826
37.	Richard Childress	15	0	1,521	7,245
38.	Bill Shirley	13	0	1,468	8,070
39.	Fred Lorenzen	8	0	1,333	19,075
40.	Wendell Scott	6	0	1,317	5,830
41.	Tommy Gale	6	0	1,298	7,197
42.	Bill Dennis	11	0	1,279	9,604
43.	G. C. Spencer	10	0	1,238	8,040
44.	Dick May	6	0	1,229	5,370
45.	Hershel McGriff	4	0	1,199	12,290
46.	Les Covey	7	0	1,128	5,070
47.	Johnny Halford	5	0	1,103	4,955
48.	Pete Hamilton	5	0	1,083	8,005
49.	Dick Brooks	14	0	1,023	14,146
50.	Eddie Yarboro	6	0	1,007	3,435

1973

AT A GLANCE

Winston Cup Champion: Benny Parsons

Notable Events: The carburetor "sleeves" are replaced by restrictor plates for the July 4 race at Daytona.

Top Newcomers: Rookie of the Year Lennie Pond, from Petersburg, Virginia (one top-5 finish, nine top-10s); Richard Childress, one top-5, two top-10s).

David Pearson enjoyed a monster year, winning 11 of the 18 races he started in the Wood Brothers Mercury. After two years in Indy-car racing, Cale Yarborough returned to NASCAR, driving the Richard Howard Chevrolet. The ride opened when Bobby Allison split with Junior Johnson, who managed the Howard team, after just one year.

Richard Petty resigned as president of the Professional Drivers Association. The PDA was formed in 1969, with Petty as president, to obtain more rights for the drivers. The PDA boycotted the inaugural race at Talladega in 1969.

Complaining about the engines Richard Petty and Buddy Baker were running, Junior Johnson said, "Those exotic engines Petty and Baker are running can't be bought. I couldn't buy one if I had a million dollars." Responding to Johnson's remarks, Richard Petty's crew chief, Maurice Petty, said, "Tell Junior to come on down here with $6,500 and we'll sell him a race-ready Hemi engine."

When NASCAR ruled that the restrictor plates, which limit the air and fuel intake in an engine, would be used starting with the Firecracker 400 at Daytona, Harry Hyde was furious. Hyde, the crew chief on Buddy Baker's K & K Insurance Dodge, said, "We are being unfairly penalized. If everybody did things like NASCAR, pro basketball would make Wilt Chamberlain play on his knees."

The controversies over rules peaked at Charlotte in early October. Charlie Glotzbach, driving a Chevrolet, put a Hoss Ellington-owned car on the pole for the first time in a Winston Cup Grand National race. The day before the National 500, however, a NASCAR inspection discovered an illegal carburetor plate on Glotzbach's engine. Forced to requalify, Glotzbach started 36th. Glotzbach and Pearson, who inherited the pole, were knocked out of

Benny Parsons in the No. 27 car in 1979.

the race in a crash on lap 46. Cale Yarborough won, but the result wasn't official until 5 p.m. the next day.

Immediately after the race, Bobby Allison filed a protest. Allison, who finished a distant third in a Chevrolet, wanted NASCAR to inspect Yarborough's Chevy and Petty's Dodge. Six hours after the race, NASCAR's Bill Gazaway said no decision had been reached. Finally, on Monday afternoon, NASCAR announced that Yarborough's victory would stand. An angry Allison, still maintaining that Yarborough and Petty were running illegal equipment, threatened to quit NASCAR. He withdrew from the next race at Rockingham. A few days later, Allison announced that he would sue NASCAR for lost earnings. Allison agreed to meet with Bill France Jr. in Atlanta. Following the meeting, in which the NASCAR president agreed to have his staff study inspection methods, Allison backed off his threats. He finished fourth in the season finale at Rockingham, behind Pearson, Baker, and Yarborough.

The season opened with Indy-car driver Mark Donohue, driving an American Motors Matador for Roger Penske, winning on the road course at Riverside, California. Petty won his fourth Daytona 500, finishing more than two laps ahead of Bobby Isaac.

In March, at North Carolina Motor Speedway in Rockingham, Pearson led 499 of the 500 laps. The only time he relinquished the lead was when he made a pit stop. A 21-car crash, described by Buddy Baker as the biggest mess he had ever seen in a race, occured early in the Winston 500 at Talladega in May. After the engine blew on Ramo Stott's Mercury, other cars skidded in the oil. Wendell Scott suffered the most serious injuries: he was hospitalized with three broken ribs, a cracked pelvis, and a lacerated arm.

The Talladega 500, in August, was a memorable event for several reasons. Larry Smith, the 1972 Grand National Rookie of the Year, died of massive head injuries and a basal skull fracture after his car hit the wall on lap 14. Jimmy Crawford, an airline pilot who had competed part-time on the Grand National circuit for several years, was encouraged by NASCAR officials not to race at the high-banked Alabama superspeedway. Crawford had been involved in several crashes. Dick Brooks, who had arrived at Talladega without a ride, drove Crawford's car to Brooks's only major victory. It would be Plymouth's last win in the series.

Parsons took a 194.35-point lead over Petty into the final race at Rockingham. On lap 13, Parsons was caught up in a wreck with Johnny Barnes. Parsons's severely damaged car appeared to be done for the day, but members of other crews helped patch the car and Parsons cruised around the track, finishing 28th. Petty dropped out on lap 133. Parsons won his first, and only, Winston Cup title by 76.15 points over Yarborough.

WINSTON CUP STANDINGS

	DRIVER	STARTS	WINS	POINTS	MONEY
1.	Benny Parsons	28	1	7,173	182,321
2.	Cale Yarborough	28	4	7,106	267,513
3.	Cecil Gordon	28	0	7,046	102,120
4.	James Hylton	28	0	6,972	82,512
5.	Richard Petty	28	6	6,877	234,389
6.	Buddy Baker	27	2	6,327	190,531
7.	Bobby Allison	27	2	6,272	161,818
8.	Walter Ballard	28	0	5,955	53,875
9.	Elmo Langley	27	0	5,826	49,542
10.	J. D. McDuffie	27	0	5,743	56,140
11.	Jabe Thomas	25	0	5,637	42,955
12.	Buddy Arrington	26	0	5,483	40,877
13.	David Pearson	18	11	5,382	228,408
14.	Henley Gray	24	0	5,215	34,112
15.	Richard Childress	25	0	5,169	37,880
16.	Frank Warren	26	0	4,992	36,551
17.	David Sisco	23	0	4,986	36,205
18.	Ed Negre	24	0	4,942	34,235
19.	Dean Dalton	26	0	4,712	35,954
20.	Charlie Roberts	24	0	4,695	32,144
21.	Bill Champion	26	0	4,447	31,828
22.	Coo Coo Marlin	21	0	4,233	29,997
23.	Lennie Pond	23	0	4,013	25,155
24.	Dave Marcis	23	0	3,973	30,253
25.	Raymond Williams	22	0	3,708	22,728
26.	Bobby Isaac	19	0	3,352	84,550
27.	Dick Brooks	14	1	3,200	55,369
28.	Darrell Waltrip	19	0	2,968	42,466
29.	Joe Frasson	14	0	2,952	25,834
30.	Vic Parsons	18	0	2,929	18,200
31.	Jim Vandiver	10	0	2,508	18,586
32.	John Sears	17	0	2,465	16,890
33.	Larry Smith	11	0	2,367	14,090
34.	Rick Newsom	12	0	1,931	8,530
35.	Donnie Allison	14	0	1,755	41,246
36.	D. K. Ulrich	11	0	1,543	3,955
37.	G. C. Spencer	10	0	1,503	12,013
38.	Mel Larson	10	0	1,182	8,235
39.	Johnny Barnes	8	0	1,174	8,585
40.	Eddie Bond	6	0	1,163	6,901
41.	Earle Canavan	5	0	1,144	4,980
42.	Earl Brooks	9	0	1,075	4,880
43.	Charlie Glotzbach	5	0	903	6,451
44.	Randy Tissat	3	0	887	4,245
45.	Ron Keselowski	5	0	879	6,060
46.	Jimmy Crawford	4	0	846	4,059
47.	Richard Brown	13	0	827	7,340
48.	Clarence Lovell	4	0	813	9,175
49.	Bill Dennis	4	0	809	4,225
50.	Jack McCoy	3	0	793	5,270

1974

AT A GLANCE

Winston Cup Champion: Richard Petty

Notable Events: The points system was altered to base points on prize money to encourage drivers to win races or finish high in each event. As it turned out, the system rewarded drivers who finished up front in the big-money races. By midseason, everyone realized the system wasn't working well and it would be changed again after the season. Also, prior to the Daytona race in February, NASCAR announced on March 18 that carburetor plates would be replaced by a new Holley carburetor on all engines larger than 366 cubic inches.

Top Newcomers: Rookie of the Year Earl Ross, one win, four top-5s, nine top-10s, eighth in the points standings; Darrell Waltrip, seven top-5 finishes, 10 top-10s.

This was the year of the Daytona 450. With the United States facing a fuel crisis, NASCAR and other racing organizations moved quickly to avoid being shut down by the federal government. Led by Bill France Sr., a committee was formed to complete a study on fuel consumption. The National Motorsports Committee compiled figures that showed auto racing ranked seventh in fuel consumption. Vacation travel was first. A government official praised the committee's findings, saying the motorsports group's figures were the best available. Responding to the government's directive to reduce fuel usage by 20 to 25 percent, the Frances cancelled the 24 Hours of Daytona and NASCAR trimmed the distances of Winston Cup races. Thus, the Daytona 450, won by Petty. By midseason, the normal race distances were restored.

Bobby Allison (No. 2) and Richard Petty (No. 43) had one of the most famous feuds in racing in the 1970s and '80s.

Petty and Cale Yarborough tied for most victories with 10 each.

The series moved to the northeast for the first time, at Pocono International Raceway in the Pennsylvania mountains. Petty won the Purolator 500, the inaugural Pocono NASCAR race, when rain halted the event with eight laps remaining. Buddy Baker, driving a Bud Moore-owned Ford, secured the first Pocono pole at 144.122 mph.

In the Winston 500 at Talladega, David Pearson beat Benny Parsons by 0.17 seconds. In the Volunteer 500 at Bristol (Tenn.), Cale Yarborough survived a car-banging duel with Baker to win by three car lengths. On the final lap, Yarborough passed Baker on the backstretch. Their cars touched several times. Afterward, Baker was not happy. "When a guy drives into the side of your car," Baker said, "[he's] not supposed to win."

At Martinsville in September, rookie Earl Ross, a 32-year-old Canadian, won his first Winston Cup race in only his 21st start. Ross, who started 11th, inherited the lead when leader Cale Yarborough's engine blew on the 184th lap.

WINSTON CUP STANDINGS

	DRIVER	STARTS	WINS	POINTS	MONEY
1.	Richard Petty	30	10	5,037	432,020
2.	Cale Yarborough	30	10	4,470	363,782
3.	David Pearson	19	7	2,389	252,819
4.	Bobby Allison	27	2	2,019	178,437
5.	Benny Parsons	30	0	1,591	185,080
6.	Dave Marcis	30	0	1,378	83,377
7.	Buddy Baker	19	0	1,016	151,025
8.	Earl Ross	21	1	1,009	81,199
9.	Cecil Gordon	30	0	1,000	66,166
10.	David Sisco	28	0	956	58,313
11.	James Hylton	29	0	924	61,385
12.	J. D. McDuffie	30	0	920	59,535
13.	Frank Warren	29	0	820	55,779
14.	Richie Panch	28	0	775	52,713
15.	Walter Ballard	27	0	748	54,039
16.	Richard Childress	29	0	735	50,249
17.	Donnie Allison	21	0	728	60,315
18.	Lennie Pond	22	0	723	55,990
19.	Darrell Waltrip	16	0	609	67,775
20.	Tony Bettenhausen Jr.	27	0	601	38,995
21.	Jackie Rogers	22	0	587	32,367
22.	Coo Coo Marlin	23	0	581	41,759
23.	Ed Negre	26	0	534	24,622
24.	Bob Burcham	20	0	445	27,923
25.	Elmo Langley	23	0	433	24,722
26.	Charlie Glotzbach	14	0	293	33,072
27.	Dick Brooks	16	0	267	22,760
28.	Joe Frasson	14	0	240	22,629
29.	George Follmer	13	0	230	53,780
30.	Buddy Arrington	16	0	221	21,510
31.	Bill Champion	18	0	207	13,480
32.	D. K. Ulrich	15	0	155	11,955
33.	Bobby Isaac	11	0	152	22,642
34.	Travis Tiller	14	0	146	11,410
35.	Roy Mayne	11	0	141	15,284
36.	Dean Dalton	14	0	125	12,375
37.	Neil Castles	14	0	123	12,479
38.	G. C. Spencer	10	0	96	12,985
39.	Ramo Stott	6	0	82	23,705
40.	Jim Vandiver	7	0	71	15,909
41.	Dan Daughtry	8	0	63	12,413
42.	Jabe Thomas	10	0	49	7,445
43.	Gary Bettenhausen	5	0	49	10,350
44.	A. J. Foyt	4	0	41	15,560
45.	Jerry Schlid	5	0	35	8,395
46.	Earle Canavan	6	0	34	6,570
47.	Dick Trickle	3	0	24	10,828
48.	Marty Robbins	4	0	23	5,734
49.	Alton Jones	5	0	20	4,080
50.	Hershel McGriff	5	0	20	8,585

1975

AT A GLANCE

Winston Cup Champion: Richard Petty

Notable Events: The current points system, devised by racing historian Bob Latford, was introduced. The previous, complicated points system was replaced with a system that awarded equal point value to all races. Bonus points also were involved. The new points structure was designed to encourage teams to enter all races.

Top Newcomers: Rookie of the Year Bruce Hill, from Topeka, Kan.: three top-5 finishes, 11 top-10s, 16th in points.

Concerned about escalating costs, NASCAR instituted an Awards and Achievement Plan. The plan actually presented appearance money. Four top teams would receive from promoters $3,000 for each superspeedway race and $2,000 for each short track event. The teams were Richard Petty, Junior Johnson (Cale Yarborough, driver), Bud Moore (Buddy Baker), and K & K Insurance (Dave Marcis). Independent teams in the top 20 in the points standings would receive $500 per superspeedway race and $250 for short track races. Johnson and Moore, without sponsors, balked at entering all 30 races.

In April, Holly Farms Poultry, based in Junior Johnson's home area of Wilkes County, North Carolina, signed on as a sponsor of Johnson's team. The deal apparently was triggered by the eye-catching television rating for the Daytona 500. ABC televised the second half of the race. Airing opposite an NBA game on CBS and an NHL game on NBC, the race produced a 10.7 rating; the NBA game drew an

8.6, and the hockey game did a 4.1. ABC also televised the Atlanta 500 live. CBS signed a deal to carry the Winston 500 at Talladega and the World 600 at Charlotte one week after each race.

Petty set a Winston Cup record with 13 victories. Baker was runner-up, with four. One of Petty's victories was in the World 600 at Charlotte, marking his first long-distance win at the 1½-mile tri-oval.

In the Daytona 500, David Pearson was leading with three laps remaining. Then he spun, allowing Benny Parsons to gain his only 500-mile win at Daytona. Elsewhere, Darrell Waltrip continued to command attention. In May, the 28-year-old Waltrip won his first race in 50 career starts on his home track in Nashville. Later, Waltrip signed with the DiGard team, owned by Mike DiProspero and Bill Gardner, after Donnie Allison was released. In October, at Richmond, Waltrip won his first race for DiGard.

During the Talladega 500 in August, NASCAR lost one of its most popular drivers when Tiny Lund died. Lund, 42, was racing in a Winston Cup event for the first time in two years. His car spun and came to a stop when it was hit on the driver's side by rookie Terry Link. Lund died of massive chest injuries.

In the Rebel 500 at Darlington in the spring, Waltrip, Bobby Allison, and his brother, Donnie, were in a close chase for the victory. Bobby outdueled Donnie and Waltrip to win. Driving for Roger Penske in a Coca-Cola-sponsored Matador, Bobby Allison won the season opener at Riverside. Pearson, seeking an unprecedented third consecutive Winston 500 victory, was unable to catch Baker, who visited victory lane for the first time since 1973. Baker called it the greatest win of his career. Dave Marcis became another first-time winner when he took the Old Dominion 500 at Martinsville in September. It was the Wisconsin native's 223rd career start. Marcis, 34, edged Benny Parsons.

WINSTON CUP STANDINGS

DRIVER	STARTS	WINS	POINTS	MONEY
1. Richard Petty	30	5	4,783	481,751
2. Dave Marcis	30	1	4,061	240,646
3. James Hylton	30	0	3,914	113,642
4. Benny Parsons	30	1	3,820	214,354
5. Richard Childress	30	0	3,818	96,780
6. Cecil Gordon	30	0	3,702	101,467
7. Darrell Waltrip	28	2	3,462	160,192
8. Elmo Langley	29	0	3,399	67,600
9. Cale Yarborough	27	3	3,295	214,691
10. Dick Brooks	25	0	3,182	93,001
11. Walter Ballard	30	0	3,151	55,696
12. Frank Warren	27	0	3,148	55,671
13. David Sisco	28	0	3,116	62,186
14. David Pearson	21	3	3,057	192,141
15. Buddy Baker	23	4	3,050	236,351
16. Bruce Hill	26	0	3,002	79,428
17. Ed Negre	29	0	2,982	49,629
18. J. D. McDuffie	26	0	2,745	50,937
19. Buddy Arrington	25	0	2,654	45,893
20. Coo Coo Marlin	23	0	2,584	60,013
21. Lennie Pond	22	0	2,540	59,265
22. Jabe Thomas	21	0	2,252	22,390
23. Carl Adams	20	0	2,182	24,865
24. Bobby Allison	19	3	2,181	122,435
25. Bruce Jacobi	15	0	1,732	29,455
26. Dean Dalton	16	0	1,486	19,430
27. D. K. Ulrich	16	0	1,453	16,525
28. Donnie Allison	14	0	1,376	45,595
29. Richie Panch	14	0	1,243	32,585
30. Jim Vandiver	13	0	1,228	24,200
31. Bill Champion	13	0	1,218	11,300
32. Earle Canavan	12	0	1,062	9,725
33. Grant Adcox	11	0	1,020	16,540
34. Joe Mihalic	10	0	957	12,910
35. Joe Frasson	9	0	939	11,975
36. Travis Tiller	10	0	922	7,780
37. Rick Newsom	10	0	877	9,370
38. Ferrel Harris	10	0	797	16,165
39. Henley Gray	9	0	747	8,785
40. G. C. Spencer	9	0	634	14,945
41. Dick May	9	0	631	11,020
42. Earl Brooks	7	0	534	4,900
43. Neil Castles	7	0	529	4,190
44. Jackie Rodgers	8	0	502	11,000
45. Harry Jefferson	5	0	455	11,395
46. Tommy Gale	5	0	437	6,570
47. Ricky Rudd	4	0	431	4,345
48. Bobby Isaac	6	0	405	6,695
49. Dick Skillen	5	0	389	4,865
50. Ray Elder	3	0	372	8,020

1976

AT A GLANCE

Winston Cup Champion: Cale Yarborough

Top Newcomers: Rookie of the Year Skip Manning, from Bogalusa, Louisiana: four top-10 finishes, 18th in points.

Qualifying for the Daytona 500 took on mysterious overtones when A.J. Foyt, Darrell Waltrip, and Dave Marcis ran six to seven mph faster than other top drivers. After a lengthy inspection, NASCAR "disallowed" their times. Inspectors apparently discovered that the fuel lines of some cars contained nitrous oxide, which provides sudden bursts of horsepower. Accepting the decision, Waltrip uttered a quote that did not go over big in

NASCAR's offices. "In Grand National racing," he said, "there are a lot of things you have to do to keep up with the competition. It's common knowledge that cheating, in one form or another, is part of it. If you don't cheat, you look like an idiot."

With several top drivers forced to requalify, the front row for the Daytona 500 was all-Iowan: Ramo Stott and Terry Ryan. Stott, from Keokuk, was a USAC and ARCA racing veteran. He had raced in 29 Winston Cup events. He finished 26th at Daytona. Ryan, from Davenport, had never competed in a major NASCAR race, but he placed sixth.

In one of the wildest finishes ever at Daytona, Richard Petty and David Pearson were dueling on the final lap. Pearson passed Petty on the backstretch, but in Turn 4 their cars met. Pearson and Petty spun into the infield just a few hundred feet from the finish line. Petty was unable to get his STP Dodge moving, but Pearson cranked up the Wood Brothers Purolator Mercury and crawled across the finish line at 15 to 20 mph for his only Daytona 500 victory.

Janet Guthrie leads the pack in the National 500 at Charlotte Motor Speedway.

Janet Guthrie made her debut in Winston Cup racing. Other women were active in NASCAR from the 1940s through the '60s, but Guthrie was the first woman in the 1970s to race in stock car racing's big league. Guthrie, 38, was a physics major at the University of Michigan. She had competed in sports car racing for more than a decade.

After failing to qualify for the Indianapolis 500, Guthrie was contacted about driving in the World 600 at Charlotte a week later. H.A. "Humpy"

Wheeler, newly named vice president and general manager of Charlotte Motor Speedway, knew a gate attraction when he saw one. Lynda Ferreri, a vice president of First Union National Bank in Charlotte, was the car owner. Guthrie qualified a Chevrolet 27th and finished 15th.

Wheeler, a former University of South Carolina football player, had been Firestone's southeastern representative. Bruton Smith, a co-founder of CMS with Curtis Turner, appointed Wheeler after gaining control of the track from Richard Howard. Wheeler was a new-breed racing promoter: he wanted fans to have fun at races and be comfortable.

On the racetracks, there were eight different winners. Cale Yarborough won his first Winston Cup points title and Junior Johnson gained his first championship as a car owner. Pearson won 10 races, one more than Yarborough, but Pearson finished ninth in the points standings because he only entered 22 races . . . Dave Marcis, driving the K & K Insurance Dodge, won three races—Richmond, Talladega and Atlanta . . . Although Richard Petty only won three races, he was runner-up to Yarborough in the points race . . . One of Petty's victories was at Rockingham in February. On the 363rd lap, Allison's car scraped Yarborough's. Allison's Mercury hit the outside wall, then lifted about 20 feet in the air. The car rolled the length of the backstretch. Although Allison was hospitalized for three days, he suffered no serious injuries . . . Presidential candidate Jimmy Carter attended the Atlanta 500. Carter, a Georgian, knew his way around the Atlanta Motor Speedway: he was a former ticket taker at the Atlanta racetrack.

WINSTON CUP STANDINGS

	DRIVER	STARTS	WINS	POINTS	MONEY
1.	Cale Yarborough	30	9	4,644	453,405
2.	Richard Petty	30	3	4,449	374,806
3.	Benny Parsons	30	2	4,304	270,043
4.	Bobby Allison	30	0	4,097	230,170
5.	Lennie Prod	30	0	3,930	159,701
6.	Dave Marcis	30	3	3,875	218,250
7.	Buddy Baker	30	1	3,745	239,922
8.	Darrell Waltrip	30	1	3,505	204,193
9.	David Pearson	22	10	3,483	346,890
10.	Dick Brooks	28	0	3,447	111,880
11.	Richard Childress	30	0	3,428	85,780
12.	J. D. McDuffie	30	0	3,400	82,240
13.	James Hylton	30	0	3,380	78,705
14.	D. K. Ulrich	30	0	3,280	69,435
15.	Cecil Gordon	30	0	3,247	73,830
16.	Frank Warren	30	0	3,240	67,732
17.	David Sisco	28	0	2,994	62,622
18.	Skip Manning	27	0	2,931	61,537
19.	Ed Negre	28	0	2,709	50,919
20.	Buddy Arrington	25	0	2,573	56,647
21.	Terry Bivins	18	0	2,099	44,070
22.	Bobby Wawak	19	0	2,062	31,415
23.	Bruce Hill	22	0	1,995	43,705
24.	Jimmy Means	19	0	1,752	20,945
25.	Dick May	18	0	1,719	29,425
26.	Walter Ballard	14	0	1,554	16,380
27.	Henley Gray	16	0	1,425	15,090
28.	Coo Coo Marlin	12	0	1,412	39,485
29.	Gary Myers	15	0	1,296	11,430
30.	Jackie Rogers	11	0	1,173	21,215
31.	Grant Adcox	11	0	1,163	25,715
32.	Neil Bonnett	14	0	1,130	31,800
33.	Tommy Gale	12	0	1,005	18,955
34.	Donnie Allison	9	1	988	48,455
35.	Joe Mihalic	9	0	981	12,925
36.	Elmo Langley	7	0	824	7,515
37.	Travis Tiller	9	0	816	6,310
38.	Sonny Easley	7	0	772	11,290
39.	Joe Frasson	9	0	707	12,075
40.	Jabe Thomas	6	0	648	6,160
41.	Bill Elliott	8	0	635	11,635
42.	Dean Dalton	6	0	633	7,245
43.	Earle Canavan	7	0	610	6,035
44.	Rick Newsom	7	0	607	5,520
45.	Tighe Scott	6	0	566	15,520
46.	Terry Ryan	5	0	558	24,940
47.	Darrell Bryant	8	0	546	11,925
48.	Buck Baker	8	0	513	12,655
49.	Chuck Bown	5	0	481	5,480
50.	Baxter Price	6	0	479	3,010

1977

AT A GLANCE

Winston Cup Champion: Cale Yarborough

Top Newcomers: Rookie of the Year Ricky Rudd, from Chesapeake, Virginia: one top-5, 10 top-10s; Neil Bonnett, two wins, five top-5 finishes, nine top-10s.

Taking his second consecutive points championship, Cale Yarborough won nine races, followed by Darrell Waltrip with six. Bonnett, a fresh face in the "Alabama Gang" that featured the Allison brothers, won two races: at Richmond in September and the season finale, at Ontario, California. Bonnett was driving for Jim Stacy.

After failing to win a race in 1976, Bobby Allison left Roger Penske's team. Penske replaced Allison with Dave Marcis. Allison decided to continue racing Matadors and acquired sponsorship from Citicorp and First National City Travelers Checks. Until '76, the last time Allison went a year without winning was 1965: in 1977, he would also go winless. Allison wasn't alone enduring an 0-fer year: Marcis also failed to win a race. After the season, Penske would leave NASCAR to concentrate on his successful Indy-car teams.

Despite squabbling within their teams, Yarborough and Waltrip won seven of the first 10 races. After finishing second at Talladega, Yarborough said he was driving "the sorriest Chevrolet on the track." Predictably, Junior Johnson was upset with his driver's comment. "If he keeps running his mouth," Johnson said, "he'll be looking for another car."

Over at the DiGard shop, former driver Darel Dieringer was hired in April as racing coordinator. Waltrip promptly won his first superspeedway race at Darlington. One month after Dieringer arrived, crew chief David Ifft quit, saying he couldn't communicate with Dieringer. Buddy Parrott replaced Ifft. Waltrip also won at Talladega in May, making DiGard 2-for-2 on superspeedways. By June, however, Dieringer was gone.

In his victory at Darlington, Waltrip showed the talent that was moving him into the Petty-Allison-Pearson-Yarborough elite level. With seven laps to go in the TranSouth 400, Waltrip was running fourth, behind Pearson, Petty, and Allison, who had relieved his brother, Donnie. When two cars collided in front of the leaders, Waltrip dashed through the wreckage and outran Allison to the caution flag. The race ended under caution. "There was a perception that nobody could beat those guys," Waltrip said. "They were the sport and no one else mattered. I knew that if you were ever going to prove yourself in this business, you had to win Darlington. Winning Darlington makes people take you seriously."

Back at Darlington in September for the Southern 500, Waltrip and Yarborough put on a memorable late-race show, passing each other several times for the lead. Just over 100 laps remained when they were racing side by side approaching three lapped cars. Neither Waltrip nor Yarborough slowed down and a five-car wreck occurred. After Yarborough finished fifth and Waltrip sixth, D.K. Ulrich, who was involved in the crash, was upset with Yarborough. The Spartanburg, South Carolina, veteran quickly advised Ulrich that Waltrip was the one who hit him. Yarborough referred to the brash Waltrip as "Jaws."

After winning at North Wilkesboro the following week, Waltrip, never one to avoid a lively verbal exchange, referred to the "Cale Scale." The scale involved degree of difficulty. Saying the race was only a 1½ or a 2, Waltrip said he wished there were another 100 laps. Waltrip wondered if Yarborough, then 38, was "getting too old."

Perhaps motivated by Waltrip's comments, Yarborough became the first driver since Herman Beam in 1962 to finish all the races he started . . . By

winning the Carolina 500 in March, Petty became the first driver to win three in a row at Rockingham.

WINSTON CUP STANDINGS

	DRIVER	STARTS	WINS	POINTS	MONEY
1.	Cale Yarborough	30	9	5,000	561,642
2.	Richard Petty	30	5	4,614	406,608
3.	Benny Parsons	30	4	4,570	359,341
4.	Darrell Waltrip	30	6	4,498	324,814
5.	Buddy Baker	30	0	3,961	224,847
6.	Dick Brooks	29	0	3,742	151,374
7.	James Hylton	30	0	3,476	108,392
8.	Bobby Allison	30	0	3,467	94,575
9.	Richard Childress	30	0	3,463	97,012
10.	Cecil Gordon	30	0	3,294	86,312
11.	Buddy Arrington	28	0	3,247	88,887
12.	J. D. McDuffie	30	0	3,236	85,227
13.	David Pearson	22	2	3,227	221,272
14.	Skip Manning	28	0	3,120	111,317
15.	D. K. Ulrich	30	0	2,901	69,677
16.	Frank Warren	29	0	2,876	67,945
17.	Ricky Rudd	25	0	2,810	75,905
18.	Neil Bonnett	23	2	2,649	122,615
19.	Jimmy Means	26	0	2,640	52,505
20.	Tighe Scott	26	0	2,628	63,225
21.	Sam Sommers	23	0	2,517	54,525
22.	Ed Negre	24	0	2,214	42,665
23.	Janet Guthrie	19	0	2,037	37,945
24.	Donnie Allison	17	2	1,970	146,435
25.	Dave Marcis	18	0	1,931	72,605
26.	Tommy Gale	18	0	1,689	39,190
27.	Dick May	13	0	1,324	21,690
28.	Henley Gray	14	0	1,214	18,610
29.	Bruce Hill	16	0	1,213	25,035
30.	Lennie Pond	14	0	1,193	49,440
31.	Butch Hartman	11	0	1,116	18,615
32.	Ferrel Harris	11	0	1,088	19,365
33.	Baxter Price	12	0	1,086	10,890
34.	Coo Coo Marlin	11	0	1,004	42,450
35.	Bill Elliott	10	0	926	20,075
36.	Gary Myers	10	0	888	10,975
37.	David Sisco	10	0	847	13,920
38.	Terry Bivins	8	0	841	14,920
39.	G. C. Spencer	8	0	785	15,755
40.	Terry Ryan	7	0	702	12,405
41.	Joe Mihalic	8	0	683	7,650
42.	Elmo Langley	7	0	634	5,855
43.	Dean Dalton	8	0	620	6,255
44.	Earl Brooks	6	0	552	3,045
45.	Bobby Wawak	8	0	522	13,455
46.	Harold Miller	6	0	470	8,480
47.	Junior Miller	5	0	467	2,475
48.	Ramo Scott	5	0	440	10,170
49.	Grant Adcox	6	0	413	8,750
50.	Sonny Easley	3	0	386	9,490

1978

AT A GLANCE

Winston Cup Champion: Cale Yarborough

Notable Events: NASCAR permits other General Motors cars to use a 350-cubic inch engine previously restricted to Chevrolets.

Top Newcomers: Rookie of the Year Ronnie Thomas, from Christianburg, Virginia: two top-10 finishes, 18th in points.

Cale Yarborough set a record with his third consecutive title. He again won the most races (10). Darrell Waltrip was runner-up, with six. Yarborough clinched the championship by winning the American 500 at North Carolina Motor Speedway. With three Winston Cup championships, Yarborough said his goal was to top Richard Petty's record of six titles.

With gas prices rising as a result of the renewed fuel crisis, NASCAR braced for the introduction of smaller cars to racing. Since the smaller cars wouldn't be in use for several more years, NASCAR extended the "used-car" rule in the Winston Cup series: four-year-old cars could still be raced. Until now, used cars could only be three years old.

Yarborough and Junior Johnson switched to Oldsmobiles, as did Benny Parsons and the L.G. DeWitt team and Buddy Baker's M.C. Anderson team. Richard Petty decided to stay with the Dodge Magnum but, after failing to finish four of the first five races, he changed his mind. Midway through the season, he switched to a Chevrolet.

Bobby Allison, driving a Bud Moore Ford, won his first Daytona 500. Ending a 67 overall-race drought, Allison outlasted Baker. Bill Elliott, a promising young Georgian, finished eighth.

At Rockingham in March, David Pearson won his 100th career Winston Cup race. In the next race, at Atlanta, Bobby Allison won again. Dave Marcis was second in a Rod Osterlund Chevrolet and Donnie Allison was third in a Hoss Ellington Chevy.

In the most exciting finish in Charlotte's 19-year history, Darrell Waltrip outdueled Donnie Allison to win the World 600. Benny Parsons and David Pearson also were in contention late in the race until Parsons spun and collected Pearson's car.

Although he had four years remaining on his contract, Waltrip strongly hinted that he wanted to leave DiGard. He was unhappy with his deal that gave him 50 percent of race earnings, plus incentives, but no post-season awards. Waltrip eyed the Oldsmobile ride with Harry Ranier, who planned to release Lennie Pond. DiGard's Bill Gardner maintained that Waltrip would have to fulfill his contract. Following a late-October meeting, Waltrip issued a surprise announcement: his contract with DiGard was extended for two years, and he would share in post-season awards.

Pond, driving a Harry Ranier Olds, won at Talladega in the fastest 500-mile race ever with an average speed of 175.700 mph. At Pocono, Waltrip edged Pearson by 0.7 seconds. In the Southern 500 at Darlington, rookie Terry Labonte finished an impressive fourth in his first Winston Cup start. Attrition removed several top cars, creating top-10 finishes for independents James Hylton (seventh), Buddy Arrington (eighth), and Ronnie Thomas (ninth).

With nine laps left in the next race at Richmond, Waltrip and Neil Bonnett evolved into a bumper-cars act. Bonnett hit the guard rail and Waltrip went on to win. As the cars returned to the pits, Bonnett slammed his Chevrolet into Waltrip's Chevy. Waltrip insisted Bonnett had cut him off. The crowd favored Bonnett in the dispute: on his way to the press box for the winner's interview, Waltrip required a police escort.

Prior to the World 600 at Charlotte, Humpy Wheeler arranged for a ride for Willy T. Ribbs, then 23 and America's most promising black driver. Ribbs was supposed to drive a Ford owned by Will Cronkrite. Since everyone thought Ribbs would need practice on a superspeedway, Wheeler set up two practice sessions. Ribbs never showed for the sessions. Cronkrite gave the ride to Dale Earnhardt, a successful local sportsman driver. With relief help from Harry Gant, Earnhardt finished 17th.

WINSTON CUP STANDINGS

DRIVER	STARTS	WINS	POINTS	MONEY
1. Cale Yarborough	30	10	4,841	623,506
3. Darrell Waltrip	30	6	4,362	413,908
4. Benny Parsons	30	3	4,350	329,993
6. Richard Petty	30	0	3,949	242,273
5. Dave Marcis	30	0	4,335	205,871
6. Richard Petty	30	0	3,949	242,273
7. Lennie Pond	28	1	3,794	181,096
8. Dick Brooks	30	0	3,769	137,590
9. Buddy Arrington	30	0	3,626	112,960
10. Richard Childress	30	0	3,566	108,702
11. J. D. McDuffie	30	0	3,255	86,857
12. Neil Bonnett	30	0	3,129	167,742
13. Tighe Scott	29	0	3,110	87,912
14. Frank Warren	30	0	3,036	68,173
15. Dick May	28	0	2,936	65,291
16. David Pearson	22	4	2,756	198,775

17.	Jimmy Means	27	0	2,756	61,725
18.	Ronnie Thomas	27	0	2,733	75,815
19.	Cecil Gordon	26	0	2,641	53,815
20.	Tommy Gale	26	0	2,639	60,765
21.	Roger Hamby	26	0	2,617	41,315
22.	D.K. Ulrich	22	0	2,452	54,550
23.	Baxter Price	24	0	2,418	36,560
24.	Buddy Baker	19	0	2,130	111,765
25	Donnie Allison	17	1	1,993	127,475
26.	James Hylton	19	0	1,965	48,045
27.	Gary Myers	19	0	1,915	22,140
28.	Ed Negre	21	0	1,857	28,995
29.	Skip Manning	17	0	1,802	55,470
30.	Grant Adcox	14	0	1,802	37,100
31.	Ricky Rudd	13	0	1,260	50,630
32.	Bruce Hill	14	0	1,214	25,770
33.	Bill Elliott	10	0	1,176	42,215
34.	Al Holbert	12	0	1,142	31,075
35.	Ferrel Harris	14	0	1,066	39,685
36.	Coo Coo Marlin	9	0	765	19,415
37.	Blackie Wangerin	10	0	760	13,515
38.	Bobby Wawak	8	0	680	5,870
39.	Terry Labonte	5	0	659	21,395
40.	Ralph Jones	7	0	634	6,305
41.	Janet Guthrie	7	0	592	17,120
42.	Earl Canavan	9	0	559	8,740
43.	Dale Earnhardt	5	0	558	20,745
44.	Roland Wlodyka	6	0	549	9,910
45.	Joe Frasson	5	0	533	9,210
46.	Nelson Oswald	6	0	501	2,955
47.	Joe Mihalic	6	0	419	6,030
48.	Jim Thirkettle	3	0	389	6,850
49.	Jimmy Insolo	3	0	369	8,665
50.	Satch Worley	4	0	368	6,205

1979

AT A GLANCE

Winston Cup Champion: Richard Petty

Top Newcomers: Dale Earnhardt (7th), Ricky Rudd (9th), and Terry Labonte (10th) crack the top 10 in points for the first time; Joe Millian finished sixth in the points standings (five top-5 finishes, 20 top-10s).

Darrell Waltrip finished with the most victories, seven, followed by Richard Petty and Bobby Allison, five apiece.

This Daytona 500 is the race that is credited for launching NASCAR's national popularity. For the first time, the race was televised live, on CBS, from start to finish. Challenging for the lead on the final lap, Cale Yarborough and Donnie Allison collided in Turn 3, spun and hit the wall. Richard Petty and Darrell Waltrip evaded trouble on the track and battled for the lead. Petty won by a car length, Waltrip was second and A.J. Foyt was third. But the action wasn't over. Allison and Yarborough climbed out of their cars near the third turn, removed their helmets,

and began arguing. Allison's brother Bobby parked his car and joined the argument. Fists started flying. Many viewers believed almost every race included action like this: they don't, but millions of fans were hooked on the sport. Petty used the victory as a springboard to his unprecedented seventh series championship. But it wasn't easy.

As a result of people watching the Daytona telecast, ticket sales soared for the next race, at Rockingham, North Carolina. Nine laps into the race, Yarborough and Donnie Allison were out front when they tangled again. Both finished the race: Yarborough was 18th, Allison 30th. Both insisted this accident had nothing to do with what occurred at Daytona, but Waltrip, never lacking an opinion, said, "Someone ought to drag Cale out of his car and whip his butt. Cale knocked the hell out of Donnie." Rookie Joe Millikan, in his fourth Winston Cup start, finished second with relief help by Richard Petty for 80 laps.

Rookie Dale Earnhardt, in his 16th Winston Cup start, won his first race, taking the Southeastern 500 at Bristol, Tennessee, by three seconds over Bobby Allison. In the Rebel 500 at Darlington, Waltrip held off Richard Petty to win. David Pearson botched a pit stop: thinking his Wood Brothers crew was only changing two tires, Pearson left the pits too soon. The crew was planning to change four tires. It was Pearson's last race for the Wood Brothers. Neil Bonnett replaced Pearson.

At Nashville in May, Millikan, driving the L.G. DeWitt Chevrolet, won his first pole position. Independent driver J.D. McDuffie, 40, led four times for 111 laps in a Chevy. McDuffie finished fifth; Millikan was 23rd in the race won by Yarborough. In the Mason-Dixon 500 at Dover, Del., Bonnett won his first race for the Wood Brothers: it was Bonnett's third career victory.

Another Petty emerged on the Winston Cup scene: Richard's son, Kyle, finished ninth in the Talladega 500. Earlier, Waltrip won his second straight World 600 at Charlotte. The Winston Cup road show returned to Texas for the first time since 1973, and the drivers wondered why they bothered: only 11,500 saw Waltrip win at Texas World Speedway. At Pocono, Yarborough gained his first super-speedway win since October 1978 at Rockingham. Earnhardt was leading on lap 98 when a tire blew on Chevrolet and he hit the wall in the tunnel turn (2). The aggressive 28-year-old broke both his collar bones. Bonnett outraced Benny Parsons to win the Firecracker 400 at Daytona by one second.

In September, David Pearson returned to Darlington, the site of his embarrassing pit-stop blunder. Filling in for the injured Earnhardt in the Rod Osterlund Chevy, the "Silver Fox" won with Bill Elliott second and Terry Labonte third.

With seven races remaining, Petty trailed Waltrip by 187 points. "King Richard" trimmed Waltrip's advantage to just 17 with three races left after Petty finished third at North Wilkesboro and Waltrip was 13th. Petty won the next race, at Rockingham, to overtake Waltrip, who was sixth. Petty led by eight points. In the next-to-last race, Waltrip inched back in front by two points as he placed fifth at Atlanta and Petty was sixth. The drivers and crews headed west, to Ontario, California. Petty finally secured his seventh title by an 11-point margin, the closest ever in Winston Cup, by finishing fifth; Waltrip was eighth.

WINSTON CUP STANDINGS

	DRIVER	STARTS	WINS	POINTS	MONEY
1.	Richard Petty	31	5	4,830	561,934
2.	Darrell Waltrip	31	7	4,819	557,012
3.	Bobby Allison	31	5	4,633	428,801

Dale Earnhardt in his rookie season of 1979.

4. Cale Yarborough	31	4	4,604	440,129
5. Benny Parsons	31	2	4,256	264,930
6. Joe Milikan	31	0	4,014	229,713
7. Dale Earnhardt	27	1	3,749	274,810
8. Richard Childress	31	0	3,735	132,922
9. Ricky Rudd	28	0	3,642	150,898
10. Terry Labonte	31	0	3,615	134,653
11. Buddy Arrington	31	0	3,589	131,833
12. D.K. Ulrich	31	0	3,508	113,458
13. J. D. McDuffie	31	0	3,473	113,478
14. James Hylton	30	0	3,405	97,428
15. Buddy Baker	26	3	3,249	342,148
16. Frank Warren	31	0	3,199	94,539
17. Ronnie Thomas	30	0	2,912	100,079
18. Tommy Gale	27	0	2,795	72,809
19. Cecil Gordon	28	0	2,737	66,275
20. Dave Marcis	25	0	2,736	56,434
21. Harry Gant	25	0	2,664	47,185
22. Dick Brooks	27	0	2,622	61,985
23. Jimmy Means	27	0	2,575	55,560
24. Donnie Allison	20	0	2,508	144,770
25. Baxter Price	24	0	2,364	45,165
26. Neil Bonnett	21	3	2,223	151,235
27. Tighe Scott	17	0	1,879	88,010
28. Bill Elliott	14	0	1,548	58,200
29. Lennie Pond	15	0	1,415	42,970
30. Dick May	19	0	1,390	26,345
31. Roger Hamby	12	0	1,231	21,000
32. David Pearson	9	1	1,203	99,180
33. Coo Coo Marlin	7	0	613	27,540
34. Bruce Hill	7	0	594	17,260
35. Blackie Wangerin	7	0	571	14,300
36. Grant Adcox	6	0	560	15,290
37. Kyle Petty	5	0	559	10,810
38. Chuck Bown	7	0	523	31,380
39. John Anderson	4	0	496	11,210
40. Ralph Jones	6	0	477	12,785
41. Earle Canavan	7	0	456	6,675
42. Slick Johnson	4	0	431	5,360
43. Nelson Oswald	6	0	431	3,610
44. Dave Watson	4	0	413	7,170
45. Al Holbert	6	0	402	14,170
46. Bobby Wawak	4	0	376	7,295
47. Jody Riley	3	0	374	11,245
48. Bill Hollar	5	0	371	2,545
49. Rick Newsom	4	0	355	5,530
50. Bill Schmitt	3	0	342	11,695

7

A DECADE OF GROWTH: CORPORATE AMERICA FALLS FOR NASCAR

Glance at a starting lineup for a Winston Cup race in the 1990s and you'll see sponsors not normally associated with auto racing: Du Pont, Kellogg's, Tide, the Family Channel, and the Cartoon Network are just a few. Why would these sponsors invest millions of dollars in racing? Two reasons: marketing and exposure.

Back in the early 1980s, it occurred to some sharp marketing and advertising people that crowds at NASCAR races were growing. Television ratings also were climbing. And the image of NASCAR drivers was appealing: on the track they were daring and occasionally exchanged angry words while defending their honor. Out of their cars, they were fan-friendly. Drivers patiently signed autographs at the tracks or at personal appearances. Unlike athletes in other sports, the names of race car drivers didn't frequently appear on police blotters. Suddenly, investing in a Winston Cup or Busch Grand National team seemed like a worthwhile, and profitable, idea to these marketing and advertising executives.

The foresight of NASCAR president Bill France, Jr. is credited by most for opening the door to many non-automotive sponsors. France studied

racing at the side of his father, NASCAR founder Bill France, Sr. In 1972, Bill Jr. succeeded his father. Throughout the 1970s, NASCAR grew. However, it still was basically a regional sport, primarily popular in the Carolinas, Virginia, Tennessee, Kentucky, Alabama, Georgia, and Florida.

After the 1979 Daytona 500, which was televised live for the first time (by CBS), more fans nationwide developed an interest in Winston Cup racing. That race at Daytona, won by Richard Petty, ended with Cale Yarborough and the Allison brothers, Bobby and Donnie, punching each other in the infield. Jim Hunter, president of Darlington Raceway in South Carolina, was working for NASCAR at the time.

"Bill France Jr. had the great vision that we needed to go after non-automotive products to expand our horizon and make more people aware of our sport," Hunter said. "Bill said these companies have the advertising and promotional budgets to help us carry our message to a bigger audience all over the country, especially in bigger markets like New York, Philadelphia, Chicago, Los Angeles, Seattle, Denver and Kansas City. Bill knew that they sell cereal everywhere. Same thing with

ELLIOT'S AMAZING RACE

It's almost impossible to pick one race as a stock car driver's single all-time best performance. So many races, so many situations, so many "what ifs" and "if onlys" to consider. So many late-race disappointments to mar what might have otherwise been a classic afternoon.

But fans of Bill Elliott generally agree that his Die-Hard 500-winning performance in July of 1987 at the Talladega Superspeedway in Alabama was the most impressive of his 40 career Winston Cup victories, all but two of them on superspeedways.

An early-race problem with his Ford's oil pump belt forced him to pit under green. He lost two and a half laps and was summarily discounted by almost everyone as a contender to win the 188-lap race. But he nevertheless returned to the track and proceeded to go as hard as he could, just hoping to make something out of nothing.

By mid-race, his break-neck pace had taken him past everyone on the track and within with one lap of the leaders. Then, to the amazement of almost everyone (including, we would learn later, Elliott himself) that frenetic pace got him past everyone another time and thus back on the lead lap.

Finally, with a pass that will stand for all time as one of the most dramatic in the sport's history, Elliott shot by Davey Allison with 38 laps remaining and led the rest of the way. His margin of victory was .15 second after being almost three miles behind at one point. He beat Allison, Dale Earnhardt, Darrell Waltrip, and Terry Labonte, all of whom were powerless to stop history as it was coming past them at close to 200 miles per hour

---

Proctor and Gamble and Tide: everybody uses detergent. These companies used NASCAR as a marketing tool for their products. As a result, NASCAR became more than a southeastern sport. It's been a phenomenal marketing success."

The major reason that NASCAR's popularity extends nationwide is television. By the mid-1990s, all Winston Cup, Busch Grand National, and Craftsman Truck Series races were being televised—on cable by ESPN, ESPN2, and The Nashville Network; and by traditional over-the-air networks CBS and ABC.

ESPN CHANGES THE FACE OF RACING

In the early 1980s, ESPN's emerging presence became a force in increasing interest in NASCAR. In October 1979, exactly one month after ESPN flickered onto the nation's television screens for the first time from its headquarters in Bristol, Connecticut, it televised its first race: a USAC sprint event from Salem, Indiana. ESPN's first live race telecast was in June 1981: an Indy-car 150-miler from Milwaukee won by Mike Mosley. He sped across the finish line first despite starting last. ESPN carried the 1985 Southern 500 from Darlington Raceway when Bill Elliott won the first Winston Million bonus.

Terry Lingner supervised ESPN's coverage of that 1979 race from Salem and remembers it well:

"Bill Fitts was the first coordinating producer at ESPN," recalled Lingner, now the head of his own production company in Indianapolis. "Bill had produced the first Super Bowl. He called in Bruce Connal and me and said our first two series were going to be boxing and something called USAC auto racing. He said, 'I don't know anything about either one. What do you want to do?' I said that since I grew up in the Midwest and loved racing, I'd be the racing guy. ESPN was, and still is, run by a lot of East Coast stick-and-ball guys. They basically turned the whole racing package over to me. I was 25 at the time. As long as they weren't getting hate mail and it wasn't going horribly, they let me grow the whole production of motor sports."

Back in the early 1980s, ESPN needed programming to fill its round-the-clock schedule. "That

ESPN needed hours was a blessing for my staff," Lingner said. "We always were given enough tools to cover races in good basic fashion. But we didn't have the budget to do what a lot of the networks were doing. We couldn't afford features so we had to work harder to make the actual race more interesting."

As racing fans learned that ESPN was providing full coverage of races, from the green to checkered flags, viewership increased. Said Lingner: "The people at ESPN had a hunch that motorsports people would be passionate." The ESPN people were right. Drivers, car owners, and promoters in NASCAR were more than willing to cooperate with ESPN and other networks.

"I grew up a bike ride away from the Indianapolis Motor Speedway," Lingner said, "but dollar for dollar, you can't beat NASCAR. I knew that, no matter what time of day or night, I could get Richard Petty or Darrell Waltrip to do something for me. It wasn't that way when I was doing Formula One or Indy car races."

BIG MONEY: THE BEER AND TOBACCO COMPANIES

By the mid-1980s, sponsors realized they could get enormous exposure through television: millions of viewers for each race would see their logos on the cars. One of these sponsors was Anheuser-Busch. Its Budweiser brand has been a familiar sight at racetracks for decades.

"Back in the 1980s and '70s, a fan had to work to find racing on TV," said Mike Hargrave, Anheuser-Busch's senior manager of sports marketing. "A lot of the markets didn't have radio coverage. As a sponsor, we were looked at as taking the sport forward for the fans. I think the fans in the '80s looked at us as more of a friend than [saying] 'Look at all the money they're making on racing.' Our initial thrust was to get to our core consumer and relate to them in a sport that they were very supportive of."

For another major brewery, Miller Brewing, the 1980s were boom years as far as their drivers winning major events. Bobby Allison won the 1988 Daytona 500 with Miller as his sponsor. Driving the Miller American car, Danny Sullivan won the 1985 Indianapolis 500 with his renowned spin-and-win maneuver. Al Holbert won the 24 Hours of Daytona and the IMSA GTP championship under Miller's banner.

While Miller likes its drivers to win, the company realizes that it's difficult to string together winning streaks. Said Mike Welsh, Miller's director of sports marketing, "With the technological advancements, it's so competitive now that it's difficult to win every race."

Welsh said that Miller is "very careful about picking our business partners." Miller is associated with the National Football League and the National Basketball Association, plus the Dallas Cowboys and the Chicago Bulls. Rusty Wallace, who drives the Miller Lite car in Winston Cup, had an off year in 1996. However, Welsh points out that Wallace is a proven driver who remains popular. "You don't have to win every race," Welsh said, "but at some point you had to win to establish yourself as a champion. In Winston Cup, there's a tremendous emotional link between the fans and drivers."

Miller, the No. 2 selling brewery in the United States behind Anheuser-Busch, previously sponsored several races in Winston Cup. Last year, its sponsorship was limited to one race at Dover Downs International Speedway in Delaware and two CART Indy-car races. Welsh said Miller concentrates on "being part of the lifestyle of our target customer. In the month leading up to a race, we work on making Miller products relevant for race fans. Once the race starts, our business is done."

Beer and racing go together like hot dogs and baseball. While there are fans who treat a weekend at the races as an opportunity for binge drinking, Welsh said Miller, like other breweries, recommends drinking in moderation. "We spend a lot of time and energy conveying responsible use of our products," he said. "We've used Rusty Wallace, Bobby Rahal, and [drag racer] Don Prudhomme in commercials, urging people not to drink and drive." Miller and other breweries want people to buy a lot of their beer, but consume it reasonably. If they don't, the brewer can come under fire.

Although the appeal of smoking has diminished over health concerns, cigarettes are another product associated with racing. The R.J. Reynolds Tobacco company has been a friend of NASCAR for decades. This year is RJR's 28th season as sponsor of the Winston Cup. In 1997, the Winston Cup champion received $1.5 million from RJR out of a total fund for the Winston Cup series of $4 million. Richard Petty, the first Winston Cup champion, collected $40,000 out of a $100,000 fund. During its years as the Winston Cup sponsor, RJR has paid out about $35 million to drivers and teams. When RJR began sponsoring the Winston Cup series, it was the first nonautomotive company to get involved in NASCAR in a major way. T. Wayne Robertson, the president of RJR's Sports Marketing Enterprises, supervises the company's sports marketing programs that include title sponsorship of the Winston 500 at Talladega. RJR funding also has paid for such improvements at racetracks as paving roads, posting signs, and building media centers.

BEYOND RJR: HOW OTHER COMPANIES HAVE TAKEN THE PLUNGE

Tide's entry into Winston Cup racing in 1987 followed two other Proctor and Gamble brands: Folger's coffee and Crisco. Folger's joined forces with the Morgan-McClure team (briefly with Joe Ruttman and then with Tim Richmond); Crisco sponsored Buddy Baker's car on a limited racing

Sponsorship, which is a huge part of racing in the '90s, really took off in the 1908s, as seen here on Alan Kulwicki's 1985.car.

schedule. Tide signed on with Darrell Waltrip's Rick Hendrick-owned car. Waltrip, at that time, was part of Hendrick's "super team" that also included drivers Geoff Bodine and Tim Richmond.

"The people at Tide liked what they had seen with the Folger's and Crisco sponsorships," said Kirby Boone, president of Sports and Promotions in Mooresville, North Carolina. Boone was involved in the negotiations with Tide from the beginning. "Scott Lutz was the Tide brand manager. He and Steve Donovan, the group vice president, were responsible for Tide getting into racing. At first, it was a southeastern regional promotion for all three Proctor and Gamble brands. Tide didn't get in it for the exposure: Tide is in close to

50 percent of United States households. They did it for marketing and hospitality."

Tide stayed with Hendrick, on Waltrip's car, through 1990. When Ricky Rudd drove for Hendrick, from 1990 through '93, Tide was the sponsor. Since '94, when Rudd formed his own team, Tide has continued as his sponsor. Even though Tide wasn't primarily seeking exposure, it received plenty in 1989 when Waltrip won the Daytona 500 and last year when Rudd won the Brickyard 400 at Indianapolis Motor Speedway.

Long before these companies began their association with NASCAR, another company showed the way for sponsors. STP was a model for other companies to follow. STP and Richard Petty are the

STP has been associated with the Petty's and car number 43 since the 1960s (shown here in 1997).

longest-running sponsor-driver relationship in NASCAR: their first contract was signed in 1972.

Back in the 1960s, STP was involved in Indy car racing and other series. When Mario Andretti won his only Indianapolis 500, in 1969, STP sponsored his car.

"If it raced, we were there," said Ralph Salvino, then STP's vice president of racing. "Cars, boats, airplanes: you name it, we were there."

Salvino began as a salesman for STP, working the West Coast. "We got involved in the grass roots of racing: the sprints, midgets, and drag races [at local tracks]. That contributed a lot to our success. We built such a strong foundation with those people." During a vacation trip to Hawaii, Darlington's Jim Hunter recalls seeing people wearing STP T-shirts.

STP began its sponsorship of Richard Petty shortly after the Detroit car manufacturers withdrew from NASCAR. "Richard was available and Andy jumped on [the deal]," Salvino said. "It was a blessing for us that the car manufacturers got out: it really opened the doors. They didn't want a sponsor's name on their cars." In 1971, the year before STP signed up Petty, Fred Lorenzen had driven an STP-sponsored Dodge.

Although other automotive-related sponsors have been involved with Winston Cup racing for a long period of time, some sponsors get involved for the short term, often three to five years. Frequently their involvement is to meet some marketing and sales objectives.

Wrangler jeans and CRC Chemicals were two of these in the late 1970s and early 1980s. Wrangler launched its sponsorship with Dale Earnhardt and the Rod Osterlund team at the end of the 1980 season, when Earnhardt clinched his first title. Wrangler stayed in until the mid-1980s. Wrangler also sponsored races at Richmond International Raceway. CRC Chemicals, based in Warminster, Pennsylvania, near Philadelphia, sponsored races at Darlington and Dover Downs International Speedway in Delaware from 1979 to 1982. CRC also sponsored the late Al Holbert, who was from Warrington, near Warminster, in Indy-car racing and the Can-Am series.

Wrangler's involvement in Winston Cup racing produced the results experienced by many sponsors. "It was a tremendous marketing tool," said Dave Fulton, who was manager of Wrangler's NASCAR special events. Fulton now works in public relations and marketing at Richmond Raceway in Virginia. "In the late '70s," Fulton said, "Wrangler was losing its market share. Wrangler was an old-line jeans manufacturer: it wasn't fashioned oriented."

Fulton said that after representatives of Blue Bell, the Greensboro, N.C.-based company that manufactured Wrangler jeans, did extensive market research about NASCAR, Robert Odear was hired to supervise the program. Odear had been a brand manager for RJR's Winston cigarettes. Odear brought in Jack Watson as director of advertising. Watson also had been a brand manager for RJR.

"Our agency in New York had created the catch-phrase 'One Tough Customer' to describe our jeans," Fulton said. "We transferred that phrase to Dale: he fit it perfectly." Also working with Wrangler was Joe Whitlock, a popular former publicist for NASCAR, Daytona International Speedway, and Charlotte Motor Speedway.

When Earnhardt joined Bud Moore's team in 1981 for two years, the Wrangler sponsorship went with them. The Blue Bell company was eventually sold in the mid 1980s to Vanity Fair, which also owned Lee jeans. That's when Wrangler left Winston Cup racing. Fulton said successful sponsors in racing spend $2.50 to $3 on advertising and promotion for every dollar they spend on the team. In other words, for every $1 million a year spent on the team, a sponsor should spend about another $3 million on advertising and promotion.

In 1976, officials of CRC Chemicals decided they wanted to challenge the manufacturers of the WD-40 spray lubricant for supremacy in the lubricant marketplace. CRC's equivalent product, 5-56, had about 11 percent of the market, whereas WD-40 controlled 80 percent. After two years of research, CRC chose motor sports as a way to increase the visibility of its products. Rich Rubinstein, now president of On Track marketing in Harrisburg, North Carolina, was hired as CRC's director of motorsports.

"WD-40's marketing strategy was to go after the end-user (general consumer) and the mass merchandiser," Rubinstein said. "CRC elected to go after the traditional market: the professional mechanic. WD-40 was a one-product company; CRC had a massive line of products. CRC said, 'We've got to get in front of the end user.' CRC was a $20 to $22 million-per-year company, too small to do TV advertising, so they looked for alternatives."

Rubinstein said CRC's research led them to motor sports in general and NASCAR in particular because NASCAR fans have tremendous brand loyalty. CRC devised a national sweepstakes program that included consumers and trade buyers. Contest winners were invited to the three 500-mile Indy car races and five Winston Cup races. Also in 1978, CRC became an associate sponsor of Richard Childress's race car. The following year, they took over full sponsorship of Childress through '81. "They saw success with what they did in '78," Rubinstein said, "and wanted to enhance it." This step led to sponsorship of races at Darlington and Dover.

In each year CRC was involved in motorsports, Rubinstein said the company had a 27 to 30 percent growth rate. Curiously, in 1982, Rubinstein said CRC started scaling down its involvement in racing. He advised the company to stay in racing, because ESPN was just increasing its coverage of racing. CRC evidently believed it had accomplished its goals in racing. CRC wasn't the first company to ride a while with NASCAR, and it won't be the last.

8

1980–1989: THIS RACE IS BROUGHT TO YOU BY

1980

AT A GLANCE

Winston Cup Champion: Dale Earnhardt

Notable Events: Prior to the April race at Martinsville, Virginia, NASCAR, seeking to reduce expenses for the teams, ruled that no tires could be changed under caution flags. Teams violating this rule would be penalized two laps.

Top Newcomers: Rookie of the Year Jody Ridley, from Chatsworth, Georgia: two top-5 finishes, 18 top-10s, seventh in points; Harry Gant, nine top-5s, 14 top-10s, 11th in points.

Dale Earnhardt won his first of seven Winston Cup titles, edging Cale Yarborough by 19 points. Earnhardt became the first Winston Cup driver to win the championship the year after earning Rookie of the Year honors. Prior to the season, Earnhardt signed a five-year contract with Rod Osterlund, a California real estate developer.

Turmoil, meanwhile, continued with the DiGard team. Crew chief Buddy Parrott, fired after the 1979 season, was rehired in January. Even though Darrell Waltrip had a contract with DiGard through 1983, he was unhappy with the team's management. When DiGard entered another car, for road racer Don Whittington, at Daytona, Waltrip's grumbles were almost as loud as the cars on the racetrack. Waltrip thought two-car teams were unfair to both drivers. "But," he added, "I'm just a lonely soldier doing my duty." Whittington failed to qualify for Daytona and later formed his own team.

Buddy Baker, driving the Ranier Racing Oldsmobile, won the Daytona 500 in record time, averaging 177.602 mph. Baker collected the largest winner's check in NASCAR history: $102,175.

In September, Cale Yarborough announced he and Junior Johnson would be splitting after eight years together. Driving for Johnson, Yarborough won three consecutive titles and 50 races. Yarborough decided he wanted to run a limited schedule. Car owner M.C. Anderson and Yarborough signed a three-year deal. Shortly after Yarborough's decision to leave Johnson, Bobby Allison said he planned to leave Bud Moore's team. Allison would succeed Baker in the Ranier Olds.

Earnhardt won at Atlanta, with rookie Rusty Wallace second in a Roger Penske Chevrolet. Earnhardt also won the next race, at Bristol. In the World 600 at Charlotte, Benny Parsons withstood the threat of Darrell Waltrip to win. Waltrip was seeking

Dale Earnhardt in his familiar No. 3 at the 1987 TranSouth 500.

his third World 600 in a row. With 120,000 fans roaring, Parsons and Waltrip swapped the lead five times during the final 25 laps. Driving the M.C. Anderson Chevrolet, Parsons finally took the lead for good with two laps remaining. His $44,850 winner's paycheck was the largest of his 11-year career.

Following the World 600 at Charlotte, Jake Elder resigned as the crew chief on Earnhardt's car. Elder rejoined DiGard after Parrott was fired again. Doug Richert, only 20 years old, was named Earnhardt's crew chief.

At Riverside, California, Waltrip overtook Neil Bonnett in the ninth turn of the last lap to win his 26th Winston Cup race. At Pocono, Richard Petty suffered a neck injury when he crashed in the tunnel turn. Doctors diagnosed the injury as a severe sprain; Petty said it was a broken neck. Bonnett, in the Wood Brothers Mercury, won the Pocono race and the next 500-miler at Talladega. Petty drove one lap at Talladega before Joe Millikan relieved him.

Terry Labonte, 23, won his first Winston Cup race, taking the Southern 500 at Darlington. Entering the final race of the season, at Ontario, California, Earnhardt led Yarborough by 29 points. Yarborough, in his last season driving for Junior Johnson, finished third at Ontario and Earnhardt was fifth. The 10th-place finisher in the points standings was Richard Childress, who would hire Earnhardt as his driver the next year.

WINSTON CUP STANDINGS

	DRIVER	STARTS	WINS	POINTS	MONEY
1.	Dale Earnhardt	31	5	4,661	671,991
2.	Cale Yarborough	31	6	4,642	567,891
3.	Benny Parsons	31	3	4,278	411,519
4.	Richard Petty	31	2	4,255	397,318
5.	Darrell Waltrip	31	5	4,239	405,711
6.	Bobby Allison	31	4	4,019	378,970
7.	Jody Riley	31	0	3,972	204,883
8.	Terry Labonte	31	1	3,766	222,502
9.	Dave Marcis	31	0	3,745	150,165
10.	Richard Childress	31	0	3,742	157,420
11.	Harry Gant	31	0	3,703	177,150
12.	Buddy Arrington	31	0	3,461	120,355
13.	James Hylton	31	0	3,449	109,230
14.	Ronnie Thomas	30	0	3,066	94,730
15.	Cecil Gordon	29	0	2,933	83,300
16.	J. D. McDuffie	31	0	2,968	82,402
18.	Tommy Gale	29	0	2,885	84,279
19.	Neil Bonnett	22	2	2,865	231,854
20.	Roger Hamby	25	0	2,606	51,534
21.	Buddy Baker	19	2	2,603	275,200
22.	Lake Speed	19	0	1,853	69,670
23.	Slick Johnson	18	0	1,851	35,460
24.	John Anderson	20	0	1,805	48,265
25.	Bobby Wawak	19	0	1,742	21,080
26.	Donnie Allison	18	0	1,730	92,640
27.	Dick Brooks	19	0	1,698	60,700
28.	Kyle Petty	15	0	1,690	36,045
29.	Baxter Price	18	0	1,689	26,615
30.	Lennie Pond	17	0	1,558	62,265
31.	Junior Miller	16	0	1,402	23,420
32.	Dick May	21	0	1,323	42,945
33.	Joe Milikan	12	0	1,274	74,765
34.	Bill Elliott	12	0	1,232	42,545
35.	Ricky Rudd	13	0	1,213	50,500
36.	Bill Elswick	12	0	1,053	15,600
37.	David Pearson	9	1	1,004	102,730
38.	D.K. Ulrich	11	0	935	23,055
39.	Tighe Scott	10	0	791	21,925
40.	Frank Warren	7	0	559	18,375
41.	Tim Richmond	5	0	527	14,925
42.	Bill Schmitt	4	0	503	21,610
43.	Buck Simmons	6	0	495	6,365
44.	Rick Newsom	6	0	483	3,830
45.	Dave Dion	4	0	441	5,015
46.	Don Whittington	7	0	429	17,610
47.	Steve Moore	4	0	412	9,040
48.	Tommy Houston	4	0	396	5,020
49.	Sterling Marlin	5	0	387	29,810
50.	Bruce Hill	6	0	348	7,540

1981

AT A GLANCE

Winston Cup Champion: Darrell Waltrip

Notable Events: With Detroit manufacturers downsizing cars, NASCAR mandated that, beginning with the Daytona 500, cars would be required to have 110-inch wheelbases. Also, when it became apparent that the Pontiac LeMans was faster than the other cars, NASCAR several times adjusted the size of spoilers, effectively discouraging use of the LeMans.

Top Newcomers: Two rookies won their first races: Ron Bouchard, at Talladega, and Morgan Shepherd, at Martinsville. Bouchard, from Fitchburg, Massachusetts, was named Rookie of the Year; Shepherd was 11th on the money list ($165,329) . . . Mark Martin won his first pole position.

Storming back from a huge points deficit midway through the season, Darrell Waltrip won his first of three championships. Waltrip, driving for Junior Johnson, dominated the series with 12 victories.

After Richard Petty won his seventh Daytona 500, crew chief Dale Inman pulled a surprise by resigning and moving to the Rod Osterlund-Dale Earnhardt team. Inman had been crew chief for 92 of Petty's 193 Winston Cup victories. In June, Osterlund sold his team to J.D. Stacy, a Kentuckian who had been in Winston Cup racing in the 1970s. Following the Talladega 500 in August, Earnhardt quit Stacy's team. The defending Winston Cup champion had not won a race in '81 (two second-place finishes were his best performances). Later in the week, Earnhardt signed on with Richard Childress, a veteran driver who was only 35, for the rest of the season. Driving a Childress-owned Pontiac, Earnhardt's best finish was fourth place, which he did twice.

Bobby Allison's season-opening victory in the Ranier Racing Chevrolet was the last Winston Cup race for the full-size cars: Allison won in a 1977 Monte Carlo. After Allison won the pole for the Daytona 500 with a speed of 194.624 mph in a LeMans, NASCAR attempted to slow down the Pontiacs and keep the fields competitive by enlarging the spoilers on all cars from 216 to 250 square inches. In the Daytona 500, Allison led 117 laps. With 28 laps remaining, Allison pitted for fuel and tires. Petty took only fuel during his stop two laps later and dashed back on the track with a 10-second lead over Allison. Petty held on to win by 3.5 seconds.

In March, prior to the Atlanta 500, NASCAR ordered another change in the spoilers: this time, different car makes would have different sized spoilers. This latest change enraged Allison and his car owner, Harry Ranier, who threatened to boycott the race. NASCAR finally allowed the Pontiacs to have a slightly larger spoiler. In the Atlanta race, Cale Yarborough won in an M.C. Anderson-owned Buick, and Allison was fourth.

At Darlington in April, Harry Gant, 41, debuted the popular Skoal Bandit Pontiac, owned by Hal Needham and actor Burt Reynolds. Gant finished runner-up to Waltrip in the race. For the Winston 500 at Talladega, Allison switched to a Buick, and won.

Jody Ridley, 38, won his first, and only, Winston Cup race at Dover Downs International Speedway in Delaware. The win also was the first for longtime Winston Cup car owner Junie Donlavey. Neil Bonnett led for 403 laps, but the engine on the Wood Brothers Ford blew with 41 laps left. Yarborough took the lead, but his engine also let go with 20 laps remaining and Ridley led the rest of the way. Ridley finished fifth in the points standings.

At Nashville, Mark Martin, a 22-year-old rookie from Arkansas, won the pole, then finished 11th in the race . . . At Michigan, Bobby Allison drove from seventh to first on the final lap to win . . . In the Firecracker 400, Yarborough passed Harry Gant on the final lap and crossed the finish line first . . . At Pocono, rivals Yarborough and Waltrip both tried to squeeze into victory lane. When Waltrip was declared the winner of the Mountain Dew 500, Yarborough insinuated that since Waltrip was sponsored by Mountain Dew, officials wanted Waltrip to win . . . Back at Michigan, seven cars, led by Richard Petty, finished within one second of each other. Petty collected his 195th career victory.

Following Neil Bonnett's win at Darlington, his first in over a year, Waltrip went on a tear, winning four races in a row: Martinsville, North Wilkesboro, Charlotte, and Rockingham. It was the first time a Winston Cup driver had won four in a row since 1976, when Cale Yarborough did it, also driving for Junior Johnson. In early June, Waltrip was 341 points off the pace in the points race. His late-season charge gave Waltrip the title by 53 points over Bobby Allison. Late in the season, Allison announced that he would be driving for the DiGard team in '82.

WINSTON CUP STANDINGS

	DRIVER	STARTS	WINS	POINTS	MONEY
1.	Darrell Waltrip	31	12	4,880	799,134
2.	Bobby Allison	31	5	4,827	680,957
3.	Harry Gant	31	0	4,210	280,047
4.	Terry Labonte	31	0	4,052	348,703
5.	Jody Riley	31	1	4,002	267,605
6.	Ricky Rudd	31	0	3,988	395,685
7.	Dale Earnhardt	31	0	3,975	353,972
8.	Richard Petty	31	3	3,880	396,072
9.	Dave Marcis	31	0	3,507	162,213
10.	Benny Parsons	31	3	3,449	311,093
11.	Buddy Arrington	31	0	3,381	133,928
12.	Kyle Petty	31	0	3,335	117,433
13.	Morgan Shepherd	29	1	3,261	170,473
14.	Jimmy Means	30	0	3,142	105,628
15.	Tommy Gale	30	0	3,140	110,518
16.	Tim Richmond	29	0	3,091	96,448
17.	J. D. McDuffie	28	0	2,996	105,499
18.	Lake Speed	27	0	2,817	94,069
19.	James Hylton	28	0	2,753	87,305
20.	Joe Milikan	23	0	2,682	148,400
21.	Ron Bouchard	22	1	2,594	152,855
22.	Neil Bonnett	22	3	2,449	181,670
23.	Cecil Gordon	25	0	2,320	55,980
24.	Cale Yarborough	18	2	2,201	150,840
25.	Richard Childress	21	0	2,144	71,125
26.	Ronnie Thomas	23	0	2,138	53,605
27.	Buddy Baker	16	0	1,904	115,095
28.	Joe Ruttman	17	0	1,851	137,275
29.	Mike Alexander	19	0	1,784	34,055
30.	Bill Elliott	13	0	1,442	70,320
31.	Bobby Wawak	14	0	1,212	21,790
32.	D.K. Ulrich	15	0	1,191	38,095
33.	Johnny Rutherford	12	0	1,140	29,045
34.	Lennie Pond	12	0	1,100	29,045
35.	Elliott Forbes-Robinson	11	0	1,020	27,350
36.	Rick Newsom	9	0	768	8,625
37.	Dick May	9	0	754	26,380
38.	Stan Barrett	10	0	718	28,540
39.	Connie Saylor	7	0	664	19,715
40.	Gary Balough	10	0	656	34,430
41.	Rick Wilson	8	0	639	15,625
42.	Mark Martin	5	0	615	13,950
43.	Bruce Hill	8	0	596	15,485
44.	Donnie Allison	6	0	527	38,745
45.	Geoff Bodine	5	0	420	15,000
46.	Joe Fields	6	0	418	7,750
47.	Jack Ingram	5	0	377	9,965
48.	Randy Ogden	4	0	367	3,905
49.	Jim Robinson	3	0	351	9,505
50.	Don Waterman	3	0	351	8,570

1982

AT A GLANCE

Winston Cup Champion: Darrell Waltrip

Top Newcomers: Rookie of the Year Geoff Bodine, from Chemung, New York: four top-5 finishes, 10 top-10s.

Waltrip repeated as champion and again won 12 races. Bobby Allison was runner-up in victories with eight.

Bobby Allison won his second Daytona 500 by 22 seconds over Cale Yarborough. Allison lost the bumper on the DiGard Buick in a scrape with Yarborough after just four laps. Tim Brewer, Yarborough's crew chief, suggested that the bumper was designed to fall off, enabling Allison's car to run faster. Gary Nelson, Allison's crew chief, reacted by wondering if Brewer had been inhaling too many fumes.

Dave Marcis won the next race, at Richmond, Virginia, in a Chevrolet. The victory was his fifth career victory; it would also be his last. Although he was still active in 1997, Marcis hadn't earned a checkered flag since. At Pocono in June, Bobby Allison was battling Tim Richmond for the lead when Allison ran out of fuel late in the race. Marcis pushed him back to the pits; Allison filled 'er up and went on to win the race ahead of Richmond in the J.D. Stacy Buick. Afterward, Robert Harrington, Richmond's team manager, was angry that Marcis, a driver sponsored by Stacy, would help Allison. A few days later, Stacy withdrew his

sponsorship of Marcis. Allison also won the July race at Pocono. Dale Earnhardt, driving the Bud Moore Ford, suffered a broken knee cap in a crash when his car went airborne. While he was learning about being a car owner, Richard Childress let Earnhardt drive for two years for the more experienced Moore.

Stacy was the focus of considerable turmoil during the season. He began the year with two cars, driven by Joe Ruttman (third at Daytona) and Jim Sauter. Stacy also sponsored five other cars, including Marcis. Early in the year, Sauter was out and Robin McCall, an 18-year-old from Texas, drove the car in three races: her best finish was 29th. In March, Ruttman quit to join the RahMoc

Darrell Waltrip in 1982.

team, owned by Bob Rahilly and Butch Mock. Tim Richmond replaced Ruttman. Shortly after Stacy split with Marcis, Stacy also zipped his wallet with the Terry Labonte-Billy Hagan team. Labonte was leading the points race even though he hadn't won a race.

Harry Gant gained his first Winston Cup victory at Martinsville in April in his 107th start. Butch Lindley, in only his sixth start, was runner-up. Waltrip passed Benny Parsons on the last lap to win the Winston 500 at Talladega. Parsons's qualifying time of 200.176 mph marked the first time a Winston Cup driver had surpassed the 200 mph barrier. Donnie Allison, racing for the first time since he was injured in the World 600 in 1981, finished sixth in a Buick.

At Dover, Bobby Allison led 486 of 500 laps and won by more than three laps over Marcis. It was the first time a driver won a Winston Cup race in a car with power steering. At Riverside, Tim Richmond won his first race, 3.8 seconds ahead of Labonte. At Michigan, Yarborough survived a last-lap "touch" with Waltrip to win. After the outcome was decided, Waltrip drove into Yarborough's car: he maintained control while Waltrip's car wound up in a puddle.

Yarborough won his record fifth Southern 500 at Darlington by 0.79 seconds over Richard Petty. Yarborough, 41, had signed with M.C. Anderson to race on a limited basis. But Anderson, a Savannah, Georgia, construction company owner, was getting the itch to compete for the 1983 championship. After the Southern 500, Yarborough was offered significantly more money to run the entire schedule in 1983. When Yarborough declined, Anderson then made a shocking announcement: he would close his shop after the season.

Waltrip won at Dover with 22-year-old Kyle Petty second . . . At Charlotte, Gant gained his first superspeedway victory . . . Waltrip also won at Martinsville and took a 37-point lead over Allison, who blew an engine for the third consecutive race . . . At Rockingham, Waltrip and Allison finished one-two, but the gap between them remained 37 points because Allison led more laps.

Allison won the Atlanta 500 and trimmed Waltrip's lead to 22 points entering the season finale at Riverside, California. Waltrip was third. Atlanta was the final race for country singer Marty Robbins, a part-time racer for years on the circuit. He died of a heart attack one month later.

Tim Richmond batted two-for-two at Riverside, Waltrip was third and Allison 16th as Waltrip pocketed back-to-back Winston Cup titles, this time by 72 points. It was Richmond's last race for Stacy: he moved to the Raymond Beadle team for '83.

WINSTON CUP STANDINGS

	DRIVER	STARTS	WINS	POINTS	MONEY
1.	Darrell Waltrip	30	12	4,489	923,151
2.	Bobby Allison	30	8	4,417	795,078
3.	Terry Labonte	30	0	4,211	398,635
4.	Harry Gant	30	2	3,877	337,582
5.	Richard Petty	30	0	3,814	465,793
6.	Dave Marcis	30	1	3,666	249,027
7.	Buddy Arrington	30	0	3,642	178,159
8.	Ron Bouchard	30	0	3,545	375,759
9.	Ricky Rudd	30	0	3,537	217,140
10.	Morgan Shepherd	29	0	3,451	166,030
11.	Jimmy Means	30	0	3,423	154,460
12.	Dale Earnhardt	30	1	3,402	400,800
13.	Jody Riley	30	0	3,333	308,664
14.	Mark Martin	30	0	3,042	142,710
15.	Kyle Petty	29	0	3,024	126,285
16.	Joe Ruttman	29	0	3,021	191,634
17.	Neil Bonnett	25	1	2,996	158,197
18.	Benny Parsons	23	0	2,892	252,267
19.	J. D. McDuffie	30	0	2,886	112,744
20.	Lake Speed	30	0	2,850	118,457
21.	Tommy Gale	26	0	2,698	101,485
22.	Geoff Bodine	25	0	2,654	247,750
23.	Buddy Baker	23	0	2,591	253,675
24.	D.K. Ulrich	25	0	2,566	78,120
25.	Bill Elliott	21	0	2,558	201,030
26.	Tim Richmond	26	2	2,497	175,980
27.	Cale Yarborough	16	3	2,022	231,590
28.	James Hylton	13	0	1,514	49,130
29.	Slick Johnson	17	0	1,261	44,190
30.	Ronnie Thomas	18	0	1,093	23,570
31.	Bobby Wawak	10	0	1,002	23,660
32.	Brad Teague	9	0	966	14,300
33.	Lennie Pond	13	0	756	45,715
34.	Rick Wilson	8	0	731	33,230
35.	Joe Milikan	8	0	678	56,230
36.	Rick Newsom	8	0	619	12,390
37.	David Pearson	6	0	613	55,945
38.	Gary Balough	5	0	564	35,735
39.	Lowell Cowell	5	0	554	26,215
40.	Philip Duffie	5	0	542	10,910
41.	H. B. Bailey	6	0	462	9,455
42.	Butch Lindley	4	0	435	16,695
43.	Dean Combs	5	0	431	7,940
44.	Delma Cowart	5	0	410	11,855
45.	Donnie Allison	9	0	406	38,180
46.	Bobby Hillin Jr.	5	0	379	9,830
47.	Roy Smith	3	0	375	26,770
48.	Dick Brooks	5	0	347	9,470
49.	Connie Saylor	7	0	335	16,225
50.	Darryl Sage	5	0	324	4,970

1983

AT A GLANCE

Winston Cup Champion: Bobby Allison

Top Newcomers: Bill Elliott, in his first full year in the series, finished third in points; Elliott won his first race; Lake Speed recorded two top-5 finishes and five top-10s.

Bending the rules, a polite way of saying cheating, has always been part of auto racing's history. Sanctioning bodies make the rules, then the racing teams do whatever they can to circumvent them. The 1983 season had several cases of, uh, creative engineering. The most notable involved Richard Petty. "The King" had won twice early in the season, then endured a slump. He continually urged his crew to provide more power in his STP Pontiac. After qualifying 20th for the October 500-miler at Charlotte, Petty raced near the lead pack. After a restart, following a caution flag on lap 293, Petty advanced to second place. Then, with 23 laps remaining of the 334-lap race, Petty sped past Darrell Waltrip and collected his 198th career victory.

During a routine post-race inspection, NASCAR officials discovered that Petty's crew had put on four left-side tires on the final pit stop, a violation of the rules. Upon further review, Petty's engine was found to measure 381.983 cubic inches, well over the 358.1 c.i. limit. NASCAR ruled that Petty could keep the victory, but the 104 points he earned were deducted from his season total—and he was fined a record $35,000. Petty denied any knowledge of the shenanigans, and his crew supported him. Crew chief Maurice Petty accepted the blame. Even Bobby Allison, one of Petty's main rivals for decades, defended Petty, saying, "Petty has shot straighter than anyone over the years. Anyone but me, that is." Petty announced, after the race at Rockingham, that he would leave Petty Enterprises and drive next season for Californian Mike Curb. Petty's son, Kyle, would continue racing for Petty Enterprises.

Allison captured his first, and only, Winston Cup title by 47 points over Darrell Waltrip. Allison and Waltrip tied for the most wins in '83, six apiece.

At Daytona, Cale Yarborough, driving a Ranier Pontiac, passed Buddy Baker on the last lap to win the 500-mile season opener. In qualifying, Yarborough had posted the first 200 mph lap at Daytona. However, he crashed on the second lap and had to start his backup car. Ricky Rudd (198.864 mph) inherited the pole. Darrell Waltrip was knocked unconscious during the race when he crashed.

At Darlington in April, Harry Gant gained his third career victory . . . At Martinsville, Waltrip won and Rudd was placed on 10-race probation. Rudd rammed his car into Joe Ruttman's car several times after the checkered flag . . . At Dover, with the race ending in a thunderstorm, Allison outraced Waltrip to the caution flag. Two spectators were killed by lightning. Allison took a 41-point lead over Gant . . . Allison won his third in a row at Pocono; he was helped when Petty and Bill Elliott ran out of fuel. It was Allison's 77th career victory . . . In the Firecracker 400 at Daytona, Buddy Baker, driving for the Wood Brothers, ended a 13-month winless slump as he gave Ford its first Winston Cup victory since the World 600 at Charlotte the year before . . . Back at Pocono in July, Tim Richmond gained his first superspeedway victory in the Blue Max Pontiac.

At Talladega, Dale Earnhardt passed Waltrip on the final lap for his second victory of the year in the Bud Moore Ford . . . Yarborough won at Michigan for his 78th career win . . . Allison won the Southern 500 at Darlington, nudged past Rudd by 0.86 seconds at Richmond, then made it three in a row by winning at Dover. His lead over Waltrip was 101 points . . . Rudd, from Chesapeake, Virginia, won at Martinsville; he was the first Virginia driver since Joe Weatherly to win at the .525-mile southern Virginia racetrack . . . Labonte took the race at Rockingham, by 0.68 seconds over Richmond, for only his second career win . . . Bill Elliott visited victory lane for the first time in Winston Cup racing when he won the season finale at Riverside.

WINSTON CUP STANDINGS

	DRIVER	STARTS	WINS	POINTS	MONEY
1.	Bobby Allison	30	6	4,667	883,010
2.	Darrell Waltrip	30	6	4,620	865,185
3.	Bill Elliott	30	1	4,279	514,030
4.	Richard Petty	30	3	4,042	508,884
5.	Terry Labonte	30	1	4,004	388,419
6.	Neil Bonnett	30	2	3,842	453,586
7.	Harry Gant	30	1	3,790	414,353
8.	Dale Earnhardt	30	2	3,732	465,203
9.	Ricky Rudd	30	2	3,693	275,400
10.	Tim Richmond	30	1	3,612	262,139
11.	Dave Marcis	30	0	3,361	306,355
12.	Joe Ruttman	30	0	3,342	223,809
13.	Kyle Petty	30	0	3,261	163,848
14.	Dick Brooks	30	0	3,230	180,556
15.	Buddy Arrington	30	0	3,158	138,429
16.	Ron Bouchard	28	0	3,113	159,173
17.	Geoff Bodine	28	0	3,019	209,611
18.	Jimmy Means	28	0	2,983	132,915
19.	Sterling Martin	30	0	2,980	148,253
20.	Morgan Shepherd	25	0	2,733	287,326
21.	Buddy Baker	21	1	2,621	216,355
22.	Ronnie Thomas	26	0	2,515	47,190
23.	Tommy Gale	28	0	2,507	88,305
24.	D.K. Ulrich	22	0	2,400	85,245
25.	Trevor Boys	23	0	2,293	87,555
26.	J. D. McDuffie	25	0	2,197	73,425
27.	Lake Speed	18	0	2,114	78,220
28.	Cale Yarborough	16	4	1,960	265,035
29.	Benny Parsons	16	0	1,657	129,760
30.	Mark Martin	16	0	1,627	99,055
31.	Ronnie Hopkins Jr.	13	0	1,147	26,455
32.	Jody Riley	10	0	1,050	45,710
33.	David Pearson	10	0	943	71,720
34.	Lennie Pond	10	0	887	41,530
35.	Ken Ragan	8	0	836	27,905
36.	Bobby Wawak	9	0	825	19,130
37.	Bobby Hillin Jr.	12	0	737	30,275
38.	Slick Johnson	10	0	705	13,665
39.	Mike Potter	11	0	662	20,375
40.	Cecil Gordon	8	0	649	17,340
41.	Rick Newsom	6	0	573	14,445
42.	Dean Combs	5	0	500	21,370
43.	Phil Parsons	5	0	458	23,850
44.	Bob Senneker	5	0	436	11,355
45.	Jerry Bowman	5	0	419	8,610
46.	Clark Dwyer	5	0	411	14,570
47.	Greg Sacks	5	0	359	8,060
48.	Rick McCray	4	0	313	3,710
49.	Delma Cowart	4	0	277	7,750
50.	Philip Duffie	4	0	265	6,480

Terry Labonte, shown here in 1997, won the first of his two Winston Cup championships in 1984.

1984

AT A GLANCE

Winston Cup Champion: Terry Labonte

Top Newcomers: Rookie of the Year Rusty Wallace: two top-5 finishes, four top-10s, 14th in points.

With perfect timing, Richard Petty, 46, won his historic 200th career race, on July 4 in the Firecracker 400 at Daytona. President Ronald Reagan watched in person. Reagan had given the command "Gentlemen, start your engines" from Air Force One on his way to Daytona. He arrived in time to watch the latter portion of the race. A wreck with three laps remaining brought out the caution flag. Realizing that the race probably would end under caution, Petty and Cale Yarborough raced back to the finish line. Petty edged Yarborough by about one foot. The more than 80,000 fans stood and cheered for the final two laps because they knew they were witnessing history: Petty's 200th. Driving the Curb Motorsports Pontiac sponsored by STP, Petty had preceded No. 200 with his 199th victory at Dover in May.

Labonte, 28, driving for Billy Hagan, only won two races, at Riverside, California, and Bristol, Tennessee. However, his consistency paid off as he used 17 top-5 finishes to top Harry Gant by 65 points and become the youngest Winston Cup champion.

Geoff Bodine, in his first year driving for the new Rick Hendrick team, won three races and finished ninth in points. With Dale Earnhardt returning to the Richard Childress stable, Ricky Rudd slipped into the Bud Moore Ford. For the first time, Junior Johnson fielded a two-car team featuring drivers

Darrell Waltrip and Neil Bonnett. Warner W. Hodgdon, the California industrialist who had purchased half-interest in four racetracks, also bought 50 percent of Johnson's team. By late in the season, Hodgdon would be reeling from severe financial losses. In January 1985, he filed for bankruptcy.

Yarborough, 43, won his second consecutive Daytona 500 with another last-lap pass: this time, he sped past Waltrip. Driving the Ranier-Lundy Chevrolet, Yarborough had set a Daytona qualifying mark of 201.848 mph. Rudd quickly established himself with the Bud Moore team by recovering from a crash at Daytona and winning the next race at Richmond. Bobby Allison won at Rockingham in the DiGard Buick. Dick Brooks, seeking his first victory since 1973, led 166 laps, but steering problems in the Junie Donlavey Ford dropped him to 23rd place. Benny Parsons, winless in nearly three years, edged Dale Earnhardt by 0.9 seconds to win the Coca-Cola 500 at Atlanta. Parson was driving the Johnny Hayes Chevrolet. Waltrip won his seventh in a row at Bristol's .533-mile track.

At Martinsville, Bodine won his first race in a Hendrick Chevrolet. The victory was the first for crew chief Harry Hyde since 1977 . . . At Talladega, Yarborough collected his 80th career victory as he beat Harry Gant by two car lengths in the Winston 500 . . . At Michigan, Bill Elliott gained his first superspeedway win. The victory was extra special because Elliott's car owner, Harry Melling, was from nearby Jackson, Michigan . . . Back at Talladega, Earnhardt roared past Terry Labonte on the final lap and won by 1.66 seconds over Buddy Baker. Labonte was third. An exhilirated Earnhardt described it as "the greatest race" he'd ever been in.

Gant won the Southern 500 at Darlington, two seconds ahead of Tim Richmond . . . Gant won again at Dover; Bobby Allison suffered a broken collarbone when his Buick hit the wall. Allison, however, did not miss any of the remaining races . . . Elliott took the Miller High Life 500 at Charlotte; Labonte led the points race by 88 over Gant . . . At North Wilkesboro, Waltrip gained his seventh victory by edging Gant by 0.5 seconds . . .

Gant was runnerup again at Rockingham, when Elliott nosed him out by just one foot . . . Elliott was involved in another close finish at Atlanta. This time, however, Earnhardt edged him by 0.56 seconds. Rookie Terry Schoonover, from Royal Palm Beach, Florida, became the first fatality at the Atlanta track when his car hit the wall on the 129th lap. Schoonover was competing in just his second Winston Cup race . . . Bodine won the season finale at Riverside for his third victory of the season. Labonte was third and Gant eighth.

WINSTON CUP STANDINGS

	DRIVER	STARTS	WINS	POINTS	MONEY
1.	Terry Labonte	30	2	4,508	767,716
2.	Harry Gant	30	3	4,443	673,060
3.	Bill Elliott	30	3	4,377	680,344
4.	Dale Earnhardt	30	2	4,265	634,671
5.	Darrell Waltrip	30	7	4,230	731,023
6.	Bobby Allison	30	2	4,094	641,049
7.	Ricky Rudd	30	1	3,918	497,779
8.	Neil Bonnett	30	0	3,802	282,533
9.	Geoff Bodine	30	3	3,734	413,748
10.	Richard Petty	30	2	3,643	257,932
11.	Ron Bouchard	30	0	3,609	246,510
12.	Tim Richmond	30	1	3,505	345,848
13.	Dave Marcis	30	0	3,416	330,766
14.	Rusty Wallace	30	0	3,316	201,739
15.	Dick Brooks	30	0	3,265	192,407
16.	Kyle Petty	30	0	3,159	329,920
17.	Trevor Boys	30	0	3,040	165,376
18.	Joe Ruttman	29	0	2,945	168,433
19.	Greg Sacks	29	0	2,545	75,184
20.	Buddy Arrington	26	0	2,504	128,802
21.	Buddy Baker	21	0	2,477	151,635
22.	Cale Yarborough	16	3	2,448	403,853
23.	Clark Dwyer	26	0	2,477	114,335
24.	Phil Parsons	22	0	2,290	90,700
25.	Jimmy Means	22	0	2,218	105,105
26.	Lake Speed	19	0	2,023	98,320
27.	Benny Parsons	14	1	1,865	241,665
28.	Mike Alexander	19	0	1,862	94,820
29.	Morgan Shepherd	20	0	1,811	59,670
30.	Ronnie Thomas	21	0	1,775	79,325
31.	Tommy Ellis	20	0	1,738	44,315
32.	Bobby Hillin Jr.	16	0	1,477	45,020
33.	Tommy Gale	16	0	1,426	69,385
34.	J. D. McDuffie	16	0	1,366	50,320
35.	Jody Riley	14	0	1,288	64,135
36.	Doug Heveron	16	0	1,265	39,950
37.	Sterling Martin	14	0	1,207	54,355
38.	Lennie Pond	12	0	923	54,200
39.	Dean Combs	12	0	903	22,385
40.	Ken Ragan	10	0	873	37,045
41.	David Pearson	11	0	812	54,125
42.	D.K. Ulrich	9	0	810	31,040
43.	Connie Saylor	8	0	367	19,675
44.	Jerry Bowman	5	0	362	6,265
45.	Elliott Forbes-Robinson	5	0	349	11,335
46.	Jeff Hooker	4	0	322	4,495
47.	Bobby Wawak	4	0	307	8,575
48.	Dick May	3	0	300	5,325
49.	Dean Roper	3	0	294	19,150
50.	Bobby Gerhart	4	0	262	7,585

1985

AT A GLANCE

Winston Cup Champion: Darrell Waltrip

Notable Events: With Fords having a clear advantage, NASCAR mandated in late April that all cars must have a roof height of 50.5 inches. Fords were required to raise their cars a half-inch and General Motors cars could lower their cars a half-inch, thereby improving their aerodynamics.

Top Newcomers: Rookie of the Year was Ken Schrader, from Fenton, Missouri: three top-10 finishes, 16th in points . . . Greg Sacks won the July 4 race at Daytona for his first, and only, victory . . . Lake Speed was second at Daytona and 11th in earnings ($300,326) . . . Bobby Hillin Jr. collected five top-10 finishes.

In only his third full season, Bill Elliott attracted unprecedented attention for the sport when he collected $1 million for winning three of the four crown-jewel events in the series. "Awesome Bill from Dawsonville" won the Daytona 500, the Winston 500, and the Southern 500. The R.J. Reynolds Co., sponsor of the Winston Cup series since 1972, offered the $1 million to the driver who could win three of the series' top four races: the World 600 at Charlotte was the fourth "crown jewel." RJR also increased the season-ending points fund by $250,000, to $750,000. Despite winning 11 races overall driving for Harry Melling, Elliott was runnerup to Darrell Waltrip in the points race by 101 points.

Elliott caught everyone's attention in qualifying for the Daytona 500 when he clocked a 205.114 mph lap in a new Coors-sponsored Thunderbird. When the race began, Elliott and Cale Yarborough, also in a T-bird, quickly moved to the front. After Yarborough's car blew an engine on the 62nd lap, the race belonged to Elliott. His only problem was on a pit stop on lap 145: NASCAR officials ordered Elliott's crew to tape the right front headlight panel, which had been loosened. The pit stop took more than twice as long as a normal 20-second stop. Still, it took Elliott just 11 laps to regain the lead. At the finish line, he was a comfortable 0.94 seconds ahead of Lake Speed in the RahMoc Pontiac.

Elliott suffered a broken leg at Rockingham in early March when his car blew a tire and he hit the wall, but he didn't miss a race. After winning three of the first eight events, Elliott arrived at Talladega for the Winston 500. This was the first race with the new rule in effect: all cars were required to have a roof height of 50.5 inches. The new rule didn't slow down Elliott's Ford: he qualified at a jaw-dropping 209.393 mph, almost four miles-an-hour faster than Yarborough. Elliott's smooth ride was jolted early in the race when smoke began flowing from his car: he needed a pit stop of more than one minute for his crew to repair a broken oil fitting. When Elliott returned to the racetrack, he was in 26th place. He then began one of the most amazing comebacks in Winston Cup history. Running laps at over 204 mph, he was back in the lead by lap 145. Elliott won by 1.72 seconds over Kyle Petty in the Wood Brothers Ford. Yarborough was third.

Waltrip interrupted Elliott's domination of the "crown jewel" events by winning the World 600 in the Junior Johnson Chevrolet; Elliott was 18th. Elliott swept both races at Pocono and Michigan. Arriving at Darlington for his last chance at the $1 million, Elliott battled Yarborough in the latter portions of the Southern 500. With Yarborough leading with 43 laps left, his Ford lost its power steering. Elliott avoided the fluid leaking out of Yarborough's car and went on to win the race and the Winston Million.

After Darlington, Elliott led the points standings by 206. However, he would win only one more race. Elliott finished the season with 11 superspeedway victories, breaking David Pearson's mark of 10 in 1973. Much to the dismay of many observers, Waltrip (three wins) took the points title by 101 points. Suggestions were made to change the point system. Bob Latford, who devised the current system, recommended awarding more points to race winners. NASCAR vetoed the idea, with Bill France Jr. noting that in the seven previous years the championship wasn't decided until the final race.

In other top races in '85, Terry Labonte, the defending points champion, didn't win his first race early until early June, at Riverside. Yarborough didn't park in victory lane until the Talladega 500 in late July. Ricky Rudd won the season finale at Riverside. At Rockingham in March, Neil Bonnett edged Harry Gant by eight inches.

Sacks's victory in the Pepsi Firecracker 400 at Daytona was remarkable for several reasons. First, he outdistanced Elliott, the runnerup, by an eye-catching 23.5 seconds. Secondly, Sacks had only 41 Winston Cup starts. Sacks was driving a Chevrolet for the DiGard team, which had been formed just 17 days before the race. His crew barely knew each other. Finally, near the end of the race, Sacks lost radio contact with Gary Nelson, his crew chief, and didn't realize he was leading. On the final lap, Sacks made an unnecessary and risky pass on Terry Labonte, who was a lap down.

WINSTON CUP STANDINGS

	DRIVER	STARTS	WINS	POINTS	MONEY
1.	Darrell Waltrip	28	3	4,292	1,318,375
2.	Bill Elliott	28	11	4,191	2,433,187
3.	Harry Gant	28	3	4,003	804,287
4.	Neil Bonnett	28	2	3,902	530,145
5.	Geoff Bodine	28	0	3,862	565,868
6.	Ricky Rudd	28	1	3,857	512,441
7.	Terry Labonte	28	1	3,683	694,510
8.	Dale Earnhardt	28	4	3,561	546,596
9.	Kyle Petty	28	0	3,528	296,367
10.	Lake Speed	28	0	3,507	300,326
11.	Tim Richmond	28	0	3,413	290,284
12.	Bobby Allison	28	0	3,312	272,536
13.	Ron Bouchard	28	0	3,267	240,304
14.	Richard Petty	28	0	3,140	306,142
15.	Bobby Hillin Jr.	28	0	3,091	145,070
16.	Ken Schrader	28	0	3,024	211,523
17.	Buddy Baker	28	0	2,986	235,480
18.	Dave Marcis	28	0	2,871	173,467
19.	Rusty Wallace	28	0	2,867	233,670
20.	Buddy Arrington	26	0	2,780	153,222
21.	Phil Parsons	28	0	2,740	104,840
22.	Clark Dwyer	28	0	2,641	128,710
23.	Jimmy Means	28	0	2,548	132,130
24.	Edie Bierschwale	26	0	2,396	102,620
25.	Greg Sacks	20	1	1,944	234,141
26.	Cale Yarborough	16	2	1,861	310,465
27.	J. D. McDuffie	23	0	1,853	84,965
28.	Trevor Boys	20	0	1,461	76,325
29.	Benny Parsons	14	0	1,427	94,450
30.	Joe Ruttman	16	0	1,410	81,425
31.	Morgan Shepherd	16	0	1,406	55,985
32.	Bobby Wawak	14	0	1,226	42,165
33.	Lennie Pond	12	0	1,107	70,640
34.	Tommy Ellis	14	0	1,100	27,695
35.	Mike Alexander	11	0	1,046	43,765
36.	David Pearson	12	0	879	55,625
37.	Sterling Martin	8	0	645	31,155
38.	Don Hume	7	0	637	22,230
39.	Ronnie Thomas	7	0	631	10,505
40.	Alan Kulwicki	5	0	509	10,230
41.	Rick Newsom	6	0	450	8,690
42.	Mike Potter	6	0	443	10,855
43.	Jerry Bowman	5	0	434	8,665
44.	Bobby Gerhart	5	0	422	7,400
45.	A. J. Foyt	7	0	410	29,750
46.	Phil Good	4	0	406	6,870
47.	Ken Ragan	7	0	356	35,995
48.	Slick Johnson	6	0	343	24,995
49.	Connie Saylor	5	0	296	8,915
50.	Jim Sauter	3	0	267	15,465

1986

AT A GLANCE

Winston Cup Champion: Dale Earnhardt

Top Newcomers: Rookie of the Year Alan Kulwicki, from Greenfield, Wisconsin: one top-5, four top-10s, 21st in points.

Prior to the end of the 1985 season, Bill France Jr. announced that "Grand National" would be dropped from the series title. From now on, the series would be known strictly as "Winston Cup." NASCAR's Sportsman series would now be the Busch Grand National series.

On the way to the second of his record-tying seven Winston Cup championships, Dale Earnhardt won five races: Darlington, Charlotte twice, Atlanta, and North Wilkesboro. Tim Richmond, driving for Rick Hendrick, was the leader in victories with seven. He finished third in the points chase. Richmond didn't start winning until Pocono in June. He was fourth in earnings, with $973,221. Darrell Waltrip was second in points, 288 behind Earnhardt.

Earnhardt's reputation as "The Intimidator" remained strong. In the season's second race, at Richmond, Waltrip tried to pass Earnhardt with three laps left. Earnhardt tapped Waltrip's right rear quarter panel, sending the Junior Johnson driver into the wall. Kyle Petty evaded the melee that also took out cars driven by Geoff Bodine and Joe Ruttman and won his first Winston Cup race. Earnhardt was fined $5,000 by NASCAR and placed on a year's probation. After Earnhardt appealed, the fine was trimmed to $3,000 and the probation was dropped.

Geoff Bodine, 0-for-1985, won the Daytona 500. He and Earnhardt were primed for a two-car dash to the finish when Earnhardt ran out of fuel and had to pit with three laps to go . . . In the season's fourth race, at Atlanta, veteran Morgan Shepherd collected his first superspeedway win. Driving an unsponsored Buick owned by Jack Beebe, Shepherd, 44, crossed the finish line 0.29 seconds ahead of Earnhardt . . . At Bristol, Rusty Wallace, 29, earned his first Winston Cup win in a Raymond Beadle-owned Pontiac. It was also the first Cup win for crew chief Barry Dodson. Wallace also won at Martinsville and was eighth in earnings ($557,354) . . . Following Bristol, Earnhardt was never passed under green-flag conditions at Darlington and won the TranSouth 500 . . . Ricky Rudd posted another home state victory at Martinsville, with rookie Alan Kulwicki placing fourth.

At Talladega, Bobby Allison, 48, became the oldest winner of a Winston Cup race by taking the Winston 500 by 0.19 seconds over Earnhardt. It was Allison's first victory in two years and also gave the Stavola Brothers, Bill and Mickey, their first Winston Cup win. Bobby Hillin Jr., driving for the Stavola brothers, won at Talladega in July for his first, and only, Winston Cup victory. Hillin, 22, originally was declared the youngest winner of a race in Winston Cup and Grand National history. Later, it was determined that Fireball Roberts and Donald Thomas were younger.

Richard Petty's start at Michigan in June was celebrated as his 1,000th Winston Cup and Grand National race. Research showed it actually was his

Alan Kulwicki in his rookie season of 1986 at Rockingham.

999th, but the ceremonies were held anyway. Petty finished 13th . . . At Dover in September, Rudd won his first superspeedway race . . . Waltrip picked up his 70th career victory at North Wilkesboro. It was his 53rd and final win driving for Junior Johnson: Waltrip announced he would be switching to the Hendrick team in '87.

The second half of the season belonged to Tim Richmond. With Harry Hyde as his crew chief, Richmond won seven of 17 races, including the Firecracker 400 and both Pocono events. After the season, Richmond was diagnosed with double pneumonia. He returned only briefly to the circuit in 1987.

WINSTON CUP STANDINGS

DRIVER	STARTS	WINS	POINTS	MONEY
1. Dale Earnhardt	29	5	4,468	1,768,880
2. Darrell Waltrip	29	3	4,180	1,099,735
3. Tim Richmond	29	7	4,174	973,221
4. Bill Elliott	29	2	3,844	1,049,142
5. Ricky Rudd	29	2	3,823	671,548
6. Rusty Wallace	29	2	3,762	557,354
7. Bobby Allison	29	1	3,698	503,095
8. Geoff Bodine	29	2	3,678	795,111
9. Bobby Hillin Jr.	29	1	3,546	448,452
10. Kyle Petty	29	1	3,537	403,242
11. Harry Gant	29	0	3,498	583,024
12. Terry Labonte	29	1	3,473	522,235
13. Neil Bonnett	28	1	3,369	485,930
14. Richard Petty	29	0	3,314	280,657
15. Joe Ruttman	29	0	3,295	259,263
16. Ken Schrader	29	0	3,052	235,904
17. Dave Marcis	29	0	2,912	220,461
18. Morgan Shepherd	27	1	2,896	244,146
19. Michael Waltrip	28	0	2,853	108,767
20. Budy Arrington	26	0	2,776	186,588
21. Alan Kulwicki	23	0	2,705	94,450
22. Jimmy Means	26	0	2,495	157,940
23. Tommy Ellis	24	0	2,393	78,310
24. Buddy Baker	17	0	1,924	138,600
25. Edie Bierschwale	24	0	1,860	98,110
26. J. D. McDuffie	20	0	1,825	106,115
27. Phil Parsons	17	0	1,742	84,680
28. Rick Wilson	17	0	1,698	88,820
29. Cale Yarborough	16	0	1,642	137,010
30. Benny Parsons	16	0	1,555	176,985
31. Ron Bouchard	17	0	1,533	106,835
32. Chet Fillip	17	0	1,433	36,110
33. Jody Ridley	12	0	1,213	84,380
34. Trevor Boys	14	0	1,064	74,645
35. Doug Heveron	13	0	1,052	74,030
36. Sterling Martin	10	0	989	113,070
37. D. K. Ulrich	10	0	804	47,795
38. Pancho Carter	9	0	706	56,335
39. Ken Ragan	7	0	627	33,890
40. Lake Speed	5	0	608	82,630
41. Greg Sacks	8	0	579	64,810
42. Ronnie Thomas	6	0	504	25,215
43. Bobby Wawak	6	0	480	10,155
44. Rodney Combs	5	0	421	12,180
45. Derrike Cope	5	0	400	8,025
46. James Hylton	4	0	386	22,090
47. Davey Allison	5	0	364	24,190
48. Mark Martin	5	0	364	20,515
49. Jim Sauter	8	0	361	52,020
50. A. J. Foyt	5	0	355	24,135

1987

AT A GLANCE

Winston Cup Champion: Dale Earnhardt

Top Newcomers: Bobby Allison's son, Davey, driving for Harry Ranier, won two races: Talladega and Dover; he also had nine top-5 finishes and 10 top-10s; he finished 21st in points.

In winning 11 races for car owner Richard Childress, Dale Earnhardt was streaky: he swept six of seven early in the season, including four in a row at Darlington, North Wilkesboro, Bristol, and Martinsville. Later, he took three consecutive races: Bristol, Darlington, and Richmond. Bill Elliott was runnerup in wins with six wins, including the Daytona 500.

Still feeling the effects of what he said was double pneumonia, Tim Richmond was unable to start the season with the Hendrick team. Rick Hendrick temporarily replaced Richmond with former Winston Cup champion Benny Parsons, and he responded by finishing second in the Daytona 500. Richmond returned for The Winston at Charlotte in May and placed third. A month later at Pocono, Richmond outran Elliott by one second to claim victory. Richmond's comeback left more than a few thick-skinned people in the garage area with tears in their eyes. The 1980 Indianapolis 500 Rookie of the Year also won the next race, at Riverside, California. However, suspicions about Richmond's condition grew at Watkins Glen, New York, in early August. On race morning, the Ohioan appeared distracted: other drivers were concerned about racing against him. Rain delayed the race one day, and Richmond finished 10th. The next race, at Michigan, would be Richmond's last start. A week after finishing 29th, he resigned from the Hendrick team. Two years later, on Aug. 13, 1989, Richmond died in a Fort Lauderdale, Florida, hospital. The cause of death was AIDS.

At the Daytona 500, Elliott won when Geoff Bodine ran out of gas with three laps to go. Bodine

Tim Richmond's Old Milwaukee Pontiac is a little worse for wear at Rockingham in 1984.

had won at Daytona under similar circumstances the previous year when Earnhardt's gas tank went dry . . . Driver furor over Earnhardt's tactics erupted again in the season's third race at Richmond. Earnhardt was running third and Harry Gant was second when "The Intimidator" bumped Gant's car, sending it into the wall. "Earnhardt is blind as a bat: he ran all over me," said an angry Gant. Earnhardt and Elliott later mixed it up during The Winston at Charlotte: both were fined by NASCAR.

By taking the Winston 500, Davey Allison, 26, became the first rookie to win a Winston Cup race since Ron Bouchard won, also at Talladega, in 1981. Driving a Ford for the Ranier Racing Team,

Allison beat Terry Labonte by 0.78 seconds. Davey's father, Bobby, winner of the race the previous year, was involved in a terrifying crash that tore away part of the grandstand fence near the start/finish line. The race was delayed for more than two hours while the fence was repaired.

In the Coca-Cola 600 at Charlotte, Kyle Petty, driving the Wood Brothers Ford, won his second Winston Cup race when several front-running cars dropped out with mechanical problems . . . At Dover, Davey Allison won. Bobby Allison led 147 laps before he blew the engine on his Buick . . . Bobby bounced back, taking the Firecracker 400 at Daytona . . . At Watkins Glen, Rusty Wallace gained his first win of the year. Patty Moise started her first Winston Cup race: she qualified 30th in a Marc Reno-owned Chevrolet, and finished 33rd.

At Dover in September, Ricky Rudd won after informing Bud Moore that he wouldn't be returning for the 1988 season . . . Two races later, Terry Labonte won at North Wilkesboro: it was his first win driving for Junior Johnson and it happened in Johnson's home area . . . Earnhardt clinched the points championship at Rockingham: after finishing second behind Elliott, Earnhardt held a 515-point lead with two races left. Elliott wound up the season by taking three of the last four races.

WINSTON CUP STANDINGS

	DRIVER	STARTS	WINS	POINTS	MONEY
1.	Dale Earnhardt	29	11	4,696	2,069,243
2.	Bill Elliott	29	6	4,207	1,599,210
3.	Terry Labonte	29	1	4,007	805,054
4.	Darrell Waltrip	29	1	3,911	511,768
5.	Rusty Wallace	29	2	3,818	690,652
6.	Ricky Rudd	29	2	3,742	653,508
7.	Kyle Petty	29	1	3,737	544,437
8.	Richard Petty	29	0	3,708	445,227
9.	Bobby Allison	29	1	3,530	515,894
10.	Ken Schrader	29	0	3,405	375,918
11.	Sterling Martin	29	0	3,381	306,412
12.	Neil Bonnett	26	0	3,352	401,541
13.	Geoff Bodine	29	0	3,328	369,889
14.	Phil Parsons	29	0	3,327	180,261
15.	Alan Kulwicki	29	0	3,238	369,889
16.	Benny Parsons	29	0	3,215	566,484
17.	Morgan Shepherd	29	0	3,099	317,034
18.	Dave Marcis	29	0	3,080	256,354
19.	Bobby Hillin Jr.	29	0	3,027	346,735
20.	Michael Waltrip	29	0	2,840	205,370
21.	Davey Allison	22	2	2,824	361,060
22.	Harry Gant	29	0	2,725	197,645
23.	Jimmy Means	28	0	2,483	154,055
24.	Buddy Baker	20	0	2,373	255,320
25.	Budy Arrington	20	0	1,885	115,300
26.	Dale Jarrett	24	0	1,840	143,405
27.	Steve Christman	20	0	1,727	54,965
28.	Rick Wilson	19	0	1,723	65,935
29.	Cale Yarborough	16	0	1,450	111,025
30.	J. D. McDuffie	17	0	1,361	45,555
31.	Lake Speed	13	0	1,345	110,810
32.	Brett Bodine	14	0	1,271	71,460
33.	Greg Sacks	16	0	1,200	54,815
34.	Edie Bierschwale	14	0	1,162	66,790
35.	Rodney Combs	14	0	1,098	90,990
36.	Tim Richmond	8	2	1,063	151,850
37.	Derrike Cope	11	0	797	33,750
38.	Mark Stahlll	9	0	687	32,850
39.	Bobby Wawak	8	0	638	22,505
40.	D. K. Ulrich	7	0	625	30,915
41.	Ken Ragan	6	0	549	30,575
42.	Connie Saylor	10	0	486	59,455
43.	Jerry Crammer	5	0	482	20,660
44.	Trevor Boys	10	0	460	59,240
45.	Mike Potter	6	0	456	13,290
46.	Slick Johnson	8	0	444	40,630
47.	Ron Bouchard	5	0	440	24,105
48.	H. B. Bailey	5	0	428	18,885
49.	A. J. Foyt	6	0	409	21,075
50.	Larry Pearson	4	0	401	18,555

1988

AT A GLANCE

Winston Cup Champion: Bill Elliott

Among Bill Elliott's six victories were Darlington, the July race at Daytona, and two at Dover. By taking four of the last five races, Rusty Wallace tied Elliott for the most wins. Wallace's fall fling included victories at Charlotte, North Wilkesboro, Rockingham, and Atlanta.

For the first time, three drivers surpassed $1 million in earnings: Elliott with $1,574,639; Wallace, $1,411,567, and Earnhardt, $1,214,089 . . . Bobby Allison, now 50, won the Daytona 500, with his son, Davey, runner-up. It was Allison's 84th career victory (NASCAR records credit Allison for 84 wins; other sources list him for 85). Later in the year, Allison suffered a life-threatening injury in a crash at Pocono.

Goodyear, the only tire supplier to NASCAR for decades, was challenged by a small company from Indiana. After a year producing tires for NASCAR's Sportsman division, the Hoosier Tire Co. moved up to Winston Cup. In the season opener, Neil Bonnett finished fourth on Hoosiers. Bonnett charged from two laps down in the next race and won at Richmond, ending a 526-race winning streak for Goodyear. The Indiana manufacturer, guided by Bob Newton, a former dirt-track racer, had caught Goodyear's attention. Throughout the summer both Goodyear and Hoosier encountered problems. All Goodyear tires were withdrawn before the July race at Pocono because they failed to pass a NASCAR test. A few weeks later, Hoosiers failed the same test at Watkins Glen. By the end of the year, drivers racing on Hoosiers had won nine of 29 races. In May 1989, Newton announced that his Hoosier Tire Co. was pulling out of Winston Cup racing. Newton cited the difficulty of a small company competing against a giant like Goodyear. Early in May, only two cars raced on Hoosiers for the Winston 500 at Talladega.

Allison gained his 85th and final career victory at Daytona by two lengths over Davey. Richard Petty's car went airborne after he was hit by A.J. Foyt: Petty's car tumbled end over end several times. Amazingly, the only injury Petty suffered was a sprained ankle and torn ligaments.

Neil Bonnett, 41, won consecutive races at Richmond and Rockingham. Driving the RahMoc Pontiac, Bonnett overcame a 30th starting position at Rockingham to beat Lake Speed by 0.62 seconds. It was the Hueytown, Alabama, driver's 18th career victory . . . At Darlington, Speed, 40, collected his first Winston Cup win. Driving an Oldsmobile, the Jackson, Mississippi, veteran finished 1.5 seconds ahead of Rusty Wallace . . . The following week at

Bristol, Bill Elliott won his first race on a short track (it was Elliott's 24th career win).

In the Winston 500 at Talladega, Phil Parsons piloted the Jackson Brothers Olds to his first victory, 0.21 seconds ahead of Bobby Allison. A.J. Foyt was fined $5,000 and suspended for six months for erratic driving on pit road. Earlier, under a caution flag, Foyt had pulled his car next to Alan Kulwicki's . . . In June, Wallace won the final race on Riverside's 2.6 mile road course.

At Pocono, Geoff Bodine halted a two-year winless streak by winning the Miller High Life 500. On the first lap, Bobby Allison's radioed to his crew that a tire on his car was losing pressure.

Bill Elliott celebrates his victory at the 1985 Daytona 500, his first step in winning the Winston Million that year.

As Allison entered the second (tunnel) turn, the car backed into the wall and wound up in the path of Jocko Maggiacomo's car. Allison's car was T-boned by Maggiacomo's. Allison suffered multiple injuries, including a cerebral concussion.

A week after Pocono, Wallace, 31, captured his first superspeedway win . . . In the next race, Elliott advanced from a 38th-place start to win the Pepsi Firecracker 400 at Daytona . . . Elliott also won the July race at Pocono, edging Rick Wilson in the Morgan-McClure Olds, to climb within three points of the leading Wallace . . . At Talladega, Ken Schrader won his first race for Hendrick Motorsports . . . The Elliott-Wallace points duel continued at Darlington as Elliott took the Southern 500 by 0.24 seconds over Wallace. Elliott led Wallace by 26 points . . . Davey Allison won the first race on Richmond's new three-quarter-mile track . . . Wallace, down two laps after having the carburetor changed early in the race at Charlotte, seized the lead with 12 laps to go and held off Darrell Waltrip by one car length. Wallace also won the next two races, at North Wilkesboro and Rockingham, and trailed Elliott by 79 points with two races remaining . . . Alan Kulwicki, driving a Ford, won his first Winston Cup event at Phoenix, then Wallace took the season finale at Atlanta. Wallace finished just 24 points behind Elliott . . . Kulwicki and Schrader were joined by two other first-time winners on the Cup circuit: Phil Parsons (Benny's younger brother) won at Talledega, while Lake Speed took the checkered flag at Darlington.

WINSTON CUP STANDINGS

	DRIVER	STARTS	WINS	POINTS	MONEY
1.	Bill Elliott	29	6	4,488	1,554,639
2.	Rusty Wallace	29	6	4,484	1,411,567
3.	Dale Earnhardt	29	3	4,256	1,214,089
4.	Terry Labonte	29	1	4,007	950,781
5.	Ken Schrader	29	1	3,858	631,544
6.	Geoff Bodine	29	1	3,779	570,643
7.	Darrell Waltrip	29	2	3,764	731,659
8.	Davey Allison	29	2	3,631	844,532
9.	Phil Parsons	29	1	3,630	532,043
10.	Sterling Martin	29	0	3,621	521,464
11.	Ricky Rudd	29	1	3,547	410,954
12.	Bobby Hillin Jr.	29	0	3,446	330,217
13.	Kyle Petty	29	0	3,296	377,092
14.	Alan Kulwicki	29	1	3,176	448,547
15.	Mark Martin	29	0	3,142	223,630
16.	Neil Bonnett	27	2	3,040	440,139
17.	Lake Speed	29	1	2,984	260,500
18.	Michael Waltrip	29	0	2,949	240,400
19.	Dave Marcis	29	0	2,854	212,485
20.	Brett Bodine	29	0	2,828	433,658
21.	Rick Wilson	28	0	2,762	209,925
22.	Richard Petty	29	0	2,644	190,155
23.	Dale Jarrett	29	0	2,622	118,640
24.	Benny Parsons	27	0	2,559	210,755
25.	Ken Bouchard	24	0	2,378	109,410
26.	Ernie Irvan	25	0	2,319	96,370
27.	Harry Gant	24	0	2,266	173,325
28.	Morgan Shepherd	23	0	2,193	197,425
29.	Buddy Baker	17	0	2,056	184,200
30.	Jimmy Means	27	0	2,045	139,290
31.	Derrike Cope	26	0	1,985	132,835
32.	Mike Alexander	16	0	1,931	200,709
33.	Bobby Allison	29	1	1,654	409,295
34.	Edie Bierschwale	20	0	1,481	59,355
35.	Rodney Combs	19	0	1,468	54,150
36.	Brad Noffsinger	17	0	1,316	54,645
37.	Greg Sacks	15	0	1,237	105,579
38.	Cale Yarborough	10	0	940	66,065
39.	Joe Ruttman	12	0	803	46,455
40.	Brad Teague	13	0	802	53,105
41.	Jimmy Horton	8	0	647	23,575
42.	A. J. Foyt	7	0	523	29,660
43.	H. B. Bailey	7	0	478	15,775
44.	Jim Sauter	9	0	463	35,040
45.	Chad Little	4	0	405	14,225
46.	Budy Arrington	4	0	352	22,165
47.	Ken Ragan	5	0	314	15,755
48.	Dana Patten	4	0	313	9,595
49.	Rick Jeffrey	4	0	307	25,535
50.	Mickey Gibbs	5	0	283	12,850

1989

AT A GLANCE

Winston Cup Champion: Rusty Wallace.

Top Newcomers: Dick Trickle, at age 47, was the Rookie of the Year. The Wisconsin Rapids, Wisconsin, veteran had raced intermittently in NASCAR while concentrating on smaller Midwestern circuits. In 89, Trickle, subbing for Mike Alexander in the Stavola Brothers ride, had six top-5 finishes and nine top-10s; he was 15th in points.

Talk about close races: Rusty Wallace edged Dale Earnhardt for his first driving title by a mere 12 points. It was the closest race since 1979 when Richard Petty finished just 11 points ahead of Darrell Waltrip. Wallace and Waltrip, the Daytona 500 winner, each won six races in '89. Earnhardt was runnerup with five.

Every sport experiences times when stars retire and new faces reign. That's what happened to Winston Cup racing in 1989. Bobby Allison, Cale Yarborough, Buddy Baker, and Benny Parsons all retired prior to the season, taking 313 Winston Cup wins and eight national titles to the front porch with them. Baker was forced to retire after

Rusty Wallace takes the checkered flag to win the Miller 400 at Michigan International Speedway in 1988.

crashing in the World 600 at Charlotte and learning three months later that he had a blood clot on the brain. All four stayed in the sport: Allison and Yarborough as car owners, and Baker and Parsons as television commentators.

Wallace started his run to the championship strong, with three wins in the first six races. Soon, however, problems surfaced between Wallace and car owner Raymond Beadle. Wallace's contract with Beadle was through 1990, but rumors in the garages indicated that the Missouri native wanted to leave at the conclusion of the 1989 season. In July, two months after Wallace insisted he was happy with the team, he filed a suit, seeking to get out of the contract after the '89 season. In the fall,

however, the suit was dropped. A new sponsor, Miller Genuine Draft beer, came on board through 1993. Wallace said he would drive the Blue Max Pontiac for Beadle the following season.

Darrell Waltrip won the Daytona 500, leading a parade of Hendrick Motorsports cars: Ken Schrader was second and Geoff Bodine fourth . . . At Darlington, Harry Gant won the TranSouth 500, ending a 90-race victory drought . . . Earnhardt won his first race of the year in mid-April at North Wilkesboro, riding on new Goodyear radial tires . . . A week later, Waltrip won at Martinsville in the last race for the Chevrolet Monte Carlo. Chevy would replace the Monte Carlos with Luminas in the next race, the Winston 500 at Talladega . . . Driving a Robert Yates-owned Ford sponsored by Texaco Havoline, Davey Allison won the Winston 500. Allison gave Ford its first victory of the year. Waltrip (fifth) and Schrader (sixth) were the highest finishing Luminas . . . By winning the Coca-Cola 600 at Charlotte, Waltrip gave himself a chance to pocket the $1 million bonus offered by the R.J. Reynolds Co.

Terry Labonte's victory at Pocono in June marked Junior Johnson's first superspeedway win since October 1986 . . . Davey Allison returned to victory lane at Daytona in July; Morgan Shepherd was runnerup and Phil Parsons was third . . . Earnhardt spoiled Waltrip's bid for the $1 million by taking the Southern 500 at Darlington; Mark Martin was second. Waltrip sputtered home 22nd after two skirmishes with the Turn 4 wall. Said the always quotable Waltrip: "I love Darlington in the spring, and I love Darlington in the fall. I love Darlington in the winner's circle, but I hate Darlington in the wall." Earnhardt stretched his points lead over Wallace to 73.

Wallace won at Richmond, with Earnhardt second. Earnhardt was first at Dover (Wallace was seventh). After Martinsville, where Wallace was fourth and Earnhardt ninth, Wallace trailed by 75 points. However, by Charlotte, Wallace was ahead by 35. In the race won by Schrader, Wallace was eighth and Earnhardt was last (engine problems). Four races to go. Earnhardt dominated the next event, at North Wilkesboro, leading 342 of the 400 laps. But a late caution created a sprint between Earnhardt and Ricky Rudd. On the last lap, they collided and Geoff Bodine won. Wallace inched ahead by 37 points. Earnhardt was furious with Rudd, saying the Virginian should be suspended for the rest of the season. Each driver accused the other of trying to force him out of the race.

Martin took the AC Delco 500 at Rockingham in a Jack Roush Ford for his first Winston Cup win (he would finish third in the point standings), with Wallace placing second after leading the most laps. Earnhardt finished 20th, after he and Wallace made contact on lap 428. Wallace took the blame for spinning Earnhardt's car. Wallace extended his points lead to 109.

At Phoenix, with 47 laps to go, Wallace tangled with Stan Barrett, a Hollywood stunt man making his fourth Winston Cup start. Wallace was relegated to a 16th-place finish; Earnhardt was sixth. All Wallace needed in the final race to clinch his first title was 18th place or higher. Earnhardt dominated the season's race in Atlanta, leading 294 of 328 laps to win. Wallace coaxed his Pontiac home 15th to capture the title.

WINSTON CUP STANDINGS

	DRIVER	STARTS	WINS	POINTS	MONEY
1.	Rusty Wallace	29	6	4,176	2,237,950
2.	Dale Earnhardt	29	5	4,164	1,432,230
3.	Mark Martin	29	1	4,053	1,016,850
4.	Darrell Waltrip	29	6	3,971	1,312,479
5.	Ken Schrader	29	1	3,876	1,037,941
6.	Bill Elliott	29	3	3,774	849,370
7.	Harry Gant	29	1	3,610	639,792
8.	Ricky Rudd	29	1	3,608	533,624
9.	Geoff Bodine	29	1	3,600	619,494
10.	Terry Labonte	29	2	3,569	703,806
11.	Davey Allison	29	2	3,481	640,956
12.	Sterling Marlin	29	0	3,422	473,267
13.	Morgan Shepherd	29	0	3,403	544,255
14.	Alan Kulwicki	29	0	3,236	501,295
15.	Dick Trickle	28	0	3,203	343,728
16.	Bobby Hillin Jr.	28	0	3,139	283,181
17.	Rick Wilson	29	0	3,119	312,402
18.	Michael Waltrip	29	0	3,057	249,233
19.	Brett Bodine	29	0	3,051	281,274
20.	Neil Bonnett	26	0	2,995	271,628
21.	Phil Parsons	29	0	2,933	285,012
22.	Ernie Irvan	29	0	2,919	155,329
23.	Larry Pearson	29	0	2,860	156,060
24.	Dale Jarrett	29	0	2,789	232,317
25.	Dave Marcis	27	0	2,715	196,161
26.	Hut Stricklin	27	0	2,705	152,504
27.	Lake Speed	24	0	2,550	201,977
28.	Derrike Cope	23	0	2,180	125,630
29.	Richard Petty	25	0	2,148	133,050
30.	Kyle Petty	19	0	2,099	117,027
31.	Jimmy Means	22	0	1,698	65,005
32.	Greg Sacks	20	0	1,565	113,535
33.	Jim Sauter	17	0	1,510	73,832
34.	Jimmy Spencer	17	0	1,445	121,065
35.	Rick Mast	13	0	1,315	128,102
36.	Edie Bierschwale	16	0	1,306	82,695
37.	Ben Hess	9	0	921	48,490
38.	Chad Little	8	0	602	44,690
39.	Butch Miller	9	0	576	22,520
40.	A. J. Foyt	7	0	527	31,995
41.	Mickey Gibbs	7	0	508	27,040
42.	Rodney Combs	9	0	470	36,090
43.	Joe Ruttman	9	0	469	64,645
44.	J. D. McDuffie	7	0	457	27,720
45.	Phil Barkdoll	4	0	378	29,050
46.	Jimmy Horton	5	0	377	19,232
47.	Dick Johnson	4	0	322	11,515
48.	Ken Bouchard	4	0	313	33,930
49.	Terry Byers	3	0	306	15,400
50.	Darin Brassfield	3	0	306	10,852

9

THE BOOM YEARS:
NASCAR IN THE '90s

New stars, new venues, new sponsors from outside motor sports: that's NASCAR in the booming 1990s. Ten years ago, people in the sport wondered if NASCAR could get much bigger. Now, many of these same people are saying there's no limit to how big major-league stock car racing can get.

Following the corporate boom of the 1980s, when major nonautomotive corporations filed into NASCAR as sponsors, disbursing checks for millions of dollars in return for tremendous exposure for their products, NASCAR expanded in the mid-'90s to the venerable Indianapolis Motor Speedway and last year to new racetracks in Texas and California. NASCAR no longer was a southeastern sport, embraced by a small portion of the nation's fans. It truly became a nationwide attraction.

As the era of Richard Petty, Bobby Allison, Cale Yarborough, David Pearson, and Buddy Baker was ending, along came Jeff Gordon, Dale Jarrett, Ernie Irvan, Mark Martin, Bobby Labonte, Jeff and Ward Burton, Ricky Craven, Johnny Benson, and Jeremy Mayfield to take the place of the well-known veteran drivers.

Away from the tracks, fans can continue their associations with racing. NASCAR Thunder mer-

chandise shops opened around the United States along with NASCAR Cafes. Thunder stores are in Atlanta; Cincinnati; Dallas; Phoenix; Winston-Salem, North Carolina; Knoxville and Chattanooga, Tennessee; and Mobile, Alabama. Additional stores are planned for Baltimore, Louisville, Chicago, Virginia Beach and Richmond, Jacksonville, and Charleston, West Virginia. The first NASCAR Cafe opened to much fanfare in Myrtle Beach, South Carolina, with a second restaurant scheduled to open in Nashville in 1998.

At the cafes, fans can eat, drink, and socialize in a racing atmosphere. The cafes simulate the racetrack scene. Surrounding the restaurant area is an entertainment concourse that reminds fans of the grandstands. One of the features on the concourse is the Papyrus NASCAR CD-ROM Racing Pod where customers can race against each other on a simulated Winston Cup track. Just in case customers aren't aware they are in a NASCAR Cafe, a stock car is suspended above the bar. Explaining the appeal of the cafes, Mark Dyer, president of NASCAR Cafe, said, "NASCAR has become a way of life. It is family, and all of the followers of the sport are part of the family."

Corporate logos are everywhere on a race day in the '90s, including on the trucks used to transport the cars.

NONTRADITIONAL OWNERS AND SPONSORS JOIN THE RACE

During the '90s, prominent people from other sports began filtering into NASCAR. Joe Gibbs, who guided the Washington Redskins to three Super Bowl championships, became a car owner with the Interstate Batteries team. Dale Jarrett was Gibbs's first driver, followed by Bobby Labonte. Gibbs continued as an NFL studio analyst for NBC Sports, but his first love is racing. Gibbs has also fielded drag racing teams.

Last year, Basketball Hall of Famer Julius Erving and ex-NFL running back Joe Washington formed a NASCAR team. The Washington-Erving

group intends to race on the Winston Cup circuit, but as of late in the year they had only announced a Busch Grand National team with Jimmy Foster as the driver. Foster is the grandson of Jim Foster, former president of NASCAR. The other partners in the team are North Carolina businessman Fields Jackson, Jr., and Kathy Thompson, a sports marketing executive.

Erving is a latecomer to racing. He didn't attend a race until last year's Daytona 500, and that visit was mainly to humor his longtime friend Washington, who played for Gibbs in Washington. It didn't take long for the famed "Doctor J" to get seriously interested in racing.

Nontraditional sponsors, such as the QVC television shopping network, have rolled into NASCAR in a big way.

"After going to my first race, I was totally turned on," he said. "I knew I had been missing something."

Although Erving and Washington had been friends for 20 years, they never had a business relationship. One day, Washington called and said, "Doc, this is the one." Erving replied, "What are you talking about?" That one visit to Daytona made Erving aware of what Washington was talking about.

Another former NBA star beat Erving into NASCAR. Brad Daugherty is a co-owner in the NASCAR Craftsman Truck series. Daugherty's driver last year was Kenny Irwin Jr., who's moving

into Winston Cup with the Robert Yates team. Unlike Erving, Daugherty knew about NASCAR from the time he was little— if the seven-footer was ever little. Daugherty attended races when he was growing up in North Carolina. His favorite driver was Richard Petty: Daugherty wore Petty's No. 43 as an NBA player.

The involvement of nontraditional NASCAR sponsors that began in the 1980s continued into the '90s. One of these sponsors in Winston Cup is the Du Pont Co. The Delaware-based company tested the racing waters as an associate sponsor with Kyle Petty in the early '90s. When customers responded favorably to that sponsorship, Du Pont moved to the

Busch Grand National series with Ricky Craven. In '93, Du Pont hit the jackpot when its automotive finishes division signed on with Hendrick Motorsports as Jeff Gordon's primary sponsor.

"Our customers kept saying we ought to be involved," said Tom Speakman, then Du Pont's marketing manager, automotive finishes division. "The first year with Kyle, we used it mainly to entertain customers." Speakman said Gordon's success has had a positive effect on Du Pont's employees. Like many corporations, Du Pont has been downsizing in the '90s. Speakman said Gordon's success "has been a rallying point for our employees: on weekends, they can root for our own car." Gordon's popularity was evident when a seventh-grade class in Ottawa was asked by a Du Pont representative what the students associated most with the company. They didn't name a Du Pont product: they said, "Jeff Gordon."

TELEVISION RATINGS SOAR

There are no Winston Cup races in Canada—fans there watch the races on television. So do many, many fans in the United States. Television ratings, like NASCAR's popularity, are soaring. On ESPN, NASCAR is second only to NFL games. Daily shows like "RPM 2Night" that update viewers on news developments in racing have added to the interest in the sport. Not long ago, racing fans outside the southeast depended on weekly racing papers for their coverage. Now, an "RPM 2Night" takes fans to the tracks every day. ABC, CBS, TNN and TBS also televise NASCAR races. Several times in 1996 on Saturday afternoons, TBS carried a couple hours of Winston Cup *practices*. Stick-and-ball fans wondered how anyone could watch race cars practicing, but NASCAR fans enjoyed the commentary and the interviews in the garage areas.

Terry Lingner has been involved with television coverage of NASCAR from ESPN's launching. Lingner, now the president of his Indianapolis-based production company, produced the coverage of ESPN's first race from Salem, Indiana, in 1979. Lingner has seen the rights fees skyrocket for Winston Cup races and others. In the 1980s, the fee for many Winston Cup races was just $75,000. Now, the fees range from $1 million up to $3 and $4 million for a Daytona 500 or a Brickyard 400.

"It would blow me away," Lingner said, "that we would pay $75,000 for a great Talladega race on a Sunday. Then, the next Saturday, we would pay $1 million for rights for a Northwestern-Wisconsin Big 10 [football] game. I thought, 'This is ridiculous: this is Richard Petty and Darrell Waltrip and we're paying $1 million for the eighth- and ninth-place teams [in the Big 10].' It's taken a long time for the market to correct itself [but] I think you've only seen about 50 percent of the potential in the whole sport."

Lingner's company produced a five-part documentary on NASCAR that will lead into the 50th anniversary celebration of NASCAR this year. The documentary will be carried on ESPN and ESPN2.

Another indication of the growing interest in NASCAR was the introduction by the *Philadelphia Daily News* last summer of a full page of NASCAR coverage every Wednesday. The *Daily News,* one of the nation's best sports sections, has traditionally covered NASCAR and Indy car races in the East, plus the Daytona and Indianapolis 500s. But the weekly full page, headlined "Up to Speed with NASCAR," was further proof that readers outside the southeast were interested in the sport.

"In the past couple of years, there has been a terrific growth and interest in NASCAR," said Mike Rathet, executive sports editor of the *Daily News.* "We started the page because we want to serve the interest in NASCAR that our readers have."

NEW TRACKS, NEW MARKETS

Shiny new racetracks are another imposing sign of NASCAR's thriving business. The 150,000-seat Texas Motor Speedway was built on the plains north of Fort Worth in familiar Bruton Smith-style. If it's Texas, it must be the biggest, or close to it. TMS is the second largest racetrack in the world: only the established Indianapolis Motor Speedway is larger.

NASCAR GOES TO JAPAN

Several dozen NASCAR drivers had a unique racing experience in November of 1996 at the Suzuka Circuitland road course in Suzuka, Japan. There, for the first time in history, a full-blown Winston Cup "exhibition" race was being staged outside North America.

The race itself was forgettable. Rusty Wallace led most of the first half, then won ahead of Dale Earnhardt and Dale Jarrett. Less than 24 hours later, the drivers, crews, owners, and media were on their way from Nagoya to Tokyo, then on to their home just in time for Thanksgiving.

They returned with one memory likely to stay with them forever. It was of thousands of Japanese fans standing behind a white line and watching politely as crewmen tuned their cars for the last practice session before the next day's race. The fans had been invited out of the grandstands and onto pit road to get a better view of the American stock cars and their drivers.

They'd been asked to stay behind the white line—so they did. Nobody brazenly ventured into the garage area. Nobody called out to the drivers or crewmen doing their work. They simply stood, pointed at what they were seeing, and spoke quietly among themselves. And when it was time to return to the grandstands, they turned on their heels and obediently went back across the track and into their seats.

"Can you image what would have happened in America if we'd let fans come that close to the garage, then asked them to stand there?" said former Busch Series champion and 1997 Winston Cup rookie David Green. "The way those people behaved that afternoon impressed me, it really did. I had a great time because we were making history over there. But I'll never forget those people standing behind that line, being polite enough and respectful enough to let us do our jobs.

"I doubt you'd ever see that kind of behavior in a garage area back home."

Smith sees the Texas market as "almost like a new frontier. Texas is opening up a giant market for more sponsorships coming into our sport. It probably ranks second in the nation as far as the home office for major companies." Prior to the opening of TMS, Smith said, "That will be the most successful speedway that's ever been built. That speedway is going to help build NASCAR more than anything I've done yet."

For the inaugural Interstate Batteries 500, TMS encountered problems with the width of part of its 1-mile racing surface and parking (heavy rains prevented the paving of some parking areas). But Smith promised that those glitches will be corrected.

Roger Penske's new California Speedway also brings NASCAR into a major market. Situated about 50 miles east of Los Angeles in Fontana, the 2-mile racetrack is near the site of the former Ontario Motor Speedway. Like TMS, the California Speedway is ultra-modern with luxury suites and all the amenities that fans at old race-

tracks didn't enjoy. Fans at the California track are referred to as "guests."

That tracks in Ontario and Riverside closed didn't discourage Penske. "In those days, racing was different," he told the weekly *NASCAR Winston Cup Scene* paper. "I raced at Riverside in the '60s and was a car owner at Ontario. Today, the momentum of the exposure that we have on a worldwide basis, the sponsors that are involved, the quality of the cars and drivers—the whole sport has taken a giant leap. What's propelled the momentum is the fact that you've got major-league companies that feel this is a medium that they can exploit their product in." Penske also noted that an important appeal of the southern California market is "this is the No. 1 retail market probably in the world. From an automotive perspective, there's more cars probably per square inch in California than there is anywhere else."

California Speedway opened with about 70,000 grandstand seats and 71 luxury suites: plans

One look at Bill Elliott's uniform tells you how important sponsorship is to NASCAR drivers in the '90s.

call for 25,000 more seats and 42 skyboxes by 1999. Gateway International Raceway, near St. Louis, opened last year with a Busch Grand National race. New Hampshire International Speedway hosted its first Winston Cup race in 1993.

Last year, Penske, the International Speedway Corp. and Bruton Smith were buying racetracks as fast as their accountants could write checks. At the end of last season, the lineup stood:

ISC: Daytona, Talladega, Darlington, Watkins Glen, and Phoenix;

Smith: Charlotte, Atlanta, Bristol, Sears Point, and Texas;

Penske: Michigan, California, and Rockingham.

Smith announced plans to build a track near Atlantic City. Almost every week there was a press conference to unveil plans for a new track. How all these tracks were going to fill dates with races was another intriguing story. Winston Cup car owners and crew chiefs are already feeling stretched to their limit. Gary DeHart, crew chief for defending Winston Cup champion Terry Labonte, resigned in September, a victim of burnout. Michael Kranefuss, co-owner of the Kmart/RC Cola-sponsored Ford driven by Jeremy Mayfield, said the stress on his staff "is my biggest concern. You can see it in terms of energy and creativity. We're already overexposed: you can't breed 1,000 more mechanics or fabricators overnight."

An exhibition race in Japan in November, started in 1996, is regarded by some as cruel and unusual punishment after such a long season, but some teams make the long trip because there is money to be made and they are aware the exposure would help NASCAR.

From a business standpoint, NASCAR no longer confines its offices to Daytona Beach. In 1997, the organization opened an office on Park Avenue in New York City to handle NASCAR's marketing activities. Further interest in NASCAR is reflected in several colleges in the South offering courses in motorsports-related subjects such as engineering, marketing, and administration. Five

universities—Duke, South Carolina, North Carolina State, North Carolina–Charlotte, and Tennessee—entered Legends cars in races at Charlotte Motor Speedway. Craig Rogers, the dean of the University of South Carolina's college of engineering, launched the idea of racing Legends cars as a way of working with the motorsports industry in the region. Rogers noted that two of the teams have women drivers, and all the teams have at least one woman on their crews.

One major reason sponsors commit to NASCAR is brand loyalty of fans. Racegoers spend several hundred dollars apiece during race weekends for hotels, restaurants, entertainment, and souvenirs. Every fan isn't committed to buying the products of companies that are NASCAR sponsors. However, in a survey by Performance Research Inc., fans were asked if, given a choice of two products with a similar price, would they select a product associated with NASCAR over one that is not. Forty-eight percent said they "almost always" choose the NASCAR product.

Typical of the devotion to NASCAR-associated products is that of Tom Foster, a retired Proctor and Gamble field representative. Foster has been attending races at Darlington for 25 years. "I buy everything I can from people who sponsor racing," he said. "If they can put their money into racing, I can help them."

Prior to the first Winston Cup race at Texas, Mike Tucker was sipping a Busch beer. The 35-year-old maintenance man from Texarkana, Arkansas, is an extreme supporter of NASCAR sponsors. "Everything I do revolves around NASCAR: I am NASCAR," Tucker told the *Dallas Morning News.*

TROUBLE BREWING?

As the 1998 season began, one of the few clouds looming over NASCAR, and all motor sports in the United States, was the tobacco issue. Under an agreement reached last June between the tobacco industry and states' attorneys general, motor sports are in danger of losing tobacco companies as sponsors. The agreement would require the RJR Nabisco Co. and three other cigarette companies to pay $368.5 billion over the next 25 years to compensate the states for the costs of treating smoking-related illness, to finance nationwide anti-smoking programs, and to underwrite health care for uninsured children. President Clinton and Congress still have to approve the agreement. RJR, which is in its 28th year sponsoring the Winston Cup series, no longer would be able to do so. Tobacco companies could not sponsor races or have their names on race cars or tracks. Jim Andrews, vice president of the IEG Sponsorship Report, a sports marketing newsletter, says tobacco companies account for about 20 percent of the total sponsorship money in motor sports. If RJR is forced to withdraw from racing, observers believe that NASCAR's soaring popularity would attract another series sponsor.

There are other concerns, as well. To make travel easier, there has been discussion about perhaps eventually dividing the Winston Cup series into East and West divisions. However, this idea has been greeted with little enthusiasm because fans of the top drivers wouldn't be happy if their favorite driver wasn't in the division in their area.

Whichever path NASCAR takes likely will be successful because its leadership has demonstrated a skilled touch at making the right decisions for the sport to prosper. As Roger Penske told *NASCAR Winston Cup Scene,* "If the competition stays as tight as it is and we can maintain the sponsorship levels, it will continue to grow. They have to keep it exciting [and] close. We've got to see different winners [and] new faces coming in. And we want to keep it as safe as we can, but yet as close as we can."

10

1990–1996: IT'S NOT JUST A SPORT, IT'S A LIFESTYLE

1990

AT A GLANCE

Winston Cup Champion: Dale Earnhardt

Top Newcomers: Rookie of the Year Rob Moroso: one top-10 finish.

Notable Events: At 50, Harry Gant becomes the oldest driver to win a Winston Cup race . . . Morgan Shepherd collects his first win since 1986.

Dale Earnhardt edged Mark Martin for his fourth Winston Cup championship by just 26 points. Entering the season finale, Earnhardt led by just six points.

The season began on another frustrating note for Earnhardt. Once again, he failed to win the Daytona 500, extending his winless streak in the series top race to 0-for-his-career. This one was unbelievably wrenching as he was leading on the last lap when he cut a tire and Derrike Cope passed him in turn three for his first victory.

In the next race at Richmond, Mark Martin beat Earnhardt by three seconds. A post-race inspection revealed that Martin had a one-inch aluminum spacer under the carburetor instead of the one-half inch spacer allowed. Martin was fined $40,000 and 46 Winston Cup points. At Rockingham, Kyle Petty won from the pole and pocketed the $228,000 pole winner's bonus that rolled over from the previous year. It was the first win for Felix Sabates as a car owner.

At Bristol, Davey Allison outdueled Martin by eight inches in the closest finish in Winston Cup history . . . In the next race, at North Wilkesboro, Brett Bodine won for the first time, by .95 of a second over Darrell Waltrip . . . Brett's older brother, Geoff, won the following race at Martinsville, marking the ninth time in NASCAR history that brothers had won consecutive races.

At Dover in June, Cope won his second race, by 1.24 seconds over Ken Schrader . . . Two weeks later at Pocono, 50-year-old Harry Gant, driving an Oldsmobile, became the oldest driver to win a Winston Cup race: he finished two seconds ahead of Rusty Wallace . . . Ricky Rudd won at Watkins Glen; Dick Trickle suffered a broken leg in a three-car practice accident.

Back at Bristol in late August, Ernie Irvan gained his first Winston Cup victory in the Morgan-McClure Chevrolet . . . In the next race, Earn-

Dale Earnhardt's icy stare is just part of the reason he's known as "The Intimidator."

	DRIVER	STARTS	WINS	POINTS	MONEY
4.	Bill Elliott	29	1	3,999	1,090,730
5.	Morgan Shepherd	29	1	3,689	666,915
6.	Rusty Wallace	29	2	3,676	954,129
7.	Ricky Rudd	29	1	3,601	573,650
8.	Alan Kulwicki	29	1	3,599	550,936
9.	Ernie Irvan	29	1	3,593	535,280
10.	Ken Schrader	29	0	3,572	769,934
11.	Kyle Petty	29	1	3,501	746,326
12.	Brett Bodine	29	1	3,440	442,681
13.	Davey Allison	29	2	3,423	640,684
14.	Sterling Marlin	29	0	3,387	369,167
15.	Terry Labonte	29	0	3,371	450,230
16.	Michael Waltrip	29	0	3,251	395,507
17.	Harry Gant	28	1	3,182	522,519
18.	Derrike Cope	29	2	3,140	569,451
19.	Bobby Hillin Jr.	29	0	3,048	339,366
20.	Darrell Waltrip	23	0	3,013	520,420
21.	Dave Marcis	29	0	2,944	242,724
22.	Dick Trickle	29	0	2,863	350,990
23.	Rick Wilson	29	0	2,666	242,067
24.	Jimmy Spencer	26	0	2,579	219,775
25.	Dale Jarrett	24	0	2,558	214,495
26.	Richard Petty	29	0	2,556	169,465
27.	Butch Miller	23	0	2,377	151,941
28.	Hut Stricklin	24	0	2,316	169,199
29.	Jimmy Means	27	0	2,271	135,165
30.	Rob Moroso	25	0	2,184	162,002
31.	Rick Mast	20	0	1,719	112,875
32.	Greg Sacks	16	0	1,663	216,148
33.	Chad Little	18	0	1,632	80,140
34.	Jack Pennington	14	0	1,278	95,860
35.	Larry Pearson	9	0	822	72,305
36.	Jimmy Horton	9	0	756	72,375
37.	Mickey Gibbs	9	0	755	38,665
38.	Mike Alexander	7	0	682	41,080
39.	Phil Parsons	9	0	632	90,010
40.	J. D. McDuffie	8	0	557	26,170
41.	Buddy Baker	8	0	498	40,085
42.	Lake Speed	6	0	479	75,537
43.	Neil Bonnett	5	0	455	62,600
44.	Mark Stahl	5	0	371	18,470
45.	Bill Venturini	4	0	349	22,970
46.	Rodney Combs	5	0	323	23,365
47.	Irv Hoerr	2	0	281	14,775
48.	Tommy Kendall	3	0	281	14,120
49.	Ted Musgrave	4	0	280	17,190
50.	Chuck Brown	3	0	276	10,150

hardt took the Southern 500 at Darlington for the third time in the last four years . . . Back at Dover, Bill Elliott, running on fumes, took his first race of the season. Martin was second and Earnhardt was third. Martin held a 21-point lead over Earnhardt in the closest points race at this stage of the season.

At Rockingham, Alan Kulwicki won in a Ford. With two races remaining, Martin's lead over Earnhardt was 45 points . . . At Phoenix, Earnhardt won and Martin finished 10th. Earnhardt inched ahead of Martin by six points . . . In the season finale at Atlanta, Morgan Shepherd, driving a Bud Moore Ford, won for the first time since 1986. Earnhardt was third and Martin sixth. Earnhardt's point margin for the championship: a mere 26 points.

Among the other important events of the year: Derrike Cope, Brett Bodine, and Ernie Irvan registered their first victories . . . Felix Sabates posted his first win as a car owner.

WINSTON CUP STANDINGS

	DRIVER	STARTS	WINS	POINTS	MONEY
1.	Dale Earnhardt	29	9	4,430	3,308,056
2.	Mark Martin	29	3	4,404	1,302,958
3.	Geoff Bodine	29	3	4,017	1,131,222

1991

AT A GLANCE

Winston Cup Champion: Dale Earnhardt.

Top Newcomers: Rookie of the Year Bobby Hamilton: four top-10 finishes.

Notable Events: Harry Gant won four races in a row.

Dale Earnhardt's repeat as Winston Cup champion was one of several major developments in '91. Davey Allison and Ernie Irvan emerged as stars in the series. At the end of the year, Bill Elliott and Harry Melling dissolved their 10-year association.

Earnhardt again was in contention to park in victory lane at the Daytona 500 for the first time, but, you guessed it: someone else grabbed Earnhardt's parking spot. Late in the race, Ernie Irvan was leading while Earnhardt and Davey Allison battled for second place. With three laps left, Allison and Earnhardt made contact, sending both their cars spinning. The race ended under caution with Irvan winning his first Daytona 500.

For the second consecutive year, Kyle Petty won the Goodwrench 500 at Rockingham from the pole. This time, Petty finished 1.1 seconds ahead of Ken Schrader . . . Schrader's quest for victory was satisfied in the next race at Atlanta. In the rain-delayed Motorcraft 500, Schrader conserved fuel and won in a Hendrick Motorsports Chevrolet . . . Michael Waltrip dominated the TranSouth 500 at Darlington, leading 280 of 367 laps. But mechanical problems in his Pontiac cost him as Ricky Rudd went on to win.

At Bristol, Rusty Wallace gained his first win for car owners Roger Penske and Don Miller . . . At North Wilkesboro, Darrell Waltrip outraced Earnhardt to win by .81 of a second and halt a 34-race losing streak . . . Earnhardt celebrated his 40th birthday by winning at Martinsville, tying him with Junior Johnson and Ned Jarrett on the all-time list with 50 wins apiece . . . Harry Gant won at Talladega in the Skoal Oldsmobile. Kyle Petty suffered a broken femur in a 22-car wreck and missed 11 races.

Davey Allison dominated the weekend at Charlotte, winning the Coca-Cola 600 and The Winston (total earnings: $462,100) . . . At Sears Point, Allison was leading on the final lap when he was tapped by Rudd's car. After Rudd took the checkered flag, officials penalized him for rough driving and awarded Allison the victory . . . Darrell Waltrip won his 81st career race at Pocono, then Allison gained his career-high third victory of the season at Michigan.

Bill Elliott's only win of the year occurred in the July race at Daytona, following the deaths of his mother and grandmother within three weeks of each other . . . In one of Earnhardt's most masterful performances, he held off the Fords of Elliott, Allison, Mark Martin, and Sterling Marlin to win the DieHard 500 at Talladega . . . NASCAR lost

one of its most popular drivers when veteran J.D. McDuffie was killed in a crash at Watkins Glen.

Dale Jarrett's first Winston Cup win, in the Champion 400 at Michigan, came in dramatic style. Jarrett and Allison raced side by side for three laps following the final caution. Exiting the final turn, their cars scraped and Jarrett won by six inches in the Wood Brothers Citgo Ford. Just two weeks before, Jarrett had announced he would be leaving the Wood Brothers team to join the newly formed team owned by Washington Redskins coach Joe Gibbs.

After Alan Kulwicki won his first race of the year at Bristol, Harry Gant launched a remarkable four-race streak that tied the modern record. Gant, 51, won at Darlington, Richmond, Dover, and Martinsville. The Martinsville victory was particularly memorable: Gant's car spun into the outside wall after he and Rusty Wallace touched. Gant was then struck by Morgan Shepherd's car. Although Gant's car was severely damaged, he overtook the field and won.

Geoff Bodine returned to Charlotte, where he broke several ribs practicing for The Winston in May, and won for Junior Johnson. The victory gave Johnson at least one win as a car owner every season since 1966. Johnson and Bodine split after the season . . . Davey Allison won the fourth time in the year at Rockingham . . . In the next-to-last race of the season, Allison won again, climbing into second place in the points standings and spoiling Earnhardt's title-clinching party. Allison trailed Earnhardt by 156 points . . . Earnhardt celebrated his fifth championship by merely starting the final race at Atlanta. Mark Martin won the race.

WINSTON CUP STANDINGS

DRIVER	STARTS	WINS	POINTS	MONEY
1. Dale Earnhardt	29	4	4,287	2,416,685
2. Ricky Rudd	29	1	4,092	1,093,765
3. Davey Allison	29	5	4,088	1,712,924
4. Harry Gant	29	5	3,985	1,194,033
5. Ernie Irvan	29	2	3,925	1,079,017
6. Mark Martin	29	1	3,914	1,039,991
7. Sterling Marlin	29	0	3,839	633,690
8. Darrell Waltrip	29	2	3,711	604,854
9. Ken Schrader	29	2	3,690	772,434
10. Rusty Wallace	29	2	3,582	502,073
11. Bill Elliott	29	1	3,535	705,605

12.	Morgan Shepherd	29	0	3,438	521,147
13.	Alan Kulwicki	29	1	3,354	595,614
14.	Geoff Bodine	27	1	3,277	625,256
15.	Michael Waltrip	29	0	3,254	440,812
16.	Hut Stricklin	29	0	3,199	426,524
17.	Dale Jarrett	29	1	3,124	444,256
18.	Terry Labonte	29	0	3,024	348,898
19.	Brett Bodine	29	0	2,980	376,220
20.	Joe Ruttman	29	0	2,938	361,661
21.	Rick Mast	29	0	2,918	344,020
22.	Bobby Hamilton	28	0	2,915	259,105
23.	Ted Musgrave	29	0	2,841	200,910
24.	Richard Petty	29	0	2,817	268,035
25.	Jimmy Spencer	29	0	2,790	283,620
26.	Rick Wilson	29	0	2,723	241,375
27.	Chad Little	28	0	2,678	184,190
28.	Derrike Cope	28	0	2,516	419,380
29.	Dave Marcis	27	0	2,374	219,760
30.	Bobby Hillin Jr.	22	0	2,317	251,645
31.	Kyle Petty	18	1	2,078	413,727
32.	Lake Speed	20	0	1,742	149,300
33.	Jimmy Means	20	0	1,562	111,210
34.	Mickey Gibbs	15	0	1,401	100,360
35.	Dick Trickle	14	0	1,258	129,125
36.	Stanley Smith	12	0	893	56,915
37.	Larry Pearson	11	0	848	56,570
38.	Wally Dallenbach Jr.	11	0	803	54,020
39.	Greg Sacks	11	0	791	84,215
40.	Buddy Baker	6	0	552	58,060

41.	Jimmy Hensley	4	0	488	32,125
42.	Eddie Bierschwale	5	0	431	55,025
43.	Jim Sauter	6	0	423	47,395
44.	Kenny Wallace	5	0	412	58,325
45.	Jeff Purvis	6	0	399	42,910
46.	Phil Barkdoll	4	0	364	41,655
47.	Mike Chase	5	0	356	22,700
48.	J. D. McDuffie	5	0	335	19,795
49.	Bill Sedgwick	3	0	324	15,150
50.	Randy Lajoie	4	0	304	23,875

1992

Alan Kulwicki's championship wasn't decided until the season's final race. In the process of winning his first title, Kulwicki dueled Davey Allison and Bill Elliott.

Dale Jarrett, shown here in 1997, claimed his first Winston Cup victory in 1991.

AT A GLANCE

Winston Cup Champion: Alan Kulwicki.

Notable Events: closest points finish in Winston Cup history . . . Richard Petty's final year as a driver . . . Bill Elliott wins four races in a row . . . Bill France, Sr. dies during the season.

Top Newcomers: Rookie of the Year Jimmy Hensley: four top-10 finishes.

At the Daytona 500, Davey Allison eluded a 14-car crash on lap 92 and led 95 of the final 100 laps to win the 500-miler for the first time. Junior Johnson's drivers, Elliott and Sterling Marlin, qualified one-two.

Elliott began his record-tying four-race winning streak at Rockingham. Elliott, driving the Budweiser Ford, nipped Kulwicki by 18 inches to win at Richmond. Elliott added victories at Atlanta and Darlington, but the consistent Allison maintained a 58-point lead over Elliott . . . At Bristol, in a race won by Kulwicki, Allison hit the wall, separating cartilage around his rib cage and knocking two vertebrae out of place . . . Still in pain, Allison won the next race at North Wilkesboro; Jimmy Hensley qualified the Texaco Ford seventh for Allison . . . Allison reinjured his rib cage in a crash at Martinsville (Mark Martin won).

At Talladega, the resilient Allison withstood Elliott's challenge for victory No. 3 of the year . . . Dale Earnhardt won his only race at Charlotte as Allison crashed again, this time as he crossed the finish line. He suffered a broken collarbone and reinjured his ribs. Allison raced the next week at Dover, but was never in contention . . . At Sears Point, Ernie Irvan steered his way to an astounding comeback. After qualifying second, Irvan was black-flagged for jumping the start of the race. Relegated to last place, Irvan began the virtually impossible task on a road course of charging to the front. On lap 67 of the 74-lap race, Irvan took the lead and held it. He dedicated the victory to NASCAR founder Bill France Sr., who died the morning of the race.

Allison won his fourth race of the year in the Miller Genuine Draft 400 at Michigan . . . In the Pepsi 400 at Daytona, President Bush helped honor Richard Petty, who led the first five laps of the race won by Irvan . . . After setting a track qualifying record in the July race at Pocono, Allison dominated the race, leading the first 140 laps. Then, on lap 149, as Allison and Darrell Waltrip exited the tunnel turn, their cars touched and Allison's car flipped several times. He was hospitalized for four days with injuries that included a broken right arm, a dislocated wrist, and a severe concussion. Worried Allison fans remembered that four years earlier at Pocono, his father, Bobby, was severely injured in a career-ending crash.

Amazingly, Davey Allison reported for duty at the next race at Talladega. He started and drove four laps before Bobby Hillin Jr. replaced him. Hillin finished third, behind Irvan and Sterling Marlin, giving Allison the points to take a one-point lead over Elliott . . . Following Kyle Petty's first road course win at Watkins Glen, the Allison family endured more grief. During practice for the Busch Grand National race at Michigan, Davey's younger brother, Clifford, died in a crash. In the Winston Cup race, Davey finished fifth.

Racing on Bristol's new concrete surface, Waltrip outraced Earnhardt and Ken Schrader for his record 12th victory on the .533-mile Tennessee oval . . . Bidding for the $1 million Winston bonus in the Southern 500 at Darlington, Allison ran in the top three. But on lap 297 of the 367-lap event, it rained. When the red flag was waved one lap later, Waltrip had won his second consecutive race and his first Southern 500.

At Richmond, aided by new crew chief Buddy Parrott, Rusty Wallace gained his first win of the year in a Pontiac . . . At Martinsville, Geoff Bodine won for the first time in a Bud Moore Ford. Bodine also won the following week at North Wilkesboro . . . At Rockingham, in the season's most dominating performance, Kyle Petty led all laps except eight. Elliott held a 70-point lead over Allison; Kulwicki was 15 points behind Allison.

With two races remaining, the traveling show went to Phoenix, where Allison won. He regained the points lead by 30 over Kulwicki, who was fourth. Allison was 40 points ahead of Elliott . . . In the final race at Atlanta, Allison needed to finish sixth or better to clinch his first title. On lap 253, a tire problem forced Ernie Irvan to lose control of his Chevrolet and Allison T-boned Irvan. Elliott and Kulwicki, both driving Fords, ran one-two for the second half of the race. Everyone realized that whoever led the most laps and received the five bonus points would win the championship. Elliott won the race, but runner-up Kulwicki led one more lap, 103 to 102, and he was the champion. After Kulwicki circled the track in the opposite direction in his "Polish victory lap," Richard Petty also took a solo farewell lap. It was "The King's" final race. Early in the race, Petty was involved in an accident that ignited flames under the hood of his STP Pontiac. Said Petty: "I wanted to go out in a blaze of glory: I just forgot the glory part."

WINSTON CUP STANDINGS

	DRIVER	STARTS	WINS	POINTS	MONEY
1.	Alan Kulwicki	29	2	4,078	2,322,561
2.	Bill Elliott	29	5	4,068	1,692,381
3.	Davey Allison	29	5	4,015	1,955,628
4.	Harry Gant	29	2	3,955	1,122,776
5.	Kyle Petty	29	2	3,945	1,107,063
6.	Mark Martin	29	2	3,887	1,000,571
7.	Ricky Rudd	29	1	3,735	793,903
8.	Terry Labonte	29	0	3,674	600,381
9.	Darrell Waltrip	29	3	3,659	876,492
10.	Sterling Marlin	29	0	3,603	649,048
11.	Ernie Irvan	29	3	3,580	996,885
12.	Dale Earnhardt	29	1	3,574	915,463
13.	Rusty Wallace	29	1	3,556	657,925
14.	Morgan Shepherd	29	0	3,549	634,222
15.	Brett Bodine	29	0	3,491	495,224
16.	Geoff Bodine	29	2	3,437	716,583
17.	Ken Schrader	29	0	3,404	639,679
18.	Ted Musgrave	29	0	3,315	449,121
19.	Dale Jarrett	29	0	3,251	418,648
20.	Dick Trickle	29	0	3,097	429,521
21.	Derrike Cope	29	0	3,033	277,215
22.	Rick Mast	29	0	2,830	350,740
23.	Michael Waltrip	29	0	2,825	410,545
24.	Wally Dallenbach Jr.	29	0	2,799	220,245
25.	Bobby Hamilton	29	0	2,787	367,065
26.	Richard Petty	29	0	2,731	348,870
27.	Hut Stricklin	28	0	2,689	336,965
28.	Jimmy Hensley	22	0	2,410	247,660
29.	Dave Marcis	29	0	2,348	218,045
30.	Greg Sacks	20	0	1,759	178,120
31.	Chad Little	19	0	1,669	145,805
32.	Jimmy Means	22	0	1,531	133,160
33.	Jimmy Spencer	12	0	1,284	183,585
34.	Bobby Hillin Jr.	13	0	1,135	102,160
35.	Stanley Smith	14	0	959	89,650
36.	Mike Potter	11	0	806	74,710
37.	Jim Sauter	9	0	729	56,045
38.	Lake Speed	9	0	726	49,545
39.	Jimmy Horton	9	0	660	50,125
40.	Bob Schacht	9	0	611	58,815
41.	Charlie Glotzbach	7	0	592	48,060
42.	James Hylton	8	0	476	37,910
43.	Andy Belmont	8	0	467	39,820
44.	Jeff Purvis	6	0	453	45,545
45.	Dave Mader III	5	0	436	69,635
46.	Jerry O'Neil	6	0	429	32,370
47.	Eddie Bierschwale	4	0	277	25,995
48.	Buddy Baker	3	0	255	49,500
49.	Rich Bickle	3	0	252	13,370
50.	Mike Wallace	3	0	249	17,415

1993

AT A GLANCE

Winston Cup Champion: Dale Earnhardt.

Notable Events: Nonracing accidents took the lives of Alan Kulwicki and Davey Allison . . . Rusty Wallace won 10 races, but was runner-up by 80 points to Earnhardt . . . Mark Martin swept four consecutive races . . . inaugural Winston Cup race at New Hampshire International Speedway.

Top Newcomers: Rookie of the Year Jeff Gordon: one pole position, seven top-5 finishes, 11 top-10s . . . Kenny Wallace: three top-10s.

Nothing that happened on the racetracks would overshadow the deaths of Alan Kulwicki and Davey Allison. Kulwicki, the defending Winston Cup champion, died in a plane crash on April 1 near the Tri-Cities Airport in Tennessee. Allison was piloting a helicopter that crashed at Talladega on July 12: he died the next day of severe head injuries. The racing world was rocked by the duel tragedies that robbed NASCAR of two of its brightest young stars.

The year began with a familiar story in the Daytona 500: Dale Earnhardt led the most laps, but he couldn't lead the last one. Approaching the white flag signalling the final lap, Earnhardt was in front, followed by rookie Jeff Gordon and Dale Jarrett. All were driving Chevrolets. Jarrett passed Gordon in the tri-oval, then eased past Earnhardt in turn one. Their cars touched, but Jarrett held on to win his first Daytona 500.

Rusty Wallace began his collection of 10 wins at Rockingham . . . at Richmond, Wallace placed second to Davey Allison: it was Allison's 19th career victory, and his last . . . the Motorcraft 500 at Atlanta was delayed a week by a blizzard. Jeff Gordon appeared headed to his first victory, but he blew a tire and scraped the wall in turn 2 with less than 15 laps remaining. Morgan Shepherd, driving the Wood Brothers Ford, gained his fourth career victory.

After winning at Bristol, Wallace paid Kulwicki a tribute by driving a "Polish victory lap," which Kulwicki was so well-known for . . . Wallace also won the next two races, at North Wilkesboro and Martinsville . . . the finish at Talladega featured a wild two-lap dash: following a red flag for a rain delay, Earnhardt led Wallace off turn four on the next-to-last lap. By the first turn of the final lap, Ernie Irvan was with Earnhardt and Wallace. When Earnhardt and Irvan made contact, Jimmy Spencer squeezed through into second place. Irvan and Spencer finished one-two. The action wasn't over, however: Earnhardt bumped the back of Wallace's Pontiac and Wallace went airborne, crossing the finish line upside down. The Winston Cup points leader suffered a concussion, broken wrist, and bruised ribs.

Most people would need a month off from work, but Wallace, in the tradition of tough race car drivers, raced the next weekend at Sears Point. He qualified sixth, and finished 38th. Just a few days after purchasing Kulwicki's team, Geoff Bodine won the race . . . at Charlotte, Earnhardt fought off a challenge from Gordon to win and take the points lead . . . in New Hampshire's debut race, Wallace advanced from his 33rd qualifying position to win his fifth event of the year. Allison finished third in his final race: his fatal helicopter crash at Talladega occurred less than 24 hours later.

At Pocono, race winner Earnhardt saluted Allison and Kulwicki by waving a No. 28 flag during a Polish victory lap . . . at Talladega, Earnhardt won in a photo finish with Irvan (margin of victory: .005 of a second). During the race, Jimmy Horton's car flipped over the first-turn wall and tumbled down a five-story high embankment. Horton was not injured. Neil Bonnett also walked away from a frightening crash that ripped a hole in the frontstretch fence.

At Watkins Glen, Mark Martin began his four-race winning streak by fending off Roush Racing teammate Wally Dallenbach . . . Martin added victories at Michigan and Bristol, then controlled the final half of the darkness-shortened Mountain Dew Southern 500. Irvan, succeeding Allison, competed for the first time in the No. 28 Yates Racing Ford. He raced up front before finishing fifth.

Jeff Gordon was Rookie of the Year in 1993.

Victories by Wallace at Richmond and Dover trimmed Earnhardt's points lead to 181 with six races remaining . . . Irvan's win at Martinsville triggered tears among crew members, marking their first trip to victory lane since Allison's death. Irvan also won at Charlotte . . . Wallace and Earnhardt finished one-two at Rockingham, leaving Earnhardt with a shrinking 72-point advantage.

At Phoenix, Wallace was running third, ahead of Earnhardt, when he blew a tire on lap 250, dooming him to a 19th-place finish. Nearing his sixth Winston Cup title, Earnhardt was fourth. He took a 126-point lead into the final race at Atlanta. All Earnhardt needed in the Hooter's 500 was a 34th-place finish or better. Wallace won at Atlanta, giving him an impressive 10 victories for the season. Earnhardt was 10th. He outdistanced Wallace by 80 points. Earnhardt won six races during the year.

	DRIVER	STARTS	WINS	POINTS	MONEY
1.	Dale Earnhardt	30	6	4,526	3,353,789
2.	Rusty Wallace	30	10	4,446	1,702,154
3.	Mark Martin	30	5	4,150	1,657,662
4.	Dale Jarrett	30	1	4,000	1,242,394
5.	Kyle Petty	30	1	3,860	914,662
6.	Ernie Irvan	29	3	3,834	1,400,468
7.	Morgan Shepherd	30	1	3,807	782,523
8.	Bill Elliott	30	0	3,774	955,859
9.	Ken Schrader	30	0	3,715	952,748
10.	Ricky Rudd	30	1	3,644	752,562
11.	Harry Gant	30	0	3,524	772,832
12.	Jimmy Spencer	30	0	3,496	686,026
13.	Darrell Waltrip	30	0	3,479	746,646
14.	Jeff Gordon	30	0	3,447	765,168
15.	Sterling Marlin	30	0	3,355	628,835
16.	Geoff Bodine	30	1	3,338	783,762
17.	Michael Waltrip	30	0	3,291	529,923
18.	Terry Labonte	30	0	3,280	531,717
19.	Bobby Labonte	30	0	3,221	395,660
20.	Brett Bodine	29	0	3,183	582,014
21.	Rick Mast	30	0	3,001	568,095
22.	Wally Dallenbach Jr.	30	0	2,978	474,340
23.	Kenny Wallace	30	0	2,893	330,325
24.	Hut Stricklin	30	0	2,866	494,600
25.	Ted Musgrave	29	0	2,853	458,615
26.	Derrike Cope	30	0	2,787	402,515
27.	Bobby Hillin Jr.	30	0	2,717	263,540
28.	Rick Wilson	29	0	2,647	299,725
29.	Phil Parsons	26	0	2,454	293,725
30.	Dick Trickle	26	0	2,224	24,065
31.	Davey Allison	16	1	2,104	513,585
32.	Jimmy Hensley	21	0	2,001	368,150
33.	Dave Marcis	23	0	1,970	202,305
34.	Lake Speed	21	0	1,956	319,800
35.	Greg Sacks	19	0	1,730	168,055
36.	Jimmy Means	18	0	1,471	148,205
37.	Bobby Hamilton	15	0	1,348	142,740
38.	Jimmy Horton	13	0	841	115,105
39.	Jeff Purvis	8	0	774	108,545
40.	Todd Bodine	10	0	715	62,245
41.	Alan Kulwicki	5	0	625	165,470
42.	P.J. Jones	6	0	498	53,370
43.	Joe Ruttman	5	0	417	70,700
44.	Joe Nemechek	5	0	389	56,580
45.	Loy Allen Jr.	5	0	362	34,695
46.	Mike Wallace	4	0	343	30,125
47.	Jim Sauter	4	0	295	48,860
48.	Rich Bickle	5	0	292	36,095
49.	Rick Carelli	3	0	258	30,125
50.	John Andretti	4	0	250	24,915

1994

AT A GLANCE

Winston Cup Champion: Dale Earnhardt.

Notable Events: Earnhardt's seventh Winston Cup title, tying him with Richard Petty for the all-time lead . . . Jeff Gordon won his first two races, including the inaugural Brickyard 400 at Indianapolis . . . Jimmy Spencer also won his first two races . . . Rusty Wallace totaled eight victories.

Top Newcomers: Rookie of the Year Jeff Burton: two top-5 finishes, three top-10s; Joe Nemechek: three top-10s; Loy Allen: first rookie to win the Daytona 500 pole.

After 18 years and 279 races, Sterling Marlin won his first Winston Cup race, and he picked the right venue for everyone to notice: the Daytona 500. Leading the final 21 laps, Marlin edged Ernie Irvan, the driver he replaced in the Morgan-McClure ride, by .19 seconds. Prior to the 500, racing lost another of its popular drivers when Neil Bonnett, 47, was killed in a practice crash. Bonnett was attempting a comeback after almost four years away from the circuit. In another fatality, Rodney Orr, 33, the defending NASCAR Goody's Dash Series champion, died in a practice accident.

Rusty Wallace dominated at Rockingham, leading 346 of 492 laps. Marlin was runner-up and Rick Mast finished a career-high third . . . Ernie Irvan won his second straight at Atlanta . . . in the TranSouth 400 at Darlington, Dale Earnhardt collected his ninth career victory on "The Track Too Tough to Tame." Only David Pearson (10) won more races at Darlington . . . Earnhardt followed up by winning at Bristol for his first short-track victory since October 1991.

In the next race, Terry Labonte won the First Union 400 at North Wilkesboro for his first victory since July 1989 . . . after finishing second to Earnhardt at Talladega, Irvan controlled the race at Sears Point. Irvan led 68 of 74 laps over the winding road course in California wine country. It was Irvan's third win of the season . . . Jeff Gordon's breakthrough in Winston Cup came at Charlotte when the 22-year-old beat Wallace by 3.91 seconds . . . at Pocono, Wallace was leading Earnhardt by 20 seconds with seven laps left when the final caution flag was unfurled. During the caution period, Gordon spun in the muddy grass. With one lap to go, the green flag came out and Wallace outgunned Earnhardt by half a second . . . Wallace also won at Michigan for his third in a row.

Jimmy Spencer, in his first season driving for Junior Johnson, won his first race, taking the Pepsi 400 at Daytona by less than a tenth of a second over Irvan . . . Ricky Rudd won at New Hampshire, extending his streak of winning at least one race a year to 12 consecutive years . . . back at Pocono for

A sight race fans thought they would never see—a NASCAR automobile on the track at the Indianapolis Motor Speedway, in this case number 21, Michael Waltrip.

the July race, Geoff Bodine, on Hoosier Tires, led 156 of the 200 laps for his first victory as an owner-driver. The next three finishers—Ward Burton, Joe Nemechek, and Jeff Burton—also rode on Hoosiers . . . Just three races after winning for the first time, Spencer visited victory lane again at Talladega. Spencer held off teammate Bill Elliott by a mere .025 of a second.

Racing history was made as the Winston Cup drivers arrived at Indianapolis Motor Speedway for the first NASCAR race to be held at the world renowned home of Indy-car racing . . . Rick Mast was the fastest qualifier in a Richard Jackson-owned Ford at 172.414 mph: it was Mast's second pole of his career . . . Jeff Gordon, who was based in nearby Pittsboro, Ind., as a teenager, won the Brickyard 400 by .53 of a second over Brett Bodine. Irvan was leading late in the race, but a flat tire knocked him out of contention.

At Watkins Glen, Mark Martin became the first Winston Cup driver to win consecutive races on the New York state road course . . . During practice for the GM Goodwrench 400 at Michigan, Irvan crashed into the turn 2 wall. He suffered a fractured skull, swelling of the brain and brain stem, and lung

injuries. For several days, there was concern that Irvan wouldn't survive. However, a few weeks later, Irvan was on the road to recovery. Kenny Wallace replaced Irvan in the Texaco Ford the rest of the season, but Irvan returned to racing in '95.

In the Southern 500, Elliott ended a 52-race losing streak despite overheating problems in his Ford. Earnhardt finished second, increasing his points lead over Wallace to 227 . . . At Richmond, Terry Labonte passed Wallace with 28 laps remaining to take his second victory of the year . . . Wallace recorded his seventh win of the year at Dover in unusual fashion: Martin held a seven-second lead over Wallace late in the race when he tangled with Rudd, who was three laps down. Martin attempted to nurse his Valvoline Ford to the finish, but finally cut a tire and careened into the wall. NASCAR planned to restart the race with one lap to go, but Marlin and Mast ran out of gas. The race ended under yellow with Wallace crossing the finish line on a flat tire.

At Charlotte, Dale Jarrett snapped a 55-race losing streak by outracing Morgan Shepherd to the finish line as the caution flag came out with one lap remaining . . . Earnhardt clinched his seventh championship the following week at Rockingham, matching Richard Petty's seven titles . . . In the season's last two races, Labonte won at Phoenix and Martin won at Atlanta . . . Martin finished second to Earnhardt, 444 points behind the champion.

WINSTON CUP STANDINGS

	DRIVER	STARTS	WINS	POINTS	MONEY
1.	Dale Earnhardt	31	4	4,694	3,400,733
2.	Mark Martin	31	2	4,250	1,678,906
3.	Rusty Wallace	31	8	4,207	1,959,072
4.	Ken Schrader	31	0	4,060	1,211,062
5.	Ricky Rudd	31	1	4,050	1,079,441

6.	Morgan Shepherd	31	0	4,029	1,119,038
7.	Terry Labonte	31	3	3,876	1,150,921
8.	Jeff Gordon	31	2	3,776	1,799,523
9.	Darrell Waltrip	31	0	3,688	854,280
10.	Bill Elliott	31	1	3,617	951,679
11.	Lake Speed	31	0	3,565	845,963
12.	Michael Waltrip	31	0	3,512	720,426
13.	Ted Musgrave	31	0	3,477	669,687
14.	Sterling Marlin	31	1	3,443	1,140,683
15.	Kyle Petty	31	0	3,339	818,832
16.	Dale Jarrett	30	1	3,298	893,754
17.	Geoff Bodine	31	3	3,297	1,287,626
18.	Rick Mast	31	0	3,238	733,361
19.	Brett Bodine	31	0	3,159	801,944
20.	Todd Bodine	30	0	3,048	504,316
21.	Bobby Labonte	31	0	3,038	550,305
22.	Ernie Irvan	20	3	3,026	1,311,522
23.	Bobby Hamilton	30	0	2,749	514,520
24.	Jeff Burton	30	0	2,726	594,700
25.	Harry Gant	30	0	2,720	556,200
26.	Hut Stricklin	29	0	2,711	333,495
27.	Joe Nemechek	29	0	2,673	386,315
28.	Steve Grissom	27	0	2,660	300,915
29.	Jimmy Spencer	29	2	2,613	479,235
30.	Derrike Cope	30	0	2,612	398,436
31.	Greg Sacks	31	0	2,593	411,728
32.	John Andretti	29	0	2,229	391,920
33.	Mike Wallace	22	0	2,191	265,115
34.	Dick Trickle	25	0	2,019	244,806
35.	Ward Burton	26	0	1,971	304,700
36.	Dave Marcis	23	0	1,910	261,650
37.	Jeremy Mayfield	20	0	1,673	226,265
38.	Wally Dallenbach Jr.	14	0	1,493	241,492
39.	Loy Allen Jr.	19	0	1,468	216,751
40.	Kenny Wallace	12	0	1,413	235,005
41.	Jimmy Hensley	17	0	1,394	203,520
42.	Chuck Brown	13	0	1,211	225,260
43.	Rich Bickle	12	0	849	115,575
44.	Bobby Hillin Jr.	9	0	749	125,340
45.	Brad Teague	8	0	548	59,990
46.	Jeff Purvis	7	0	484	78,755
47.	Billy Standridge	8	0	404	56,405
48.	Randy Lajoie	3	0	312	30,565
49.	Rick Carellli	4	0	283	31,975
50.	Phil Parsons	3	0	243	21,415

1995

AT A GLANCE

Winston Cup Champion: Jeff Gordon.

Notable Events: Sterling Marlin winning a second consecutive Daytona 500 and finishing a career-high third in the points standings . . . Ted Musgrave (seventh) and Bobby Labonte (10th) cracking the top 10 in points for the first time . . . Ernie Irvan returning from his near-fatal crash the year before.

Top Newcomers: Rookie of the Year Rick Craven: four top-10 finishes; Jeremy Mayfield: one top-10; Robert Pressley: one top-10.

Jeff Gordon overtook Sterling Marlin midway in the season and went on to his first championship. Driving the Du Pont Chevrolet, Gordon won seven races and eight poles.

By winning two in a row at Daytona in the Kodak Film Chevrolet, Marlin joined Richard Petty and Cale Yarborough as the only drivers to win the prestigious 500 in back-to-back seasons . . . Gordon won his first race of the year at Rockingham . . . in the next race, Terry Labonte took his second Richmond event in a row. Following a winless spell of nearly five years, Labonte now had three victories in his last 11 races driving the Kellogg's Chevy.

Marlin won at Darlington, then, at Bristol, Gordon gained his third win of the year and his first short-track victory . . . Dale Earnhardt's triumph at North Wilkesboro gave him at least one win for 14 consecutive years . . . Rusty Wallace's victory at Martinsville was Ford's first of the year and his third in a row at the .526-mile Virginia track . . . Mark Martin's win at Talladega was the first of four during '95 for the Arkansas native.

At Sears Point, Earnhardt recorded his first road-course victory in 36 races . . . the Coca- Cola 600 at Charlotte turned into Labonte Family Day. Bobby won his first Winston Cup race and older brother Terry was runner-up. The last time brothers finished one-two at Charlotte was in '71 when Bobby Allison was first and Donnie was second . . . at Dover, Kyle Petty overcame a 37th starting position, avoided a 17-car crash on lap two, and rang up his first win in 60 starts. No driver had won at Dover from such a distant starting berth.

At Pocono, Terry Labonte took advantage of a rare mistake by Hendrick Motorsports teammate Jeff Gordon for victory. Gordon had led 124 laps, but on the final restart, with seven lefts to go, he missed a shift . . . at Michigan, Bobby Labonte nudged ahead of Gordon by .23 seconds after dueling for the final 60 laps . . . in the summer race at Daytona, Gordon, 23, became the event's youngest winner . . . Gordon won again at New Hampshire, and assumed the points lead: he would not relinquish it the rest of the year.

Dale Jarrett arrived at Pocono in July with six straight 23rd-or-worse finishes. He ended the slump, and a 20-race losing streak, by winning for the first time for car owner Robert Yates . . . at Talladega, Marlin won from the pole and collected $219,425, including the $121,600 bonus from

Sterling Marlin won his second straight Daytona 500 in 1995, only the third driver to pull off that feat.

racing at North Wilkesboro was an emotional time: Irvan led 30 laps and finished sixth in the Tyson Holly Farms 400 won by Martin . . . at Rockingham, Ward Burton and car owner Bill Davis met on the victory stand for the first time after just seven races together. Earnhardt left the historic North Carolina track 162 points behind Gordon.

At Phoenix, Ricky Rudd, in the Tide Ford, extended his streak to 13 years with at least one victory. Earnhardt was third and Gordon fifth: Gordon's points lead was 147 . . . Earnhardt won the NAPA 500 at Atlanta and led the most laps, but Gordon, who faded to 32nd place, still won the title by 34 points.

Unocal for winning from the pole . . . Earnhardt also had a memorable payday at Indianapolis, banking $565,600 after leading the last 27 laps.

Mark Martin won his third in a row at Watkins Glen, then polesitter Bobby Labonte went two-for-two at Michigan. Again, brother Terry was runner-up . . . Terry's second career victory at Bristol, and his first since 1984, was hardly routine. As he and Earnhardt battled on the final lap, Earnhardt tapped Labonte's car exiting turn four and near the finish line. Labonte crashed head-on into the frontstretch wall, but was not injured. Talk about getting a bang out of winning. . . .

Gordon won the Southern 500 for his sixth victory of the year . . . at Dover, he was in control, leading 400 of the 500 laps and boosting his points lead over Earnhardt to 309. Bobby Hamilton was second for his best career finish . . . Ernie Irvan's return to

WINSTON CUP STANDINGS

	DRIVER	STARTS	WINS	POINTS	MONEY
1.	Jeff Gordon	31	7	4,614	4,347,343
2.	Dale Earnhardt	31	5	4,580	3,154,241
3.	Sterling Marlin	31	3	4,361	2,253,502
4.	Mark Martin	31	4	4,320	1,893,519
5.	Rusty Wallace	31	2	4,240	1,642,837
6.	Terry Labonte	31	3	4,146	1,558,659
7.	Ted Musgrave	31	0	3,949	1,147,445
8.	Bill Elliott	31	0	3,746	996,816
9.	Ricky Rudd	31	1	3,734	1,337,703
10.	Bobby Labonte	31	3	3,718	1,413,682
11.	Morgan Shepherd	31	0	3,618	996,374
12.	Michael Waltrip	31	0	3,601	898,338
13.	Dale Jarrett	31	1	3,584	1,363,158
14.	Bobby Hamilton	31	0	3,576	804,505
15.	Derrike Cope	31	0	3,384	683,075
16.	Geoff Bodine	31	0	3,357	1,011,090
17.	Ken Schrader	31	0	3,221	886,566
18.	John Andretti	31	0	3,140	593,542
19.	Darrell Waltrip	31	0	3,075	850,632
20.	Brett Bodine	31	0	2,958	893,029
21.	Rick Mast	31	0	2,984	749,550
22.	Ward Burton	29	1	2,926	634,655
23.	Lake Speed	31	0	2,921	529,435
24.	Ricky Craven	31	0	2,883	597,054
25.	Dick Trickle	31	0	2,875	694,920
26.	Jimmy Spencer	29	0	2,809	504,560
27.	Steve Grissom	29	0	2,757	509,047
28.	Joe Nemechek	29	0	2,742	428,925
29.	Robert Pressley	31	0	2,663	695,875
30.	Kyle Petty	30	1	2,635	698,875
31.	Jeremy Mayfield	27	0	2,637	436,805
32.	Jeff Burton	29	0	2,556	628,270
33.	Todd Bodine	28	0	2,372	664,620
34.	Mike Wallace	26	0	2,175	428,006
35.	Dave Marcis	28	0	2,126	337,853
36.	Hut Stricklin	24	0	2,052	486,065
37.	Bobby Hillin Jr.	18	0	1,888	244,270
38.	Elton Sawyer	20	0	1,499	416,490
39.	Greg Sacks	20	0	1,349	323,720
40.	Randy Lajoie	14	0	1,133	281,945
41.	Loy Allen Jr.	11	0	890	186,670
42.	Kenny Wallace	11	0	878	151,700
43.	Chuck Brown	9	0	818	99,995
44.	Jimmy Hensley	9	0	558	161,025
45.	Rich Bickle	8	0	538	153,250
46.	Davey Jones	7	0	520	109,925
47.	Jeff Purvis	7	0	391	93,875
48.	Ernie Irvan	3	0	354	54,875
49	Steve Kinser	5	0	287	105,224
50.	Wally Dallenbach Jr.	2	0	221	63,900

1996

AT A GLANCE

Winston Cup Champion: Terry Labonte.

Notable Events: Jeff Gordon, at age 25, won more races (10) and poles (5) than any other driver. Bobby Hamilton won his first Winston Cup race, providing Richard Petty with his first victory as a car owner.

Top Newcomers: Rookie of the Year Johnny Benson (one pole, one top-5 finish, six top-10s).

The long wait ended for Terry Labonte. The veteran Texan captured his second Winston Cup title; his first was in 1984. Labonte only won two races in the Kellogg's Chevrolet, but his consistency paid off as he finished 37 points ahead of teammate Jeff Gordon.

The Daytona 500 developed into a high-speed chase between Dale Jarrett and Dale Earnhardt. Jarrett, making his first start for the Robert Yates Racing team, prevailed by .12 of a second. Ken Schrader was third in his best finish of the season.

Earnhardt quickly shook off the frustration of continuing his Daytona 0-for-the-career streak by winning at Rockingham . . . in the next race at Richmond, Jeff Gordon put his 42nd- and 40th-place finishes in the first two races behind him and won the Pontiac Excitement 400 . . . Earnhardt won the Purolator 500 at Atlanta; his eighth victory surpassed Cale Yarborough for the most victories in the track's history. No one guessed that it would be Earnhardt's last stop in victory lane for the season.

At North Wilkesboro, Terry Labonte celebrated tying Richard Petty's record of 513 consecutive starts by winning from the pole . . . at Talladega, Sterling Marlin's .22-second win over Jarrett was marred by crashes that caused injuries to Bill Elliott and Ricky Craven. Elliott suffered a broken left leg in his accident: he would be sidelined until the July race at Daytona. Craven's Chevrolet flipped high in the air, tangling with the top of the fence.

In the Save Mart 300 at Sears Point, Rusty Wallace took his sixth career road-course victory . . . by

winning the Coca-Cola 600 at Charlotte, Jarrett became eligible for the Winston Million if he could win the Southern 500 at Darlington . . . in a rain-shortened Pepsi 400 at Daytona, Marlin won again on the 2½-mile superspeedway . . . Ernie Irvan, less than two years after his nearly fatal practice crash at Michigan, registered a 5.7-second victory over Jarrett, his Yates Racing teammate . . . at Pocono, Rusty Wallace led a Ford sweep of the first four places (Ricky Rudd, Jarrett, and Irvan followed Wallace across the line). It was the first time all season that Chevrolet didn't finish at least second.

Earnhardt experienced his worst crash ever in the DieHard 500 at Talladega, suffering a broken sternum and collarbone in a race won by Gordon . . . in the Brickyard 400, teammates Jarrett and Irvan swapped the lead twice in the last 62 laps. Eventually, Jarrett seized the lead and won as the race ended under caution. Irvan was runner-up. Earnhardt started the race, then was relieved by Mike Skinner, who finished 15th.

At Watkins Glen, Geoff Bodine won for the first time since October 1994. No winner at the Glen had ever started as far back as Bodine, 13th. Earnhardt, still in pain from his crash at Talladega, proved again how tough he is by qualifying fastest and leading the most laps (54) before finishing sixth . . . at Michigan, although Jarrett only led the final eight laps, he won his fourth race of the year . . . Rusty Wallace, in the Miller-sponsored Ford, took his fifth victory of the season at Bristol.

Gordon, growing into the Darlington dominator, won his third in a row at the famed South Carolina track in the Southern 500. Hut Stricklin, 0-for-217 starts, controlled much of the race before settling for second place. Jarrett's bid for the Winston Million expired when he slid in some oil while leading on lap 46 . . . at Richmond, Irvan won his second race of the year . . . Gordon added his third in a row at Dover, then also won at Martinsville for his ninth victory of the season. He led Terry Labonte by 81 points.

In the final Winston Cup race to be held at North Wilkesboro, Gordon gained his 10th and final win of '96 . . . Labonte picked the right time to win his first race at Charlotte: by taking the UAW-GM Quality 500, Labonte narrowed Gordon's edge in points to just one. Gordon was 31st in the race . . . Ricky Rudd's victory at Rockingham made it 14 years in a row with at least one win. Labonte's third-place finish boosted him 32 points ahead of Gordon.

Bobby Hamilton's first career win in the Dura-Lube 500 at Phoenix was a special moment: it was the first time the No. 43 STP car had been in victory lane since Richard Petty's last win in 1984. Labonte, driving with a broken left hand suffered in a practice crash, was third and Gordon finished fifth. With one race left, Labonte held a 47-point lead over Gordon . . . the season's final race was a

memorable day for the Labonte family: Bobby won his only race of the year and Terry clinched his second points title. Winning from the pole in the Joe Gibbs-owned Chevy, Bobby earned the Unocal bonus for a total payday of $274,900. Terry was fifth and Gordon third, giving Terry the title by just 37 points. The championship also made Rick Hendrick the first car owner in the modern era to win consecutive titles with different drivers.

WINSTON CUP STANDINGS

DRIVER	STARTS	WINS	POINTS	MONEY
1. Terry Labonte	31	2	4,657	4,030,648
2. Jeff Gordon	31	10	4,620	3,428,485
3. Dale Jarrett	31	4	4,568	2,985,418
4. Dale Earnhardt	31	2	4,327	2,285,926

Terry Labonte drove the Kelloggs' Corn Flakes car to his second NASCAR championship in 1996.

Rank	Driver	Starts	Wins	Points	Money
5.	Mark Martin	31	0	4,278	1,887,396
6.	Ricky Rudd	31	1	3,845	1,503,025
7.	Rusty Wallace	31	5	3,717	1,665,315
8.	Sterling Marlin	31	2	3,682	1,588,425
9.	Bobby Hamilton	31	1	3,639	1,151,235
10.	Ernie Irvan	31	2	3,632	1,683,313
11.	Bobby Labonte	31	1	3,590	1,475,196
12.	Ken Schrader	31	0	3,540	1,089,603
13.	Jeff Burton	30	0	3,538	884,303
14.	Michael Waltrip	31	0	3,535	1,182,811
15.	Jimmy Spencer	31	0	3,476	1,090,876
16.	Ted Musgrave	31	0	3,466	961,512
17.	Geoff Bodine	31	1	3,218	1,031,762
18.	Rick Mast	31	0	3,190	924,559
19.	Morgan Shepherd	31	0	3,133	719,059
20.	Ricky Craven	31	0	3,078	941,959
21.	Johnny Benson Jr.	30	0	3,004	947,080
22.	Hut Stricklin	31	0	2,854	631,055
23.	Lake Speed	31	0	2,834	817,175
24.	Brett Bodine	30	0	2,814	767,716
25.	Wally Dallenbach Jr.	30	0	2,786	837,001
26.	Jeremy Mayfield	30	0	2,721	592,853
27.	Kyle Petty	28	0	2,696	689,041
28.	Kenny Wallace	30	0	2,694	457,665
29.	Darrell Waltrip	31	0	2,657	740,185
30.	Bill Elliott	24	0	2,627	716,506
31.	John Andretti	30	0	2,621	688,511
32.	Robert Pressley	30	0	2,485	690,465
33.	Ward Burton	27	0	2,411	873,619
34.	Joe Nemechek	29	0	2,391	666,247
35.	Derrike Cope	29	0	2,374	675,781
36.	Dick Trickle	26	0	2,131	404,927
37.	Bobby Hillin Jr.	26	0	2,128	395,224
38.	Dave Marcis	27	0	2,047	435,177
39.	Steve Grissom	13	0	1,188	314,983
40.	Todd Bodine	10	0	991	198,525
41.	Mike Wallace	11	0	799	169,082
42.	Greg Sacks	9	0	710	207,755
43.	Elton Sawyer	9	0	705	129,618
44.	Chad Littlle	9	0	627	164,752
45.	Loy Allen Jr.	9	0	603	130,667
46.	Gary Bradberry	9	0	591	155,785
47.	Mike Skinner	5	0	529	65,850
48.	Jeff Purvis	4	0	328	91,127
49.	Jeff Green	4	0	247	46,875
50.	Randy MacDonald	3	0	228	33,910

11

1997 RACE RESULTS

RACE 1—DAYTONA 500

Daytona International Speedway
Daytona Beach Florida
Feb. 18
Winner: Jeff Gordon.

Led by Gordon, Hendrick Motorsports drivers finished one-two-three. Defending points champion Terry Labonte was second and Ricky Craven, in his first Winston Cup start for Hendrick, was third . . . Gordon's victory was his first in the Daytona 500; at 25 years, six months, and 12 days, he became the youngest driver ever to win the Super Bowl of stock car racing . . . Richard Petty was 26 when he won at Daytona in 1964 . . . Gordon avoided a crash that damaged the cars of contenders Dale Jarrett and Ernie Irvan on lap 189 of the 200-lap race. Dale Earnhardt's car hit the wall and flipped when Gordon passed him exiting turn 2 . . . with five laps remaining, Gordon passed leader Bill Elliott on the apron in turn one. Later, Gordon said he would have driven on the grass if he had to . . . the race finished under caution following an 11-car crash on lap 196 . . . Earnhardt, frustrated again in his 19th attempt to win the Daytona 500, led 48 laps . . . Mark Martin led 52 laps . . . pole-sitter Mike Skinner, a rookie, finished 12th.

Daytona 500

Average speed: 148.295 mph
Time of race: 3 hours, 22 minutes, 18 seconds
Margin of victory: under caution

FINISH	DRIVER	CAR
1.	Jeff Gordon	Chevy
2.	Terry Labonte	Chevy
3.	Ricky Craven	Chevy
4.	Bill Elliott	Ford
5.	Sterling Marlin	Chevy
6.	Jeremy Mayfield	Ford
7.	Mark Martin	Ford
8.	Ward Burton	Pont.
9.	Ricky Rudd	Ford
10.	Darrell Waltrip	Chevy
11.	Jeff Burton	Ford
12.	Mike Skinner	Chevy
13.	Ted Musgrave	Ford
14.	Kyle Petty	Pont.
15.	Bobby Hamilton	Pont.
16.	Robby Gordon	Chevy
17.	Dave Marcis	Chevy
18.	Brett Bodine	Ford
19.	Hut Stricklin	Ford
20.	Ernie Irvan	Ford
21.	Bobby Labonte	Pont.
22.	Kenny Wallace	Ford
23.	Dale Jarrett	Ford
24.	Lake Speed	Ford
25.	John Andretti	Ford
26.	Loy Allen	Ford
27.	Joe Nemechek	Chevy
28.	Johnny Benson	Pont.
29.	Morgan Shepherd	Pont.
30.	Dick Trickle	Ford
31.	Dale Earnhardt	Chevy
32.	Michael Waltrip	Ford
33.	Ken Schradrer	Chevy
34.	Geoff Bodine	Ford
35.	Jimmy Spencer	Ford
36.	Derrike Cope	Pont.
37.	Greg Sacks	Ford
38.	Bobby Hillin	Ford
39.	Robert Pressley	Chevy
40.	Steve Grissom	Chevy
41.	Rusty Wallace	Ford
42.	Wally Dallenbach	Chevy

Led by Bill Elliott in the McDonald's car, a pack heads out of the turn at Daytona.

RACE 2—GOODWRENCH SERVICE 400

North Carolina Motor Speedway
Rockingham, North Carolina
Feb. 23

Winner: Jeff Gordon

After dominating all afternoon and looking like a shoo-in for victory, Dale Jarrett found himself trailing Gordon at the checkered flag, behind by 2.43 seconds, about two dozen car lengths . . . Jarrett led four times for 323 laps, far and away more

than anybody else . . . Gordon's No. 24 Chevrolet came on late, after his crew tinkered with his car on almost every stop . . . He finally found better traction in the high groove and went by Jarrett with only 43 laps left, and they were the only laps he led all day . . . He beat Jarrett, Jeff Burton, Ricky Rudd, and fifth-place Ricky Craven . . . Pole-sitter Mark Martin led twice for 22 laps before finishing well back with engine problems . . . Gordon was the first driver in 21 years (the last was David Pearson in 1976) to open the season with back-to-back victories.

GM Goodwrench 400

Average speed: 125.927 mph
Time of race: 3 hours, 17 minutes, 35 seconds
Margin of victory: 2.43 seconds

FINISH	DRIVER	CAR
1.	Jeff Gordon	Chevy
2.	Dale Jarrett	Ford
3.	Jeff Burton	Ford
4.	Ricky Rudd	Ford
5.	Ricky Craven	Chevy
6.	Rusty Wallace	Ford
7.	Terry Labonte	Chevy
8.	Geoff Bodine	Ford
9.	Ernie Irvan	Ford
10.	Morgan Shepherd	Pont.
11.	Dale Earnhardt	Chevy
12.	Ted Musgrave	Ford
13.	Mark Martin	Ford
14.	Bobby Labonte	Pont.
15.	Lake Speed	Ford
16.	Jeremy Mayfield	Ford
17.	Brett Bodine	Ford
18.	Ken Schrader	Chevy
19.	Dick Trickle	Ford
20.	Sterling Marlin	Chevy
21.	Rick Mast	Ford
22.	Bill Elliott	Ford
23.	Ward Burton	Pont.
24.	Steve Grissom	Chevy
25.	Mike Skinner	Chevy
26.	Michael Waltrip	Ford
27.	Johnny Benson	Pont.
28.	Bobby Hamilton	Pont.
29.	Kyle Petty	Pont.
30.	Dave Marcis	Chevy
31.	Derrike Cope	Pont.
32.	Darrell Waltrip	Chevy
33.	Robby Gordon	Chevy
34.	John Andretti	Ford
35.	Joe Nemechek	Chevy
36.	Hut Stricklin	Ford
37.	Robert Pressley	Chevy
38.	David Green	Chevy
39.	Greg Sacks	Ford
40.	Jimmy Spencer	Ford
41.	Kenny Wallace	Ford
42.	Bobby Hillin	Ford
43.	Loy Allen	Ford

RACE 3—PONTIAC EXCITEMENT 400

Richmond International Raceway
Richmond, Virginia
March 2
Winner: Rusty Wallace

Question: what could be better than winning an early-season race to immediately relieve some of the sponsor's pressure? Answer: doing it without the appearance that you might have used an illegal engine to do it . . . That was the case at RIR, where Wallace beat Geoff Bodine, Dale Jarrett, Jeff Gordon, and Bobby Hamilton in the first of the season's six short-track races . . . Wallace led three times for 135 laps, including the final three laps after re-passing Jarrett, who had just passed to lead laps 393-397 . . . But the engine in Wallace's No. 2 Ford car measured slightly too large in post-race inspection and NASCAR said the results would not be official until the next day . . . Upon further examination, the engine was ruled close enough and the victory allowed to stand.

Pontiac Excitement 400

Average speed: 108.499 miles per hour
Time of race: 2 hours, 45 minutes, 54 seconds
Margin of victory: .441 seconds

FINISH	DRIVER	CAR
1.	Rusty Wallace	Ford
2.	Geoff Bodine	Ford
3.	Dale Jarrett	Ford
4.	Jeff Gordon	Chevy
5.	Bobby Hamilton	Pont
6.	Ricky Rudd	Ford
7.	Terry Labonte	Chevy
8.	Bobby Labonte	Pont.
9.	Johnny Benson	Pont.
10.	Kyle Petty	Pont.
11.	Steve Grissom	Chevy
12.	Lake Speed	Ford
13.	Mark Martin	Ford
14.	Ricky Craven	Chevy
15.	Bill Elliott	Ford
16.	Darrell Waltrip	Chevy
17.	Jeremy Mayfield	Ford
18.	Rick Mast	Ford
19.	Sterling Marlin	Chevy
20.	Ted Musgrave	Ford
21.	Robert Pressley	Chevy
22.	Jimmy Spencer	Ford
23.	Brett Bodine	Ford
24.	Ward Burton	Pont.
25.	Dale Earnhardt	Chevy
26.	Mike Skinner	Chevy
27.	Michael Waltrip	Ford
28.	Robby Gordon	Chevy
29.	Dick Trickle	Ford
30.	Derrike Cope	Pont.
31.	John Andretti	Ford
32.	Hut Stricklin	Ford
33.	David Green	Chevy
34.	Chad Little	Pont.
35.	Ken Schrader	Chevy
36.	Ernie Irvan	Ford
36.	Dave Marcis	Chevy
38.	Gary Bradberry	Ford
39.	Joe Nemechek	Chevy
40.	Kenny Wallace	Ford
41.	Bobby Hillin	Ford
42.	Jeff Burton	Ford
43.	Morgan Shepherd	Pont.

RACE 4—PRIMESTAR 500

Atlanta Motor Speedway
Hampton, Georgia
March 9
Winner: Dale Jarrett

After being so strong and competitive (and finishing second) at Rockingham and Richmond, Jarrett finally had something to show for his No. 88 Ford team's efforts . . . He led six times for 242 of the 328 in winning ahead of Ernie Irvan, Morgan Shepherd, Bobby Labonte, and Jeff Burton . . . The race was stopped 52 minutes for track repairs at lap 281, after Steve Grissom crashed hard into the backstretch concrete wall and bounced back toward the line of oncoming traffic . . . Pole-sitter Robby Gordon led twice for 42 early laps and finished 14th, the best showing of his young Winston Cup career.

PRIMESTAR 500

Average speed: 132.730
Time of race: 3 hours, 45 minutes, 7 seconds
Margin of victory: 1.38 seconds

FINISH	DRIVER	CAR
1.	Dale Jarrett	Ford
2.	Ernie Irvan	Ford
3.	Morgan Shepherd	Pont.
4.	Bobby Labonte	Pont.
5.	Jeff Burton	Ford
6.	Mark Martin	Ford
7.	Michael Waltrip	Ford
8.	Dale Earnhardt	Chevy
9.	Terry Labonte	Chevy
10.	Bobby Hamilton	Pont.
11.	Johnny Benson	Pont.
12.	Ward Burton	Pont.
13.	Kyle Petty	Pont.
14.	Robby Gordon	Chevy
15.	John Andretti	Ford
16.	Darrell Waltrip	Chevy
17.	Rick Mast	Ford
18.	Brett Bodine	Ford
19.	Chad Little	Pont.
20.	Geoff Bodine	Ford
21.	Mike Skinner	Chevy
22.	Lake Speed	Ford
23.	Sterling Marlin	Chevy
24.	David Green	Chevy
25.	Ken Schrader	Chevy
26.	Mike Wallace	Chevy
27.	Greg Sacks	Ford
28.	Dick Trickle	Ford
29.	Kenny Wallace	Ford
30.	Ricky Rudd	Ford

Hut Stricklin (No. 8) and Lake Speed (No. 9) get tangled up at the Daytona 500.

31.	Rusty Wallace	Ford
32.	Jimmy Spencer	Ford
33.	Steve Grissom	Chevy
34.	Ted Musgrave	Ford
35.	Ricky Craven	Chevy
36.	B. Standridge	Ford
37.	JeremyMayfield	Ford
38.	Bill Elliott	Ford
39.	Joe Nemechek	Chevy
40.	Gary Bradberry	Ford
41.	Hut Stricklin	Ford
42.	Jeff Gordon	Chevy

RACE 5—TRANSOUTH FINANCIAL 400

Darlington Raceway
Darlington, South Carolina
March 23
Winner: Dale Jarrett

Jarrett would have been an instant millionaire if he'd done as well at Darlington in September of '96 as he did in the spring of '97 . . . As it was, his overpowering victory in the TranSouth 400 extended his early-season hot streak . . . After starting from the pole in the No. 88 Ford, he led three times for 164 of the 293 laps, including the final 128 . . . Ted Musgrave was second, followed by Jeff Gordon, Jeff Burton, and Bobby Labonte . . . The treacherous "Lady in Black" was on good behavior as only 5 of the 43 starters were eliminated in accidents . . . The victory allowed Jarrett to maintain his points lead ahead of Gordon, Terry and Bobby Labonte, and Burton.

TRANSOUTH FINANCIAL 400

Average speed: 141.4. 10 mph
Time of race: 3 hours, 18 minutes, 12 seconds
Margin of victory: 0.169 seconds

FINISH	DRIVER	CAR
1.	Dale Jarrett	Ford
2.	Ted Musgrave	Ford
3.	Jeff Gordon	Chevy
4.	Jeff Burton	Ford
5.	Bobby Labonte	Pont.
6.	Rusty Wallace	Ford
7.	Michael Waltrip	Ford
8.	Ken Schrader	Chevy
9.	Geoff Bodine	Ford
10.	Johnny Benson	Pont.
11.	Darrell Waltrip	Chevy
12.	Morgan Shepherd	Pont.
13.	Terry Labonte	Chevy
14.	Kenny Wallace	Ford
15.	Dale Earnhardt	Chevy
16.	Bill Elliott	Ford
17.	Jeremy Mayfield	Ford
18.	Ward Burton	Pont.
19.	Rick Mast	Ford
20.	Derrike Cope	Pont.
21.	Ernie Irvan	Ford
22.	Jimmy Spencer	Ford
23.	Ricky Rudd	Ford
24.	Mark Martin	Ford
25.	John Andretti	Ford
26.	Hut Stricklin	Ford
27.	Chad Little	Pont.
28.	Dave Marcis	Chevy
29.	Greg Sacks	Ford
30.	Mike Skinner	Chevy
31.	Phil Parsons	Chevy
32.	Sterling Marlin	Chevy
33.	Kyle Petty	Pont.
34.	Robby Gordon	Chevy
35.	Brett Bodine	Ford
36.	Lake Speed	Ford
37.	Bobby Hamilton	Pont
38.	Gary Bradberry	Ford
39.	Robert Pressley	Chevy
40.	Ricky Craven	Chevy
41.	David Green	Chevy
42.	Bobby Hillin	Ford
43.	Mike Wallace	Chevy

RACE 6—INTERSTATE BATTERIES 500

Texas Motor Speedway

Ft. Worth, Texas

April 6

Winner: Jeff Burton

Burton led the final 58 laps to win his first Winston Cup race and the inaugural event at Texas Motor Speedway before 150,000 fans . . . Dale Jarrett was second, 4.067 seconds behind Burton . . . Burton, driving a Jack Roush-owned Ford, overcame falling a lap down after the second pit stop . . . running second late in the race, Burton was pursuing Todd Bodine, who was filling in for the injured Ricky Craven. On lap 277, Burton tried to pass Bodine on the inside in turn 2. Bodine's car hit the wall, bringing out the 10th and final caution flag. Burton led the rest of the way . . . Texan Terry Labonte led 79 laps midway through the race; he finished fourth, behind younger brother Bobby . . . with qualifying rained out, the drivers started in order of their Winston Cup points standings.

Interstate Batteries 500

Average speed: 125.105 miles per hour
Time of race: 4 hours, 17 seconds
Margin of victory: 4.067 seconds

FINISH	DRIVER	CAR
1.	Jeff Burton	Ford
2.	Dale Jarrett	Ford
3.	Bobby Labonte	Pont.
4.	Terry Labonte	Chevy
5.	Ricky Rudd	Ford
6.	Dale Earnhardt	Chevy
7.	Ward Burton	Pont
8.	Sterling Marlin	Chevy
9.	Michael Waltrip	Ford
10.	Steve Grissom	Chevy
11.	Bill Elliott	Ford
12.	John Andretti	Ford
13.	Kenny Wallace	Ford
14.	Geoff Bodine	Ford
15.	Dave Marcis	Chev
16.	Lake Speed	Ford
17.	Mike Wallace	Chevy
18.	Ken Schrader	Chevy
19.	Brett Bodine	Ford
20.	Bobby Hamilton	Pont.
21.	Billy Standridge	Ford
22.	Mike Skinner	Chevy
23.	Dick Trickle	Ford
24.	Morgan Shepherd	Pont.
25.	Todd Bodine	Chevy
26.	Chad Little	Pont.
27.	Kyle Petty	Pont.
28.	Johnny Benson	Pont.
29.	Joe Nemechek	Chevy
30.	Jeff Gordon	Chevy
31.	Rick Mast	Ford
32.	Jeremy Mayfield	Ford
33.	Hut Stricklin	Ford
34.	Robby Gordon	Chevy
35.	Ted Musgrave	Ford
36.	Ernie Irvan	Ford
37.	Rusty Wallace	Ford
38.	Mark Martin	Ford
39.	Jimmy Spencer	Ford
40.	Greg Sacks	Ford
41.	Derrike Cope	Pont.
42.	Bobby Hillin Jr.	Ford
43.	Darrell Waltrip	Chevy

RACE 7—FOOD CITY 500

Bristol Motor Speedway

Bristol, Tennessee

April 13

Winner: Jeff Gordon

With the money just sitting there for the taking, Gordon bumped Rusty Wallace aside in the last turn on the last lap in the year's most exciting finish . . .

Wallace had won the pole and led four times for 229 of the 500 laps (including 415-499), but was no match when Gordon's No. 24 Chevrolet came roaring by . . . Wallace managed to recover just long enough to hold back third-place Terry Labonte . . . Dale Jarrett and Mark Martin were fourth and fifth, among 14 drivers on the lead lap . . . The race was typical of Bristol: an afternoon of beating and banging interrupted by occasional spells of good racing . . . There were 20 cautions for 132 laps and 20 of the 43 starters were listed on the incident report, seven of them more than once.

Food City 500

Average speed: 75.035 miles per hour
Time of race: 3 hours, 33 minutes, 6 seconds
Margin of victory: 0.499 seconds

FINISH	DRIVER	CAR
1.	Jeff Gordon	Chevy
2.	Rusty Wallace	Ford
3.	Terry Labonte	Chevy
4.	Dale Jarrett	Ford
5.	Mark Martin	Ford
6.	Dale Earnhardt	Chevy
7.	Bill Elliott	Ford
8.	Chad Little	Pont.
9.	Jeremy Mayfield	Ford
10.	Brett Bodine	Ford
11.	Dick Trickle	Ford
12.	Ken Schrader	Chevy
13.	Bobby Hamilton	Pont.
14.	Robert Pressley	Chevy
15.	Jimmy Spencer	Ford
16.	Derrike Cope	Pont.
17.	Rick Mast	Ford
18.	Ward Burton	Pont.
19.	Joe Nemechek	Chevy
20.	Sterling Marlin	Chevy
21.	Michael Waltrip	Ford
22.	David Green	Chevy
23.	Ed Berrier	Chevy
24.	John Andretti	Ford
25.	Darrell Waltrip	Chevy
26.	Hut Stricklin	Ford
27.	Ricky Rudd	Ford
28.	Morgan Shepherd	Pont.
29.	Kyle Petty	Pont.
30.	Dave Marcis	Chevy
31.	Johnny Benson	Pont.
32.	Steve Grissom	Chevy
33.	Geoff Bodine	Ford
34.	Bobby Labonte	Pont.
35.	Mike Skinner	Chevy
36.	Lake Speed	Ford
37.	Gary Bradberry	Ford
38.	Ted Musgrave	Ford
39.	Ernie Irvan	Ford
40.	Jack Sprague	Chevy
41.	Kenny Wallace	Ford
42.	Jeff Burton	Ford
43.	Robby Gordon	Pont.

RACE 8—GOODY'S 500

Martinsville Speedway
Martinsville, Virginia
April 20
Winner: Jeff Gordon

Talk about your dominating, one-sided, no-contest race . . . Gordon started from fourth on the grid, took the lead for the first time after just 22 laps and spent most of the rest of the afternoon in the lead . . . His No. 24 Chevrolet led twice for 431 of the 500 laps: laps 22-327 and laps 366-500, losing the lead only because of scheduled pit stops . . . He beat Bobby Hamilton, Mark Martin, Terry Labonte, and Rusty Wallace after a late caution bunched the field and gave everybody one last chance . . . It wasn't close, and his fourth victory of the season was never in serious doubt . . . Pole-sitter Kenny Wallace didn't lead, but finished a lead-lap sixth.

Goody's 500

Average speed: 70.920 mph
Time of race: 3 hours, 44 minutes, 30 seconds
Margin of victory: 1.047 seconds

FINISH	DRIVER	CAR
1.	Jeff Gordon	Chevy
2.	Bobby Hamilton	Pont.
3.	Mark Martin	Ford
4.	Terry Labonte	Chevy
5.	Rusty Wallace	Ford
6.	Kenny Wallace	Ford
7.	Jeremy Mayfield	Ford
8.	Bobby Labonte	Pont.
9.	Darrell Waltrip	Chevy
10.	Ken Schrader	Chevy
11.	Jimmy Spencer	Ford
12.	Dale Earnhardt	Chevy
13.	Ricky Rudd	Ford
14.	Hut Stricklin	Ford
15.	Jeff Burton	Ford
16.	Dale Jarrett	Ford
17.	Johnny Benson	Pont.
18.	Ward Burton	Pont.
19.	Joe Nemechek	Chevy
20.	Steve Grissom	Chevy
21.	Sterling Marlin	Chevy
22.	Ricky Craven	Chevy
23.	Robert Pressley	Chevy
24.	Ted Musgrave	Ford
25.	Lake Speed	Ford
26.	Michael Waltrip	Ford
27.	Brett Bodine	Ford
28.	John Andretti	Ford
29.	Geoff Bodine	Ford
30.	Dick Trickle	Ford
31.	Ernie Irvan	Ford
32.	Mike Skinner	Chevy
33.	Bobby Hillin	Ford
34.	Derrike Cope	Pont.
35.	Morgan Shepherd	Pont.
36.	Rick Mast	Ford
37.	Bill Elliott	Ford
38.	Dave Marcis	Chevy
39.	Mike Wallace	Ford
40.	Kyle Petty	Pont.
41.	Robby Gordon	Pont.
42.	Chad Little	Pont.

RACE 9—SAVE MART SUPERMARKETS 300

Sears Point
Sonoma, California

May 4

Winner: Mark Martin.

Martin ended his 42-race winless drought in dominating style: starting from the pole in a Ford, he led 69 of the 74 laps on the 2.52-mile course . . . he beat Jeff Gordon by 0.563 of a second for his 19th career victory . . . Terry Labonte was third . . . Martin's last victory was at Charlotte in October 1995 . . . Rusty Wallace passed Martin on the fourth lap, but two laps later Martin regained the lead when Wallace slid off the course . . . Gordon attempted to pass Martin on the final lap on the last turn, but Martin held him off . . . Gordon's second-place finish was his best ever on a road course, as was Dale Jarrett's fourth place . . . veteran Darrell Waltrip's fifth-place finish was his first top five since the '95 season.

Save Mart Supermarkets 300

Average speed: 75.788 mph.
Time of race: 2 hours, 27 minutes, 38 seconds.
Margin of victory: 0.536 seconds

FINISH	DRIVER	CAR
1.	Mark Martin	Ford
2.	Jeff Gordon	Chevy
3.	Terry Labonte	Chevy
4.	Dale Jarrett	Ford
5.	Darrell Waltrip	Chevy
6.	Brett Bodine	Ford
7.	Michael Waltrip	Ford
8.	Ernie Irvan	Ford
9.	Jeff Burton	Ford
10.	Ward Burton	Pont.
11.	Ted Musgrave	Ford
12.	Dale Earnhardt	Chevy
13.	Kyle Petty	Pont.
14.	Jimmy Spencer	Ford
15.	W. Dallenbach	Chevy
16.	Mike Skinner	Chevy
17.	Steve Grissom	Chevy
18.	Derrike Cope	Pont.
19.	Bobby Hamilton	Pont
20.	Bobby Labonte	Pont.
21.	Johnny Benson	Pont.
22.	Mike Wallace	Chevy
23.	Morgan Shepherd	Pont.
24.	Butch Gilliland	Ford
25.	Dave Marcis	Chevy
26.	Sterling Marlin	Chevy
27.	Jeremy Mayfield	Ford
28.	Tom Hubert	Ford
29.	Hut Stricklin	Ford
30.	John Andretti	Ford
31.	Ken Schrader	Chevy
32.	Bill Elliott	Ford
33.	Sean Woodside	Pont.
34.	Ricky Rudd	Ford
35.	Bobby Hillin	Ford
36.	Kenny Wallace	Ford
37.	Jeff Davis	Ford
38.	Larry Gunselman	Ford
39.	Ricky Craven	Chevy
40.	Rusty Wallace	Ford
41.	Robby Gordon	Chevy
42.	Lance Hooper	Ford
43.	Gary Bradberry	Ford
44.	Geoff Bodine	Ford

RACE 10—WINSTON 500

Talladega Superspeedway
Talladega, Alabama
May 10

Winner: Mark Martin

Without question, this rescheduled-by-rain Saturday afternoon race was the surprise race of the year, not because Martin won, but because they ran 188 caution-free laps on a track that generally has at least one or two major pileups . . . Martin won by .146 seconds ahead of Dale Earnhardt, who suffered painful injuries in a spectacular crash here the previous summer and hadn't run especially well since . . . Martin and his No. 6 Ford led three times for 47 laps, second to Earnhardt's eight times for 53 laps . . . Bobby Labonte was third, pole-sitter John Andretti fourth, and Jeff Gordon fifth . . . Only six of the 43 starters did not finish, all with engine problems . . . It was the first caution-free race in track history.

Winston 500

Average speed: 188.354 mph (New NASCAR Record)
Time of race: 2 hours, 39 minutes, 18 seconds
Margin of victory: .146 seconds

FINISH	DRIVER	CAR
1.	Mark Martin	Ford
2.	Dale Earnhardt	Chevy
3.	Bobby Labonte	Pont.
4.	John Andretti	Ford
5.	Jeff Gordon	Chevy
6.	Terry Labonte	Chevy
7.	Jimmy Spencer	Ford
8.	Jeff Burton	Ford
9.	Johnny Benson	Pont.
10.	Ernie Irvan	Ford
11.	Ricky Rudd	Ford
12.	Ken Schrader	Chevy
13.	Derrike Cope	Pont.
14.	Michael Waltrip	Ford
15.	Dick Trickle	Ford
16.	Mike Skinner	Chevy
17.	Wally Dallenbach	Chevy
18.	Bill Elliott	Ford
19.	Joe Nemechek	Pont.
20.	Bobby Hillin	Ford
21.	Lake Speed	Ford
22.	Rick Mast	Ford
23.	Jeremy Mayfield	Ford
24.	Ted Musgrave	Ford
25.	Greg Sacks	Ford
26.	Kenny Wallace	Ford
27.	Ricky Craven	Chevy
28.	Morgan Shepherd	Pont.
29.	Robert Pressley	Chevy
30.	Dave Marcis	Chevy
31.	Bobby Hamilton	Pont
32.	Darrell Waltrip	Chevy
33.	Brett Bodine	Ford
34.	Chad Little	Pont.
35.	Dale Jarrett	Ford
36.	Hut Stricklin	Ford
37.	Rusty Wallace	Ford
38.	David Green	Chevy
39.	Sterling Marlin	Chevy
40.	Kyle Petty	Pont.

41.	Steve Grissom	Chevy	
42.	Ward Burton	Pont.	
43.	Geoff Bodine	Ford	

38.	Kenny Wallace	Ford	
40.	Sterling Marlin	Chevy	
41.	Robby Gordon	Chevy	
42.	Todd Bodine	Ford	

RACE 11—COCA-COLA 600

Charlotte Motor Speedway
Concord, North Carolina
May 25
Winner: Jeff Gordon

The year's longest day was made even longer by rain that delayed the twilight start, then stopped the race twice, the second time for three hours near the halfway mark . . . Mercifully, NASCAR officials called a halt at 12:59 Monday morning, a full 67 laps and 100 miles shy of its advertised distance . . . Gordon and his No. 24 Chevrolet won another leg (their second in three tries) of the Winston Million program, beating Rusty Wallace, Mark Martin, Bill Elliott, and Jeff Burton . . . He led just four times for 44 of the 333 laps, but among them were the last 17 . . . He took the lead by passing Wallace on the outside, where few people had dared run all night.

Coca-Cola 600

Average speed: 136.745 miles per hour
Time of race: 3 hours, 34 minutes, 02 seconds
Margin of victory: .468 seconds

FINISH	DRIVER	CAR
1.	Jeff Gordon	Chevy
2.	Rusty Wallace	Ford
3.	Mark Martin	Ford
4.	Bill Elliott	Ford
5.	Jeff Burton	Ford
6.	Bobby Labonte	Pont.
7.	Dale Earnhardt	Chevy
8.	Terry Labonte	Chevy
9.	Morgan Shepherd	Pont.
10.	Ricky Rudd	Ford
11.	Steve Grissom	Chevy
12.	Derrike Cope	Pont.
13.	Ernie Irvan	Ford
14.	Kyle Petty	Pont.
15.	Johnny Benson	Pont.
16.	David Green	Chevy
17.	Michael Waltrip	Ford
18.	Jimmy Spencer	Ford
19.	Joe Nemechek	Chevy
20.	Rick Mast	Ford
21.	Darrell Waltrip	Chevy
22.	Jeff Green	Chevy
23.	Ted Musgrave	Ford
24.	Lake Speed	Ford
25.	Hut Stricklin	Ford
26.	Brett Bodine	Ford
27.	Dale Jarrett	Ford
28.	Jeremy Mayfield	Ford
29.	Bobby Hamilton	Pont.
30.	John Andretti	Ford
31.	Gary Bradberry	Ford
32.	B. Standridge	Ford
33.	Dick Trickle	Ford
34.	Mike Skinner	Chevy
35.	Wally Dallenbach	Chevy
36.	Ward Burton	Pont.
37.	Ricky Craven	Chevy
38.	Ken Schrader	Chevy

RACE 12—MILLER 500

Dover Downs International Speedway
Dover, Delaware
June 1
Winner: Ricky Rudd.

Rudd, in a Ford, extended his streak of winning at least one race a year to 15 by being patient . . . Dale Jarrett led 255 laps of the last scheduled 500-lap race at Dover before engine problems in his Ford spoiled his day on lap 463 . . . 13 laps earlier, Jarrett survived a bump by Jeff Gordon, who was forced to park his Chevrolet . . . when Jarrett lost the lead, his teammate, Ernie Irvan, moved in front for 10 laps. However, with no one near him, Irvan spun and crashed in turn 1 with 29 laps to go. Irvan said he hit an oil slick on the track . . . Rudd led only twice for 31 laps, but he was in front for the final 29 laps . . . Rudd's only concern then was holding off Mark Martin. Stalking Rudd over the last 10 laps, Martin's Ford was almost attached to Rudd's car. Rudd crossed the finish line just .0091 of a second ahead of Martin . . . pole-sitter Bobby Labonte faded to a 40th-place finish.

Miller 500

Average speed: 114.635 miles per hour
Time of race: 4 hours, 21 minutes, 42 seconds
Margin of victory: .091 seconds

FINISH	DRIVER	CAR
1.	Ricky Rudd	Ford
2.	Mark Martin	Ford
3.	Jeff Burton	Ford
4.	Jeremy Mayfield	Ford
5.	Kyle Petty	Pont.
6.	Ken Schrader	Chevy
7.	Michael Waltrip	Ford
8.	Bill Elliott	Ford
9.	Mike Skinner	Chevy
10.	Sterling Marlin	Chevy
11.	Ted Musgrave	Ford
12.	Rick Mast	Ford
13.	Ricky Craven	Chevy
14.	Terry Labonte	Chevy
15.	Joe Nemechek	Chevy
16.	Dale Earnhardt	Chevy
17.	Bobby Hamilton	Pont.
18.	David Green	Chevy
19.	Hut Stricklin	Ford
20.	Derrike Cope	Pont.
21.	Johnny Benson	Pont.
22.	Jimmy Spencer	Ford
23.	Mike Wallace	Chevy
24.	Steve Grissom	Chevy
25.	Dave Marcis	Chevy
26.	Jeff Gordon	Chevy
27.	Kenny Wallace	Ford

28.	Darrell Waltrip	Chevy
29.	John Andretti	Ford
30.	Ernie Irvan	Ford
31.	Chad Little	Pont.
32.	Dale Jarrett	Ford
33.	Brett Bodine	Ford
34.	Ward Burton	Pont.
35.	Gary Bradberry	Ford
36.	W. Dallenbach	Chevy
37.	Jeff Green	Chevy
38.	Morgan Shepherd	Pont.
39.	Rusty Wallace	Ford
40.	Bobby Labonte	Pont.
41.	Dick Trickle	Ford
42.	Geoff Bodine	Ford
43.	Bobby Hillin	Ford

RACE 13—POCONO 500

Pocono Raceway
Pocono, Pennsylvania
June 8
Winner: Jeff Gordon.

Overcoming a flat tire on his Chevrolet early in the race, Gordon won his sixth race of the year and took the points lead. He and teammate Terry Labonte each had 1,955 points, but Gordon's six victories (to none for Labonte) gave him the lead . . . Jeff Burton, in a Ford, was runnerup, 1.415 seconds off the pace . . . Gordon took the lead on lap 133 and held it until No. 174, when he pitted . . . when leader Ted Musgrave stopped for fuel on lap 184, Gordon regained the lead for good . . . Ward Burton led the most laps (60). However, he blew an engine on his Pontiac on lap 141 of the 200-lap race and finished 38th . . . pole-sitter Bobby Hamilton, also in a Pontiac, led the first 19 laps, but his car was taken out in an accident on lap 129, relegating him to 39th place.

Dale Earnhardt (No. 3) takes the lead at Dover.

Pocono 500

Average speed: 139.828 mph
Time of race: 3 hours, 24 minutes, 33 seconds
Margin of victory: 1.415 seconds

FINISH	DRIVER	CAR
1.	Jeff Gordon	Chevy
2.	Jeff Burton	Ford
3.	Dale Jarrett	Ford
4.	Mark Martin	Ford
5.	Jeremy Mayfield	Ford
6.	Ted Musgrave	Ford
7.	Darrell Waltrip	Chevy
8.	Geoff Bodine	Ford
9.	Terry Labonte	Chevy
10.	Dale Earnhardt	Chevy
11.	Derrike Cope	Pont.
12.	Morgan Shepherd	Pont.
13.	Michael Waltrip	Ford
14.	Kyle Petty	Pont.
15.	Sterling Marlin	Chevy
16.	Ricky Craven	Chevy
17.	Wally Dallenbach	Chevy
18.	Steve Grissom	Chevy
19.	Jimmy Spencer	Ford
20.	Rick Mast	Ford
21.	Ricky Rudd	Ford
22.	Rusty Wallace	Ford
23.	Ken Schrader	Chevy
24.	Hut Stricklin	Ford
25.	Brett Bodine	Ford
26.	Dick Trickle	Ford
27.	Johnny Benson	Pont.
28.	David Green	Chevy
29.	Ernie Irvan	Ford
30.	Mike Wallace	Chevy
31.	Bobby Labonte	Pont.
32.	Bill Elliott	Ford
33.	Gary Bradberry	Ford
34.	Kenny Wallace	Ford
35.	Jeff Green	Chevy
36.	Joe Nemechek	Chevy
37.	Bobby Hillin	Ford
38.	Ward Burton	Pont.
39.	Bobby Hamilton	Pont.
40.	John Andretti	Ford
41.	Mike Skinner	Chevy
42.	Greg Sacks	Chevy

RACE 14—MILLER 400

Michigan International Speedway
Brooklyn, Michigan
June 15
Winner: Ernie Irvan.

Returning to the site of his life-threatening practice crash in 1994, Irvan benefitted from a quick final pit stop to beat Bill Elliott by 2.964 seconds. In gaining his 15th career Winston Cup victory, an emotional Irvan won for the first time since Richmond in '96 . . . Thinking about the significance of winning at Michigan, Irvan said, "I was getting a little teary eyed. It's real hard to drive with tears in your eyes." . . . Irvan was only the 20th fastest qualifier and he spun on the second lap . . . the race featured some of the year's best competition, with cars frequently side-by-side three-wide

. . . Irvan's first lead came on lap 163, when he passed Elliott . . . on lap 176, Irvan pitted, followed by Elliott two laps later. Irvan's Robert Yates-team crew was seconds faster than Elliott's . . . Ted Musgrave led the most laps (68) . . . pole-sitter Dale Jarrett finished sixth.

Miller 400

Average speed: 153.338 mph
Time of race: 2 hours, 36 minutes
Margin of victory: 2.964 seconds

FINISH	DRIVER	CAR
1.	Ernie Irvan	Ford
2.	Bill Elliott	Ford
3.	Mark Martin	Ford
4.	Ted Musgrave	Ford
5.	Jeff Gordon	Chevy
6.	Dale Jarrett	Ford
7.	Dale Earnhardt	Chevy
8.	Derrike Cope	Pont.
9.	Bobby Labonte	Pont.
10.	Johnny Benson	Pont.
11.	Lake Speed	Ford
12.	Jeremy Mayfield	Ford
13.	Ricky Rudd	Ford
14.	Jeff Burton	Ford
15.	Jimmy Spencer	Ford
16.	Michael Waltrip	Ford
17.	Sterling Marlin	Chevy
18.	Ricky Craven	Chevy
19.	Brett Bodine	Ford
20.	W. Dallenbach	Chevy
21.	Rick Wilson	Ford
22.	Hut Stricklin	Ford
23.	Dick Trickle	Ford
24.	Darrell Waltrip	Chevy
25.	Chad Little	Pont.
26.	Kyle Petty	Pont.
27.	Ken Schrader	Chevy
28.	David Green	Chevy
29.	Rusty Wallace	Ford
30.	Rick Mast	Ford
31.	Jeff Green	Chevy
32.	Bobby Hamilton	Pont.
33.	Billy Standridge	Ford
34.	Dave Marcis	Chevy
35.	Ward Burton	Pont.
36.	Jerry Nadeau	Pont.
37.	John Andretti	Ford
38.	Steve Grissom	Chevy
39.	Terry Labonte	Chevy
40.	Geoff Bodine	Ford
41.	Joe Nemechek	Chevy
42.	Mike Skinner	Chevy
43.	Kenny Wallace	Ford

RACE 15—CALIFORNIA 500 BY NAPA

California Speedway
Fontana, California
June 22
Winner: Jeff Gordon.

Aided by the fuel-management advice of crew chief Ray Evernham, Gordon celebrated winning the first Winston Cup race at the new Cal-

IRVAN'S MIRACLE

Saturday morning, Aug. 17, 1994.

The 2-mile Michigan International Speedway near Brooklyn.

Practice for the following afternoon's GM Goodwrench 400 NASCAR Winston Cup race.

At approximately 10:30, Ernie Irvan took his No. 28 Texaco Havoline-sponsored Ford Thunderbird out for a brief test session. He'd made only a handful of laps when the right-front tire blew, sending his car hard into the Turn 2 outside retaining wall.

The force of the impact created major critical internal injuries. There was a closed head wound, plus chest and rib injuries. He was airlifted to a hospital in Jackson, put on a ventilator and given perhaps a 10 percent chance of living through the night.

Slightly more than 14 months later, Ernie Irvan was back racing a self-owned truck in the NASCAR Craftsman Series. Nine months after that, he won a 300-lap Winston Cup race at Loudon, New Hampshire, then added a second 1996 victory two months later at Richmond, Virginia.

And in June of 1997, back at the track that had almost taken his life, Ernie Irvan won a 400-mile Winston Cup race.

Ten percent chance of simply making it through the night, they'd said at the time.

If he does live, others agreed, he'll be lucky to be able to get around on his own and do the most simple of chores.

Racing, they agreed, was out of the question, a preposterous and foolish hope, given all he'd been through.

Which brings us to the point of the story:

It's been said for years that coaches and doctors and athletic trainers can measure everything about an athlete except his heart and willpower.

Miracle of miracle, thy name is Ernie Irvan.

---

ifornia Speedway by proving that there's more to winning than just going fast. Gordon coaxed every drop of gas from his Chevrolet to edge teammate Terry Labonte by 1.074 seconds. Gordon ran out of fuel on the victory lap and had to cut across the infield grass to make it to victory lane . . . Gordon led 113 of the race's 250 laps, including 42 of the final 48 laps . . . Gordon took the lead from Mark Martin on lap 240 . . . Martin finished 10th . . . Ricky Rudd was third and Ted Musgrave was fourth. . . . Pole-sitter Joe Nemechek finished 18th . . . The event marked the return of Winston Cup racing to southern California for the first time since 1988, when the last race was held at Riverside International Raceway.

California 500 by NAPA

Average speed: 155.025 mph
Time of race: 3 hours, 13 minutes, 31 seconds.
Margin of victory: 1.074 seconds

FINISH	DRIVER	CAR
1.	Jeff Gordon	Chevy
2.	Terry Labonte	Chevy
3.	Ricky Rudd	Ford
4.	Ted Musgrave	Ford
5.	Jimmy Spencer	Ford
6.	Bobby Labonte	Pont.
7.	Jeff Green	Chevy
8.	Dale Jarrett	Ford
9.	Ricky Craven	Chevy
10.	Mark Martin	Ford
11.	Michael Waltrip	Ford
12.	Jeremy Mayfield	Ford
13.	Johnny Benson	Pont.
14.	Rusty Wallace	Ford
15.	Darrell Waltrip	Chevy
16.	Dale Earnhardt	Chevy
17.	Steve Grissom	Chevy
18.	Joe Nemechek	Chevy
19.	Chad Little	Pont.
20.	Lake Speed	Ford
21.	John Andretti	Ford
22.	Dick Trickle	Ford
23.	Bobby Hamilton	Pont.
24.	Morgan Shepherd	Ford
25.	David Green	Chevy
26.	Brett Bodine	Ford
27.	Greg Sacks	Chevy
28.	Ward Burton	Pont.
29.	Derrike Cope	Pont.
30.	Jeff Burton	Ford
31.	Kyle Petty	Pont.
32.	Bill Elliott	Ford
33.	Mike Skinner	Chevy
34.	Ken Schrader	Chevy
35.	Geoff Bodine	Ford
36.	Sterling Marlin	Chevy
37.	Ernie Irvan	Ford
38.	Jerry Nadeau	Pont.
39.	W. Dallenbach	Chevy
40.	Dave Marcis	Chevy
41.	Rick Mast	Ford
42.	Hut Stricklin	Ford

RACE 16—PEPSI 400

Daytona International Speedway
Daytona Beach, Florida
July 5
Winner: John Andretti.

Andretti's first Winston Cup victory was worth the wait. The win, by just 0.029 of a second over Terry Labonte, occurred on the famed track where his uncle, Mario, won the Daytona 500 in 1967. And it gave Cale Yarborough, one of NASCAR's greatest drivers, his first win in 293 races as a car owner . . . talk about frantic finishes: four laps from the end, a multi-car crash caused the final caution pause. Andretti raced back to the start/finish line ahead of the pace. As the leader when the green and white flags were waved for the last lap, Andretti stayed in front. He missed another multi-car crash behind him . . . Andretti, who started third, credited fellow Ford driver Bill Elliott for earlier helping him pass Mark Martin for the lead . . . Andretti led 112 of the 160 laps . . . Mike Skinner, the pole-sitter for the Daytona 500, also started from the pole in the Pepsi 400, but he finished a disappointing 41st.

Pepsi 400

Average speed: 157.791 mph.
Time of race: 2 hours, 32 minutes, 6 seconds
Margin of victory: .029 seconds

FINISH	DRIVER	CAR
1.	John Andretti	Ford
2.	Terry Labonte	Chevy
3.	Sterling Marlin	Chevy
4.	Dale Earnhardt	Chevy
5.	Dale Jarrett	Ford
6.	Rusty Wallace	Ford
7.	Kyle Petty	Pont.
8.	Jeff Burton	Ford
9.	Ernie Irvan	Ford
10.	Bobby Labonte	Pont.
11.	Kenny Wallace	Ford
12.	Ted Musgrave	Ford
13.	Jeremy Mayfield	Ford
14.	Darrell Waltrip	Chevy
15.	Ken Schrader	Chevy
16.	Johnny Benson	Pont.
17.	Dave Marcis	Chevy
18.	Rick Mast	Ford
19.	David Green	Chevy
20.	Bobby Hamilton	Pont.
21.	Jeff Gordon	Chevy
22.	Robby Gordon	Chevy
23.	Brett Bodine	Ford
24.	Joe Nemechek	Chevy
25.	Dick Trickle	Ford
26.	Ward Burton	Pont.
27.	Mark Martin	Ford
28.	Derrike Cope	Pont.
29.	Lake Speed	Ford
30.	Jerry Nadeau	Pont.
31.	Jimmy Spencer	Ford
32.	Morgan Shepherd	Ford
33.	Bill Elliott	Ford
34.	Ricky Rudd	Ford
35.	Michael Waltrip	Ford
36.	Hut Stricklin	Ford
37.	Ricky Craven	Chevy
38.	Steve Grissom	Chevy
39.	Wally Dallenbach	Chevy
40.	Billy Standridge	Ford
41.	Mike Skinner	Chevy
42.	Chad Little	Pont.

RACE 17—JIFFY LUBE 300

New Hampshire International Speedway
Loudon, New Hampshire
July 13
Winner: Jeff Burton.

Burton's second victory of the season helped soothe memories of his Winston Cup debut at New Hampshire in 1993 when he crashed twice and finished 37th . . . This time, Burton was a comfortable 5.392 seconds ahead of runnerup Dale Earnhardt . . . Burton didn't lead until lap 174, when pacesetter Dale Jarrett pitted. Burton made a pit stop one lap later, yielding the lead to John Andretti. Burton took the lead again on lap 195 during a pit stop for the second caution period . . . Ernie Irvan and Dale Earnhardt staged a battle for second, with an engine problem forcing Irvan to finally bow out 50 laps from the finish . . . Rusty Wallace was third and Steve Grissom posted his best finish of the season in fourth . . . with only two caution flags for 10 laps, Burton set a track record, averaging 117.194 mph . . . Dale Jarrett led 91 laps and Bobby Hamilton was in front for 43 laps . . . pole-sitter Ken Schrader finished 11th.

Jiffy Lube 300

Average speed: 117.194 miles per hour
Time of race: 2 hours, 42 minutes, 35 seconds
Margin of victory: 5.392 seconds

FINISH	DRIVER	CAR
1.	Jeff Burton	Ford
2.	Dale Earnhardt	Chevy
3.	Rusty Wallace	Ford
4.	Steve Grissom	Chevy
5.	Mark Martin	Ford
6.	Bill Elliott	Ford
7.	Terry Labonte	Chevy
8.	Ernie Irvan	Ford
9.	Ricky Rudd	Ford
10.	Geoff Bodine	Ford
11.	Ken Schrader	Chevy
12.	Jimmy Spencer	Ford
13.	Kyle Petty	Pont.
14.	John Andretti	Ford
15.	Hut Stricklin	Ford
16.	Ricky Craven	Chevy
17.	Jeremy Mayfield	Ford
18.	Johnny Benson	Pont.

FINISH	DRIVER	CAR
19.	Kenny Wallace	Ford
20.	Derrike Cope	Pont.
21.	Mike Skinner	Chevy
22.	Sterling Marlin	Chevy
23.	Jeff Gordon	Chevy
24.	David Green	Chevy
25.	Dick Trickle	Ford
26.	Ted Musgrave	Ford
27.	Bobby Labonte	Pont.
28.	Rick Mast	Ford
29.	Michael Waltrip	Ford
30.	Chad Little	Pont.
31.	Bobby Hamilton	Pont.
32.	Jeff Green	Chevy
33.	Darrell Waltrip	Chevy
34.	Robby Gordon	Chevy
35.	Dave Marcis	Chevy
36.	Ward Burton	Pont.
37.	Morgan Shepherd	Ford
38.	Dale Jarrett	Ford
39.	Jerry Nadeau	Pont.
40.	Joe Nemechek	Chevy
41.	Randy MacDonald	Chevy
42.	Brett Bodine	Ford

RACE 18—PENNSYLVANIA 500

Pocono Raceway
Pocono, Pennsylvania
July 20
Winner: Dale Jarrett.

With two victories in '97, Dale Jarrett wasn't exactly in a slump when he returned to the Pocono Mountains. However, he hadn't won since March. Fortunately for Jarrett, his Robert Yates team provided him with what he called "the best engine" he'd ever had in a race car . . . Driving a Ford, Jarrett led 108 of the 200 laps . . . Jeff Gordon led 53 laps, but he conceded that Jarrett had the better car . . . once again, pit strategy influenced the outcome. Making his final pit stop on lap 165, Jarrett took four tires whereas the other contenders put on only right-side tires . . . Roush Racing teammates finished third (Jeff Burton), fourth (Ted Musgrave), and fifth (Mark Martin) in Fords . . . rookie Mike Skinner's sixth-place was his best of the season . . . pole-sitter Joe Nemechek was 21st.

Pennsylvania 500

Average speed: 142.068.
Time of race: 3 hours, 31 minutes, 10 seconds.
Margin of victory: 2.99 seconds

FINISH	DRIVER	CAR
1.	Dale Jarrett	Ford
2.	Jeff Gordon	Chevy
3.	Jeff Burton	Ford
4.	Ted Musgrave	Ford
5.	Mark Martin	Ford
6.	Mike Skinner	Chevy
7.	Jimmy Spencer	Ford
8.	Kyle Petty	Pont.
9.	Jeremy Mayfield	Ford

FINISH	DRIVER	CAR
10.	Bill Elliott	Ford
11.	Bobby Labonte	Pont.
12.	Dale Earnhardt	Chevy
13.	Johnny Benson	Pont.
14.	Ken Schrader	Chevy
15.	Ward Burton	Pont.
16.	Derrike Cope	Pont.
17.	Geoff Bodine	Ford
18.	Ricky Craven	Chevy
19.	Dick Trickle	Ford
20.	Sterling Marlin	Chevy
21.	Joe Nemechek	Chevy
22.	Michael Waltrip	Ford
23.	Hut Stricklin	Ford
24.	John Andretti	Ford
25.	Rick Mast	Ford
26.	Darrell Waltrip	Chevy
27.	Morgan Shepherd	Ford
28.	Chad Little	Pont.
29.	Brett Bodine	Ford
30.	Steve Grissom	Chevy
31.	Jeff Green	Chevy
32.	Bobby Hamilton	Pont.
33.	Jerry Nadeau	Pont.
34.	Kenny Wallace	Ford
35.	Terry Labonte	Chevy
36.	Ricky Rudd	Ford
37.	Rusty Wallace	Ford
38.	Wally Dallenbach	Chevy
39.	David Green	Chevy
40.	Ernie Irvan	Ford
41.	Dave Marcis	Chevy
42.	Robby Gordon	Chevy

RACE 19—BRICKYARD 400

Indianapolis Motor Speedway
Indianapolis, Indiana
Aug. 2
Winner: Ricky Rudd.

Rudd took perhaps the biggest gamble of his career and it paid off with a huge winner's check for $571,000. Rudd's payday was the second largest in NASCAR history: Jeff Gordon collected $613,000 in the first Brickyard 400 in 1994 . . . Rudd and crew chief Jim Long gambled that he could complete the race without a final pit stop for fuel that the other contenders would need . . . following the sixth and final caution on lap 156, caused by Rich Bickle's car hitting the wall in turn 3, the race went green on lap 158: just three laps to the finish. A burst by Rudd put him 10 laps ahead of Bobby Labonte. While other cars scraped fenders jockeying for final positions, Rudd won by 0.183 of a second over Labonte. Dale Jarrett was third and Gordon was fourth . . . Rudd's victory was an uplifting day for a single-car owner/driver . . . Rudd's two wins in '97 marked the first time he was a double winner since 1987 when he drove for Bud Moore . . . there was no dominant driver in the race: pole-sitter Ernie Irvan led the most laps, the first 39. Jarrett was next with 31, followed by Gordon (25), Jeff Burton (21), and Rudd (15). Irvan wound up 10th.

Brickyard 400

Average speed: 130.828 mph
Time of race: 3 hours, 3 minutes, 26.8. 41 seconds
Margin of victory: 0.18 seconds

FINISH	DRIVER	CAR
1.	Ricky Rudd	Ford
2.	Bobby Labonte	Pont.
3.	Dale Jarrett	Ford
4.	Jeff Gordon	Chevy
5.	Jeremy Mayfield	Ford
6.	Mark Martin	Ford
7.	Johnny Benson	Pont.
8.	Bill Elliott	Ford
9.	Mike Skinner	Chevy
10.	Ernie Irvan	Ford
11.	Ken Schrader	Chevy
12.	Lake Speed	Ford
13.	Kyle Petty	Pont.
14.	Darrell Waltrip	Chevy
15.	Jeff Burton	Ford
16.	Ricky Craven	Chevy
17.	John Andretti	Ford
18.	Brett Bodine	Ford
19.	Ward Burton	Pont.
20.	Bobby Hamilton	Pont.
21.	Rick Wilson	Ford
22.	Ron Barfield	Ford
23.	Rick Mast	Ford
24.	Jimmy Spencer	Ford
25.	Jeff Green	Chevy
26.	Steve Grissom	Chevy
27.	Ed Berrier	Chevy
28.	Robby Gordon	Chevy
29.	Dale Earnhardt	Chevy
30.	Kenny Wallace	Ford
31.	Greg Sacks	Chevy
32.	Joe Nemechek	Chevy
33.	Ted Musgrave	Ford
34.	Rich Bickle	Chevy
35.	David Green	Chevy
36.	Wally Dallenbach	Chevy
37.	Jeff Purvis	Chevy
38.	Rusty Wallace	Ford

Jeff Gordon (No. 24) and Dale Jarrett (No. 88) battle it out at Pocono. Jarrett eventually blew by Gordon to claim the victory.

39.	Michael Waltrip	Ford
40.	Terry Labonte	Chevy
41.	Derrike Cope	Pont.
42.	Chad Little	Pont.
43.	Sterling Marlin	Chevy

RACE 20—THE BUD AT THE GLEN

Watkins Glen
Watkins Glen, New York
Aug. 10
Winner: Jeff Gordon.

The road-course breakthrough victory that eluded Gordon finally was added to his glittering resume . . . Gordon won by 1.350 seconds over Geoff Bodine, the defending race champion who is from the Watkins Glen area . . . Gordon called the accomplishment "one of the most satisfying wins I've ever had." . . . Rusty Wallace, who also challenged Gordon, was third. . . . It was Gordon's eighth victory of the season . . . Gordon, who qualified 11th, didn't lead until lap 53 of the 90-lap race, but he led the final 28 laps . . . Bodine led by as much as five seconds midway in the race. Then, on lap 53, Gordon passed Bodine in turn 10 . . . Early in the race, Dale Jarrett (15 laps) and Joe Nemechek (10) were among the nine leaders . . . Robby Gordon finished a career-best fourth in a Chevrolet . . . Bodine's brother, Todd, was the surprising fastest qualifier: he finished 35th.

Bud at the Glen

Average speed: 91.294 mph.
Time of race: 2 hours, 24 minutes, 55 seconds
Margin of victory: 1.35 seconds

FINISH	DRIVER	CAR
1.	Jeff Gordon	Chevy
2.	Geoff Bodine	Ford
3.	Rusty Wallace	Ford
4.	Robby Gordon	Chevy
5.	Mark Martin	Ford
6.	Ted Musgrave	Ford
7.	Bill Elliott	Ford
8.	Terry Labonte	Chevy
9.	Steve Grissom	Chevy
10.	Wally Dallenbach	Chevy
11.	Johnny Benson	Pont.
12.	Joe Nemechek	Chevy
13.	Sterling Marlin	Chevy
14.	Ken Schrader	Chevy
15.	Jeremy Mayfield	Ford
16.	Dale Earnhardt	Chevy
17.	Ricky Craven	Chevy
18.	Darrell Waltrip	Chevy
19.	Mike Skinner	Chevy
20.	John Andretti	Ford
21.	Ernie Irvan	Ford
22.	David Green	Chevy
23.	Rick Mast	Ford
24.	Lance Hooper	Pont.
25.	Michael Waltrip	Ford
26.	Kyle Petty	Pont.
27.	Kenny Wallace	Ford
28.	Bobby Hamilton	Pont.
29.	Jeff Burton	Ford
30.	Jeff Green	Chevy
31.	Dorsey Schroeder	Ford
32.	Dale Jarrett	Ford
33.	Steve Park	Chevy
34.	Jimmy Spencer	Ford
35.	Todd Bodine	Chevy
36.	Hut Stricklin	Ford
37.	Bobby Labonte	Pont.
38.	Derrike Cope	Pont.
39.	Brett Bodine	Ford
40.	Ricky Rudd	Ford
41.	Ward Burton	Pont.
42.	Chad Little	Pont.

RACE 21—DEVILBISS 400

Michigan International Speedway
Brooklyn, Michigan
Aug. 17
Winner: Mark Martin.

Any driver who falls two laps down in a Winston Cup race is a longshot to win. On this day, however, it wouldn't have been wise to bet against Mark Martin . . . Aided by Roush Racing teammate Jeff Burton, Martin stormed back to win by 2.009 seconds over Jeff Gordon . . . Martin, normally a stoic sort, proclaimed his comeback as "pretty awesome." . . . Burton was leading on lap 105 when a caution period was ordered for rain. His crew chief, veteran Buddy Parrott, told Burton to help Martin get back on the lead lap. Burton slowed, permitting Martin to pass him and regain the lost lap . . . Earlier, Martin's car cut a rear tire, sending him spinning in turn 2 on lap 86. A 52-second pit stop followed, putting him two laps down . . . Martin's victory was his third of the year, the 21st of his career, and his third at Michigan . . . Martin trimmed Gordon's lead in the points standings to 99 . . . pole-sitter Johnny Benson, a Michigan native, finished 24th in a Pontiac.

DeVilbiss 400

Average speed: 126.88 mph.
Time of race: 3 hours, 9 minutes, 9 seconds
Margin of victory: 2.009 seconds

FINISH	DRIVER	CAR
1.	Mark Martin	Ford
2.	Jeff Gordon	Chevy
3.	Ted Musgrave	Ford
4.	Ernie Irvan	Ford
5.	Dale Jarrett	Ford
6.	Bobby Labonte	Pont.
7.	Bill Elliott	Ford
8.	Jeff Burton	Ford
9.	Dale Earnhardt	Chevy

10.	Terry Labonte	Chevy
11.	Geoff Bodine	Ford
12.	Ricky Craven	Chevy
13.	Rusty Wallace	Ford
14.	Ken Schrader	Chevy
15.	Darrell Waltrip	Chevy
16.	Derrike Cope	Pont.
17.	Robby Gordon	Chevy
18.	Jeff Green	Chevy
19.	Jimmy Spencer	Ford
20.	David Green	Chevy
21.	Lake Speed	Ford
22.	Michael Waltrip	Ford
23.	Kyle Petty	Pont.
24.	Johnny Benson	Pont.
25.	Steve Grissom	Chevy
26.	Bobby Hamilton	Pont.
27.	Joe Nemechek	Chevy
28.	Ward Burton	Pont.
29.	Ricky Rudd	Ford
30.	Mike Skinner	Chevy
31.	Brett Bodine	Ford
32.	Kenny Wallace	Ford
33.	Jeremy Mayfield	Ford
34.	Lance Hooper	Pont.
35.	John Andretti	Ford
36.	Hut Stricklin	Ford
37.	Gary Bradberry	Ford
38.	Rick Mast	Ford
39.	Dick Trickle	Ford
40.	Morgan Shepherd	Ford
41.	Wally Dallenbach	Chevy
42.	Chad Little	Pont.
43.	Sterling Marlin	Chevy

RACE 22—GOODY'S 500

Bristol Motor Speedway
Bristol, Tennessee
Aug. 23
Winner: Dale Jarrett

After winning two of the first five races and being among the top-10 in six of the next 10 races, Jarrett had been in something of a slump . . . He and his No. 88 Ford snapped it in the second of the season's three night races, leading four times for 220 of the 500 laps on the steeply banked half-mile . . . He beat Mark Martin, Dick Trickle, Jeff Burton, and Steve Grissom, passing Martin for the lead seconds before a caution waved for oil on the track . . . Among the wall-banging casualties: Dale Earnhardt, Darrell Waltrip, pole-sitter Kenny Wallace, Kyle Petty, Bill Elliott, Bobby Labonte, Jeff Gordon, and David Green, who suffered a broken right shoulder . . . All told, 23 of the 42 entries were listed at least once on the incident report.

Goody's 500

Average speed: 80.010 mph.
Time of race: 3 hours, 19 minutes, 51 seconds
Margin of victory: 0.102 seconds

FINISH	DRIVER	CAR
1.	Dale Jarrett	Ford
2.	Mark Martin	Ford

3.	Dick Trickle	Ford
4.	Jeff Burton	Ford
5.	Steve Grissom	Chevy
6.	Ken Schrader	Chevy
7.	Terry Labonte	Chevy
8.	Bobby Labonte	Pont.
9.	Geoff Bodine	Ford
10.	Sterling Marlin	Chevy
11.	John Andretti	Ford
12.	Rusty Wallace	Ford
13.	Ricky Craven	Chevy
14.	Dale Earnhardt	Chevy
15.	Ted Musgrave	Ford
16.	Bill Elliott	Ford
17.	Ward Burton	Pont.
18.	Johnny Benson	Pont.
19.	Ricky Rudd	Ford
20.	Chad Little	Pont.
21.	Jeff Green	Chevy
22.	Bobby Hamilton	Pont.
23.	Hut Stricklin	Ford
24.	Lance Hooper	Pont.
25.	Michael Waltrip	Ford
26.	Wally Dallenbach	Chevy
27.	Jimmy Spencer	Ford
28.	Ed Berrier	Chevy
29.	Lake Speed	Ford
30.	Jeremy Mayfield	Ford
31.	Brett Bodine	Ford
32.	Derrike Cope	Pont.
33.	Rick Mast	Ford
34.	Mike Skinner	Chevy
35.	Jeff Gordon	Chevy
36.	Kyle Petty	Pont.
37.	Gary Bradberry	Ford
38.	Joe Nemechek	Chevy
39.	Kenny Wallace	Ford
40.	David Green	Chevy
41.	Ernie Irvan	Ford
42.	Darrell Waltrip	Chevy

RACE 23—MOUNTAIN DEW SOUTHERN 500

Darlington Raceway
Darlington, South Carolina
Aug. 31
Winner: Jeff Gordon

Only Dale Earnhardt's spooky opening-lap blackout could upstage Gordon's victory that produced the Winston Million cash bonus from R.J. Reynolds Inc. . . . While Gordon's No. 24 Chevrolet was nipping Jeff Burton in a frantic last-lap battle for the victory, Earnhardt was in a nearby hospital for tests to determine why he was woozy and disoriented, and had double-vision when the race began . . . Meanwhile, Gordon was beating Burton, Dale Jarrett, Bill Elliott, and Ricky Rudd . . . Gordon got RJR's million because he'd also won the Daytona 500 and Coca-Cola World 600, two of the other three races (with the Winston 500) that made up the special promotion . . . Gordon led only twice for 115 laps, fewer than Elliott's three times in front for 181 laps, but more than held his own in a fender-banging duel with Burton in the final laps.

Mountain Dew Southern 500

Average speed: 121.149 mph
Time of race: 4 hours, 8 minutes, 17 seconds.
Margin of victory: 0.144 seconds

FINISH	DRIVER	CAR
1.	Jeff Gordon	Chevy
2.	Jeff Burton	Ford
3.	Dale Jarrett	Ford
4.	Bill Elliott	Ford
5.	Rick Rudd	Ford
6.	Terry Labonte	Chevy
7.	Bobby Labonte	Pont.
8.	Mark Martin	Ford
9.	Michael Waltrip	Ford
10.	Ken Schrader	Chevy
11.	Chad Little	Pont.
12.	Geoff Bodine	Ford
13.	Dick Trickle	Ford
14.	Derrike Cope	Pont.
15.	Brett Bodine	Ford
16.	Jeremy Mayfield	Ford
17.	Hut Stricklin	Ford
18.	Lake Speed	Ford
19.	Johnny Benson	Pont.
20.	Bobby Hamilton	Pont.
21.	Steve Grissom	Chevy
22.	Robby Gordon	Chevy
23.	Joe Nemechek	Chevy
24.	Kenny Wallace	Ford
25.	Gary Bradberry	Ford
26.	Darrell Waltrip	Chevy
27.	Ward Burton	Pont.
28.	Jimmy Spencer	Ford
29.	Ted Musgrave	Ford
30.	Dale Earnhardt	Chevy
31.	Ricky Craven	Chevy
32.	Kyle Petty	Pont.
33.	Ernie Irvan	Ford
34.	Rick Mast	Ford
35.	Lance Hooper	Pont.
36.	Mike Skinner	Chevy
37.	John Andretti	Ford
38.	Jeff Purvis	Chevy
39.	Jeff Green	Chevy
40.	Sterling Marlin	Chevy
41.	Wally Dallenbach	Chevy
42.	Todd Bodine	Chevy
43.	Rusty Wallace	Ford

RACE 24—EXIDE NASCAR SELECT BATTERIES 400

Richmond
Richmond, Virginia
Sept. 6
Winner: Dale Jarrett

Jarrett slipped past Jeff Burton with 40 laps remaining to claim his second straight short-track victory and fifth win of the season . . . once he made the pass, Jarrett just pulled away the rest of the race, eventually winning by 1.790 seconds over Burton . . . the win was his 13th career Winston Cup victory . . . moved up from 23rd on the starting grid on the 3/4-mile track . . . remained in third in the season's Winston Cup standings, but gained 15 points on leader Jeff Gordon . . . credits his crew and his ability to ease through traffic as the keys to

victory . . . Burton led the most laps, leading three times for 234 laps . . . Jarrett averages a track-record 108.707 mph while winning.

Exide NASCAR Select Batteries 400

Average speed: 108.707 mph (new track record)
Time of race: 2 hours, 45 minutes, 35 seconds (new track record)
Margin of victory: 1.790 secconds

FINISH	DRIVER	CAR
1.	Dale Jarrett	Ford
2.	Jeff Burton	Ford
3.	Jeff Gordon	Chevy
4.	Geoff Bodine	Ford
5.	Rusty Wallace	Ford
6.	Joe Nemechek	Chevy
7.	Ward Burton	Pont.
8.	Kenny Irwin Jr.	Ford
9.	Ted Musgrave	Ford
10.	Jeremy Mayfield	Ford
11.	Jimmy Spencer	Ford
12.	Steve Grissom	Chevy
13.	Johnny Benson	Pont.
14.	Ken Schrader	Chevy
15.	Dale Earnhardt	Chevy
16.	Derrike Cope	Pont.
17.	Terry Labonte	Chevy
18.	Ricky Craven	Chevy
19.	Dick Trickle	Ford
20.	Kyle Petty	Pont.
21.	Brett Bodine	Ford
22.	John Andretti	Ford
23.	Ernie Irvan	Ford
24.	Kenny Wallace	Ford
25.	Mark Martin	Ford
26.	Rick Mast	Ford
27.	Hut Stricklin	Ford
28.	Ricky Rudd	Ford
29.	Mike Skinner	Chevy
30.	Bill Elliott	Ford
31.	Jeff Green	Chevy
32.	Darrell Waltrip	Chevy
33.	Lance Hooper	Pont.
34.	Bobby Labonte	Pont.
35.	Michael Waltrip	Ford
36.	Lake Speed	Ford
37.	David Green	Chevy
38.	Bobby Hamilton	Pont.
39.	Sterling Marlin	Chevy
40.	Chad Little	Pont.
41.	Wally Dallenbach	Chevy
42.	Robby Gordon	Chevy

RACE 25—CMT 300

New Hampshire International Speedway
Loudon, New Hampshire
Sept. 14
Winner: Jeff Gordon.

Gordon's 10th victory of the year wasn't particularly dramatic, but it was typical Gordon: run near the front for the first half of the race, then make a move and rely on crew chief Ray Evernham and the "Rainbow Warriors" for sharp pit work . . . Gordon became the first driver to log consecutive 10-win Winston Cup seasons since Darrell Waltrip in 1981-82 . . . Gordon edged Ernie Irvan by 0.209 of a second . . . Bobby Hamilton was third, followed by Steve Grissom and Gordon's Hendrick Motorsports teammate, Ricky Craven . . . Craven, a native of Maine, was a popular front-runner, leading 61 laps early in the race. Craven led a total of 85 laps . . . Gordon paced the most laps, 137 of 300, but he didn't lead until lap 149 . . . Irvan passed him on lap 223, but three laps later the third caution flag of the race was unfurled when Hut Stricklin spun . . . Gordon led the rest of the way to extend his points lead over Mark Martin to 139 . . . pole-sitter Ken Schrader was 37th.

CMT 300

Average speed: 100.376 mph
Time of race: 3 hours, 9 minutes, 44 seconds
Margin of victory: 0.209 seconds

FINISH	DRIVER	CAR
1.	Jeff Gordon	Chevy
2.	Ernie Irvan	Ford
3.	Bobby Hamilton	Pont.
4.	Steve Grissom	Chevy
5.	Ricky Craven	Chevy
6.	Dale Jarrett	Ford
7.	Jimmy Spencer	Ford
8.	Dale Earnhardt	Chevy
9.	Mark Martin	Ford
10.	Hut Stricklin	Ford
11.	Bill Elliott	Ford
12.	Kyle Petty	Pont.
13.	Joe Nemechek	Chevy
14.	Jeff Burton	Ford
15.	Bobby Labonte	Pont.
16.	Geoff Bodine	Ford
17.	John Andretti	Ford
18.	Lake Speed	Ford
19.	Johnny Benson	Pont.
20.	Rick Mast	Ford
21.	Rusty Wallace	Ford
22.	Derrike Cope	Pont.
23.	Dick Trickle	Ford
24.	Ward Burton	Pont.
25.	Robby Gordon	Chevy
26.	Jeremy Mayfield	Ford
27.	Kenny Wallace	Ford
28.	Chad Little	Pont.
29.	Dave Marcis	Chevy
30.	Ted Musgrave	Ford
31.	Wally Dallenbach	Chevy
32.	Darrell Waltrip	Chevy
33.	Brett Bodine	Ford
34.	Gary Bradberry	Ford
35.	Mike Skinner	Chevy
36.	Michael Waltrip	Ford
37.	Ken Schrader	Chevy
38.	Jeff Green	Chevy
39.	Sterling Marlin	Chevy
40.	David Green	Chevy
41.	Terry Labonte	Chevy
42.	Ricky Rudd	Ford
43.	Robert Pressley	Ford

RACE 26—MBNA 400

Dover Downs International Speedway
Dover, Delaware
Sept. 21
Winner: Mark Martin.

Dale Earnhardt enjoys a lighter moment at Dover.

At the end of the first 400-miler at Dover's "Monster Mile," Martin was saying nice things about Jack Roush, and not just because Roush is his boss. Martin credited Roush for the successful fuel strategy that gave the Arkansas native his fourth win of the season and 22nd of his Winston Cup career . . . the race evolved into a two-driver battle: Martin led four times for 194 laps; Kyle Petty was in front three times for 191 laps . . . Petty, who led Martin by as much as 15 seconds late in the race, had to pit for fuel on lap 380 while Martin stayed on the track . . . Petty, driving a Pontiac, finished third in his best finish of the season . . . Dale Earnhardt, still winless in his last 53 races but improving in the second half of '97, was runnerup, a distant 10.334 seconds behind Martin . . . After the race, Jeff Gordon's advantage in the points race was 105 points over Martin.

MBNA 400

Average speed: 142.719 mph
Time of race: 3. hours, 50 seconds
Margin of victory: 10.334 seconds

FINISH	DRIVER	CAR
1.	Mark Martin	Ford
2.	Dale Earnhardt	Chevy
3.	Kyle Petty	Pont.
4.	Bobby Labonte	Pont.
5.	Dale Jarrett	Ford
6.	Ricky Rudd	Ford
7.	Jeff Gordon	Chevy

8.	Bill Elliott	Ford
9.	Ernie Irvan	Ford
10.	Rick Mast	Ford
11.	Jeff Burton	Ford
12.	Ken Schrader	Chevy
13.	Bobby Hamilton	Pont.
14.	Geoff Bodine	Ford
15.	John Andretti	Ford
16.	Rusty Wallace	Ford
17.	Hut Stricklin	Ford
18.	Dick Trickle	Ford
19.	Mike Skinner	Chevy
20.	Joe Nemechek	Chevy
21.	Steve Grissom	Chevy
22.	Ward Burton	Pont.
23.	Jeremy Mayfield	Ford
24.	Ted Musgrave	Ford
25.	David Green	Chevy
26.	Brett Bodine	Ford
27.	Sterling Marlin	Chevy
28.	Johnny Benson	Pont.
29.	Chad Little	Pont.
30.	Derrike Cope	Pont.
31.	Morgan Shepherd	Pont.
32.	Darrell Waltrip	Chevy
33.	Robby Gordon	Chevy
34.	Dave Marcis	Chevy
35.	Gary Bradberry	Ford
36.	Jimmy Spencer	Ford
37.	Terry Labonte	Chevy
38.	Kenny Wallace	Ford
39.	Robert Pressley	Ford
40.	Jeff Green	Chevy
41.	Ricky Craven	Chevy
42.	Michael Waltrip	Ford

RACE 27—HANES 500

Martinsville Speedway
Martinsville, Virginia
Sept. 29
Winner: Jeff Burton

It wasn't exactly a hometown victory, but it was as close as he could get . . . Burton, from 80 miles away in South Boston, Virginia, beat Dale Earnhardt, Bobby Hamilton, Jeff Gordon, and Bill Elliott in the last of the year's six short-track races . . . Driving the No. 99 Ford, he led three times for 92 of the 500 laps, including the final 22 after Rusty Wallace was black-flagged for jumping the restart after the day's last caution period . . . Wallace, who led three times for 225 laps, finished 15th, the last driver on the lead lap after his stop-and-go penalty under green . . . Pole-sitter Ward Burton, the winner's brother, led four times for 71 laps before finishing seventh in the race, rescheduled for Monday after day-long rain Sunday.

Hanes 500

Average speed: 73.078 mph
Time of race: 3 hours, 35 minutes, 56 seconds
Margin of victory: 0.778 seconds

FINISH	DRIVER	CAR
1.	Jeff Burton	Ford
2.	Dale Earnhardt	Chevy

3.	Bobby Hamilton	Pont.
4.	Jeff Gordon	Chevy
5.	Bill Elliott	Ford
6.	Kenny Wallace	Ford
7.	Ward Burton	Pont.
8.	Ricky Craven	Chevy
9.	Ken Schrader	Chevy
10.	Ernie Irvan	Ford
11.	Mark Martin	Ford
12.	Dale Jarrett	Ford
13.	Ricky Rudd	Ford
14.	Lake Speed	Ford
15.	Rusty Wallace	Ford
16.	Hut Stricklin	Ford
17.	Brett Bodine	Ford
18.	Jeremy Mayfield	Ford
19.	Johnny Benson	Pont.
20.	David Green	Chevy
21.	Ted Musgrave	Ford
22.	Terry Labonte	Chevy
23.	Rick Mast	Ford
24.	Darrell Waltrip	Chevy
25.	Joe Nemechek	Chevy
26.	Kyle Petty	Pont.
27.	Bobby Labonte	Pont.
28.	Geoff Bodine	Ford
29.	John Andretti	Ford
30.	Jeff Green	Chevy
31.	Mike Skinner	Chevy
32.	Michael Waltrip	Ford
33.	Jimmy Spencer	Ford
34.	Wally Dallenbach	Chevy
35.	Chad Little	Pont.
36.	Derrike Cope	Pont.
37.	Kenny Irwin	Ford
38.	Robert Pressley	Ford
39.	Sterling Marlin	Chevy
40.	Steve Grissom	Chevy
41.	Steve Park	Chevy
42.	Dick Trickle	Ford

RACE 28—GM/UAW TEAMWORK 500

Charlotte Motor Speedway
Concord, North Carolina
Oct. 5
Winner: Dale Jarrett

Despite getting his sixth victory, Jarrett didn't gain much ground on Jeff Gordon and Mark Martin for the series championship . . . Jarrett's No. 88 Ford led five times for 85 laps (including the final 57) in winning ahead of outside pole-sitter Bobby Labonte, Dale Earnhardt, Martin, and Gordon . . . Pole-sitter Geoff Bodine crashed out early, along with Jimmy Spencer and Ricky Rudd . . . Labonte led the most laps (three time for 144) as Pontiacs continued to show well after recent rules changes . . . And Earnhardt flashed signs of renewed life, leading three times for 31 laps and hanging with the leaders all afternoon . . . Jarrett's car was best on long green-flag runs, and the final 163 caution-free laps played into his hands perfectly.

WALTRIP'S STREAK ENDS

Darrell Waltrip was 716-for-716 when he arrived at the Charlotte Motor Speedway for the UAW-GW Teamwork 500 in October of 1997. Never in his long and illustrious career had the three-time Winston Cup champion (and 84-race winner) failed to qualify for a Winston Cup race. He'd missed a handful because of injuries and taken provisionals to start some others, but never had he failed to qualify one way or another.

Until Oct. 2, that is.

Somewhat typically for that stage in his career, Waltrip was only 48th-fastest out of 50 in the first qualifying session on Wednesday night. Since the second qualifying session was scheduled for the heat of Thursday afternoon, hardly anyone thought any of the drivers relegated to the second session would crack the top 38 and make the field on speed.

That meant Waltrip could stand on his Wednesday night time and feel secure about getting a past champion's provisional into the 500-mile. The only problem was that Kenny Wallace, Lake Speed, and Ernie Irvan went out and qualified faster than anybody expected them to.

Their unexpected success dropped 36th-fastest Terry Labonte down to 39th, one position outside the all-important top 38. Suddenly, Waltrip's 716-for-716 streak was in jeopardy because Labonte was eligible for the past champion's provisional that Waltrip had been counting on. And when NASCAR doled out its owner-point provisionals a few minutes later, they went to Jeremy Mayfield, Kyle Petty, Bobby Hamilton, and Ricky Craven.

And there was Waltrip, on the outside looking in, speechless. Both, it should be noted, for the first time in his career.

GM/UAW Teamwork 500

Average speed: 144.323 miles per hour
Time of race: 3 hour, 28 minutes, 17 seconds
Margin of victory: 4.142 seconds

FINISH	DRIVER	CAR
1.	Dale Jarrett	Ford
2.	Bobby Labonte	Pont.
3.	Dale Earnhardt	Chevy
4.	Mark Martin	Ford
5.	Jeff Gordon	Chevy
6.	Jeff Burton	Ford
7.	Bill Elliott	Ford
8.	Ward Burton	Pont.
9.	Kyle Petty	Pont.
10.	Johnny Benson	Pont.
11.	Terry Labonte	Ford
12.	Rusty Wallace	Ford
13.	Steve Grissom	Chevy
14.	Dick Trickle	Ford
15.	Ken Schrader	Chevy
16.	Joe Nemechek	Chevy
17.	Ted Musgrave	Ford
18.	Ernie Irvan	Ford
19.	Rick Wilson	Ford
20.	Sterling Marlin	Chevy
21.	Bobby Hamilton	Pont.
22.	Morgan Shepherd	Pont.
23.	Chad Little	Pont.
24.	Michael Waltrip	Ford
25.	Ricky Craven	Chevy
26.	Todd Bodine	Chevy
27.	Jeremy Mayfield	Ford
28.	Kenny Wallace	Ford
29.	Jeff Green	Chevy
30.	Brett Bodine	Ford
31.	David Green	Chevy
32.	John Andretti	Ford
33.	Derrike Cope	Pont.
34.	Gary Bradberry	Chevy
35.	Hut Stricklin	Ford
36.	Robert Pressley	Ford
37.	Wally Dallenbach	Chevy
38.	Lake Speed	Ford
39.	Jeff Purvis	Chevy
40.	Kevin Lepage	Chevy
41.	Ricky Rudd	Ford
42.	Jimmy Spencer	Ford
43.	Geoff Bodine	Ford

RACE 29—DIEHARD 500

Talladega Superspeedway
Talladega, Alabama
Oct. 12
Winner: Terry Labonte

The defending series champion got his first 1997 victory by passing his brother, Bobby, and Ken Schrader in the final laps . . . All told, 16 drivers swapped the lead 32 times in a race marked by a backstretch accident that eliminated or heavily damaged almost two dozen cars, including points-leader Jeff Gordon, second-place Mark Martin, and third-place Dale Jarrett . . . Labonte was making his first start with new crew chief Randy Dorton, who replaced Gary DeHart after the Charlotte race . . . The No. 5 Chevrolet qualified sixth and stayed among the leaders all afternoon . . . Labonte won ahead of his brother, Bobby, with John Andretti, Schrader, and pole-sitter Ernie Irvan the rest of the top five.

DieHard 500

Average speed: 156.601 miles per hour
Time of race: 3 hours, 11 minutes, 36 seconds
Margin of victory: .146 of a second

FINISH	DRIVER	CAR
1.	Terry Labonte	Chevy
2.	Bobby Labonte	Pont.
3.	John Andretti	Ford
4.	Ken Schrader	Chevy
5.	Ernie Irvan	Ford
6.	Ricky Craven	Chevy
7.	Kyle Petty	Pont.
8.	Geoff Bodine	Ford
9.	Rick Mast	Ford
10.	Rusty Wallace	Ford
11.	Ted Musgrave	Ford
12.	Morgan Shepherd	Pont.
13.	Bill Elliott	Ford
14.	Jeff Burton	Ford
15.	Kenny Wallace	Ford
16.	David Green	Chevy
17.	Kevin Lepage	Chevy
18.	Derrike Cope	Pont.
19.	Johnny Benson	Pont.
20.	Bobby Hamilton	Pont.
21.	Dale Jarrett	Ford
22.	Brett Bodine	Ford
23.	Dick Trickle	Ford
24.	Jimmy Spencer	Ford
25.	Dave Marcis	Chevy
26.	Jeremy Mayfield	Ford
27.	Robert Pressley	Ford
28.	Michael Waltrip	Ford
29.	Dale Earnhardt	Chevy
30.	Mark Martin	Ford
31.	Joe Nemechek	Chevy
32.	Steve Grissom	Chevy
33.	Mike Skinner	Chevy
34.	Ricky Rudd	Ford
35.	Jeff Gordon	Chevy
36.	Lake Speed	Ford
37.	Darrell Waltrip	Chevy
38.	Sterling Marlin	Chevy
39.	Greg Sacks	Chevy
40.	Chad Little	Pont.
41.	Wally Dallenbach	Chevy
42.	Billy Standridge	Ford

RACE 30—AC DELCO 400

North Carolina Motor Speedway
Rockingham, North Carolina
Oct. 27
Winner: Bobby Hamilton

Hamilton's second career victory came almost a year after his first, and like that one at Phoenix, this one came on a one-mile track . . . A late caution helped Hamilton, whose Richard Petty-owned Pontiac was fast on short runs with fresh tires . . . Until Greg Sacks stalled, it looked like Dale Jarrett and Ricky Craven might finish 1-2 ahead of Hamilton . . . After each took four tires, Craven passed Jarrett for the lead, then Hamilton and the No. 43 Pontiac passed them both and drove off . . . Jarrett passed Craven for second on the last lap, with points-leader Jeff Gordon fourth and Dick Trickle fifth

after winning a stirring late-race battle with a none-too-happy Mark Martin . . . The race was run on Monday morning, following rain on Sunday.

AC Delco 400

Average speed: 121.730 miles per hour
Time of race: 3 hours, 17 minutes, 00 seconds
Margin of victory: .941 of a second

FINISH	DRIVER	CAR
1.	Bobby Hamilton	Pont.
2.	Dale Jarrett	Ford
3.	Ricky Craven	Chevy
4.	Jeff Gordon	Chevy
5.	Dick Trickle	Ford
6.	Mark Martin	Ford
7.	Terry Labonte	Chevy
8.	Dale Earnhardt	Chevy
9.	Sterling Marlin	Chevy
10.	Joe Nemechek	Chevy
11.	Bobby Labonte	Pont.
12.	Bill Elliott	Ford
13.	Robert Pressley	Ford
14.	Michael Waltrip	Ford
15.	Jeremy Mayfield	Ford
16.	Chad Little	Pont.
17.	Lake Speed	Ford
18.	Rusty Wallace	Ford
19.	Geoff Bodine	Ford
20.	Derrike Cope	Pont.
21.	Jeff Green	Chevy
22.	Kyle Petty	Pont.
23.	Mike Skinner	Chevy
24.	Steve Grissom	Chevy
25.	Hut Stricklin	Ford
26.	Ward Burton	Pont.
27.	David Green	Chevy
28.	Ernie Irvan	Ford
29.	Darrell Waltrip	Chevy
30.	Ken Schrader	Chevy
31.	John Andretti	Ford
32.	Ted Musgrave	Ford
33.	Steve Park	Chevy
34.	Morgan Shepherd	Pont.
35.	Wally Dallenbach	Chevy
36.	Johnny Benson	Pont.
37.	Kenny Wallace	Ford
38.	Jeff Burton	Ford
39.	Greg Sacks	Chevy
40.	Ricky Rudd	Ford
41.	Gary Bradberry	Ford
42.	Rick Mast	Ford
43.	Jimmy Spencer	Ford

RACE 31—DURA-LUBE 500

Phoenix International Raceway
Phoenix, Arizona
November 2
Winner: Dale Jarrett

In the next-to-last race at Phoenix, Jarrett stormed back from 17th, with 174 laps remaining, to win his career-high seventh race of the season . . . Jarrett passed Rusty Wallace on lap 240 of the 312-lap race . . . Gordon, hampered by handling and tire problems, placed 17th and saw his points lead over Jarrett trimmed to 77 . . . Jar-

Lake Speed's day is over at the 1997 Daytona 500.

rett actually leapfrogged over Mark Martin and into second place in the standings . . . it was Gordon's second flat tire in three races . . . Wallace led the most laps, twice for 117 . . . Bobby Hamilton, Ken Schrader, and Dale Earnhardt rounded out the top five.

Dure-Lube 500

Average speed: 110.824 mph
Time of race: 2 hours, 48 minutes, 54 seconds
Margin of victory: 2.105-seconds

FINISH	DRIVER	CAR
1.	Dale Jarrett	Ford
2.	Rusty Wallace	Ford
3.	Bobby Hamilton	Pontiac
4.	Ken Schrader	Chevrolet
4.	Dale Earnhardt	Chevrolet
6.	Mark Martin	Ford
7.	Johnny Benson	Pontiac
8.	Steve Grissom	Chevrolet
9.	Kyle Petty	Pontiac
10.	Geoff Bodine	Ford
11.	Terry Labonte	Chevrolet
12.	Darrell Waltrip	Chevrolet
13.	Jeff Burton	Ford
14.	Jimmy Spencer	Ford
14.	Bill Elliott	Ford
16.	Derrike Cope	Pontiac
17.	Jeff Gordon	Chevrolet
18.	Ernie Irvan	Ford
19.	Jeremy Mayfield	Ford
20.	Kenny Irwin	Ford
21.	Greg Sacks	Chevrolet
22.	Ted Musgrave	Ford
23.	Bobby Labonte	Pontiac
24.	Joe Nemechek	Chevrolet
25.	Chad Little	Pontiac
26.	Michael Waltrip	Ford
27.	Sterling Marlin	Chevrolet
28.	Mike Skinner	Chevrolet
29.	David Green	Chevrolet
30.	Hut Stricklin	Ford
31.	Rick Mast	Ford
32.	Jeff Green	Chevrolet
33.	Brett Bodine	Ford
34.	Dave Marcis	Chevrolet
34.	Kenny Wallace	Ford
36.	Ricky Rudd	Ford
37.	Lake Speed	Ford
38.	Robert Pressley	Ford
39.	John Andretti	Ford
40.	Dick Trickle	Ford
41.	Steve Park	Chevrolet
42.	Ward Burton	Pontiac
43.	Ricky Craven	Chevrolet

RACE 32—NAPA 500

Atlanta Motor Speedway
Atlanta, Georgia
November 16
Winner: Bobby Labonte

Gordon maintained the suspense in the season finale at Atlanta . . . he needed to finish 18th or higher to clinch his second points championship in three years . . . qualifying was rained out on Friday . . . before qualifying on Saturday, Gordon was scuffing the tires on his Chevrolet when he lost control and struck Bobby Hamilton's car on pit road . . . forced to switch to a backup car, Gordon qualified a disappointing 37th . . . he still managed to finish 17th, while Jarrett and Martin were second and third respectively . . . Gordon's final points margin was just 14 over Jarrett and 29   over Martin . . . it was the closes three-way finish in Winston Cup history . . . Gordon celebrated by dancing on the roof of his Du Pont Automotive Finishes Chevy . . . Bobby Labonte won the race for the second year in a row.

NAPA 500

Average speed: 159.904 mph
Time of race: 3 hours, 7 minutes, 48 seconds
Margin of victory: 3.801 seconds

FINISH	DRIVER	CAR
1.	Bobby Labonte	Pontiac
2.	Dale Jarrett	Ford
3.	Mark Martin	Ford
4.	Jeff Green	Chevrolet
4.	Derrike Cope	Pontiac
6.	Kyle Petty	Pontiac
7.	Bobby Hamilton	Pontiac
8.	Joe Nemechek	Chevrolet
9.	Ward Burton	Pontiac
10.	Johnny Benson	Pontiac
11.	Sterling Marlin	Chevrolet
12.	Ernie Irvan	Ford
13.	Michael Waltrip	Ford
14.	Dick Trickle	Ford
14.	Steve Park	Chevrolet
16.	Dale Earnhardt	Chevrolet
17.	Jeff Gordon	Chevrolet
18.	Chad Little	Pontiac
19.	Jeremy Mayfield	Ford
20.	Ken Schrader	Chevrolet
21.	Terry Labonte	Chevrolet
22.	John Andretti	Ford
23.	Mike Skinner	Chevrolet
24.	Jimmy Spencer	Ford
24.	Kenny Irwin	Ford
26.	Lake Speed	Ford
27.	Morgan Shepherd	Pontiac
28.	Steve Grissom	Chevrolet
29.	Kevin Lepage	Chevrolet
30.	Kenny Wallace	Ford
31.	Ted Musgrave	Ford
32.	Rusty Wallace	Ford
33.	Geoff Bodine	Ford
34.	Jeff Burton	Ford
34.	Rick Mast	Ford
36.	Bill Elliott	Ford
37.	Ricky Rudd	Ford
38.	Wally Dallenbach	Chevrolet
39.	Ricky Craven	Chevrolet
40.	Darrell Waltrip	Chevrolet
41.	Brett Bodine	Ford
42.	Gary Bradberry	Ford
43.	Buckshot Jones	Pontiac

12

TWENTY EVENTS THAT CHANGED NASCAR

1. THE BIRTH OF NASCAR IN DAYTONA BEACH

Stock car racing was unkempt and ill-mannered until part-time racer and full-time promoter Bill France, Sr. stepped into the breech. On Dec. 14, 1947, shortly after his National Championship Stock Car Circuit ended its inaugural season, he chaired a three-day meeting at the Streamline Hotel in Daytona Beach to unite warring factions. When the meeting adjourned, NASCAR was established with a uniform set of rules, a points system designed to crown a single national champion, a driver's benevolent fund, and a full schedule of Modified races for 1948.

2. THE FIRST STRICTLY STOCK RACE

It took Bill France, Sr. 15 months to realize the public wanted to see racing among passengers cars like those they drove. His Modified series had thrived in 1948, but "Strictly Stock" hadn't come close to catching on. Never one to duck a challenge, France scheduled a 200-lapper for street-legal, showroom-stock, family cars on June 19, 1949, on a 3/4-mile dirt track in Charlotte, North Carolina. It carried a $5,000 purse, attracted a full

33-car field, and drew upwards of 15,000 fans. It was that last figure that convinced France that "Strictly Stock"—later renamed Grand National, then Winston Cup—might just make it after all.

3. HAROLD BRASINGTON BUILDS DARLINGTON SPEEDWAY

It's been said the most dangerous race fan in American is one with 100 acres and a bulldozer. Harold Brasington, a peanut farmer from Darlington, South Carolina, didn't have 100 acres, but he had earth-moving equipment and enough money to buy some land west of town. In 1948, after returning from the Indianapolis 500, he began building Darlington Raceway and planning NASCAR's first 500-mile race. More than 25,000 fans watched Johnny Mantz win the inaugural Southern 500 on Labor Day of 1950, a race that quieted those who said stock cars couldn't run 500 miles.

4. THE SHORT-LIVED PRESENCE OF CARL KIEKHAEFER

Even though millionaire Carl Kiekhaefer was in stock car racing for only two seasons, he had an enormous impact. He was the first owner to: 1) field

IT'S A FAMILY AFFAIR

Never has a Daytona 500 had the heart-stirring emotion of the 1988 race. Its finish featured a 48-year-old veteran in the No. 22 Buick Regal against a 25-year-old upstart in the No. 28 Ford Thunderbird.

They raced hard throughout the final handful of laps, neither giving an inch and neither taking anything that wasn't rightfully his. The younger driver made a bold move to pass his more-experienced rival in the last turn on the last lap, but came up several car-lengths short. At the end, the 48-year-old former champion had his third and last Daytona 500 triumph (it turned to be the last of his 83 career victories) and the 25-year-old upstart had a memory he'd never forget.

And when it was over, Davey Allison walked to victory lane at Daytona International Speedway to hug and congratulate his father Bobby on a victory well-earned and a family moment to be savored for all time.

---

multiple entries, ranging between two and seven cars for most of two years; 2) transport his cars in enclosed trailers, similiar to the rigs used today; 3) outfit team members in matching uniforms; 4) demand discipline and dignity from his employees; and 5) bring a major national sponsor to the sport.

With high-visibility backing from his own Mercury Marine Outboards company, his well-financed, well-prepared, and expertly-driven cars won 52 of 90 races in the 1955 and 1956 seasons. Many have said he was 30 years ahead of his time, that the approach he used in the 1950s was similiar to that of modern-era owners Rick Hendrick, Jack Roush, Robert Yates, and Felix Sabates. More than anything, Kiekhaefer showed that nothing was impossible to someone with deep pockets.

5. THE OPENING OF DAYTONA INTERNATIONAL SPEEDWAY

It took Bill France, Sr. six years to plan, finance, and build the Daytona International Speedway. As early as 1953, while successfully promoting events on the beach/highway course south of Daytona Beach, he longed for a permanent, paved superspeedway on the mainland. He didn't have $3 million to build it himself and the city failed in repeated attempts to sell municipal bonds.

Finally, in November of 1957, France created a corporation and scraped up $27,000 for a down payment toward a 50-year lease of 450 acres west of the local airport. He designed the speedway with high-banked turns and a D-shaped frontstretch, using dirt from a 44-acre infield lake for the banking. The first Daytona 500 in 1959 saw Lee Petty and Johnny Beauchamp in a photo finish, and NASCAR spent three days poring over still and movie pictures before deciding that Petty was the winner.

6. NASCAR'S FIRST SUPER SPEEDWAY BUILDING BOOM

Darlington Raceway opened in 1950 and Daytona International Speedway nine years later, and hardly anyone could dare call that a meaningful growth spurt. But two high-profile superspeedways and a popular short track opened in the early 60s, giving the fledgling NASCAR series three more places to run.

The 1½-mile Charlotte Motor Speedway opened on June 19, 1960 with an unprecedented 400-lap, 600-mile race. Six weeks later, south of Atlanta in rural Hampton, Georgia, the 1½-mile Atlanta International Raceway opened with a 200-lap, 300-mile race. Charlotte and Atlanta were important because they reinforced the growing feeling that stock car racing was more than just a passing fancy. A year later, in extreme eastern Tennessee, the half-mile Bristol Raceway opened with a 500-lap race, an annual event that has become one of the most popular on the circuit.

7. RICHARD PETTY'S 27-WIN SEASON OF 1967

Richard Petty was an full-blown star when the 1967 season rolled around. Perhaps appropriately, he

The 1964 Plymouth that Richard Petty drove to victory at Daytona.

got his 49th career victory in that year's opening race, then added 26 more victories in the next 10 months. His unprecedented assault on the record book showed 27 wins in 48 starts, 11 other top-fives, one more top-10, and 31 front-row qualifying efforts.

But he was more than just a big winner and the series champion. His easy-going manner, boyish appearance, and warm relationship with fans made him NASCAR's most popular star. He became stock car racing's best goodwill ambassador, the perfect driver to deliver the sport into the consciousness of the country.

8. NASCAR'S SECOND SUPER SPEEDWAY BUILDING BOOM

By 1968, fully 20 years after it was incorporated, NASCAR still had only six paved superspeedways: Atlanta, Charlotte, Darlington, Daytona Beach, Rockingham, North Carolina (a 1-mile track opened in 1965), the 2.52-mile road course at Riverside, California, and the 1½-mile track at Trenton, New Jersey. Most races were contested on paved tracks measuring between one-third and one-half mile, with a smattering of dirt tracks still on the schedule.

Things began changing in the late 1960s and continued into the early- to mid-'70s. A 2-mile track at Brooklyn, Michigan, opened in June of 1969 and a 1-mile track opened three weeks later in Dover, Delaware. In September, Bill France opened his new 2.66-mile track in eastern Alabama, near Talladega. Later that fall, a 2-mile track opened at College Station, Texas.

The boom continued in 1971, with a 2½-mile track opening in Ontario, California, just east of Los Angeles. The growth spurt finally topped out in 1974 when a 2½-mile track opened in Pocono, Pennsylvania, 85 miles north of Philadelphia and 100 miles from New York City.

Suddenly, stock car racing was gaining a foothold all over America. In addition to its Southern roots, the sport had two tracks on the West Coast. There was a huge track in Texas, another near car-crazy Detroit, and three in the Northeast. Truly, NASCAR racing was going big-time.

9. THE 1969 BOYCOTT AT TALLADEGA

Bill France, Sr. had survived one threat when he kept the Teamsters Union out of NASCAR in 1960. He faced another highly-visible, emotional challenge nine years later during the opening weekend at his 2.66-mile Alabama International Motor Speedway near Talladega.

There, in September, many of his top stars balked at running the Talladega 500. They said Firestone and Goodyear tires weren't built for 190 miles per hour, and asked France to postpone the race until better tires could be built. When he refused, many top drivers loaded up and went home. France filled the grid with a handful of front-line cars and several dozen backmarkers and Grand American cars. The race went off without incident, perhaps because France ordered caution periods often enough to prevent tire problems. An unknown driver named Richard Brickhouse won at 153.778 mph, almost 46 mph slower than Charlie Glotzbach's pole speed.

10. THE R.J. REYNOLDS CO. BECOMES SERIES SPONSOR

Without meaning to, a decision by federal lawmakers may have given stock car racing one of its biggest boosts. In 1969, inspired by medical research linking tobacco to cancer, the Food and Drug Administration urged Congress to ban all tobacco advertising on television. The ban went into effect in 1970, and within weeks, team owner Junior Johnson went to Winston-Salem, North Carolina, to ask the R.J. Reynolds Co. to spend its television budget on his race team.

RJR did better than that—it decided to sponsor the entire series. Within a year—at RJR's urg-ing—the schedule was reduced from between 45 and 50 races to approximately 30, each carrying equal weight toward the championship. NASCAR dropped the name "Grand National" and renamed its premier division "Winston Cup" in gratitude for the $100,000 RJR poured into the 1971 post-season point fund. All told, the company has poured $37.2 million into the point fund since 1971 and spent perhaps that much more on special events and promotions.

It may not be a marriage made in heaven, but it doesn't miss it by much.

11. BILL FRANCE, SR. RETIRES IN 1972

In January of 1972, after heading up the world's most successful sanctioning body for 25 years, Bill France, Sr. retired as president of NASCAR. He handed the keys to sons Bill and Jim, and moved over to the International Speedway Corporation, parent company of the family-owned speedways in Daytona Beach and Talladega.

Much like the late Judge Kenesaw Mountain Landis in baseball and the late Pete Rozelle in football, Bill France led his sport through some of its most trying times. He brought order, discipline, and respectability in the early days when it didn't seem anyone could do that. He guided the sport through its infancy, withstood the Teamsters' threat in the early '60s, built massive speedways in Florida and Alabama, kept the Detroit automakers from having their way regarding rules, and introduced Corporate America to stock car racing.

12. THE FIRST LIVE, START-TO-FINISH TELECAST OF A NASCAR RACE

The 1979 Daytona 500 is most often mentioned as the turning point in national awareness and acceptance of stock car racing. On February 18, with CBS-TV broadcasting the race into every nook and cranny of America for the first time, leader Donnie Allison and second-place Cale Yarborough wrecked on the backstretch on the last lap. Seconds later, Richard Petty won his sixth Daytona 500 and Yarborough began fighting with Donnie and his brother, Bobby, on the apron in Turn 3.

With much of the East Coast forced inside by horrible weather, CBS's coverage of the 500 and its memorable finish exposed NASCAR to tens of millions of new fans. Those who chart such things still contend that the willingness of Corporate America to do business with NASCAR and its teams stemmed from that afternoon when the rest of the country discovered what the Southeast had known for years.

13. NASCAR TAKES ITS AWARDS BANQUET TO NEW YORK CITY

For years, stock car racing crowned its national champion and distributed its major awards each February during a modest little dinner in Daytona Beach during Speed Week. But in 1982 someone finally realized there was nothing special about doing it there when everybody had to be there anyway. So NASCAR brazenly took its banquet to New York City.

With the R.J. Reynolds Co. and team sponsors picking up most of the tab, drivers, crewmen, team owners, track operators, sponsor VIPs, and a handful of media gathered in December at The Waldorf-Astoria in midtown Manhattan. The event didn't attract much attention from the mainstream sports media, but the weekend was important because NASCAR had finally demonstrated that it was something more than a regional sport filled with rubes who didn't know one fork from another.

14. RICHARD PETTY'S 200TH CAREER VICTORY

NASCAR's most famous driver couldn't have picked a better stage for his final victory. Richard Petty had been chasing win number 200 since May of 1983, when he got his 197th at Talladega. He got 198 near Charlotte in the fall, a victory some felt was tainted because his car failed post-race tech inspection. But all was forgotten—if not totally forgiven—when Petty won 199 at Dover in June.

On July 4, at Daytona Beach, with President Ronald Reagan watching from Bill France's private suite, Petty posted career victory 200. He did it by surviving a late-race, side-by-side bumping duel with Cale Yarborough back around to the race-ending caution flag. Afterward, Petty went to France's suite to talk politics with Reagan. Almost overlooked in the hoopla was the fact that Yarborough mistakenly pitted on the last lap and handed second-place to Harry Gant.

15. THE FIRST WINSTON ALL-STAR RACE

Everybody else had an all-star game—baseball, basketball, hockey, and football—so why not NASCAR? That question led to a joint announcement in December of 1984 that NASCAR, the R.J. Reynolds Co., and Charlotte Motor Speedway would stage stock car racing's inaugural all-star race in May of 1985. The field was limited to the 12 drivers who'd won a Winston Cup race during 1984, and would be 70 laps around the 1½-mile track.

The race was run the day before the World 600 and was a good one. Darrell Waltrip passed Harry Gant on the last lap, then took the checkered flag an instant before his engine expired. (There was suspicion a'plenty that Waltrip intentionally blew the engine to keep inspectors from getting a good look.) Eleven of the 12 starters were running at the end, all of them on the lead lap.

A footnote: CMS promoter Humpy Wheeler chartered a jet to bring in several dozen writers from the Indianapolis Motor Speedway, scene of the next day's Indy 500. The move ensured widespread press coverage of the race.

16. BILL ELLIOTT WINS THE WINSTON MILLION

The groundwork for one of racing's greatest moments was laid in December of 1984 at the Winston Cup Awards Banquet in New York. There, in The Waldorf-Astoria, representatives of R.J. Reynolds Co. offered a $1 million bonus to anyone who could win three of the tour's Crown Jewel races: the Daytona 500, the Winston 500, the World 600, and the Southern 500.

Bill Elliott did it that very first summer in 1985, taking the Daytona 500 in February and the Winston 500 in May. He faltered badly at the World 600 in May, but won the Labor Day weekend Southern 500 when leader Cale Yarborough was forced into an unscheduled late-race pit stop for power steering repairs. Several days later, stock car racing got a mighty boost when Elliott was on the cover of *Sports Illustrated* magazine, a first for NASCAR racing. Twelve years later, Jeff Gordon duplicated Elliott's feat by winning at Daytona, Charlotte, and Darlington, but Elliot's win is the one that made NASCAR a national cover boy.

17. THE FIRST NIGHT RACE AT CHARLOTTE MOTOR SPEEDWAY

Bruton Smith and Humpy Wheeler have always been ahead of their time. Smith is the wealthy president of Charlotte Motor Speedway and Wheeler is his innovative promoter/general manager. They realized early-on that while television on Sunday afternoon was good for racing, television on prime time would be even better. To that end, they announced plans in 1992 to light their 1½-mile track so it would be suitable for nighttime telecasts.

Amidst great hype and hoopla, Musco Lighting of Iowa turned night into day for the 1992 Winston all-star race. In one of the most surreal few seconds in NASCAR history, leader Dale Earn-

Bill Elliott completed the Winston Million with this win at Darlington in the 1985 Southern 500.

hardt and second-place Kyle Petty banged together in Turn 3 on the last lap. That helped Davey Allison catch and pass Petty at the finish, a split-second before he crashed hard in Turn 1. If anyone had doubted the wisdom of lighting CMS, it was snuffed right then and there.

18. RICHARD PETTY RETIRES

It'll never rank up there with Lou Gehrig's farewell speech or Bob Cousy's tearful goodbye in Boston Garden, but Richard Petty's 1992 season-long "Fan Appreciation Tour" brought enormous publicity and deep emotion to stock car racing. The seven-time champion announced in 1991 that '92 would be his last season—although he'd always be around as owner and revered star and spokesman emeritus.

His last season was far from satisfying. He managed an outside pole in his final Daytona International Speedway appearance in July, but couldn't earn even one top-10 finish throughout the 29-race season. He crashed near the start of the season- and career-ending race outside Atlanta in November, but returned at half-speed in the final laps so he could be running at the finish.

Petty left records that likely will stand forever: 1,177 starts, 127 poles, 200 victories, 549 top-5 finishes, 693 top-10s, 7 championships, a 27-victory 1967 season, and a 10-race winning streak

Bruton Smith, president of Charlotte Motor Speedway, looks out over his track.

that same year. More importantly, he left 35 years of smiles and memories, figures not even Gehrig or Cousy could approach.

A footnote: an up-and-coming youngster began his Winston Cup career the same afternoon Petty closed his with a 35th-place run. The kid's name was Jeff Gordon, and he finished 31st.

19. THE FIRST BRICKYARD 400

When hell freezes over.

That was the date most people figured NASCAR would run a Winston Cup race at the Indianapolis Motor Speedway. Well, let the record show it happened on August 6, 1994, when more than 300,000 fans watched hometown hero Jeff Gordon make history by winning the 160-lap, 400-mile race.

It seemed natural that America's most popular racing series would race on the world's most famous track. But it might not have happened if NASCAR founder Bill France, Sr. and IMS savior Tony Hulman had still been alive to veto the deal. But their successors—Bill France, Jr. and Tony George—were more receptive, realizing the enormous potential of a stock car race at the Brickyard. In the end, the question remained: Who came out better, NASCAR or the Speedway?

Really, though, did it matter?

Jeff Gordon is the latest in NASCAR's seemingly endless supply of fan-friendly stars.

20. THE NEVER-ENDING PARADE OF STARS

It says here that NASCAR is so fabulously popular because it always has 8 to 10 American-born and reared drivers who possess star quality.

In the '50s, they were Lee Petty, Curtis Turner, the Flock brothers (Tim, Bob, and Fonty), Buck Baker, Herb Thomas, Fireball Roberts, Speedy Thompson, and Junior Johnson.

In the '60s, Richard Petty, Fred Lorenzen, the Allison brother (Donnie and Bobby), Bobby Isaac, David Pearson, Ned Jarrett, Dick Hutcherson, Marvin Panch, Jim Paschal, and the late Roberts, Joe Weatherly, and LeeRoy Yarbrough.

In the '70s, the Allisons, Petty, Pearson, Isaac, Cale Yarborough, Buddy Baker, Benny Parsons, and Darrell Waltrip.

In the '80s, Waltrip, Yarborough, Bobby Allison, Harry Gant, Dale Earnhardt, Neil Bonnett, Bill Elliott, Ricky Rudd, Geoff Bodine, Terry Labonte, Rusty Wallace, and the late Tim Richmond.

And in the '90s, Earnhardt, Elliott, Rudd, Bodine, Labonte, Wallace, Gant, Dale Jarrett, Ernie Irvan, Sterling Marlin, Mark Martin, and the late Davey Allison and Alan Kulwicki.

13

WHAT IS NASCAR?

What began 50 years ago as an innovative regional racing series created by one man has developed into the fastest growing sport in the United States. It also is a huge money-making and marketing machine.

How huge? Jim Andrews, vice president of the Chicago-based IEG Sponsorship Report, says that corporations will spend more than $440 million in NASCAR this year. Joyce Julius, president of Julius Associates, Inc., a sports marketing firm in Dearborn, Michigan, says the measured ad images from the Winston Cup series in 1996 were worth almost $900 million in sponsor exposure. NASCAR is big business. Really big business. NASCAR and the International Speedway Corp. are $2-billion-a-year businesses. ISC owns five racetracks: Daytona, Talladega, Darlington, Watkins Glen, and Phoenix.

Bill France, Sr. organized NASCAR, and his son, Bill Jr., has had the vision to take NASCAR out of the Southeast to tracks across the nation and into corporate boardrooms. Joe Gibbs, the former Washington Redskins coach, has been in the Winston Cup series since the early '90s. Referring to Bill France, Jr., Gibbs said, "One reason this sport is growing is, it's run by one person. You don't have

these board meetings that other sports have. It's one guy: here's the rules; if you don't like it, get out."

The Winston Cup series is stock car racing's major league and NASCAR's premier attraction. There will be 33 Winston Cup races in 1998, one more than a year ago. A race has been added at the Las Vegas Motor Speedway on March 1. In addition to Winston Cup, 11 other series race under NASCAR's umbrella. NASCAR sanctions about 2,000 events in these series, which produced purses of more than $70 million in 1997. The Busch Grand National series, in baseball terms the Triple A level of stock car racing, expanded from 26 to 30 races in '97. And the Craftsman Truck Series increased by one event, to 27. The other series under NASCAR are the Winston West; the Busch series, Grand National North; Featherlite Modified; Slim Jim All-Pro; Goody's Dash; Reb-Co Northwest Tour; Featherlite Southwest Tour; Busch All-Star Tour; and the Winston Racing Series.

Racing is what NASCAR does, but in the 1990s marketing and merchandising also are high priorities for the organization. Last year, NASCAR opened an office on Park Avenue in New York City and named Steve Schiffman, a former executive

LEAVING DAYTONA!?

Can you imagine stock car racing's most important event moving to Palm Beach, Florida? Or France, his family and their NASCAR empire moving farther south than it is now?

For a few days in 1953, it looked like it might happen.

NASCAR founder and long-time president Bill France was the guest of several Palm Beach civic and business leaders in the fall of 53. A few months earlier he had suggested that Daytona Beach help him build a 2.5-mile, high-banked paved track to host several major events each year. When he didn't see much hope for cooperation, he went to Palm Beach in a chartered DC-3.

He spent the day being wined and dined by civic and business leaders. They were willing (anxious, in fact) to make concessions for NASCAR and its annual Speed Week program to move from Daytona Beach to an oval near Boca Raton. And they wanted France to relocate NASCAR's offices to their area.

Ever the politician, France held his counsel. He told the Palm Beach group he couldn't give an answer on the spot, but promised one within days. In his heart he knew full well his trip to Palm Beach would generate great concern in Daytona Beach, where civic leaders saw Speed Week as the social and economic highlight of the winter.

France, of course, never seriously considered deserting his adopted hometown. He thanked the folks in Palm Beach and promptly turned his attention back to building his dream speedway—which finally opened six years later.

with Kraft Foods, as vice president of strategic marketing. NASCAR on Park Avenue: what would Fireball Roberts and the sport's other pioneers think? Schiffman directs sales efforts focusing on sponsorships. Schiffman works with Ken Clapp, who is vice president of marketing development. Clapp, a 20-year NASCAR employee, handles business with West Coast-based companies.

NASCAR Thunder stores, selling licensed NASCAR merchandise, have opened in Atlanta,

Bill France, Jr.

Louisville, Winston-Salem, Knoxville, Dallas, and Cincinnati. The first NASCAR Cafe restaurant opened in Myrtle Beach, South Carolina, with others on the way. There's more: the first NASCAR SpeedPark will be built in Las Vegas, enabling fans to race in go-kart type cars built by Roush Industries. The vehicles will resemble Winston Cup or Craftsman series trucks. NASCAR Silicon Motor Speedway, an interactive indoor driving center, opened in the Mall of America, in Bloomington, Minnesota, last September. The Silicon Motor Speedway features state-of-the-art stock car simulators that give fans an authentic racing experience at close to 200 mph. LBE Technologies, Inc., based in Cupertino, Calif., created the NASCAR Silicon Speedway. The NASCAR Online website is one of the nation's most popular, providing daily updates, features, and opportunities to chat with drivers, owners, and crew personnel.

Guiding all these coast-to-coast series and business ventures is Bill France, Jr. Learning every phase of racing from his father, "Big Bill," Bill Jr. keeps a firm hand on NASCAR. He isn't as visible as some commissioners in sports are, but everyone knows who runs NASCAR. Under his watch, Winston Cup racing continues to expand annually.

Daytona USA, a multi-million dollar attraction featuring interactive and historical exhibits, opened a few years ago on the grounds of Daytona International Speedway, and now draws close to 500,000 visitors yearly.

Talking about his father, Brian France, NASCAR's vice president of marketing and corporate communications, told *Racer Magazine:* "He knows how to build a race car, he understands the rule book (and) he's up on marketing. He's more well-rounded than anybody else in the business."

France is a vigorous 62, but he knows he can't continue forever as head of NASCAR. Waiting, and working, in the wings are Brian and his sister, Lesa Kennedy. Lesa is executive vice president of the International Speedway Corp. Like his father, Brian learned about racing from the ground up. When he was in high school, he visited Daytona International Speedway seeking a job. His grandfather, Bill France, Sr., advised him to walk around the grounds and check on anything that "wasn't working right." Brian made a list of problems. When he returned, his grandather said, "Great, now get started fixing all those things."

Brian and Lesa work well together. "Our skills are complementary," Lesa says. "Brian is very adept at the marketing side of the business." And Lesa, Brian says, "is probably a better organizer in terms of getting teams of people together."

While Lesa and Brian are considered frontrunners to succeed their father, the decision is not carved in a racing tire stashed somewhere in Daytona. Says Brian: "My father has said all along he's going to put the best person in charge to grow the sport. It may not necessarily be a France family member."

Brian attended the University of Central Florida. Lesa, an outstanding gymnast, graduated from Duke. Lesa and her husband, Bruce, a plastic surgeon, have a five-year-old son, Ben.

BIOGRAPHIES

Bill France, Jr.

Succeeded his father, NASCAR founder Bill France, Sr., in 1972 . . . growing up in the formative

Mike Helton

years of stock car racing, Bill Jr. learned every detail of the sport from his father . . . Bill Jr. has promoted, scored, and flagged races. He also raced in a few NASCAR events in the 1950s . . . also is chairman and chief executive officer of the International Speedway Corp., which owns the tracks at Daytona, Darlington, Talladega, Watkins Glen, and Phoenix . . . born in Washington, D.C . . . .when he was two, the family moved to Daytona Beach . . . .played basketball at Seabreeze High and attended the University of Florida . . . served two years in the Navy . . . enjoys fishing . . . he and his wife, Betty Jane, have two children: Lesa and Brian.

Jim France

President of the International Speedway Corp., and executive vice president and secretary of NASCAR . . . younger brother of Bill France Jr . . . .active in Legends racing series . . . '92 BF Goodrich Legends Cars national champion . . . formerly raced dirt bikes . . . strong supporter of motorcycle racing in the United States . . . was a starter for the U.S. Motorcycle Grand Prix in the late 1960s . . . served in the Army in Vietnam . . . he and his wife, Sharon, have three children: Jamie, Jennifer, and Amy.

Mike Helton

NASCAR's vice president for competition since January 1994 . . . formerly general manager and president of Talladega Superspeedway . . . began his career in racing as public relations director at Atlanta International Speedway in 1980 . . . born and raised in Bristol, Virginia . . . .graduate of King College in Bristol, Tennessee . . . .Helton, 44, and his wife, Lynda, have two children: Richey and Tina.

Gary Nelson

Winston Cup series director . . . from Redlands, California . . . .attracted to racing when he and friends would ride their dirt bikes 15 miles from their homes to Riverside International Raceway . . . learned about cars from his father, who fixed up used cars . . . began racing career "sweeping floors" for the DiGard team . . . worked his way up to crew chief . . . his teams won 21 races, including 16 with Bobby Allison as driver . . . won 1983 Winston Cup championship with Allison . . . joined NASCAR in 91 as successor to Dick Beaty . . .

Gary Nelson

Nelson, 44, and his wife, Christine, have two children: William and Zachary.

14

TRYIN' TO MAKE THE SHOW: BUSCH GRAND NATIONAL

Seems like every sport has it—a feeder system that uncovers the next young superstar and keeps talented newcomers heading to the big leagues. The National Football League has those Saturday afternoon semi-pro leagues (you know, the ones run by the NCAA) as its private training ground, a place to nurture and develop the next Troy Aikman, Barry Sanders, Bruce Smith, and Jerry Rice. It's worked pretty well for years and, best of all, it's free and wildly popular. Similarly, the National Basketball Association has big-time college hoops and, to a lesser extent, some minor leagues as its training ground. (Shame on you for thinking Michael and Patrick and Grant just floated down right out of high school).

And don't forget Major League Baseball and the National Hockey League—they have high schools, the NCAA, and their own minor league systems to find and train future talent. Almost everybody who's anybody has spent some time in the minors, waiting for the day they're called up to The Show.

But what about NASCAR and its major league Winston Cup series? Where will Bill France, Jr. find the next Dale Earnhardt or Jeff Gordon? How does big-time stock car racing develop the next wave of Ricky Rudds, Dale Jarretts, and Mark Mar-

tins? At a time when some NASCAR-watchers fear the supply of marketable talent is getting dangerously low, where are the next superstars who'll take Winston Cup into the next century?

In the Busch-sponsored Grand National Series, that's where.

Even though NASCAR and long-time patron Anheuser-Busch have changed the name several times, the Busch Series traces its roots to 1950. That's when NASCAR founder Bill France, Sr. named his second-level series the Sportsman Division. It was created as a lower-profile, more relaxed, and relatively inexpensive alternative to the fledgling Strictly Stock Division that eventually became Winston Cup. "Sportsman" was renamed "Late Model Sportsman" in 1968, then renamed "Grand National" in 1982. Budweiser was its primary sponsor for several years before the good folks at Anheuser-Busch headquarters in St. Louis decided to make Busch brand the series' sponsor instead of Budweiser.

THE STARTING POINT

With few exceptions, every one of NASCAR's leading Winston Cup drivers have spent time on the farm. Gordon raced several seasons with team owner Bill Davis before getting an unexpected call from Rick Hendrick to join his Winston Cup team. "It was great experience, invaluable experience, something I really learned from," the two-time champion said of his years in a Busch car. "Winston Cup is so difficult and competitive, it's good to have had a series that helped prepare for that. It helped me in so many ways, and I look back on those days as a tremendous learning experience."

Dale Jarrett raced his own Busch Series car for years before getting his first full-time Cup ride with the Cale Yarborough-owned team. Dale Earnhardt started in the old Late Model Sportsman division (where his late father, Ralph, had been a two-time champion). Likewise, Mark Martin, the Burton brothers (Jeff and Ward), Bobby Labonte, Johnny Benson, Michael Waltrip, Jimmy Spencer, the Bodine brothers (Geoff, Brett, and Todd), Ricky Craven, Steve Grissom, Rick Mast, Mike and Kenny Wallace, and Joe Nemechek also spent time in NASCAR's minor league en route to a shot in Winston Cup.

There have been a few exceptions. Rudd went directly from go-karts to Winston Cup and skipped the minor leagues altogether. Likewise, Terry Labonte started in Winston Cup without any Late Model Sportsman or Busch Series schooling. Jeremy Mayfield, Lake Speed, Rusty Wallace, Bill Elliott, Kyle Petty, and John Andretti are others who have made their mark in Winston Cup with only a minimum of schooling in either the Busch Series or a similar short-track series.

For years, young drivers dreaming of making it into NASCAR's upper level had few options. They could walk right in and try starting at the top—a costly, risky, and perhaps unwise route (and, not surprisingly, one NASCAR no longer allows)—or they could start in a lower level at weekly short track races in hopes of getting to Late Model Sportsman, then Winston Cup. When NASCAR created its Busch Series in 1982, it eased the transition from those 1/3-mile Friday night bullrings to the Saturday afternoon superspeedway races.

Late Model Sportsman cars of the '60s and '70s weren't nearly as fast, sophisticated or costly as Cup cars. They ran mostly 100- or 200-lap races at backwater short tracks that didn't have Winston Cup dates. The atmosphere generally was low-key (competitive, certainly, but not like at a Cup race), the purse was modest, and the media attention almost nonexistent. But that circuit of weekend races wasn't the ideal training ground.

Tracks were so widely scattered that the best drivers in New England might never face the best in the Carolinas. Competition was diluted even more since every track operated on Friday or Saturday night, leaving promoters little choice but to offer under-the-table deal money to attract stars to their tracks. What's more, a local backmarker might discover where the regional stars were going, then make plans to be somewhere else. More often than not, the national Late Model Sportsman champion was the driver who started the most races and finished the best. The level of competition seldom had anything to do with it.

CROWNING A TRUE NATIONAL CHAMPION

That changed with the advent of the Busch Series. Instead of between 55 and 65 races for the national short-track championship, NASCAR created a touring series of 28 to 32 points-paying races and called it Grand National. Except for the cost and the tracks it visited, it was similiar to Winston Cup. (To stay alive when NASCAR scrapped the unwieldy Late Model division in 1981, local short tracks replaced it with their own Late Model Stock Car class.)

In the Grand National series, the same drivers ran each race, a refreshing change that brought an end to the deal money era that had created hard feelings among mid- and lower-level drivers. And instead of racing under varying track rules and conditions so prevalent under the old system, Grand National rules were uniform throughout the nation. The same group of inspectors and officials worked every event and NASCAR even created a separate marketing and public relations division for the series.

Just as Winston Cup began growing and spreading its wings in the '80s and '90s, the Busch-sponsored Grand National Series began coming of age, too. It began by running more Saturday afternoon races in support of Sunday afternoon Cup shows, a tactic that brought more Cup drivers into Busch racing. (After all, another few hours of "live practice" before the next day's feature never hurt anyone). With more Cup drivers came larger crowds, which led to larger purses, which led to more teams, which led to more sponsors, which led to an even healthier series that saw media and PR attention increase more than anyone could have imagined a few years before.

In 1996, for example, the Busch Series ran 17 same-weekend shows in support of a Winston Cup event the next day. It went to three other tracks (Loudon, New Hampshire; Watkins Glen, New York; and Fontana, California) where Cup cars also race, but on non-Winston Cup weekends as "stand-alone" events. And in a dramatic turnabout from the early years, the series visited only four tracks (Nashville; South Boston, Virginia; Hickory, North Carolina; and Myrtle Beach, South Carolina) that could be considered traditional, old-time, weekly short tracks. And, now that purses have gone up so dramatically, it looks for all the world like South Boston and Myrtle Beach won't return to the 1998 schedule.

Whether that's good or bad depends on your outlook. Old-timers who still embrace the close-quarter racing typical on 1/4-mile, 1/3-mile and 5/8ths-mile tracks bemoan the loss of traditional venues like Hickory, South Boston, Langley Speedway (in Hampton, Virginia), Volusia County (Florida) Speedway, and Lanier, Georgia. If they want to watch a superspeedway race, they say, they'll simply go to a Cup race on Sunday afternoon. The Busch Series, they argue, was never designed as a condensed version of Winston Cup.

Others argue that the ever-increasing cost of racing demands bigger sponsors, more TV and contingency money, and larger purses. That can only be generated by running longer races at larger venues that have more seats, more room for radio and TV coverage, and more hospitality and catering facilities to entertain sponsors. Besides, supporters add, why not visit major markets like Las Vegas, Miami, St. Louis, Milwaukee, and Nashville. Each of those cities has an acceptable stock car racing venue, but with the exception of Las Vegas in 1998, none of them has a Winston Cup race. The only way to improve the series, say Busch fans, is to expose it to new markets, new sponsors, and new fans.

BOOM TIMES FOR BUSCH

They must be right, because the series has never been healthier. It drew more than 100,000 for the 1997 season-opening race in Daytona Beach, Fla., and a similiar number for an early-season race at a new track in Fort Worth, Texas. More than 75,000 watched a late-summer race at Bristol, Tennessee., a spring race at Talladega, Alabama, and a May race at Charlotte, North Carolina. Near-sellout crowds jammed into Hickory, North Carolina; Clermont, Indiana; Dover, Deleware; Myrtle Beach; and Richmond, Virginia. All told, the series was expected to attract almost three million fans in 1997.

That's in stark contrast to the half-million or so who watched Grand National races in its formative years, between 1982 and, say, 1988. Much of the schedule in those days included races at rough little backwoods tracks that always seemed to be looking backward rather than forward. Among them: the old standbys at Hickory, South Boston, Myrtle Beach, and Hampton, plus tracks at Rougemont, North Carolina; Radford, Virginia; Asheville, North Carolina; Asheboro, North Carolina; Gainesville, Georgia; Greenville, South Carolina; Oxford, Maine; Barberville, Florida; and Jefferson, Georgia.

None of the drivers who ran in the inaugural Budweiser-sponsored Grand National season of 1982 are still active racers. The top four in points that year—Jack Ingram, Sam Ard, Tommy Ellis, and Tommy Houston—have long-since retired. Likewise, series regulars Ronnie Silver, L.D. Ottinger, Bosco Lowe, Joe Thurman, Larry Pol-

Randy LaJoie, who claimed his second consecutive Busch Grand National title in 1997.

been able to reestablish himself in either series. Rob Moroso, the '88 champion, died in a highway accident in 1990, the year he was named Winston Cup rookie of the year. Ellis, the '89 champion, quit in the early 1990s and 1990 champion Chuck Bown went to Winston Cup, got hurt at the Pocono, Pennsylvania, track then found a home in the Craftsman Truck series when he couldn't find a ride in the Busch or Cup series.

Every champion between 1991 and 1995 has made the jump to Winston Cup: Bobby Labonte ('91) is with Joe Gibbs, Joe Nemechek ('92) is with Felix Sabates, Steve Grissom ('93) is with Larry Hedrick, David Green ('94) is with Buz McCall, and Johnny Benson ('95) is with Chuck Rider. Two-time champion Randy LaJoie ('96 and '97) made an early-'90s foray from Busch Series to Winston Cup, came back, then won his consecutive Busch titles with Bill Baumgardner, the man who helped Benson claim the 1995 title.

lard, and Mike Alexander haven't raced in years. For many, the hassle of towing their race car to far-away races and trying to make every event to stay in the championship hunt proved too much. For others, the cost of "tour racing" and keeping up with the better-financed teams simply went beyond their means.

Two-time champion Larry Pearson ('86 and '87) went from Busch Series to Winston Cup, but came back a few years later. Since then, he hasn't

To the casual fan, a Busch car racing around Daytona International Speedway looks a lot like a Winston Cup car. Its wheelbase is five inches shorter (105 vs. the 110 of a Cup car) and it's tuned with a 9.5-to-1 compression ratio engine (Cup cars run 14-to-1). Busch cars weigh 100 pounds less (3,300 vs. 3,400 lbs.) and its engine generates about 520 horsepower, roughly 200 to 230 less than a Cup car. Speeds are comparable at most tracks since the Busch car's weight and wheelbase almost make up for its weaker engine.

The future of the Busch Series depends largely on what NASCAR sees as its role. Is it to provide an intermediate stepping stone for young drivers headed from weekly short tracks to Winston Cup, or is its role to give superspeedway promoters an attractive Saturday afternoon support race? What does NASCAR plan for its Craftsman Truck series, a touring division that many feel is the sanctioning body's fair-haired favorite, as seen in its incredible growth in only three years.

Whatever happens, this much is evident: Bill France, Sr. would be stunned to see what his old "Sportsman Division" has become. Come to think of it, even those who've been around since the Busch Series was created in 1982 are pretty stunned by how far it's come in 16 years.

1997 RESULTS: LAJOIE LEADS THE WAY

Randy LaJoie won the 1997 title by 266 points over Todd Bodine and by 301 over rookie of the year Steve Park. Mike McLaughlin and Elliott Sadler rounded out the top five in points, followed by Phil Parsons, Buckshot Jones, Elton Sawyer, Tim Fedewa, and Hermie Sadler.

LaJoie led all series regulars with five victories in 30 starts, but Winston Cup star Mark Martin upstaged that with six victories in only 15 starts. Elliott Sadler and Park each won three times, and McLaughlin and Winston Cup drivers Jeff Burton, Joe Nemechek, and Jimmy Spencer each won twice. Single victories went to Bodine, Joe Bessey, Jeff Green, and Winston Cup drivers Bobby Labonte and Dick Trickle.

Career starts

Tommy Houston	417
Dale Jarrett	311
Elton Sawyer	292
Jack Ingram	275
Jimmy Hensley	254
Larry Pearson	245
Rick Mast	242
Tommy Ellis	234
Steve Grissom	216
L.D. Ottinger	206

Career poles

Tommy Ellis	28
Sam Ard	24
Mark Martin	19
Tommy Houston	18
David Green	18
Brett Bodine	16
Jimmy Hensley	15
Dale Jarrett	14
Harry Gant	14
Geoff Bodine	13

Career victories

Mark Martin	32
Jack Ingram	26
Tommy Houston	24
Sam Ard	22
Tommy Ellis	22
Dale Earnhardt	21
Harry Gant	21
Larry Pearson	15
Morgan Shepherd	15
Darrell Waltrip	13

15

NO MORE JOKES: THE CRAFTSMAN
TRUCK SERIES COMES OF AGE

At first, the idea seemed too "red-necky" for even the most devoted motorsports fan to take seriously. Truck racing? Did they say truck racing, as in pickup truck racing? Man, you gotta be kidding.

No, they weren't kidding. That's exactly what they meant. Adding to the almost endless variety of motorsports in America, several off-road racers from Southern California had come up with this crazy idea of putting the body of a street-legal pickup truck atop the chassis and rollcage of a Winston Cup car and seeing what happened.

But first they had to endure the outbreak of jokes that made light of what they thought was a perfectly good idea. For example:

1) By NASCAR rules, each truck would carry a gun rack in its rear window, right back there with the Confederate flag. Whether the rack carried guns and whether any of them were loaded would be determined by the chief steward and/or each driver's probation officer;

2) Each driver would carry his favorite dog and make him hang out the right-side window. The dog would be walked during pit stops,

but only in the presence of a crewman with a pooper-scooper. Drivers would be penalized a lap for each "deposit" left untended;

3) Each truck would carry two of three NASCAR-approved bumper stickers. Drivers would chose between RUSH IS RIGHT; the bandy-legged and grizzled old Confederate vet saying FORGET HELL; or the one urging fans to SEE ROCK CITY. The bumper sticker warning IF YOU CAN READ THIS YOU'RE TOO DAMNED CLOSE would be optional for night races;

4) And all trucks would haul a load of peat moss and fertilizer during spring races, then switch to a cord of firewood for fall races. For races on holiday weekends, the load had to include an inner tube and a cooler of Bud Lite.

Funny stuff, huh? But seriously now...

SUPERTRUCKS TAKE THE TRACK

Veteran off-road racers Dick Landfield, Jimmy Smith, Jim Venable, and Scoop Vessels didn't think their dream of racing pickup trucks on paved, oval speedways was the least bit strange. They liked it so much, in fact, they built a prototype in the fall of 1993 and went to NASCAR in February of 1994 with a request to sanction several demonstration races. Three months later, during the Winston Cup weekend at Sonoma, California, NASCAR president Bill France stepped to the microphone and announced creation of the SuperTruck Series by Craftsman, later renamed the Craftsman Truck Series.

The first of four exhibition races was run at Mesa Marin Speedway in Bakersfield, California in July of 1994. Later that year, NASCAR announced a 20-race schedule for 1995, a scheduled that featured a total purse of $1.6 million and

a television contract to broadcast the full schedule. Suddenly, all the "red-necky" jokes about gun racks, dogs, and bumper stickers were a thing of the past.

Seldom has any NASCAR-sanctioned series grown faster or been accepted more openly than the Craftsman Truck series. Many races in that inaugural year of 1995 were either sold out or close to it, and the media attention was more than anyone at NASCAR could have expected. It was almost like every Craftsman-related meeting at NASCAR headquarters in Daytona Beach began and ended with this mantra: "It must not fail. We can't let it fail. It will not fail."

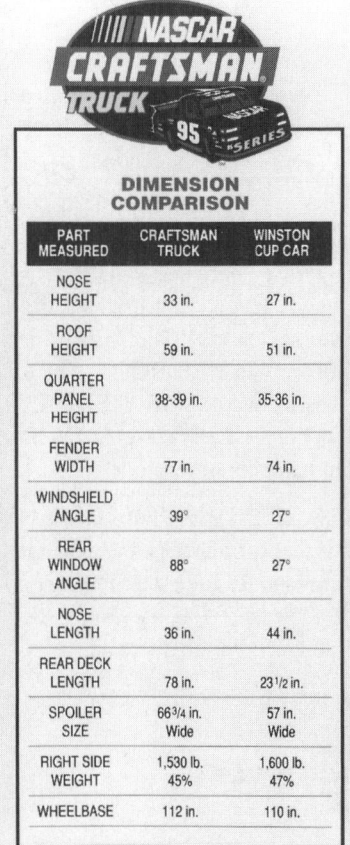

DIMENSION COMPARISON

PART MEASURED	CRAFTSMAN TRUCK	WINSTON CUP CAR
NOSE HEIGHT	33 in.	27 in.
ROOF HEIGHT	59 in.	51 in.
QUARTER PANEL HEIGHT	38-39 in.	35-36 in.
FENDER WIDTH	77 in.	74 in.
WINDSHIELD ANGLE	39°	27°
REAR WINDOW ANGLE	88°	27°
NOSE LENGTH	36 in.	44 in.
REAR DECK LENGTH	78 in.	23 1/2 in.
SPOILER SIZE	66 3/4 in. Wide	57 in. Wide
RIGHT SIDE WEIGHT	1,530 lb. 45%	1,600 lb. 47%
WHEELBASE	112 in.	110 in.

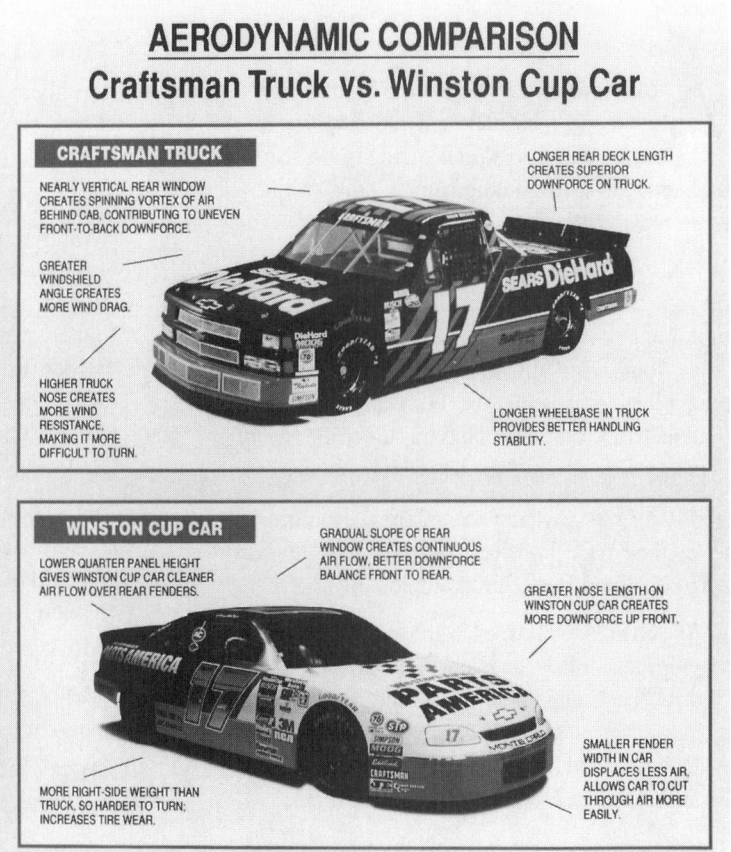

AERODYNAMIC COMPARISON
Craftsman Truck vs. Winston Cup Car

CRAFTSMAN TRUCK

NEARLY VERTICAL REAR WINDOW CREATES SPINNING VORTEX OF AIR BEHIND CAB, CONTRIBUTING TO UNEVEN FRONT-TO-BACK DOWNFORCE.

GREATER WINDSHIELD ANGLE CREATES MORE WIND DRAG.

HIGHER TRUCK NOSE CREATES MORE WIND RESISTANCE, MAKING IT MORE DIFFICULT TO TURN.

LONGER REAR DECK LENGTH CREATES SUPERIOR DOWNFORCE ON TRUCK.

LONGER WHEELBASE IN TRUCK PROVIDES BETTER HANDLING STABILITY.

WINSTON CUP CAR

LOWER QUARTER PANEL HEIGHT GIVES WINSTON CUP CAR CLEANER AIR FLOW OVER REAR FENDERS.

GRADUAL SLOPE OF REAR WINDOW CREATES CONTINUOUS AIR FLOW, BETTER DOWNFORCE BALANCE FRONT TO REAR.

GREATER NOSE LENGTH ON WINSTON CUP CAR CREATES MORE DOWNFORCE UP FRONT.

SMALLER FENDER WIDTH IN CAR DISPLACES LESS AIR, ALLOWS CAR TO CUT THROUGH AIR MORE EASILY.

MORE RIGHT-SIDE WEIGHT THAN TRUCK, SO HARDER TO TURN; INCREASES TIRE WEAR.

Credit: Sears Craftsman / '97

A comparison of a Craftsman truck and a Winston Cup car.

NASCAR gave the fledgling series its own radio network, offered extraordinary coverage in its membership publications, and made sure no motorsports fan in America could ever say, "Duh, I never knew they raced pickup trucks." So enthusiastic was NASCAR over the trucks that many Busch Grand National teams developed some hard feelings over the attention the new circuit was receiving. Grand National had been the "second banana" to Winston Cup for so many years, and now they were even further back in the pecking order. Suddenly and without apology, they were shunted to the kitchen so the upstart truck series could come into the dining room and have some tea.

SKINNER TAKES THE FIRST TITLE

The first full season of 1995 featured 20 races at 15 tracks (Phoenix got three and Bakersfield two) in 13 states. The schedule ranged from 1-mile ovals at Phoenix and Milwaukee, Wisconsin, to the 1/3-mile track at Santa Clarita, California. And just to make things interesting, the tour went road racing at Topeka, Kansas, and Sonoma, California. Mike Skinner, driving for Winston Cup team owner Richard Childress, won eight poles and eight races to claim the first championship by 126 points over Joe Ruttman. The post-season awards banquet was a posh affair at The Fairmont Hotel in San Francisco.

Mike Skinner, now the driver of the No. 31 car on the Winston Cup circuit, won the first truck season championship ever.

Skinner beat Winston Cup star Terry Labonte in the series' first-ever "points race" at Phoenix in February of 1995. Driving Chevrolet trucks, he also won twice more at Phoenix, and once each at Odessa, Missouri; Louisville; Milwaukee; Clermont, Indiana; and Bakersfield. Other winners that first year were Ron Hornaday with six victories, Ruttman with two, and one-time winners Ken Schrader, Terry Labonte, Mike Bliss, and Butch Miller.

No question about it, truck racing was on its way. The 1996 schedule was expanded to 24 races at 23 tracks (Phoenix got two) in 18 states, including stops in the extreme corners of the country. The tour ran its first 1½-mile tracks (at Homestead, Florida, and Las Vegas), returned to the road courses at Topeka and Sonoma, and added the famed Watkins Glen road circuit in upstate New York. More than Winston Cup or Grand National, it became evident nearly from the start that truck racing would test man and machine on almost every conceivable type of track, with a cross-country schedule only a World of Outlaw racer could love.

Ron Hornaday, in Chevrolets owned by Winston Cup star Dale Earnhardt, won two poles and four races (Portland, Louisville, Watkins Glen, and Loudon, New Hamphsire) en route to winning the 1996 title by 53 points over Jack Sprague. Like all championship drivers, he occasionally concentrated more on scoring points (19 consecutive top-ten finishes to open the season) than in racing flat-out for the victory. Skinner won eight races, Sprague five, Dave Rezendes three, Mike Bliss two, and Mark Martin and Rick Carelli one each.

There was no letup in 1997. In fact, the schedule was expanded to 26 races at 25 tracks in 19 states. The purse grew to more than $6 million, impressive when you realize the long-established Busch Series raced for just $10 million. But it also ran a half-dozen "major superspeedway" Saturday afternoon races as preludes to Winston Cup races. The trucks visited the brand-new superspeedways at Fort Worth, Texas (1½ miles) and Fontana, California (2 miles), and the 1-mile Disney World Speedway in Orlando. Jack Sprague, who finished second in 1996, broke through and won the championship by a series-record 232 points over Rich Bickle, who ended up just one point ahead of third-place Joe Ruttman. The rest of the top 10 included Hornaday, Jay Sauter, Rick Carelli, Jimmy Hensley, Chuck Bown, and Kenny Irwin.

Hornaday was the series' big winner, taking seven checkered flags in 26 starts. Ruttman won five races (including three of the last five), Sprague and Bickle each won three, and Irwin won two. One-time winners included Bliss, Sauter, Bob Keselowski, Tony Raines, Randy Tolsma, and Ron Fellows.

And in one of the year's strangest races, Jimmy Hensley won the pole and led the first 200 laps of a 200-lap race at Clermont, Indiana—but still finished third. Series rules dictate that all races must end under green, and Hensley was leading the 200th lap under caution. He had a flat tire under caution and slipped back when the race was restarted for a two-lap dash to the finish.

After three years, then, it's obvious that Landfield, Smith, Venable, and Vessels knew their stuff when they presented their "trucking" idea to NASCAR during Speed Week in 1994. The jokes are gone, replaced once and for all by overflowing grandstands, solid TV and radio ratings, and involvement by some of NASCAR's most respected owners, drivers, crewmen, sponsors, and manufacturers.

REACHING NEW HEIGHTS

"This series has risen in only 18 months to a level it took Winston Cup 20 years to reach," France said at the inaugural series awards banquet. "It can only be described as a national phenomenon." NASCAR vice-president Dennis Huth called the truck series "a natural entertainment and marketing opportunity since 89 percent of all truck owners enjoy some sort of motorsports."

But why does it work? What is there about pickup trucks on ovals or road courses that draws American race fans in ever-increasing numbers? Certainly it's more than an "entertainment and marketing opportunity." Ask around and you'll get several answers:

Don't pooh-pooh the novelty of truck racing. Only the most discerning NASCAR-watcher can tell the difference in a Ford Thunderbird dressed out in Winston Cup livery and a Ford Thunderbird on the Busch Grand National tour. There are differences, to be sure, but a Cup car and a Busch car remain so close that to see one race on Saturday afternoon is almost to see the other race on Sunday afternoon. There are, on the other hand, no similarities whatsoever in a Cup (or Busch) car and a Craftsman truck. They look different and they sound different, and fans don't need to look twice to realize that.

Another factor is the fierce loyalty of truck buyers. In the fall of 1996, for the first time in American automotive history, the sale of light and heavy trucks (combined with sport utility vehicles) accounted for 50 percent of the country's new vehicle registrations. As the Craftsman information booklet proudly explains, half the new cars in this country aren't cars at all. While passenger car sales have declined in recent years, the market for full-sized pickups is the largest segment of the truck industry.

Another reason is the competition among brands. General Motors and Ford are bitter rivals in Winston Cup and Busch Grand National, but you have to go to the Craftsman Truck series to see the presence of Chrysler. Each of the Big Three manufacturers has a truck body similiar to one of its corporate rival. It's been proven that fans in the stands readily identify with "their" brand over the others. It's been a decade since Mopar was a player in NASCAR, and the presence of Dodge Ram trucks has rekindled emotions for the once-suffering and now flourishing Chrysler.

And don't discount the gentle persuasion that France and his people applied to convince owners like Childress, Jack Roush, Richard Petty, and Rick Hendrick to get involved. From there, it was easier to convince Winston Cup drivers like Earnhardt, Schrader, Labonte, Darrell Waltrip, Geoff Bodine, Johnny Benson, A.J. Foyt, Harry Gant,

Ernie Irvan, Bobby Hamilton, and Jimmy Hensley to get involved in the series.

Much like the Busch Series, the Craftsman tour has already started sending its "graduates" into Winston Cup. Skinner went from 1995 champion and 1996 third-place driver to a place as Earnhardt's teammate on Childress' team. Irwin, with limited truck credentials, was selected by Robert Yates (and, certainly, Ford and Texaco) to replace Ernie Irvan for the 1998 Cup season. And Bickle spent only two years in trucks before becoming Darrell Waltrip's driver of choice for the 98 Cup season.

Pickup trucks on ovals and road courses? Why not? After all, there was a time when people didn't think stock CARS would make it.

Career starts

Bill Sedgwick	76
Bob Keselowski	75
Rick Carelli	70
Ron Hornaday	70
Butch Miller	70
Joe Ruttman	70
Jack Sprague	70
Mike Bliss	69
Dave Rezendes	59
Jimmy Hensley	53

Career victories

Ron Hornaday	20
Mike Skinner	16
Jack Sprague	10
Joe Ruttman	8
Rich Bickle	5
Mike Bliss	4
Kenny Irwin	4
Dave Rezendes	3
Rick Carelli	2

Career poles

Mike Skinner	15
Jack Sprague	12
Ron Hornaday	11
Mike Bliss	10
Rich Bickle	9
Joe Ruttman	5
Jimmy Hensley	4

16

DRIVER REGISTER

RUSTY WALLACE

Born: Aug. 14, 1956
St. Louis, MO
Resides: Lake Norman, NC
Wife: Patti.
Children: Greg, 17;
Katie, 13; Stephen, 10

No. 2 Miller Lite Ford

Career highlights 1989 Winston Cup titlist, edging Dale Earnhardt by 12 points . . . runner-up in '88 and '93 . . . 15-year winning streak . . . won the inaugural NASCAR race in Japan in '96 . . . rated one of the top all-time Winston Cup road racers . . . first Winston Cup win was at Bristol, in '86 . . . Winston Cup Rookie of the Year in '84 . . . USAC Rookie of the Year in '79 . . . ASA national champion in '83 . . . '91 IROC titlist . . . finished second in his first Winston Cup race at Atlanta in '80, driving a car owned by Roger Penske. Penske and Don Miller are co-owners of his current Winston Cup car . . . has pilot's license and owns fleet of planes . . . drag racing fan . . . four dogs are named Sadoe, Winston, Miller, and Gadget . . . father was a champion racer in the St. Louis area.

YEAR	RANK	EVENTS	POLES	WINS	TOP 10	MONEY
1980	57	2	0	0	0	22,860
1981	64	4	0	0	1	12,895
1982	65	3	0	0	0	7,655
1983	NR	0	0	0	0	1,100
1984	14	30	0	0	4	201,739
1985	19	28	0	0	8	233,670
1986	6	29	0	2	16	557,354
1987	5	29	1	2	16	690,652
1988	2	29	2	6	23	1,411,567
1989	1	29	4	6	20	2,237,950
1990	6	29	2	2	16	954,129
1991	10	29	2	2	14	502,073
1992	13	29	1	1	12	657,925
1993	2	30	3	10	21	1,705,154
1994	3	31	2	8	20	1,959,072
1995	5	31	0	2	19	1,642,837
1996	7	31	0	5	18	1,665,315
1997	9	32	1	1	12	1,505,260
Lifetime		425	18	47	221	$15,966,207

DALE EARNHARDT

Born: April 29, 1951.
Kannapolis, NC
Resides: Mooresville, NC
Wife: Teresa.
Children: Kerry Dale, 28;
Kelley King, 25; Ralph Dale
Jr., 23; Taylor Nicole, 9

No. 3 GM Goodwrench Chevrolet

Career highlights seven-time Winston Cup champion, tying Richard Petty for most championships . . . runner-up in '89 and '95 . . . considered by many the greatest stock car driver of all time . . . nicknamed "The Intimidator" for his aggressive driving style . . . not the driver most rivals want to see in their rear-view mirrors with a race on the line . . . sixth on the all-time Winston Cup victory list with 70 . . . has driven Richard Childress-owned cars since 1984 . . . broke into Winston Cup racing driving for Rod Osterlund in '79 . . . responded by winning Rookie of the Year honors . . . won the Winston Cup title the next season . . . first win was at Bristol in only his 16th start . . . father, Ralph, was the 1956 NASCAR Sportsman champion . . . hobbies include hunting and fishing . . . owns two Hatteras boats and a Lear jet . . . favorite baseball team: Atlanta Braves.

YEAR	RANK	EVENTS	POLES	WINS	TOP 10	MONEY
1975	NR	1	0	0	0	2,425
1976	103	2	0	0	0	3,085
1977	117	1	0	0	0	1,375
1978	43	5	0	0	1	20,745
1979	7	27	4	1	17	274,810
1980	1	31	0	5	24	671,991
1981	7	31	0	0	17	353,972
1982	12	30	1	1	12	400,880
1983	8	30	0	2	16	465,203
1984	4	30	0	2	24	634,671
1985	8	28	1	4	16	546,596
1986	1	29	1	5	23	1,768,880
1987	1	29	1	11	24	2,069,243
1988	3	29	0	3	19	1,214,089
1989	2	29	0	5	19	1,432,230
1990	1	29	4	9	23	3,308,054
1991	1	29	0	4	24	2,416,685
1992	12	29	1	1	15	915,463
1993	1	30	2	6	21	3,353,789
1994	1	31	2	4	25	3,400,733
1995	2	31	3	5	23	3,154,241
1996	4	31	2	2	17	2,285,926
1997	5	32	0	0	16	1,663,019
Lifetime		574	22	70	370	$30,358,107

Dale Earnhardt's pit crew works hard to get him back on the track as quickly as they can.

BOBBY HAMILTON

Born: May 29, 1957
Nashville, TN
Resides: Mount Juliet, TN
Wife: Debbie
Children: Bobby, Jr.

No. 4 Kodak Film Chevrolet

Career highlights won his first Winston Cup race at Phoenix in 1996 driving the STP Pontiac for Richard Petty; the victory was the first for Petty Enterprises since 1983 . . . in '96 surpassed $1 million in earnings for the first time . . . 1991 Winston Cup Rookie of the Year . . . enjoys reading about racing history . . . former Nashville Speedway champion . . . drove a car in the movie *Days of Thunder,* starring Tom Cruise and Robert Duvall . . . grandfather and father built race cars for the late singer/racer Marty Robbins.

YEAR	RANK	EVENTS	POLES	WINS	TOP 10	MONEY
1989	89	1	0	0	0	3,075
1990	66	3	0	0	0	13,065
1991	22	28	0	0	4	259,105
1992	25	29	0	0	2	367,065
1993	37	15	0	0	1	142,740
1994	23	30	0	0	1	514,520
1995	14	31	0	0	10	804,505
1996	9	31	2	1	11	1,151,235
1997	16	32	2	1	8	1,350,335
Lifetime		200	4	2	37	$4,605,645

TERRY LABONTE

Born: Nov. 16, 1956
Corpus Christi, TX
Resides: Thomasville, NC
Wife: Kim.
Children: Justin, 16;
Kristen, 14

No. 5 Kellogg's Chevrolet

Career highlights two-time Winston Cup champion (1984 and '96) . . . NASCAR's "Ironman" with 569 consecutive starts . . . broke Richard Petty's mark of 513 consecutive starts during the '96 season . . . season finale in '96 at Atlanta was a memorable day for the Labonte family: Terry clinched his second title and younger brother Bobby won his first Winston Cup race . . . the 12 seasons between championships is the longest span in Winston Cup history . . . first Winston Cup victory was in '80 in the Southern 500 at Darlington, driving for Billy Hagan . . . spent 11 full seasons with Hagan Racing . . . started racing quarter-midgets in Texas in '64 . . . three victories in '94, in his first season driving for Hendrick Motorsports, were his first since '89 when he was the IROC series champion . . . .won the '90 Christmas 400K in Melbourne, Australia.

YEAR	RANK	EVENTS	POLES	WINS	TOP 10	MONEY
1978	39	5	0	0	3	21,395
1979	10	31	0	0	13	134,653
1980	8	31	0	1	16	222,502
1981	4	31	2	0	18	348,703
1982	3	30	2	0	21	398,635
1983	5	30	3	1	20	388,419
1984	1	30	2	2	24	767,716
1985	7	28	4	1	17	694,510
1986	12	29	1	1	10	522,235
1987	3	29	4	1	22	805,054
1988	4	29	1	1	18	950,781
1989	10	29	0	2	11	703,806
1990	15	29	0	0	9	450,230
1991	18	29	1	0	7	348,898
1992	8	29	0	0	16	600,381
1993	18	30	0	0	10	531,717
1994	7	31	0	3	14	1,150,921
1995	6	31	1	3	17	1,558,659
1996	1	31	4	2	24	4,030,648
1997	6	32	1	1	12	1,951,844
Lifetime		574	26	19	301	$16,581,707

MARK MARTIN

Born: Jan. 9, 1959
Batesville, AR
Resides: Daytona Beach, FL
Wife: Arlene.
Children: Amy, 25; Rachel and Heather, 23; Stacey, 19; Matthew Clyde, 5

No. 6 Valvoline Ford

Career highlights '97 was one of the best years of his career as he finished third in the Winston Cup standings . . . runner-up to Dale Earnhardt in points in '90 by just 26 points . . . winless '96 season was his first since gaining his first victory in '89 . . . IROC championship last season was his third . . . runner-up to Geoff Bodine in the '82 Winston Cup Rookie of the Year balloting . . . first victory was at North Carolina Motor Speedway in Rockingham in '89 . . . four-time ASA champion . . . devoted body builder: frequently works out before sunrise . . . favorite actress: Jodie Foster . . . favorite actor:

Mark Martin (No.6) and Jeff Gordon (No. 24) fought it out all season (along with Dale Jarrett) for the Winston Cup championship. Here they go head-to-head at Dover.

Arnold Schwarzenegger . . . favorite singers: Stevie Nicks, Melissa Etheridge, and Tanya Tucker.

YEAR	RANK	EVENTS	POLES	WINS	TOP 10	MONEY
1981	42	5	2	0	2	13,950
1982	14	30	0	0	8	142,710
1983	30	16	0	0	3	99,665
1986	48	5	0	0	0	20,515
1987	101T	1	0	0	0	3,550
1988	15	29	1	0	10	223,630
1989	3	29	6	1	18	1,016,850
1990	2	29	3	3	23	1,302,958
1991	6	29	5	1	17	1,039,991
1992	6	29	1	2	17	1,000,571
1993	3	30	5	5	19	1,657,662
1994	2	31	1	2	20	1,678,906
1995	4	31	4	4	22	1,893,519
1996	5	31	4	0	23	1,887,396
1997	3	32	3	4	24	1,877,130
Lifetime		357	35	22	206	$13,859,003

GEOFF BODINE

Born: April 18, 1949.
Elmira, NY
Resides: Julian, NC
Children: Matthew, 26; Barry, 20

No. 7 Ford

Career highlights won the Daytona 500 in 1986 . . . Winston Cup Rookie of the Year in '82 . . . older brother of Brett and Todd . . . purchased the late Alan Kulwicki's team in May '93 . . . first Winston Cup victory was at Martinsville in '84 . . . innovative thinker: introduced power steering in Winston Cup at Martinsville in '81 . . . founder of USA Bobsled Project, a sleeker bodsled for the '94 USA bobsled team . . . '87 IROC titlist . . . runner-up in national modified standings in '77 . . . board member of the Make-A-Wish Foundation . . . favorite NFL team: Dallas.

YEAR	RANK	EVENTS	POLES	WINS	TOP 10	MONEY
1979	81	3	0	0	0	4,820
1981	45	5	0	0	1	15,000
1982	22	25	2	0	10	247,750
1983	17	28	1	0	9	209,611
1984	9	30	3	3	14	413,748
1985	5	28	3	0	14	565,868
1986	8	29	8	2	15	795,111
1987	13	29	2	0	10	449,816
1988	6	29	3	1	16	570,643
1989	9	29	3	1	11	619,494
1990	3	29	2	3	19	1,131,222
1991	14	27	2	1	12	625,256
1992	16	29	0	2	11	716,583
1993	16	30	1	1	9	783,762
1994	17	31	5	3	10	1,287,762
1995	16	31	0	0	4	1,011,090
1996	17	31	0	1	6	1,031,762
1997	22	29	2	0	10	1,021,114
Lifetime		472	37	18	181	$11,406,484

HUT STRICKLIN

Born: June 24, 1961
Birmingham, AL
Resides: Mt. Ulla, NC
Wife: Pam.
Children: Taylor, 9; Tabitha, 4

No. 8 Circuit City Chevrolet

Career highlights best career finishes are seconds at Michigan in '91 and the Southern 500 at Darlington in '96 . . . in the '91 Michigan race, won by Davey Allison, Hut was driving for Davey's father, Winston Cup legend Bobby . . . now driving for the Stavola Brothers; previously drove for Kenny Bernstein and Travis Carter . . . Alabama limited sportsman champion in '78 and '79 . . . Winston Racing Series titlist in '82 and '84 . . . as the NASCAR Dash series winner in '86 he won 9 of 17 races plus 10 poles . . . began attending races with his father, Waymond Sr., who owned a wrecker service and worked at local tracks . . . wife, Pam, is the daughter of former Winston Cup driver Donnie Allison . . . hobbies include restoring old cars . . . favorite actor: Richard Gere.

YEAR	RANK	EVENTS	POLES	WINS	TOP 10	MONEY
1987	58	3	0	0	0	6,085
1989	26	27	0	0	4	152,504
1990	28	24	0	0	2	169,199
1991	16	29	0	0	7	426,524
1992	27	28	0	0	4	336,965
1993	24	30	0	0	2	494,600
1994	26	29	0	0	1	333,495
1995	36	24	1	0	5	486,065
1996	22	31	0	0	1	631,055
1997	34	29	0	0	1	802,904
Lifetime		254	1	0	27	$3,839,396

LAKE SPEED

Born: Jan. 17, 1948.
Jackson, MS
Resides: Kannapolis, NC
Wife: Rice.
Children: Lake Jr., 25; Sara Ann, 10; Maurie Ray, 8; Christopher, 7.

No. 9 Cartoon Network Ford

Career highlights beginning his fourth year driving for car owner Harry Melling . . . has spent most of his career driving his own cars . . . only victory was in the '88 TranSouth 500 at Darlington . . . runner-up in '85 Daytona 500 . . . drove for Hoss Ellington in '83 and '84 and credits engine builder Runt Pittman during those years for helping him improve as a driver . . . only driver on the Winston Cup circuit from Mississippi . . . if he weren't a racer, he'd probably be a commercial real-estate salesman . . . enjoys water and snow skiing, and working with horses.

YEARS	RANK	EVENTS	POLES	WINS	TOP 10	MONEY
1980	22	19	0	0	5	70,640
1981	18	27	0	0	6	95,690
1982	20	30	0	0	5	118,457
1983	27	18	0	0	5	78,220
1984	26	19	0	0	7	98,320
1985	10	28	0	0	14	300,326
1986	40	5	0	0	2	82,800
1987	31	13	0	0	5	110,810
1988	17	29	0	1	7	260,500
1989	27	24	0	0	5	201,977
1990	42	6	0	0	0	75,537
1991	32	20	0	0	0	149,300
1992	38	9	0	0	0	52,645
1993	34	21	0	0	1	319,800
1994	11	31	0	0	9	845,963
1995	23	31	0	0	2	529,445
1996	23	31	0	0	2	817,175
1997	35	25	0	0	0	715,074
Lifetime		386	0	1	75	$4,922,669

RICKY RUDD

Born: Sept. 12, 1956.
Chesapeake, VA
Resides: Cornelius, NC
Wife: Linda.
Children: Landon Lee, 3.

No. 10 Tide Ford

Career highlights has won at least one race every year since 1983 . . . won Brickyard 400 at Indianapolis last year . . . runner-up in points to Dale Earnhardt in '91 . . . has finished in the top 10 points standings every year since '81 except in '88 . . . Winston Cup Rookie of the Year in '77 . . . first win was at Riverside, California, in '83 . . . excels at racing on road courses . . . '92 IROC champion . . . if he weren't racing, he'd be an airline pilot . . . favorite movie: "Forrest Gump" . . . favorite actor: "Gump" star Tom Hanks . . . Washington Redskins fan . . . enjoys Elton John's music.

YEAR	RANK	EVENTS	POLES	WINES	TOP 10	MONEY
1975	47	4	0	0	1	4,345
1976	53	4	0	0	1	7,525
1977	17	25	0	0	10	75,905
1978	31	13	0	0	4	50,630
1979	9	28	0	0	17	150,898
1980	35	13	0	0	13	50,500
1981	6	31	3	0	17	395,685
1982	9	30	2	0	13	217,140
1983	9	30	4	2	14	275,400
1984	7	30	4	1	16	497,779
1985	6	28	0	1	19	512,441
1986	5	29	1	2	17	671,548
1987	6	29	0	2	13	653,508
1988	11	29	2	1	11	410,954
1989	8	29	0	1	15	533,624
1990	7	29	2	1	15	573,650
1991	2	29	1	1	17	1,093,765
1992	7	29	1	1	18	793,903
1993	10	30	0	1	14	752,562
1994	5	31	1	1	15	1,079,441
1995	9	31	2	1	16	1,337,703
1996	6	31	0	1	16	1,503,025
1997	17	32	0	2	11	1,863,040
Lifetime		594	23	19	293	$13,504,971

BRETT BODINE

Born: Jan. 11, 1959
Elmira, NY
Resides: Davidson, NC
Wife: Diane.
Children: Heidi, 20.

No. 11 Ford

Career highlights 1997 was his second as an owner/driver . . . purchased his team from Junior Johnson late in '95 . . . drove for Johnson in '95 after five-year tour with Kenny Bernstein . . . started racing full time in Winston Cup in '88 with Bud Moore after successful Busch Grand National career . . . runner-up for the '86 Grand National championship . . . began racing at the Chemung (NY) Speedrome . . . raced modifieds in the Northeast from 1980 through '84 . . . in his Winston Cup debut, won the pole for the '87 Winston Open driving for Hoss Ellington . . . first victory was at North Wilkesboro in '90 . . . middle brother of the racing Bodines . . . graduate of New York State University at Alfred with an associate degree in mechanical engineering.

YEAR	RANK	EVENTS	POLES	WINS	TOP 10	MONEY
1986	92T	1	0	0	0	10,100
1987	32	14	0	0	0	51,145
1988	20	29	0	0	5	433,658
1989	19	29	0	0	6	281,274

YEAR	RANK	EVENTS	POLES	WINS	TOP 10	MONEY
1990	12	29	1	1	9	422,681
1991	19	29	1	0	6	376,220
1992	15	29	1	0	13	495,224
1993	20	29	2	0	9	582,014
1994	19	31	0	0	6	801,944
1995	20	31	0	0	2	893,029
1996	24	30	0	0	1	767,716
1997	29	31	0	0	2	936,694
Lifetime		312	5	1	59	$6,071,699

MORGAN SHEPHERD

Born: Oct. 21, 1941
Ferguson, NC
Resides: Conover, NC
Wife: Cindy.
Children: Debbie, 35;
Crystal, 33; Terri, 32; Morgan Jr., 30;
Cynthia, 28; Shanda Renee, 11.

No. 14 R & L Carriers Pontiac

Career highlights three of his four Winston Cup victories were at Atlanta . . . last win was in '93 in Atlanta, driving for the Wood Brothers . . . in '96, finished out of the top 15 in points for the first time since '88 . . . fourth rookie to win a Winston Cup race in '81 . . . oldest driver (by six days over Dick Trickle) on the Winston Cup circuit . . . NASCAR National Sportsman (now Grand National) champion in '80 . . . could take apart an automobile motor and put it back together when he was 11 . . . credits car owner Cliff Stewart with giving him his biggest racing break . . . relaxes by roller skating and dancing . . . big boxing fan: George Foreman is one of his favorite people in sports . . . pet collection includes a racoon named Citgo.

YEAR	RANK	EVENTS	POLES	WINS	TOP 10	MONEY
1970	90	3	0	0	0	965
1977	53	3	0	0	1	7,465
1978	75	2	0	0	0	8,115
1979	NR	0	0	0	0	256
1981	13	29	1	1	10	170,473
1982	10	29	2	0	9	166,030
1983	20	25	0	0	13	287,326
1984	29	20	0	0	1	59,670
1985	31	16	0	0	2	55,985
1986	18	27	0	1	8	244,146
1987	17	29	1	0	11	317,034
1988	28	23	2	0	6	197,425
1989	13	29	1	0	13	544,255
1990	5	29	0	1	16	666,915
1991	12	29	0	0	14	521,147
1992	14	29	0	0	11	634,222
1993	7	30	0	1	15	782,523
1994	6	31	0	0	16	1,119,038
1995	11	31	0	0	10	966,374
1996	19	31	0	0	5	719,059
1997	38	32	0	0	3	662,999
Lifetime		477	7	4	168	$8,031,421

TED MUSGRAVE

Born: Dec. 18, 1955
Evanston, IL
Resides: Troutman, NC
Wife: Debi.
Children: Ted Jr., 19;
Justin, 16; Brittany, 6.

No. 16 Primestar Ford

Career highlights finished 12th in points last year . . . won the pole for the final Winston Cup race at North Wilkesboro in '96 . . . runner-up in '91 Winston Cup Rookie of the Year standings . . . began racing on Wisconsin short tracks, where his father also raced . . . '87 ASA Rookie of the Year . . . after driving career ends, wants to be a Winston Cup crew chief . . . favorite actress: Michelle Pfeiffer . . . favorite actor: Clint Eastwood . . . restores vintage vehicles as a hobby.

YEAR	RANK	EVENTS	POLES	WINS	TOP 10	MONEY
1990	49	4	0	0	0	17,190
1991	23	29	0	0	0	200,910
1992	18	29	0	0	7	449,121
1993	25	29	0	0	5	458,615
1994	13	31	3	0	8	669,687
1995	7	31	1	0	13	1,147,445
1996	16	31	1	0	7	961,512
1997	12	32	0	0	8	1,128,404
Lifetime		216	5	0	48	$5,032,884

DARRELL WALTRIP

Born: Feb. 5, 1947
Owensboro, KY
Resides: Franklin, TN
Wife: Stevie.
Children: Jessica Leigh, 10;
Sarah Kaitlyn, 5.

No. 17 Fox Network Chevrolet

Career highlights three-time Winston Cup champion (1981, '82, '85) . . . his 84 victories are the most of the model era . . . tied with Bobby Allison for third place on the all-time win list . . . won the '89 Daytona 500 . . . only five-time winner of the Coca-Cola 600 at Charlotte . . . first three-time winner of the American Driver of the Year award ('79, '81, '82) . . . chosen Tennessee Professional Athlete of the Year in '79 . . . nicknamed "Jaws" when he was younger, for his brashness . . . now, he's "ol' D.W." . . . older brother of Michael Wal-

Nerves of steel are required by today's drivers, who often travel at speeds near 200 mph while less than a foot behind the car ahead of them.

trip . . . informative and entertaining television analyst for races . . . if he weren't a race car driver, he'd be a trial lawyer . . . drove in the Late Model Sportsman division at Kentucky short tracks before moving to Winston Cup . . . favorite NFL team: Kansas City . . . favorite actress: Demi Moore . . . favorite actor: Clint Eastwood . . . favorite movie: "Patton." . . . favortie singers: Travis Tritt, Neil Diamond, and Vern Gosdin . . .

YEAR	RANK	EVENTS	POLES	WINS	TOP 10	MONEY
1972	56	5	0	0	3	8,615
1973	28	19	0	0	5	42,466
1974	19	16	1	0	11	67,775
1975	7	28	2	2	14	160,192
1976	8	30	3	1	12	204,193
1977	4	30	3	6	14	324,814
1978	3	30	2	6	20	413,908
1979	2	31	5	7	22	557,012
1980	5	31	5	5	17	405,711
1981	1	31	11	12	25	799,134
1982	1	30	7	12	20	923,151
1983	2	30	7	6	25	865,185
1984	5	30	4	7	20	731,023
1985	1	28	4	3	21	1,318,375
1986	2	29	1	3	22	1,099,735
1987	4	29	0	1	16	511,768
1988	7	29	2	2	14	731,659
1989	4	29	0	6	18	1,312,479
1990	20	23	0	0	12	520,420
1991	8	29	0	2	17	604,854
1992	9	29	1	3	13	876,492
1993	13	30	0	0	10	746,646
1994	9	31	0	0	13	854,280
1995	19	31	1	0	8	850,632
1996	29	31	0	0	2	740,185
1997	26	31	0	0	4	946,179
Lifetime		720	59	84	388	$16,620,883

BOBBY LABONTE

Born: May 8, 1964.
Corpus Christi, TX
Resides: Trinity, NC
Wife: Donna.
Children: Tyler, 3

No. 18 Interstate Batteries Pontiac

Career highlights won his only race in '96 in the season finale at Atlanta, the same day older brother Terry clinched his second Winston Cup title . . . in fourth season driving for former Washington Redskins coach Joe Gibbs . . . spent two seasons with the Bill Davis team . . . runner-up to Jeff Gordon in the '93 Winston Cup Rookie of the Year standings . . . Busch Grand National champion in '91 . . . finished just three points behind '92 Grand National titlist Joe Nemechek . . . owns Grand National car:

his driver, David Green, won the '94 BGN championship . . . began racing at Texas short tracks . . . favorite actress: Demi Moore . . . favorite actors: Mel Gibson and Tommy Lee Jones . . . favorite comedian: Steve Martin . . . enjoys working with computers.

YEAR	RANK	EVENTS	POLES	WINS	TOP 10	MONEY
1991	66	2	0	0	0	8,350
1993	19	30	1	0	6	395,660
1994	21	31	0	0	14	550,305
1995	10	31	2	3	14	1,413,682
1996	11	31	4	1	14	1,475,196
1997	7	32	3	1	18	1,943,239
Lifetime		157	10	5	54	$5,786,432

JEFF GREEN

Born: Sept. 6, 1962
Owensboro, KY
Resides: Owensboro, KY
Wife: Michelle

No. 20 Cartoon Network Chevrolet

Career highlights inherited the Cartoon Network Chevy ride from Robert Pressley last season . . . younger brother of drivers David and Mark Green . . . finished fourth in the 1996 Busch Grand National standings . . . drove for Dale and Teresa Earnhardt in the Grand National series . . . started in racing with go-karts, then moved up to stock cars at Kentucky Motor Speedway near Owensboro . . . dominated the '91 season at Nashville Speedway.

YEAR	RANK	EVENTS	POLES	WINS	TOP 10	MONEY
1996	66	2	0	0	0	8,350
1997	39	20	0	0	2	434,685
Lifetime		145	7	4	38	$4,277,878

MICHAEL WALTRIP

Born: April 30, 1963.
Owensboro, KY
Resides: Sherrills Ford, NC
Wife: Elizabeth "Buffy."
Children: Caitlin, 7; Margaret Carol, 1.

No. 21 Citgo Ford

Career highlights drives for the Wood Brothers, Winston Cup pioneers . . . won the '96 Winston nonpoints race at Charlotte . . . still seeking his first victory in 13th full Winston Cup season . . . best career finish: second at Pocono in '88 . . . fielding a second Busch Grand National team this year, with Patty Moise as driver . . . younger brother of three-time Winston Cup champion Darrell Waltrip . . . started racing on Kentucky short tracks . . . NASCAR Dash series champion in '83 . . . first Winston Cup pole at Dover in '91 . . . lived with Richard and Kyle Petty when he started racing in North Carolina . . . plays basketball and golf in his spare time . . . owns a '73 Cadillac Eldorado and an '81 Beechcraft Baron.

YEAR	RANK	EVENTS	POLES	WINS	TOP 10	MONEY
1985	57	5	0	0	0	9,540
1986	19	28	0	0	0	108,767
1987	20	29	0	0	1	205,370
1988	18	29	0	0	3	240,400
1989	18	29	0	0	5	249,233
1990	16	29	0	0	10	395,507
1991	15	29	2	0	12	440,812
1992	23	29	0	0	2	410,545
1993	17	30	0	0	5	529,923
1994	12	31	0	0	9	720,426
1995	12	31	0	0	8	898,338
1996	14	31	0	0	11	1,182,811
1997	18	32	0	0	6	1,015,384
Lifetime		362	2	0	72	$6,407,056

WARD BURTON

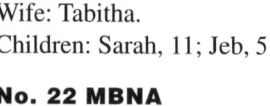

Born: Oct. 25, 1961
Danville, VA
Resides: South Boston, VA
Wife: Tabitha.
Children: Sarah, 11; Jeb, 5

No. 22 MBNA America Pontiac

Career highlights during rookie Winston Cup season in '94 was the fastest qualifier for the fall race at Charlotte and finished runner-up at Pocono . . . older brother of Winston Cup driver Jeff Burton . . . started racing go-karts at age 8, moved on to street stock and late model stocks at tracks near his South Boston, Virginia, home . . . in rookie Busch Grand National season in '90 registered three top-10 finishes for car owner Mike Swaim . . . graduated from Hargrave Military Academy, where he was on the rifle team . . . attended Elon College for 2½ years . . . sponsors the Ward Burton Wildlife Foundation at Patrick Henry School for Boys and Girls.

YEAR	RANK	EVENTS	POLES	WINS	TOP 10	MONEY
1994	35	26	1	0	2	304,700
1995	22	29	0	1	6	634,655
1996	33	27	1	0	4	873,619
1997	24	31	1	0	7	977,044
Lifetime		113	3	1	19	$2,790,018

JIMMY SPENCER

Born: Feb. 15, 1957.
Berwick, PA
Resides: Huntersville, NC
Wife: Pat.
Children: James, 11; Katrina, 9

No. 23 Winston Ford

Career highlights drives for Travis Carter . . . previously drove for two NASCAR legends: Junior Johnson and Bobby Allison . . . gained both his Winston Cup victories, in the summer races at Talladega and Daytona, with Johnson in '94 . . . first Winston Cup pole: North Wilkesboro in '94 . . . surpassed $1 million in earnings for the first time in '96 . . . earned Sears DieHard Racer award in '96 for completing the most miles . . . won Winston Open at Charlotte in '96 . . . nicknamed "Mr. Excitement" during his short-track driving days . . . two-time Winston Modified national champion ('86 and '87).

YEAR	RANK	EVENTS	POLES	WINS	TOP 10	MONEY
1989	34	17	0	0	3	121,065
1990	24	26	0	0	2	219,775
1991	25	29	0	0	6	283,620
1992	33	12	0	0	3	186,085
1993	12	30	0	0	10	686,026
1994	29	29	1	2	4	479,235
1995	26	29	0	0	4	479,235
1996	15	31	0	0	9	1,090,876
1997	20	32	0	0	4	1,016,109
Lifetime		235	1	2	49	$4,589,651

JEFF GORDON

Born: Aug. 4, 1971
Vallejo, CA
Resides: Mooresville, NC
Wife: Brooke

No. 24 Du Pont Refinishes Chevrolet

Career highlights won his second Winston Cup championship in 1997 . . . at 24 became the youngest Winston Cup point champion when he won the 1995 title . . . runner-up to teammate Terry Labonte in '96 . . . won last year's Daytona 500 . . . one of the most visible people in all of sports . . . tamed Darlington by winning three consecutive races at the fabled racetrack . . . added to his Darlington achievements by winning last year's Southern 500 and collecting the Winston Million bonus . . . active in bone-marrow donor drive: car owner Rick Hendrick was diagnosed with leukemia early last year . . . '95 Winston Cup title was Hendrick's first after fielding cars in the series since '84 . . . began racing go-karts and quarter-midgets at age 5 . . . '79 and '81 national quarter-midget champion . . . '91 USAC Silver Crown winner . . . has more than 500 short-track victories . . . '91 Busch Grand National Rookie of the Year . . . won a record 11 Grand National poles in '92 . . . stepfather, John Bickford, moved family to Midwest so Jeff, then 13, could race . . . wife, Brooke, is a former Miss Winston . . . relaxes by skiing, playing golf, racquetball, and video games.

YEARS	RANK	EVENTS	POLES	WINS	TOP 10	MONEY
1992	79T	1	0	0	0	6,285
1993	14	30	1	0	11	765,168
1994	8	31	1	2	14	1,799,523
1995	1	31	8	7	23	4,347,343
1996	2	31	5	10	24	3,428,485
1997	1	32	1	10	23	4,201,227
Lifetime		156	16	29	95	$14,548,031

KENNY IRWIN, JR.

Born: Aug. 5, 1969
Indianapolis, IN
Resides: Indianapolis, IN
Single

No. 28 Texaco Havoline Ford

Career highlights promising Winston Cup rookie . . . succeeds Ernie Irvan in the No. 28 Ford . . . Said Tim Stephens, of the Liberty Racing team: "Everybody has been looking for the next Jeff Gordon: we think we found him." . . . second fastest qualifier in last year's September race at Richmond; driving a David Blair Ford, Irwin led 12 laps before finishing eighth . . . Irwin likes the Richmond track: in only his second NASCAR Craftsman Truck series start in '96, he won the

pole position . . . another young NASCAR driver with an open-wheel racing background . . . '96 USAC Skoal National midget series champion . . . goal was always to race in Winston Cup. No career statistics: no previous Winston Cup record.

DERRIKE COPE

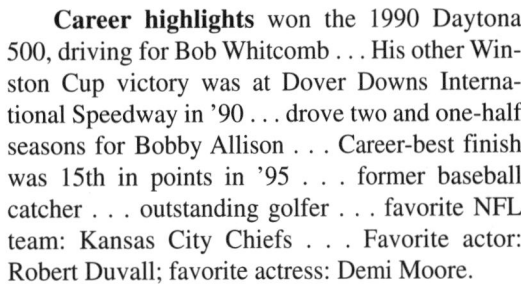

Born: Nov. 3, 1958
San Diego, CA
Resides: Huntersville, NC
Wife: Renee

No. 30 Jiffy-Lube Pontiac

Career highlights won the 1990 Daytona 500, driving for Bob Whitcomb . . . His other Winston Cup victory was at Dover Downs International Speedway in '90 . . . drove two and one-half seasons for Bobby Allison . . . Career-best finish was 15th in points in '95 . . . former baseball catcher . . . outstanding golfer . . . favorite NFL team: Kansas City Chiefs . . . Favorite actor: Robert Duvall; favorite actress: Demi Moore.

YEAR	RANK	EVENTS	POLES	WINS	TOP 10	MONEY
1982	101	1	0	0	0	625
1984	57	3	0	0	0	6,500
1985	55	2	0	0	0	7,100
1986	45	5	0	0	1	8,025
1987	37	11	0	0	0	33,750
1988	31	26	0	0	0	132,835
1989	29	23	0	0	4	125,630
1990	18	29	0	2	6	569,451
1991	28	28	0	0	2	419,380
1992	21	29	0	0	3	277,215
1993	26	30	0	0	1	402,515
1994	30	30	0	0	2	398,436
1995	15	31	0	0	8	683,075
1996	35	29	0	0	3	675,781
1997	27	31	0	0	2	707,404
Lifetime		308	0	2	32	$4,447,722

MIKE SKINNER

Born: June 28, 1957
Ontario, CA
Resides: Sophia, NC
Wife: Beth
Children: Jamie, 20;
Dustin, 12

No. 31 Lowe's Chevrolet

Career highlights won the Daytona 500 pole last year in his first full season racing in Winston

Cup . . . champion of the first NASCAR Craftsman Truck Series championship in 1995 . . . won eight races in each of his two seasons in the truck series . . . took 10 poles in his first truck season, five in his second season . . . played baseball and basketball in high school in California . . . outstanding pool player . . . owns three horses . . . favorite movie: *Grumpier Old Men;* favorite actor: Clint Eastwood.

YEAR	RANK	EVENTS	POLES	WINES	TOP 10	MONEY
1986	61	3	0	0	0	4,255
1990	96	1	0	0	0	2,825
1991	64T	2	0	0	0	8,505
1992	59	2	0	0	0	13,450
1993	80	1	0	0	0	5,180
1994	72T	1	0	0	0	9,550
1996	47	5	0	0	0	65,850
1997	30	31	2	0	3	791,819
Lifetime		46	2	0	3	$901,434

KEN SCHRADER

Born: May 29, 1955
St. Louis, MO
Resides: Concord, NC
Wife: Ann
Children: Dorothy, 8; Sheldon, 2

No. 33 Skoal Chevrolet

Career highlights spent eight years driving for Hendrick Motorsports before joining Andy Petree's team . . . won three consecutive Daytona 500 pole positions from 1988 to '90 . . . known as a strong qualifier: in 1993 he won six poles . . . 1985 Winston Cup Rookie of the Year driving for Junie Donlavey . . . first Winston Cup victory was in the DieHard 500 in 1988 at Talladega . . . drove USAC midgets, sprint cars, and Silver Crown cars . . . 1982 Silver Crown champion . . . '83 sprint titlist . . . father was a racer . . . for years he was one of the busiest drivers on the circuit, racing almost any time, anywhere . . . favorite movie: "The Sting" . . . favorite singer: Garth Brooks . . . favorite baseball team: St. Louis Cardinals . . . hobbies include collecting old trucks and cars.

YEAR	RANK	EVENTS	POLES	WINS	TOP 10	MONEY
1984	53	5	0	0	0	16,425
1985	16	28	0	0	3	211,523
1986	16	29	0	0	4	235,904

1987	10	29	1	0	10	375,918
1988	5	29	2	1	17	631,544
1989	5	29	4	1	14	1,037,941
1990	10	29	3	0	14	769,934
1991	9	29	0	2	18	772,434
1992	17	29	1	0	14	639,679
1993	9	30	6	0	15	952,748
1994	4	31	0	0	18	1,211,062
1995	17	31	1	0	10	886,566
1996	12	31	0	0	10	1,089,603
1997	10	32	2	0	8	1,109,782
Lifetime		391	20	4	152	$9,941,063

TODD BODINE

Born: Feb. 27, 1964.
Elmira, NY
Resides: Davidson, NC
Wife: Lynn

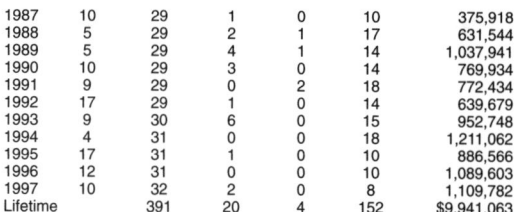

No. 35 Tabasco Pontiac

Career highlights returns to Winston Cup after a successful '97 season in the Busch Grand National series where he was runner-up to Randy LaJoie . . . youngest of the three racing Bodine brothers . . . drove a full Winston Cup schedule for Butch Mock in 1994 and 10 races for Mock in '95 . . . had two top-five finishes in '94 . . . Winston Cup debut was in '92 at his home track, Watkins Glen, New York . . . 14th driver in Busch Grand National series to win more than $1 million in his career . . . father and grandfather owned the Chemung (NY) Speedrome . . . Todd built race cars before he started racing them . . . eats pasta the night before every race.

YEAR	RANK	EVENTS	POLES	WINS	TOP 10	MONEY
1992	87T	1	0	0	0	3,485
1993	40	10	0	0	0	63,245
1994	20	30	0	0	7	504,316
1995	33	28	0	0	3	664,620
1996	40	10	0	0	1	198,525
1997	52	5	1	0	0	125,845
Lifetime		84	1	0	11	$1,560,036

ERNIE IRVAN

Born: Jan. 13, 1959
Salinas, CA
Resides: Concord, NC
Wife: Kim
Children: Jordan, 4

No. 36 Skittles Pontiac

Career highlights joined the MB2 Skittles-sponsored team after four and one-half seasons with the Robert Yates team . . . succeeded the late Davey Allison as the driver of Yates's No. 28 Texaco/Havoline car . . . survived life-threatening practice crash at Michigan in August 1994 . . . returned to the circuit at North Wilkesboro (N.C.) on Oct. 1, 1995: led 30 laps and finished sixth . . . won at New Hampshire and Richmond in '96 . . . won last year's June race at Michigan with tears in his eyes . . . winner of the '91 Daytona 500 . . . top finish in the points standings was fifth in '91 . . . runnerup to Ken Bouchard in the '88 Winston Cup Rookie of the Year standings . . . played football and tennis in high school . . . father helped him build his first race car . . . enjoys listening to James Taylor music.

YEAR	RANK	EVENTS	POLES	WINS	TOP 10	MONEY
1987	52	5	0	0	1	23,050
1988	26	25	0	0	0	96,370
1989	22	29	0	0	4	155,329
1990	9	29	3	1	13	535,280
1991	5	29	1	2	19	1,079,017
1992	11	29	3	3	11	996,885
1993	6	29	4	3	14	1,400,468
1994	22	20	5	3	15	1,311,522
1995	48	3	0	0	2	54,875
1996	10	31	1	2	16	1,683,313
1997	14	32	2	1	13	1,492,739
Lifetime		261	19	15	108	$8,828,848

JEREMY MAYFIELD

Born: May 27, 1969
Owensboro, KY
Resides: Cornelius, NC
Wife: Christina.

No. 37 Kmart Ford

Career highlights won the pole at Talladega in '96 while driving for the Cale Yarborough-owned team . . . was "traded" to the Kranefuss-Haas team later in '96 for John Andretti . . . first pole position was in '96 at the July Talladega race . . . '93 ARCA Rookie of the Year . . . inspired by Owensboro, Kentucky native Darrell Waltrip to begin a racing career . . . Mayfield moved to Nashville at an early age . . . Favorite movie: *Rocky* . . . Favorite actress: Heather Locklear . . . favorite actor: Clint Eastwood . . . favorite singer: Garth Brooks.

YEAR	RANK	EVENTS	POLES	WINS	TOP 10	MONEY
1993	74T	1	0	0	0	4,830
1994	37	20	0	0	0	226,265
1995	31	27	0	0	1	436,875
1996	26	30	1	0	2	592,853
1997	13	32	0	0	8	943,794
Lifetime		110	1	0	11	$2,204,547

STERLING MARLIN

Born: June 30, 1957
Franklin, TN
Resides: Columbia, TN
Wife: Paula
Children: Steadman, 17; Sutherln, 7

No. 40 Coors Light Chevrolet

Career highlights two-time winner of the Daytona 500 (1994 and '95) . . . his first career victory was in the '94 Daytona 500 . . . also won the '96 summer race at Daytona . . . best '97 finish was third in the Pepsi 400 at Daytona . . . moved to the Felix Sabates team after four seasons with Morgan-McClure . . . has finished in the top 10 in points five times . . . '83 Winston Cup Rookie of the Year . . . outstanding high school football player . . . big fan of the University of Tennessee football team . . . father, "Coo Coo," is a former Winston Cup driver . . . Sterling's Winston Cup debut was in '76 when he substituted for his father, who had a broken shoulder . . . collects Civil War artifacts.

YEAR	RANK	EVENTS	POLES	WINS	TOP 10	MONEY
1976	101	1	0	0	0	565
1978	67	2	0	0	1	10,320
1979	85	1	0	0	0	505
1980	49	5	0	0	2	29,810
1981	93	2	0	0	0	1,955
1982	NR	1	0	0	0	4,015
1983	19	30	0	0	1	148,253
1984	37	14	0	0	2	54,355
1985	37	8	0	0	0	31,155
1986	36	10	0	0	4	113,070
1987	11	29	0	0	8	306,412
1988	10	29	0	0	13	521,464
1989	12	29	0	0	13	473,267
1990	14	29	0	0	10	369,167
1991	7	29	2	0	15	633,690
1992	10	29	5	0	13	649,048
1993	15	30	0	0	8	628,835
1994	14	31	1	1	11	1,140,683
1995	3	31	1	3	22	2,253,502
1996	8	31	0	2	10	1,588,425
1997	25	32	0	0	6	1,287,570
Lifetime		403	9	6	140	$10,246,066

Derrike Cope (No. 36) pulls ahead of Sterling Marlin (the Coors Light car) in a 1997 race at Dover.

STEVE GRISSOM

Born: June 26, 1963
Gadsden, AL
Resides: Concord, NC
Wife: Susan
Children: Kyle, 8

No. 41 Kodiak Chevrolet

Career highlights runner-up to Jeff Burton in the 1994 Winston Cup Rookie of the Year balloting . . . began racing on Alabama dirt tracks, following in his father's racing tracks . . . won 11 Busch Grand National races . . . won '85 All-Pro series

before moving to the Grand National series in '87 . . . Winston Cup debut was in '90 driving one race for Dick Moroso . . . captain of high school football team: was offered a scholarship to the University of Alabama; also played basketball and baseball . . . enjoys riding dirt bikes with son Kyle.

YEAR	RANK	EVENTS	POLES	WINS	TOP 10	MONEY
1990	78T	1	0	0	0	4,275
1993	74T	1	0	0	0	6,485
1994	28	27	0	0	3	300,915
1995	27	29	0	0	4	509,047
1996	39	13	0	0	2	314,983
1997	21	31	0	0	6	1,045,374
Lifetime		102	0	0	15	$2,181,079

JOE NEMECHEK

Born: Sept. 26, 1963
Naples, FL
Resides: Mooresville, NC
Wife: Andrea
Children: John Hunter, 1

No. 42 Bell South Chevrolet

Career highlights owned his team for two seasons prior to joining Felix Sabates . . . 1990 Busch Grand National Rookie of the Year . . . majored in mechanical engineering at Florida Institute of Technology . . . began racing in motorcross at age 13, winning more than 300 races over six years . . . started racing stock cars in '86 . . . All-Pro late model series champion and Rookie of the Year in '89 . . . driving for Larry Hedrick, finished third in '94 Winston Cup Rookie of the Year chase, just 13 points behind Jeff Burton . . . younger brother, John, was killed at Las Vegas last year during a NASCAR Craftsman Truck series race . . . Joe played four sports in high school . . . hobbies include boating and fishing . . . favorite NFL team: Miami Dolphins.

YEAR	RANK	EVENTS	POLES	WINS	TOP 10	MONEY
1993	44	5	0	0	0	56,580
1994	27	29	0	0	3	389,565
1995	28	29	0	0	4	428,925
1996	34	29	0	0	2	666,247
1997	28	30	2	0	3	732,194
Lifetime		122	2	0	12	$2,273,511

JOHN ANDRETTI

Born: March 12, 1963
Bethlehem, PA
Resides: Mooresville, NC
Wife: Nancy
Children: Jarett, 5; Olivia, 2

No. 43 STP Pontiac

Career highlights won first Winston Cup race last year at Daytona in July . . . gained first pole in the Winston 500 at Talladega . . . former Indy car driver . . . first Indy car victory was in Australia in '91 . . . Talk about long-distance driving: in '94, finished 10th in the Indy 500 and 36th in the Coca-Cola 600 at Charlotte on the same day . . . nephew of racing legend Mario Andretti and cousin of Indy car driver

Michael Andretti . . . co-driving with Mario and Michael, placed sixth in the 24 Hours of LeMans in '88 . . . his father, Aldo, is Mario's brother . . . has degree in business management from Moravian College in Bethlehem . . . godfather is A.J. Foyt . . .

YEAR	RANK	EVENTS	POLES	WINS	TOP 10	MONEY
1993	50	4	0	0	0	24,915
1994	32	29	0	0	0	391,920
1995	18	31	1	0	5	593,542
1996	31	30	0	0	3	688,511
1997	23	32	1	1	3	1,115,725
Lifetime		126	2	1	11	$2,824,791

KYLE PETTY

Born: June 2, 1960
Randleman, NC
Resides: High Point, NC
Wife: Patti.
Children: Adam, 17; Austin, 15; Montgomery Lee, 12

No. 44 Hot Wheels Pontiac

Career highlights Son of racing legend Richard Petty . . . Kyle's the first third-generation driver to win a Winston Cup race: grandfather Lee won his first in 1949 . . . Kyle is the first Petty to win $1 million in a season (1992) . . . returned to Petty Enterprises last year after four seasons with Felix Sabates . . . career-best in points standings: fifth in '92 and '93 . . . in '79, won an ARCA 200-miler at Daytona in his first race on a closed course . . . organizes an annual cross-country charity motorcyle ride . . . won the 1993 Daytona 500 pole . . . has recorded country music songs.

YEAR	RANK	EVENTS	POLES	WINS	TOP 10	MONEY
1980	28	15	0	0	6	36,350
1981	12	31	0	0	10	117,433
1982	15	29	0	0	4	126,285
1983	13	30	0	0	2	163,848
1984	16	30	0	0	6	329,920
1985	9	28	0	0	12	296,367
1986	10	29	0	1	14	403,242
1987	7	29	0	1	13	544,437
1988	13	29	0	1	8	377,092
1989	30	19	0	0	5	117,022
1990	11	29	2	1	4	746,326
1991	31	18	2	1	4	413,727
1992	5	29	3	2	17	1,107,063
1993	5	30	1	1	15	914,662
1994	15	31	0	0	7	818,832
1995	30	30	0	1	5	698,875
1996	27	28	0	0	2	689,041
1997	15	32	0	0	9	834,639
Lifetime		501	8	8	155	$8,745,971

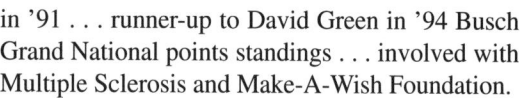

WALLY DALLENBACH

Born: May 23, 1963
Basalt, CO
Resides: Greensboro, NC
Wife: Robin.
Children: Jacob, 7; Wyatt, 5

No. 46 First Union Chevrolet

Career highlights best career finish was second in the '93 Bud at the Glen . . . finished third at Sears Point in '96 . . . drove one season ('96) for NASCAR pioneer Bud Moore . . . four-time winner of the 24 Hours of Daytona . . . would be a professional hunter in Africa if he weren't racing . . . wife, Robin, also is a race-car driver . . . father, Wally Sr., is a former Indy-car driver who served for many years as chief steward for the CART Indy car series. He is now special assistant to CART president Andrew Craig.

YEAR	RANK	EVENTS	POLES	WINS	TOP 10	MONEY
1991	38	11	0	0	0	54,020
1992	24	29	0	0	1	220,245
1993	22	30	0	0	4	474,340
1994	38	14	0	0	3	241,492
1995	50	2	0	0	1	63,900
1996	25	30	0	0	3	837,001
1997	41	22	0	0	1	461,279
Lifetime		138	0	0	13	$2,352,277

RICKY CRAVEN

Born: May 24, 1966
Newburgh, ME.
Resides: Concord, NC
Wife: Cathleen
Children: Riley Diane, 6; Richard Everett, 1

No. 50 Budweiser Chevrolet

Career highlights third in last year's Daytona 500, giving Hendrick Motorsports a sweep of the first three places . . . was injured while practicing for the inaugural Winston Cup race at Texas Motor Speedway . . . previously drove two seasons for Larry Hedrick . . . won his first two Winston Cup poles in '96 . . . Daytona 500 finish last year matched his best career finishes at Rockingham and Darlington in '96 . . . NASCAR Busch North titlist

in '91 . . . runner-up to David Green in '94 Busch Grand National points standings . . . involved with Multiple Sclerosis and Make-A-Wish Foundation.

YEAR	RANK	EVENTS	POLES	WINS	TOP 10	MONEY
1991	82T	1	0	0	0	3,750
1995	24	31	0	0	4	597,054
1996	20	31	2	0	5	941,959
1997	19	30	0	0	7	1,139,860
Lifetime		93	2	0	16	$2,682,623

DAVE MARCIS

Born: March 1, 1941
Wausau, WI
Resides: Avery's Creek, NC
Wife: Helen
Children: Shawn Marie, Richard

No. 71 Realtree Camouflage Chevrolet

Career highlights has five career Winston Cup victories: first was in Martinsville in 1975; last was in '82 at Richmond . . . runner-up to Richard Petty in the '75 points race . . . first Winston Cup race was the 1968 Daytona 500 . . . has competed in 29 consecutive Daytona 500s . . . wears black leather hard-soled shoes when he is racing . . . product of Wisconsin short tracks . . . father owned a garage: Dave's first attraction to racing occurred when he drove his father's cars in a field near the garage . . . hopes to run a fishing resort and/or restaurant when he retires from racing.

YEAR	RANK	EVENTS	POLES	WINS	TOP 10	MONEY
1968	34	10	0	0	2	8,199
1969	19	37	0	0	11	32,383
1970	9	47	0	0	15	41,111
1971	21	29	2	0	14	37,582
1972	15	27	0	0	11	45,012
1973	24	23	0	0	6	30,253
1974	6	30	0	0	18	83,377
1975	2	30	4	1	18	240,646
1976	6	30	7	3	16	218,250
1977	25	18	0	0	7	72,605
1978	5	30	0	0	24	205,871
1979	20	25	0	0	6	56,434
1980	9	31	0	0	14	249,027
1981	9	31	1	0	9	162,213
1982	6	30	0	1	14	249,027
1983	11	30	0	0	7	306,355
1984	13	30	0	0	9	330,766
1985	18	28	0	0	5	173,467
1986	17	29	0	0	4	220,461
1987	18	29	0	0	7	256,354
1988	19	29	0	0	2	212,485
1989	25	27	0	0	1	196,161
1990	21	29	0	0	0	242,724

1991	29	27	0	0	1	219,760
1992	29	29	0	0	0	218,045
1993	33	23	0	0	0	202,305
1994	36	23	0	0	1	261,650
1995	35	28	0	0	0	337,853
1996	38	27	0	0	0	435,177
1997	42	19	0	0	0	427,364
Lifetime		835	14	5	222	$5,674,055

RICK MAST

Born: March 4, 1957
Lexington, VA
Resides: Rockbridge Baths, VA
Wife: Sharon
Children: Ricky 14; twins Katie and Sarah, 1

No. 75 Remington Arms Ford

Career highlights won the pole for the inaugural Brickyard 400 at Indianapolis Motor Speedway in 1994 . . . first pole was at Atlanta in '92 in Richard Petty's final race . . . top career finish was second at Rockingham in the fall '94 race despite hitting the wall . . . best '96 finish was fourth at Martinsville . . . drove for Richard Jackson for six years . . . started racing at age 16 . . . father and uncle owned race cars and local race tracks . . . won nine Busch Grand National races . . . played high school basketball . . . has a business administration degree from Blue Ridge (Virginia) Community College.

YEAR	RANK	EVENTS	POLES	WINS	TOP 10	MONEY
1988	NR	2	0	0	0	9,190
1989	35	13	0	0	1	128,102
1990	31	20	0	0	1	112,875
1991	21	29	0	0	3	344,020
1992	22	29	1	0	5	350,740
1993	21	30	0	0	5	568,095
1994	18	31	1	0	10	733,361
1995	21	31	1	0	3	749,550
1996	18	31	0	0	5	924,559
1997	32	29	0	0	2	829,339
Lifetime		245	3	0	31	$4,749,829

ROBERT PRESSLEY

Born: April 8, 1959
Washington, D.C.
Resides: Asheville, NC
Wife: Gina
Children: Coleman, 9; Shelby, 3

No. 77 Jasper Motorsports Ford

Career highlights spent the 1995 and '96 seasons driving for Leo Jackson . . . best career finish: fourth at North Wilkesboro in '96 . . . runnerup in '95 Winston Cup Rookie of the Year points to Ricky Craven . . . track champion at New Asheville (N.C.) Speedway and Greenville-Pickens (S.C.) Speedway . . . father, Bob, continues to race on short tracks in the Carolinas . . . Robert and NBA center Brad Daugherty formed a Busch Grand National team in '88 . . . brother, Charley, is a crew chief for Hedrick Motorsports . . . favorite actress: Goldie Hawn . . . favorite actors: Andy Griffith and Don Knotts . . . favorite singers: Alan Jackson and Janet Jackson.

YEAR	RANK	EVENTS	POLES	WINS	TOP 10	MONEY
1994	57	3	0	0	0	39,485
1995	29	31	0	0	1	695,875
1996	32	30	0	0	3	690,465
1997	43	14	0	0	0	252,478
Lifetime		78	0	0	4	1,678,303

KENNY WALLACE

Born: Aug. 23, 1963
St. Louis, MO
Resides: Concord, NC
Wife: Kim.
Children: Brooke, 10; Brandy, 8; Brittany, 7

No. 81 Square D Ford.

Career highlights substituted for injured Ernie Irvan in Robert Yates car for final 10 races in '94 . . . best career finish was fourth at Martinsville in '94 . . . top finish last year also was at Martinsville, sixth in the spring race . . . Busch Grand National Rookie of the Year in '89 . . . runner-up for Grand National championship in '91 . . . '86 ASA Rookie of the Year . . . known for his sense of humor: voted class clown in high school . . . younger brother of Rusty Wallace . . . built a go-kart track in backyard: holds night on the track races during race weekends at Charlotte . . . favorite baseball team: St. Louis Cardinals . . . favorite baseball player: Ozzie Smith.

YEAR	RANK	EVENTS	POLES	WINS	TOP 10	MONEY
1990	81T	1	0	0	0	6,050
1991	44	5	0	0	0	58,325

YEAR	RANK	EVENTS	POLES	WINS	TOP 10	MONEY
1993	23	30	0	0	3	330,325
1994	40	12	0	0	3	235,005
1995	42	11	0	0	0	151,700
1996	28	30	0	0	2	457,665
1997	33	31	2	0	2	926,501
Lifetime		120	2	0	10	$2,165,571

DALE JARRETT

Born: Nov. 26, 1956
Newton, NC
Resides: Hickory, NC
Wife: Kelley.
Children: Jason, 21; Natalee, 9; Karsyn, 7; Zachary, 2

No. 88 Quality Care Ford

Career highlights last year was his best season, as he finished second in the points standings and posted a career-high seven victories . . . in '96 became the first driver to win the Daytona 500 and Brickyard 400 in the same season . . . also won the 1993 Daytona 500 . . . had a chance to be only the second driver to win the $1 million Winston Million: he started on the pole in the Southern 500 at Darlington, but skidded in another car's oil and finished 14th . . . drove three seasons for former NFL coach Joe Gibbs . . . son of two-time Winston Cup champion Ned Jarrett . . . Dale is an excellent golfer and was an all-conference selection in football and basketball in high school.

YEARS	RANK	EVENTS	POLES	WINS	TOP 10	MONEY
1984	72	3	0	0	0	7,305
1986	107T	1	0	0	0	990
1987	26	24	0	0	2	143,405
1988	23	29	0	0	1	118,640
1989	24	29	0	0	5	232,317
1990	25	24	0	0	7	214,495
1991	17	29	0	1	8	444,256
1992	19	29	0	0	8	418,648
1993	4	30	0	1	18	1,242,394
1994	16	30	0	1	9	893,754
1995	13	31	1	1	14	1,363,158
1996	3	31	2	4	21	2,985,418
1997	2	32	3	7	23	2,512,382
Lifetime		322	6	15	116	10,577,162

DICK TRICKLE

Born: Oct. 27, 1941
Wisconsin Rapids, WI
Resides: Iron Station, NC
Wife: Darlene.
Children: Victoria, Todd, Chad

No. 90 Helig-Meyers/Simmons Ford

Career highlights 1989 Winston Cup Rookie of the Year, at age 48 . . . replaced the injured Mike Alexander in the Stavola Brothers car in '89 . . . won first, and only, pole at Dover in '90 in his 55th Winston Cup attempt . . . won '90 Winston Open . . . popular midwestern driver who has more than 1,200 feature victories . . . attended first race when he was 10; made his racing debut in 1959 as an 18-year-old . . . favorite sports team: Green Bay Packers . . . favorite athlete: Bart Starr . . . enjoys working on his property when he has time.

YEAR	RANK	EVENTS	POLES	WINS	TOP 10	MONEY
1970	NR	2	0	0	0	1,415
1973	81	1	0	0	1	3,385
1974	47	3	0	0	3	10,828
1975	113	1	0	0	0	1,705
1976	105T	1	0	0	0	1,225
1977	98T	1	0	0	0	1,100
1978	108	1	0	0	0	910
1984	87	1	0	0	0	7,500
1985	55	3	0	0	1	8,650
1986	55	2	0	0	9	19,175
1989	15	28	0	0	4	343,728
1990	22	29	1	0	4	350,990
1991	35	14	0	0	1	129,125
1992	20	29	0	0	9	429,521
1993	30	26	0	0	2	240,165
1994	34	25	0	0	1	244,806
1995	25	31	0	0	1	694,920
1996	36	26	0	0	1	404,927
1997	31	28	0	0	2	656,189
Lifetime		252	1	0	35	$3,550,264

BILL ELLIOTT

Born: Oct. 8, 1955
Cumming, GA
Resides: Blairsville, GA.
Wife: Cindy
Children: Starr, Chase

No. 94 McDonald's Ford

Career highlights won record 11 superspeedway races in 1985, the year he also was the first driver to collect the Winston Million bonus for winning three of the series "crown jewels:" the Daytona and Winston 500s and the Southern 500 at Darlington . . . voted Most Popular Driver a record 11 times . . . 1988 Winston Cup champion . . . three-time runner-up in points ('85, '87 and '92) . . . first full Winston Cup season was 1983 . . . drove 10 seasons for Harry Melling, then three for Junior Johnson . . . voted American Driver of the Year twice, in 1985 and '88 . . . recorded fastest official time in a stock car, 212.809 mph, qualifying for the '87 Winston 500 at Talladega . . . began racing on Georgia's short tracks with brothers Dan and Ernie . . . flies his own aircraft . . . Favorite movie: *Stroker Ace.*

YEAR	RANK	EVENTS	POLES	WINS	TOP 10	MONEY
1976	41	8	0	0	0	11,635
1977	35	10	0	0	2	20,075
1978	33	10	0	0	5	42,215
1979	28	14	0	0	5	58,215
1980	34	12	0	0	4	44,005
1981	30	13	1	0	6	70,320
1982	25	21	1	0	9	201,030
1983	3	30	0	1	22	514,030
1984	3	30	4	3	24	680,344
1985	2	28	11	11	18	2,433,187
1986	4	29	4	2	16	1,049,142
1987	2	29	8	6	20	1,599,210
1988	1	29	6	6	22	1,554,639
1989	6	29	2	3	14	849,370
1990	4	29	2	1	16	1,090,730
1991	11	29	2	1	12	705,605
1992	2	29	2	5	17	1,692,381
1993	8	30	2	0	15	955,859
1994	10	31	1	1	12	951,679
1995	8	31	2	0	11	996,816
1996	30	24	0	0	6	716,506
1997	8	32	1	0	14	1,377,607
Lifetime		527	49	40	271	17,614,540

DAVID GREEN

Born: Jan. 28, 1958
Owensboro, KY
Resides: Archdale, NC
Wife: Diane

No. 96 Catepillar Chevrolet

Career highlights Winston Cup rookie last year . . . suffered a broken left shoulder in a crash at Bristol . . . Busch Grand National champion in 1994, runner-up in '96 . . . finished second to Jeff Gordon in '91 Busch Rookie of the Year standings . . . in his first season of racing, he won four of his first five races at the short track in Owensboro, home town of Darrell Waltrip . . . spent the '92 season working as a mechanic with Bobby Labonte's Busch team . . . brothers Jeff and Mark race in the Grand National series . . . favorite sports team: Chicago Bulls.

CHAD LITTLE

Born: April 23, 1962
Spokane, WA
Resides: Charlotte, NC
Wife: Donna

No. 97 John Deere Pontiac

Career highlights spent three seasons in the Busch Grand National series before returning to Winston Cup . . . team last year was co-owned by veteran NFL quarterback Mark Rypien . . . first Grand National victory was in the Goody's 300 at Daytona in 1995 . . . 1987 Winston West titlist . . . has marketing degree from Washington State and law degree from Gonzaga University Law School . . . all-city running back in high school.

YEAR	RANK	EVENTS	POLES	WINS	TOP 10	MONEY
1986	70	2	0	0	0	6,065
1987	59	2	0	0	0	8,810
1988	45	4	0	0	0	14,225
1989	38	8	0	0	0	44,690
1990	33	18	0	0	0	80,140
1991	27	28	0	0	1	184,190
1992	31	19	0	0	1	145,805
1993	51	3	0	0	0	41,040
1994	53	2	0	0	0	30,805
1995	53	2	0	0	0	22,775
1996	44	9	0	0	0	164,752
1997	36	29	0	0	1	555,914
Lifetime		123	0	0	3	$1,299,211

JEFF BURTON

Born: June 29, 1967
South Boston, VA
Resides: Huntersville, NC
Wife: Kim
Children: Kimberle

No. 99 Exide Batteries Ford

Career highlights won first Winston Cup race in the inaugural race at Texas Motor Speedway last year . . . followed that with a win at New Hampshire . . . won first Winston Cup pole at Michigan in '96 . . . younger brother of Ward Burton . . . developed racing itch at age five watching Ward race go-karts at a track in their home town of South Boston . . . worked his way up from short-track racing to the Busch Grand National series in '88, where he won five races in his rookie season . . . outstanding athlete in high school: played basketball and soccer . . . favorite sports team: Duke University's basketball squad.

YEAR	RANK	EVENTS	POLES	WINS	TOP 10	MONEY
1993	83T	1	0	0	0	9,550
1994	24	30	0	0	3	594,700
1995	32	29	0	0	2	628,270
1996	13	30	1	0	12	884,303
1997	4	32	0	3	18	1,858,234
Lifetime		122	1	3	35	$3,975,057

17

HALL OF FAME DRIVER REGISTER

BOBBY ALLISON

Born: Dec. 3, 1937

Hueytown, AL

Career highlights: forced to retire after serious crash midway through the 1988 season: 717 starts between 1961 and career-ending accident at Pocono . . . won 57 poles and 84 races, including 44 on superspeedways currently on the schedule . . . among his major victories: seven at Dover; six each at Riverside, Charlotte, and Daytona Beach; five each at Atlanta and Darlington; four each at Bristol, Michigan, Talladega, Rockingham and North Wilkesboro; three at Pocono; two at Ontario; and one at Nashville . . . 1983 Winston Cup champion and six-time most popular driver . . . three-time ('71, '72, and '83) NASCAR driver of the year . . . lost two sons to accidents, Clifford in a Busch Series practice session in Michigan and Davey in a helicopter crash at the Talladega Superspeedway in 1993 . . . struggled to field a competitive team after the 1988 crash left him unable to continue racing and financially strapped . . . finally gave up after the 1996 season.

YEAR	RANK	EVENTS	POLES	WINS	TOP 10	MONEY
1961	106	4	0	0	0	650
1965	34	8	0	0	3	4780
1966	10	33	4	3	15	23,420
1967	4	45	2	6	27	58,250
1968	11	37	2	2	20	52,288
1969	20	27	1	5	15	69,483
1970	2	46	5	3	35	149,745
1971	4	42	9	11	31	254,316
1972	2	31	12	10	27	348,939
1973	7	27	6	2	16	161,818
1974	4	27	3	2	17	178,437
1975	24	19	3	3	10	126,735
1976	4	30	2	0	19	230,170
1977	8	30	0	0	15	94,575
1978	2	30	1	5	22	411,517
1979	3	31	3	5	22	428,801
1980	6	31	2	4	18	378,970
1981	2	31	2	5	26	680,957
1982	2	30	1	8	20	795,078
1983	1	30	0	6	25	883,010
1984	6	30	0	2	18	641,049
1985	12	28	0	0	11	272,536
1986	7	29	0	1	15	503,095
1987	9	29	1	1	13	515,894
1988	33	13	0	1	6	409,295
Lifetime		718	59	85	446	$7,673,808

DAVEY ALLISON

Born: Feb. 25, 1961

Died: July 13, 1993

Hueytown, AL

Career highlights: was the 1987 rookie of the year after starting out in ARCA and Daytona Dash cars . . . won two races and had eight other top-10s in rookie year with owner Robert Yates . . . started 191 races, had 14 poles and 19 victories, including a Daytona 500, Coca-Cola World 600, GM-UAW Teamwork 500, a Mountain Dew Southern 500;

Bobby Allison flashes the No. 1 sign at Daytona in 1972.

won three times at Michigan, twice each at Richmond, Talladega, Rockingham, and Phoenix, and once each at Watkins Glen, Bristol, and North Wilkesboro . . . 1992 NASCAR driver of the year . . . killed in helicopter accident on infield at Talladega in July of 1993.

YEAR	RANK	EVENTS	POLES	WINS	TOP 10	MONEY
1985	71	3	0	0	1	11,715
1986	47	5	0	0	1	8,070
1987	21	22	5	2	10	361,060
1988	8	29	3	2	16	844,532
1989	11	29	1	2	13	640,956
1990	13	29	0	2	10	640,684
1991	3	29	3	5	16	1,712,924
1992	3	29	2	5	17	1,955,628
1993	31	16	0	1	8	513,585
Lifetime		191	14	19	92	6,689,154

DONNIE ALLISON

Born: Sept. 7, 1939
Hueytown, AL

Career highlights: retired during the 1988 season: made 242 Winston Cup starts between 1966 and 1988 . . . won 18 poles and 10 races, including three superspeedway triumphs at Charlotte, two each at Talladega and Rockingham, and one each at Daytona Beach and Atlanta . . . 1967 Winston Cup rookie of the year . . . finished fourth and was rookie of the race in the 1970 Indy 500 . . . was critically injured in a crash at Charlotte in 1981, a crash that effectively ended his career . . . was part of what was arguably the most important race in NASCAR history, the 1979 Daytona 500 in which he and Cale Yarborough crashed on the last lap in the first major race ever televised live from start to finish.

YEAR	RANK	EVENTS	POLES	WINS	TOP 10	MONEY
1966	64	2	0	0	1	2,180
1967	16	20	0	0	6	17,614
1968	25	13	1	1	8	50,815
1969	24	16	2	1	11	78,055
1970	40	19	1	3	12	96,081
1971	29	13	5	1	9	69,995
1972	36	10	0	0	3	16,826
1973	35	14	0	0	5	41,246
1974	17	21	2	0	10	60,315
1975	28	14	2	0	6	49,080
1976	34	9	0	1	5	48,455
1977	24	17	3	2	10	146,435
1978	25	17	0	1	8	127,475
1979	24	20	1	0	10	144,770
1980	26	18	1	0	6	92,640
1981	44	6	0	0	1	38,745
1982	41	9	0	0	3	38,180
1983	NR	2	0	0	0	6,375
1986	114T	1	0	0	0	1,840
1987	NR		0	0	0	1,050
1988	81	1	0	0	0	6,700
Lifetime		242	18	10	115	1,134,872

BUCK BAKER

Born March 4, 1919

Charlotte, NC

Career highlights: finally retired during the 1976 season: two-time ('56 and '57) series champion was one of NASCAR's biggest stars in its formative years . . . only NASCAR driver to compete in the '40s, '50s, '60s, '70s, and '80s before finally retiring . . . won 44 poles and 46 races, including three at Darlington and the first NASCAR race at Watkins Glen in 1957 . . . found it hard to retire, running several of NASCAR's lesser series in the '70s and picking up some second-rate Winston Cup rides into the '80s.

YEAR	RANK	EVENTS	POLES	WINS	TOP 10	MONEY
1949	48	2	0	0	0	50
1950	12	9	1	0	5	2,145
1951	23	11	0	0	5	1,800
1952	12	14	2	1	6	3,187
1953	4	33	4	4	25	18,167
1954	3	34	7	4	28	19,368
1955	2	42	2	3	34	19,771
1956	1	48	12	14	39	34,077
1957	1	40	16	10	38	30,764
1958	2	44	3	3	35	25,841
1959	5	35	4	1	19	11,061
1960	4	37	2	2	24	38,399
1961	10	42	1	1	15	13,697
1962	13	37	0	0	14	12,787
1963	11	47	0	1	30	18,616
1964	9	34	0	2	18	43,781
1965	17	31	0	0	12	21,580
1966	21	36	0	0	14	14,900
1967	27	21	0	0	5	7,730
1968	40	17	0	0	3	3,580
1969	NR	1	0	0	0	1,300
1970	NR	1	0	0	0	610
1971	NR	6	0	0	2	2,345
1972	NR	5	0	0	0	3,255
1973	101	1	0	0	0	670
1976	48	8	0	0	1	12,655
Lifetime		636	44	46	378	$362,136

BUDDY BAKER

Born: Jan. 25, 1941

Charlotte, NC

Career highlights: retired after a few races into the 1992 season: first NASCAR racer to reach more than 200 miles per hour, running 200.47 in a Dodge Daytona at Talladega in March of 1970 . . . was at his best on long and fast superspeedways, where he got 17 of his 19 career victories . . . among them were four each at Talladega and Charlotte; two each at Atlanta, Darlington, and Daytona Beach; and one each at Michigan, Ontario, and College Station . . . finally retired in the early '90s to pursue career in radio and TV.

YEAR	RANK	EVENTS	POLES	WINS	TOP 10	MONEY
1959	26	12	0	0	5	1,705
1960	38	15	0	0	1	1,745
1961	31	14	0	0	2	4,965
1962	23	31	0	0	10	7,578
1963	52	8	0	0	2	2,665
1964	31	33	0	0	7	8,460
1965	9	42	0	0	17	26,837
1966	22	41	1	0	7	21,335
1967	15	20	0	1	7	46,950
1968	13	38	4	1	18	56,023
1969	22	18	3	0	11	63,525
1970	24	18	1	1	8	63,778
1971	15	19	1	1	16	115,150
1972	24	17	1	2	9	103,140
1973	6	27	5	2	20	190,531
1974	7	19	2	0	12	151,025
1975	15	23	3	4	13	236,351
1976	7	30	2	1	16	239,922
1977	5	30	0	0	18	224,847
1978	24	19	1	0	8	111,765
1979	15	26	7	3	15	342,148
1980	21	19	6	2	12	275,200
1981	27	16	0	0	9	115,095
1982	23	23	1	0	11	253,480
1983	21	21	1	1	12	216,355
1984	21	21	1	0	12	151,635
1985	17	28	0	0	7	235,480
1986	24	17	0	0	6	138,600
1987	24	20	0	0	10	255,320
1988	29	17	0	0	7	184,200
1990	41	8	0	0	0	40,085
1991	40	6	0	0	0	58,060
1992	48	3	0	0	0	49,500
1994	NR	0	0	0	0	1,850
Lifetime		699	40	19	311	3,995,500

NEIL BONNETT

Born: July 30, 1946
Died: Feb. 11, 1994
Bessemer, AL

Career highlights: a member of the "Alabama Gang" that also included three Allisons and veteran short-track star Red Farmer . . . won 20 poles and 18 races in 363 career starts from 1974 through the 1993 season . . . among his major victories: three each at Rockingham and Atlanta, two each at Dover and Charlotte, and one each at Darlington, Daytona Beach, Pocono, Talladega, and Ontario . . . also won short-track races at Richmond and North Wilkesboro . . . drove for such noted owners as Butch Mock, Junior Johnson, and the Wood brothers . . . was one of the tour's most popular and quotable drivers and one of its most avid outdoorsmen . . . died while practicing for the Daytona 500.

YEAR	RANK	EVENTS	POLES	WINS	TOP 10	MONEY
1974	87	2	0	0	0	2,560
1975	NR	2	0	0	0	2,705
1976	32	14	1	0	4	32,275
1977	18	23	6	2	9	112,615
1978	12	30	3	0	12	162,742
1979	26	21	4	3	6	151,235
1980	19	22	0	2	13	231,854
1981	22	22	1	3	8	181,670
1982	17	25	0	1	10	158,197
1983	6	30	4	2	17	453,586
1984	8	30	0	0	16	282,533
1985	4	28	1	2	7	530,145
1986	13	28	0	1	12	485,930
1987	12	26	0	0	15	401,541
1988	16	27	0	2	7	440,139
1989	20	26	0	0	11	271,628
1990	43	5	0	0	0	62,600
1993	67T	2	0	0	0	14,515
Lifetime		363	20	18	156	3,998,470

RED BYRON

Born: March 12, 1915
Died: Nov. 11, 1960
Anniston, AL

Career highlights: NASCAR's very first Winston Cup champion drove in six of the eight races contested in 1949 . . . he was third in the season-opener in Charlotte, won three weeks later on the highway/beach course in Daytona Beach, was 22nd at Hillsborough, third at Langhorne, skipped the race at Hamburg, won at Martinsville in September, skipped the Oct. 2 race in Pittsburgh, then

was 16th in the season finale at North Wilkesboro . . . he beat Lee Petty by 117.5 points for the championship . . . a B-29 flight engineer in World War II, he was critically wounded when his plane was shot down and spent 27 months in a hospital . . . he returned to racing in 1946 and promptly won his first race on the highway/beach course . . . later, he'd win three more on that same course.

YEAR	RANK	EVENTS	POLES	WINS	TOP 10	MONEY
1949	1	6	1	2	4	5,800
1950	NR	4	1	0	3	3,325
1951	NR	5	0	0	2	975
Lifetime		15	2	2	9	10,100

DAREL DIERINGER

Born: June 1, 1926
Died: Oct. 28, 1989
Indianapolis, IN

Career highlights: won 11 poles and seven races, among them Riverside in 1963, Augusta in 1964, a Daytona qualifier in 1965, Monroe, Weaverville, the Southern 500 of 1966 (with owner Bud Moore), and at North Wilkesboro in 1967 . . . was seventh in points in '63 and third in '65 . . . beat Richard Petty, David Pearson, Marvin Panch, and Fred Lorenzen at Darlington.

YEAR	RANK	EVENTS	POLES	WINS	TOP 10	MONEY
1957	59	9	0	0	3	1,210
1958	131	2	0	0	0	110
1961	35	7	0	0	2	3,150
1962	33	14	1	0	3	5,000
1963	7	20	0	1	15	29,725
1964	11	27	1	1	13	20,685
1965	3	35	2	1	15	52,214
1966	12	25	0	3	9	52,530
1967	12	19	6	1	9	34,710
1968	21	18	1	0	8	28,215
1969	NR	1	0	0	0	250
1975	54	4	0	0	2	10,530
Lifetime		181	11	7	79	241,054

FONTY FLOCK

Born: March 21, 1921
Died: July 15, 1972
Decatur, GA

Career highlights: one of four siblings to race in the late '40s, throughout the '50s and into

Neil Bonnett (no. 72) passes David Pearson (No. 21) on the outside at Darlington in 1980.

the '60s . . . others were brothers Bob and Tim, and sister Ethel . . . won 30 poles and 19 races in 154 career starts between 1949 and 1957 . . . he briefly quit NASCAR in 1954, but returned for two more full seasons . . . among his most impressive triumphs: Langhorne, the 1952 Southern 500 at Darlington, a 100-miler on the 1-mile track at Raleigh, and a 250-miler at the 1.5-mile track at LeHi, Arkansas . . . finished second in the very first Winston Cup race, held in Charlotte, in 1949.

YEAR	RANK	EVENTS	POLES	WINS	TOP 10	MONEY
1949	5	6	0	0	3	2,015
1950	14	7	2	1	3	2,195
1951	2	34	12	8	22	15,200
1952	4	29	7	2	17	19,112
1953	5	33	3	4	17	17,756
1954	NR	5	0	0	2	1,000
1955	11	31	7	3	14	13,100
1956	50	7	2	1	4	1,780
1957	63	2	0	0	1	1,600
Lifetime		154	33	19	83	73,758

TIM FLOCK

Born: May 11, 1924
Atlanta, GA

Career highlights: two-time ('52 and '55) series champion won 37 poles and 40 races in 187 starts between 1949 and 1961 . . . best season was '55 when he won 18 races and had 15 other top-10 finishes in 38 starts . . . was fifth in the first Winston Cup race at Charlotte in 1949 . . . won 18 races between 1950 and 1953, then sat out the '54 season after being disqualified from an apparent victory at Daytona Beach in February of that year . . . returned the next season and won 18 races and the championship for owner Carl Kiekhaefer . . . won back-to-back races an incredible 11 times in his career . . . major victories included a 100-miler at a 1-mile track in Atlanta and a 250-miler at a 1-mile track in Detroit . . . the tour's most popular driver in 1955.

YEAR	RANK	EVENTS	POLES	WINS	TOP 10	MONEY
1949	8	5	0	0	3	1,510
1950	16	12	1	1	7	3,980
1951	3	30	6	7	21	14,545
1952	1	33	4	8	25	22,890
1953	6	26	4	1	18	8,282
1954	35	5	1	0	3	1,050
1955	1	39	18	18	33	37,780
1956	9	22	5	4	14	15,769
1957	93	1	0	0	0	135
1958	NR	3	0	0	0	410
1959	31	2	0	0	1	850
1960	63	2	0	0	1	850
1961	NR	7	0	0	3	1,605
Lifetime		187	39	39	127	109,656

A.J. FOYT.

Born: January 16, 1935
Houston, TX

Career highlights: the four-time Indy 500 winner's last Winston Cup attempt was at the inaugural Brickyard 400 in 1994: made it a habit in the late '60s and early '70s to win a major NASCAR superspeedway race with some degree of regularity . . . among his seven victories are three at Daytona Beach, two at Ontario, and one each at Atlanta and Riverside . . . three of his victories came with the Wood brothers, the others with Ray Nichels, Banjo Matthews, and Jack Bowsher . . . went from fifth to third on the last lap of the 1979 Daytona 500 when Cale Yarborough and Donnie Allison wrecked on the backstretch.

YEAR	RANK	EVENTS	POLES	WINS	TOP 10	MONEY
1963	NR	5	0	0	2	8,850
1964	NR	6	0	1	2	15,950
1965	NR	4	0	1	3	12,040
1966	NR	4	0	0	0	2,390
1967	NR	7	0	0	2	8,035
1968	NR	4	0	0	1	4,975
1969	NR	4	1	0	3	17,375
1970	NR	3	0	1	1	21,210
1971	NR	7	4	2	4	88,574
1972	NR	6	3	2	5	101,340
1973	NR	3	0	0	1	8,555
1974	44	4	0	0	2	17,110
1975	NR	7	0	0	1	17,155
1976	NR	5	1	0	1	15,610
1977	NR	6	1	0	3	29,200
1978	NR	2	0	0	1	24,875
1979	NR	2	0	0	2	41,690
1980	101	1	0	0	0	3,575
1981	59	3	0	0	1	9,210
1982	70	2	0	0	0	9,405
1983	76	3	0	0	0	22,935
1984	76	3	0	0	0	8,830
1985	45	7	0	0	1	29,750
1986	50	5	0	0	0	24,135
1987	49	6	0	0	0	21,075
1988	42	7	0	0	0	29,660
1989	40	7	0	0	0	31,995
1990	62	3	0	0	0	26,725
1992	70	1	0	0	0	23,055
1993	NR	0	0	0	0	2,400
1994	70T	1	0	0	0	29,000
Lifetime		128	10	7	36	706,684

HARRY GANT

Born: Jan. 10, 1940
Taylorsville, NC

Career highlights: became a fan favorite in 1982 with win at Martinsville after nine runner-up finishes . . . ran 474 Winston Cup races and earned 17 poles and 18 victories, including four straight (Darlington, Richmond, Dover, and Martinsville) before a second-place finish at North Wilkesboro in the fall of 1991 . . . won three other races at both Dover and Darlington, two others at Martinsville, plus two at Pocono, and one each at Michigan, Talladega, North Wilkesboro, and Charlotte . . . was an accomplished weekly short-track and Busch Series racer before he went to Cup, and did some truck racing after leaving Cup racing in 1994 . . . was the '91 NASCAR driver of the year.

YEAR	RANK	EVENTS	POLES	WINS	TOP 10	MONEY
1973	85	1	0	0	0	2,260
1974	64	3	0	0	1	4,784
1975	105T	1	0	0	0	1,130
1976	84	1	0	0	1	5,430
1977	100T	1	0	0	0	1,460
1978	53	5	0	0	1	14,150
1979	21	25	1	0	5	47,185
1980	11	31	0	0	14	177,150
1981	3	31	3	0	18	280,047
1982	4	30	1	2	16	337,582
1983	7	30	0	1	16	414,353
1984	2	30	3	3	23	673,060
1985	3	28	3	3	19	804,287
1986	11	29	2	0	13	583,024
1987	22	29	1	0	4	197,645
1988	27	24	0	0	3	173,325
1989	7	29	0	1	14	639,792
1990	17	28	0	1	9	522,519
1991	4	29	1	5	17	1,194,033
1992	4	29	0	2	15	1,122,776
1993	11	30	1	0	12	772,832
1994	25	30	1	0	7	556,020
Lifetime		474	17	18	208	$8,524,844

DICK HUTCHERSON

Born: Nov. 30, 1931

Keokuk, IA

Career highlights: one of several successful NASCAR drivers from the state of Iowa . . . (his brother, Ron, was another, along with Tiny Lund and Ramo Stott) . . . "Hutch" was an outstanding short-track racer in the mid-'60s, winning 22 poles and 14 races between 1964 and 1968 . . . he was part of the Ford factory team that dominated the '65 season, then battled the Chrysler products the next few seasons . . . was co-driver with Dick Brooks in the 24 Hours of LeMans in 1976, the only time a Winston Cup team has entered the twice-around-the-clock race . . . retired from full-schedule racing in the late '60s to concentrate on his chassis-building business in Charlotte; retired after the 1967 season.

YEAR	RANK	EVENTS	POLES	WINS	TOP 10	MONEY
1964	76	4	2	0	2	1,585
1965	2	52	9	9	37	57,851
1966	28	14	2	3	9	22,985
1967	3	33	9	2	25	85,160
Lifetime		103	22	14	73	$167,581

JAMES HYLTON

Born: Aug. 26, 1935

Inman, SC

Career highlights: never won a championship and won only two races (Richmond in '70 and Talladega in '72), but was always near the top in points . . . the 66 rookie of the year was second in points in '66, '67, and '71, and was top-5 in six other seasons . . . became a driver after being chief mechanic for Rex White and Ned Jarrett . . . never had the solid financial backing to win races, but always seemed to find a way to finish in the top-10; continues to try to run every now and then, with very little success.

YEAR	RANK	EVENTS	POLES	WINS	TOP 10	MONEY
1964	NR	3	0	0	0	350
1966	2	41	1	0	32	38,723
1967	2	46	1	0	39	49,732
1968	7	41	0	0	28	32,608
1969	3	52	0	0	39	114,416
1970	3	47	1	1	39	78,201
1971	2	46	1	0	37	90,282
1972	3	31	0	1	23	126,705
1973	4	28	0	0	11	82,512
1974	11	29	0	0	8	61,385
1975	3	30	0	0	16	113,642
1976	13	30	0	0	5	78,705
1977	7	30	0	0	11	108,392
1978	26	19	0	0	4	48,045
1979	14	30	0	0	5	98,333
1980	13	31	0	0	4	109,230
1981	19	28	0	0	0	87,305
1982	28	13	0	0	0	50,630
1983	NR	2	0	0	0	12,105
1985	NR	1	0	0	0	3,945
1986	46	4	0	0	0	22,090
1987	79	2	0	0	0	2,550
1989	74	2	0	0	0	3,775
1990	NR	1	0	0	0	2,800
1991	54	4	0	0	0	14,190
1992	42	8	0	0	0	37,910
1993	64T	2	0	0	0	17,295
1995	NR	0	0	0	0	3,950
Lifetime		601	4	2	301	$1,489,806

BOBBY ISAAC

Born: Aug. 1, 1934

Died: Aug. 14, 1977

Catawba, NC

Career highlights: drove the No. 71 Dodges owned by Nord Krauskopf and prepared by Harry Hyde to the 1970 NASCAR championship and driver of the year award; won 13 poles and 11 races that year, proving his 20-pole, 17-win (and most popular driver) season of 1969 was no fluke; among his 37 career victories were a 125-mile qualifier and 400-miler at Daytona Beach, a 500-miler at Rockingham, a 400-miler at College Station, and short-track triumphs at Martinsville, North Wilkesboro, and Nashville . . . once retired in the middle of a 500-miler at Talladega when (according to him) he heard voices warning him to quit . . . stayed out of racing for a few years, then died of a heart attack during a Saturday night short-track race at Hickory, N.C. in the summer of 1977.

YEAR	RANK	EVENTS	POLES	WINS	TOP 10	MONEY
1961	158T	1	0	0	0	50
1963	28	27	0	0	7	9,529
1964	18	19	0	1	7	26,733
1965	75	4	1	0	1	1,860
1966	53	9	0	0	3	5,530
1967	14	12	0	0	5	24,475
1968	2	49	3	3	36	60,342
1969	6	50	20	17	33	92,074
1970	1	47	13	11	38	199,600
1971	23	25	5	4	17	106,526
1972	19	27	8	1	10	133,257
1973	26	19	0	0	6	84,550
1974	33	11	0	0	5	22,642
1975	48	6	0	0	1	6,695
1976	114	2	0	0	1	4,190
Lifetime		308	50	37	170	$778,053

NED JARRETT

Born: Oct. 12, 1932

Neton, NC

Career highlights:: two-time ('61 and '65) series champion, but is probably better known to latter-day fans as Dale's father and outstanding radio/TV commentator . . . graduated to Winston Cup after outstanding career in short-track and Sportsman racing . . . ran the Cup circuit for only 13 years, beginning as a part-timer in 1953 and quitting after the 1966 season . . . won 35 poles and 50 races, including 15 wins in '64 and 13 (with 13 runnerup finishes) the next year . . . his first two career victories came back-to-back, on Aug. 1, 1959, at Myrtle Beach and the next day at Charlotte . . . most notable victories were a 400-miler at Atlanta in '64 and the '65 Southern 500 at Darlington . . . remains one of the most popular and well-respected of the drivers who helped NASCAR become what it is . . . retired after the 1966 season.

YEAR	RANK	EVENTS	POLES	WINS	TOP 10	MONEY
1953	68	2	0	0	0	125
1954	147	2	0	0	0	25
1955	173	3	0	0	0	260
1956	166	2	0	0	0	60
1957	169	1	0	0	0	50
1959	37	17	0	2	7	3,860
1960	5	40	5	5	26	25,438
1961	1	46	4	1	34	41,056
1962	3	52	4	6	35	43,444
1963	4	53	4	8	39	45,844
1964	2	59	9	15	45	71,925
1965	1	54	9	13	45	93,625
1966	13	21	0	0	8	23,255
Lifetime		352	35	50	239	$348,967

JUNIOR JOHNSON

Born: June 28, 1931

Ronda, NC

Career highlights: one of NASCAR's most successful, most popular, best-known, most beloved, and most controversial figures . . . did hard time in an Ohio prison for moonshining in his native Wilkes County, NC . . . became a racer after going to early-'50s event at nearby North Wilkesboro Speedway . . . started 313 races between 1953 and 1966, winning 47 poles and 50 features . . . his resume features two victories each at North Wilkesboro, Martinsville, and Charlotte; and one each at Atlanta, Bristol, Darlington, Daytona Beach, and

Richmond . . . one of the sport's most successful team-owners, he fielded cars that won for LeeRoy Yarbrough, Cale Yarborough, Bobby Allison, Darrell Waltrip, Charlie Glotzbach, Terry Labonte, Geoff Bodine, Bill Elliott, Jimmy Spencer, Neil Bonnett, and Terry Labonte . . . helped Yarborough win three Winston Cup titles and was the owner of record for Waltrip's '81, '82, and '85 championships . . . sold his team in the mid-'90s to spend more time with his wife and infant son . . . retired from driving after the 1966 season, then retired as an owner after the 1995 season.

YEAR	RANK	EVENTS	POLES	WINS	TOP 10	MONEY
1953	NR	1	0	0	0	110
1954	55	4	1	0	1	550
1955	6	36	2	5	18	13,803
1956	38	13	1	0	1	1,350
1957	154	1	0	0	0	50
1958	8	27	0	6	16	13,809
1959	11	28	1	5	15	9,675
1960	7	34	3	3	18	38,990
1961	6	41	10	7	22	28,541
1962	20	23	2	1	8	34,841
1963	12	33	9	7	14	67,351
1964	14	29	5	3	15	26,975
1965	12	36	10	13	19	62,216
1966	49	7	3	0	1	3,610
Lifetime		313	47	50	148	$301,871

ALAN KULWICKI

Born: Dec. 14, 1954

Died:April 1, 1993

Greenfield, WI

Career highlights: the '86 rookie of the year and '92 Winston Cup champion came from his native Wisconsin in '85, determined to graduate from ASA into NASCAR racing . . . he drove for himself and often served as his own crew chief, leading NASCAR watchers to say he'd never make it . . . he proved them wrong, winning 24 poles and five race before dying in a plane crash four months after accepting the Winston Cup trophy in New York . . . won at Phoenix in '88, Rockingham in '90, Bristol in '91, and Pocono and Bristol in '92 . . . came from 278 points behind in the final six races to win the '92 championship by 10 points, closest margin in NASCAR history.

YEAR	RANK	EVENTS	POLES	WINS	TOP 10	MONEY
1985	40	5	0	0	0	10,290
1986	21	23	0	0	4	94,450

1987	15	29	3	0	9	369,889
1988	14	29	4	1	9	448,547
1989	14	29	6	0	9	501,295
1990	8	29	1	1	13	550,936
1991	13	29	4	1	11	595,614
1992	1	29	6	2	17	2,322,561
1993	41	5	0	0	3	165,470
Lifetime		207	24	5	75	$5,059,052

FRED LORENZEN

Born: Dec. 30, 1934
Elmhurst, IL

Career highlights: came from the Chicago suburb of Elmhurst to become one of stock car racing's most successful and popular drivers . . . won 33 poles and 26 races in 158 starts dating from 1956 through 1972 . . . came to NASCAR after winning USAC championships in '58 and '59, but struggled through the 1960 season before winning three races in '61 and two in '62 . . . exploded on the scene in '63 with six victories and 23 top-10s (and a then-record $122,587) in only 29 starts . . . won eight more races (and had 10 more top-10s) in only 16 starts the next year . . . among his major victories: five at Martinsville, four each at Atlanta and Charlotte, three at Bristol, two at Darlington, and one each at Daytona Beach, Rockingham, and North Wilkesboro . . . last victory came at Daytona Beach in February of 1967 . . . won most popular driver awards in '63 and '65 . . . cited ulcers and stress as the reasons for leaving NASCAR that season and returning to Illinois . . . made a handful of starts in the early '70s before retiring for good after the 1972 season.

YEAR	RANK	EVENTS	POLES	WINS	TOP 10	MONEY
1956	120	7	0	0	0	235
1960	15	10	0	0	5	9,136
1961	19	15	4	3	6	30,395
1962	7	19	3	2	12	46,100
1963	3	29	9	6	23	122,588
1964	13	16	7	8	10	73,860
1965	13	17	6	4	6	80,615
1966	23	11	2	2	6	37,305
1967	29	5	0	1	2	19,125
1970	54	7	1	0	1	12,610
1971	45	14	1	0	9	45,100
1972	39	8	0	0	4	19,505
Lifetime		158	33	26	84	$496,574

TINY LUND

Born: March 3, 1936
Died: Aug. 17, 1975
Cross, SC

Career highlights: came from Iowa in the 60s, looking for fame and fortune in NASCAR racing . . . best-known for winning the 1963 Daytona 500 after pulling injured driver Marvin Panch from his wrecked sports car several days before the 500 . . . the Wood brothers rewarded Lund by letting him drive while Panch was hospitalized . . . Lund won the 500, one of only three career victories . . . he also won at Columbia in 1965 and won a combination Grand American East and Winston Cup race at North Wilkesboro in 1971 . . . won the 1968 Grand American "pony car" championship and was an outstanding Busch Series star when it was called Late Model Sportsman . . . died in a crash at Talladega in 1975.

YEAR	RANK	EVENTS	POLES	WINS	TOP 10	MONEY
1955	217	1	0	0	0	60
1956	19	21	0	0	8	2,811
1957	11	32	3	0	15	6,424
1958	25	22	2	0	7	3,155
1959	20	27	0	0	10	4,941
1960	32	8	0	0	2	2,440
1961	23	10	0	0	2	5,545
1962	34	10	0	0	0	2,880
1963	10	22	0	1	12	49,397
1964	20	22	0	0	9	9,913
1965	21	30	0	1	17	11,750
1966	29	31	1	1	10	11,880
1967	19	19	0	0	5	17,332
1968	22	17	0	0	10	17,785
1969	NR	1	0	0	1	1,675
1970	NR	5	0	0	2	11,365
1971	NR	15	0	2	9	18,965
1972	104	4	0	0	0	2,345
1973	94	5	0	0	0	4,420
1975	116	1	0	0	0	620
Lifetime		303	6	5	119	$185,703

RALPH MOODY

Born: Sept. 10, 1917
Taunton, MA

Career highlights: a capable driver in his own right (five poles and seven feature victories in the '50s), he became better known and more successful as a car and engine builder, and team owner . . . he and business partner John Holman enjoyed success with Nelson Stacy, Curtis Turner, Joe Weatherly, Fred Lorenzen, Fireball Roberts, David Pearson, and Bobby Allison . . . they teamed with various drivers for dozens of victories, all of them in Ford products . . . their racing shop near Charlotte was among the first to sell "purpose-built" stock car chassis for racing.

YEAR	RANK	EVENTS	POLES	WINS	TOP 10	MONEY
1956	8	35	5	4	21	15,493
1957	NR	10	0	1	5	2,905
1959	NR	1	0	0	1	200
1962	137	1	0	0	0	75
Lifetime		47	5	5	27	18,673

BUD MOORE

Born: 1924

Spartansburg, SC

Career highlights: remains active with his Bud Moore Engineering team . . . a World War II hero, he returned to build and field winning cars for some of stock car racing's greatest early-era stars . . . the list includes Joe Weatherly, Billy Wade, and Darel Dieringer . . . later, after several years of Trans-Am success, he returned to NASCAR with David Pearson, Donnie Allison, LeeRoy Yarbrough, Darrell Waltrip, Buddy Baker, Bobby Allison, Dale Earnhardt, Ricky Rudd, Benny Parsons, Brett Bodine, Morgan Shepherd, Geoff Bodine, Lake Speed, Wally Dallenbach, and Morgan Shepherd . . . all told, has 43 poles and 63 victories, including most of the major superspeedway events.

MARVIN PANCH

Born: May 28, 1926

Oakland, CA

Career highlights: won 21 poles and 17 races in 216 career starts between 1951 and 1966 . . . won once in '56 and six times in '57 . . . won once more in '61 and '63, three times in '64, four times in '65 (including twice at Atlanta and once at Watkins Glen), then won his last race at Charlotte in May of 1966 . . . his son, Richie, followed him into racing and was killed when a private plane crashed in 1985 . . . retired after the 1966 season.

YEAR	RANK	EVENTS	POLES	WINS	TOP 10	MONEY
1951	36	3	0	0	2	1,075
1953	60	2	0	0	0	160
1954	17	10	1	0	7	4,747
1955	14	10	0	0	4	4,385
1956	10	20	1	1	13	11,520
1957	2	42	4	6	27	24,307
1958	18	11	2	0	5	4,114
1959	66	4	0	0	0	1,050
1960	26	11	0	0	1	3,225
1961	18	9	1	1	6	30,478
1962	9	17	0	0	8	26,746
1963	13	12	2	1	12	39,102
1964	10	31	5	3	21	34,836
1965	5	20	5	4	14	64,027
1966	17	14	0	1	6	38,432
Lifetime		216	21	17	126	288,204

BENNY PARSONS

Born: July 12, 1941

Ellerbe, NC

Career highlights: former cab driver in his adopted hometown of Detroit, Parsons came to NASCAR after winning the '68 and '69 ARCA championships, which made him ineligible to run for NASCAR's '70 rookie of the year award . . . undeterred, he won the '73 Winston Cup title for owner L.G. DeWitt, overcoming a vicious crash in the season finale at Rockingham to beat Cale Yarborough by 67 points . . . Parsons won 20 poles and 21 races in his 526-race career that extended from 1964 through 1988 . . . his major triumphs: three at Nashville; two each at Dover, Charlotte, Ontario, and Richmond; and one each at Atlanta, Bristol, Darlington, Daytona Beach, Michigan, Pocono, North Wilkesboro, Riverside, and College Station . . . retired after the 1988 season to continue with his career in radio and television.

YEAR	RANK	EVENTS	POLES	WINS	TOP 10	MONEY
1964	120	1	0	0	0	250
1969	56	4	0	0	3	7,650
1970	8	45	1	0	23	59,402
1971	11	35	0	1	18	55,896
1972	5	31	0	0	19	102,043
1973	1	28	0	1	21	182,321
1974	5	30	0	0	14	185,080
1975	4	30	3	1	17	214,354
1976	3	30	2	2	23	270,043
1977	3	30	3	4	22	359,341
1978	4	30	2	3	21	329,993
1979	5	31	1	2	21	264,930
1980	3	31	2	3	21	411,519
1981	10	31	0	3	12	311,093
1982	18	23	3	0	13	252,267
1983	29	16	0	0	5	129,760
1984	27	14	2	1	10	241,665
1985	29	14	0	0	6	94,450
1986	30	16	1	0	4	176,985
1987	16	29	0	0	9	566,848
1988	24	27	0	0	1	210,755
Lifetime		526	20	21	283	4,426,287

JIM PASCHAL

Born: Dec. 5, 1926

High Point, NC

Career highlights: one of the most successful Winston Cup drivers in the '50s and '60s, he won

12 poles and 25 races, all but two of them (the Coca-Cola World 600s of '64 and '67) on short tracks . . . won five Grand American races in an AMC Javelin in 1969.

YEAR	RANK	EVENTS	POLES	WINS	TOP 10	MONEY
1949	NR	1	0	0	0	0
1950	24	6	0	0	2	850
1951	15	16	0	0	7	2,450
1952	18	15	0	0	7	1,483
1953	7	24	1	1	9	5,571
1954	7	27	2	1	11	5,451
1955	8	36	2	3	20	10,586
1956	5	42	1	1	27	17,204
1957	10	35	0	0	17	7,079
1958	42	6	1	1	4	1,670
1959	25	6	0	0	4	2,980
1960	9	10	0	0	7	15,096
1961	9	23	1	2	16	18,100
1962	6	39	0	4	21	27,348
1963	19	32	1	5	18	20,979
1964	7	22	0	1	15	60,116
1965	35	10	0	0	4	7,805
1966	14	18	2	2	10	30,985
1967	6	45	1	4	25	60,123
1968	104	1	0	0	0	275
1970	NR	1	0	0	0	1,800
1971	NR	6	0	0	3	4,215
1972	NR	1	0	0	0	1,825
Lifetime		422	12	25	230	303,991

DAVID PEARSON

Born: Dec. 22, 1934
Spartanburg, SC

Career highlights: the driver Richard Petty called "the best there's even been" did it all during his career . . . '60 rookie of the year, three-time ('66, '68, and '69) series champion, 113-time pole winner and 105-time race winner . . . was equally good on road courses (three victories at Riverside, one at Bridgehampton), superspeedways (48 victories) and short tracks (54 victories) . . . also won 23 dirt-track races . . . won at least once at almost every major venue: 10 times at Darlington; nine at Michigan; six at Daytona Beach; five each at Bristol, Dover and Rockingham; four each at Charlotte and Atlanta; three each at Riverside and Talladega; and one each at Martinsville, Pocono, Nashville, and Ontario . . . '73 NASCAR driver of the year . . . retired during the 1986 season.

YEAR	RANK	EVENTS	POLES	WINS	TOP 10	MONEY
1960	23	22	1	0	7	5,030
1961	13	19	1	3	8	51,911
1962	10	12	0	0	7	19,032
1963	8	41	2	0	19	24,986
1964	3	61	12	8	42	45,542
1965	40	14	1	2	11	8,925
1966	1	42	7	15	34	78,194
1967	7	22	2	2	13	72,651
1968	1	48	14	16	38	133,065
1969	1	51	14	11	44	229,760
1970	23	19	2	1	11	87,493
1971	51	17	2	2	9	32,010
1972	20	17	4	6	13	142,440
1973	13	18	8	11	14	228,408
1974	3	19	11	7	15	252,819
1975	14	21	7	3	14	192,141
1976	9	22	8	10	18	346,890
1977	13	22	5	2	16	221,272
1978	16	22	7	4	11	198,775
1979	32	9	2	1	5	99,180
1980	37	9	1	1	5	102,730
1981	70	6	1	0	2	17,150
1982	37	6	2	0	2	55,945
1983	33	10	0	0	3	71,720
1984	41	11	1	0	3	54,125
1985	36	12	0	0	1	55,625
1986	82	2	0	0	1	8,405
Lifetime		574	113	105	366	2,836,224

LEE PETTY

Born: March 14, 1914
Randleman, NC

Career highlights: won NASCAR championships in '54, '58, and '59, won the inaugural Daytona 500, and fathered seven-time champion and 200-time race winner Richard. Not a bad career . . . was among stock car racing's first stars, competing full time from 1949 through the opening days of the 1961 season, when his car sailed over the Turn 4 wall at Daytona International Speedway, almost killing him . . . won 18 poles and 54 races in 427 career starts . . . only superspeedway victory was the '59 Daytona 500 . . . best year was '59, when he won 11 of 42 races . . . last victory was at Jacksonville in November of 1960, which is listed within NASCAR's 1961 records . . . was the tour's most popular driver in '53 and '54 . . . retired in 1964, but had run only nine races since a serious crash at Daytona Beach in 1961.

YEAR	RANK	EVENTS	POLES	WINS	TOP 10	MONEY
1949	2	6	0	1	5	3,855
1950	3	17	0	1	13	7,120
1951	4	32	0	1	19	7,400
1952	3	32	0	3	27	16,876
1953	2	36	0	5	32	18,447
1954	1	34	3	7	32	21,127
1955	3	42	1	6	30	18,920
1956	4	47	1	2	28	15,338
1957	4	41	3	4	33	18,326
1958	1	50	4	7	43	26,565
1959	1	42	2	11	35	49,220
1960	6	39	3	5	30	31,283
1961	104	3	1	1	2	1,260
1962	73	1	0	0	1	750
1963	82	3	0	0	2	600
1964	109	2	0	0	0	250
Lifetime		427	18	54	332	237,337

RICHARD PETTY

Born: July 2, 1937
Randleman, NC

Career highlights: Where do you begin? . . . seven-time champion, winning the Cup in '64, '67, '71, '72, '74, '75, and '79 . . . won a record 127 poles and 200 races in a 1,184-race career that helped make the sport the attraction it is today . . . once won 10 straight races and 27 in a season (1967) . . . '74, '75, and '79 driver of the year and most popular driver in '62, '64, '68, and '70, then '74 through '78 . . . list of major victories is impressive: 15 each at North Wilkesboro and Martinsville; 11 at Rockingham; 10 at Daytona Beach; nine at Nashville; seven at Dover; six at Atlanta; five at Riverside; four each at Charlotte and Michigan; three each at College Station, Bristol, and Darlington; and two each at Pocono and Talladega . . . his 1970 spring crash at Darlington and 1988 Daytona 500 crash rank among the most spectacular in NASCAR history . . . has been associated with STP since 1972 . . . retired after the 1992 season:.

YEAR	RANK	EVENTS	POLES	WINS	TOP 10	MONEY
1958	37	9	0	0	1	760
1959	15	21	0	0	9	8,111
1960	2	40	2	3	30	41,873
1961	8	42	2	2	23	25,239
1962	2	52	4	8	39	60,764
1963	2	54	8	14	39	55,964
1964	1	61	9	9	43	114,772
1965	38	14	7	4	10	16,450

A common sight in the 1970s: Richard Petty's red and blue STP logo leading the way.

YEAR	RANK	EVENTS	POLES	WINS	TOP 10	MONEY
1966	3	39	16	8	22	94,666
1967	1	48	19	27	40	150,197
1968	3	49	12	16	35	99,535
1969	2	50	6	10	38	129,906
1970	4	40	9	18	31	151,124
1971	1	46	9	21	41	351,071
1972	1	31	3	8	28	339,405
1973	5	28	3	6	17	234,389
1974	1	30	7	10	23	432,020
1975	1	30	3	13	24	481,751
1976	2	30	1	3	22	374,806
1977	2	30	5	5	23	406,608
1978	6	30	0	0	17	242,273
1979	1	31	1	5	25	561,934
1980	4	31	0	2	19	397,318
1981	8	31	0	3	16	396,072
1982	5	30	0	0	16	465,793
1983	4	30	0	3	21	508,884
1984	10	30	0	2	13	257,932
1985	14	28	0	0	13	306,142
1986	14	29	0	0	11	280,657
1987	8	29	0	0	14	445,227
1988	22	29	0	0	5	190,155
1989	29	25	0	0	0	133,050
1990	26	29	0	0	1	169,465
1991	24	29	0	0	1	268,035
1992	26	29	0	0	0	348,870
Lifetime		1184	126	200	712	8,541,218

DICK RATHMANN

Born: Jan. 6, 1924

Los Angeles, CA

Career highlights: won 10 poles and 13 races between and 1951 and 1955, including Martinsville, three in a row at Langhorne, Darlington, and Daytona, then Daytona again in the 1952 season . . . won five more races in '53 (including two at Langhorne) and three more (including back-to-back spring races at Oakland and North Wilkesboro) in '54 . . . was fifth in points in '52, third in '53, fourth in '54, and 18th in '55, when he ran fewer than half the races.

YEAR	RANK	EVENTS	POLES	WINS	TOP 10	MONEY
1951	8	15	0	0	7	3,225
1952	5	27	2	5	14	11,248
1953	3	34	1	5	24	20,245
1954	4	32	4	3	26	16,264
1955	18	20	3	0	8	4,368
Lifetime		128	10	13	79	55,350

BILL REXFORD

Born: March 14, 1927

Died: April 18, 1994

Conowango Valley, NY

Career highlights: the youngest champion in Winston Cup history, he was just 21 when he won the 1950 title by winning one race, that being at Canfield, Ohio, on May 30 . . . it was the only victory of his career, which leaned more toward Indy-car racing after his brief moment of fame . . . as it was, he won the '50 title only because Lee Petty and Red Byron lost their points for driving in non-NASCAR races . . . and Fireball Roberts might have beaten Rexford instead of finishing second if he'd taken it easy in the season-finale after Rexford had fallen out . . . instead, Roberts blew up and finished poorly, and Rexford won the title by 110 points.

YEAR	RANK	EVENTS	POLES	WINS	TOP 10	MONEY
1949	12	3	0	0	2	785
1950	1	17	0	1	11	5,800
1951	72	11	1	0	1	450
1952	NR	3	0	0	1	150
1953	NR	2	0	0	2	350
Lifetime		36	1	1	17	7,535

TIM RICHMOND

Born: June 7, 1955

Died: Aug. 13, 1989

Ashland, OH

Career highlights: one of the most popular and flamboyant drivers to ever sit in a stock car . . . had a brief (185 races) but bittersweet career (14 poles and 13 wins) between 1980 and his last start for Hendrick Motorsports in 1987 . . . came to NASCAR after being rookie of the race in the 1980 Indianapolis 500 . . . all but one of his Winston Cup wins (the exception being Richmond in 1986) came on superspeedways: four each at Pocono and Riverside, two at Charlotte, and one each at Darlington, Daytona Beach and Watkins Glen . . . became embroiled with NASCAR over his medical status prior to the 1988 season . . . NASCAR wouldn't let him race without medical clearance, and Richmond didn't want to take a physical because he knew it would show he had AIDS, which caused his death in 1989.

YEAR	RANK	EVENTS	POLES	WINS	TOP 10	MONEY
1980	41	5	0	0	0	14,925
1981	16	29	0	0	6	96,448
1982	26	26	1	2	12	191,830
1983	10	30	4	1	15	262,139
1984	12	30	0	1	11	345,848
1985	11	28	0	0	13	290,284
1986	3	29	8	7	17	973,221
1987	36	8	1	2	4	151,850
Lifetime		185	14	13	78	2,316,545

Tim Richmond in the Folger's car shoots past Bill Elliott at Michigan International Speedway in 1986.

FIREBALL ROBERTS

Born: Jan. 29, 1929
Died: July 7, 1964
Daytona Beach, FL

Career highlights: he never won a series championship (he was second in 1950), but he was one of the best and most popular racers in NASCAR history . . . won 35 poles and 35 races in 206 career starts between 1950 and 1964, when he died from injuries received in a fiery crash at Charlotte . . . his major victories included four each at Daytona Beach and Darlington, and one at Atlanta, plus successes at Bristol and Martinsville . . . got his nickname not because of racing, but because he was an outstanding baseball pitcher . . . was the '57 season's most popular driver and had five top-10 finishes in the points between '57 and '63.

YEAR	RANK	EVENTS	POLES	WIN	TOP 10	MONEY
1950	2	9	1	1	5	6,800
1951	12	9	0	0	3	1,685
1952	59	7	0	0	1	199
1953	132	2	0	0	0	365
1954	22	5	0	0	2	1,080
1955	201	2	1	0	0	140
1956	7	33	3	5	22	14,742
1957	6	42	4	8	27	19,829
1958	11	10	0	6	9	32,219
1959	16	8	3	1	4	10,865
1960	9	9	6	2	3	19,895
1961	5	22	6	2	14	50,267
1962	8	19	9	3	12	66,152
1963	5	20	2	4	14	73,060
1964	27	9	0	1	6	28,345
Lifetime		206	35	33	122	325,643

WENDELL SCOTT

Born: Aug. 29, 1921
Died: Dec. 23, 1990
Danville, VA

Career highlights: the only African-American to find any success at all in Winston Cup racing . . . won one pole and the Dec. 1, 1963 race at Jacksonville, a race originally given to Buck Baker before Scott correctly pointed out a scoring error . . . a native of Danville, Virginia, he was recruited by short-track promoters who thought the novelty of having a black driver would boost attendance . . . raced for most of the '60s and into the '70s, finally retiring after suffering major injuries in a crash at Talladega in '73 . . . his life and times were the basis of the film "Greased Lightening" which starred Richard Pryor . . . was sixth in season-ending points in '66, then 10th, 9th, and 9th the next three seasons.

YEAR	RANK	EVENTS	POLES	WINS	TOP 10	MONEY
1961	32	23	0	0	5	3,240
1962	22	41	1	0	19	7,133
1963	15	47	0	0	15	10,966
1964	12	56	0	1	25	16,495
1965	11	52	0	0	21	18,639
1966	6	45	0	0	17	23,052
1967	10	45	0	0	11	19,510
1968	9	48	0	0	10	20,498
1969	9	51	0	0	11	47,451
1970	14	41	0	0	9	28,518
1971	19	37	0	0	4	21,701
1972	40	6	0	0	0	5,830
1973	61	3	0	0	0	3,530
Lifetime		495	1	1	137	226,563

JACK SMITH

Born: May 24, 1924
Sandy Springs, GA

Career highlights: won 24 poles and 21 races during his 263-race career that began in 1949 and ended in 1964 . . . among his most important wins: the 1962 Firecracker 250 at Daytona Beach, plus victories at Bristol, North Wilkesboro, on the road course at Bridgehampton, a 100-mile qualifier at Daytona Beach and at Martinsville . . . best season was '62, when he won five races and was fourth in points.

YEAR	RANK	EVENTS	POLES	WINS	TOP 10	MONEY
1949	58	1	0	0	0	50
1950	32	3	0	0	1	775
1951	39	7	0	0	2	1,275
1952	34	8	1	0	2	820
1954	64	6	0	0	1	500
1955	141	2	0	0	2	400
1956	21	15	0	1	6	3,825
1957	5	39	2	4	25	14,562
1958	5	39	4	2	21	12,634
1959	8	21	3	4	12	13,290
1960	14	13	4	3	7	24,721
1961	7	25	0	2	12	21,410
1962	4	51	7	5	35	34,748
1963	24	29	2	0	11	8,885
1964	81	4	1	0	2	1,575
Lifetime		263	24	21	141	139,470

MARSHALL TEAGUE

Born: Feb. 17, 1922
Died: Feb. 11, 1959
Daytona Beach, FL

Career highlights: died attempting to set a speed record at the new Daytona International Speedway . . . a Daytona Beach native and successful and popular beach racer, he won five of the first 14 Winston Cup races in '51 in Hudson Hornets and two of the first three in '52, also in Hudsons . . . left NASCAR to go IndyCar racing for most of the '50s, but couldn't resist the lure of coming back home when Bill France opened his 2.5-mile track in February of 1959.

YEAR	RANK	EVENTS	POLES	WINS	TOP 10	MONEY
1949	62T	1	0	0	0	50
1950	119	3	0	0	0	50
1951	NR	15	1	5	9	7,410
1952	NR	4	1	2	2	2,550
Lifetime		23	2	7	11	$10,060

HERB THOMAS

Born: April 6, 1923
Olivia, NC

Career highlights: two-time ('51 and '53) series champion likely would have won a third if he hadn't been hurt late in 1956 and missed the last three races . . . as it was, he finished second that year to Buck Baker, the third time ('52, '54, and '56) he'd been runner-up . . . he won 38 poles and 48 races in his 230-start career that began in 1949 and ended in 1962 . . . won the 1951, 1954, and 1955 Southern 500s, and the 1950 and 1954 races at Martinsville.

YEAR	RANK	EVENTS	POLES	WINS	TOP 10	MONEY
1949	25	4	0	0	1	225
1950	11	13	0	1	6	2,645
1951	1	36	4	7	18	20,850
1952	2	32	10	8	22	18,965
1953	1	37	12	12	31	28,910
1954	2	34	8	12	27	30,975
1955	5	23	2	3	15	18,024
1956	3	48	2	5	36	19,352
1957	148	2	0	0	0	25
1962	97	1	0	0	0	200
Lifetime		230	38	48	156	$139,944

SPEEDY THOMPSON

Born: April 3, 1926
Died: April 2, 1972
Monroe, NC

Career highlights: the man with the near-perfect racing name won 18 poles and 20 races in his 198-start Winston Cup career . . . his first win was at Macon in the fall of '53, his last at Richmond in the fall of '60 . . . among his most important victories: North Wilkesboro, Martinsville, the '57 Southern 500 at Darlington, twice at Richmond, and the 1960 National 400 at Charlotte . . . was third in points for four consecutive seasons: '56, '57, '58, and '59, then was 25th in '60 . . . most of his success came in '55 and '56, when he won 10 races driving for team owner Carl Kiekhaefer . . . to prove it wasn't all Kiekhaefer, though, Thompson won four races in '58 in his own cars . . . died of a heart attack while racing at the Metrolina Speedway in Charlotte, NC, just one day short of his 46th birthday.

YEAR	RANK	EVENTS	POLES	WINS	TOP 10	MONEY
1950	NR	1	0	0	0	0
1951	75	3	0	0	1	325
1952	37	2	0	0	0	305
1953	11	7	0	2	7	6,547
1954	23	7	0	0	3	1,165
1955	15	15	0	2	5	7,090
1956	2	42	6	8	29	27,169
1957	3	38	4	2	22	26,841
1958	3	38	7	4	24	17,295
1959	3	29	1	0	9	6,816
1960	25	9	0	2	5	18,035
1961	63	3	0	0	0	1,100
1962	41	3	0	0	1	1,400
1971	NR	1	0	0	0	1,800
Lifetime		198	18	20	106	$115,888

CURTIS TURNER

Born: April 12, 1924
Died: Oct. 4, 1970

Career highlights: one of NASCAR's earliest stars and among its most controversial drivers . . . won 17 poles and 17 races in his career, which spanned 1949 through 1968 . . . he won the fourth Winston Cup race of its inaugural season of 1949, then won 16 more, almost all of them during the '50s . . . he was suspended from competition by NASCAR president Bill France, Sr. in 1960 because he tried to organize the drivers for the Teamsters Union . . . was the first president of the Charlotte Motor Speedway, and needed a loan from the Teamsters in 1960 to repay creditors . . . when France got wind of it, he banned Turner until late in the 1965 season . . . in a storybook comeback, Turner won the first 500-mile race at the North Carolina Motor Speedway on Halloween Day of 1965 . . . died in a plane crash in 1970.

YEAR	RANK	EVENTS	POLES	WINS	TOP 10	MONEY
1949	6	6	1	1	4	2,675
1950	5	16	4	4	7	8,190
1951	NR	12	0	3	5	3,980
1952	50	7	0	0	1	290
1953	10	19	3	1	5	4,347
1954	9	10	1	1	8	10,120
1955	34	9	0	0	4	2,605
1956	20	13	0	1	5	14,541
1957	22	10	1	0	4	4,830
1958	20	17	1	3	10	10,029
1959	24	10	1	2	4	3,845
1960	36	9	1	0	1	3,220
1961	NR	8	0	0	2	6,090
1965	39	7	0	1	3	18,175
1966	24	21	2	0	6	16,920
1967	71	4	2	0	0	7,875
1968	47	6	0	0	4	5,850
Lifetime		184	17	17	73	$122,155

JOE WEATHERLY

Born: May 29, 1922
Died: Jan. 19, 1964
Norfolk, VA

Career highlights: two-time ('62 and '63) series champion graduated from motorcycles in the '50s to become one of NASCAR's most popular and successful stars . . . won 19 poles and 24 races in 230 career starts, many of them on rough and tumble short dirt tracks . . . among his major victories: the 1960 and 1963 Rebel 300s at Darlington, and 1961 National 400 at Charlotte . . . nicknamed "The Clown Prince" for his free-spirited nature, he died when his head hit the retaining wall when his car slid into it at Riverside . . . one of the first NASCAR drivers to have his own plane and he delighted in terrorizing unsuspecting passengers . . . 1961's most popular driver, he was fourth in points that year, which was the season before he won his first championship.

YEAR	RANK	EVENTS	POLES	WINS	TOP 10	MONEY
1952	51	1	0	0	0	150
1954	102	1	0	0	1	200
1955	47	6	0	0	4	2,575
1956	16	17	1	0	12	5,251
1957	50	14	0	0	7	5,340
1958	28	15	1	1	7	6,330
1959	18	17	0	0	10	9,816
1960	20	24	0	3	11	20,124
1961	4	25	4	9	18	47,079
1962	1	52	7	9	45	70,743
1963	1	53	6	3	35	74,624
1964	48	5	0	0	3	5,290
Lifetime		230	19	25	153	$247,522

BOB WELBORN

Born: May 5, 1928
Died: 1997
Denton, NC

Career highlights: won seven poles and nine races, all but one of them on short tracks between '57 and '59 . . . the lone exception was in 1959, the first race (a 100-mile qualifier) at the new Daytona International Speedway . . . also won twice at Martinsville and twice at Fayetteville, and once each at Greensboro, Winston-Salem, and Myrtle Beach.

YEAR	RANK	EVENTS	POLES	WINS	TOP 10	MONEY
1952	81	3	0	0	0	90
1953	24	11	0	0	6	1,210
1954	51	12	0	0	3	1,125
1955	4	32	1	0	25	10,147
1956	84	6	0	0	2	650
1957	NR	4	0	1	3	5,050
1958	149	18	1	5	15	13,270
1959	17	29	5	3	13	9,370
1960	16	15	0	0	10	6,194
1961	14	14	0	0	7	13,487
1962	15	25	0	0	12	10,347
1963	40	11	0	0	4	4,830
1964	78	3	0	0	2	805
Lifetime		183	7	9	102	$76,575

REX WHITE

Born: Aug. 17, 1929
Spartanburg, SC

Career highlights: won 36 poles and 28 races in his 233-race career dating from 1956 through the 1964 season . . . was the 1960 NASCAR champion with six victories, 25 top-5 finishes, and 35 top-10s in 40 starts . . . his only superspeedway victory was his last victory, the 1962 Dixie 400 at Atlanta Motor Speedway, where he led only the final three laps in beating Joe Weatherly and Marvin Panch thanks to better fuel efficiency . . . career totals include two victories each at Martinsville and North Wilkesboro and one at Richmond . . . he followed his championship season with a second-place points finish in 1961, fifth in 1962, and ninth in 1963, when he was 0-for-25.

YEAR	RANK	EVENTS	POLES	WINS	TOP 10	MONEY
1956	11	24	1	0	14	5,334
1957	21	9	1	0	6	3,870
1958	7	22	7	2	17	12,233
1959	10	23	5	5	13	12,360
1960	1	40	3	6	35	57,525
1961	2	47	7	7	38	56,395
1962	5	37	9	8	23	36,246
1963	9	25	3	0	14	27,241
1964	28	6	0	0	3	12,310
Lifetime		233	36	28	163	$223,514

GLEN WOOD

Born: July 18, 1925
Stuart, VA

Career highlights: won four times, then became full-time director (with his brother Leonard) of the family-owned team that still bears their name . . . the Wood brothers have fielded winning cars for such luminaries as Speedy Thompson, Marvin Panch, Tiny Lund, Dan Gurney, Curtis Turner, Cale Yarborough, Parnelli Jones, Donnie Allison, A.J. Foyt, Neil Bonnett, Kyle Petty, Buddy Baker, Dale Jarrett, and Morgan Shepherd . . . enjoyed greatest success (43 of their 96 victories) with David Pearson between '72 and '79 . . . the team has won almost every major NASCAR race at least once, including its victory in the 1996 Winston all-star race with Michael Waltrip . . . retired as a driver after running a very limited schedule throughout the '50s and early '60s.

YEAR	RANK	EVENTS	POLES	WINS	TOP 10	MONEY
1953	64	2	0	0	0	125
1954	215T	1	0	0	0	0

1955	242T	1	0	0	0	0
1956	246T	2	0	0	0	50
1957	74	6	0	0	1	1,670
1958	NR	10	3	0	7	3,120
1959	57	20	3	0	13	6,875
1960	103	9	4	3	7	5,260
1961	65	6	1	0	3	2,000
1963	73	3	2	1	2	1,070
1964	100	2	1	0	1	530
Lifetime		62	14	4	34	$20,700

CALE YARBOROUGH

Born: March 27, 1939
Timmonsville, SC

Career highlights: won three consecutive championships ('76, '77, '78) with team-owner Junior Johnson and was second in Johnson-owned cars in '73, '74, and '80 . . . started 559 races between 1957 and 1988, when he retired after eight years of a partial schedule . . . won 70 poles and 83 races, fifth on the all-time victory list . . . among his triumphs: nine at Bristol; eight each at Michigan and Daytona Beach (four in the 500, four in the 400); seven each at Rockingham, Nashville, and Atlanta; six at Martinsville; five each at North Wilkesboro and Darlington; three each at Riverside, Richmond, Talladega, Dover, and Charlotte; two at Pocono; and one at College Station . . . also raced in the Indy 500 . . . retired after the 1988 season.

YEAR	RANK	EVENTS	POLES	WINS	TOP 10	MONEY
1957	159	1	0	0	0	100
1959	110	1	0	0	0	150
1960	132	1	0	0	0	85

Cale Yarborough (No. 11) and Donnie Allison (No. 1) nearly scrape paint at the Firecracker 400 in 1979.

YEAR	RANK	EVENTS	POLES	WINS	TOP 10	MONEY
1961	NR	1	0	0	0	200
1962	50	8	0	0	1	2,725
1963	25	18	0	0	7	5,550
1964	19	24	0	0	9	10,378
1965	10	46	0	1	21	26,587
1966	18	14	0	0	7	28,130
1967	20	16	4	2	8	57,312
1968	17	21	4	6	12	138,052
1969	23	19	6	2	8	75,065
1970	34	19	5	3	13	117,600
1971	NR	4	0	0	1	3,844
1972	51	5	0	0	4	11,667
1973	2	28	5	4	19	267,513
1974	2	30	3	10	22	363,782
1975	9	27	3	3	13	214,691
1976	1	30	2	9	23	453,405
1977	1	30	3	9	27	561,642
1978	1	30	8	10	24	623,506
1979	4	31	1	4	22	440,129
1980	2	31	14	6	22	567,891
1981	24	18	2	2	10	150,840
1982	27	16	2	3	8	231,590
1983	28	16	3	4	8	265,035
1984	22	16	4	3	10	403,853
1985	26	16	0	2	7	310,465
1986	29	16	1	0	5	137,010
1987	29	16	0	0	4	111,025
1988	38	10	0	0	3	66,065
Lifetime		559	70	83	318	$5,645,887

LEEROY YARBROUGH

Born: Sept. 17, 1938
Died: Dec. 7, 1984
Jacksonville, FL

Career highlights: had an undistinguished Winston Cup career until the late '60s, when he teamed up with crew chief Herb Nab and team-owner Junior Johnson . . . won seven major races in '69 (twice each at Darlington and Daytona Beach and once each at Charlotte, Rockingham, and Atlanta) and won a then-record $193,211 . . . all told, won 10 poles and 14 races in 198-race career from 1960 through 1972 . . . other super-speedway victories came at Charlotte in '66 and '70, Daytona Beach in '67, and Atlanta in '68 . . . contracted Rocky Mountain spotted fever in the '70s and died in a nursing home in 1984.

YEAR	RANK	EVENTS	POLES	WINS	TOP 10	MONEY
1960	137	1	0	0	0	225
1962	36	12	0	0	1	3,485
1963	26	14	1	0	5	6,680
1964	15	34	0	2	15	16,630
1965	37	14	0	0	3	5,905
1966	26	9	2	1	4	23,980
1967	37	15	0	1	4	15,575
1968	16	26	6	2	16	87,920
1969	16	30	0	7	21	193,211
1970	43	19	1	1	11	61,980
1971	73	6	0	0	3	9,260
1972	34	18	0	0	9	40,920
Lifetime		198	10	14	92	$465,771

OTHER PERSONALITIES OF NOTE

Mario Andretti: he did everything else, so why not NASCAR? Won the 1967 Daytona 500 in a Holman-Moody No. 11 Ford, one of the few races Richard Petty didn't win that season.

Johnny Beauchamp: involved in the controversial 1959 Daytona 500 finish with Lee Petty . . . only career victories in 23 starts came at Atlanta in March of 1959 and Nashville in August of 1960.

Ron Bouchard: the 1981 rookie of the year (and former great Modified star) beat Darrell Waltrip and Terry Labonte in a photo finish to win at Talladega in the fall of 1981. His brother, Ken, was 1988 rookie of the year, but didn't last long in Winston Cup.

Richard Brickhouse: journeyman driver in the late '60s whose only victory was in the 1969 fall race at Talladega, a race most of the sport's top stars boycotted because of concerns over the reliability of tires.

Dick Brooks: 1969 Winston Cup rookie of the year struggled for years before getting his first (and only) victory in the summer of 1973 at Talladega.

Mark Donohue: Indy 500 winner and Formula 1 racer won the 1973 season-opening race at Riverside.

Bill Gardner: better-known half of the Gardner/Mike DiProsperio team that created DiGard Racing in the late '70s . . . it fielded cars for Donnie Allison, Darrell Waltrip and Ricky Rudd before finally folding in the early '80s.

Charlie Glotzbach: won 12 poles and four races, three of the four races on superspeedways: once each at Michigan, Charlotte, Daytona Beach (a 125-mile qualifier) and Bristol between 1968 and 1971.

Paul Goldsmith: won nine poles and nine races between '56 and '66, among them Langhorne, on both the highway/beach course and the 2.5-mile paved superspeedway in Daytona Beach, and at Richmond, Rockingham, Bristol, and a 1-mile paved track at Raleigh.

Pete Hamilton: 1968 rookie of the year came to Winston Cup after successful Sportsman career . . . won the 1970 Daytona 500, both races that year at Talladega, plus a Daytona 125-mile qualifying race in 1971.

Bobby Johns: won two poles and two races (Bristol and Atlanta) in a career that began in the late '50s and ended in the late '60s.

Joe Lee Johnson: won inaugural Coca-Cola World 600 at the Charlotte Motor Speedway, the only victory of his career.

Carl Kiekhaefer: came into NASCAR in 1955 and 1956 with multi-car teams that won most of the races and back-to-back championships with first Tim Flock, then Buck Baker.

Nord Krauskopf: his K&K Insurance Co. was long-time sponsor of Bobby Isaac, Buddy Baker, and Dave Marcis in No. 71 Dodges . . . Isaac won the 1970 title in Krauskopf-owned cars.

Johnny Mantz: only NASCAR victory was in the inaugural (1950) Mountain Dew Southern 500 in a car co-owned by Bill France, Curtis Turner, Hubert Westmoreland, and Alvin Hawkins.

Banjo Matthews: an outstanding Modified/Sportsman driver in the '50s and '60s, he won three Winston Cup poles but no races . . . became better known as a successful team-owner (winning several races with Donnie Allison) and one of the sport's best car-builder and chassis technicians.

J.D. McDuffie: one of the sport's most determined independent drivers, one with enthusiasm and ambition, but very limited resources . . . never won a race, but won the pole at Dover in 1978 . . . died in the opening laps at Watkins Glen in 1991.

Hershel McGriff: one of stock car racing's pioneers who did (and continues to do) just about everything . . . ran in the first Southern 500, is a veteran of the Mexican Road Race (teaming with Bill France, Sr) . . . got all four of his victories late in the '54 season: San Mateo, Macon, Charlotte, and North Wilkesboro . . . retired to return to the Northwest to tend his lumber business . . . stayed active into the '90s with rides in the Winston West and Craftsman Truck series . . . was among the American drivers to take a Winston Cup-type car to the 24 Hours of LeMans in 1976.

Sam McQuagg: was the 1965 Winston Cup rookie of the year . . . only victory was in 1966 Pepsi 400 at Daytona Beach

Rob Moroso: 1989 Busch Series champion and 1990 Winston Cup rookie of the year died in a highway accident late in the 1990 season.

Cotton Owens: won 11 poles and nine races in the late '50s and early '60s . . . later became known as one of NASCAR's most innovative and successful team owners once he retired from driving.

Rod Osterlund: wealthy California businessman gave Dale Earnhardt his first full-time ride in 1979 . . . Earnhardt was rookie of the year that season and won the first of his seven championships for Osterlund in '80 . . . when Osterlund shut down his team during the '81 season, Earnhardt drove briefly for J.D. Stacy before moving to Richard Childress for the last 11 races of the season.

Raymond Parks: owner and engine-builder on the car Red Byron drove to NASCAR's very first championship in 1949.

Lennie Pond: the 1973 rookie of the year (he beat Darrell Waltrip) got his only career victory in the summer race at Talladega in 1978.

Jim Reed: won seven races in the late '50s, including the 1959 Mountain Dew Southern 500 at Darlington.

Jody Ridley: the 1980 Winston Cup rookie of the year got his only career victory at Dover in the spring of 1981.

Earl Ross: native of Canada was 1974 rookie of the year and won at Martinsville in the fall of 1974 for owner Junior Johnson.

Nelson Stacy: got all four of his career victories in a 54-week span: a 500-miler at Darlington in September of 1961, a 300 at Darlington in May of 1962, a 600-miler two weeks later at Charlotte, then a 500-lap short-track race at Martinsville in September.

Billy Wade: got all four of his career victories during a four-race swing into New Jersey and New York in July of 1964: Old Bridge, NJ; Bridge-hampton, NY; Islip, NY; and Watkins Glen.

18

TEAM DIRECTORY

DALE EARNHARDT, INC.

No. 1 Chevrolet Monte
  Carlo
Driver: Steve Park
Owner: Dale and Teresa
  Earnhardt
Crew Chief: Philippe Lopez
Sponsor: Pennzoil
Address: 1675 Coddle Creek Hwy.
Mooresville, NC 28115-8245

About Dale Earnhardt: seven-time Winston Cup champion, tying Richard Petty for most championships . . . runner-up in '89 and '95 . . . considered by many the greatest stock car driver of all time . . . nicknamed "The Intimidator" for his aggressive driving style . . . not the driver most rivals want to see in their rear-view mirrors with a race on the line . . . sixth on the all-time Winston Cup victory list with 70 . . . has driven Richard Childress-owned cars since 1984 . . . broke into Winston Cup racing driving for Rod Osterlund in '79 . . . responded by winning Rookie of the Year honors . . . won the Winston Cup title the next season . . . first win was at Bristol in only his 16th start . . . father, Ralph, was the 1956 NASCAR Sports-

man champion . . . hobbies include hunting and fishing . . . owns two Hatteras boats and a Lear jet . . . favorite baseball team: Atlanta Braves . . . Dale and Teresa also own a Busch Grand National team and expect to have their son Dale Earnhardt, Jr. drive for them in 1998.

PENSKE RACING SOUTH

No. 2 Ford Taurus
Driver: Rusty Wallace
Owner: Roger Penske
Crew Chief:
  Robin Pemberton
Sponsor: Miller Lite
Address: 136 Knob Hill Rd.
Mooresville, NC 28115
Phone: (704)664-2300

About Roger Penske: If it involves major-league motorsports in America, you can bet Roger Penske has been involved. After an outstanding career as a sports car racer, he became an Indy-car team owner in 1969 with the late Mark Donohue. Through the years the Indy-car division of Penske Racing has won 116 poles, 96 races, 21 races of 500 miles, nine CART championships, 11 Indy 500 poles and 10 Indy 500 victories. His Indy-car lineup has included Donohue, David Hobbs, Gary Bettenhaussen, Bobby Allison, Mike Hiss, Tom Sneva, Mario Andretti, Rick Mears, Bobby Unser, Bill Alsup, Kevin Cogan, Al Unser, Danny Sullivan, Emerson Fittipaldi, Paul Tracy and Al Unser Jr. He began his Winston Cup involvement in 1972 on a limited basis with Donohue, Dave Marcis and Donnie Allison. He also fielded cars for George Follmer, Bobby Allison, Neil Bonnett and Bettenhaussen through 1977, and fielded a car for Wallace in the 1980 season-finale near Atlanta. Penske returned to NASCAR in 1991 with a team built around Wallace, a team that's won 29 races and often challenged for the series championship. As if that's not enough of a load, Penske owns speedways in Michigan, Pennsylvania, North Carolina and California, and is looking to build in Colorado.

RICHARD CHILDRESS RACING

No. 3 Chevrolet.
Driver: Dale Earnhardt.
Owner: Richard Childress.
Crew Chief: Larry
    McReynolds.
Sponsor: GM Goodwrench Service.
Address: P.O. Box 1189
    236 Industrial Drive
    Welcome, NC 27374
Phone: (910)731-3334

About Richard Childress: a former racer, he finished in the top 10 in points five times (best finish: fifth, in 1975). While he was still racing in Winston Cup, he signed Dale Earnhardt in 1981. Together, they have won six Winston Cup titles. Retired as a driver in '81 . . . as an owner, expanded to the NASCAR Crafstman Truck series in 1995 . . . With Mike Skinner driving, the Childress team won the first truck series title . . . Childress also owns 200 acres of farmland and is the principle owner in a merchandise and apparel business . . . some employees

have been with Childress Racing for more than 20 years . . . Childress and his wife, Judy, have one daughter: Tina Lynn Dillon. Tina's husband, Mike, drives in the Busch Grand National series.

MORGAN-MCCLURE MOTORSPORTS

No. 4 Chevrolet
    Monte Carlo
Driver: Bobby Hamilton
Owner: Larry McClure
Crew Chief: Robert larkins
Sponsor: Kodak Gold Film
Address: 25139 Lee Highway
    Abingdon, VA 24211
Phone: (540)628-3683

About Larry McClure: On most teams with hyphenated owners— in this case, the other owner is Charles Morgan—it's generally left for one to be the "front" man. Larry McClure is it: active, highly visible, deeply involved and passionate about the team he co-founded in 1983. He and Morgan went through five drivers before hiring Ernie Irvan in 1990. They were a potent combo until Irvan left late in the 1993 season to drive for Robert Yates Racing. The Morgan-McClure team used three drivers the rest of '93, then hired Sterling Marlin in 1994. All told, the team has four victories at Talladega, three in the Daytona 500, two in the Pepsi 400, and one each at Bristol, Watkins, Darlington and Sonoma, all with Kodak backing. Hamilton joins the team this year after three seasons with Petty Enterprises.

HENDRICK MOTORSPORTS

No. 5 Chevrolet
    Monte Carlo
Driver: Terry Labonte
Owner: Rick Hendrick
Crew Chief: Andy Graves
Sponsor: Kellogg's Corn Flakes
Address: 4414 Papa Joe Hendrick Blvd.
    Harrisburg, NC 28075
Phone: (704)455-3400

About Rick Hendrick: Few owners in the 50-year history of NASCAR have gone through the highs and lows that Rick Hendrick has experienced in the past few years. On one hand, he's been plagued with extensive legal and medical problems that have often seemed almost insurmountable. On the other, his organization won the 1995 and 1997 NASCAR titles with Jeff Gordon, and the 1996 title with Terry Labonte. That, in addition to winning 43 races in the decade of the '90s while fielding full-schedule teams for such stars as Darrell Waltrip, Ken Schrader, Ricky Rudd, Ricky Craven, Gordon and Labonte. The empire that is Hendrick Motorsports began taking shape in 1984, when Hendrick—owner of several dozen automobile dealerships—started a team with Geoff Bodine. Since then, 18 others have driven for Hendrick, and they've produced 75 poles, 70 victories, two championships and more than $50 million in earnings.

ROUSH RACING

No. 6 Ford Taurus
Driver: Mark Martin
Owner: Jack Roush
Crew Chief: Jimmy Fennig
Sponsor: Valvoline
Address: 122 Knob Hill Rd.
   Mooressville, NC 28115
Phone: (704)664-3800

About Jack Roush: One of the most innovative and single-minded owners in stock car racing began with a modest one-team effort in 1988 with journeyman driver Mark Martin. Four years later, Roush added a second car for Wally Dallenbach (replaced after two years by Ted Musgrave), added a third car for Jeff Burton in 1996, and will add Chad Little and Johnny Benson to his stable this year. In addition, Michigan-based Roush Racing fields a Craftsman Truck team for Joe Ruttman, an SCCA Trans-Am team for Tom Kendall and builds engines for the Indy Racing League. In addition to its Winston Cup success, Roush Racing once won 10 consecutive IMSA GTO 24-hour races at Daytona Beach and has dominated Trans-Am in recent years.

MATTEI MOTORSPORTS

No. 7 Ford Taurus
Driver: Geoff Bodine
Owner: Jim Mattei
Crew Chief: Tim Brewer
Sponsor: To be announced
Address: 6007 Victory Lane
   Harrisburg, NC 28075
Phone: (704)483-9340

About Jim Mattea: Purchased majority ownership of the team in August 1997 . . . venture capital investor from Dallas, Texas . . . serves on several corporate and charitable boards around the country . . . son Jim serves as business manager of the team . . . born December 28, 1949 in Mobile, Alabama . . . resides in Dallas . . . has another son, Scott

STAVOLA BROTHERS RACING

No. 8 Chevrolet
   Monte Carlo
Driver: Hut Stricklin
Owner: Billy and Mickey Stavola
Crew Chief: Bill Ingle
Sponsor: Circuit City
Address: Highway 49 North
   Harrisburg, NC 28075
Phone: (704)455-6461

About The Stavolas: The need for speed is old hat for the Stavolas, a pair of New Jersey-based businessmen. Mickey used to race Jersey Speed Skiffs in powerboat competition and Billy is a national-caliber ice boat racer. In addition, they own successful thoroughbred racing and breeding stables in New Jersey and Florida. They discovered stock car racing in 1983 during a Winston Cup 500-miler at Pocono, Pennsylvania. They began sponsoring Bobby Hillin, a relationship that lasted through the 1990 season, then added Bobby Allison to their team in 1986. When Allison suffered career-ending injuries in 1988 (ironically, after winning that year's Daytona 500), the Stavolas hired Mike Alexander to be Hillin's teammate. When Alexander suffered career-ending injuries in 1988, they hired Dick Trickle as Hillin's teammate. Hillin was replaced by

BUD MOORE: CAR OWNER, WAR HERO

Bud Moore had never been so scared in all his life. He would have been (in his own words) "a damned fool" if he hadn't been scared on the morning of June 7, 1944. Walter (Bud) Moore, you see, was about to get a close-up and personal look at World War II from the ramp of an Army landing craft powering ashore on a beach in the French province of Normandy.

As the war raged, Moore was just a teen-age farm boy from upstate South Carolina. He volunteered when he became of age and sailed from New York to near Liverpool, where his Army infantry unit was told to prepare for the D-Day invasion. The man who would later field cars that won dozens of races and the 1962 Winston Cup championship for Joe Weatherly proved to be as

good a soldier as he was to become an owner/mechanic.

He made it ashore without serious incident and settled in with his unit. Later that summer he flushed out several Germans hiding in a farm house and preparing an ambush site. He received several combat commendations and a battlefield promotion, and returned to South Carolina a war hero.

Years later, his Spartanburg-based team won races with Weatherly, Billy Wade, Darel Dieringer, Buddy Baker, Bobby Allison, Benny Parsons, Dale Earnhardt, Ricky Rudd, Morgan Shepherd, and Geoff Bodine.

And so far as we know, not a shot was fired in anger.

Rick Wilson in 1990, then Trickle replaced him for 1992. Sterling Marlin drove the car in 1993, then Jeff Burton in 1994 and 1995 before Hut Stricklin got the call for the 1996 season.

MELLING RACING INC.

No. 9 Ford Taurus
Driver: Lake Speed
Owner: Harry Melling
Crew Chief: Jeff Buice
Sponsor: The Cartoon Network
Address: 2004 Pitts School Rd
   Concord, NC 28027
Phone: (704)786-4635

About Harry Melling: It's hard to say where Bill Elliott would be today if not for Harry Melling. In 1982, when the family-run Elliott team was struggling to survive, Melling stepped up and offered to help their low-budget Ford team. The rest is history: the Elliotts won 40 poles and 34 races and the 1988 championship, and became one of the sport's most popular and well-respected teams. Melling Racing hasn't been the same since Elliott left after 1991 to drive for Junior Johnson. He and Melling Oil Pump sponsored 10 drivers (some for only a race or two)

from 1992 through 1994, then settled on Lake Speed. The team spent most of 1997 without a full-time sponsor (a much-ballyhooed deal with the University of Nebraska fell through), but should fare better this year with The Cartoon Network.

RUDD PERFORMANCE MOTORSPORTS

No. 10 Ford Taurus
Driver: Ricky Rudd
Owner: Ricky Rudd
Crew Chief: Jim Long
Sponsor: Tide
Address: 292 Rolling Hills Rd.
   Mooresville, NC 28115
Phone: (704)664-4372

About Ricky Rudd: Few NASCAR-watchers would have guessed in 1993 that Ricky Rudd would become as successful an owner/driver as he has. After spending most of his career driving for others—among them: Junie Donlavey, DiGard Racing, Richard Childress, Bud Moore, Kenny Bernstein, and Rick Hendrick—the Virginia native left Hendrick after 1993 to create his own Tide-backed Ford team. He's won at least one race and been top-10 in points every year as an owner/driver, and extended his annual winning streak to 15 years by winning twice in 1997, including the Brickyard 400. A successful go-kart racer growing up, he moved to stock cars in 1975 after outdriving his brother, Al, in a private test session at a short track in Hampton, Virginia.

BODINE/EVANS MOTORSPORTS

No. 11 Ford Taurus
Driver: Brett Bodine
Owner: Andy Evans/
  Brett Bodine
Crew Chief:
  Donnie Richeson
Sponsor: To be announced
Address: 304 Performance Rd
  Mooresville, NC 28115
Phone: (704)664-1111

About Evans/Bodine: 1997 was his second as an owner/driver . . . purchased his team from Junior Johnson late in '95 . . . drove for Johnson in '95 after five-year tour with Kenny Bernstein . . . started racing full time in Winston Cup in '88 with Bud Moore after successful Busch Grand National career . . . runner-up for the '86 Grand National championship . . . began racing at the Chemung (NY) Speedrome . . . raced modifieds in the Northeast from 1980 through '84 . . . in his Winston Cup debut, won the pole for the '87 Winston Open driving for Hoss Ellington . . . first victory was at North Wilkesboro in '90 . . . middle brother of the racing Bodines . . . graduate of New York State University at Alfred with an associate degree in mechanical engineering. . . . resides in Davidson, North Carolina with wife Diane and daughter Heidi.

PRECISION PRODUCTS RACING

No. 14 Pontiac Grand Prix
Driver: Morgan Shepherd
Owner: Richard Jackson
Crew Chief: Ed Jones
Sponsor: R&L Carriers

Address: Highway 16 North
  Denver, NC 28037
Phone: (704)483-9340

About Richard Jackson: After years of tinkering with short-track cars at weekly tracks around western North Carolina, the Jackson brothers—Richard and Leo—created a Winston Cup team in 1985 for the Parsons brothers—Benny and Phil. They stayed a foursome for two years, until Benny left for other opportunities in NASCAR. The Jacksons won at Talladega in 1988 with Phil, shortly before Leo left to form a separate team for Harry Gant. Richard kept Phil one more season, then hired Terry Labonte for 1990 and Rick Mast for the next six seasons. When Mast left for another team, Richard hired Morgan Shepherd. It's an on-again, off-again relationship that finally appears solid going into 1998.

ROUSH RACING

No. 16 Ford Taurus
Driver: Ted Musgrave
Owner: Jack Roush
Crew Chief: James Ince
Sponsor: Primestar
Address: Highway 29 South
  Liberty, NC 27298
Phone: (910)622-5160

About Jack Roush: See No. 6 Mark Martin/Valvoline

DARRELL WALTRIP MOTORSPORTS

No. 17 Chevrolet
  Monte Carlo
Driver: Darrell Waltrip
Owner: Darrell Waltrip
Crew Chief: To be announced
Sponsor: Fox network
Address: 16780 Hudspeth Rd.
  Harrisburg, NC 28075
Phone: (704)455-3117

About Darrell Waltrip: One of NASCAR's most successful drivers and its most colorful and articulate spokesman hasn't enjoyed nearly as much success as an owner/driver. After getting the first of his 83 victories in a self-owned car in 1975, Waltrip spent the next 15 years driving for DiGard Racing, Junior Johnson and Rick Hendrick. He won 26 races with DiGard, 43 races and three Winston Cup titles with Johnson, then six races with Hendrick. He broke away after the 1990 season to form his own team and promptly won two races in '91 and three more in '92. But he hasn't won since September of '92, and announced last year that 1997 would be his final full year as a driver. That appears to have changed, and he's now talking about running the full 1998 schedule as well as fielding a second full-schedule team for Rich Bickle.

JOE GIBBS RACING

No. 18 Pontiac Grand Prix
Driver: Bobby Labonte
Owner: Joe Gibbs
Crew Chief: Jimmy Makar
Sponsor: Interstate Batteries
Address: 9900 Twin Lakes
    Parkway
    Charlotte, NC 28269
Phone: (704)875-2895

About Joe Gibbs: One of NASCAR's best-known and most popular owners is better known to tens of millions of Americans as former head coach of the Washington Redskins. A native of North Carolina, his family moved to California when he was still in grade school. He grew up near car-crazy San Diego and became an avid fan of all types of motorsports. After working as an assistant coach at the college and professional level, he became head coach of the Redskins prior to the 1981 season. They were a combined 140-65 in the regular season and playoffs in his 12 years, including Super Bowl appearances after the 1982 (beat Miami), 1983 (lost to Oakland), 1987 (beat Denver), and 1991 (beat Buffalo) seasons. He retired after the 1992 season to devote his full attention to the Winston Cup team he created in 1992 for Dale Jarrett.

WOOD BROTHERS RACING TEAM

No. 21 Ford Taurus
Driver: Michael Waltrip
Owner: Glen Wood
Crew Chiefs: Eddie and
    Len Wood
Sponsor: Citgo Petroleum
Address: 21 Performance Dr.
    Stuart, VA 24171
Phone: (540)694-2121

About Glen Wood: Since 1953, when he finished 30th at Martinsville and 20th at Raleigh in Lincolns prepared by his brothers, Glen Wood has been an important part of NASCAR racing. He competed until 1965, when he and his family began fielding cars for some of racing's biggest names: Dan Gurney, Curtis Turner, Parnelli Jones, A.J. Foyt, LeeRoy Yarbrough, Cale Yarborough, and Marvin Panch. Later, the Ford team featured David Pearson, Neil Bonnett, Buddy Baker, Kyle Petty, Dale Jarrett, and Morgan Shepherd before Michael Waltrip came aboard in 1996. The organization's record is among the most impressive in NASCAR history: 907 starts, 116 poles, 96 victories (the most recent in 1993 by Shepherd near Atlanta) and almost $12 million in winnings.

BILL DAVIS RACING INC.

No. 22 Pontiac Grand Prix
Driver: Ward Burton
Owner: Bill Davis
Crew Chief: Chris Hussey
Sponsor: MBNA America Bank
Address: 301 Old Thomasville Rd.
    High Point, NC 27260
Phone: (910)887-2222

About Bill Davis: After several years as a Busch Series team-owner, Bill Davis made the move to Winston Cup for 1993. Ex-Busch champ Bobby Labonte drove two seasons, then Randy LaJoie, Jimmy Hensley and Wally Dallenbach shared time in 1995 before Ward Burton came aboard for the final 9 races, including a fall victory at Rockingham. Burton stayed with the Pontiac team in '96 and '97, and is back again this year. Davis was encouraged to graduate to Winston Cup after a couple of pretty decent drivers did well in his Busch Series cars in the late '80s and early '90s. Mark Martin won one each in '88, '89, and '90, and Jeff Gordon won three races for Davis in '93 before Rick Hendrick snatched him for his Winston Cup team.

TEAM WINSTON

No. 23 Ford Taurus
Driver: Jimmy Spencer
Owner: Travis Carter
Crew Chief: Donnie Wingo
Sponsor: Winston Cigarettes
Address: U.S. Highway 421
   South
   Hamptonville, NC 27020
Phone: (910)468-6896

About Travis Carter: It didn't take very long for Travis Carter to make his mark in NASCAR racing. With hardly any experience at all, he was named crew chief of the L.G. DeWitt-owned team that won the 1973 Winston Cup for Benny Parsons. Five years later, Carter was again the Cup-winning crew chief, this time with Cale Yarborough and team owner Junior Johnson. In addition to Parsons and Yarborough, he's worked with Bobby Allison, Dave Marcis, Stan Barrett, Harry Gant, Morgan Shepherd, Rick Mast, Butch Miller and Hut Stricklin. He's had two stints with Spencer—all of 1991 and part of 1992, then again beginning in 1995. Carter has been part of 41 poles and 31 victories as crew chief, and two championships. His record as a team-owner is more modest: 168 starts, no poles and no victories with Mast, Miller, Stricklin and Spencer.

HENDRICK MOTORSPORTS

No. 24 Chevrolet Monte Carlo
Driver: Jeff Gordon
Owner: Rick Hendrick
Crew Chief: Ray Evernham

Sponsor: DuPont
   Refinishing
Address: 4433 Papa Joe
   Hendrick Blvd.
   Harrisburg, NC 28075
Phone: (704)455-3400

About Rick Hendrick: See No. 5 Terry Labonte/Kellogg's Corn Flakes entry

ROUSH RACING

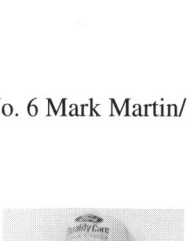

No. 26 Ford Taurus
Driver: Johnny Benson
Owner: Jack Roush
Crew Chief: To be
   announced
Sponsor:
Address: Highway 29 South
   Liberty, NC 27298
Phone: (910)622-5160

About Jack Roush: See No. 6 Mark Martin/Valvoline entry

ROBERT YATES RACING

No. 28 Ford Taurus
Driver: Kenny Irwin
Owner: Robert Yates
Crew Chief: Marc Reno
Sponsor: Texaco Havoline
Address: 115 Dwelle St.; Charlotte, NC 28208
Phone: 704-392-8184

About Robert Yates: It was in the early '60s when Robert Yates realized his place in life would likely be automotive. He'd done some drag racing around Charlotte, NC, but was more smitten by roundy-round racing at paved and dirt tracks in the Carolinas. He was hired by the potent Holman-Moody team in 1968 and built engines for the Junior Johnson team in the early '70s. He worked at DiGard Racing for 10 years, providing engines for Darrell Waltrip, Ricky Rudd, Bobby Allison and Greg Sacks. He became general manager of the Harry Ranier-owned team in 1986, then bought it two years later with Davey Allison as his driver.

Tragedy struck twice: Allison died in a helicopter crash in 1993 and Irvan suffered life-threatening injuries in a practice session in Michigan in 1994. Yates hired Dale Jarrett for the 1995 season and fielded a second team when Irvan returned in the fall of that year. They were teammates throughout 1996 and 1997, when Yates chose not to renew his contract with Irvan and, instead, hired promising newcomer Kenny Irwin. All told, Robert Yates Racing has won 33 races with Allison, Jarrett, and Irvan . . . Yates, 54, is the ninth, and youngest, child of a prominent Southern Baptist minister in Charlotte . . . twin brother, Richard, is the business manager for Yates Racing . . . Robert and his wife, Carolyn, have two children: Doug and Amy.

DIAMOND RIDGE MOTORSPORTS

No. 29 Chevrolet Monte Carlo
Driver: Jeff Green
Owner: Gary Bechtel
Crew Chief: Wes Ward
Sponsor: To be announced
Address: 5901 Orr Rd.
    Charlotte, NC 28213
Phone: (704)598-5295

About Gary Bechtel: Founded Diamond Ridge Motor Sports in November 1993 . . . serves as owner and president of the company . . . former president of Bechtel Civil Company . . . became interested in NASCAR after meeting fellow owners Rick Hendrick and Felix Sabates and attending races while living in Charlotte, North Carolina from 1985 to 1990 . . . fielded car on a limited basis for Phil Parsons on the Winston Cup circuit in 1990 . . . also fielded a Winston West team with John Krebs before joining Winston Cup full-time in 1994 . . . graduate of the University of the Pacific in California . . . has three children: Brian, Blake, and Carly.

BAHARI RACING

No. 30 Pontiac Grand Prix
Driver: Derrike Cope
Owner: Chuck
    Rider/Lowrance Harry
Crew Chief: Doug Hewitt

Sponsor: Gumout
Address: 208 Rolling
    Hills Rd.
    Mooresville, NC 28115
Phone: (704)664-6670

About Rider/Harry: You can take this one to the bank: there will be wide-spread cheering and not the first sign of resentment when the Bahari Racing team finally gets its first Winston Cup victory. Chuck Rider and business partner Lowrance Harry (they founded a chain of auto parts and small-engine stores) have been at it since 1987. They've made thousands of friends along the way, both inside and outside the racing community. They formed their race team in 1987 for Michael Waltrip, and they were together for 266 races spread over nine years. Johnny Benson drove their yellow No. 30 Pontiacs for two years (and was '96 rookie of the year) before leaving to become Jack Roush's fifth driver. Derrike Cope, former Daytona 500 champion, will drive the No. 30 Pontiacs this year.

RICHARD CHILDRESS RACING

No. 31 Chevrolet
Driver: Mike Skinner
Owner: Richard Childress
Crew Chief: Kevin Hamlin
Sponsor: Lowe's Home Improvement Warehouse
Address: P.O. Box 1189
    Welcome, NC 27374-1189
Phone: (910)731-3334

About Richard Childress: See No. 3 Dale Earnhardt/GM Goodwrench Service entry.

ANDY PETREE RACING

No. 33 Chevrolet
Driver: Ken Schrader
Owner: Andy Petree
Crew Chief: Andy Petree
Sponsor: Skoal/U.S.
    Tobacco

Address: P.O. Box 325
  908 Upward Rd.
  East Flat Rock, NC 28726
Phone: (704)698-0335

About Andy Petree: Purchased Lee Jackson Motorsports in October 1996 after serving as crew chief for Dale Earnhardt. With Earnhardt, Petree won two Winston Cup championships (1993 and 94) and 15 races . . . returned to Lee Jackson's team in 96: first worked for Jackson as a mechanic in '82 . . . Robert Pressley was the team's driver during the 96 season . . . first victory as crew chief was in 1988 when Phil Parsons won at Talladega . . . was crew chief for Harry Gant from 1989 to '92. In '91, Gant won four consecutive races . . . born in Newton, NC, near Hickory Motor Speedway, Petree, 39, attended his first race with an uncle. "I loved it before I ever saw the cars going around the track," Petree said. "Just hearing the motors as we approached the gates was a thrill." . . . Petree and his second wife, Patrice, have two children: Joey, 16, and Justin, 11.

ISM MOTORSPORTS

No. 35 Pontiac
Driver: Todd Bodine
Owner: L.G. "Bob" Hancher, Jr.
Crew Chief: Pat Tryson
Sponsor: Tabasco Pepper Sauce
Address: 103 Center Lane
  Huntersville, NC 28078 (team address will
  change early in 1998)
Phone: (704)947-0035.

About Bob Hancher: Serves as president of International Sports Management, owner of Team Tabasco . . . a former athlete at the University of Iowa, the 6 foot, 5 inch, 275-pound Hancher is an imposing figure . . . a businessman based in Noblesville, Ind . . . .his interest in racing developed when he was a marketing executive for the Raynor garage door company. Indianapolis Motor Speedway purchased doors from Raynor, which eventually sponsored Dennis Firestone in the Indy 500 . . . as an importer for Pi Research's "Intelligent Information" computer package, Hancher worked with tops teams in NASCAR, Indy car, Formula One and IMSA . . . he and his wife Gretchen have been married for 22 years.

MB2 MOTORSPORTS

No. 36 Pontiac
Driver: Ernie Irvan
Owner: Nelson Bowers,
  Tom Beard, Read Morton, Jr.
Crew Chief:
  Ryan Pemberton
Sponsor: Skittles
Address: 185 McKenzie Rd.
  Mooresville, NC 28115
Phone:(704)664-7416

About the MB2 owners: "How Bout Them Dawgs!" should be inscribed on the side of the No. 36 car: Nelson Bowers, Tom Beard and Read Morton are all University of Georgia graduates . . . Bowers is founder, chairman and CEO of Bowers Transportation Group, a chain of multi-franchised automobile dealerships based in Chattanooga, Tenn . . . Bowers attended Georgia on a football scholarship . . . In 1976, at age 30, he became a franchised Volvo dealer in Chattanooga . . . Today, the Bowers Group consists of 14 franchises in seven locations in the Chattanooga market . . . Bowers and his wife, Pam, have two children: Courtney and Rick . . . Beard is an investment banker with Stephens, Inc., an Arkansas-based banking and brokerage firm . . . the native Georgian served as an Army infantry officer . . . from 1976 through '80 Beard was deputy assistant to President Jimmy Carter . . . Beard and his wife, Frances, have three sons: Brooks, Hayes and Casey . . . Morton is senior partner and head of the corporate department of the Atlanta law firm of Cashin, Morton and Mullis . . . his primary areas are corporate, business transactions and corporate finance . . . he and his wife, Margaret, have two children: Frances and Billy.

KRANEFUSS/ PENSKE RACING

No. 37 Ford
Driver: Jeremy Mayfield
Owner: Michael Kranefuss
  and ROger Penske
Crew Chief: Paul Andrews

Sponsor: Kmart
Address: 163 Rolling Hills Rd.
   Mooresville, NC 28115
Phone:(704)663-3700

About Michael Kranefuss and Carl Haas:
Before they formed their Winston Cup association
in 1994, they were both winners . . . Under the
leadership of Kranefuss, Ford's racing program
was rebuilt into the world's most diverse motorsports program. When he retired in '93, Ford was
the only auto manufacturer involved in Winston
Cup, CART Indy car, Formula One and the World
Rally Championship . . . In Winston Cup, Ford tied
for the manufacturer's title in '91 after not having
won it since '69. Bill Elliott ('88) and Alan Kulwicki ('92) won Winston Cup driving championships in Fords . . . A native of Germany, Kranefuss joined Ford Motor Co. in 1968 as assistant
manager of Ford's newly formed Germany compe-
titions department . . . he moved to the United
States in 1980 and is now a U.S. citizen . . . he and
his wife, Immy, have two sons: Daniel and Phillip
. . . Since '74 Haas has won 15 championships in
CART, Can-Am and other racing series . . . his drivers have included Mario and Michael Andretti,
Jackie Stewart and Nigel Mansell . . . Haas and
actor Paul Newman have been partners in a CART
Indy car team since '83 . . . Haas also operates the
Milwaukee Mile, the nation's oldest major racing
facility . . . Haas, based in suburban Chicago, is a
prominent distributor of racing equipment.

TEAM SABCO

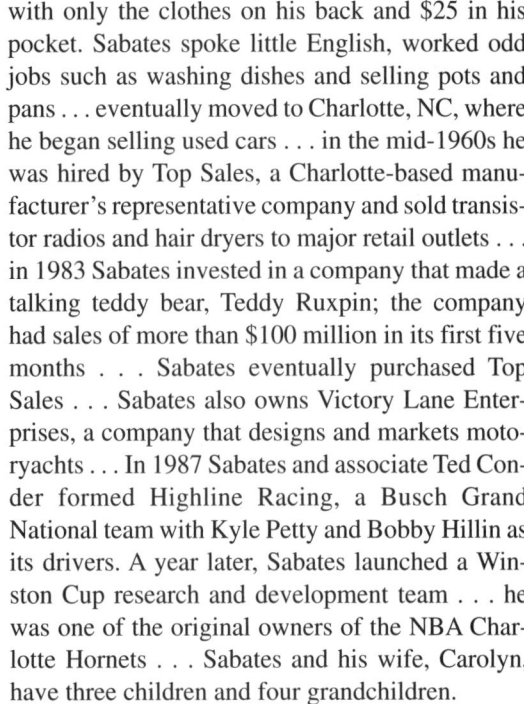

No. 40 Chevrolet
Driver: Sterling Marlin
Owner: Felix Sabates
Crew Chief: Buddy Barnes
Sponsor: Coors Light/Coors
   Original
Address: 114 Meadow Hill Circle
   Mooresville, NC 28115
Phone: (704)662-9642.

About Felix Sabates: One of the most
intriguing success stories in American sports . . .
born in Cuba, Sabates fled to Miami, Fla., at age 16
with only the clothes on his back and $25 in his
pocket. Sabates spoke little English, worked odd
jobs such as washing dishes and selling pots and
pans . . . eventually moved to Charlotte, NC, where
he began selling used cars . . . in the mid-1960s he
was hired by Top Sales, a Charlotte-based manufacturer's representative company and sold transis-
tor radios and hair dryers to major retail outlets . . .
in 1983 Sabates invested in a company that made a
talking teddy bear, Teddy Ruxpin; the company
had sales of more than $100 million in its first five
months . . . Sabates eventually purchased Top
Sales . . . Sabates also owns Victory Lane Enterprises, a company that designs and markets moto-
ryachts . . . In 1987 Sabates and associate Ted Con-
der formed Highline Racing, a Busch Grand
National team with Kyle Petty and Bobby Hillin as
its drivers. A year later, Sabates launched a Winston Cup research and development team . . . he
was one of the original owners of the NBA Charlotte Hornets . . . Sabates and his wife, Carolyn,
have three children and four grandchildren.

LARRY HEDRICK MOTORSPORTS

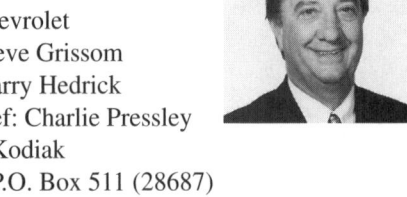

No. 41 Chevrolet
Driver: Steve Grissom
Owner: Larry Hedrick
Crew Chief: Charlie Pressley
Sponsor: Kodiak
Address: P.O. Box 511 (28687)
   114 Victory Lane
   Statesville, NC 28677
Phone: (704)881-0410

About Larry Hedrick: formed Hedrick
Motorsports in 1990 . . . Larry Pearson drove 11
races for Hedrick in '91 . . . Greg Sacks, Dave Marcis, and Hut Stricklin were the drivers in '92, followed by Phil Parsons and Dick Trickle the following year . . . Joe Nemechek was Hedrick's driver in
'94, then Ricky Craven won Winston Cup Rookie of
the Year honors in '95. Craven returned in '96, winning two pole positions . . . Hedrick, 51, is president
and owner of several businesses in North Carolina,
including Hedrick Motors, Inc., Tarheel Auction

and Realty and the Class A Kannapolis Boll Weevils baseball team . . . Hedrick established Statesville Auto Auction in 1976; he sold it to Manheim Auctions in '93 . . . Hedrick is involved in many community projects in Iredell County . . . he and his wife, Sue, have two children: Chris and Suzanne.

TEAM SABCO

No. 42 Chevrolet
Driver: Joe Nemechek
Owner: Felix Sabates
Crew Chief: Scott Eggleston
Sponsor: BellSouth
Address: 114 Meadow
    Hill Circle
    Mooresville, NC 28115
Phone: (704)662-9642

About Sabates: See No. 40 Sterling Marlin/ Coors Light/Coors Original entry.

PETTY ENTERPRISES

No. 43 Pontiac
Driver: John Andretti
Owner: Richard Petty
Crew Chief: Robbie Loomis
Sponsor: STP
Address: 311 Branson Mill Rd.
    Randleman, NC 27317
Phone: (910)498-3745

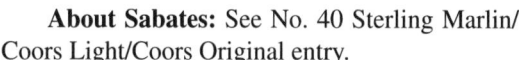

About Richard Petty: one of the most popular drivers ever in any racing series . . . holds the record (200) for most Winston Cup race victories and most Daytona 500 wins (7) . . . shares with Dale Earnhardt the mark for most Winston Cup titles (7) . . . only driver to win the Daytona 500 in four different makes of cars: Plymouth, Dodge, Oldsmobile, and Buick . . . his fender-denting duels with Bobby Allison, Cale Yarborough, David Pearson and others are at the core of NASCAR's history . . . President Bush helped Petty celebrate his 55th birthday at Daytona in 1992, the year he retired as a driver . . . President Reagan attended the Firecracker 400 at Daytona in '84 when Petty won his final race . . . followed his father, Lee, into Winston Cup racing . . . early in

Richard's career he won a convertible division race by a few inches, but the runner-up protested; officials upheld the protest and gave the victory to the second-place finisher, Lee Petty . . . Richard's trademarks include a cowboy hat and sunglasses . . . has served as a county commissioner in Randolph County, N.C. . . . The No. 43 car and STP have been associated since 1972 . . . nicknamed "King Richard" . . . he and his wife, Lynda, have four children: Kyle, Sharon, Lisa, and Rebecca.

PE-2

No. 44 Pontiac
Driver: Kyle Petty
Owners: Richard Petty and
    Kyle Petty
Crew Chief: Bobby Kennedy
Sponsor: Mattel Hot
    Wheels/Spree
Address: 7571 Flowes Store Rd.
    Concord, NC 28025
Phone: (704)788-4400.

About the Pettys: For information on Richard, see the No. 43 car above. Kyle Petty is the son of racing legend Richard . . . Kyle's the first third-generation driver to win a Winston Cup race: grandfather Lee won his first in 1949 . . . Kyle is the first Petty to win $1 million in a season (1992) . . . returned to Petty Enterprises last year after four seasons with Felix Sabates . . . career-best in points standings: fifth in '92 and '93 . . . in '79, won an ARCA 200-miler at Daytona in his first race on a closed course . . . organizes an annual cross-country charity motorcycle ride . . . won the 1993 Daytona 500 pole . . . has recorded country music songs.

TEAM SABCO

No. 46 Chevrolet
Driver: Wally Dallenbach, Jr.
Owner: Felix Sabates
Crew Chief: To be
    announced
Sponsor: First Union Corp.

Address: 114 Meadow Hill Circle
   Mooresville, NC 28115
Phone: (704)662-9642.

About Sabates: see No. 40 Sterling Marlin/ Coors Light/Coors Original entry.

HENDRICK MOTORSPORTS

No. 50 Chevrolet
   Monte Carlo
Driver: Ricky Craven
Owner: Rick Hendrick
Crew Chief: Tony Furr
Sponsor: Budweiser
Address: 4423 Papa Joe Hendrick Blvd.
   Harrisburg, NC 28075
Phone: (704)455-3400

About Rick Hendrick: See No. 5 Terry Labonte/Kellogg's Corn Flakes entry

MARCIS AUTO RACING

No. 71 Chevrolet
Driver: Dave Marcis
Owner: Helen Marcis
Crew Chief: Joe Piete
Sponsor: Realtree
   Camouflage
Address: P.O. Box 645
   Skyland, NC 28776
Phone: 704 684-7170

About Helen and Dave Marcis: Dave has five career Winston Cup victories: first was in Martinsville in 1975; last was in '82 at Richmond . . . runner-up to Richard Petty in the '75 points race . . . first Winston Cup race was the 1968 Daytona 500 . . . has competed in 29 consecutive Daytona 500s . . . wears black leather hard-soled shoes when he is racing . . . product of Wisconsin short tracks . . . father owned a garage: Dave's first attraction to racing occurred when he drove his father's cars in a field near the garage . . . hopes to run a fishing resort and/or restaurant when he retires from racing.

BUTCH MOCK MOTORSPORTS, INC.

No. 75 Ford
Driver: Rick Mast
Owner: Butch Mock
Crew Chief: David
   Charpentier
Sponsor: Remington Arms. Co.
Address: 217 Rolling Hills Rd.
   Mooresville, NC 28115
Phone: (704)663-7572

About Butch Mock: Born and raised in Miami, Florida . . . .worked in construction with his father, then owned a welding and fabrication business . . . raced at local short tracks on Saturday nights; track champion at Hialeah Speedway in the early 1970s . . . saw his first NASCAR race in 1977 . . . formed Rahmoc Racing a year later with his friend, Bob Rahilly. Rahilly built race cars and Mock drove them in '78 in what is now the Busch Grand National series . . . for several years Mock relinquished his seat to several drivers . . . Joe Ruttman drove the car in '82 . . . In '83, Neil Bonnett won five races, including the World 600 at Charlotte and the Atlanta Journal 500 . . . Recalls Mock: "When we won that first Winston Cup race, I felt like my career was complete." . . . Driving for Rahmoc, Bonnett won the first Winston Cup race outside the United States, in Australia in '88 . . . Morgan Shepherd, Rick Wilson and Dick Trickle also drove for Rahmoc . . . the Mock-Rahilly association ended in '92 . . . Todd Bodine was Mock's driver in 1994 and '95 . . . Shepherd returned in '96 . . . Mock's hobbies include collecting vintage hot rods, motorcycle riding, and deep-sea fishing.

JASPER MOTORSPORTS

No. 77 Ford
Driver: Robert Pressley
Owners: Doug Bawel, Mark Wallace,
   Mark Harrah
Crew Chief: Michael McSwain
Sponsors: Jasper Engines and Transmissions/
   Federal & Mogul

Address: 110 Knob Hill Rd.
   Mooresville, NC 28115
Phone: (704)662-6222.

About Bawel, Wallace and Harrah: Doug Bawel has been involved in the automotive business since he began selling cars at a Ford dealership while he was a student at the University of Evansville. Bawel joined Jasper Engines and Transmissions as a sales trainee and worked his way up as advertising manager, sales manager and vice president before he was elected president in 1987. He and his associates purchased the company from founder Alvin Ruxer in '87 . . . Jasper sponsored Ken Ragan in Winston Cup in '89 . . . in '93 Bawel became a partner with DK Ulrich, fielding a Ford for Greg Sacks in '94. Davy Jones and Bobby Hillin Jr. later drove for Jasper . . . in '95, Bawel bought Ulrich's interest in Japser Motorsports and formed a partnership with Wallace and Harrah. They are owners of Jasper distributorships, Wallace in Atlanta and Harrah in Greensboro, NC

FILMAR RACING

No. 81 Ford
Driver: Kenny Wallace
Owner: Filbert Martocci
Crew Chief: Newt Moore (interim)
Sponsor: Square D Co.
Address: 2730 Zion Church Rd.
   Concord, NC 28025
Phone: (704)786-8000.

About Filbert Martocci: Originally from Baltimore, moved to Nashville in the early 1960s . . . first racing association was sponsoring a local driver in 1975 at the Nashville Motor Speedway . . . since then, has sponsored and invested in stock cars, USAC sprint cars and IHRA funny cars. Dal Denton, one of his drivers, won the 1988 IHRA Top Alcohol Funny Car championship . . . formed Filmar Racing in 1988 with Bobby Hamilton in the Busch Grand National series . . . later drivers included David Green and Jeff Burton . . . Square D, based in Palatine, Ill., is a leading manufacturer of electrical distribution, industrial control, and automatic products, systems, and services for elec-

tricity. The company's products are used at many NASCAR facilities.

ROBERT YATES RACING

No. 88 Ford
Driver: Dale Jarrett
Owner: Robert Yates
Crew Chief: Todd Parrott
Sponsor: Quality Care/Ford
   Credit
Address: 115 Dwelle St.
   Charlotte, NC 28208
Phone: (704)392-8184.

About Robert Yates: See No. 28 Kenny Irwin/Texaco Havoline entry.

DONLAVEY RACING

No. 90 Ford
Driver: Dick Trickle
Owner: W.C. "Junie"
   Donlavey
Crew Chief:
   Tommy Baldwin
Sponsor: Heilig-Meyers Furniture/
   Simmons Beautyrest
Address: 5011 Old Midlothian Pike
   Richmond, VA 23224
Phone: (804)233-8592.

About Junie Donlavey: One of the most popular people in Winston Cup racing . . . has been in racing for six decades . . . has just one Winston Cup victory in almost 800 races: Jody Ridley won at Dover Downs in 1981 . . . Ken Schrader, driving a Donlavey car, won a 125-mile qualifying race at Daytona in '87 . . . during his career, Donlavey, 73, has had more than 150 drivers, including 65 in the Winston Cup series . . . three of his drivers were Winston Cup Rookies of the Year: Bill Dennis (1970), Ridley ('80) and Schrader ('85) . . . first driver was Hank Stanley in 1949 in the modified division . . . entered a car in the inaugural Southern 500 at Darlington: Bob Apperson was the driver, with Runt Harris in relief . . . entered a Winston

SOMETIMES NICE GUYS FINISH FIRST

Every dog, of course, has his day. Some may have to wait longer than others, but with time and patience and hard work and fortune, good things eventually happen to every race team.

So it was that on May 17, 1981, at the 1-mile Dover Downs International Speedway, the best of all possible things finally happened for long-time and much-beloved Winston Cup team-owner Junie Donlavey. After 356 career starts dating to 1950, the Richmond, Virginia, man about whom nothing bad has ever been spoken finally saw his car win its first (and most likely, only) Winston Cup race in the Mason-Dixon 500

Jody Ridley, a tough-as-nails little short-track star from Chatsworth, Georgia, started 11th that Sunday afternoon in a Ford sponsored by Trux-more Industries. He was a nonfactor most of the day, a day in which Neil Bonnett and Cale Yarborough swapped the lead eight times before both fell out with mechanical problems. Bonnett led laps 196 to 459, then Yarborough led 460 until his car, too, quit 20 laps later.

Ridley was two laps down at the time, so the scoring was held while he caught up. Once in front, he stayed there, leading the final 20 laps and winning by 22 seconds—that's almost a full lap—ahead of Bobby Allison, the only other driver on the lead lap.

Donlavey has been around NASCAR for most of its 50 years and has more friends than any of us can imagine. He's a quiet and respectful man, always full of good cheer, and possessing perhaps the most well-balanced and realistic outlook of any owner in the business. That's why his victory with Ridley at Dover was unanimously cheered by everyone in the garage area.

"These are my friends and this is my family," he said that afternoon so long ago. "Having them congratulate my team means the world to me. Winning is nice, but having this many friends is even nicer."

Cup car in the 24 Hours of LeMans in 1976 with Dick Brooks and Dick Hutcherson as two of the drivers . . . received the Bill France Award of Excellence at Pocono Raceway last summer for his contributions to racing . . . has no outside business: racing is his business . . . he and his wife, Phyllis, have three children: Linda, Beverly, and Richard.

BILL ELLIOTT RACING TEAM

No. 94 Ford
Driver: Bill Elliott
Owner: Bill Elliott Racing
Crew Chief: Mike Beam
Sponsor: McDonald's
Address: P.O. Box 665
   2367 Elliott Family Parkway S.
   Dawsonville, Ga. 30534.
Phone: (706) 265-6666
Also: P.O. Box 456
   Hickory, NC 28603
Phone: (704)345-6102

About Bill Elliott: Won record 11 superspeedway races in 1985, the year he also was the first driver to collect the Winston Million bonus for winning three of the series "crown jewels:" the Daytona and Winston 500s and the Southern 500 at Darlington . . . voted Most Popular Driver a record 11 times . . . 1988 Winston Cup champion . . . three-time runner-up in points ('85, '87 and '92) . . . first full Winston Cup season was 1983 . . . drove ten seasons for Harry Melling, then three for Junior Johnson . . . voted American Driver of the Year twice, in 1985 and '88 . . . recorded fastest official time in a stock car, 212.809 mph qualifying for the '87 Winston 500 at Talladega . . . began racing on Georgia's short tracks with brothers Dan and Ernie . . . flies his own aircraft . . . Favorite movie: *Stroker Ace.*

AMERICAN EQUIPMENT RACING

No. 96 Chevrolet.
Driver: David Green.
Owner: Howard "Buz" McCall, Jr.
Crew Chief: Butch Enners.
Sponsor: Caterpillar.

Address: 7701-C North Tryon St.
   Charlotte, NC 28262
Phone: (704)510-0002.

About Buz McCall: Former successful Trans-Am series owner who moved to the Busch Grand National series, with driver Ward Burton, in 1995. David Green drove for McCall's Busch team in '96 before stepping up to Winston Cup . . . McCall's Trans-Am teams won four championships in a row: Scott Sharp in '91 and '93, Jack Baldwin in '92 and Scott Pruett in '94 . . . McCall, 51, is a former racer: in '89 he co-drove a GTO car with Baldwin . . . McCall is president of the American Equipment Co., based in Boca Raton, Fla. The company specializes in railroad equipment . . . as a 14-year-old, after telling his mother than he and friends were going camping, hitch-hiked from Boca Raton to Daytona to watch his first Firecracker 400 . . . in 1969, a year after graduating from Florida State University, he joined the Army Reserves as a combat engineer, and was called to active duty . . . on his first date with his future wife, Pat, then a junior at the University of Connecticut, they attended a race at the Norwood (Mass.) Speedway . . . the couple has two children: Brad and Kelly.

ROUSH RACING

No. 97 Ford Taurus
Driver: Chad Little
Owner: Jack Roush
Crew Chief: Skip Eyler
Sponsor: John Deere
Address: 177 Knob Hill Rd.
   Mooresville, NC 28115
Phone: (704)664-8097

About Jack Roush: See No. 6 Mark Martin/Valvoline entry

CALE YARBOROUGH MOTORSPORTS

No. 98 Ford Taurus
Driver: Greg Sacks
Owner: Cale Yarborough

Crew Chief: Mike Hillman
Sponsor: Thorn Apple Valley
   Premium Meats
Address: 4200 Stough Rd.
   Concord, NC 28027
Phone: (704)792-9800.

About Cale Yarborough: the three-time Winston Cup champion retired in 1988 . . . the year before, he purchased Jack Beebe's team . . . Dale Jarrett (in '89) and Dick Trickle ('90) were Yarborough's first full-time drivers . . . several drivers were behind the wheel of Yarborough's cars until Derrike Cope drove the full '93 schedule . . . after Cope was released during the '94 season, Jeremy Mayfield occupied the seat until after the '96 Southern 500 when John Andretti replaced him . . . Yarborough's '83 career Winston Cup victories are fourth on the all-time list . . . four-time winner of the Daytona 500 (1968, '77, '83, '84) . . . he's also proud that he won five Winston Cup races at Darlington, "The Track Too Tough to Tame," in his home state . . . he also raced on the Indy-car circuit . . . Commenting on Yarborough's aggressive driving style, former driver and car owner Junior Johnson said, "When you strap Cale into the car, it's like adding 20 horsepower." . . . Yarborough still resides in Timmonsville, SC, where he grew up . . . he and his wife, Betty Jo, have three children: Julie, Kelley, and B.J.

ROUSH RACING

No. 99 Ford Taurus
Driver: Jeff Burton
Owner: Jack Roush
Crew Chief: Frank Stoddard
Sponsor: Exide Batteries
Address: 122 Knob Hill Rd.
   Mooresville, NC 28115
Phone: (704)664-3800

About Jack Roush: See No. 6 Mark Martin/Valvoline entry

19

HOW TO WATCH A NASCAR RACE

At home somewhere in North Carolina:

HE: Hey, honey, I'm home and I've got good news. Great news, in fact.

SHE: Oh, great, this oughtta be good. The last time you came home bragging about good news it cost us $147 and 36 hours in jail. No, thanks, I don't want to go see another time-share condo near Bayonne.

HE: No, no, I don't want to do that, either. This is different, honey, this is something new and exciting, something we've always talked about doing but never had the chance.

SHE: OK, what's the deal? What's got you so revved up?

HE: Racing's got me revved up. Look here—two prime tickets to the Daytona 500. All expenses paid, too. I won 'em in a raffle down at the plant. How about them apples—we're going to Daytona Beach!

SHE: Like I said: 'Oh, great, this oughtta be good.' The question now is, what do we need to carry with us and what are we gonna see when we get there?

It's safe to say that words to that effect are spoken thousands of times each year as NASCAR attracts tens of thousands of new fans. To be sure, an afternoon at the races requires more than just a ticket and a few bucks for cold beer. Maybe this session of Winston Cup Racing 101 will help you understand what you'll see and give you some hints about what to watch for.

By the time you graduate you'll have gone from a wide-eyed freshman who didn't know Darrell Waltrip from Darryl Hannah (trust us, it's not even close) to an honor graduate who can speak with authority when somebody at work asks what's all the fuss about something called a carburetor restrictor plate.

Lesson 1: An afternoon in Daytona Beach—or Darlington, or Richmond—isn't anything like a leisurely, laid-back day at Wrigley Field, Fenway Park, or Camden Yard. By their very nature, unmuffled, normally-aspirated V-8 racing motors that generate 750-horsepower are loud. Ear-piercing, sternum-rattling, "what-did-you-say?" loud. Even under caution, the growl of 40 souped-up racing engines just itching to kick loose and stretch their legs can be unsettling.

We suggest you invest a dollar or two in a set of earplugs. You can't walk 10 feet through Souvenir Alley at any track without seeing dozens of displays with various styles and sizes of plugs. It's a small price to pay for not having a throbbing headache the next day. Besides, it'll make your afternoon immeasurably more pleasant. (Footnote: If you're into headaches and ringing ears, then ignore this suggestion and save yourself a buck. But don't say we didn't warn you).

Lesson 2: Buy one of the track's overpriced programs and spend some time studying the entry list and qualifying results. Feel free to be bummed out — but only a little — if the driver you've taken a liking to didn't qualify well. Conversely, don't start gloating and counting your pool winnings if the guy qualified well and seems to be faster than Jack the Bear.

You see, there's often a huge difference in how a driver qualified on Friday or Saturday and how he races on Sunday. Some drivers simply aren't very good at going out by themselves and running around an empty track with nothing but the clock to beat. They qualify poorly, then run much better during the race, when the spirit of competition is greater. Changing weather or track conditions often affect how a car performs on raceday versus how it qualified. Also, crews often use their best motor for practice and qualifying, but don't feel confident enough to use it for more than 500 miles. And cars are set up (balanced) and geared far differently for qualifying than they are for the race.

Look carefully for longshots. It's inevitable that a "name" driver will qualify poorly almost every weekend, then put on a great charge toward the front come Sunday afternoon. It works the other way, too: journeymen drivers given almost no chance of winning often qualify well enough to turn everyone's head. It's interesting and exciting to watch not only the progress of the star coming from the back, but the fortunes of the struggling longshot who might just be looking for his first career victory after an especially good qualifying effort.

Watching someone working his way from the 30s, through the 20s and teens, and into the top-10 is more fun than watching the pole-sitter lead from the start. Remember, some of NASCAR's best racing is often back in the pack. Get your eyes off the front of the pack and you might be surprised at how tough the backmarkers are racing amongst themselves.

Lesson 3: What are the chances Dallas Cowboys coach Barry Switzer will let you eavesdrop as he talks strategy with Troy Aikman in the final seconds of the Super Bowl? Slim to none, right? And do you think Chicago Bulls coach Phil Jackson would ever invite you to hang around the bench while he chats with Michael Jordan? No way, no how.

But NASCAR teams give you complete freedom to listen in while they make plans, discuss how their car is running and try to figure out how to win the race with pit strategy. Is this a great country or what?

The trick is to buy a scanner, a perfectly legal type of citizens' band radio. Good ones will set you back a couple of hundred bucks, maybe more if you opt for the upper-level model with all the bells and whistles. Check 'em out at the national-chain radio and electronic shops for prices better than at the race track. Be sure the one you buy has several hundred bands and channels, and make doubly sure you have everything you need i.e., battery charger, carrying case, headset straps, spare power pack, etc.) before going to the track.

Find someone — they're almost everywhere within the racing family — with a list of team frequencies. Ask if he or she will program your scanner so you'll KNOW it's right. It doesn't take long, and most veterans delight in showing rookies the ropes. Test the unit the night before the race, then charge its battery overnight. And don't forget the list of frequencies so you can dial up your favorite drivers.

It's amazing what you might hear during a long race. Subjects range from what changes are needed during the next pit stop to the latest rumor about who might be looking to change teams. Under caution you might hear a crewman relaying the latest NFL scores or asking the driver where he'd like to have dinner after the race. And you'll probably hear a driver or two speak ill of NASCAR's officials, especially if a pit road penalty has just been imposed.

Most of the time, though, it's all business. The car's loose going in the turns and tight coming out, the driver might say. The crew chief might offer advice or ask if the driver has any suggestions. The crew chief might give the driver a countdown to his next pit stop and let him know what service he can expect. The dialogue often gets somewhat technical, but hang tough and you'll catch on. It's great fun listening to the driver and crew plot strategy, then watching it play out with the race's outcome in the balance. (Footnote: Some of the conversations —even that from devout, born-again Christians — might be unsuitable for small or impressionable children. Parental discretion is advised, especially after something has gone wrong.)

Lesson 4: It's a little-known fact that all racing is a timed game, just as football and basketball and hockey are timed games. The only real difference is that stick-and-ball sports use minutes and seconds kept on a clock. Racing uses laps, and records them on a lap-counter. It's pretty simple: the first driver to complete the prescribed number of laps wins, regardless of how long it takes. Everyone else is placed on the payoff sheet in the order of how quickly they finished the laps they ran.

Only recently has NASCAR adopted an automated scoring system. From 1948 until a few years ago, each driver's scorer had a yellow pencil (with eraser) and a scorecard. The scorecard had as many blocks as the race had laps, and the scorer noted the race's elapsed time each time the driver crossed the scoring line. The winner was the driver with the lowest elapsed time in the last block. Today, each car has a transponder programmed to automatically record and download its elapsed time of each lap. Just in case, though, scorers flip a switch that records their car's elapsed time after each lap.

Here's a can't-miss suggestion: use a digital stopwatch to check several of your favorite driver's laps. Then, compare them to the lap times of his closest pursuer. Time your guy in passing situations, while he's running alone (or reasonably alone), then in drafting situations. Notice whether he prefers to draft ahead or behind a specific brand of car, and whether he likes drafting with his brother or a long-time friend, or with a teammate.

If you're close enough for a clear view, time his pit stops. Not just how long his car is stopped, but the slowing down and speeding up time, too. It's not simply the time getting serviced that's so important — it's the TOTAL time to slow down, get stopped in the pit box, get serviced, then get out of the pits and back to speed.

Lesson 5: Things you should know that don't seem to make sense at first glance.

Question: What's with that erratic swerving left to right (and right to left) before the race starts and before restarts?

Answer: Warm tires grip the track and offer better traction than cold tires. Drivers intentionally scuff their tires under caution and before green flags to pound some heat into them. And the hard to-and-fro steering also helps clean the tires of debris they may have picked up at slower speeds. (It's like scuffing your shoes after you step on something yucky as you approach the front door at home).

Question: Why do drivers who have just made a two-tire pit stop often come back a lap or so later for two more fresh tires? Why didn't he take four tires in the first place?

Answer: Because the tire he or the crew thought was going down wasn't going down at all. Maybe he felt a slight vibration and thought it was from the right-front tire. He made a quick stop for right-sides, only to realize when he got back on the track that it was a left-side tire all along. So he has to make another costly stop for left-sides tires.

Question: Why do cars sometimes slow abruptly, then just as quickly pick up speed and go on their merry way, apparently no worse for wear?

Answer: Winston Cup cars have two ignition systems. Occasionally, the primary system will lose power, causing the car to slow and maybe even cut off. But the switch that activates the backup system is within reach of the driver. It might take a second or two — which looks like an eternity on the track —for the driver to reach over and activate the backup that brings the car back to life.

Question: Why does someone with a small can stand behind the left-rear of the car during pit stops?

Answer: To catch any fuel that might spill during the refueling process. Once the car's 22-gallon fuel cell is filled, any excess on subsequent pit stops backs up through a hose leading to a small pipe sticking out the left-rear of the car. The "catch-can man" collects the excess, then pours it back into one of his team's 11-gallon dumpcans.

Question: How can a race-long backmarker suddenly start passing the leaders like they had V-6s and he had a V-8?

Answer: Probably because he's got four fresh tires and the leaders have worn tires. As soon as they take fresh tires, they'll return to the front of the pack and blow him back into the weeds. For a few laps, though, the guy headed for a 15th-place finish can brag that he was the fastest thing on the track.

Question: What's with that fishing net deal in the driver's side window opening?

Answer: You can thank Richard Petty for the safety net that keeps a driver's arm and hand inside if his car goes over. Petty dislocated his left shoulder and missed several races after almost being thrown out the left-side window during his famous flip and roll at Darlington, S.C., in 1970. There's a small gap at the front of the net so a crewman can hand the driver a cup of water of Gatorade during pit stops.

Question: Why is everybody in the stands wearing some sort of headset?

Answer: Most likely, half of them are scanners. The other half are head-hugger radios, and chances are better than good than the fans in question are not listening to a political debate on National Public Radio. Since every race is broadcast, fans get double duty from the head-huggers: a play-by-play (with insider information and driver comments) and ear protection.

Question: Who are those guys in team uniforms standing together atop the grandstand or above the race track's NASCAR control/press box?

Answer: They're spotters, and it's their vitally-important job to coach their driver from green to checkered. They tell him which groove seems to be working best, whether he's clear to make a move in tight traffic, and which lane to pick — high, low or the middle — to dodge an accident or debris. The spotter often has a better feel for the scoring and is able to remind his driver which drivers to ignore and which ones to race hard.

Question: Why don't they race in the rain like other sanctioning bodies? Are they wimps, or what?

Answer: Not hardly. Unlike Formula 1, Professional Sports Car, Trans-Am, and CART Indycar road racing, NASCAR has neither water-repelling grooved tires nor a tradition of racing in the rain. The thinking seems to be, why make your paying customers sit in the rain when a clear day is usually just around the corner? And can you imagine trying to convince drivers to race door to door and bumper to bumper in a rainstorm at Daytona Beach or Talladega?

There's been talk between NASCAR and Goodyear about rain tires for Watkins Glen and Sears Point, but it doesn't loom as a high-priority issue. To be sure, the current batch of treadless Goodyear Eagles used in Winston Cup racing lose most of their grip at the mere scent of moisture. They're absolutely useless on a damp track, never mind a wet one.

Question: Why do drivers lower their left-side window net after an accident, even when they may not be ready to get out?

Answer: It's often difficult for rescue workers rushing toward an accident scene to tell exactly how seriously — if, indeed, at all — a driver might be. Several years ago, NASCAR and its competitors agreed that lowering the window net would serve as a preliminary signal that the driver was conscious and in no immediate peril. In the case of several cars at an accident scene, rescue workers would immediately tend to the drivers who had not yet lowered their window net.

Question: Why do cars that are beat and battered and missing much of their sheet metal go back out after losing countless laps in the garage?

Answer: In one word — money. Drivers earn post-season bonuses based on their point standings. Points are earned by how well they finish, and even two or three finish positions (which could bring between six and 15 points) could prove the difference in tens of thousands of dollars in post-season awards.

Say, for example, Mark Martin, Bill Elliott, Rusty Wallace, Elton Sawyer, and Geoff Bodine crash together at lap 145 of a 400-lap race. Their cars are towed to the garage, where the Martin, Wallace, and Bodine crews don't bother with repairs. But even though they lose 50 laps, Sawyer and Elliott get their cars back together enough to finish the race.

The final rundown shows Martin, Wallace, and Bodine 39th, 40th and 41st, worth less than 50 points. Despite being 50-some laps behind, Sawyer and Elliott finish 27th and 28th, and get almost twice as many points as the drivers in the same wreck. That effort was worth $25,000 to Elliott, who finished 14 points and one position ahead of Wallace in the final standings.

Question: In 50 words or less, explain drafting.

Answer: The tailgating car runs faster because it's in the vacuum created by the front car. The front car runs faster because the air flow that usually comes off its roof and buffets the rear deck and spoiler goes back to the second car, thus making both of them more stable.

Question: In 50 words or less, explain carburetor restrictor plates.

Answer: How about 75 words?

NASCAR tries to control speeds at Daytona Beach and Talladega by limiting the cubic feet per minute of air and fuel drawn through the four-barrel carburetor into the intake for combustion. They limit the mixture by placing a steel plate with four round openings between the carburetor and the intake. The openings line up with the carburetor's four openings, but are smaller and thus limit the volume of air and fuel available for combustion.

Question: What's more important, the team or the driver?

Answer: What came first, the chicken or the egg? How high is high? Who put the bop in the bop-she-bop-she-bop? Is there intelligent life on earth?

In other words, who knows?

Jeff Gordon, with a good team on a good day, is almost unbeatable. Would, say, Loy Allen be just as good on that same team on that same good day? Your guess is a good as anybody's.

Better yet, would Jeff Gordon on a mediocre team on a good day be better than, say, Rick Wilson on a good team on a good day? Once again, your guess is as good as anybody's.

Dale Earnhardt didn't do much in the handful of pickup rides he had before going full-time with Rod Osterlund in 1979. But he won with Osterlund, and with Bud Moore, before going to Richard Childress, where he's often looked unbeatable. But would he have won six more championships with Osterlund, as he did with Childress? Hard to say.

NASCAR watchers often put a 65-35 or 70-30 ratio on the importance of team and crew chief to driver. Not surprisingly, a good driver on a good team will enjoy greater success than a mediocre driver on a mediocre team. But what about a mediocre driver on a good team, and what about a good driver on a mediocre team?

Clearly, they are questions better suited for Winston Cup Racing 402.

20

LIFE IN THE PITS

At first, nobody paid much attention or gave much thought to the role of pit stops during the early years of NASCAR. For one thing, most of the Strictly Stock (then Grand National, then Winston Cup) races were only 100 to 150 miles, so crews didn't need to do much more than occasionally change tires and add fuel. Out of inactivity, it seemed, came apathy.

The other factor was that NASCAR's early cars were strictly stock in more than just name. There wasn't much a pit crew could do because the rule book didn't allow much freedom or innovation. Crews were pretty much limited to cosmetic changes if their car crashed. They loosened lug nuts with tire irons, twisted open stock fuel caps while refueling cars and generally didn't worry about how long any of it was taking.

That began to change when Darlington Raceway opened with the sport's first 500-mile race in 1950. And it changed even more dramatically in the '60s as more superspeedways were built and races were scheduled for up to an unimaginable 600 miles. With more miles to run and more tires and gas to be used, teams began realizing that the quicker they got in and out of the pits, the quicker they'd get to the checkered flag.

And it was during the early '60s when cars went from street-legal, showroom-fresh family sedans to cars that looked stock but had the inner workings of a purpose-built race car. The newer cars sported all manner of adjustable parts and pieces to enhance performance and give crews something to tinker with.

The Wood brothers of Stuart, Virginia, raised pit work from an "oh, by the way" afterthought to something resembling an art form. Their pit work became so famous that Graham Hill recruited them to Indianapolis to service his car during the 1965 Indianapolis 500. When he won the race by spending far less time for service than anyone else, their legend was born and pit stops came into their own.

EVERY SECOND COUNTS

It has come to this in the past 20 years: half-seconds are so precious that some teams hire physical-fitness experts to train their crewmen during the week to keep them sharp for their Sunday jobs. And many competitive teams have on-site gyms so crewmen can maintain their strength and flexibility.

Almost every team films pit stops, whether under green- or yellow-flag conditions, then

Pit crews of the 1970s were a little more casual than the high-tech teams of the '90s. Here, Benny Parsons takes on new tires in a 1977 race.

studs and tighten the lug nuts with the distinctive BLAT BLAT BLAT BLAT BLAT of their wrenches. The instant they're finished, the jackman twists the handle to lower the car.

The changers sprint around the car while flipping the switch back to "LOOSEN" on their wrenches. They drop to their knees and start removing the five lug nuts on the two left-side tires. The jackman gets the car off the ground just as the last lug nuts spin off. The carriers reach in to help the changers hoist their tire up on the hub.

While the tires are being changed, two other crewmen are refueling the car. NASCAR fuel cells hold 22 gallons and each team's dump cans hold 11 gallons. The gas man jams the aviation-style refueling nozzle into the gaping mouth of the spring-loaded fuel hose and lets gravity do the rest. He empties one can, tosses it aside (only seven crewmen may cross the wall to perform service), then takes the second can from another crewman. A crewman with a catch can follows the car for a few yards to catch fuel that spurts from the overflow as the car accelerates.

It's taken less than 20 seconds to change four 40-pound tires and empty two 11-gallon cans of fuel, each weighing 18 pounds. The windshield and radiator grill have been cleaned, and somebody has handed the driver a cup of water or soda. If the driver asked, someone might have bent the rear spoiler up a little bit or added pressure to the rear springs with a wedge adjustment.

GOOD CREWS ARE REWARDED

It is not the thankless job it used to be. Indeed, drivers know better than to overlook their crew's pit work during victory lane speeches. When races are routinely won by fractions of seconds, the difference in being first and, say, fifth could be the time

reviews them on the spot. They mount a small camera on the end of a long pole attached to the mobile tool chest. The camera points directly into the pit box below and starts working when the car enters.

This is what the camera sees during a four-tire-and-gas stop: One crewman dashes around the front of the car and slides a manually-operated pneumatic jack beneath an arrow painted midway along the car's right-side rockerpanel. With two mighty pumps of the handle, the right-side tires come several inches off the ground. By then, the front- and rear-tire carriers have delivered fresh tires to two crewmen on their knees, air wrenches poised to spring into action.

If things are going smoothly, a crewman with an air-wrench has loosened five lug nuts and is removing the worn right-front tire. At the same time, another crewman is doing the same to the right-rear tire. The jackman—his primary duty completed for the time being—stands poised to help either of the changers. When the tires are in place and things look to be in hand, the carriers sprint around the car for the left-side tires.

Within seconds, the tire changers change the direction of their wrenches from "LOOSEN" to "TIGHTEN." They hoist the fresh tires on the wheel

GET A HAIRCUT, SON

It was one of the most vicious licks Kyle Petty had ever taken in a race car. Maybe even worse than the one that broke his leg at Talladega, in 1991. Certainly, it took longer to unfold.

This was at the Indianapolis Motor Speedway in the 1996 Brickyard 400 Winston Cup race. Early in the going Petty's Pontiac Grand Prix blew a right-front tire in Turn 4. The car veered to the right, slammed the outside wall, bounced back cross the track and was hit by Sterling Marlin. That impact knocked Petty's car back against the outside wall—which sent it back across the track and into the inside wall.

Dazed but otherwise unhurt, Petty clambered from the bashed-in car and lay on the edge of pit road to catch his breath. That's when his second set of problems began.

Petty screamed in agony when the rescue workers began lifting him onto the gurney for the ambulance ride to the infield care center.

What is it, someone asked. Is it your ribs that are hurting?

No, Petty said.

Seconds later, as they began lifting him a second time, Petty cried out again.

Is it your leg or your arm, one of the rescue workers asked? Is it your neck or your back? What's hurting?

My hair, Petty said. Somebody's been standing on my ponytail while y'all've been trying to pick me up.

---

one crewman stumbled just a bit during his team's final green-flag pit stop with 50 laps remaining.

NASCAR pit work is not for the weak, the easily-frazzled, or the faint of heart. Service stops are always hectic and frequently dangerous, and hardly a race passes when someone isn't bumped or brushed by a passing car, or is sent sprawling from contact from one of his own teammates. Don Miller of the Roger Penske team lost a leg during a pit stop at Talladega in the '70s. Randy Owens, Richard Petty's brother-in-law and a member of the STP team, died when a pressurized water tank exploded at Talladega as he tried to use it. And Mike Rich, a young member of Bill Elliott's team, died when Ricky Rudd slid into him during a pit stop at Atlanta in the late '80s.

The next year, NASCAR made a simple, no-nonsense rule designed to prevent a similar tragedy. It imposed a pit road speed limit (different at each track, depending on its length) and initiated stiff penalties for speeding into or out of the pits. Since that rule was introduced, there have been no major incidents along pit road.

The contribution of pit crewmen might last no more than 90 seconds out of several hours, but what crucial seconds they are. Look at it like this: at racing speed, one second at the Daytona International Speedway is equal to about 100 yards of real estate. And where would you rather try to make up that deficit: chasing the leader on the race track or beating him by two seconds in the pits?

As Ted Musgrave brings the No. 16 car into the pits, his crew springs into action, heading for the right-side tires first.

After the jackman has lifted the car, two tire-carriers and two tire-changers work to change the two right-side tires, then head to the left side.

After finishing the right-side tires, the tire changers sprint to the left side of the car, carrying the air wrench used to loosen the lug nuts.

The gas man handles the heavy 11=gallon dump cans that fill the car's fuel cells. Each car holds 22 gallons.

21

SAFETY FIRST:
NASCAR PROTECTS ITS DRIVERS

The down and dirty on stock car racing is that it's dangerous. At times, terribly so. No ifs, ands or buts about it, NASCAR racing at any level isn't your sedate afternoon of golf or a spirited set of tennis. Little wonder: you can't dangle several million dollars in front of 44 highly competitive men encapsulated in heavy, full-bodied, well-padded and powerful race cars, then tell them to race for several hours without running into each other or hitting a wall or two along the way

Right from the beginning, nobody ever said it wouldn't be dangerous. Maybe not as dangerous as wading ashore at Normandy like Bud Moore did in 1944 or as dangerous as hauling moonshine along Thunder Road, as Junior Johnson did so many moonless Carolina nights in the 1950s. And maybe not even as dangerous as being a sky-diving daredevil like Cale Yarborough was in his younger days, after rattlesnake hunting grew boring. But make no mistake, you could get seriously killed in a stock car race.

To his credit, though, NASCAR founder Bill France knew early-on that the marketability of his drivers was his greatest asset. Not the races themselves. Not his member-tracks and certainly not

their promoters. Fans queued up to see drivers, so NASCAR obliged them with rules that allow struggling drivers to start an event even if they haven't qualified on speed. There are race-by-race and post-season incentives that encourage teams to run every event, and there's even a rule allowing injured or ailing drivers to start a race, get a substitute driver almost immediately, yet still earn points for how the car finishes.

DISASTERS LEAD TO NEW SAFETY FEATURES

But despite the organization's long-standing concern with driver and team safety, there are times when things go horribly wrong.

There wasn't anything anybody on this earth could do for Little Joe. He was dead where he slumped, killed instantly, it looked at first glance, by a savage blow to the left side of his head. A jagged crack down that side of his helmet was grim evidence that he hadn't stood a chance against the concrete wall adjacent the Esses at Riverside International Raceway that Sunday afternoon in January of 1964.

Bobby Allison gets up into the wall of Turn 4 during the Firecracker 400 at Daytona in 1978.

Joe Weatherly was a two-time NASCAR champion when he died early that year, a memorable season that would see two other star drivers killed. Weatherly was among the tour's most popular characters, equal parts fearless racer and relentless party-goer. His death on the Riverside road course sent shock waves through the close-knit racing fraternity. It also moved NASCAR to review its safety standards, especially those relating to the cockpit of its race cars.

Weatherly, you see, was wearing only a lap safety belt that day. Like many other drivers, he didn't especially like the shoulder harness that had been developed years before and was available almost everywhere. At 41 and not as spry as he

once had been, he was concerned that the multi-buckled harness might delay him getting from a car, especially one upside-down or burning. So he wore the single-strand lap belt that did nothing to keep his left shoulder and head inside the car when it skittered off the track and glanced against the concrete wall that took his life.

Fast forward six years to May of 1970 at the Darlington Raceway in South Carolina. There, in one of stock car racing's most famous single-car accidents, Richard Petty's No. 43 Plymouth loses purchase in Turn 4, slaps the outside wall and careens across the track toward the inside retaining wall along pit road. With no steering and no brakes—both were damaged by the first impact

WHEN TRAGEDY STRIKES

At its best, big-time stock car racing is a grand and glorious exercise. Skilled and cunning men driving fast cars just inches from each other at speeds once thought unimaginable. Few sports offer the color and spectacle of motorsports while offering up such an engaging and gracious cast of characters.

At its worst, it is unspeakably cruel. Here is a list of the drivers who have been killed during a NASCAR race:

Larry Mann at Langhorne, Pennsylvania, in September of 1954.

Frank Arford at Langhorne, Pennsylvania, in June of 1955.

Lou Figaro at North Wilkesboro, North Carolina, in 1954.

John McVitty at Langhorne, Pennsylvania, in April of 1956.

Clint McHugh at LeHi, Arkansas, in June of 1956.

Thomas Priddy at LeHi, Arkansas, in June of 1956.

Billy Myers at Darlington, South Carolina, in September of 1957.

Joe Weatherly at Riverside, California, in January of 1964.

Fireball Roberts at Charlotte, North Carolina, in July of 1964 from injuries received in May.

Buren Skeen, at Darlington in September of 1965.

Tab Prince at Daytona Beach, Florida, in February of 1970.

Friday Hassler at Daytona Beach, Florida, in February of 1972.

Larry Smith at Talladega, Alabama, in August of 1973.

Tiny Lund at Talladega, Alabama, in August of 1975.

Ricky Knott at Daytona Beach, Florida, in February of 1972.

Terry Schoonover at Atlanta, Georgia, in November 1984.

Grant Adcox at Atlanta in November of 1989.

J.D. McDuffie at Watkins Glen, New York, in August of 1991.

May they rest in peace.

---

and utterly useless—what happens next is nothing short of a miracle.

The blue and white Plymouth hits the inside wall a mighty blow, almost head-on and almost at full speed. It begins to rise like a leaf in the wind, seemingly with a mind of its own—but uncertain exactly what it wanted to do. Finally, it begins a series of barrel rolls down the frontstretch. Three. Four. Five. Side to roof to side to roof to wheels, and back to roof. Six times, then seven.

TV clips and still photos show Petty's left arm and shoulder flopping wildly outside the window opening. The sequence looks very much like something from a rodeo, where the cowboy is trying to ride the bull for eight seconds. He's holding on with his right hand while the other is being snatched and jerked around. He has about as much chance on that bull as Petty did in his Plymouth.

And then it's over. The car stops on its roof, all four wheels still moving slowly as rescue workers get to the sport's most beloved star. There's a mass of red something-or-other hanging out the window, leading onlookers to immediately wonder if it's the slump of his left arm. But no! Petty crawls from the car holding his left shoulder—to which an arm remains attached. "Danged shoulder," he tells cousin/crew chief Dale Inman. "I hurt my danged shoulder."

And the mass of red something-or-other by the window? It was simply a chew rag, a clean shop rag that Petty often soaked in cold water and sucked on between pit stops. As for blood and guts: not a trace.

Still, NASCAR had seen enough. Shortly after Petty's crash, the sanctioning body decided to mandate window nets to cover the driver's side opening in all cars. Resembling netting from a tennis court, it covered the opening and virtually ensured that arms, hands, shoulders and heads would remain inside the car, almost no matter how serious the impact or how many times the car flipped. Weatherly, one might reasonably assume, would have survived Riverside if such a safety net had been in place in January of 1964. And Petty likely wouldn't have suffered even a dislocated shoulder if he'd had a window net on his car in 1970.

NASCAR PROTECTS ITS STARS

Because of its concern for driver safety, it should come as no surprise that NASCAR has always gone to great lengths to protect its stars once they're inside their cars. It wasn't long after Fireball Roberts died of crash and fire-related injuries in the summer of 1964 that officials encouraged the Firestone Tire and Rubber Co. to begin working on a military-style rubber fuel bladder in hopes of reducing or eliminating altogether the danger of fire.

Roberts' car was carrying almost a full load of fuel when it spun on the backstretch at Lap 7 of the World 600 in May of 1964. It backed into an opening in the concrete wall separating the backstretch from the inside, then flipped and burst into flames. A well-conditioned 35, he survived the impact and the immediate ravages of fire after respected rival Ned Jarrett helped pull him from the car. But Roberts died six weeks later from burn-related complications, including blood poisoning and pneumonia. Less than a year later, with that tragedy still a fresh and disturbing memory, Firestone introduces its Racesafe Fuel Cell.

The third death of the 1964 season spurred interest and development of yet another safety device. Jimmy Pardue, the pole-sitter for the selfsame World 600 that had taken Roberts' life, was conducting a tire test for Goodyear at the Charlotte Motor Speedway in September of that year. Seconds after running a reported 149 miles per hour—much faster than the existing track record—a tire exploded and he crashed through the Turn 3 steel railing.

There was almost no chance he could have survived. His Plymouth tore down 48 feet of rail-

ing, then went airborne for almost 150 yards. The car landed nose-first against a chain-link fence at the bottom of a 75-foot embankment. Pardue was taken to a nearby hospital, where he lingered for slightly less than three hours before dying from a crushed chest and extensive brain trauma. He died at 33, and had two NASCAR victories on his resume: at Richmond, Virginia, in 1962 and at Moyock, North Carolina, in 1963.

In 1966, too late to help Jimmy Pardue or Billy Wade (who, ironically, had died testing tires at Daytona Beach in January of 1965) Goodyear unveiled the safety inner liner. Although the new development didn't keep tires from blowing out or puncturing, it lessened the chances of a catastrophic failure. More importantly, it gave drivers a few precious extra seconds of warning that something was amiss, time to perhaps slow and control their car. And as Jimmy Pardue and Billy Wade might have told you, a few seconds might have been all they needed.

Throughout NASCAR's early years and into the 60s, the cars on the race tracks looked very much like their cousins on the showroom floor or parked by church on Sunday morning. Early on, France had insisted that while safety was always a prime concern, he wanted his race cars to appear as stock as possible. By that he meant inside and out.

So it was that race cars throughout the 50s and into the early 60s still raced with headlights and windshield wipers. Even though the headlights and rear lights might be taped over, they were on the car in their factory position just the same. The cars of those days had working glass in the side windows, bench or bucket seats (depending on the street version), a functional instrument panel, door handles, and factory-installed gas caps. A few models even sported vinyl roofs, something of a fashion statement in the early-to-mid-60s.

"I'll tell you how street stock they were," said Richard Petty, a seven-time series champion and 200-time race winner. "There was many a time Daddy loaded me and Maurice and Mamma in the family car, drove it to a race, put us out, raced that same car, then loaded everybody back up and took us back home in it. Later on he started towing the family car to races and towing it back, but it was as street-legal and stock as it could be back in the 50s and early 60s."

Glen Wood, part of the famous Wood brothers team, recalled the time he and his brothers went to a local junk yard to salvage a battered Ford for the fall of 1960 race at the new Charlotte Motor Speedway. "Speedy Thompson won that race in a street car we got from a junk yard and turned into a race car," Wood said. "It started to turn a little more toward real race cars in the mid-to-late-60s, but not when Speedy won for us at Charlotte. That was a wrecked street car that we'd cleaned up and straightened out and taken to Charlotte. It was as stock as it could be."

Herb Thomas, the NASCAR champion in 1951 and 1953, recalled when drivers first chained the driver's side door to the door post so it wouldn't fly open in an accident. "We'd use rope or chain, anything to keep it secured," he said. "We'd open the door and get in, then reach back and tie the rope or loop the chain around the window opening and the door post. Back then, we didn't have any idea they'd someday hand-build race cars from the ground up like they do now. We didn't know a thing about rollcages or fuel cells or things like that."

Ron Bouchard (No. 98) and Bill Elliott (No. 9) trade a little paint when they come face-to-face at Richmond in 1986.

HOLMAN-MOODY SETS THE PACE

Indeed, safety features were primitive in the 50s and early-60s, but reasonably effective. Safety rollcages had been around for years, with refinements and modifications coming almost annually. At first, the "cage" was simply a single rollover bar bolted to the chassis and curving behind and above the driver's head. Later, reinforcing bars were positioned here and there within the cockpit, often without apparent rhyme or reason except for the bars throughout the driver's-side door.

In time, teams quit converting showroom stock passenger cars (often, as in the case of the Wood brothers, from junkyards) into racing cars.

Instead, they began buying purpose-built chassis, then buying only the factory-stamped sheet metal and glass needed to complete their cars. The famous Holman-Moody shop in Charlotte was the first to build racing chassis with rollcage. When teams realized how strong the H-M chassis and rollcages were, everyone began building their cars the same way. From that evolved the current NASCAR rollcage that has absorbed so much punishment without serious incident.

"Holman-Moody started with a unitized 65 Ford Fairlane chassis from the factory," said Junie Donlavey, a Winston Cup team owner for almost 50 years. "Then they put a complete rollcage on it

Neil Bonnet (No.5), Roland Wlodkya (No. 98), Lennie Pond (No. 54), and Cale Yarborough (No. 11) bring out the yellow flag at the 1978 Southeastern 500 in Bristol, Tennessee.

to make it almost like one piece. Then they put on the stock suspension parts like NASCAR required, then the fuel cell and sheet metal. Nobody knew much about aerodynamics back then, so whatever shape the street version had, that was what the race car looked like.

"There's no question but that what Holman-Moody did back then got the ball rolling to where we are now. The unitized-body construction they came up with in '66 and '67 really changed the face of the sport. I'm sure a lot of people are alive today because of what Holman-Moody and their people did."

Example I: Dick Brooks, Phil Parsons, Ricky Craven, Rusty Wallace, Dale Earnhardt, Rick Mast, Ken Schrader, Jimmy Horton, Mark Martin, Bill Elliott, Bobby Allison, Jimmy Spencer, and Kyle Petty have survived spectacular, high-speed accidents at the Talladega (Alabama) Speedway in the past 20 years.

Example II: Richard Petty, Walter Ballard, Darrell Waltrip, Rusty Wallace, Dale Earnhardt, David Pearson, Cale Yarborough, Donnie Allison, Ken Schrader, Randy LaJoie, Ricky Rudd, and John Anderson have limped away from similar accidents at the Daytona International Speedway.

Example III: Bobby Allison at Pocono and Rockingham, Tim Richmond and Dale Earnhardt at Pocono, Davey Allison at Pocono, Steve Grissom at Atlanta, Donnie Allison at Charlotte, Cale Yarborough at Darlington, Richard Petty at Darlington, Pocono and Sears Point, Rusty Wallace at Bristol, David Green at Bristol and Wendell Scott at Talladega.

TODAY'S CARS: THE SAFEST IN RACING

Today's race-ready NASCAR cars are perhaps the world's safest racing machines. Several hundred feet of steel tubing surrounds the driver, all of it designed to absorb and distribute the force of impact, thus making him safe regardless of the angle of impact. While fires occasionally flare up as part of an accident, most are from broken fuel or oil lines, not from exploding or ruptured fuel cells.

And all cars have on-board fire suppression systems designed to snuff any flames in the cockpit.

Even though cars are more aerodynamic than ever, the laws of physics often are suspended when cars get airborne. After Rusty Wallace took a couple of rides at Talladega and Daytona Beach (where, it is said, radar at the nearby airport briefly tracked him), team owner Jack Roush designed roof and cowl flaps in hopes of keeping it from happening again. The flaps are designed to lay flat and be unobtrusive so long as the car is maintaining a straight-ahead attitude.

But the flaps pop up and act as reverse spoilers on the left- and right-rear of the roof and in front of the windshield if the car loops around and begins sliding backward. At today's super-fast speeds around Talladega and Daytona Beach, it's only a matter of seconds before air rushing beneath a backward-sliding car lifts it off the ground, usually with frightening consequences. More than once in recent years, cars that otherwise might have taken off over here and landed over there in parts and pieces have simply settled back down on all fours, thanks to roof flaps.

NASCAR and its inspectors are ever vigilant. In 1996, when Dale Earnhardt had a horrendous and potentially-fatal crash at Talladega, officials found something they liked. They noticed that even though Earnhardt's No. 3 Chevrolet Monte Carlo was knocked into the frontstretch wall and flopped on its side before being T-boned (a crash in which the front or rear end of one car collides with the side or top of another) in the center of its roof, the roof didn't cave in on him.

Earnhardt suffered a broken shoulder blade and bruised sternum, but his head was never in danger from above. Inspectors credited that to an extra rollbar the Richard Childress Racing team had installed vertically in the middle of the front windshield. It extended from beneath the dashboard to where the roof and windshield met, and may have kept the roof from caving in on Earnhardt's head. Within weeks, NASCAR let its crew chiefs know they should install just such a rollbar. It was optional the balance of 1996, then mandatory for all cars in 1997.

In the early 90s, as tire giant Goodyear battled industry upstart Hoosier for the hearts and checkbooks of many teams, another cockpit safety feature emerged. Several "name" drivers blew tires and crashed hard during the so-called "Tire War." When Ricky Rudd and Harry Gant fell victim to leg injuries at Charlotte, NASCAR suggested a rigid piece of steel be extended along the left side of the driver's seat, then down along the outside of the left leg. It offered additional protection in case of a T-bone in the driver's-side door, second to fire among things drivers fear the most.

RESTRICTOR PLATE RACING

Among those other fearsome things is restrictor-plate racing at the Talladega Superspeedway and the Daytona International Speedway. For that, you can blame innovative engine-builders and sheet metal fabricators.

Restrictor plates are equal parts safety feature and ticking time bomb. The idea behind the device is to restrict the amount of fuel and air sucked through the four-barrel carburetor of a Winston Cup engine into the intake manifold and down into the combustion chamber. The mixture is restricted by a small steel plate that fits snugly between the bottom of the carburetor and the top of the intake.

The plate has four holes that line up with the four holes in the bottom of the carburetor. But here's the rub: the four holes in the restrictor plate are slightly smaller than the four holes in the bottom of the carburetor. So instead of a free-flowing mixture of air and fuel from the carburetor, through its four barrels and into the intake, the mixture is limited by the size of the holes in the restrictor plate.

Think of it in this everyday context: you can dump untold amounts of gas or water or sand into the big end of a funnel, but the rate at which the substance comes out the bottom end is limited by the size of its opening. The trickle of whatever went in the big end is similar to how drivers feel when they stomp their car's gas pedal and expect a burst of power. Instead, they get a trickle that seems to take forever to take effect.

Restrictor plates are nothing new, but they're as unpopular and widely-cursed now as when they first appeared in the early 70s. Qualifying speeds at the Daytona International Speedway jumped from 190-plus mph for the 1969 Daytona 500 to 194-plus for the 1970 race. At the same time, qualifying speeds at the new Talladega track were in the 199 mph range. There was concern that tire technology wasn't keeping up with speeds, so NASCAR introduced restrictor plates.

Controversial? Absolutely. Unpopular? No question about it. But they did what they were supposed to do. The pole speed for the 1971 Daytona 500 was a mere 182.744 mph, more than 11 mph slower than the previous year. And the qualifying speeds at Talladega dropped from the 199s into the 186 mph range. Officials finally got rid of the dreaded plates in the mid-70s, when engine displacement went from 427 cubic inches to 358 and cars began being downsized.

The plates being used today are the result of a harrowing crash Bobby Allison had at Talladega in May of 1987. On that day, in the Winston 500, the engine in his 200 mph, red and gold No. 22 Miller High Life-sponsored Buick exploded as he approached the start/finish line. A shard of metal from the bell housing punctured a rear tire, and Allison was helpless to keep his car under control. It spun around, then lifted like a candy wrapper and sailed into the catch-fencing separating the race track from the paying customers along the main frontstretch grandstands. It tore down several hundred feet of fencing and came perilously close to bringing down the flag stand and its two workers.

That the car didn't clear the fence and do catastrophic damage in the grandstand itself can be credited only to good fortune and the grace of God. Moments after seeing how close it had come to a major disaster, NASCAR officials began planning to revive the dreaded restrictor plates. They had dodged a serious bullet that afternoon, and everybody went home that night knowing how lucky they had been. As it was, several fans suffered minor injuries from flying debris.

Scenes like this one at Daytona in 1997 are common when restrictor plates are used.

Restrictor plates were mandated shortly after that horrific accident, but only for the super-fast tracks at Talladega and Daytona Beach. And while plates have effectively slowed cars, they have done nothing to keep them on the ground. Rusty Wallace has been through two high-flying accidents in recent years and Jimmy Spencer, Bill Elliott, and Ken Schrader have seen their cars take off and rise above the height of the retaining wall.

Clearly, restrictor plates are a double-edged sword. Granted, they keep speeds at a somewhat manageable level, which means there's less likelihood that one might take off and endanger spectators. But plates also keep cars bunched together

because engine-builders can't produce enough OOMPH! for their car to drive away from anyone else. Drivers complain that restrictor plates not only kill speed, but also steals much of their engine's response time when they need a quick burst of speed. Almost everyone agrees that being bunched together in 15- to 25-car packs at almost 200 mph for several hundred miles is an invitation to wreck.

And thus, almost invariably, they do. Someone in the middle of the pack gets frustrated and impatient, and tries a move that likely would have worked on an unrestricted track where cars are more lively and responsive. But the move doesn't work at Talladega or Daytona Beach, where his eight-cylinder, 600-horsepower racing engine suddenly responds with all the speed and acceleration of a Yugo trying to get on the freeway.

Engine-builders hate plates because they stifle the never-ending search for horsepower. Crew chiefs hate them because they always seem to disrupt a team's carefully-designed game plan. Team owners hate them because of the inordinate amount of research and development (not to mention money) needed to prepare for just four races a year. And drivers hate them because they create inherently dangerous situations.

On the other hand, almost everyone involved in NASCAR understands that the sport as they know it—indeed, life as they know it—might have changed for all time if Bobby Allison's No. 22 Buick had cleared the frontstretch catch-fence at Talladega that Sunday afternoon in 1987 and settled in amongst the paying customers.

There, but for the grace of God . . . .

22

ENTERTAINING CLIENTS: COMPANIES LOVE NASCAR SPONSORSHIP

A basic magic formula for sponsorship in auto racing would be:

Talented driver + shrewd car owner + skilled crew + money = winning

Ah, but the formula doesn't always produce the perfect result. As George Steinbrenner has learned in baseball, you can't always buy a winning team.

A racing team can have all four ingredients and still not win as many races as it thinks it should. Sometimes a top driver cannot escape bad luck on the track: swerving away from accidents caused by others is occasionally unavoidable for even the best drivers. Also, sometimes a top driver makes mistakes. The best—the Jeff Gordons, Dale Jarretts, Mark Martins, Terry Labontes, and Dale Earnhardts—make fewer errors than many of their rivals, but when you're racing at 160 mph to 190 mph, it's impossible to be mistake-free for the entire season.

Nevertheless, if a company invests in racing to ride with a winner, it's wise to form an association with a top driver, crew, and owner. For some companies, however, winning isn't the major reason they get into racing. They're just looking for exposure or a way to entertain employees and customers. Sometimes, company executives are simply racing fans who want to be part of the exciting scene at the tracks hosting Winston Cup races.

IT AIN'T CHEAP

An investment in Winston Cup doesn't come from the petty cash drawer. It costs anywhere from $3 million to $5 million a year to sponsor a team (most teams have primary sponsors and associate sponsors). For some of the top Winston Cup teams, the price is even higher, to include salaries of marquee drivers. Title sponsorships for races cost from $500,000 to more than $1 million.

For oil companies and breweries, it's easier to justify the costs of Winston Cup racing than it is for smaller companies. Interstate Batteries, for example, didn't jump into Winston Cup until the early 1990s.

"We're not a Texaco or a Du Pont," R. Tom Miller, the president and chief executive officer of Interstate Batteries, told the *Fort Worth Star-Telegram* prior to the inaugural Winston Cup 500-mile race at Texas Motor Speedway last year. "It

SPONSORS DON'T ALWAYS HAVE THE FINAL SAY

Latter-day fans might find it hard to believe that Richard Petty's race cars haven't always been red and blue. There was a time when "Petty blue" was his color of choice and anyone who didn't like it had to deal with the entire family.

Andy Granatelli didn't like it, and he told Petty so when they met early in 1972 season to talk about STP becoming Petty's major sponsor. Their meeting in Chicago went well and everything seemed set until Granatelli casually mentioned that the car would, of course, be painted STP red.

No, Petty said, it'll still be Petty blue.

The debate raged until Petty abruptly stood to leave. He was determined to stay blue and would forget the deal before he changed his car's color. Granatelli offered a compromise: half red and half blue, with a $50,000 bonus coming to Petty the day he told his paint shop to skip the blue and make it red all over.

Years later, someone jabbed at Petty by reminding him he never got his $50,000. He didn't miss a beat in jabbing back, "And I never got rid of Petty blue, either, did I?"

---

took some serious soul-searching to roll the dice and dedicate so much of our promotion money to one area."

Interstate Batteries is based in Fort Worth. The company sponsored the race at TMS in addition to bankrolling the Winston Cup car driven by Bobby Labonte. Miller said the decision to get involved in Winston Cup eventually was "a natural" for Interstate. "If you look at the demographics of the NASCAR audience, they're mechanical people. A lot are in the automotive trade."

Miller said Interstate is the second most-recognized battery brand in America, trailing only Sears' DieHard, which sponsors a 500-mile race at Talladega, Alabama. According to Miller, Interstate's annual revenues are more than $400 million, an increase of more than $100 million since

its Winston Cup involvement. "NASCAR has been a tremendous asset," Miller said, "and it's gotten us to a level that would've taken a lot more time and a lot more money."

Miller knew his company was on the right track with racing sponsorship in 1990. Miller and his staff were attending a convention of distributors in Nashville, Tennessee. "When people heard that we were going to sponsor a team (in a lower-level series), the whole place just erupted." Miller turned to his brother, Interstate chairman Norman Miller, and said, "I guess we've stumbled onto something here."

OIL COMPANIES ARE HIGH-PROFILE

Two of the most prominent and successful auto-related sponsors in NASCAR are Texaco and Valvoline. Texaco Havoline sponsors the No. 28 car owned by Robert Yates. Davey Allison drove No. 28 Ford until he died in a helicopter crash in 1993. Ernie Irvan succeeded Allison until the end of 1997. Rookie Kenny Irwin, a product of the Craftsman Truck series and the U.S. Auto Club's midget and Silver Crown series, will be behind the wheel of No. 28 this season. Mark Martin, driver of the No. 6 Valvoline Ford, has raced for Jack Roush's team for 10 seasons.

Texaco and Valvoline pour millions of dollars into these sponsorships each year. Financially backing a top Winston Cup team costs a sponsor $5 to $6 million annually. For this money, these sponsors expects results.

"The key is having a car that runs up front," said Chuck Kosich, Texaco's vice president of advertising worldwide. "A lot of sponsors don't get this, and I'm glad they don't. If they're only in it for internal reasons, for employee morale or for entertaining customers, that's fine. You don't need to run up front."

Valvoline was in Winston Cup and Indy-car racing in the 1980s. After Neil Bonnett was injured in a crash, Valvoline withdrew from the Winston Cup series in 1989. Mark Coughlin, director of

Like Valvoline, Texaco wants its driver to win races and run up front, but the Houston-based company also uses Winston Cup racing as a sales stimulator. Kosich says that in 1996 Texaco entertained 16,000 customers and their families at NASCAR and Indy car races. Many of these customers are purchasing managers. "A few weeks later," Kosich said, "when a salesman calls on them, it makes sales easier."

Kosich said Texaco's marketing focuses on people whose cars "are more than just transportation. They go to races, they read racing magazines, they watch races on television." Research has shown Texaco and other sponsors that NASCAR fans and Indy car fans are often two distinct groups. "NASCAR fans seems to be more do-it-yourselfers," Kosich said. "Indy car fans are more involved in the technology. We have to reach them both."

Texaco's pitch has been that the oil a consumer can buy off the shelf is the same oil the company's racing teams use in their race cars. Kosich said Texaco chemists said the motor oil they developed will protect engines when they start, guard against heat, and clean the engine. "When we asked consumers if they would buy a motor oil like that," Kosich said, "They said, 'yes, but you have to prove you're not lying.' The hook of our advertising has been that this is the same motor oil used by the race teams we sponsor."

Valvoline's Coughlin also emphasized how important advertising and marketing is for an oil company. "In the oil category," he said, "there isn't a high degree of loyalty to a brand. You only change

Ernie Irvan drove the No. 28 Texaco Havoline car until the end of 1997. Rookie Kenny Irwin will take over the reigns in 1998.

Valvoline's sports marketing program, said that when the Lexington, Kentucky-based company planned its return to Winston Cup, it wanted to be with a winner. "We decided that if we were going to be involved, we needed to be with a front-running team," Coughlin said. At the time, Coughlin said there weren't any top teams that didn't have an oil company affiliation, so Valvoline went with Mark Martin as an associate sponsor in 1990 (Folger's coffee was the primary sponsor). Valvoline became a full sponsor of Martin's car two years later.

your oil every 3,000 miles or every three months. It depends on how you hit them promotionally, or what day of the week you hit them with a message that they might be attuned to. That's why, for us, running up front is everything. We feel it has some direct backspin on the perception of our brand. A lot of people don't understand: they think that spending $3 million to plaster your name on the side of a car will automatically make the cash register ring. That's just the start of it. In NASCAR, especially, you need to be a top-five runner in order to get some of that return on the investment. It's like advertising: you can't say that a spot on the Super Bowl telecast is going to sell that much more product for you."

Coughlin added that the initial investment in a sponsorship is just the beginning. "For every dollar that you pay the race team, you've got to put at least $1 or $2 behind it to really get everything out of it," he said.

THIS BUD'S FOR YOU

Anheuser-Busch has been a presence in NASCAR as a car and race sponsor since the 1970s. Budweiser has sponsored Junior Johnson's Winston Cup cars. For years, Busch has sponsored the Grand National series and a popular pre-Daytona 500 race. Although Anheuser-Busch has withdrawn its title sponsorship of all Winston Cup races except The Bud at the Glen, Mike Hargrave, Anheuser-Busch's senior manager of sports marketing, says the company's commitment to motorsports is greater than ever. Budweiser sponsors Ricky Craven's Hendrick Motorsports car.

"In the '80s," Hargrave said, "we jumped out in front with race sponsorship, along with Miller and some others. We're the official beer of the series, and we still have the pole award program. From a dollars standpoint, we have much more money dedicated out of our marketing program to motorsports than we've ever had. No longer do you just buy something, put your name on it, and your day is done. We now have to drive our team, series, and official beer sponsorships into the marketplace with print, TV, radio and point-of-sale (advertising)."

The primary way that breweries and other sponsors measure if their investments are paying off is in increased sales of their products.

"At the beginning, we could see from the money that we were investing that it was worthwhile," Hargrave said. "There were some very loyal fans there and the dollars made sense. If you put money in their sport, they will support you. That really hasn't changed in NASCAR, but it's getting more sophisticated. Just being the friendly sponsor no longer cuts it. Now, when we put up a display, with NASCAR on it, in the marketplace, we have to ask if the store owner wants that. Our retailers are demanding it, and the only reason they would demand it is because their customers are demanding it. We're focused more on street level than we used to be. We used to look at the big picture: the bigger the logo, the better. Now we say, how does this association help drive sales? Like everybody else, we also use television ratings and attendance figures."

With millions of dollars invested in racing, it's understandable that sponsors require driver approval. A sponsor wants a driver who runs up front, wins his (or her) share of races, is comfortable with sponsors. The levels of approval vary among sponsors.

Said Coughlin: "I get very involved in driver selection. We don't leave it to the team owner: our contracts say we have to mutually agree on who the driver will be. We want a driver who will continually run up front and one who will have an out-of-car presence. We don't want somebody who everybody loves to hate."

Kosich indicated that Texaco trusts Robert Yates's judgment. "We can't be unreasonable in denying (his) choice," Kosich said, "but we do have to approve it. We'll do a background check and have the driver take a physical exam."

Car owner Michael Kranefuss was in the middle of an unusual "trade" during the 1996 Winston Cup season. He and driver John Andretti weren't happy with the team's performance. Andretti wanted out from the Kmart/RC Cola team, and

Kranefuss was able to accommodate him by letting him go to Cale Yarborough's RCA-sponsored team. Kranefuss acquired Yarborough's driver, Jeremy Mayfield.

"I'm completely open with our sponsors," Kranefuss said. "It's better to tell them what's going on. I told them the relationship between Andretti and (crew chief) Tim Brewer had gone south and we had to make a change. Jeremy wanted out of his contract, so Cale and I talked. (The sponsors) knew everything that was going on."

WORKING THE ROOM: THE DRIVER AS SPOKESPERSON

By the early '1980s, as more major sponsors climbed onto the emerging NASCAR bandwagon, it became important for drivers to be articulate. They didn't have to sound like graduates of Harvard or Yale, or even Possum Trot Community College. But they did have to present themselves professionally with the executives of the companies interested in sponsoring them. Most of these executives understood they weren't hiring prep school graduates wearing button-down blue shirts and blazers: all the companies wanted were talented drivers who could socialize nicely. Smile, shake hands, tell a few racing stories like "Let me tell you what it's like racing against Earnhardt out there..." Presidents and vice presidents, who were confined to offices and spent much of their time in meetings, were mesmerized by what the drivers said.

Several years ago, Ricky Rudd, now the owner-driver for the Tide Ford, said, "The No. 1 thing sponsors today want is for the driver to be competitive. The No. 2 thing they want is for you to speak well."

Winning races is the primary objective of drivers. Keeping the sponsor happy is high on a driver's priority list. Darrell Waltrip once said, "The guy who does it the best gets paid the most. You're of no value to a sponsor unless you can talk." Added Mark Martin: "For some of us, (the talking) is the hard part. Driving the car is what we started out doing. Our goal was being big winners, not great talkers."

Prior to races, many promoters bring drivers to their areas for media sessions. These meetings, held several days before the race (usually at a local restaurant), require the driver to be sociable and interesting. Questions range from the nuts-and-bolts of racing to offering their opinions on the state of NASCAR to their hobbies. The better the answers, the more attention the stories will receive in the area newspapers and on television and radio.

Kellogg's is a nonautomotive sponsor that has moved into NASCAR in a major way. In 1990, Kellogg's competed in three races, with Chuck Bown as its driver. Kellogg's was with Larry Hedrick's team for the next two years, then signed with Terry Labonte in 1993 when he was still driving for Billy Hagan. Since '94, Kellogg's has backed Labonte as a member of the powerful Hendrick Motorsports team.

Bill Nielsen, the director of promotional development and licensing for Kellogg's, said the cereal company began its involvement in NASCAR at the request of its sales people in the South.

"Grocery chains in the South merchandise around NASCAR races," Nielsen said. "Our sales guys said we had to do something: it was killing us that we weren't involved. We weren't being included in displays, at the end of aisles, that attract customers." Nielsen said the response to the three-race deal with Bown was "enormous."

When Labonte was looking for a new sponsor, Nielsen said the conservative Kellogg's company was eager to sign him up "because Terry Labonte is Kellogg's: he's clean-cut, a family man, and he's not a loudmouth." The deal paid off for Kellogg's and Labonte when he won the 1996 Winston Cup championship.

Nielsen believes that Kellogg's joined the NASCAR club at the right time. "In a few years, we believe this sport will be pushing football as the most popular sport in America," Nielsen said. Nielsen pointed to the exciting finish of the Southern 500 at Darlington Raceway in September 1997, when Jeff Gordon edged Jeff Burton to win the $1 million Winston bonus. "I told my wife, 'This is why people love racing,'" Nielsen recalled. "For 400 laps or so, it was okay. Then, for the last two laps, Jeff Gordon and Jeff Burton were doing everything they could to win the race. They weren't worrying about their next paycheck. These guys are like golfers: they're independent businessmen. If they don't win, they won't make as much money."

Although top drivers aren't as accessible as they used to be, for the most part they manage to maintain a positive relationship with fans. "When we bring Terry Labonte to an event," Nielsen said, "people line up for three hours ahead of time. Sometimes, we have to go back in the line and tell them they probably won't get an autograph because Terry's time will be up. They say, 'That's okay, we'll wait. We just want to see him and wave to him.' The drivers relationship with the public is very important. People want to identify with celebrities."

Like others in racing, Nielsen is concerned that eventually drivers may develop attitudes like other athletes whose salaries are soaring. "My fear," Nielsen said, "is that the drivers won't be as accessible to the fans as they are now. Dale Earnhardt and Jeff Gordon are making from $10 million to $20 million a year. Sometimes, when you start making that kind of money, you say, 'I don't have to do all these things (with the public).' "

Ricky Rudd, driver of the Tide Ford, says sponsors today expect two things out of their drivers: to be competitive and to speak well when representing the product.

While sponsor/car owner relationships are strictly business, there are some lighter moments. After Harry Ranier encountered some financial problems, Yates said he would buy the team and keep Davey Allison as the driver. However, he needed a multi-year contract. Said Kosich: "Robert told us he could only afford to do it if he had a one-year contract extension. He's so honest. I went down the hall to my boss, Glenn Tilton, and told him what Robert said. Glenn thought for a few moments, then said, 'We really like Davey, don't we?' I said, 'Yes.' Glenn said, 'Tell him we won't just give him one year; we'll give *three* years. Robert was so happy."

When Kranefuss, the former head of Ford Motorsports, and partner Carl Haas wanted to get into NASCAR, closing a deal with Kmart as a sponsor was relatively easy. Kmart has sponsored Haas's Indy cars for years. Kranefuss invited Ron Flotho, then president of Kmart's Super K stores, to Michigan for a race in 1994. After Flotho spent some time around the race track, he said to Kranefuss, "This is our crowd."

Kmart went through some reorganization and now, Kranefuss says, the company is "completely committed" to racing. Kranefuss said that Kmart is one of the top sellers of NASCAR sponsors products. Warren Flick, Kmart current president, spends time in the pits at races. "He's not a racer," Kranefuss said. "He's in it to increase Kmart business. But we're grateful that he gets close to the races in the pits. He wants us to run up front, but he understands how competitive Winston Cup racing is. If one little thing is missing, you won't be up front."

QVC, the shopping network, was selling NASCAR products on its network before it became a sponsor of Geoff Bodine's car in 1996. The overwhelming response to NASCAR goods rang the bells at QVC's headquarters in West Chester, Pennsylvania. "It was kind of a no-brainer," said Doug Rose, QVC's marketing director. "The fan of NASCAR has money to spend (and) more people are coming to QVC (to find NASCAR products)." (QVC curtailed its sponsorship of Bodine's car after the 1997 season. Rose said QVC would continue in the sport in other areas).

7-UP ANYONE?

Richard Petty was among the drivers who boycotted the inaugural Talladega 500 in September of 1969. Like many others, he was fearful that the tires built by Goodyear and Firestone for the 2.66-mile, high-banked, super-fast track wouldn't stand up to the 200 mph speeds. After trying unsuccessfully to convince NASCAR president Bill France to postpone the race until the tire companies could do their homework, Petty and many other top-name drivers pulled out on Saturday afternoon and went home.

One of his associate sponsors at the time was 7-Up, and company was deep into its "Uncola" advertising campaign at the time. That led one NASCAR-watcher to quip as Petty left that afternoon: "There goes Richard Petty, the Unracer."

NEW KIDS ON THE BLOCK

One of the new sponsors in NASCAR is MCI. The telephone company isn't supporting a racing team, as it does in Indy car racing: MCI is the official timing and scoring system in NASCAR. MCI sees its relationship in NASCAR as good business.

"We think racing is a winning environment," said Andy Deas, the general manager of MCI's racing program. "There are a number of large accounts in the United States that we may be able to get. Racing gives us a different entree. When you talk with a CEO at an event, you hope it can turn into business for MCI."

As an example, Deas said if MCI gets the telephone accounts for a car manufacturer, then MCI is able to put "X" millions back into a racing program. "It's a win-win situation," Deas said. In the CART Indy car series, after MCI acquired Toyota's telephone business, MCI sponsored Max Papis's car.

Deas, who is from Liverpool, England, is familiar with Indy car racing from his days (and nights) as vice president of sponsorship and sales. Deas said NASCAR's appeal includes the three to four million in live attendance at races, the on-site sales opportunities, and the television audiences that more than double Indy car TV ratings.

Deas sees room for improvement in NASCAR. "CART is a little more professional in its (marketing) presentation," Deas said. "Too often in NASCAR, they say, 'Sure, we'll put your logo on the car,' then they walk away."

Valvoline, like other companies in racing, doesn't limit its involvement in racing simply to painting its name on a car. "We look at this program as a platform to do a lot of other things," said Mark Coughlin. "We can set up sales promotions, incentive programs, and hospitality for customers. We also do product development on the racetrack."

While MCI is a new logo around the racetracks, TranSouth Financial has been associated with Darlington Raceway in South Carolina since 1981. TranSouth was founded in the Palmetto state 50 years ago. TranSouth is now owned by The Associates, based in Dallas. Ken Stephenson, former president of TranSouth and currently president of Specialized Branch Operations of The Associates, grew up as a racing fan in North Carolina. He attended the inaugural race at North Carolina Motor Speedway in Rockingham in 1960.

"The company started seeing [in the early '80s] how there was a love for the sport and what it generated in the way of excitement and customer appeal," said Stephenson. "In 1983, we started sponsoring the Winston Cup [spring] event."

TranSouth began its sponsorship program with a campaign that was launched 90 days prior to the spring race at Darlington. For the last four years, Stephenson said TranSouth's association at Darlington has become year-round. "It's been a great business friendship and partnership because of the customers it brings to our company as well as Darlington, and the employees it effects," Stephenson said. "I'm trying to create a stronger bond between the customer and the company that does the sponsorship. I think we've had a huge impact just looking at the television ratings on our race the last couple years. We're trying to get the people to understand who TranSouth is. When they

see TranSouth, hopefully they'll think about Darlington Raceway and a company they can receive financial services from."

For last year's TranSouth race, the company ran a sweepstakes with a Ford Thunderbird as the grand prize. Three winners from the company's branch divisions were flown to Darlington. Each selected a set of car keys out of a hat. One of the keys started the T-bird. For the Mountain Dew Southern 500, TranSouth conducted a "Fantasy Day at Darlington." The winner, Deborah McCormick, of Winter Haven, Florida, rode in the pace car, met the drivers, and had her picture taken with winner Jeff Gordon. Talk about a collector's item: that's the day Gordon won the $1 million Winston bonus.

When McCormick was notified that she won, she had forgotten even filling out the card. Her trip to Darlington was her first live Winston Cup race. "I really enjoyed it," she said. "It's so different from what you see on TV: I had no idea the track was angled like that. I makes you realize what the drivers go through." McCormick said she might have trouble keeping her photo of Jeff Gordon because her 12-year-old niece, Tonya Leopard, is a Gordon fan.

Another financial services company in NASCAR is MBNA America Bank. MBNA sponsors both Winston Cup and Busch Grand National races at Dover Downs International Speedway. MBNA's association with NASCAR was a natural since more than 400,000 NASCAR fans hold credit cards issued by MBNA. The cards bear either the NASCAR emblem or the image of a driver. MBNA also sponsors Ward Burton's Winston Cup car. David Elgena, MBNA's executive vice president of motorsports, said sponsoring the races at Dover Downs is "a natural extension of MBNA's very successful niche marketing efforts in NASCAR." MBNA employs more than 8,000 people in Delaware.

Banks, cereal companies, cable networks . . . almost everyone except butchers, bakers and candlestick makers wants to sponsor race cars. And don't be surprised if someone from that latter group eventually winds up as a sponsor.

23

TRACK DIRECTORY

On the Winston Cup circuit, the tracks are where it all happens. Side-by-side, front grill to back bumper, the best drivers in the world race around the track at nearly 200 mph, secure in the knowledge that the tracks they are racing are among the best maintained and safest surfaces in all of racing. Lives depend on it, week in and week out.

Each of the tracks has its own personality, its own special features that distinguish it from the other 19 courses on the Winston Cup circuit. To the casual observer, the tracks might look the same—ribbons of concrete and asphalt upon which the cars pass by at amazing speeds. NASCAR fans know that nothing could be further from the truth. There's the season-opening race at Daytona, the 2½-mile superspeedway where speeds once topped 200 mph until restrictor plates were added for safety. Thirty-one races later, it's time to end the season at Atlanta Motor Speedway, another lightning fast track that was completely overhauled in time for the 1997 season.

In between, there's the "track too tough to tame" at Darlington and the "monster mile" at Dover; the "World's Fastest Half-Mile" at Bristol and the "Mecca of Motorsports" at Charlotte; the tight, ½-mile bullring at Martinsville and the superspeedway that drives like a road course at Pocono; the history and huge crowds of Indianapolis and the shiny newness and almost as-huge crowds of the Texas Speedway. In the end, there is a little something for everyone at the tracks of the Winston Cup.

As a result, the fans flock to the track. NASCAR is the biggest spectator sport in America these days, with attendance increasing every year. Nearly every track on the circuit has undergone renovations and expansion in recent years to add more seats to let more fans in on the fun. In most regions where tracks are located, they are the largest sporting venues of any type, with many seating more than 100,000 people. The Brickyard at Indianapolis can accommodate more than 300,000 people.

So, get out there and join the fun. Use this handy directory to find the track nearest you and plan a vacation around a NASCAR race. The directory includes a phone number to call for tickets, information on where the track is located, numbers to call for lodging information, and ideas on other things to do when you're in town for a race.

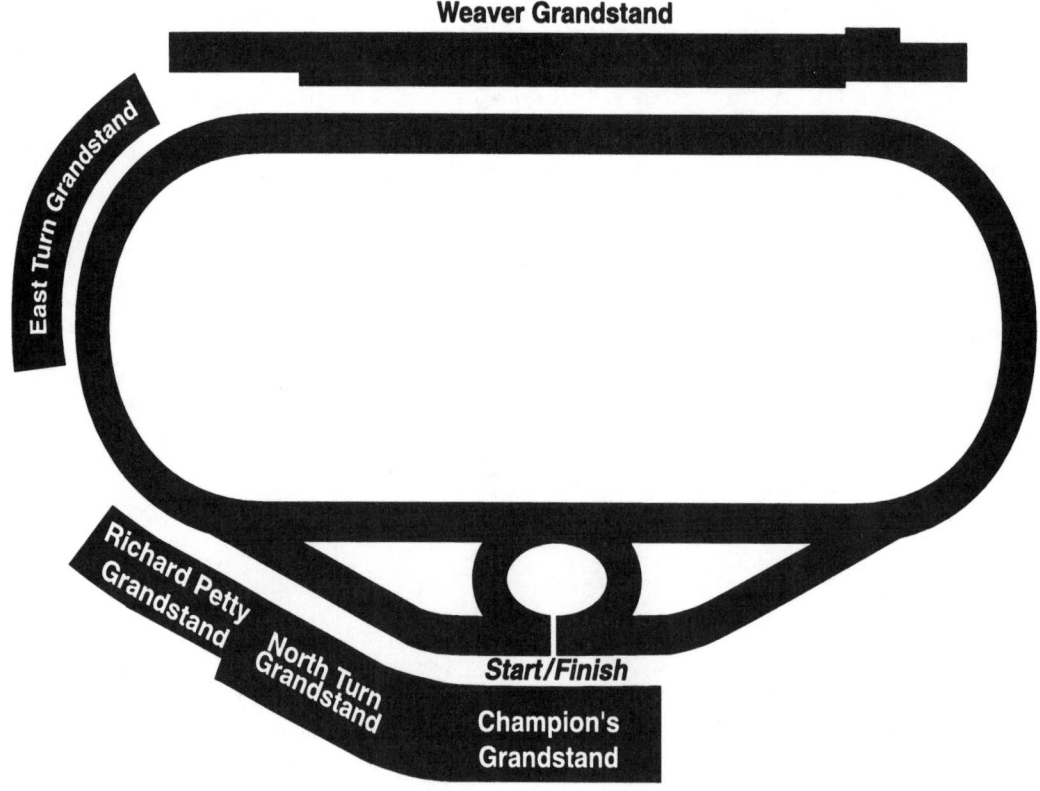

Weaver Grandstand

East Turn Grandstand

Richard Petty Grandstand

North Turn Grandstand

Start/Finish

Champion's Grandstand

ATLANTA MOTOR SPEEDWAY

Completely remodeled as of last November, Atlanta's Motor Speedway now resembles Bruton Smith's tracks at Charlotte and Texas. The track was completely overhauled in time for the 1997 race schedule. A new main grandstand has been built and the pits have been moved across the infield. Other improvements included a new press box, infield media center, control tower, scoring stand, infield hospital, garage area, and two pedestrian tunnels on the front stretch. The biggest change, though, was the conversion of the track from a 1.522-mile oval to a 1.54-mile quad oval.

How to get there

The track is in Hampton, Georgia, some 25 miles south of Atlanta. From the north, take I-75 to Exit 70 and follow Georgia 20 eight miles west to the track.

Who to contact

Speedway Motorsports Inc.
PO Box 500
Highways 19 & 41
Hampton, GA 30228
Phone: (770) 946-4211

Where to stay

For area lodging information, call the Henry County Chamber of Commerce at (770) 957-5786.

To order tickets

Call (770) 946-4211

Things to do

The first NASCAR retail store, NASCAR Thunder, is located in the Gwinnett Place Mall, I-85 at Exit 40, Atlanta. The store sells driver, team, and NASCAR-branded merchandise, and has a 12-screen video wall and one of Bill Elliott's Winston Cup cars. Call (770) 232-2808.

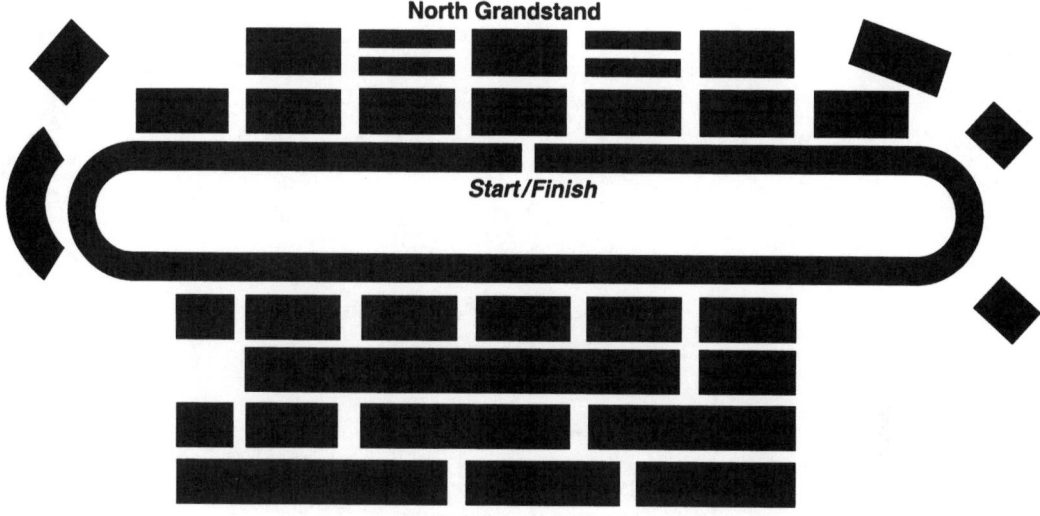

North Grandstand

Start/Finish

South Grandstand

BRISTOL MOTOR SPEEDWAY

One of the shortest tracks on the Winston Cup schedule, Bristol is also said to be one of the most exciting—especially in August when the cars race under the lights. Called "The World's Fastest Half-Mile," the track underwent significant renovations in 1997 to make it more fan friendly. Driving Bristol's bullring has been compared to flying a jet fighter inside a high school gymnasium, and the place is just as noisy because the tall grandstands hold the noise inside the Bristol bowl. Some advice: seats in one of the turns are the most desirable, and earplugs are mandatory. Seating capacity was nearly doubled, from 71,000 to 130,000.

How to get there

Bristol Motor Speedway is on Volunteer Parkway, Highway 11E, seven miles southwest of Bristol, Tennessee. It is accessible from I-81, I-181, or the Bristol Beltway.

Who to contact

Speedway Motorsports Inc.
PO Box 3966
Bristol, TN 37625
Phone: (423) 764-1161

Where to stay

Call the Bristol Chamber of Commerce at (423)989-4850, or for information on camping at the track, call (423) 764-1161.

To order tickets

Call (423) 764-1161

Things to do

Family nights and driver and show car appearances are often held in the area in the weeks leading up the race.

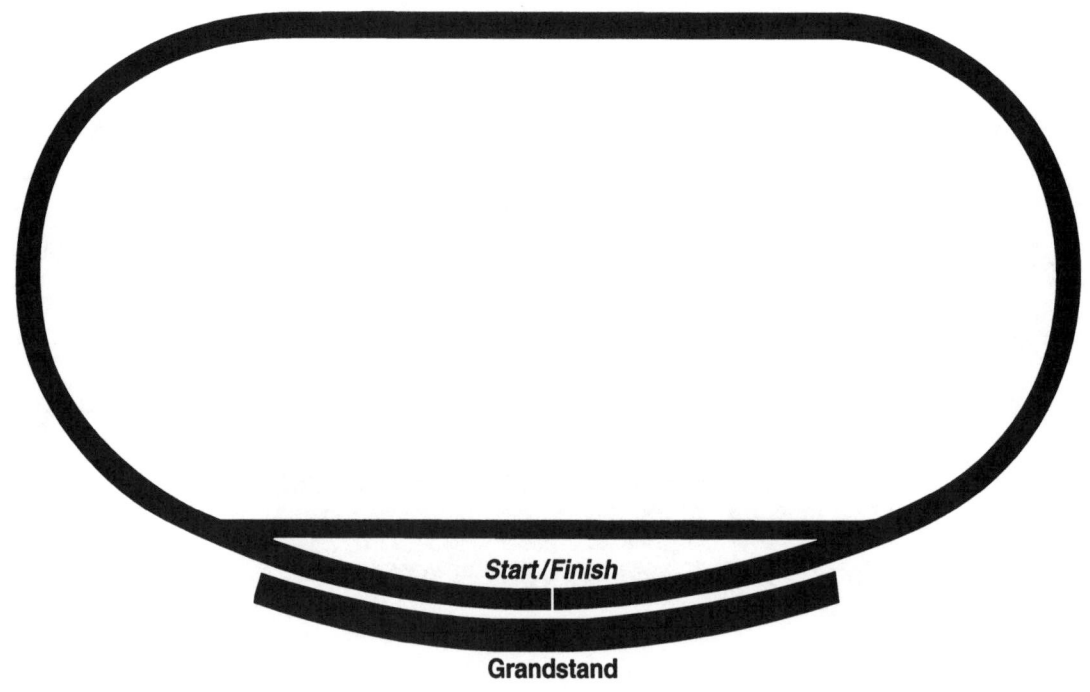

Start/Finish

Grandstand

CALIFORNIA SPEEDWAY

This track is modeled after owner Roger Penske's Michigan International Speedway, although the turns are banked four degrees less than at Michigan (14 as opposed to 18). A void was created in the Los Angeles area with the demise of both the Ontario Motor Speedway and the Riverside International Raceway in the 1980s. Roger Penske filled that void when he and investor Bill France, Jr. constructed the California Speedway. Built on 475 acres of what was once a steel mill. Seats 68,000 with room for 12,000 in the infield.

How to get there

The track is in Fontana, some 40 miles east of downtown Los Angeles, near the Ontario International Airport. It is one mile north of I-10 and three miles east of I-15. A Metrolink train station also allows access from major nearby cities.

Who to contact

Penske Motorsports Inc.
300 Cherry Ave.
Fontana, CA 92335-9300
Phone: (909) 428-3929

Where to stay

For lodging information, call the Fontana Chamber of Commerce at (909) 822-4433.

To order tickets

Call (800) 944-RACE (7223).

Things to do

The NHRA Historical Service Center, a drag racing museum, is located just west of the Pomona NHRA Fairplex. Call (909) 593-3151. The Petersen Automotive Museum at 6060 Wilshire Blvd. in Los Angeles is one of the newest and finest automotive displays in the world. Call (213) 930-CARS (2277).

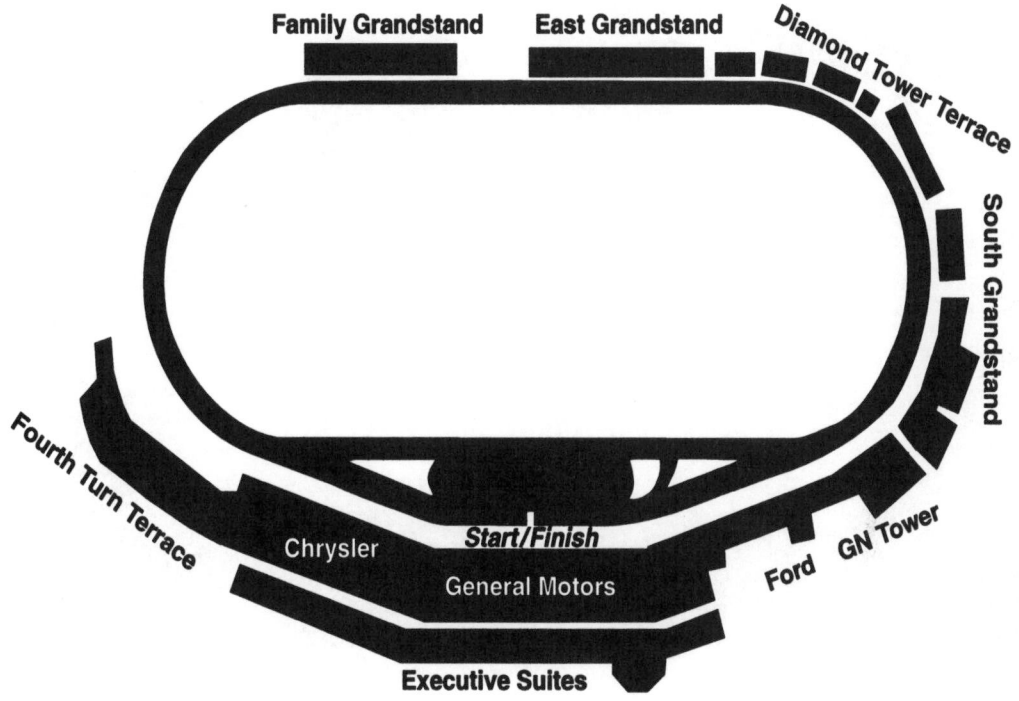

Family Grandstand   East Grandstand   Diamond Tower Terrace

South Grandstand

Fourth Turn Terrace

Chrysler   Start/Finish

General Motors

Ford   GN Tower

Executive Suites

CHARLOTTE MOTOR SPEEDWAY

Designed by stock car racer Curtis Turner and owned by Bruton Smith and Humpy Wheeler, the Charlotte Motor Speedway more closely resembles a motorsports showplace than a racing facility. In fact, the track is known as the "Mecca of Motorsports." The racetrack features condominiums outside Turn One and an exclusive dining facility, the Speedway Club, high above the start/finish line. Many drivers and teams live in and around the Charlotte area. The track seats 112,000 and hosts Legends, SCCA, and other motorsports events in addition to NASCAR.

How to get there

The racetrack is 12 miles northeast of Charlotte, North Carolina, at Concord. It is east of I-85 on Highway 29.

Who to contact

Speedway Motorsports Inc.
PO Box 600
Concord, NC 28026-0600
Phone: (704) 455-3200

Where to stay

For lodging information, call the Charlotte Convention and Visitors Bureau at (704) 331-2700 or (800) 231-4636.

To order tickets

Call: (704) 455-3200.

Things to do

Most of the Winston Cup teams are based in Charlotte, and many open their facilities for tours. Richard Childress's shop in Welcome, and Richard Petty's in Randleman, have their own museums.

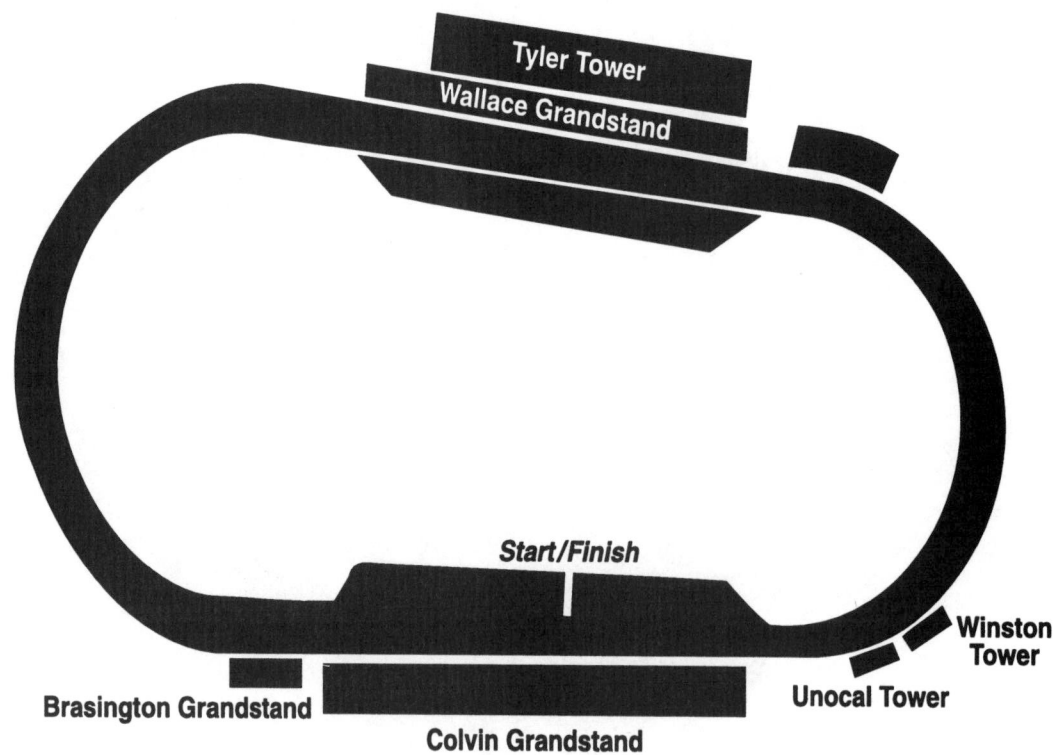

DARLINGTON RACEWAY

Dubbed "the track too tough to tame", Darlington Raceway will become even more difficult this year. Instead of having to earn their "Darlington Stripes" as they rub their fenders along the wall in the decreasing radius of Turn Four, the drivers will have to contend with Turn Two, as the start/finish line has been moved to the middle of what used to be the backstrech. The change marks the first alteration in the Darlington track since it opened in 1950 as the first superspeedway. New grandstands and new parking areas make it easier for fans to enjoy the action.

How to get there

Darlington is 10 miles north of Florence, South Carolina, near the junction of I-20 and I-95, some 70 miles from Myrtle Beach. The racetrack is two miles west of Darlington on South Carolina Highway 151-34.

Who to contact

International Speedway Corp.

Where to stay

For motel information, call the Darlington County Chamber of Commerce at (803) 393-2641 or the PeeDee Tourism Commission at (803) 669-0950.

To order tickets

Call Phone: (803) 395-8499.

Things to do

Adjacent to the racetrack is the NMPA Stock Car Hall of Fame/Joe Weatherly Museum, which salutes the history of NASCAR and Darlington, the sport's first superspeedway.

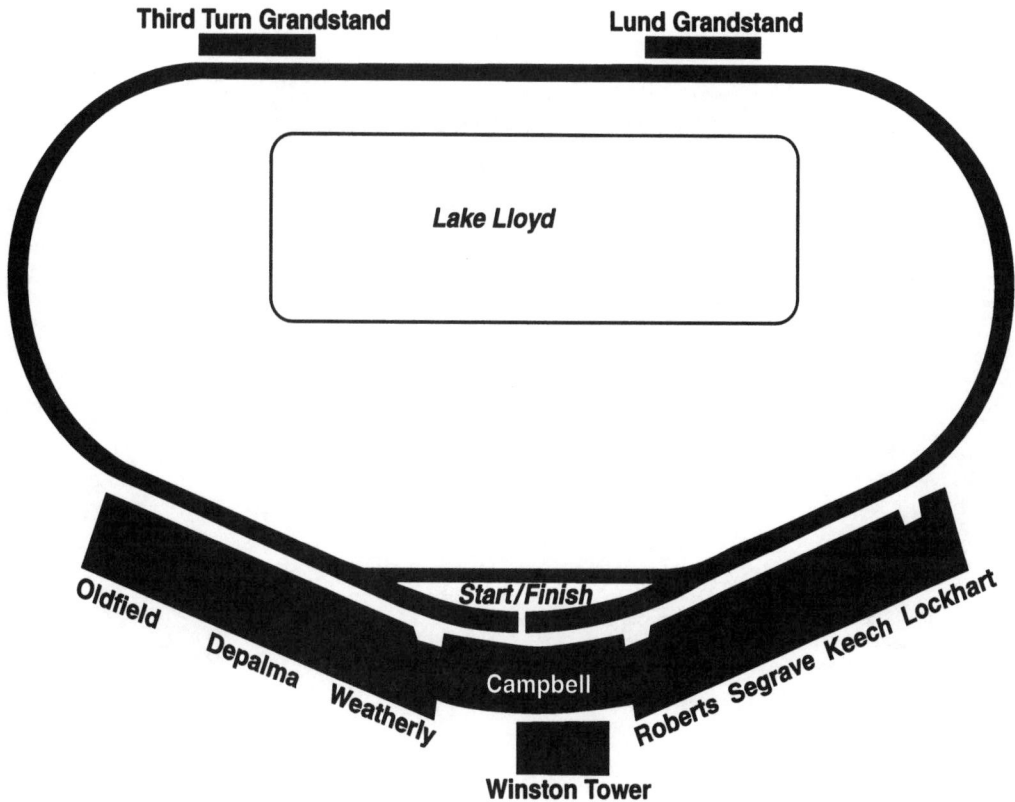

Third Turn Grandstand   Lund Grandstand

Lake Lloyd

Oldfield Depalma Weatherly   Campbell   Start/Finish   Roberts Segrave Keech Lockhart

Winston Tower

DAYTONA INTERNATIONAL SPEEDWAY

Self-proclaimed the "World Center of Racing," Daytona remains the most famous venue for racing. Stock car competition in Daytona predates even the races at Indianapolis, and people have been gathering here since 1902 to see how fast their cars could go. As late as 1958, stock cars raced on a circuit that was part paved road, part beach. Then NASCAR founder Bill France, Jr. built his high-banked, D-shaped oval speedway in 1959. The infield includes the 44-acre Lake Lloyd, a man-made lake that was formed when dirt was removed to help build the famous 31-degree high bank turns.

How to get there

The Speedway is 35 miles northeast of Orlando and 65 miles south of Jacksonville, or one mile east of I-95 on U.S. 92, adjacent to Daytona Regional Airport.

Who to contact

International Speedway Corp.
1801 W. International Speedway Blvd.
Daytona Beach, FL 32114
Phone: (904) 254-2700

Where to stay

Call the Greater Daytona Beach Convention and Visitors Bureau at (800) 854-1234.

To order tickets

Call (904) 253-7223.

Things to do

DAYTONA USA, a multimillion dollar interactive motorsports attraction and tourist destination, opened last July on the Speedway grounds. Call (904) 947-6800.

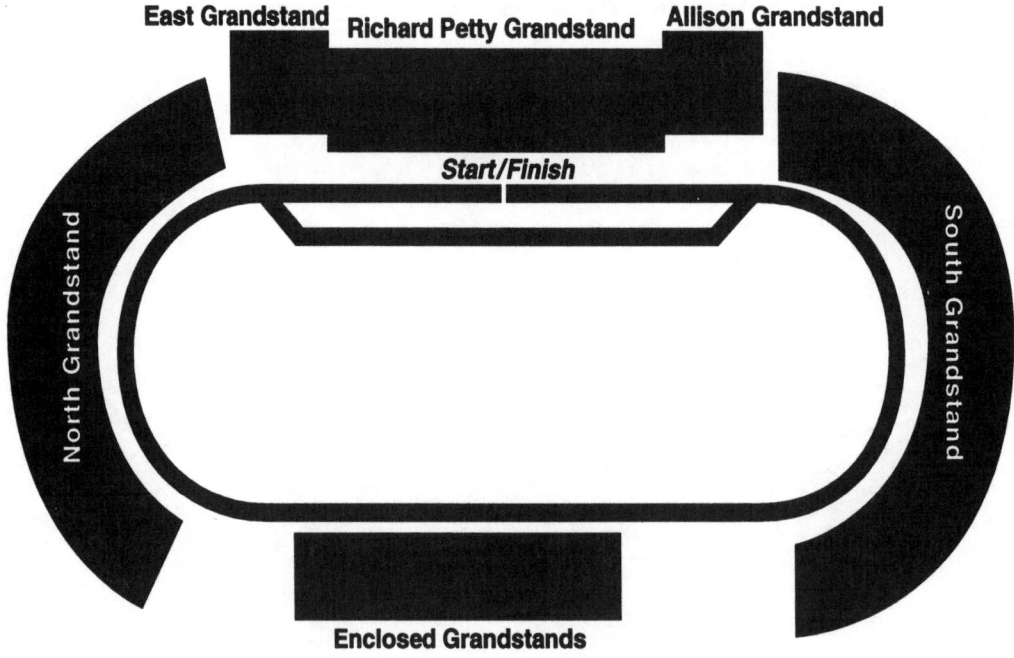

East Grandstand   Richard Petty Grandstand   Allison Grandstand

North Grandstand

South Grandstand

Start/Finish

Enclosed Grandstands

DOVER DOWNS INTERNATIONAL SPEEDWAY

The track known as "The Monster Mile" because of the physical demands it places on drivers expanded in 1997 and hopes to grow to 170,000 seats by the year 2004. The track is considered one of the most treacherous on the circuit, both for the drivers and for the cars. Two races are held at the track each year. The fall race has been shortened from 500 to 400 miles, but the high-banked curves and dead-straight straightaways will leave the drivers no time to relax.

How to get there

The track is one mile north of Dover, Delaware, on U.S. 13. Dover is about 65 miles from Philadelphia and 75 miles from Baltimore.

Who to contact

Denis McGlynn is president and Jerry Dunning is the general manager.

PO Box 843
Dover, DE 19903
Phone: (302) 674-4600

Where to stay

Call the Central Delaware Chamber of Commerce at (302) 734-7514.

To order tickets

Call (800) 441-RACE (7223) or (302) 734-RACE.

Things to do

Dover Downs Slots, a casino with restaurants, is located on the track grounds and features simulcast horse race wagering (you must be 21 to enter the Slots, 18 to attend simulcasts).

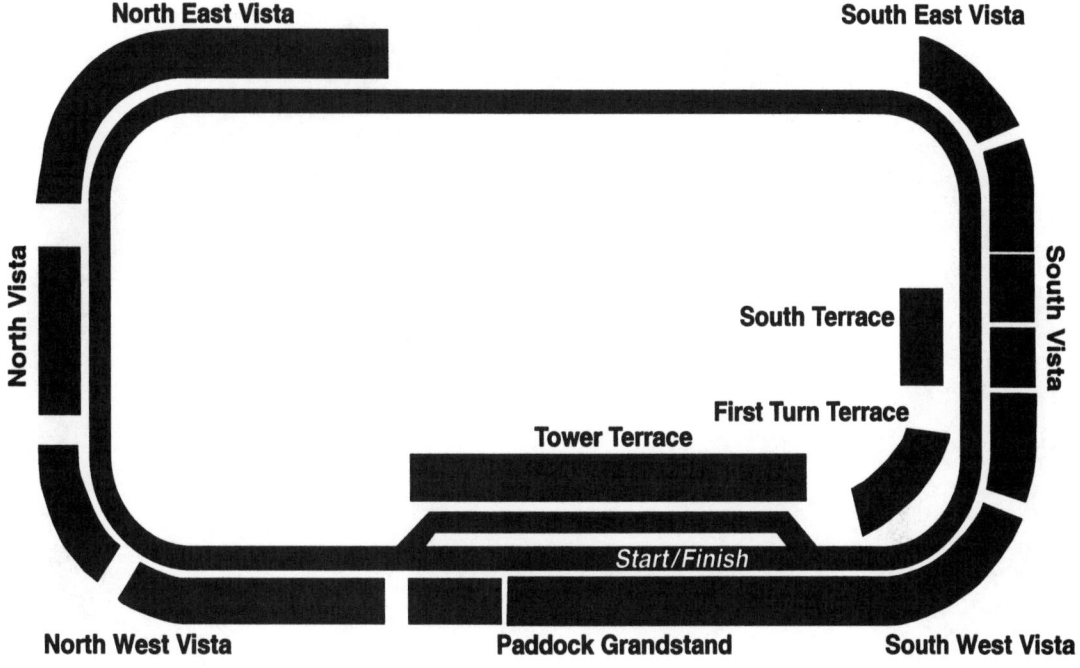

North East Vista

South East Vista

North Vista

South Vista

South Terrace

First Turn Terrace

Tower Terrace

Start/Finish

North West Vista

Paddock Grandstand

South West Vista

INDIANAPOLIS MOTOR SPEEDWAY

Most people thought that hell would freeze over before NASCAR would ever hold a race at Indianapolis, but the Brickyard 400 has become so popular, people wonder why the powers that be waited so long. Jeff Gordon won the inaugural race in 1994. Known as the Brickyard for the 3.2 million bricks that were used to pave the track when it's original tar and crushed stone surface crumbled. Most of the bricks remain in place today under the track's modern ashphalt surface. The Speedway is the largest sporting venue in the country, with room for more than 300,000 fans.

How to get there

The speedway is in a town called Speedway, and it is located at the northeast corner of 16th St. and Georgetown Rd., seven miles northwest of downtown Indianapolis.

Who to contact

The Indianapolis Motor Speedway Corp.
4790 W. 16th St.
Indianapolis, IN 46222
Phone: (317) 481-8500

Where to stay

Call the Indianapolis City Center at (317) 237-5200 or the Indianapolis Convention and Visitors Association at (800) 323-INDY (4269).

To order tickets

Tickets to both races are sold by mail order. Write to PO Box 24152, Speedway, IN 46224.

Things to do

The Speedway grounds include the Brickyard Crossing Golf Resort and Inn, and the IMS Hall of Fame Museum.

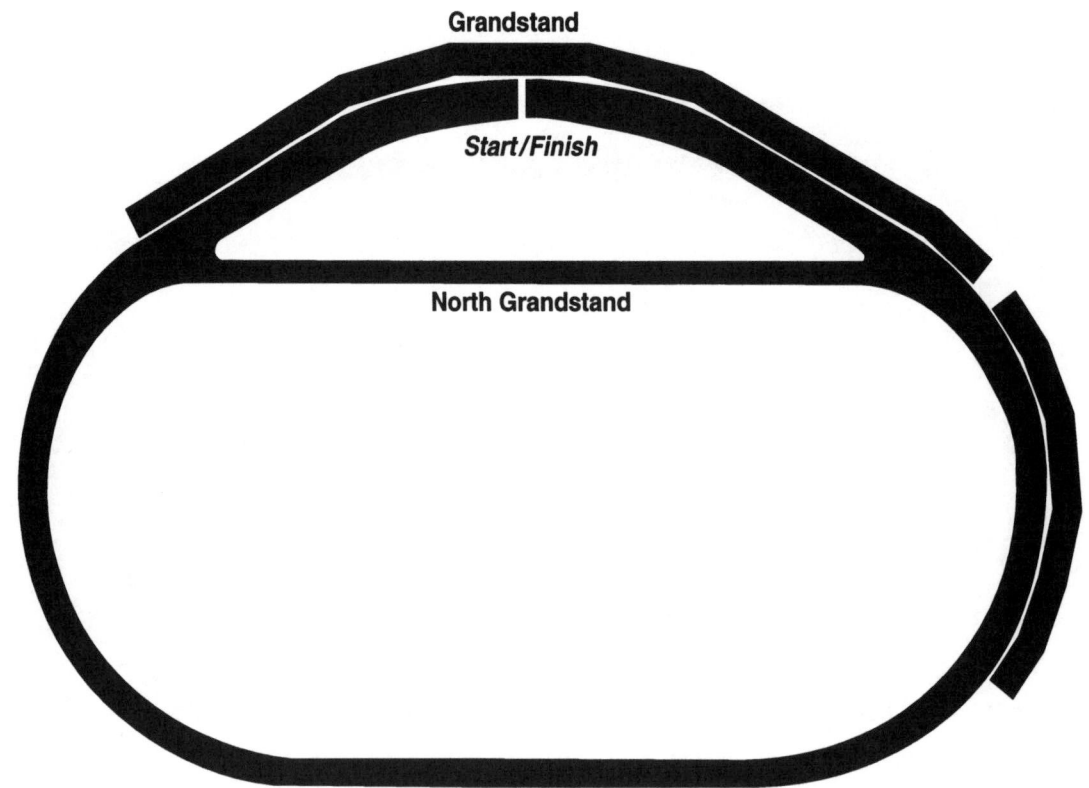

Grandstand

Start/Finish

North Grandstand

LAS VEGAS MOTOR SPEEDWAY

With some of the money to build the track coming from Las Vegas casinos, it's no surprise that the track is somewhat outrageous. The Speedway includes two drag strips, two road courses, and three ovals, including a 1.5 mile loop with banking that enables drivers to stay on the throttle all the way around. Some NASCAR drivers who have tested the track consider it to be the best track in the country. It will make its NASCAR debut as part of the 1998 season.

How to get there

The track is eight miles north of downtown Las Vegas and 11 miles from the center of the Strip. From McCarran International Airport, take I-15 north to Speedway Blvd.

Who to contact

Richie Clyne is the owner and president. Ray Wilkings is general manager.

7000 Las Vegas Blvd. North
Las Vegas, NV 89115
Phone: (702) 644-4444

Where to stay

For lodging information, call the Las Vegas Convention and Visitors Authority's Visitors Information Center at (702) 892-7576.

To order tickets

Call (702) 644-4443

Things to do

Speedway owner Richie Clyne also is director of the Imperial Palace Auto Connection, on the fifth floor of the Imperial Palace Casino, 3535 Las Vegas Blvd. South. The museum may be known for its celebrity cars and dictators' vehicles, but it also has a huge collection of Duesenbergs and other cars of significance.

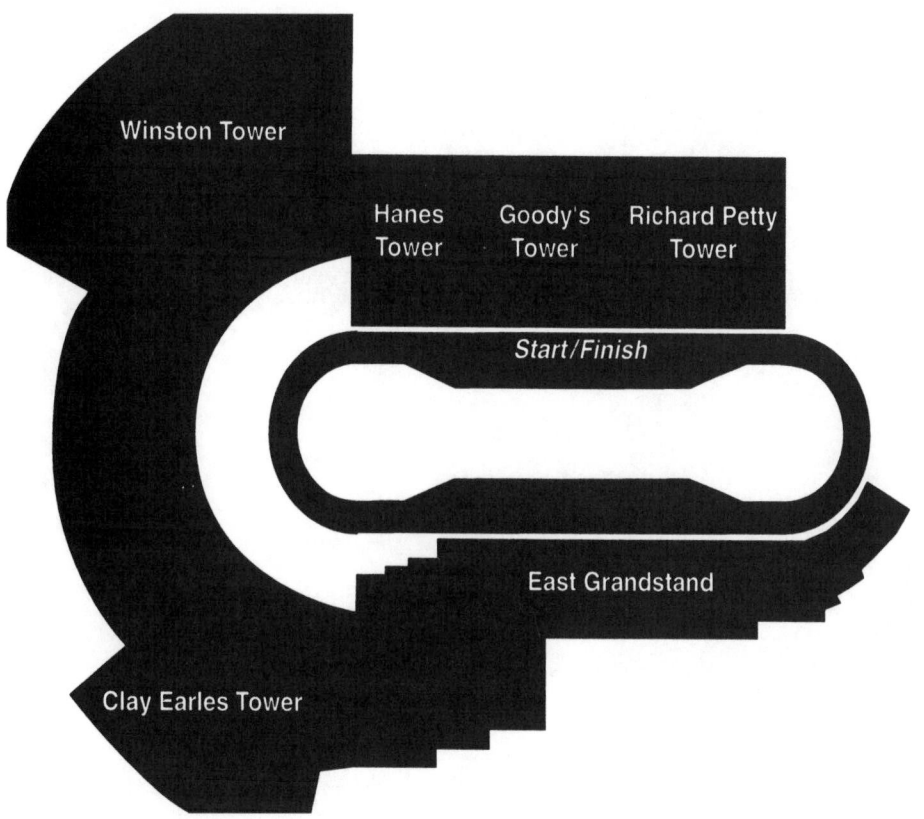

Winston Tower

Hanes Tower   Goody's Tower   Richard Petty Tower

Start/Finish

East Grandstand

Clay Earles Tower

MARTINSVILLE SPEEDWAY

Martinsville Speedway celebrated its 50th anniversary in 1997. It is the only track that has been a part of NASCAR Grand National and Winston Cup racing since the very beginning. It started as a dirt track before being paved. Red Byron won the first race ever held there. Aside from being repaved, the 0.526-mile oval hasn't changed much since its conception. "Two drag strips with short turns," is how Martinsville, the shortest track still hosting Winston Cup races, is usually described.

How to get there

The track is two miles south of Martinsville, Virginia, on U.S. 220 South Business Route. It is a 45-minute drive from the Greensboro Airport; take Route 68 to U.S. 220 north.

Who to contact

H. Clay Earles, who built the track in 1947, is chairman of the board and CEO. Earles' grandson, W. Clay Campbell, is president and general manager.

PO Box 3311
U.S. 220 South Business Route
Martinsville, VA 24112
Phone: (540) 956-3151

Where to stay

For lodging information, call the Martinsville/Henry County Chamber of Commerce at (540) 632-6401.

To order tickets

Call (540) 956-3151

Things to do

The Wood Brothers Racing Museum is at Stuart, about 30 miles west of the racetrack on U.S. 58. Call (540) 694-2121.

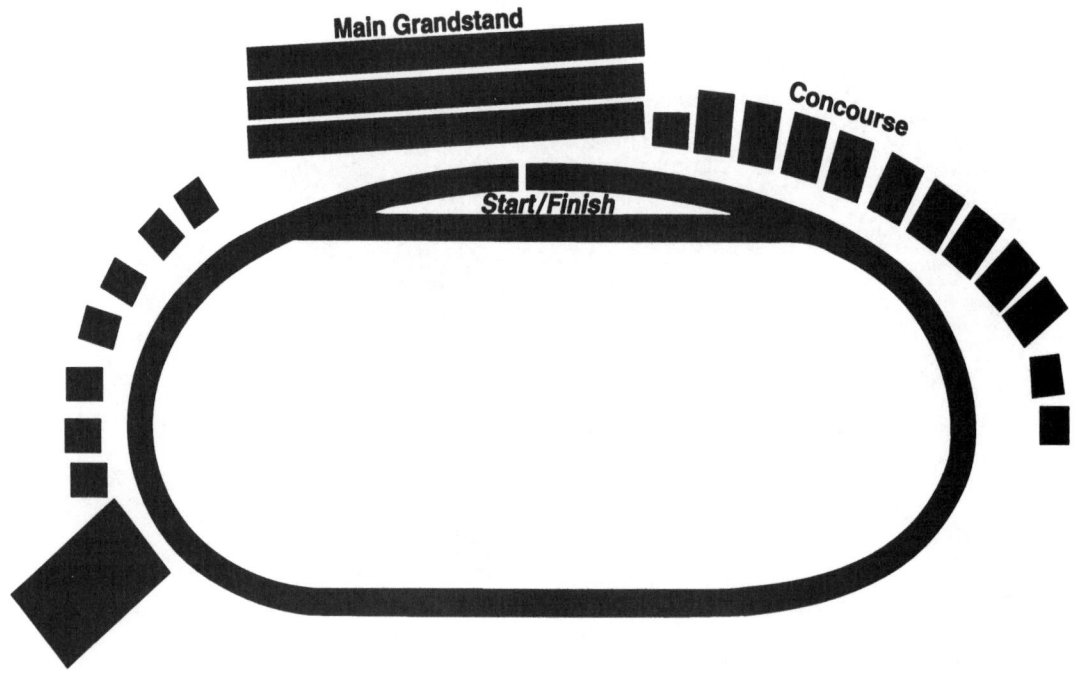

MICHIGAN SPEEDWAY

Charlie Moneypenny and Sterling Moss designed this track, which is know for it wide straightaways and high-banked turns, which together make three- and four-abreast racing common. Moneypenny also designed Daytona and employed many of the same engineering ideas at Michigan. The 18-degree banking at Michigan, which many drivers consider to be the best in the world, got even better after being bought by Penske in 1973. The latest upgrade was a larger grandstand overlooking Turn 4. If you look closely from Michigan's grandstands, you can still see the remnant of a road course where Trans-Am, Can-Am, and F5000 cars once raced.

How to get there

Michigan Speedway is 65 miles southwest of downtown Detroit, at the intersection of U.S. 12 and Brooklyn Road.

Who to contact

Penske Motorsports Inc.
12626 U.S. 12
Brooklyn, MI 49230-9068
Phone: (517) 592-6666

To order tickets

Call (800) 354- 1010.

Things to do

The Henry Ford Museum/Greenfield Village is about 50 miles northeast of the track at 20900 Oakwood Blvd., Dearborn. Call (313) 271-1620. The R.E. Olds Transportation Museum is about 50 miles north of the track at 240 Museum Dr., Lansing. Call (517) 372-0422.

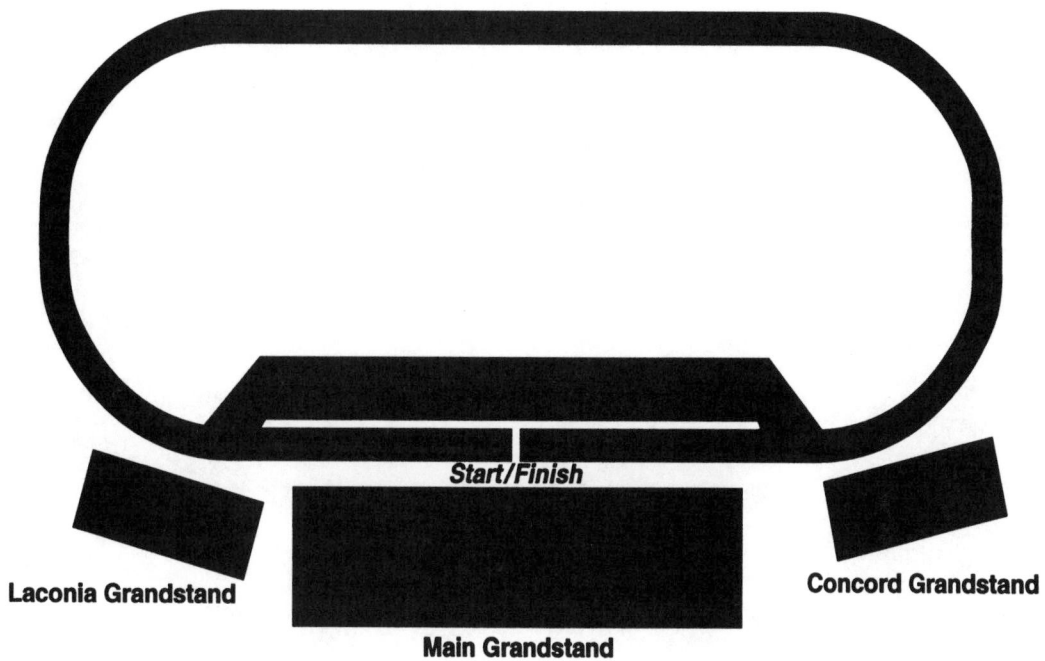

Start/Finish

Laconia Grandstand

Main Grandstand

Concord Grandstand

NEW HAMPSHIRE INTERNATIONAL SPEEDWAY

Bob Bahre, hoping to bring major league racing to New England, bought the site of the former Bryar Motorsports Park and built this one-mile oval track—with no guarantee that anyone would race there. The gamble paid off big. New Hampshire hosted two Winston Cup races last season and an Indy Racing League competition. To gain approval to build the racetrack, Bahre had to personally by the town of Loudon a new fire truck with a ladder high enough to reach the top of the grandstands and press box.

How to get there

The track is on Route 106 in Loudon, New Hampshire, about 70 miles north of Boston.

Who to contact

Bob Bahre is chairman of the board and his son, Gary, is president.

PO Box 7888
Loudon, NH 03301
Phone: (603) 783-4744

Where to stay

For lodging information, call the Concord Chamber of Commerce at (603) 224-2508.

To order tickets

Call (603) 783-4931

Things to do

The July Winston Cup weekend begins on Wednesday with Race Fever night in Concord. The Governor's charity breakfast is Thursday morning in Laconia (tickets are available through the race track), and a charity golf tournament is played Thursday afternoon at Laconia.

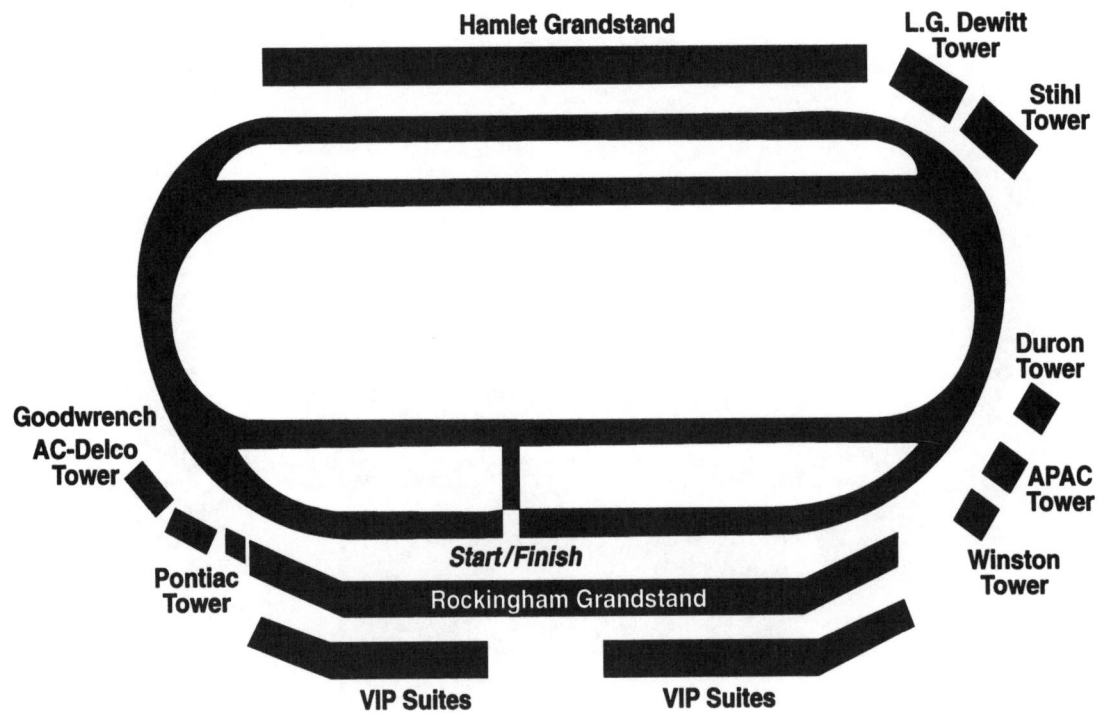

NORTH CAROLINA MOTOR SPEEDWAY AT ROCKINGHAM

Usually refered to as just Rockingham, or, the Rock, this speedway was built by Harold Brasington (responsible for the first Southern superspeedway at Darlington, NC) and North Carolina trucking company owner L.G. DeWitt. The track opened in 1965, and has since become one the most recognized venues in stock car racing. It is the site of the first and last NASCAR races to be held in North Carolina each season, and in October, it hosts the UNOCAL 76/RockinghamWorld Pit Crew Competition, which crowns the world's fastest pit crew.

How to get there

The racetrack is on U.S. 1, about 10 miles north of Rockingham and 20 miles south of Southern Pines.

Who to contact

Carrie DeWitt is chairman of the board and Jo DeWitt Wilson is president and chief executive.

PO Box 500
Rockingham, NC 28380-0500
Phone: (910) 582-2861

Where to stay

For lodging information in Richmond County, call (910) 895-9058. In the Sandhills area, call (910) 692-3926.

To order tickets

Call (910) 582-2861

Things to do

The Pinehurst-Southern Pines area is one of the county's top golfing meccas.

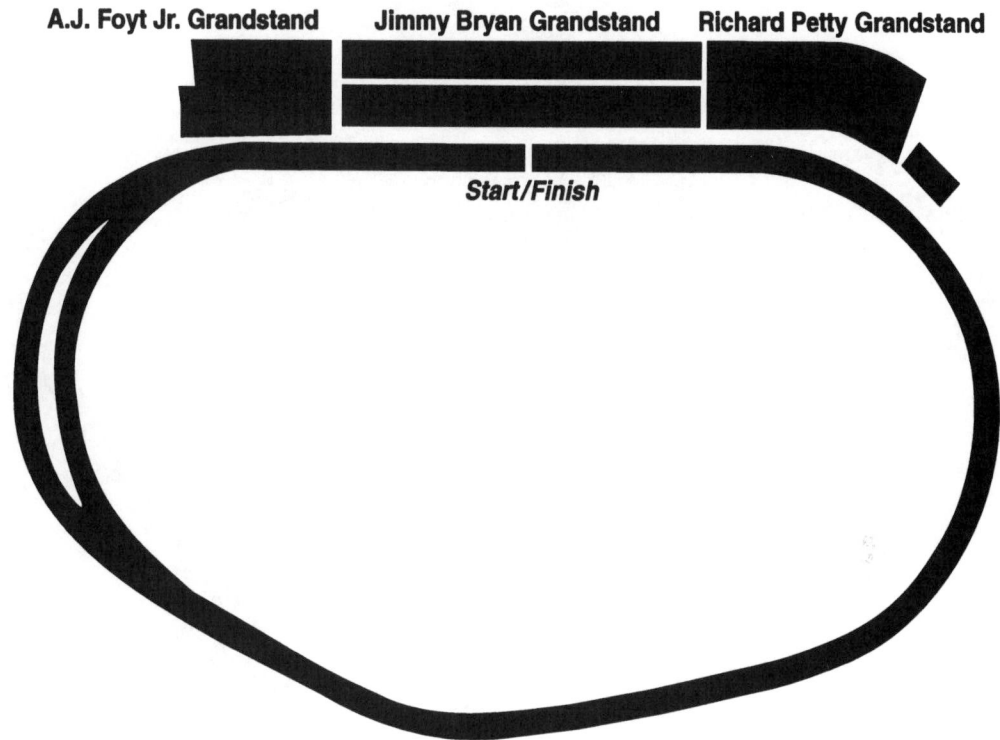

A.J. Foyt Jr. Grandstand   **Jimmy Bryan Grandstand**   **Richard Petty Grandstand**

Start/Finish

PHOENIX INTERNATIONAL RACEWAY

Phoenix International Raceway is considerd to be the fastest one-mile oval track in the world. In addition to NASCAR, it is host to the Copper World Classic every winter, a proving ground for up-and-comers hoping to eventually make appearences at Indy or NASCAR races. Rumor has it that the best seats in the house are on the hillside above Turn Four, and they're at general admission prices. Fans are treated to races on one tough track: serious banking into Turn One, a tight Turn Two, a dogleg going to Turn Three, and a Turn Four that propels drivers on the start/finish straight. The track is located at the base of the Estrella Mountains, near the Salt and Gila Rivers.

How to get there

Phoenix International Raceway is southwest of the city, about 23 miles west on I-10 to the 115th Ave. Exit, then six miles south again.

Who to contact

Emmett "Buddy" Jobe is owner and president.

PO Box 13088
Phoenix, AZ 85002
Phone: (602) 252-3833

Where to stay

For lodging information, call the Phoenix and Valley of the Sun Convention and Visitors Bureau at (602) 254-6500.

To order tickets

Call the track at (602) 252-2227 or Dillard's Box Office at (800) 638-4253.

Things to do

The Bob Bondurant School of High Performance Driving is based at Firebird International Raceway, just southeast of Phoenix. Call (520) 796-1111.

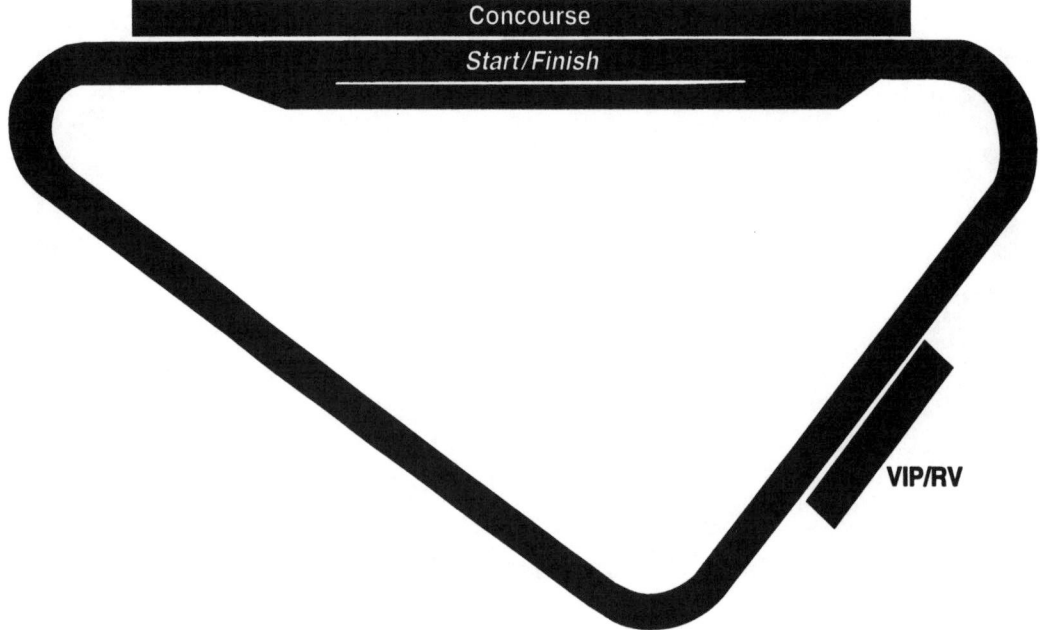

Terrace Club
Terrace Vista
Terrace

Concourse

Start/Finish

VIP/RV

POCONO RACEWAY

Pocono Raceway is one of the most competitive, and one of the most unique, tracks on the NASCAR circuit. Its 2½-mile tri-oval features three turns, each with a different degree of banking, and three straights, each with a different length. That combination produces fender-to-fender action in the turns and 200 mph duels down the straightaways. Because of the unique layout, Pocono is often called the "superspeedway that drives like a road course."

How to get there

Pocono Raceway is in the Pocono Mountains resort area, off State Highway 115, south of I-80, and about 90 miles north of Philadelphia.

Who to contact

Dr. Joseph Mattioli is chairman and president.

PO Box 500
Long Pond, PA 18344
Phone: (717) 646-2300

Where to stay

For lodging information, call the Pocono Mountains Vacation Bureau at (800) POCONOS (762-6667).

To order tickets

Call (800) RACEWAY (722-3929)

Things to do

The JEM Classic Car Museum is on Route 443 in Andreas, Pennsylvania. Call (717) 386-3554. The Boyertown Museum of Historic Vehicles is at 28 Warnick St., in Boyertown. Call (610) 367-2090.

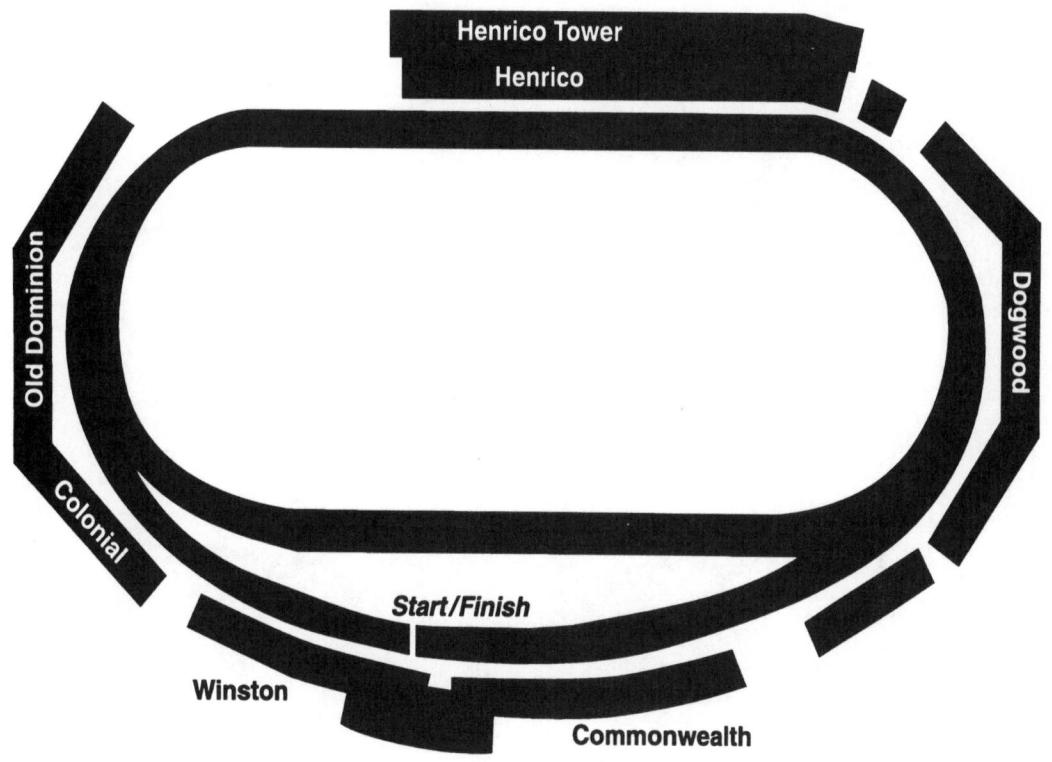

Henrico Tower
Henrico

Old Dominion

Dogwood

Colonial

Start/Finish

Winston

Commonwealth

RICHMOND INTERNATIONAL RACEWAY

Richmond has hosted NASCAR races since 1953, although it was a popular race destination for several years before that. Originally a dirt track (part of the Atlantic Rural Exposition of 1948), it was paved in 1968 and bought by Richmond International Raceway Inc. In 1988 it was expanded from a half-mile to three-quarters of a mile. The racing surface is 60 feet wide with 14 degrees of banking in the turns, combining the intimacy of a short oval with the racing style of a superspeedway. Grandstands hold 83,000 people.

How to get there

The racetrack is near the intersection of I-95 and I-64, on Strawberry Hill in the Virginia State Fairgrounds near downtown Richmond.

Who to contact

PO Box 9257
Richmond, VA 23227
Phone: (804) 345-RACE (7223)

Where to stay

For lodging information, send a self-addressed stamped envelope (with 55 cents of postage) for the track's "Fan Friendly Guide," to PO Box 9257, Richmond, VA 23227-9257.

To order tickets

Call (800) 345-RACE (7223).

Things to do

Drive to Washington, D.C., and visit the Smithsonian's National Museum of American History, where the vehicles on display include Henry Ford's original Model T and the STP Pontiac in which Richard Petty won his 200th race.

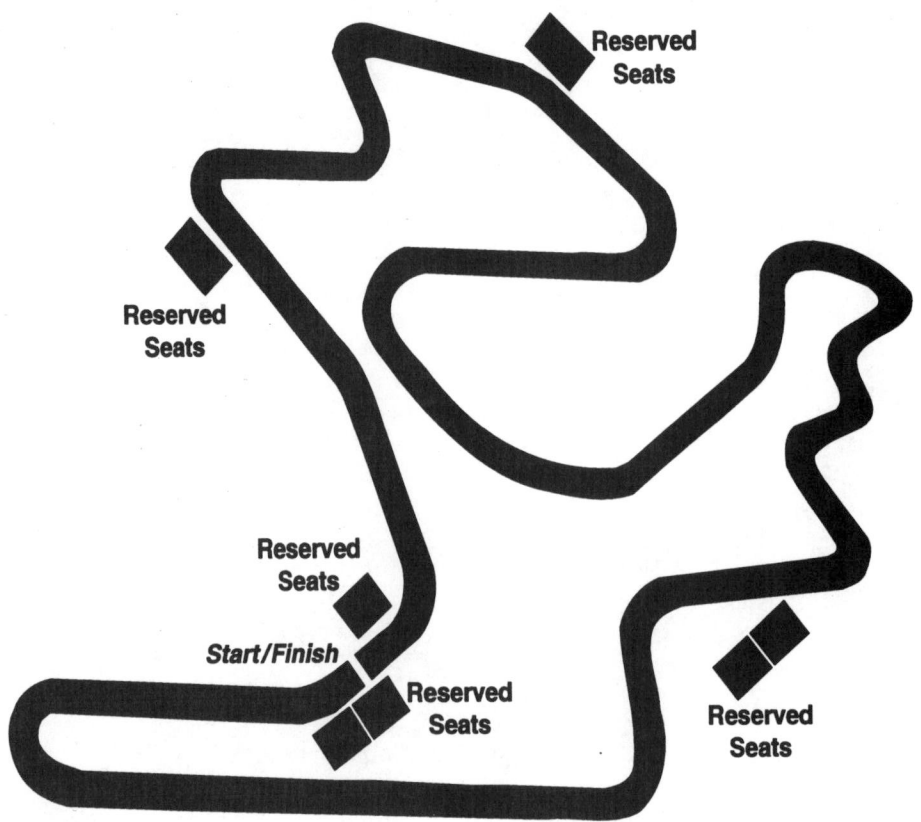

SEARS POINT RACEWAY

Sears Point, host to Winston Cup and NHRA events, is part of the Bruton Smith empire which includes tracks at Charlotte, Atlanta, and Bristol to name only a few. Smith also has plans to build a new oval in the Quad Cities area of northern Illinois-Iowa. Renovations and improvements are planned for Sears Point in the near future.The twisting and turning 2.52-mile, twelve turn road course closed for a few years before reopening in 1973. Last-lap duels to the finish line are common at Sears Point.

How to get there

The raceway is at the intersection of California Routes 37 and 121, 40 miles north of San Francisco and just west of Napa.

Who to contact

Owned by Brenda Raceways Corp., Speedway Motorsports Inc. operates the track under a long-term lease, and has the option to buy the track after three years.

Routes 37 & 121
Sonoma, CA 95476
Phone: (707) 938-8448

Where to stay

Call (800) 870-7223 For lodging information.

To order tickets

Call (800) 870-7223.

Things to do

The Blackhawk Automotive Museum is at 3700 Blackhawk Plaza Circle, Danville. Call (510) 736-2280. Martin Swig's Automobilia store is at 1701 Van Ness Ave., San Francisco. Call (415) 561-8400. The only Ferrari factory in the United States is at 596 Redwood Highway, Mill Valley. Call (415) 380-9700.

Gentlemen, start your engines! The green flag drops to start the Daytona 500 and kick off the 1997 Winston Cup season.

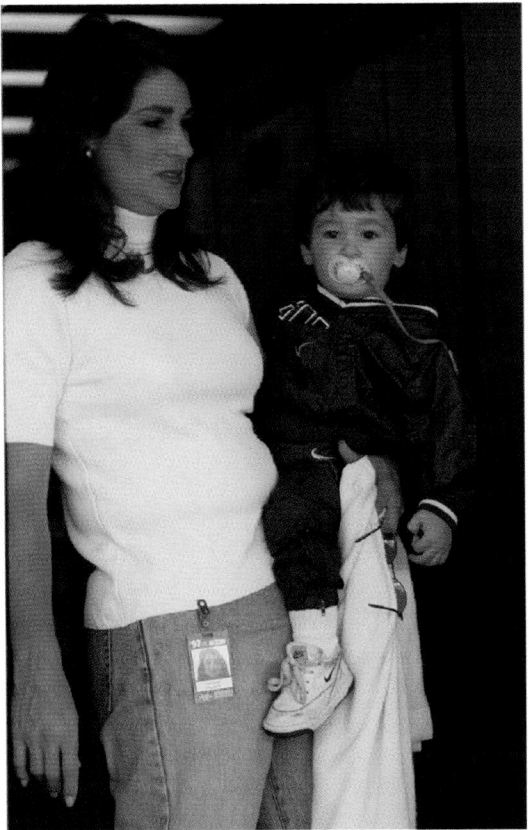

Dale Earnhardt's pit crew stays in touch with its driver through radio communication. Fans with scanners can listen in at the track.

Bill Elliott's wife Cindy and their son Chase in the garage area. Close family ties are an important part of the NASCAR tradition.

Ernie Irvan (28) avoids trouble as Dale Earnhardt (3) hits the wall while another car spins onto the grass apron at Daytona.

Mark Martin's third-place Winston Cup finish gave owner Jack Roush (above) reason to smile in '97.

◄ Today's high tech engines are nothing like those used in NASCAR's early years. Getting an engine ready for a race means hours of preparation.

Robert Yates, owner of the No. 88 Quality Care Ford that Dale Jarrett drove to a second-place Winston Cup finish.

Many fans show up early on race ➤ day to check out the souvenir stands and other attractions that give a big race a carnival-like atmosphere.

◀ *Ernie Irvan's car is reflected in the glossy finish of one of his competitors'. The colors, sounds, and excitement associated with a NASCAR race are what draw many fans to the sport.*

Ward Burton's crew hustles to get him back on the racetrack. To the untrained eye, a pit stop is nothing but chaos, but in reality, every man has a very specific role to fill.

Ray Evernham, crew chief for Jeff Gordon, in a reflective mood before a race.

Ernie Irvan takes the No. 28 Texaco Havoline car in for a pit stop. Good tires are a must if a driver hopes to win any race.

Mark Martin (No. 6) might have led Jeff Gordon (No. 24) in this race at Pocono, but in the end, Gordon had the last laugh when he won the Winston Cup season championship.

Dale Jarrett relaxing before a race. A 500-mile race is a grueling physical and mental challenge, so drivers relax whenever they can.

Jeff Gordon's jackman sprints for the pit wall as the other crew members put the finishing touches on this pit stop.

Members of the Jasper Motorsports team prepare Robert Pressley's No. 77 car for the race. Finding just the right engine settings before the race is crucial.

Terry Labonte, two-time Winston
Cup champion and current driver
of the Kellogg's Corn Flakes car.
Big-name sponsors have flocked
to NASCAR in recent years.

Bill Elliott's crew races to change the tires and get Elliot back in the race. Pit
stops are dangerous business, so all members of the crew have to stay
sharp and do their jobs well.

Lucky fans on the infield revvin' up for a day of action. The infield is usually home to the most diehard fans and some
of the biggest prerace parties.

Jeff Gordon (No. 24) and Mark Martin (No. 6) lead the pack towards the starting grid at the MBNA 400 at Dover Downs International Speedway. Seconds after the cars start out in this organized, side-by-side pattern, it will be every

man for himself by the time they reach the first turn. Most fans know that the moments following the green flag are the most dangerous time in any race, since the cars are so tightly bunched.

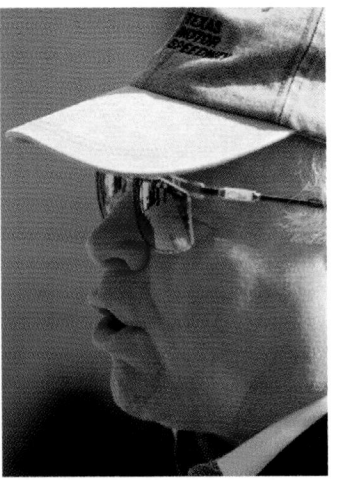

Bruton Smith, NASCAR pioneer and owner of tracks in Charlotte, Atlanta, and Texas.

Steve Grissom signs a hat while Terry Labonte looks on. NASCAR drivers are among the friendliest and most accessible athletes in professional sports.

Every second is crucial during pit stops—many races are won by a few seconds or less, so the three seconds saved on a pit stop can translate into big dollars at the finish line. Here, Mike Skinner's crew works to get him back on the track.

Robby Loomis is the crew chief for the most famous team in racing history—the Petty Enterprises team owned by NASCAR legend Richard Petty.

Dale Jarrett, who dueled Jeff ➤ Gordon right down to the last race before finishing second in Winston Cup points, hangs loose with a crew member.

Jeff Gordon's calm, cool demeanor on and off the track is one of the big reasons he's already won two NASCAR Winston Cup titles.

◀ All the horsepower in the world doesn't matter if the engine won't run. Dale Earnhardt's crew uses a little people power to get its man back to the garage.

Jeff Gordon (left) and crew chief Ray Evernham seem to be pondering strategies and possible outcomes.

Bill Elliott, a fan favorite, will be even busier on race days next year when he teams with Miami Dolphin's quarterback Dan Marino to field a new NASCAR team while still driving his own car.

Fans salute as Ernie Irvan's Texaco Havoline car passes by. Beer and baseball caps are common sights at every NASCAR race.

Nope, that's not Bobby Hamilton. It's actually Rusty Wallace and crew chief Robin Pemberton relaxing before a race.

Fans fly their favorite's colors at Pocono. Flags, t-shirts, and baseball caps are just a few of the ways NASCAR fans demonstrate fierce loyalty for their favorite drivers.

Steve Grissom (41), Mike Skinner (31), and John Andretti (98) jockey for position in close quarters at Pocono. Seeing drivers inches apart, at speeds approaching 200 mph, is one of the most exciting parts of NASCAR racing.

Jimmy Makar, Bobby Labonte's crew chief.

Ted Musgrave gets a little help from his friends as his car gets rolled out of the customized transport truck. ➤

Michael Waltrip is one half of the racing Waltrip brothers (older brother Darrell is the other).

◄ Pre-and post-race inspections are one of the key steps in every Winston Cup race as NASCAR officials try to make sure that everyone plays by the same set of rules.

Terry Labonte shares a moment with rival car owner Richard Childress. Most car owners are very actively involved at the track on race day.

Car owner Bud Moore relaxes in the garage area. Combine a three- or four-hour race with all the pre-race preparation and post-race packing up, and a day at the track can be a long one for the owners and team members.

Johnny Benson (No. 30) heads out of pit road just as Terry Labonte pulls in for a fresh set of tires and a full tank of gas. As a race nears its end, drivers try to sneak in for one final pit stop that will carry them to the finish line.

Jeff Gordon (in the DuPont car) clinches victory at the 1997 Daytona 500 as the yellow caution flag comes out on lap 196 of the 200-lap race. The caution lasted for the last four laps, giving team owner Rick Hendrick an unprecedented 1-2-3 sweep as Terry Labonte (the Corn Flakes car) and Ricky Craven (the Bud car) followed Gordon across the finish line.

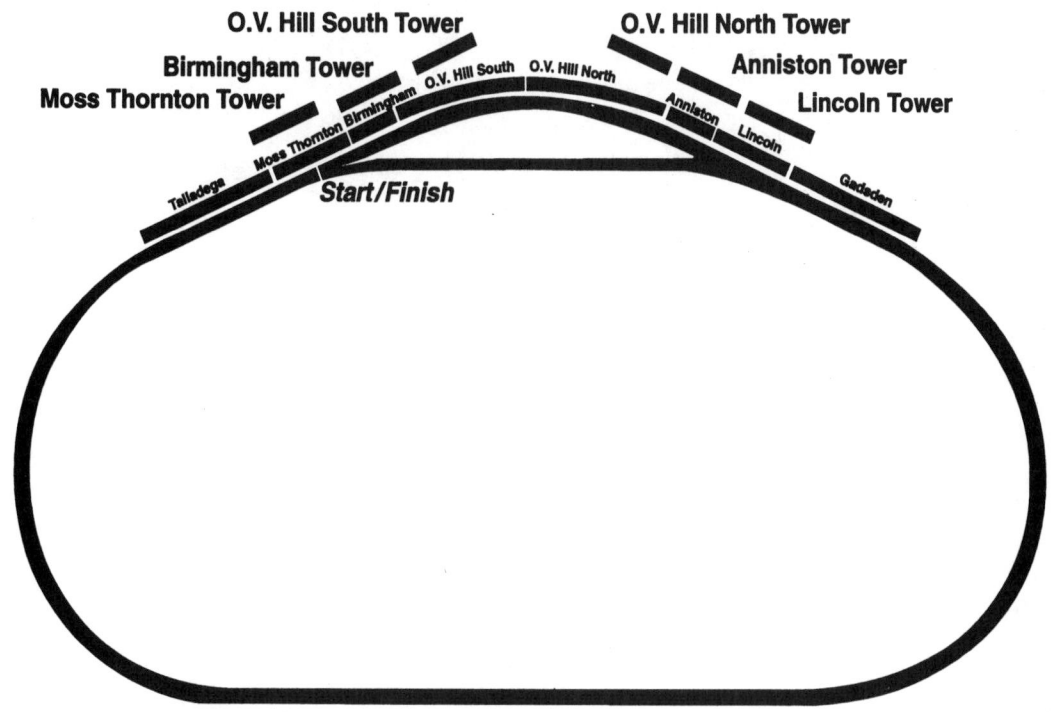

O.V. Hill South Tower
O.V. Hill North Tower
Birmingham Tower
Anniston Tower
Moss Thornton Tower
Lincoln Tower
O.V. Hill South
O.V. Hill North
Moss Thornton
Birmingham
Anniston
Lincoln
Talladega
Gadsden
Start/Finish

TALLADEGA SUPERSPEEDWAY

Talladega is the biggest, fastest, and most competitive motorsports venue in the world. In the days before restrictor plates, cars qualified at more than 212 mph at Talladega. Spectacular crashes were the order of the day, and several drivers were killed at the track. It is still the fastest track on the circuit. Mark Donohue set a world record of 221.160 for a close course at Talladega on Aug. 9, 1975; that mark stood until 1986, when Rick Mears broke it in an IndyCar at Michigan Speedway. In 1987, Bill Elliott established a world stock car speed record when he ran at 212.809 mph in qualifying for the Winston 500.

How to get there

Talladega Superspeedway is 40 miles east of Birmingham (take exit 168 on I-20), 90 miles west of Atlanta (take exit 173 on I-20), and 120 miles south of Chattanooga (take exit 181 on I-59 in Gadsen, then go south on Alabama 77 to Speedway Blvd.).

Who to contact

International Speedway Corp.
PO Box 777
Talladega, AL 35161
Phone: (205) 362-2261

Where to stay

For lodging information in Birmingham, call (800) 458-8085.

To order tickets

Call (205) 362-9064.

Things to do

The International Motorsports Hall of Fame & Museum is on the speedway grounds.

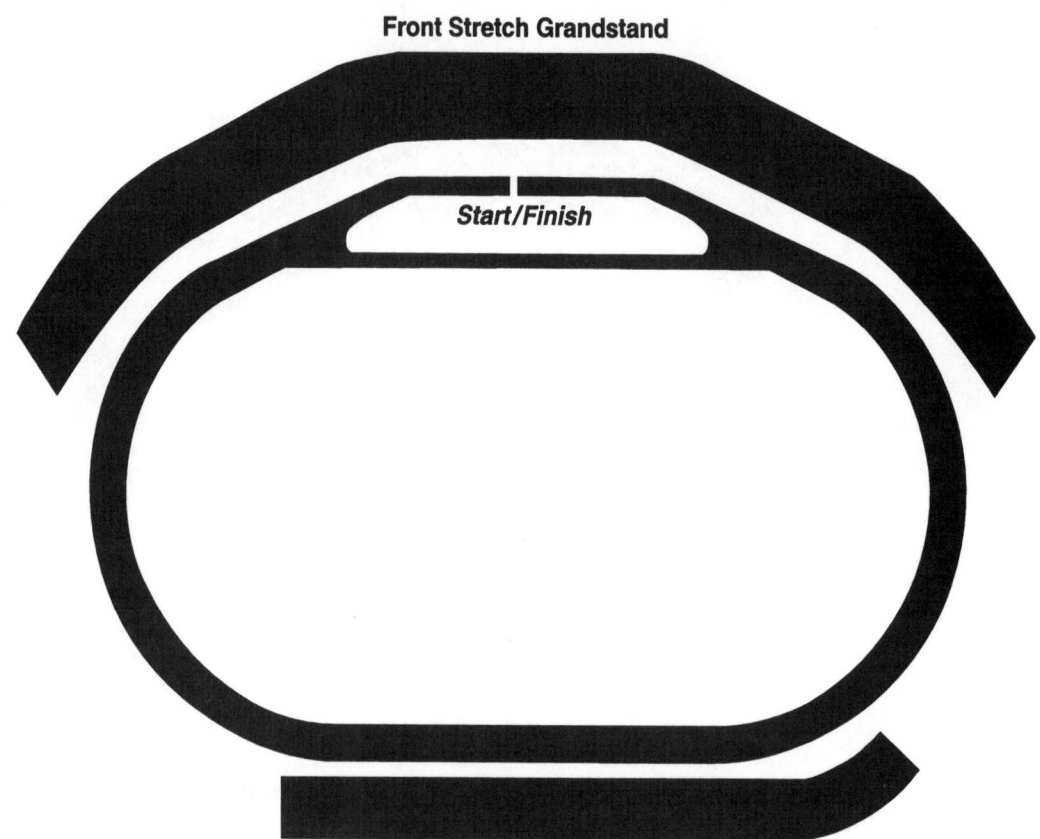

Front Stretch Grandstand

Start/Finish

Back Stretch Grandstand

TEXAS INTERNATIONAL RACEWAY

This 1½-mile trioval is patterned after Bruton Smith's original track, the Charlotte Motor Speedway. It features more than 150,000 seats, which makes it the second largest sporting venue in the country, behind the Indianapolis Motor Speedway. This, plus the track's unusual banking (8 degrees in its lower lanes and 24 in the high groove, with 5 degree banking in the straightaways) should make this a favorite track in years to come. Also features the one thing that every new arena must have, no matter what the sport—200 luxury suites. The track also has lights.

How to get there

Texas International Raceway is north of Fort Worth and west of Dallas/Fort Worth International Airport, at the intersection of I-35 and Texas 114.

Who to contact

Speedway Motorsports Inc.
PO Box 500
Fort Worth, TX 76101-2500
Phone: (817) 215-8500

Where to stay

Call Fort Worth Visitors Information at (888) 397-7333, or the Dallas Convention and Visitor's Bureau at (214) 746-6677.

To order tickets

Tickets are sold only through the mail. Write to: PO Box 500, Fort Worth, TX 76101.

Things to do

The Texas Motorplex, south of Dallas in Ennis, Texas, is host to two NHRA national events, and also holds run-what-you-brung bracket races every weekend.

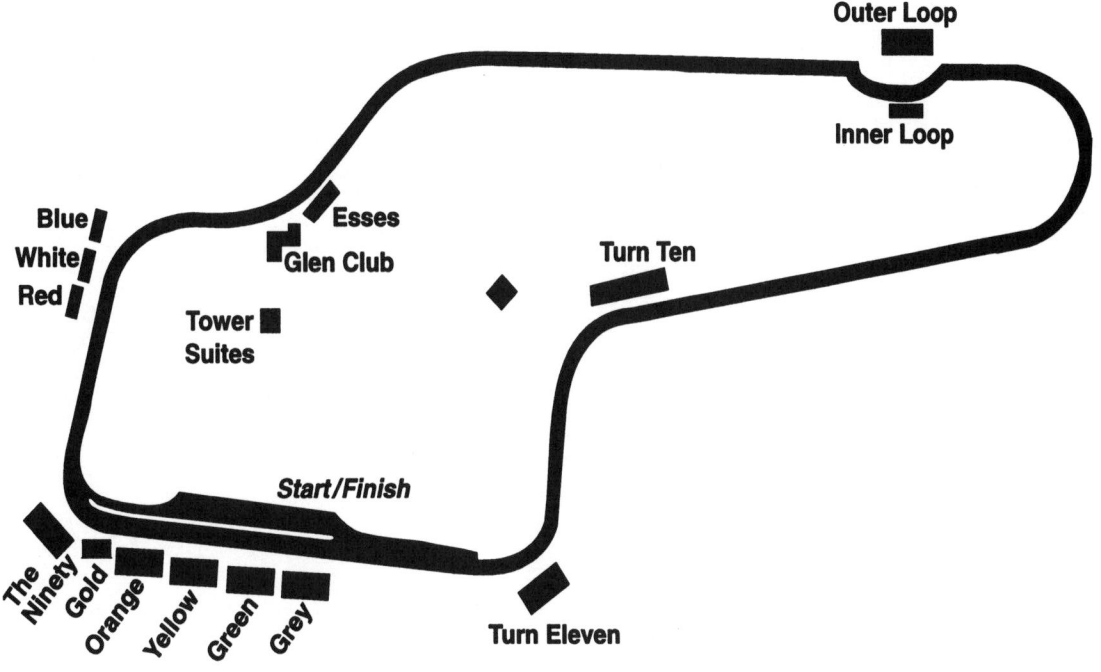

WATKINS GLEN INTERNATIONAL

Watkins Glen is the cradle of modern road racing. In 1948 Cameron Argetsinger, a law student, laid out a 6.6-mile course in and around the village of Watkins Glen at the foot of Lake Seneca. The race was moved to another spot outside of town in 1956, and was home to the U.S. Grand Prix for years. Now, Watkins Glen International hosts an annual Winston Cup weekend and a six-hour sports car endurance race. The NASCAR race is a unique experience for fans and drivers alike in that 7 of the course's 11 turns are right-hand turns, which is not the norm in NASCAR. Considered to be one of the best spectator tracks on the NASCAR circuit.

How to get there

The track is 18 miles northeast of Corning, New York, or five miles southwest of Watkins Glen. It is two miles west of New York Route 414 on County Route 16.

Who to contact

Co-owned by Corning Enterprises and the International Speedway Corp.

PO Box 500
Watkins Glen, NY 14891
Phone: (607) 535-2486

Where to stay

For lodging information, call the Chamber of Commerce at (800) 607-4552.

To order tickets

Call (607) 535-2481.

Things to do

The Walk of Fame in downtown Watkins Glen honors the history of the street and road racing circuits, and the Collier Brothers Memorial Alcove in the Watkins Glen Library has an extensive racing and automobile collection.

24

NASCAR NATION

Across the United States, on any given weekend throughout the racing season, NASCAR fans can be found cheering on their favorite driver, either in person or on televison. Perhaps no sport in America has fans that are so loyal and so knowledgeable about the sport. Some examples:

- On a cool, overcast early June afternoon, Julia Foster is sitting in a chair outside a camper in the infield at Pocono Raceway. Asked what she enjoys most about the races, Foster smiles and says, "Watching Jeff Gordon win."

  Foster is from Bethany, Pennsylvania, in the northeast corner of the state. Born in England, Foster has been in the United States for 10 years. Her friend, Jimmy Bates, is a Bill Elliott fan. Bates drives a truck for a construction company; Foster works in advertising.

  Explaining how she became interested in racing, Foster said, "I watched a race or two with Jimmy and got into it. When I call England, I tell them, 'Watch it!' In England, the football (soccer) fans can be dangerous. Here, people like different drivers, but they joke with you about it. They all get along."

- Danny Massengill has been attending races since 1964. His first race was at Charlotte, when Glenn "Fireball" Roberts, one of NASCAR's legendary drivers, was killed.

  Massengill's business also keep him in touch with racing fans and teams. He operates a convenience store and Phillips 66 service center just off Exit 90 of Interstate 95, halfway between the Virginia and South Carolina borders. "We sell a lot of NASCAR products here," he said.

  Massengill, 48, attends up to five races a year: the two at North Carolina Motor Speedway in Rockingham, plus Richmond, Martinsville and, sometimes, Daytona. He has a collection of eight millimeter movies he has filmed of races as far back as the early 1970s.

  Although he worries about the rising cost of tickets and the difficulty in getting good seats, Massengill enjoys racing as much as he ever did. "When they race side by side, it's as exciting for me now as it was 20 years ago," he said. "The smell of the racetrack and the noise: it's just something that makes your blood pump harder in your veins."

Massengill's favorite driver is Dale Earnhardt. During Earnhardt's 0-for-1997 slump, Massengill never lost faith in Earnhardt.

Although Richard Petty is a fellow North Carolinian, Massengill was never a fan of "The King." Said Massengill: "I never liked him as a driver because I liked Cale Yarborough and Bobby Allison. But as a person, I liked Richard. I supported him when he ran for (North Carolina) Secretary of State. I paid $125 for a plate of barbecue (as a Petty fund raiser)."

• Tom Foster is another loyal racing fan from the South: Taylors, South Carolina, to be precise. Foster, 58, has missed only one race at venerable Darlington Raceway in 25 years. He had a good reason for missing that one race: he had suffered a stroke.

"I got out of the hospital the Sunday before the race," recalled the former field representative for Proctor and Gamble. "I asked the doctor if I could go to the race the next Sunday, and he said, 'Absolutely not.'"

Foster and his wife, Christine, enjoy the family atmosphere at Darlington's races. The Fosters have parked their camper in the same place outside the track for 25 years. They are joined by friends from North Carolina and Virginia. "The lady that owns the park always has a barbecue," Foster said. "Everybody in the park brings a covered dish."

FROM SEA TO SHINING SEA

Across the country, there are hundreds of thousands of more fans like the Fosters and Massengill. They fill the grandstands and infields at racetracks from California to New Hampshire, from Michigan to Florida. These fans are attracted by the speed, the noise, and atmosphere of NASCAR races. Tour any racetrack and you'll see families spending time together. You'll also see women: 40 percent of NASCAR fans are women.

The infield scene at most racetracks is basically the same: people arrive in campers and motor homes two or three days ahead of a race. Frequently, you'll see colorfully painted school buses that groups use for the weekend. These fans, like those in the campers and motor homes, bring their own food, soft drinks, and beer and enjoy the outdoors. There are still areas in infields and places outside racetracks where a man wouldn't want his wife or daughter to roam unescorted. But generally, the crowds at races are well behaved. You'll see youngsters and adults tossing frisbees and footballs. And you never know what you'll discover in the infield: at the September race at New Hampshire International Speedway in 1997, Dawn Urquhart, a nurse manager at the University of Rochester Medical Center, brought along her family *and* the family pets, four parrots and four dogs. "We call it the petting zoo," Urquhart said.

At the first Winston Cup race at the California Speedway in 1997, Robert Mixon made the trip from Texas. He paid $50 for an infield parking space, and immediately made friends. "Nice track, nice folks out here," he said. Nearby, Trent Kyllo of Denver was praising the facilities and the fans behavior at the Roger Penske-owned track. "When it came time to be quiet (between midnight and 6 a.m.), everyone was quiet except for the people doing the course work," he said.

Harry F. Stone III, a Johnson County, Texas resident, points out that staying in the infield solves the traffic headache: getting in and out of a racetrack at a Winston Cup race can take hours. "It's much more comfortable to spend the night out there where you don't have to fight traffic every day," said Stone, a trucking company owner. "Plus, you get to meet a bunch of good people who become your neighbors."

Infield parking at the new Texas Motor Speedway costs between $350 and $800 for a season pass. The most sought after spots along the backstretch cost $800. "Probably your most die-hard fans are in the infield," said Bill Young, owner of an oil-related business in Wichita, Kansas. "You're right in the middle of the action." Young flies an Earnhardt flag from his motor home.

Robert James has been attending races at Darlington since the 1960s. James, 50, is an operator in a textile mill. He lives in Hartsville, South Carolina, only a 20-minute ride from Darlington.

"Fonty Flock used to drive with one hand," James recalled. "He'd have his other arm out the window, with a cigar in his hand. Back then, you were a Chevrolet man, or a Ford man. You pulled for the car, not the driver. The rivalries were like (South) Carolina-Clemson, Alabama-Auburn, or Florida-Florida State (in football)."

James's favorite drivers are Earnhardt and Jeff Gordon. "I don't like (Rusty) Wallace or (Geoff) Bodine," he said. With his son, Brian and his friends, James watches the races from the infield Azalea Terrace in the third turn at Darlington. "My brother, Allen, talked me into going to the infield,"

James said. "It was rough at first; now, it's not as bad as it used to be."

Prior to Hurricane Hugo in 1989, James sat in box seats at Darlington. After the hurricane destroyed some of the grandstands, James moved to what he termed "decent seats. But I couldn't handle it: I weigh 250 pounds. You sit shoulder to shoulder. There was no room for a cooler, and people were continually getting up to go to the bathroom."

Keith Parker, a UPS supervisor who lives in Greensboro, North Carolina, began attending races in the mid 1980s. He has been to races at Charlotte, Rockingham, Darlington, and Martinsvlle. "The personalities and the competition between General Motors and Ford appeal to me," said Parker, a

Full grandstands like this one at Pocono Raceway are common at NASCAR races.

Chevrolet fan. Jeff Gordon, Dale Earnhardt, and Ken Schrader are Parker's favorite drivers. Gordon and Earnhardt were central figures in three of Parker's most memorable races. "One year at Martinsville, Earnhardt was hit from behind, spun 360 degrees and only lost one place," Parker said. "I was at Charlotte when Gordon won his first race, and I was at Darlington when he won the Winston Million."

Joe Garrett, a self-employed carpenter from Abingdon, Virginia, and his wife, Jean, have attended every race at Charlotte since the speedway opened in 1960. Joe spent 25 years serving on the rescue squad at Bristol Motor Speedway. His most memorable race was the 1964 event at Charlotte when Fireball Roberts was killed. "I hate to see people wreck, but that race sticks in my mind because of (Ned) Jarrett's true display of heroism and bravery," Garrett said. After Roberts's car crashed and exploded, Jarrett, now a NASCAR television commentator, parked his car and tried to free Roberts. "That isn't my favorite race," Garrett said. "It's just one that I won't ever forget."

It was easy to tell that Matthew Baum is a racing fan: outside the north grandstand at Dover Downs International Speedway in Delaware, Baum was carrying a scanner and headphones to listen to the pit crews as they talked to their drivers during the race. Baum, from York, Pennsylvania, has been attending Winston Cup races at Dover and Pocono for the last 10 years. He's an Earnhardt fan; his son,

Fans aren't shy about showing who they like and, in this case, don't like.

Devlin, 16, is a Rusty Wallace fan. The bearded Baum was wearing a black Earnhardt T-shirt and jeans. For Baum, racing's appeal is "the speed and the competition, on the track and in the pits."

Baum, a welder for the Harley Davidson Co. in York, worries that NASCAR might be getting too popular. Nodding toward the white limousines parked nearby, he said, "Tracks like North Wilkesboro are the heart and soul of racing. They can build tracks like Texas as big as they want, but they won't compare to a Dover."

Debbie and Diane Nelson, from Old Bridge, New Jersey, are among NASCAR's 35 to 40 percent female fans. Said Debbie, prior to a race at Dover: "I like the sound, the colors. It's a great rush. Another thing that makes it fun is, we know someone on Michael Waltrip's crew."

It is not uncommon to see colorful renovated buses in the infields at Winston Cup races. Instead of carrying students, they are renovated to make room for food and cooking equipment, beverages, television sets, and perhaps sleeping quarters. The bright red "Pocono Princess" makes an appearance every summer at Pocono Raceway. The bus is a project organized by some men from the Lehighton Fire Company. Tim Beers (how's that for a racing fan's name?), who keeps the bus in the off-season, said the Princess also is used for Christmas caroling. Beers said the group includes carpenters, welders, and prison guards.

The track infield is the place to be for on- and off-track action.

WHO WATCHES NASCAR?

NASCAR fans are everywhere and they come from different backgrounds. Data gathered by Performance Research, in Newport, Rhode Island, shows that 81 percent of NASCAR fans own their owns homes and 73 percent are married. The most common income bracket for fans is $35,000 to $50,000 (26 percent). The next most common bracket is $50,000 to $75,000 (22 percent). Research also shows that 42 percent of NASCAR fans are high school graduates, 18 percent are college graduates (27 percent have attended college).

Although there are no Winston Cup races in Connecticut, Charlie Mordenti, Dave Cronin and Lenny Dorosh are fans. They grew up attending races at Connecticut short tracks. Since 1985, they've been attending races at Dover. Mordenti, from Oakville, Connecticut, likes "the speed, the sound, the smells." And, he added, "The people are friendly." He also likes the drivers because "they give their time to charities, and they don't charge for autographs."

Weekends at the races allow these fans in their 30s and 40s to act young again. Said Dorosh: "We get together and make fools of ourselves. We've been going to races since before we were married. Now, the races are my getaway. My wife asks, 'When are you leaving?'"

Dover Downs seems to be a popular getaway weekend for people from Connecticut. Parked near each other for last September's race were Houston Vaughn and his family, from New Britain, Connecticut, and the Bourgoins, from Cromwell, Connecticut. The Vaughns and Bourgoins don't know each other, but they have two likes in common: racing and the outdoors.

Relaxing in the shade under an awning at his motor home parked outside the racetrack, Houston Vaughn, 50, said he and the family attend about six races a year. "I've been going to races since I was five," said Houston, a machinist. "We've been coming here for 14 years." The Vaughns — wife, Sandra, and sons Steven and Houston Jr. — bring motorbikes, enabling them to leave the racetrack area and visit restaurants and shopping malls.

Racegoers pay $40 to park their mobile homes at Dover for the weekend. The Vaughns watch the races from the top row of the grandstands in Turn 4. They said they have relatives who also attend the races at Dover, but they rarely see each other on a race weekend. That's understandable when there are more than 100,000 people on the site for a race.

At the Bourgoin motor home, Diane was sitting in the sun while Roger was in the shade keeping an eye on their dog, Toby, a miniature collie. Roger's brother, Don, also was enjoying the sun. The Bourgoins attend races at Dover, New Hampshire and Daytona. They also watch every Winston Cup race on television. Diane, a mail courier, is a Jeff Gordon fan. Hearing Gordon's name, Don looked at her, smiled and said loudly, "Earnhardt! She's new to this: she's still learning." Roger said Toby the collie is a Mark Martin fan.

Kris and Pierre Pearson were among the 150,000 fans at the inaugural Winston Cup race at Texas Motor Speedway near Fort Worth in April last year. The couple, from New Hampton, Iowa, attend two to three races a year. They enjoy the speed, the noise and the fans. "Ninety percent of the fans are nice and easy to get along with," Kris said. Kris manages a J.C. Penney catalog store in New Hampton; Pierre is a truck driver. Said Kris: "I'm a Dale Earnhardt fan: I get very verbal."

Larry and Kathy Sarnecki didn't have far to travel to attend the first Winston Cup race last April at the Texas Motor Speedway. The Sarneckis are from nearby Arlington. "I've always liked automobiles and racing," Larry said. The Sarneckis lived outside of Chicago before moving to Texas. "I like the sound and the excitement: to see them racing side-by-side at 190 miles an hour is exciting," Larry said. "Plus, the drivers seem like decent people." Larry has raced go-karts with his sons. Said Kathy: "I'm getting to be a fan."

Gathered outside a motor home at TMS were Deborah and John Ticer and Rhonda and Steve Horton. Although it was several hours before the race, this group was getting in a racing mood. Deborah was smoking a cigar, and the others were sipping cold beverages.

Deborah, from Midland, Texas, said she likes racing "because you can feel the power of the cars in your chest. It's fast, loud, exciting, and safe." Rhonda said she appreciates the accessibility of the drivers. "When the drivers are here, they make themselves available," she said. "I have a jacket autographed by (the late) Alan Kulwicki and Davey Allison. Every driver I asked to sign the jacket did it." Deborah also likes the friendliness of the drivers. "They're not like the Cowboys," she said.

The Ticers and the Hortons enjoy the social aspects of attending races. They've been to Phoenix and Indianapolis. "NASCAR fans are the best," said Steve. "Indy car fans are snooty."

Later in the summer, the Hortons experienced what it's like to hurry around a racetrack in a Winston Cup car. When a driving school from North Carolina visited Texas Motor Speedway, Rhonda and Steve each took a ride with an instructor behind the wheel. "Once you've gone around a banked track at 150 miles an hour, you get a new feeling for what the drivers do," Rhonda said.

The Interstate Batteries 500 at Texas had attracted Dr. Mark Altgelt, a retired dentist, and his family to their first race. On Sunday morning, they were relaxing in chairs outside their motor home. "I love cars," said Mark. "I've driven some (sports cars). I've watched a lot of NASCAR and drag racing on TV. NASCAR has a lot of appeal because the cars don't look like computers with four tires. I enjoy watching the efficiency in the pits."

Marty Dunn, from Stony Point, New York, is standing behind the grandstands at Pocono Raceway, watching his 3-year-old son pile stones into a Ricky Craven hat. From the top row of the stands, a couple loudmouth fans are screaming at Jeff Gordon, calling him a "bum." Says Dunn: "I like Gordon, but I don't wear his hat because I don't want it to look like I'm on his bandwagon." Dunn is wearing a Kyle Petty charity tour hat. Dunn's brother, Jimmy, is an Earnhardt fan.

Dunn, a public utility worker, has been to Winston Cup races at Charlotte and Bristol, Tennessee. "I'm a drag racing fan, and I like racing at

the local dirt tracks," he says. For Winston Cup racing, Dunn chooses a couple teams and follows them for the year. "It's like following a baseball team," he says.

Dave Nagy also is training some young racing fans. Nagy, an auto worker from Normal, Illinois, brought his sons, David, 6, and Danny, 5, to the Brickyard 400 at Indianapolis Motor Speedway. Dad is an Earnhardt fan: he was wearing a black Earnhardt shirt and a black Earnhardt bandana under his hat. "When the boys were babies," Nagy said, "we woke up to feed them at 2 o'clock in the morning and watched replays of the races on ESPN. That's how they became fans."

Fans are from all walks of life: name the profession, blue-collar or white-collar, and you'll probably find NASCAR fans. Glenn Kenton, an attorney with Richards, Layton and Finger in Wilmington, Delaware, grew up in downstate Delaware. He was aware of NASCAR through the races at Dover Downs. But it wasn't until the Du Pont Co. hit the jackpot by sponsoring Jeff Gordon that Kenton started attending races. He has spent time in Gordon's pits, and has access to the Du Pont suite at Dover Downs. However, the former Delaware Secretary of State prefers watching the races from outside the suite. That's where he can experience what Denis McGlynn, president of Dover Downs, describes as a major appeal of Winston Cup racing: "Until you have the cars come by you at 170 miles an hour and suck the air out of your lungs and make your bones vibrate, you can't really appreciate what the physical experience is of watching a car race." Despite NASCAR's soaring popularity, Kenton says many of his friends haven't caught the racing fever. Smiling like an insider, Kenton says, "They still don't get it."

Jim McGovern, a Mark Martin fan, has been attending races at Dover Downs and Pocono since the 1970s. "I started when the Indy-car circuit raced at Langhorne (Pennsylvania), Trenton (New Jersey) and Pocono," said McGovern, a composing-room worker at the *Philadelphia Daily News and Inquirer.* "When the Indy cars stopped coming to Pocono, a friend got me interested in going to Dover, and I enjoyed it." To McGovern, who also officiates high school football games, the appeal of racing is the cars. "Stock cars are an American tradition," he said. "Most of the fans grew up around cars: they worked on them before they became so sophisticated."

Souvenir sales at Winston Cup races are similar to other sports: T-shirts, hats and jackets representing drivers and racetracks are available. Among the most unusual items on sale at tracks are tires. Used tires.

Billy Ladd, from North Wilkesboro, North Carolina, sells used tires at Texas Motor Speedway. "We come here with 400 tires, and we'll sell every one of them." Ladd doesn't wonder what his customers do with the tires. "As long as they give me $20, I don't care what they do with them," he said.

25

RESOURCES

NASCAR ON FILM

Movies

The Big Wheel (1949) Old story retold fairly well. Rooney is a young son determined to travel in his father's tracks as a race car driver, even when dad buys the farm on the oval. Good acting and direction keep this a cut above average.★★

Car Crash (19??) Organized crime hits stock car racing head on to produce crashing bore.★

Days of Thunder (1990) "Top Gun" in race cars! Cruise follows the same formula he has followed for several years now (with the notable exception of "Born on the Fourth of July.") Cruise and Towne co-wrote the screenplay concerning a young kid bursting with talent and raw energy who must learn to deal with his mentor, his girlfriend, and eventually the bad guy. First film that featured cameras that were actually on the race cars. If you like Cruise or race cars then this is the movie for you. ★★

Eat My Dust (1976) Teenage son of a California sheriff steals the best stock cars from a race track to take the town's heartthrob for a joy ride. Subsequently he leads the town on a wild car chase. Brainless but fast-paced.★★

Grandview U.S.A. (1984) A low-key look at low-rent middle America, centering on a foxy local speedway owner and the derby-obsessed boys she attracts. Pre-"Dirty Dancing" choreography from Patrick Swayze and wife Lisa Niemi.★★

Greased Lightning (1977) The story of the first black auto racing champion, Wendell Scott, who had to overcome racial prejudice to achieve his success. Slightly-better-than-average Pryor comedy vehicle.★★★

The Last American Hero (1973) The true story of how former moonshine runner Junior Johnson became one of the fastest race car drivers in the history of the sport. Entertaining slice of life chronicling whiskey running and stock car racing, with Bridges superb in the lead. Based on a series of articles written by Tom Wolfe.★★★

Red Line (1996) Stock-car racer Jim (Chad McQueen) loses his sponsorship, turns to petty crime to settle his debts, and winds up in trouble with the mob when he hooks up with a couple of hoods to steal some diamonds.★

Red Line 7000 (1965) High stakes auto racers drive hot cars and date pretty women. Excellent racing footage in an otherwise routine four-wheel fest. ★★

Richard Petty Story (1972) The biography of race car driver Petty, played by himself, and his various achievements on the track. ★

Six Pack (1982) The Gambler goes auto racing. Kenny Rogers, in his theatrical debut, stars as Brewster Baker, a former stock car driver. He returns to the racing circuit with the help of six larcenous orphans (the six-pack, get it?) adept at stripping cars. Kinda cute if you're in the mood for sugar-powered race car story. ★

Speedway (1968) Elvis the stock car driver finds himself being chased by Nancy (Sinatra) the IRS agent during an important race. Will Sinatra keep to the business at hand? Or will the King melt her heart? Some cameos by real-life auto racers, including Richard Petty and Cale Yarborough. Watch for a young Terri Garr. Movie number 27 for Elvis. ★★

Stroker Ace (1983) Flamboyant stock car driver tries to break an iron-clad promotional contract signed with a greedy fried-chicken magnate. Off duty, he ogles blondes as dopey as he is. One of the worst from Burt Reynolds—and that's saying something. ★

Documentaries

A.J. Foyt: Champion for Life

Release Date: 199?
Run Time: 55
Description: A biography of race-car driver Foyt, whose career almost ended his life in 1990. Includes racing footage from Indy, Daytona, and LeMans as well as interviews with Foyt's friends and family.

All-American Crashes

Release Date: 1990
Run Time: 60
Description: See the most gut-wrenching racing crashes in history.

BUDDY'S BIG SCENE

Let the record show there's never been a good movie about stock race racing. (Well, *Thunder in Carolina* with Rory Calhoun and Alan Hale comes close, although it is not currently available on video). The list of embarrassing mediocrity stretches from *Days of Thunder* to *Speedway*, from *The Last American Hero* to *Greased Lightning*, and from *Six Pack* to *Stroker Ace* or *Redline 7,000*.

But there's been one unforgettable line in all those flops, and it came from Buddy Baker (playing himself) in the otherwise forgettable *The Richard Petty Story*.

It was delivered during a scene in which Baker and Richard Petty were confronted by the dastardly villain the night before The Big Race. After issuing an "I'll get you" threat to Petty, the villain turned on his heels and strode away, confident he's made his point and feeling oh, so good about himself.

At which point Baker deadpanned his famous line in his unmistakable voice about two octaves above soprano: "He makes me so mad I could just spit."

So he did.

The Art of Speed

Release Date: 1991
Run Time: 50
Description: Documentary of the car racing legend Richard Petty. Included are interviews with his family and footage of numerous racing highlights since the early days of the sport.

Beyond the Finish Line, Vol. 1 and 2

Release Date: 1988
Run Time: 54
Description: A host of racing legends are featured, including the likes of Bill Stroppe, Parnelli Jones, Jack Roush, Bob Glidden, Mark Oswald, Pete Halsmer, Steve Saleen, Robert Yates, Bill Elliott, Richard Petty and many more.

Bill Elliot: Racing into History

Release Date: 1988
Run Time: 45
Description: An overview of Elliot's career from his beginnings in 1976 to his 1988 Winston Cup Championship season. Includes interviews with Elliot, his family and his crew.

Champions of the Checkered Flag

Release Date: 1990
Run Time: 30
Description: A look behind the scenes at two stock car racing heroes, Geoff Bodine and Greg Sacks.

Circuit

Release Date: 1985
Run Time: 90
Description: A documentary look at the world of high speed racing, with interviews with drivers and lots of high-speed track footage.

Crash & Burn

Release Date: 1990
Run Time: ?
Description: It's thrills, spills and chills from racing's greatest crashes and flips.

A Crash Course in Racing

Release Date: 1990
Run Time: 48
Description: Hosted by A.J. Foyt, four time Indy winner; with Phil Parsons, Harry Gant, and Benny Parsons. Learn first hand how to be a more informed racing fan. See 14 of the most dramatic crashes in NASCAR history. Learn how to spot wrecks before they happen, why hand signals at 200 mph save lives, and how television cameras can help you pick a winner.

Darrell Waltrip Explains NASCAR Racing

Release Date: 1987
Run Time: 30
Description: An instruction in stock car racing from the champ of the Grand National Stock Car race circuit.

Daytona: Drama, Danger and Dedication

Release Date: 1991
Run Time: 90
Description: Racing legends like Cale Yarborough, Bill Elliot and Richard Petty discuss the best of the Daytona 500 from 1979 through 1991.

The Daytona 500: 1971

Release Date: 1971
Run Time: 30
Description: A classic auto race in which the lead changes more than twenty times, with six cars running nose to tail at 200 m.p.h.

Driven by a Dream

Release Date: 1990
Run Time: 28
Description: In May of 1983, stock car racer Phil Parsons was almost killed after 14 flips at over 200 m.p.h. Five years later, he won at that very same track. An insider's view of what it takes to make it in stock car racing.

Driven to Excellence

Release Date: 199?
Run Time: ?
Description: Examines why automobile racing is so popular.

Hard Drivin'

Release Date: 1960
Run Time: 92
Description: Rowdy action featuring Southern stock car drivers with well shot race scenes from the Southern 500.

Legends: The Statesmen of the Racing World

Release Date: 1994
Run Time: 30
Description: Profiles NASCAR drivers Ned Jarrett and "Fearless Freddie" Lorenzen.

Making of "Days of Thunder": NASCAR Goes to Hollywood

Release Date: 1991

Run Time: 40
Description: See how the exciting race scenes were filmed in "Days of Thunder" in this fast-paced documentary.

The NASCAR Story, Volume One: From Thunder Road to Victory Lane: 1947 - 1958

Run Time: 65
Description Covers the origins of stock car racing, from the early races on the beach at Daytona to the first NASCAR supersrtars, such as the Flock brothers and Lee Petty.

The NASCAR Story, Volume Two: Superstars and Superspeedways: 1959–1971

Run Time: 65
Description Covers the birth of Daytona International Speedway, races at Darlington and Martinsville, and historical footage of NASCAR greats Junior Johnson, Bud Moore, Ned Jarrett, and Richard Petty.

The NASCAR Story, Volume Three: Four Star Battle for the Winston Cup: 1972 - 1979

Run Time: 65
Description Covers the beginning of NASCAR's "Modern Era" in 1972 and highlights four of the best drivers of all-time: Richard Petty, David Pearson, Bobby Allison, and Cale Yarborough. Includes coverage of the famous Petty-Allison feud and Yarborough's record three straight Winston Cup championships.

The NASCAR Story, Volume Four: The Thunder Rolls On: 1980 - 1994

Run Time: 65
Description Covers the start of Dale Earnhardt's career, Richard Petty's 200th career win, Bill Elliott's Winston Million, and the rise and tragic fall of Tim Richmond, Alan Kulwicki, and Davey Allison.

NASCAR Video: Alan Kulwicki: Champion of Dreams

Release Date: 1994
Run Time: 30

Description: Tribute to Winston cup champion Kulwicki who died in May, 1993. Details the story of his career from his rookie of the year status in 1986 to his work with sponsors and other personal moments. Little on-the-track action.

The NASCAR Video: Collector's Series, Vol. 1

Release Date: 1991
Run Time: 60
Description: This volume of the racing history series looks at Daytona's beginnings, profiles Richard Petty and Dale Earnhardt, offers driving tips and much more.

The NASCAR Video: Collector's Series, Vol. 2

Release Date: 1991
Run Time: 60
Description: Volume two of NASCAR's video magazine. This issue focuses on the top ten drivers of all time, profiles driver Ernie Irvan and much more.

The NASCAR Video: Collector's Series, Vol. 3

Release Date: 1991
Run Time: 60
Description: This volume of the series looks at what it means to own your own race car, profiles women drivers, looks at Joe Weatherly and Chad Little, offers racing tips and much more.

The '93 NASCAR Year in Review

Run Time: 70
Description Recaps the 1993 Winston Cup season, including race footage from every race. Covers Dale Earnhardt's sixth Winston Cup title and the untimely deaths of Alan Kulwicki and Davey Allison.

The '94 NASCAR Year in Review

Run Time: 70
Description Recaps the 1994 Winston Cup season, including race footage from every race. Covers Dale Earnhardt's record-tying seventh Winston Cup championship and the inaugural Brickyard 400.

Dale Earnhardt heads into the pits with the back end of his car a little worse for wear.

The '95 NASCAR Year in Review

Run Time: 70
Description Recaps the 1995 Winston Cup season, including race footage from every race. Covers Jeff Gordon's first Winston Cup Championship.

The '96 NASCAR Year in Review

Run Time: 70
Description Recaps the 1996 Winston Cup season, including race footage from all 31 races. Covers Terry Labonte's second Winston Cup championship.

Popular Mechanics: 20 Great Stock-Car Finishes

Release Date: 1990

Description: Rare footage of classic races is supplemented by a close-up look at the mechanics of winning cars.

Record Breaking

Release Date: 1991
Run Time: 23
Description: Sam Posey hosts this look at record breaking auto speeds by A.J. Foyt and other racing greats.

Richard Petty

Release Date: 1991
Run Time: 30
Description: The legend of stock car racing is

ALL IN THE FAMILY

Few sports instill in its competitors and fans the same sense of family and community and togetherness as stock car racing. The reasons are many and varied, but perhaps none as important as this: since each driver routinely places his life in the hands of others, there forms an indelible bond that may sometimes be bent, but hardly ever breaks.

As much as anything, that sense of family explains why hardly anyone raised a serious fuss when CBS-TV let former two-time NASCAR champion Ned Jarrett unashamedly root on his son, Dale, in the final laps of the 1993 Daytona 500 at the Daytona International Speedway.

The elder Jarrett's over-the-air call of the final laps will stand for all time as a tribute not only to the moment itself, but to the special relationship between motorsports and its ever-expanding generations of fans.

"Come on, Dale. Go, baby, go. Alright! Come on.

"I know he's got it to the floorboard; he can't do any more.

"Come on.

"Take her to the inside; don't let 'em get to the inside of you coming around this turn.

"Here he comes, Earnhardt.

"It's the Dale and Dale show as they come off Turn 4.

"You know who I'm pulling for, it's Dale Jarrett.

"Bring her to the inside, Dale; don't let him get down there.

"He's gonna make it.

"Dale Jarrett's gonna win the Daytona 500.

"Alright!

"Oh, look at Martha. Oh, dear, can you believe it?

"Oh, man."

---

honored here through interviews and footage from his many victories.

Rusty Wallace: In the Driver's Seat

Run Time: 70
Description Ride along with Rusty Wallace for an inside look at life in the high speed world of NASCAR. Includes exclusive behind-the-scenes looks at life in the pits and in a Winston Cup garage.

Southern 500 Auto Race, 1963-1979

Release Date: 198?
Run Time: 30
Description: The highlights and on-location reports of the Southern 500 auto races from 1963 to 1979 are presented in these seventeen individual programs.

Sports Hour #20

Release Date: 198?
Run Time: 56
Description: "Time Crunch," a documentary about the 1972 Indy 500, is featured with partici-

pants such as Andy Granatelli. "Faces of Racing" is also included, with the likes of Cale Yarborough, Parnelli Jones, Dan Gurney and A.J. Foyt.

Stock Car Memories: Darlington— Southern 500

Release Date: 1955
Run Time: 55
Description: Vintage racing footage pitting the independents against the factory teams and featuring racing greats like Herb Thomas, Buck Baker, Tim & Fonty Flock and Fireball Roberts, among others.

Stock Cars Grow Up: NASCAR

Release Date: 1959
Run Time: 55
Description: The history of road racing from the 1930s to the 1960s. Includes exciting race footage with the biggest pileup in automotive history and clips featuring Cotton Owens, Fred Lorenzen, Joe Weatherly and more.

Terry Labonte: Turning Iron Into Gold

Run Time: 45

Description Covers Terry Labonte's 1996 championship season in complete detail, including interviews with Labonte and exclusive home movie footage. Also covers his memorable side-by-side victory lap with his brother Bobby in Atlanta.

The Top Ten Drivers of All Time

Release Date: 19??

Description: Part of the NASCAR Collector's Series, hosted by Benny Parson. Top ten drivers in the history of Stock Car racing talk about some of their greatest racing moments.

A Week in the Life of a Race Team

Release Date: 19??

Description: Part of the NASCAR Collector's Series. Highlights the teamwork and dedication needed by a race team to be successful in NASCAR Winston Cup Competition. Follows the activities of a Winston Cup racing team.

NASCAR IN PRINT

Books

Assael, Shaun. *Wide Open: Days & Nights on the Nascar Tour.* Ballantine Books, Inc., February 1998.

Benson, Michael. *Stock Car Spectacular.* Random House Value Publishing, Inc., March 1995.

Berggren, Dick. *Stock Car Racing.* Smithmark Publishers, Inc., June 1995.

Bledsoe, Jerry. *The World's Number One, Flat-Out, All-Time Great, Stock Car Racing Book.* Down Home Press, February 1995.

Bodine, Geoff. *NASCAR for Dummies.* IDG Books Worldwide, April 1998.

Bongard, Tim. *Richard Petty: The Cars of King: The Story of Richard Petty's & the Development of Stock Racing in America.* Sagamore Publishing, Inc., September 1997.

Breslauer, Ken. *Stock Car Racing Collectibles: Fifty Years of NASCAR Memorabilia.* David Bull Publishing, Inc., November 1997.

Buchanan, Keith. *Stock Car Trivia Encyclopedia: The ABC's of Racing!* Premium Press America, April 1996.

Buchanan, Lee. *NASCAR Racing Strategies & Secrets.* Sybex, Inc., October 1995.

Burt, Bill. *Behind the Scenes at NASCAR.* Motorbooks International, Publishers & Wholesalers, March 1997.

Craft, John. *The Anatomy & Development of the Stock Car.* Motorbooks International, Publishers & Wholesalers, December 1993.

Craft, John. *Legends of Stock Car Racing.* Motorbooks International, Publishers & Wholesalers, July 1995.

Dregni, Michael. *Stock Car Racing.* Capstone Press, Inc., January 1994.

Dregni, Michael. *Stock Car Racing.* Children's Press, 1994.

Dunter, Don. *American Stock Car Racers & Portraits of NASCAR Greats.* Motorbooks International, Publishers & Wholesalers, October 1997.

Emanuel, Dave F. *The Buick Stage II V-6 Racing Engine: The Complete Preparation Guide for NASCAR, Grand National, & Short Track Racing.* Performance Publishing, November 1987.

Emmons, Bob. *Building the Hobby Stock-Street Stock Car.* Steve Smith Autosports, November 1979.

Fielden, Greg. *The Stock Car Racing Encyclopedia.* Macmillan Publishing Company, Inc., January 1997.

Freeman, Criswell. *Book of Stock Car Wisdom.* Walnut Grove Press, 1996.

Gaillard, Frye. *Kyle at 200 M.P.H.: A Sizzling Season in the Petty-NASCAR Dynasty.* Saint Martin's Press, Inc., May 1995.

Garrison, Joe. *Dirt Stock Car Fabrication & Preparation.* Steve Smith Autosports, May 1996.

Gilliam, Mark. *Racin' : The NASCAR Winston Cup Stock Car Racing Series.* Howell Press, April 1989.

Golenbock, Peter. *American Zoom: Stock Car Racing From the Dirt Tracks to Daytona.* Macmillan Publishing Company, Inc., September 1994.

Hagstrom, Robert G. Jr. *The Nascar Way.* John Wiley & Sons, Inc., February 1998.

Howell, Mark D. *From Moonshine to Madison Avenue: A Cultural History of the NASCAR Winston Cup Series.* Bowling Green University Popular Press, June 1997.

Huff, Richard M. *Behind the Wall: New Edition Captures Terry Labonte's 1996 NASCAR Season.* Bonus Books, Inc., March 1997.

Huff, Richard. *Behind the Wall : A Season On the NASCAR Circuit.* Bonus Books, Inc., August 1994.

Huff, Richard. *The Insider's Guide to Stock Car Racing: NASCAR Racing: America's Fastest-Growing Sport.* Bonus Books, Inc., May 1997.

Lindsey, Dave. *The Great American Stock Car Racing Trivia Book.* Premium Press America, July 1994.

MacKnight, Nigel. *Showroom Stock Race Car Preparation.* Motorbooks International, Publishers & Wholesalers, October 1992.

Martin, Ronda J. *Stock Car Legends: The Laughs, Practical Jokes, & Fun Stories from Racing's Greats!* Premium Press America, October 1994.

Until the smoke clears, as shown here at Daytona, it's often hard to tell who's racing day has come to an end.

Mauk, Jonathan Van Dorn. *The Gallery of Legends Book: An Historical Overview of Racing in the Daytona Beach Florida Area From 1903-1995 covering World Land Speed Records, Stock Car, Sports Car & Motorcycle Racing.* International Speedway Corporation, May 1995.

Mayes, Angie. *Great American Stock Car Racing.* Premium Press America, June 1997.

McCulloch, Jim. *How to Tell if You're a Real Race Fan: A Guidebook for Stock Car Fans.* Stone-Brook Publishing, July 1996.

McKenna, A. T. *Stock Car Racing.* Abdo & Daughters Publishing, September 1998.

NASCAR 50th Anniversary Book. Harper Collins, February 1998.

NASCAR Pocket - Race Planner. Competitive Motorsports Products, Inc., September 1997.

Nascar Yearbook & Press Guide. National Association for Stock Car Auto Racing, February 1992.

National Speedway Directory. Slideways Publications, 1997.

Norman, Skip. *Super Stock Factory Musclecars.* Motorbooks International, Publishers & Wholesalers, December 1992.

Riggs, D. Randy. *Flat-Out Racing: An Insider's Look at the World of Stock Car Racing.* Michael Friedman Publishing Group, Inc., March 1995.

Riley, Gail B. *Top 10 NASCAR Drivers.* Enslow Publishers, Inc., November 1995.

Schnitzer, George C. Jr. *Stock Car Fun & Games: Puzzles, Word Games, & More!* Premium Press America, September 1996.

Sumner, Jim L. *A History of Sports in North Carolina.* North Carolina Division of Archives & History, March 1990.

Vehorn, Frank. *A Farewell to the King: A Personal Look Back at the Career of Richard Petty, Stock Car Racing's Winningest & Most Popular Driver.* Down Home Press, May 1992.

Walker, Mark. *NASCAR Racing 2: The Champion's Handbook.* Prima Publishing, May 1997.

Young, Jesse. *Stock Cars.* Capstone Press, Inc., September 1994.

Periodicals

Auto Racing Digest

Century Publishing Co.
990 Grove St.
Evanston, IL 60201-4370
Phone: (847)491-6440
Fax: (847)491-0867
Description: Magazine covering auto racing.

AutoWeek

Crain Communications, Inc.
1400 Woodbridge Ave.
Detroit, MI 48207-3187
Phone: (313)446-6000
Toll-free: 800-722-7798
Fax: (313)393-0347
Description: Magazine for car enthusiasts includes news coverage and features on vehicles, personalities, and events. Provides coverage of Formula One, CART, NASCAR, and IMSA races.

Inside NASCAR

The Quarton Group
888 W. Big Beaver, Ste. 600
Troy, MI 48084
Phone: (248) 362-7400
Description: Monthly magazine covering NASCAR from an insider's point of view. Includes interviews, features, trivia, and more.

NASCAR Newsletter

National Association for Stock Car Auto Racing
1801 W. International Speedway Blvd.
Daytona Beach, FL 32114-1243
Phone: (904)253-0611
Fax: (904)252-8804

Description: Consists of articles covering NASCAR racing across the U.S. and Canada. Reports race-results, and features innovations in the sport. Recurring features include news of members and a calendar of events. Illustrations: black and white photographs.

National Speed Sport News

National Speed Sport News
6509 Hudspeth Rd.
P.O. Box 1210
Harrisburg, NC 28075-1210
Phone: (704)455-2531
Fax: (704)455-2605
Description: Newspaper featuring auto racing, sport cars, and motors.

On Track

O.T. Publishing. Inc.
815 Pilot Rd. No. F
Las Vegas, NV 89119
Toll-free: 800-228-0787
Description: Auto racing magazine. Subtitle: The Auto Racing Magazine of Record

Road & Track

1499 Monrovia Ave.
Newport Beach, CA 92663
Phone: (714)720-5300
Fax: (714)631-2757
Description: Automotive magazine.

Southern MotoRacing

Southern Motor Racing
1049 Northwest Blvd.
PO Box 500
Winston-Salem, NC 27102
Phone: (910) 723-5227
Description: Tabloid covering auto racing.

Speedway Scene

Hockomock Publishing
50 Washington St.
PO Box 300
North Easton, MA 02356
Phone: (508)238-7016
Fax: (508)230-2381

Description: Tabloid covering circle track racing from Winston Cup to local events.

Stock Car Racing

65 Parker St., Ste. 2
Newburyport, MA 01950
Phone: (508)463-3787
Fax: (508)463-3250
Description: Magazine covering stock car racing.

Winston Cup Scene

American City Business Journals
First Citizen Plaza
128 S. Tryon, Ste. 2300
Charlotte, NC 28202
Phone: (704)375-7404
Toll-free: 800-704-3757
Fax: (704)371-3299
Description: Trade paper covering the NASCAR Winston Cup and Busch Series circuits.

NASCAR ORGANIZATIONS

Associations

National Association for Stock Car Auto Racing (NASCAR)

PO Box 2875
1801 Volusia Ave.
Daytona Beach, FL 32120-2875
Phone: (904) 253-0611
Fax: (904) 258-7646
Contact: William C. France, President
Description: Sanctions and supervises stock car races. Compiles statistics and issues publications.

National Motorsports Press Association (NMPA)

PO Box 500
Darlington, SC 29532
Phone: (803) 395-8821
Contact: Russell Branham, Exec. Sec.
Description: Individuals covering automobiles and automobile racing for news media; participants in

the automotive field. Purposes are to: promote better quality in motorsports news coverage; serve as a medium of exchange for ideas; promote a better understanding of motorsports among participants, officials, and fans; recognize and honor those persons whose achievements are outstanding in the field of motorsports participation and motorsports news coverage. Maintains Stock Car Hall of Fame and Joe Weatherly Museum at Darlington Raceway.

American Auto Racing Writers and Broadcasters Association (AARWBA)

c/o Dusty Brandel
922 N. Pass Ave.
Burbank, CA 91505
Phone: (818) 842-7005
Contact: Dusty Brandel, Pres.
Description: Persons who write, broadcast, or photograph auto racing. Seeks to: upgrade coverage of auto racing; promote the stature of racing; secure better facilities for writers. Conducts contests for-top race stories, photography, and broadcasts.

National Association of Auto Racing Memorabilia Collectors (NAARMC)

PO Box 12226
St. Petersburg, FL 33733
Phone: (813) 895-3482
Fax: (813) 895-3389
Contact: Ken C. Breslauer, Pres.
Description: Collectors, hobbyists, and historians interested in auto racing memorabilia who participate in the annual Day Before the 500 Meet in Indianapolis, IN. Encourages and facilitates trading, buying, and selling among members. Maintains speakers' bureau.

Fan Clubs

Bobby Allison Racing Team Club

6616 Walmsley Blvd.
Richmond, VA 23224

John Andretti Fan Club

P.O. Box 59244
Indianapolis, IN 46259

Troy Beebe Fan Club

P.O. Box 10976
Bakersfield, CA 93389-0976

Johnny Benson Fan Club

3102 Bird NE
Grand Rapids, MI 49505

Rich Bickle Fan Club

3700 Teaberry Court
Charlotte, NC 28227

Geoff Bodine Fan Club

P.O. Box 1790
Monroe, NC 28111-1790

Todd Bodine Fan Club

217 Rolling Hills Raod
Mooresville, NC 28115

Ward Burton Fan Club

P.O. Box 1473
South Boston, VA 24592

Johny Chapman Fan Club

P.O. Box 516
Stony Point, NC 28678

Sammy Coghill Fan Club

1236 58th Ave North
St. Petersburg, FL 33703

Derrike Cope Fan Club

P.O. Box 1542
Cornelius, NC 28031

Ricky Craven Fan Club

P.O. Box 1610
Statesville, NC 28687-1610

Bobby Dotter Fan Club

118 Stutts Road
Mooresville, NC 28115

Dale Earnhardt Fan Club

5301-A West W.T. Harris Blvd
Charlotte, NC 28269
Telephone: (800) 342-7612

Bill Elliott Fan Club

P.O. Box 248
Dawsonville, GA 30534

Tim Fedewa Fan Club

P.O. Box 609
Harrison, MI 48625

Harry Gant Fan Club

Route 3, Box 587
Taylorsville, NC 28681

Jeff Gordon National Fan Club

P.O. Box 515
Williams, AZ 86046-0515
Fax: (602) 635-2583

David Green Fan Club

P.O. Box 4821
Archdale, NC 27263-4821

Steve Grissom Fan Club

3110 S.R. 54 #198
Lutz, FL 33549

Doug Heveron Fan Club

P.O. Box 250
Denver, NC 28037

Brad Hietala Fan Club

85 North Street
Entfield, CT 06082-3933

Andy Hillenburg Fan Club

P.O. Box 160
Harrisburg, NC 28075-0160

Bobby Hillin Fan Club

135 Longfield Drive
Mooresville, NC 28115

Ernie Irvan Fan Club

1027 Central Drive
Concord, NC 28027

Dale Jarrett Fan Club

P.O.Box 564
Conover, NC 28613

Jason Keller Fan Club

P.O. Box 14748
Greenville, SC 29610

Bobby Labonte Fan Club

105 Gettysburg Court
Simpsonville, SC 29681

Terry Labonte Fan Club

P.O. Box 4617
Archdale, NC 27263

Randy LaJoie Fan Club

P.O. Box 3478
Westport, CT 06880

Ron LeMaster, Jr.

3705 Brandon Road
Huntington, WV 25704

Tracy Leslie Fan Club

8530 Cliff Cameron Drive
Charlotte, NC 28269

Chad Little Fan Club

P.O. Box 562323
Charlotte, NC 28256

Curtis Markham Fan Club

433 Bostwick Lane
Gathersburg, MD 20878

Sterling Marlin Fan Club

1116 West 7th Street, Suite 62
Columbia, TN 38401

Mark Martin Fan Club

P.O. Box 68
Ash Flat, AR 72513

Rick Mast Fan Club

Route 6, Box 224A
Lexington, VA 24450
Phone: (540) 463-4855
Fax: (540) 463-3814

Ted Musgrave Fan Club

P.O. Box 1089
Liberty, NC 27298

NASCAR Fan Membership

Attn: Accounting Dept.
P.O. Box 2875
Daytona Beach, FL 32120-2875

Joe Nemechek Fan Club

P.O. Box 1131
Mooresville, NC 28115

Steve Park Fan Club

P.O. Box 172
E. Northport, NY 11731-0172

Larry Pearson Fan Club

P.O. Box 1788
Kernerville, NC 27285

Kyle Petty Fan Club

8318 Pineville-Matthews Road,
Suite #708-119
Charlotte, NC 28226
Fax: (704) 544-9863

Richard Petty Fan Club

1028 East 22nd Street
Kannapolis, NC 28083

Robert Pressley Fan Club

P.O. Box 46361
Washington, DC 20050-6361
Phone: (703) 440-8735
E-Mail: rpfanclub@aol.com

Jeff Purvis Fan Club

900 Providence Blvd.
Clarksville, TN 37042

Jody Ridley Fan Club

1700 South Dixie Highway
Dalton, GA 30721

Shawna Robinson Fan Club

P.O. Box 221769
Charlotte, NC 28222

Ricky Rudd Fan Club, Inc.

P.O. Box 7586
Richmond, VA 23231

Hermie Sadler Fan Club

P.O. Box 871
Emporia, VA 23847

Elton Sawyer/Patty Moise

P.O. Box 77919
Greensboro, NC 27417

Ken Schrader Fan Club

P.O. Box 599
Licking, MO 65542

Bob Senneker Fan Club

P.O. Box 140984
Grand Rapids, MI 49514-0984

Dennis Setzer Fan Club

159 Bevan Drive
Mooresville, NC 28115

NASCAR ON THE WEB

Pole-Sitters

American Racing 'Zine

http://www.racecar.com/index.html

Straightforward site provides current race and qualifying results, point standings, and the NASCAR schedule, all in easy-to-read table format. Also includes Shoptalk discussion forum and a photo gallery.

Daytona USA/International Speedway Corp.

http://www.daytonausa.com

News, headlines, and information on International Speedway Corporation-owned tracks such as Daytona International Speedway, Darlington, Phoenix International Raceway, Talladega Superspeedway, Tucson Raceway Park, Metro-Dade Homestead Motorsports Complex, and Watkins Glen.

ESPN Auto Racing

http://espnet.sportszone.com/car/

No bells and whistles here, just plenty of info. Recent headlines, stats, standings, notes. Does include some all-time NASCAR lists and stats in the Almanac section. Good nuts-and-bolts source for quick info. Also includes news on Indy car, F-1, and drag racing.

goracing.com

http://www.goracing.com/

Nice graphics and bright look highlight this site filled with the usual results, car and driver profiles, news, and stats. Online shopping is available at the Racer Mall. Game room features demos of motor sports games, as well as racing-related image puzzles and word games. Covers all types of auto racing.

Hundreds of NASCAR Links

http://members.aol.com/BrkydRacer/COOLLINK
   S.HTML

Pretty much what the name implies. Eight search engines help you find all the track, event, driver, sponsor, collectibles, and NASCAR sites you could want.

iRace

http://www.irace.com/

Online racing 'zine covers the whole spectrum of auto racing: NASCAR, CART, IRL, NHRA, F-1, ACA, ARCA, Trans-Am, IROC, etc. Features the usual headlines, features, results, and stats. Lots of info in a nice presentation.

Motor Racing Network Radio

http://www.mrnnet.com

Official site of the Motor Racing Network, which broadcasts most Winston Cup, Busch Grand National, and Craftsman Truck Series events. Includes a list of MRN affiliates, broadcast schedules, "Nascar Live" and "Nascar Today" radio show archives.

Motorsports Hall of Fame

http://www.mshf.com/index.html

Official site of the Motorsports Hall of Fame and Museum, which is concerned with all forms of motorsports, including stock cars, open wheel and Indy cars, power boats, motorcycles, and air vehicles. Hall of Fame section includes profiles of most of the inductees. Museum section highlights selected vehicles and exhibits. Gift Shop allows browsers to buy selected merchandise, and the Information Desk tells about the Hall and provides membership registration.

MotorSports Image MS Online

http://www.msimage.com/

Yet another well done site with requisite information: results, standings, schedules, team and driver information, and photo gallery. Nice graphics and presentation.

NandO Racing News

http://www2.nando.net/newsroom/sports/oth/199
   5/oth/car/feat/car.html

News and headlines from Raleigh, NC News and Observer newspaper covering the world of auto racing. Includes NASCAR (including Buch Grand National and Craftsman Truck Series), CART, IRL, F-1, and NHRA. Archive goes back two weeks.

NASCAR Collectibles For Sale or Trade

http://www.angelfire.com/tn/harrygantcollector/in
   dex.html

Lists NASCAR items the host has for sale or trade, with short description and prices. Also includes links to other collectibles sites.

NASCAR.COM

http://www.nascar.com/

The official NASCAR site. Includes headlines, standings, schedules, and rankings for the Winston Cup, Busch Grand National, and Craftsman Truck seasons. Provides results, as well as audio and visual clips, from previous races. Also has driver and team profiles, sponsors live chats with drivers and other personnel, and offers insight into the jobs of behind-the-scenes workers. Garage section offers information on rules, specs, technical reports, and inspections. This site has just about everything for the NASCAR fan, except extensive links.

The red and blue No. 43 STP car is perhaps the most famous in all of auto racing thanks to the legendary Richard Petty, who drove the car to victory 200 times. He currently owns the No. 43 STP team.

NASCAR Driver Fan Clubs

http://www.ianet.net/~ron/fan.html

Straightforward listing of driver fan clubs, includes contact and cost information

NASCARweb

http://web.infoave.net/~klanglois/

Another NASCAR info-fest with the usual news, features, stats, standings, driver and track profiles, MRN radio stations, and NASCAR facts. Enjoyable site seems to be co-sponsored by NASCAR and South Carolina tourism department.

ovaltrack.com

http://www.ovaltrack.com/

Links to other NASCAR-related site. Good starting point if you're looking for NASCAR on the web.

RaceComm

http://www.racecomm.com/

Has the standard results and standings, along with a couple of nice touches, such as; a section that explains the reasons for the different flags used in a race, a listing of the radio frequencies used by drivers and their teams, complete list of seasonal champions going back to 1949, and the Manufacturer's Championship point standings.

RaceZine

http://www.primenet.com/~bobwest/index.html

Online racing magazines offers extensive links to other racing sites, as well as a number of newsgroups.Includes an image archive and trivia questions. Retrospective section highlights historical racing events and personalities. Coverage is not limited to just NASCAR.

The Racing Zone

http://racingzone.com/

Mostly a subscription site that lets you sign up to receive NASCAR news updates automatically via e-mail.

Rasberry Hill Stock Car Racing Stock Market Game

http://www.raspberryhill.com/stockcar.html

Fantasy league/stock market game allows players to "buy and sell stock" in NASCAR drivers. Results are based on actual Winston Cup, Busch Grand National, and Craftsman Truck Series race results and standings. Entry is free and prizes are awarded.

rec.auto.sports.nascar
Image Archive

http://www2.msstate.edu/~rls3/rasn.html

Collection of downloadable racing photos from people in the r.a.s.n. newsgroup.

Speednet

http://www.starnews.com/speednet/nasdir.html

Highlight is a searchable NASCAR story database. Also includes the usual race and TV schedules, track and driver information, results and standings. A message forum lets fans discuss the sport. Also provides information on fan clubs. Site has lots to see and makes it all pretty easy to find.

SpeedWorld

http://www.speedworld.net/

In addition to the usual results, standings, schedules, and rankings, this ad-heavy site has a section devoted to the celebration of NASCAR's 50th anniversary, as well as classified ads, chat rooms, message boards, and extensive links to sites of interest for fans and racing professionals.

The Super Fan Data Bank

http://www.raceshop.com/press-box/
    winston_stats/index.html

Searchable database for race results, statistics, and reports, as well as driver information. Extensive and easy to use.

USA Today Sagarin's NASCAR Ratings

http://www.usatoday.com/sports/motor/smnasag.
    htm

Jeff Sagarin presents his ratings of NASCAR drivers. Ratings take into account driver's finishing position, the number of drivers in each race, driver's races started, and the total number of races in the circuit.

The Valvoline Racing Team

http://www.valvoline.com/racing/

Official site for the Valvoline Racing Team, which includes NASCAR driver Mark Martin and CART driver Gil De Ferran. Highlights include the Internet Racing Game, a trivia game where players answer questions to collect points; and Racing USA, a section dedicated to the history of auto racing in the United States.

Winston Cup Today

http://www.raceshop.com/wct/

RealAudio clips of the weekly 30-minute and daily 5-minute Winston Cup Today radio show. Includes archive of past shows. Victory Lane section offers a weekly contest in which participants guess the winner and average speed of the week's upcoming race. Winners receive prizes, usually a t-shirt. Pit

Stop section offers a discussion area, as well as Q &A. Links to a NASCAR fantasy league called Fantasy Cup Racing.

Best of the Rest

Miscellaneous and Fan Sites

Brickyard 400
http://www.brickyard.com/400/

Christopher's NASCAR Page
http://www.cs.gasou.edu/~cdis/nascar/

Everything Else Is Just a Game
http://www.geocities.com/MotorCity/Downs/6659/

Gary McGriff's NASCAR Page
http://fly.hiwaay.net/~gmcgriff/nascar.htm

Guide to NASCAR Racing
http://gaia.ecs.csus.edu/~huftyl/

Jason's Mustang and NASCAR Page
http://www.geocities.com/MotorCity/7356/

Joe King's NASCAR Pit Stop
http://www.geocities.com/MotorCity/Speed-way/2496/

Kids and the Hood
http://www.wrldpwr.com/kids/

My Temple d'NASCAR
http://www.ianet.net/~rbarnes/NASCAR.html

NASCAR—The Best Sport on Earth
http://www.ianet.net/~ron/Nascar.html

NASCAR Fans Website
http://www.nascarfans.com/

NASCAR Northwest Tour Page
http://www.aa.net/~cawsey/

Osbone's NASCAR Page
http://www4.ncsu.edu/eos/users/b/bowilder/www/nascar/index.html

Paul's NASCAR Page
http://members.aol.com/flpmps/paul1.htm

Richard Friedrich's NASCAR Page
http://www2.wavetech.net/~rrf/nascar/hpnascar.html

Rob Armstrong's NASCAR Page
http://www.geocities.com/~the-bandit/nascar.html

Rocky's Pitstop
http://www.tff.net/special/nascar/

Shakey's Super Nascar Page
http://www.pitt.edu/~jbbst13/nascar/nascar.html

Stooge's Nascar Page
http://www.geocities.com/MotorCity/1071/

Driver Sites

Keilman's Ward Burton Page
http://members.aol.com/wardburt0n/doc.html

TJ's Jeff Burton Page
http://www.geocities.com/Colosseum/9769/jburton.html

Derrike Cope Fan Club
http://www.nol.net/~jeffcope/derrikecope/

Unofficial Wally Dallenbach Page
http://home.earthlink.net/~wdaniel/dallenbach/

Derek's Dale Earnhardt Page
http://www.geocities.com/MotorCity/Downs/1347/

InTheFlesh's Bill Elliott Page
http://members.aol.com/intheflesh/main.html

#24 All the Way
http://www.geocities.com/MotorCity/Downs/7324/

Bo's Jeff Gordon Page
http://www.geocities.com/Colosseum/Arena/7646/

Official Jeff Gordon Website
http://www.jeffgordon.com/

Jeff Gordon National Fan Club
http://www.jeffgordonfanclub.com/

Sunday Thunder
http://www.geocities.com/MotorCity/6024/index.html

J.F.G. Haters of America Page
http://www.geocities.com/MotorCity/Downs/4870/

NASCAR Fans Against Jeff Gordon Page
http://home.klis.com/~brobertsjr/nfajg.htm

Ernie Irvan Fan Page
http://www.geocities.com/MotorCity/Speedway/2836/

Dale Jarrett Fan Page
http://www.geocities.com/MotorCity/6132/index.html

A.M. Bulin's Bobby Labonte Fan Page
http://www.geocities.com/MotorCity/Speedway/1864/

Seann's Sterling Marlin Page
http://www.geocities.com/MotorCity/8731/

Unofficial Mark Martin Fan Page
http://www.ovaltrack.com/martin/martin1.htm

Josh's Unofficial Mark Martin Page
http://www.newwave.net/~dlinville/index2.html

Ultimate Jeremy Mayfield Site
http://members.aol.com/holli9537/index.htm

Adam Justice's Kyle Petty Page
http://www.geocities.com/MotorCity/7554/

Kyle Heinzman's Tribute to Kyle Petty
http://www.geocities.com/MotorCity/Speedway/1744/

Matt Eighmey's Kyle Petty Page
http://members.aol.com/MEighmey44/kyle.html

REV Speedway
http://www.revspeedway.com/index.htm

Official Ricky Rudd Page
http://www.RickyRudd.com/

Kenny Schrader Fan Page
http://users.deltanet.com/users/jayzeb/kenny.html

Kenny Schrader Skoal Bandit #33
http://www.the-bandit.com/

Wermuth Racing Dick Trickle Page
http://members.aol.com/wormfire/main.htm

Darrell Waltrip Motorsports
http://www.dw17.com/

Darrell Waltrip Fan Page
http://www.red-comet.com/waltrip/

Team Sites

Parker Racin, Inc.
http://www.parkerracing.com/

Sadler Racing
http://www.sadlerwc95.com/

Schultz Racing Team
http://www.schultzracing.com/

Skittles Racing Team
http://www.skittles.com/

Thunderbird Racing Page
http://www.ARMAnet.com/racing/racing.html

26

CAREER AND SINGLE-SEASON RECORDS—DRIVERS AND OWNERS

CAREER RECORDS—DRIVERS

RACES STARTED

1.	Richard Petty	1,184
2.	Dave Marcis	835
3.	Darrell Waltrip	720
4.	Bobby Allison	718
5.	Buddy Baker	699
6.	J.D. McDuffie	653
7.	Buck Baker	636
8.	James Hylton	601
9.	Ricky Rudd	594
10.	David Pearson	574
11.	Dale Earnhardt	574
	Terry Labonte	574
13.	Buddy Arrington	560
14.	Cale Yarborough	559
15.	Elmo Langley	536
16.	Bill Elliott	527
17.	Benny Parsons	526
18.	Kyle Petty	501
19.	Neil Castles	497
	Wendell Scott	495
21.	Harry Gant	477
22.	Jimmy Means	475
23.	Geoff Bodine	472
24.	Morgan Shepherd	468
25.	Cecil Gordon	450

WINS

1.	Richard Petty	200
2.	David Pearson	105
3.	Bobby Allison	84
	Darrell Waltrip	84
5.	Cale Yarborough	83
6.	Dale Earnhardt	70
7.	Lee Petty	54
8.	Ned Jarrett	50
	Junior Johnson	50
10.	Herb Thomas	48
	Rusty Wallace	47
12.	Buck Baker	46
13.	Bill Elliott	40
14.	Tim Flock	39
15.	Bobby Isaac	37
16.	Fireball Roberts	33
	Jeff Gordon	29
18.	Rex White	28
19.	Fred Lorenzen	26
20.	Jim Paschal	25

Joe Weatherly	25	
Mark Martin	22	
23. Benny Parsons	21	
Jack Smith	21	
25. Speedy Thompson	20	
26. Davey Allison	19	
Buddy Baker	19	
Fonty Flock	19	
Terry Labonte	19	
Ricky Rudd	19	
31. Geoff Bodine	18	
Neil Bonnett	18	
Harry Gant	18	
34. Marvin Panch	17	
Curtis Turner	17	
Ernie Irvan	15	
37. Dale Jarrett	15	
38. Dick Hutherson	14	
LeeRoy Yarborough	14	
40. Dick Rathmann	13	
Tim Richmond	13	
42. Donnie Allison	10	
43. Paul Goldsmith	9	
Cotton Owens	9	
Bob Welborn	9	
Kyle Petty	8	
47. Darel Dieringer	7	
A. J. Foyt	7	
Jim Reed	7	
Marshall Teague	7	
51. Sterling Marlin	6	
52. Dan Gurney	5	
Alan Kulwicki	5	
Bobby Labonte	5	
Tiny Lund	5	
Dave Marcis	5	
Ralph Moody	5	
58. Lloyd Dane	4	
Bob Flock	4	
Charlie Glotzbach	4	
Eddie Gray	4	
Pete Hamilton	4	
Parnelli Jones	4	
Hershel McGriff	4	
Eddie Pagan	4	
Ken Schrader	4	
Morgan Shepherd	4	

Nelson Stacy	4
Billy Wade	4
Glen Wood	4
71. Bill Blair	3
Jeff Burton	3
Dick Linder	3
Frank Mundy	3
Gwyn Staley	3
77. Johnny Beauchamp	2
Red Byron	2
Derrike Cope	2
Ray Elder	2
Bobby Hamilton	2
James Hylton	2
Bobby Johns	2
Joe Lee Johnson	2
Al Keller	2
Elmo Langley	2
Danny Letner	2
Billy Myers	2
Jimmy Pardue	2
Tom Pistone	2
Marvin Porter	2
Gober Sosebee	2
Jimmy Spencer	2
Emmanuel Zervokis	2

TOP 5 FINISHES

1. Richard Petty	555	
2. Bobby Allison	336	
3. David Pearson	301	
4. Darrell Waltrip	275	
5 Dale Earnhardt	256	
6. Cale Yarborough	255	
7. Buck Baker	246	
8. Lee Petty	231	
9. Buddy Baker	202	
10. Benny Parsons	199	
11. Ned Jarrett	185	
12. Terry Labonte	166	
13. Bill Elliott	151	
14. Jim Paschal	149	
Ricky Rudd	149	
16. Rusty Wallace	142	
17 James Hylton	140	

18. Bobby Isaac	134
19. Mark Martin	131
20. Harry Gant	123
21. Herb Thomas	122
22. Junior Johnson	121
23. Rex White	110
24. Joe Weatherly	105
25. Tim Flock	102

TOP 10 FINISHES

1. Richard Petty	712
2. Bobby Allison	446
3. Darrell Waltrip	388
4. Buck Baker	372
5. Dale Earnhardt	370
6. David Pearson	366
7. Lee Petty	332
8. Cale Yarborough	318
9. Buddy Baker	311
10. Terry Labonte	309
11. James Hylton	301
12. Ricky Rudd	293
13. Benny Parsons	283
14. Bill Elliott	271
15. Ned Jarrett	239
16. Jim Paschal	230
17. Dave Marcis	222
18. Rusty Wallace	221
19. Harry Gant	208
20. Mark Martin	206
21. Elmo Langley	193
22. Geoff Bodine	181
23. Neil Castles	178
24. Bobby Isaac	170
25. Morgan Shepherd	168

POLES

1. Richard Petty	126
2. David Pearson	113
3. Cale Yarborough	70
4. Bobby Allison	59
Darrell Waltrip	59
6. Bobby Isaac	50

GONE FISHIN'

The only thing the late Neil Bonnett loved more than his family and racing was bass fishing. He loved it so much he had a state-of-the-art bass boat with an engine that was much larger and quite a bit faster than was needed. There was, however, a method to the Alabama native's fishing madness.

Bonnett's best racing buddy was Dale Earnhardt, and they often went out together in Bonnett's souped-up bass boat. Once (as the story goes) Bonnett opened it up on a huge lake to show Earnhardt just how fast the boat would go.

Later, he conceded he didn't need a boat that fast, but allowed as how it was nice to have the extra OOMPH! if he needed it."After all," Bonnett told Earnhardt, "If you hook one of them big suckers at 100 mile an hour it'll take the fight right out of em."

7. Bill Elliott	49
8. Junior Johnson	47
9. Buck Baker	44
10. Buddy Baker	40
11. Tim Flock	39
12. Herb Thomas	38
13. Geoff Bodine	37
14. Rex White	36
15. Ned Jarrett	35
Mark Martin	35
Fireball Roberts	35
18. Fonty Flock	33
Fred Lorenzen	33
20. Terry Labonte	25
21. Alan Kulwicki	24
Jack Smith	24
23. Ricky Rudd	23
24. Dale Earnhardt	22
Dick Hutcherson	22

WINNINGS

1. Dale Earnhardt	29,897,490
2. Bill Elliott	17,634,592

3. Terry Labonte	16,437,247	18. Bobby Allison	7,673,808
4. Darrell Waltrip	16,128,230	19. Davey Allison	6,689,154
5. Rusty Wallace	15,925,295	20. Michael Waltrip	6,393,056
6. Jeff Gordon	14,528,031	21. Brett Bodine	6,061,199
7. Mark Martin	13,807,347	22. Cale Yarborough	5,645,887
8. Ricky Rudd	13,389,379	23. Dave Marcis	5,477,823
9. Geoff Bodine	11,456,664	24. Alan Kulwicki	5,059,052
10. Dale Jarrett	10,565,202	25. Derrick Cope	4,447,722
11. Sterling Martin	10,228,227		
12. Ken Schrader	9,902,568		
13. Ernie Irvan	8,830,048		
14. Kyle Petty	8,711,379		
15. Richard Petty	8,541,218		
16. Harry Gant	8,524,844		
17. Morgan Shepherd	8,064,248		

LAPS COMPLETED

1. Richard Petty	307,836
2. Dave Marcis	218,486
3. Darrell Waltrip	214,555
4. Bobby Allison	197,438

Ricky Rudd, who drives the Tide car, is in the top ten in career Winston Cup winnings.

5.	Dale Earnhardt	173,474
6.	Ricky Rudd	172,509
7	Terry Labonte	169,667
8.	James Hylton	160,733
9.	Bill Elliott	156,269
10.	Buddy Baker	151,129
11.	J. D. McDuffie	148,694
12.	Buddy Arrington	147,899
13.	Cale Yarborough	144,552
14.	Kyle Petty	143,535
15.	David Pearson	135,020
16.	Benny Parsons	134,540
17.	Geoff Bodine	134,106
18.	Harry Gant	133,629
19.	Morgan Shepherd	127,322
20.	Rusty Wallace	124,266
21.	Elmo Langley	119,706
22.	Sterling Marlin	114,337
23.	Ken Schrader	114,849
24.	Jimmy Means	113,945
25.	Cecil Gordon	112,908

LAPS LED

1.	Richard Petty	52,194
2.	Cale Yarborough	31,776
3.	Bobby Allison	27,539
4.	David Pearson	25,425
5.	Dale Earnhardt	24,833
6.	Darrell Waltrip	23,006
7.	Rusty Wallace	13,967
8.	Bobby Isaac	13,229
9.	Junior Johnson	12,651
10.	Bill Elliott	10,242
11.	Buddy Baker	9,748
12.	Ned Jarrett	9,468
13.	Geoff Bodine	8,627
14.	Harry Gant	8,445
15.	Fred Lorenzen	8,131
16.	Jeff Gordon	7,247
17.	Tim Flock	6,937
18.	Benny Parsons	6,860
19.	Mark Martin	6,657
20.	Neil Bonnett	6,382
21.	Ricky Rudd	6,238

22.	Herb Thomas	6,197
23.	Terry Labonte	6,090
24.	Fireball Roberts	5,970
25.	Buck Baker	5,662

RACES LED

1.	Richard Petty	599
2.	Bobby Allison	414
3.	Darrell Waltrip	393
4.	Dale Earnhardt	366
5.	Cale Yarborough	340
6.	David Pearson	329
7.	Buddy Baker	242
8.	Bill Elliott	213
9.	Geoff Bodine	211
	Terry Labonte	211
11.	Rusty Wallace	193
12.	Harry Gant	192
	Benny Parsons	192
14.	Dave Marcis	186
15.	Ricky Rudd	175
16.	Mark Martin	162
17.	Neil Bonnett	155
	Bobby Isaac	155
19.	Junior Johnson	138
20.	Ken Schrader	122
21.	Ernie Irvan	116
22.	Ned Jarrett	111
23.	Donnie Allison	105
24.	Buck Baker	104
	Morgan Shepherd	104

CONSECUTIVE RACES LED

1.	Bobby Allison	39	1971-72
2.	Darrell Waltrip	25	1981-82
	Cale Yarborough	25	1976
4.	Richard Petty	22	1972-73
	Cale Yarborough	22	1977-78
6.	Dale Earnhardt	20	1986-87
	Dale Earnhardt	20	1987-88
8.	Jeff Gordon	19	1995
9.	Geoff Bodine	17	1986
	David Pearson	17	1969

11. Richard Petty	16	1974
Darrell Waltrip	16	1980-81
Cale Yarborough	16	1978
14. Bobby Isaac	15	1972
Richard Petty	15	1971
16. Bobby Allison	14	1981
Bill Elliott	14	1988
Tim Flock	14	1955
Terry Labonte	14	1984-85
Richard Petty	14	1971-72
Darrell Waltrip	14	1978
Darrell Waltrip	14	1979
Darrell Waltrip	14	1982
Darrell Waltrip	14	1985-86
Cale Yarborough	14	1974
Cale Yarborough	14	1978-79
Cale Yarborough	14	1980

CONSECUTIVE RACES STARTED

1. Terry Labonte	569
2. Dale Earnhardt	546
3. Richard Petty	513
4. Ricky Rudd	507
5. Darrell Waltrip	431
6. Bill Elliott	427
7. Rusty Wallace	416
8. Ken Schrader	386
9. Bobby Allison	374
10. Michael Waltrip	356
11. Sterling Marlin	329
12. Benny Parsons	321
13. Mark Martin	300
14. Dave Marcis	284
15. Harry Gant	264
16. Richard Childress	256
17. Dale Jarrett	251
18. Morgan Shepherd	240
19. Darrell Waltrip	216
20. Geoff Bodine	212
21. Kyle Petty	208
22. Buddy Arrington	205
23. Brett Bodine	198
24. J. D. McDuffie	195
25. Cecil Gordon	193

CONSECUTIVE RACES WON

1. Richard Petty	10	1967
2. Bobby Allison	5	1971
Richard Petty	5	1971
4. Dale Earnhardt	4	1987
Bill Elliott	4	1992
Harry Gant	4	1991
Mark Martin	4	1993
David Pearson	4	1966
David Pearson	4	1968
Billy Wade	4	1964
Darrell Waltrip	4	1981
Cale Yarborough	4	1976

CONSECUTIVE YEARS RACING

1. Richard Petty	35	1958-92
2. Buddy Baker	30	1959-88
Dave Marcis	30	1968-97
Cale Yarborough	30	1959-88
5. A. J. Foyt	28	1963-90
6. David Pearson	27	1960-86
7. Elmo Langley	26	1954-79
J. D. McDuffie	26	1966-91
Darrell Waltrip	26	1972-97
10. Buddy Arrington	25	1964-88
Buck Baker	25	1949-73
12. Bobby Allison	24	1965-88
13. Dale Earnhardt	23	1975-97
Ricky Rudd	23	1975-97
15. Bill Elliott	22	1976-97
Harry Gant	22	1973-94
17. Terry Labonte	20	1978-97
Sterling Marlin	20	1978-97
Benny Parsons	20	1969-88
Jim Paschal	20	1949-68
G.C. Spencer	20	1958-77
22. Tiny Lund	19	1955-73
Kyle Petty	18	1979-97
Bill Schmitt	19	1975-93
25. Donnie Allison	18	1966-83
James Hylton	18	1966-83
Jimmy Means	18	1976-93
Frank Warren	18	1963-80

NOT-SO-SPARKLING DEBUTS

From such humble beginnings did great careers emerge. Notice how some of NASCAR's most successful drivers fared in their Winston Cup debut:

- Richard Petty was 17th (out of 19 starters) at Toronto, Ontario, Canada in 1958.
- David Pearson finished 17th at Daytona Beach in 1960.
- Darrell Waltrip was 38th at Talladega in 1972.
- Cale Yarborough was 42nd at Darlington in 1957.
- Bobby Allison was 31st at Daytona Beach in 1961.
- Dale Earnhardt finished 22nd at Charlotte in 1975.
- Jeff Burton qualified sixth, then finished 37th in the 1993 race at Loudon, New Hampshire
- Sterling Marlin was 29th in a field of 30 at Nashville in the spring of 1976.

- Bill Elliott was 33rd at Rockingham in 1976.
- Jeff Gordon was 31st near Atlanta in 1992.
- Mark Martin was 27th at North Wilkesboro in 1981.
- Geoff Bodine was 29th in the Daytona 500 of 1979.
- Dale Jarrett was 14th (eight laps behind) at Martinsville in 1984.

And how about these signs of things to come:

- Rusty Wallace was second in his first Winston Cup race. It was the 1980 spring race near Atlanta, and he was driving for team-owner Roger Penske.
- Terry Labonte was fourth in his Cup debut, at Darlington on Labor Day of 1978, driving for Bill Hagan.
- Ricky Rudd was 11th in his first race, at Rockingham in the spring of 1975.

PERFORMANCE POINTS* (1949-1997)

1. Richard Petty	3,645	
2. David Pearson	2,045	
3. Bobby Allison	1,933	
4. Darrell Waltrip	1,644	
5. Cale Yarborough	1,559	
6. Dale Earnhardt	1,485	
7. Lee Petty	1,269	
8. Buck Baker	1,262	
9. Ned Jarrett	1,044	
10. Buddy Baker	916	
11. Rusty Wallace	875	
12. Benny Parsons	866	
13. Bill Elliott	845	
14. Herb Thomas	796	
15. Bobby Isaac	795	
16. Terry Labonte	783	
17. Junior Johnson	778	
18. Jim Paschal	755	
19. Mark Martin	678	
Ricky Rudd	678	
21. Tim Flock	645	
22. Rex White	637	
23. Harry Gant	618	
24. Joe Weatherly	590	
25. Fireball Roberts	577	

*Points are based on an International Point System on 10-6-4-3-2-1 breakdown for the first six finishers in every event. It is the most effectivce method of ranking individuals based on performance.

SINGLE-SEASON RECORDS—DRIVERS

WINS

1. Richard Petty	1967	27
2. Richard Petty	1971	21

3. Tim Flock	1955	18
Richard Petty	1970	18
5. Bobby Isaac	1969	17
6. David Pearson	1968	16
Richard Petty	1968	16
8. Ned Jarrett	1964	15
David Pearson	1966	15
10. Buck Baker	1956	14
Richard Petty	1963	14
12. Ned Jarrett	1965	13
Junior Johnson	1965	13
Richard Petty	1975	13
15. Herb Thomas	1953	12
Herb Thomas	1954	12
Darrell Waltrip	1981	12
Darrell Waltrip	1982	12
19. Bobby Allison	1971	11
Dale Earnhardt	1987	11
Bill Elliott	1985	11
Bobby Isaac	1970	11
David Pearson	1969	11
David Pearson	1973	11
Lee Petty	1959	11

MONEY

1. Jeff Gordon	1995	$4,347,343
2. Jeff Gordon	1997	4,201,227
3. Terry Labonte	1996	4,030,648
4. Jeff Gordon	1996	3,428,485
5. Dale Earnhardt	1994	3,400,733
6. Dale Earnhardt	1993	3,353,789
7. Dale Earnhardt	1990	3,308,056
8..Dale Earnhardt	1995	3,154,241
9. Dale Jarrett	1996	2,985,415
10. Dale Jarrett	1997	2,512,382
11. Bill Eliott	1985	2,433,187
12. Dale Earnhardt	1991	2,416,685
13. Alan Kulwicki	1992	2,322,561
14. Dale Earnhardt	1996	2,285,926
15. Sterling Martin	1995	2,253,502
16. Rusty Wallace	1989	2,237,950
17. Dale Earnhardt	1987	2,069,243
18. Rusty Wallace	1989	1,959,072
19. Davey Allison	1992	1,955,628

20. Terry Labonte	1997	1,951,844
21. Bobby Labonte	1997	1,943,239
22. Mark Martin	1995	1,893,519
23. Mark Martin	1996	1,887,396
24. Mark Martin	1997	1,877,139
25. Ricky Rudd	1997	1,863,040

LAPS LED

1. Richard Petty	1967	5,537
2. Bobby Isaac	1969	5,072
3. Richard Petty	1970	5,007
4. Richard Petty	1971	4,932
5. Bobby Allison	1972	4,343
6. Richard Petty	1968	4,242
7. Junior Johnson	1965	3,998
8. David Pearson	1968	3,950
9. Cale Yarborough	1976	3,791
10. Cale Yarborough	1974	3,630
11. Cale Yarborough	1978	3,587
12. Bobby Allison	1971	3,582
13. Richard Petty	1964	3,534
14. Tim Flock	1955	3,495
15. Dale Earnhardt	1987	3,358
16. Ned Jarrett	1964	3,304
17. Cale Yarborough	1977	3,218
18. Bobby Isaac	1970	3,188
19. David Pearson	1966	3,174
20. Cale Yarborough	1973	3,167
21. Richard Petty	1975	3,158
22. Richard Petty	1974	3,100
23. Darrell Waltrip	1982	3,027
24. David Pearson	1969	3,018
25. Richard Petty	1966	2,924

MILES LED

1. Bobby Allison	1972	4,117
2. Bobby Allison	1971	4,042
3. Cale Yarborough	1978	3,867
4. Richard Petty	1971	3,721
5. Richard Petty	1967	3,666
6. Richard Petty	1970	3,633
7. Cale Yarborough	1976	3,576

8. Jeff Gordon	1995	3,458
9. Dale Earnhardt	1987	3,399
10. Cale Yarborough	1974	3,374
11. Richard Petty	1975	3,319
12. David Pearson	1973	3,275
13. Richard Petty	1974	3,256
14. Bobby Allison	1982	3,217
15. Dale Earnhardt	1990	3,203
16. Bill Elliott	1985	3,188
17. Cale Yarborough	1980	3,155
18. Richard Petty	1964	3,065
19. Cale Yarborough	1977	3,054
20. Cale Yarborough	1973	2,727
21. Bobby Isaac	1969	2,688
22. Darrell Waltrip	1982	2,672
23. Darrell Waltrip	1979	2,629
24. Dale Earnhardt	1989	2,624
25. Rusty Wallace	1989	2,549

LAPS COMPLETED

1. David Pearson	1969	14,270
2. Richard Petty	1964	14,041
3. Richard Petty	1971	13,739
4. James Hylton	1969	13,540
5. Ned Jarrett	1965	13,525
6. Ned Jarrett	1964	13,325
7. David Pearson	1964	13,225
8. David Pearson	1968	13,097
9. Bobby Isaac	1968	12,947
10. James Hylton	1971	12,785
11. Richard Petty	1967	12,739
12. Bobby Isaac	1970	12,726
13. James Hylton	1970	12,712
14. Neil Castles	1969	12,661
15. Richard Petty	1969	12,589
16. Elmo Langley	1969	12,531
17. Cecil Gordon	1971	12,468
18. Bobby Allison	1970	12,452
19. Joe Weatherly	1962	12,431
20. Bobby Isaac	1969	12,308
21. Richard Petty	1968	12,254
22. Richard Petty	1963	12,183
23. Jabe Thomas	1969	12,025
24. Clyde Lynn	1968	12,013
25. Wendell Scott	1969	11,856

MILES DRIVEN

1. Richard Petty	1971	12,870
2. James Hylton	1971	12,718
3. Dale Jarrett	1997	12,651
4. Johnny Benson	1997	12,510
5. Dale Earnhardt	1997	12,509
6. Bill Elliott	1997	12,433
7. Jeff Burton	1997	12,426
8. Ken Schrader	1997	12,370
9. Mark Martin	1997	12,359
10. Bobby Labonte	1997	12,347
11. Jeremy Mayfield	1997	12,332
12. Terry labonte	1997	12,303
13. Bobby Hamilton	1997	12,272
14. Bobby Allison	1971	12,122
16. Ted Musgrave	1997	12,100
15. Ricky Rudd	1994	12,046
17. Michael Waltrip	1997	12,946
18. Cecil Gordon	1971	12,034
19. Darrell Waltrip	1994	12,026
20. Richard Petty	1972	11,996
21. Jeff Gordon	1997	11,988
22. John Andretti	1997	11,972
23. Kyle Petty	1997	11,962
24. Morgan Shepherd	1994	11,950
25. Sterling Marlin	1995	11,936
26. Ted Musgrave	1995	11,822
27. Dale Earnhardt	1993	11,808
28. Bobby Allison	1972	11,801
29. Darrell Waltrip	1979	11,768
30. Ken Schrader	1994	11,740

POLES

1. Bobby Isaac	1969	20
2. Richard Petty	1967	19
3. Tim Flock	1955	18
4. Richard Petty	1966	16
5. Cale Yarborough	1980	14
David Pearson	1969	14
7. Bobby Isaac	1970	13
8. Bobby Allison	1972	12
Buck Baker	1956	12
Fonty Flock	1951	12

David Pearson	1964	12
David Pearson	1968	12
Richard Petty	1968	12
Herb Thomas	1953	12
15. Bill Elliott	1985	11
David Pearson	1974	11
Darrell Waltrip	1981	11
18. Junior Johnson	1961	10
Junior Johnson	1965	10
Herb Thomas	1952	10

TOP 5 FINISHES

1. Ned Jarrett	1965	42
David Pearson	1969	42
3. Ned Jarrett	1964	40
4. Joe Weatherly	1962	39
5. Richard Petty	1967	38
Richard Petty	1971	38
7. Richard Petty	1964	37
8. David Pearson	1968	36
9. Tim Flock	1955	32
Dick Hutcherson	1965	32
Boby Isaac	1970	32
Ned Jarrett	1963	32
Richard Petty	1962	32
14. Buck Baker	1956	31
Richard Petty	1968	31
Richard Petty	1969	31
17. Bobby Allison	1970	30
Buck Baker	1957	30
Richard Petty	1963	30
20. Bobby Isaac	1969	29
David Pearson	1964	29
Rex White	1961	29
23. Lee Petty	1958	28
24. Bobby Allison	1971	27
James Hylton	1969	27
Bobby Isaac	1968	27
Lee Petty	1959	27
Richard Petty	1970	27
Jack Smith	1962	27
Herb Thomas	1953	27

TOP 10 FINISHES

1. Ned Jarrett	1964	45
Ned Jarrett	1965	45
Joe Weatherly	1962	45
4. David Pearson	1969	44
5. Lee Petty	1958	43
Richard Petty	1964	43
7. David Pearson	1964	42
8. Richard Petty	1971	41
9. Richard Petty	1967	40
10. Buck Baker	1956	39
James Hylton	1967	39
James Hylton	1969	39
James Hylton	1970	39
Ned Jarrett	1963	39
Richard Petty	1962	39
Richard Petty	1963	39
17. Buck Baker	1957	38
Bobby Isaac	1970	38
David Pearson	1968	38
Richard Petty	1969	38
Rex White	1961	38
22. Dick Hutcherson	1965	37
James Hylton	1971	37
24. Bobby Isaac	1968	36
Herb Thomas	1956	36

RACES LED

1. Richard Petty	1967	41
Richard Petty	1971	41
3. David Pearson	1969	39
4. Bobby Isaac	1969	38
5. David Pearson	1968	37
6. Bobby Isaac	1970	35
Richard Petty	1968	35
8. Tim Flck	1955	33
Richard Petty	1964	33
10. Richard Petty	1969	32
Richard Petty	1970	32
12. Bobby Allison	1971	31
David Pearson	1964	31
14. Bobby Allison	1972	30
Ned Jarrett	1964	30
Junior Johnson	1965	30

Richard Petty	1972	30
18. Jeff Gordon	1995	29
Ned Jarrett	1965	29
Richard Petty	1963	29
21. Darrell Waltrip	1980	28
Cale Yarborough	1976	28
Cale Yarborough	1977	28
Cale Yarborough	1978	28
Cale Yarborough	1980	28

WIN PERCENT (10 STARTS MINIMUM)

1. David Pearson	1973	61%
2. Fireball Roberts	1958	60%
3. Richard Petty	1967	56%
4. Fred Lorenzen	1964	50%
5. Tim Flock	1955	46%
Richard Petty	1971	46%
7. David Pearson	1976	45%
Richard Petty	1971	45%
9. Richard Petty	1975	43%
10. Darrell Waltrip	1982	40%
11. Bill Elliott	1985	39%
Darrell Waltrip	1982	39%
13. Dale Earnhardt	1987	38%
14. David Pearson	1974	37%
15. Junior Johnson	1965	36%
Joe Weatherly	1961	36%
David Pearson	1966	36%
18. David Pearson	1972	35%
Herb Thomas	1954	35%
20. Bobby Isaac	1969	34%
21. David Pearson	1968	33%
Richard Petty	1974	33%
Marshall Teague	1951	33%
Rusty Wallace	1993	33%
Cale Yarborough	1974	33%
Cale Yarborough	1978	33%

CAREER RECORDS—OWNERS

RACES STARTED

1. Petty Enterprises		1,667
2. Wood Bros.		928

3. Bud Moore		911
4. Junior Johnson		750
5. Junie Donlavey		745
6. Richard Childress		692
7. Elmo Langley		675
8. Dave Marcis		646
9. James Hylton		634
10. Buddy Arrington		584
11. Billy Hagan		546
12. Buck Baker		525
13. L. G. DeWitt		521
14. J D McDuffie		488
15. Rick Hendrick		479
16. Henley Gray		476
17. D. K. Ulrich		469
18. Wendell Scott		465
19. G. C. Spencer		451
20. Jimmy Means		435
21. Don Robertson		431
22. Bobby Allison		429
23. Harry Melling		414
24. Cecil Gordon		406
25 Stavola Brothers		397

WINS

1. Petty Enterprises		267
2. Junior Johnson		119
3. Wood Bros.		97
4. Holman-Moody		93
5. Rick Hendrick		71
6. Bud Moore		63
7. Richard Childress		63
8. Carl Kiekhaefer		52
9. Herb Thomas		44
10. Nord Krauskopf		43
DiGard		43
12. Cotton Owens		39
13. Robert Yates		35
14. Harry Melling		34
Roger Penske		34
16. Bondy Long		31
17. Rex White		26
18. Jack Roush		25
19. Harry Ranier		24
20. Frank Christian		22

21. Pete DePaolo	21
Richard Howard	21
23. Rex Lovette	20
Ted Chester	20
Raymond Beadle	20

TOP 5 FINISHES

1. Petty Enterprises	877
2. Junior Johnson	417
3. Rick Hendrick	328
4. Wood Bros.	323
5. Bud Moore	308
6. Holman-Moody	281
7. Richard Childress	218
8. Cotton Owens	179
9. L. G. DeWitt	177
10. Nord Krauskopf	171
11. Jack Roush	162
12. Buck Baker	159
13. DiGard	158
14. Robert Yates	127
15. Roger Penske	121
16. Herb Thomas	118
17. Carl Kiekhaefer	116
18. Bondy Long	115
19. Harry Melling	114
20. Harry Ranier	107
21. Bobby Allison	101
Billy Hagan	101
23. James Hylton	94
24. Rex White	89
25. Frank Christian	85

TOP 10 FINISHES

1. Petty Enterprises	1,203
2. Junior Johnson	556
3. Rick Hendrick	543
4. Wood Bros.	483
5. Bud Moore	476
6. Richard Childress	376
7. Holman-Moody	331
8. Buck Baker	330

9. L. G. DeWitt	315
10. Jack Roush	262
11. Cotton Owens	246
12. James Hylton	237
13. Billy Hagan	236
14. Junie Donlavey	216
15. Nord Krauskopf	214
16. DiGard	211
17. Harry Melling	180
18. Roger Penske	178
Robert Yates	178
20. Herb Thomas	158
21. Bobby Allison	155
Wendell Scott	155
23. Harry Ranier	146
24. Carl Kiekhaefer	138
25. Bondy Long	136

POLES

1. Petty Enterprises	152
2. Wood Bros.	118
3. Junior Johnson	106
4. Holman-Moody	83
5. Rick Hendrick	76
6. Nord Krauskopf	67
7. Carl Kiekhaefer	50
8. Bud Moore	48
9. Harry Melling	40
10. Harry Ranier	39
Jack Roush	39
12. Cotton Owens	36
13. Herb Thomas	34
14. Frank Christian	31
15. Bondy Long	28
16. Richard Childress	26\
DiGard	26
Rex White	26
18. Alan Kulwicki	24
20. Richard Howard	23
21. Jack Smith	22
22. Rex Lovette	21
Robert Yates	21
23. Bobby Allison	20
24. Pete DePaolo	18
Ray Fox	18

26.	Roger Penske	17
27.	Smokey Yunick	16
	Buck Baker	16
30.	Billy Hagan	15

LAPS COMPLETED

1.	Petty Enterprises	481,509
2.	Rick Hendrick	316,409
3.	Junior Johnson	295,136
4.	Wood Bros.	253,847
5.	Bud Moore	253,664
6.	Richard Childress	208,364
7.	Junie Donlavey	200,377
8.	James Hylton	171,126
9.	Dave Marcis	170,210
10.	Elmo Langley	165,647
11.	Jack Roush	162,420
12.	Billy Hagan	157,574
13.	Buddy Arrington	156,200
14.	Stavola Brothers	147,793
15.	L. G. DeWitt	135,176
16.	Buck Baker	133,944
17.	Harry Melling	122,898
18.	Holman-Moody	120,432
19.	J. D. McDuffie	119,110
20.	Don Robertson	116,035
21.	Bobby Allison	110,474
22.	Jimmy Means	109,180
23.	Rahmoc	107,849
24.	Cecil Gordon	107,152
25.	D.K. Ulrich	107,070

LAPS LED

1.	Petty Enterprises	60,049
2.	Junior Johnson	40,377
3.	Holman-Moody	24,412
4.	Wood Bros.	24,295
5.	Richard Childress	21,868
6.	Rick Hendrick	20,439
7.	Bud Moore	17,110
8.	Nord Krauskopf	15,705
9.	DiGard	14,277

10.	Robert Yates	10,432
11.	Roger Penske	10,415
12.	Richard Howard	10,209
13.	Cotton Owens	9,560
14.	Carl Kiekhaefer	8,255
15.	Harry Melling	8,132
16.	Jack Roush	7,619
17.	Bondy Long	7,381
18.	Harry Ranier	7,029
19.	Rex Lovette	6,741
20.	Raymond Beadle	5,968
21.	Herb Thomas	5,899
22.	Bobby Allison	5,495
23.	Hal Needham	4,962
24.	Ray Fox	4,709
25.	L. G. DeWitt	4,344

RACES LED

1.	Petty Enterprises	728
2.	Junior Johnson	510
3.	Wood Bros.	401
4.	Bud Moore	335
5.	Rick Hendrick	323
6.	Richard Childress	319
7.	Holman-Moody	243
8.	DiGard	227
9.	Nord Krauskopf	198
10.	Jack Roush	167
11.	Cotton Owens	157
12.	Robert Yates	154
13.	Harry Melling	153
14.	Roger Penske	152
15.	Harry Ranier	147
16.	Billy Hagan	146
17.	L. G. DeWitt	128
18.	Dave Marcis	120
19.	Raymond Beadle	114
20.	Bobby Allison	112
	Morgan/McClure	112
22.	Hal Needham	111
23.	Hoss Ellington	99
24.	Bondy Long	90
25.	Banjo Matthews	77

SINGLE-SEASON RECORDS—OWNERS

1. Carl Kiekhaefer	1956	30
2. Petty Enterprises	1967	27
3. Carl Kiekhaefer	1955	22
Petty Enterprises	1971	22
5. Petty Enterprises	1970	19
Petty Enterprises	1963	19
7. Holman-Moody	1968	17
Nord Krauskopf	1969	17
9. Petty Enterprises	1968	16
10. Cotton Owens	1966	15
11. Bondy Long	1964	14
12. Petty Enterprises	1975	13
Rex Lovette	1965	13
Holoman-Moody	1965	13
Bondy Long	1965	13
16. Junior Johnson	1982	12
Junior Johnson	1981	12
Rick Hendrick	1996	12
Herb Thomas	1954	12
Herb Thomas	1953	12
21. Wood Bros.	1973	11
Harry Melling	1985	11
Holman-Moody	1963	11
Richard Childress	1987	11
Petty Enterprises	1959	11
Nord Krauskopf	1970	11
Holman-Moody	1969	11
Petty Enterprises	1962	11
Rick Hendrick	1997	11

LAPS LED

1. Petty Enterprises	1971	5,625
2. Petty Enterprises	1967	5,538
3. Petty Enterprises	1970	5,140
4. Nord Krauskopf	1969	5,072
5. Howard/Johnson	1972	4,398
6. Holman-Moody	1968	4,287
7. Petty Enterprises	1968	4,242
8. Carl Kiekhaefer	1968	4,228
9. Rex Lovette	1965	4,170
10. Carl Kiekhaefer	1955	4,027
11. Junior Johnson	1976	3,791
12. Petty Enterprises	1964	3,710
13. Junior Johnson	1978	3,587
14. Richard Childress	1987	3,358
15. Rick Hendrick	1996	3,334
16. Holman-Moody	1963	3,276
16. Rick Hendrick	1995	3,276
18. Junior Johnson	1977	3,218
19. Nord Krauskopf	1970	3,188
20. Cotton Owens	1966	3,174
21. Howard/Johnson	1973	3,167
22. Petty Enterprises	1975	3,158
23. Petty Enterprises	1974	3,100
24. Holman-Moody	1965	3,086
25. Bondy Long	1964	3,071

MILES LED

1. Petty Enterprises	1971	4,691
2. Petty Enterprises	1970	4,286
3. Rick Hendrick	1995	4,194
4. Howard/Johnson	1972	4,117
5. Junior Johnson	1978	3,867
6. Rick Hendrick	1996	3,697
7. Petty Enterprises	1967	3,669
8. Rick Hendrick	1986	3,646
9. Junior Johnson	1976	3,576
10. Holman-Moody	1971	3,468
11. Richard Childress	1987	3,399
12. Petty Enterprises	1964	3,347
13. Petty Enterprises	1975	3,319
14. Wood Bros.	1973	3,275
15. Petty Enterprises	1974	3,256
16. DiGard	1982	3,217
17. Richard Childress	1990	3,203
18. Robert Yates	1997	3,190
19. Harry Melling	1985	3,188
20. Junior Johnson	1980	3,155
21. Junior Johnson	1977	3,054
22. Carl Kiekhaefer	1956	3,026
23. Wood Bros.	1972	2,873
24. Carl Kiekhaefer	1956	2,769
25. Richard Howard	1973	2,727

1. Rick Hendrick	1990	30,006
2. Jack Roush	1997	28,240
3. Rick Hendrick	1996	28,156
4. Rick Hendrick	1994	28,130
5. Rick Hendrick	1989	27,745
6. Rick Hendrick	1988	27,205
7. Rick Hendrick	1995	27,031
8. Jack Roush	1996	27,008
9. Rick Hendrick	1997	26,943
10. Rick Hendrick	1993	26,059
11. Rick Hendrick	1987	24,996
12. Petty Enterprises	1963	22,021
13. Buck Baker	1965	21,684
14. Carl Kiekaefer	1956	20,937
15. Petty Enterprises	1964	20,386
16. Cotton Owens	1964	20,382
17. Buck Baker	1966	20,340
18. Bill Seifert	1969	20,047
19. Petty Enterprises	1960	19,035
20. Jack Roush	1995	18,973
21. Junior Johnson	1984	18,590
22. Robert Yates	1997	18,528
23. Jack Roush	1994	18,474
24. Stavola Brothers	1988	18,363
25. Petty Enterprises	1971	18,353

MILES DRIVEN

1. Jack Roush	1997	36,887
2. Rick Hendrick	1990	36,777
3. Rick Hendrick	1997	34,895
4. Rick Hendrick	1994	34,601
5. Rick Hendrick	1996	33,883
6. Rick Hendrick	1989	33,292
7. Rick Hendrick	1995	33,150
8. Jack Roush	1996	33,005
9. Rick Hendrick	1988	32,906
10. Rick Hendrick	1987	31,979
11. Rick Hendrick	1993	31,717
12. Robert Yates	1997	24,251
13. Jack Roush	1995	23,249
14. Richard Childress	1997	23,001
15. Stavola Brothers	1988	21,945
16. Jack Roush	1994	21,908

17. Junior Johnson	1991	21,881
18. Junior Johnson	1992	21,868
19. Felix Sabates	1993	21,737
20. Junior Johnson	1992	21,546
21. Robert Yates	1996	21,400
22. Rick Hendrick	1991	21,268
23. Junior Johnson	1984	21,259
24. Rick Hendrick	1989	21,162
25. Junior Johnson	1994	20,900

POLES

1. Carl Kiekhaefer	1955	25
Carl Kiekhaefer	1956	25
3. Nord Krauskopf	1969	20
4. Petty Enterprises	1967	19
5. Rick Hendrick	1986	16
Petty Enterprises	1966	16
7. Holman-Moody	1965	15
8. Junior Johnson	1980	14
Holman-Moody	1969	14
10. Nord Krauskopf	1970	13
11. Howard/Johnson	1972	12
Frank Christian	1951	12
Holman-Moody	1968	12
Petty Enterprises	1968	12
Cotton Owens	1964	12
16. Wood Bros.	1974	11
Harry Melling	1985	11
Herb Thomas	1952	11
Junior Johnson	1981	11
Herb Thomas	1953	11
Rex Lovette	1965	11
Petty Enterprises	1970	11
23. Rick Hendrick	1995	10
Petty Enterprises	1971	10
Bondy Long	1965	10

TOP 5 FINISHES

1. Carl Kiekhaefer	1956	74
2. Petty Enterprises	1963	51
3. Petty Enterprises	1971	50
4. Petty Enterprises	1964	49
5. Rick Hendrick	1996	45

6. Petty Enterprises	1967	43	
Holman-Moody	1965	43	
8. Carl Kiekhaefer	1955	42	
Holman-Moody	1965	42	
10. Pete Depaolo	1956	41	
Petty Enterprises	1960	41	
Bondy Long	1965	41	
13. Petty Enterprises	1962	40	
14. Cotton Owens	1964	39	
15. Holman-Moody	1968	38	
Bud Moore	1962	38	
Bondy Long	1964	38	
18. Holman-Moody	1963	37	
19. Rick Hendrick	1997	34	
Petty Enterprises	1970	34	
Jack Roush	1997	34	
22. Pete DePaolo	1957	33	
Rick Hendrick	1989	33	
Rick Hendrick	1995	33	
Petty Enterprises	1959	33	

TOP 10 FINISHES

1. Carl Kiekhaefer	1956	92
2. Petty Enterprises	1960	70
3. Petty Enterprises	1963	65
4. Pete DePaolo	1956	61
5. Petty Enterprises	1964	60
6. Cotton Owens	1964	59
7. Rick Hendrick	1996	58
8. Petty Enterprises	1971	56
Buck Baker	1965	56
10. Petty Enterprises	1962	54
11. Rick Hendrick	1997	50
Rick Hendrick	1995	50
Jack Roush	1997	50
14. Holman-Moody	1963	49
Holman-Moody	1965	49
16. Rick Hendrick	1988	47
Petty Enterprises	1958	47
18. Rick Hendrick	1994	46
Carl Kiekhaefer	1955	46
20. Rick Hendrick	1990	45
Petty Enterprises	1967	45
Bondy Long	1965	45
23. Petty Enterprises	1959	44

Bud Moore	1962	44
Holman-Moody	1969	44

RACES LED

1. Rick Hendrick	1997	44
Petty Enterprises	1971	44
3. Jack Roush	1997	43
4. Petty Enterprises	1967	42
5. Carl Kiekhaefer	1956	40
Holman-Moody	1969	40
7. Holman-Moody	1968	38
Nord Krauskopf	1969	38
9. Robert Yates	1997	37
10. Petty Enterprises	1970	36
11. Carl Kiekhaefer	1955	35
Nord Krauskopf	1970	35
Petty Enterprises	1968	35
Petty Enterprises	1964	35
15. Holman-Moody	1965	34
16. Cotton Owens	1964	33
17. Petty Enterprises	1969	32
Petty Enterprises	1963	32
19. Petty Enterprises	1972	31
Rick Hendrick	1996	31
Rex Lovette	1965	31
22. Howard/Johnson	1972	30
Rick Hendrick	1995	30
24. Holman-Moody	1971	29
Bondy Long	1965	29

WIN PERCENTAGE

1. Wood Bros.	1973	61%
2. Carl Kiekhaefer	1956	59%
3. Carl Kiekhaefer	1955	56%
4. Pete DePaolo	1957	56%
5. Petty Enterprises	1967	55%
6. Petty Enterprises	1970	49%
7. Petty Enterprises	1971	47%
8. Wood Bros.	1976	45%
9. Petty Enterprises	1975	43%
10. Holman-Moody	1964	41%
11. Richard Howard	1974	40%
Junior Johnson	1982	40%

13. Harry Melling	1985	39%
Wood Bros.	1972	39%
Junior Johnson	1981	39%
Rick Hendrick	1996	39%
17. Holman-Moody	1963	38%
Richard Childress	1987	38%
19. Wood Bros.	1974	37%
20. Holman-Moody	1968	36%
Cotton Owens	1966	36%

22. Marshall Teague	1951	35%
Herb Thomas	1954	35%
Rex Lovette	1965	35%
Wood Bros.	1965	35%
Wood Bros.	1968	35%
Bud Moore	1961	35%
Petty Enterprises	1963	35%

27

RACE RESULTS: 1949-1996

This chapter contains race results for every NASCAR Strictly Stock, Grand National, and Winston Cup race run through the 1996 season. Between the years 1949 and 1971, as many as 60 races were held in a single season and records were not kept as tightly as they are today. For this reason, only the race winner is listed for those years. Starting in 1972, when R.J. Reynolds took over as primary sponsor and the Winston Cup circuit was created, the season was shortened to a more manageable number of approximately 30 races. Complete race results are included from 1971 to 1996, including a listing of all finishers, time of race, average speed, and, when available, margin of victory. 1997 race-by-race results are included in Chapter 11, "1997 Race Results."

1949

RACE WINNERS

RACE	DRIVER	CAR
Charlotte NC	Jim Roper	Lincoln
Daytona Beach FL	Red Byron	Olds
Hillsboro NC	Bob Flock	Olds
Langhorne PA	Curtis Turner	Olds
Hamburg NY	Jack White	Lincoln
Martinsville VA	Red Byron	Olds
Heidelberg PA	Lee Petty	Plymouth
N Wilkesboro NC	Bob Flock	Olds

1950

RACE WINNERS

RACE	DRIVER	CAR
Daytona Beach FL	Harold Kite	Lincoln
Charlotte NC	Tim Flock	Lincoln
Langhorne PA	Curtis Turner	Olds
Martinsville	Curtis Turner	Olds
Canfield OH	Bill Rexford	Olds
Vernon NY	Bill Blair	Mercury
Dayton OH	Jimmy Florian	Ford
Rochester NY	Curtis Turner	Olds
Charlotte NC	Curtis Turner	Olds
Hillsboro NC	Fireball Roberts	Olds
Dayton OH	Dick Linder	Olds
Hamburg NY	Dick Linder	Olds
Darlington SC	Johnny Mantz	Plymouth
Langhorne PA	Fonty Flock	Olds
N Wilkesboro NC	Leon Sales	Plymouth
Vernon NY	Dick Linder	Olds
Martinsville VA	Herb Thomas	Plymouth
Winchester IN	Lloyd Moore	Mercury
Hillsboro NC	Lee Petty	Plymouth

1951

RACE WINNERS

RACE	DRIVER	CAR
Dayton Beach FL	Marshall Teague	Hudson
Charlotte NC	Curtis Turner	Nash
Mobile AL	Tim Flock	Olds

Gardena CA	Marshall Teague	Hudson
Hillsboro NC	Fonty Flock	Olds
Phoenix AZ	Marshall Teague	Hudson
N Wilkesboro NC	Fonty Flock	Olds
Martinsville VA	Curtis Turner	Olds
Canfield OH	Marshall Teague	Hudson
Columbus OH	Tim Flock	Olds
Columbia SC	Frank Mundy	Studebake
Dayton OH	Curtis Turner	Olds
Gardena CA	Lou Figaro	Hudson
Grand Rapids MI	Marshall Teague	Hudson
Bainbridge OH	Fonty Flock	Olds
Heidelberg PA	Herb Thomas	Olds
Weaverville NC	Fonty Flock	Olds
Rochester NY	Lee Petty	Plymouth
Altamont NY	Fonty Flock	Olds
Detroit MI	Tommy Thompson	Chrysler
Toledo OH	Tim Flock	Olds
Morristown NJ	Tim Flock	Olds
Greenville SC	Bob Flock	Olds
Darlington SC	Herb Thomas	Hudson
Columbia SC	Tim Flock	Olds
Macon GA	Herb Thomas	Hudson
Langhorne PA	Herb Thomas	Hudson
Charlotte NC	Herb Thomas	Hudson
Dayton OH	Fonty Flock	Olds
Wilson NC	Fonty Flock	Olds
Hillsboro NC	Herb Thomas	Hudson
Thompson CT	Neil Cole	Olds
Shippenville PA	Tim Flock	Olds
Martinsville VA	Frank Mundy	Olds
Oakland CA	Marvin Burke	Mercury
N Wilkesboro NC	Fonty Flock	Olds
Hanford CA	Danny Weinberg	Studebake
Jacksonville FL	Herb Thomas	Hudson
Atlanta GA	Tim Flock	Hudson
Gardena CA	Bill Norton	Mercury
Mobile AL	Frank Mundy	Studebake

1952

RACE WINNERS

RACE	DRIVER	CAR
W Palm Beach FL	Fim Flock	Hudson
Daytona Beach FL	Marshall Teague	Hudson
Jacksonville FL	Marshall Teague	Hudson
N Wilkesboro NC	Herb Thomas	Hudson
Martinsville VA	Dick Rathmann	Hudson
Columbia SC	Buck Baker	Hudson
Atlanta GA	Bill Blair	Olds
Macon GA	Herb Thomas	Hudson
Langhorne PA	Dick Rathmann	Hudson
Darlington	Dick Rathmann	Hudson
Dayton OH	Dick Rathmann	Hudson
Canfield OH	Herb Thomas	Hudson
Augusta GA	Gober Sosebee	Chrysler
Toledo OH	Tim Flock	Hudson
Hillsboro NC	Tim Flock	Hudson
Charlotte NC	Herb Thomas	Hudson
Detroit MI	Tim Flock	Hudson
Niagara Falls ONT	Buddy Shuman	Hudson
Oswego NY	Tim Flock	Hudson
Monroe MI	Tim Flock	Hudson
Morristown NJ	Lee Petty	Plymouth
South Bend IN	Tim Flock	Hudson
Rochester NY	Tim Flock	Hudson
Weaverville NC	Bob Flock	Hudson
Darlington SC	Fonty Flock	Olds
Macon GA	Lee Petty	Plymouth
Langhorne PA	Lee Petty	Plymouth
Dayton OH	Dick Rathmann	Hudson
Wilson NC	Herb Thomas	Hudson
Hillsboro NC	Fonty Flock	Olds
Martinsville VA	Herb Thomas	Hudson
N Wilkesboro NC	Herb Thomas	Hudson
Atlanta GA	Donald Thomas	Hudson
W Palm Beach FL	Herb Thomas	Hudson

1953

RACE WINNERS

RACE	DRIVER	CAR
W Palm Beach FL	Lee Petty	Dodge
Daytona Beach FL	Bill Blair	Olds
Spring Lake NC	Herb Thomas	Hudson
N Wilkesboro NC	Herb Thomas	Hudson
Charlotte NC	Dick Passwater	Olds
Richmond VA	Lee Petty	Dodge
Macon GA	Dick Rathmann	Hudson
Langhorne PA	Buck Baker	Olds
Columbia SC	Buck Baker	Olds
Hickory NC	Tim Flock	Hudson
Martinsville VA	Lee Petty	Dodge
Columbus OH	Herb Thomas	Hudson
Raleigh NC	Fonty Flock	Hudson
Shreveport LA	Lee Petty	Dodge
Pensacola FL	Herb Thomas	Hudson
Langhorne PA	Dick Rathmann	Hudson
High Point NC	Herb Thomas	Hudson
Wilson NC	Fonty Flock	Hudson
Rochester NY	Herb Thomas	Hudson
Spartanburg SC	Lee Petty	Dodge
Morristown NJ	Dick Rathmann	Hudson
Atlanta GA	Herb Thomas	Hudson
Rapid City SD	Herb Thomas	Hudson
N Platte NE	Dick Rathmann	Hudson
Davenport IA	Herb Thomas	Hudson
Hillsboro NC	Curtis Turner	Olds
Weaverville NC	Fonty Flock	Hudson
Norfolk VA	Herb Thomas	Hudson
Hickory NC	Fonty Flock	Hudson
Darlington SC	Buck Baker	Olds
Macon GA	Speedy Thompson	Olds
Langhorne PA	Dick Rathmann	Hudson
Bloomsburg PA	Herb Thomas	Hudson
Wilson NC	Herb Thomas	Hudson
N Wilkesboro NC	Speedy Thompson	Olds
Martinsville VA	Jim Paschal	Dodge
Atlanta GA	Buck Baker	Olds

1954

RACE WINNERS

RACE	DRIVER	CAR
W Palm Beach FL	Herb Thomas	Hudson
Daytona Beach FL	Lee Petty	Chrysler
Jacksonville FL	Herb Thomas	Hudson
Atlanta GA	Herb Thomas	Hudson
Savannah GA	Al Keller	Hudson
Oakland CA	Dick Rathmann	Hudson
N Wilkesboro NC	Dick Rathmann	Hudson
Hillsboro NC	Herb Thomas	Hudson
Macon GA	Gober Sosebee	Olds
Langhorne PA	Herb Thomas	Hudson
Wilson NC	Buck Baker	Olds
Martinsville VA	Jim Paschal	Olds
Sharon PA	Lee Petty	Chrysler
Raleigh NC	Herb Thomas	Hudson
Charlotte NC	Buck Baker	Olds
Gardena CA	John Soares	Dodge
Columbia SC	Curtis Turner	Olds
Linden NJ	Al Keller	Jaguar
Hickory NC	Herb Thomas	Hudson
Rochester NY	Lee Petty	Chrysler
Mechanicsburg PA	Herb Thomas	Hudson
Spartanburg SC	Herb Thomas	Hudson
Weaverville NC	Herb Thomas	Hudson
Willow Springs IL	Dick Rathmann	Hudson
Grand Rapids MI	Lee Petty	Chrysler

Morristown NJ	Buck Baker	Olds
Oakland CA	Danny Letner	Hudson
Charlotte NC	Lee Petty	Chrysler
San Mateo CA	Hershell McGriff	Olds
Corbin KY	Lee Petty	Chrysler
Darlington SC	Herb Thomas	Hudson
Macon GA	Hershel McGriff	Olds
Charlotte NC	Hershel McGriff	Olds
Langhorne PA	Herb Thomas	Hudson
LeHi AR	Buck Baker	Olds
Martinsville VA	Lee Petty	Chrysler
N Wilkesboro NC	Hershel McGriff	Olds

1955

RACE WINNERS

RACE	DRIVER	CAR
High Point NC	Lee Petty	Chrysler
W Palm Beach FL	Herb Thomas	Hudson
Jacksonville FL	Lee Petty	Chrysler
Daytona Beach FL	Tim Flock	Chrysler
Savannah GA	Lee Petty	Chrysler
Columbia SC	Fonty Flock	Chevrolet
Hillsboro NC	Jim Paschal	Olds
N Wilkesboro NC	Buck Baker	Olds
Montgomery AL	Tim Flock	Chrysler
Langhorne PA	Tim Flock	Chrusler
Charlotte NC	Buck Baker	Buick
Hickory NC	Junior Johnson	Olds
Phoenix AZ	Tim Flock	Chrysler
Tucson AZ	Danny Letner	Olds
Martinsville VA	Tim Flock	Chrysler
Richmond VA	Tim Flock	Chrysler
Raleigh NC	Junior Johnson	Olds
Winston Salem NC	Lee Petty	Chrysler
New Oxford PA	Junior Johnson	Olds
Rochester NY	Tim Flock	Chrysler
Fonda NY	Junior Johnson	Olds
Plattsburg NY	Lee Petty	Chrysler
Charlotte NC	Tim Flock	Chrysler
Spartanburg SC	Tim Flock	Chrysler
Columbia SC	Jim Paschal	Olds
Weaverville NC	Tim Flock	Chrysler
Morristown NJ	Tim Flock	Chrysler
Altamont NY	Junior Johnson	Olds
Syracuse NY	Tim Flock	Chrysler
San Mateo CA	Tim Flock	Chrysler
Charlotte NC	Jim Paschal	Olds
Winston-Salem NC	Lee Petty	Dodge
LeHi AR	Fonty Flock	Chrysler
Raleigh NC	Herb Thomas	Buick
Darlington SC	Heb Thomas	Chevrolet
Montgomery AL	Tim Flock	Chrysler
Langhorne PA	Tim Flock	Chrysler
Raleigh NC	Fonty Flock	Chrysler
Greenville SC	Tim Flock	Chrysler
LeHi AR	Speedy Thompson	Ford
Columbia SC	Tim Flock	Chrysler
Martinsville VA	Speedy Thompson	Chrysler
Las Vegas NV	Norm Nelson	Chrysler
N Wilkesboro NC	Buck Baker	Ford
Hillsboro NC	Tim Flock	Chrysler

1956

RACE WINNERS

RACE	DRIVER	CAR
Hickory NC	Tim Flock	Chrysler
Charlotte NC	Fonty Flock	Chrysler

Lancaster CA	Chuck Stevenson	Ford
W Palm Beach FL	Herb Thomas	Chevrolet
Phoenix AZ	Buck Baker	Chrysler
Daytona Beach FL	Tim Flock	Chrysler
W Palm Beach FL	Billy Myers	Mercury
Wilson NC	Herb Thomas	Chevrolet
Atlanta GA	Buck Baker	Chrysler
N Wilkesboro NC	Tim Flock	Chrysler
Longhorne PA	Buck Baker	Chrysler
Richmond VA	Buck Baker	Dodge
Columbia SC	Speedy Thompson	Dodge
Concord NC	Speedy Thompson	Chrysler
Greenville SC	Buck Baker	Dodge
Hickory NC	Speedy Thompson	Chrysler
Hillsboro NC	Buck Baker	Chrysler
Martinsville VA	Buck Baker	Dodge
Abbottstown PA	Buck Baker	Dodge
Charlotte NC	Speedy Thompson	Chrysler
Portland OR	Herb Thomas	Chrysler
Eureka CA	Herb Thomas	Chrysler
Syracuse NY	Buck Baker	Chrysler
Merced CA	Herb Thomas	Chrysler
LeHi AR	Ralph Moody	Ford
Charlotte NC	Speedy Thompson	Chrysler
Rochester NY	Speedy Thompson	Chrysler
Portland OR	John Kieper	Olds
Weaverville NC	Lee Petty	Dodge
Raleigh NC	Fireball Roberts	Ford
Spartanburg SC	Lee Petty	Dodge
Sacramento CA	Lloyd Dane	Mercury
Chicago IL	Fireball Roberts	Ford
Shelby NC	Speedy Thompson	Dodge
Montgomery AL	Marvin Panch	Ford
Oklahoma City OK	Jim Paschal	Mercury
Elkhart Lake WI	Tim Flock	Mercury
Old Bridge NJ	Ralph Moody	Ford
San Mateo CA	Eddie Pagan	Ford
Norfolk VA	Billy Myers	Mercury
Spartanburg SC	Ralph Moody	Ford
Myrtle Beach SC	Fireball Roberts	Ford
Portland OR	Royce Haggerty	Dodge
Darlington SC	Curtis Turner	Ford
Montgomery AL	Buck Baker	Chrysler
Charlotte NC	Ralph Moody	Ford
Langhorne PA	Paul Goldsmith	Chevrolet
Portland OR	Lloyd Dane	Ford
Columbia SC	Buck Baker	Dodge
Hillsboro NC	Fireball Roberts	Ford
Newport TN	Fireball Roberts	Ford
Charlotte NC	Buck Baker	Chrysler
Shelby NC	Buck Baker	Chrysler
Martinsville VA	Jack Smith	Dodge
Hickory NC	Speedy Thompson	Chrysler
Wilson NC	Buck Baker	Chrysler

1957

RACE WINNERS

RACE	DRIVER	CAR
Lancaster CA	Marvin Panch	Ford
Concord NC	Marvin Panch	Ford
Titusville FL	Fireball Roberts	Ford
Daytona Beach FL	Cotton Owens	Pontiac
Concord NC	Jack Smith	Chevrolet
Wilson NC	Ralph Moody	Ford
Hillsboro NC	Buck Baker	Chevrolet
Weaverville NC	Buck Baker	Chevrolet
N Wilkesboro NC	Fireball Roberts	Ford
Langhorne PA	Fireball Roberts	Ford
Charlotte NC	Fireball Roberts	Ford
Spartanburg SC	Marvin Panch	Ford
Greensboro NC	Paul Goldsmith	Ford
Portland OR	Art Watts	Ford
Shelby NC	Fireball Roberts	Ford
Richmond VA	Paul Goldsmith	Ford
Martinsville VA	Buck Baker	Chevrolet
Portland OR	Eddie Pagan	Ford
Eureka CA	Lloyd Dane	Ford

New Oxford PA	Buck Baker	Chevrolet
Lancaster SC	Paul Goldsmith	Ford
Los Angeles CA	Eddie Pagan	Ford
Newport TN	Fireball Roberts	Ford
Columbia SC	Jack Smith	Chevrolet
Sacramento CA	Bill Amick	Ford
Spartanburg SC	Lee Petty	Olds
Jacksonville NC	Buck Baker	Chevrolet
Raleigh NC	Paul Goldsmith	Ford
Charlotte NC	Marvin Panch	Ford
LeHi AR	Marvin Panch	Pontiac
Portland OR	Eddie Pagan	Ford
Hickory NC	Jack Smith	Chevrolet
Norfolk VA	Buck Baker	Chevrolet
Lancaster SC	Speedy Thompson	Chevrolet
Watkins Glen NY	Buck Baker	Chevrolet
Bremerton WA	Parnelli Jones	Ford
New Oxford PA	Marvin Panch	Ford
Old Bridge NJ	Lee Petty	Olds
Myrtle Beach SC	Gwyn Staley	Chevrolet
Darlington SC	Speedy Thompson	Chevrolet
Syracuse NY	Gwyn Staley	Chevrolet
Weaverville NC	Lee Petty	Olds
Sacramento CA	Danny Graves	Chevrolet
San Jose CA	Marvin Porter	Ford
Langhorne PA	Gwyn Staley	Chevrolet
Columbia SC	Buck Baker	Chevrolet
Shelby NC	Buck Baker	Chevrolet
Charlotte NC	Lee Petty	Olds
Martinsville VA	Bob Welborn	Chevrolet
Newberry SC	Fireballl Roberts	Ford
Concord NC	Fireball Roberts	Ford
N Wilkesboro NC	Jack Smith	Chevrolet
Greensboro NC	Buck Baker	Chevrolet

1958

RACE WINNERS

RACE	WINNER	CAR
Fayetteville, NC	Rex White	Chevrolet
Daytona Beach, FL	Paul Goldsmith	Pontiac
Charlotte, NC	Lee Petty	Oldsmobile
Fayetteville, NC	Curtis Turner	Ford
Wilson, NC	Lee Petty	Oldsmobile
Hillsborough, NC	Buck Baker	Chevrolet
Fayetteville, NC	Bob Welborn	Chevrolet
Columbia, SC	Speedy Thompson	Chevrolet
Spartanburg, SC	Speedy Thompson	Chevrolet
Atlanta, GA	Curtis Turner	Ford
Charlotte, NC	Curtis Turner	Ford
Martinsville, VA	Bob Welborn	Chevrolet
Manassas, VA	Frankie Schneider	Chevrolet
Old Bridge, NJ	Jim Reed	Ford
Greenville, SC	Jack Smith	Chevrolet
Greensboro, NC	Bob Welborn	Chevrolet
Roanoke, VA	Jim Reed	Ford
N Wilkesboro, NC	Junior Johnson	Ford
Winston-Salem, NC	Bob Welborn	Chevrolet
Trenton, NJ	Fireball Roberts	Chevrolet
Riverside, CA	Eddie Gray	Ford
Columbia, SC	Junior Johnson	Ford
Bradford, PA	Junior Johnson	Ford
Reading, PA	Junior Johnson	Ford
New Oxford, PA	Lee Petty	Oldsmobile
Hickory, NC	Lee Petty	Oldsmobile
Weaverville, NC	Rex White	Chevrolet
Raleigh, NC	Fireball Roberts	Chevrolet
Asheville, NC	Jim Paschal	Chevrolet
Busti, NY	Shortly Rollins	Ford
Toronto, CAN	Lee Petty	Olds
Buffalo, NY	Jim Reed	Ford
Rochester, NY	Cotton Owens	Pontiac
Belmar, NJ	Jim Reed	Chevrolet
Bridgehampton, NY	Jack Smith	Chevrolet
Columbia, SC	Speedy Thompson	Chevrolet
Nashville, TN	Joe Weatherly	Ford
Weaverville, NC	Fireball Roberts	Chevrolet
Winston-Salem, NC	Lee Petty	Oldsmobile

Myrtle Beach, SC	Bob Welborn	Chevrolet
Darlington, SC	Fireball Roberts	Chevrolet
Charlotte, NC	Buck Baker	Chevrolet
Birmingham, AL	Fireball Roberts	Chevrolet
Sacramento, CA	Parnelli Jones	Ford
Gastonia, NC	Buck Baker	Chevrolet
Richmond, VA	Speedy Thompson	Chevrolet
Hillsborough, NC	Joe Eubanks	Pontiac
Salisbury, NC	Lee Petty	Oldsmobile
Martinsville	Fireball Roberts	Chevrolet
N Wilkesboro, NC	Junior Johnson	Ford
Atlanta, GA	Junior Johnson	Ford

1959

RACE WINNERS

RACE	WINNER	CAR
Fayetteville, NC	Bob Welborn	Chevrolet
Daytona Beach, FL	Bob Welborn	Chevrolet
Daytona Beach, FL	Lee Petty	Oldsmobile
Hillsborough, NC	Curtis Turner	Ford
Atlanta, GA	Johnny Beauchamp	Ford
Wilson, NC	Junior Johnson	Ford
Winston-Salem, NC	Jim Reed	Ford
Columbia, SC	Jack Smith	Chevrolet
N Wilkesboro, NC	Lee Petty	Olds
Reading, PA	Junior Johnson	Ford
Hickory, NC	Junior Johnson	Ford
Martinsville, VA	Lee Petty	Olds
Trenton, NJ	Tom Pistone	Ford
Charlotte, NC	Lee Petty	Olds
Nashville, TN	Rex White	Chevrolet
Los Angeles, CA	Parnelli Jones	Ford
Spartanburg, SC	Jack Smith	Chevrolet
Greenville, SC	Junior Johnson	Ford
Atlanta, GA	Lee Petty	Plymouth
Columbia, SC	Lee Petty	Plymouth
Wilson, NC	Junior Johnson	Ford
Richmond, VA	Tom Pistone	Ford
Winston-Salem	Rex White	Chevrolet
Weaverville, NC	Rex White	Chevrolet
Daytona Beach, FL	Fireball Roberts	Pontiac
Pittsburgh, PA	Jim Reed	Chevrolet
Charlotte, NC	Jack Smith	Chevrolet
Myrtle Beach, SC	Ned Jarrett	Ford
Charlotte, NC	Ned Jarrett	Ford
Nashville, TN	Joe Lee Johnson	Chevrolet
Weaverville, NC	Bob Welborn	Chevrolet
Winston-Salem, NC	Rex White	Chevrolet
Greenville, SC	Buck Baker	Chevrolet
Columbia, SC	Lee Petty	Chevrolet
Darlington, SC	Jim Reed	Chevrolet
Hickory, NC	Lee Petty	Chevrolet
Richmond, VA	Cotton Ownes	Ford
Sacramento, CA	Eddie Gray	Ford
Hillsborough, NC	Lee Petty	Plymouth
Martinsville, VA	Roy White	Chevrolet
Weaverville, NC	Lee Petty	Plymouth
N Wilkesboro, NC	Lee Petty	Plymouth
Charlotte, NC	Jack Smith	Chevrolet

1960

RACE WINNERS

RACE	WINNER	CAR
Charlotte, NC	Jack Smith	Chevrolet
Columbia, SC	Ned Jarrett	Ford
Daytona Beach, FL	Fireball Roberts	Pontiac

Daytona Beach, FL	Jack Smith	Pontiac
Daytona Beach, FL	Junior Johnson	Chevrolet
Charlotte, NC	Richard Petty	Plymouth
N Wilkesboro, NC	Lee Petty	Plymouth
Phoenix, AZ	John Rostek	Ford
Columbia, SC	Rex White	Chevrolet
Martinsville, VA	Richard Petty	Plymouth
Hickory, NC	Joe Weatherly	Ford
Wilson, NC	Joe Weatherly	Ford
Winston-Salem, NC	Glen Wood	Ford
Greenville, SC	Ned Jarrett	Ford
Weaverville, NC	Lee Petty	Plymouth
Darlington, SC	Joe Weatherly	Ford
Spartanburg, SC	Ned Jarrett	Ford
Hillsborough, NC	Lee Petty	Plymouth
Richmond, VA	Lee Petty	Plymouth
Hanford, CA	Marvin Porter	Ford
Concord, NC	Joe Lee Johnson	Chevrolet
Winston-Salem, NC	Glen Wood	Ford
Daytona Beach, FL	Jack Smith	Pontiac
Pittsburgh, PA	Lee Petty	Plymouth
Montgomery, NY	Rex White	Chevrolet
Myrtle Beach, SC	Buck Baker	Chevrolet
Hampton, GA	Fireball Roberts	Pontiac
Birmingham, AL	Ned Jarrett	Ford
Nashville, TN	Johnny Beauchamp	Chevrolet
Weaverville, NC	Rex White	Chevrolet
Spartanburg, SC	Cotton Owens	Pontiac
Columbia, SC	Rex White	Chevrolet
South Boston, VA	Junior Johnson	Chevrolet
Winston-Salem, NC	Glen Wood	Ford
Darlington, SC	Buck Baker	Pontiac
Hickory, NC	Junior Johnson	Chevrolet
Sacramento, CA	Jim Cook	Dodge
Sumter, SC	Ned Jarrett	Ford
Hillsborough, NC	Richard Petty	Plymouth
Martinsville, VA	Rex White	Chevrolet
N Wilkesboro, NC	Rex White	Chevrolet
Concord, NC	Speedy Thompson	Ford
Richmond, VA	Speedy Thompson	Ford
Hampton, GA	Bobby Johns	Pontiac

Bud Moore, World War II hero and legendary NASCAR car owner.

1961

RACE WINNERS

RACE	WINNER	CAR
Charlotte, NC	Joe Weatherly	Ford
Jacksonville, FL	Lee Petty	Plymouth
Daytona Beach, FL	Fireball Roberts	Pontiac
Daytona Beach, FL	Joe Weatherly	Pontiac
Daytona Beach, FL	Marvin Panch	Pontiac
Spartanburg, SC	Cotton Owens	Pontiac
Weaverville, NC	Rex White	Chevrolet
Hanford, CA	Fireball Roberts	Pontiac
Hampton, GA	Bob Burdick	Pontiac
Greenville, SC	Emanuel Zervakis	Chevrolet
Hillsborough, NC	Cotton Owens	Pontiac
Winston Salem, NC	Rex White	Chevrolet
Martinsville, VA	Fred Lorenzen	Ford
N Wilkesboro, NC	Rex White	Chevrolet
Columbia, SC	Cotton Owens	Pontiac
Hickory, NC	Junior Johnson	Pontiac
Richmond, VA	Richard Petty	Plymouth
Martinsville, VA	Junior Johnson	Pontiac
Darlington, SC	Fred Lorenzen	Ford
Concord, NC	Richard Petty	Plymouth
Concord, NC	Joe Weatherly	Pontiac
Riverside, CA	Lloyd Dane	Chevrolet
Los Angeles, CA	Eddie Gray	Ford
Concord, NC	David Pearson	Pontiac
Spartanburg, SC	Jim Paschal	Pontiac
Birmingham, AL	Ned Jarrett	Chevrolet
Greenville, SC	Jack Smith	Pontiac
Winston-Salem, NC	Rex White	Chevrolet
Norwood MA	Emanuel Zervakis	Chevrolet
Hartsville, SC	Buck Baker	Chrysler
Roanoke, VA	Junior Johnson	Pontiac
Daytona Beach, FL	David Pearson	Pontiac
Hampton, GA	Fred Lorenzen	Ford
Columbia, SC	Cotton Owens	Pontiac
Myrtle Beach, SC	Joe Weatherly	Pontiac
Nashville, TN	Jim Paschal	Pontiac
Bristol, TN	Jack Smith	Pontiac
Winston-Salem, NC	Rex White	Chevrolet
Weaverville, NC	Junior Johnson	Pontiac
Richmond, VA	Junior Johnson	Pontiac
South Boston	Junior Johnson	Pontiac
Darlington, SC	Nelson Stacy	Ford
Hickory, NC	Rex White	Chevrolet
Richmond, VA	Joe Weatherly	Pontiac
Sacramento, CA	Eddie Gray	Ford
Hampton, GA	David Pearson	Pontiac
Martinsville, VA	Joe Weatherly	Pontiac
N Wilkesboro, NC	Rex White	Chevrolet
Concord, NC	Joe Weatherly	Pontiac
Bristol, TN	Joe Weatherly	Pontiac
Greenville, SC	Junior Johnson	Pontiac
Hillsborough, NC	Joe Weatherly	Pontiac

1962

RACE WINNERS

RACE	WINNER	CAR
Concord, NC	Jack Smith	Pontiac
Weaverville, NC	Rex White	Chevrolet

Daytona Beach, FL	Fireball Roberts	Pontiac
Daytona Beach, FL	Joe Weatherly	Pontiac
Daytona Beach, FL	Fireball Roberts	Pontiac
Concord, NC	Joe Weatherly	Pontiac
Weaverville, NC	Joe Weatherly	Pontiac
Savannah, GA	Jack Smith	Pontiac
Hillsborough, NC	Rex White	Chevrolet
Richmond, VA	Rex White	Chevrolet
Columbia, SC	Ned Jarrett	Chevrolet
N Wilkesboro, NC	Richard Petty	Plymouth
Greenville, SC	Ned Jarrett	Chevrolet
Myrtle Beach, SC	Jack Smith	Pontiac
Martinsville, VA	Richard Petty	Plymouth
Winston-Salem, NC	Rex White	Chevrolet
Bristol, TN	Bobby Johns	Pontiac
Richmond, VA	Jimmy Pardue	Pontiac
Hickory, NC	Jack Smith	Pontiac
Concord, NC	Joe Weatherly	Pontiac
Darlington, SC	Nelson Stacy	Ford
Spartanburg, NC	Ned Jarrett	Chevrolet
Concord, NC	Nelson Stacy	Ford
Hampton, GA	Fred Lorenzen	Ford
Winston-Salem, NC	Johnny Allen	Pontiac
Augusta, GA	Joe Weatherly	Pontiac
Richmond, VA	Jim Paschal	Pontiac
South Boston, VA	Rex White	Cevrolet
Daytona Beach, FL	Fireball Roberts	Pontiac
Columbia, SC	Rex White	Chevrolet
Asheville, NC	Jack Smith	Pontiac
Greenville, SC	Richard Petty	Plymouth
Augusta, GA	Joe Weatherly	Pontiac
Savannah, GA	Joe Weatherly	Pontiac
Myrtle Beach, SC	Ned Jarrett	Chevrolet
Bristol, TN	Jim Paschal	Plymouth
Chattanooga, TN	Joe Weatherly	Pontiac
Nashville, TN	Jim Paschal	Plymouth
Huntsville, AL	Richard Petty	Plymouth
Weaverville, NC	Jim Paschal	Plymouth
Roanoke, VA	Richard Petty	Plymouth
Winston-Salem, NC	Richard Petty	Plymouth
Spartanburg, SC	Richard Petty	Plymouth
Valdosta, GA	Ned Jarrett	Chevrolet
Darlington, SC	Larry Frank	Ford
Hickory, NC	Rex White	Chevrolet
Richmond, VA	Joe Weatherly	Pontiac
Moyock, NC	Ned Jarrett	Chevrolet
Augusta, GA	Fred Lorenzen	Ford
Martinsville, VA	Nelson Stacy	Ford
N Wilkesboro, NC	Richard Petty	Plymouth
Concord, NC	Junior Johnson	Pontiac
Hampton, GA	Rex White	Chevrolet
Randleman, NC	Jim Paschal	Plymouth
Darlington, SC	Joe Weatherly	Pontiac
Manassas, VA	Richard Petty	Plymouth
Richmond, VA	Ned Jarrett	Ford
Concord, NC	Fred Lorenzen	Ford
Birmingham, AL	Richard Petty	Plymouth
Hampton, GA	Junior Johnson	Chevrolet
Daytona Beach, FL	Fireball Roberts	Ford
Myrtle Beach, SC	Ned Jarrett	Ford
Savannah, GA	Ned Jarrett	Ford
Moyock, NC	Jimmy Pardue	Ford
Winston-Salem, NC	Glen Wood	Ford
Asheville, NC	Ned Jarrett	Ford
Old Bridge, NJ	Fireball Roberts	Ford
Bridgehampton, NY	Richard Petty	Plymouth
Bristol, TN	Fred Lorenzen	Ford
Greenville, SC	Richard Petty	Plymouth
Nashville, TN	Jim Paschal	Plymouth
Columbia, SC	Richard Petty	Plymouth
Weaverville, NC	Fred Lorenzen	Ford
Spartanburg, NC	Ned Jarrett	Ford
Winston-Salem, NC	Junior Johnson	Plymouth
Huntington, WV	Fred Lorenzen	Ford
Darlington, SC	Fireball Roberts	Ford
Hickory, NC	Junior Johnson	Chevrolet
Richmond, VA	Ned Jarrett	Ford
Martinsville, VA	Fred Lorenzen	Ford
Moyock, NC	Ned Jarrett	Ford
N Wilkesboro, NC	Marvin Panch	Ford
Randleman, NC	Richard Petty	Plymouth
Concord, NC	Junior Johnson	Chevrolet
South Boston, VA	Richard Petty	Plymouth
Hillsborough, NC	Joe Weatherly	Pontiac
Riverside, CA	Darel Dieringer	Mercury

1963

RACE WINNERS

RACE	WINNER	CAR
Birmingham, AL	Jim Paschal	Plymouth
Tampa, FL	Richard Petty	Plymouth
Randleman, NC	Jim Paschal	Plymouth
Riverside, CA	Dan Gurney	Ford
Daytona Beach, FL	Junior Johnson	Chevrolet
Daytona Beach, FL	Johnny Rutherford	Chevrolet
Daytona Beach, FL	Tiny Lund	Ford
Spartanburg, NC	Richard Petty	Plymouth
Weaverville, NC	Richard Petty	Plymouth
Hillsborough, NC	Junior Johnson	Chevrolet
Hampton, GA	Fred Lorenzen	Ford
Hickory, NC	Junior Johnson	Chevrolet
Bristol, TN	Fireball Roberts	Ford
Augusta, GA	Ned Jarrett	Ford
Richmond, VA	Joe Weatherly	Pontiac
Greenville, SC	Buck Baker	Pontiac
South Boston, VA	Richard Petty	Plymouth
Winston-Salem, NC	Jim Paschal	Plymouth
Martinsville, VA	Richard Petty	Plymouth
N. Wilkesboro, NC	Richard Petty	Plymouth
Columbia, SC	Richard Petty	Plymouth

1964

RACE WINNERS

RACE	WINNER	CAR
Concord, NC	Ned Jarrett	Ford
Augusta, GA	Fireball Roberts	Ford
Jacksonville, FL	Wendell Scott	Chevrolet
Savannah, GA	Richard Petty	Plymouth
Riverside, CA	Dan Gurney	Ford
Daytona Beach, FL	Junior Johnson	Dodge
Daytona Beach, FL	Richard Petty	Plymouth
Richmond, VA	David Pearson	Dodge
Bristol, TN	Fred Lorenzen	Ford
Greenville, SC	David Pearson	Dodge
Winston-Salem, NC	Marvin Panch	Ford
Hampton, GA	Fred Lorenzen	Ford
Weaverville, NC	Marvin Panch	Ford
Hillsborough, NC	David Pearson	Dodge
Spartanburgh, SC	Ned Jarrett	Ford
Columbia, SC	Ned Jarrett	Ford
Wilkesboro, NC	Fred Lorenzen	Ford
Martinsville, VA	Fred Lorenzen	Ford
Savannah, GA	LeeRoy Yarbrough	Plymouth
Darlington, SC	Fred Lorenzen	Ford
Hampton, VA	Ned Jarrett	Ford
Hickory, NC	Ned Jarrett	Ford
South Boston, VA	Richard Petty	Plymouth
Concord, NC	Jim Paschal	Plymouth
Greenville, SC	LeeRoy Yarbrough	Poymouth
Asheville, NC	Ned Jarrett	Ford
Hampton, GA	Ned Jarrett	Ford
Concord, NC	Richard Petty	Plymouth
Nashville, TN	Richard Petty	Plymouth
Chattanooga	David Pearson	Dodge
Birmingham, AL	Ned Jarrett	Ford
Valdosta, GA	Buck Baker	Dodge
Spartanburg, SC	Richard Petty	Plymouth
Daytona Beach, FL	A.J. Foyt	Dodge
Manassas, VA	Ned Jarrett	Ford
Old Bridge, NJ	Billy Wade	Mercury
Bridgehampton, NY	Billy Wade	Mercury
Islip, NY	Billy Wade	Mercury

Watkins Glen, NY	Billy Wade	Mercury
Oxford, PA	David Pearson	Dodge
Bristol, TN	Fred Lorenzen	Ford
Nashville, TN	Richard Petty	Plymouth
Myrtle Beach, SC	David Pearson	Dodge
Weaverville, NC	Ned Jarrett	Ford
Moyock, NC	Ned Jarrett	Ford
Huntington, WV	Richard Petty	Plymouth
Columbia, SC	David Pearson	Dodge
Winston-Salem, NC	Junior Johnson	Ford
Roanoke, VA	Junior Johnson	Ford
Darlington, SC	Buck Baker	Dodge
Hickory, NC	David Pearson	Dodge
Richmond, VA	Cotton Owens	Dodge
Manassas, VA	Ned Jarrett	Ford
Hillsborough, NC	Ned Jarrett	Ford
Martinsville, VA	Fred Lorenzen	Ford
Savannah, GA	Ned Jarrett	Ford
N Wilkesboro, NC	Marvin Panch	Ford
Concord, NC	Fred Lorenzen	Ford
Harris, NC	Richard Petty	Plymouth
Augusta, GA	Darel Dieringer	Mercury
Jacksonville, NC	Ned Jarrett	Ford

1965

RACE WINNERS

RACE	WINNER	CAR
Riverside, CA	Dan Gurney	Ford
Daytona Beach, FL	Darel Dieringer	Mercury
Daytona Beach, FL	Junior Johnson	Ford
Daytona Beach, FL	Fred Lorenzen	Ford
Spartanburg, SC	Ned Jarrett	Ford
Weaverville, NC	Ned Jarrett	Ford
Richmond, VA	Junior Johnson	Ford
Hillsborough, NC	Ned Jarrett	Ford
Hampton, GA	Marvin Panch	Ford
Greenville, SC	Dick Hutcherson	Ford
N Wilkesboro, NC	Junior Johnson	Ford
Martinsville, VA	Fred Lorenzen	Ford
Columbia, SC	Tiny Lund	Ford
Bristol, NC	Junior Johnson	Ford
Darlington, SC	Junior Johnson	Ford
Hampton, VA	Ned Jarrett	Ford
Winston-Salem, NC	Junior Johnson	Ford
Hickory, NC	Junior Johnson	Ford
Concord, NC	Fred Lorenzen	Ford
Shelby, NC	Ned Jarrett	Ford
Ashville, NC	Junior Johnson	Ford
Harris, NC	Ned Jarrett	Ford
Nashville, TN	Dick Hutcherson	Ford
Birmingham, AL	Ned Jarrett	Ford
Hampton, GA	Marvin Panch	Ford
Greenville, SC	Dick Hutcherson	Ford
Myrtle Beach, SC	Dick Hutcherson	Ford
Valdosta, GA	Cale Yarborough	Ford
Daytona Beach, FL	A.J. Foyt	Ford
Manassas, VA	Junior Johnson	Ford
Old Bridge, NJ	Junior Johnson	Ford
Islip, NY	Marvin Panch	Ford
Watkins Glen, NY	Marvin Panch	Ford
Bristol, TN	Ned Jarrett	Ford
Nashville, TN	Richard Petty	Plymouth
Shelby, NC	Ned Jarrett	Ford
Weaverville, NC	Richard Petty	Plymouth
Maryville, TN	Dick Hutcherson	Ford
Spartanburg, SC	Ned Jarrett	Ford
Augusta, GA	Dick Hutcherson	Ford
Columbia, SC	David Pearson	Dodge
Moyock, NC	Dick Hutcherson	Ford
Beltsville, MD	Ned Jarrett	Ford
Winston-Salem, NC	Junior Johnson	Ford
Darlington, SC	Ned Jarrett	Ford
Hickory, NC	Richard Petty	Plymouth
New Oxford, PA	Dick Hutcherson	Ford
Manassas, VA	Richard Petty	Plymouth
Richmond, VA	David Pearson	Dodge
Martinsville, VA	Junior Johnson	Ford

N Wilkesboro, NC	Junior Johnson	Ford
Concord, NC	Fred Lorenzen	Ford
Hillsborough, NC	Dick Hutcherson	Ford
Rockingham, NC	Curtis Turner	Ford
Moyock, NC	Ned Jarrett	Ford

1966

RACE WINNERS

RACE	WINNER	CAR
Augusta, GA	Richard Petty	Plymouth
Riverside, CA	Dan Gurney	Ford
Daytona Beach, FL	Paul Goldsmith	Plymouth
Daytona Beach, FL	Earl Balmer	Dodge
Daytona Beach, FL	Richard Petty	Plymouth
Rockingham, NC	Paul Goldsmith	Plymouth
Bristol, TN	Dick Hutcherson	Ford
Hampton, GA	Jim Hurtubise	Plymouth
Hickory, NC	David Pearson	Dodge
Columbia, SC	David Pearson	Dodge
Greenville, SC	David Pearson	Dodge
Winston-Salem, NC	David Pearson	Dodge
N Wilkesboro, NC	Jim Paschal	Plymouth
Martinsville, VA	Jim Paschal	Plymouth
Darlington, SC	Richard Petty	Plymouth
Hampton, VA	Richard Petty	Plymouth
Macon, GA	Richard Petty	Plymouth
Monroe, NC	Darel Dieringer	Ford
Richmond, VA	David Pearson	Dodge
Concord, NC	Marvin Panch	Plymouth
Moyock, NC	David Pearson	Dodge
Ashville, NC	David Pearson	Dodge
Spartanburg, SC	Elmo Langley	Ford
Maryville, TN	David Pearson	Dodge
Weaverville, NC	Richard Petty	Plymouth
Beltsville, MD	Tiny Lund	Ford
Greenville, SC	David Pearson	Dodge
Daytona Bearch, FL	Sam McQuagg	Dodge
Manassas, VA	Elmo Langley	Ford
Bridgehampton, NY	David Pearson	Dodge
Oxford ME	Bobby Allison	Chevrolet
Fonda, NY	David Pearson	Dodge
Islip, NY	Bobby Allison	Chevrolet
Briston, TN	Paul Goldsmith	Plymouth
Maryville, TN	Paul Lewis	Plymouth
Nashville, TN	Richard Petty	Plymouth
Hampton, GA	Richard Petty	Plymouth
Columbia, SC	David Pearson	Dodge
Weaverville, NC	Darel Dieringer	Mercury
Beltsville, MD	Bobby Allison	Chevrolet
Winston-Salem, NC	David Pearson	Dodge
Darliangton, SC	Darel Dieringer	Mercury
Hickory, NC	David Pearson	Dodge
Richmond, VA	David Pearson	Dodge
Hillsborough, NC	Dick Hutcherson	Ford
Martinsville, VA	Fred Lorenzen	Ford
N Wilkesboro, NC	Dick Hutcherson	Ford
Concord, NC	LeeRoy Yarbrough	Dodge
Rockingham, NC	Fred Lorenzen	Ford

1967

RACE WINNERS

RACE	WINNER	CAR
Augusta, GA	Richard Petty	Plymouth
Riverside, CA	Parnelli Jones	Ford

Daytona Beach, FL	Fred Lorenzen	Ford
Daytona Beach, FL	Mario Andretti	Ford
Weaverville, NC	Richard Petty	Plymouth
Bristol, TN	David Pearson	Dodge
Greenville, SC	David Pearson	Dodge
Winston-Salem, NC	Bobby Allison	Chevrolet
Hampton, GA	Cale Yearborough	Ford
Columbia, SC	Richard Petty	Plymouth
Hickoary, NC	Richard Petty	Plymouth
N Wilkesboro, NC	Darel Dieringer	Ford
Martinsville, VA	Richard Petty	Plymouth
Savannah, GA	Bobby Allison	Chevrolet
Richmond VA	Richard Petty	Plymouth
Darlington, SC	Richard Petty	Plymouth
Beltsville, MD	Jim Paschal	Plymouth
Hampton, VA	Richard Petty	Plymouth
Concord, NC	Jim Paschal	Plymouth
Asheville, NC	Jim Paschal	Plymouth
Macon, GA	Richard Petty	Plymouth
Maryville, TN	Richard Petty	Plymouth
Birmingham, AL	Bobby Allison	Dodge
Rockingham, NC	Richard Petty	Plymouth
Greenville, SC	Richard Petty	Plymouth
Montgomery, AL	Jim Paschal	Plymouth
Daytona Beach, FL	Cale Yarborough	Ford
Trenton, NJ	Richard Petty	Plymouth
Oxford ME	Bobby Allison	Chevrolet
Fonda, NY	Richard Petty	Plymouth
Islip, NY	Richard Petty	Plymouth
Bristol, NY	Richard Petty	Plymouth
Maryville, TN	Dick Hutcherson	Ford
Nashville, TN	Richard Petty	Plymouth
Hampton, GA	Dick Hutcherson	Ford
Winston-Salem, NC	Richard Petty	Plymouth
Columbia, SC	Richard Petty	Plymouth
Savannah, GA	Richard Petty	Plymouth
Darlington, SC	Richard Petty	Plymouth
Hickory, NC	Richard Petty	Plymouth
Richmond, VA	Richard Petty	Plymouth
Beltsville, MD	Richard Petty	Plymouth
Hillsborough, NC	Richard Petty	Plymouth
Martinsville, VA	Richard Petty	Plymouth
N Wilkesboro, NC	Richard Petty	Plymouth
Concord, NC	Buddy Baker	Dodge
Rockingham, NC	Bobby Allison	Ford
Weaverville, NC	Bobby Allison	Ford

Oxford ME	Richard Petty	Plymouth
Fond, NY	Richard Petty	Plymouth
Trenton, NJ	LeeRoy Yarbrough	Ford
Bristol, TN	David Pearson	Ford
Maryville, TN	Richard Petty	Plymouth
Nashville, TN	David Pearson	Ford
Hampton, GA	LeeRoy Yarbrough	Ford
Columbia, SC	David Pearson	Ford
Winston-Salem, NC	David Pearson	Ford
Weaverville, NC	David Pearson	Ford
Hampton, VA	David Pearson	Ford
South Boston, VA	Richard Petty	Plymouth
Darlington, SC	Cale Yarborough	Mercury
Hickory, NC	David Pearson	Ford
Richmond, VA	Richard Petty	Plymouth
Beltsville, MD	Bobby Isaac	Dodge
Hillsborough, NC	Richard Petty	Plymouth
Martinsville, VA	Richard Petty	Plymouth
N Wilkesboro, NC	Richard Petty	Plymouth
Augusta, GA	David Pearson	Ford
Concord, NC	Charlie Glotzbach	Dodge
Rockingham, NC	Richard Petty	Plymouth
Jefferson, GA	Cale Yarborough	Mercury

1968

RACE WINNERS

RACE	WINNER	CAR
Macon, GA	Bobby Allison	Ford
Montgomery, AL	Richard Petty	Plymouth
Riverside, CA	Dan Gurney	Ford
Daytona Beach, FL	Cale Yarborough	Mercury
Bristol, TN	David Pearson	Ford
Richmond, VA	David Pearson	Ford
Hampton, GA	Cale Yarborough	Mercury
Hickory, NC	Richard Petty	Plymouth
Greenville, SC	Richard Petty	Plymouth
Columbia, SC	Bobby Isaac	Dodge
N Wilkesboro, NC	David Pearson	Ford
Martinsville, VA	Cale Yarborough	Mercury
Augusta, GA	Bobby Isaac	Dodge
Weaverville, NC	David Pearson	Ford
Darlington, SC	David Pearson	Ford
Beltsville, MD	David Pearson	Ford
Hampton, VA	David Pearson	Ford
Concord, NC	Buddy Baker	Dodge
Asheville, NC	Richard Petty	Plymouth
Macon, GA	David Pearson	Ford
Maryville, TN	Richard Petty	Plymouth
Birmingham, AL	Richard Petty	Plymouth
Rockingham, NC	Donnie Allison	Ford
Greenville, SC	Richard Petty	Plymouth
Daytona Beach, FL	Cale Yarborough	Mercury
Islip, NY	Bobby Allison	Chevrolet

1969

RACE WINNERS

RACE	WINNER	CAR
Macon, GA	Richard Petty	Plymouth
Montgomery, AL	Bobby Allison	Plymouth
Riverside, CA	Richard Petty	Ford
Daytona Beach, FL	David Pearson	Ford
Daytona Beach, FL	Bobby Isaac	Dodge
Daytona Beach, FL	LeeRoy Yarbrough	Ford
Rockingham, NC	David Pearson	Ford
Augusta, GA	David Pearson	Ford
Briston, TN	Bobby Allison	Dodge
Hampton, GA	Cale Yarborough	Mercury
Columbia, SC	Bobby Isaac	Dodge
Hickory, NC	Bobby Isaac	Dodge
Greenville, SC	Bobby Isaac	Dodge
Richmond, VA	David Pearson	Ford
N. Wilkesboro, NC	Bobby Allison	Dodge
Martinsville, VA	Richard Petty	Ford
Weaverville, NC	Bobby Isaac	Dodge
Darlington, SC	LeeRoy Yarbrough	Mercury
Beltsville, MD	Bobby Isaac	Dodge
Hampton, VA	David Pearson	Ford
Concord, NC	LeeRoy Yarbrough	Mercury
Macon, GA	Bobby Isaac	Dodge
Maryville, TN	Bobby Isaac	Dodge
Brooklyn, MI	Cale Yarborough	Mercury
Kingsport, TN	Richard Petty	Ford
Greenville, SC	Bobby Isaac	Dodge
Raleigh, NC	David Pearson	Ford
Daytona Beach, FL	LeeRoy Yarbrough	Ford
Dover, DE	Richard Petty	Ford
Thompson, CT	David Pearson	Ford
Trenton, NJ	David Pearson	Ford
Beltsville, MD	Richard Petty	Ford
Bristol, TN	David Pearson	Ford
Nashville, TN	Richard Petty	Ford
Maryville, TN	Richard Petty	Ford
Hampton, GA	LeeRoy Yarbrough	Ford
Brooklyn, MI	David Pearson	Ford
South Boston, VA	Bobby Isaac	Dodge
Winston-Salem, NC	Richard Petty	Ford
Weaverville Nc	Bobby Isaac	Dodge
Darlington, SC	LeeRoy Yarbrough	Ford
Hickory, NC	Bobby Isaac	Dodge
Richmond, VA	Bobby Allison	Dodge
Talladega, AL	Richard Brickhouse	Dodge
Columbia, SC	Bobby Isaac	Dodge
Martinsville, VA	Richard Petty	Ford
N Wilkesboro, NC	David Pearson	Ford
Concord, NC	Dannie Allison	Ford
Savannah, GA	Bobby Isaac	Dodge

Augusta, GA	Bobby Isaac	Dodge
Rockingham, NC	LeeRoy Yarbrough	Ford
Jefferson, GA	Bobby Isaac	Dodge
Macon, GA	Bobby Isaac	Dodge
College Station, TX	Bobby Isaac	Dodge

1970

RACE WINNERS

RACE	WINNER	CAR
Riverside, CA	A.J. Foyt	Ford
Daytona Beach, FL	Cale Yarborough	Mercury
Daytona Beach, FL	Charlie Glotzbach	Dodge
Datona Beach, FL	Pete Hamilton	Plymouth
Richmond, VA	James Hylton	Ford
Rockingham, NC	Richard Petty	Plymouth
Savannah, GA	Richard Petty	Plymouth
Hampton, GA	Bobby Allison	Dodge
Bristol, TN	Donnie Allison	Ford
Talladega, AL	Pete Hamilton	Plymouth
N Wilkesboro, NC	Richard Petty	Plymouth
Columbia, SC	Richard Petty	Plymouth
Darlington, SC	David Pearson	Ford
Beltsville, MD	Bobby Isaac	Dodge
Hampton, VA	Bobby Isaac	Dodge
Concord, NC	Donnie Allison	Ford
Maryville, TN	Bobby Issac	Dodge
Martinsville, VA	Bobby Issac	Dodge
Brooklyn, MI	Cale Yarborough	Mercury
Riverside, CA	Richard Petty	Plymouth
Hickory, NC	Bobby Isaac	Dodge
Kingsport, TN	Richard Petty	Plymouth
Greenville, SC	Bobby Isaac	Dodge
Daytona Beach, FL	Donnie Allison	Ford
Malta, NY	Richard Petty	Plymouth
Thompson, CT	Bobby Isaac	Dodge
Trenton, NJ	Richard Petty	Plymouth
Bristol, TN	Bobby Allison	Dodge
Maryville, TN	Richard Petty	Plymouth
Nashville, TN	Bobby Isaac	Dodge
Hampton, GA	Richard Petty	Plymouth
Columbia, SC	Bobby Isaac	Dodge
Ona, WV	Richard Petty	Plymouth
Brooklyn, MI	Charlie Glotzbach	Dodge
Talladega, AL	Pete Hamilton	Plymouth
Winston-Salem, NC	Richard Petty	Plymouth
South Boston, VA	Richard Petty	Plymouth
Darlington, SC	Buddy Baker	Dodge
Hickory, NC	Bobby Isaac	Dodge
Richmond, VA	Richard Petty	Plymouth
Dover, DE	Richard Petty	Plymouth
Raleigh, NC	Richard Petty	Plymouth
N Wilkesboro, NC	Bobby Isaac	Dodge
Concord, NC	LeeRoy Yarbrough	Mercury
Martinsville, VA	Richard Petty	Plymouth
Macon, GA	Richard Petty	Plymouth
Rockingham, NC	Cale Yarborough	Mercury
Hampton, VA	Bobby Allison	Dodge

1971

RACE WINNERS

RACE	WINNER	CAR
Riverside, CA	Ray Elder	Dodge
Daytona Beach, FL	Pete Hamilton	Plymouth
Daytona Beach, FL	David Pearson	Mercury

Daytona Beach, FL	Richard Petty	Plymouth
Ontario, CA	A.J. Foyt	Mercury
Richmond, VA	Richard Petty	Plymouth
Rockingham, NC	Richard Petty	Plymouth
Hickory, NC	Richard Petty	Plymouth
Bristol, TN	David Pearson	Ford
Hampton, GA	A.J. Foyt	Mercury
Columbia, SC	Richard Petty	Plymouth
Greenville, SC	Bobby Isaac	Dodge
Maryville, TN	Richard Petty	Plymouth
N Wilkesboro, NC	Richard Petty	Plymouth
Martinsville, VA	Richard Petty	Plymouth
Darlington, SC	Buddy Baker	Dodge
South Boston, VA	Benny Parsons	Ford
Talladega, AL	Donnie Allison	Mercury
Asheville, NC	Richard Petty	Plymouth
Kinsport, TN	Bobby Isaac	Dodge
Concord, NC	Bobby Allison	Mercury
Dover, DE	Bobby Allison	Mercury
Brooklyn, MI	Bobby Allison	Mercury
Riverside, CA	Bobby Allison	Dodge
Houston, TX	Bobby Allison	Dodge
Greenville, SC	Richard Petty	Plymouth
Daytona Beach, FL	Bobby Isaac	Dodge
Bristol, TN	Charlie Glotzbach	Chevrolet
Malta, NY	Richard Petty	Plymouth
Islip, NY	Richard Petty	Plymouth
Trenton, NJ	Richard Petty	Plymouth
Nashville, TN	Richard Petty	Plymouth
Hampton, GA	Richard Petty	Plymouth
Winston-Salem, NC	Bobby Allison	Mustang
West Ona, WV	Richard Petty	Plymouth
Brooklyn, MI	Bobby Allison	Mercury
Talladega, AL	Bobby Allison	Mercury
Columbia, SC	Richard Petty	Plymouth
Hickory, SC	Tiny Lund	Camaro
Darlington, SC	Bobby Allison	Mercury
Martinsville, VA	Bobby Isaac	Dodge
Concord, NC	Bobby Allison	Mercury
Dover, DE	Richard Petty	Plymouth
Rockingham, NC	Richard Petty	Plymouth
Macon, GA	Bobby Allison	Ford
Richmond, VA	Richard Petty	Plymouth
North Wilkesboro, NC	Tiny Lund	Camaro
College Station, TX	Richard Petty	Plymouth

1972

WINSTON WESTERN 500

Time of Race: 3 hours, 45 minutes, 11 seconds
Average Speed: 104.018 mph

FINISH	DRIVER	CAR
1	Richard Petty	Plymouth
2	Bobby Allison	Chevrolet
3	Bobby Isaac	Dodge
4	Ray Elder	Dodge
5	Hershel McGriff	Plymouth
6	Kevin Terris	Plymouth
7	James Hylton	Ford
8	Elmo Langley	Ford
9	Friday Hassler	Chevrolet
10	Cecil Gordon	Mercury
11	John Soares, Jr.	Dodge
12	Carl Joyner	Chevrolet
13	Dick Bown	Plymouth
14	Walter Ballard	Ford
15	Raymond Williams	Ford
16	Don Noel	Dodge
17	Charlie Roberts	Ford
18	J.D. McDuffie	Chevrolet
19	Johnny Anderson	Chevrolet
20	Ivan Baldwin	Chevrolet
21	Henley Gray	Ford
22	Jerry Oliver	Olds

23	Dick Kranzler	Chevrolet
24	Larry Esau	Chevrolet
25	Frank James	Chevrolet
26	David Pearson	Ford
27	Ed Negre	Ford
28	A.J. Foyt	Mercury
29	Frank Warren	Dodge
30	Jim Danielson	Mercury
31	David Ray Boggs	Dodge
32	Chuck Bown	Plymouth
33	Paul Dority	Dodge
34	Ron Keselowski	Dodge
35	Ron Gautsche	Ford
36	Jack McCoy	Dodge
37	Neil Castles	Dodge
38	Joe Frasson	Dodge
39	Mark Donohue	Matador
40	Benny Parsons	Ford

DAYTONA 500

Time of Race: 3 hours, 5 minutes, 42 seconds
Average Speed: 161.650 mph

FINISH	DRIVER	CAR
1	A.J. Foyt	Mercury
2	Charlie Glotzbach	Dodge
3	Jim Vandiver	Dodge
4	Benny Parsons	Mercury
5	James Hylton	Ford
6	Jabe Thomas	Plymouth
7	David Sisco	Chevrolet
8	Jabe Thomas	Plymouth
9	John Sears	Plymouth
10	Vic Elford	Plymouth
11	Tommy Gale	Mercury
12	Elmo Langley	Ford
13	Richard Brown	Chevrolet
14	Henley Gray	Ford
15	George Althiede	Dodge
16	Bobby Allison	Chevrolet
17	Ben Arnold	Ford
18	Frank Warren	Dodge
19	David Ray Boggs	Dodge
20	Dr. Ed Hessert	Dodge
21	Larry Dickson	Ford
22	Jim Hurtubise	Chevrolet
23	Bill Dennis	Ford
24	J.D. McDuffie	Chevrolet
25	Coo Marlin	Chevrolet
26	Richard Petty	Plymouth
27	Dave Marcis	Dodge
28	Ron Keselowski	Dodge
29	Bill Seifert	Ford
30	Red Farmer	Ford
31	Jimmy Finger	Ford
32	Buddy Arington	Plymouth
33	Bobby Isaac	Dodge
34	Buddy Baker	Dodge
35	Mark Donohue	Matador
36	Walter Ballard	Ford
37	Ramo Stott	Dodge
38	Bill Champion	Ford
39	Cecil Gordon	Mercury
40	Raymond Williams	Ford

RICHMOND 500

Time of Race: 3 hours, 32 minutes, 12 seconds
Average Speed: 76.258 mph

FINISH	DRIVER	CAR
1	Richard Petty	Plymouth
2	Bobby Allison	Chevrolet
3	Bobby Isaac	Dodge

4	Dave Marcis	Dodge
5	Bill Dennis	Ford
6	James Hylton	Dodge
7	Elmo Langley	Ford
8	Benny Parsons	Ford
9	Cecil Gordon	Mercury
10	John Sears	Dodge
11	Neil Castles	Dodge
12	J.D. McDuffie	Chevrolet
13	Eddie Yarboro	Plymouth
14	Richard Brown	Chevrolet
15	Frank Warren	Plymouth
16	Phil Finney	Chevrolet
17	Jabe Thomas	Plymouth
18	David Ray Boggs	Dodge
19	Bill Seifert	Ford
20	Bill Champion	Ford
21	Walter Ballard	Plymouth
22	Bill Shirey	Plymouth
23	Raymond Williams	Ford
24	Ron Keselowski	Dodge
25	Dean Dalton	Mercury
26	Dub Simpson	Chevrolet
27	Les Covey	Chevrolet
28	Jim Vandiver	Dodge
29	Richard Childress	Chevrolet
30	Ed Negre	Chevrolet

MILLER HIGH LIFE 500

Time of Race: 3 hours, 56 minutes, 4 seconds
Average Speed: 127.082 mph

FINISH	DRIVER	CAR
1	A.J. Foyt	Mercury
2	Bobby Allison	Chevrolet
3	Buddy Baker	Dodge
4	Richard Petty	Plymouth
5	Ray Elder	Dodge
6	Hershel McGriff	Plymouth
7	James Hylton	Ford
8	Marty Robbins	Dodge
9	Elmo Langley	Ford
10	Ramo Stott	Plymouth
11	Jimmy Finger	Ford
12	Jack McCoy	Dodge
13	John Soares, Jr.	Dodge
14	Benny Parsons	Mercury
15	Bill Burns	Dodge
16	Cliff Garner	Ford
17	Johnny Anderson	Chevrolet
18	Dick Bown	Plymouth
19	J.C. Danielson	Mercury
20	Bill Champion	Ford
21	Ben Arnold	Ford
22	Kevin Terris	Plymouth
23	J.D. McDuffie	Chevrolet
24	Mike James	Chevrolet
25	Dean Dalton	Mercury
26	Raymond Williams	Ford
27	Jim Whitt	Ford
28	George Althiede	Dodge
29	Bob Kauf	Chevrolet
30	Carl Adams	Ford
31	Henley Gray	Ford
32	Charlie Roberts	Ford
33	Chuck Bown	Plymouth
34	Les Louder	Chevrolet
35	Ron Gausche	Ford
36	Cecil Gordon	Mercury
37	Dick Kranzler	Chevrolet
38	Don White	Plymouth
39	Gene Romero	Plymouth
40	T.T. Tallas	Ford
41	Red Farmer	Ford
42	Earle Canavan	Plymouth
43	Frank Warren	Dodge
44	Mark Donohue	Matador
45	Bobby Isaac	Dodge
46	Bill Osborne	Ford
47	Walter Ballard	Ford

48	Don Noel	Ford
49	George Follmer	Dodge
50	David Ray Boggs	Dodge
51	Jim Vandiver	Dodge

CAROLINA 500

Time of Race: 4 hours, 23 minutes, 50 seconds
Average Speed: 113.895 mph

FINISH	DRIVER	CAR
1	Bobby Isaac	Dodge
2	Richard Petty	Plymouth
3	Jim Vandiver	Dodge
4	LeeRoy Yarbrough	Ford
5	Dave Marcis	Dodge
6	James Hylton	Mercury
7	Benny Parsons	Ford
8	Buddy Arrington	Dodge
9	Elmo Langley	Ford
10	Neil Castles	Dodge
11	Larry Smith	Ford
12	Joe Frasson	Dodge
13	Jabe Thomas	Plymouth
14	Ed Negre	Dodge
15	Ben Arnold	Ford
16	John Sears	Plymouth
17	David Ray Boggs	Dodge
18	Dean Dalton	Mercury
19	Frank Warren	Dodge
20	Henley Gray	Ford
21	H.B. Bailey	Ford
22	George Althiede	Dodge
23	Richard Brown	Chevrolet
24	Charlie Roberts	Ford
25	Ron Keselowski	Dodge
26	Cecil Gordon	Ford
27	Bobby Allison	Chevrolet
28	Johnny Halford	Plymouth
29	Bill Champion	Ford
30	G.C. Spencer	Plymouth
31	Bill Shirey	Plymouth
32	Walter Ballard	Chevrolet
33	Les Covey	Chevrolet
34	Buddy Baker	Dodge
35	Raymond Williams	Ford
36	Buck Baker	Chevrolet
37	Richard Childress	Chevrolet
38	Dub Simpson	Chevrolet
39	Bobby Mausgrover	Dodge
40	Jackie Oliver	Ford

ATLANTA 500

Time of Race: 3 hours, 53 minutes, 37 seconds
Average Speed: 128.214 mph

FINISH	DRIVER	CAR
1	Bobby Allison	Chevrolet
2	A.J. Foyt	Mercury
3	Bobby Isaac	Dodge
4	David Pearson	Ford
5	Donnie Allison	Chevrolet
6	Richard Petty	Plymouth
7	Benny Parsons	Ford
8	Buddy Baker	Dodge
9	LeeRoy Yarbrough	Ford
10	James Hylton	Ford
11	Buddy Arrington	Dodge
12	Coo Coo Marlin	Chevrolet
13	Richard Brown	Chevrolet
14	G.C. Spencer	Plymouth
15	Mark Donohue	Matador
16	Bill Dennis	Plymouth
17	Cecil Gordon	Mercury

18	Ed Negre	Dodge
19	Jabe Thomas	Plymouth
20	Charlie Roberts	Ford
21	John Sears	Plymouth
22	George Althiede	Dodge
23	Dave Marcis	Dodge
24	Henley Gray	Ford
25	Frank Warren	Dodge
26	Walter Ballard	Ford
27	Tommy Gale	Mercury
28	Dean Dalton	Mercury
29	Ben Arnold	Ford
30	Joe Frasson	Dodge
31	Red Farmer	Ford
32	Jim Vandiver	Dodge
33	Raymond Williams	Ford
34	Elmo Langley	Ford
35	Dick May	Ford
36	Ron Keselowski	Dodge
37	David Sisco	Chevrolet
38	Larry Smith	Ford
39	Lem Blankenship	Dodge
40	Dick Brooks	Ford

SOUTHEASTERN 500

Time of Race: 2 hours, 50 minutes, 18 seconds
Average Speed: 92.826 mph

FINISH	DRIVER	CAR
1	Bobby Allison	Chevrolet
2	Bobby Isaac	Dodge
3	Richard Petty	Plymouth
4	LeeRoy Yarbrough	Ford
5	Cecil Gordon	Mercury
6	Coo Coo Marlin	Chevrolet
7	Elmo Langley	Ford
8	James Hylton	Ford
9	G.C. Spencer	Plymouth
10	Jabe Thomas	Plymouth
11	Walter Ballard	Ford
12	Henley Gray	Ford
13	Dean Dalton	Mercury
14	Charlie Roberts	Ford
15	Frank Warren	Plymouth
16	Bill Champion	Ford
17	Jim Vandiver	Dodge
18	Richard Childress	Chevrolet
19	J.D. McDuffie	Chevrolet
20	David Ray Boggs	Dodge
21	Benny Parsons	Mercury
22	Ed Negre	Dodge
23	David Sisco	Chevrolet
24	Raymond Williams	Ford
25	John Sears	Plymouth
26	Dave Marcis	Dodge
27	Ben Arnold	Ford
28	George Althiede	Dodge
29	Ronnie Daniels	Chevrolet
30	Richard Brown	Chevrolet

REBEL 400

Time of Race: 3 hours, 13 minutes, 0 seconds
Average Speed: 124.406 mph

FINISH	DRIVER	CAR
1	David Pearson	Mercury
2	Richard Petty	Plymouth
3	Joe Frasson	Dodge
4	Benny Parsons	Mercury
5	James Hylton	Ford
6	Buddy Arrington	Dodge
7	Bobby Allison	Chevrolet
8	John Sears	Plymouth

FINISH	DRIVER	CAR
9	Jabe Thomas	Plymouth
10	Cecil Gordon	Mercury
11	Bill Champion	Ford
12	Dean Dalton	Mercury
13	Elmo Langley	Ford
14	Raymond Williams	Ford
15	Charlie Roberts	Ford
16	Jim Vandiver	Dodge
17	Ben Arnold	Ford
18	Walter Ballard	Mercury
19	J.D. McDuffie	Chevrolet
20	Buddy Baker	Dodge
21	Frank Warren	Dodge
22	Jackie Oliver	Ford
23	Bill Dennis	Plymouth
24	Ed Negre	Dodge
25	Dave Marcis	Dodge
26	LeeRoy Yarbrough	Ford
27	Bobby Mausgrover	Dodge
28	Bobby Isaac	Dodge
29	Fred Lorenzon	Ford
30	Buck Baker	Chevrolet
31	Neil Castles	Dodge
32	H.B. Bailey	Ford
33	Larry Smith	Ford
34	Henley Gray	Ford
35	Dick Brooks	Pontiac
36	G.C. Spencer	Plymouth

GWYN STALEY MEMORIAL

Time of Race: 2 hours, 53 minutes, 19 seconds
Average Speed: 88.381

FINISH	DRIVER	CAR
1	Richard Petty	Plymouth
2	Bobby Allison	Chevrolet
3	Bobby Isaac	Dodge
4	James Hylton	Ford
5	Benny Parsons	Mercury
6	LeeRoy Yarbrough	Dodge
7	Dave Marcis	Dodge
8	Larry Smith	Ford
9	Walter Ballard	Mercury
10	John Sears	Plymouth
11	Dub Simpson	Chevrolet
12	Raymond Williams	Ford
13	Neil Castles	Dodge
14	Richard Brown	Chevrolet
15	Dean Dalton	Mercury
16	Charlie Roberts	Ford
17	Henley Gray	Ford
18	Cecil Gordon	Mercury
19	Ben Arnold	Ford
20	Frank Warren	Plymouth
21	Buck Baker	Chevrolet
22	Ed Negre	Dodge
23	Bill Champion	Ford
24	Elmo Langley	Ford
25	J.D. McDuffie	Chevrolet
26	Jim Vandiver	Dodge
27	Richard Childress	Chevrolet
28	Jabe Thomas	Plymouth
29	Eddie Yarboro	Plymouth
30	Bill Dennis	Plymouth

VIRGINIA 500

Time of Race: 3 hours, 37 minutes, 0 seconds
Average Speed: 72.657 mph

FINISH	DRIVER	CAR
1	Richard Petty	Plymouth
2	Bobby Allison	Chevrolet
3	Dave Marcis	Dodge

FINISH	DRIVER	CAR
4	Cecil Gordon	Mercury
5	Richard Brown	Chevrolet
6	Bill Champion	Ford
7	James Hylton	Ford
8	David Pearson	Ford
9	Walter Ballard	Mercury
10	Raymond Williams	Ford
11	Elmo Langley	Ford
12	Neil Castles	Dodge
13	J.D. McDuffie	Chevrolet
14	Dean Dalton	Mercury
15	Henley Gray	Ford
16	Wendell Scott	Ford
17	Eddie Yarboro	Plymouth
18	Frank Warren	Plymouth
19	Bobby Isaac	Dodge
20	Benny Parsons	Mercury
21	Les Covey	Chevrolet
22	John Sears	Plymouth
23	LeeRoy Yarbrough	Mercury
24	Charlie Roberts	Ford
25	Bill Dennis	Plymouth
26	Bill Shirey	Plymouth
27	Buddy Arrington	Dodge
28	Charlie Glotzbach	Plymouth
29	Richard Childress	Chevrolet
30	Ed Negre	Dodge
31	Jabe Thomas	Plymouth
32	Jim Vandiver	Chevrolet
33	Jimmy Hensley	Ford
34	Earl Brooks	Ford
35	Larry Smith	Ford
36	David Ray Boggs	Dodge

WINSTON 500

Time of Race: 3 hours, 43 minutes, 15 seconds
Average Speed: 136.400 mph

FINISH	DRIVER	CAR
1	David Pearson	Mercury
2	Bobby Isaac	Dodge
3	Buddy Baker	Dodge
4	Fred Lorenzen	Ford
5	Richard Petty	Dodge
6	Joe Frasson	Dodge
7	LeeRoy Yarbrough	Mercury
8	Dick Brooks	Ford
9	Frank Warren	Dodge
10	Benny Parsons	Mercury
11	Dave Marcis	Dodge
12	David Ray Boggs	Dodge
13	Jabe Thomas	Plymouth
14	Cecil Gordon	Mercury
15	Ed Negre	Dodge
16	Jimmy Crawford	Plymouth
17	Ben Arnold	Ford
18	Ron Keselowski	Dodge
19	Walter Ballard	Mercury
20	Larry Smith	Ford
21	John Sears	Plymouth
22	Dean Dalton	Mercury
23	Bobby Mausgrover	Dodge
24	Elmo Langley	Ford
25	Henley Gray	Ford
26	Raymond Williams	Ford
27	Richard Brown	Chevrolet
28	Donnie Allison	Chevrolet
29	Dub Simpson	Chevrolet
30	Bill Champion	Mercury
31	Buddy Arrington	Dodge
32	Clarence Lovell	Ford
33	James Hylton	Ford
34	J.D. McDuffie	Chevrolet
35	Coo Coo Marlin	Chevrolet
36	Jim Vandiver	Dodge
37	David Sisco	Chevrolet
38	Darrell Waltrip	Mercury
39	Red Farmer	Ford
40	Buck Baker	Chevrolet

41	Wayne Smith	Chevrolet
42	Roy Mayne	Chevrolet
43	Charlie Roberts	Ford
44	Jackie Oliver	Ford
45	Bobby Allison	Chevrolet
46	Bill Dennis	Plymouth
47	Neil Castles	Dodge
48	Robert Wales	Dodge
49	Bill Ward	Ford
50	Marty Robbins	Dodge

WORLD 600

Time of Race: 4 hours, 13 minutes, 4 seconds
Average Speed: 142.255 mph

FINISH	DRIVER	CAR
1	Buddy Baker	Dodge
2	Bobby Allison	Chevrolet
3	Charlie Glotzbach	Dodge
4	Benny Parsons	Mercury
5	LeeRoy Yarbrough	Mercury
6	Larry Smith	Ford
7	Buddy Arrington	Dodge
8	Cecil Gordon	Mercury
9	Frank Warren	Dodge
10	Ben Arnold	Ford
11	Elmo Langley	Mercury
12	Ron Keselowski	Dodge
13	Raymond Williams	Ford
14	Jabe Thomas	Plymouth
15	Walter Ballard	Mercury
16	Jim Paschal	Chevrolet
17	Dean Dalton	Mercury
18	Fred Lorenzen	Ford
19	Richard Petty	Dodge
20	James Hylton	Ford
21	Joe Frasson	Dodge
22	Wendell Scott	Chevrolet
23	Bobby Isaac	Dodge
24	John Sears	Plymouth
25	David Pearson	Mercury
26	Bill Champion	Ford
27	Clarence Lovell	Ford
28	Coo Coo Marlin	Chevrolet
29	Ken Rush	Dodge
30	Richard Brown	Chevrolet
31	Dave Marcis	Matador
32	Jackie Oliver	Ford
33	J.D. McDuffie	Chevrolet
34	Donnie Allison	Ford
35	Neil Castles	Dodge
36	Dick Brooks	Ford
37	Wayne Smith	Chevrolet
38	David Ray Boggs	Dodge
39	G.C. Spencer	Plymouth
40	Jim Vandiver	Dodge

MASON-DIXON 500

Time of Race: 4 hours, 12 minutes, 40 seconds
Average Speed: 118.019 mph

FINISH	DRIVER	CAR
1	Bobby Allison	Chevrolet
2	Richard Petty	Dodge
3	LeeRoy Yarbrough	Mercury
4	Jackie Oliver	Ford
5	John Sears	Plymouth
6	Benny Parsons	Ford
7	James Hylton	Ford
8	Cecil Gordon	Mercury
9	Ron Keselowski	Dodge
10	Paul Tyler	Mercury
11	J.D. McDuffie	Chevrolet
12	Charlie Roberts	Ford
13	Dean Dalton	Mercury
14	Bobby Isaac	Dodge
15	Jabe Thomas	Plymouth
16	Walter Ballard	Mercury
17	Bill Champion	Ford
18	Ronnie Daniel	Chevrolet
19	Frank Warren	Dodge
20	Wendell Scott	Ford
21	Richard Brown	Chevrolet
22	Jim Vandiver	Dodge
23	Bill Shirey	Plymouth
24	Coo Coo Marlin	Chevrolet
25	Elmo Langley	Ford
26	Ben Arnold	Ford
27	Dick May	Ford
28	Les Covey	Chevrolet
29	Neil Castles	Dodge
30	Earl Brooks	Ford
31	Ed Negre	Dodge
32	James Cox	Plymouth
33	David Ray Boggs	Dodge
34	Larry Smith	Ford
35	Earle Canavan	Plymouth
36	Dave Marcis	Dodge
37	Richard Childress	Chevrolet
38	Raymond Williams	Ford
39	Henley Gray	Ford
40	Clarence Lovell	Ford

MOTOR STATE 400

Time of Race: 2 hours, 43 minutes, 40 seconds
Average Speed: 146.639 mph

FINISH	DRIVER	CAR
1	David Pearson	Mercury
2	Bobby Allison	Chevrolet
3	Richard Petty	Dodge
4	James Hylton	Ford
5	Ron Keselowski	Dodge
6	Larry Smith	Ford
7	Ben Arnold	Ford
8	Dean Dalton	Mercury
9	Buddy Arrington	Dodge
10	Bill Champion	Mercury
11	Cecil Gordon	Mercury
12	Walter Ballard	Mercury
13	John Sears	Plymouth
14	Raymond Williams	Ford
15	David Sisco	Chevrolet
16	J.D. McDuffie	Chevrolet
17	Johnny Halford	Plymouth
18	Dick May	Ford
19	Richard Childress	Plymouth
20	Doc Faustina	Plymouth
21	Ed Negre	Dodge
22	Pete Hamilton	Plymouth
23	Les Covey	Chevrolet
24	Jabe Thomas	Plymouth
25	Benny Parsons	Mercury
26	Bobby Isaac	Dodge
27	Dick Brooks	Ford
28	LeeRoy Yarbrough	Mercury
29	Elmo Langley	Ford
30	Dave Marcis	Mercury
31	Bill Shirey	Plymouth
32	Charlie Roberts	Ford
33	Donnie Allison	Ford
34	Richard Brown	Chevrolet
35	Joe Frasson	Dodge
36	Frank Warren	Dodge
37	Earl Brooks	Ford
38	Bobby Mausgrover	Dodge
39	Bill Siefert	Dodge
40	Neil Castles	Dodge

GOLDEN STATE 400

Time of Race: 4 hours, 3 minutes, 32 seconds
Average Speed: 98.781 mph

FINISH	DRIVER	CAR
1	Ray Elder	Dodge
2	Benny Parsons	Mercury
3	Donnie Allison	Matador
4	James Hylton	Ford
5	Carl Joiner	Chevrolet
6	Bobby Allison	Chrysler
7	Carl Adams	Ford
8	Cecil Gordon	Mercury
9	Frank James	Chevrolet
10	Dick May	Ford
11	Charlie Roberts	Ford
12	Hershel McGriff	Plymouth
13	Dick Bown	Plymouth
14	Chuck Bown	Plymouth
15	Henley Gray	Ford
16	Dick Kranzler	Chevrolet
17	Kevin Torrie	Plymouth
18	Paul Dorrity	Chevrolet
19	Jim Insolo	Chevrolet
20	Bill Butts	Dodge
21	Bobby Isaac	Dodge
22	Dean Dalton	Mercury
23	Richard Petty	Plymouth
24	Bill Champion	Ford
25	Walter Ballard	Mercury
26	Ray Johnstone	Oldsmobile
27	Johnny Anderson	Chevrolet
28	J.D. McDuffie	Chevrolet
29	John Hren	Chevrolet
30	Clem Proctor	Oldsmobile
31	Sonny Easley	Chevrolet
32	Dick Gulstrand	Chevrolet
33	Dick Brooks	Ford
34	Sam Stanley	Ford
35	John Soares, Jr.	Dodge
36	Tru Cheek	Ford
37	Ed Negre	Dodge
38	Jack McCoy	Dodge
39	Bob Kauf	Chevrolet
40	Mike James	Chevrolet

LONE STAR 500

Time of Race: 4 3ours, 26 minutes, 4 seconds
Average Speed: 1442.185 mph

FINISH	DRIVER	CAR
1	Richard Petty	Plymouth
2	Bobby Allison	Chevrolet
3	Coo Coo Marlin	Chevrolet
4	Benny Parsons	Mercury
5	Bobby Isaac	Dodge
6	James Hylton	Ford
7	Larry Smith	Ford
8	Ben Arnold	Ford
9	Dean Dalton	Mercury
10	Bill Champion	Ford
11	H.B. Bailey	Pontiac
12	Tiny Lund	Chevrolet
13	Dave Marcis	Dodge
14	Raymond Williams	Ford
15	Cecil Gordon	Mercury
16	Jabe Thomas	Plymouth
17	Charlie Roberts	Ford
18	Paul Jett	Ford
19	Clarence Lovell	Ford
20	Dick May	Ford
21	John Sears	Plymouth
22	Les Covey	Chevrolet
23	Frank Warren	Dodge
24	Joe Frasson	Dodge
25	Ronnie Chumley	Chevrolet
26	Jim White	Ford

FINISH	DRIVER	CAR
27	J.D. McDuffie	Chevrolet
28	Ed Negre	Dodge
29	Elmo Langley	Ford
30	David Ray Boggs	Dodge
31	Richard Childress	Chevrolet
32	Wendell Scott	Ford
33	Walter Ballard	Mercury
34	Doc Faustina	Plymouth
35	Dick Brooks	Ford
36	Jackie Oliver	Ford
37	Neil Castles	Dodge
38	D.K. Ulrich	Ford
39	Henley Gray	Ford
40	Marty Robbins	Dodge
41	LeeRoy Yarbrough	Ford
42	Johnny Anderson	Chevrolet
43	Ron Keselowski	Dodge
44	Bill Shirey	Plymouth

FIRECRACKER 400

Time of Race: 2 hours, 29 minutes, 14 seconds
Average Speed: 160.821

FINISH	DRIVER	CAR
1	David Pearson	Mercury
2	Richard Petty	Dodge
3	Bobby Allison	Chevrolet
4	Coo Coo Marlin	Chevrolet
5	James Hylton	Ford
6	LeeRoy Yarbrough	Mercury
7	Ron Keselowski	Dodge
8	Donnie Allison	Ford
9	Wayne Smith	Chevrolet
10	Johnny Halford	Plymouth
11	Cecil Gordon	Mercury
12	Charlie Roberts	Ford
13	Dave Marcis	Dodge
14	Richard Brown	Chevrolet
15	Mel Larson	Plymouth
16	Ben Arnold	Ford
17	Buddy Arrington	Dodge
18	Bill Champion	Mercury
19	Jabe Thomas	Plymouth
20	George Althiede	Dodge
21	Frank Warren	Dodge
22	Henley Gray	Ford
23	Walter Ballard	Mercury
24	Buddy Baker	Dodge
25	Jakie Oliver	Ford
26	David Ray Boggs	Dodge
27	Bobby Isaac	Dodge
28	J.D. McDuffie	Chevrolet
29	David Sisco	Chevrolet
30	Clarence Lovell	Ford
31	Dean Dalton	Mercury
32	John Sears	Plymouth
33	Pete Hamilton	Plymouth
34	Bill Shirley	Plymouth
35	Elmo Langley	Ford
36	Benny Parsons	Mercury
37	Neil Castles	Dodge
38	Larry Smith	Ford
39	Roy Mayne	Chevrolet
40	Joe Frasson	Dodge

VOLUNTEER 500

Time of Race: 2 hours, 30 minutes, 28 seconds
Average Speed: 92.735 mph

FINISH	DRIVER	CAR
1	Bobby Allison	Chevrolet
2	Richard Petty	Plymouth
3	Dave Marcis	Dodge
4	Benny Parsons	Mercury

FINISH	DRIVER	CAR
5	J.D. McDuffie	Dodge
6	John Sears	Plymouth
7	Raymond Williams	Ford
8	Cecil Gordon	Mercury
9	Walter Ballard	Mercury
10	Ben Arnold	Ford
11	Elmo Langley	Ford
12	James Hylton	Ford
13	Bill Champion	Ford
14	Charlie Roberts	Ford
15	Jabe Thomas	Plymouth
16	Henley Gray	Ford
17	Ed Negre	Dodge
18	Bobby Isaac	Dodge
19	LeeRoy Yarbrough	Ford
20	Dean Dalton	Mercury
21	Bob Brown	Chevrolet
22	Coo Coo Marlin	Chevrolet
23	David Ray Boggs	Dodge
24	David Sisco	Chevrolet
25	Johnny Halford	Plymouth
26	Richard Childress	Chevrolet
27	Ron Keselowski	Dodge
28	G.C. Spencer	Plymouth
29	Frank Warren	Dodge
30	Richard Brown	Chevrolet

NORTHERN 300

Time of Race: 2 hours, 57 minutes, 41 seconds
Average Speed: 114.030 mph

FINISH	DRIVER	CAR
1	Bobby Allison	Chevrolet
2	Bobby Isaac	Dodge
3	Richard Petty	Plymouth
4	Fred Lorenzen	Ford
5	Cecil Gordon	Mercury
6	James Hylton	Ford
7	Larry Smith	Ford
8	Benny Parsons	Mercury
9	Raymond Williams	Ford
10	Walter Ballard	Mercury
11	Elmo Langley	Ford
12	Dean Dalton	Mercury
13	Bob Greeley	Plymouth
14	Charlie Roberts	Ford
15	Jabe Thomas	Plymouth
16	J.D. McDuffie	Chevrolet
17	Ed Negre	Dodge
18	Richard Childress	Chevrolet
19	D.K. Ulrich	Ford
20	Wendell Scott	Ford
21	Frank Warren	Dodge
22	David Ray Boggs	Dodge
23	Earl Brooks	Ford
24	Bill Champion	Ford
25	Dave Marcis	Dodge
26	Fred Drake	Pontiac
27	Neil Castles	Dodge
28	Dr. Ed Hassert	Plymouth
29	Henley Gray	Ford
30	Bill Shirey	Plymouth
31	John Sears	Plymouth
32	Earle Canavan	Plymouth
33	A.J. Cox	Dodge

DIXIE 500

Time of Race: 3 hours, 47 minutes, 8 seconds
Average Speed: 131.295 mph

FINISH	DRIVER	CAR
1	Bobby Allison	Chevrolet
2	Richard Petty	Dodge
3	David Pearson	Mercury
4	Benny Parsons	Mercury

FINISH	DRIVER	CAR
5	LeeRoy Yarbrough	Ford
6	Fred Lorenzen	Chevrolet
7	Dave Marcis	Dodge
8	Darrell Waltrip	Mercury
9	Cecil Gordon	Mercury
10	Walter Ballard	Mercury
11	John Sears	Plymouth
12	Ben Arnold	Ford
13	Buddy Arrington	Dodge
14	Charlie Roberts	Ford
15	Johnny Halford	Plymouth
16	Ron Keselowski	Dodge
17	Bill Champion	Mercury
18	Raymond Williams	Ford
19	Bobby Mausgrover	Ford
20	Elmo Langley	Ford
21	Eddie Yarboro	Plymouth
22	Neil Castles	Dodge
23	Frank Warren	Dodge
24	Clarence Lovell	Ford
25	Ed Negre	Dodge
26	David Ray Boggs	Dodge
27	Richard Brown	Chevrolet
28	Joe Frasson	Dodge
29	Coo Coo Marlin	Chevrolet
30	Henley Gray	Ford
31	Bobby Isaac	Dodge
32	Donnie Allison	Ford
33	Doc Faustina	Plymouth
34	Jabe Thomas	Plymouth
35	James Hylton	Ford
36	Larry Smith	Ford
37	Dean Dalton	Mercury
38	Dick Brooks	Ford
39	Dub Simpson	Chevrolet
40	G.C. Spencer	Plymouth

TALLADEGA 500

Time of Race: 3 hours, 22 minutes, 9 seconds
Average Speed: 146.728 mph

FINISH	DRIVER	CAR
1	James Hylton	Mercury
2	Ramo Stott	Ford
3	Bobby Allison	Chevrolet
4	Red Farmer	Ford
5	Buddy Arrington	Dodge
6	Ben Arnold	Ford
7	Richard Petty	Dodge
8	Henley Gray	Ford
9	Raymond Williams	Ford
10	Paul Jett	Ford
11	John Sears	Plymouth
12	Dean Dalton	Mercury
13	David Ray Boggs	Dodge
14	Elmo Langley	Ford
15	Walter Ballard	Mercury
16	Coo Coo Marlin	Chevrolet
17	David Sisco	Chevrolet
18	George Althiede	Dodge
19	Pete Hamilton	Plymouth
20	Fred Lorenzen	Chevrolet
21	Bill Champion	Mercury
22	Buddy Baker	Dodge
23	Richard Brown	Chevrolet
24	Clarence Lovell	Ford
25	Benny Parsons	Mercury
26	David Pearson	Mercury
27	Darrell Waltrip	Mercury
28	Tommy Gale	Mercury
29	Paul Tyler	Mercury
30	Mel Larson	Plymouth
31	Donnie Allison	Plymouth
32	Charlie Roberts	Ford
33	LeeRoy Yarbrough	Ford
34	Frank Warren	Dodge
35	Jabe Thomas	Plymouth
36	J.D. McDuffie	Chevrolet
37	Larry Smith	Ford
38	Bobby Mausgrover	Ford
39	Ed Negre	Dodge
40	Dick Brooks	Ford

41	Joe Frasson	Dodge
42	Bobby Isaac	Dodge
43	Cecil Gordon	Mercury
44	Ron Keselowski	Dodge
45	Don Faustina	Plymouth
46	Dave Marcis	Dodge
47	Bill Shirey	Plymouth
48	Neil Castles	Plymouth
49	Roy Mayne	Chevrolet
50	Robert Wales	Dodge

YANKEE 400

Time of race: 2 hours, 58 minutes, 31 seconds
Average speed: 134.416 mph

FINISH	DRIVER	CAR
1	David Pearson	Mercury
2	Bobby Allison	Chevrolet
3	Bobby Isaac	Dodge
4	Richard Petty	Dodge
5	Cale Yarborough	Mercury
6	James Hylton	Ford
7	Benny Parsons	Mercury
8	Bill Seifert	Mercury
9	Dave Marcis	Matador
10	Larry Smith	Ford
11	Walter Ballard	Mercury
12	Elmo Langley	Ford
13	David Sisco	Chevrolet
14	Clarence Lovell	Ford
15	Cecil Gordon	Mercury
16	John Sears	Plymouth
17	Mel Larson	Plymouth
18	Ben Arnold	Ford
19	Bill Champion	Ford
20	Raymond Williams	Ford
21	Jabe Thomas	Plymouth
22	Ed Negre	Dodge
23	Dean Dalton	Mercury
24	Henley Gray	Ford
25	Dick May	Dodge
26	Charlie Roberts	Ford
27	Doc Faustina	Plymouth
28	Frank Warren	Dodge
29	J.D. McDuffie	Chevrolet
30	Joe Frasson	Dodge
31	David Ray Boggs	Dodge
32	Ron Keselowski	Dodge
33	Buddy Arrington	Dodge
34	Coo Coo Marlin	Chevrolet
35	George Altheide	Dodge
36	Jim Vandiver	Dodge
37	Ron Grana	Chevrolet
38	G.C. Spencer	Plymouth
39	Earle Canavan	Plymouth
40	Dick Brooks	Ford

NASHVILLE 420

Time of Race: 2 hours, 42 minutes, 14 seconds
Average Speed: 92.678 mph

FINISH	DRIVER	CAR
1	Bobby Allison	Chevrolet
2	Richard Petty	Plymouth
3	Darrell Waltrip	Mercury
4	Benny Parsons	Mercury
5	Elmo Langley	Ford
6	Cecil Gordon	Mercury
7	Henley Gray	Ford
8	James Hylton	Ford
9	Walter Ballard	Mercury
10	J.D. McDuffie	Chevrolet
11	D.K. Ulrich	Ford
12	John Sears	Plymouth
13	Earl Brooks	Ford
14	Frank Warren	Plymouth

15	David Ray Boggs	Dodge
16	Richard Childress	Chevrolet
17	David Sisco	Chevrolet
18	Raymond Williams	Ford
19	Charlie Roberts	Ford
20	Ben Arnold	Ford
21	Bob Brown	Chevrolet
22	Jabe Thomas	Plymouth
23	Dean Dalton	Mercury
24	George Althiede	Dodge
25	Bill Champion	Ford
26	Coo Coo Marlin	Chevrolet
27	Bobby Isaac	Dodge
28	LeeRoy Yarbrough	Ford

SOUTHERN 500

Time of Race: 4 hours, 4 minutes, 14 seconds
Average Speed: 122.655 mph

FINISH	DRIVER	CAR
1	Bobby Allison	Chevrolet
2	David Pearson	Mercury
3	Richard Petty	Dodge
4	Fred Lorenzen	Chevrolet
5	H.B. Bailey	Pontiac
6	Buddy Arrington	Dodge
7	Dave Marcis	Matador
8	Jim Vandiver	Dodge
9	Marty Robbins	Dodge
10	Coo Coo Marlin	Chevrolet
11	James Hylton	Mercury
12	Walter Ballard	Mercury
13	Bill Champion	Ford
14	Ed Negre	Dodge
15	J.D. McDuffie	Dodge
16	Tommy Gale	Mercury
17	Frank Warren	Dodge
18	David Ray Boggs	Dodge
19	G.C. Spencer	Plymouth
20	Jabe Thomas	Plymouth
21	Dean Dalton	Mercury
22	Elmo Langley	Ford
23	Neil Castles	Plymouth
24	Henley Gray	Ford
25	Larry Smith	Ford
26	Buck Baker	Chevrolet
27	Eddie Yarboro	Plymouth
28	Cecil Gordon	Mercury
29	Buddy Baker	Dodge
30	John Sears	Plymouth
31	Paul Tyler	Mercury
32	Dick Brooks	Mercury
33	Clarence Lovell	Ford
34	Ron Keselowski	Dodge
35	Benny Parsons	Mercury
36	Ben Arnold	Ford
37	Joe Frasson	Dodge
38	Donnie Allison	Ford
39	LeeRoy Yarbrough	Ford
40	Bobby Isaac	Dodge

CAPITAL CITY 500

Time of Race: 3 hours, 34 minutes, 14 seconds
Average Speed: 75.899 mph

FINISH	DRIVER	CAR
1	Richard Petty	Plymouth
2	Bobby Allison	Chevrolet
3	Bill Dennis	Chevrolet
4	James Hylton	Ford
5	Dave Marcis	Dodge
6	Bill Champion	Ford
7	Ben Arnold	Ford
8	Dean Dalton	Mercury
9	Jabe Thomas	Plymouth
10	Buddy Arrington	Dodge

11	Raymond Williams	Ford
12	Walter Ballard	Mercury
13	John Sears	Plymouth
14	Henley Gray	Ford
15	Ed Negre	Dodge
16	Eddie Yarboro	Plymouth
17	Buddy Baker	Dodge
18	Frank Warren	Dodge
19	Larry Smith	Ford
20	Cecil Gordon	Mercury
21	Neil Castles	Plymouth
22	Elmo Langley	Ford
23	Benny Parsons	Mercury
24	David Pearson	Ford
25	Richard Childress	Chevrolet
26	David Ray Boggs	Dodge
27	Charlie Roberts	Ford
28	Ron Keselowski	Dodge
29	George Althiede	Dodge
30	J.D. McDuffie	Plymouth

DELAWARE 500

Time of Race: 4 hours, 8 minutes, 57 seconds
Average Speed: 120.508 mph

FINISH	DRIVER	CAR
1	David Pearson	Mercury
2	Richard Petty	Plymouth
3	Ramo Stott	Ford
4	James Hylton	Ford
5	Cecil Gordon	Mercury
6	Ben Arnold	Ford
7	Elmo Langley	Ford
8	Walter Ballard	Mercury
9	Dean Dalton	Mercury
10	Charlie Roberts	Ford
11	Buddy Baker	Dodge
12	Jabe Thomas	Plymouth
13	Paul Tyler	Mercury
14	D.K. Ulrich	Ford
15	Earle Canavan	Plymouth
16	Wendell Scott	Ford
17	Ed Negre	Dodge
18	Bill Shirey	Plymouth
19	Henley Gray	Ford
20	Bobby Allison	Chevrolet
21	Les Covey	Chevrolet
22	Raymond Williams	Ford
23	Ron Keselowski	Dodge
24	J.D. McDuffie	Chevrolet
25	Frank Warren	Dodge
26	Clarence Lovell	Ford
27	Buddy Arrington	Dodge
28	John Sears	Plymouth
29	Earl Brooks	Ford
30	Larry Smith	Ford
31	Harry Schilling	Chevrolet
32	Neil Castles	Plymouth
33	Richard Childress	Chevrolet
34	Benny Parsons	Mercury
35	Bill Champion	Ford
36	Coo Coo Marlin	Chevrolet
37	Dave Marcis	Matador
38	David Ray Boggs	Dodge
39	Bill Seifert	Mercury
40	George Althiede	Dodge

OLD DOMINION 500

Time of Race: 3 hours, 45 minutes, 2 seconds
Average Speed: 69.989 mph

FINISH	DRIVER	CAR
1	Richard Petty	Plymouth
2	Bobby Allison	Chevrolet
3	David Pearson	Mercury
4	Buddy Baker	Dodge

5	Jimmy Hensley	Ford
6	Benny Parsons	Mercury
7	Buddy Arrington	Dodge
8	James Hylton	Ford
9	Elmo Langley	Ford
10	Cecil Gordon	Mercury
11	Coo Coo Marlin	Chevrolet
12	Bill Champion	Ford
13	Raymond Williams	Ford
14	J.D. McDuffie	Chevrolet
15	John Sears	Plymouth
16	Ben Arnold	Ford
17	Neil Castles	Plymouth
18	Ed Negre	Dodge
19	Charlie Roberts	Ford
20	Walter Ballard	Mercury
21	Jabe Thomas	Plymouth
22	James Cox	Plymouth
23	Henley Gray	Ford
24	David Ray Boggs	Dodge
25	Ray Hendrick	Dodge
26	Tiny Lund	Chevrolet
27	Fred Lorenzen	Chevrolet
28	Dean Dalton	Mercury
29	Dave Marcis	Matador
30	LeeRoy Yarbrough	Ford
31	Bill Dennis	Chevrolet
32	Frank Warren	Dodge
33	Richard Childress	Chevrolet
34	Larry Smith	Ford
35	Bobby Isaac	Ford
36	Bill Shirey	Plymouth

WILKES 400

Time of Race: 2 hours, 38 minutes, 33 seconds
Average Speed: 95.818 mph

FINISH	DRIVER	CAR
1	Richard Petty	Plymouth
2	Bobby Allison	Chevrolet
3	Buddy Baker	Dodge
4	Benny Parsons	Mercury
5	John Sears	Chevrolet
6	Dave Marcis	Plymouth
7	Cecil Gordon	Mercury
8	Elmo Langley	Ford
9	Vic Parsons	Ford
10	Raymond Williams	Ford
11	Buddy Arrington	Dodge
12	Jabe Thomas	Plymouth
13	Ben Arnold	Ford
14	Bill Champion	Ford
15	Dean Dalton	Mercury
16	Frank Warren	Dodge
17	James Hylton	Ford
18	Max Berrier	Ford
19	Walter Ballard	Mercury
20	Bill Shirey	Plymouth
21	Charlie Roberts	Ford
22	Ed Negre	Dodge
23	J.D. McDuffie	Chevrolet
24	David Ray Boggs	Dodge
25	Richard Childress	Chevrolet
26	Tiny Lund	Chevrolet
27	Henley Gray	Plymouth
28	Larry Smith	Ford
29	Ron Keselowski	Dodge
30	Coo Coo Marlin	Chevrolet

NATIONAL 500

Time of Race: 3 hours, 45 minutes, 37 seconds
Average Speed: 133.234 mph

FINISH	DRIVER	CAR
1	Bobby Allison	Chevrolet
2	Buddy Baker	Dodge

3	David Pearson	Mercury
4	A.J. Foyt	Mercury
5	Butch Hartman	Ford
6	Darrell Waltrip	Mercury
7	James Hylton	Mercury
8	Buddy Arrington	Dodge
9	Joe Frasson	Dodge
10	Richard Petty	Dodge
11	Larry Smith	Ford
12	Ron Keselowski	Dodge
13	Raymond Williams	Ford
14	Ben Arnold	Ford
15	Neil Castles	Plymouth
16	John Sears	Plymouth
17	Cecil Gordon	Mercury
18	Bill Champion	Mercury
19	Walter BAllard	Mercury
20	David Ray Boggs	Mercury
21	Frank Warren	Dodge
22	Henley Gray	Ford
23	Tommy Gale	Mercury
24	Dean Dalton	Mercury
25	Donnie Allison	Ford
26	Dave Marcis	Matador
27	Roger McCluskey	Dodge
28	Bobby Isaac	Chevrolet
29	Bill Dennis	Chevrolet
30	Harry Schilling	Chevrolet
31	Earle Canavan	Plymouth
32	Pete Hamilton	Plymouth
33	Jim Vandiver	Dodge
34	Coo Coo Marlin	Chevrolet
35	Elmo Langley	Ford
36	G.C. Spencer	Dodge
37	Jabe Thomas	Chevrolet
38	Benny Parsons	Mercury
39	Cale Yarborough	Chevrolet
40	Dick Brooks	Mercury
41	Richard Brown	Ford
42	Gordon Johncock	Plymouth
43	Bobby Unser	Chevrolet
44	Ed Negre	Dodge

AMERICAN 500

Time of Race: 4 hours, 13 minutes, 49 seconds
Average Speed: 116.275 mph

FINISH	DRIVER	CAR
1	Bobby Allison	Chevrolet
2	Richard Petty	Plymouth
3	Buddy Baker	Dodge
4	David Pearson	Mercury
5	Pete Hamilton	Plymouth
6	Cale Yarborough	Chevrolet
7	Dave Marcis	Matador
8	Larry Smith	Ford
9	David Sisco	Chevrolet
10	Buddy Arrington	Dodge
11	John Sears	Plymouth
12	Clarence Lovell	Ford
13	Elmo Langley	Ford
14	Ben Arnold	Ford
15	Walter Ballard	Mercury
16	Dean Dalton	Mercury
17	Ed Negre	Dodge
18	Charlie Roberts	Ford
19	James Hylton	Ford
20	Cecil Gordon	Mercury
21	Joe Frasson	Dodge
22	Raymond Williams	Ford
23	Jabe Thomas	Plymouth
24	J.D. McDuffie	Chevrolet
25	Frank Warren	Dodge
26	Marty Robbins	Dodge
27	Coo Coo Marlin	Chevrolet
28	Bill Champion	Mercury
29	Roy Mayne	Plymouth
30	Jim Vandiver	Dodge
31	Neil Castles	Plymouth
32	Bill Dennis	Chevrolet

33	Ron Keselowski	Dodge
34	Dick Brooks	Ford
35	Benny Parsons	Mercury
36	Bobby Isaac	Chevrolet
37	Henley Gray	Mercury
38	Tiny Lund	Chevrolet
39	Tommy Gale	Mercury
40	Ron Hutcherson	Ford

TEXAS 500

Time of Race: 3 hours, 24 minutes, 0 seconds
Average Speed: 147.059 mph

FINISH	DRIVER	CAR
1	Buddy Baker	Dodge
2	A.J. Foyt	Mercury
3	Richard Petty	Dodge
4	Bobby Allison	Chevrolet
5	Hershel McGriff	Plymouth
6	Benny Parsons	Mercury
7	Coo Coo Marlin	Chevrolet
8	Cecil Gordon	Mercury
9	Cale Yarborough	Chevrolet
10	Joe Frasson	Dodge
11	James Hylton	Mercury
12	Dave Marcis	Dodge
13	Ramo Stott	Ford
14	J.D. McDuffie	Chevrolet
15	Ben Arnold	Ford
16	John Sears	Plymouth
17	Dick Brooks	Ford
18	Walter Ballard	Mercury
19	Jim Whitt	Ford
20	Dean Dalton	Mercury
21	Raymond Williams	Ford
22	Rick Newsom	Ford
23	Harry Schilling	Chevrolet
24	Elmo Langley	Ford
25	Ed Negre	Dodge
26	Johnny Rutherford	Ford
27	David Sisco	Chevrolet
28	Charlie Roberts	Ford
29	Bill Shirey	Dodge
30	Mel Larson	Plymouth
31	Larry Smith	Ford
32	Paul Feldner	Plymouth
33	Clarence Lovell	Ford
34	Buddy Arrington	Dodge
35	Gordon Johncock	Plymouth
36	H.B. Balley	Pontiac
37	Jabe Thomas	Plymouth
38	Frank Warren	Dodge
39	Henley Gray	Ford
40	Bill Hollar	Mercury
41	Ron Keselowski	Dodge
42	Earle Canavan	Plymouth
43	Bill Champion	Ford
44	Bill Seifert	Mercury

1973

WINSTON WESTERN 500

Time of Race: 4 hours, 48 minutes, 33 seconds
Average Speed: 104.055 mph

FINISH	DRIVER	CAR
1	Mark Donohue	Matador
2	Bobby Allison	Chevrolet

3	Ray Elder	Dodge
4	Bobby Unser	Ford
5	Jimmy Insolo	Chevrolet
6	Jack McCoy	Dodge
7	Elmo Langley	Ford
8	Richard White	Ford
9	J.C. Danielson	Mercury
10	Henley Gray	Mercury
11	Charlie Roberts	Ford
12	James Hylton	Mercury
13	Carl Adams	Ford
14	Benny Parsons	Chevrolet
15	Gerald Thompson	Pontiac
16	Bill Champion	Ford
17	Dick Bown	Dodge
18	Jim White	Chevrolet
19	Walter Ballard	Plymouth
20	Cecil Gordon	Chevrolet
21	Richard Petty	Dodge
22	David Pearson	Mercury
23	Hershel McGriff	Plymouth
24	Gale Yarborough	Chevrolet
25	Sonny Easley	Ford
26	John Soares, Jr.	Dodge
27	Bobby Isaac	Dodge
28	Johnny Anderson	Chevrolet
29	Chuck Bown	Dodge
30	John Hren	Chevrolet
31	Glen Francis	Chevrolet
32	J.D. McDuffie	Chevrolet
33	Carl Joiner	Chevrolet
34	Harry Jefferson	Ford
35	Buddy Baker	Dodge
36	Hugh Pearson	Chevrolet
37	Bob Kauf	Chevrolet
38	Clem Proctor	Ford
39	Jerry Grant	Chevrolet
40	Dave Marcis	Dodge

DAYTONA 500

Time of Race: 3 hours, 10 minutes, 50 seconds
Average Speed: 157.205 mph

FINISH	DRIVER	CAR
1	Richard Petty	Dodge
2	Bobby Isaac	Ford
3	Dick Brooks	Dodge
4	A.J. Foyt	Chevrolet
5	Hershel McGriff	Plymouth
6	Buddy Baker	Dodge
7	James Hylton	Mercury
8	Ramo Stott	Mercury
9	Buddy Arrington	Dodge
10	Vic Parsons	Mercury
11	David Sisco	Chevrolet
12	Darrell Waltrip	Mercury
13	Joe Frasson	Dodge
14	Larry Smith	Mercury
15	Jabe Thomas	Dodge
16	Frank Warren	Dodge
17	Ed Negre	Mercury
18	Ray Elder	Dodge
19	Walter Ballard	Chevrolet
20	Ron Keselowski	Dodge
21	Cecil Gordon	Chevrolet
22	Cale Yarborough	Chevrolet
23	Maynard Troyer	Ford
24	John A. Utsman	Dodge
25	Bobby Allison	Chevrolet
26	J.D. McDuffie	Chevrolet
27	Dave Marcis	Matador
28	Jim Vandiver	Dodge
29	Coo Coo Marlin	Chevrolet
30	Benny Parsons	Chevrolet
31	John Sears	Dodge
32	Red Farmer	Ford
33	David Pearson	Mercury
34	Marty Robbins	Dodge
35	Bill Dennis	Chevrolet

36	Tiny Lund	Chevrolet
37	Neil Castles	Dodge
38	Gordon Johncock	Chevrolet
39	Earl Ross	Chevrolet
40	Pete Hamilton	Plymouth

RICHMOND 500

Time of Race: 3 hours, 37 minutes, 29 seconds
Average Speed: 74.764 mph

FINISH	DRIVER	CAR
1	Richard Petty	Dodge
2	Buddy Baker	Dodge
3	Cale Yarborough	Chevrolet
4	Bobby Isaac	Ford
5	Dave Marcis	Dodge
6	Bill Dennis	Chevrolet
7	Lennie Pond	Chevrolet
8	Cecil Gordon	Chevrolet
9	James Hylton	Mercury
10	Benny Parsons	Chevrolet
11	Walter Ballard	Mercury
12	Elmo Langley	Ford
13	Jabe Thomas	Dodge
14	Bill Champion	Ford
15	Bobby Allison	Chevrolet
16	Henley Gray	Ford
17	Buddy Arrington	Dodge
18	Charlie Roberts	Ford
19	John Sears	Dodge
20	Richard Brown	Chevrolet
21	Sonny Hutchins	Chevrolet
22	Frank Warren	Dodge
23	Tiny Lund	Chevrolet
24	Neil Castles	Dodge
25	Donnie Allison	Chevrolet
26	Ray Hendrick	Mercury
27	Dean Dalton	Mercury
28	David Sisco	Chevrolet
29	J.D. McDufle	Chevrolet
30	Vic Parsons	Mercury

CAROLINA 500

Time of Race: 4 hours, 13 minutes, 1 second
Average Speed: 107.205 mph

FINISH	DRIVER	CAR
1	David Pearson	Mercury
2	Cale Yarborough	Chevrolet
3	Buddy Baker	Dodge
4	Bobby Allison	Chevrolet
5	Dick Brooks	Ford
6	Darrell Waltrip	Mercury
7	Jim Vandiver	Dodge
8	Joe Frasson	Dodge
9	Richard Childress	Chevrolet
10	Bill Dennis	Chevrolet
11	James Hylton	Mercury
12	Buddy Arrington	Plymouth
13	Jabe Thomas	Dodge
14	Coo Coo Marlin	Chevrolet
15	Frank Warren	Dodge
16	Ed Negre	Dodge
17	Charlie Roberts	Ford
18	Henley Gray	Ford
19	Larry Smith	Mercury
20	Lennie Pond	Chevrolet
21	Elmo Langley	Ford
22	Cecil Gordon	Chevrolet
23	Richard Petty	Dodge
24	David Sisco	Chevrolet
25	Gordon Johncock	Chevrolet

26	Dean Dalton	Mercury
27	Buck Baker	Chevrolet
28	Eddie Bond	Dodge
29	J.D. McDuffie	Chevrolet
30	Bobby Isaac	Ford
31	Benny Parsons	Chevrolet
32	Bill Champion	Mercury
33	John A. Utsman	Dodge
34	Vic Parsons	Mercury
35	Raymond Williams	Ford
36	Neil Castles	Dodge
37	Dave Marcis	Matador
38	Clarence Lovell	Chevrolet
39	Walter Ballard	Mercury
40	Tiny Lund	Chevrolet

SOUTHEASTERN 500

Time of Race: 2 hours, 57 minutes, 43 seconds
Average Speed: 88.952 mph

FINISH	DRIVER	CAR
1	Cale Yarborough	Chevrolet
2	Richard Petty	Dodge
3	Bobby Allison	Chevrolet
4	Dave Marcis	Dodge
5	Benny Parsons	Mercury
6	Lennie Pond	Chevrolet
7	Coo Coo Marlin	Chevrolet
8	James Hylton	Mercury
9	Vic Parsons	Ford
10	John A. Utsman	Dodge
11	David Sisco	Chevrolet
12	Elmo Langley	Ford
13	John Sears	Dodge
14	Buddy Arrington	Plymouth
15	Bobby Isaac	Ford
16	Richard Brown	Chevrolet
17	Walter Ballard	Mercury
18	Charlie Roberts	Ford
19	Henley Gray	Ford
20	Richard Childress	Chevrolet
21	J.D. McDuffie	Chevrolet
22	Jabe Thomas	Dodge
23	Bill Champion	Ford
24	Donnie Allison	Chevrolet
25	Buddy Baker	Dodge
26	Frank Warren	Dodge
27	Dean Dalton	Mercury
28	Raymond Williams	Ford
29	Cecil Gordon	Chevrolet
30	Darrell Waltrip	Mercury

ATLANTA 500

Time of Race: 3 hours, 34 minutes, 52 seconds
Average Speed: 139.351 mph

FINISH	DRIVER	CAR
1	David Pearson	Mercury
2	Bobby Isaac	Ford
3	Benny Parsons	Chevrolet
4	Buddy Baker	Dodge
5	Cale Yarborough	Chevrolet
6	Coo Coo Marlin	Chevrolet
7	Dick Brooks	Mercury
8	Cecil Gordon	Chevrolet
9	Clarence Lovell	Chevrolet
10	Jim Vandiver	Dodge
11	Gordon Johncock	Chevrolet
12	Dave Marcis	Dodge
13	Richard Childress	Chevrolet
14	Walter Ballard	Mercury

15	Buddy Arrington	Plymouth
16	Frank Warren	Dodge
17	Raymond Williams	Ford
18	Charles Barrett	Ford
19	Johnny Barnes	Mercury
20	Larry Smith	Mercury
21	James Hylton	Mercury
22	Earle Canavan	Plymouth
23	Dean Dalton	Mercury
24	Ed Negre	Mercury
25	Charlie Roberts	Ford
26	Elmo Langley	Ford
27	A.J. Foyt	Chevrolet
28	Joe Frasson	Dodge
29	Bill Champion	Mercury
30	Mark Donahue	Matador
31	Ron Keselowski	Dodge
32	Roy Mayne	Dodge
33	Darrell Waltrip	Mercury
34	Richard Petty	Dodge
35	Bobby Allison	Chevrolet
36	John Sears	Dodge
37	Bobby Mausgrover	Chevrolet
38	Tiny Lund	Chevrolet
39	Pete Hamilton	Plymouth
40	Tony Bettenhausen	Dodge

GWYN STALEY MEMORIAL

Time of Race: 2 hours, 34 minutes, 17 seconds
Average Speed: 97.224 mph

FINISH	DRIVER	CAR
1	Richard Petty	Dodge
2	Benny Parsons	Chevrolet
3	Buddy Baker	Dodge
4	Bobby Allison	Chevrolet
5	Cecil Gordon	Chevrolet
6	Cale Yarborough	Chevrolet
7	Lennie Pond	Chevrolet
8	James Hylton	Mercury
9	Donnie Allison	Chevrolet
10	Yvon DuHamal	Ford
11	John Sears	Dodge
12	Vic Parsons	Ford
13	Elmo Langley	Ford
14	Bill Champion	Ford
15	Earl Brooks	Ford
16	Richard Childress	Chevrolet
17	Dean Dalton	Mercury
18	Walter Ballard	Mercury
19	Ed Negre	Mercury
20	Dave Marcis	Dodge
21	Frank Warren	Dodge
22	Neil Castles	Dodge
23	J.D. McDuffie	Chevrolet
24	Henley Gray	Mercury
25	Buddy Arrington	Dodge
26	Raymond Williams	Ford
27	Charlie Roberts	Ford
28	Bobby Isaac	Ford
29	Jabe Thomas	Dodge
30	Rick Newsom	Ford

REBEL 500

Time of Race: 4 hours, 4 minutes, 14 seconds
Average Speed: 122.655 mph

FINISH	DRIVER	CAR
1	David Pearson	Mercury
2	Benny Parsons	Chevrolet
3	Bobby Allison	Chevrolet
4	Richard Childress	Chevrolet

5	J.D. McDuffie	Chevrolet
6	Dean Dalton	Mercury
7	Richard Petty	Dodge
8	Buddy Baker	Dodge
9	Roy Mayne	Dodge
10	Raymond Williams	Ford
11	Dick Brooks	Ford
12	Earle Canavan	Plymouth
13	Buddy Arrington	Dodge
14	Wendell Scott	Ford
15	G.C. Spencer	Dodge
16	Jabe Thomas	Mercury
17	Richie Panch	Mercury
18	Johnny Barnes	Mercury
19	Cale Yarborough	Chevrolet
20	Ed Negre	Mercury
21	Cecil Gordon	Chevrolet
22	John Sears	Dodge
23	James Hytron	Mercury
24	Darrell Waltrip	Mercury
25	Walter Ballard	Mercury
26	Charlie Roberts	Ford
27	Paul Tyler	Mercury
28	Vic Parsons	Ford
29	David Ray Boggs	Dodge
30	Clarence Lovell	Mercury
31	Charlie Glotzbach	Chevrolet
32	Frank Warren	Dodge
33	Bobby Isaac	Ford
34	Joe Frasson	Dodge
35	Elmo Langley	Ford
36	Lennie Pond	Chevrolet
37	Larry Smith	Mercury
38	Earl Brooks	Ford
39	Bill Champion	Mercury
40	Dave Marcis	Dodge

VIRGINIA 500

Time of Race: 3 hours, 44 minutes, 28 seconds
Average Speed: 70.251 mph

FINISH	DRIVER	CAR
1	David Pearson	Mercury
2	Cale Yarborough	Chevrolet
3	Bobby Isaac	Ford
4	Buddy Baker	Dodge
5	Cecil Gordon	Chevrolet
6	Benny Parsons	Chevrolet
7	Jimmy Hensley	Mercury
8	Walter Ballard	Mercury
9	Vic Parsons	Ford
10	James Hylton	Ford
11	Elmo Langley	Ford
12	Rick Newsom	Ford
13	J.D. McDuffie	Chevrolet
14	Henley Gray	Ford
15	Earl Brooks	Ford
16	Frank Warren	Ford
17	Bill Dennis	Chevrolet
18	Buddy Arrington	Dodge
19	Lennie Pond	Chevrolet
20	Charlie Roberts	Ford
21	Richard Petty	Dodge
22	Ed Negre	Mercury
23	Ronnie Daniels	Chevrolet
24	Richard Childress	Chevrolet
25	David Sisco	Chevrolet
26	Dave Marcis	Matador
27	Donnie Allison	Chevrolet
28	John Sears	Dodge
29	Dean Dalton	Mercury
30	Jabe Thomas	Dodge
31	Raymond Williams	Ford
32	Bobby Allison	Chevrolet
33	Richard Brown	Chevrolet
34	Bill Champion	Ford

WINSTON 500

Time of Race: 3 hours, 47 minutes, 23 seconds
Average Speed: 131.958 mph

FINISH	DRIVER	CAR
1	David Pearson	Mercury
2	Donnie Allison	Chevrolet
3	Benny Parsons	Chevrolet
4	Clarence Lovell	Chevrolet
5	Cecil Gordon	Chevrolet
6	Coo Coo Marlin	Chevrolet
7	Dick Simon	Dodge
8	Jim Vandiver	Dodge
9	Vic Parsons	Mercury
10	Charles Barrett	Ford
11	Ed Negre	Dodge
12	Eddie Bond	Dodge
13	Tommy Gale	Mercury
14	Earl Ross	Chevrolet
15	Jabe Thomas	Dodge
16	Dean Dalton	Mercury
17	Dave Marcis	Dodge
18	J.D. McDuffie	Chevrolet
19	Elmo Langley	Ford
20	John Sears	Dodge
21	Dick May	Mercury
22	Richard Childress	Chevrolet
23	Dick Brooks	Plymouth
24	Frank Warren	Dodge
25	Paul Tyler	Mercury
26	Bobby Isaac	Ford
27	Johnny Barnes	Mercury
28	Raymond Williams	Ford
29	Mel Larson	Chevrolet
30	Rony Bettenhausen	Chevrolet
31	Darrell Waltrip	Mercury
32	Red Farmer	Ford
33	D.K. Ulrich	Ford
34	Henley Gray	Mercury
35	Richard Petty	Dodge
36	David Sisco	Chevrolet
37	Bill Champion	Mercury
38	Gordon Johncock	Chevrolet
39	Alton Jones	Chevrolet
40	Buddy Baker	Dodge
41	Cale Yarborough	Chevrolet
42	Bobby Allison	Chevrolet
43	Joe Frasson	Dodge
44	Ramo Stott	Mercury
45	James Hylton	Mercury
46	Lennie Pond	Chevrolet
47	Slick Gardner	Mercury
48	Walter Ballard	Mercury
49	Buddy Arrington	Plymouth
50	Ron Keselowski	Dodge
51	Bill Ward	Chevrolet
52	Ben Arnold	Mercury
53	Charlie Roberts	Ford
54	Bobby Mausgrover	Ford
55	Wendell Scott	Mercury
56	Earl Brooks	Ford
57	Ronnie Daniel	Chevrolet
58	Larry Smith	Mercury
59	Eddie Yarboro	Dodge
60	Richard Brown	Chevrolet

MUSIC CITY 420

Time of Race: 2 hours, 34 minutes, 48seconds
Average Speed: 98.419 mph

FINISH	DRIVER	CAR
1	Cale Yarborough	Chevrolet
2	Benny Parsons	Chevrolet
3	Buddy Baker	Dodge
4	Cecil Gordon	Chevrolet
5	Bobby Allison	Chevrolet
6	Coo Coo Marlin	Chevrolet

FINISH	DRIVER	CAR
7	Bobby Isaac	Ford
8	David Sisco	Chevrolet
9	J.D. McDuffie	Chevrolet
10	Vic Parsons	Ford
11	Dave Marcis	Dodge
12	James Hylton	Mercury
13	Richard Petty	Dodge
14	Buddy Arrington	Dodge
15	Dean Dalton	Mercury
16	Rick Newsom	Ford
17	Elmo Langley	Ford
18	Jabe Thomas	Dodge
19	Bob Brown	Chevrolet
20	Frank Warren	Dodge
21	Charlie Roberts	Ford
22	Walter Ballard	Mercury
23	Richard Childress	Chevrolet
24	Darrell Waltrip	Mercury
25	Henley Gray	Ford
26	Alton Jones	Chevrolet
27	Ed Negre	Mercury
28	Bobby Poole	Mercury

WORLD 600

Time of Race: 4 hours, 26 minutes, 53 seconds
Average Speed: 134.890 mph

FINISH	DRIVER	CAR
1	Buddy Baker	Dodge
2	David Pearson	Mercury
3	Cale Yarborough	Chevrolet
4	Bobby Isaac	Ford
5	Benny Parsons	Chevrolet
6	Jim Vandiver	Dodge
7	Darrell Waltrip	Mercury
8	Cecil Gordon	Chevrolet
9	Dick Brooks	Ford
10	David Sisco	Chevrolet
11	Richard Childress	Chevrolet
12	James Hylton	Mercury
13	Richard Petty	Dodge
14	Elmo Langley	Ford
15	Larry Smith	Mercury
16	Bill Champion	Ford
17	Raymond Williams	Ford
18	Walter Ballard	Mercury
19	Ed Negre	Dodge
20	Charlie Blanton	Dodge
21	J.D. McDuffie	Chevrolet
22	Billy Scott	Chevrolet
23	Frank Warren	Dodge
24	Charlie Glotzbach	Chevrolet
25	Joe Frasson	Dodge
26	Vic Parsons	Ford
27	Charles Barrett	Ford
28	Dave Marcis	Matador
29	G.C. Spencer	Dodge
30	Dean Dalton	Mercury
31	Jabe Thomas	Dodge
32	Buddy Arrington	Plymouth
33	Coo Coo Marlin	Chevrolet
34	Neil Castles	Dodge
35	Paul Tyler	Mercury
36	Tiny Lund	Chevrolet
37	Peter Gregg	Dodge
38	Lennie Pond	Chevrolet
39	Richard Brown	Chevrolet
40	Alton Jones	Chevrolet

MASON-DIXON 500

Time of Race: 4 hours, 10 minutes, 32 seconds
Average Speed: 119.745 mph

FINISH	DRIVER	CAR
1	David Pearson	Mercury
2	Cale Yarborough	Chevrolet
3	Bobby Allison	Chevrolet
4	Richard Petty	Dodge
5	Cecil Gordon	Chevrolet
6	Benny Parsons	Chevrolet
7	Buddy Baker	Dodge
8	Dave Marcis	Matador
9	Dean Dalton	Mercury
10	David Sisco	Chevrolet
11	Jabe Thomas	Dodge
12	James Hylton	Mercury
13	Henley Gray	Mercury
14	Charlie Roberts	Ford
15	Bill Hollar	Mercury
16	Jimmy Crawford	Plymouth
17	Elmo Langley	Ford
18	Richard Childress	Chevrolet
19	J.D. McDuffie	Chevrolet
20	Lennie Pond	Chevrolet
21	Buddy Arrington	Dodge
22	John Sears	Dodge
23	Paul Tyler	Mercury
24	Frank Warren	Dodge
25	Raymond Williams	Ford
26	G.C. Spencer	Dodge
27	D.K. Ulrich	Ford
28	Walter Ballard	Mercury
29	Bobby Isaac	Ford
30	Vic Parsons	Ford
31	Bill Champion	Mercury
32	Mel Larson	Chevrolet
33	Ed Negre	Dodge
34	Earle Canavan	Plymouth
35	Coo Coo Marlin	Chevrolet
36	Richard Brown	Chevrolet
37	Neil Castles	Dodge
38	Donnie Allison	Chevrolet
39	Rick Newsom	Ford
40	Eddie Pettyjohn	Mercury

TUBORG 400

Time of Race: 4 hours, 0 minutes, 0 seconds
Average Speed: 100.215 mph

FINISH	DRIVER	CAR
1	Bobby Allison	Chevrolet
2	Richard Petty	Dodge
3	Benny Parsons	Chevrolet
4	Jimmy Insolo	Chevrolet
5	Cecil Gordon	Chevrolet
6	Richard White	Ford
7	Hershel McGriff	Plymouth
8	James Hylton	Ford
9	Jack McCoy	Dodge
10	Chuck Bown	Dodge
11	Bill Champion	Mercury
12	J.D. McDuffie	Chevrolet
13	Larry Smith	Mercury
14	Leon Fox	Chevrolet
15	Walter Ballard	Mercury
16	George Behlman	Chevrolet
17	Richard Childress	Chevrolet
18	Glen Francis	Chevrolet
19	Elmo Langley	Ford
20	Mike James	Chevrolet
21	Johnny Anderson	Chevrolet
22	Carl Adams	Ford
23	Don Nool	Ford
24	Cale Yarborough	Chevrolet
25	Dick Kranzler	Chevrolet
26	Jack Simpson	Chevrolet
27	Henley Gray	Mercury
28	Hugh Pearson	Chevrolet
29	Sonny Easley	Ford
30	Ron Hornaday	Chevrolet
31	John Soares, Jr.	Dodge
32	Dick Bown	Dodge
33	Bobby Isaac	Ford
34	Ronnie Aldeman	Chevrolet
35	Nels Miller	Chevrolet
36	Ray Elder	Dodge
37	Jim Whitt	Chevrolet
38	Buddy Baker	Dodge

ANDRETTI TELLS IT LIKE IT IS

Trust an Andretti to pop off the perfect squelch at the perfect time. In this case, it was Mario in the post-race interview after he'd won the 1967 Daytona 500 in a No. 11 Ford owned and prepared by the potent Holman-Moody team.

During the race Andretti was all over the place. He'd run a lap up near the wall, the next one down near the apron of the track and the next one somewhere in the middle. There was method to his madness, though, since nobody chasing him down the stretch had any idea what line he might take next.

Someone asked in the interview why he'd been so erratic for the whole 200-lap, 500-mile race? "Well," Andretti reported answered after his first and only NASCAR victory, "that's why they paved the whole thing, isn't it?"

| 39 | Chuck Wahl | Chevrolet |
| 40 | Dean Dalton | Mercury |

FIRECRACKER 400

Time of Race: 2 hours, 31 minutes, 27 seconds
Average Speed: 168.488 mph

FINISH	DRIVER	CAR
1	David Pearson	Mercury
2	Richard Petty	Dodge
3	Buddy Baker	Dodge
4	Gordon Johncock	Chevrolet
5	Benny Parsons	Chevrolet
6	Dave Marcis	Dodge
7	Vic Parsons	Ford
8	Marty Robbins	Dodge
9	Dick Brooks	Ford
10	Joe Frasson	Dodge
11	David Sisco	Chevrolet
12	James Hylton	Mercury
13	Cecil Gordon	Chevrolet
14	G.C. Spencer	Dodge
15	Roy Mayne	Dodge
16	Elmo Langley	Ford
17	Dean Dalton	Mercury
18	Buddy Arrington	Plymouth
19	Frank Warren	Dodge
20	Lennie Pond	Chevrolet
21	Larry Smith	Mercury
22	Raymond Williams	Ford
23	Henley Gray	Mercury
24	Bill Champion	Mercury
25	Darrell Waltrip	Mercury
26	Walter Ballard	Mercury
27	Richard Childress	Chevrolet
28	Donnie Allison	Chevrolet
29	Ed Negre	Dodge
30	Bobby Allison	Chevrolet
31	Jabe Thomas	Dodge
32	Jim Vandiver	Dodge
33	John Sears	Dodge
34	Ed Sczech	Chevrolet
35	Dick Simon	Dodge

36	Cale Yarborough	Chevrolet
37	A.J. Foyt	Chevrolet
38	Coo Coo Marlin	Chevrolet
39	Bobby Isaac	Ford
40	J.D. McDuffie	Chevrolet

VOLUNTEER 500

Time of Race: 2 hours, 53 minutes, 4 seconds
Average Speed: 912.342 mph

FINISH	DRIVER	CAR
1	Benny Parsons	Chevrolet
2	L.D. Ottinger	Chevrolet
3	Cecil Gordon	Chevrolet
4	Lennie Pond	Chevrolet
5	J.D. McDuffie	Chevrolet
6	Ed Negre	Dodge
7	Raymond Williams	Ford
8	James Hylton	Mercury
9	Elmo Langley	Ford
10	Henley Gray	Mercury
11	David Sisco	Chevrolet
12	Rick Newsom	Ford
13	Jabe Thomas	Dodge
14	Walter Ballard	Mercury
15	Frank Warren	Dodge
16	Ronnie Daniel	Chevrolet
17	Charlie Roberts	Ford
18	Bill Champion	Mercury
19	Cale Yarborough	Chevrolet
20	Bobby Allison	Chevrolet
21	Richard Petty	Dodge
22	Bobby Isaac	Ford
23	Dean Dalton	Mercury
24	D.K. Ulrich	Ford
25	Richard Childress	Chevrolet
26	Richard Brown	Chevrolet
27	Coo Coo Marlin	Chevrolet
28	Dave Marcis	Matador
29	G.C. Spencer	Dodge
30	Buddy Arrington	Dodge

DIXIE 500

Time of Race: 3 hours, 50 minutes, 1 seconds
Average Speed: 130.211 mph

FINISH	DRIVER	CAR
1	David Pearson	Mercury
2	Cale Yarborough	Chevrolet
3	Donnie Allison	Chevrolet
4	Joe Frasson	Dodge
5	Jody Ridley	Mercury
6	Lennie Pond	Chevrolet
7	J.D. McDuffie	Chevrolet
8	G.C. Spencer	Dodge
9	Jabe Thomas	Dodge
10	Larry Smith	Mercury
11	Buddy Arrington	Dodge
12	Rick Newsom	Ford
13	Henley Gray	Ford
14	Frank Warren	Dodge
15	Walter Ballard	Mercury
16	Randy Tissot	Chevrolet
17	Bill Champion	Mercury
18	Ed Negre	Dodge
19	Charlie Robert	Ford
20	Raymond Williams	Ford
21	James Hylton	Ford
22	Dean Dalton	Mercury
23	Richard Childress	Chevrolet
24	Cecil Gordon	Chevrolet
25	Benny Parsons	Chevrolet
26	David Sisco	Chevrolet
27	Bobby Allison	Chevrolet
28	Ed Sczech	Chevrolet
29	Vic Parsons	Ford

FINISH	DRIVER	CAR
30	Coo Coo Marlin	Chevrolet
31	Darrell Waltrip	Mercury
32	Dave Marcis	Dodge
33	Richard Petty	Dodge
34	Buddy Baker	Dodge
35	Bobby Isaac	Ford
36	John Sears	Dodge
37	Tommy Gale	Mercury
38	Elmo Langley	Ford
39	H.B. Bailey	Pontiac
40	Charlie Barrett	Ford

TALLADEGA 500

Time of Race: 3 hours, 26 minutes, 17 seconds
Average Speed: 187.084 mph

FINISH	DRIVER	CAR
1	Dick Brooks	Plymouth
2	Buddy Baker	Dodge
3	David Pearson	Mercury
4	James Hylton	Mercury
5	David Sisco	Chevrolet
6	Cale Yarborough	Chevrolet
7	Darrell Waltrip	Mercury
8	Cecil Gordon	Mercury
9	Walter Ballard	Mercury
10	L.D. Ottinger	Chevrolet
11	J.D. McDuffie	Chevrolet
12	Dave Marcis	Dodge
13	Bobby Isaac	Ford
14	Richard Petty	Dodge
15	Frank Warren	Dodge
16	Jabe Thomas	Dodge
17	Dean Dalton	Mercury
18	Bill Ward	Chevrolet
19	Alton Jones	Chevrolet
20	Randy Tissot	Chevrolet
21	Elmo Langley	Ford
22	Bill Champion	Mercury
23	Eddie Bond	Dodge
24	Bobby Mausgrover	Chevrolet
25	Ed Negre	Dodge
26	Donnie Allison	Chevrolet
27	Buddy Arrington	Plymouth
28	Henley Gray	Mercury
29	Bobby Allison	Chevrolet
30	Johnny Barnes	Mercury
31	Richard Childress	Chevrolet
32	Red Farmer	Ford
33	Ed Sczech	Chevrolet
34	Bob Davis	Dodge
35	Jim Vandiver	Dodge
36	Marty Robbins	Dodge
37	Jody Ridley	Mercury
38	Benny Parsons	Chevrolet
39	D.K. Ulrich	Ford
40	Coo Coo Marlin	Chevrolet
41	Phil Fhinney	Chevrolet
42	Charlie Roberts	Ford
43	Joe Frasson	Dodge
44	Mel Larson	Dodge
45	Ramo Stott	Chevrolet
46	Raymond Williams	Ford
47	Lennie Pond	Chevrolet
48	Tommy Gale	Mercury
49	Larry Smith	Mercury
50	Paul Tyler	Mercury

NASHVILLE 420

Time of Race: 2 hours, 48 minutes, 12 seconds
Average Speed: 89.310 mph

FINISH	DRIVER	CAR
1	Buddy Baker	Dodge
2	Richard Petty	Dodge

FINISH	DRIVER	CAR
3	Coo Coo Marlin	Chevrolet
4	David Sisco	Chevrolet
5	Ed Negre	Dodge
6	James Hylton	Mercury
7	Walter Ballard	Mercury
8	Cecil Gordon	Chevrolet
9	Alton Jones	Chevrolet
10	Bill Champion	Ford
11	Rick Newsom	Ford
12	Buddy Arrington	Dodge
13	Henley Gray	Mercury
14	Cale Yarborough	Chevrolet
15	Frank Warren	Ford
16	Earl Brooks	Ford
17	Charlie Roberts	Ford
18	J.D. McDuffie	Chevrolet
19	Benny Parsons	Chevrolet
20	Richard Childress	Chevrolet
21	Elmo Langley	Ford
22	Bobby Allison	Chevrolet
23	Lennie Pond	Chevrolet
24	Darrell Waltrip	Chevrolet
25	Richard Brown	Chevrolet
26	Jabe Thomas	Mercury
27	Dean Dalton	Mercury
28	Dick May	Ford
29	Vic Parsons	Ford
30	Raymond Williams	Ford
31	Mel Larson	Dodge
32	Dick Brooks	Mercury
33	Bob Brown	Chevrolet

SOUTHERN 500

Time of Race: 3 hours, 44 minutes, 25 seconds
Average Speed: 134.033 mph

FINISH	DRIVER	CAR
1	Cale Yarborough	Chevrolet
2	David Pearson	Mercury
3	Buddy Baker	Dodge
4	Richard Petty	Dodge
5	Benny Parsons	Chevrolet
6	Bobby Allison	Chevrolet
7	Coo Coo Marlin	Chevrolet
8	Darrell Waltrip	Ford
9	Dick Brooks	Chevrolet
10	J.D. McDuffie	Chevrolet
11	Cecil Gordon	Chevrolet
12	James Hylton	Mercury
13	Jabe Thomas	Dodge
14	Buddy Arrington	Dodge
15	Randy Tissot	Chevrolet
16	Charlie Roberts	Chevrolet
17	Walter Ballard	Mercury
18	D.K. Ulrich	Ford
19	Dean Dalton	Mercury
20	Henley Gray	Mercury
21	Mel Larson	Dodge
22	Bill Champion	Mercury
23	Joe Frasson	Dodge
24	Frank Warren	Dodge
25	Raymond Williams	Ford
26	Ed Negre	Dodge
27	Jim Vandiver	Dodge
28	David Sisco	Chevrolet
29	Bud Moore	Mercury
30	Charlie Glotzbach	Chevrolet
31	Elmo Langley	Ford
32	Dick May	Mercury
33	Richie Panch	Ford
34	Vic Parsons	Ford
35	Johnny Barnes	Mercury
36	Tommy Gale	Mercury
37	Lennie Pond	Chevrolet
38	Richard Brown	Chevrolet
39	G.C. Spencer	Dodge
40	Richard Childress	Chevrolet

CAPITAL CITY 500

Time of Race: 4 hours, 13 minutes, 17 seconds
Average Speed: 83.215 mph

FINISH	DRIVER	CAR
1	Richard Petty	Dodge
2	Cale Yarborough	Chevrolet
3	Bobby Allison	Chevrolet
4	Benny Parsons	Chevrolet
5	Buddy Arrington	Dodge
6	Walter Ballard	Mercury
7	Cecil Gordon	Chevrolet
8	James Hylton	Mercury
9	Henley Gray	Mercury
10	Raymond Williams	Ford
11	Charlie Roberts	Ford
12	Richard Childress	Chevrolet
13	Rick Newsom	Ford
14	Frank Warren	Dodge
15	Elmo Langley	Ford
16	David Sisco	Chevrolet
17	Buddy Baker	Dodge
18	Jabe Thomas	Dodge
19	Mel Larson	Dodge
20	John Sears	Dodge
21	Ed Negre	Dodge
22	Earl Brooks	Ford
23	Ronnie Daniels	Chevrolet
24	Dick May	Mercury
25	D.K. Ulrich	Ford
26	Darrell Waltrip	Ford
27	Dick Brooks	Mercury
28	Lennie Pond	Chevrolet
29	J.D. McDuffie	Chevrolet
30	Bill Champion	Ford
31	Dean Dalton	Mercury
32	Vic Parsons	Ford
33	Richard Brown	Chevrolet
34	Baxter Price	Chevrolet

DELAWARE 500

Time of Race: 4 hours, 25 minutes, 50 seconds
Average Speed: 112.852 mph

FINISH	DRIVER	CAR
1	David Pearson	Mercury
2	Bobby Allison	Chevrolet
3	Buddy Baker	Dodge
4	Benny Parsons	Chevrolet
5	J.D. McDuffie	Chevrolet
6	Coo Coo Marlin	Chevrolet
7	Richard Petty	Dodge
8	Elmo Langley	Ford
9	Lennie Pond	Chevrolet
10	Eddie Pettyjohn	Mercury
11	Ed Negre	Dodge
12	Donnie Allison	Chevrolet
13	Mel Larson	Dodge
14	Jabe Thomas	Dodge
15	Rick Newsom	Ford
16	Richard Childress	Chevrolet
17	Walter Ballard	Mercury
18	Bobby Mausgrover	Chevrolet
19	James Hylton	Chevrolet
20	Darrell Waltrip	Chevrolet
21	Henley Gray	Mercury
22	Charlie Roberts	Chevrolet
23	Raymond Williams	Ford
24	Earle Canavan	Plymouth
25	Cale Yarborough	Chevrolet
26	Jimmy Carwford	Plymouth
27	Cecil Gordon	Chevrolet
28	Johnny Barnes	Mercury
29	David Sisco	Chevrolet
30	G.C. Spencer	Dodge
31	John Sears	Dodge

32	Ron Keselowski	Dodge
33	Earl Brooks	Ford
34	Dean Dalton	Mercury
35	D.K. Ulrich	Ford
36	Vic Parsons	Chevrolet
37	Frank Warren	Dodge
38	Toby Tobias	Mercury
39	Bill Champion	Mercury
40	Buddy Arrington	Dodge

WILKES 400

Time of Race: 2 hours, 37 minutes, 34 seconds
Average Speed: 95.198 mph

FINISH	DRIVER	CAR
1	Bobby Allison	Chevrolet
2	Richard Petty	Dodge
3	Cale Yarborough	Chevrolet
4	Buddy Baker	Dodge
5	Benny Parsons	Chevrolet
6	Lennie Pond	Chevrolet
7	Dave Marcis	Dodge
8	Dick Brooks	Mercury
9	Cecil Gordon	Chevrolet
10	J.D. McDuffie	Chevrolet
11	Coo Coo Marlin	Chevrolet
12	James Hylton	Mercury
13	Walter Ballard	Mercury
14	Elmo Langley	Ford
15	Henley Gray	Mercury
16	Jabe Thomas	Dodge
17	Richard Childress	Chevrolet
18	Raymond Williams	Ford
19	Dean Dalton	Ford
20	Mel Larson	Dodge
21	Frank Warren	Dodge
22	Ed Negre	Dodge
23	D.K. Ulrich	Ford
24	Earl Brooks	Ford
25	Buddy Arrington	Dodge
26	Charlie Roberts	Chevrolet
27	David Sisco	Chevrolet
28	John Sears	Dodge
29	Bill Champion	Mercury
30	Darrell Waltrip	Ford

OLD DOMINION 500

Time of Race: 3 hours, 48 minutes, 51 seconds
Average Speed: 68.831 mph

FINISH	DRIVER	CAR
1	Richard Petty	Dodge
2	Cale Yarborough	Chevrolet
3	Bobby Allison	Chevrolet
4	Buddy Baker	Dodge
5	Jack McCoy	Dodge
6	Benny Parsons	Chevrolet
7	Cecil Gordon	Chevrolet
8	James Hylton	Mercury
9	Buddy Arrington	Dodge
10	J.D. McDuffie	Chevrolet
11	Ray Hendrick	Mercury
12	John Sears	Dodge
13	Elmo Langley	Ford
14	Henley Gray	Mercury
15	Frank Warren	Dodge
16	Jabe Thomas	Dodge
17	Mel Larson	Dodge
18	Walter Ballard	Mercury
19	Earl Brooks	Ford
20	Dean Dalton	Ford
21	D.K. Ulrich	Ford
22	Charlie Roberts	Chevrolet

23	Coo Coo Marlin	Chevrolet
24	Ronnie Daniel	Chevrolet
25	Richard Childress	Chevrolet
26	Ed Negre	Dodge
27	Pee Wee Wentz	Chevrolet
28	David Sisco	Chevrolet
29	Raymond Williams	Ford
30	Lennie Pond	Chevrolet
31	David Pearson	Mercury
32	Rick Newsom	Ford
33	Dave Marcis	Dodge
34	Donnie Allison	Chevrolet
35	Richard Brown	Chevrolet
36	Bill Champion	Ford

NATIONAL 500

Time of Race: 3 hours, 26 minutes, 58 seconds
Average Speed: 145.240 mph

FINISH	DRIVER	CAR
1	Cale Yarborough	Chevrolet
2	Richard Petty	Dodge
3	Bobby Allison	Chevrolet
4	Benny Parsons	Chevrolet
5	Dick Trickle	Chevrolet
6	Lennie Pond	Chevrolet
7	Buddy Arrington	Plymouth
8	Elmo Langley	Ford
9	Cecil Gordon	Chevrolet
10	Henley Gray	Mercury
11	Harry Gant	Ford
12	Wendell Scott	Dodge
13	James Hylton	Chevrolet
14	Charlie Roberts	Chevrolet
15	Johnny Barnes	Mercury
16	Jimmy Crawford	Plymouth
17	Jim Vandiver	Dodge
18	Richard Childress	Chevrolet
19	Coo Coo Marlin	Chevrolet
20	Eddie Bond	Dodge
21	David Sisco	Chevrolet
22	Joe Frasson	Dodge
23	Walter Ballard	Mercury
24	Dave Marcis	Matador
25	Jabe Thomas	Dodge
26	Bill Champion	Mercury
27	Ed Negre	Chevrolet
28	L.D. Ottinger	Chevrolet
29	J.D. McDuffie	Chevrolet
30	Dean Dalton	Mercury
31	Neil Castles	Dodge
32	Donnie Allison	Chevrolet
33	Raymond Williams	Ford
34	Dick Brooks	Dodge
35	Frank Warren	Dodge
36	David Pearson	Mercury
37	Charlie Glotzbach	Chevrolet
38	Darrell Waltrip	Ford
39	G.C. Spencer	Dodge
40	Wayne Andrews	Mercury
41	Buddy Baker	Dodge

AMERICAN 500

Time of Race: 4 hours, 14 minutes, 57 seconds
Average Speed: 117.749 mph

FINISH	DRIVER	CAR
1	David Pearson	Mercury
2	Buddy Baker	Dodge
3	Cale Yarborough	Chevrolet
4	Bobby Allison	Chevrolet
5	Dave Marcis	Matador
6	Donnie Allison	Chevrolet
7	Dick Brooks	Dodge
8	Charlie Glotzbach	Mercury

9	Lennie Pond	Chevrolet
10	Coo Coo Marlin	Chevrolet
11	Cecil Gordon	Chevrolet
12	Elmo Langley	Ford
13	Johnny Rutherford	Chevrolet
14	Richard Childress	Chevrolet
15	David Sisco	Chevrolet
16	Tony Bettenhausen	Chevrolet
17	Henley Gray	Mercury
18	Jabe Thomas	Dodge
19	James Hylton	Chevrolet
20	J.D. McDuffie	Chevrolet
21	Ed Negre	Dodge
22	Walter Ballard	Mercury
23	Dean Dalton	Mercury
24	Buddy Arrington	Plymouth
25	Gordon Johncock	Chevrolet
26	PeeWee Wentz	Chevrolet
27	Darrell Waltrip	Ford
28	Benny Parsons	Chevrolet
29	Eddie Bond	Dodge
30	Bill Champion	Mercury
31	Jody Ridley	Ford
32	Jim Vandiver	Dodge
33	John Sears	Dodge
34	Charlie Roberts	Chevrolet
35	Richard Petty	Dodge
36	Richie Panch	Ford
37	Paul Tyler	Dodge
38	Neil Castles	Dodge
39	Richard Brown	Chevrolet
40	Joe Frasson	Dodge
41	G.C. Spencer	Dodge
42	Johnny Barnes	Mercury
43	Frank Warren	Ford

1974

WINSTON WESTERN 500

Time of Race: 4 hours, 56 minutes, 52 seconds
Average Speed: 101.40 Mph

FINISH	DRIVER	CAR
1	Cale Yarborough	Chevrolet
2	Richard Petty	Dodge
3	David Pearson	Mercury
4	Benny Parsons	Chevrolet
5	Bobby Allison	Chevrolet
6	Donnie Allison	Chevrolet
7	Gary Bettenhausen	Matador
8	Cecil Gordon	Chevrolet
9	Richie Panch	Chevrolet
10	Hershel McGriff	Dodge
11	J.C. Danielson	Mercury
12	Sonny Easley	Ford
13	Carl Adams	Ford
14	Dick May	Mercury
15	Elmo Langley	Ford
16	Charlie Roberts	Ford
17	Tony Bettenhausen	Chevrolet
18	George Follmer	Ford
19	Richard White	Ford
20	John Anderson	Chevrolet
21	Jack McCoy	Dodge
22	J.D. McDuffie	Chevrolet
23	Jim Insolo	Chevrolet
24	Odie Robertson	Chevrolet
25	Jim Gilliam	Chevrolet
26	Bill Osborne	Chevrolet
27	Harry Jefferson	Ford
28	Dave Marcis	Dodge
29	George Esau	Chevrolet
30	Jerry Grant	Chevrolet
31	Dick Brown	Dodge

32	Don Pruitt	Chevrolet
33	Ross Surgenor	Chevrolet
34	Ray Elder	Dodge
35	Chuck Bown	Dodge

DAYTONA 500

Time of Race: 3 hours, 11 minutes, 38 seconds
Average Speed: 140.894 Mph

FINISH	DRIVER	CAR
1	Richard Petty	Dodge
2	Cale Yarborough	Chevrolet
3	Ramo Stott	Chevrolet
4	CooCoo Marlin	Chevrolet
5	A.J. Foyt	Chevrolet
6	Donnie Allison	Chevrolet
7	Darrell Waltrip	Chevrolet
8	Bobby Isaac	Chevrolet
9	Dick Brooks	Dodge
10	Walter Ballard	Chevrolet
11	Earl Ross	Chevrolet
12	Gary Bettenhausen	Matador
13	Cecil Gordon	Chevrolet
14	Dave Marcis	Dodge
15	David Sisco	Chevrolet
16	James Hylton	Chevrolet
17	Bob Burchem	Chevrolet
18	Richie Panch	Ford
19	Jimmy Crawford	Plymouth
20	George Follmer	Ford
21	Bill Dennis	Ford
22	Benny Parsons	Chevrolet
23	Lennie Pond	Chevrolet
24	Johnny Rutherford	Chevrolet
25	Jim Hurtubise	Chevrolet
26	Joe Frasson	Dodge
27	Jim Vandiver	Dodge
28	J.D. McDuffie	Chevrolet
29	L.D. Ottinger	Chevrolet
30	Bobby Allison	Chevrolet
31	Dick Simon	Dodge
32	Jackie Rogers	Chevrolet
33	Tony Bettenhausen	Chevrolet
34	Frank Warren	Dodge
35	David Pearson	Mercury
36	Charlie Glotzbach	Chevrolet
37	Joe Mihalic	Chevrolet
38	Dan Daughtry	Ford
39	Hershel McGriff	Dodge
40	Richard Childress	Chevrolet

RICHMOND 500

Time of Race: 3 hours, 2 minutes, 2 seconds
Average Speed: 80.095 Mph

FINISH	DRIVER	CAR
1	Bobby Allison	Chevrolet
2	Richard Petty	Dodge
3	Cale Yarborough	Chevrolet
4	Lennie Pond	Chevrolet
5	Dave Marcis	Dodge
6	James Hylton	Chevrolet
7	J.D. McDuffie	Chevrolet
8	Bill Dennis	Ford
9	Elmo Langley	Ford
10	Buddy Arrington	Plymouth
11	Cecil Gordon	Chevrolet
12	Tony Bettenhausen	Chevrolet
13	Benny Parsons	Chevrolet
14	Jimmy Hensley	Chevrolet
15	Neil Castles	Dodge
16	Richard Childress	Chevrolet
17	Donnie Allison	Chevrolet
18	Travis Tiller	Dodge
19	Walter Ballard	Chevrolet
20	Frank Warren	Dodge

21	Richie Panch	Chevrolet
22	D.K. Ulrich	Chevrolet
23	David Sisco	Chevrolet
24	Ed Negre	Dodge
25	Jerry Hufflin	Chevrolet
26	Jabe Thomas	Dodge
27	Bill Champion	Ford
28	Dean Dalton	Chevrolet

CAROLINA 500

Time of Race: 3 hours, 42 minutes, 50 seconds
Average Speed: 121.622 Mph

FINISH	DRIVER	CAR
1	Richard Petty	Dodge
2	Cale Yarborough	Chevrolet
3	Bobby Allison	Chevrolet
4	Charlie Glotzbach	Chevrolet
5	George Follmer	Ford
6	Walter Ballard	Chevrolet
7	Bill Dennis	Ford
8	Dave Marcis	Dodge
9	Lennie Pond	Chevrolet
10	James Hylton	Chevrolet
11	Bob Burcham	Chevrolet
12	Dick Brooks	Dodge
13	J.D. McDuffie	Chevrolet
14	Richie Panch	Chevrolet
15	Jackie Rogers	Chevrolet
16	Buddy Arrington	Plymouth
17	Joe Mihalic	Chevrolet
18	Grant Adcox	Chevrolet
19	Tony Bettenhausen	Chevrolet
20	Frank Warren	Dodge
21	Richard Skillen	Chevrolet
22	Ed Negre	Dodge
23	Benny Parsons	Chevrolet
24	CooCoo Marlin	Chevrolet
25	Darrell Waltrip	Chevrolet
26	Jimmy Crawford	Plymouth
27	Donnie Allison	Chevrolet
28	Charlie Blanton	Dodge
29	Cecil Gordon	Chevrolet
30	Roy Mayne	Dodge
31	David Sisco	Chevrolet
32	Hershel McGriff	Dodge
33	Dean Dalton	Chevrolet
34	David Pearson	Mercury
35	Neil Castles	Dodge
36	Richard Childress	Chevrolet
37	Joe Frasson	Dodge
38	Elmo Langley	Ford
39	G.C. Spencer	Dodge
40	Charlie Roberts	Ford

SOUTHEASTERN 500

Time of Race: 3 hours, 42 minutes, 50 seconds
Average Speed: 64.533 Mph

FINISH	DRIVER	CAR
1	Cale Yarborough	Chevrolet
2	Bobby Isaac	Chevrolet
3	Richard Petty	Dodge
3	Benny Parsons	Chevrolet
4	Bobby Allison	Chevrolet
5	Donnie Allison	Chevrolet
6	Cecil Gordon	Chevrolet
7	Joe Mihalic	Chevorlet
8	James Hylton	Chevrolet
9	Alton Jones	Chevrolet
10	CooCoo Marlin	Chevrolet
11	Ed Negre	Dodge
12	J.D. McDuffie	Chevrolet
13	Frank Warren	Dodge
14	Walter Ballard	Chevrolet
15	Bobby Fleming	Chevrolet

16	Elmo Langley	Ford
17	David Sisco	Chevrolet
18	Bill Champion	Ford
19	Travis Tiller	Dodge
20	Richard Childress	Chevrolet
21	Buddy Arrington	Plymouth
22	Dave Marcis	Dodge
23	Richard Petty	Dodge
24	Dean Dalton	Chevrolet
25	L.D. Ottinger	Chevrolet
26	Lennie Pond	Chevrolet
27	Richie Panch	Chevrolet
28	George Follmer	Ford
29	Tony Bettenhausen	Chevrolet
30	Jabe Thomas	Dodge

ATLANTA 500

Time of Race: 3 hours, 1 minute, 26 seconds
Average Speed: 136.910 Mph

FINISH	DRIVER	CAR
1	Cale Yarborough	Chevrolet
2	David Pearson	Mercury
3	Buddy Baker	Dodge
4	George Follmer	Ford
5	Donnie Allison	Chevrolet
6	Richard Petty	Dodge
7	Darrell Waltrip	Chevrolet
8	Bob Burcham	Chevrolet
9	Gary Bettenhausen	Matador
10	Lennie Pond	Chevrolet
11	Charlie Glotzbach	Chevrolet
12	James Hylton	Chevrolet
13	Earl Ross	Chevrolet
14	David Sisco	Chevrolet
15	J.D. McDuffie	Chevrolet
16	Jackie Rogers	Chevrolet
17	Frank Warren	Dodge
18	Carl Adams	Ford
19	Joe Frasson	Dodge
20	Dave Marcis	Dodge
21	Roy Mayne	Dodge
22	Ed Negre	Dodge
23	Jim Hurtubise	Chevrolet
24	Dick Brooks	Dodge
25	Grant Adcox	Chevrolet
26	Bobby Allison	Chevrolet
27	Richard Childress	Chevrolet
28	CooCoo Marlin	Chevrolet
29	Benny Parsons	Chevrolet
30	G.C. Spencer	Dodge
31	John Martin	Dodge
32	Dan Daughtry	Ford
33	Jody Ridley	Ford
34	Cecil Gordon	Chevrolet
35	Travis Tiller	Dodge
36	Richie Panch	Chevrolet

REBEL 500

Time of Race: 3 hours, 50 minutes, 6 seconds
Average Speed: 150.689 Mph

FINISH	DRIVER	CAR
1	David Pearson	Mercury
2	Bobby Allison	Chevrolet
3	Buddy Baker	Dodge
4	Donnie Allison	Chevrolet
5	Cale Yarborough	Chevrolet
6	Dave Marcis	Dodge
7	Sam McQuagg	Chevrolet
8	Joe Frasson	Dodge
9	Darrell Waltrip	Chevrolet
10	Bob Burcham	Chevrolet
11	Cecil Gordon	Chevrolet
12	Earl Ross	Chevrolet

13	David Sisco	Chevrolet
14	Jackie Rogers	Chevrolet
15	Roy Mayne	Dodge
16	Buddy Arrington	Plymouth
17	Frank Warren	Dodge
18	Tony Bettenhausen	Chevrolet
19	CooCoo Marlin	Chevrolet
20	Richard Petty	Dodge
21	Lennie Pond	Chevrolet
22	George Follmer	Ford
23	Randy Tissot	Chevrolet
24	Ed Negre	Dodge
25	Richard Skillen	Chevrolet
26	James Hylton	Chevrolet
27	Johnny Barnes	Dodge
28	Bill Champion	Ford
29	Dick Brooks	Dodge
30	J.D. McDuffie	Chevrolet
31	Pee Wee Wentz	Chevrolet
32	Benny Parsons	Chevrolet
33	Bobby Isaac	Chevrolet
34	Neil Castles	Dodge
35	Charlie Roberts	Ford
36	G.C. Spencer	Dodge
37	Richie Panch	Chevrolet
38	Elmo Langley	Ford
39	Richard Childress	Chevrolet
40	Walter Ballard	Chevrolet

GWYN STALEY 400

Time of Race: 2 hours, 20 minutes, 20 seconds
Average Speed: 96.200 Mph

FINISH	DRIVER	CAR
1	Richard Petty	Dodge
2	Cale Yarborough	Chevrolet
3	Bobby Allison	Chevrolet
4	Benny Parsons	Chevrolet
5	Lennie Pond	Chevrolet
6	George Follmer	Ford
7	Donnie Allison	Chevrolet
8	J.D. McDuffie	Chevrolet
9	Harry Gant	Ford
10	Dave Marcis	Dodge
11	Cecil Gordon	Chevrolet
12	Walter Ballard	Chevrolet
13	Elmo Langley	Ford
14	Tony Bettenhausen	Chevrolet
15	David Sisco	Chevrolet
16	Neil Castles	Dodge
17	Ed Negre	Dodge
18	Richie Panch	Chevrolet
19	Frank Warren	Dodge
20	Jabe Thomas	Dodge
21	D.K. Ulrich	Chevrolet
22	Richard Childress	Chevrolet
23	Jerry Hufflin	Chevrolet
24	Dick Brooks	Dodge
25	Bill Champion	Ford
26	Marv Acton	Chevrolet
27	Buddy Arrington	Plymouth
28	James Hylton	Chevrolet
29	Dean Dalton	Chevrolet
30	Ronnie Childress	Chevrolet

VIRGINIA 500

Time of Race: 3 hours, 22 minutes, 41 seconds
Average Speed: 70.427 Mph

FINISH	DRIVER	CAR
1	Cale Yarborough	Chevrolet
2	Richard Petty	Dodge
3	Bobby Allison	Chevrolet
4	Benny Parsons	Chevrolet
5	Lennie Pond	Chevrolet

6	Jimmy Hensley	Ford
7	James Hylton	Chevrolet
8	Dave Marcis	Dodge
9	J.D. McDuffie	Chevrolet
10	Richard Childress	Chevrolet
11	Walter Ballard	Chevrolet
12	CooCoo Marlin	Chevrolet
13	Richie Panch	Chevrolet
14	Dean Dalton	Chevrolet
15	Cecil Gordon	Chevrolet
16	Frank Warren	Dodge
17	Buddy Arrington	Plymouth
18	David Sisco	Chevrolet
19	Jabe Thomas	Dodge
20	Travis Tiller	Dodge
21	Ernie Shaw	Chevrolet
22	George Follmer	Ford
23	Donnie Allison	Chevrolet
24	Bill Champion	Ford
25	Bobby Isaac	Chevrolet
26	Ed Negre	Dodge
27	Elmo Langley	Ford
28	Neil Castles	Dodge
29	Tony Bettenhausen	Chevrolet
30	Bobby Fleming	Chevrolet

WINSTON 500

Time of Race: 3 hours, 28 minutes, 09 seconds
Average Speed: 130.220 Mph

FINISH	DRIVER	CAR
1	David Pearson	Mercury
2	Benny Parsons	Chevrolet
3	Richard Petty	Dodge
4	Charlie Glotzbach	Chevrolet
5	Lennie Pond	Chevrolet
6	Dave Marcis	Dodge
7	CooCoo Marlin	Chevrolet
8	Sam McQuagg	Chevrolet
9	Cale Yarborough	Chevrolet
10	Bob Burcham	Chevrolet
11	Richard Childress	Chevrolet
12	Hershel McGriff	Dodge
13	Roy Mayne	Dodge
14	James Hylton	Chevrolet
15	Marty Robbins	Dodge
16	Jim Vandiver	Dodge
17	Jackie Rogers	Chevrolet
18	Frank Warren	Dodge
19	J.D. McDuffie	Chevrolet
20	Iggy Katona	Chevrolet
21	Cecil Gordon	Chevrolet
22	Carl Adams	Ford
23	Elmo Langley	Ford
24	Walter Ballard	Chevrolet
25	Joe Frasson	Dodge
26	D.K. Ulrich	Chevrolet
27	Red Farmer	Ford
28	George Follmer	Ford
29	Dick Brooks	Dodge
30	Tony Bettenhausen	Chevrolet
31	Bobby Allison	Chevrolet
32	Randy Tissot	Chevrolet
33	Buddy Baker	Dodge
34	Ed Negre	Dodge
35	Travis Tiller	Dodge
36	Donnie Allison	Chevrolet
37	Gary Bettenhausen	Matador
38	Grant Adcox	Chevrolet
39	David Sisco	Chevrolet
40	Jerry Schild	Chevrolet
41	John Ray	Dodge
42	John Martin	Dodge
43	Terry Link	Pontiac
44	Richie Panch	Chevrolet
45	Neil Bonnett	Chevrolet
46	Buddy Arrington	Plymouth
47	Alton Jones	Chevrolet
48	Dan Daughtry	Ford
49	Dean Dalton	Chevrolet
50	Earl Ross	Chevrolet

MUSIC CITY USA 420

Time of Race: 3 hours, 6 minutes, 31 seconds
Average Speed: 84.240 Mph

FINISH	DRIVER	CAR
1	Richard Petty	Dodge
2	Donnie Allison	Chevrolet
3	Darrell Waltrip	Chevrolet
4	Bob Burcham	Chevrolet
5	Dave Marcis	Dodge
6	George Follmer	Ford
7	J.D. McDuffie	Chevrolet
8	David Sisco	Chevrolet
9	CooCoo Marlin	Chevrolet
10	Buddy Arrington	Plymouth
11	Lennie Pond	Chevrolet
12	Elmo Langley	Ford
13	Henley Gray	Chevrolet
14	Cale Yarborough	Chevrolet
15	Dean Dalton	Chevrolet
16	Benny Parsons	Chevrolet
17	D.K. Ulrich	Chevrolet
18	Frank Warren	Dodge
19	Jack Donohue	Chevrolet
20	Bobby Allison	Chevrolet
21	Walter Ballard	Chevrolet
22	Jerry Sisco	Chevrolet
23	Tony Bettenhausen	Chevrolet
24	James Hylton	Chevrolet
25	Cecil Gordon	Chevrolet
26	Richard Childress	Chevrolet
27	Alton Jones	Chevrolet
28	Richie Panch	Chevrolet

MASON-DIXON 500

Time of Race: 3 hours, 54 minutes, 40 seconds
Average Speed: 119.99 Mph

FINISH	DRIVER	CAR
1	Cale Yarborough	Chevrolet
2	David Pearson	Chevrolet
3	Richard Petty	Dodge
4	Benny Parsons	Chevrolet
5	George Follmer	Ford
6	Lennie Pond	Chevrolet
7	Dave Marcis	Dodge
8	Jackie Rogers	Chevrolet
9	Ramo Stott	Chevrolet
10	James Hylton	Chevrolet
11	J.D. McDuffie	Chevrolet
12	Buddy Arrington	Plymouth
13	Dean Dalton	Chevrolet
14	Ed Negre	Dodge
15	Frank Warren	Dodge
16	Earle Canavan	Plymouth
17	D.K. Ulrich	Chevrolet
18	Elmo Langley	Ford
19	Bill Champion	Ford
20	Darrell Waltrip	Chevrolet
21	Richard Childress	Chevrolet
22	Walter Ballard	Chevrolet
23	Travis Tiller	Dodge
24	Dave Sisco	Chevrolet
25	Jabe Thomas	Dodge
26	Ernie Shaw	Chevrolet
27	Cecil Gordon	Chevrolet
28	Bobby Allison	Chevrolet
29	Jack Donohue	Chevrolet
30	Donnie Allison	Chevrolet
31	G.C. Spencer	Dodge
32	Ed Pettyjohn	Ford
33	Jim Bray	Chevrolet
34	Tony Bettenhausen	Chevrolet
35	Richard Brown	Pontiac

WORLD 600

Time of Race: 3 hours, 58 minutes, 21 seconds
Average Speed: 135.720 Mph

FINISH	DRIVER	CAR
1	David Pearson	Mercury
2	Richard Petty	Dodge
3	Bobby Allison	Chevrolet
4	Darrell Waltrip	Chevrolet
5	Earl Ross	Chevrolet
6	Dave Marcis	Dodge
7	Dick Trickle	Dodge
8	Jim Vandiver	Dodge
9	Dave Sisco	Chevrolet
10	J.D. McDuffie	Chevrolet
11	Cale Yarborough	Chevrolet
12	Walter Ballard	Chevrolet
13	Roy Mayne	Dodge
14	Harry Gant	Ford
15	James Hylton	Chevrolet
16	Neil Castles	Dodge
17	Frank Warren	Dodge
18	Richard Skillen	Chevrolet
19	Buddy Arrington	Plymouth
20	Lennie Pond	Chevrolet
21	Tony Bettenhausen	Chevrolet
22	Buddy Baker	Dodge
23	Richie Panch	Chevrolet
24	Billy Scott	Chevrolet
25	G.C. Spencer	Dodge
26	Travis Tiller	Dodge
27	Dick Brooks	Dodge
28	Cecil Gordon	Chevrolet
29	Dan Daughtry	Ford
30	Donnie Allison	Chevrolet
31	Benny Parsons	Chevrolet
32	Sam McQuagg	Chevrolet
33	Bobby Isaac	Chevrolet
34	Richard Childress	Chevrolet
35	Randy Tissot	Chevrolet
36	Bob Burcham	Chevrolet
37	Charlie Glotzbach	Chevrolet
38	CooCoo Marlin	Chevrolet
39	Jackie Rogers	Chevrolet
40	Joe Frasson	Dodge

TUBORG 400

Time of Race: 3 hours, 31 minutes, 40 seconds
Average Speed: 102.489 Mph

FINISH	DRIVER	CAR
1	Cale Yarborough	Chevrolet
2	Bobby Allison	Chevrolet
3	Benny Parsons	Chevrolet
4	Cecil Gordon	Chevrolet
5	Frank Warren	Dodge
6	James Hylton	Chevrolet
7	Sonny Easley	Ford
8	Chuck Wahl	Chevrolet
9	Eddie Bradshaw	Chevrolet
10	Don Reynolds	Chevrolet
11	Buck Peralta	Ford
12	Ross Sergenor	Chevrolet
13	Glen Frances	Chevrolet
14	Leon Fox	Chevrolet
15	Richard Childress	Chevrolet
16	Jack Simpson	Chevrolet
17	J.D. McDuffie	Chevrolet
18	Markey James	Ford
19	Hugh Pearson	Chevrolet
20	Chuck Bown	Dodge
21	Walt Price	Chevrolet
22	Jim Insolo	Chevrolet
23	Ed Negre	Dodge
24	Harry Schilling	Chevrolet
25	Richard Petty	Dodge
26	Gary Mathews	Chevrolet

FINISH	DRIVER	CAR
27	Dave Marcis	Dodge
28	John Anderson	Chevrolet
29	George Behlman	Chevrolet
30	Dick Brown	Dodge
31	Tony Bettenhausen	Chevrolet
32	Jim Lee	Chevrolet
33	George Follmer	Matador
34	Jack McCoy	Dodge
35	Hershel McGriff	Chevrolet

MOTORSTATE 400

Time of Race: 2 hours, 48 minutes, 46 seconds
Average Speed: 127.098 Mph

FINISH	DRIVER	CAR
1	Richard Petty	Dodge
2	Earl Ross	Chevrolet
3	David Pearson	Mercury
4	Gary Bettenhausen	Matador
5	Marty Robbins	Dodge
6	Richard Childress	Chevrolet
7	David Sisco	Chevrolet
8	Dave Marcis	Dodge
9	Richie Panch	Chevrolet
10	Cecil Gordon	Chevrolet
11	Jackie Rogers	Chevrolet
12	Buddy Arrington	Plymouth
13	Coo Coo Marlin	Chevrolet
14	Frank Warren	Dodge
15	D.K. Ulrich	Chevrolet
16	Bob Burcham	Chevrolet
17	J. D. McDuffie	Chevrolet
18	Joe Frasson	Dodge
19	Dick Brooks	Dodge
20	Donnie Allison	Chevrolet
21	Dean Dalton	Chevrolet
22	Henley Gray	Chevrolet
23	Bobby Allison	Chevrolet
24	Ron Keselowski	Dodge
25	Benny Parsons	Chevrolet
26	Lennie Pond	Chevrolet
27	Cale Yarborough	Chevrolet
28	Jabe Thomas	Dodge
29	Travis Tiller	Dodge
30	Buddy Baker	Ford
31	Ed Negre	Dodge
32	James Hylton	Chevrolet
33	Bill Champion	Ford
34	Neil Castles	Dodge
35	Walter Ballard	Chevrolet
36	Tony Bettenhausen	Chevrolet

FIRECRACKER 400

Time of Race: 2 hours, 53 minutes, 32 seconds
Average Speed: 138.301 Mph

FINISH	DRIVER	CAR
1	David Pearson	Mercury
2	Richard Petty	Dodge
3	Buddy Baker	Ford
4	Cale Yarborough	Chevrolet
5	Bobby Allison	Chevrolet
6	Bobby Isaac	Chevrolet
7	Lennie Pond	Chevrolet
8	Jackie Rogers	Chevrolet
9	David Sisco	Chevrolet
10	Cecil Gordon	Chevrolet
11	J. D. McDuffie	Chevrolet
12	Dean Dalton	Chevrolet
13	Earl Ross	Chevrolet
14	Tony Bettenhausen	Chevrolet
15	Dick Brooks	Dodge
16	Frank Warren	Dodge
17	Joe Frasson	Dodge

18	Coo Coo Marlin	Chevrolet
19	Dave Marcis	Dodge
20	Walter Ballard	Chevrolet
21	Buddy Arrington	Plymouth
22	Charlie Glotzbach	Ford
23	Richard Childress	Chevrolet
24	Darrell Waltrip	Chevrolet
25	Roy Mayne	Dodge
26	Ed Negre	Dodge
27	Benny Parsons	Chevrolet
28	Ron Keselowski	Dodge
29	A.J. Foyt	Chevrolet
30	G.C. Spencer	Dodge
31	Dan Daughtry	Ford
32	James Hylton	Chevrolet
33	Donnie Allison	Chevrolet
34	Richie Panch	Chevrolet
35	Jim Vandiver	Dodge
36	Jim Crawford	Plymouth
37	L.D. Ottinger	Chevrolet
38	Bob Burcham	Chevrolet
39	Johnny Rutherford	Chevrolet
40	Bill Champion	Ford

VOLUNTEER 500

Time of Race: 3 hours, 31 minutes, 59 seconds
Average Speed: 75.430

FINISH	DRIVER	CAR
1	Cale Yarborough	Chevrolet
2	Buddy Baker	Ford
3	Richard Petty	Dodge
4	Charlie Glotzbach	Ford
5	Bobby Allison	Chevrolet
6	Cecil Gordon	Chevrolet
7	Dick Brooks	Dodge
8	Buddy Arrington	Plymouth
9	Dave Marcis	Dodge
10	Walter Ballard	Chevrolet
11	J. D. McDuffie	Chevrolet
12	Coo Coo Marlin	Chevrolet
13	Ed Negre	Dodge
14	Bob Burcham	Chevrolet
15	Richie Panch	Chevrolet
16	Earl Ross	Chevrolet
17	Benny Parsons	Chevrolet
18	Ernie Shaw	Chevrolet
19	David Sisco	Chevrolet
20	James Hylton	Chevrolet
21	Frank Warren	Dodge
22	Bill Champion	Ford
23	D.K. Ulrich	Chevrolet
24	Richard Childress	Chevrolet
25	L.D. Ottinger	Chevrolet
26	Tony Bettenhausen	Chevrolet
27	Elmo Langley	Ford
28	Dean Dalton	Chevrolet
29	Roy Mayne	Dodge
30	Jackie Rogers	Chevrolet

NASHVILLE 420

Time of Race: 3 hours, 10 minutes, 40 seconds
Average Speed: 76.368

FINISH	DRIVER	CAR
1	Cale Yarborough	Chevrolet
2	Bobby Allison	Chevrolet
3	Darrell Waltrip	Chevrolet
4	David Sisco	Chevrolet
5	Alton Jones	Chevrolet
6	Charlie Glotzbach	Ford
7	Benny Parsons	Chevrolet
8	Earl Ross	Chevrolet
9	Buddy Arrington	Plymouth
10	Richie Panch	Chevrolet

11	Tony Bettenhausen	Chevrolet
12	D.K. Ulrich	Chevrolet
13	Richard Petty	Dodge
14	Henley Gray	Chevrolet
15	Dean Dalton	Chevrolet
16	Ernie Shaw	Chevrolet
17	Bobby Ore	Chevrolet
18	Elmo Langley	Ford
19	Dick Simpson	Chevrolet
20	Cecil Gordon	Chevrolet
21	Dave Marcis	Dodge
22	James Hylton	Chevrolet
23	Richard Childress	Chevrolet
24	Roy Mayne	Dodge
25	Buddy Baker	Ford
26	Walter Ballard	Chevrolet
27	J. D. McDuffie	Chevrolet
28	Coo Coo Marlin	Chevrolet
29	Ed Negre	Dodge
30	Frank Warren	Dodge

DIXIE 500

Time of Race: 3 hours, 42 minutes, 31 seconds
Average Speed: 131.651 Mph

FINISH	DRIVER	CAR
1	Richard Petty	Dodge
2	David Pearson	Mercury
3	Buddy Baker	Ford
4	Darrell Waltrip	Chevrolet
5	Lennie Pond	Chevrolet
6	Dave Marcis	Dodge
7	Joe Frasson	Dodge
8	Benny Parsons	Chevrolet
9	Coo Coo Marlin	Chevrolet
10	Cecil Gordon	Chevrolet
11	Richard Childress	Chevrolet
12	David Sisco	Chevrolet
13	Walter Ballard	Chevrolet
14	Cale Yarborough	Chevrolet
15	Buddy Arrington	Plymouth
16	Elmo Langley	Ford
17	Frank Warren	Dodge
18	Jackie Rogers	Chevrolet
19	J. D. McDuffie	Chevrolet
20	Earl Ross	Chevrolet
21	G.C. Spencer	Dodge
22	Bob Burcham	Chevrolet
23	James Hylton	Chevrolet
24	Tony Bettenhausen	Chevrolet
25	Ed Negre	Dodge
26	Charlie Glotzbach	Ford
27	Richie Panch	Chevrolet
28	Bobby Allison	Chevrolet
29	Dean Dalton	Chevrolet
30	Donnie Allison	Chevrolet
31	Jimmy Crawford	Plymouth
32	Roy Mayne	Dodge
33	Bill Champion	Ford
34	Bobby Isaac	Chevrolet
35	Neil Castles	Dodge

PUROLATOR 500

Time of Race: 4 hours, 09 minutes, 09 seconds
Average Speed: 115.593

FINISH	DRIVER	CAR
1	Richard Petty	Dodge
2	Buddy Baker	Ford
3	Cale Yarborough	Chevrolet
4	David Pearson	Mercury
5	Benny Parsons	Chevrolet
6	Dave Marcis	Dodge
7	Cecil Gordon	Chevrolet
8	Jan Opperman	Chevrolet
9	Jackie Rogers	Chevrolet

10	Ken Brightbill	Chevrolet
11	David Sisco	Chevrolet
12	Richard Childress	Chevrolet
13	Earl Ross	Chevrolet
14	Earle Canavan	Plymouth
15	Bob Burcham	Chevrolet
16	Buddy Arrington	Plymouth
17	D.K. Ulrich	Chevrolet
18	Elmo Langley	Ford
19	Frank Warren	Dodge
20	Ed Negre	Dodge
21	Bobby Allison	Chevrolet
22	Bill Champion	Ford
23	John Martin	Dodge
24	Travis Tiller	Dodge
25	J. D. McDuffie	Chevrolet
26	Richie Panch	Chevrolet
27	Tony Bettenhausen	Chevrolet
28	Larry Richardson	Chevrolet
29	Walter Ballard	Chevrolet
30	Lennie Pond	Chevrolet
31	Roy Mayne	Dodge
32	Dean Dalton	Chevrolet
33	Neil Castles	Dodge
34	James Hylton	Chevrolet
35	Jim Bray	Chevrolet

TALLADEGA 500

Time of Race: 3 hours, 21 minutes, 52 seconds
Average Speed: 148.637 mph

FINISH	DRIVER	CAR
1	Richard Petty	Dodge
2	David Pearson	Mercury
3	Bobby Allison	Matador
4	Cale Yarborough	Chevrolet
5	Benny Parsons	Chevrolet
6	Buddy Baker	Ford
7	Ramo Stott	Chevrolet
8	Bobby Isaac	Chevrolet
9	Marty Robbins	Dodge
10	Earl Ross	Dodge
11	Dave Marcis	Dodge
12	James Hylton	Chevrolet
13	Richard Childress	Chevrolet
14	Ed Negre	Dodge
15	Cecil Gordon	Chevrolet
16	Jerry Schield	Chevrolet
17	Frank Warren	Dodge
18	Dick May	Ford
19	Roy Mayne	Dodge
20	Elmo Langley	Ford
21	Jackie Rogers	Chevrolet
22	John Ray	Dodge
23	Red Farmer	Ford
24	J.D. McDuffie	Chevrolet
25	Jerry Hansen	Chevrolet
26	Alton Jones	Chevrolet
27	Bob Burcham	Chevrolet
28	David Sisco	Chevrolet
29	Dick Brooks	Dodge
30	D.K. Ulrich	Chevrolet
31	Phil Finney	Chevrolet
32	Tony Bettenhausen	Chevrolet
33	Jim Vandiver	Dodge
34	Charlie Glotzbach	Ford
35	CooCoo Marlin	Chevrolet
36	Bill Champion	Ford
37	Terry Link	Pontiac
38	Travis Tiller	Dodge
39	Neil Bonnett	Chevrolet
40	Donnie Allison	Chevrolet
41	Dan Daughtry	Ford
42	Joe Frasson	Dodge
43	Richie Panch	Ford
44	Darrell Waltrip	Chevrolet
45	A.J. Reno	Chevrolet
46	Neil Castles	Dodge
47	Johnny Barnes	Ford
48	Walter Ballard	Chevrolet

YANKEE 400

Time of Race: 3 hours, 23 seconds
Average Speed: 133.045 mph

FINISH	DRIVER	CAR
1	David Pearson	Mercury
2	Richard Petty	Dodge
3	Cale Yarborough	Dodge
4	Buddy Baker	Ford
5	Bobby Allison	Matador
6	Earl Ross	Chevrolet
7	Dave Marcis	Dodge
8	Dick Brooks	Dodge
9	David Sisco	Chevrolet
10	Richie Panch	Chevrolet
11	CooCoo Marlin	Chevrolet
12	Cecil Gordon	Chevrolet
13	J.D. McDuffie	Chevrolet
14	Bob Burcham	Chevrolet
15	Earle Canavan	Plymouth
16	Elmo Langley	Ford
17	Travis Tiller	Dodge
18	Clyde Dagit	Dodge
19	Bob Whitlow	Dodge
20	Frank Warren	Dodge
21	Ed Negre	Chevrolet
22	Benny Parsons	Chevrolet
23	Joe Frasson	Dodge
24	Walter Ballard	Chevrolet
25	Tony Bettenhausen	Chevrolet
26	Jerry Hansen	Chevrolet
27	Richard Childress	Chevrolet
28	D.K. Ulrich	Dodge
29	Ron Keselowski	Dodge
30	Bill Champion	Ford
31	Jackie Rogers	Chevrolet
32	Jabe Thomas	Dodge
33	John Banks	Dodge
34	Jim Bray	Chevrolet
35	James Hylton	Chevrolet
36	Gary Myers	Chevrolet

SOUTHERN 500

Time of Race: 3 hours, 30 minutes, 48 seconds
Average Speed: 111.075 Mph

FINISH	DRIVER	CAR
1	Cale Yarborough	Chevrolet
2	Darrell Waltrip	Chevrolet
3	David Sisco	Chevrolet
4	Dave Marcis	Dodge
5	James Hylton	Chevrolet
6	G.C. Spencer	Dodge
7	Jackie Rogers	Chevrolet
8	Jerry Schild	Chevrolet
9	Joe Frasson	Dodge
10	PeeWee Wentz	Plymouth
11	Tony Bettenhausen	Chevrolet
12	Frank Warren	Dodge
13	Lennie Pond	Chevrolet
14	Charlie Glotzbach	Ford
15	Jim Vandiver	Dodge
16	Walter Ballard	Dodge
17	J.D. McDuffie	Chevrolet
18	Richard Childress	Chevrolet
19	Cecil Gordon	Chevrolet
20	Elmo Langley	Ford
21	Ed Negre	Dodge
22	Earl Ross	Chevrolet
23	Earle Canavan	Plymouth
24	Richie Panch	Chevrolet
25	David Pearson	Mercury
26	Benny Parsons	Chevrolet
27	Bob Burcham	Chevrolet
28	Ramo Stott	Chevrolet
29	CooCoo Marlin	Chevrolet

FINISH	DRIVER	CAR
30	Bobby Allison	Matador
31	Bill Champion	Ford
32	Henley Gray	Chevrolet
33	Buddy Baker	Ford
34	Dick Brooks	Dodge
35	Richard Petty	Dodge
36	Neil Castles	Dodge
37	Bobby Isaac	Chevrolet
38	Jerry Hansen	Chevrolet
39	Roy Mayne	Dodge
40	Earl Brooks	Dodge

CAPITAL CITY 500

Time of Race: 4 hours, 12 minutes, 22 seconds
Average Speed: 64.430 Mph

FINISH	DRIVER	CAR
1	Richard Petty	Dodge
2	Benny Parsons	Chevrolet
3	Richie Panch	Chevrolet
4	Charlie Glotzbach	Ford
5	Walter Ballard	Chevrolet
6	Elmo Langley	Ford
7	Tony Bettenhausen	Chevrolet
8	J.D. Duffie	Chevrolet
9	Cecil Gordon	Chevrolet
10	Lennie Ford	Chevrolet
11	Bill Champion	Ford
12	Travis Tiller	Dodge
13	Dave Marcis	Dodge
14	Bob Burcham	Ford
15	Earl Ross	Chevrolet
16	Dick Brooks	Dodge
17	David Sisco	Chevrolet
18	CooCoo Marlin	Chevrolet
19	Frank Warren	Dodge
20	Ed Negre	Dodge
21	Cale Yarborough	Chevrolet
22	Jackie Rogers	Chevrolet
23	James Hylton	Chevrolet
24	Richard Childress	Chevrolet
25	Johnny Barnes	Chevrolet
26	George England	Chevrolet
27	Joey Arrington	Plymouth

DELAWARE 500

Time of Race: 4 hours, 23 minutes, 59 seconds
Average Speed: 113.64 Mph

FINISH	DRIVER	CAR
1	Richard Petty	Dodge
2	Buddy Baker	Ford
3	Earl Ross	Chevrolet
4	Benny Parsons	Chevrolet
5	Dave Marcis	Dodge
6	David Sisco	Dodge
7	Cecil Gordon	Chevrolet
8	Kenny Brightbill	Chevrolet
9	Henley Gray	Chevrolet
10	Walter Ballard	Chevrolet
11	Ed Negre	Dodge
12	J.D. McDuffie	Chevrolet
13	Bobby Allison	Matador
14	Rick Newsom	Ford
15	Tony Bettenhausen	Chevrolet
16	Frank Warren	Dodge
17	Earle Canavan	Plymouth
18	Richard Childress	Chevrolet
19	James Hylton	Chevrolet
20	Richie Panch	Chevrolet
21	Jim Bray	Chevrolet
22	Elmo Langley	Ford
23	Joe Mihalic	Chevrolet

FINISH	DRIVER	CAR
24	Eddie Pettyjohn	Ford
25	CooCoo Marlin	Chevrolet
26	D.K. Ulrich	Chevrolet
27	George England	Chevrolet
28	Cale Yarborough	Chevrolet
29	Bob Burcham	Chevrolet
30	David Pearson	Mercury
31	Donnie Allison	Chevrolet
32	Lennie Pond	Chevrolet
33	Jackie Rogers	Chevrolet
34	Gary Myers	Chevrolet
35	Darrell Waltrip	Chevrolet
36	Travis Tiller	Dodge
37	G.C. Spencer	Dodge
38	Bill Champion	Ford
39	Larry Manning	Plymouth
40	Johnny Barnes	Chevrolet

WILKES 400

Time of Race: 3 hours, 5 minutes, 41 seconds
Average Speed: 80.782 Mph

FINISH	DRIVER	CAR
1	Cale Yarborough	Chevrolet
2	Richard Petty	Dodge
3	Buddy Baker	Ford
4	Earl Ross	Chevrolet
5	Dave Marcis	Dodge
6	Bobby Isaac	Chevrolet
7	Richard Childress	Chevrolet
8	Jackie Rogers	Chevrolet
9	Walter Ballard	Chevrolet
10	David Sisco	Chevrolet
11	CooCoo Marlin	Chevrolet
12	Joey Arrington	Plymouth
13	Benny Parsons	Chevrolet
14	D.K. Ulrich	Chevrolet
15	Charlie Glotzbach	Ford
16	Travis Tiller	Dodge
17	Richie Panch	Chevrolet
18	Frank Warren	Dodge
19	Bob Burcham	Chevrolet
20	Jabe Thomas	Chevrolet
21	Neil Castles	Dodge
22	Rick Newsom	Ford
23	J.D. McDuffie	Chevrolet
24	James Hylton	Chevrolet
25	Tony Bettenhausen	Chevrolet
26	Elmo Langley	Ford
27	Cecil Gordon	Chevrolet
28	Bill Champion	Ford
29	George England	Chevrolet
30	Ed Negre	Dodge

OLD DOMINION 500

Time of Race: 3 hours, 58 minutes, 3 seconds
Average Speed: 66.232 Mph

FINISH	DRIVER	CAR
1	Earl Ross	Chevrolet
2	Buddy Baker	Ford
3	Donnie Allison	Chevrolet
4	Dave Marcis	Dodge
5	Richie Panch	Chevrolet
6	James Hylton	Chevrolet
7	Elmo Langley	Ford
8	Frank Warren	Dodge
9	Satch Worley	Plymouth
10	Jabe Thomas	Chevrolet
11	Cale Yarborough	Chevrolet
12	Lennie Pond	Chevrolet
13	D.K. Ulrich	Chevrolet
14	Tony Bettenhausen	Chevrolet
15	Benny Parsons	Chevrolet

FINISH	DRIVER	CAR
16	J.D. McDuffie	Chevrolet
17	Ed Negre	Dodge
18	Ray Hendrick	Dodge
19	Jimmy Hensley	Dodge
20	Dave Sisco	Chevrolet
21	Sonny Hutchins	Chevrolet
22	CooCoo Marlin	Chevrolet
23	Pee Wee Wentz	Chevrolet
24	Richard Childress	Chevrolet
25	Walter Ballard	Chevrolet
26	Cecil Gordon	Chevrolet
27	Randy Hutchison	Ford
28	Jackie Rogers	Chevrolet
29	Richard Petty	Dodge
30	Paul Radford	Ford

NATIONAL 500

Time of Race: 4 hours, 10 minutes, 41 seconds
Average Speed: 119.912 Mph

FINISH	DRIVER	CAR
1	David Pearson	Mercury
2	Richard Petty	Dodge
3	Darrell Waltrip	Chevrolet
4	Donnie Allison	Chevrolet
5	Bobby Allison	Matador
6	Lennie Pond	Chevrolet
7	Harry Jefferson	Ford
8	Dick Trickle	Dodge
9	Bob Burcham	Chevrolet
10	Dan Daughtry	Ford
11	James Hylton	Chevrolet
12	Walter Ballard	Chevrolet
13	David Sisco	Chevrolet
14	Richie Panch	Chevrolet
15	Cecil Gordon	Chevrolet
16	Ron Keselowski	Dodge
17	Ed Negre	Dodge
18	Grant Adcox	Chevrolet
19	Ramo Stott	Chevrolet
20	Earl Ross	Chevrolet
21	J.D. McDuffie	Chevrolet
22	CooCoo Marlin	Chevrolet
23	Cale Yarborough	Chevrolet
24	Johnny Rutherford	Chevrolet
25	Frank Warren	Dodge
26	A.J. Foyt	Chevrolet
27	Benny Parsons	Chevrolet
28	Jackie Rogers	Chevrolet
29	Wally Dallenback	Dodge
30	Charlie Glotzbach	Ford
31	Dave Marcis	Dodge
32	Bobby Isaac	Dodge
33	Elmo Langley	Ford
34	Jerry Schild	Chevrolet
35	Harry Gant	Dodge
36	Dick Brooks	Dodge
37	Buddy Baker	Ford
38	Joe Frasson	Dodge
39	Jim Vandiver	Dodge
40	Neil Castles	Dodge
41	Richard Childress	Chevrolet
42	Marty Robbins	Dodge

AMERICAN 500

Time of Race: 4 hours, 13 minutes, 21 seconds
Average Speed: 118.493 Mph

FINISH	DRIVER	CAR
1	David Pearson	Mercury
2	Cale Yarborough	Chevrolet
3	Richard Petty	Dodge
4	Bobby Allison	Matador
5	Darrell Waltrip	Chevrolet

FINISH	DRIVER	CAR
6	Donnie Allison	Chevrolet
7	Dick Trickle	Mercury
8	Earl Ross	Chevrolet
9	Benny Parsons	Chevrolet
10	Jackie Rogers	Chevrolet
11	Lennie Pond	Chevrolet
12	CooCoo Marlin	Chevrolet
13	Jerry Schild	Chevrolet
14	Bob Burcham	Chevrolet
15	Walter Ballard	Chevrolet
16	Joe Mihalic	Chevrolet
17	Joe Millikan	Plymouth
18	James Hylton	Chevrolet
19	J.D. McDuffie	Chevrolet
20	Tony Bettenhausen	Chevrolet
21	Cecil Gordon	Chevrolet
22	Bill Champion	Ford
23	Frank Warren	Dodge
24	Richard Childress	Chevrolet
25	Elmo Langley	Ford
26	David Sisco	Chevrolet
27	Richie Panch	Chevrolet
28	Ed Negre	Dodge
29	Dave Marcis	Dodge
30	Jody Ridley	Ford
31	Dick Brooks	Chevrolet
32	Harry Jefferson	Ford
33	Neil Castles	Dodge
34	Buddy Baker	Ford
35	G.C. Spencer	Dodge
36	Joe Frasson	Dodge

LA TIMES 500

Time of Race: 3 hours, 42 minutes, 17 seconds
Average Speed: 134.963

FINISH	DRIVER	CAR
1	Bobby Allison	Matador
2	David Pearson	Mercury
3	Cale Yarborough	Chevrolet
4	A.J. Foyt	Chevrolet
5	Buddy Baker	Ford
6	Darrell Waltrip	Chevrolet
7	Ramo Stott	Chevrolet
8	Earl Ross	Chevrolet
9	Richie Panch	Chevrolet
10	J.D. McDuffie	Chevrolet
11	David Sisco	Chevrolet
12	Richard Childress	Chevrolet
13	Bruce Hill	Chevrolet
14	James Hylton	Chevrolet
15	Richard Petty	Dodge
16	Walter Ballard	Chevrolet
17	Dave Marcis	Ford
18	Don Reynolds	Chevrolet
19	Jim Insolo	Chevrolet
20	Chuck Wahl	Chevrolet
21	Frank Warren	Dodge
22	Glen Francis	Chevrolet
23	Ed Negre	Dodge
24	D.K. Ulrich	Chevrolet
25	Jackie Rogers	Chevrolet
26	Sonny Easley	Ford
27	Don Hall	Chevrolet
28	Bill Osborne	Ford
29	Cecil Gordon	Chevrolet
30	Earle Canavan	Plymouth
31	Walt Price	Chevrolet
32	George Follmer	Ford
33	Jack McCoy	Dodge
34	Harry Jefferson	Ford
35	Benny Parsons	Ford
36	Ray Elder	Dodge
37	Hugh Pearson	Chevrolet
38	John Martin	Chevrolet
39	Chuck Bown	Plymouth
40	Carl Adams	Ford

1975

WINSTON WESTERN 500

Time of Race: 5 hours, 4 minutes, 26 seconds
Average Speed: 98.627 Mph

FINISH	DRIVER	CAR
1	Bobby Allison	Matador
2	David Pearson	Mercury
3	Cecil Gordon	Chevrolet
4	Dave Marcis	Dodge
5	Elmo Langley	Ford
6	James Hylton	Chevrolet
7	Richard Petty	Dodge
8	Gary Mathews	Chevrolet
9	Ed Negre	Dodge
10	Hershel McGriff	Chevrolet
11	Richard Childress	Chevrolet
12	Don Puskarich	Chevrolet
13	Ray Elder	Dodge
14	J.D. McDuffie	Chevrolet
15	Larry Esau	Chevrolet
16	Bill Osborne	Ford
17	Chuck Wahl	Chevrolet
18	Bill Schmitt	Chevrolet
19	Richard White	Chevrolet
20	Don Reynolds	Chevrolet
21	Sonny Easley	Ford
22	Ron Esau	Chevrolet
23	Hugh Pearson	Chevrolet
24	Benny Parsons	Chevrolet
25	Glen Francis	Chevrolet
26	Pete Torres	Ford
27	Chuck Bown	Dodge
28	Chuck Little	Ford
29	G.T. Tallas	Ford
30	Dick Bown	Chevrolet
31	Walter Ballard	Chevrolet
32	Harry Jefferson	Ford
33	Jim Insolo	Chevrolet
34	Carl Adams	Ford
35	Ivan Baldwin	Dodge

DAYTONA 500

Time of Race: 3 hours, 15 minutes, 15 seconds
Average Speed: 153.649 Mph

FINISH	DRIVER	CAR
1	Benny Parsons	Chevrolet
2	Bobby Allison	Matador
3	Cale Yarborough	Chevrolet
4	David Pearson	Mercury
5	Ramo Stott	Chevrolet
6	Dave Marcis	Dodge
7	Richard Petty	Dodge
8	Richie Panch	Chevrolet
9	G.C. Spencer	Dodge
10	James Hylton	Chevrolet
11	A.J. Foyt	Chevrolet
12	Bruce Jacobi	Chevrolet
13	Bob Burcham	Ford
14	Ed Negre	Dodge
15	Cecil Gordon	Chevrolet
16	Ferrel Harris	Dodge
17	CooCoo Marlin	Chevrolet
18	Richard Childress	Chevrolet
19	Lennie Pond	Chevrolet
20	Buddy Baker	Ford
21	David Sisco	Chevrolet
22	Dick Brooks	Ford
23	Tom Gale	Ford
24	George Follmer	Chevrolet

25	Walter Ballard	Chevrolet
26	Darrell Waltrip	Chevrolet
27	Johnny Rutherford	Chevrolet
28	Donnie Allison	Chevrolet
29	Randy Tissot	Chevrolet
30	Hershel McGriff	Chevrolet
31	Rick Newsom	Ford
32	Bruce Hill	Chevrolet
33	J.D. McDuffie	Chevrolet
34	Joe Mihalic	Chevrolet
35	Jim Vandiver	Dodge
36	Dick Trickle	Mercury
37	Grant Adcox	Chevrolet
38	Dan Daughtry	Ford
39	Marty Robbins	Dodge
40	Warren Tope	Ford

RICHMOND 500

Time of Race: 3 hours, 37 minutes, 3 seconds
Average Speed: 74.913 Mph

FINISH	DRIVER	CAR
1	Richard Petty	Dodge
2	Lennie Pond	Chevrolet
3	Benny Parsons	Chevrolet
4	Dick Brooks	Ford
5	Elmo Langley	Ford
6	Buddy Arrington	Dodge
7	Cecil Gordon	Chevrolet
8	David Sisco	Chevrolet
9	Richard Childress	Chevrolet
10	Ed Negre	Dodge
11	Bruce Hill	Chevrolet
12	Jabe Thomas	Dodge
13	Earle Canavan	Dodge
14	James Hylton	Chevrolet
15	Darrell Waltrip	Chevrolet
16	Dave Marcis	Dodge
17	Frank Warren	Dodge
18	Neil Castles	Dodge
19	Walter Ballard	Ford
20	Dick May	Chevrolet
21	Bill Champion	Chevrolet
22	Rick Newsom	Ford

CAROLINA 500

Time of Race: 4 hours, 15 minutes, 18 seconds
Average Speed: 117.588 Mph

FINISH	DRIVER	CAR
1	Cale Yarborough	Chevrolet
2	David Pearson	Mercury
3	Richard Petty	Dodge
4	Dick Brooks	Ford
5	Bruce Hill	Chevrolet
6	Richard Childress	Chevrolet
7	Ed Negre	Dodge
8	James Hylton	Chevrolet
9	Buddy Arrington	Dodge
10	Dean Dalton	Ford
11	Ricky Rudd	Ford
12	Elmo Langley	Ford
13	Carl Adams	Ford
14	David Sisco	Chevrolet
15	Clyde Dagit	Dodge
16	Travis Tiller	Dodge
17	Walter Ballard	Chevrolet
18	Frank Warren	Dodge
19	Rick Newsom	Ford
20	Cecil Gordon	Chevrolet
21	Darrell Waltrip	Chevrolet
22	Benny Parsons	Chevrolet
23	Lennie Pond	Chevrolet
24	Dave Marcis	Dodge
25	Buddy Baker	Ford

FINISH	DRIVER	CAR
26	CooCoo Marlin	Chevrolet
27	Jabe Thomas	Chevrolet
28	Donnie Allison	Chevrolet
29	Bobby Isaac	Chevrolet
30	Richard Skillen	Chevrolet
31	Earle Canavan	Dodge

SOUTHEASTERN 500

Time of Race: 2 hours, 43 minutes, 53 seconds
Average Speed: 97.053 Mph

FINISH	DRIVER	CAR
1	Richard Petty	Dodge
2	Benny Parsons	Chevrolet
3	Buddy Baker	Ford
4	Cecil Gordon	Chevrolet
5	James Hylton	Chevrolet
6	Darrell Waltrip	Chevrolet
7	David Sisco	Chevrolet
8	Dave Marcis	Dodge
9	Richard Childress	Chevrolet
10	Ricky Rudd	Ford
11	D.K. Ulrich	Chevrolet
12	Frank Warren	Dodge
13	Ed Negre	Dodge
14	Jabe Thomas	Chevrolet
15	Buddy Arrington	Plymouth
16	Henley Gray	Chevrolet
17	Elmo Langley	Ford
18	Walter Ballard	Chevrolet
19	Dick Brooks	Ford
20	Cale Yarborough	Chevrolet
21	Travis Tiller	Dodge
22	Joe Frasson	Dodge
23	Earle Canavan	Dodge

ATLANTA 500

Time of Race: 3 hours, 44 minutes, 6 seconds
Average Speed: 133.496 Mph

FINISH	DRIVER	CAR
1	Richard Petty	Dodge
2	Buddy Baker	Ford
3	David Pearson	Mercury
4	Dick Brooks	Ford
5	Darrell Waltrip	Chevrolet
6	Donnie Allison	Chevrolet
7	CooCoo Marlin	Chevrolet
8	Cecil Gordon	Chevrolet
9	Harry Jefferson	Ford
10	Lennie Pond	Chevrolet
11	Ferrel Harris	Dodge
12	Frank Warren	Dodge
13	James Hylton	Chevrolet
14	Skip Manning	Chevrolet
15	Richard Childress	Chevrolet
16	Carl Adams	Ford
17	Elmo Langley	Ford
18	Warren Tope	Ford
19	Henley Gray	Chevrolet
20	Rick Newsom	Ford
21	Grant Adcox	Chevrolet
22	Cale Yarborough	Chevrolet
23	Bruce Hill	Chevrolet
24	Walter Ballard	Chevrolet
25	Ricky Rudd	Ford
26	Jim Vandiver	Dodge
27	Dave Marcis	Dodge
28	Benny Parsons	Chevrolet
29	Jody Ridley	Ford
30	Bobby Allison	Matador
31	David Sisco	Chevrolet
32	Johnny Rutherford	Chevrolet
33	Joe Mihalic	Chevrolet
34	Richie Panch	Chevrolet
35	A.J. Foyt	Chevrolet
36	G.C. Spencer	Dodge

GWYN STALEY 400

Time of Race: 2 hours, 46 minutes, 39 seconds
Average Speed: 90.009 Mph

FINISH	DRIVER	CAR
1	Richard Petty	Dodge
2	Cale Yarborough	Chevrolet
3	Buddy Baker	Ford
4	Dave Marcis	Dodge
5	Lennie Pond	Chevrolet
6	Benny Parsons	Chevrolet
7	Darrell Waltrip	Chevrolet
8	Dick Brooks	Ford
9	Cecil Gordon	Chevrolet
10	Walter Ballard	Chevrolet
11	James Hylton	Chevrolet
12	Frank Warren	Dodge
13	J.D. McDuffie	Chevrolet
14	Joe Mihalic	Chevrolet
15	Jabe Thomas	Chevrolet
16	Bruce Hill	Chevrolet
17	Richard Childress	Chevrolet
18	Carl Adams	Ford
19	Ed Negre	Dodge
20	Buddy Arrington	Plymouth
21	Travis Tiller	Dodge
22	Neil Castles	Dodge
23	David Sisco	Chevrolet
24	Rick Newsom	Ford
25	Earle Canavan	Dodge
26	Charlie Griffin	Dodge
27	Elmo Langley	Ford
28	Ricky Rudd	Ford

REBEL 500

Time of Race: 4 hours, 15 minutes, 41 seconds
Average Speed: 117.597 Mph

FINISH	DRIVER	CAR
1	Bobby Allison	Matador
2	Darrell Waltrip	Chevrolet
3	Donnie Allison	Chevrolet
4	Dave Marcis	Dodge
5	CooCoo Marlin	Chevrolet
6	Benny Parsons	Chevrolet
7	David Pearson	Mercury
8	James Hylton	Chevrolet
9	Bruce Jacobi	Chevrolet
10	Buddy Arrington	Plymouth
11	J.D. McDuffie	Chevrolet
12	Carl Adams	Ford
13	Joe Mihalic	Chevrolet
14	Ferrel Harris	Dodge
15	Bruce Hill	Chevrolet
16	Frank Warren	Dodge
17	Earle Canavan	Dodge
18	Walter Ballard	Chevrolet
19	Buddy Baker	Ford
20	Elmo Langley	Ford
21	Cecil Gordon	Chevrolet
22	Richard Childress	Chevrolet
23	Richard Skillen	Chevrolet
24	G.C. Spencer	Dodge
25	Dick Brooks	Ford
26	Richard Petty	Dodge
27	Lennie Pond	Chevrolet
28	David Sisco	Chevrolet
29	Randy Tissot	Chevrolet
30	Neil Castles	Dodge
31	Ed Negre	Dodge
32	Dean Dalton	Ford
33	Rick Newsom	Ford
34	Bill Champion	Ford
35	Jabe Thomas	Chevrolet
36	Cale Yarborough	Chevrolet

VIRGINIA 500

Time of Race: 3 hours, 47 minutes, 15 seconds
Average Speed: 69.282 Mph

FINISH	DRIVER	CAR
1	Richard Petty	Dodge
2	Darrell Waltrip	Chevrolet
3	Cale Yarborough	Chevrolet
4	Bobby Allison	Matador
5	Dave Marcis	Dodge
6	Benny Parsons	Chevrolet
7	Jimmy Hensley	Chevrolet
8	Dick Brooks	Ford
9	Richard Childress	Chevrolet
10	James Hylton	Chevrolet
11	Elmo Langley	Ford
12	Carl Adams	Ford
13	Ed Negre	Ford
14	Buddy Arrington	Plymouth
15	Walter Ballard	Chevrolet
16	Bill Champion	Ford
17	Richie Panch	Chevrolet
18	Frank Warren	Dodge
19	Buddy Baker	Ford
20	David Pearson	Mercury
21	Donnie Allison	Chevrolet
22	Jabe Thomas	Chevrolet
23	Cecil Gordon	Chevrolet
24	Travis Tiller	Dodge
25	Lennie Pond	Chevrolet
26	David Sisco	Chevrolet
27	Joey Arrington	Dodge
28	J.D. McDuffie	Chevrolet
29	Richard Brown	Pontiac
30	Dean Dalton	Dodge

WINSTON 500

Time of Race: 3 hours, 26 minutes, 59 seconds
Average Speed: 144.948 Mph

FINISH	DRIVER	CAR
1	Buddy Baker	Ford
2	David Pearson	Mercury
3	Dick Brooks	Ford
4	Darrell Waltrip	Chevrolet
5	CooCoo Marlin	Chevrolet
6	Harry Jefferson	Ford
7	Grant Adcox	Chevrolet
8	Bruce Jacobi	Chevrolet
9	Joe Mihalic	Chevrolet
10	Richard Childress	Chevrolet
11	Bill Champion	Ford
12	Walter Ballard	Chevrolet
13	Dave Marcis	Dodge
14	Elmo Langley	Ford
15	Skip Manning	Chevrolet
16	David Sisco	Chevrolet
17	Earle Canavan	Dodge
18	Joe Frasson	Pontiac
19	Richard Petty	Dodge
20	Tom Williams	Chevrolet
21	Cecil Gordon	Chevrolet
22	G.C. Spencer	Dodge
23	Travis Tiller	Dodge
24	Frank Warren	Dodge
25	Jabe Thomas	Dodge
26	Lennie Pond	Chevrolet
27	Jim Vandiver	Dodge
28	Randy Tissot	Chevrolet
29	J.D. McDuffie	Chevrolet
30	Ramo Stott	Chevrolet
31	Marty Robbins	Dodge
32	Ed Negre	Ford
33	James Hylton	Chevrolet
34	William Miller	Chevrolet
35	Bobby Allison	Matador
36	Gordon Johncock	Chevrolet
37	Red Farmer	Ford

FINISH	DRIVER	CAR
38	Buddy Arrington	Plymouth
39	Dean Dalton	Dodge
40	Cale Yarborough	Chevrolet
41	Rick Newsom	Ford
42	Donnie Allison	Chevrolet
43	Benny Parsons	Chevrolet
44	Carl Adams	Ford
45	Ferrel Harris	Dodge
46	Dan Daughtry	Ford
47	Bruce Hill	Chevrolet
48	John Ray	Chevrolet
49	Richie Panch	Chevrolet
50	John Banks	Dodge

MUSIC CITY USA 420

Time of Race: 2 hours, 39 minutes, 45 seconds
Average Speed: 94.107 Mph

FINISH	DRIVER	CAR
1	Darrell Waltrip	Chevrolet
2	Benny Parsons	Chevrolet
3	CooCoo Marlin	Chevrolet
4	Dave Marcis	Dodge
5	Cecil Gordon	Chevrolet
6	Alton Jones	Chevrolet
7	Richard Petty	Dodge
8	David Sisco	Chevrolet
9	James Hylton	Chevrolet
10	Walter Ballard	Chevrolet
11	J.D. McDuffie	Chevrolet
12	Frank Warren	Dodge
13	Rick Newsom	Ford
14	Cale Yarborough	Chevrolet
15	Elmo Langley	Ford
16	Richard Childress	Chevrolet
17	Earle Canavan	Dodge
18	Bill Champion	Ford
19	Jabe Thomas	Chevrolet
20	Baxter Price	Chevrolet
21	Paul Dean Holt	Ford
22	Earl Brooks	Dodge
23	Bruce Hill	Chevrolet
24	Ed Negre	Dodge
25	Richard Brown	Pontiac
26	Travis Tiller	Dodge
27	Joey Arrington	Dodge
28	Buddy Arrington	Plymouth

MASON-DIXON 500

Time of Race: 4 hours, 57 minutes, 32 seconds
Average Speed: 100.82 Mph

FINISH	DRIVER	CAR
1	David Pearson	Mercury
2	Cecil Gordon	Chevrolet
3	Richard Petty	Dodge
4	James Hylton	Chevrolet
5	David Sisco	Chevrolet
6	CooCoo Marlin	Chevrolet
7	Kenny Brightbill	Ford
8	Bruce Hill	Chevrolet
9	Henley Gray	Chevrolet
10	Jabe Thomas	Chevrolet
11	Buddy Baker	Ford
12	Elmo Langley	Ford
13	Buddy Arrington	Plymouth
14	Joe Frasson	Dodge
15	Frank Warren	Dodge
16	Richard Childress	Chevrolet
17	Dean Dalton	Ford
18	J.D. McDuffie	Chevrolet
19	Bill Champion	Ford
20	Dave Marcis	Dodge
21	John Harkins	Dodge
22	Darrell Waltrip	Chevrolet
23	Benny Parsons	Chevrolet

FINISH	DRIVER	CAR
24	Travis Tiller	Dodge
25	Walter Ballard	Chevrolet
26	Earl Brooks	Dodge
27	Cale Yarborough	Chevrolet
28	Donnie Allison	Chevrolet
29	Dick Brooks	Ford
30	D.K. Ulrich	Chevrolet
31	Ed Negre	Dodge
32	Joey Arrington	Dodge
33	Lennie Pond	Chevrolet
34	Earle Canavan	Dodge
35	Dick May	Dodge

WORLD 600

Time of Race: 4 hours, 7 minutes, 42 seconds
Average Speed: 145.327 Mph

FINISH	DRIVER	CAR
1	Richard Petty	Dodge
2	Cale Yarborough	Chevrolet
3	David Pearson	Mercury
4	Darrell Waltrip	Chevrolet
5	Buddy Baker	Ford
6	Charlie Glotzbach	Chevrolet
7	Dick Brooks	Ford
8	Richie Panch	Chevrolet
9	Donnie Allison	Chevrolet
10	Walter Ballard	Chevrolet
11	J.D. McDuffie	Chevrolet
12	Darel Dieringer	Chevrolet
13	Earl Ross	Ford
14	Jackie Rogers	Chevrolet
15	Jim Vandiver	Dodge
16	Bruce Jacobi	Chevrolet
17	Dean Dalton	Ford
18	Bruce Hill	Chevrolet
19	Frank Warren	Dodge
20	James Hylton	Chevrolet
21	Harry Jefferson	Ford
22	Dale Earnhardt	Dodge
23	Richard Childress	Chevrolet
24	Elmo Langley	Ford
25	Richard Skillen	Chevrolet
26	Buddy Arrington	Plymouth
27	David Sisco	Chevrolet
28	Joe Frasson	Chevrolet
29	Bill Champion	Ford
30	Travis Tiller	Dodge
31	Harry Gant	Chevrolet
32	Ed Negre	Dodge
33	Randy Bethea	Chevrolet
34	Dave Marcis	Dodge
35	Bobby Isaac	Chevrolet
36	Lennie Pond	Chevrolet
37	Cecil Gordon	Chevrolet
38	G.C. Spencer	Dodge
39	Benny Parsons	Chevrolet
40	CooCoo Marlin	Chevrolet

TUBORG 400

Time of Race: 3 hours, 58 minutes, 4 seconds
Average Speed: 101.028 Mph

FINISH	DRIVER	CAR
1	Richard Petty	Dodge
2	Bobby Allison	Matador
3	Benny Parsons	Chevrolet
4	Ray Elder	Dodge
5	Dave Marcis	Dodge
6	Chuck Wahl	Chevrolet
7	J.D. McDuffie	Chevrolet
8	Bill Schmitt	Chevrolet
9	Richard Childress	Chevrolet
10	Gene Rinker	Chevrolet
11	Glen Francis	Chevrolet
12	Elmo Langley	Ford
13	James Hylton	Chevrolet

FINISH	DRIVER	CAR
14	Jim Boyd	Dodge
15	Gary Mathews	Chevrolet
16	Pete Torres	Ford
17	Frank Warren	Dodge
18	Cecil Gordon	Chevrolet
19	Hershel McGriff	Chevrolet
20	John Kieper	Chevrolet
21	Darrell Waltrip	Chevrolet
22	Carl Joiner	Chevrolet
23	Carl Adams	Ford
24	Walter Ballard	Chevrolet
25	Ed Bradshaw	Chevrolet
26	Bill Osborne	Ford
27	Jim Insolo	Chevrolet
28	Ed Negre	Dodge
29	George Follmer	Chevrolet
30	Sonny Easley	Ford
31	John Soares	Dodge
32	Don Puskarich	Chevrolet
33	Ted Fritz	Chevrolet
34	Chuck Bown	Dodge
35	Ivan Baldwin	Dodge

MOTOR STATE 400

Time of Race: 3 hours, 2 minutes, 39 seconds
Average Speed: 131.398 Mph

FINISH	DRIVER	CAR
1	David Pearson	Mercury
2	Richard Petty	Dodge
3	Dave Marcis	Dodge
4	Cale Yarborough	Chevrolet
5	Darrell Waltrip	Chevrolet
6	Richie Panch	Chevrolet
7	Dick Brooks	Ford
8	David Sisco	Chevrolet
9	James Hylton	Chevrolet
10	Richard Childress	Chevrolet
11	Walter Ballard	Chevrolet
12	CooCoo Marlin	Chevrolet
13	Ferrel Harris	Dodge
14	Elmo Langley	Chevrolet
15	Buddy Arrington	Plymouth
16	Frank Warren	Dodge
17	Salt Walther	Chevrolet
18	J.D. McDuffie	Chevrolet
19	Dean Dalton	Ford
20	John Banks	Dodge
21	Carl Adams	Ford
22	Bobby Allison	Matador
23	Travis Tiller	Dodge
24	John Ray	Chevrolet
25	Bruce Jacobi	Chevrolet
26	D.K. Ulrich	Chevrolet
27	Ed Negre	Dodge
28	William Miller	Chevrolet
29	Grand Adcox	Chevrolet
30	Bruce Hill	Chevrolet
31	Joe Frasson	Dodge
32	Mel Larson	Chevrolet
33	Cecil Gordon	Chevrolet
34	Benny Parsons	Chevrolet
35	Donnie Allison	Chevrolet
36	Rick Newsom	Ford

FIRECRACKER 400

Time of Race: 2 hours, 31 minutes, 32 seconds
Average Speed: 158.381 Mph

FINISH	DRIVER	CAR
1	Richard Petty	Dodge
2	Buddy Baker	Ford
3	Dave Marcis	Dodge
4	Darrell Waltrip	Chevrolet
5	Donnie Allison	Chevrolet
6	Dick Brooks	Ford
7	Bruce Hill	Chevrolet

8	Benny Parsons	Chevrolet
9	Carl Adams	Ford
10	Darel Dieringer	Ford
11	James Hylton	Chevrolet
12	Ed Negre	Dodge
13	Richard Childress	Chevrolet
14	Jim Vandiver	Dodge
15	Skip Manning	Chevrolet
16	Randy Tissot	Chevrolet
17	Frank Warren	Dodge
18	Tommy Gale	Ford
19	Jackie Rogers	Chevrolet
20	David Pearson	Mercury
21	Buddy Arrington	Plymouth
22	J.D. McDuffie	Chevrolet
23	Dick May	Chevrolet
24	A.J. Foyt	Chevrolet
25	Elmo Langley	Ford
26	Cale Yarborough	Chevrolet
27	Joe Mihalic	Chevrolet
28	Richie Panch	Chevrolet
29	Cecil Gordon	Chevrolet
30	John Ray	Chevrolet
31	Walter Ballard	Chevrolet
32	Bruce Jacobi	Chevrolet
33	David Sisco	Chevrolet
34	CooCoo Marlin	Chevrolet
35	Bobby Allison	Matador
36	Grant Adcox	Chevrolet
37	Salt Walther	Chevrolet
38	Lennie Pond	Chevrolet
39	G.C. Spencer	Dodge
40	Johnny Rutherford	Chevrolet

NASHVILLE 420

Time of Race: 2 hours, 47 minutes, 16 seconds
Average Speed: 89.792 Mph

FINISH	DRIVER	CAR
1	Cale Yarborough	Chevrolet
2	Richard Petty	Dodge
3	Dave Marcis	Dodge
4	Benny Parsons	Chevrolet
5	Cecil Gordon	Chevrolet
6	Richard Childress	Chevrolet
7	David Sisco	Chevrolet
8	Carl Adams	Ford
9	J.D. McDuffie	Chevrolet
10	Elmo Langley	Ford
11	James Hylton	Chevrolet
12	Alton Jones	Chevrolet
13	Bruce Hill	Chevrolet
14	Neil Bonnett	Chevrolet
15	Ed Negre	Dodge
16	Frank Warren	Dodge
17	Richard Brown	Pontiac
18	Walter Ballard	Chevrolet
19	Bruce Jacobi	Chevrolet
20	D.K. Ulrich	Chevrolet
21	Jabe Thomas	Chevrolet
22	Baxter Price	Chevrolet
23	Earl Brooks	Dodge
24	Paul Dean Holt	Ford
25	Buddy Arrington	Plymouth
26	CooCoo Marlin	Chevrolet
27	Grant Adcox	Chevrolet
28	Darrell Waltrip	Chevrolet
29	Neil Castles	Chevrolet
30	Bill Champion	Ford

PUROLATOR 500

Time of Race: 4 hours, 29 minutes, 50 seconds
Average Speed: 111.179 Mph

FINISH	DRIVER	CAR
1	David Pearson	Mercury
2	Richard Petty	Dodge

3	Buddy Baker	Ford
4	Benny Parsons	Chevrolet
5	Richard Childress	Chevrolet
6	Carl Adams	Ford
7	CooCoo Marlin	Chevrolet
8	Bruce Hill	Chevrolet
9	James Hylton	Chevrolet
10	Cecil Gordon	Chevrolet
11	Bruce Jacobi	Chevrolet
12	Buddy Arrington	Plymouth
13	Walter Ballard	Ford
14	Ed Negre	Dodge
15	D.K. Ulrich	Chevrolet
16	Frank Warren	Dodge
17	Dick May	Dodge
18	Baxter Price	Chevrolet
19	David Sisco	Chevrolet
20	Jabe Thomas	Chevrolet
21	Joe Mihalic	Chevrolet
22	Doc Faustina	Dodge
23	Carl Van Horn	Chevrolet
24	Elmo Langley	Ford
25	Dave Marcis	Dodge
26	Earl Brooks	Dodge
27	J.D. McDuffie	Chevrolet
28	Tome Gale	Ford
29	Earle Canavan	Dodge
30	Jackie Rogers	Chevrolet
31	Bobby Allison	Matador
32	George Wiltshire	Dodge
33	Richie Panch	Chevrolet
34	Darrell Waltrip	Chevrolet
35	Cale Yarborough	Chevrolet

TALLADEGA 500

Time of Race: 3 hours, 49 minutes, 14 seconds
Average Speed: 130.892 Mph

FINISH	DRIVER	CAR
1	Buddy Baker	Ford
2	Richard Petty	Dodge
3	Donnie Allison	Chevrolet
4	Dave Marcis	Dodge
5	CooCoo Marlin	Chevrolet
6	Benny Parsons	Chevrolet
7	James Hylton	Chevrolet
8	Joe Frasson	Chevrolet
9	Jackie Rogers	Chevrolet
10	Cecil Gordon	Chevrolet
11	Dean Dalton	Ford
12	Bruce Jacobi	Chevrolet
13	Richard Childress	Chevrolet
14	Elmo Langley	Ford
15	Ferrel Harris	Dodge
16	Jabe Thomas	Chevrolet
17	Frank Warren	Dodge
18	Ed Negre	Dodge
19	Billy Joe Hagan	Chevrolet
20	Jeff Handy	Chevrolet
21	A.J. Reno	Ford
22	Earl Brooks	Chevrolet
23	Carl Adams	Ford
24	Buddy Arrington	Plymouth
25	D.K. Ulrich	Chevrolet
26	Joe Mihalic	Chevrolet
27	David Sisco	Chevrolet
28	Bill Ward	Chevrolet
29	Bobby Allison	Matador
30	Bill Champion	Ford
31	Bruce Hill	Chevrolet
32	Lennie Pond	Chevrolet
33	Jim Vandiver	Dodge
34	Grant Adcox	Chevrolet
35	Neil Bonnett	Chevrolet
36	Harold Miller	Chevrolet
37	Darel Dieringer	Ford
38	Dick Brooks	Ford
39	David Pearson	Mercury
40	John Ray	Chevrolet
41	Cale Yarborough	Chevrolet
42	Darrell Waltrip	Chevrolet

43	Richie Panch	Chevrolet
44	Red Farmer	Ford
45	J.D. McDuffie	Chevrolet
46	Tiny Lund	Dodge
47	Terry Link	Pontiac
48	Walter Ballard	Chevrolet
49	G.C. Spencer	Dodge
50	Randy Tissot	Chevrolet

CHAMPION SPARK PLUG 400

Time of Race: 3 hours, 43 minutes, 5 seconds
Average Speed: 107.583 Mph

FINISH	DRIVER	CAR
1	Richard Petty	Dodge
2	David Pearson	Mercury
3	Cale Yarborough	Chevrolet
4	Bobby Allison	Matador
5	Dave Marcis	Dodge
6	Buddy Baker	Ford
7	Darrell Waltrip	Chevrolet
8	Bruce Hill	Chevrolet
9	Terry Bivens	Chevrolet
10	Dean Dalton	Ford
11	Walter Ballard	Chevrolet
12	David Sisco	Chevrolet
13	Cecil Gordon	Chevrolet
14	Grant Adcox	Chevrolet
15	Bruce Jacobi	Chevrolet
16	Ferrel Harris	Dodge
17	James Hylton	Chevrolet
18	Elmo Langley	Ford
19	Dick May	Chevrolet
20	Dick Brooks	Ford
21	D.K. Ulrich	Chevrolet
22	Buddy Arrington	Plymouth
23	Jabe Thomas	Chevrolet
24	Harold Miller	Chevrolet
25	Richie Panch	Chevrolet
26	Frank Warren	Dodge
27	Henley Gray	Chevrolet
28	J.D. McDuffie	Chevrolet
29	Carl Adams	Ford
30	A.J. Foyt	Chevrolet
31	Richard Childress	Chevrolet
32	Earle Canavan	Dodge
33	Ed Negre	Dodge
34	Benny Parsons	Chevrolet
35	CooCoo Marlin	Chevrolet
36	Jackie Rogers	Chevrolet

SOUTHERN 500

Time of Race: 4 hours, 17 minutes, 28 seconds
Average Speed: 116.825 Mph

FINISH	DRIVER	CAR
1	Bobby Allison	Matador
2	Richard Petty	Dodge
3	David Sisco	Chevrolet
4	Jim Vandiver	Dodge
5	Bruce Hill	Chevrolet
6	Cecil Gordon	Chevrolet
7	Richard Childress	Chevrolet
8	Dick May	Chevrolet
9	Bruce Jacobi	Chevrolet
10	Elmo Langley	Ford
11	Skip Manning	Chevrolet
12	Jabe Thomas	Chevrolet
13	Grant Adcox	Chevrolet
14	Frank Warren	Dodge
15	Randy Tissot	Chevrolet
16	D.K. Ulrich	Chevrolet
17	Buddy Arrington	Plymouth
18	Ferrel Harris	Dodge
19	Cale Yarborough	Chevrolet
20	Benny Parsons	Chevrolet
21	Lennie Pond	Chevrolet

22	Tom Gale	Ford
23	James Hylton	Chevrolet
24	Dave Marcis	Dodge
25	Walter Ballard	Chevrolet
26	Dick Brooks	Ford
27	David Pearson	Mercury
28	Buddy Baker	Ford
29	Bill Champion	Chevrolet
30	Ed Negre	Chevrolet
31	G.C. Spencer	Dodge
32	Dean Dalton	Ford
33	J.D. McDuffie	Chevrolet
34	Darrell Waltrip	Chevrolet
35	Earle Canavan	Dodge
36	Henley Gray	Chevrolet
37	Dick Skillen	Chevrolet
38	Jackie Rogers	Chevrolet
39	CooCoo Marlin	Chevrolet
40	H.B. Bailey	Pontiac

DELAWARE 500

Time of Race: 4 hours, 29 minutes, 22 seconds
Average Speed: 111.372 Mph

>FINISH	DRIVER	CAR
1	Richard Petty	Dodge
2	Dick Brooks	Ford
3	Benny Parsons	Chevrolet
4	Cale Yarborough	Chevrolet
5	Bruce Hill	Chevrolet
6	Richard Childress	Chevrolet
7	James Hylton	Chevrolet
8	J.D. McDuffie	Chevrolet
9	Dean Dalton	Ford
10	D.K. Ulrich	Chevrolet
11	Ed Negre	Dodge
12	Rick Newsom	Chevrolet
13	Jabe Thomas	Chevrolet
14	Walter Ballard	Chevrolet
15	Randy Tissott	Chevrolet
16	Frank Warren	Dodge
17	David Sisco	Chevrolet
18	Buddy Arrington	Plymouth
19	Henley Gray	Chevrolet
20	Lennie Pond	Chevrolet
21	Terry Bivens	Chevrolet
22	Bruce Jacobi	Chevrolet
23	Bill Hollar	Chevrolet
24	Elmo Langley	Ford
25	Earle Canavan	Dodge
26	David Pearson	Mercury
27	Darrell Waltrip	Chevrolet
28	Bobby Allison	Matador
29	Cecil Gordon	Chevrolet
30	Dave Marcis	Dodge
31	CooCoo Marlin	Chevrolet
32	Joe Mihalic	Chevrolet
33	Buddy Baker	Ford
34	Earl Brooks	Dodge
35	Tom Gale	Ford
36	Joe Frasson	Dodge
37	Dick May	Ford

WILKES 400

Time of Race: 2 hours, 48 minutes, 34 seconds
Average Speed: 88.986 Mph

FINISH	DRIVER	CAR
1	Richard Petty	Dodge
2	Cale Yarborough	Chevrolet
3	Darrell Waltrip	Chevrolet
4	Buddy Baker	Ford
5	Lennie Pond	Chevrolet
6	Benny Parsons	Chevrolet
7	J.D. McDuffie	Chevrolet
8	Richard Childress	Chevrolet

9	Jim Vandiver	Dodge
10	Bruce Hill	Chevrolet
11	Dick Brooks	Ford
12	CooCoo Marlin	Chevrolet
13	James Hylton	Chevrolet
14	Elmo Langley	Ford
15	Dean Dalton	Ford
16	Cecil Gordon	Chevrolet
17	Ed Negre	Dodge
18	Buddy Arrington	Plymouth
19	David Sisco	Chevrolet
20	Carl Adams	Ford
21	Bill Champion	Ford
22	Bill Hollar	Chevrolet
23	D.K. Ulrich	Chevrolet
24	Frank Warren	Dodge
25	Walter Ballard	Chevrolet
26	Jabe Thomas	Chevrolet
27	Dave Marcis	Dodge
28	Charlie Griffith	Dodge
29	Henley Gray	Chevrolet
30	Richard Brown	Pontiac

OLD DOMINION 500

Time of Race: 3 hours, 27 minutes, 47 seconds
Average Speed: 75.800 Mph

FINISH	DRIVER	CAR
1	Dave Marcis	Dodge
2	Benny Parsons	Chevrolet
3	Bobby Allison	Matador
4	Richard Childress	Chevrolet
5	Richie Panch	Chevrolet
6	Dick Brooks	Ford
7	Carl Adams	Ford
8	Jim Vandiver	Dodge
9	Cecil Gordon	Chevrolet
10	Elmo Langley	Ford
11	Buddy Arrington	Plymouth
12	Frank Warren	Ford
13	James Hylton	Chevrolet
14	Walter Ballard	Chevrolet
15	Jabe Thomas	Chevrolet
16	Joe Mihalic	Chevrolet
17	Darrell Waltrip	Chevrolet
18	Buddy Baker	Ford
19	Cale Yarborough	Chevrolet
20	David Sisco	Chevrolet
21	Ed Negre	Ford
22	Richard Petty	Dodge
23	David Pearson	Mercury
24	Lennie Pond	Chevrolet
25	Bruce Hill	Chevrolet
26	Chuck Bown	Chevrolet
27	Jimmy Hensley	Chevrolet
28	D.K. Ulrich	Chevrolet
29	CooCoo Marlin	Chevrolet
30	J.D. McDuffie	Chevrolet

NATIONAL 500

Time of Race: 3 hours, 47 minutes, 22 seconds
Average Speed: 132.209 Mph

FINISH	DRIVER	CAR
1	Richard Petty	Dodge
2	David Pearson	Mercury
3	Buddy Baker	Ford
4	Benny Parsons	Chevrolet
5	Cecil Gordon	Chevrolet
6	James Hylton	Chevrolet
7	Darel Dieringer	Ford
8	Richard Childress	Chevrolet
9	J.D. McDuffie	Chevrolet
10	Elmo Langley	Ford
11	Hershel McGriff	Dodge
12	Chuck Bown	Chevrolet
13	Joe Frasson	Chevrolet

14	Frank Warren	Dodge
15	David Sisco	Chevrolet
16	Grant Adcox	Chevrolet
17	Buddy Arrington	Chevrolet
18	Bob Burcham	Chevrolet
19	Cale Yarborough	Chevrolet
20	Jabe Thomas	Chevrolet
21	A.J. Foyt	Chevrolet
22	Lennie Pond	Chevrolet
23	Jim Vandiver	Dodge
24	Darrell Waltrip	Chevrolet
25	Richie Panch	Chevrolet
26	Dave Marcis	Dodge
27	Bruce Hill	Chevrolet
28	Harry Jefferson	Ford
29	Jackie Rogers	Chevrolet
30	Ed Negre	Dodge
31	Bobby Allison	Matador
32	G.C. Spencer	Dodge
33	Donnie Allison	Chevrolet
34	Johnny Rutherford	Chevrolet
35	Dick Brooks	Ford
36	Charlie Glotzbach	Chevrolet
37	Bobby Isaac	Mercury
38	Skip Manning	Chevrolet
39	Jim Insolo	Chevrolet
40	Neil Castles	Chevrolet
41	Walter Ballard	Chevrolet
42	CooCoo Marlin	Chevrolet

CAPITAL CITY 500

Time of Race: 3 hours, 18 minutes, 34 seconds
Average Speed: 81.886 Mph

FINISH	DRIVER	CAR
1	Darrell Waltrip	Chevrolet
2	Lennie Pond	Chevrolet
3	Dick Brooks	Ford
4	Cecil Gordon	Chevrolet
5	J.D. McDuffie	Chevrolet
6	James Hylton	Chevrolet
7	Elmo Langley	Ford
8	Bruce Hill	Chevrolet
9	CooCoo Marlin	Chevrolet
10	Jabe Thomas	Chevrolet
11	Carl Adams	Ford
12	Buddy Arrington	Plymouth
13	D.K. Ulrich	Chevrolet
14	Frank Warren	Dodge
15	Walter Ballard	Chevrolet
16	Bill Hollar	Chevrolet
17	Earl Brooks	Dodge
18	Benny Parsons	Chevrolet
19	Dean Dalton	Ford
20	Bruce Jacobi	Chevrolet
21	Richard Childress	Chevrolet
22	Ed Negre	Dodge
23	Dave Marcis	Dodge
24	David Sisco	Chevrolet
25	Bill Champion	Ford
26	Cale Yarborough	Chevrolet
27	Jim Vandiver	Dodge
28	Richard Petty	Dodge

AMERICAN 500

Time of Race: 4 hours, 9 minutes, 54 seconds
Average Speed: 120.135 Mph

FINISH	DRIVER	CAR
1	Cale Yarborough	Chevrolet
2	Bobby Allison	Matador
3	Dave Marcis	Dodge
4	Lennie Pond	Chevrolet
5	A.J. Foyt	Chevrolet
6	Bruce Hill	Chevrolet
7	Bobby Isaac	Chevrolet

8	Jim Vandiver	Dodge
9	Donnie Allison	Chevrolet
10	CooCoo Marlin	Chevrolet
11	Walter Ballard	Chevrolet
12	Ed Negre	Dodge
13	Buddy Arrington	Plymouth
14	Frank Warren	Dodge
15	James Hylton	Chevrolet
16	Bruce Jacobi	Chevrolet
17	Dick May	Chevrolet
18	Jabe Thomas	Chevrolet
19	Glen McDuffie	Chevrolet
20	J.D. McDuffie	Chevrolet
21	Richard Childress	Chevrolet
22	Ferrel Harris	Dodge
23	Elmo Langley	Ford
24	Benny Parsons	Chevrolet
25	David Pearson	Mercury
26	David Sisco	Chevrolet
27	Richard Skillen	Chevrolet
28	Buddy Baker	Ford
29	Dick Brooks	Ford
30	Cecil Gordon	Chevrolet
31	D.K. Ulrich	Chevrolet
32	Darrell Waltrip	Chevrolet
33	Henley Gray	Chevrolet
34	Neil Castles	Chevrolet
35	Richard Petty	Dodge
36	Jackie Rogers	Chevrolet
37	Joe Frasson	Chevrolet

VOLUNTEER 500

Time of Race: 2 hours, 44 minutes, 49 seconds
Average Speed: 97.016 Mph

FINISH	DRIVER	CAR
1	Richard Petty	Dodge
2	Lennie Pond	Chevrolet
3	Darrell Waltrip	Chevrolet
4	Dave Marcis	Dodge
5	Benny Parsons	Chevrolet
6	Dick Brooks	Ford
7	CooCoo Marlin	Chevrolet
8	Cecil Gordon	Chevrolet
9	James Hylton	Chevrolet
10	Bruce Hill	Chevrolet
11	Ed Negre	Dodge
12	Walter Ballard	Chevrolet
13	Richard Childress	Chevrolet
14	Carl Adams	Ford
15	Buddy Arrington	Plymouth
16	David Sisco	Chevrolet
17	Bill Champion	Ford
18	Jabe Thomas	Chevrolet
19	Elmo Langley	Ford
20	Cale Yarborough	Chevrolet
21	Dick May	Chevrolet
22	Frank Warren	Dodge
23	Bobby Isaac	Chevrolet
24	Buddy Baker	Ford
25	Grant Adcox	Chevrolet
26	Joe Frasson	Chevrolet
27	D.K. Ulrich	Chevrolet
28	Travis Tiller	Dodge
29	Dean Dalton	Ford
30	J.D. McDuffie	Chevrolet

DIXIE 500

Time of Race: 3 hours, 48 minutes, 40 seconds
Average Speed: 130.900 Mph

FINISH	DRIVER	CAR
1	Buddy Baker	Ford
2	Dave Marcis	Dodge
3	Richard Petty	Dodge
4	David Pearson	Mercury

5	Cale Yarborough	Chevrolet
6	Lennie Pond	Chevrolet
7	Dick Brooks	Ford
8	CooCoo Marlin	Chevrolet
9	Cecil Gordon	Chevrolet
10	Ed Negre	Dodge
11	Jody Ridley	Ford
12	Richard Childress	Chevrolet
13	Bruce Hill	Chevrolet
14	Bruce Jacobi	Chevrolet
15	Elmo Langley	Chevrolet
16	Carl Adams	Ford
17	Walter Ballard	Chevrolet
18	J.D. McDuffie	Chevrolet
19	Benny Parsons	Chevrolet
20	Buddy Arrington	Plymouth
21	John Banks	Dodge
22	James Hylton	Chevrolet
23	Bob Burcham	Chevrolet
24	Ferrel Harris	Dodge
25	Frank Warren	Dodge
26	Bobby Allison	Matador
27	Donnie Allison	Chevrolet
28	Jim Vandiver	Dodge
29	David Sisco	Chevrolet
30	Bobby Isaac	Chevrolet
31	Neil Castles	Chevrolet
32	Dean Dalton	Ford
33	D.K. Ulrich	Chevrolet
34	Harold Miller	Chevrolet
35	Richie Panch	Mercury
36	Darrell Waltrip	Chevrolet

L.A. TIMES 500

Time of Race: 3 hours, 33 minutes, 12 seconds
Average Speed: 140.712 mph (New record)

FINISH	DRIVER	CAR
1	Buddy Baker	Ford
2	David Pearson	Mercury
3	Dave Marcis	Dodge
4	Cale Yarborough	Chevrolet
5	Bobby Allison	Matador
6	Lennie Pond	Chevrolet
7	Jim Insolo	Chevrolet
8	Dick Brooks	Ford
9	James Hylton	Chevrolet
10	Richard Childress	Chevrolet
11	Don Hall	Chevrolet
12	David Sisco	Chevrolet
13	D.K. Ulrich	Chevrolet
14	A.J. Foyt	Chevrolet
15	Don Hoffman	Chevrolet
16	Richard Petty	Dodge
17	Frank Warren	Dodge
18	Hugh Pearson	Chevrolet
19	Cecil Gordon	Chevrolet
20	Walter Ballard	Chevrolet
21	J.D. McDuffie	Chevrolet
22	Elmo Langley	Chevrolet
23	Tom Williams	Chevrolet
24	John Kieper	Chevrolet
25	Ray Elder	Dodge
26	Bruce Hill	Chevrolet
27	Jim Boyd	Dodge
28	Carl Adams	Ford
29	Roy Smith	Chevrolet
30	John Martin	Dodge
31	Hershel McGriff	Chevrolet
32	Jim Thurkettle	Chevrolet
33	Bill Schmitt	Chevrolet
34	Benny Parsons	Chevrolet
35	Chuck Wahl	Chevrolet
36	Richie Panch	Mercury
37	Don Puskarich	Dodge
38	Chuck Bown	Dodge
39	Sonny Easley	Ford
40	Ed Negre	Dodge

1976

WINSTON WESTERN 500

Time of Race: 5 hours, 2 minute, 44 seconds
Average Speed: 99.180 MPH

FINISH	DRIVER	CAR
1	David Pearson	Mercury
2	Cale Yarborough	Chevrolet
3	Jim Insolo	Chevrolet
4	Ray Elder	Dodge
5	Benny Parsons	Chevrolet
6	Lennie Pond	Chevrolet
7	Richard Childress	Chevrolet
8	Dave Marcis	Dodge
9	James Hylton	Chevrolet
10	Bill Schmitt	Chevrolet
11	Frank Warren	Dodge
12	D.K. Ulrich	Chevrolet
13	Larry Esau	Chevrolet
14	Ron Esau	Chevrolet
15	Bobby Allison	Matador
16	Chuck Bown	Dodge
17	Gary Mathews	Dodge
18	Ed Bradshaw	Chevrolet
19	J.D. McDuffie	Chevrolet
20	Carl Joiner	Chevrolet
21	Darrell Waltrip	Chevrolet
22	Chuck Wahl	Chevrolet
23	Cecil Gordon	Chevrolet
24	Hugh Pearson	Chevrolet
25	Richard Petty	Dodge
26	Bill Polich	Chevrolet
27	Don Puskarich	Chevrolet
28	Buddy Baker	Ford
29	Gary Johnson	Dodge
30	Hershel McGriff	Chevrolet
31	John Ray	Ford
32	Sonny Easley	Ford
33	Dick Brooks	Chevrolet
34	Sam Beler	Ford
35	Harry Jefferson	Ford

DAYTONA 500

Time of Race: 3 hours, 17 minutes, 8 seconds
Average Speed: 152.181 MPH

FINISH	DRIVER	CAR
1	David Pearson	Mercury
2	Richard Petty	Dodge
3	Benny Parsons	Chevrolet
4	Lennie Pond	Chevrolet
5	Neil Bonnett	Chevrolet
6	Terry Ryan	Chevrolet
7	J.D. McDuffie	Chevrolet
8	Terry Bivins	Chevrolet
9	Richard Childress	Chevrolet
10	Frank Warren	Dodge
11	Buddy Arrington	Dodge
12	Salt Walther	Chevrolet
13	Ed Negre	Dodge
14	Joe Frasson	Chevrolet
15	Jackie Rogers	Chevrolet
16	Jim Hurtubise	Chevrolet
17	Joe Mihalic	Chevrolet
18	Cecil Gordon	Chevrolet
19	D.K. Ulrich	Chevrolet
20	Roy Smith	Chevrolet
21	CooCoo Marlin	Chevrolet
22	A.J. Foyt	Chevrolet
23	James Hylton	Chevrolet
24	Jim Lee Capps	Chevrolet
25	Bobby Allison	Mercury

FINISH	DRIVER	CAR
26	Ramo Stott	Chevrolet
27	Dave Marcis	Dodge
28	John Ray	Chevrolet
29	David Sisco	Chevrolet
30	Skip Manning	Dodge
31	Richard Skillen	Chevrolet
32	Darrell Waltrip	Chevrolet
33	Buddy Baker	Ford
34	David Hobbs	Chevrolet
35	Tighe Scott	Chevrolet
36	Bruce Hill	Chevrolet
37	Tom Williams	Chevrolet
38	Dick May	Chevrolet
39	Earl Ross	Chevrolet
40	Jimmy Means	Chevrolet
41	Dick Brooks	Ford
42	Cale Yarborough	Chevrolet

CAROLINA 500

Time of Race: 4 hours, 24 minutes, 8 seconds
Average Speed: 113.665 MPH

FINISH	DRIVER	CAR
1	Richard Petty	Dodge
2	Darrell Waltrip	Chevrolet
3	Cale Yarborough	Chevrolet
4	Buddy Baker	Ford
5	Benny Parsons	Chevrolet
6	Bobby Isaac	Chevrolet
7	Grant Adcox	Chevrolet
8	CooCoo Marlin	Chevrolet
9	Ed Negre	Dodge
10	J.D. McDuffie	Chevrolet
11	Darrell Bryant	Chevrolet
12	Jackie Rogers	Chevrolet
13	Terry Bivins	Chevrolet
14	John Utsman	Dodge
15	Tom Gale	Ford
16	Dick May	Chevrolet
17	D.K. Ulrich	Chevrolet
18	Travis Tiller	Dodge
19	James Hylton	Chevrolet
20	David Sisco	Chevrolet
21	Bobby Allison	Mercury
22	Bruce Hill	Chevrolet
23	Richard Childress	Chevrolet
24	Dick Brooks	Ford
25	Walter Ballard	Chevrolet
26	Dave Marcis	Dodge
27	Glen McDuffie	Chevrolet
28	Frank Warren	Dodge
29	David Pearson	Mercury
30	Lennie Pond	Chevrolet
31	Buddy Arrington	Dodge
32	A.J. Foyt	Chevrolet
33	Bill Elliott	Ford
34	Cecil Gordon	Chevrolet
35	Skip Manning	Chevrolet
36	Henley Gray	Chevrolet

RICHMOND 400

Time of Race: 2 hours, 58 minutes, 44 seconds
Average Speed: 72.792 MPH

FINISH	DRIVER	CAR
1	Dave Marcis	Dodge
2	Richard Petty	Dodge
3	Bobby Allison	Mercury
4	Cale Yarborough	Chevrolet
5	Terry Bivins	Chevrolet
6	Richard Childress	Chevrolet
7	Cecil Gordon	Chevrolet
8	David Sisco	Chevrolet
9	Benny Parsons	Chevrolet
10	Elmo Langley	Ford

11	Buddy Arrington	Plymouth
12	Joe Mihalic	Chevrolet
13	Ed Negre	Dodge
14	Walter Ballard	Chevrolet
15	James Hylton	Chevrolet
16	Ernie Shaw	Chevrolet
17	Travis Tiller	Dodge
18	Earle Canavan	Dodge
19	Frank Warren	Dodge
20	D.K. Ulrich	Chevrolet
21	J.D. McDuffie	Chevrolet
22	Richard Brown	Pontiac
23	Lennie Pond	Chevrolet
24	Darrell Waltrip	Chevrolet
25	Neil Castles	Chevrolet
26	Dick Brooks	Ford
27	Jabe Thomas	Chevrolet
28	Bill Champion	Ford
29	Buddy Baker	Ford
30	Skip Manning	Chevrolet

14	Bob Burcham	Chevrolet
15	Frank Warren	Dodge
16	Cecil Gordon	Chevrolet
17	Skip Manning	Chevrolet
18	Bruce Hill	Chevrolet
19	John Utsman	Dodge
20	Darrell Bryant	Chevrolet
21	D.K. Ulrich	Chevrolet
22	Jerry Sisco	Chevrolet
23	Henley Gray	Chevrolet
24	Walter Ballard	Chevrolet
25	Buddy Baker	Ford
26	Terry Bivins	Chevrolet
27	J.D. McDuffie	Chevrolet
28	Richard Petty	Dodge
29	Bobby Allison	Mercury
30	Buddy Arrington	Dodge
31	James Hylton	Chevrolet
32	Dave Marcis	Dodge
33	Jimmy Capps	Chevrolet
34	Jimmy Means	Chevrolet
35	Tom Gale	Ford
36	Bill Elliott	Ford

SOUTHEASTERN 500

Time of Race: 2 hours, 26 minutes, 24 seconds
Average Speed: 87.377 MPH

FINISH	DRIVER	CAR
1	Cale Yarborough	Chevrolet
2	Darrell Waltrip	Chevrolet
3	Benny Parsons	Chevrolet
4	Dave Marcis	Dodge
5	Bobby Allison	Mercury
6	Dick Brooks	Ford
7	James Hylton	Chevrolet
8	Ed Negre	Dodge
9	Buddy Arrington	Plymouth
10	J.D. McDuffie	Chevrolet
11	Jerry Sisco	Chevrolet
12	Skip Manning	Chevrolet
13	Jabe Thomas	Chevrolet
14	Frank Warren	Dodge
15	Elmo Langley	Ford
16	Baxter Price	Chevrolet
17	Earle Canavan	Dodge
18	Travis Tiller	Dodge
19	Walter Ballard	Chevrolet
20	Richard Childress	Chevrolet
21	Buddy Baker	Ford
22	Lennie Pond	Chevrolet
23	David Sisco	Chevrolet
24	Terry Bivins	Chevrolet
25	D.K. Ulrich	Chevrolet
26	Joe Mihalic	Chevrolet
27	Richard Petty	Dodge
28	Cecil Gordon	Chevrolet
29	Bill Champion	Ford
30	Henley Gray	Chevrolet

GWYN STALEY 400

Time of Race: 2 hours, 34 minutes, 52 seconds
Average Speed: 96.858 MPH

FINISH	DRIVER	CAR
1	Cale Yarborough	Chevrolet
2	Richard Petty	Dodge
3	Bobby Allison	Mercury
4	Benny Parsons	Chevrolet
5	J. D. McDuffie	Chevrolet
6	Lennie Pond	Chevrolet
7	Dick Brooks	Ford
8	Dave Marcis	Dodge
9	Richard Childress	Chevrolet
10	Walter Ballard	Chevrolet
11	Skip Manning	Chevrolet
12	Cecil Gordon	Chevrolet
13	James Hylton	Chevrolet
14	Junior Miller	Chevrolet
15	Elmo Langley	Ford
16	Bill Champion	Ford
17	Ed Negre	Dodge
18	Buddy Arrington	Plymouth
19	D. K. Ulrich	Chevrolet
20	Frank Warren	Dodge
21	Jabe Thomas	Chevrolet
22	Darrell Waltrip	Chevrolet
23	Baxter Price	Chevrolet
24	Richard Brown	Pontiac
25	Neil Castles	Dodge
26	Buddy Baker	Ford
27	David Sisco	Chevrolet
28	Jeff Handy	Chevrolet

ATLANTA 500

Time of Race: 3 hours, 52 minutes, 16 seconds
Average Speed: 128.904 MPH

FINISH	DRIVER	CAR
1	David Pearson	Mercury
2	Benny Parsons	Chevrolet
3	Cale Yarborough	Chevrolet
4	Lennie Pond	Chevrolet
5	Darrell Waltrip	Chevrolet
6	CooCoo Marlin	Chevrolet
7	Dick Brooks	Ford
8	Neil Bonnett	Chevrolet
9	David Sisco	Chevrolet
10	Jackie Rogers	Chevrolet
11	Richard Childress	Chevrolet
12	Grant Adcox	Chevrolet
13	Ed Negre	Dodge

REBEL 500

Time of Race: 4 hours, 4 minutes, 36 seconds
Average Speed: 122.973 MPH

FINISH	DRIVER	CAR
1	David Pearson	Mercury
2	Buddy Baker	Ford
3	Benny Parsons	Chevrolet
4	Lennie Pond	Chevrolet
5	Dave Marcis	Dodge
6	Buck Baker	Ford
7	Grant Adcox	Chevrolet
8	Joe Frasson	Chevrolet
9	Richard Childress	Chevrolet
10	Bruce Hill	Chevrolet
11	Cecil Gordon	Chevrolet
12	John Utsman	Dodge

13	David Sisco	Chevrolet
14	Skip Manning	Chevrolet
15	Dick May	Chevrolet
16	D. K. Ulrich	Chevrolet
17	Frank Warren	Dodge
18	Bobby Allison	Mercury
19	Earle Canavan	Dodge
20	Earl Brooks	Chevrolet
21	Dick Skillen	Chevrolet
22	Tom Gale	Ford
23	Richard Petty	Dodge
24	Buddy Arrington	Dodge
25	Cale Yarborough	Chevrolet
26	Jerry Sisco	Chevrolet
27	J. D. McDuffie	Chevrolet
28	Ed Negre	Dodge
29	Henley Gray	Chevrolet
30	Neil Bonnett	Chevrolet
31	Darrell Waltrip	Chevrolet
32	James Hylton	Chevrolet
33	Bob Burcham	Chevrolet
34	Donnie Allison	Chevrolet
35	Dick Brooks	Ford
36	Darrell Bryant	Chevrolet

VIRGINIA 500

Time of Race: 3 hours, 39 minutes, 43 seconds
Average Speed: 71.759 MPH

FINISH	DRIVER	CAR
1	Darrell Waltrip	Chevrolet
2	Cale Yarborough	Chevrolet
3	David Pearson	Mercury
4	Richard Petty	Dodge
5	Dick Brooks	Ford
6	Bobby Allison	Mercury
7	Bruce Hill	Chevrolet
8	Richard Childress	Chevrolet
9	Walter Ballard	Chevrolet
10	Cecil Gordon	Chevrolet
11	Gary Myers	Chevrolet
12	James Hylton	Chevrolet
13	Elmo Langley	Ford
14	Jabe Thomas	Chevrolet
15	Bruce Blodgett	Dodge
16	D. K. Ulrich	Chevrolet
17	Skip Manning	Chevrolet
18	Rick Newsom	Ford
19	Neil Bonnett	Chevrolet
20	Benny Parsons	Chevrolet
21	Dave Marcis	Dodge
22	Lennie Pond	Chevrolet
23	J. D. McDuffie	Chevrolet
24	David Sisci	Chevrolet
25	Jimmy Hensley	Chevrolet
26	Travis Tiller	Dodge
27	Buddy Baker	Ford
28	Buddy Arrington	Dodge
29	Frank Warren	Dodge
30	Ed Negre	Chevrolet

WINSTON 500

Time of Race: 2 hours, 56 minutes, 37 seconds
Average Speed: 169.887 MPH

FINISH	DRIVER	CAR
1	Buddy Baker	Ford
2	Cale Yarborough	Chevrolet
3	Bobby Allison	Mercury
4	Richard Petty	Dodge
5	Terry Ryan	Chevrolet
6	Cecil Gordon	Chevrolet
7	Donnie Allison	Chevrolet
8	Bruce Hill	Chevrolet
9	Dave Marcis	Dodge
10	Frank Warren	Dodge

11	Lennie Pond	Chevrolet
12	Dick Brooks	Ford
13	Jim Vandiver	Dodge
14	David Sisco	Chevrolet
15	John Utsman	Dodge
16	Skip Manning	Chevrolet
17	Tighe Scott	Chevrolet
18	Tom Gale	Ford
19	Grant Adcox	Chevrolet
20	D. K. Ulrich	Chevrolet
21	Dick Skillen	Chevrolet
22	Buddy Arrington	Dodge
23	Ricky Rudd	Chevrolet
24	Richard Childress	Chevrolet
25	Ferrel Harris	Dodge
26	Benny Parsons	Chevrolet
27	J. D. McDuffie	Chevrolet
28	James Hylton	Chevrolet
29	Bob Wawak	Chevrolet
30	Bob Burcham	Chevrolet
31	Jimmy Means	Chevrolet
32	Ed Negre	Chevrolet
33	Darrell Waltrip	Chevrolet
34	Buck Baker	Chevrolet
35	Gary Myers	Chevrolet
36	Joe Frasson	Chevrolet
37	David Pearson	Mercury
38	Bill Elliott	Ford
39	Neil Bonnett	Chevrolet
40	Darrell Bryant	Chevrolet

MUSIC CITY USA 420

Time of Race: 2 hours, 57 minutes, 43 seconds
Average Speed: 84.512 MPH

FINISH	DRIVER	CAR
1	Cale Yarborough	Chevrolet
2	Richard Petty	Dodge
3	Benny Parsons	Chevrolet
4	Buddy Baker	Ford
5	Bobby Allison	Mercury
6	Lennie Pond	Chevrolet
7	Dave Marcis	Dodge
8	Walter Ballard	Chevrolet
9	David Sisco	Chevrolet
10	Frank Warren	Dodge
11	D. K. Ulrich	Chevrolet
12	Darrell Waltrip	Chevrolet
13	Elmo Langley	Ford
14	Cecil Gordon	Chevrolet
15	Jimmy Means	Chevrolet
16	Buck Baker	Chevrolet
17	Richard Childress	Chevrolet
18	James Hylton	Chevrolet
19	Ed Negre	Dodge
20	J. D. McDuffie	Chevrolet
21	Jabe Thomas	Chevrolet
22	Skip Manning	Chevrolet
23	Bruce Hill	Chevrolet
24	Baxter Price	Chevrolet
25	Henley Gray	Chevrolet
26	Buddy Arrington	Dodge
27	Gary Myers	Chevrolet
28	Walter Wallace	Chevrolet
29	Sterling Marlin	Chevrolet
30	Rick Newsom	Ford

MASON-DIXON 500

Time of Race: 4 hours, 19 minutes, 53 seconds
Average Speed: 115.436 MPH

FINISH	DRIVER	CAR
1	Benny Parsons	Chevrolet
2	David Pearson	Mercury
3	Dave Marcis	Dodge
4	Bobby Allison	Mercury

5	Buddy Baker	Ford
6	Richard Petty	Dodge
7	Dick Brooks	Ford
8	Lennie Pond	Chevrolet
9	Darrell Bryant	Chevrolet
10	Richard Childress	Chevrolet
11	Skip Manning	Chevrolet
12	D. K. Ulrich	Chevrolet
13	Frank Warren	Dodge
14	Jabe Thomas	Chevrolet
15	J. D. McDuffie	Chevrolet
16	Walter Ballard	Chevrolet
17	James Hylton	Chevrolet
18	Joe Mihalic	Chevrolet
19	Budd Hagelin	Dodge
20	Rick Newsom	Ford
21	Baxter Price	Chevrolet
22	David Sisco	Chevrolet
23	Travis Tiller	Dodge
24	Doc Faustina	Dodge
25	Gary Myers	Chevrolet
26	Bobby Wawak	Chevrolet
27	Cale Yarborough	Chevrolet
28	Buck Baker	Chevrolet
29	Dean Dalton	Chevrolet
30	Darrell Waltrip	Chevrolet
31	Buddy Arrington	Dodge
32	Earl Brooks	Ford
33	Ricky Rudd	Chevrolet
34	Ed Negre	Dodge
35	Donnie Allison	Chevrolet
36	Cecil Gordon	Chevrolet
37	Tom Gale	Ford
38	Neil Castles	Chevrolet
39	Bruce Hill	Chevrolet

WORLD 600

Time of Race: 4 hours, 22 minutes, 6 seconds
Average Speed: 137.352 MPH

FINISH	DRIVER	CAR
1	David Pearson	Mercury
2	Richard Petty	Dodge
3	Cale Yarborough	Chevrolet
4	Bobby Allison	Mercury
5	Benny Parsons	Chevrolet
6	Donnie Allison	Chevrolet
7	Dick Brooks	Ford
8	Lennie Pond	Chevrolet
9	Harry Gant	Chevrolet
10	David Sisco	Chevrolet
11	Darrell Waltrip	Chevrolet
12	Grant Adcox	Chevrolet
13	James Hylton	Chevrolet
14	Buddy Arrington	Dodge
15	Janet Guthrie	Chevrolet
16	D. K. Ulrich	Chevrolet
17	Richard Childress	Chevrolet
18	Frank Warren	Dodge
19	Darrell Bryant	Chevrolet
20	Cecil Gordon	Chevrolet
21	Dick May	Chevrolet
22	Walter Ballard	Chevrolet
23	Bill Elliott	Ford
24	Sam Sommers	Chevrolet
25	J. D. McDuffie	Chevrolet
26	Bobby Wawak	Chevrolet
27	Ed Negre	Dodge
28	Buddy Baker	Ford
29	Dave Marcis	Dodge
30	Gary Myers	Chevrolet
31	Dale Earnhardt	Chevrolet
32	Dick Trickle	Ford
33	Skip Manning	Chevrolet
34	Charlie Glotzbach	Chevrolet
35	Bob Burcham	Chevrolet
36	Jackie Rogers	Chevrolet
37	Bruce Hill	Chevrolet
38	Bobby Isaac	Chevrolet
39	Jimmy Means	Chevrolet
40	Terry Ryan	Chevrolet

RIVERSIDE 400

Time of Race: 2 hours, 20 minutes, 31 seconds
Average Speed: 106.279 MPH

FINISH	DRIVER	CAR
1	David Pearson	Mercury
2	Bobby Allison	Mercury
3	Benny Parsons	Chevrolet
4	Ray Elder	Dodge
5	Buddy Baker	Ford
6	Darrell Waltrip	Chevrolet
7	Cale Yarborough	Chevrolet
8	Jim Insolo	Chevrolet
9	Richard Petty	Dodge
10	Dave Marcis	Dodge
11	Richard Childress	Chevrolet
12	Cecil Gordon	Chevrolet
13	Chuck Wahl	Chevrolet
14	J. D. McDuffie	Chevrolet
15	Eddie Bradshaw	Chevrolet
16	James Hylton	Chevrolet
17	Bill Polich	Chevrolet
18	Don Reynolds	Chevrolet
19	Chuck Bown	Chevrolet
20	Frank Warren	Dodge
21	Don Puskarich	Chevrolet
22	John Dineen	Ford
23	Gary Johnson	Chevrolet
24	Ed Negre	Dodge
25	Lennie Pond	Chevrolet
26	D. K. Ulrich	Chevrolet
27	Roy Smith	Chevrolet
28	J. C. Danielson	Dodge
29	Neil Bonnett	Chevrolet
30	Hugh Pearson	Chevrolet
31	Rusty Sanders	Chevrolet
32	John Hamson	Chevrolet
33	Ernie Stierly	Chevrolet
34	Jim Thirkettle	Chevrolet
35	Ron Esau	Ford

CAM2 MOTOR OIL 400

Time of Race: 2 hours, 50 minutes, 2 seconds
Average Speed: 141.148 MPH

FINISH	DRIVER	CAR
1	David Pearson	Mercury
2	Cale Yarborough	Chevrolet
3	Bobby Allison	Mercury
4	Richard Petty	Dodge
5	Buddy Baker	Ford
6	Dick Brooks	Ford
7	Lennie Pond	Chevrolet
8	David Sisco	Chevrolet
9	Jackie Rogers	Chevrolet
10	Cecil Gordon	Chevrolet
11	Buddy Arrington	Dodge
12	D. K. Ulrich	Chevrolet
13	Coo Coo Marlin	Chevrolet
14	Dick May	Chevrolet
15	Tighe Scott	Chevrolet
16	J. D. McDuffie	Chevrolet
17	Ed Negre	Dodge
18	Richard Childress	Chevrolet
19	Benny Parsons	Chevrolet
20	Skip Manning	Chevrolet
21	Tom Gale	Ford
22	Travis Tiller	Dodge
23	Jimmy Means	Chevrolet
24	Frank Warren	Dodge
25	Bruce Hill	Chevrolet
26	Bobby Wawak	Chevrolet
27	Gary Myers	Chevrolet
28	Bill Elliott	Ford
29	Darrell Waltrip	Chevrolet
30	Dave Marcis	Dodge
31	Walter Ballard	Chevrolet

32	Terry Ryan	Chevrolet
33	Henley Gray	Chevrolet
34	Earle Canavan	Dodge
35	James Hylton	Chevrolet
36	Joe Frasson	Chevrolet

FIRECRACKER 400

Time of Race: 2 hours, 29 minutes, 6 seconds
Average Speed: 160.966 MPH

FINISH	DRIVER	CAR
1	Cale Yarborough	Chevrolet
2	David Pearson	Mercury
3	Bobby Allison	Mercury
4	A. J. Foyt	Chevrolet
5	Dave Marcis	Dodge
6	Coo Coo Martin	Chevrolet
7	Benny Parsons	Chevrolet
8	Dick Brooks	Ford
9	David Sisco	Chevrolet
10	Ricky Rudd	Chevrolet
11	Jimmy Means	Chevrolet
12	Richard Childress	Chevrolet
13	Frank Warren	Dodge
14	Bobby Wawak	Chevrolet
15	Janet Guthrie	Chevrolet
16	D. K. Ulrich	Chevrolet
17	Dick Skillen	Chevrolet
18	Harold Miller	Chevrolet
19	Bill Elliott	Ford
20	John Rutherford	Chevrolet
21	Jimmy Capps	Chevrolet
22	Richard Petty	Dodge
23	Joe Mihalic	Chevrolet
24	J. D. McDuffie	Chevrolet
25	Bruce Hill	Chevrolet
26	James Hylton	Chevrolet
27	Dick May	Chevrolet
28	Ferrel Harris	Dodge
29	Tom Gale	Chevrolet
30	Grant Adcox	Chevrolet
31	Skip Manning	Chevrolet
32	Lennie Pond	Chevrolet
33	Neil Bonnett	Chevrolet
34	Cecil Gordon	Chevrolet
35	Buddy Baker	Ford
36	Buck Baker	Chevrolet
37	Ed Negre	Chevrolet
38	Jackie Rogers	Chevrolet
39	Darrell Waltrip	Chevrolet
40	Buddy Arrington	Dodge

NASHVILLE 420

Time of Race: 2 hours, 52 minutes, 49 seconds
Average Speed: 86.908 MPH

FINISH	DRIVER	CAR
1	Benny Parsons	Chevrolet
2	Richard Petty	Dodge
3	Darrell Waltrip	Chevrolet
4	Lennie Pond	Chevrolet
5	Cale Yarborough	Chevrolet
6	Dave Marcis	Dodge
7	Bobby Allison	Mercury
8	Coo Coo Marlin	Chevrolet
9	Skip Manning	Chevrolet
10	Bobby Wawak	Chevrolet
11	James Hylton	Chevrolet
12	Frank Warren	Dodge
13	J. D. McDuffie	Chevrolet
14	Bill Elliott	Ford
15	Cecil Gordon	Chevrolet
16	David Sisco	Chevrolet
17	D. K. Ulrich	Chevrolet
18	Walter Wallace	Chevrolet

High-technology plays an important role in the pit area of every team.

19	Gary Myers	Chevrolet
20	Walter Ballard	Chevrolet
21	Dick May	Chevrolet
22	Terry Bivins	Chevrolet
23	Buddy Baker	Ford
24	Jimmy Means	Chevrolet
25	Ed Negre	Dodge
26	Buddy Arrington	Dodge
27	Bruce Hill	Chevrolet
28	Richard Childress	Chevrolet
29	Dick Brooks	Ford
30	Joe Frasson	Chevrolet

PUROLATOR 500

Time of Race: 4 hours, 18 minutes, 54 seconds
Average Speed: 115.875 MPH

FINISH	DRIVER	CAR
1	Richard Petty	Dodge
2	Buddy Baker	Ford
3	Benny Parsons	Chevrolet
4	David Pearson	Mercury
5	Lennie Pond	Chevrolet
6	Cecil Gordon	Chevrolet
7	Buddy Arrington	Plymouth
8	Jackie Rogers	Chevrolet
9	Richard Childress	Chevrolet
10	David Sisco	Chevrolet
11	Ed Negre	Dodge
12	Skip Manning	Chevrolet
13	Joe Mihalic	Chevrolet
14	Bobby Wawak	Chevrolet
15	Dean Dalton	Chevrolet
16	Frank Warren	Dodge
17	James Hylton	Chevrolet
18	Dick May	Chevrolet
19	Terry Bivins	Chevrolet
20	Henley Gray	Chevrolet
21	J. D. McDuffie	Chevrolet
22	Dave Marcis	Dodge
23	Jimmy Means	Chevrolet
24	Bobby Allison	Mercury

FINISH	DRIVER	CAR
25	Cale Yarborough	Chevrolet
26	Darrell Waltrip	Chevrolet
27	Gary Myers	Chevrolet
28	Baxter Price	Chevrolet
29	Bruce Hill	Chevrolet
30	Tighe Scott	Chevrolet
31	Dick Brooks	Ford
32	Bill Elliott	Ford
33	Travis Tiller	Dodge
34	Tom Gale	Ford
35	Darrell Bryant	Chevrolet
36	Earle Canavan	Dodge
37	Walter Ballard	Dodge
38	D. K. Ulrich	Chevrolet
39	Bill Hollar	Chevrolet
40	Joe Frasson	Chevrolet

TALLADEGA 500

Time of Race: 3 hours, 10 minutes, 27 seconds
Average Speed: 157.547 MPH

FINISH	DRIVER	CAR
1	Dave Marcis	Dodge
2	Buddy Baker	Ford
3	Dick Brooks	Ford
4	James Hylton	Chevrolet
5	Lennie Pond	Chevrolet
6	Tighe Scott	Chevrolet
7	J. D. McDuffie	Chevrolet
8	Richard Childress	Chevrolet
9	Skip Manning	Chevrolet
10	Jimmy Capps	Chevrolet
11	Jimmy Means	Chevrolet
12	Frank Warren	Dodge
13	Joe Mihalic	Chevrolet
14	Harold Miller	Chevrolet
15	Jackie Rogers	Chevrolet
16	Buck Baker	Chevrolet
17	Henley Gray	Chevrolet
18	Grant Adcox	Chevrolet
19	Dick May	Chevrolet
20	Richard Petty	Dodge
21	D. K. Ulrich	Chevrolet
22	A. J. Foyt	Chevrolet
23	Bobby Allison	Mercury
24	Bobby Wawak	Chevrolet
25	G. C. Spencer	Dodge
26	Cale Yarborough	Chevrolet
27	Ed Negre	Dodge
28	David Pearson	Mercury
29	Cecil Gordon	Chevrolet
30	Dick Skillen	Chevrolet
31	David Sisco	Chevrolet
32	Bruce Hill	Chevrolet
33	Buddy Arrington	Dodge
34	Coo Coo Marlin	Chevrolet
35	Bob Burcham	Chevrolet
36	Sam Sommers	Chevrolet
37	Darrell Waltrip	Chevrolet
38	Neil Bonnett	Chevrolet
39	Benny Parsons	Chevrolet
40	Tom Gale	Ford

CHAMPION SPARK PLUG 400

Time of Race: 2 hours, 51 minutes, 20 seconds
Average Speed: 140.078 MPH

FINISH	DRIVER	CAR
1	David Pearson	Mercury
2	Cale Yarborough	Chevrolet
3	Richard Petty	Dodge
4	Bobby Allison	Mercury
5	Dave Marcis	Dodge
6	Neil Bonnett	Chevrolet
7	D. K. Ulrich	Chevrolet
8	J. D. McDuffie	Chevrolet
9	Benny Parsons	Chevrolet

FINISH	DRIVER	CAR
10	Bobby Wawak	Chevrolet
11	Henley Gray	Chevrolet
12	Coo Coo Marlin	Chevrolet
13	Richard Childress	Chevrolet
14	Skip Manning	Chevrolet
15	Terry Bivins	Ford
16	Dick May	Chevrolet
17	David Hobbs	Ford
18	Dean Dalton	Chevrolet
19	Bruce Hill	Chevrolet
20	Harold Miller	Chevrolet
21	James Hylton	Chevrolet
22	Joe Mihalic	Chevrolet
23	Frank Warren	Dodge
24	Jimmy Means	Chevrolet
25	Lennie Pond	Chevrolet
26	Cecil Gordon	Chevrolet
27	Darrell Waltrip	Chevrolet
28	Joe Frasson	Chevrolet
29	Dick Brooks	Ford
30	Ed Negre	Dodge
31	Buddy Baker	Ford
32	David Sisco	Chevrolet
33	John Haver	Chevrolet
34	G. C. Spencer	Dodge
35	Jackie Rogers	Chevrolet
36	Tighe Scott	Chevrolet

VOLUNTEER 400

Time of Race: 2 hours, 8 minutes, 59 seconds
Average Speed: 99.175 MPH

FINISH	DRIVER	CAR
1	Cale Yarborough	Chevrolet
2	Richard Petty	Dodge
3	Darrell Waltrip	Chevrolet
4	Benny Parsons	Chevrolet
5	Buddy Baker	Ford
6	Bobby Allison	Mercury
7	Dick Brooks	Ford
8	Lennie Pond	Chevrolet
9	Bobby Wawak	Chevrolet
10	Richard Childress	Chevrolet
11	D. K. Ulrich	Chevrolet
12	Terry Bivins	Chevrolet
13	James Hylton	Chevrolet
14	David Sisco	Chevrolet
15	Henley Gray	Chevrolet
16	Dick May	Chevrolet
17	Buddy Arrington	Plymouth
18	Skip Manning	Chevrolet
19	Jimmy Means	Chevrolet
20	Frank Warren	Dodge
21	Cecil Gordon	Chevrolet
22	Dave Marcis	Dodge
23	J. D. McDuffie	Chevrolet
24	Clyde Lynn	Ford
25	Elmo Langley	Ford
26	Walter Ballard	Chevrolet
27	Gary Myers	Chevrolet
28	Dean Dalton	Chevrolet
29	Ed Negre	Dodge
30	Joe Frasson	Chevrolet

SOUTHERN 500

Time of Race: 4 hours, 9 minutes, 33 seconds
Average Speed: 120.534 MPH

FINISH	DRIVER	CAR
1	David Pearson	Mercury
2	Richard Petty	Dodge
3	Darrell Waltrip	Chevrolet
4	Dave Marcis	Dodge
5	Lennie Pond	Chevrolet
6	Dick Brooks	Ford
7	Benny Parsons	Chevrolet
8	Coo Coo Marlin	Chevrolet

9	Bobby Allison	Mercury
10	Bobby Wawak	Chevrolet
11	Dean Dalton	Chevrolet
12	Cecil Gordon	Chevrolet
13	Grant Adcox	Chevrolet
14	Terry Bivins	Chevrolet
15	Jackie Rogers	Chevrolet
16	D. K. Ulrich	Chevrolet
17	Buck Baker	Chevrolet
18	Jimmy Means	Chevrolet
19	Frank Warren	Dodge
20	James Hylton	Chevrolet
21	Henley Gray	Chevrolet
22	Bruce Hill	Chevrolet
23	Cale Yarborough	Chevrolet
24	Neil Bonnett	Chevrolet
25	J. D. McDuffie	Chevrolet
26	Ed Negre	Dodge
27	Gary Myers	Chevrolet
28	Dick May	Dodge
29	Earle Canavan	Dodge
30	Sam Sommers	Chevrolet
31	Buddy Baker	Ford
32	Skip Manning	Chevrolet
33	Donnie Allison	Chevrolet
34	Joe Frasson	Chevrolet
35	Buddy Arrington	Dodge
36	Richard Childress	Chevrolet
37	Bruce Jacobi	Ford
38	Rick Newsom	Chevrolet
39	David Sisco	Chevrolet
40	Darrell Bryant	Chevrolet

CAPITAL CITY 400

Time of Race: 2 hours, 46 minutes, 47 seconds
Average Speed: 77.993 MPH

FINISH	DRIVER	CAR
1	Cale Yarborough	Chevrolet
2	Bobby Allison	Mercury
3	Richard Petty	Dodge
4	Darrell Waltrip	Chevrolet
5	Buddy Baker	Ford
6	Lennie Pond	Chevrolet
7	Dave Marcis	Dodge
8	Dick Brooks	Ford
9	Terry Bivins	Chevrolet
10	Bobby Wawak	Chevrolet
11	J. D. McDuffie	Chevrolet
12	Henley Gray	Chevrolet
13	Cecil Gordon	Chevrolet
14	Dean Dalton	Chevrolet
15	Elmo Langley	Ford
16	James Hylton	Chevrolet
17	D. K. Ulrich	Chevrolet
18	Buddy Arrington	Dodge
19	Dick May	Chevrolet
20	Earl Brooks	Chevrolet
21	Gary Myers	Chevrolet
22	Walter Ballard	Chevrolet
23	David Sisco	Chevrolet
24	Jimmy Means	Chevrolet
25	Richard Childress	Chevrolet
26	Frank Warren	Dodge
27	Ed Negre	Dodge
28	Travis Tiller	Dodge
29	Benny Parsons	Chevrolet
30	Larry Lamay	Chevrolet

DELAWARE 500

Time of Race: 4 hours, 19 minutes, 12 seconds
Average Speed: 115.740 MPH

FINISH	DRIVER	CAR
1	Cale Yarborough	Chevrolet
2	Richard Petty	Dodge
3	David Pearson	Mercury

4	Bobby Allison	Mercury
5	Buddy Baker	Ford
6	Dick Brooks	Ford
7	J. D. McDuffie	Chevrolet
8	D. K. Ulrich	Chevrolet
9	James Hylton	Chevrolet
10	Buddy Arrington	Dodge
11	David Sisco	Chevrolet
12	Skip Manning	Chevrolet
13	Henley Gray	Chevrolet
14	Dave Marcis	Dodge
15	Ed Negre	Dodge
16	Walter Ballard	Chevrolet
17	Dick May	Chevrolet
18	Joe Mihalic	Chevrolet
19	Jack Donohue	Chevrolet
20	Richard Childress	Chevrolet
21	Tommy Ellis	Ford
22	Bobby Wawak	Chevrolet
23	Frank Warren	Dodge
24	Earle Canavan	Dodge
25	Tom Gale	Ford
26	Benny Parsons	Chevrolet
27	Jimmy Means	Chevrolet
28	Bruce Jacobi	Chevrolet
29	Gary Myers	Chevrolet
30	Rick Newsom	Ford
31	Darrell Waltrip	Chevrolet
32	Terry Bivins	Chevrolet
33	Janet Guthrie	Chevrolet
34	Lennie Pond	Chevrolet
35	Cecil Gordon	Chevrolet
36	Bruce Hill	Chevrolet

OLD DOMINION 500

Time of Race: 2 hours, 22 minutes, 15 seconds
Average Speed: 75.370 MPH

FINISH	DRIVER	CAR
1	Cale Yarborough	Chevrolet
2	Darrell Waltrip	Chevrolet
3	Buddy Baker	Ford
4	Richard Petty	Dodge
5	Benny Parsons	Chevrolet
6	Dick Brooks	Ford
7	Jimmy Hensley	Chevrolet
8	Terry Bivins	Chevrolet
9	Sonny Easley	Ford
10	Richard Childress	Chevrolet
11	Buddy Arrington	Dodge
12	Dave Marcis	Dodge
13	D. K. Ulrich	Chevrolet
14	Frank Warren	Chevrolet
15	Cecil Gordon	Chevrolet
16	David Sisco	Chevrolet
17	Dick May	Chevrolet
18	James Hylton	Chevrolet
19	David Pearson	Mercury
20	Jimmy Means	Chevrolet
21	J. D. McDuffie	Chevrolet
22	Ed Negre	Ford
23	Skip Manning	Chevrolet
24	Rick Newsom	Ford
25	Bobby Wawak	Chevrolet
26	Gary Myers	Chevrolet
27	Bobby Allison	Mercury
28	Chuck Bown	Chevrolet
29	Lennie Pond	Chevrolet
30	Bruce Hill	Chevrolet

WILKES 400

Time of Race: 2 hours, 35 minutes, 38 seconds
Average Speed: 96.380 MPH

FINISH	DRIVER	CAR
1	Cale Yarborough	Chevrolet
2	Benny Parsons	Chevrolet

FINISH	DRIVER	CAR
3	Richard Petty	Dodge
4	Buddy Baker	Ford
5	Lennie Pond	Chevrolet
6	Dick Brooks	Ford
7	J. D. McDuffie	Chevrolet
8	Bobby Wawak	Chevrolet
9	Terry Bivins	Chevrolet
10	Sonny Easley	Ford
11	James Hylton	Chevrolet
12	Buddy Arrington	Plymouth
13	Cecil Gordon	Chevrolet
14	David Sisco	Chevrolet
15	Junior Miller	Chevrolet
16	Larry Lamay	Chevrolet
17	Dave Marcis	Dodge
18	Gary Myers	Chevrolet
19	Henley Gray	Chevrolet
20	Dick May	Chevrolet
21	Skip Manning	Ford
22	Frank Warren	Dodge
23	Richard Childress	Chevrolet
24	Darrell Waltrip	Chevrolet
25	Ed Negre	Dodge
26	D. K. Ulrich	Chevrolet
27	Jimmy Means	Chevrolet
28	Neil Bonnett	Chevrolet
29	Bobby Allison	Mercury
30	Richard Brown	Pontiac

NATIONAL 500

Time of Race: 3 hours, 32 minutes, 51 seconds
Average Speed: 141.226 MPH

FINISH	DRIVER	CAR
1	Donnie Allison	Chevrolet
2	Cale Yarborough	Chevrolet
3	Bobby Allison	Mercury
4	Buddy Baker	Ford
5	Benny Parsons	Chevrolet
6	David Pearson	Mercury
7	Lennie Pond	Chevrolet
8	Richard Petty	Dodge
9	Dick Brooks	Ford
10	Bobby Wawak	Chevrolet
11	Darrell Waltrip	Chevrolet
12	Buddy Arrington	Dodge
13	Skip Manning	Chevrolet
14	Grant Adcox	Chevrolet
15	Richard Childress	Chevrolet
16	Ricky Rudd	Chevrolet
17	G. C. Spencer	Dodge
18	James Hylton	Chevrolet
19	David Sisco	Chevrolet
20	Earl Brooks	Chevrolet
21	Bill Dennis	Chevrolet
22	Janet Guthrie	Chevrolet
23	J. D. McDuffie	Chevrolet
24	Buck Baker	Chevrolet
25	Terry Bivins	Chevrolet
26	Frank Warren	Dodge
27	Bruce Jacobi	Chevrolet
28	Cecil Gordon	Chevrolet
29	Dave Marcis	Dodge
30	D. K. Ulrich	Chevrolet
31	Johnny Rutherford	Chevrolet
32	Coo Coo Marlin	Chevrolet
33	Sonny Easley	Ford
34	Bruce Hill	Chevrolet
35	Neil Bonnett	Chevrolet
36	Sam Sommers	Chevrolet
37	Ed Negre	Dodge
38	A. J. Foyt	Chevrolet
39	Gordon Johncock	Dodge
40	Al Holbert	Ford

AMERICAN 500

Time of Race: 4 hours, 15 minutes, 1 seconds
Average Speed: 117.718 MPH

FINISH	DRIVER	CAR
1	Richard Petty	Dodge
2	Lennie Pond	Chevrolet
3	Darrell Waltrip	Chevrolet
4	Bobby Allison	Mercury
5	Cale Yarborough	Chevrolet
6	David Pearson	Mercury
7	Donnie Allison	Chevrolet
8	Dick Brooks	Ford
9	Skip Manning	Chevrolet
10	Coo Coo Marlin	Chevrolet
11	Sonny Easley	Ford
12	Grant Adcox	Chevrolet
13	Ed Negre	Dodge
14	D. K. Ulrich	Chevrolet
15	Cecil Gordon	Chevrolet
16	Buddy Arrington	Dodge
17	Terry Bivins	Chevrolet
18	Rick Newsom	Ford
19	Jackie Rogers	Chevrolet
20	David Sisco	Chevrolet
21	Jack Donohue	Chevrolet
22	Frank Warren	Chevrolet
23	Jimmy Means	Chevrolet
24	Tom Gale	Ford
25	Dave Marcis	Dodge
26	J. D. McDuffie	Chevrolet
27	Richard Childress	Chevrolet
28	Buddy Baker	Ford
29	James Hylton	Dodge
30	Dick May	Chevrolet
31	Benny Parsons	Chevrolet
32	Travis Tiller	Dodge
33	Bobby Wawak	Chevrolet
34	Gary Myers	Chevrolet
35	Bruce Hill	Chevrolet
36	Henley Gray	Dodge

DIXIE 500

Time of Race: 3 hours, 55 minutes, 7 seconds
Average Speed: 127.396 MPH

FINISH	DRIVER	CAR
1	Dave Marcis	Dodge
2	David Pearson	Mercury
3	Donnie Allison	Chevrolet
4	Cale Yarborough	Chevrolet
5	Buddy Baker	Ford
6	Benny Parsons	Chevrolet
7	Darrell Waltrip	Chevrolet
8	Neil Bonnett	Chevrolet
9	Sam Sommers	Chevrolet
10	Bobby Wawak	Chevrolet
11	Bruce Hill	Chevrolet
12	James Hylton	Chevrolet
13	J. D. McDuffie	Chevrolet
14	Skip Manning	Chevrolet
15	Sonny Easley	Ford
16	Gene Felton	Ford
17	Jimmy Means	Chevrolet
18	D. K. Ulrich	Chevrolet
19	Dale Earnhardt	Chevrolet
20	Grant Adcox	Chevrolet
21	Richie Panch	Ford
22	Terry Bivins	Chevrolet
23	Cecil Gordon	Chevrolet
24	Lennie Pond	Chevrolet
25	Richard Childress	Chevrolet
26	Bobby Allison	Mercury
27	Frank Warren	Dodge
28	Richard Petty	Dodge
29	Dick Brooks	Ford
30	Coo Coo Marlin	Chevrolet
31	Chuck Bown	Chevrolet
32	Dick May	Chevrolet
33	David Sisco	Chevrolet
34	Billy McGinnis	Chevrolet
35	G. C. Spencer	Dodge
36	Jack Donohue	Chevrolet

LOS ANGELES TIMES 500

Time of Race: 3 hours, 38 minutes, 49 seconds
Average Speed: 137.101 MPH

FINISH	DRIVER	CAR
1	David Pearson	Mercury
2	Lennie Pond	Chevrolet
3	Benny Parsons	Chevrolet
4	Dick Brooks	Ford
5	James Hylton	Chevrolet
6	Bobby Wawak	Chevrolet
7	Terry Bivins	Chevrolet
8	Skip Manning	Chevrolet
9	Terry Ryan	Chevrolet
10	Bruce Hill	Chevrolet
11	J. D. McDuffie	Chevrolet
12	Ed Negre	Dodge
13	Larry Phillips	Ford
14	Sonny Easley	Ford
15	Don Puskarich	Chevrolet
16	Cecil Gordon	Chevrolet
17	Tom Gale	Ford
18	Frank Warren	Dodge
19	Chuck Bown	Chevrolet
20	Janet Guthrie	Chevrolet
21	Jim Insolo	Chevrolet
22	Mike Hiss	Chevrolet
23	Cale Yarborough	Chevrolet
24	Dave Marcis	Dodge
25	D. K. Ulrich	Chevrolet
26	Bill Schmitt	Chevrolet
27	Richard Petty	Dodge
28	Glen Francis	Chevrolet
29	Jim Thirkettle	Chevrolet
30	David Sisco	Chevrolet
31	Carl Joiner	Chevrolet
32	Hershel McGriff	Chevrolet
33	Bobby Allison	Mercury
34	Donnie Allison	Chevrolet
35	John Kleper	Chevrolet
36	Richard Childress	Chevrolet
37	Dick May	Chevrolet
38	Roy Smith	Chevrolet
39	Buddy Baker	Ford
40	Darrell Waltrip	Chevrolet

1977

WINSTON WESTERN 500

Time of Race: 2 hours, 54 minutes, 46 seconds
Average Speed: 107.038 Mph

FINISH	DRIVER	CAR
1	David Pearson	Mercury
2	Cale Yarborough	Chevrolet
3	Richard Petty	Dodge
4	Dave Marcis	Chevrolet
5	Sonny Easley	Ford
6	Richard Childress	Chevrolet
7	Hershel McGriff	Chevrolet
8	Hugh Pearson	Chevrolet
9	Darrell Waltrip	Chevrolet
10	Eddie Bradshaw	Chevrolet
11	Cecil Gordon	Chevrolet
12	Buddy Baker	Ford
13	Chuck Bown	Chevrolet
14	James Hylton	Chevrolet
15	D. K. Ulrich	Chevrolet
16	Jim Thirkettle	Chevrolet
17	Neil Bonnett	Dodge
18	Bobby Wawak	Chevrolet
19	Bill Schmitt	Chevrolet

20	Gary Johnson	Chevrolet
21	Benny Parsons	Chevrolet
22	Roy Smith	Chevrolet
23	Norm Palmer	Dodge
24	Gary Mathews	Plymouth
25	Frank Warren	Dodge
26	Chuck Wahl	Chevrolet
27	Ed Negre	Dodge
28	Bill Baker	Chevrolet
29	J. D. McDuffie	Chevrolet
30	Don Puskarich	Chevrolet
31	Carl Joiner	Chevrolet
32	Henley Gray	Chevrolet
33	Glen Francis	Chevrolet
34	Jim Insolo	Chevrolet
35	Bobby Allison	Matador

DAYTONA 500

Time of Race: 3 hours, 15 minutes, 48 seconds
Average Speed: 153.218 Mph

FINISH	DRIVER	CAR
1	Cale Yarborough	Chevrolet
2	Benny Parsons	Chevrolet
3	Buddy Baker	Ford
4	Coo Coo Marlin	Chevrolet
5	Dick Brooks	Ford
6	A. J. Foyt	Chevrolet
7	Darrell Waltrip	Chevrolet
8	Jimmy Means	Chevrolet
9	Bob Burcham	Chevrolet
10	James Hylton	Chevrolet
11	Frank Warren	Dodge
12	Janet Guthrie	Chevrolet
13	J. D. McDuffie	Chevrolet
14	D. K. Ulrich	Chevrolet
15	Bobby Allison	Matador
16	Tighe Scott	Chevrolet
17	Cecil Gordon	Chevrolet
18	Terry Ryan	Chevrolet
19	Walter Ballard	Chevrolet
20	Jim Vandiver	Dodge
21	David Pearson	Mercury
22	Ricky Rudd	Chevrolet
23	Richard Childress	Chevrolet
24	Salt Walther	Chevrolet
25	Bruce Hill	Chevrolet
26	Richard Petty	Dodge
27	Ramo Stott	Chevrolet
28	Dave Marcis	Mercury
29	Ed Negre	Dodge
30	Donnie Allison	Chevrolet
31	Sam Sommers	Chevrolet
32	Ron Hutcherson	Chevrolet
33	Jimmy Capps	Chevrolet
34	Grant Adcox	Chevrolet
35	Jim Hurtubise	Chevrolet
36	Skip Manning	Chevrolet
37	Neil Bonnett	Dodge
38	Buddy Arrington	Dodge
39	Roy Smith	Chevrolet
40	E. Forbes-Robinson	Dodge
41	Johnny Rutherford	Chevrolet
42	Bobby Wawak	Chevrolet

RICHMOND 400

Time of Race: 1 Hour, 49 minutes, 1 second
Average Speed: 73.084 Mph

FINISH	DRIVER	CAR
1	Cale Yarborough	Chevrolet
2	Darrell Waltrip	Chevrolet
3	Benny Parsons	Chevrolet
4	Dave Marcis	Chevrolet
5	Bobby Allison	Matador
6	Richard Petty	Dodge

7	Neil Bonnett	Dodge
8	James Hylton	Chevrolet
9	Buddy Baker	Ford
10	Richard Childress	Chevrolet
11	Tighe Scott	Chevrolet
12	Janet Guthrie	Chevrolet
13	Cecil Gordon	Chevrolet
14	Terry Bivins	Chevrolet
15	Ed Negre	Dodge
16	J. D. McDuffie	Chevrolet
17	Junior Miller	Chevrolet
18	Skip Manning	Chevrolet
19	Henley Gray	Chevrolet
20	Elmo Langley	Ford
21	Robin Schildknecht	Chevrolet
22	Walter Ballard	Chevrolet
23	Rick Newsom	Ford
24	Buddy Arrington	Dodge
25	Earl Brooks	Chevrolet
26	Ricky Rudd	Ford
27	Dick Brooks	Ford
28	D. K. Ulrich	Chevrolet
29	Jimmy Means	Chevrolet
30	Frank Warren	Dodge

CAROLINA 500

Time of Race: 5 hours, 6 minutes, 46 seconds
Average Speed: 97.86 Mph

FINISH	DRIVER	CAR
1	Richard Petty	Dodge
2	Darrell Waltrip	Chevrolet
3	Donnie Allison	Chevrolet
4	Buddy Baker	Ford
5	Neil Bonnett	Dodge
6	Cale Yarborough	Chevrolet
7	Sam Sommers	Chevrolet
8	Skip Manning	Chevrolet
9	James Hylton	Chevrolet
10	Cecil Gordon	Chevrolet
11	Gary Myers	Chevrolet
12	Benny Parsons	Chevrolet
13	Ed Negre	Dodge
14	Buddy Arrington	Dodge
15	J. D. McDuffie	Chevrolet
16	Henley Gray	Chevrolet
17	Richard Childress	Chevrolet
18	Jimmy Lee Capps	Chevrolet
19	Ricky Rudd	Chevrolet
20	E. Forbes-Robinson	Dodge
21	Tom Gale	Ford
22	Dick Brooks	Ford
23	D. K. Ulrich	Chevrolet
24	Dave Marcis	Chevrolet
25	Earl Brooks	Chevrolet
26	Terry Bivins	Chevrolet
27	Bobby Allison	Matador
28	Jimmy Means	Chevrolet
29	Joe Mihalic	Chevrolet
30	Bill Elliott	Ford
31	Junior Miller	Chevrolet
32	David Pearson	Mercury
33	Tighe Scott	Chevrolet
34	Lennie Pond	Chevrolet
35	Frank Warren	Dodge
36	Bruce Hill	Chevrolet

ATLANTA 500

Time of Race: 3 hours, 27 minutes, 51 seconds
Average Speed: 144.093 Mph

FINISH	DRIVER	CAR
1	Richard Petty	Dodge
2	David Pearson	Mercury
3	Cale Yarborough	Chevrolet
4	Donnie Allison	Chevrolet

5	Buddy Baker	Ford
6	Dave Marcis	Chevrolet
7	Darrell Waltrip	Chevrolet
8	Coo Coo Marlin	Chevrolet
9	Lennie Pond	Chevrolet
10	Bruce Hill	Chevrolet
11	Buddy Arrington	Dodge
12	Neil Bonnett	Dodge
13	Sam Sommers	Chevrolet
14	Jody Ridley	Mercury
15	Ramo Stott	Chevrolet
16	Cecil Gordon	Chevrolet
17	Harold Miller	Chevrolet
18	Jimmy Capps	Chevrolet
19	Richard Childress	Chevrolet
20	Jimmy Means	Chevrolet
21	G. C. Spencer	Dodge
22	Tom Gale	Ford
23	Dick Brooks	Ford
24	Terry Bivins	Chevrolet
25	Tighe Scott	Chevrolet
26	Benny Parsons	Chevrolet
27	Frank Warren	Dodge
28	Skip Manning	Chevrolet
29	D. K. Ulrich	Chevrolet
30	Janet Guthrie	Chevrolet
31	J. D. McDuffie	Chevrolet
32	Bill Elliott	Ford
33	Henley Gray	Chevrolet
34	A. J. Foyt	Chevrolet
35	Phil Finney	Chevrolet
36	E. Forbes-Robinson	Dodge
37	Dean Dalton	Chevrolet
38	James Hylton	Chevrolet
39	Ed Negre	Chevrolet
40	Johnny Rutherford	Chevrolet
41	Bobby Allison	Matador
42	Jim Hurtubise	Ford

GWYN STALEY 400

Time of Race: 2 hours, 48 minutes, 38 seconds
Average Speed: 88.950 Mph

FINISH	DRIVER	CAR
1	Cale Yarborough	Chevrolet
2	Richard Petty	Dodge
3	Benny Parsons	Chevrolet
4	Buddy Baker	Ford
5	Bobby Allison	Matador
6	Dick Brooks	Ford
7	Darrell Waltrip	Chevrolet
8	Richard Childress	Chevrolet
9	James Hylton	Chevrolet
10	Buddy Arrington	Dodge
11	Gary Myers	Chevrolet
12	Dave Marcis	Chevrolet
13	Cecil Gordon	Chevrolet
14	Henley Gray	Ford
15	Robin Schildnecht	Chevrolet
16	Frank Warren	Dodge
17	Terry Bivins	Chevrolet
18	Junior Miller	Chevrolet
19	David Sisco	Chevrolet
20	D. K. Ulrich	Chevrolet
21	Neil Bonnett	Dodge
22	J. D. McDuffie	Chevrolet
23	Tighe Scott	Chevrolet
24	Larry LeMay	Chevrolet
25	Earl Brooks	Chevrolet
26	Skip Manning	Chevrolet
27	Jimmy Means	Chevrolet
28	Ed Negre	Dodge
29	Rick Newsom	Ford

REBEL 500

Time of Race: 3 hours, 53 minutes, 18 seconds
Average Speed: 128.817 Mph

FINISH	DRIVER	CAR
1	Darrell Waltrip	Chevrolet
2	Donnie Allison	Chevrolet
3	Richard Petty	Dodge
4	David Pearson	Mercury
5	Benny Parsons	Chevrolet
6	Dave Marcis	Chevrolet
7	Buddy Baker	Ford
8	G. C. Spencer	Dodge
9	Dick Brooks	Ford
10	Bruce Hill	Chevrolet
11	Butch Hartman	Chevrolet
12	Cecil Gordon	Chevrolet
13	Sam Sommers	Chevrolet
14	Buddy Arrington	Dodge
15	Gary Myers	Chevrolet
16	Cale Yarborough	Chevrolet
17	Richard Childress	Chevrolet
18	Ferrel Harris	Chevrolet
19	J. D. McDuffie	Chevrolet
20	Jimmy Means	Chevrolet
21	Tom Gale	Ford
22	Ricky Rudd	Chevrolet
23	Skip Manning	Chevrolet
24	Ed Negre	Dodge
25	Joe Mihalic	Chevrolet
26	Tighe Scott	Chevrolet
27	Frank Warren	Dodge
28	Henley Gray	Chevrolet
29	Bobby Allison	Matador
30	Terry Bivins	Chevrolet
31	Lennie Pond	Chevrolet
32	James Hylton	Chevrolet
33	Neil Bonnett	Dodge
34	D. K. Ulrich	Chevrolet
35	Dean Dalton	Chevrolet
36	Earle Canavan	Dodge

SOUTHEASTERN 500

Time of Race: 2 hours, 38 minutes, 20 seconds
Average Speed: 100.989 Mph

FINISH	DRIVER	CAR
1	Cale Yarborough	Chevrolet
2	Dick Brooks	Ford
3	Richard Petty	Dodge
4	Neil Bonnett	Dodge
5	Benny Parsons	Chevrolet
6	Bobby Allison	Matador
7	James Hylton	Chevrolet
8	Richard Childress	Chevrolet
9	Jimmy Means	Chevrolet
10	Ricky Rudd	Chevrolet
11	Janet Guthrie	Chevrolet
12	Skip Manning	Chevrolet
13	Frank Warren	Dodge
14	Buddy Arrington	Dodge
15	Sam Sommers	Chevrolet
16	Elmo Langley	Ford
17	Cecil Gordon	Chevrolet
18	Ferrel Harris	Chevrolet
19	Darrell Waltrip	Chevrolet
20	J. D. McDuffie	Chevrolet
21	Dave Marcis	Chevrolet
22	David Sisco	Chevrolet
23	Henley Gray	Chevrolet
24	Junior Miller	Chevrolet
25	Ed Negre	Dodge
26	D. K. Ulrich	Chevrolet
27	Rick Newsom	Ford
28	Tighe Scott	Chevrolet
29	Buddy Baker	Ford
30	Larry LeMay	Chevrolet

VIRGINIA 500

Time of Race: 2 hours, 36 minutes, 26 seconds
Average Speed: 77.405 Mph

FINISH	DRIVER	CAR
1	Cale Yarborough	Chevrolet
2	Benny Parsons	Chevrolet
3	Richard Petty	Dodge
4	Lennie Pond	Chevrolet
5	David Pearson	Mercury
6	Dick Brooks	Ford
7	Bruce Hill	Chevrolet
8	Jimmy Means	Chevrolet
9	J. D. McDuffie	Chevrolet
10	Richard Childress	Chevrolet
11	Terry Bivins	Chevrolet
12	Neil Bonnett	Dodge
13	Cecil Gordon	Chevrolet
14	Tighe Scott	Chevrolet
15	D. K. Ulrich	Chevrolet
16	Ferrel Harris	Chevrolet
17	James Hylton	Chevrolet
18	Henley Gray	Chevrolet
19	Bobby Allison	Matador
20	Dave Marcis	Chevrolet
21	Darrell Waltrip	Chevrolet
22	Jimmy Hensley	Chevrolet
23	Tom Gale	Ford
24	Buddy Baker	Ford
25	Ed Negre	Dodge
26	Donnie Allison	Chevrolet
27	Skip Manning	Chevrolet
28	Sam Sommers	Chevrolet
29	Gary Myers	Chevrolet
30	Bobby Wawak	Chevrolet

WINSTON 500

Time of Race: 3 hours, 1 minute, 59 seconds
Average Speed: 164.877 Mph

FINISH	DRIVER	CAR
1	Darrell Waltrip	Chevrolet
2	Cale Yarborough	Chevrolet
3	Benny Parsons	Chevrolet
4	Donnie Allison	Chevrolet
5	Dave Marcis	Mercury
6	Ron Hutcherson	Chevrolet
7	Dick Brooks	Ford
8	Coo Coo Marlin	Chevrolet
9	Terry Bivins	Chevrolet
10	Sam Sommers	Chevrolet
11	Ramo Stott	Chevrolet
12	Peter Knab	Chevrolet
13	Frank Warren	Dodge
14	Ferrel Harris	Chevrolet
15	Tom Gale	Ford
16	Cecil Gordon	Chevrolet
17	Tighe Scott	Chevrolet
18	James Hylton	Chevrolet
19	Buddy Arrington	Dodge
20	Richard Petty	Dodge
21	Richard Childress	Chevrolet
22	David Pearson	Mercury
23	Skip Manning	Chevrolet
24	Joe Frasson	Chevrolet
25	Butch Hartman	Chevrolet
26	J. D. McDuffie	Chevrolet
27	Bruce Hill	Chevrolet
28	Ricky Rudd	Chevrolet
29	Neil Bonnett	Dodge
30	David Sisco	Chevrolet
31	D. K. Ulrich	Chevrolet
32	Janet Guthrie	Chevrolet
33	Buddy Baker	Ford
34	Jimmy Means	Chevrolet
35	Terry Ryan	Chevrolet
36	Richard Skillen	Chevrolet
37	Grant Adcox	Chevrolet
38	A. J. Foyt	Chevrolet
39	Henley Gray	Dodge
40	Bobby Allison	Matador
41	Ed Negre	Dodge

MUSIC CITY USA 420

Time of Race: 2 hours, 51 minutes, 40 seconds
Average Speed: 87.490 Mph

FINISH	DRIVER	CAR
1	Benny Parsons	Chevrolet
2	Cale Yarborough	Chevrolet
3	Darrell Waltrip	Chevrolet
4	Dave Marcis	Chevrolet
5	Richard Petty	Dodge
6	Buddy Baker	Ford
7	Bobby Allison	Matador
8	Coo Coo Marlin	Chevrolet
9	Jimmy Means	Chevrolet
10	Ricky Rudd	Chevrolet
11	James Hylton	Chevrolet
12	Gary Myers	Chevrolet
13	Cecil Gordon	Chevrolet
14	D. K. Ulrich	Chevrolet
15	Buddy Arrington	Dodge
16	Rick Newsom	Ford
17	Earl Brooks	Chevrolet
18	Ralph Jones	Ford
19	David Sisco	Chevrolet
20	Ferrel Harris	Chevrolet
21	Skip Manning	Chevrolet
22	Dick Brooks	Ford
23	Elmo Langley	Chevrolet
24	J. D. McDuffie	Chevrolet
25	Henley Gray	Chevrolet
26	Richard Childress	Chevrolet
27	Terry Ryan	Chevrolet
28	Paul Dean Holt	Ford
29	Frank Warren	Dodge
30	Dean Dalton	Chevrolet

MASON-DIXON 500

Time of Race: 4 hours, 3 minutes, 26 seconds
Average Speed: 123.327 Mph

FINISH	DRIVER	CAR
1	Cale Yarborough	Chevrolet
2	David Pearson	Mercury
3	Richard Petty	Dodge
4	Darrell Waltrip	Chevrolet
5	Dick Brooks	Ford
6	Benny Parsons	Chevrolet
7	Lennie Pond	Chevrolet
8	Bobby Allison	Matador
9	Buddy Baker	Ford
10	Morgan Shepherd	Mercury
11	Buddy Arrington	Dodge
12	Cecil Gordon	Chevrolet
13	J. D. McDuffie	Chevrolet
14	Tighe Scott	Chevrolet
15	Ed Negre	Dodge
16	Dick May	Ford
17	Skip Manning	Chevrolet
18	Tom Gale	Ford
19	Ferrel Harris	Chevrolet
20	D. K. Ulrich	Chevrolet
21	Richard Childress	Chevrolet
22	Gary Myers	Chevrolet
23	Earle Canavan	Dodge
24	Baxter Price	Chevrolet
25	Earl Brooks	Chevrolet
26	Frank Warren	Dodge
27	Ricky Rudd	Chevrolet
28	Rick Newsom	Ford
29	Jimmy Means	Chevrolet
30	David Sisco	Chevrolet
31	Elmo Langley	Chevrolet
32	Henley Gray	Chevrolet
33	James Hylton	Chevrolet
34	Dean Dalton	Chevrolet
35	Bruce Hill	Chevrolet
36	Raymond Williams	Ford

WORLD 600

Time of Race: 4 hours, 21 minutes, 29 seconds
Average Speed: 137.676 Mph

FINISH	DRIVER	CAR
1	Richard Petty	Dodge
2	David Pearson	Mercury
3	Benny Parsons	Chevrolet
4	Lennie Pond	Chevrolet
5	Buddy Baker	Ford
6	Darrell Waltrip	Chevrolet
7	Neil Bonnett	Dodge
8	Dick Brooks	Ford
9	Sam Sommers	Chevrolet
10	Skip Manning	Chevrolet
11	Ron Hutcherson	Chevrolet
12	Coo Coo Marlin	Chevrolet
13	Morgan Shepherd	Mercury
14	Richard Childress	Chevrolet
15	Bill Elliott	Ford
16	Tighe Scott	Chevrolet
17	Ricky Rudd	Chevrolet
18	Buddy Arrington	Dodge
19	Jimmy Means	Chevrolet
20	G. C. Spencer	Dodge
21	Dick May	Ford
22	Cecil Gordon	Chevrolet
23	Butch Hartman	Chevrolet
24	Cale Yarborough	Chevrolet
25	J. D. McDuffie	Chevrolet
26	Frank Warren	Dodge
27	Harold Miller	Chevrolet
28	James Hylton	Chevrolet
29	Terry Ryan	Chevrolet
30	Harry Gant	Chevrolet
31	Bruce Hill	Chevrolet
32	David Sisco	Chevrolet
33	Donnie Allison	Chevrolet
34	D. K. Ulrich	Chevrolet
35	Ed Negre	Dodge
36	Dave Marcis	Mercury
37	Tom Gale	Ford
38	Henley Gray	Chevrolet
39	Bobby Allison	Matador
40	Ramo Stott	Chevrolet

NAPA RIVERSIDE 400

Time of Race: 2 hours, 22 minutes, 12 seconds
Average Speed: 105.021 Mph

FINISH	DRIVER	CAR
1	Richard Petty	Dodge
2	David Pearson	Mercury
3	Cale Yarborough	Chevrolet
4	Jim Insolo	Ford
5	Buddy Baker	Ford
6	Norm Palmer	Dodge
7	Sonny Easley	Ford
8	Richard Childress	Chevrolet
9	Cecil Gordon	Chevrolet
10	Skip Manning	Chevrolet
11	D. K. Ulrich	Chevrolet
12	Dick Brooks	Ford
13	John Dineen	Ford
14	James Hylton	Chevrolet
15	Frank Warren	Dodge
16	Bill Baker	Chevrolet
17	Bobby Allison	Matador
18	Chuck Wahl	Chevrolet
19	Buddy Arrington	Dodge
20	Ernie Stierly	Chevrolet
21	Harry Goularte	Chevrolet
22	Richard White	Chevrolet
23	Roy Smith	Chevrolet
24	Jim Thirkettle	Chevrolet
25	Chuck Bown	Chevrolet

FINISH	DRIVER	CAR
26	Darrell Waltrip	Chevrolet
27	Benny Parsons	Chevrolet
28	Don Puskarich	Chevrolet
29	Gary Johnson	Chevrolet
30	Bill Schmitt	Chevrolet
31	Sumner McKnight	Chevrolet
32	Ray Elder	Plymouth
33	J. D. McDuffie	Chevrolet
34	Hershel McGriff	Chevrolet
35	Don Noel	Chevrolet

CAM 2 MOTOR OIL 400

Time of Race: 2 hours, 57 minutes, 44 seconds
Average Speed: 135.033 Mph

FINISH	DRIVER	CAR
1	Cale Yarborough	Chevrolet
2	Richard Petty	Dodge
3	Benny Parsons	Chevrolet
4	Dave Marcis	Chevrolet
5	David Pearson	Mercury
6	Buddy Baker	Ford
7	Dick Brooks	Ford
8	Sam Sommers	Chevrolet
9	Butch Hartman	Chevrolet
10	Bobby Allison	Matador
11	James Hylton	Chevrolet
12	Bill Seifert	Ford
13	Marty Robbins	Dodge
14	Jimmy Means	Chevrolet
15	Bill Elliott	Ford
16	D. K. Ulrich	Chevrolet
17	Terry Ryan	Chevrolet
18	Bobby Wawak	Chevrolet
19	Buddy Arrington	Dodge
20	J. D. McDuffie	Chevrolet
21	Cecil Gordon	Chevrolet
22	Henley Gray	Chevrolet
23	Tom Gale	Ford
24	Donnie Allison	Chevrolet
25	David Sisco	Chevrolet
26	Janet Guthrie	Chevrolet
27	Skip Manning	Chevrolet
28	Ricky Rudd	Chevrolet
29	Roland Wlodyka	Chevrolet
30	Frank Warren	Dodge
31	Tighe Scott	Chevrolet
32	Bruce Hill	Chevrolet
33	John Kennedy	Ford
34	Richard Childress	Chevrolet
35	Darrell Waltrip	Chevrolet
36	Ferrel Harris	Chevrolet

FIRECRACKER 400

Time of Race: 2 hours, 48 minutes, 10 seconds
Average Speed: 142.716 Mph

FINISH	DRIVER	CAR
1	Richard Petty	Dodge
2	Darrell Waltrip	Chevrolet
3	Benny Parsons	Chevrolet
4	David Pearson	Mercury
5	A.J. Foyt	Chevrolet
6	Donnie Allison	Chevrolet
7	Buddy Baker	Ford
8	Neil Bonnett	Dodge
9	Dick Brooks	Ford
10	Sam Sommers	Chevrolet
11	Cecil Gordon	Chevrolet
12	Terry Ryan	Chevrolet
13	Coo Coo Marlin	Chevrolet
14	G. C. Spencer	Dodge
15	Jim Hurtubise	Chevrolet

Darrell Waltrip tries to explain just what happened to him out on the track.

FINISH	DRIVER	CAR
16	Skip Manning	Chevrolet
17	Bobby Allison	Matador
18	Butch Hartman	Chevrolet
19	Richard Childress	Chevrolet
20	Jimmy Means	Chevrolet
21	Frank Warren	Dodge
22	Buddy Arrington	Dodge
23	Cale Yarborough	Chevrolet
24	J. D. McDuffie	Chevrolet
25	Baxter Price	Chevrolet
26	Grant Adcox	Chevrolet
27	Tighe Scott	Chevrolet
28	Harold Miller	Chevrolet
29	Ron Hutcherson	Chevrolet
30	Bruce Hill	Chevrolet
31	Lella Lombardi	Chevrolet
32	Ramo Stott	Chevrolet
33	Lennie Pond	Chevrolet
34	David Sisco	Chevrolet
35	Bill Elliott	Ford
36	Ricky Rudd	Chevrolet
37	Christine Beckers	Ford
38	Tom Gale	Ford
39	James Hylton	Chevrolet
40	Janet Guthrie	Chevrolet
41	D. K. Ulrich	Chevrolet

NASHVILLE 420

Time of Race: 3 hours, 10 minutes, 09 seconds
Average Speed: 78.999 Mph

FINISH	DRIVER	CAR
1	Darrell Waltrip	Chevrolet
2	Bobby Allison	Matador
3	Richard Petty	Dodge
4	Cale Yarborough	Chevrolet
5	Dick Brooks	Ford
6	Buddy Baker	Ford
7	Skip Manning	Chevrolet
8	J. D. McDuffie	Chevrolet

FINISH	DRIVER	CAR
9	Buddy Arrington	Dodge
10	Ricky Rudd	Chevrolet
11	Coo Coo Marlin	Chevrolet
12	Frank Warren	Dodge
13	Tighe Scott	Chevrolet
14	D. K. Ulrich	Chevrolet
15	Janet Guthrie	Chevrolet
16	Baxter Price	Chevrolet
17	Henley Gray	Chevrolet
18	Benny Parsons	Chevrolet
19	James Hylton	Chevrolet
20	Cecil Gordon	Chevrolet
21	Neil Bonnett	Dodge
22	David Sisco	Chevrolet
23	Ralph Jones	Ford
24	Sam Sommers	Chevrolet
25	Grant Adcox	Chevrolet
26	Gary Myers	Chevrolet
27	Richard Childress	Chevrolet
28	Elmo Langley	Ford
29	Jimmy Means	Chevrolet
30	Mike Kempton	Chevrolet

COCA-COLA 500

Time of Race: 3 hours, 53 minutes, 41 seconds
Average Speed: 128.379 Mph

FINISH	DRIVER	CAR
1	Benny Parsons	Chevrolet
2	Richard Petty	Dodge
3	Darrell Waltrip	Chevrolet
4	Bobby Allison	Matador
5	Dick Brooks	Ford
6	Cale Yarborough	Chevrolet
7	Ricky Rudd	Chevrolet
8	Skip Manning	Chevrolet
9	Butch Hartman	Chevrolet
10	James Hylton	Chevrolet
11	Janet Guthrie	Chevrolet
12	Kenny Brightbill	Mercury
13	Tighe Scott	Chevrolet
14	J. D. McDuffie	Chevrolet
15	Buddy Arrington	Dodge
16	Ed Negre	Dodge
17	Richard Childress	Chevrolet
18	Joe Mihalic	Chevrolet
19	Frank Warren	Dodge
20	Jimmy Means	Chevrolet
21	Cecil Gordon	Chevrolet
22	Baxter Price	Chevrolet
23	Nestor Peles	Chevrolet
24	Dick May	Ford
25	Tom Gale	Ford
26	C. Maggiacomo	Matador
27	Buddy Baker	Ford
28	David Pearson	Mercury
29	Greg Heller	Ford
30	Gary Myers	Chevrolet
31	Roland Wlodyka	Chevrolet
32	Sam Sommers	Chevrolet
33	Ronnie Thomas	Chevrolet
34	D. K. Ulrich	Chevrolet
35	Earle Canavan	Dodge

TALLADEGA 500

Time of Race: 3 hours, 4 minutes, 37 seconds
Average Speed: 162.524 Mph

FINISH	DRIVER	CAR
1	Donnie Allison	Chevrolet
2	Cale Yarborough	Chevrolet
3	Skip Manning	Chevrolet

FINISH	DRIVER	CAR
4	Ricky Rudd	Chevrolet
5	Lennie Pond	Chevrolet
6	Buddy Baker	Ford
7	Bobby Allison	Matador
8	J. D. McDuffie	Chevrolet
9	James Hylton	Chevrolet
10	Frank Warren	Dodge
11	Richard Petty	Dodge
12	Buddy Arrington	Dodge
13	Harold Miller	Chevrolet
14	Tom Gale	Ford
15	Grant Adcox	Chevrolet
16	Cecil Gordon	Chevrolet
17	Dick May	Chevrolet
18	D. K. Ulrich	Chevrolet
19	Steve Moore	Chevrolet
20	Richard Childress	Chevrolet
21	Johnny Rutherford	Chevrolet
22	Darrell Waltrip	Chevrolet
23	Bill Elliott	Mercury
24	Benny Parsons	Chevrolet
25	Neil Bonnett	Dodge
26	Sam Sommers	Chevrolet
27	Tighe Scott	Chevrolet
28	David Sisco	Chevrolet
29	Butch Hartman	Chevrolet
30	Jim Raptis	Chevrolet
31	G. C. Spencer	Dodge
32	Joe Mihalic	Chevrolet
33	Peter Knab	Chevrolet
34	Janet Guthrie	Chevrolet
35	Bruce Hill	Chevrolet
36	Jimmy Means	Chevrolet
37	David Pearson	Mercury
38	Marty Robbins	Dodge
39	Dick Brooks	Ford
40	Coo Coo Marlin	Chevrolet

CHAMPION SPARK PLUG 400

Time of Race: 2 hours, 53 minutes, 59 seconds
Average Speed: 137.944 Mph

FINISH	DRIVER	CAR
1	Darrell Waltrip	Chevrolet
2	David Pearson	Mercury
3	Benny Parsons	Chevrolet
4	Sam Sommers	Chevrolet
5	Cale Yarborough	Chevrolet
6	Dick Brooks	Ford
7	Ricky Rudd	Chevrolet
8	Richard Petty	Dodge
9	Terry Ryan	Chevrolet
10	Janet Guthrie	Chevrolet
11	Tighe Scott	Chevrolet
12	Skip Manning	Chevrolet
13	Bruce Hill	Chevrolet
14	Buddy Arrington	Dodge
15	Bobby Wawak	Chevrolet
16	James Hylton	Chevrolet
17	Jimmy Means	Chevrolet
18	D. K. Ulrich	Chevrolet
19	Cecil Gordon	Chevrolet
20	J. D. McDuffie	Chevrolet
21	Dean Dalton	Chevrolet
22	Dave Marcis	Chevrolet
23	Frank Warren	Dodge
24	Joe Mihalic	Chevrolet
25	Butch Hartman	Chevrolet
26	Bobby Allison	Matador
27	C. Maggiacomo	Matador
28	Harold Miller	Chevrolet
29	Bill Elliott	Mercury
30	Buddy Baker	Ford
31	Ed Negre	Dodge
32	Tom Gale	Ford
33	Richard Childress	Chevrolet
34	Baxter Price	Chevrolet
35	Elmo Langley	Dodge
36	Earle Canavan	Dodge

VOLUNTEER 400

Time of Race: 2 hours, 40 minutes, 27 seconds
Average Speed: 79.726 Mph

FINISH	DRIVER	CAR
1	Cale Yarborough	Chevrolet
2	Darrell Waltrip	Chevrolet
3	Benny Parsons	Chevrolet
4	Dick Brooks	Ford
5	Tighe Scott	Chevrolet
6	Janet Guthrie	Chevrolet
7	Skip Manning	Chevrolet
8	Richard Childress	Chevrolet
9	James Hylton	Chevrolet
10	Buddy Arrington	Dodge
11	D. K. Ulrich	Chevrolet
12	Ed Negre	Dodge
13	Frank Warren	Dodge
14	Ferrel Harris	Chevrolet
15	Buddy Baker	Ford
16	Ricky Rudd	Chevrolet
17	Neil Bonnett	Dodge
18	J. D. McDuffie	Chevrolet
19	Ralph Jones	Ford
20	Sam Sommers	Chevrolet
21	Travis Tiller	Dodge
22	Richard Petty	Dodge
23	Dean Dalton	Ford
24	Dick May	Chevrolet
25	Earl Brooks	Chevrolet
26	Baxter Price	Chevrolet
27	Jimmy Means	Chevrolet
28	Bobby Allison	Matador
29	Cecil Gordon	Chevrolet

SOUTHERN 500

Time of Race: 4 hours, 41 minutes, 48 seconds
Average Speed: 106.797 Mph

FINISH	DRIVER	CAR
1	David Pearson	Mercury
2	Donnie Allison	Chevrolet
3	Buddy Baker	Ford
4	Richard Petty	Dodge
5	Cale Yarborough	Chevrolet
6	Darrell Waltrip	Chevrolet
7	Ricky Rudd	Chevrolet
8	Richard Childress	Chevrolet
9	Bruce Hill	Chevrolet
10	Bill Elliott	Ford
11	Ed Negre	Dodge
12	J. D. McDuffie	Chevrolet
13	James Hylton	Chevrolet
14	Buddy Arrington	Dodge
15	Gary Myers	Chevrolet
16	Janet Guthrie	Chevrolet
17	Frank Warren	Dodge
18	Tom Gale	Ford
19	Cecil Gordon	Chevrolet
20	Mike Kempton	Chevrolet
21	Baxter Price	Chevrolet
22	Bobby Wawak	Chevrolet
23	Earle Canavan	Dodge
24	Terry Bivins	Chevrolet
25	Benny Parsons	Chevrolet
26	Coo Coo Marlin	Chevrolet
27	D. K. Ulrich	Chevrolet
28	Lennie Pond	Chevrolet
29	Sam Sommers	Chevrolet
30	Ralph Jones	Ford
31	Dick May	Ford
32	Tighe Scott	Chevrolet
33	Ferrel Harris	Chevrolet
34	Dick Brooks	Ford
35	Butch Hartman	Chevrolet
36	Roland Wlodyka	Chevrolet

37	G. C. Spencer	Dodge
38	Skip Manning	Chevrolet
39	Bobby Allison	Matador
40	Joe Mihalic	Chevrolet

CAPITAL CITY 400

Time of Race: 2 hours, 41 minutes, 18 seconds
Average Speed: 80.644 Mph

FINISH	DRIVER	CAR
1	Neil Bonnett	Dodge
2	Richard Petty	Dodge
3	Benny Parsons	Chevrolet
4	Cale Yarborough	Chevrolet
5	Lennie Pond	Chevrolet
6	Bobby Allison	Matador
7	Darrell Waltrip	Chevrolet
8	Dick Brooks	Ford
9	James Hylton	Chevrolet
10	Jimmy Means	Chevrolet
11	Ricky Rudd	Chevrolet
12	Janet Guthrie	Chevrolet
13	J. D. McDuffie	Chevrolet
14	D. K. Ulrich	Chevrolet
15	Skip Manning	Chevrolet
16	Ed Negre	Dodge
17	Cecil Gordon	Chevrolet
18	Tighe Scott	Chevrolet
19	Dick May	Chevrolet
20	Frank Warren	Dodge
21	Baxter Price	Chevrolet
22	Ferrel Harris	Chevrolet
23	Marv Acton	Chevrolet
24	Tom Gale	Ford
25	Buddy Arrington	Dodge
26	Richard Childress	Chevrolet
27	Buddy Baker	Ford
28	Rick Newsom	Chevrolet

DELAWARE 500

Time of Race: 4 hours, 21 minutes, 32 seconds
Average Speed: 114.706 Mph

FINISH	DRIVER	CAR
1	Benny Parsons	Chevrolet
2	David Pearson	Mercury
3	Cale Yarborough	Chevrolet
4	Donnie Allison	Chevrolet
5	Darrell Waltrip	Chevrolet
6	Buddy Baker	Ford
7	Richard Childress	Chevrolet
8	Dick Brooks	Ford
9	Bobby Allison	Matador
10	Sam Sommers	Chevrolet
11	Janet Guthrie	Chevrolet
12	J. D. McDuffie	Chevrolet
13	Buddy Arrington	Dodge
14	Jimmy Means	Chevrolet
15	Ed Negre	Dodge
16	James Hylton	Chevrolet
17	Neil Bonnett	Dodge
18	Joe Mihalic	Chevrolet
19	Skip Manning	Chevrolet
20	Dick May	Chevrolet
21	Cecil Gordon	Chevrolet
22	Frank Warren	Dodge
23	Richard Petty	Dodge
24	Tighe Scott	Chevrolet
25	Ronnie Thomas	Chevrolet
26	Tom Gale	Ford
27	Rick Newsom	Chevrolet
28	C. Maggiacomo	Matador
29	Dean Dalton	Dodge
30	Lennie Pond	Chevrolet

31	D. K. Ulrich	Chevrolet
32	Ricky Rudd	Chevrolet
33	Bill Seifert	Chevrolet
34	Gary Myers	Chevrolet
35	Nestor Peles	Chevrolet
36	Steve Stolarek	Chevrolet
37	Baxter Price	Chevrolet
38	Marv Acton	Chevrolet
39	Jim Hurtubise	Ford
40	Kenny Brightbill	Mercury

OLD DOMINION 500

Time of Race: 3 hours, 34 minutes, 40 seconds
Average Speed: 73.447 Mph

FINISH	DRIVER	CAR
1	Cale Yarborough	Chevrolet
2	Benny Parsons	Chevrolet
3	David Pearson	Mercury
4	Richard Petty	Dodge
5	Sam Sommers	Chevrolet
6	Jimmy Hensley	Chevrolet
7	Buddy Arrington	Dodge
8	James Hylton	Chevrolet
9	Jimmy Means	Chevrolet
10	Darrell Waltrip	Chevrolet
11	Frank Warren	Dodge
12	D. K. Ulrich	Chevrolet
13	Skip Manning	Chevrolet
14	Dick May	Chevrolet
15	Richard Childress	Chevrolet
16	Elmo Langley	Ford
17	J. D. McDuffie	Chevrolet
18	Cecil Gordon	Chevrolet
19	Ronnie Thomas	Chevrolet
20	Tighe Scott	Chevrolet
21	Buddy Baker	Ford
22	Neil Bonnett	Dodge
23	Bobby Allison	Matador
24	Ed Negre	Dodge
25	Lennie Pond	Chevrolet
26	Dick Brooks	Ford
27	Ricky Rudd	Chevrolet
28	Donnie Allison	Chevrolet
29	Travis Tiller	Dodge
30	Baxter Price	Chevrolet

WILKES 400

Time of Race: 2 hours, 52 minutes, 59 seconds
Average Speed: 86.713 Mph

FINISH	DRIVER	CAR
1	Darrell Waltrip	Chevrolet
2	Cale Yarborough	Chevrolet
3	Neil Bonnett	Dodge
4	Bobby Allison	Matador
5	Benny Parsons	Chevrolet
6	Richard Childress	Chevrolet
7	Ricky Rudd	Chevrolet
8	Dick Brooks	Ford
9	Buddy Baker	Ford
10	Buddy Arrington	Dodge
11	Jimmy Means	Chevrolet
12	James Hylton	Chevrolet
13	Skip Manning	Ford
14	Sam Sommers	Chevrolet
15	Cecil Gordon	Chevrolet
16	Walter Ballard	Chevrolet
17	Ed Negre	Dodge
18	Baxter Price	Chevrolet
19	Roger Hamby	Chevrolet
20	Dick May	Chevrolet
21	Frank Warren	Dodge
22	D. K. Ulrich	Chevrolet
23	J. D. McDuffie	Chevrolet

24	Richard Petty	Dodge
25	Ferrel Harris	Chevrolet
26	Junior Miller	Chevrolet

NAPA NATIONAL 500

Time of Race: 3 hours, 30 minutes, 32 seconds
Average Speed: 142.780 Mph

FINISH	DRIVER	CAR
1	Benny Parsons	Chevrolet
2	Cale Yarborough	Chevrolet
3	David Pearson	Mercury
4	Buddy Baker	Ford
5	Darrell Waltrip	Chevrolet
6	Dick Brooks	Ford
7	A. J. Foyt	Chevrolet
8	Neil Bonnett	Dodge
9	Janet Guthrie	Chevrolet
10	Bill Elliott	Mercury
11	Ron Hutcherson	Chevrolet
12	Coo Coo Marlin	Chevrolet
13	Dick May	Chevrolet
14	James Hylton	Chevrolet
15	J. D. McDuffie	Chevrolet
16	Richard Childress	Chevrolet
17	Buddy Arrington	Dodge
18	G. C. Spencer	Dodge
19	D. K. Ulrich	Chevrolet
20	Peter Knab	Chevrolet
21	Tom Gale	Ford
22	Ed Negre	Dodge
23	Dave Marcis	Chevrolet
24	Ricky Rudd	Chevrolet
25	Tighe Scott	Chevrolet
26	Bobby Allison	Matador
27	Tom Sneva	Dodge
28	Jimmy Means	Chevrolet
29	Dick Trickle	Chevrolet
30	Lennie Pond	Chevrolet
31	Butch Hartman	Chevrolet
32	Richard Petty	Dodge
33	Frank Warren	Dodge
34	Sam Sommers	Chevrolet
35	Skip Manning	Chevrolet
36	Donnie Allison	Chevrolet
37	Cecil Gordon	Chevrolet
38	Dale Earnhardt	Chevrolet
39	Roland Wlodyka	Chevrolet
40	Jim Raptis	Chevrolet
41	Bruce Hill	Chevrolet

AMERICAN 500

Time of Race: 4 hours, 24 minutes, 18 seconds
Average Speed: 113.584 Mph

FINISH	DRIVER	CAR
1	Donnie Allison	Chevrolet
2	Richard Petty	Dodge
3	Darrell Waltrip	Chevrolet
4	Cale Yarborough	Chevrolet
5	Dick Brooks	Ford
6	Bobby Allison	Matador
7	Benny Parsons	Chevrolet
8	Skip Manning	Chevrolet
9	Janet Guthrie	Chevrolet
10	J. D. McDuffie	Chevrolet
11	Bobby Wawak	Chevrolet
12	Buddy Arrington	Dodge
13	James Hylton	Chevrolet
14	Dick May	Chevrolet
15	Tom Gale	Ford
16	Baxter Price	Chevrolet
17	Sam Sommers	Chevrolet
18	Richard Childress	Chevrolet
19	Dean Dalton	Ford

FINISH	DRIVER	CAR
20	Randy Myers	Chevrolet
21	Joe Mihalic	Chevrolet
22	Jimmy Means	Chevrolet
23	Cecil Gordon	Chevrolet
24	Ed Negre	Dodge
25	Ricky Rudd	Chevrolet
26	Bruce Hill	Chevrolet
27	David Pearson	Mercury
28	Neil Bonnett	Dodge
29	Buddy Baker	Ford
30	Ronnie Thomas	Chevrolet
31	Dave Marcis	Chevrolet
32	Travis Tiller	Chevrolet
33	D. K. Ulrich	Chevrolet
34	Tighe Scott	Chevrolet
35	Frank Warren	Dodge
36	Lennie Pond	Chevrolet

DIXIE 500

Time of Race: 3 hours, 42 minutes, 23 seconds
Average Speed: 110.052 Mph

FINISH	DRIVER	CAR
1	Darrell Waltrip	Chevrolet
2	David Pearson	Mercury
3	Benny Parsons	Chevrolet
4	Donnie Allison	Chevrolet
5	Cale Yarborough	Chevrolet
6	Richard Petty	Dodge
7	Buddy Baker	Ford
8	Ricky Rudd	Chevrolet
9	Bobby Allison	Matador
10	Coo Coo Marlin	Chevrolet
11	Bill Elliott	Mercury
12	Butch Hartman	Chevrolet
13	Skip Manning	Chevrolet
14	Billy McGinnis	Chevrolet
15	Bruce Hill	Chevrolet
16	Janet Guthrie	Chevrolet
17	Buddy Arrington	Dodge
18	D. K. Ulrich	Chevrolet
19	Tighe Scott	Chevrolet
20	Cecil Gordon	Chevrolet
21	Richard Childress	Chevrolet
22	Grant Adcox	Chevrolet
23	Frank Warren	Dodge
24	Ervin Wangerin	Mercury
25	G. C. Spencer	Dodge
26	James Hylton	Chevrolet
27	J. D. McDuffie	Chevrolet
28	Sam Sommers	Chevrolet
29	Bobby Wawak	Chevrolet
30	Harold Miller	Chevrolet
31	Roger Hamby	Chevrolet
32	Dick May	Chevrolet
33	Morgan Shepherd	Mercury
34	Bob Burcham	Chevrolet
35	Ed Negre	Dodge
36	Dave Marcis	Chevrolet
37	Dick Brooks	Ford
38	Neil Bonnett	Dodge
39	Jim Raptis	Chevrolet
40	Jimmy Means	Chevrolet

LOS ANGELES TIMES 500

Time of Race: 3 hours, 53 minutes, 50 seconds
Average Speed: 128.296 Mph

FINISH	DRIVER	CAR
1	Neil Bonnett	Dodge
2	Richard Petty	Dodge
3	Cale Yarborough	Chevrolet
4	Buddy Baker	Ford
5	David Pearson	Mercury
6	Dick Brooks	Ford

FINISH	DRIVER	CAR
7	Bobby Allison	Matador
8	Ricky Rudd	Chevrolet
9	James Hylton	Chevrolet
10	Richard Childress	Chevrolet
11	A. J. Foyt	Chevrolet
12	Benny Parsons	Chevrolet
13	Joe Ruttman	Ford
14	Dave Marcis	Chevrolet
15	Roland Wlodyka	Chevrolet
16	Frank Warren	Dodge
17	Tighe Scott	Chevrolet
18	Harry Jefferson	Ford
19	Buddy Arrington	Ford
20	J. D. McDuffie	Chevrolet
21	D. K. Ulrich	Chevrolet
22	Tom Gale	Ford
23	Bill Osborne	Chevrolet
24	Janet Guthrie	Chevrolet
25	Richard White	Chevrolet
26	Sonny Easley	Ford
27	Ed Negre	Dodge
28	John Borneman	Chevrolet
29	Darrell Waltrip	Chevrolet
30	Don Graham	Chevrolet
31	Ron McGee	Chevrolet
32	Cecil Gordon	Chevrolet
33	V. Giamformaggio	Chevrolet
34	Norm Palmer	Dodge
35	Ernie Stierly	Chevrolet
36	John Kieper	Chevrolet
37	Eddie Bradshaw	Chevrolet
38	Sam Sommers	Chevrolet
39	Chuck Bown	Chevrolet
40	Roger McCluskey	Chevrolet
41	Bill Schmitt	Chevrolet
42	Donnie Allison	Chevrolet

1978

WINSTON WESTERN 500

Time of Race: 3 hours, 2 minutes, 55 seconds
Average Speed: 102.269 mph

FINISH	DRIVER	CAR
1	Cale Yarborough	Oldsmobile
2	Benny Parsons	Chevrolet
3	David Pearson	Mercury
4	Neil Bonnett	Dodge
5	Dave Marcis	Chevrolet
6	Hershel McGriff	Ford
7	Jim Insolo	Chevrolet
8	Al Holbert	Chevrolet
9	Roy Smith	Chevrolet
10	D. K. Ulrich	Chevrolet
11	Buddy Arrington	Ford
12	Rick McCray	Dodge
13	Frank Warren	Dodge
14	Norm Palmer	Dodge
15	Dick Brooks	Ford
16	Richard Petty	Dodge
17	Jim Thirkettle	Buick
18	Tighe Scott	Chevrolet
19	Ernie Stierly	Chevrolet
20	Richard Childress	Chevrolet
21	Skip Manning	Chevrolet
22	Jack Simpson	Chevrolet
23	Darrell Waltrip	Chevrolet
24	Richard White	Chevrolet
25	Cecil Gordon	Chevrolet
26	Rocky Moran	Chevrolet
27	John Borneman	Chevrolet
28	J. D. McDuffie	Chevrolet
29	V. Giamformaggio	Chevrolet
30	Bobby Allison	Ford

31	Don Puskarich	Chevrolet
32	Bill Schmitt	Chevrolet
33	Eddie Bradshaw	Chevrolet
34	Ray Elder	Dodge
35	Gary Johnson	Chevrolet

DAYTONA 500

Time of Race: 3 hours, 07 minutes, 49 seconds
Average Speed: 159.730 mph

FINISH	DRIVER	CAR
1	Bobby Allison	Ford
2	Cale Yarborough	Oldsmobile
3	Benny Parsons	Oldsmobile
4	Ron Hutcherson	Buick
5	Dick Brooks	Mercury
6	Dave Marcis	Chevrolet
7	Buddy Baker	Oldsmobile
8	Bill Elliott	Mercury
9	Ferrel Harris	Dodge
10	Lennie Pond	Oldsmobile
11	Tighe Scott	Oldsmobile
12	Skip Manning	Buick
13	Richard Childress	Oldsmobile
14	Grant Adcox	Chevrolet
15	Roger Hamby	Chevrolet
16	Buddy Arrington	Dodge
17	D. K. Ulrich	Chevrolet
18	Dick May	Ford
19	Roland Wlodyka	Buick
20	Jerry Jolly	Chevrolet
21	Cecil Gordon	Chevrolet
22	Claude Ballot-Lena	Dodge
23	Jimmy Lee Capps	Chevrolet
24	Frank Warren	Dodge
25	Tom Gale	Ford
26	Coo Coo Marlin	Chevrolet
27	Neil Bonnett	Dodge
28	Darrell Waltrip	Chevrolet
29	Al Holbert	Chevrolet
30	J. D. McDuffie	Chevrolet
31	Joe Mihalic	Oldsmobile
32	A. J. Foyt	Buick
33	Richard Petty	Dodge
34	David Pearson	Mercury
35	Jimmy Means	Chevrolet
36	Blackie Wangerin	Mercury
37	Ricky Rudd	Chevrolet
38	Jim Vandiver	Chevrolet
39	Donnie Allison	Oldsmobile
40	Morgan Shepherd	Mercury
41	Harry Gant	Buick

RICHMOND 400

Time of Race: 2 hours, 41 minutes, 59 seconds
Average Speed: 80.304 mph@error?:A

FINISH	DRIVER	CAR
1	Benny Parsons	Chevrolet
2	Lennie Pond	Chevrolet
3	Cale Yarborough	Oldsmobile
4	Darrell Waltrip	Chevrolet
5	Dick Brooks	Ford
6	Bobby Allison	Ford
7	Dave Marcis	Chevrolet
8	Richard Childress	Chevrolet
9	Neil Bonnett	Dodge
10	Tighe Scott	Chevrolet
11	James Hylton	Chevrolet
12	Jimmy Means	Chevrolet
13	Skip Manning	Chevrolet
14	Frank Warren	Dodge
15	Buddy Arrington	Dodge
16	D. K. Ulrich	Chevrolet
17	Cecil Gordon	Chevrolet

18	Ronnie Thomas	Chevrolet
19	Jimmy Lee Capps	Chevrolet
20	Baxter Price	Chevrolet
21	Ed Negre	Dodge
22	Richard Petty	Dodge
23	Tom Gale	Ford
24	Earle Canavan	Dodge
25	Roger Hamby	Chevrolet
26	Roland Wlodyka	Chevrolet
27	J. D. McDuffie	Chevrolet
28	Woody Fisher	Chevrolet
29	Dick May	Chevrolet
30	Nelson Oswald	Chevrolet

CAROLINA 500

Time of Race: 4 hours, 17 minutes, 17 seconds
Average Speed: 116.681 mph

FINISH	DRIVER	CAR
1	David Pearson	Mercury
2	Bobby Allison	Ford
3	Benny Parsons	Chevrolet
4	Richard Petty	Dodge
5	Lennie Pond	Chevrolet
6	Neil Bonnett	Dodge
7	Skip Manning	Chevrolet
8	Richard Childress	Chevrolet
9	Buddy Arrington	Dodge
10	Jimmy Means	Chevrolet
11	Dave Marcis	Chevrolet
12	Frank Warren	Dodge
13	Ronnie Thomas	Chevrolet
14	Tom Gale	Ford
15	James Hylton	Chevrolet
16	Joe Frasson	Chevrolet
17	Dick May	Chevrolet
18	Cale Yarborough	Oldsmobile
19	Joe Mihalic	Oldsmobile
20	Ralph Jones	Ford
21	Darrell Waltrip	Chevrolet
22	Cecil Gordon	Chevrolet
23	Baxter Price	Chevrolet
24	Earle Canavan	Dodge
25	J. D. McDuffie	Chevrolet
26	D. K. Ulrich	Chevrolet
27	Roger Hamby	Chevrolet
28	Dick Brooks	Ford
29	Ed Negre	Dodge
30	Grand Adcox	Chevrolet
31	Donnie Allison	Chevrolet
32	Roland Wlodyka	Chevrolet
33	Buddy Baker	Chevrolet
34	Tighe Scott	Chevrolet
35	Jimmy Lee Capps	Chevrolet
36	Woody Fisher	Chevrolet

ATLANTA 500

Time of Race: 3 hours, 30 minutes, 10 seconds
Average Speed: 142.520 mph

FINISH	DRIVER	CAR
1	Bobby Allison	Ford
2	Dave Marcis	Chevrolet
3	Donnie Allison	Chevrolet
4	Cale Yarborough	Oldsmobile
5	Lennie Pond	Chevrolet
6	Dick Brooks	Ford
7	Grant Adcox	Chevrolet
8	Connie Saylor	Dodge
9	Bruce Hill	Oldsmobile
10	Janet Guthrie	Chevrolet
11	D. K. Ulrich	Chevrolet
12	Sam Sommers	Chevrolet
13	Benny Parsons	Chevrolet
14	Buddy Arrington	Dodge

15	Richard Childress	Oldsmobile
16	J. D. McDuffie	Chevrolet
17	Cecil Gordon	Chevrolet
18	Roland Wlodyka	Chevrolet
19	Frank Warren	Dodge
20	Woody Fisher	Chevrolet
21	David Pearson	Mercury
22	Tom Gale	Ford
23	Skip Manning	Chevrolet
24	Ronnie Thomas	Chevrolet
25	Ed Negre	Dodge
26	Richard Petty	Dodge
27	Buddy Baker	Oldsmobile
28	Billy McGinnis	Chevrolet
29	Blackie Wangerin	Mercury
30	Chuck Bown	Chevrolet
31	Al Holbert	Chevrolet
32	Jimmy Means	Chevrolet
33	Neil Bonnett	Dodge
34	Tighe Scott	Oldsmobile
35	Darrell Waltrip	Chevrolet
36	Butch Hartman	Chevrolet
37	Roger Hamby	Chevrolet
38	Bill Elliott	Mercury
39	Coo Coo Marlin	Chevrolet
40	John Utsman	Chevrolet

SOUTHEASTERN 500

Time of Race: 2 hours, 53 minutes, 3 seconds
Average Speed: 92.401 mph

FINISH	DRIVER	CAR
1	Darrell Waltrip	Chevrolet
2	Benny Parsons	Oldsmobile
3	Dave Marcis	Chevrolet
4	Cale Yarborough	Oldsmobile
5	Lennie Pond	Chevrolet
6	Richard Childress	Oldsmobile
7	James Hylton	Chevrolet
8	Buddy Arrington	Dodge
9	Tighe Scott	Chevrolet
10	Ed Negre	Dodge
11	D. K. Ulrich	Chevrolet
12	Dick May	Chevrolet
13	Frank Warren	Dodge
14	Lynn Carroll	Chevrolet
15	Skip Manning	Chevrolet
16	Baxter Price	Chevrolet
17	Roger Hamby	Oldsmobile
18	Cecil Gordon	Chevrolet
19	Dick Brooks	Ford
20	Ronnie Thomas	Chevrolet
21	Bobby Allison	Ford
22	Tom Gale	Ford
23	Jimmy Means	Chevrolet
24	Joe Mihalic	Chevrolet
25	Richard Petty	Dodge
26	Neil Bonnett	Dodge
27	Roland Wlodyka	Chevrolet
28	J. D. McDuffie	Chevrolet
29	Bobby Wawak	Chevrolet

REBEL 500

Time of Race: 3 hours, 55 minutes, 50 seconds
Average Speed: 127.544 mph

FINISH	DRIVER	CAR
1	Benny Parsons	Chevrolet
2	Darrell Waltrip	Chevrolet
3	Lennie Pond	Oldsmobile
4	Dave Marcis	Chevrolet
5	Richard Petty	Dodge
6	Buddy Baker	Chevrolet
7	Al Holbert	Chevrolet

8	Skip Manning	Chevrolet
9	Bill Elliott	Mercury
10	Ricky Rudd	Chevrolet
11	J. D. McDuffie	Chevrolet
12	Jimmy Means	Chevrolet
13	Roger Hamby	Chevrolet
14	Bobby Allison	Ford
15	Cale Yarborough	Oldsmobile
16	Baxter Price	Chevrolet
17	Frank Warren	Dodge
18	Buddy Arrington	Dodge
19	Blackie Wangerin	Mercury
20	D. K. Ulrich	Chevrolet
21	Tom Gale	Ford
22	Earle Canavan	Dodge
23	Donnie Allison	Chevrolet
24	Joe Frasson	Chevrolet
25	Grant Adcox	Chevrolet
26	Joe Mihalic	Chevrolet
27	Sam Sommers	Chevrolet
28	Richard Childress	Oldsmobile
29	David Pearson	Mercury
30	Chuck Bown	Chevrolet
31	Ronnie Thomas	Chevrolet
32	Neil Bonnett	Dodge
33	Cecil Gordon	Chevrolet
34	Tighe Scott	Chevrolet
35	Dick Brooks	Ford
36	Dick May	Chevrolet

STALEY 400

Time of Race: 2 hours, 42 minutes, 26 seconds
Average Speed: 92.345 mph

FINISH	DRIVER	CAR
1	Darrell Waltrip	Chevrolet
2	Richard Petty	Dodge
3	Benny Parsons	Chevrolet
4	Lennie Pond	Chevrolet
5	Dave Marcis	Chevrolet
6	Bobby Allison	Ford
7	J. D. McDuffie	Chevrolet
8	Dick Brooks	Ford
9	Skip Manning	Chevrolet
10	Richard Childress	Oldsmobile
11	Buddy Arrington	Dodge
12	James Hylton	Chevrolet
13	D. K. Ulrich	Chevrolet
14	Jimmy Means	Chevrolet
15	Ed Negre	Dodge
16	Joe Booher	Chevrolet
17	Cecil Gordon	Chevrolet
18	Dick May	Chevrolet
19	Baxter Price	Chevrolet
20	Gary Myers	Chevrolet
21	Ronnie Thomas	Chevrolet
22	Frank Warren	Dodge
23	Roger Hamby	Chevrolet
24	Neil Bonnett	Dodge
25	Tighe Scott	Chevrolet
26	Cale Yarborough	Oldsmobile
27	Tom Gale	Ford
28	Bill Hollar	Chevrolet
29	John Kennedy	Ford

VIRGINIA 500

Time of Race: 3 hours, 22 minutes
Average Speed: 77.971 mph - New Record

FINISH	DRIVER	CAR
1	Darrell Waltrip	Chevrolet
2	Neil Bonnett	Dodge
3	Richard Petty	Dodge
4	Dave Marcis	Chevrolet

FINISH	DRIVER	CAR
5	Buddy Arrington	Dodge
6	Bobby Allison	Ford
7	James Hylton	Chevrolet
8	Richard Childress	Oldsmobile
9	Cecil Gordon	Chevrolet
10	Jimmy Means	Chevrolet
11	Baxter Price	Chevrolet
12	Bobby Wawak	Chevrolet
13	D.K. Ulrich	Chevrolet
14	Roger Hamby	Chevrolet
15	Benny Parsons	Chevrolet
16	Cale Yarborough	Oldsmobile
17	Tom Gale	Ford
18	Lennie Pond	Chevrolet
19	Ed Negre	Dodge
20	Ronnie Thomas	Chevrolet
21	David Pearson	Mercury
22	Frank Warren	Dodge
23	Skip Manning	Chevrolet
24	Chuck Bown	Chevrolet
25	Tighe Scott	Chevrolet
26	J.D. McDuffie	Chevrolet
27	Dick Brooks	Ford
28	Dick May	Chevrolet
29	John Kennedy	Ford
30	Gary Myers	Chevrolet

WINSTON 500

Time of Race: 3 hours, 7 minutes, 53 seconds
Average Speed: 159.699 mph

FINISH	DRIVER	CAR
1	Cale Yarborough	Oldsmobile
2	Buddy Baker	Oldsmobile
3	A.J. Foyt	Buick
4	Skip Manning	Buick
5	Grant Adcox	Chevrolet
6	Bill Elliott	Mercury
7	Ferrel Harris	Dodge
8	Dave Marcis	Chevrolet
9	Richard Childress	Oldsmobile
10	James Hylton	Olds
11	Richard Petty	Dodge
12	Buddy Arrington	Dodge
13	Tighe Scott	Oldsmobile
14	Ronnie Thomas	Chevrolet
15	Dick Brooks	Mercury
16	Tom Gale	Ford
17	D.K. Ulrich	Chevrolet
18	Claude Ballot-Lena	Dodge
19	Roger Hamby	Oldsmobile
20	Baxter Price	Chevrolet
21	Lennie Pond	Oldsmobile
22	Darrell Waltrip	Chevrolet
23	Dick May	Chevrolet
24	Donnie Allison	Chevrolet
25	Cecil Gordon	Chevrolet
26	Jimmy Means	Chevrolet
27	Ricky Rudd	Buick
28	Ed Negre	Dodge
29	Frank Warren	Dodge
30	Blackie Wangerin	Mercury
31	Benny Parsons	Oldsmobile
32	John Utsman	Chevrolet
33	Chuck Bown	Chervrolet
34	Ron Hutcherson	Buick
35	David Pearson	Mercury
36	Bruce Hill	Oldsmobile
37	Frank Hill	Chrvrolet
38	Bobby Allison	Ford
39	Neil Bonnett	Oldsmobile
40	J.D. McDuffie	Chevrolet
41	Coo Coo Marlin	Chevrolet

MASON-DIXON 500

Time of Race: 4 hours, 20 minutes, 12 seconds
Average Speed: 138.355 mph

FINISH	DRIVER	CAR
1	David Pearson	Mercury
2	Cale Yarborough	Oldsmobile
3	Lennie Pond	Chevrolet
4	Benny Parsons	Chevrolet
5	Neil Bonnett	Dodge
6	Darrell Waltrip	Chevrolet
7	Richard Petty	Dodge
8	Bobby Allison	Ford
9	Dick Brooks	Ford
10	Al Holbert	Chevrolet
11	Tighe Scott	Chevrolet
12	Skip Manning	Buick
13	Buddy Arrington	Dodge
14	Satch Worley	Chevrolet
15	Dave Marcis	Chevrolet
16	D.K. Ulrich	Chevrolet
17	Jimmy Means	Chevrolet
18	Tom Gale	Ford
19	Bruce Hill	Oldsmobile
20	Earle Canavan	Dodge
21	Dick May	Chevrolet
22	Baxter Price	Chevrolet
23	Buddy Baker	Chevrolet
24	Nestor Peles	Chevrolet
25	Cecil Gordon	Chevrolet
26	Gary Myers	Chevrolet
27	Frank Warren	Dodge
28	Bobby Wawak	Chevrolet
29	Greg Heller	Ford
30	Joe Mihalic	Chevrolet
31	Roger Hamby	Chevrolet
32	Ronnie Thomas	Chevrolet
33	Richard Childress	Oldsmobile
34	J.D. McDuffie	Chevrolet
35	Ed Negre	Dodge
36	Bill Hollar	Chevrolet
37	Elmo Langley	Chevrolet
38	Nelson Oswald	Chevrolet
39	Wayne Morgan	Chevrolet
40	Dave Dion	Ford

WORLD 600

Time of Race: 4 hours, 20 minutes, 12 seconds
Average Speed: 138.355 mph
Margin of Victory: 1 car length (finished under caution)

FINISH	DRIVER	CAR
1	Darrell Waltrip	Chevrolet
2	Donnie Allison	Chevrolet
3	Bobby Allison	Ford
4	Cale Yarborough	Oldsmobile
5	David Pearson	Mercury
6	Benny Parsons	Oldsmobile
7	Buddy Baker	Chevrolet
8	Richard Petty	Dodge
9	Sterling Marlin	Chevrolet
10	Bruce Hill	Oldsmobile
11	Grant Adcox	Chevrolet
12	Morgan Shepherd	Mercury
13	Dick May	Ford
14	Bill Elliott	Mercury
15	Buddy Arrington	Dodge
16	John Utsman	Chevrolet
17	Dale Earnhardt	Ford
18	Gary Myers	Chevrolet
19	Dick Brooks	Mercury
20	Richard Childress	Oldsmobile
21	Roland Wlodyka	Chevrolet
22	J.D. McDuffie	Chevrolet
23	Frank Warren	Chevrolet
24	Tom Gale	Ford
25	Baxter Price	Chevrolet
26	Skip Manning	Chevrolet
27	Jim Vandiver	Chevrolet
28	Ricky Rudd	Chevrolet
29	D.K. Ulrich	Chevrolet
30	Ronnie Thomas	Chevrolet

FINISH	DRIVER	CAR
31	Tighe Scott	Oldsmobile
32	Dave Marcis	Chevrolet
33	Lennie Pond	Oldsmobile
34	Connie Saylor	Dodge
35	Neil Bonnett	Oldsmobile
36	Harry Gant	Chevrolet
37	Jimmy Means	Chevrolet
38	Al Holbert	Oldsmobile
39	Ron Hutcherson	Buick
40	Jerry Jolly	Chevrolet

MUSIC CITY USA 420

Time of Race: 2 hours, 51 minutes, 34 seconds
Average Speed: 87.541 mph

FINISH	DRIVER	CAR
1	Cale Yarborough	Oldsmobile
2	Lennie Pond	Chevrolet
3	Richard Petty	Dodge
4	Dave Marcis	Chevrolet
5	Neil Bonnett	Dodge
6	Grant Adcox	Chevrolet
7	Tighe Scott	Chevrolet
8	Richard Childress	Oldsmobile
9	Buddy Arrington	Dodge
10	D.K. Ulrich	Chevrolet
11	James Hylton	Chevrolet
12	J.D. McDuffie	Chevrolet
13	Bobby Wawak	Chevrolet
14	Dick Brooks	Ford
15	Ronnie Thomas	Chevrolet
16	Frank Warren	Dodge
17	Baxter Price	Chevrolet
18	Dick May	Chevrolet
19	Cecil Gordon	Chevrolet
20	Benny Parsons	Chevrolet
21	Bobby Allison	Ford
22	Coo Coo Marlin	Chevrolet
23	Roger Hamby	Oldsmobile
24	Ralph Jones	Ford
25	Bruce Hill	Oldsmobile
26	Darrell Waltrip	Chevrolet
27	Ed Negre	Dodge
28	Gary Myers	Chevrolet
29	Richard Waters	Chevrolet
30	Jimmy Means	Chevrolet

NAPA RIVERSIDE 400

Time of Race: 2 hours, 23 minutes, 10 seconds
Average Speed: 104.311 mph
Margin of Victory: 29 seconds

FINISH	DRIVER	CAR
1	Benny Parsons	Chevrolet
2	Richard Petty	Dodge
3	Bobby Allison	Ford
4	Dave Marcis	Chevrolet
5	Cale Yarborough	Oldsmobile
6	Ray Elder	Dodge
7	Lennie Pond	Chevrolet
8	Bill Schmitt	Oldsmobile
9	Jim Thirkettle	Buick
10	Neil Bonnett	Dodge
11	Tighe Scott	Chevrolet
12	Cecil Gordon	Chevrolet
13	Rick McCray	Chevrolet
14	D.K. Ulrich	Chevrolet
15	Richard Childress	Oldsmobile
16	Darrell Waltrip	Chevrolet
17	Hershel McGriff	Chevrolet
18	Buddy Arrington	Ford
19	Harry Goularte	Chevrolet
20	Richard White	Chevrolet
21	Dick May	Chevrolet
22	Don Graham	Chevrolet

FINISH	DRIVER	CAR
23	John Borneman	Chevrolet
24	J.D. McDuffie	Chevrolet
25	Ronnie Thomas	Chevrolet
26	Dick Brooks	Ford
27	David Pearson	Mercury
28	Chuck Wahl	Chevrolet
29	Frank Warren	Dodge
30	Rocky Moran	Buick
31	Ernie Stierly	Chevrolet
32	Jim Insolo	Oldsmobile
33	Don Noel	Chevrolet
34	Bill Baker	Buick
35	Norm Palmer	Dodge

GABRIEL 400

Time of Race: 2 hours, 40 minutes, 28 seconds
Average Speed: 149.563 mph
Margin of Victory: 12 seconds

FINISH	DRIVER	CAR
1	Cale Yarborough	Oldsmobile
2	David Pearson	Mercury
3	Benny Parsons	Oldsmobile
4	Dave Marcis	Chevrolet
5	Donnie Allison	Chevrolet
6	Richard Petty	Dodge
7	Dick Brooks	Ford
8	Buddy Baker	Chevrolet
9	Ricky Rudd	Chevrolet
10	Richard Childress	Oldsmobile
11	Tighe Scott	Oldsmobile
12	Buddy Arrington	Dodge
13	J.D. McDuffie	Chevrolet
14	D.K. Ulrich	Chevrolet
15	Jimmy Means	Chevrolet
16	Skip Manning	Chevrolet
17	Cecil Gordon	Chevrolet
18	Ronnie Thomas	Chevrolet
19	Dick May	Chevrolet
20	Frank Warren	Dodge
21	Tom Gale	Chevrolet
22	Grant Adcox	Chevrolet
23	Gary Myers	Chevrolet
24	Bobby Allison	Ford
25	Lennie Pond	Oldsmobile
26	Baxter Price	Chevrolet
27	Roger Hamby	Oldsmobile
28	Darrell Waltrip	Chevrolet
29	Bruce Hill	Oldsmobile
30	John Kennedy	Ford
31	Al Holbert	Chevrolet
32	Blackie Wangerin	Mercury
33	Earle Canavan	Dodge
34	Joe Booher	Chevrolet
35	Ed Negre	Dodge
36	Neil Bonnett	Dodge

FIRECRACKER 400

Time of Race: 2 hours, 35 minutes, 30 seconds
Average Speed: 154.340 mph
Margin of Victory: One car length

FINISH	DRIVER	CAR
1	David Pearson	Mercury
2	Cale Yarborough	Oldsmobile
3	Darrell Waltrip	Chevrolet
4	Richard Petty	Dodge
5	Lennie Pond	Chevrolet
6	Dave Marcis	Chevrolet
7	Dale Earnhardt	Ford
8	Ferrel Harris	Chevrolet
9	Bill Elliott	Mercury
10	Tighe Scott	Oldsmobile
11	Janet Guthrie	Chevrolet
12	J.D. McDuffie	Chevrolet

13	Jimmy Means	Chevrolet
14	Joe Frasson	Chevrolet
15	Tom Gale	Ford
16	Dick May	Chevrolet
17	Frank Warren	Dodge
18	Satch Worley	Oldsmobile
19	D.K. Ulrich	Chevrolet
20	Baxter Price	Chevrolet
21	Ricky Rudd	Buick
22	Grant Adcox	Chevrolet
23	Neil Bonnett	Chevrolet
24	Richard Childress	Oldsmobile
25	Ronnie Thomas	Chevrolet
26	Benny Parsons	Oldsmobile
27	Bobby Allison	Ford
28	Paul Fess	Chevrolet
29	Raymond Williams	Buick
30	Al Holbert	Oldsmobile
31	Blackie Wangerin	Mercury
32	Cecil Gordon	Chevrolet
33	Donnie Allison	Chevrolet
34	Buddy Arrington	Dodge
35	Claude Ballot-Lena	Dodge
36	Dick Brooks	Mercury
37	Buddy Baker	Oldsmobile
38	Coo Coo Marlin	Chevrolet
39	Skip Manning	Buick
40	Bruce Hill	Oldsmobile

NASHVILLE 420

Time of Race: 2 hours, 48 minutes, 54 seconds
Average Speed: 88.924 mph
Margin of Victory: 2 laps

FINISH	DRIVER	CAR
1	Cale Yarborough	Oldsmobile
2	Darrell Waltrip	Chevrolet
3	Richard Childress	Oldsmobile
4	Dave Marcis	Chevrolet
5	J.D. McDuffie	Chevrolet
6	Benny Parsons	Chevrolet
7	Bobby Allison	Ford
8	Dick Brooks	Ford
9	Farrel Harris	Chevrolet
10	Ronnie Thomas	Chevrolet
11	Grant Adcox	Chevrolet
12	Buddy Arrington	Dodge
13	Frank Warren	Dodge
14	Bruce Hill	Oldsmobile
15	Gary Myers	Chevrolet
16	Elmo Langley	Ford
17	Roger Hamby	Chevrolet
18	Dick May	Chevrolet
19	Cecil Gordon	Chevrolet
20	D.K. Ulrich	Chevrolet
21	Ralph Jones	Ford
22	Tighe Scott	Chevrolet
23	Richard Petty	Dodge
24	Jimmy Means	Chevrolet
25	Sterling Marlin	Chevrolet
26	Lennie Pond	Chevrolet
27	Baxter Price	Chevrolet
28	Neil Bonnett	Chevrolet
29	Bobby Fisher	Chevrolet
30	Walter Ballard	Chevrolet

COCA-COLA 500

Time of Race: 3 hours, 30 minutes, 28 seconds
Average Speed: 142.540 mph - New Record
Margin of Victory: second

FINISH	DRIVER	CAR
1	Darrell Waltrip	Chevrolet
2	David Pearson	Mercury
3	Bobby Allison	Ford

4	Dave Marcis	Chevrolet
5	Buddy Baker	Chevrolet
6	Ricky Rudd	Chevrolet
7	Dick Brooks	Mercury
8	Tighe Scott	Chevrolet
9	Satch Worley	Oldsmobile
10	J.D. McDuffie	Chevrolet
11	Dick May	Ford
12	Al Holbert	Chevrolet
13	Jimmy Means	Chevrolet
14	Buddy Arrington	Dodge
15	Blackie Wangerin	Mercury
16	Tom Gale	Ford
17	Bruce Hill	Oldsmobile
18	Frank Warren	Dodge
19	Gary Myers	Chevrolet
20	Ferrel Harris	Chevrolet
21	Nestor Peles	Chevrolet
22	Joe Booher	Chevrolet
23	Kenny Brightbill	Mercury
24	Richard Childress	Oldsmobile
25	D.K. Ulrich	Chevrolet
26	Cale Yarborough	Oldsmobile
27	Roger Hamby	Chevrolet
28	Baxter Price	Chevrolet
29	Benny Parsons	Chevrolet
30	Richard Petty	Dodge
31	Janet Guthrie	Chevrolet
32	Joe Mihalic	Chevrolet
33	Ronnie Thomas	Chevrolet
34	Bobby Wawak	Ford
35	Donnie Allison	Oldsmobile
36	Neil Bonnett	Chevrolet
37	Jocko Maggiacomo	Matador
38	Dave Dion	Ford
39	James Hylton	Chevrolet
40	Cecil Gordon	Chevrolet

TALLADEGA 500

Time of Race: 2 hours, 51 minutes, 43 seconds
Average Speed: 174.700 mph - New Record
Margin of Victory: 1 foot

FINISH	DRIVER	CAR
1	Lennie Pond	Oldsmobile
2	Donnie Allison	Oldsmobile
3	Benny Parsons	Oldsmobile
4	Cale Yarborough	Oldsmobile
5	David Pearson	Mercury
6	Bobby Allison	Ford
7	Richard Petty	Dodge
8	Neil Bonnett	Chevrolet
9	Dick Brooks	Mercury
10	Tighe Scott	Oldsmobile
11	Ferrel Harris	Chevrolet
12	Dale Earnhardt	Ford
13	Bill Elliott	Mercury
14	Dave Marcis	Oldsmobile
15	Buddy Arrington	Dodge
16	Dick May	Chevrolet
17	J.D. McDuffie	Chevrolet
18	Marty Robbins	Dodge
19	D.K. Ulrich	Chevrolet
20	Tom Gale	Ford
21	Gary Myers	Chevrolet
22	Grant Adcox	Chevrolet
23	Baxter Price	Chevrolet
24	Ronnie Thomas	Chevrolet
25	Richard Childress	Oldsmobile
26	Coo Coo Marlin	Chevrolet
27	Steve Moore	Chevrolet
28	Buddy Baker	Oldsmobile
29	Janet Guthrie	Buick
30	Al Holbert	Oldsmobile
31	Earle Canavan	Dodge
32	Jimmy Means	Chevrolet
33	Frank Warren	Dodge
34	Darrell Waltrip	Chevrolet
35	Bruce Hill	Oldsmobile
36	Roger Hamby	Chevrolet

FAMILY TIES ONLY GO SO FAR

Lee Petty was generally accepted as one of the most refined and gentlemanly of the early stars of NASCAR racing. He played fair, so he expected everyone else to play fair, too. Beat him if you could, but you'd better be honest about it. He didn't take kindly to people trying to take away what was rightfully his.

That extended all the way to his son, too.

Richard Petty had been racing for about a year when he took his first checkered flag. It was June 14, 1959 at Lakewood Speedway, a 1-mile dirt-track in Atlanta, Georgia. The event was a 150-lap race among a full field of 40 cars. Lee Petty drew 37th on the grid (rain forced race officials to cancel time trials) and Richard drew 27th. Lee was in a hard-top Oldsmobile, Richard in an Oldsmobile convertible.

Moments after Richard took what would have been his first victory, a call came that someone back in the pack had protested the scoring and demanded a thorough recheck. It turned out to be Lee Petty, and he was convinced that while his son had run a hard, clean and fair race, he was also convinced that his son had finished second to him.

Turns out he was right. It took an hour for officials to figure out that instead of finishing ahead of his father, Richard was behind him in second-place. Buck Baker was third, Curtis Turner fourth and Tom Pistone fifth, the first driver two laps down. Instead of Richard getting his first career victory, Lee ended up with his 42nd.

Years later, Richard spoke of the incident with not the slightest bit of rancor. "Daddy didn't want me to get anything that wasn't mine," he said. "I hadn't earned that win, so he was right, I shouldn't have gotten it. The most important thing was that the Petty team ran 1-2. It didn't matter which one was first and which one was second. Back then, that's just the way it was."

37	Claude Ballot-Lena	Dodge
38	Skip Manning	Buick
39	Ricky Rudd	Chevrolet
40	Blackie Wangerin	Mercury
41	James Hylton	Buick

CHAMPION SPARK PLUG 400

Time of Race: 3 hours, 5 minutes, 14 seconds
Average Speed: 129.566 mph
Margin of Victory: 10 feet

FINISH	DRIVER	CAR
1	David Pearson	Mercury
2	Cale Yarborough	Oldsmobile
3	Darrell Waltrip	Chevrolet
4	Dave Marcis	Chevrolet
5	Bobby Allison	Ford
6	Dick Brooks	Mercury
7	J.D. McDuffie	Chevrolet
8	Lennie Pond	Oldsmobile
9	Neil Bonnett	Oldsmobile
10	Ferrel Harris	Chevrolet
11	Dick May	Chevrolet
12	Buddy Arrington	Dodge
13	Benny Parsons	Oldsmobile
14	Richard Petty	Chevrolet
15	Jimmy Means	Chevrolet
16	Tom Gale	Ford
17	Cecil Gordon	Chevrolet
18	Ed Negre	Dodge
19	Tighe Scott	Chevrolet
20	Gary Myers	Chevrolet
21	Baxter Price	Chevrolet
22	Joey Arrington	Dodge
23	D.K. Ulrich	Chevrolet
24	Frank Warren	Dodge
25	Blackie Wangerin	Mercury

26	Ronnie Thomas	Chevrolet
27	Janet Guthrie	Buick
28	Ricky Rudd	Chevrolet
29	Donnie Allison	Oldsmobile
30	Roger Hamby	Chevrolet
31	Richard Childress	Oldsmobile
32	Earle Canavan	Dodge
33	Mel Larson	Oldsmobile
34	Bruce Hill	Oldsmobile
35	James Hylton	Chevrolet
36	Buddy Baker	Oldsmobile

VOLUNTEER 500

Time of Race: 3 hours, 25 minutes
Average Speed: 88.628 mph
Margin of Victory: 15 seconds

FINISH	DRIVER	CAR
1	Cale Yarborough	Oldsmobile
2	Benny Parsons	Oldsmobile
3	Darrell Waltrip	Chevrolet
4	Dick Brooks	Ford
5	Richard Petty	Chevrolet
6	Dave Marcis	Chevrolet
7	Richard Childress	Oldsmobile
8	J.D. McDuffie	Chevrolet
9	D.K. Ulrich	Chevrolet
10	Roger Hamby	Chevrolet
11	Ronnie Thomas	Chevrolet
12	Buddy Arrington	Dodge
13	Cecil Gordon	Chevrolet
14	Gary Myers	Chevrolet
15	Frank Warren	Dodge
16	Baxter Price	Chevrolet
17	James Hylton	Chevrolet
18	Ferrel Harris	Chevrolet
19	Jimmy Means	Chevrolet

FINISH	DRIVER	CAR
20	Neil Bonnett	Chevrolet
21	Tom Gale	Ford
22	Bobby Allison	Ford
23	Tighe Scott	Chevrolet
24	Nelson Oswald	Chevrolet
25	Dick May	Chevrolet
26	Lennie Pond	Oldsmobile
27	Ralph Jones	Ford
28	Bobby Wawak	Chevrolet
29	Ed Negre	Dodge
30	Bil Green	Chevrolet

SOUTHERN 500

Time of Race: 4 hours, 17 minutes, 46 seconds
Average Speed: 116.828 mph
Margin of Victory: .05 seconds

FINISH	DRIVER	CAR
1	Cale Yarborough	Oldsmobile
2	Darrell Waltrip	Chevrolet
3	Richard Petty	Chevrolet
4	Terry Labonte	Chevrolet
5	Bobby Allison	Ford
6	Bill Elliott	Mercury
7	James Hylton	Chevrolet
8	Buddy Arrington	Dodge
9	Ronnie Thomas	Chevrolet
10	Benny Parsons	Chevrolet
11	Jimmy Means	Chevrolet
12	Frank Warren	Dodge
13	Tom Gale	Ford
14	Gary Myers	Chevrolet
15	Baxter Price	Chevrolet
16	Dale Earnhardt	Ford
17	Joe Frasson	Chevrolet
18	Ralph Jones	Ford
19	Roger Hamby	Chevrolet
20	J.D. McDuffie	Chevrolet
21	Ed Negre	Chrysler
22	Bob Burcham	Chevrolet
23	Tighe Scott	Chevrolet
24	Donnie Allison	Chevrolet
25	Dick Brooks	Mercury
26	Lennie Pond	Chevrolet
27	Richard Childress	Oldsmobile
28	David Pearson	Mercury
29	D.K. Ulrich	Chevrolet
30	Coo Coo Marlin	Chevrolet
31	Grant Adcox	Chevrolet
32	Buddy Baker	Chevrolet
33	Blackie Wangerin	Mercury
34	Neil Bonnett	Chevrolet
35	Dave Marcis	Chevrolet
36	Ricky Rudd	Chevrolet
37	Bobby Wawak	Chevrolet
38	Dick May	Ford
39	Earle Canavan	Dodge
40	Bruce Hill	Oldsmobile

CAPITAL CITY 400

Time of Race: 2 hours, 43 minutes, 19 seconds
Average Speed: 79.568 mph
Margin of Victory: 1 second

FINISH	DRIVER	CAR
1	Darrell Waltrip	Chevrolet
2	Bobby Allison	Ford
3	Neil Bonnett	Chevrolet
4	Cale Yarborough	Oldsmobile
5	Dick Brooks	Ford
6	Benny Parsons	Chevrolet
7	Terry Labonte	Chevrolet
8	J.D. McDuffie	Chevrolet
9	Dave Marcis	Chevrolet

FINISH	DRIVER	CAR
10	Roger Hamby	Chevrolet
11	Richard Childress	Oldsmobile
12	Lennie Pond	Chevrolet
13	Jimmy Means	Chevrolet
14	Ronnie Thomas	Chevrolet
15	Dick May	Dodge
16	Buddy Arrington	Dodge
17	Cecil Gordon	Chevrolet
18	James Hylton	Chevrolet
19	Joey Arrington	Dodge
20	Richard Petty	Chevrolet
21	Gary Myers	Chevrolet
22	Baxter Price	Chevrolet
23	Frank Warren	Dodge
24	Tom Gale	Ford
25	Nelson Oswald	Chevrolet
26	Dave Dion	Ford
27	Tighe Scott	Chevrolet
28	Ferrel Harris	Chevrolet
29	Wayne Morgan	Chevrolet
30	Ed Negre	Chrysler

DELAWARE 500

Time of Race: 4 hours, 11 minutes, 20 seconds
Average Speed: 119.323 mph
Margin of Victory: 19.7 seconds

FINISH	DRIVER	CAR
1	Bobby Allison	Ford
2	Cale Yarborough	Oldsmobile
3	Buddy Baker	Chevrolet
4	David Pearson	Mercury
5	Darrell Waltrip	Chevrolet
6	Dick Brooks	Ford
7	Lennie Pond	Oldsmobile
8	Dave Marcis	Chevrolet
9	Donnie Allison	Oldsmobile
10	Dick May	Chevrolet
11	Ronnie Thomas	Chevrolet
12	Richard Childress	Oldsmobile
13	Al Holbert	Chevrolet
14	Cecil Gordon	Chevrolet
15	Ed Negre	Dodge
16	Earle Canavan	Dodge
17	Tom Gale	Ford
18	Roger Hamby	Oldsmobile
19	Nestor Peles	Chevrolet
20	Gary Myers	Chevrolet
21	Frank Warren	Dodge
22	Buddy Arrington	Dodge
23	Baxter Price	Chevrolet
24	Nelson Oswald	Chevrolet
25	Tighe Scott	Chevrolet
26	Benny Parsons	Chevrolet
27	Richard Petty	Chevrolet
28	Dave Dion	Ford
29	Neil Bonnett	Oldsmobile
30	Ralph Jones	Ford
31	Joey Arrington	Dodge
32	Jimmy Means	Chevrolet
33	J.D. McDuffie	Chevrolet
34	James Hylton	Chevrolet
35	Louis Gatto	Chevrolet
36	Ferrel Haris	Chrysler
37	Jabe Thomas	Chevrolet

OLD DOMINION 500

Time of Race: 3 hours, 18 minutes, 54 seconds
Average Speed: 79.185 mph
Margin of Victory: car length

FINISH	DRIVER	CAR
1	Cale Yarborough	Oldsmobile
2	Darrell Waltrip	Chevrolet

3	Benny Parsons	Chevrolet
4	Neil Bonnett	Chevrolet
5	Lennie Pond	Chevrolet
6	Richard Petty	Chevrolet
7	Bobby Allison	Ford
8	Dave Marcis	Chevrolet
9	Terry Labonte	Chevrolet
10	Buddy Arrington	Dodge
11	James Hylton	Chevrolet
12	Richard Childress	Oldsmobile
13	Dick Brooks	Ford
14	Satch Worley	Oldsmobile
15	Gary Myers	Chevrolet
16	Ronnie Thomas	Chevrolet
17	Dick May	Buick
18	Ed Negre	Dodge
19	Baxter Price	Chevrolet
20	Ferrel Harris	Chevrolet
21	Frank Warren	Dodge
22	J.D. McDuffie	Chevrolet
23	Jimmy Means	Chevrolet
24	Roger Hamby	Chevrolet
25	David Pearson	Mercury
26	Buddy Baker	Chevrolet
27	Tom Gale	Ford
28	Harry Gant	Chevrolet
29	Tighe Scott	Chevrolet
30	Cecil Gordon	Chevrolet

WILKES 400

Time of Race: 2 hours, 23 minutes, 18 seconds
Average Speed: 97.847 mph
Margin of Victory: 10 seconds

FINISH	DRIVER	CAR
1	Cale Yarborough	Oldsmobile
2	Darrell Waltrip	Chevrolet
3	Bobby Allison	Ford
4	Richard Petty	Chevrolet
5	Neil Bonnett	Chevrolet
6	Benny Parsons	Chevrolet
7	Lennie Pond	Chevrolet
8	Dave Marcis	Chevrolet
9	Dick Brooks	Ford
10	Tighe Scott	Chevrolet
11	J.D. McDuffie	Chevrolet
12	Roger Hamby	Chevrolet
13	Buddy Arrington	Dodge
14	Richard Childress	Oldsmobile
15	Junior Miller	Chevrolet
16	James Hylton	Chevrolet
17	Tom Gale	Ford
18	Nelson Oswald	Chevrolet
19	Ronnie Thomas	Chevrolet
20	Ed Negre	Dodge
21	Baxter Price	Chevrolet
22	Gary Myers	Chevrolet
23	Jimmy Means	Chevrolet
24	Frank Warren	Dodge
25	Dick May	Buick
26	Cecil Gordon	Chevrolet
27	John Kennedy	Ford

NAPA NATIONAL 500

Time of Race: 3 hours, 31 minutes, 57 seconds
Average Speed: 141.826 mph
Margin of Victory: 30.2 seconds

FINISH	DRIVER	CAR
1	Bobby Allison	Ford
2	Darrell Waltrip	Chevrolet
3	Dave Marcis	Chevrolet
4	Donnie Allison	Chevrolet

5	David Pearson	Mercury
6	Lennie Pond	Chevrolet
7	Coo Coo Marlin	Chevrolet
8	Dick May	Ford
9	Richard Childress	Oldsmobile
10	Dick Brooks	Mercury
11	J.D. McDuffie	Chevrolet
12	Tighe Scott	Chevrolet
13	Bruce Hill	Oldsmobile
14	Buddy Arrington	Dodge
15	James Hylton	Chevrolet
16	Connie Saylor	Dodge
17	Bill Elliott	Mercury
18	Roger Hamby	Chervolet
19	Harry Gant	Chevrolet
20	Glenn Jarrett	Oldsmobile
21	Ed Negre	Chrysler
22	Cale Yarborough	Oldsmobile
23	Ricky Rudd	Chevrolet
24	Terry Labonte	Chevrolet
25	Frank Warren	Dodge
26	Butch Mock	Chevrolet
27	Richard Petty	Chevrolet
28	Benny Parsons	Oldsmobile
29	Baxter Price	Ford
30	Neil Bonnett	Chevrolet
31	Tommy Gale	Ford
32	John Utsman	Chevrolet
33	Grant Adcox	Chevrolet
34	Buddy Baker	Chevrolet
35	Janet Guthrie	Buick
36	Jerry Jolly	Buick
37	Bill Dennis	Chevrolet
38	Skip Manning	Chevrolet
39	Dick Trickle	Ford
40	Bobby Fisher	Chevrolet

AMERICAN 500

Time of Race: 4 hours, 15 minutes, 58 seconds
Average Speed: 117.288 mph
Margin of Victory: 2 laps & 21 seconds

FINISH	DRIVER	CAR
1	Cale Yarborough	Oldsmobile
2	Bobby Allison	Ford
3	Darrell Waltrip	Chevrolet
4	Benny Parsons	Chevrolet
5	Dick Brooks	Ford
6	Richard Petty	Chevrolet
7	Lennie Pond	Chevrolet
8	Dave Marcis	Chevrolet
9	Buddy Arrington	Dodge
10	Richard Childress	Oldsmobile
11	Dick May	Chevrolet
12	J.D. McDuffie	Chevrolet
13	Jimmy Means	Chevrolet
14	James Hylton	Chevrolet
15	Cecil Gordon	Oldsmobile
16	Frank Warren	Dodge
17	Gary Myers	Chevrolet
18	Tom Gale	Ford
19	Baxter Price	Chevrolet
20	Donnie Allison	Chevrolet
21	Tighe Scott	Chevrolet
22	Buddy Baker	Chevrolet
23	Joe Frasson	Buick
24	David Pearson	Mercury
25	Ricky Rudd	Chevrolet
26	Roger Hamby	Chevrolet
27	Bobby Wawak	Chevrolet
28	Junior Miller	Chevrolet
29	Elmo Langley	Buick
30	Johnny Halford	Chevrolet
31	Neil Bonnett	Chevrolet
32	Charlie Blanton	Chevrolet
33	Ronnie Thomas	Chevrolet
34	Ferrel Harris	Chevrolet
35	Ed Negre	Dodge
36	Bill Hollar	Chevrolet

DIXIE 500

Time of Race: 4 hours, 43 seconds
Average Speed: 124.312 mph
Margin of Victory: 2 car length

FINISH	DRIVER	CAR
1	Donnie Allison	Chevrolet
2	Richard Petty	Chevrolet
3	Dave Marcis	Chevrolet
4	Dale Earnhardt	Chevrolet
5	Benny Parsons	Oldsmobile
6	Bobby Allison	Ford
7	Harry Gant	Chevrolet
8	Cale Yarborough	Oldsmobile
9	Ricky Rudd	Chevrolet
10	Coo Coo Marlin	Chevrolet
11	Roger Hamby	Chevrolet
12	Dick Brooks	Mercury
13	Terry Labonte	Chevrolet
14	J.D. McDuffie	Chevrolet
15	Ronnie Thomas	Chevrolet
16	Buddy Arrington	Dodge
17	Dave Watson	Chevrolet
18	Cecil Gordon	Oldsmobile
19	Dick May	Chevrolet
20	Ferrel Harris	Chevrolet
21	Buddy Baker	Chevrolet
22	Tighe Scott	Oldsmobile
23	Jimmy Means	Chevrolet
24	Butch Mock	Chevrolet
25	Skip Manning	Mercury
26	Ed Negre	Chrysler
27	Gary Myers	Chevrolet
28	Darrell Waltrip	Chevrolet
29	Ralph Jones	Ford
30	Richard Childress	Oldsmobile
31	Tom Gale	Chevrolet
32	David Pearson	Mercury
33	Frank Warren	Dodge
34	Neil Bonnett	Chevrolet
35	Al Holbert	Chevrolet
36	Bruce Hill	Oldsmobile
37	Bill Elliott	Oldsmobile
38	Grant Adcox	Chevrolet
39	Lennie Pond	Chevrolet
40	John Kennedy	Ford

LOS ANGELES TIMES 500

Time of Race: 3 hours, 37 minutes, 44 seconds
Average Speed: 137.783 mph
Margin of Victory: 1.7 seconds

FINISH	DRIVER	CAR
1	Bobby Allison	Ford
2	Cale Yarborough	Oldsmobile
3	Donnie Allison	Chevrolet
4	Buddy Baker	Chevrolet
5	Darrell Waltrip	Chevrolet
6	Lennie Pond	Chevrolet
7	Jim Insolo	Chevrolet
8	Benny Parsons	Chevrolet
9	Dick Brooks	Mercury
10	Jim Thirkettle	Buick
11	Richard Childress	Oldsmobile
12	Roger Hamby	Chevrolet
13	Janet Guthrie	Buick
14	Bill Schmitt	Oldsmobile
15	Cecil Gordon	Oldsmobile
16	James Hylton	Oldsmobile
17	Tom Gale	Ford
18	Richard White	Chevrolet
19	Ferrel Harris	Chevrolet
20	Rocky Moran	Buick
21	Ed Negre	Chrysler
22	Jimmy Means	Chevrolet
23	Frank Warren	Dodge
24	Gary Myers	Chevrolet

FINISH	DRIVER	CAR
25	John Borneman	Chevrolet
26	J.D. McDuffie	Chevrolet
27	Dave Marcis	Chevrolet
28	Don Noel	Chevrolet
29	Mel Larson	Buick
30	Ronnie Thomas	Chevrolet
31	Dick May	Chevrolet
32	Steve Pfeifer	Chevrolet
33	Harry Goularte	Chevrolet
34	Richard Petty	Chevrolet
35	Buddy Arrington	Ford
36	Chuck Wahl	Chevrolet
37	Neil Bonnett	Chevrolet
38	David Pearson	Mercury
39	Rick McCray	Chevrolet
40	Ray Elder	Dodge

1979

WINSTON WESTERN 500

Time of Race: 2 hours, 53 minutes, 30 seconds
Average Speed: 107.820 MPH
Margin of Victory: 32.9 seconds

FINISH	DRIVER	CAR
1	Darrell Waltrip	Chevrolet
2	David Pearson	Mercury
3	Cale Yarborough	Oldsmobile
4	Bill Schmitt	Oldsmobile
5	Donnie Allison	Chevrolet
6	Joe Millikan	Chevrolet
7	Buddy Baker	Chevrolet
8	Jim Thirkettle	Buick
9	Tim Williamson	Chevrolet
10	Harry Gant	Chevrolet
11	James Hylton	Chevrolet
12	Ronnie Thomas	Chevrolet
13	Vince Giamformaggio	Chevrolet
14	D. K. Ulrich	Buick
15	Richard Childress	Oldsmobile
16	Jim Insolo	Oldsmobile
17	J. D. McDuffie	Chevrolet
18	Buddy Arrington	Ford
19	Bobby Allison	Ford
20	Al Holbert	Chevrolet
21	Dale Earnhardt	Chevrolet
22	Don Graham	Chevrolet
23	Harry Goularte	Chevrolet
24	Dave Marcis	Chevrolet
25	Cecil Gordon	Oldsmobile
26	Benny Parsons	Chevrolet
27	Frank Warren	Dodge
28	Don Puskarich	Chevrolet
29	Richard White	Chevrolet
30	Jim Robinson	Chevrolet
31	Don Noel	Chevrolet
32	Richard Petty	Chevrolet
33	Dick Brooks	Oldsmobile
34	Neil Bonnett	Chevrolet
35	Terry Labonte	Chevrolet

DAYTONA 500

Time of Race: 3 hours, 28 minutes, 22 seconds
Average Speed: 143.977 MPH
Margin of Victory: One car length

FINISH	DRIVER	CAR
1	Richard Petty	Oldsmobile
2	Darrell Waltrip	Oldsmobile

3	A. J. Foyt	Oldsmobile
4	Donnie Allison	Oldsmobile
5	Cale Yarborough	Oldsmobile
6	Tighe Scott	Buick
7	Chuck Bown	Buick
8	Dale Earnhardt	Buick
9	Coo Coo Marlin	Chevrolet
10	Frank Warren	Dodge
11	Bobby Allison	Ford
12	Buddy Arrington	Dodge
13	D. K. Ulrich	Buick
14	Bill Dennis	Chevrolet
15	Ralph Jones	Ford
16	Terry Labonte	Buick
17	Richard Childress	Oldsmobile
18	Benny Parsons	Oldsmobile
19	Bruce Hill	Oldsmobile
20	Blackie Wangerin	Mercury
21	Bobby Wawak	Oldsmobile
22	Paul Fess	Oldsmobile
23	Grant Adcox	Chevrolet
24	Dave Marcis	Chevrolet
25	J. D. McDuffie	Oldsmobile
26	Dave Watson	Chevrolet
27	Dick Brooks	Oldsmobile
28	John Utsman	Chevrolet
29	Geoff Bodine	Oldsmobile
30	Lennie Pond	Oldsmobile
31	Ricky Rudd	Mercury
32	Neil Bonnett	Oldsmobile
33	Harry Gant	Oldsmobile
34	Ronnie Thomas	Chevrolet
35	Gary Balough	Oldsmobile
36	Joe Millikan	Oldsmobile
37	David Pearson	Mercury
38	Skip Manning	Oldsmobile
39	Butch Mock	Buick
40	Buddy Baker	Oldsmobile
41	Jim Vandiver	Oldsmobile

CAROLINA 500

Time of Race: 4 hours, 6 minutes, 30 seconds
Average Speed: 121.727 MPH
Margin of Victory: 52 seconds

FINISH	DRIVER	CAR
1	Bobby Allison	Ford
2	Joe Millikan	Chevrolet
3	Dick Brooks	Oldsmobile
4	Tighe Scott	Buick
5	Richard Childress	Chevrolet
6	D. K. Ulrich	Buick
7	James Hylton	Chevrolet
8	Dave Watson	Chevrolet
9	Frank Warren	Dodge
10	Benny Parsons	Chevrolet
11	Cecil Gordon	Oldsmobile
12	Dale Earnhardt	Chevrolet
13	Tommy Gale	Ford
14	Baxter Price	Chevrolet
15	Terry Labonte	Buick
16	Dave Marcis	Chevrolet
17	Darrell Waltrip	Chevrolet
18	Cale Yarborough	Oldsmobile
19	Buddy Arrington	Dodge
20	Dick May	Chevrolet
21	Roger Hamby	Chevrolet
22	Geoff Bodine	Oldsmobile
23	David Pearson	Mercury
24	Jimmy Means	Chevrolet
25	J. D. McDuffie	Chevrolet
26	Harry Gant	Chevrolet
27	Slick Johnson	Chevrolet
28	Nelson Oswald	Chevrolet
29	Ronnie Thomas	Chevrolet
30	Donnie Allison	Chevrolet
31	Buddy Baker	Chevrolet
32	Richard Petty	Chevrolet
33	Neil Bonnett	Oldsmobile
34	Ricky Rudd	Ford
35	Bill Hollar	Chevrolet

RICHMOND 400

Time of Race: 2 hours, 35 minutes, 34 seconds
Average Speed: 83.608 MPH
Margin of Victory: 6 seconds

FINISH	DRIVER	CAR
1	Cale Yarborough	Oldsmobile
2	Bobby Allison	Ford
3	Darrell Waltrip	Chevrolet
4	Benny Parsons	Chevrolet
5	Richard Petty	Chevrolet
6	Joe Millikan	Chevrolet
7	J. D. McDuffie	Chevrolet
8	Terry Labonte	Chevrolet
9	Donnie Allison	Chevrolet
10	D. K. Ulrich	Buick
11	Ricky Rudd	Ford
12	James Hylton	Chevrolet
13	Dale Earnhardt	Chevrolet
14	Lennie Pond	Oldsmobile
15	Buddy Arrington	Dodge
16	Dave Marcis	Chevrolet
17	Ronnie Thomas	Buick
18	Dave Watson	Chevrolet
19	Dave Dion	Ford
20	Joe Fields	Chevrolet
21	Frank Warren	Dodge
22	Tommy Gale	Ford
23	Baxter Price	Chevrolet
24	Bill Hollar	Chevrolet
25	Cecil Gordon	Oldsmobile
26	Richard Childress	Chevrolet
27	Jimmy Means	Chevrolet
28	Dick Brooks	Oldsmobile
29	Buddy Baker	Chevrolet
30	Roger Hamby	Chevrolet

ATLANTA 500

Time of Race: 3 hours, 41 minutes, 47 seconds
Average Speed: 135.136 MPH
Margin of Victory: 6 seconds

FINISH	DRIVER	CAR
1	Buddy Baker	Oldsmobile
2	Bobby Allison	Ford
3	Darrell Waltrip	Chevrolet
4	Cale Yarborough	Oldsmobile
5	Benny Parsons	Chevrolet
6	Dave Marcis	Chevrolet
7	Donnie Allison	Chevrolet
8	Joe Millikan	Oldsmobile
9	Ricky Rudd	Mercury
10	Dick Brooks	Oldsmobile
11	Richard Petty	Oldsmobile
12	Dale Earnhardt	Buick
13	James Hylton	Chevrolet
14	D. K. Ulrich	Buick
15	Bruce Hill	Oldsmobile
16	Chuck Bown	Buick
17	J. D. McDuffie	Oldsmobile
18	David Pearson	Mercury
19	Baxter Price	Chevrolet
20	Richard Childress	Oldsmobile
21	Tommy Gale	Ford
22	Frank Warren	Dodge
23	Cecil Gordon	Oldsmobile
24	Dick May	Chevrolet
25	Terry Labonte	Chevrolet
26	Roger Hamby	Chevrolet
27	Claude Ballot-Lena	Oldsmobile
28	Grant Adcox	Chevrolet
29	Buddy Arrington	Dodge
30	Blackie Wangerin	Mercury
31	Ralph Jones	Ford
32	Dave Watson	Chevrolet
33	Jimmy Means	Chevrolet

34	Ronnie Thomas	Buick
35	Geoff Bodine	Oldsmobile
36	Bill Elliott	Mercury
37	Tighe Scott	Buick
38	Coo Coo Marlin	Chevrolet
39	John Kennedy	Chevrolet
40	Keith Davis	Chevrolet

NORTHWESTERN BANK 400

Time of Race: 2 hours, 49 minutes, 41 seconds
Average Speed: 88.400 MPH
Margin of Victory: 5 seconds

FINISH	DRIVER	CAR
1	Bobby Allison	Ford
2	Richard Petty	Chevrolet
3	Benny Parsons	Chevrolet
4	Dale Earnhardt	Chevrolet
5	Darrell Waltrip	Chevrolet
6	J. D. McDuffie	Chevrolet
7	Richard Childress	Chevrolet
8	Buddy Baker	Chevrolet
9	Cale Yarborough	Oldsmobile
10	Joe Millikan	Chevrolet
11	Donnie Allison	Chevrolet
12	Dave Marcis	Chevrolet
13	Dick Brooks	Oldsmobile
14	Ricky Rudd	Ford
15	Terry Labonte	Chevrolet
16	James Hylton	Chevrolet
17	Frank Warren	Dodge
18	D. K. Ulrich	Buick
19	Roger Hamby	Chevrolet
20	Tommy Gale	Ford
21	Dick May	Chevrolet
22	Cecil Gordon	Oldsmobile
23	Baxter Price	Chevrolet
24	Slick Johnson	Chevrolet
25	Buddy Arrington	Dodge
26	Nelson Oswald	Chevrolet
27	Earl Brooks	Dodge
28	Ronnie Thomas	Buick
29	Bill Hollar	Chevrolet
30	Jimmy Means	Chevrolet

SOUTHEASTERN 500

Time of Race: 2 hours, 55 minutes, 39 seconds
Average Speed: 91.033 MPH
Margin of Victory: 3 seconds

FINISH	DRIVER	CAR
1	Dale Earnhardt	Chevrolet
2	Bobby Allison	Ford
3	Darrell Waltrip	Chevrolet
4	Richard Petty	Oldsmobile
5	Benny Parsons	Oldsmobile
6	Donnie Allison	Chevrolet
7	Terry Labonte	Chevrolet
8	Joe Millikan	Chevrolet
9	James Hylton	Chevrolet
10	Ricky Rudd	Ford
11	Richard Childress	Chevrolet
12	D. K. Ulrich	Chevrolet
13	Buddy Arrington	Dodge
14	Roger Hamby	Oldsmobile
15	Cecil Gordon	Oldsmobile
16	Mike Potter	Chevrolet
17	Dave Marcis	Chevrolet
18	Tommy Gale	Ford
19	Baxter Price	Chevrolet
20	Frank Warren	Dodge
21	Harry Gant	Oldsmobile
22	Dick Brooks	Oldsmobile

23	Ronnie Thomas	Chevrolet
24	Cale Yarborough	Oldsmobile
25	Buddy Baker	Chevrolet
26	J. D. McDuffie	Chevrolet
27	Dick May	Chevrolet
28	Jimmy Means	Chevrolet
29	Bobby Wawak	Chevrolet
30	Ralph Jones	Ford

CRC CHEMICALS REBEL 500

Time of Race: 4 hours, 7 minutes, 7 seconds
Average Speed: 121.721 MPH
Margin of Victory: One half car length

FINISH	DRIVER	CAR
1	Darrell Waltrip	Chevrolet
2	Richard Petty	Chevrolet
3	Donnie Allison	Chevrolet
4	Benny Parsons	Chevrolet
5	Buddy Baker	Chevrolet
6	Cale Yarborough	Oldsmobile
7	Bill Elliott	Mercury
8	Ricky Rudd	Mercury
9	Dick Brooks	Oldsmobile
10	Joe Millikan	Chevrolet
11	Lennie Pond	Chevrolet
12	D. K. Ulrich	Chevrolet
13	Neil Bonnett	Oldsmobile
14	Butch Hartman	Chevrolet
15	James Hylton	Chevrolet
16	Richard Childress	Chevrolet
17	Frank Warren	Dodge
18	Ed Negre	Chrysler
19	J. D. McDuffie	Chevrolet
20	Baxter Price	Chevrolet
21	Al Holbert	Chevrolet
22	David Pearson	Mercury
23	Dale Earnhardt	Chevrolet
24	Ronnie Thomas	Chevrolet
25	Buddy Arrington	Dodge
26	Bobby Allison	Ford
27	Dave Marcis	Chevrolet
28	Bobby Wawak	Chevrolet
29	Terry Labonte	Chevrolet
30	Jimmy Means	Chevrolet
31	Cecil Gordon	Oldsmobile
32	Roger Hamby	Oldsmobile
33	Dick May	Chevrolet
34	Tommy Gale	Ford
35	Earle Canavan	Dodge
36	Travis Tiller	Dodge

VIRGINIA 500

Time of Race: 3 hours, 25 minutes, 43 seconds
Average Speed: 76.562 MPH
Margin of Victory: 4 seconds

FINISH	DRIVER	CAR
1	Richard Petty	Chevrolet
2	Buddy Baker	Chevrolet
3	Darrell Waltrip	Chevrolet
4	Bobby Allison	Ford
5	Joe Maillikan	Chevrolet
6	Harry Gant	Chevrolet
7	James Hylton	Chevrolet
8	Dale Earnhardt	Chevrolet
9	Terry Labonte	Chevrolet
10	J. D. McDuffie	Chevrolet
11	Cale Yarborough	Oldsmobile
12	Ricky Rudd	Ford
13	Tighe Scott	Buick
14	Richard Childress	Chevrolet
15	D. K. Ulrich	Chevrolet

16	Tommy Gale	Ford
17	Cecil Gordon	Oldsmobile
18	Frank Warren	Dodge
19	Benny Parsons	Chevrolet
20	Ronnie Thomas	Chevrolet
21	Dick Brooks	Oldsmobile
22	Buddy Arrington	Dodge
23	Chuck Bown	Buick
24	Baxter Price	Chevrolet
25	Neil Bonnett	Mercury
26	Dave Marcis	Chevrolet
27	Donnie Allison	Chevrolet
28	Jimmy Means	Chevrolet
29	Lennie Pond	Chevrolet
30	Dick May	Chevrolet

WINSTON 500

Time of Race: 3 hours, 13 minutes, 52 seconds
Average Speed: 154.770 MPH
Margin of Victory: 1 Lap and 50 seconds

FINISH	DRIVER	CAR
1	Bobby Allison	Ford
2	Darrell Waltrip	Oldsmobile
3	Buddy Arrington	Dodge
4	Richard Petty	Oldsmobile
5	Joe Millikan	Oldsmobile
6	Bill Elliott	Mercury
7	Tommy Gale	Ford
8	Frank Warren	Dodge
9	Terry Labonte	Buick
10	Coo Coo Marlin	Chevrolet
11	Cecil Gordon	Oldsmobile
12	Jimmy Means	Chevrolet
13	Ed Negre	Chrysler
14	Dave Marcis	Chevrolet
15	James Hylton	Oldsmobile
16	Kevin Housby	Chevrolet
17	Neil Bonnett	Mercury
18	Connie Saylor	Oldsmobile
19	Jimmy Finger	Buick
20	Dick May	Chevrolet
21	D. K. Ulrich	Buick
22	Jerry Jolly	Ford
23	Donnie Allison	Oldsmobile
24	Richard Childress	Oldsmobile
25	Ronnie Thomas	Buick
26	Baxter Price	Chevrolet
27	Ricky Rudd	Mercury
28	Blackie Wangerin	Mercury
29	Wayne Broome	Oldsmobile
30	Keith Davis	Oldsmobile
31	J. D. McDuffie	Chevrolet
32	Buddy Baker	Oldsmobile
33	Cale Yarborough	Oldsmobile
34	Benny Parsons	Oldsmobile
35	Tighe Scott	Buick
36	Dale Earnhardt	Buick
37	Dick Brooks	Oldsmobile
38	Lennie Pond	Oldsmobile
39	Harry Gant	Oldsmobile
40	Travis Tiller	Dodge

SUN-DROP MUSIC CITY USA 420

Time of Race: 2 hours, 49 minutes, 25 seconds
Average Speed: 88.652 MPH
Margin of Victory: 3 seconds

FINISH	DRIVER	CAR
1	Cale Yarborough	Oldsmobile
2	Richard Petty	Chevrolet
3	Bobby Allison	Ford
4	Dale Earnhardt	Chevrolet

5	J. D. McDuffie	Chevrolet
6	Richard Childress	Chevrolet
7	Benny Parsons	Chevrolet
8	Buddy Baker	Chevrolet
9	Terry Labonte	Chevrolet
10	Ricky Rudd	Ford
11	Jimmy Means	Chevrolet
12	Steve Spencer	Buick
13	Tommy Gale	Ford
14	Bobby Wawak	Chevrolet
15	Al Elmore	Chevrolet
16	D. K. Ulrich	Oldsmobile
17	Ronnie Thomas	Chevrolet
18	Mike Kempton	Chevrolet
19	Baxter Price	Chevrolet
20	Frank Warren	Dodge
21	Darrell Waltrip	Chevrolet
22	James Hylton	Chevrolet
23	Joe Millikan	Chevrolet
24	Darrell Busham	Mercury
25	Nelson Oswald	Chevrolet
26	Buddy Arrington	Dodge
27	Dick Brooks	Chevrolet
28	Harry Gant	Chevrolet

MASON-DIXON 500

Time of Race: 4 hours, 29 minutes, 37 seconds
Average Speed: 111.269 MPH
Margin of Victory: 2 Car lengths

FINISH	DRIVER	CAR
1	Neil Bonnett	Mercury
2	Cale Yarborough	Chevrolet
3	Buddy Baker	Chevrolet
4	Bobby Allison	Ford
5	Dale Earnhardt	Chevrolet
6	Terry Labonte	Chevrolet
7	Benny Parsons	Chevrolet
8	Joe Millikan	Chevrolet
9	Lennie Pond	Chevrolet
10	Buddy Arrington	Dodge
11	Dick May	Buick
12	D. K. Ulrich	Chevrolet
13	J.D. McDuffie	Chevrolet
14	Ricky Rudd	Ford
15	Baxter Price	Chevrolet
16	Ronnie Thomas	Chevrolet
17	James Hylton	Chevrolet
18	Darrell Waltrip	Chevrolet
19	Tommy Gale	Ford
20	Steve Peles	Chevrolet
21	Frank Warren	Dodge
22	Nelson Oswald	Chevrolet
23	Cecil Gordon	Oldsmobile
24	Tighe Scott	Bucik
25	Harry Gant	Chevrolet
26	Joey Arrington	Dodge
27	Louis Gatto	Chevrolet
28	Elmo Langley	Chevrolet
29	Richard Childress	Chevrolet
30	Richard Petty	Oldsmobile
31	Jimmy Means	Chevrolet

WORLD 600

Time of Race: 4 hours, 23 minutes, 24 seconds
Average Speed: 136.674 MPH
Margin of Victory: 7 seconds

FINISH	DRIVER	CAR
1	Darrell Waltrip	Chevrolet
2	Richard Petty	Chevrolet
3	Dale Earnhardt	Chevrolet
4	Cale Yarborough	Oldsmobile

5	Benny Parsons	Chevrolet
6	Ricky Rudd	Mercury
7	Terry Labonte	Chevrolet
8	Al Holbert	Chevrolet
9	Lennie Pond	Chevrolet
10	Richard Childress	Oldsmobile
11	Grant Adcox	Oldsmobile
12	Buddy Arrington	Dodge
13	J. D. McDuffie	Chevrolet
14	Ronnie Thomas	Chevrolet
15	Blackie Wangerin	Mercury
16	Tighe Scott	Buick
17	Cecil Gordon	Oldsmobile
18	D. K. Ulrich	Chevrolet
19	Jim Vandiver	Oldsmobile
20	Tommy Gale	Ford
21	Frank Warren	Dodge
22	Bobby Allison	Ford
23	Harry Gant	Chevrolet
24	Bruce Hill	Buick
25	Neil Bonnett	Mercury
26	Dave Marcis	Chevrolet
27	Joe Millikan	Chevrolet
28	Bill Dennis	Chevrolet
29	Glenn Jarrett	Chevrolet
30	Coo Coo Marlin	Chevrolet
31	Bobby Fisher	Buick
32	Skip Manning	Chevrolet
33	James Hylton	Chevrolet
34	Connie Saylor	Oldsmobile
35	Travis Tiller	Dodge
36	Buddy Baker	Chevrolet
37	Donnie Allison	Chevrolet
38	Bill Elliott	Mercury
39	Dick Brooks	Oldsmobile
40	Chuck Bown	Buick

TEXAS 400

Time of Race: 2 hours, 33 minutes, 39 seconds
Average Speed: 156.216 MPH
Margin of Victory: 1 Lap & 1 second

FINISH	DRIVER	CAR
1	Darrell Waltrip	Chevrolet
2	Bobby Allison	Ford
3	Buddy Baker	Chevrolet
4	Cale Yarborough	Chevrolet
5	Terry Labonte	Chevrolet
6	Richard Petty	Chevrolet
7	Richard Childress	Oldsmobile
8	Joe Millikan	Chevrolet
9	Buddy Arrington	Dodge
10	James Hylton	Chevrolet
11	John Rezek	Oldsmobile
12	Dale Earnhardt	Chevrolet
13	Bruce Hill	Buick
14	J. D. McDuffie	Chevrolet
15	D. K. Ulrich	Buick
16	H. B. Bailey	Pontiac
17	Billy Hagan	Chevrolet
18	Earle Canavan	Dodge
19	Frank Warren	Dodge
20	Tommy Gale	Ford
21	Cecil Gordon	Oldsmobile
22	Mike Potter	Chevrolet
23	Jimmy Means	Chevrolet
24	Jim Hurlbert	Ford
25	Benny Parsons	Chevrolet
26	Ronnie Thomas	Chevrolet
27	Baxter Price	Chevrolet
28	Ricky Rudd	Mercury
29	Mike Kempton	Chevrolet
30	Dick May	Oldsmobile
31	Lennie Pond	Chevrolet
32	Bill Meazell	Chevrolet
33	John Haver	Chevrolet
34	Jimmy Finger	Buick

NAPA RIVERSIDE 400

Time of Race: 2 hours, 23 minutes, 58 seconds
Average Speed: 103.732 MPH
Margin of Victory: 33 seconds

FINISH	DRIVER	CAR
1	Bobby Allison	Ford
2	Darrell Waltrip	Chevrolet
3	Richard Petty	Chevrolet
4	Cale Yarborough	Chevrolet
5	Benny Parsons	Chevrolet
6	Richard Childress	Oldsmobile
7	J. D. McDuffie	Chevrolet
8	Norm Palmer	Dodge
9	Buddy Arrington	Ford
10	Joe Millikan	Chevrolet
11	Cecil Gordon	Oldsmobile
12	Hal Callentine	Oldsmobile
13	Dale Earnhardt	Chevrolet
14	James Hylton	Chevrolet
15	Ed Hale	Chevrolet
16	Richard White	Chevrolet
17	Baxter Price	Chevrolet
18	Terry Labonte	Chevrolet
19	Dick Whalen	Chevrolet
20	John Borneman	Chevrolet
21	Jim Robinson	Chevrolet
22	Frank Warren	Dodge
23	Ronnie Thomas	Chevrolet
24	Robert Tartagila	Chevrolet
25	Jimmy Insolo	Oldsmobile
26	Tim Williamson	Chevrolet
27	Rick McCray	Buick
28	Neil Bonnett	Mercury
29	Dick Kranzier	Chevrolet
30	Bill Schmitt	Oldsmobile
31	Jimmy Means	Chevrolet
32	Steve Pfeifer	Chevrolet
33	D. K. Ulrich	Chevrolet
34	Chris Monoleos	Chevrolet
35	Elmo Langley	Ford

GABRIEL 400

Time of Race: 2 hours, 56 minutes, 44 seconds
Average Speed: 135.798 MPH
Margin of Victory: 1 second

FINISH	DRIVER	CAR
1	Buddy Baker	Chevrolet
2	Donnie Allison	Chevrolet
3	Cale Yarborough	Oldsmobile
4	Neil Bonnett	Mercury
5	Richard Petty	Chevrolet
6	Dale Earnhardt	Chevrolet
7	Bobby Allison	Ford
8	Ricky Rudd	Mercury
9	Tighe Scott	Buick
10	Dick Brooks	Chevrolet
11	Lennie Pond	Chevrolet
12	Bill Elliott	Mercury
13	Darrell Waltrip	Chevrolet
14	J. D. McDuffie	Chevrolet
15	Buddy Arrington	Dodge
16	Jimmy Means	Chevrolet
17	Harry Gant	Chevrolet
18	John Kennedy	Chevrolet
19	Sandy Satullo	Buick
20	James Hylton	Chevrolet
21	D. K. Ulrich	Buick
22	Frank Warren	Dodge
23	Richard Childress	Oldsmobile
24	Bob Burcham	Chevrolet
25	Terry Labonte	Chevrolet
26	Dave Marcis	Chevrolet
27	Ronnie Thomas	Chevrolet

28	David Sosebee	Chevrolet
29	Roger Hamby	Chevrolet
30	Joe Millikan	Chevrolet
31	Benny Parsons	Chevrolet
32	Paul Fess	Oldsmobile
33	Tommy Gale	Ford
34	Bill Green	Chevrolet
35	Marty Robbins	Dodge
36	Bill Seifert	Oldsmobile

FIRECRACKER 400

Time of Race: 2 hours, 18 minutes, 49 seconds
Average Speed: 172.890 MPH
Margin of Victory: 1 second

FINISH	DRIVER	CAR
1	Neil Bonnett	Mercury
2	Benny Parsons	Oldsmobile
3	Dale Earnhardt	Oldsmobile
4	Darrell Waltrip	Oldsmobile
5	Richard Petty	Oldsmobile
6	Chuck Bown	Buick
7	Harry Gant	Oldsmobile
8	Joe Millikan	Oldsmobile
9	Dick Brooks	Oldsmobile
10	A. J. Foyt	Oldsmobile
11	Bill Elliott	Mercury
12	Donnie Allison	Chevrolet
13	Ricky Rudd	Mercury
14	Tighe Scott	Buick
15	Buddy Arrington	Dodge
16	Gary Balough	Oldsmobile
17	Dave Marcis	Chevrolet
18	D. K. Ulrich	Buick
19	James Hylton	Chevrolet
20	Cale Yarborough	Oldsmobile
21	J. D. McDuffie	Chevrolet
22	Jimmy Means	Chevrolet
23	Rick Newsom	Oldsmobile
24	Blackie Wangerin	Mercury
25	Coo Coo Marlin	Chevrolet
26	Roger Hamby	Oldsmobile
27	Tommy Gale	Ford
28	Lennie Pond	Oldsmobile
29	Terry Labonte	Buick
30	Bobby Allison	Ford
31	Claude Ballot-Lena	Oldsmobile
32	Al Holbert	Chevrolet
33	Grant Adcox	Oldsmobile
34	Buddy Baker	Oldsmobile
35	Cecil Gordon	Oldsmobile
36	Travis Tiller	Dodge
37	Richard Childress	Oldsmobile
38	Sandy Satullo	Buick
39	Jimmy Finger	Buick
40	Frank Warren	Dodge
41	Bruce Hill	Buick

BUSCH NASHVILLE 420

Time of Race: 2 hours, 42 minutes, 51 seconds
Average Speed: 92.227 MPH
Margin of Victory: 1 Lap & 1 second

FINISH	DRIVER	CAR
1	Darrell Waltrip	Chevrolet
2	Cale Yarborough	Chevrolet
3	Dale Earnhardt	Chevrolet
4	Benny Parsons	Chevrolet
5	Richard Petty	Chevrolet
6	James Hylton	Chevrolet
7	Richard Childress	Chevrolet
8	J. D. McDuffie	Chevrolet
9	Ronnie Thomas	Chevrolet
10	Jimmy Means	Chevrolet
11	Cecil Gordon	Oldsmobile
12	Waye Watercutter	Chevrolet

13	Roger Hamby	Oldsmobile
14	Frank Warren	Dodge
15	Sterling Marlin	Chevrolet
16	Bobby Allison	Ford
17	Buddy Arrington	Dodge
18	Baxter Price	Chevrolet
19	Dick Brooks	Chevrolet
20	Steve Spencer	Chevrolet
21	Joe Millikan	Chevrolet
22	Harry Gant	Chevrolet
23	D. K. Ulrich	Chevrolet
24	Ralph Jones	Ford
25	Terry Labonte	Chevrolet
26	Henry Jones	Chevrolet
27	Nelson Oswald	Chevrolet
28	Tommy Gale	Ford
29	Dick May	Chevrolet
30	Jimmy Hindman	Ford

COCA-COLA 500

Time of Race: 4 hours, 20 minutes, 24 seconds
Average Speed: 115.207 MPH
Margin of Victory: 1 second

FINISH	DRIVER	CAR
1	Cale Yarborough	Chevrolet
2	Richard Petty	Chevrolet
3	Buddy Baker	Chevrolet
4	Benny Parsons	Chevrolet
5	Ricky Rudd	Mercury
6	Joe Millikan	Chevrolet
7	Darrell Waltrip	Chevrolet
8	Neil Bonnett	Mercury
9	Bobby Allison	Ford
10	Tighe Scott	Buick
11	D. K. Ulrich	Chevrolet
12	Richard Childress	Chevrolet
13	J. D. McDuffie	Chevrolet
14	Ronnie Thomas	
15	Harry Gant	Chevrolet
16	Jimmy Means	Chevrolet
17	Tommy Gale	Ford
18	Cecil Gordon	Oldsmobile
19	Frank Warren	Dodge
20	Dick Brooks	Chevrolet
21	Steve Peles	Chevrolet
22	Buddy Arrington	Dodge
23	Terry Labonte	Chevrolet
24	Jocko Maggiacomo	Oldsmobile
25	Nelson Oswald	Chevrolet
26	Rick Newsom	Oldsmobile
27	Earle Canavan	Dodge
28	Dick May	Ford
29	Dale Earnhardt	Chevrolet
30	Wayne Broome	Oldsmobile
31	Baxter Price	Chevrolet
32	Wayne Watercutter	Chevrolet
33	James Hylton	Chevrolet
34	Lennie Pond	Oldsmobile
35	Gary Balough	Oldsmobile
36	Louis Gatto	Chevrolet
37	Al Holbert	Chevrolet
38	Roger Hamby	Oldsmobile
39	Steve Gray	Chevrolet

TALLADEGA 500

Time of Race: 3 hours, 6 minutes, 6 seconds
Average Speed: 161.229 MPH
Margin of Victory: 62 seconds

FINISH	DRIVER	CAR
1	Darrell Waltrip	Oldsmobile
2	David Pearson	Oldsmobile
3	Ricky Rudd	Mercury
4	Richard Petty	Oldsmobile

5	Jody Ridley	Mercury
6	Tighe Scott	Buick
7	Harry Gant	Oldsmobile
8	Buddy Arrington	Dodge
9	Kyle Petty	Dodge
10	Richard Childress	Oldsmobile
11	Dick Brooks	Oldsmobile
12	Bill Elliott	Mercury
13	Jimmy Means	Chevrolet
14	Bob Burcham	Chevrolet
15	Rick Newsom	Oldsmobile
16	Bruce Hill	Oldsmobile
17	Steve Moore	Chevrolet
18	J. D. McDuffie	Chevrolet
19	Grant Adcox	Oldsmobile
20	James Hylton	Oldsmobile
21	Benny Parsons	Oldsmobile
22	Ronnie Thomas	Buick
23	Frank Warren	Dodge
24	Cale Yarborough	Oldsmobile
25	Joe Millikan	Oldsmobile
26	Baxter Price	Oldsmobile
27	D. K. Ulrich	Buick
28	Bobby Allison	Ford
29	Coo Coo Marlin	Chevrolet
30	Donnie Allison	Chevrolet
31	Dave Marcis	Chevrolet
32	Marty Robbins	Dodge
33	Terry Labonte	Buick
34	Neil Bonnett	Mercury
35	Jack Ingram	Oldsmobile
36	Tommy Gale	Ford
37	Blackie Wangerin	Mercury
38	Al Holbert	Oldsmobile
39	Buddy Baker	Oldsmobile
40	Cecil Gordon	Oldsmobile
41	Dick May	Oldsmobile

CHAMPION SPARK PLUG 400

Time of Race: 3 hours, 4 minutes, 5 seconds
Average Speed: 130.376 MPH
Margin of Victory: 1 second

FINISH	DRIVER	CAR
1	Richard Petty	Chevrolet
2	Buddy Baker	Chevrolet
3	Benny Parsons	Chevrolet
4	David Pearson	Chevrolet
5	John Anderson	Chevrolet
6	Joe Millikan	Chevrolet
7	Ricky Rudd	Mercury
8	Tighe Scott	Buick
9	J. D. McDuffie	Chevrolet
10	Richard Childress	Oldsmobile
11	Bill Elliott	Mercury
12	James Hylton	Chevrolet
13	Kyle Petty	Dodge
14	Tommy Gale	Ford
15	John Kennedy	Chevrolet
16	Frank Warren	Dodge
17	Cale Yarborough	Chevrolet
18	Cecil Gordon	Oldsmobile
19	Darrell Waltrip	Chevrolet
20	Buddy Arrington	Dodge
21	Baxter Price	Oldsmobile
22	Jimmy Means	Chevrolet
23	Bobby Allison	Ford
24	Ronnie Thomas	Chevrolet
25	Harry Gant	Chevrolet
26	Terry Labonte	Chevrolet
27	Marty Robbins	Dodge
28	D. K. Ulrich	Buick
29	Dick Brooks	Chevrolet
30	Dave Marcis	Chevrolet
31	Lennie Pond	Chevrolet
32	Al Rudd, Jr.	Chevrolet
33	Neil Bonnett	Mercury
34	Earle Canavan	Dodge
35	H. B. Bailey	Pontiac
36	Blackie Wangerin	Mercury

VOLUNTEER 500

Time of Race: 2 hours, 54 minutes, 46 seconds
Average Speed: 91.493 MPH
Margin of Victory: 3 second

FINISH	DRIVER	CAR
1	Darrell Waltrip	Chevrolet
2	Richard Petty	Chevrolet
3	Bobby Allison	Ford
4	Benny Parsons	Chevrolet
5	Cale Yarborough	Chevrolet
6	Joe Millikan	Oldsmobile
7	David Pearson	Chevrolet
8	Terry Labonte	Chevrolet
9	Ricky Rudd	Chevrolet
10	Bill Elliott	Chevrolet
11	Richard Childress	Chevrolet
12	D. K. Ulrich	Chevrolet
13	James Hylton	Chevrolet
14	Buddy Arrington	Dodge
15	Tommy Gale	Ford
16	Harry Gant	Chevrolet
17	Frank Warren	Dodge
18	Dave Marcis	Chevrolet
19	Jimmy Means	Chevrolet
20	Dick Brooks	Oldsmobile
21	Dick May	Chevrolet
22	Cecil Gordon	Oldsmobile
23	Mike Potter	Chevrolet
24	Baxter Price	Chevrolet
25	Jack Ingram	Chevrolet
26	J. D. McDuffie	Chevrolet
27	Ronnie Thomas	Chevrolet
28	Melvin Revis	Chevrolet
29	Henry Jones	Chevrolet
30	John Kennedy	Chevrolet

SOUTHERN 500

Time of Race: 3 hours, 58 minutes, 14 seconds
Average Speed: 126.259 MPH
Margin of Victory: 2 Laps & 4 seconds

FINISH	DRIVER	CAR
1	David Pearson	Chevrolet
2	Bill Elliott	Mercury
3	Terry Labonte	Chevrolet
4	Buddy Baker	Chevrolet
5	Benny Parsons	Chevrolet
6	Dave Marcis	Chevrolet
7	Dick Brooks	Chevrolet
8	Ricky Rudd	Mercury
9	Richard Petty	Chevrolet
10	Bobby Allison	Ford
11	Darrell Waltrip	Chevrolet
12	Harry Gant	Chevrolet
13	D. K. Ulrich	Buick
14	Buddy Arrington	Dodge
15	Joe Millikan	Chevrolet
16	Jimmy Means	Chevrolet
17	Chuck Bown	Buick
18	J. D. McDuffie	Chevrolet
19	Cale Yarborough	Chevrolet
20	Ed Negre	Chrysler
21	Tommy Gale	Ford
22	Frank Warren	Dodge
23	Baxter Price	Chevrolet
24	Ronnie Thomas	Chevrolet
25	Lennie Pond	Chevrolet
26	Cecil Gordon	Oldsmobile
27	H. B. Bailey	Pontiac
28	Jim Vandiver	Chevrolet
29	Richard Childress	Chevrolet
30	Jack Ingram	Oldsmobile
31	Donnie Allison	Chevrolet
32	Neil Bonnett	Mercury

33	Billy Smith	Ford
34	Dick May	Ford
35	Tighe Scott	Buick
36	Coo Coo Marlin	Chevrolet
37	Ralph Jones	Ford
38	James Hylton	Chevrolet
39	Earle Canavan	Dodge
40	Ferrel Harris	Ford

CAPITAL CITY 400

Time of Race: 2 hours, 41 minutes, 23 seconds
Average Speed: 80.604 MPH
Margin of Victory: 11 seconds

FINISH	DRIVER	CAR
1	Bobby Allison	Ford
2	Darrell Waltrip	Chevrolet
3	Ricky Rudd	Ford
4	Dale Earnhardt	Chevrolet
5	Cale Yarborough	Oldsmobile
6	Richard Petty	Chevrolet
7	Dave Marcis	Chevrolet
8	Benny Parsons	Chevrolet
9	Harry Gant	Chevrolet
10	Joe Millikan	Chevrolet
11	Bill Elliott	Chevrolet
12	D. K. Ulrich	Chevrolet
13	Buddy Arrington	Dodge
14	J. D. McDuffie	Chevrolet
15	Richard Childress	Chevrolet
16	Billy Elswick	Oldsmobile
17	Terry Labonte	Chevrolet
18	Cecil Gordon	Oldsmobile
19	Baxter Price	Chevrolet
20	Jimmy Means	Chevrolet
21	James Hylton	Chevrolet
22	Earle Canavan	Dodge
23	Ronnie Thomas	Chevrolet
24	Tommy Gale	Ford
25	Lennie Pond	Chevrolet
26	Frank Warren	Dodge

CRC CHEMICALS 500

Time of Race: 4 hours, 22 minutes, 19 seconds
Average Speed: 114.366 MPH
Margin of Victory: Car length

FINISH	DRIVER	CAR
1	Richard Petty	Chevrolet
2	Donnie Allison	Chevrolet
3	Cale Yarborough	Chevrolet
4	Buddy Baker	Chevrolet
5	Joe Millikan	Chevrolet
6	Bobby Allison	Ford
7	Dave Marcis	Chevrolet
8	Ricky Rudd	Ford
9	Dale Earnhardt	Chevrolet
10	Tighe Scott	Buick
11	John Anderson	Chevrolet
12	D. K. Ulrich	Chevrolet
13	Richard Childress	Chevrolet
14	James Hylton	Oldsmobile
15	Tommy Gale	Ford
16	Jimmy Means	Chevrolet
17	Roger Hamby	Chevrolet
18	Frank Warren	Dodge
19	Nester Peles	Oldsmobile
20	Cecil Gordon	Oldsmobile
21	Neil Bonnett	Mercury
22	Benny Parsons	Chevrolet
23	Lennie Pond	Chevrolet
24	Ronnie Thomas	Chevrolet
25	Terry Labonte	Chevrolet

26	Dick Brooks	Chevrolet
27	J. D. McDuffie	Chevrolet
28	Harry Gant	Chevrolet
29	Darrell Waltrip	Chevrolet
30	Bill Hollar	Chevrolet
31	Baxter Price	Chevrolet
32	Buddy Arrington	Dodge
33	Earle Canavan	Dodge
34	Dick May	Oldsmobile
35	Rick Newsom	Oldsmobile
36	Jeff Halverson	Chevrolet

OLD DOMINION 500

Time of Race: 3 hours, 29 minutes, 40 seconds
Average Speed: 75.119 MPH
Margin of Victory: 18 seconds

FINISH	DRIVER	CAR
1	Buddy Baker	Chevrolet
2	Richard Petty	Chevrolet
3	Joe Millikan	Chevrolet
4	Bobby Allison	Ford
5	Dave Marcis	Chevrolet
6	Ricky Rudd	Ford
7	Buddy Arrington	Dodge
8	Cale Yarborough	Oldsmobile
9	Terry Labonte	Chevrolet
10	D. K. Ulrich	Chevrolet
11	Darrell Waltrip	Chevrolet
12	Harry Gant	Chevrolet
13	Richard Childress	Chevrolet
14	Baxter Price	Chevrolet
15	Dick Brooks	Chevrolet
16	Frank Warren	Dodge
17	Jimmy Means	Chevrolet
18	Neil Bonnett	Mercury
19	Roger Hamby	Chevrolet
20	Ronnie Thomas	Chevrolet
21	J. D. McDuffie	Chevrolet
22	Tommy Gale	Ford
23	James Hylton	Chevrolet
24	Cecil Gordon	Oldsmobile
25	Dick May	Chevrolet
26	Dave Dion	Chevrolet
27	Benny Parsons	Chevrolet
28	Butch Lindley	Chevrolet
29	Dale Earnhardt	Chevrolet
30	Bill Hollar	Chevrolet

NAPA NATIONAL 500

Time of Race: 3 hours, 43 minutes, 53 seconds
Average Speed: 134.266 MPH
Margin of Victory: 1 Lap and 5 seconds

FINISH	DRIVER	CAR
1	Cale Yarborough	Chevrolet
2	Bobby Allison	Ford
3	Darrell Waltrip	Chevrolet
4	Richard Petty	Chevrolet
5	Donnie Allison	Chevrolet
6	Benny Parsons	Chevrolet
7	Bill Elliott	Mercury
8	Dick Brooks	Chevrolet
9	D. K. Ulrich	Buick
10	Dale Earnhardt	Chevrolet
11	Ricky Rudd	Mercury
12	Buddy Arrington	Dodge
13	Tighe Scott	Buick
14	Richard Childress	Chevrolet
15	Terry Labonte	Chevrolet
16	John Anderson	Chevrolet
17	Dick May	Ford
18	Kyle Petty	Dodge

19	Frank Warren	Pontiac
20	Harry Gant	Chevrolet
21	Tommy Gale	Ford
22	J.D. McDuffie	Chevrolet
23	James Hylton	Chevrolet
24	Baxter Price	Oldsmobile
25	Buddy Baker	Chevrolet
26	Jody Ridley	Mercury
27	David Sosebee	Chevrolet
28	John Rezek	Oldsmobile
29	Joe Millikan	Chevrolet
30	Steve Pfeifer	Chevrolet
31	Neil Bonnett	Mercury
32	Cecil Gordon	Chevrolet
33	Chuck Bown	Chevrolet
34	Jim Vandiver	Oldsmobile
35	Bobby Brack	Chevrolet
36	Jack Ingram	Chevrolet
37	Dave Marcis	Chevrolet
38	Ronnie Thomas	Chevrolet
39	Richard Brickhouse	Oldsmobile
40	Jimmy Means	Chevrolet

7	Richard Childress	Chevrolet
8	Ronnie Thomas	Chevrolet
9	Dave Marcis	Chevrolet
10	Slick Johnson	Chevrolet
11	James Hylton	Chevrolet
12	Tommy Gale	Ford
13	Cecil Gordon	Oldsmobile
14	Bill Elswick	Oldsmobile
15	Dick Brooks	Chevrolet
16	Freddy Smith	Chevrolet
17	Buddy Arrington	Dodge
18	Joe Millikan	Chevrolet
19	Bobby Allison	Ford
20	Ricky Rudd	Ford
21	Harry Gant	Chevrolet
22	Baxter Price	Oldsmobile
23	Bill Elliott	Chevrolet
24	Frank Warren	Dodge
25	J. D. McDuffie	Chevrolet
26	Dick May	Chevrolet
27	Terry Labonte	Chevrolet
28	D. K. Ulrich	Buick
29	Neil Bonnett	Mercury
30	Randy Ogden	Chevrolet
31	Jimmy Means	Chevrolet
32	Glenn Jarrett	Chevrolet
33	Buddy Baker	Chevrolet
34	Travis Tiller	Buick
35	Mike Potter	Chevrolet
36	Bub Strickler	Oldsmobile
37	Tighe Scott	Buick

HOLLY FARMS 400

Time of Race: 2 hours, 44 minutes, 1 second
Average Speed: 91.454 MPH
Margin of Victory: 1/4 Car length

FINISH	DRIVER	CAR
1	Benny Parsons	Chevrolet
2	Bobby Allison	Ford
3	Richard Petty	Chevrolet
4	Dale Earnhardt	Chevrolet
5	Ricky Rudd	Ford
6	Terry Labonte	Chevrolet
7	Ronnie Thomas	Chevrolet
8	D. K. Ulrich	Chevrolet
9	Buddy Arrington	Dodge
10	Richard Childress	Chevrolet
11	James Hylton	Chevrolet
12	Roger Hamby	Chevrolet
13	Darrell Waltrip	Chevrolet
14	Harry Gant	Chevrolet
15	Joe Millikan	Chevrolet
16	Ernie Shaw	Chevrolet
17	Baxter Price	Chevrolet
18	Cecil Gordon	Buick
19	Bill Elswick	Oldsmobile
20	Cale Yarborough	Oldsmobile
21	Dave Marcis	Chevrolet
22	Larry Iseley	Chevrolet
23	John Kennedy	Chevrolet
24	Jimmy Means	Chevrolet
25	Dick May	Oldsmobile
26	Frank Warren	Dodge
27	Tommy Gale	Ford
28	J. D. McDuffie	Chevrolet
29	Henry Jones	Chevrolet

AMERICAN 500

Time of Race: 4 hours, 37 minutes, 4 seconds
Average Speed: 108.356 MPH
Margin of Victory: 17 seconds

FINISH	DRIVER	CAR
1	Richard Petty	Chevrolet
2	Benny Parsons	Chevrolet
3	Cale Yarborough	Chevrolet
4	Donnie Allison	Chevrolet
5	Dale Earnhardt	Chevrolet
6	Darrell Waltrip	Chevrolet

DIXIE 500

Time of Race: 3 hours, 33 minutes, 46 seconds
Average Speed: 140.120 MPH
Margin of Victory: Car length

FINISH	DRIVER	CAR
1	Neil Bonnett	Mercury
2	Dale Earnhardt	Chevrolet
3	Cale Yarborough	Oldsmobile
4	Bobby Allison	Ford
5	Darrell Waltrip	Chevrolet
6	Richard Petty	Chevrolet
7	Terry Labonte	Chevrolet
8	Ricky Rudd	Mercury
9	Joe Millikan	Chevrolet
10	Jody Ridley	Mercury
11	Harry Gant	Oldsmobile
12	J. D. McDuffie	Chevrolet
13	Slick Johnson	Chevrolet
14	Buck Simmons	Chevrolet
15	Richard Childress	Chevrolet
16	James Hylton	Chevrolet
17	Buddy Arrington	Dodge
18	Freddy Smith	Chevrolet
19	Jimmy Means	Chevrolet
20	H. B. Bailey	Pontiac
21	Frank Warren	Dodge
22	Tommy Gale	Ford
23	Dave Marcis	Chevrolet
24	John Anderson	Chevrolet
25	D. K. Ulrich	Buick
26	Wayne Watercutter	Chevrolet
27	Grant Adcox	Buick
28	Ronnie Thomas	Chevrolet
29	Tighe Scott	Buick
30	Ralph Jones	Ford
31	Benny Parsons	Chevrolet
32	Kyle Petty	Dodge
33	David Sosebee	Chevrolet
34	Steve Pfeifer	Chevrolet
35	Donnie Allison	Chevrolet
36	John Rezek	Oldsmobile
37	Randy Ogden	Chevrolet
38	Cecil Gordon	Oldsmobile
39	Buddy Baker	Chevrolet
40	Dick Brooks	Chevrolet
41	Dick May	Chevrolet

LOS ANGELES TIMES 500

Time of Race: 3 hours, 45 minutes, 52 seconds
Average Speed: 132.822 MPH
Margin of Victory: 42 seconds

FINISH	DRIVER	CAR
1	Benny Parsons	Chevrolet
2	Bobby Allison	Ford
3	Cale Yarborough	Oldsmobile
4	Buddy Baker	Chevrolet
5	Richard Petty	Chevrolet
6	Neil Bonnett	Mercury
7	Dick Brooks	Chevrolet
8	Darrell Waltrip	Chevrolet
9	Dale Earnhardt	Chevrolet
10	Ricky Rudd	Mercury
11	Donnie Allison	Chevrolet
12	Joe Millikan	Chevrolet
13	Terry Labonte	Oldsmobile
14	Kyle Petty	Chevrolet
15	Bruce Hill	Oldsmobile
16	Richard Childress	Chevrolet
17	Dave Marcis	Chevrolet
18	Bill Schmitt	Oldsmobile
19	Buddy Arrington	Dodge
20	Harry Gant	Chevrolet
21	Roy Smith	Oldsmobile
22	Tim Williamson	Chevrolet
23	Hal Callantine	Oldsmobile
24	Cecil Gordon	Oldsmobile
25	Frank Warren	Dodge
26	James Hylton	Chevrolet
27	Ronnie Thomas	Chevrolet
28	Randy Ogden	Chevrolet
29	Buck Simmons	Chevrolet
30	Richard White	Chevrolet
31	J. D. McDuffie	Chevrolet
32	Jim Robinson	Chevrolet
33	D. K. Ulrich	Chevrolet
34	Tommy Gale	Ford
35	John Rezek	Buick
36	Jimmy Insolo	Oldsmobile
37	Vince Giamformaggio	Chevrolet

1980

WINSTON WESTERN 500

Time of Race: 3 hours, 16 minutes, 58 seconds
Average Speed: 94.974 mph
Margin of Victory: 2.97 seconds

FINISH	DRIVER	CAR
1	Darrell Waltrip	Chevrolet
2	Dale Earnhardt	Chevrolet
3	Richard Petty	Chevrolet
4	Joe Millikan	Chevrolet
5	Bill Schmitt	Oldsmobile
6	Richard Childress	Chevrolet
7	Terry Labonte	Chevrolet
8	Bill Whittington	Chevrolet
9	Don Whittington	Chevrolet
10	Ronnie Thomas	Chevrolet
11	James Hylton	Chevrolet
12	Harry Gant	Oldsmobile
13	Roy Smith	Chevrolet
14	Buddy Arrington	Dodge
15	JD McDuffie	Chevrolet
16	Jody Ridley	Ford
17	Dave Marcis	Chevrolet
18	Bobby Allison	Ford
19	Don Puskarich	Chevrolet

20	Vince Giamformaggio	Chevrolet
21	Jimmy Means	Chevrolet
22	Dick Brooks	Chevrolet
23	Cale Yarborough	Chevrolet
24	Jim Robinson	Chevrolet
25	Chuck Wahl	Chevrolet
26	Hershel McGriff	Dodge
27	Steve Pfeifer	Chevrolet
28	Dan Gurney	Chevrolet
29	Lake Speed	Oldsmobile
30	Randy Ogden	Chevrolet
31	John Borneman	Chevrolet
32	Dick May	Dodge
33	Benny Parsons	Chevrolet
34	Neil Bonnett	Mercury
35	Rick McCray	Buick
36	Chuck Bown	Chevrolet
37	Bill Osborne	Chevrolet

DAYTONA 500

Time of Race: 2 hours, 48 minutes, 55 seconds
Average Speed: 177.602 mph - New Record
Margin of Victory: 12 seconds (finished under caution)

FINISH	DRIVER	CAR
1	Buddy Baker	Oldsmobile
2	Bobby Allison	Mercury
3	Neil Bonnett	Mercury
4	Dale Earnhardt	Oldsmobile
5	Benny Parsons	Oldsmobile
6	Terry Labonte	Oldsmobile
7	Donnie Allison	Oldsmobile
8	Sterling Marlin	Chevrolet
9	Lennie Pond	Buick
10	Jody Ridley	Ford
11	Janet Guthrie	Chevrolet
12	Bill Elliott	Mercury
13	Richard Childress	Oldsmobile
14	Slick Johnson	Chevrolet
15	Jimmy Means	Buick
16	Don Whittington	Chevrolet
17	Joe Booher	Buick
18	John Anderson	Oldsmobile
19	Cale Yarborough	Oldsmobile
20	Tommy Gale	Ford
21	Cecil Gordon	Oldsmobile
22	Dave Marcis	Oldsmobile
23	Bill Schmitt	Oldsmobile
24	Bill Elswick	Oldsmobile
25	Richard Petty	Oldsmobile
26	James Hylton	Oldsmobile
27	JD McDuffie	Buick
28	John Utsman	Chevrolet
29	Ronnie Thomas	Buick
30	Kevin Housby	Oldsmobile
31	A.J. Foyt	Oldsmobile
32	Bill Whittington	Buick
33	Bruce Hill	Oldsmobile
34	Joe Millikan	Oldsmobile
35	Chuck Bown	Oldsmobile
36	Dick Brooks	Oldsmobile
37	Jim Vandiver	Oldsmobile
38	James Hurlbert	Dodge
39	Tighe Scott	Buick
40	Darrell Waltrip	Oldsmobile
41	Buddy Arrington	Dodge
42	Harry Gant	Oldsmobile

RICHMOND 400

Time of Race: 3 hours, 12 minutes, 8 seconds
Average Speed: 67.703 mph
Margin of Victory: 1.2 seconds

FINISH	DRVER	CAR
1	Darrell Waltrip	Chevrolet
2	Bobby Allison	Ford

3	Richard Petty	Chevrolet
4	Dave Marcis	Chevrolet
5	Dale Earnhardt	Chevrolet
6	Buddy Arrington	Dodge
7	James Hylton	Chevrolet
8	Cecil Gordon	Oldsmobile
9	J.D. McDuffie	Chevrolet
10	Bobby Wawak	Chevrolet
11	Joe Booher	Chevrolet
12	Harry Gant	Chevrolet
13	Joey Arrington	Dodge
14	Bub Strickler	Chevrolet
15	Bill Elswick	Chevrolet
16	Roger Hamby	Chevrolet
17	Tommy Houston	Chevrolet
18	Jody Ridley	Ford
19	Rick Newsom	Chevrolet
20	Dick May	Chevrolet
21	Tommy Gale	Ford
22	Richard Childress	Oldsmobile
23	Bill Hollar	Chevrolet
24	Terry Labonte	Chevrolet
25	Cale Yarborough	Chevrolet
26	Ronnie Thomas	Chevrolet
27	Joe Millikan	Chevrolet
28	Benny Parsons	Chevrolet
29	Dick Brooks	Chevrolet
30	Jimmy Means	Chevrolet
31	Baxter Price	Chevrolet

CAROLINA 500

Time of Race: 4 hours, 36 minutes, 6 seconds
Average Speed: 108.735 mph
Margin of Victory: 3 seconds

FINISH	DRIVER	CAR
1	Cale Yarborough	Oldsmobile
2	Richard Petty	Chevrolet
3	Dale Earnhardt	Chevrolet
4	Darrell Waltrip	Chevrolet
5	Donnie Allison	Chevrolet
6	Neil Bonnett	Mercury
7	Bobby Allison	Ford
8	Harry Gant	Chevrolet
9	Dave Marcis	Chevrolet
10	Terry Labonte	Chevrolet
11	Ronnie Thomas	Chevrolet
12	Ricky Rudd	Chevrolet
13	James Hylton	Chevrolet
14	Richard Childress	Chevrolet
15	Buddy Baker	Chevrolet
16	Dick Brooks	Chevrolet
17	Bobby Wawak	Chevrolet
18	Roger Hamby	Chevrolet
19	Dick May	Dodge
20	Jimmy Means	Chevrolet
21	Benny Parsons	Chevrlolet
22	Buck Simmons	Chevrolet
23	Bill Elswick	Chevrolet
24	John Anderson	Chevrolet
25	Buddy Arrington	Dodge
26	Tommy Gale	Ford
27	Baxter Price	Oldsmobile
28	Joe Millikan	Oldsmobile
29	Jody Ridley	Ford
30	Slick Johnson	Chevrolet
31	Kyle Petty	Chevrolet
32	J.D. McDuffie	Chevrolet
33	Cecil Gordon	Oldsmobile
34	Randy Ogden	Chevrolet
35	Bill Osborne	Chevrolet
36	Mike Potter	Chevrolet
37	Tighe Scott	Buick
38	Junior Miller	Chevrolet

ATLANTA 500

Time of Race: 3 hours, 42 minutes, 32 seconds
Average Speed: 134.080 mph
Margin of Victory: 9 seconds

FINISH	DRIVER	CAR
1	Dale Earnhardt	Chevrolet
2	Rusty Wallace	Chevrolet
3	Bobby Allison	Ford
4	Dave Marcis	Oldsmobile
5	Dick Brooks	Chevrolet
6	Jody Ridley	Ford
7	Buddy Baker	Oldsmobile
8	Cale Yarborough	Chevrolet
9	J.D. McDuffie	Chevrolet
10	Slick Johnson	Chevrolet
11	Lake Speed	Chevrolet
12	Jimmy Means	Chevrolet
13	Richard Childress	Oldsmobile
14	Kyle Petty	Chevrolet
15	Terry Labonte	Chevrolet
16	Harry Gant	Chevrolet
17	Kevin Housby	Oldsmobile
18	Tommy Gale	Ford
19	Buddy Arrington	Dodge
20	Frank Warren	Dodge
21	Baxter Price	Oldsmobile
22	Ronnie Thomas	Chevrolet
23	Lennie Pond	Chevrolet
24	Cecil Gordon	Oldsmobile
25	Ralph Jones	Ford
26	Donnie Allison	Chevrolet
27	Bruce Hill	Oldsmobile
28	Darell Waltrip	Chevrolet
29	Bill Elliott	Mercury
30	Benny Parsons	Chevrolet
31	Ricky Rudd	Chevrolet
32	Tighe Scott	Buick
33	Richard Petty	Chevrolet
34	Roger Hamby	Chevrolet
35	Joe Booner	Buick
36	Rick Newson	Oldsmobile
37	Joe Millikan	Chevrolet
38	Don Whittington	Oldsmobile
39	James Hylton	Chevrolet
40	Buick Simmons	Chevrolet
41	Neil Bonnett	Mercury
42	Randy Ogden	Chevrolet

VALLEYDALE SOUTHEASTERN 500

Time of Race: 2 hours, 44 minutes, 53 seconds
Average Speed: 96.977 mph
Margin of Victory: 8 seconds

FINISH	DRIVER	CAR
1	Dale Earnhardt	Chevrolet
2	Darrell Waltrip	Chevrolet
3	Bobby Allison	Ford
4	Benny Parsons	Chevroler
5	Cale Yarborough	Chevrolet
6	Joe Millikan	Chevrolet
7	Harry Gant	Chevrolet
8	Richard Petty	Chevrolet
9	Dave Marcis	Chevrolet
10	Terry Labonte	Chevrolet
11	Jody Ridley	Ford
12	Ronnie Thomas	Chevrolet
13	J.D. McDuffie	Chevrolet
14	James Hylton	Chevrolet
15	Tommy Houston	Chevrolet
16	Dick May	Chevrolet
17	Tommy Gale	Ford
18	Roger Hamby	Chevrolet
19	Bill Elswick	Chevrolet
20	John Utsman	Chevrolet
21	Buddy Arrington	Dodge
22	Cecil Gordon	Oldsmobile
23	Baxter Price	Chevrolet
24	Jimmy Means	Chevrolet
25	Junior Miller	Chevrolet
26	Slick Johnson	Chevrolet
27	Dick Brooks	Chevrolet
28	Travis Tiller	Dodge

29	Richard Childress	Oldsmobile
30	Mike Potter	Chevrolet
31	Bobby Wawak	Chevrolet
32	Buck Simmons	Chevrolet

CRC CHEMICALS REBEL 500

Time of Race: 2 hours, 23 minutes, 49 seconds
Average Speed: 112.397 mph
Margin of Victory: 3 seconds

FINISH	DRIVER	CAR
1	David Pearson	Chevrolet
2	Benny Parsons	Chevrolet
3	Harry Gant	Chevrolet
4	Darrell Waltrip	Chevrolet
5	Dick Brooks	Chevrolet
6	Lennie Pond	Chevrolet
7	Joe Millikan	Chevrolet
8	Lake Speed	Chevrolet
9	Richard Petty	Chevrolet
10	Jody Ridley	Ford
11	Sterling Marlin	Oldsmobile
12	Cale Yarborough	Chevrolet
13	Bobby Wawak	Chevrolet
14	Buddy Arrington	Dodge
15	Tommy Gale	Ford
16	Roger Hamby	Chevrolet
17	John Anderson	Chevrolet
18	James Hylton	Chevrolet
19	Ricky Rudd	Chevrolet
20	Bill Elswick	Chevrolet
21	Richard Childress	Oldsmobile
22	J.D. McDuffie	Chevrolet
23	Dave Marcis	Chevrolet
24	Dick May	Chevrolet
25	Slick Johnson	Chevrolet
26	Ronnie Thomas	Chevrolet
27	Buck Simmons	Chevrolet
28	Jimmy Means	Chevrolet
29	Dale Earnhardt	Chevrolet
30	Bobby Allison	Ford
31	Baxter Price	Chevrolet
32	Terry Labonte	Chevrolet
33	Melvin Revis	Chevrolet
34	Cecil Gordon	Chrysler
35	Buddy Baker	Chevrolet
36	Neil Bonnett	Mercury

NORTHWESTERN BANK 400

Time of Race: 2 hours, 37 minutes, 4 seconds
Average Speed: 95.501 mph
Margin of Victory: 1 lap - 5 seconds

FINISH	DRIVER	CAR
1	Richard Petty	Chevrolet
2	Harry Gant	Chevrolet
3	Bobby allison	Ford
4	Cale Yarborough	Chevrolet
5	Benny Parsons	Chevrolet
6	Dale Earnhardt	Chevrolet
7	Jody Ridley	Ford
8	Kyle Petty	Chevrolet
9	Slick Johnson	Chevrolet
10	Joe Millikan	Chevrolet
11	Richard Childress	Chevrolet
12	Darrell Waltrip	Chevrolet
13	Buddy Arrington	Dodge
14	Jimmy Means	Chevrolet
15	Dick May	Chevrolet
16	Bobby Wawak	Chevrolet
17	James Hylton	Chevrolet
18	Jeff McDuffie	Buick
19	Baxter Price	Chevrolet
20	Rick Newsom	Chevrolet

21	Dave Marcis	Chevrolet
22	Terry Labonte	Chevrolet
23	Ronnie Thomas	Chevrolet
24	Bill Elswick	Chevrolet
25	Roger Hamby	Chevrolet
26	D.K. Ulrich	Chevrolet
27	Dick Brooks	Chevrolet
28	John Anderson	Chevrolet
29	Tommy Gale	Ford
30	J.D. McDuffie	Chevrolet
31	Tommy Houston	Chevrolet

VIRGINIA 500

Time of Race: 3 hours, 48 minutes, 6 seconds
Average Speed: 69.049 mp
Margin of Victory: 9 seconds (finished under caution)

FINISH	DRIVER	CAR
1	Darrell Waltrip	Chevrolet
2	Benny Parsons	Chevrolet
3	Richard Petty	Chevrolet
4	Cale Yarborough	Chevrolet
5	Joe Millikan	Chevrolet
6	Neil Bonnett	Mercury
7	Jody Ridley	Ford
8	Dave Marcis	Chevrolet
9	Slick Johnson	Chevrolet
10	Buddy Arrington	Chevrolet
11	Richard Childress	Chevrolet
12	Jimmy Means	Chevrolet
13	Dale Earnhardt	Chevrolet
14	Junior Miller	Chevrolet
15	Kyle Petty	Chevrolet
16	Buck Simmons	Chevrolet
17	Cecil Gordon	Oldsmobile
18	James Hylton	Chevrolet
19	Baxter Price	Chevrolet
20	Dick May	Chevrolet
21	Harry Gant	Chevrolet
22	Rnnie Thomas	Chevrolet
23	Terry Labonte	Chevrolet
24	Buddy Baker	Chevrolet
25	Bobby Allison	Ford
26	Dick Brooks	Chevrolet
27	Bill Elswick	Chevrolet
28	D.K. Ulrich	Chevrolet
29	Tommy Gale	Ford
30	J.D. McDuffie	Chevrolet
31	Bobby Wawak	Chevrolet
32	Rick Newsom	Oldsmobile

WINSTON 500

Time of Race: 2 hours, 56 minutes
Average Speed: 170.481 mph
Margin of Victory: 3 feet

FINISH	DRIVER	CAR
1	Buddy Baker	Oldsmobile
2	Dale Earnhardt	Oldsmobile
3	David Pearson	Oldsmobile
4	Lennie Pond	Oldsmobile
5	Tighe Scott	Oldsmobile
6	Cale Yarborough	Oldsmobile
7	Lake Speed	Chevrolet
8	Benny Parsons	Oldsmobile
9	Dick Brooks	Oldsmobile
10	Jody Ridley	Mercury
11	Coo Coo Marlin	Chevrolet
12	Richard Childress	Oldsmobile
13	James Hylton	Chevrolet
14	Steve Moore	Chevrolet
15	Dick May	Dodge
16	Tommy Gale	Ford

17	Roger Hamby	Chevrolet
18	Buddy Arrington	Dodge
19	Frank Warren	Dodge
20	Ronnie Thomas	Buick
21	Bill Elliott	Mercury
22	Gary Baker	Chevrolet
23	Cecil Gordon	Oldsmobile
24	Buick Simmons	Oldsmobile
25	Donnie Allison	Oldsmobile
26	John Anderson	Buick
27	Neil Bonnett	Mercury
28	Dick Skillen	Buick
29	Dave Marcis	Oldsmobile
30	Bobby Wawak	Dodge
31	Richard Petty	Oldsmobile
32	Terry Labonte	Oldsmobile
33	Marty Robbins	Dodge
34	Don Whittington	Oldsmobile
35	Bill Elswick	Oldsmobile
36	Bruce Hill	Oldsmobile
37	Harry Gant	Oldsmobile
38	Phil Finney	Oldsmobile
39	Jim Vandiver	Oldsmobile
40	Bobby Allison	Mercury
41	J.D. McDuffie	Buick
42	Darrell Waltrip	Oldsmobile

MUSIC CITY 420

Time of Race: 2 hours, 47 minutes, 52 seconds
Average Speed: 89.471 mph
Margin of Victory: One car length

FINISH	DRIVER	CAR
1	Richard Petty	Chevrolet
2	Benny Parsons	Chevrolet
3	Cale Yarborough	Chevrolet
4	Darrell Waltrip	Chevrolet
5	Bobby Allison	Ford
6	Dale Earnhardt	Chevrolet
7	Terry Labonte	Chevrolet
8	Jody Ridley	Ford
9	Harry Gant	Chevrolet
10	Mike Alexander	Chevrolet
11	Dave Marcis	Chevrolet
12	Jimmy Means	Chevrolet
13	James Hylton	Chevrolet
14	Don Spouse	Chevrolet
15	Tommy Gale	Ford
16	Junior Miller	Chevrolet
17	Dick May	Chevrolet
18	Bobby Wawak	Chevrolet
19	Cecil Gordon	Oldsmobile
20	J.D. McDuffie	Chevrolet
21	Ronnie Thomas	Chevrolet
22	Baxter Price	Chevrolet
23	Roger Hamby	Chevrolet
24	John Anderson	Chevrolet
25	Slick Johnson	Chevrolet
26	Rick Newsom	Oldsmobile
27	Buddy Arrington	Dodge
28	Steve Spencer	Chevrolet
29	Richard Childress	Chevrolet
30	Dick Brooks	Chevrolet

MASON-DIXON 500

Time of Race: 4 hours, 23 minutes, 28 seconds
Average Speed: 113.866 mph
Margin of Victory: 26 seconds

FINISH	DRIVER	CAR
1	Bobby Allison	Ford
2	Richard Petty	Chevrolet
3	Buddy Baker	Chevrolet

4	Harry Gant	Chevrolet
5	Terry Labonte	Chevrolet
6	Jody Ridley	Ford
7	Dick May	Chevrolet
8	Richard Childress	Chevrolet
9	Cecil Gordon	Oldsmobile
10	Dale Earnhardt	Chevrolet
11	Ronnie Thomas	Buick
12	Tommy Gale	Ford
13	Roger Hamby	Chevrolet
14	Baxter Price	Chevrolet
15	Jim Ingram	Chevrolet
16	Cale Yarborough	Chevrolet
17	Dick Brooks	Chevrolet
18	Neil Bonnett	Mercury
19	James Hylton	Chevrolet
20	Darrell Waltrip	Chevrolet
21	Kyle Petty	Chevrolet
22	Benny Parsons	Chevrolet
23	Tighe Scott	Chevrolet
24	Jocko Maggiacomo	Oldsmobile
25	Dave Marcis	Chevrolet
26	Buddy Arrington	Dodge
27	Jimmy Means	Chevrolet
28	Nestor Peles	Oldsmobile
29	Bobby Wawak	Chevrolet
30	Bill Elswick	Chevrolet
31	Junior Miller	Chevrolet
32	Rick Newsom	Oldsmobile
33	J.D. McDuffie	Chevrolet
34	D.K. Ulrich	Chevrolet

WORLD 600

Time of Race: 5 hours, 1 minute, 51 seconds
Average Speed: 119.265 mph
Margin of Victory: car length

FINISH	DRIVER	CAR
1	Benny Parsons	Chevrolet
2	Darrell Waltrip	Chevrolet
3	Terry Labonte	Chevrolet
4	Richard Petty	Chevrolet
5	Neil Bonnett	Mercury
6	David Pearson	Chevrolet
7	Kyle Petty	Chevrolet
8	Jim Vandiver	Oldsmobile
9	Ricky Rudd	Chevrolet
10	Buddy Arrington	Dodge
11	Richard Chldress	Oldsmobile
12	Jody Ridley	Mercury
13	Blackie Wangerin	Mercury
14	Jimmy Means	Chevrolet
15	Dick Brooks	Chevrolet
16	Sterling Marlin	Oldsmobile
17	Cale Yarborough	Chevrolet
18	John Anderson	Chevrolet
19	Connie Saylor	Chevrolet
20	Dale Earnhardt	Chevrolet
21	Baxter Price	Oldsmobile
22	Ronnie Thomas	Chevrolet
23	James Hylton	Chevrolet
24	Tommy Houston	Chevrolet
25	Bobby Wawak	Buick
26	Bobby Allison	Mercury
27	Billy Harvey	Oldsmobile
28	Harry Gant	Chevrolet
29	Dave Marcis	Oldsmobile
30	J.D. McDuffie	Chevrolet
31	Donnie Allison	Chevrolet
32	Slick Johnson	Chevrolet
33	Tommy Gale	Ford
34	Bill Elswick	Chevrolet
35	Steve Moore	Chevrolet
36	Tighe Scott	Oldsmobile
37	Cecil Gordon	Oldsmobile
38	Bruce Hill	Oldsmobile
39	Buddy Baker	Buick
40	John Greenwood	Chevrolet
41	Lennie Pond	Chevrolet
42	Bill Elliott	Mercury

NASCAR 400

Time of Race: 2 hours, 30 minutes, 54 seconds
Average Speed: 159.046 mph - New Record
Margin of Victory: 1 lap - 14 seconds

FINISH	DRIVER	CAR
1	Cale Yarborough	Chevrolet
2	Richard Petty	Chevrolet
3	Bobby Allison	Ford
4	Darrell Waltrip	Chevrolet
5	Terry Labonte	Chevrolet
6	Richard Childress	Chevrolet
7	Dave Marcis	Oldsmobile
8	Harry Gant	Chevrolet
9	Dale Earnhardt	Chevrolet
10	James Hylton	Chevrolet
11	Ronnie Thomas	Chevrolet
12	Lake Speed	Chevrolet
13	Jimmy Finger	Buick
14	Cecil Gordon	Oldsmobile
15	D.K. Ulrich	Chevrolet
16	Dick May	Buick
17	Frank Warren	Dodge
18	Baxter Price	Chevrolet
19	Jimmy Means	Chevrolet
20	Nelson Oswald	Buick
21	Henry Jones	Oldsmobile
22	Roger Hamby	Chevrolet
23	Benny Parsons	Chevrolet
24	Bobby Wawak	Buick
25	Tommy Gale	Ford
26	Jody Ridley	Ford
27	Dick Brooks	Chevrolet
28	Buddy Arrington	Dodge
29	J.D. McDuffie	Chevrolet
30	Slick Johnson	Chevrolet
31	Randy Ogden	Chevrolet

WARNER W. HODGDON 400

Time of Race: 2 hours, 26 minutes, 38 seconds
Average Speed: 101.846 mph
Margin of Victory: 1 car length

FINISH	DRIVER	CAR
1	Darrell Waltrip	Chevrolet
2	Neil Bonnett	Mercury
3	Benny Parsons	Chevrolet
4	Cale Uarborough	Chevrolet
5	Dale Earnhardt	Chevrolet
6	Dave Marcis	Chevrolet
7	Harry Gant	Chevrolet
8	Richard Petty	Chevrolet
9	J.D. McDuffie	Chevrolet
10	Cecil Gordon	Oldsmobile
11	Jody Ridley	Ford
12	James Hylton	Chevrolet
13	Bill Schmitt	Oldsmobile
14	Buddy Arrington	Dodge
15	Bobby Allison	Ford
16	Ronnie Thomas	Chevrolet
17	Don Puskarich	Chevrolet
18	Richard Childress	Chevrolet
19	Joe Booher	Dodge
20	Jim Robinson	Chevrolet
21	Steve Pfeifer	Chevrolet
22	Bobby Wawak	Buick
23	Roger Hamby	Chevrolet
24	Hershel McGriff	Chevrolet
25	Don Waterman	Oldsmobile
26	Lake Speed	Chevrolet
27	Jim Hopkinson	Chevrolet
28	Roy Smith	Oldsmobile
29	Ed Hale	Chevrolet
30	Donnie Allison	Chevrolet
31	Dick Brooks	Chevrolet

32	Rick McCray	Buick
33	Terry Labonte	Chevrolet
34	John Borneman	Chevrolet
35	Don Whittington	Chevrolet
36	D.K. Ulrich	Chevrolet

GABRIEL 400

Time of Race: 3 hours, 2 minutes, 5 seconds
Average Speed: 131.808 mph
Margin of Victory: 1 car length

FINISH	DRIVER	CAR
1	Benny Parsons	Chevrolet
2	Cale Yarborough	Chevrolet
3	Buddy Baker	Chevrolet
4	Neil Bonnett	Mercury
5	Richard Petty	Chevrolet
6	Jody Ridley	Ford
7	Kyle Petty	Chevrolet
8	Bobby Allison	Ford
9	Bill Elliott	Mercury
10	Tighe Scott	Chevrolet
11	Terry Labonte	Chevrolet
12	Dale Earnhardt	Chevrolet
13	John Anderson	Chevrolet
14	Richard Childress	Chevrolet
15	J.D. McDuffie	Chevrolet
16	Wayne Watercutter	Oldsmobile
17	Lake Speed	Chevrolet
18	Mike Potter	Chevrolet
19	Tom Gale	Chevrolet
20	Cecil Gordon	Oldsmobile
21	Roger Hamby	Chevrolet
22	Jimmy Means	Chevrolet
23	Buddy Arrington	Dodge
24	James Hylton	Chevrolet
25	David Pearson	Chevrolet
26	Darrell Waltrip	Chevrolet
27	Baxter Price	Oldsmobile
28	Harry Gant	Chevrolet
29	Bobby Wawak	Buick
30	Ronnie Thomas	Chevrolet
31	Chuck Bown	Oldsmobile
32	Ricky Rudd	Chevrolet
33	Dick Brooks	Chevrolet
34	Junior Miller	Chevrolet
35	Dave Marcis	Chevrolet
36	Donnie Allison	Chevrolet
37	Henry Jones	Oldsmobile

FIRECRACKER 400

Time of Race: 2 hours, 18 minutes, 21 seconds
Average Speed: 173.473 mph
Margin of Victory: 1 second

FINISH	DRIVER	CAR
1	Bobby Allison	Mercury
2	David Pearson	Odsmobile
3	Dale Earnhardt	Oldsmobile
4	Buddy Baker	Oldsmobile
5	Richard Petty	Oldsmobile
6	Benny Parsons	Oldsmobile
7	Jody Ridley	Mercury
8	Richard Childress	Oldsmobile
9	John Anderson	Buick
10	Buddy Arrington	Dodge
11	Lennie Pond	Buick
12	Bill Elliott	Mercury
13	Ricky Rudd	Oldsmobile
14	Coo Coo Marlin	Chevrolet
15	Rick Wilson	Oldsmobile
16	Harry Gant	Oldsmobile
17	RonnieThomas	Oldsmobile

18	Steve Moore	Chevrolet
19	Donnie Allison	Oldsmobile
20	Phil Finney	Oldsmobile
21	John Greenwood	Oldsmobile
22	Don Whittington	Oldsmobile
23	J.D. McDuffie	Buick
24	James Hylton	Oldsmobile
25	James Vandiver	Oldsmobile
26	Jimmy Means	Buick
27	Roger Hamby	Chevrolet
28	Timmy Gale	Ford
29	Cecil Gordon	Oldsmobile
30	Marty Robbins	Dodge
31	Darrell Waltrip	Oldsmobile
32	Terry Labonte	Oldsmobile
33	Dave Marcis	Oldsmobile
34	Neil Bonnett	Mercury
35	Bruce Hill	Oldsmobile
36	Tighe Scott	Oldsmobile
37	Chuck Bown	Oldsmobile
38	Lake Speed	Chevrolet
39	Connie Saylor	Chevrolet
40	Cale Yarborough	Oldsmobile

BUSCH NASHVILLE 420

Time of Race: 2 hours, 40 minutes, 5 seconds
Average Speed: 93.821 mph
Margin of Victory: 1 second

FINISH	DRIVER	CAR
1	Dale Earnhardt	Chevrolet
2	Cale Yarborough	Chevrolet
3	Benny Parsons	Chevrolet
4	Darrell Waltrip	Chevrolet
5	Richard Petty	Chevrolet
6	Bobby Allison	Ford
7	Sterling Marlin	Chevrolet
8	Jody Ridley	Ford
9	Richard Childress	Chevrolet
10	Buddy Arrington	Dodge
11	J.D. McDuffie	Chevrolet
12	John Anderson	Chevrolet
13	Slick Johnson	Chevrolet
14	Dave Marcis	Chevrolet
15	Roger Hamby	Chevrolet
16	Jimmy Means	Chevrolet
17	James Hylton	Chevrolet
18	Tommy Gale	Ford
19	Baxter Price	Chevrolet
20	Junior Miller	Chevrolet
21	Cecil Gordon	Buick
22	Terry Labonte	Chevrolet
23	Bobby Wawak	Buick
24	Don Sprouse	Chevrolet
25	Steve Spencer	Chevrolet
26	Ronnie Thomas	Chevrolet
27	Donnie Allison	Chevrolet
28	Ricky Rudd	Chevrolet
29	Harry Gant	Chevrolet
30	Dick May	Dodge

COCA-COLA 500

Time of Race: 4 hours, 1 minute, 10 seconds
Average Speed: 124.395 mph
Margin of Victory: second

FINISH	DRIVER	CAR
1	Neil Bonnett	Mercury
2	Buddy Baker	Buick
3	Cale Yarborough	Chevrolet
4	Dale Earnhardt	Chevrolet
5	Harry Gant	Chevrolet
6	Terry Labonte	Chevrolet
7	Kyle Petty	Chevrolet

8	Dave Marcis	Chevrolet
9	Richard Childress	Chevrolet
10	Ricky Rudd	Chevrolet
11	Billy Harvey	Chevrolet
12	Tim Richmond	Chevrolet
13	Buddy Arrington	Dodge
14	Jimmy Means	Chevrolet
15	James Hylton	Chevrolet
16	Cecil Gordon	Oldsmobile
17	Dave Dion	Ford
18	Jody Ridley	Ford
19	Tommy Gale	Ford
20	Benny Parsons	Chevrolet
21	Junior Miller	Chevrolet
22	Baxter Price	Chevrolet
23	Ronnie Thomas	Chevrolet
24	Roger Hamby	Chevrolet
25	Ken Hemphill	Chevrolet
26	Darrell Waltrip	Chevrolet
27	Bob Riley	Chevrolet
28	Janet Guthrie	Ford
29	Dick May	Chevrolet
30	Lake Speed	Chevrolet
31	Slick Johnson	Chevrolet
32	Tighe Scott	Chevrolet
33	Richard Petty	Chevrolet
34	Bobby Allison	Ford
35	Chuck Bown	Oldsmobile
36	J.D. McDuffie	Chevrolet
37	Henry Jones	Oldsmobile
38	Nelson Oswald	Buick
39	Jocko Maggiacomo	Oldsmobile
40	Travis Tiller	Oldsmobile

TALLADEGA 500

Time of Race: 2 hours, 59 minutes, 47 seconds
Average Speed: 166.894 mph
Margin of Victory: 1 second

FINISH	DRIVER	CAR
1	Neil Bonnett	Mercury
2	Cale Yarborough	Oldsmobile
3	Dale Earnhardt	Oldsmobile
4	Benny Parsons	Oldsmobile
5	Harry Gant	Oldsmobile
6	Richard Childress	Oldsmobile
7	Bill Elliott	Mercury
8	Lake Speed	Chevrolet
9	Kyle Petty	Chevrolet
10	Dick May	Buick
11	Darrell Waltrip	Oldsmobi;e
12	Harry Dinwiddie	Buick
13	Marty Robbins	Dodge
14	James Hylton	Oldsmobile
15	Jimmy Means	Chevrolet
16	Billy Harvey	Oldsmobile
17	David Pearson	Oldsmobile
18	Richard Petty	Oldsmobile
19	Slick Johnson	Chevrolet
20	Ricky Rudd	Oldsmobile
21	Ronnie Thomas	Oldsmobile
22	Roger Hamby	Chevrolet
23	Cecil Gordon	Oldsmobile
24	Bobby Wawak	Buick
25	J.D. McDuffie	Buick
26	Donnie Allison	Oldsmobile
27	Baxter Price	Oldsmobile
28	Lennie Pond	Oldsmobile
29	Tommy Gale	Ford
30	Jody Ridley	Mercury
31	Terry Labonte	Oldsmobile
32	Buddy Baker	Oldsmobile
33	Frank Warren	Dodge
34	Tighe Scott	Oldsmobile
35	Bobby Allison	Mercury
36	Rick Wilson	Oldsmobile
37	Coo Coo Marlin	Chevrolet
38	Buddy Arrington	Dodge
39	Dave Marcis	Oldsmobile
40	Ferrel Harris	Chevrolet
41	Bruce Hill	Oldsmobile

CHAMPION SPARK PLUG 400

Time of Race: 2 hours, 45 minutes, 7 seconds
Average Speed: 145.352 mph
Margin of Victory: 1 second

FINISH	DRIVER	CAR
1	Cale Yarborough	Chevrolet
2	Neil Bonnett	Mercury
3	Donnie Allison	Chevrolet
4	Darrell Waltrip	Chevrolet
5	Richard Petty	Chevrolet
6	Buddy Baker	Chevrolet
7	Bobby Allison	Mercury
8	Benny Parsons	Chevrolet
9	Bill Elliott	Mercury
10	Kenny Hemphill	Chevrolet
11	Terry Labonte	Chevrolet
12	Kyle Petty	Chevrolet
13	Buddy Arrington	Dodge
14	Jimmy Means	Chevrolet
15	D. K. Ulrich	Chevrolet
16	Lake Speed	Chevrolet
17	Billy Harvey	Chevrolet
18	Jody Ridley	Mercury
19	Dick May	Chevrolet
20	J.D. McDuffie	Chevrolet
21	Cecil Gordon	Oldsmobile
22	Tommy Gale	Ford
23	Bruce Jacobi	Ford
24	Wayne Watercutter	Oldsmobile
25	James Hylton	Oldsmobile
26	Dave Marcis	Chevrolet
27	Richard Childress	Chevrolet
28	Stuart Huffman	Buick
29	Ronnie Thomas	Buicl
30	Roger Hamby	Chevrolet
31	Frank Warren	Dodge
32	Baxter Price	Oldsmobile
33	Bobby Wawak	Buick
34	Ricky Rudd	Chevrolet
35	Dale Earnhardt	Chevrolet
36	John Anderson	Chevrolet
37	Harry Gant	Chevrolet

BUSCH VOLUNTEER 500

Time of Race: 3 hours, 3 minutes, 51 seconds
Average Speed: 86.973 mph
Margin of Victory: 1 second

FINISH	DRIVER	CAR
1	Cale Yarborough	Chevrolet
2	Dale Earnhardt	Chevrolet
3	Darrell Waltrip	Chevrolet
4	Richard Petty	Chevrolet
5	Benny Parsons	Chevrolet
6	Bobby Allison	Ford
7	Dave Marcis	Chevrolet
8	Lennie Pond	Oldsmobile
9	Richard Childress	Chevrolet
10	D.K. Ulrich	Chevrolet
11	J.D. McDuffie	Chevrolet
12	Jody Ridley	Mercury
13	Tommy Gale	Ford
14	Harry Gant	Chevrolet
15	John Anderson	Chevrolet
16	Roger Hamby	Chevrolet
17	James Hylton	Chevrolet
18	Baxter Price	Chevrolet
19	Cecil Gordon	Oldsmobile
20	Buddy Arrington	Dodge
21	Bub Strickler	Oldsmobile
22	Jimmy Means	Chevrolet
23	Terry Labonte	Chevrolet
24	Stuart Huffman	Buick
25	Steve Spencer	Chevrolet
26	Dick May	Buick
27	Junior Miller	Chevrolet
28	Ricky Rudd	Chevrolet

| 29 | Ronnie Thomas | Chevrolet |
| 30 | Bobby Sands | Chevrolet |

SOUTHERN 500

Time of Race: 4 hours, 21 minutes, 5 seconds (Red flagged 1 hour 12 minutes, because of rain)
Average Speed: 115.210 mph
Margin of Victory: - 3 feet (Finished under caution)

FINISH	DRIVER	CAR
1	Terry Labonte	Chevrolet
2	David Pearson	Chevrolet
3	Harry Gant	Chevrolet
4	Benny Parsons	Chevrolet
5	Neil Bonnett	Mercury
6	Bobby Allison	Ford
7	Dale Earnhardt	Chevrolet
8	Dave Marcis	Chevrolet
9	Richard Petty	Chevrolet
10	Dick Brooks	Chevrolet
11	Chuck Bown	Chevrolet
12	Richard Childress	Chevrolet
13	D.K. Ulrich	Chevrolet
14	Connie Saylor	Chevrolet
15	Slick Johnson	Chevrolet
16	Jimmy Means	Chevrolet
17	Buddy Arrington	Dodge
18	J.D. McDuffie	Chevrolet
19	Cecil Gordon	Oldsmobile
20	Ferrel Harris	Dodge
21	James Hylton	Chevrolet
22	Ronnie Thomas	Chevrolet
23	Frank Warren	Dodge
24	Ralph Jones	Ford
25	Darrell Waltrip	Chevrolet
26	Buddy Baker	Chevrolet
27	Lake Speed	Chevrolet
28	Dick May	Buick
29	Cale Yarborough	Chevrolet
30	Jody Ridley	Ford
31	Tommy Gale	Ford
32	Donnie Allison	Chevrolet
33	Bill Elliott	Mercury
34	Ricky Rudd	Chevrolet
35	Roger Hamby	Chevrolet
36	John Anderson	Chevrolet
37	Blackie Wangerin	Mercury
38	Don Whittington	Chevrolet
39	Bobby Wawak	Buick
40	Lennie Pond	Chevrolet
41	Kenny Hemphill	Chevrolet

CAPITAL CITY 400

Time of Race: 2 hours, 43 minutes, 10 seconds
Average Speed: 79.722 mph
Margin of Victory: 2 seconds

FINISH	DRIVER	CAR
1	Bobby Allison	Ford
2	Richard Petty	Chevrolet
3	Lennie Pond	Chevrolet
4	Dale Earnhardt	Chevrolet
5	Jody Ridley	Ford
6	Darrell Waltrip	Chevrolet
7	Dave Marcis	Chevrolet
8	Terry Labonte	Chevrolet
9	Dave Dion	Ford
10	Benny Parsons	Chevrolet
11	Richard Childress	Chevrolet
12	Buddy Arrington	Dodge
13	Jimmy Means	Chevrolet
14	Bill Elswick	Oldsmobile
15	Don Sprouse	Chevrolet
16	Roger Hamby	Chevrolet
17	James Hylton	Chevrolet
18	Cecil Gordon	Oldsmobile

EARLY PIONEERS

Here's a little-know fact about NASCAR stock car racing: a lady started 13th and finished 14th in the very first Winston Cup race. Not only that, two other ladies were regular competitors in the first year of what was then known as Strictly Stock.

Sara Christian raced in the inaugural Cup race at the half-mile dirt Charlotte Speedway on June 19, 1949. She started the No. 71 Ford owned by her husband, Frank, then got out and let Bob Flock drive the final 90 or so laps.

Three weeks later, Christian was joined by Ethel Mobley and Louise Smith in the field for a 166-mile race on the beach and highway course in Daytona Beach. Christian finished sixth in her Ford, Mobley was 11th in a Cadillac, and Smith was 20th in a Ford after surviving a rollover in the early laps.

Christian and Smith raced later that year at Hillsborough, North Carolina (Christian was 23rd, Smith 27th), then all three of them competed at Langhorne, Pennsylvania, where Christian was sixth, Smith 16th, and Mobley 44th. Christian finished the season with starts at Pittsburgh (fifth) and North Wilkesboro, where she finished 12th.

For the season, she started six races, had one top-five and two top-10s, and finished 13th in points. In later years, other women would get far more attention than Christian, Smith, and Mobley, but isn't that always the way it is with pioneers?

19	Tommy Gale	Ford
20	Harry Gant	Chevrolet
21	Eddie Dickerson	Dodge
22	Ronnie Thomas	Chevrolet
23	Junior Miller	Chevrolet
24	Baxter Price	Chevrolet
25	D.K. Ulrich	Chevrolet
26	Cale Yarborough	Oldsmobile
27	Bobby Wawak	Chevrolet
28	Bub Strickler	Chevrolet
29	J.D. McDuffie	Chevrolet
30	Bobby Allison	Chevrolet
31	Tim Richmond	Chevrolet
32	John Anderson	Chevrolet
33	Kenny Hemphill	Chevrolet
34	Dale Earnhardt	Chevrolet
35	Bub Strickler	Chevrolet
36	Tommy Gale	Ford
37	Richard Childress	Chevrolet
38	J.D. McDuffie	Chevrolet
39	Bob Riley	Chevrolet
40	Steve Gray	Buick

CRC CHEMICALS 500

Time of Race: 4 hours, 18 minutes, 34 seconds
Average Speed: 116.024 mph
Margin of Victory: 47/100 of a second

FINISH	DRIVER	CAR
1	Darrell Waltrip	Chevrolet
2	Harry Gant	Chevrolet
3	Buddy Baker	Chevrolet
4	Cale Yarborough	Chevrolet
5	Benny Parsons	Chevrolet
6	Neil Bonnett	Mercury
7	Donnie Allison	Chevrolet
8	Lennie Pond	Chevrolet
9	Jody Ridley	Ford
10	Ronnie Thomas	Chevrolet
11	Lake Speed	Chevrolet
12	Dave Marcis	Chevrolet
13	Buddy Arrington	Dodge
14	Dave Dion	Ford
15	Cecil Gordon	Oldsmobile
16	Joe Booher	Chevrolet
17	Richard Petty	Chevrolet
18	Joel Stowe	Chevrolet
19	James Hylton	Chevrolet
20	Roger Hamby	Chevrolet
21	John Callis	Ford
22	Eddie Dickerson	Dodge
23	Kyle Petty	Chevrolet
24	Dick May	Dodge
25	Frank Warren	Dodge
26	Travis Tiller	Oldsmobile
27	Jimmy Means	Chevrolet
28	Terry Labonte	Chevrolet
29	Junior Miller	Chevrolet

HOLLY FARMS 400

Time of Race: 3 hours, 18 minutes, 39 seconds
Average Speed: 75.510 mph
Margin of Victory: second

FINISH	DRIVER	CAR
1	Bobby Allison	Ford
2	Darrell Waltrip	Chevrolet
3	Dave Marcis	Chevrolet
4	Harry Gant	Chevrolet
5	Dale Earnhardt	Chevrolet
6	Benny Parsons	Chevrolet
7	Terry Labonte	Chevrolet
8	Slick Johnson	Chevrolet
9	Jody Ridley	Ford
10	Cale Yarborough	Oldsmobile
11	Bobby Wawak	Chevrolet
12	Jimmy Means	Chevrolet
13	Junior Miller	Chevrolet
14	Cecil Gordon	Oldsmobile
15	James Hylton	Chevrolet
16	Joel Stowe	Oldsmobile
17	Jeff McDuffie	Buick
18	Richard Petty	Chevrolet
19	Richard Childress	Chevrolet
20	Tommy Gale	Ford
21	Lake Speed	Chevrolet
22	Roger Hamby	Chevrolet
23	Bub Strickler	Chevrolet
24	J.D. McDuffie	Chevrolet
25	Ronnie Thomas	Chevrolet
26	Buddy Arrington	Dodge
27	John Anderson	Chevrolet
28	Lennie Pond	Chevrolet
29	Dick May	Chevrolet
30	D.K. Ulrich	Chevrolet

OLD DOMINION 500

Time of Race: 3 hours, 46 minutes, 7 secons
Average Speed: 69.654 mph
Margin of Victory: 1 second

FINISH	DRIVER	CAR
1	Dale Earnhardt	Chevrolet
2	Buddy Baker	Chevrolet
3	Cale Yarborough	Oldsmobile
4	Benny Parsons	Chevrolet
5	Dave Marcis	Chevrolet
6	Donnie Allison	Chevrolet
7	Terry Labonte	Chevrolet
8	Buddy Arrington	Dodge
9	Jody Ridley	Ford
10	James Hylton	Chevrolet
11	Tommy Gale	Ford
12	Tim Richmond	Chevrolet
13	Cecil Gordon	Oldsmobile
14	Roger Hamby	Chevrolet
15	Richard Petty	Chevrolet
16	John Anderson	Buick
17	Junior Miller	Chevrolet
18	Ronnie Thomas	Chevrolet
19	Neil Bonnett	Mercury
20	Lake Speed	Chevrolet
21	Darrell Waltrip	Chevrolet
22	Bobby Allison	Ford
23	Don Sprouse	Chevrolet
24	Slick Johnson	Chevrolet
25	Richard Childress	Chevrolet
26	J.D. McDuffie	Chevrolet
27	Kyle Petty	Oldsmobile
28	Lennie Pond	Chevrolet
29	Harry Gant	Chevrolet
30	Jimmy Means	Chevrolet
31	Dave Dion	Ford

NATIONAL 500

Time of Race: 3 hours, 42 minutes, 16 seconds
Average Speed: 135.243 mph
Margin of Victory: 1 seconds

FINISH	DRIVER	CAR
1	Dale Earnhardt	Chevrolet
2	Cale Yarborough	Chevrolet
3	Buddy Baker	Buick
4	Ricky Rudd	Chevrolet
5	Donnie Allison	Chevrolet
6	Bill Elliott	Mercury
7	Lake Speed	Chevrolet
8	Jody Ridley	Mercury
9	Kyle Petty	Chevrolet
10	Dick Brooks	Chevrolet
11	Richard Childress	Chevrolet
12	Tim Richmond	Chevrolet
13	Buddy Arrington	Dodge
14	Rusty Wallace	Chevrolet
15	Kenny Hemphill	Chevrolet
16	Harry Gant	Chevrolet
17	Dick May	Dodge
18	Darrell Waltrip	Chevrolet
19	Dave Marcis	Oldsmobile
20	J.D. McDuffie	Chevrolet
21	James Hylton	Chevrolet
22	Tommy Gale	Ford
23	Connie Saylor	Chevrolet
24	Cecil Gordon	Oldsmobile
25	Chuck Bown	Chevrolet
26	Junior Miller	Chevrolet
27	Richard Petty	Chevrolet
28	Roger Hamby	Chevrolet
29	Bobby Allison	Mercury
30	Neil Bonnett	Mercury
31	Terry Labonte	Chevrolet

32	Marty Robbins	Chevrolet
33	Benny Parsons	Chevrolet
34	Lennie Pond	Chevrolet
35	John Anderson	Chevrolet
36	Sterling Marlin	Chevrolet
37	Rick Wilson	Chevrolet
38	David Pearson	Chevrolet
39	Mike Miller	Ford
40	Slick Johnson	Chevrolet
41	Jim Sauter	Chevrolet

AMERICAN 500

Time of Race: 4 hours, 22 minutes, 59 seconds
Average Speed: 114.159 mph
Margin of Victory: 3 car lengths

FINISH	DRIVER	CAR
1	Cale Yarborough	Chevrolet
2	Harry Gant	Chevrolet
3	Darrell Waltrip	Chevrolet
4	Terry Labonte	Chevrolet
5	Jody Ridley	Ford
6	Dave Marcis	Chevrolet
7	Richard Childress	Chevrolet
8	Slick Johnson	Chevrolet
9	James Hylton	Chevrolet
10	Ronnie Thomas	Chevrolet
11	Stan Barrett	Chevrolet
12	Buddy Arrington	Dodge
13	Jimmy Means	Chevrolet
14	Richard Petty	Chevrolet
15	Cecil Gordon	Oldsmobile
16	Dick May	Chevrolet
17	Roger Hamby	Chevrolet
18	Dale Earnhardt	Chevrolet
19	Jeff McDuffie	Buick
20	Tom Gale	Ford
21	J.D. McDuffie	Chevrolet
22	Donnie Allison	Chevrolet
23	Benny Parsons	Chevrolet
24	Joe Millikan	Chevrolet
25	Neil Bonnett	Mercury
26	Bobby Allison	Ford
27	Buddy Baker	Chevrolet
28	Lake Speed	Chevrolet
29	Lennie Pond	Chevrolet
30	Ernie Cline	Chevrolet
31	Dick Brooks	Chevrolet
32	John Anderson	Chevrolet
33	Junior Miller	Chevrolet
34	Glenn Jarrett	Chevrolet
35	Kyle Petty	Chevrolet
36	Bill Elswick	Oldsmobile

ATLANTA JOURNAL 500

Time of Race: 3 hours, 48 minutes, 19 seconds
Average Speed: 131.190 mph
Margin of Victory: 2.01 seconds

FINISH	DRIVER	CAR
1	Cale Yarborough	Chevrolet
2	Neil Bonnett	Mercury
3	Dale Earnhardt	Chevrolet
4	Buddy Baker	Buick
5	Terry Labonte	Chevrolet
6	Jody Ridley	Ford
7	Lennie Pond	Chevrolet
8	Ronnie Thomas	Chevrolet
9	Richard Childress	Chevrolet
10	Stan Barrett	Chevrolet
11	Buddy Arrington	Dodge
12	Roger Hamby	Chevrolet
13	Steve Moore	Chevrolet

14	James Hylton	Chevrolet
15	Tommy Gale	Ford
16	Charlie Chamblee	Buick
17	J.D. McDuffie	Chevrolet
18	Bill Elliott	Mercury
19	Clay Young	Oldsmobile
20	Jimmy Means	Chevrolet
21	Richard Petty	Chevrolet
22	Dave Marcis	Chevrolet
23	Joe Millikan	Chevrolet
24	Lake Speed	Chevrolet
25	Cecil Gordon	Chevrolet
26	Darrell Waltrip	Chevrolet
27	Connie Saylor	Chevrolet
28	Mike Miller	Ford
29	Tim Richmond	Chevrolet
30	Travis Tiller	Oldsmobile
31	David Pearson	Oldsmobile
32	Benny Parsons	Chevrolet
33	John Anderson	Chevrolet
34	Blackie Wangerin	Mercury
35	Junior Miller	Chevrolet
36	Harry Gant	Chevrolet
37	Donnie Allison	Chevrolet
38	Bobby Allison	Mercury
39	Gary Balough	Chevrolet
40	John Callis	Ford

LOS ANGELES TIMES 500

Time of Race: 3 hours, 51 minutes, 46 seconds
Average Speed: 129.441 mph
Margin of Victory: 6 seconds

FINISH	DRIVER	CAR
1	Benny Parsons	Chevrolet
2	Neil Bonnett	Mercury
3	Cale Yarborough	Chevrolet
4	Bobby Allison	Ford
5	Dale Earnhardt	Chevrolet
6	Lake Speed	Chevrolet
7	Joe Millikan	Chevrolet
8	Terry Labonte	Chevrolet
9	John Anderson	Chevrolet
10	Buddy Arrington	Dodge
11	Bill Schmitt	Oldsmobile
12	Glen Jarrett	Chevrolet
13	Stan Barrett	Chevrolet
14	J.D. McDuffie	Chevrolet
15	Dave Marcis	Chevrolet
16	Tom Gale	Ford
17	Cecil Gordon	Oldsmobile
18	Jody Ridley	Ford
19	Rick McCray	Buick
20	Don Waterman	Oldsmobile
21	Richard Childress	Chevrolet
22	Henry Jones	Buick
23	Hershel McGriff	Chevrolet
24	James Hylton	Chevrolet
25	Darrell Waltrip	Chevrolet
26	Kevin Housby	Chevrolet
27	Chuck Bown	Dodge
28	Jim Robinson	Chevrolet
29	Lennie Pond	Chevrolet
30	Richard Petty	Chevrolet
31	Jimmy Means	Chevrolet
32	Glen Francis	Chevrolet
33	Kyle Petty	Chevrolet
34	Joe Booher	Dodge
35	Glen Ward	Chevrolet
36	Roy Smith	Oldsmobile
37	D.K. Ulrich	Chevrolet
38	Ronnie Thomas	Chevrolet
39	Donnie Allison	Chevrolet
40	Joe Ruttman	Oldsmobile
41	Harry Gant	Chevrolet
42	Don Puskarich	Chevrolet

1981

WINSTON WESTERN 500

Time of Race: 3 hours, 16 minutes, 18 seconds
Average Speed: 95.263 mph
Margin of Victory: 173 seconds

FINISH	DRIVER	CAR
1	Bobby Allison	Chevrolet
2	Terry Labonte	Chevrolet
3	Dale Earnhardt	Pontiac
4	Richard Childress	Chevrolet
5	Richard Petty	Chevrolet
6	Jim Robinson	Chevrolet
7	Jody Ridley	Ford
8	Elliott Forbes-Robinson	Buick
9	Buddy Arrington	Dodge
10	Don Waterman	Oldsmobile
11	James Hylton	Chevrolet
12	John Borneman	Chevrolet
13	Joe Millikan	Chevrolet
14	Don Whittington	Chevrolet
15	Harry Gant	Chevrolet
16	Benny Parsons	Ford
17	Darrell Waltrip	Chevrolet
18	Jimmy Means	Chevrolet
19	Ricky Rudd	Chevrolet
20	Kyle Petty	Chevrolet
21	Bob Bondurant	Oldsmobile
22	Bill Schmitt	Buick
23	J. D. McDuffie	Chevrolet
24	Steve Pfeifer	Chevrolet
25	John Gunn	Chevrolet
26	Rick McCray	Chevrolet
27	Neil Bonnett	Ford
28	Dave Marcis	Chevrolet
29	Tim Richmond	Chevrolet
30	Jim Insolo	Buick
31	Roy Smith	Oldsmobile
32	Don Puskarich	Chevrolet
33	Hershel McGriff	Dodge
34	Lake Speed	Chevrolet
35	Robert Tartaglia	Chevrolet
36	Cecil Gordon	Oldsmobile

DAYTONA 500

Time of Race: 2 hours, 56 minutes, 50 seconds
Average Speed: 169.651 mph
Margin of Victory: 3 seconds

FINISH	DRIVER	CAR
1	Richard Petty	Buick
2	Bobby Allison	Pontiac
3	Ricky Rudd	Oldsmobile
4	Buddy Baker	Oldsmobile
5	Dale Earnhardt	Pontiac
6	Bill Elliott	Ford
7	Jody Ridley	Ford
8	Cale Yarborough	Oldsmobile
9	Joe Millikan	Buick
10	Johnny Rutherford	Pontiac
11	Bill Elswick	Oldsmobile
12	Donnie Allison	Oldsmobile
13	Stan Barrett	Pontiac
14	Don Whittington	Oldsmobile
15	Dave Marcis	Oldsmobile
16	Dick Brooks	Buick
17	Tommy Gale	Ford
18	Ronnie Sanders	Buick
19	Glenn Jarrett	Buick
20	Don Sprouse	Oldsmobile

21	Jimmy Means	Pontiac
22	Geoff Bodine	Pontiac
23	Harry Gant	Buick
24	J. D. McDuffie	Pontiac
25	Elliott Forbes-Robinson	Buick
26	Buddy Arrington	Dodge
27	Lennie Pond	Buick
28	Ronnie Thomas	Pontiac
29	David Pearson	Chevrolet
30	Tim Richmond	Buick
31	Benny Parsons	Ford
32	Kyle Petty	Buick
33	Neil Bonnett	Ford
34	James Hylton	Pontiac
35	A. J. Foyt	Oldsmobile
36	Darrell Waltrip	Buick
37	Cecil Gordon	Buick
38	Richard Childress	Pontiac
39	Bruce Hill	Buick
40	Terry Labonte	Buick
41	Billy Harvey	Pontiac
42	Blackie Wangerin	Ford

RICHMOND 500

Time of Race: 2 hours, 49 minutes, 53 seconds
Average Speed: 76.570 mph
Margin of Victory: 5 seconds

FINISH	DRIVER	CAR
1	Darrell Waltrip	Buick
2	Ricky Rudd	Oldsmobile
3	Richard Petty	Buick
4	Morgan Shepherd	Pontiac
5	Benny Parsons	Ford
6	Harry Gant	Buick
7	Dale Earnhardt	Pontiac
8	Jody Ridley	Ford
9	Joe Millikan	Buick
10	J. D. McDuffie	Pontiac
11	Lennie Pond	Buick
12	Lake Speed	Oldsmobile
13	Richard Childress	Pontiac
14	Jimmy Means	Pontiac
15	Don Sprouse	Oldsmobile
16	Buddy Arrington	Dodge
17	Tim Richmond	Buick
18	Tommy Gale	Oldsmobile
19	Cecil Gordon	Buick
20	Henry Jones	Buick
21	Ronnie Thomas	Pontiac
22	Dave Marcis	Dodge
23	Bobby Allison	Chevrolet
24	Kyle Petty	Buick
25	Glenn Jarrett	Chevrolet
26	Terry Labonte	Buick
27	Rick Newsom	Chevrolet
28	Joe Fields	Pontiac
29	James Hylton	Pontiac
30	Baxter Price	Buick

CAROLINA 500

Time of Race: 4 hours, 21 minutes, 59 seconds
Average Speed: 114.594 mph
Margin of Victory: 5 seconds

FINISH	DRIVER	CAR
1	Darrell Waltrip	Buick
2	Cale Yarborough	Buick
3	Richard Petty	Buick
4	Neil Bonnett	Ford
5	Buddy Baker	Oldsmobile
6	Bobby Allison	Pontiac
7	Joe Millikan	Chevrolet

8	Kyle Petty	Buick
9	Lake Speed	Buick
10	Elliott Forbes-Robinson	Buick
11	Ronnie Thomas	Pontiac
12	Johnnie Rutherford	Pontiac
13	Mike Alexander	Oldsmobile
14	Bobby Wawak	Buick
15	Dave Marcis	Dodge
16	Tim Richmond	Buick
17	Jody Ridley	Oldsmobile
18	Harry Gant	Buick
19	Tommy Gale	Ford
20	James Hylton	Pontiac
21	Terry Labonte	Buick
22	Richard Childress	Pontiac
23	Cecil Gordon	Buick
24	Benny Parsons	Ford
25	Slick Johnson	Chevrolet
26	Dale Earnhardt	Pontiac
27	Glenn Jarrett	Chevrolet
28	Morgan Shepherd	Pontiac
29	Jimmy Means	Pontiac
30	David Pearson	Chevrolet
31	Ricky Rudd	Oldsmobile
32	Rick Newsom	Chevrolet
33	J. D. McDuffie	Pontiac
34	Donnie Allison	Oldsmobile
35	Rick Wilson	Oldsmobile
36	Stan Barrett	Pontiac
37	Buddy Arrington	Dodge

COCA-COLA 500

Time of Race: 3 hours, 44 minutes, 10 seconds
Average Speed: 133.619 mph
Margin of Victory: 33 seconds

FINISH	DRIVER	CAR
1	Cale Yarborough	Buick
2	Harry Gant	Buick
3	Dale Earnhardt	Pontiac
4	Bobby Allison	Pontiac
5	Benny Parsons	Ford
6	Jody Ridley	Ford
7	A. J. Foyt	Oldsmobile
8	Morgan Shepherd	Pontiac
9	Bill Elliott	Ford
10	Joe Ruttman	Buick
11	J. D. McDuffie	Pontiac
12	Johnny Rutherford	Pontiac
13	Bill Elswick	Buick
14	Buddy Arrington	Dodge
15	Joe Millikan	Buick
16	Stan Barrett	Pontiac
17	Richard Childress	Pontiac
18	Tommy Gale	Ford
19	Terry Labonte	Buick
20	Rick Newsom	Chevrolet
21	Jimmy Means	Pontiac
22	Ricky Rudd	Buick
23	Bruce Hill	Buick
24	Dick May	Oldsmobile
25	James Hylton	Pontiac
26	Tim Richmond	Buick
27	Dave Marcis	Oldsmobile
28	Neil Bonnett	Ford
29	Donnie Allison	Oldsmobile
30	Steve Spencer	Buick
31	Ronnie Thomas	Pontiac
32	David Pearson	Chevrolet
33	Mike Alexander	Buick
34	Slick Johnson	Chevrolet
35	Lake Speed	Buick
36	Darrell Waltrip	Buick
37	Cecil Gordon	Buick
38	Richard Petty	Buick
39	Elliott Forbes-Robinson	Buick
40	Buddy Baker	Oldsmobile
41	Kyle Petty	Buick
42	Bobby Wawak	Pontiac

VALLEYDALE 500

Time of Race: 2 hours, 58 minutes, 36 seconds
Average Speed: 89.530 mph
Margin of Victory: 25 seconds

FINISH	DRIVER	CAR
1	Darrell Waltrip	Buick
2	Ricky Rudd	Oldsmobile
3	Bobby Allison	Pontiac
4	Morgan Shepherd	Pontiac
5	Benny Parsons	Ford
6	Jody Ridley	Ford
7	Terry Labonte	Buick
8	Harry Gant	Pontiac
9	Lake Speed	Oldsmobile
10	Tim Richmond	Buick
11	Kyle Petty	Buick
12	Mike Alexander	Oldsmobile
13	Buddy Arrington	Dodge
14	Jimmy Means	Chevrolet
15	Tom Gale	Ford
16	Richard Childress	Pontiac
17	Joe Millikan	Buick
18	Ronnie Thomas	Pontiac
19	D. K. Ulrich	Buick
20	Steve Spencer	Chevrolet
21	Cecil Gordon	Buick
22	J. D. McDuffie	Pontiac
23	Rick Newsom	Chevrolet
24	Ron Bouchard	Buick
25	Butch Lindley	Chevrolet
26	Bruce Hill	Buick
27	Elliott Forbes-Robinson	Oldsmobile
28	Dale Earnhardt	Pontiac
29	Richard Petty	Buick
30	Ernie Cline	Pontiac
31	Dave Marcis	Chevrolet

NORTHWESTERN BANK 400

Time of Race: 2 hours, 55 minutes, 41 seconds
Average Speed: 85.381 mph
Margin of Victory: 3 seconds

FINISH	DRIVER	CAR
1	Richard Petty	Buick
2	Bobby Allison	Pontiac
3	Darrell Waltrip	Buick
4	Dave Marcis	Chevrolet
5	Harry Gant	Oldsmobile
6	Ricky Rudd	Buick
7	Terry Labonte	Buick
8	Ron Bouchard	Buick
9	Morgan Shepherd	Pontiac
10	Dale Earnhardt	Pontiac
11	Mike Alexander	Oldsmobile
12	Ronnie Thomas	Pontiac
13	D. K. Ulrich	Buick
14	Jimmy Means	Chevrolet
15	James Hylton	Pontiac
16	J. D. McDuffie	Pontiac
17	Richard Childress	Pontiac
18	Tim Richmond	Buick
19	Tommy Gale	Ford
20	Tommy Houston	Buick
21	Benny Parsons	Ford
22	Kyle Petty	Buick
23	Lake Speed	Oldsmobile
24	Butch Lindley	Chevrolet
25	Joe Fields	Oldsmobile
26	Joe Millikan	Chevrolet
27	Mark Martin	Pontiac
28	Jody Ridley	Ford
29	Buddy Arrington	Dodge
30	Bobby Wawak	Buick
31	Cecil Gordon	Buick

CRC CHEMICALS REBEL 500

Time of Race: 3 hours, 57 minutes, 24 seconds
Average Speed: 126.703 mph
Margin of Victory: Car length

FINISH	DRIVER	CAR
1	Darrell Waltrip	Buick
2	Harry Gant	Pontiac
3	Dave Marcis	Chevrolet
4	Bill Elliott	Ford
5	Benny Parsons	Ford
6	Buddy Baker	Buick
7	Jody Ridley	Ford
8	David Pearson	Chevrolet
9	Bobby Allison	Buick
10	Joe Millikan	Buick
11	Ricky Rudd	Buick
12	Tim Richmond	Buick
13	Buddy Arrington	Dodge
14	Terry Labonte	Buick
15	Dick Brooks	Buick
16	J. D. McDuffie	Pontiac
17	Dale Earnhardt	Pontiac
18	Tommy Gale	Ford
19	James Hylton	Pontiac
20	Ronnie Thomas	Buick
21	Cecil Gordon	Buick
22	D. K. Ulrich	Buick
23	Jimmy Means	Pontiac
24	Bobby Wawak	Buick
25	Kyle Petty	Buick
26	Cale Yarborough	Buick
27	Ron Bouchard	Buick
28	Johnny Rutherford	Pontiac
29	Neil Bonnett	Ford
30	Geoff Bodine	Pontiac
31	Richard Childress	Pontiac
32	Slick Johnson	Chevrolet
33	Richard Petty	Buick
34	Morgan Shepherd	Pontiac
35	Mike Potter	Chevrolet
36	Mike Alexander	Buick

VIRGINIA 500

Time of Race: 3 hours, 30 minutes, 10 seconds
Average Speed: 75.019 mph
Margin of Victory: 15 seconds

FINISH	DRIVER	CAR
1	Morgan Shepherd	Pontiac
2	Neil Bonnett	Ford
3	Ricky Rudd	Buick
4	Harry Gant	Oldsmobile
5	Terry Labonte	Buick
6	Jody Ridley	Ford
7	Lake Speed	Oldsmobile
8	Buddy Arrington	Dodge
9	Ron Bouchard	Pontiac
10	Mike Alexander	Oldsmobile
11	Dave Marcis	Chevrolet
12	Jimmy Means	Pontiac
13	Bobby Allison	Pontiac
14	Tim Richmond	Buick
15	Kyle Petty	Buick
16	Joe Fields	Buick
17	James Hylton	Pontiac
18	Tommy Gale	Buick
19	Bobby Wawak	Buick
20	Tommy Houston	Chevrolet
21	Cale Yarborough	Buick
22	Richard Childress	Pontiac
23	Benny Parsons	Ford
24	Cecil Gordon	Buick
25	Dale Earnhardt	Pontiac
26	Darrell Waltrip	Buick

27	Butch Lindley	Chevrolet
28	Richard Petty	Buick
29	Joe Millikan	Buick
30	J. D. McDuffie	Pontiac
31	Ronnie Thomas	Pontiac

WINSTON 500

Time of Race: 3 hours, 20 minutes, 52 seconds
Average Speed: 149.376 mph
Margin of Victory: 1 Foot

FINISH	DRIVER	CAR
1	Bobby Allison	Buick
2	Buddy Baker	Buick
3	Darrell Waltrip	Buick
4	Ricky Rudd	Oldsmobile
5	Donnie Allison	Oldsmobile
6	Tim Richmond	Buick
7	Terry Labonte	Buick
8	Dale Earnhardt	Pontiac
9	Dick May	Dodge
10	Bobby Wawak	Buick
11	Tommy Gale	Ford
12	Tommy Houston	Buick
13	Richard Childress	Pontiac
14	Dave Marcis	Buick
15	Cecil Gordon	Buick
16	E. Forbes-Robinson	Buick
17	Buddy Arrington	Dodge
18	Lake Speed	Buick
19	James Hylton	Pontiac
20	Ron Bouchard	Buick
21	Mike Alexander	Buick
22	J. D. McDuffie	Pontiac
23	Morgan Shepherd	Pontiac
24	Cale Yarborough	Buick
25	Rick Wilson	Oldsmobile
26	Ronnie Thomas	Buick
27	Jimmy Means	Pontiac
28	Bruce Hill	Buick
29	Joe Ruttman	Buick
30	Kyle Petty	Buick
31	Jody Ridley	Ford
32	Neil Bonnett	Ford
33	Rick Newsom	Chevrolet
34	Harry Gant	Pontiac
35	Stan Barrett	Pontiac
36	Benny Parsons	Ford
37	Connie Saylor	Oldsmobile
38	Joe Millikan	Oldsmobile
39	Richard Petty	Buick
40	Bill Elliott	Ford

MELLING TOOL 420

Time of Race: 2 hours, 47 minutes, 2 seconds
Average Speed: 89.756 mph
Margin of Victory: 1 Car length

FINISH	DRIVER	CAR
1	Benny Parsons	Ford
2	Darrell Waltrip	Buick
3	Bobby Allison	Pontiac
4	Richard Petty	Buick
5	Ricky Rudd	Buick
6	Terry Labonte	Buick
7	Kyle Petty	Buick
8	Morgan Shepherd	Pontiac
9	Buddy Arrington	Dodge
10	Dave Marcis	Chevrolet
11	Mike Alexander	Buick
12	Tim Richmond	Buick
13	Richard Childress	Pontiac
14	Jimmy Means	Chevrolet

15	Mike Potter	Chevrolet
16	J. D. McDuffie	Pontiac
17	Tommy Gale	Ford
18	Bobby Wawak	Buick
19	Cecil Gordon	Pontiac
20	Dale Earnhardt	Pontiac
21	James Hylton	Pontiac
22	Harry Gant	Oldsmobile
23	D. K. Ulrich	Buick
24	Lake Speed	Pontiac
25	Jody Ridley	Ford
26	Charley Chamblee	Pontiac
27	Mark Martin	Pontiac

MASON-DIXON 500

Time of Race: 4 hours, 17 minutes, 18 seconds
Average Speed: 116.595 mph
Margin of Victory: 22 seconds

FINISH	DRIVER	CAR
1	Jody Ridley	Ford
2	Bobby Allison	Buick
3	Dale Earnhardt	Pontiac
4	D. K. Ulrich	Buick
5	Ricky Rudd	Buick
6	Morgan Shepherd	Pontiac
7	Buddy Arrington	Dodge
8	Terry Labonte	Buick
9	Jimmy Means	Pontiac
10	Cale Yarborough	Buick
11	Donnie Allison	Oldsmobile
12	Darrell Waltrip	Buick
13	Neil Bonnett	Ford
14	Tommy Gale	Buick
15	Cecil Gordon	Buick
16	Harry Gant	Chevrolet
17	Richard Childress	Pontiac
18	James Hylton	Pontiac
19	Richard Petty	Buick
20	Kyle Petty	Buick
21	Mike Alexander	Oldsmobile
22	Joe Fields	Buick
23	J. D. McDuffie	Pontiac
24	Ronnie Thomas	Pontiac
25	David Pearson	Oldsmobile
26	Junior Miller	Oldsmobile
27	Ron Bouchard	Buick
28	Lowell Cowell	Chevrolet
29	Elmo Langley	Oldsmobile
30	Bob Riley	Buick
31	Dave Marcis	Chevrolet
32	Benny Parsons	Ford

WORLD 600

Time of Race: 4 hours, 38 minutes, 22 seconds
Average Speed: 129.326 mph
Margin of Victory: 9 seconds

FINISH	DRIVER	CAR
1	Bobby Allison	Buick
2	Harry Gant	Chevrolet
3	Cale Yarborough	Buick
4	Ricky Rudd	Buick
5	Kyle Petty	Buick
6	Morgan Shepherd	Pontiac
7	Joe Ruttman	Buick
8	Joe Millikan	Chevrolet
9	Darrell Waltrip	Buick
10	E. Forbes-Robinson	Buick
11	Lennie Pond	Buick
12	Connie Saylor	Oldsmobile
13	J. D. McDuffie	Pontiac
14	Terry Labonte	Buick

DINNER WITH THE MARLIN FAMILY

They swear this happened, so who are we to dispute Sterling Marlin and his father, Coo Coo? Besides, whether true or exaggerated, it's still a good story:

It seems father and son had finally agreed it was high time for Sterling to graduate from the short tracks of Tennessee and Alabama to a NASCAR superspeedway. Specifically, the massive and intimidating 2.66-mile, high-banked track at Talladega.

The only problem was working the words "Sterling" and "Talladega race" into the same sentence, then slipping it past family boss lady Eula Faye Marlin during their dinner time conversation.

It happened (so they claim) something like this back in the early '80s:

Coo Coo: These sure are good collard greens, Eula Faye. Don't you agree, son?

Sterling: Yes, sir, Daddy, they sure are. Good collard greens, no doubt about it.

Coo Coo: No doubt about it at all Sterling's gonna run the Talladega race pass the mashed potatoes and gravy, please and, by the way, they sure are good collard greens, Eula Faye, and by the way, Sterling's gonna run Talladega.

Where it should be noted, he eventually won the 1995 DieHard 500 and the 1996 Winston 500.

15	Buddy Arrington	Dodge
16	James Hylton	Pontiac
17	Tommy Gale	Ford
18	Dale Earnhardt	Pontiac
19	Richard Childress	Pontiac
20	Jody Ridley	Ford
21	Bill Dennis	Buick
22	Ronnie Thomas	Pontiac
23	Jimmy Means	Pontiac
24	Richard Petty	Buick
25	Dick May	Buick
26	Ron Bouchard	Buick
27	Mike Alexander	Buick
28	Lake Speed	Oldsmobile
29	Neil Bonnett	Ford
30	Rusty Wallace	Pontiac
31	Bobby Wawak	Buick
32	Stan Barrett	Pontiac
33	Buddy Baker	Oldsmobile
34	Jack Ingram	Ford
35	Dave Marcis	Dodge
36	Dick Brooks	Buick
37	Benny Parsons	Ford
38	Donnie Allison	Oldsmobile
39	Chuck Bown	Buick
40	Bill Elliott	Ford
41	Bruce Hill	Buick
42	Rick Wilson	Oldsmobile

BUDWEISER NASCAR 400

Time of Race: 3 hours, 1 minute, 10 seconds
Average Speed: 132.475 mph
Margin of Victory: 51 seconds

FINISH	DRIVER	CAR
1	Benny Parsons	Ford
2	Dale Earnhardt	Pontiac
3	Bobby Allison	Buick
4	Richard Petty	Buick
5	Dave Marcis	Buick
6	Jody Riley	Ford
7	Tim Richmond	Oldsmobile
8	Lake Speed	Oldsmobile
9	Joe Ruttman	Buick
10	Harry Gant	Pontiac
11	J. D. McDuffie	Pontiac

12	Tommy Gale	Ford
13	Buddy Arrington	Dodge
14	Richard Childress	Pontiac
15	H. B. Bailey	Pontiac
16	Dick May	Buick
17	Lowell Cowell	Oldsmobile
18	Cecil Gordon	Buick
19	Jimmy Means	Pontiac
20	Ronnie Thomas	Pontiac
21	Rick Baldwin	Buick
22	Randy Ogden	Oldsmobile
23	Terry Labonte	Buick
24	Ricky Rudd	Oldsmobile
25	James Hylton	Pontiac
26	Bobby Wawak	Buick
27	Roger Hamby	Chevrolet
28	Rick Newsom	Chevrolet
29	Kyle Petty	Buick
30	Darrell Waltrip	Buick
31	Morgan Shepherd	Pontiac
32	D. K. Ulrich	Buick
33	Kirk Shelmerdine	Pontiac
34	Baxter Price	Chevrolet

WARNER W. HODGDON 400

Time of Race: 2 hours, 39 minutes, 30 seconds
Average Speed: 93.597 mph
Margin of Victory: 1 Car length

FINISH	DRIVER	CAR
1	Darrell Waltrip	Buick
2	Dale Earnhardt	Pontiac
3	Richard Petty	Buick
4	Neil Bonnett	Ford
5	Ricky Rudd	Buick
6	Kyle Petty	Buick
7	Jody Ridley	Ford
8	Roy Smith	Buick
9	Dave Marcis	Chevrolet
10	Jim Robinson	Oldsmobile
11	Stan Barrett	Pontiac
12	J. D. McDuffie	Pontiac
13	Cecil Gordon	Buick
14	Steve Pfeifer	Chevrolet
15	Randy Ogden	Oldsmobile
16	Rick O'Dell	Buick

17	Don Puskarich	Oldsmobile
18	Richard Childress	Pontiac
19	James Hylton	Pontiac
20	Benny Parsons	Ford
21	Morgan Shepherd	Pontiac
22	Terry Labonte	Buick
23	Don Waterman	Buick
24	Bill Schmitt	Buick
25	Hershel McGriff	Buick
26	Buddy Arrington	Dodge
27	D. K. Ulrich	Oldsmobile
28	Jimmy Means	Pontiac
29	Bobby Allison	Buick
30	Tommy Gale	Buick
31	Harry Gant	Chevrolet
32	Jim Bown	Oldsmobile
33	Tim Richmond	Buick
34	Ronnie Thomas	Pontiac
35	E. Forbes-Robinson	Buick
36	Jim Insolo	Buick

GABRIEL 400

Time of Race: 3 hours, 3 minutes, 47 seconds
Average Speed: 130.589 mph
Margin of Victory: 1 Car length

FINISH	DRIVER`	CAR
1	Bobby Allison	Buick
2	Harry Gant	Pontiac
3	Benny Parsons	Ford
4	Jody Ridley	Ford
5	Dale Earnhardt	Pontiac
6	Richard Petty	Buick
7	Darrell Waltrip	Buick
8	Cale Yarborough	Buick
9	Neil Bonnett	Ford
10	Ron Bouchard	Buick
11	Terry Labonte	Buick
12	Buddy Arrington	Dodge
13	Buddy Baker	Buick
14	Tim Richmond	Oldsmobile
15	Morgan Shepherd	Pontiac
16	Lake Speed	Buick
17	Johnny Rutherford	Pontiac
18	Stan Barrett	Pontiac
19	Richard Childress	Pontiac
20	D. K. Ulrich	Oldsmobile
21	Kyle Petty	Buick
22	J. D. McDuffie	Pontiac
23	James Hylton	Pontiac
24	Joe Booher	Buick
25	Ronnie Thomas	Pontiac
26	Mike Potter	Buick
27	Cecil Gordon	Buick
28	Jimmy Means	Pontiac
29	Dave Marcis	Buick
30	Ricky Rudd	Buick
31	Joe Millikan	Chevrolet
32	Mike Alexander`	Buick
33	Bobby Wawak	Buick
34	Randy Ogden	Oldsmobile
35	Bill Elliott	Ford
36	Tommy Gale	Ford
37	Rick Wilson	Oldsmobile

FIRECRACKER 400

Time of Race: 2 hours, 48 minutes, 32 seconds
Average Speed: 142.588 mph
Margin of Victory:

FINISH	DRIVER	CAR
1	Cale Yarborough	Buick
2	Harry Gant	Buick

3	Richard Petty	Buick
4	Buddy Baker	Oldsmobile
5	Johnny Rutherford	Pontiac
6	Kyle Petty	Buick
7	Mike Alexander	Buick
8	Terry Labonte	Buick
9	Ron Bouchard	Buick
10	Darrell Waltrip	Buick
11	Lennie Pond	Buick
12	J. D. McDuffie	Pontiac
13	Dave Marcis	Buick
14	Connie Saylor	Oldsmobile
15	Tim Richmond	Buick
16	Bruce Hill	Buick
17	Buddy Arrington	Dodge
18	Jimmy Means	Pontiac
19	Tommy Gale	Ford
20	Morgan Shepherd	Pontiac
21	Richard Childress	Pontiac
22	James Hylton	Pontiac
23	E. Forbes-Robinson	Buick
24	Bill Elswick	Buick
25	Cecil Gordon	Buick
26	Stan Barrett	Pontiac
27	Tommy Houston	Oldsmobile
28	Bobby Allison	Buick
29	Joe Ruttman	Buick
30	Neil Bonnett	Ford
31	Dick May	Buick
32	A. J. Foyt	Oldsmobile
33	Lake Speed	Buick
34	Bill Elliott	Ford
35	Dale Earnhardt	Pontiac
36	Kevin Housby	Oldsmobile
37	Jack Ingram	Ford
38	Jody Ridley	Ford
39	Benny Parsons	Ford
40	Ricky Rudd	Oldsmobile
41	Billy Harvey	Pontiac
42	Rick Wilson	Oldsmobile

BUSCH NASHVILLE 420

Time of Race: 2 hours, 46 minutes, 47 seconds
Average Speed: 90.052 mph
Margin of Victory: Half a car length

FINISH	DRIVER	CAR
1	Darrell Waltrip	Buick
2	Bobby Allison	Buick
3	Benny Parsons	Ford
4	Ricky Rudd	Chevrolet
5	Terry Labonte	Buick
6	Kyle Petty	Buick
7	Dale Earnhardt	Pontiac
8	Harry Gant	Pontiac
9	Richard Petty	Buick
10	Jody Ridley	Ford
11	Mark Martin	Pontiac
12	Tim Richmond	Chevrolet
13	Morgan Shepherd	Pontiac
14	Ronnie Thomas	Pontiac
15	Jimmy Means	Buick
16	James Hylton	Pontiac
17	Richard Childress	Pontiac
18	Steve Spencer	Buick
19	Tommy Houston	Chevrolet
20	J. D. McDuffie	Pontiac
21	Tommy Gale	Ford
22	Lake Speed	Oldsmobile
23	D. K. Ulrich	Buick
24	Randy Ogden	Oldsmobile
25	Dave Marcis	Chrysler
26	Sterling Marlin	Buick
27	Mike Alexander	Buick
28	Buddy Arrington	Dodge
29	Cecil Gordon	Buick
30	Donald Satterfield	Chevrolet

MOUNTAIN DEW 500

Time of Race: 4 hours, 11 minutes, 52 seconds
Average Speed: 119.111 mph
Margin of Victory: 1 Car length

FINISH	DRIVER	CAR
1	Darrell Waltrip	Buick
2	Richard Petty	Buick
3	Benny Parsons	Ford
4	Harry Gant	Pontiac
5	Cale Yarborough	Buick
6	Ricky Rudd	Chevrolet
7	Buddy Baker	Buick
8	Kyle Petty	Buick
9	Tim Richmond	Oldsmobile
10	Ron Bouchard	Buick
11	Dale Earnhardt	Pontiac
12	Gary Balough	Chevrolet
13	Terry Labonte	Buick
14	Stan Barrett	Pontiac
15	Jody Ridley	Ford
16	Buddy Arrington	Dodge
17	Mike Alexander	Buick
18	J. D. McDuffie	Pontiac
19	Jimmy Means	Pontiac
20	Joe Booher	Buick
21	Cecil Gordon	Buick
22	James Hylton	Pontiac
23	Richard Childress	Pontiac
24	Al Loquasto	Buick
25	Bobby Allison	Buick
26	Rick Newson	Chevrolet
27	Lake Speed	Oldsmobile
28	Lowell Cowell	Chevrolet
29	Morgan Shepherd	Pontiac
30	Bruce Jacobi	Buick
31	Tommy Gale	Ford
32	Bob Riley	Pontiac
33	Dave Marcis	Buick]
34	Neil Bonnett	Ford
35	Ronnie Thomas	Pontiac

TALLADEGA 500

Time of Race: 3 hours, 11 minutes, 24 seconds
Average Speed: 156. 737 mph
Margin of Victory: 2 Feet

FINISH	DRIVER	CAR
1	Ron Bouchard	Buick
2	Darrell Waltrip	Buick
3	Terry Labonte	Buick
4	Harry Gant	Buick
5	Bobby Allison	Buick
6	Lake Speed	Buick
7	Kyle Petty	Buick
8	Jody Ridley	Ford
9	Stan Barrett	Pontiac
10	Dave Marcis	Buick
11	Bill Elliott	Ford
12	E. Forbes-Robinson	Buick
13	Benny Parsons	Ford
14	Terry Herman	Buick
15	Dick May	Buick
16	Jimmy Means	Pontiac
17	Cecil Gordon	Buick
18	Tommy Gale	Ford
19	Bobby Wawak	Buick
20	Rick Wilson	Oldsmobile
21	Rusty Wallace	Pontiac
22	Joe Ruttman	Buick
23	Ricky Rudd	Buick
24	Lennie Pond	Buick
25	Gary Balough	Buick
26	Richard Childress	Pontiac
27	Mike Potter	Buick

FINISH	DRIVER	CAR
28	Cale Yarborough	Buick
29	Dale Earnhardt	Pontiac
30	Bruce Hill	Buick
31	Sandy Satullo	Buick
32	Buddy Baker	Buick
33	Connie Saylor	Oldsmobile
34	Tim Richmond	Buick
35	Mike Alexander	Buick
36	Morgan Shepherd	Pontiac
37	Neil Bonnett	Ford
38	Jack Ingram	Ford
39	James Hylton	Buick
40	Richard Petty	Buick
41	Buddy Arrington	Chrysler
42	Joe Booher	Pontiac

CHAMPION SPARK PLUG 400

Time of Race: 3 hours, 14 minutes, 24 seconds
Average Speed: 123.457 mph
Margin Of Victory: 1 Car Length

FINISH	DRIVER	CAR
1	Richard Petty	Buick
2	Darrell Waltrip	Buick
3	Ricky Rudd	Chevrolet
4	Harry Gant	Pontiac
5	Buddy Baker	Buick
6	Joe Ruttman	Pontiac
7	Bobby Allison	Buick
8	Bill Elliott	Ford
9	Dale Earnhardt	Pontiac
10	Mike Alexander	Buick
11	Dave Marcis	Buick
12	Jody Ridley	Ford
13	Johnny Rutherford	Pontiac
14	Terry Labonte	Buick
15	Lake Speed	Buick
16	J. D. McDuffie	Pontiac
17	Cale Yarborough	Buick
18	Gary Balough	Buick
19	Kyle Petty	Buick
20	Rick Knoop	Buick
21	Tommy Gale	Ford
22	Joe Booher	Buick
23	Joe Millikan	Pontiac
24	Cecil Gordon	Buick
25	Jimmy Means	Pontiac
26	Benny Parsons	Ford
27	James Hylton	Pontiac
28	Neil Bonnett	Ford
29	Ron Bouchard	Buick
30	Tim Richmond	Buick
31	Bobby Wawak	Buick
32	Bob Schacht	Oldsmobile
33	Bruce Hill	Buick
34	Morgan Shepherd	Buick
35	Buddy Arrington	Dodge
36	Dick May	Buick

BUSCH 500

Time of Race: 3 hours, 8 minutes, 44 seconds
Average Speed: 84.723 mph
Margin of Victory: 1 Lap (finished under caution)

FINISH	DRIVER	CAR
1	Darrell Waltrip	Buick
2	Ricky Rudd	Chevrolet
3	Terry Labonte	Buick
4	Bobby Allison	Buick
5	Ron Bouchard	Buick
6	Benny Parsons	Ford
7	Lake Speed	Oldsmobile
8	Tim Richmond	Oldsmobile

9	Dave Marcis	Buick
10	Buddy Arrington	Dodge
11	Harry Gant	Pontiac
12	Jimmy Means	Pontiac
13	J. D. McDuffie	Pontiac
14	Lennie Pond	Buick
15	James Hylton	Pontiac
17	Joe Millikan	Pontiac
18	Ronnie Thomas	Pontiac
19	Morgan Shepherd	Buick
20	Jody Ridley	Ford
21	Joe Ruttman	Pontiac
22	Rick Newsom	Chevrolet
23	E. Forbes-Robinson	Buick
24	Richard Petty	Buick
25	Mike Alexander	Buick
26	Mike Potter	Chevrolet
27	Dale Earnhardt	Pontiac
28	Kyle Petty	Buick
29	Joel Stowe	Pontiac
30	Cecil Gordon	Buick

SOUTHERN 500

Time of Race: 3 hours, 57 minutes, 57 seconds
Average Speed: 126.410 mph
Margin of Victory: 1 Car Length

FINISH	DRIVER	CAR
1	Neil Bonnett	Ford
2	Darrell Waltrip	Buick
3	Dave Marcis	Buick
4	Terry Labonte	Buick
5	Buddy Baker	Buick
6	Dale Earnhardt	Pontiac
7	Bill Elliott	Ford
8	David Pearson	Buick
9	Bobby Allison	Chevrolet
10	Cale Yarborough	Buick
11	Ron Bouchard	Buick
12	Jody Ridley	Ford
13	Lake Speed	Buick
14	Harry Gant	Pontiac
15	Joe Ruttman	Pontiac
16	Morgan Shepherd	Buick
17	Lennie Pond	Buick
18	Joe Millikan	Pontiac
19	Dick May	Dodge
20	Mike Alexander	Oldsmobile
21	J. D. McDuffie	Pontiac
22	Tim Richmond	Buick
23	Ricky Rudd	Chevrolet
24	Bobby Wawak	Buick
25	Gary Balough`	Buick
26	James Hylton	Pontiac
27	Ronnie Thomas	Pontiac
28	Mike Potter	Buick
29	Tommy Gale	Ford
30	Richard Petty	Buick
31	D. K. Ulrich	Buick
32	Jack Ingram	Ford
33	Johnny Rutherford	Pontiac
34	Kyle Petty	Buick
35	Slick Johnson	Buick
36	H. B. Bailey	Pontiac
37	Budy Arrington	Dodge
38	Jimmy Means	Pontiac
39	Benny Parsons	Ford
40	Connie Saylor	Oldsmobile

WRANGLER SANFORSET 400

Time of Race: 3 hours, 5 minutes, 50 seconds
Average Speed: 69.998 mph
Margin of Victory: 1 Car Length

FINISH	DRIVER	CAR
1	Benny Parsons	Ford
2	Harry Gant	Pontiac
3	Darrell Waltrip	Buick
4	Terry Labonte	Buick
5	Bobby Allison	Buick
6	Dale Earnhardt	Pontiac
7	Mark Martin	Pontiac
8	Joe Millikan	Pontiac
9	Jody Ridley	Ford
10	Gary Balough	Buick
11	Richard Petty	Buick
12	Ricky Rudd	Chevrolet
13	Buddy Arrington	Dodge
14	Tim Richmond	Buick
15	Joe Fields	Buick
16	Jimmy Means	Pontiac
17	Tommy Gale	Ford
18	James Hylton	Pontiac
19	Dave Marcis	Chevrolet
20	Lake Speed	Oldsmobile
21	D. K. Ulrich	Buick
22	Kyle Petty	Buick
23	Cecil Gordon	Buick
24	Ronnie Thomas	Chevrolet
25	Ron Bouchard	Buick
26	Tommy Ellis	Chevrolet
27	Lennie Pond	Buick
28	Dave Dion	Ford
29	Morgan Shepherd	Buick
30	Joe Ruttman	Pontiac
31	Johnny Rutherford	Pontiac
32	Mike Alexander	Buick

CRC CHEMICALS 500

Time of Race: 4 hours, 10 minutes, 55 seconds
Average Speed: 119.561 mph
Margin of Victory: 1 Lap, 15 seconds

FINISH	DRIVER	CAR
1	Neil Bonnett	Ford
2	Darrell Waltrip	Buick
3	Bobby Allison	Buick
4	Ron Bouchard	Buick
5	Ricky Rudd	Chevrolet
6	Joe Ruttman	Pontiac
7	Kyle Petty	Buick
8	Dave Marcis	Chevrolet
9	Tim Richmond	Buick
10	Richard Petty	Buick
11	Jody Ridley	Ford
12	Morgan Shepherd	Buick
13	Cale Yarborough	Buick
14	Buddy Arrington	Dodge
15	Dale Earnhardt	Pontiac
16	Lennie Pond	Buick
17	Gary Balough	Buick
18	D. K. Ulrich	Buick
19	Jimmy Means	Pontiac
20	Ronnie Thomas	Pontiac
21	Joe Millikan	Pontiac
22	Lowell Cowell	Chevrolet
23	Harry Gant	Pontiac
24	Tommy Gale	Ford
25	Dick May	Buick
26	Cecil Gordon	Chevrolet
27	Lake Speed	Buick
28	J. D. McDuffie	Pontiac
29	Terry Labonte	Buick
30	Robert Schacht	Oldsmobile
31	Jocko Maggiacomo	Oldsmobile
32	James Hylton	Pontiac
33	Bob Riley	Pontiac
34	Benny Parsons	Ford

OLD DOMINION 500

Time of Race: 3 hours, 44 minutes, 57 seconds
Average Speed: 70.089 mph
Margin of Victory: 9 seconds

FINISH	DRIVER	CAR
1	Darrell Waltrip	Buick
2	Harry Gant	Pontiac
3	Mark Martin	Pontiac
4	Neil Bonnett	Ford
5	Joe Millikan	Pontiac
6	Ron Bouchard	Buick
7	Jimmy Hensley	Buick
8	Ricky Rudd	Chevrolet
9	Terry Labonte	Buick
10	Bobby Allison	Buick
11	Buddy Arrington	Dodge
12	Tommy Houston	Chevrolet
13	Tom Gale	Ford
14	Dave Marcis	Chevrolet
15	Jimmy Means	Pontiac
16	Bob McElwee	Buick
17	Joe Ruttman	Buick
18	Richard Petty	Buick
19	Kyle Petty	Buick
20	Tim Richmond	Buick
21	Jody Ridley	Ford
22	Lake Speed	Buick
23	Geoff Bodine	Buick
24	Benny Parsons	Ford
25	Lennie Pond	Buick
26	Dale Earnhardt	Pontiac
27	Ronnie Thomas	Pontiac
28	Morgan Shepherd	Pontiac
29	Buddy Baker	Buick
30	Tommy Ellis	Chevrolet

HOLLY FARMS 400

Time of Race: 2 hours, 41 minutes, 08 seconds
Average Speed: 93.091 mph
Margin of Victory: 1 Lap, 10 seconds

FINISH	DRIVER	CAR
1	Darrell Waltrip	Buick
2	Bobby Allison	Buick
3	Joe Millikan	Pontiac
4	Dale Earnhardt	Pontiac
5	Ron Bouchard	Buick
6	Morgan Shepherd	Buick
7	Jody Ridley	Ford
8	Bob McElwee	Buick
9	Jimmy Means	Chevrolet
10	Buddy Arrington	Dodge
11	Tommy Houston	Oldsmobile
12	J. D. McDuffie	Pontiac
13	Tim Richmond	Buick
14	Tommy Gale	Ford
15	James Hylton	Pontiac
16	Dave Marcis	Chevrolet
17	Ronnie Thomas	Pontiac
18	Kyle Petty	Buick
19	Cecil Gordon	Buick
20	Junior Miller	Oldsmobile
21	Richard Petty	Buick
22	Rick Newsom	Chevrolet
23	Lennie Pond	Buick
24	Harry Gant	Pontiac
25	Ricky Rudd	Chevrolet
26	Joe Ruttman	Pontiac
27	Lake Speed	Oldsmobile
28	Dean Combs	Buick
29	Benny Parsons	Ford
30	Terry Labonte	Buick

NATIONAL 500

Time of Race: 4 hours, 15 minutes, 52 seconds
Average Speed: 117.483 mph
Margin of Victory: 32 seconds

FINISH	DRIVER	CAR
1	Darrell Waltrip	Buick
2	Bobby Allison	Chevrolet
3	Ricky Rudd	Chevrolet
4	Tommy Ellis	Chevrolet
5	Ron Bouchard	Buick
6	Rusty Wallace	Buick
7	Geoff Bodine	Buick
8	Morgan Shepherd	Buick
9	Jack Ingram	Ford
10	Buddy Arrington	Dodge
11	Connie Saylor	Oldsmobile
12	Jimmy Means	Dodge
13	Rick Wilson	Oldsmobile
14	D. K. Ulrich	Buick
15	Jody Ridley	Ford
16	H. B. Bailey	Pontiac
17	J. D. McDuffie	Pontiac
18	Tim Richmond	Buick
19	Joe Ruttman	Buick
20	Kyle Petty	Buick
21	Bob Senneker	Pontiac
22	Tommy Gale	Ford
23	Terry Labonte	Buick
24	Gary Balough	Buick
25	Dale Earnhardt	Pontiac
26	Charlie Glotzbach	Buick
27	Johnny Rutherford	Buick
28	Sterling Marlin	Chevrolet
29	Neil Bonnett	Ford
30	Richard Petty	Buick
31	Cale Yarborough	Buick
32	Ronnie Thomas	Buick
33	Bill Elliott	Ford
34	Lake Speed	Buick
35	Joe Millikan	Pontiac
36	Bobby Wawak	Buick
37	Buddy Baker	Buick
38	Benny Parsons	Ford
39	John Anderson	Buick
40	Dave Marcis	Buick
41	Harry Gant	Pontiac

AMERICAN 500

Time of Race: 4 hours, 39 minutes, 32 seconds
Average Speed: 107.399 mph
Margin of Victory: One Half Car Length

FINISH	DRIVER	CAR
1	Darrell Waltrip	Buick
2	Bobby Allison	Buick
3	Harry Gant	Pontiac
4	Richard Petty	Buick
5	Joe Ruttman	Pontiac
6	Benny Parsons	Ford
7	Terry Labonte	Buick
8	Bill Elliott	Ford
9	Dale Earnhardt	Pontiac
10	Jody Ridley	Ford
11	Ron Bouchard	Buick
12	Dave Marcis	Chevrolet
13	Tommy Gale	Ford
14	Buddy Arrington	Dodge
15	Cecil Gordon	Buick
16	Buddy Baker	Buick
17	D. K. Ulrich	Buick
18	Ricky Rudd	Chevrolet
19	Joe Millikan	Pontiac
20	Jimmy Means	Pontiac
21	Dick Brooks	Ford

22	Tim Richmond	Buick
23	Joe Fields	Buick
24	John Anderson	Buick
25	Cale Yarborough	Buick
26	James Hylton	Pontiac
27	Morgan Shepherd	Buick
28	Chuck Bown	Buick
29	Johnny Rutherford	Buick
30	J. D. McDuffie	Pontiac
31	Lake Speed	Oldsmobile
32	Gary Balough`	Buick
33	Don Hume	Buick
34	Dean Combs	Buick
35	Neil Bonnett	Ford
36	Lennie Pond	Buick
37	Kyle Petty	Buick

ATLANTA JOURNAL 500

Time of Race: 3 hours, 49 minutes, 43 seconds
Average Speed: 130.391 mph
Margin of Victory: One Half Car Length

FINISH	DRIVER	CAR
1	Neil Bonnett	Ford
2	Darrell Waltrip	Buick
3	Cale Yarborough	Buick
4	Bobby Allison	Buick
5	Jody Ridley	Ford
6	Bill Elliott	Ford
7	Terry Labonte	Buick
8	Kyle Petty	Buick
9	Buddy Baker	Buick
10	Joe Millikan	Pontiac
11	Rick Wilson	Oldsmobile
12	Connie Saylor	Oldsmobile
13	Dick Brooks	Ford
14	Lake Speed	Buick
15	Chuck Bown	Buick
16	John Anderson	Buick
17	Buddy Arrington	Dodge
18	Delma Cowart	Buick
19	James Hylton	Buick
20	Harry Gant	Pontiac
21	Tim Richmond	Buick
22	Tommy Gale	Ford
23	J. D. McDuffie	Pontiac
24	Dale Earnhardt	Pontiac
25	Joe Ruttman	Buick
26	Richard Petty	Buick
27	D. K. Ulrich	Buick
28	Dave Marcis	Buick
29	Rusty Wallace	Buick
30	Geoff Bodine	Buick
31	Morgan Shepherd	Buick
32	Travis Tiller	Chevrolet
33	Tommy Ellis	Chevrolet
34	Gary Balough	Buick
35	Jimmy Means	Pontiac
36	Benny Parsons	Ford
37	Johnny Rutherford	Buick
38	Ricky Rudd	Buick
40	H. B. Bailey	Pontiac

WINSTON WESTERN 500

Time of Race: 3 hours, 16 minutes, 19 seconds
Average Speed: 95.288 mph
Margin of Victory: 2 Car Lengths

FINISH	DRIVER	CAR
1	Bobby Allison	Buick
2	Joe Ruttman	Buick
3	Terry Labonte	Buick
4	Dale Earnhardt	Pontiac

5	Joe Millikan	Pontiac
6	Darrell Waltrip	Buick
7	Richard Petty	Buick
8	Harry Gant	Pontiac
9	Jody Ridley	Ford
10	Ron Bouchard	Buick
11	J. D. McDuffie	Pontiac
12	Gary Kershaw	Buick
13	Morgan Shepherd	Buick
14	Bill Schmitt	Buick
15	Don Waterman	Buick
16	Lake Speed	Buick
17	James Hylton	Buick
18	Bob Bondurant	Pontiac
19	Gary Balough	Buick
20	Tim Richmond	Buick
21	Don Puskarich	Oldsmobile
22	Gene Thonesen	Buick
23	Mark Stahl	Ford
24	Buddy Arrington	Dodge
25	Dave Marcis	Pontiac
26	Tommy Gale	Dodge
27	Benny Parsons	Ford
28	Chuck Pittenger	Buick
29	Scott Miller	Pontiac
30	Roy Smith	Buick
31	Terry Herman	Buick
32	Jim Robinson	Oldsmobile
33	Neil Bonnett	Ford
34	Pat Mintey	Chevrolet
35	Don Whittington	Oldsmobile
36	Jim Bown	Buick
37	Kyle Petty	Buick
38	Hershel McGriff	Buick
39	Richard Childress	Buick
40	Ricky Rudd	Buick

1982

DAYTONA 500

Time of Race: 3 hours, 14minutes, 49 seconds
Average Speed: 153.991 mph
Margin of Victory: 23 seconds

FINISH	DRIVER	CAR
1	Bobby Allison	Buick
2	Cale Yarborough	Buick
3	Joe Ruttman	Buick
4	Terry Labonte	Buick
5	Bill Elliott	Ford
6	Ron Bouchard	Buick
7	Harry Gant	Buick
8	Buddy Baker	Buick
9	Jody Ridley	Ford0
10	Roy Smith	Pontiac
11	Gary Balough	Pontiac
12	Jim Sauter	Buick
13	J.D. McDuffie	Pontiac
14	Lowell Cowell	Buick
15	Buddy Arrington	Dodge
16	Tommy Gale	Ford
17	Jimmy Means	Buick
18	Rick Wilson	Oldsmobile
19	Morgan Shepherd	Buick
20	Darrell Waltrip	Buick
21	A.J. Foyt	Oldsmobile
22	Tom Sneva	Buick
23	Kyle Petty	Pontiac
24	Dave Marcis	Buick
25	Neil Bonnett	Ford
26	Benny Parsons	Pontiac
27	Richard Petty	Pontiac
28	E. Forbes-Robinson	Buick
29	Tighe Scott	Buick
30	Mark Martin	Buick

31	Stan Barrett	Buick
32	Bobby Wawak	Buick
33	Delma Cowart	Buick
34	Donnie Allison	Buick
35	Ricky Rudd	Pontiac
36	Dale Earnhardt	Ford
37	Rusty Wallace	Buick
38	Dick Brooks	Ford
39	Billie Harvey	Buick
40	Joe Millikan	Pontiac
41	Lake Speed	Buick
42	Geoff Bodine	Buick

RICHMOND 400

Time of Race: 1 hour 51 minutes, 30 seconds
Average Speed: 72.914 mph
Margin of Victory: 12 seconds

FINISH	DRIVER	CAR
1	Dave Marcis	Chevrolet
2	Richard Petty	Pontiac
3	Benny Parsons	Pontiac
4	Dale Earnhardt	Ford
5	Terry Labonte	Chevrolet
6	Joe Millikan	Pontiac
7	Neil Bonnett	Ford
8	Bobby Allison	Chevrolet
9	Ron Bouchard	Buick
10	Morgan Shepherd	Buick
11	Tommy Ellis	Chevrolet
12	Bill Elliott	Ford
13	Jody Ridley	Ford
14	Buddy Arrington	Dodge
15	Joe Ruttman	Buick
16	Bob Schacht	Oldsmobile
17	Slick Johnson	Pontiac
18	Jimmy Means	Chevrolet
19	Lake Speed	Buick
20	Kyle Petty	Pontiac
21	Tommy Gale	Ford
22	Ricky Rudd	Pontiac
23	J.D. McDuffie	Pontiac
24	Lennie Pond	Buick
25	Tommy Houston	Buick
26	Mark Martin	Pontiac
27	Darrell Waltrip	Buick
28	Joe Fields	Buick
29	D.K. Ulrich	Buick
30	Harry Gant	Buick
31	Tom Sneva	Buick
32	Gary Balough	Buick

VALLEYDALE 500

Time of Race: 2 hours, 49 minutes, 52 seconds
Average Speed: 94.025 mph
Margin of Victory: 13 seconds

FINISH	DRIVER	CAR
1	Darrell Waltrip	Buick
2	Dale Earnhardt	Ford
3	Morgan Shepherd	Buick
4	Terry Labonte	Chevrolet
5	Bobby Allison	Chevorlet
6	Harry Gant	Buick
7	Richard Petty	Pontiac
8	Ron Bouchard	Buick
9	Benny Parsons	Pontiac
10	Dave Marcis	Chevrolet
11	Kyle Petty	Pontiac
12	Brad Teague	Chevrolet
13	Joe Millikan	Pontiac
14	Mark Martin	Pontiac

15	Buddy Arrington	Dodge
16	Jimmy Means	Pontiac
17	Tommy Gale	Ford
18	Joe Ruttman	Buick
19	J.D. McDuffie	Pontiac
20	Jody Ridley	Ford
21	Slick Johnson	Pontiac
22	Neil Bonnett	Buick
23	Gary Balough	Buick
24	Johnny McFadden	Buick
25	Ronnie Thomas	Pontiac
26	D.K. Ulrich	Buick
27	Ricky Rudd	Pontiac
28	Dick Brooks	Ford
29	Lake Speed	Buick
30	Dick May	Buick

COCA-COLA 500

Time of Race: 3 hours, 29 minutes, 58 secons
Average Speed: 124.824 mph
Margin of Victory: 2 inches

FINISH	DRIVER	CAR
1	Darrell Waltrip	Buick
2	Richard Petty	Pontiac
3	Cale Yarborough	Buick
4	Benny Parsons	Pontiac
5	Harry Gant	Buick
6	Morgan Shepherd	Buick
7	Gary Balough	Buick
8	Terry Labonte	Buick
9	Rick Wilson	Oldsmobile
10	Jim Sauter	Buick
11	Donnie Allison	Buick
12	Dave Marcis	Buick
13	Brad Teague	Chevrolet
14	Buddy Arrington	Dodge
15	Tom Sneva	Buick
16	Jimmy Means	Buick
17	Jody Ridley	Ford
18	Steve Moore	Pontiac
19	Mark Martin	Buick
20	Dick May	Pontiac
21	Bill Elliott	Ford
22	Bobby Allison	Buick
23	Delma Cowart	Buick
24	Joe Millikan	Pontiac
25	Ricky Rudd	Pontiac
26	Kyle Petty	Pontiac
27	Neil Bonnett	Ford
28	Dale Earnhardt	Ford
29	Joe Ruttman	Buick
30	Buddy Baker	Buick
31	Connie Saylor	Oldsmobile
32	D.K. Ulrich	Buick
33	Lake Speed	Buick
34	Dick Brooks	Ford
35	Rusty Wallace	Buick
36	Ron Bouchard	Buick
37	Tommy Gale	Ford
38	J.D. McDuffie	Pontiac
39	A.J. Foyt	Oldsmobile
40	E. Forbes-Robinson	Buick

WARNER W. HODGDON CAROLINA 500

Time of Race: 4 hours, 35 minutes, 27 seconds
Average Speed: 108.992 mph
Margin of Victory: 1 lap, 1 car length

FINISH	DRIVER	CAR
1	Cale Yarborough	Buick
2	Terry Labonte	Chevrolet

3	Benny Parsons	Pontiac
4	Bobby Allison	Chevrolet
5	Morgan Shepherd	Buick
6	Joe Millikan	Pontiac
7	Darrell Waltrip	Buick
8	Harry Gant	Buick
9	Buddy Arrington	Dodge
10	J.D. McDuffie	Pontiac
11	Tommy Gale	Ford
12	Gary Balough	Buick
13	Dick May	Buick
14	Buddy Baker	Buick
15	Ricky Rudd	Pontiac
16	Ron Bouchard	Buick
17	Jimmy Means	Pontiac
18	Slick Johnson	Buick
19	Neil Bonnett	Ford
20	Ronnie Thomas	Pontiac
21	Dave Marcis	Chevrolet
22	Donnie Allison	Buick
23	Bill Elliott	Ford
24	Joe Ruttman	Buick
25	Dale Earnhardt	Ford
26	D.K. Ulrich	Buick
27	Kyle Petty	Pontiac
28	Bobby Wawak	Buick
29	Ernie Cline	Pontiac
30	Richard Petty	Pontiac
31	Tim Richmond	Ford
32	Mark Martin	Buick
33	Jody Ridley	Ford
34	Lake Speed	Buick

CRC CHEMICALS REBEL 500

Time of Race: 4 hours, 3 minutes, 27 seconds
Average Speed: 123.554 mph
Margin of Victory: 1 car length

FINISH	DRIVER	CAR
1	Dale Earnhardt	Ford
2	Cale Yarborough	Buick
3	Bill Elliott	Ford
4	Benny Parsons	Pontiac
5	Tim Richmond	Buick
6	Terry Labonte	Buick
7	Mark Martin	Buick
8	Buddy Arrington	Dodge
9	Donnie Allison	Buick
10	Lennie Pond	Buick
11	Jimmy Means	Buick
12	Tommy Gale	Ford
13	Ronnie Thomas	Pontiac
14	Rick Newsom	Chevrolet
15	D.K. Ulrich	Buick
16	Joe Millikan	Pontiac
17	Lake Speed	Buick
18	Kyle Petty	Pontiac
19	Harry Gant	Buick
20	Dick May	Buick
21	Bobby Wawak	Chevrolet
22	Jody Ridley	Ford
23	Darrell Waltrip	Buick
24	Neil Bonnett	Ford
25	Bobby Allison	Chevrolet
26	Slick Johnson	Buick
27	Dave Marcis	Buick
28	John Anderson	Buick
29	Ricky Rudd	Pontiac
30	Morgan Shepherd	Buick
31	Richard Petty	Pontiac
32	Dick Brooks	Ford
33	Jim Sauter	Buick
34	Ron Bouchard	Buick
35	H.B. Bailey	Pontiac
36	J.D. McDuffie	Pontiac
37	Buddy Baker	Buick

NORTHWESTERN BANK 400

Time of Race: 2 hours, 33 minutes, 37 seconds
Average Speed: 97.646 mph
Margin of Victory: 1 car length

FINISH	DRIVER	CAR
1	Darrell Waltrip	Buick
2	Terry Labonte	Chevrolet
3	Dale Earnhardt	Ford
4	Benny Parsons	Pontiac
5	Richard Petty	Pontiac
6	Harry Gant	Buick
7	Morgan Shepherd	Buick
8	Bobby Allison	Chevrolet
9	Ricky Rudd	Pontiac
10	Neil Bonnett	Buick
11	Tim Richmond	Buick
12	Joe Ruttman	Buick
13	Ron Bouchard	Buick
14	Kyle Petty	Pontiac
15	Geoff Bodine	Pontiac
16	Buddy Arrington	Dodge
17	Jody Ridley	Ford
18	Jimmy Means	Buick
19	D.K. Ulrich	Buick
20	J.D. McDuffie	Pontiac
21	Bobby Hillin	Buick
22	Brad Teague	Chevrolet
23	Ronnie Thomas	Pontiac
24	Lake Speed	Buick
25	Mark Martin	Pontiac
26	Lennie Pond	Buick
27	Bob Schacht	Oldsmobile
28	Butch Lindley	Buick
29	Dave Marcis	Chevrolet
30	Slick Johnson	Pontiac

VIRGINIA NATIONAL BANK 500

Time of Race: 3 hours, 30 minutes, 1 second
Average Speed: 75.073 mph
Margin of Victory: 1 lap, 1 second

FINISH	DRIVER	CAR
1	Harry Gant	Buick
2	Butch Lindley	Buick
3	Neil Bonnett	Ford
4	Ricky Rudd	Pontiac
5	Darrell Waltrip	Buick
6	Dave Marcis	Chevrolet
7	Mark Martin	Pontiac
8	Buddy Arrington	Dodge
9	Jimmy Hensley	Buick
10	Slick Johnson	Pontiac
11	Brad Teague	Chevrolet
12	Jody Ridley	Ford
13	Jimmy Means	Buick
14	Joe Ruttman	Buick
15	Richard Petty	Pontiac
16	J.D. McDuffie	Pontiac
17	Bobby Allison	Chevrolet
18	Tim Richmond	Buick
19	Ron Bouchard	Buick
20	Terry Labonte	Chevrolet
21	Bob Schacht	Oldsmobile
22	Lennie Pond	Buick
23	Dale Earnhardt	Ford
24	Lake Speed	Buick
25	Geoff Bodine	Pontiac
26	Morgan Shepherd	Buick
27	Kyle Petty	Pontiac
28	Buddy Baker	Buick
29	Benny Parsons	Pontiac
30	Donnie Allison	Buick
31	D.K. Ulrich	Buick

WINSTON 500

Time of Race: 3 hours, 11 minutes, 19 seconds
Average Speed: 156.697 mph
Margin of Victory: 1 car length

FINISH	DRIVER	CAR
1	Darrell Waltrip	Buick
2	Terry Labonte	Buick
3	Benny Parsons	Pontiac
4	Kyle Petty	Pontiac
5	Morgan Shepherd	Buick
6	Donnie Allison	Buick
7	Tim Richmond	Buick
8	Dale Earnhardt	Ford
9	Jimmy Means	Buick
10	Mark Martin	Buick
11	Buddy Arrington	Dodge
12	Slick Johnson	Buick
13	Bobby Allison	Buick
14	Harry Gant	Buick
15	D.K. Ulrich	Buick
16	Tommy Gale	Ford
17	Philip Duffie	Buick
18	J.D. McDuffie	Pontiac
19	Neil Bonnett	Ford
20	John Anderson	Buick
21	Lowell Cowell	Buick
22	Joe Ruttman	Pontiac
23	Ferrel Harris	Buick
24	Ricky Rudd	Pontiac
25	Buddy Baker	Buick
26	Bill Elliott	Ford
27	Richard Petty	Pontiac
28	Bill Scott	Buick
29	Elliott Forbes-Robinson	Buick
30	Dave Marcis	Buick
31	Lennie Pond	Buick
32	Rick Wilson	Oldsmobile
33	Geoff Bodine	Pontiac
34	Lake Speed	Buick
35	Steve Moore	Pontiac
36	Ron Bouchard	Buick
37	Cale Yarborough	Buick
38	Jody Ridley	Ford
39	L.W. Wright	Chevrolet
40	David Simko	Pontiac

CRACKER BARREL 420

Time of Race: 2 hours, 59 minutes, 52 seconds
Average Speed: 83.502 mph
Margin of Victory: One lap, three seconds

FINISH	DRIVER	CAR
1	Darrell Waltrip	Buick
2	Terry Labonte	Chevrolet
3	Ron Bouchard	Buick
4	Joe Ruttman	Buick
5	Neil Bonnett	Buick
6	Bobby Allison	Chevrolet
7	Tim Richmond	Buick
8	Dave Marcis	Chevrolet
9	Richard Petty	Pontiac
10	Dale Earnhardt	Ford
11	Bill Elliott	Ford
12	Mark Martin	Buick
13	Jody Ridley	Ford
14	Buddy Arrington	Dodge
15	Morgan Shepherd	Buick
16	Tommy Gale	Ford
17	James Hylton	Pontiac
18	J.D. McDuffie	Pontiac
19	Ricky Rudd	Pontiac
20	Brad Teague	Chevrolet
21	Geoff Bodine	Pontiac
22	Benny Parsons	Pontiac
23	Jimmy Means	Buick

FINISH	DRIVER	CAR
24	Ronnie Thomas	Pontiac
25	Slick Johnson	Buick
26	D.K. Ulrich	Buick
27	Kyle Petty	Pontiac
28	Bob Jarvis	Buick
29	Harry Gant	Buick
30	Lake Speed	Pontiac

MASON-DIXON 500

Time of Race: 4 hours, 9 minutes, 43 seconds
Average Speed: 120.136 mph
Margin of Victory: 3 laps, 6 seconds

FINISH	DRIVER	CAR
1	Bobby Allison	Chevrolet
2	Dave Marcis	Chevrolet
3	Dale Earnhardt	Ford
4	Terry Labonte	Chevrolet
5	Mark Martin	Buick
6	Ron Bouchard	Buick
7	Morgan Shepherd	Buick
8	Donnie Allison	Buick
9	Tim Richmond	Buick
10	Lake Speed	Pontiac
11	Buddy Arrington	Dodge
12	James Hylton	Pontiac
13	Tommy Gale	Ford
14	D.K. Ulrich	Buick
15	Darrell Waltrip	Buick
16	Slick Johnson	Buick
17	Jody Ridley	Ford
18	Joe Ruttman	Pontiac
19	Neil Bonnett	Ford
20	Benny Parsons	Pontiac
21	Geoff Bodine	Pontiac
22	Ricky Rudd	Pontiac
23	Ronnie Thomas	Buick
24	Richard Petty	Pontiac
25	Brad Teague	Pontiac
26	Jocko Maggiacomo	Oldsmobile
27	J.D. McDuffie	Pontiac
28	Jimmy Walker	Ford
29	Kyle Petty	Pontiac
30	Harry Gant	Buick
31	Jimmy Means	Pontiac
32	John Callis	Pontiac

WORLD 600

Time of Race: 4 hours, 36 minutes, 48 seconds
Average Speed: 130.058 mph
Margin of Victory: 2 car length

FINISH	DRIVER	CAR
1	Neil Bonnett	Ford
2	Bill Elliott	Ford
3	Bobby Allison	Buick
4	Cale Yarborough	Buick
5	Buddy Baker	Buick
6	Jody Ridley	Ford
7	Ricky Rudd	Pontiac
8	Richard Petty	Pontiac
9	Dave Marcis	Buick
10	Ron Bouchard	Buick
11	Buddy Arrington	Dodge
12	Lake Speed	Buick
13	Harry Gant	Buick
14	Jimmy Means	Buick
15	Connie Saylor	Oldsmobile
16	Bosco Lowe	Buick
17	Kyle Petty	Pontiac
18	Slick Johnson	Buick
19	Morgan Shepherd	Buick
20	Bobby Wawak	Buick

21	David Pearson	Buick
22	Darrell Waltrip	Buick
23	Tommy Gale	Buick
24	Brad Teague	Chevrolet
25	Geoff Bodine	Pontiac
26	H.B. Bailey	Pontiac
27	Mark Martin	Pontiac
28	D.K. Ulrich	Buick
29	Rusty Wallace	Buick
30	Dale Earnhardt	Ford
31	Lennie Pond	Buick
32	Delma Cowart	Buick
33	J.D. McDuffie	Pontiac
34	Terry Labonte	Buick
35	Steve Moore	Pontiac
36	Rick Wilson	Buick
37	Donnie Allison	Buick
38	Dean Combs	Buick
39	Benny Parsons	Pontiac
40	Tim Richmond	Buick
41	Joe Ruttman	Buick
42	John Anderson	Buick

VAN SCOY DIAMOND MINE 500

Time of Race: 4 hours, 24 minutes, 8 seconds
Average Speed: 113.579 mph
Margin of Victory: 3 seconds

FINISH	DRIVER	CAR
1	Bobby Allison	Buick
2	Tim Richmond	Buick
3	Benny Parsons	Pontiac
4	Harry Gant	Buick
5	Terry Labonte	Chevrolet
6	Ricky Rudd	Pontiac
7	Richard Petty	Pontiac
8	Geoff Bodine	Pontiac
9	Jody Ridley	Ford
10	Dave Marcis	Chevrolet
11	Kyle Petty	Pontiac
12	Buddy Arrington	Dodge
13	Darrell Waltrip	Buick
14	Bobby Wawak	Buick
15	D.K. Ulrich	Buick
16	Al Loquasto	Buick
17	Rick Newsom	Chevrolet
18	Tommy Gale	Ford
19	Bill Elliott	Ford
20	Lake Speed	Buick
21	Lowell Cowell	Buick
22	Buddy Baker	Buick
23	Ronnie Thomas	Buick
24	Jimmy Means	Buick
25	Brad Teague	Chevrolet
26	Mark Martin	Buick
27	Steve Gray	Buick
28	Cale Yarborough	Buick
29	Slick Johnson	Buick
30	Joe Ruttman	Buick
31	Ron Bouchard	Buick
32	Jocko Maggiacano	Oldsmobile
33	J.D. McDuffie	Pontiac
34	Dale Earnhardt	Ford
35	Morgan Shepherd	Buick
36	Bobby Hillin	Buick
37	Jimmy Walker	Ford

BUDWEISER 400

Time of Race: 2 hours, 23 minutes, 51 seconds
Average Speed: 103.816 mph
Margin of Victory: 4 seconds

FINISH	DRIVER	CAR
1	Tim Richmond	Buick
2	Terry Labonte	Buick

3	Geoff Bodine	Pontiac
4	Dale Earnhardt	Ford
5	Neil Bonnett	Ford
6	Roy Smith	Buick
7	Jody Ridley	Ford
8	Mark Martin	Buick
9	Ron Bouchard	Buick
10	Jim Reich	Chevrolet
11	Don Waterman	Buick
12	Kyle Petty	Pontiac
13	Scott Miller	Pontiac
14	Rick McCray	Pontiac
15	Buddy Arrington	Dodge
16	D.K. Ulrich	Buick
17	Jim Bown	Buick
18	Jimmy Means	Buick
19	John Krebs	Pontiac
20	Don Puskarich	Buick
21	Randy Becker	Dodge
22	Mark Stahl	Ford
23	Benny Parsons	Pontiac
24	Bill Schmitt	Buick
25	J.D. McDuffie	Pontiac
26	Joe Ruttman	Pontiac
27	Bobby Allison	Chevrolet
28	Jim Robinson	Oldsmobile
29	Ricky Rudd	Pontiac
30	Dave Marcis	Pontiac
31	Lake Speed	Buick
32	Darrell Waltrip	Buick
33	Hershel McGriff	Buick
34	Jimmie Lee	Buick
35	Harry Gant	Buick
36	Richard Petty	Pontiac

GABRIEL 400

Time of Race: 3 hours, 23 minutes, 13 seconds
Average Speed: 118.101 mph
Margin of Victory: 3 car lengths

FINISH	DRIVER	CAR
1	Cale Yarborough	Buick
2	Darrell Waltrip	Buick
3	Bill Elliott	Ford
4	Bobby Allison	Buick
5	Ricky Rudd	Pontiac
6	Kyle Petty	Pontiac
7	Dale Earnhardt	Ford
8	Morgan Shepherd	Buick
9	Geoff Bodine	Pontiac
10	Harry Gant	Buick
11	Neil Bonnett	Ford
12	Ron Bouchard	Buick
13	Joe Ruttman	Buick
14	Dave Marcis	Buick
15	Buddy Arrington	Dodge
16	Bobby Hillin	Buick
17	Dean Combs	Buick
18	Tom Gale	Ford
19	Dick May	Buick
20	Jimmy Means	Buick
21	H.B. Bailey	Pontiac
22	D.K. Ulrich	Buick
23	James Hylton	Buick
24	Dennis DeVea	Buick
25	Tim Richmond	Buick
26	Richard Petty	Pontiac
27	Jody Ridley	Ford
28	Terry Labonte	Buick
29	Robin McCall	Buick
30	Slick Johnson	Buick
31	Buddy Baker	Pontiac
32	Benny Parsons	Buick
33	Mark Martin	Pontiac
34	Lake Speed	Buick
35	Ronnie Thomas	Pontiac
36	David Pearson	Buick
37	J.D. McDuffie	Pontiac

FIRECRACKER 400

Time of Race: 2 hours, 27 minutes, 9 seconds
Average Speed: 163.099
Margin of Victory: car length

FINISH	DRIVER	CAR
1	Bobby Allison	Buick
2	Bill Elliott	Ford
3	Ron Bouchard	Buick
4	Morgan Shepherd	Buick
5	David Pearson	Buick
6	Geoff Bodine	Pontiac
7	Ricky Rudd	Pontiac
8	Buddy Baker	Pontiac
9	Lake Speed	Buick
10	Dave Marcis	Buick
11	J.D. McDuffie	Pontiac
12	Buddy Arrington	Dodge
13	Lowell Cowell	Oldsmobile
14	Tommy Gale	Ford
15	Jody Ridley	Ford
16	Lennie Pond	Buick
17	Delma Cowart	Buick
18	Philip Duffie	Buick
19	James Hylton	Buick
20	Bobby Hillin	Buick
21	Jimmy Means	Buick
22	Cale Yarborough	Buick
23	Tim Richmond	Buick
24	Harry Gant	Buick
25	Richard Petty	Pontiac
26	Travis Tiller	Buick
27	Terry Labonte	Buick
28	Benny Parsons	Buick
29	Dale Earnhardt	Ford
30	Blackie Wangerin	Ford
31	Mark Martin	Pontiac
32	Neil Bonnett	Ford
33	Rick Wilson	Buick
34	Slick Johnson	Buick
35	Dr. Bob Jarvis	Buick
36	Darrell Waltrip	Buick
37	Marty Robbins	Buick
38	Kyle Petty	Buick
39	Connie Saylor	Oldsmobile
40	Joe Ruttman	Buick

BUSCH NASHVILLE 420

Time of Race: 2 hours, 53 minutes, 35 seconds
Average Speed: 86.524 mph
Margin of Victory: 1 Lap

FINISH	DRIVER	CAR
1	Darrell Waltrip	Buick
2	Terry Labonte	Chevrolet
3	Harry Gant	Buick
4	Ricky Rudd	Pontiac
5	Tim Richmond	Buick
6	Geoff Bodine	Pontiac
7	Richard Petty	Pontiac
8	Jody Ridley	Ford
9	Dale Earnhardt	Ford
10	Ron Bouchard	Buick
11	Dave Marcis	Chevrolet
12	Joe Ruttman	Buick
13	Lake Speed	Buick
14	Jimmy Means	Chevrolet
15	Mark Martin	Pontiac
16	Darryl Sage	Chevrolet
17	D.K. Ulrich	Buick
18	Tommy Gale	Ford
19	Bobby Allison	Chevrolet
20	James Hylton	Pontiac
21	Bill Elliott	Ford
22	Buddy Arrington	Dodge

23	Kyle Petty	Pontiac
24	Buddy Baker	Pontiac
25	J.D. McDuffie	Pontiac
26	Morgan Shepherd	Buick
27	Lennie Pond	Buick
28	Slick Johnson	Buick

MOUNTAIN DEW 500

Time of Race: 4 hours, 19 minutes, 45 seconds
Average Speed: 115.496 mph
Margin of Victory: 17 seconds

FINISH	DRIVER	CAR
1	Bobby Allison	Buick
2	Richard Petty	Pontiac
3	Terry Labonte	Buick
4	Ron Bouchard	Buick
5	Buddy Baker	Pontiac
6	Darrell Waltrip	Buick
7	Joe Ruttman	Buick
8	Dave Marcis	Buick
9	Buddy Arrington	Dodge
10	Mark Martin	Pontiac
11	Geoff Bodine	Pontiac
12	James Hylton	Pontiac
13	Rick Newsom	Chevrolet
14	Cecil Gordon	Buick
15	Kyle Petty	Buick
16	J.D. McDuffie	Pontiac
17	Jimmy Means	Pontiac
18	Charlie Baker	Buick
19	Bobby Wawak	Buick
20	Mike Potter	Buick
21	Joe Booher	Buick
22	Harry Gant	Buick
23	Tommy Gale	Ford
24	Tim Richmond	Buick
25	Dale Earnhardt	Ford
26	Cale Yarborough	Buick
27	John Callis	Pontiac
28	Morgan Shepherd	Buick
29	Al Loquasto	Buick
30	Bill Elliott	Ford
31	Ricky Rudd	Pontiac
32	Ronnie Thomas	Buick
33	Lake Speed	Buick
34	Jocko Maggiacomo	Oldsmobile
35	Tom Hessert	Pontiac
36	Jody Ridley	Ford

TALLADEGA 500

Time of Race: 2 hours, 58 minutes, 26 seconds
Average Speed: 168.157 mph
Margin of Victory: 1 car length

FINISH	DRIVER	CAR
1	Darrell Waltrip	Buick
2	Buddy Baker	Pontiac
3	Richard Petty	Pontiac
4	Cale Yarborough	Buick
5	Terry Labonte	Buick
6	Bill Elliott	Ford
7	Tim Richmond	Buick
8	Morgan Shepherd	Buick
9	Ricky Rudd	Pontiac
10	Bobby Allison	Pontiac
11	Joe Ruttman	Buick
12	Mark Martin	Pontiac
13	Dave Marcis	Buick
14	Jody Ridley	Ford
15	Geoff Bodine	Pontiac
16	Neil Bonnett	Ford

FINISH	DRIVER	CAR
17	Jimmy Means	Buick
18	Lowell Cowell	Oldsmobile
19	Bobby Hillin	Buick
20	Buddy Arrington	Dodge
21	Lake Speed	Buick
22	J.D. McDuffie	Pontiac
23	Philip Duffie	Buick
24	Al Loquasto	Buick
25	James Hylton	Buick
26	Bobby Wawak	Buick
27	Rick Wilson	Buick
28	Travis Tiller	Buick
29	Tommy Gale	Ford
30	Delma Cowart	Buick
31	Charlie Baker	Buick
32	Slick Johnson	Buick
33	Bob Slawinski	Buick
34	Ron Bouchard	Buick
35	Dale Earnhardt	Ford
36	Lennie Pond	Buick
37	Connie Saylor	Oldsmobile
38	Harry Gant	Buick
39	Kyle Petty	Buick
40	Jim Hurlbert	Buick

CHAMPION SPARK PLUG 400

Time of Race: 2 hours, 45 minutes, 53 seconds
Average Speed: 136.454
Margin of Victory: 3/4 car length

FINISH	DRIVER	CAR
1	Bobby Allison	Buick
2	Richard Petty	Pontiac
3	Harry Gant	Buick
4	Geoff Bodine	Pontiac
5	Benny Parsons	Buick
6	Buddy Arrington	Chrysler
7	Darrell Waltrip	Buick
8	Dave Marcis	Buick
9	Neil Bonnett	Ford
10	Ron Bouchard	Buick
11	Jimmy Means	Buick
12	Lake Speed	Buick
13	Dean Combs	Buick
14	Ricky Rudd	Pontiac
15	Kyle Petty	Pontiac
16	J.D. McDuffie	Pontiac
17	Ronnie Thomas	Pontiac
18	Joe Booher	Buick
19	Charlie Baker	Buick
20	Tom Gale	Ford
21	Terry Labonte	Buick
22	James Hylton	Chevrolet
23	Tim Richmond	Buick
24	Tony Bettenhausen	Buick
25	Buddy Baker	Pontiac
26	Jody Ridley	Ford
27	Bill Elliott	Ford
28	Cale Yarborough	Buick
29	Dave Simko	Buick
30	Dale Earnhardt	Ford
31	David Pearson	Buick
32	Morgan Shepherd	Buick
33	Robin McCall	Buick
34	Mark Martin	Pontiac
35	H.B. Bailey	Pontiac
36	Al Loquasto	Buick
37	Earle Canavan	Oldsmobile
38	Joe Ruttman	Buick

BUSCH 500

Time of Race: 2 hours, 49 minutes, 32 seconds
Average Speed: 94.318 mph
Margin of Victory: 3 car length

FINISH	DRIVER	CAR
1	Darrell Waltrip	Buick
2	Bobby Allison	Chevrolet
3	Harry Gant	Buick
4	Terry Labonte	Buick
5	Morgan Shepherd	Buick
6	Dale Earnhardt	Ford
7	Ricky Rudd	Pontiac
8	Jody Ridley	Ford
9	Buddy Baker	Pontiac
10	Geoff Bodine	Pontiac
11	Mark Martin	Pontiac
12	Ron Bouchard	Oldsmobile
13	Lake Speed	Buick
14	Jimmy Means	Chevrolet
15	Brad Teague	Chevrolet
16	Buddy Arrington	Dodge
17	Darryl Sage	Chevrolet
18	D.K. Ulrich	Buick
19	Tommy Gale	Ford
20	Connie Saylor	Buick
21	Dave Marcis	Buick
22	J.D. McDuffie	Pontiac
23	James Hylton	Pontiac
24	Joe Ruttman	Buick
25	Tim Richmond	Buick
26	Richard Petty	Pontiac
27	Al Laquasto	Buick
28	Ronnie Thomas	Pontiac
29	Rick Newsom	Chevrolet
30	Kyle Petty	Pontiac

SOUTHERN 500

Time of Race: 4 hours, 21 minutes, 0 seconds
Average Speed: 115.224 mph
Margin of Victory: 1 car length

FINISH	DRIVER	CAR
1	Cale Yarborough	Buick
2	Richard Petty	Pontiac
3	Dale Earnhardt	Ford
4	Bill Elliott	Ford
5	Buddy Baker	Pontiac
6	Lake Speed	Buick
7	Geoff Bodine	Pontiac
8	Benny Parsons	Buick
9	Buddy Arrington	Dodge
10	Dave Marcis	Chevrolet
11	Harry Gant	Buick
12	Connie Saylor	Oldsmobile
13	Joe Ruttman	Buick
14	Kyle Petty	Buick
15	Dick May	Buick
16	J.D. McDuffie	Pontiac
17	Philip Duffie	Buick
18	Joe Millikan	Pontiac
19	Rick Newsom	Chevrolet
20	Bobby Allison	Buick
21	Bobby Wawak	Chevrolet
22	Mark Martin	Buick
23	Jimmy Means	Pontiac
24	Darrell Waltrip	Buick
25	Tommy Gale	Ford
26	Ron Bouchard	Buick
27	D.K. Ulrich	Buick
28	Jody Ridley	Ford
29	H.B. Bailey	Pontiac
30	Tim Richmond	Buick
31	Ricky Rudd	Pontiac
32	Slick Johnson	Buick
33	Mike Potter	Oldsmobile
34	Neil Bonnett	Ford
35	Terry Labonte	Chevrolet
36	Morgan Shepherd	Buick
37	David Pearson	Buick
38	Ronnie Thomas	Pontiac
39	Earle Canavan	Buick
40	Lennie Pond	Buick

Dale Jarrett finished second to Jeff Gordon in the 1997 Winston Cup points race.

WRANGLER SANFORSET 400

Time of Race: 2 hours, 37 minutes, 6 seconds
Average Speed: 82.800 mph
Margin of Victory: 17 seconds

FINISH	DRIVER	CAR
1	Bobby Allison	Chevrolet
2	Tim Richmond	Buick
3	Darrell Waltrip	Buick
4	Ricky Rudd	Pontiac
5	Neil Bonnett	Ford
6	Terry Labonte	Buick
7	Harry Gant	Buick
8	Dave Marcis	Chevrolet
9	Buddy Baker	Pontiac
10	Speed Lake	Pontiac
11	Tommy Ellis	Chevrolet
12	Morgan Shepherd	Buick
13	Richard Petty	Pontiac
14	Kyle Petty	Pontiac
15	Ron Bouchard	Oldsmobile
16	Buddy Arrington	Dodge
17	James Hylton	Chevrolet
18	Darryl Sage	Chevrolet
19	Jimmy Means	Buick
20	D.K. Ulrich	Buick
21	Tommy Gale	Ford
22	Joe Fields	Buick
23	Ronnie Thomas	Pontiac
24	Butch Lindley	Buick
25	Jody Ridley	Ford

26	Mark Martin	Buick
27	Dale Earnhardt	Ford
28	Geoff Bodine	Pontiac
29	Jimmy Hensley	Buick
30	J.D. McDuffie	Pontiac
31	Joe Ruttman	Buick

CRC CHEMICALS 500

Time of Race: 4 hours, 38 minutes, 42.5 seconds
Average Speed: 107.642 mph
Margin of Victory: 1 car length

FINISH	DRIVER	CAR
1	Darrell Waltrip	Buick
2	Kyle Petty	Pontiac
3	Bill Elliott	Ford
4	Geoff Bodine	Pontiac
5	Benny Parsons	Buick
6	Dave Marcis	Chevrolet
7	Buddy Arrington	Dodge
8	Ron Bouchard	Buick
9	Tim Richmond	Buick
10	Bobby Allison	Chevrolet
11	Ricky Rudd	Pontiac
12	Harry Gant	Buick
13	J.D. McDuffie	Pontiac
14	Tommy Gale	Ford
15	James Hylton	Chevrolet
16	Cecil Gordon	Buick
17	Jimmy Means	Pontiac
18	Joe Ruttman	Buick
19	D.K. Ulrich	Buick
20	Dale Earnhardt	Ford
21	Neil Bonnett	Ford
22	Lake Speed	Pontiac
23	Dick May	Buick
24	Morgan Shepherd	Buick
25	Jody Ridley	Ford
26	John Callis	Pontiac
27	Terry Labonte	Chevrolet
28	Jocko Maggiacomo	Oldsmobile
29	Buddy Baker	Pontiac
30	Richard Petty	Pontiac
31	Ronnie Thomas	Pontiac
32	J.R. Charbonneau	Buick
33	Mark Martin	Pontiac
34	Dr. Gil Roth	Oldsmobile
35	Rick Newsom	Chevrolet

HOLLY FARMS 400

Time of Race: 2 hours, 32 minutes, 57 seconds
Average Speed: 98.071
Margin of Victory: 14 seconds

FINISH	DRIVER	CAR
1	Darrell Waltrip	Buick
2	Harry Gant	Buick
3	Terry Labonte	Chevrolet
4	Richard Petty	Pontiac
5	Geoff Bodine	Pontiac
6	Joe Ruttman	Buick
7	Ron Bouchard	Buick
8	Lake Speed	Pontiac
9	Jody Ridley	Ford
10	Kyle Petty	Pontiac
11	Dave Marcis	Chevrolet
12	Mark Martin	Buick
13	Morgan Shepherd	Buick
14	Jimmy Means	Pontiac
15	D.K. Ulrich	Buick
16	Jeff McDuffie	Pontiac
17	James Hylton	Chevrolet
18	Cecil Gordon	Buick
19	Tommy Gale	Ford
20	Dale Earnhardt	Ford

21	Buddy Arrington	Dodge
22	Tim Richmond	Buick
23	Bobby Allison	Chevrolet
24	Buddy Baker	Pontiac
25	Ricky Rudd	Pontiac
26	Dean Combs	Buick
27	Joel Stowe	Buick
28	Jimmy Walker	Ford
29	Ronnie Thomas	Pontiac
30	J.D. McDuffie	Pontiac

NATIONAL 500

Time of Race: 3 hours, 39 minutes, 5 seconds
Average Speed: 137.208 mph
Margin of Victory: 2 seconds

FINISH	DRIVER	CAR
1	Harry Gant	Buick
2	Bill Elliott	Ford
3	David Pearson	Buick
4	Joe Ruttman	Buick
5	Benny Parsons	Buick
6	Buddy Baker	Pontiac
7	Jody Ridley	Ford
8	Richard Petty	Pontiac
9	Bobby Allison	Buick
10	Rick Wilson	Oldsmobile
11	Jimmy Means	Buick
12	Rick Baldwin	Dodge
13	Geoff Bodine	Pontiac
14	Darrell Waltrip	Buick
15	D.K. Ulrich	Buick
16	Terry Labonte	Buick
17	John Anderson	Buick
18	J.D. McDuffie	Pontiac
19	Tim Richmond	Buick
20	Lennie Pond	Buick
21	Lake Speed	Buick
22	Buddy Arrington	Chrysler
23	Sterling Marlin	Oldsmobile
24	Dick Brooks	Pontiac
25	Dale Earnhardt	Ford
26	H.B. Bailey	Pontiac
27	Richard Brickhouse	Pontiac
28	Neil Bonnett	Ford
29	Kyle Petty	Buick
30	Morgan Shepherd	Buick
31	Ricky Rudd	Pontiac
32	Dave Marcis	Buick
33	Cale Yarborough	Buick
34	Dean Combs	Buick
35	Ron Bouchard	Oldsmobile
36	Tommy Gale	Ford
37	Ronnie Thomas	Pontiac
38	Mark Martin	Buick
39	Connie Saylor	Oldsmobile
40	Travis Tiller	Buick

OLD DOMINION 500

Time of Race: 3 hours, 41 minutes, 5 seconds
Average Speed: 71.315 mph
Margin of Victory: 2 seconds

FINISH	DRIVER	CAR
1	Darrell Waltrip	Buick
2	Ricky Rudd	Pontiac
3	Richard Petty	Pontiac
4	Terry Labonte	Chevrolet
5	Joe Ruttman	Buick
6	Buddy Baker	Pontiac
7	Jody Ridley	Ford
8	Harry Gant	Buick
9	Jimmy Means	Chevrolet
10	Buddy Arrington	Dodge
11	Geoff Bodine	Pontiac
12	D.K. Ulrich	Buick

13	Tim Richmond	Buick
14	Ron Bouchard	Buick
15	J.D. McDuffie	Buick
16	James Hylton	Chevrolet
17	Tommy Gale	Ford
18	Morgan Shepherd	Buick
19	Bobby Allison	Chevrolet
20	Mark Martin	Buick
21	Kyle Petty	Pontiac
22	Neil Bonnett	Ford
23	Jimmy Hensley	Buick
24	Joe Fields	Buick
25	Ronnie Thomas	Pontiac
26	Butch Lindley	Miller Buick
27	Dale Earnhardt	Ford
28	Dave Marcis	Chevrolet
29	Lake Speed	Pontiac
30	Darryl Sage	Chevrolet
31	Rick Newsom	Chevrolet

WARNER W. HODGDON AMERICAN 500

Time of Race: 4 hours, 20 minutes, 47 seconds
Average Speed: 115.122 mph
Margin of Victory: 9.5 seconds

FINISH	DRIVER	CAR
1	Darrell Waltrip	Buick
2	Bobby Allison	Chevrolet
3	Neil Bonnett	Ford
4	Terry Labonte	Buick
5	Morgan Shepherd	Buick
6	Richard Petty	Pontiac
7	Buddy Baker	Pontiac
8	Ron Bouchard	Buick
9	Lennie Pond	Chevrolet
10	D.K. Ulrich	Buick
11	Dave Marcis	Chevrolet
12	Bill Elliott	Ford
13	Bobby Wawak	Buick
14	Dale Earnhardt	Ford
15	Jimmy Means	Chevrolet
16	Tommy Gale	Ford
17	Tim Richmond	Buick
18	Joe Ruttman	Buick
19	Slick Johnson	Buick
20	Randy Baker	Pontiac
21	Richard Brickhouse	Pontiac
22	J.D. McDuffie	Pontiac
23	Buddy Arrington	Dodge
24	Mark Martin	Buick
25	Cale Yarborough	Buick
26	Joe Millikan	Buick
27	Geoff Bodine	Pontiac
28	Ricky Rudd	Pontiac
29	Kyle Petty	Pontiac
30	Ronnie Thomas	Pontiac
31	Jody Ridley	Ford
32	Harry Gant	Buick
33	Lake Speed	Pontiac
34	Benny Parsons	Buick
35	Rick Newsom	Chevrolet

ATLANTA JOURNAL 500

Time of Race: 3 hours, 48 minutes, 451 seconds
Average Speed: 130.884 mph
Margin of Victory: .5 seconds

FINISH	DRIVER	CAR
1	Bobby Allison	Buick
2	Harry Gant	Buick
3	Darrell Waltrip	Buick
4	Tim Richmond	Buick
5	Joe Ruttman	Buick
6	Dave Marcis	Buick
7	Ricky Rudd	Pontiac
8	Terry Labonte	Buick

9	Rodney Combs	Buick
10	Mark Martin	Buick
11	Neil Bonnett	Ford
12	Lennie Pond	Chevrolet
13	Jimmy Means	Chevrolet
14	Buddy Arrington	Chrysler
15	Richard Petty	Pontiac
16	Philip Duffie	Buick
17	Bobby Wawak	Chevrolet
18	Travis Tiller	Buick
19	Geoff Bodine	Pontiac
20	Benny Parsons	Buick
21	Buddy Baker	Pontiac
22	Darryl Sage	Chevrolet
23	D.K. Ulrich	Buick
24	Bill Elliott	Ford
25	Morgan Shepherd	Buick
26	Tommy Gale	Ford
27	Rick Wilson	Oldsmobile
28	Jody Ridley	Ford
29	Lake Speed	Pontiac
30	J.D. McDuffie	Pontiac
31	Kyle Petty	Pontiac
32	Ron Bouchard	Buick
33	Marty Robbins	Buick
34	Dale Earnhardt	Ford
35	Cale Yarborough	Buick
36	Jerry Bowman	Oldsmobile
37	Dick May	Buick
38	Donnie Allison	Oldsmobile
39	Glenn Jarrett	Ford
40	Steve Moore	Pontiac

WINSTON WESTERN 500

Time of Race: 3 hours, 7 minutes, 24 seconds
Average Speed: 99.823 mph
Margin of Victory: 7 seconds

FINISH	DRIVER	CAR
1	Tim Richmond	Buick
2	Ricky Rudd	Pontiac
3	Darrell Waltrip	Buick
4	Neil Bonnett	Ford
5	Mark Martin	Buick
6	Ron Bouchard	Buick
7	Benny Parsons	Buick
8	Morgan Shepherd	Buick
9	Jody Ridley	Ford
10	Jim Bown	Buick
11	Geoff Bodine	Pontiac
12	Jimmy Means	Pontiac
13	Terry Herman	Buick
14	Glen Francis	Pontiac
15	D.K. Ulrich	Buick
16	Bobby Allison	Pontiac
17	Cecil Gordon	Buick
18	J.D. McDuffie	Buick
19	Jim Reich	Chevrolet
20	Jim Robinson	Oldsmobile
21	Bill Schmitt	Buick
22	Trevor Boys	Pontiac
23	Jimmie Lee	Buick
24	Roy Smith	Buick
25	Bill Elliott	Ford
26	Harry Gant	Buick
27	Terry Labonte	Buick
28	Hershel McGriff	Buick
29	Dave Marcis	Pontiac
30	Jimmy Insolo	Pontiac
31	Richard Petty	Pontiac
32	Lake Speed	Pontiac
33	Don Waterman	Buick
34	Rick McCray	Pontiac
35	Buddy Arrington	Chrysler
36	Derrike Cope	Ford
37	John Krebs	Pontiac
38	Randy Baker	Chrysler
39	Mark Stahl	Ford
40	Joe Ruttman	Pontiac
41	Kevin Terris	Buick
42	Dale Earnhardt	Ford

1983

DAYTONA 500

Time of Race: 3 hours, 12 minutes, 20 seconds
Average Speed: 155.979 mph
Margin of Victory: One car length

FINISH	DRIVER	CAR
1	Cale Yarborough	Pontiac
2	Bill Elliott	Ford
3	Buddy Baker	Ford
4	Joe Ruttman	Chevrolet
5	Dick Brooks	Ford
6	Terry Labonte	Chevrolet
7	Tom Sneva	Chevrolet
8	David Pearson	Chevrolet
9	Bobby Allison	Chevrolet
10	Jody Ridley	Buick
11	A. J. Foyt	Chevrolet
12	Lennie Pond	Buick
13	Phil Parsons	Buick
14	Jimmy Means	Buick
15	Dean Roper	Pontiac
16	Buddy Arrington	Chrysler
17	Ronnie Thomas	Pontiac
18	Jim Sauter	Chevrolet
19	Ronnie Hopkins	Buick
20	Rick Baldwin	Dodge
21	Clark Dwyer	Chevrolet
22	Neil Bonnett	Chevrolet
23	James Hylton	Chevrolet
24	Ricky Rudd	Chevrolet
25	Lake Speed	Chevrolet
26	Ron Bouchard	Buick
27	Tommy Gale	Ford
28	Mark Martin	Buick
29	J. D. McDuffie	Pontiac
30	Geoff Bodine	Pontiac
31	Delma Cowart	Buick
32	Dave Marcis	Chevrolet
33	Kyle Petty	Pontiac
34	Sterling Marlin	Chevrolet
35	Dale Earnhardt	Ford
36	Darrell Waltrip	Chevrolet
37	Harry Gant	Buick
38	Richard Petty	Pontiac
39	Bosco Lowe	Buick
40	E. Forbes-Robinson	Buick
41	Tim Richmond	Pontiac
42	Benny Parsons	Buick

RICHMOND 400

Time of Race: 2 hours, 43 minutes, 45 seconds
Average Speed: 79.584 mph
Margin of Victory: Four car lengths

FINISH	DRIVER	CAR
1	Bobby Allison	Chevrolet
2	Dale Earnhardt	Ford
3	Neil Bonnett	Chevrolet
4	Geoff Bodine	Pontiac
5	Harry Gant	Buick
6	Bill Elliott	Ford
7	Joe Ruttman	Buick
8	Richard Petty	Pontiac
9	Dave Marcis	Chevrolet
10	Buddy Baker	Ford
11	Butch Lindley	Buick
12	Ron Bouchard	Buick
13	Dick Brooks	Ford
14	Kyle Petty	Pontiac
15	Lake Speed	Chevrolet

FINISH	DRIVER	CAR
16	Jimmy Means	Chevrolet
17	Tim Richmond	Pontiac
18	Sterling Marlin	Pontiac
19	Jim Sauter	Buick
20	Buddy Arrington	Dodge
21	James Hylton	Chevrolet
22	Terry Labonte	Chevrolet
23	Ronnie Thomas	Pontiac
24	Mark Martin	Buick
25	J.D. McDuffie	Pontiac
26	Joe Fields	Buick
27	Slick Johnson	Buick
28	Ricky Rudd	Chevrolet
29	Darrell Waltrip	Chevrolet
30	Dave Dion	Ford
31	Morgan Shepherd	Ford
32	Tommy Gale	Buick

WARNER W. HODGDON CAROLINA 500

Time of Race: 4 hours, 25 minutes, 30 seconds
Average Speed: 113.055 mph
Margin of Victory: car length

FINISH	DRIVER	CAR
1	Richard Petty	Pontiac
2	Bill Elliott	Ford
3	Darrell Waltrip	Chevrolet
4	Lake Speed	Chevrolet
5	Harry Gant	Buick
6	Ricky Rudd	Chevrolet
7	Tim Richmond	Pontiac
8	Dick Brooks	Ford
9	Cale Yarborough	Chevrolet
10	Bobby Allison	Chevrolet
11	Mark Martin	Buick
12	Neil Bonnett	Chevrolet
13	Sterling Marlin	Pontiac
14	Jimmy Means	Pontiac
15	Kyle Petty	Pontiac
16	Bobby Wawak	Buick
17	Ronnie Hopkins	Buick
18	D. K. Ulrich	Buick
19	Geoff Bodine	Pontiac
20	Ron Bouchard	Buicl
21	Tommy Gale	Ford
22	Buddy Arrington	Chrysler
23	Slick Johnson	Buick
24	Terry Labonte	Chevrolet
25	Bobby Hillin	Buick
26	Jim Sauter	Buick
27	Ronnie Thomas	Pontiac
28	Rick Newsom	Chevrolet
29	Joe Ruttman	Buick
30	J. D. McDuffie	Pontiac
31	Lennie Pond	Pontiac
32	Buddy Baker	Ford
33	Dale Earnhardt	Ford
34	Dave Marcis	Chevrolet
35	Ernie Cline	Pontiac

COCA-COLA 500

Time of Race: 4 hours, 1 minute, 27 seconds
Average Speed: 124.055 mph
Margin of Victory: 2.5 seconds

FINISH	DRIVER	CAR
1	Cale Yarborough	Chevrolet
2	Neil Bonnett	Chevrolet
3	Buddy Baker	Ford
4	Joe Ruttman	Buick
5	Richard Petty	Pontiac
6	Dick Brooks	Ford

FINISH	DRIVER	CAR
7	Mark Martin	Buick
8	Terry Labonte	Chevrolet
9	Tim Richmond	Pontiac
10	Ricky Rudd	Chevrolet
11	Harry Gant	Buick
12	Ron Bouchard	Buick
13	Dave Marcis	Chevrolet
14	Benny Parsons	Buick
15	Lake Speed	Chevrolet
16	Buddy Arrington	Dodge
17	Jody Ridley	Buick
18	Bobby Wawak	Buick
19	Bobby Hillin	Buick
20	Darryl Sage	Chevrolet
21	Ronnie Hopkins	Buick
22	H. B. Bailey	Pontiac
23	Tommy Gale	Ford
24	Ronnie Thomas	Pontiac
25	Bobby Allison	Buick
26	Eddie Bierschwale	Buick
27	Ken Ragan	Buick
28	Bob Senneker	Pontiac
29	Jim Sauter	Chevrolet
30	Bill Elliott	Ford
31	Sterling Marlin	Chevrolet
32	Jimmy Means	Buick
33	Dale Earnhardt	Ford
34	Slick Johnson	Buick
35	Kyle Petty	Pontiac
36	J. D. McDuffie	Buick
37	David Simko	Oldsmobile
38	A. J. Foyt	Chevrolet
39	Jim Vandiver	Chrysler
40	Darrell Waltrip	Chevrolet
41	Geoff Bodine	Pontiac

TRANSOUTH 500

Time of Race: 3 hours, 50 minutes, 5 seconds
Average Speed: 130.406 mph
Margin of Victory: .5 seconds

FINISH	DRIVER	CAR
1	Harry Gant	Buick
2	Darrell Waltrip	Chevrolet
3	Mark Martin	Buick
4	Ricky Rudd	Chevrolet
5	Bill Elliott	Ford
6	Cale Yarborough	Chevrolet
7	Neil Bonnett	Chevrolet
8	Bobby Allison	Buick
9	Geoff Bodine	Pontiac
10	D. K. Ulrich	Buick
11	Sterling Marlin	Chevrolet
12	Jimmy Means	Pontiac
13	Dale Earnhardt	Ford
14	Tommy Gale	Ford
15	Travis Tiller	Buick
16	Bobby Wawak	Buick
17	J. D. McDuffie	Pontiac
18	Ron Bouchard	Buick
19	Dick Brooks	Ford
20	Joe Ruttman	Buick
21	Dick May	Buick
22	David Pearson	Chevrolet
23	Buddy Arrington	Dodge
24	Ronnie Thomas	Pontiac
25	Richard Petty	Pontiac
26	Cecil Gordon	Chrysler
27	Jody Ridley	Buick
28	Lake Speed	Chevrolet
29	Slick Johnson	Buick
30	Ronnie Hopkins	Chevrolet
31	Kyle Petty	Pontiac
32	Buddy Baker	Ford
33	Dave Marcis	Chevrolet
34	Benny Parsons	Buick
35	Tim Richmond	Pontiac
36	Terry Labonte	Chevrolet

NORTHWESTERN BANK 400

Time of Race: 2 hours, 44 minutes, 3 seconds
Average Speed: 91.436 mph
Margin of Victory: 8 seconds

FINISH	DRIVER	CAR
1	Darrell Waltrip	Chevrolet
2	Bobby Allison	Buick
3	Harry Gant	Buick
4	Neil Bonnett	Chevrolet
5	Geoff Bodine	Pontiac
6	Terry Labonte	Chevrolet
7	Joe Ruttman	Buick
8	Lake Speed	Chevrolet
9	Dave Marcis	Chevrolet
10	Richard Petty	Pontiac
11	Ron Bouchard	Buick
12	Lennie Pond	Chevrolet
13	D. K. Ulrich	Buick
14	Jimmy Means	Chevrolet
15	Buddy Arrington	Chrysler
16	Bobby Hillin	Buick
17	Ronnie Thomas	Pontiac
18	Joe Millikan	Ford
19	Tommy Gale	Ford
20	Dick Brooks	Ford
21	Bill Elliott	Ford
22	Sterling Marlin	Pontiac
23	Rick McCray	Pontiac
24	Ronnie Hopkins	Chevrolet
25	Slick Johnson	Buick
26	Mark Martin	Buick
27	Ricky Rudd	Chevrolet
28	Tim Richmond	Pontiac
29	Dale Earnhardt	Ford
30	Kyle Petty	Pontiac

VIRGINIA NATIONAL BANK 500

Time of Race: 3 hours, 57 minutes, 14 seconds
Average Speed: 66.460 mph
Margin of Victory: .5 seconds

FINISH	DRIVER	CAR
1	Darrell Waltrip	Chevrolet
2	Harry Gant	Buick
3	Bobby Allison	Buick
4	Joe Ruttman	Buick
5	Ricky Rudd	Chevrolet
6	Terry Labonte	Chevrolet
7	Ron Bouchard	Buick
8	Dick Brooks	Ford
9	Buddy Arrington	Dodge
10	Jimmy Means	Chevrolet
11	Kyle Petty	Pontiac
12	Sterling Marlin	Pontiac
13	D. K. Ulrich	Ford
14	Lennie Pond	Chevrolet
15	Tim Richmond	Pontiac
16	Neil Bonnett	Chevrolet
17	Richard Petty	Pontiac
18	Ronnie Thomas	Pontiac
19	Dave Marcis	Chevrolet
20	Rick Newsom	Buick
21	Bill Elliott	Ford
22	Tommy Gale	Buick
23	Lake Speed	Chevrolet
24	Rick McCray	Pontiac
25	Geoff Bodine	Pontiac
26	Dale Earnhardt	Ford
27	Mark Martin	Buick
28	Slick Johnson	Buick
29	Trevor Boys	Chevrolet
30	Ronnie Hopkins	Buick
31	Buddy Baker	Ford
32	Morgan Shepherd	Buick

WINSTON 500

Time of Race: 3 hours, 14 minutes, 55 seconds
Average Speed: 153.936 mph
Margin of Victory: 1 car length

FINISH	DRIVER	CAR
1	Richard Petty	Pontiac
2	Benny Parsons	Buick
3	Lake Speed	Chevrolet
4	Harry Gant	Buick
5	Bill Elliott	Ford
6	Terry Labonte	Chevrolet
7	Jimmy Means	Buick
8	Ricky Rudd	Chevrolet
9	Dave Marcis	Chevrolet
10	Bobby Allison	Buick
11	Joe Ruttman	Chevrolet
12	Ken Ragan	Buick
13	Tommy Gale	Ford
14	Dick Brooks	Ford
15	Neil Bonnett	Chevrolet
16	Cecil Gordon	Chrysler
17	Morgan Shepherd	Buick
18	Dean Roper	Pontiac
19	Lennie Pond	Chevrolet
20	Ron Bouchard	Buick
21	Geoff Bodine	Pontiac
22	Steve Moore	Pontiac
23	Buddy Arrington	Chrysler
24	Dale Earnhardt	Ford
25	Buddy Baker	Ford
26	Lowell Cowell	Oldsmobile
27	Tim Richmond	Pontiac
28	Phil Parsons	Pontiac
29	Cale Yarborough	Chevrolet
30	Kyle Petty	Pontiac
31	David Pearson	Chevrolet
32	Jody Ridley	Buick
33	Darrell Waltrip	Chevrolet
34	A. J. Foyt	Chevrolet
35	Ronnie Thomas	Pontiac
36	Mark Martin	Chevrolet
37	Rick Wilson	Buick
38	Philip Duffie	Buick
39	Clark Dwyer	Chevrolet
40	Connie Saylor	Oldsmobile
41	Sterling Marlin	Chevrolet
42	Rick Baldwin	Buick

MARTY ROBBINS 420

Time of Race: 3 hours, 32 minutes, 23 seconds
Average Speed: 70.717 mph
Margin of Victory: 1 lap, 4 seconds

FINISH	DRIVER	CAR
1	Darrell Warltrip	Chevrolet
2	Bobby Allison	Buick
3	Harry Gant	Buick
4	Morgan Shepherd	Buick
5	Bill Elliott	Ford
6	Richard Petty	Pontiac
7	Joe Ruttman	Buick
8	Terry Labonte	Chevrolet
9	Ron Bouchard	Buick
10	Tim Richmond	Pontiac
11	Sterling Marlin	Pontiac
12	Jimmy Means	Chevrolet
13	Neil Bonnett	Chevrolet
14	Ricky Rudd	Chevrolet
15	Ronnie Thomas	Pontiac
16	Buddy Arrington	Chrysler
17	Kyle Petty	Pontiac
18	J. D. McDuffie	Pontiac
19	Trevor Boys	Chevrolet
20	Geoff Bodine	Pontiac
21	Mark Martin	Buick

22	Steve Gray	Buick
23	Rick Newsom	Buick
24	Dale Earnhardt	Ford
25	Dick Brooks	Ford
26	Darryl Sage	Chevrolet
27	Dave Marcis	Chevrolet
28	Tommy Gale	Ford
29	Ronnie Hopkins	Chevrolet

15	Ronnie Thomas	Pontiac
16	Buddy Arrington	Chrysler
17	Ronnie Hopkins	Buick
18	Sterling Marlin	Pontiac
19	Rick Newsom	Buick
20	Tommy Gale	Ford
21	Dick Brooks	Ford
22	Trevor Boys	Chevrolet
23	Joe Ruttman	Pontiac
24	J. D. McDuffie	Pontiac
25	Geoff Bodine	Pontiac
26	Ricky Rudd	Chevrolet
27	Harry Gant	Buick
28	Mike Potter	Buick

MASON-DIXON 500

Time of Race: 4 hours, 21 minutes, 13 seconds
Average Speed: 114.847 mph
Margin of Victory: 2 seconds

FINISH	DRIVER	CAR
1	Bobby Allison	Buick
2	Darrell Waltrip	Chevrolet
3	Joe Ruttman	Buick
4	Bill Elliott	Ford
5	Buddy Baker	Ford
6	Morgan Shepherd	Buick
7	Richard Petty	Pontiac
8	Dale Earnhardt	Ford
9	Harry Gant	Buick
10	Sterling Marlin	Pontiac
11	Kyle Petty	Pontiac
12	Jimmy Means	Pontiac
13	Jerry Bowman	Ford
14	Rick Newsom	Chevrolet
15	Dick Brooks	Ford
16	Dave Marcis	Chevrolet
17	Jimmy Ingle	Buick
18	D. K. Ulrich	Buick
19	Buddy Arrington	Chrysler
20	John Callis	
21	Cecil Gordon	Chrysler
22	Cale Yarborough	Chevrolet
23	J. D. McDuffie	Pontiac
24	Ricky Rudd	Chevrolet
25	Ronnie Thomas	Pontiac
26	Ronnie Hopkins	Chevrolet
27	Tommy Gale	Ford
28	Neil Bonnett	Chevrolet
29	Benny Parsons	Buick
30	Tim Richmond	Pontiac
31	Terry Labonte	Chevrolet
32	Trevor Boys	Chevrolet
33	Dick May	Ford
34	Ron Bouchard	Buick
35	Geoff Bodine	Pontiac
36	Jocko Maggiacomo	Oldsmobile

VALLEYDALE 500

Time of Race: 2 hours, 51 minutes, 7 seconds
Average Speed: 93.445 mph
Margin of Victory: 2 seconds

FINISH	DRIVER	CAR
1	Darrell Waltrip	Chevrolet
2	Bobby Allison	Buick
3	Morgan Shepherd	Buick
4	Neil Bonnett	Chevrolet
5	Richard Petty	Pontiac
6	Terry Labonte	Chevrolet
7	Ron Bouchard	Buick
8	Bill Elliott	Ford
9	Dale Earnhardt	Ford
10	Tim Richmond	Pontiac
11	Kyle Petty	Pontiac
12	Dave Marcis	Chevrolet
13	D. K. Ulrich	Buick
14	Jimmy Means	Chevrolet

WORLD 600

Time of Race: 4 hours, 15 minutes, 51 seconds
Average Speed: 140.707 mph
Margin of Victory: 1 second

FINISH	DRIVER	CAR
1	Neil Bonnett	Chevrolet
2	Richard Petty	Pontiac
3	Bobby Allison	Buick
4	Darrell Waltrip	Chevrolet
5	Dale Earnhardt	Ford
6	Lake Speed	Chevrolet
7	Buddy Baker	Ford
8	Kyle Petty	Pontiac
9	Morgan Shepherd	Buick
10	Dave Marcis	Chevrolet
11	Bobby Hillin	Buick
12	Buddy Arrington	Chrysler
13	Dean Combs	Buick
14	Joe Ruttman	Chevrolet
15	Tommy Ellis	Buick
16	Bill Elliott	Ford
17	Ken Ragan	Buick
18	Bobby Wawak	Chevrolet
19	Sterling Marlin	Chevrolet
20	Trevor Boys	Chevrolet
21	Jim Vandiver	Chrysler
22	H. B. Bailey	Pontiac
23	D. K. Ulrich	Chevrolet
24	Slick Johnson	Buick
25	Harry Gant	Buick
26	J. D. McDuffie	Pontiac
27	Bob Senneker	Pontiac
28	Cale Yarborough	Chevrolet
29	Mark Martin	Chevrolet
30	Philip Duffie	Buick
31	Rick Newsom	Chevrolet
32	Ricky Rudd	Chevrolet
33	Terry Labonte	Chevrolet
34	Benny Parsons	Buick
35	Tommy Gale	Ford
36	Geoff Bodine	Pontiac
37	Dick Brooks	Ford
38	Jimmy Means	Buick
39	David Pearson	Chevrolet
40	Tim Richmond	Pontiac
41	Ron Bouchard	Buick

BUDWEISER 400

Time of Race: 2 hours, 49 minutes, 35 seconds
Average Speed: 88.063 mph
Margin of Victory: 7 seconds

FINISH	DRIVER	CAR
1	Ricky Rudd	Chevrolet
2	Bill Elliott	Ford

3	Harry Gant	Buick
4	Dale Earnhardt	Ford
5	Dick Brooks	Ford
6	Kyle Petty	Pontiac
7	Darrell Waltrip	Chevrolet
8	Morgan Shepherd	Buick
9	Bill Schmitt	Chevrolet
10	Richard Petty	Pontiac
11	Jim Robinson	Oldsmobile
12	Dave Marcis	Pontiac
13	Neil Bonnett	Chevrolet
14	Glen Francis	Pontiac
15	Summer McKnight	Chevrolet
16	D. K. Ulrich	Buick
17	Buddy Arrington	Chrysler
18	Jimmy Means	Chevrolet
19	Bob Kennedy	Chevrolet
20	Don Waterman	Buick
21	Stephen Wheeler	Buick
22	Bobby Allison	Buick
23	Jim Bown	Buick
24	J. D. McDuffie	Pontiac
25	Sterling Marlin	Pontiac
26	Hershel McGriff	Buick
27	Rick McCray	Pontiac
28	Tim Richmond	Pontiac
29	Geoff Bodine	Pontiac
30	Scott Miller	Pontiac
31	Terry Labonte	Chevrolet
32	Trevor Boys	Chevrolet
33	Ronnie Thomas	Pontiac
34	Joe Ruttman	Buick
35	Ron Esau	Buick
36	Randy Becker	Buick
37	Pat Mintey	Pontiac

VAN SCOY DIAMOND MINE 500

Time of Race: 3 hours, 53 minutes, 13 seconds
Average Speed: 128.636 mph
Margin of Victory: 9.56 seconds

FINISH	DRIVER	CAR
1	Bobby Allison	Buick
2	Darrell Waltrip	Chevrolet
3	Richard Petty	Pontiac
4	Tim Richmond	Pontiac
5	Benny Parsons	Buick
6	Bill Elliott	Chevrolet
7	Neil Bonnett	Ford
8	Dale Earnhardt	Ford
9	Terry Labonte	Chevrolet
10	Joe Ruttman	Pontiac
11	Dave Marcis	Chevrolet
12	Lake Speed	Chevrolet
13	Kyle Petty	Pontiac
14	Trevor Boys	Chevrolet
15	Morgan Shepherd	Buick
16	D. K. Ulrich	Buick
17	Buddy Arrington	Dodge
18	Harry Gant	Buick
19	J. D. McDuffie	Pontiac
20	Jimmy Means	Chevrolet
21	Ronnie Thomas	Pontiac
22	Mike Potter	Buick
23	Cecil Gordon	Chrysler
24	Steve Gra;y	Buick
25	Tommy Gale	Ford
26	Ronnie Hopkins	Chevrolet
27	Cale Yarborough	Chevrolet
28	Dick Brooks	Ford
29	Sterling Marlin	Pontiac
30	Geoff Bodine	Pontiac
31	Ricky Rudd	Chevrolet
32	Bob Riley	Pontiac
33	John Callis	Chevrolet
34	Ron Bouchard	Buick
35	Jocko Maggiacomo	Buick
36	Jerry Bowman	Ford
37	Bobby Hillin	Buick
38	Bobby Gerhart	Buick

GABRIEL 400

Time of Race: 2 hours, 53 minutes, 0 seconds
Average Speed: 138.728 mph
Margin of Victory: 1.01 seconds

FINISH	DRIVER	CAR
1	Cale Yarborough	Chevrolet
2	Bobby Allison	Buick
3	Tim Richmond	Pontiac
4	Darrell Waltrip	Chevrolet
5	Terry Labonte	Chevrolet
6	Ricky Rudd	Chevrolet
7	Buddy Baker	Ford
8	Harry Gant	Buick
9	Geoff Bodine	Buick
10	Morgan Shepherd	Buick
11	Richard Petty	Pontiac
12	Dick Brooks	Ford
13	Benny Parsons	Buick
14	Bob Senneker	Pontiac
15	Dale Earnhardt	Ford
16	Kyle Petty	Pontiac
17	Ronnie Hopkins	Chevrolet
18	Trevor Boys	Chevrolet
19	Lake Speed	Chevrolet
20	Sterling Marlin	Pontiac
21	Jimmy Means	Buick
22	D. K. Ulrich	Chevrolet
23	Steve Moore	Pontiac
24	Ronnie Thomas	Pontiac
25	Bill Elliott	Ford
26	Tommy Gale	Ford
27	Mark Martin	Oldsmobile
28	Ron Bouchard	Buick
29	Buddy Arrington	Chrysler
30	Dave Marcis	Chevrolet
31	Neil Bonnett	Chevrolet
32	Tom Sneva	Chevrolet
33	Joe Ruttman	Buick
34	J. D. McDuffie	Pontiac
35	David Pearson	Chevrolet
36	Rick Baldwin	Chrysler
37	Bobby Wawak	Buick

FIRECRACKER 400

Time of Race: 2 hours, 23 minutes, 20 seconds
Average Speed: 167.442 mph
Margin of Victory: 29 seconds

FINISH	DRIVER	CAR
1	Buddy Baker	Ford
2	Morgan Shepherd	Buick
3	David Pearson	Chevrolet
4	Ron Bouchard	Buick
5	Terry Labonte	Chevrolet
6	Geoff Bodine	Pontiac
7	Bill Elliott	Ford
8	Jody Ridley	Buick
9	Dale Earnhardt	Ford
10	Lennie Pond	Buick
11	Harry Gant	Buick
12	Ken Ragan	Chevrolet
13	Dave Marcis	Chevrolet
14	Bobby Allison	Buick
15	Bobby Hillin	Buick
16	Sterling Marlin	Chevrolet
17	Trevor Boys	Chevrolet
18	Connie Saylor	Chevrolet
19	Mark Martin	Oldsmobile
20	Darrell Waltrip	Chevrolet
21	Ricky Rudd	Chevrolet
22	Cecil Gordon	Chrysler
23	Tommy Gale	Ford

24	Ronnie Thomas	Pontiac
25	Clark Dwyer	Chevrolet
26	Benny Parsons	Chevrolet
27	Bobby Wawak	Chevrolet
28	Neil Bonnett	Chevrolet
29	Lake Speed	Chevrolet
30	Kyle Petty	Pontiac
31	Tim Richmond	Pontiac
32	Dick Brooks	Ford
33	Richard Petty	Pontiac
34	Buddy Arrington	Chrysler
35	Delma Cowart	Buick
36	Jimmy Means	Buick
37	Joe Ruttman	Chevrolet
38	Greg Sacks	Chevrolet
39	Blackie Wangerin	Ford
40	Cale Yarborough	Chevrolet

BUSCH NASHVILLE 420

Time of Race: 2 hours, 55 minutes, 12 seconds
Average Speed: 85.726 mph
Margin of Victory: 11 seconds

FINISH	DRIVER	CAR
1	Dale Earnhardt	Ford
2	Darrell Waltrip	Chevrolet
3	Tim Richmond	Pontiac
4	Bobby Allison	Buick
5	Ricky Rudd	Chevrolet
6	Neil Bonnett	Chevrolet
7	Bill Elliott	Ford
8	Harry Gant	Buick
9	Dave Marcis	Chevrolet
10	Morgan Shepherd	Buick
11	Terry Labonte	Chevrolet
12	Jimmy Means	Chevrolet
13	Trevor Boys	Chevrolet
14	Dick Brooks	Ford
15	Sterling Marlin	Pontiac
16	Geoff Bodine	Pontiac
17	J. D. McDuffie	Pontiac
18	Al Elmore	Buick
19	Richard Petty	Pontiac
20	Kyle Petty	Pontiac
21	Steve Gray	Buick
22	Joe Ruttman	Pontiac
23	Ronnie Thomas	Pontiac
24	Buddy Arrington	Chrysler
25	Don Satterfield	Buick
26	Darryl Sage	Chevrolet
27	Ron Bouchard	Buick
28	Tommy Gale	Ford
29	James Walker	Ford
30	D. K. Ulrich	Buick

LIKE COLA 500

Time of Race: 4 hours, 21 minutes, 17 seconds
Average Speed: 114.818 mph
Margin of Victory: 2 seconds

FINISH	DRIVER	CAR
1	Tim Richmond	Pontiac
2	Darrell Waltrip	Chevrolet
3	Bobby Allison	Buick
4	Neil Bonnett	Chevrolet
5	Harry Gant	Buick
6	Bill Elliott	Ford
7	Ricky Rudd	Chevrolet
8	Dave Marcis	Chevrolet
9	Joe Ruttman	Buick
10	Richard Petty	Pontiac
11	Kyle Petty	Pontiac

12	Terry Labonte	Chevrolet
13	Ron Bouchard	Buick
14	Trevor Boys	Chevrolet
15	Dick Brooks	Ford
16	Bobby Hillin	Buick
17	D. K. Ulrich	Pontiac
18	Sterling Marlin	Pontiac
19	Morgan Shepherd	Buick
20	Ronnie Thomas	Pontiac
21	Mike Potter	Oldsmobile
22	Al Elmore	Buick
23	Cecil Gordon	Chrysler
24	Tommy Gale	Ford
25	J. D. McDuffie	Pontiac
26	Jocko Maggiacomo	Oldsmobile
27	Bobby Wawak	Buick
28	Jerry Bowman	Ford
29	Greg Sacks	Chevrolet
30	Dale Earnhardt	Ford
31	Benny Parsons	Chevrolet
32	Buddy Arrington	Dodge
33	Dick May	Buick
34	Bobby Gerhart	Buick
35	Jimmy Means	Pontiac
36	Glenn Jarrett	Ford
37	Slick Johnson	Buick
38	Bob Riley	Pontiac
39	Geoff Bodine	Pontiac
40	Clark Dwyer	Chevrolet

TALLADEGA 500

Time of Race: 2 hours, 55 minutes, 52 seconds
Average Speed: 170.611 mph
Margin of Victory: One-half car length

FINISH	DRIVER	CAR
1	Dale Earnhardt	Ford
2	Darrell Waltrip	Chevrolet
3	Tim Richmond	Pontiac
4	Richard Petty	Pontiac
5	Harry Gant	Buick
6	Geoff Bodine	Pontiac
7	Dick Brooks	Ford
8	Bill Elliott	Ford
9	Bobby Allison	Chevrolet
10	Mark Martin	Chevrolet
11	Kyle Petty	Pontiac
12	Ron Bouchard	Buick
13	Bobby Hillin	Buick
14	Ken Ragan	Chevrolet
15	Joe Ruttman	Chevrolet
16	Ricky Rudd	Chevrolet
17	Trevor Boys	Chevrolet
18	Buddy Arrington	Dodge
19	Al Elmore	Chevrolet
20	Ronnie Thomas	Pontiac
21	Sterling Marlin	Chevrolet
22	Benny Parsons	Chevrolet
23	J. D. McDuffie	Pontiac
24	Cale Yarborough	Chevrolet
25	David Pearson	Chevrolet
26	Lake Speed	Chevrolet
27	Morgan Shepherd	Buick
28	Buddy Baker	Ford
29	Terry Labonte	Chevrolet
30	Mike Potter	Oldsmobile
31	Jody Ridley	Chevrolet
32	Dave Marcis	Chevrolet
33	Cecil Gordon	Chrysler
34	Bobby Wawak	Chevrolet
35	Neil Bonnett	Chevrolet
36	Grant Adcox	Chevrolet
37	Billie Harvey	Buick
38	Tommy Gale	Ford
39	Travis Tiller	Chevrolet
40	Richard Skillen	Pontiac

NASCAR FANS FORGIVE AND FORGET

The NASCAR family has a near-endless capacity for forgiveness. Junior Johnson served hard time for moonshining, then returned from a federal prison in Ohio to become one of stock car racing's most beloved stars. And with few exceptions, fans are quick to overlook a driver's personal transgressions, even when they spill onto the front pages of newspapers. That willingness to forgive and forget even extended to the sport's all-time most popular driver.

By 1983, Richard Petty had been a revered figure for almost 20 years. In the eyes of many fans, he was a man who could do no wrong. He already had seven Winston Cup championship trophies, had won 197 races, and was generally considered a gentleman and a sportsman in every respect. Not even a clear-cut episode of cheating that helped him win a 500-mile race was going to change that.

On Oct. 9, 1983, at the Charlotte Motor Speedway, Petty took the checkered flag ahead of Darrell Waltrip, Benny Parsons, Terry Labonte, and Tim Richmond in the Miller High Life 500. Driving his familiar red-and blue No. 43 Pontiac, he started 20th, and led only the final 13 laps of the 334-lap event. His margin of victory over Waltrip was an unusually-comfortable four seconds.

Nobody thought anything was unusual until NASCAR's technical inspectors began speaking in whispered tones and huddling over their engine-measuring tools. Red flags went up when Petty was called out of the post-race interview and asked to go the inspection station. There, officials told him the engine in his car was oversized and that the last set of tires he'd used were improperly mounted. The tires were a minor point; the oversized engine wasn't.

After hours, of agonizing debate and endless meetings, NASCAR announced that the victory would stand. It's not right, they reasoned, for fans to watch a race in person, then discover on late-night TV or in the next day's newspaper that what they'd seen wasn't really what they'd seen after all. No matter how he gets it, they explained, the winner is always the winner.

So the victory would stand—it was Petty's 198th—but his team would lose 104 championship points and $25,000 from what would have been a payoff of $65,000. Later, it was learned that Maurice Petty had built an oversized engine in hopes of beating teams he suspected of using illegal engines to beat his brother.

As for the impact it had on Richard's career—it was merely a blip on the radar screen of fan adoration. Less than a year later, after getting No. 199 at Dover, Del. in June, Petty got his 200th and last victory at Daytona Beach.

And who was there to greet him like a long-lost pal? None other than President Ronald Reagan, a man who had skirted the rules a time or two himself.

CHAMPION SPARK PLUG 400

Time of Race: 2 hours, 42 minutes, 42 seconds
Average Speed: 147.511 mph
Margin of Victory: .5 seconds

FINISH	DRIVER	CAR
1	Cale Yarborough	Chevrolet
2	Darrell Waltrip	Chevrolet
3	Bill Elliott	Ford
4	Terry Labonte	Chevrolet
5	Tim Richmond	Pontiac
6	Richard Petty	Pontiac
7	Dale Earnhardt	Ford
8	Lake Speed	Chevrolet
9	David Pearson	Chevrolet
10	Buddy Baker	Ford
11	Dave Marcis	Chevrolet
12	Ron Bouchard	Buick
13	Benny Parsons	Chevrolet
14	Kyle Petty	Pontiac
15	Jody Ridley	Chevrolet
16	Bob Senneker	Pontiac
17	Greg Sacks	Chevrolet
18	Mark Martin	Oldsmobile
19	Trevor Boys	Chevrolet
20	Dean Combs	Buick
21	Dick Brooks	Ford
22	Lennie Pond	Chevrolet
23	Buddy Arrington	Dodge
24	Joe Ruttman	Chevrolet
25	Bobby Hillin	Buick
26	Eddie Bierschwale	Buick
27	Ricky Rudd	Chevrolet
28	Tommy Gale	Ford
29	Sterling Marlin	Chevrolet
30	Harry Gant	Buick
31	Phil Parsons	Chevrolet
32	J. D. McDuffie	Pontiac
33	D. K. Ulrich	Pontiac
34	Bobby Allison	Buick
35	Neil Bonnett	Chevrolet
36	Geoff Bodine	Pontiac
37	Morgan Shepherd	Buick

BUSCH 500

Time of Race: 2 hours, 29 minutes, 50 seconds
Average Speed: 89.430 mph
Margin of Victory: 1 car length

FINISH	DRIVER	CAR
1	Darrell Waltrip	Chevrolet
2	Dale Earnhardt	Ford
3	Bobby Allison	Buick
4	Geoff Bodine	Pontiac
5	Terry Labonte	Chevrolet
6	Harry Gant	Buick
7	Ron Bouchard	Buick
8	Morgan Shepherd	Buick
9	Richard Petty	Pontiac
10	Neil Bonnett	Chevrolet
11	Kyle Petty	Pontiac
12	Ronnie Thomas	Pontiac
13	Buddy Arrington	Chrysler
14	Ricky Rudd	Chevrolet
15	Sterling Marlin	Pontiac
16	Al Elmore	Buick
17	Trevor Boys	Chevrolet
18	Joe Ruttman	Pontiac
19	Don Satterfield	Buick
20	Dave Marcis	Chevrolet
21	Dick Brooks	Ford
22	Tim Richmond	Pontiac
23	Tommy Gale	Ford
24	Mike Potter	Pontiac
25	J.D. McDuffie	Pontiac
26	Jimmy Means	Chevrolet
27	Bill Elliott	Ford
28	Ronnie Hopkins	Chevrolet
29	Johnny McFadden	Buick

SOUTHERN 500

Time of Race: 4 hours, 3 minutes, 52 seconds
Average Speed: 123.343 mph
Margin of Victory: 7 seconds

FINISH	DRIVER	CAR
1	Bobby Allison	Buick
2	Bill Elliott	Ford
3	Darrell Waltrip	Chevrolet
4	Neil Bonnett	Chevrolet
5	Terry Labonte	Chevrolet
6	Buddy Baker	Ford
7	Cale Yarborough	Chevrolet
8	Benny Parsons	Chevrolet
9	Morgan Shepherd	Buick
10	David Pearson	Chevrolet
11	Dale Earnhardt	Ford
12	Richard Petty	Pontiac
13	Geoff Bodine	Pontiac
14	Dave Marcis	Chevrolet
15	Lake Speed	Chevrolet
16	D.K. Ulrich	Buick
17	Mark Martin	Oldsmobile
18	Buddy Arrington	Dodge
19	Ken Ragan	Chevrolet
20	Jimmy Means	Chevrolet
21	Bobby Wawak	Chevrolet
22	Harry Gant	Buick
23	Dick May	Ford
24	Sterling Marlin	Pontiac
25	Ricky Rudd	Chevrolet
26	Tim Richmond	Pontiac
27	Slick Johnson	Buick
28	Trevor Boys	Chevrolet
29	Tommy Gale	Ford
30	Ronnie Thomas	Poantiac
31	Dick Brooks	Ford
32	Ron Bouchard	Buick
33	Jody Ridley	Chevrolet
34	Philip Duffie	Buick
35	Kyle Petty	Pontiac

36	Mike Potter	Oldsmobile
37	J.D. McDuffie	Pontiac
38	Joe Ruttman	Pontiac
39	Lennie Pond	Buick
40	Ronnie Hopkins	Chevrolet
41	Bobby Hillin	Buick

WRANGLER SANFORSET 400

Time of Race: 2 hours, 43 minutes, 8 seconds
Average Speed: 79.381 mph
Margin of Victory: 2 seconds

FINISH	DRIVER	CAR
1	Bobby Allison	Buick
2	Ricky Rudd	Chevrolet
3	Darrell Waltrip	Chevrolet
4	Bill Elliott	Ford
5	Terry Labonte	Chevrolet
6	Richard Petty	Pontiac
7	Buddy Baker	Ford
8	Neil Bonnett	Chevrolet
9	Trevor Boys	Chevrolet
10	D.K. Ulrich	Buick
11	J.D. McDuffie	Pontiac
12	Kyle Petty	Pontiac
13	Dick Brooks	Ford
14	Buddy Arrington	Dodge
15	Joe Fields	Buick
16	Morgan Shepherd	Buick
17	Ronnie Thomas	Pontiac
18	Dave Marcis	Chevrolet
19	Mike Potter	Pontiac
20	Harry Gant	Buick
21	Geoff Bodine	Pontiac
22	Dale Earnhardt	Ford
23	Tim Richmond	Pontiac
24	Jimmy Means	Chevrolet
25	Ron Bouchard	Buick
26	Sterling Marlin	Pontiac
27	Joe Ruttman	Pontiac
28	Lennie Pond	Buick
29	Don Satterfield	Buick
30	Tommy Gale	Ford

BUDWEISER 500

Time of Race: 4 hours, 18 minutes, 45 seconds
Average Speed: 116.077 mph
Margin of Victory: 1 car length

FINISH	DRIVER	CAR
1	Bobby Allison	Buick
2	Geoff Bodine	Pontiac
3	Tim Richmond	Pontiac
4	Terry Labonte	Chevrolet
5	Darrell Waltrip	Chevrolet
6	Morgan Shepherd	Buick
7	Neil Bonnett	Chevrolet
8	Bill Elliott	Ford
9	Richard Petty	Pontiac
10	Clark Dwyer	Chevrolet
11	Bobby Hillin	Buick
12	D.K. Ulrich	Buick
13	Ricky Rudd	Chevrolet
14	Joe Fields	Buick
15	Cecil Gordon	Chrysler
16	Ron Bouchard	Buick
17	Harry Gant	Buick
18	Jimmy Ingalls	Buick
19	Laurent Rioux	Chevrolet
20	Joe Ruttman	Pontiac
21	Jimmy Means	Chevrolet
22	Dave Marcis	Chevrolet
23	Buddy Arrington	Dodge
24	Ronnie Thomas	Pontiac
25	Buddy Baker	Ford

26	Kyle Petty	Pontiac
27	Sterling Marlin	Pontiac
28	Tommy Gale	Pontiac
29	Bob Riley	Pontiac
30	Jerry Bowman	Ford
31	Trevor Boys	Chevrolet
32	Dick Brooks	Ford
33	Dean Combs	Buick
34	Natz Peters	Buick
35	Dale Earnhardt	Ford
36	J.D. McDuffie	Pontiac

GOODY'S 500

Time of Race: 3 hours, 27 minutes, 16 seconds
Average Speed: 76.134 mph
Margin of Victory: 4.5 seconds

FINISH	DRIVER	CAR
1	Ricky Rudd	Chevrolet
2	Bobby Allison	Buick
3	Darrell Waltrip	Chevrolet
4	Dale Earnhardt	Ford
5	Geoff Bodine	Pontiac
6	Neil Bonnett	Chevrolet
7	Joe Ruttman	Buick
8	Harry Gant	Buick
9	Richard Petty	Pontiac
10	Buddy Arrington	Dodge
11	Trevor Boys	Chevrolet
12	Kyle Petty	Pontiac
13	J.D. McDuffie	Pontiac
14	Bill Elliott	Ford
15	Jimmy Means	Chevrolet
16	Dick Brooks	Ford
17	Laurent Rioux	Chevrolet
18	D.K. Ulrich	Buick
19	Tommy Gale	Ford
20	Mike Potter	Pontiac
21	Ronnie Thomas	Pontiac
22	Buddy Baker	Ford
23	Mark Stahl	Ford
24	Terry Labonte	Chevrolet
25	Butch Lindley	Buick
26	Tim Richmond	Pontiac
27	Sterling Marlin	Pontiac
28	Dave Marcis	Chevrolet
29	Morgan Shepherd	Buick

HOLLY FARMS 400

Time of Race: 2 hours, 28 minutes, 56 seconds
Average Speed: 100.716 mph
Margin of Victory: 3 seconds

FINISH	DRIVER	CAR
1	Darrell Waltrip	Chevrolet
2	Dale Earnhardt	Ford
3	Bobby Allison	Buick
4	Bill Elliott	Ford
5	Terry Labonte	Chevrolet
6	Ricky Rudd	Chevrolet
7	Ron Bouchard	Buick
8	Morgan Shepherd	Buick
9	Harry Gant	Buick
10	Tim Richmond	Pontiac
11	Geoff Bodine	Pontiac
12	Richard Petty	Pontiac
13	Neil Bonnett	Chevrolet
14	Joe Ruttman	Buick
15	Dick Brooks	Ford
16	Kyle Petty	Pontiac
17	Sterling Marlin	Pontiac
18	Buddy Arrington	Chrysler
19	Trevor Boys	Chevrolet
20	D.K. Ulrich	Buick
21	Ronnie Thomas	Pontiac

22	Jimmy Means	Chevrolet
23	Mark Stahl	Ford
24	Tommy Gale	Ford
25	Dave Marcis	Chevrolet
26	J.D. McDuffie	Pontiac
27	Jimmy Walker	Ford
28	Johnny McFadden	Buick
29	Mike Potter	Pontiac
30	Ed Baugess	Chevrolet

MILLER HIGH LIFE 500

Time of Race: 3 hours, 34 minutes, 43 seconds
Average Speed: 139.998 mph
Margin of Victory: 4 seconds

FINISH	DRIVER	CAR
1	Richard Petty	Pontiac
2	Darrell Waltrip	Chevrolet
3	Benny Parsons	Chevrolet
4	Terry Labonte	Chevrolet
5	Tim Richmond	Pontiac
6	Buddy Baker	Ford
7	Bobby Allison	Buick
8	Bill Elliott	Ford
9	Ricky Rudd	Chevrolet
10	Cale Yarborough	Chevrolet
11	Lake Speed	Chevrolet
12	Jody Ridley	Chevrolet
13	Joe Ruttman	Chevrolet
14	Dale Earnhardt	Ford
15	Ron Bouchard	Buick
16	Trevor Boys	Chevrolet
17	Dave Marcis	Oldsmobile
18	Kyle Petty	Pontiac
19	Phil Parsons	Chevrolet
20	D.K. Ulrich	Chevrolet
21	Jim Sauter	Chevrolet
22	Rodney Combs	Buick
23	Jimmy Means	Chevrolet
24	John Anderson	Chevrolet
25	Morgan Shepherd	Buick
26	Neil Bonnett	Chevrolet
27	Phil Duffie	Buick
28	Geoff Bodine	Pontiac
29	Harry Gant	Buick
30	Greg Sacks	Chevrolet
31	Tommy Gale	Ford
32	Dean Combs	Oldsmobile
33	Mark Martin	Chevrolet
34	Buddy Arrington	Chrysler
35	Delma Cowart	Chevrolet
36	Bobby Hillin	Buick
37	Dick Brooks	Ford
38	Ken Ragan	Chevrolet
39	David Pearson	Chevrolet
40	Sterling Marlin	Chevrolet

WARNER W. HODGDON AMERICAN 500

Time of Race: 4 hours, 11 minutes, 36 seconds
Average Speed: 119.324 mph
Margin of Victory: 1 second

FINISH	DRIVER	CAR
1	Terry Labonte	Chevrolet
2	Tim Richmond	Pontiac
3	Ricky Rudd	Chevrolet
4	Neil Bonnett	Chevrolet
5	Darrell Waltrip	Chevrolet
6	Ron Bouchard	Buick
7	Dave Marcis	Chevrolet
8	Lennie Pond	Buick
9	Jimmy Means	Chevrolet
10	Tommy Gale	Ford
11	D.K. Ulrich	Chevrolet
12	Buddy Arrington	Dodge

FINISH	DRIVER	CAR
13	Rick Baldwin	Chrysler
14	J.D. McDuffie	Pontiac
15	Sterling Marlin	Pontiac
16	Bobby Allison	Buick
17	Dale Earnhardt	Ford
18	Dick Brooks	Ford
19	Ronnie Thomas	Pontiac
20	Slick Johnson	Chevrolet
21	Bill Elliott	Ford
22	Dick May	Ford
23	Harry Gant	Buick
24	Kyle Petty	Pontiac
25	Jerry Bowman	Ford
26	Richard Petty	Pontiac
27	Morgan Shepherd	Buick
28	Lake Speed	Chevrolet
29	Buddy Baker	Ford
30	Joe Ruttman	Pontiac
31	Mike Potter	Pontiac
32	Trevor Boys	Chevrolet
33	Geoff Bodine	Pontiac
34	Blackie Wangerin	Ford
35	Johnny McFadden	Buick
36	Cale Yarborough	Chevrolet

ATLANTA JOURNAL 500

Time of Race: 3 hours, 37 minutes, 37 seconds
Average Speed: 137.643 mph
Margin of Victory: second

FINISH	DRIVER	CAR
1	Neil Bonnett	Chevrolet
2	Buddy Baker	Ford
3	Bobby Allison	Buick
4	Terry Labonte	Chevrolet
5	Richard Petty	Pontiac
6	Bill Elliott	Ford
7	Morgan Shepherd	Buick
8	Dean Combs	Oldsmobile
9	Darrell Waltrip	Chevrolet
10	Jody Ridley	Chevrolet
11	Trevor Boys	Chevrolet
12	Lake Speed	Chevrolet
13	Dave Marcis	Oldsmobile
14	Buddy Arrington	Chrysler
15	Bob Senneker	Pontiac
16	Sterling Marlin	Chevrolet
17	Ken Ragan	Chevrolet
18	Jimmy Means	Chevrolet
19	Tommy Gale	Ford
20	Kyle Petty	Pontiac
21	D.K. Ulrich	Chevrolet
22	Mike Potter	Pontiac
23	Cale Yarborough	Chevrolet
24	Delma Cowart	Buick
25	Benny Parsons	Chevrolet
26	Ricky Rudd	Chevrolet
27	Rick Baldwin	Chrysler
28	Phil Parsons	Chevrolet
29	Tim Richmond	Pontiac
30	Joe Ruttman	Pontiac
31	Dick Brooks	Ford
32	J.D. McDuffie	Pontiac
33	Dale Earnhardt	Ford
34	Eddie Bierschwale	Buick
35	Ron Bouchard	Buick
36	Donnie Allison	Pontiac
37	Harry Gant	Buick
38	Greg Sacks	Chevrolet
39	Joe Booher	Buick

WINSTON WESTERN 500

Time of Race: 3 hours, 15 minutes, 9 seconds
Average Speed: 95.859 mph
Margin of Victory: 3 seconds

FINISH	DRIVER	CAR
1	Bill Elliott	Ford
2	Benny Parsons	Chevrolet
3	Neil Bonnett	Chevrolet
4	Dale Earnhardt	Ford
5	Tim Richmond	Pontiac
6	Darrell Waltrip	Chevrolet
7	Terry Labonte	Chevrolet
8	Hershel McGriff	Buick
9	Bobby Allison	Buick
10	Richard Petty	Pontiac
11	Ron Bouchard	Buick
12	Dave Marcis	Oldsmobile
13	Kyle Petty	Pontiac
14	Donnie Allison	Pontiac
15	Randy Becker	Buick
16	Jimmy Means	Chevrolet
17	Sterling Marlin	Pontiac
18	Doug Wheller	Buick
19	Sumner McNight	Chevrolet
20	Buddy Baker	Ford
21	Jim Robinson	Oldsmobile
22	Scott Miller	Pontiac
23	Buddy Arrington	Dodge
24	Trevor Boys	Chevrolet
25	Don Waterman	Buick
26	D.K. Ulrich	Ford
27	Ronnie Thomas	Pontiac
28	Glen Francis	Pontiac
29	Pat Mintey	Chevrolet
30	J.D. McDuffie	Pontiac
31	Harry Gant	Buick
32	John Krebs	Oldsmobile
33	Morgan Shepherd	Buick
34	Dick Brooks	Ford
35	Jim Bown	Buick
36	Roy Smith	Buick
37	Ricky Rudd	Chevrolet
38	Ron Esau	Buick
39	Rick McCay	Pontiac
40	Bill Schmitt	Chevrolet
41	Joe Ruttman	Pontiac
42	Jimmy Insolo	Buick

1984

DAYTONA 500

Time of Race: 3 hours, 18 minutes, 41 seconds
Average Speed: 15.994 mph
Margin of Victory: 8 car lengths

FINISH	DRIVER	CAR
1	Cale Yarborough	Chevrolet
2	Dale Earnhardt	Chevrolet
3	Darrell Waltrip	Chevrolet
4	Neil Bonnett	Chevrolet
5	Bill Elliott	Ford
6	Harry Gant	Chevrolet
7	Ricky Rudd	Ford
8	Geoff Bodine	Chevrolet
9	David Pearson	Chevrolet
10	Jody Ridley	Chevrolet
11	Phil Parsons	Chevrolet
12	Terry Labonte	Chevrolet
13	Lennie Pond	Chevrolet
14	Ken Ragan	Chevrolet
15	Sterling Marlin	Chevrolet
16	Dean Roper	Pontiac
17	Jimmy Means	Chevrolet
18	Greg Sacks	Chevrolet

19	Dean Combs	Oldsmobile
20	Clark Dwyer	Chevrolet
21	Mike Alexander	Oldsmobile
22	Connie Saylor	Chevrolet
23	Doug Heveron	Chevrolet
24	Ronnie Thomas	Chevrolet
25	Buddy Arrington	Chrysler
26	Dick Brooks	Ford
27	Ron Bouchard	Buick
28	Joe Ruttman	Chevrolet
29	Benny Parsons	Chevrolet
30	Rusty Wallace	Pontiac
31	Richard Petty	Pontiac
32	Tommy Gale	Ford
33	Tim Richmond	Pontiac
34	Bobby Allison	Buick
35	Bobby Hillin	Chevrolet
36	Dick Trickle	Chevrolet
37	Lake Speed	Chevrolet
38	Buddy Baker	Ford
39	A.J. Foyt	Oldsmobile
40	Kyle Petty	Ford
41	Trevor Boys	Chevrolet
42	Dave Marcis	Pontiac

MILLER HIGH LIFE 400

Time of Race: 2 hours, 9 minutes, 31 seconds
Average Speed: 76.736 mph
Margin of Victory: 1 second

FINISH	DRIVER	CAR
1	Ricky Rudd	Ford
2	Darrell Waltrip	Chevrolet
3	Terry Labonte	Chevrolet
4	Bill Elliott	Ford
5	Neil Bonnett	Chevrolet
6	Dale Earnhardt	Chevrolet
7	Tim Richmond	Pontiac
8	Harry Gant	Chevrolet
9	Geoff Bodine	Chevrolet
10	Joe Ruttman	Chevrolet
11	Dave Marcis	Chevrolet
12	Lake Speed	Chevrolet
13	Morgan Shepherd	Buick
14	Cale Yarborough	Chevrolet
15	Richard Petty	Ford
16	Rusty Wallace	Pontiac
17	Kyle Petty	Ford
18	Phil Parsons	Chevrolet
19	Dick Brooks	Ford
20	Lennie Pond	Chevrolet
21	Mike Alexander	Oldsmobile
22	Jimmy Hensley	Ford
23	J.D. McDuffie	Pontiac
24	Greg Sacks	Chevrolet
25	Dean Combs	Oldsmobile
26	Trevor Boys	Chevrolet
27	Clark Dwyer	Pontiac
28	Jimmy Means	Chevrolet
29	Ron Bouchard	Buick
30	Bobby Allison	Buick
31	Ronnie Thomas	Chevrolet
32	David Pearson	Chevrolet

WARNER W. HODGDON CAROLINA 500

Time of Race: 4 hours, 3 minutes, 55 seconds
Average Speed: 122.931 mph
Margin of Victory: car length

FINISH	DRIVER	CAR
1	Bobby Allison	Buick
2	Terry Labonte	Chevrolet
3	Lake Speed	Chevrolet
4	Richard Petty	Pontiac
5	Buddy Baker	Ford

6	Geoff Bodine	Chevrolet
7	Ricky Rudd	Ford
8	Bill Elliott	Ford
9	Dave Marcis	Pontiac
10	Darrell Waltrip	Chevrolet
11	Mike Alexander	Oldsmobile
12	Clark Dwyer	Chevrolet
13	Jimmy Means	Pontiac
14	Dale Earnhardt	Chevrolet
15	Buddy Arrington	Chrysler
16	J.D. McDuffie	Pontiac
17	Joe Ruttman	Chevrolet
18	Mark Stahl	Ford
19	Trevor Boys	Chevrolet
20	Laurent Rioux	Chevrolet
21	Ron Bouchard	Buick
22	D.K. Ulrich	Chevrolet
23	Dick Brooks	Ford
24	Harry Gant	Chevrolet
25	Lennie Pond	Chevrolet
26	Rusty Wallace	Pontiac
27	Tim Richmond	Pontiac
28	Neil Bonnett	Chevrolet
29	Rick Newsom	Buick
30	Tommy Gale	Ford
31	Kyle Petty	Ford
32	Ronnie Thomas	Chevrolet
33	Connie Saylor	Pontiac
34	Greg Sacks	Chevrolet
35	Sterling Marlin	Buick
36	Blackie Wangerin	Ford

COCA-COLA 500

Time of Race: 3 hours, 26 minutes, 39 seconds
Average Speed: 144-945 mph
Margin of Victory: seconds

FINISH	DRIVER	CAR
1	Benny Parsons	Chevrolet
2	Dale Earnhardt	Chevrolet
3	Cale Yarborough	Chevrolet
4	Richard Petty	Pontiac
5	Bobby Allison	Buick
6	Harry Gant	Chevrolet
7	Terry Labonte	Chevrolet
8	Ricky Rudd	Ford
9	Lake Speed	Chevrolet
10	Darrell Waltrip	Chevrolet
11	Bill Elliott	Ford
12	Ron Bouchard	Buick
13	Geoff Bodine	Chevrolet
14	Dick Brooks	Ford
15	Trevor Boys	Chevrolet
16	Greg Sacks	Chevrolet
17	Jim Sauter	Chevrolet
18	Dave Marcis	Pontiac
19	Rusty Wallace	Pontiac
20	Buddy Arrington	Dodge
21	Ken Ragan	Chevrolet
22	H.B. Bailey	Pontiac
23	Buddy Baker	Ford
24	Tommy Gale	Ford
25	Ronnie Thomas	Chevrolet
26	Don Hume	Oldsmobile
27	Jody Ridley	Chevrolet
28	Joe Ruttman	Chevrolet
29	Phil Parsons	Chevrolet
30	Doug Heverson	Chevrolet
31	Mike Anderson	Oldsmobile
32	Dean Combs	Oldsmobile
33	Neil Bonnett	Chevrolet
34	Tim Richmond	Pontiac
35	A.J. Foyt	Oldsmobile
36	Delma Cowart	Buick
37	Bobby Hillin	Chevrolet
38	Kyle Petty	Ford
39	Lennie Pond	Chevrolet
40	Clark Dwyer	Pontiac

VALLEYDALE 500

Time of Race: 2 hours, 50 minutes, 10 seconds
Average Speed: 93.967 mph
Margin of Victory: 2 seconds

FINISH	DRIVER	CAR
1	Darrell Waltrip	Chevrolet
2	Terry Labonte	Chevrolet
3	Ron Bouchard	Buick
4	Dave Marcis	Pontiac
5	Tim Richmond	Pontiac
6	Ricky Rudd	Ford
7	Dale Earnhardt	Ford
8	Richard Petty	Pontiac
9	Bill Elliott	Ford
10	Joe Ruttman	Chevrolet
11	Neil Bonnett	Chevrolet
12	Rusty Wallace	Pontiac
13	Phil Parsons	Chevrolet
14	Doug Heveron	Chevrolet
15	Ronnie Thomas	Chevrolet
16	Trevor Boys	Chevrolet
17	Jimmy Means	Pontiac
18	Clark Dwyer	Chevrolet
19	Bobby Allison	Buick
20	Tommy Gale	Ford
21	J.D. McDuffie	Pontiac
22	Buddy Arrington	Dodge
23	Harry Gant	Chevrolet
24	D.K. Ulrich	Chevrolet
25	Geoff Bodine	Chevrolet
26	Kyle Petty	Ford
27	Morgan Shepherd	Buick
28	Tommy Ellis	Chevrolet
29	Mike Alexander	Oldsmobile
30	Dick Brooks	Ford

NORTHWESTERN BANK 400

Time of Race: 2 hours, 33 minutes, 19 seconds
Average Speed: 97.83 mph
Margin of Victory: second

FINISH	DRIVER	CAR
1	Tim Richmond	Pontiac
2	Harry Gant	Chevrolet
3	Ricky Rudd	Ford
4	Terry Labonte	Chevrolet
5	Kyle Petty	Ford
6	Darrell Waltrip	Chevrolet
7	Ron Bouchard	Buick
8	Dale Earnhardt	Chevrolet
9	Neil Bonnett	Chevrolet
10	Bill Elliott	Ford
11	Dick Brooks	Ford
12	Richard Petty	Pontiac
13	Dave Marcis	Pontiac
14	Geoff Bodine	Chevrolet
15	Phil Parsons	Chrysler
16	Clark Dwyer	Pontiac
17	Trevor Boys	Chevrolet
18	Greg Sacks	Chevrolet
19	D.K. Ulrich	Buick
20	Buddy Arrington	Chrysler
21	Mike Alexander	Oldsmobile
22	Bobby Allison	Buick
23	Tommy Gale	Ford
24	J.D. McDuffie	Pontiac
25	Jimmy Means	Chevrolet
26	Ronnie Thomas	Chevrolet
27	Brent Elliott	Buick
28	Rusty Wallace	Pontiac
29	Tommy Ellis	Chevrolet
30	Joe Ruttman	Chevrolet
31	Dean Combs	Oldsmobile

TRANSOUTH 500

Time of Race: 4 hours, 18 minutes, 16 seconds
Average Speed: 119.925 mph
Margin of Victory: 2 seconds

FINISH	DRIVER	CAR
1	Darrell Waltrip	Chevrolet
2	Terry Labonte	Chevrolet
3	Bill Elliott	Ford
4	Cale Yarborough	Chevrolet
5	Dale Earnhardt	Chevrolet
6	Harry Gant	Chevrolet
7	Richard Petty	Pontiac
8	Phil Parsons	Chevrolet
9	Ricky Rudd	Ford
10	Neil Bonnett	Chevrolet
11	Buddy Arrington	Dodge
12	Bobby Hillin	Buick
13	Dave Marcis	Pontiac
14	Jimmy Means	Pontiac
15	Clark Dwyer	Pontiac
16	Trevor Boys	Chevrolet
17	Ron Bouchard	Buick
18	Tommy Gale	Ford
19	Joe Ruttman	Chevrolet
20	Bobby Allison	Buick
21	Greg Sacks	Chevrolet
22	Lake Speed	Chevrolet
23	Tommy Ellis	Chevrolet
24	Kyle Petty	Ford
25	Connie Saylor	Pontiac
26	Morgan Shepherd	Chevrolet
27	Benny Parsons	Chevrolet
28	Ronnie Thomas	Chevrolet
29	D.K. Ulrich	Buick
30	Rusty Wallace	Pontiac
31	Dick Brooks	Ford
32	Mike Alexander	Oldsmobile
33	Buddy Baker	Ford
34	Tim Richmond	Pontiac
35	Geoff Bodine	Chevrolet
36	Jody Ridley	Chevrolet
37	David Pearson	Chevrolet
38	Lennie Pond	Buick

SOVRAN BANK 500

Time of Race: 3 hours, 35 minutes, 23 seconds
Average Speed: 73.264 mph
Margin of Victory: 6 seconds

FINISH	DRIVER	CAR
1	Geoff Bodine	Chevrolet
2	Ron Bouchard	Buick
3	Darrell Waltrip	Chevrolet
4	Bobby Allison	Buick
5	Neil Bonnett	Chevrolet
6	Joe Ruttman	Chevrolet
7	Bill Elliott	Ford
8	Kyle Petty	Ford
9	Dale Earnhardt	Chevrolet
10	Buddy Baker	Ford
11	Dick Brooks	Ford
12	Richard Petty	Pontiac
13	Harry Gant	Chevrolet
14	Dale Jarrett	Chevrolet
15	Rusty Wallace	Pontiac
16	Phil Parsons	Chevrolet
17	Greg Sacks	Chevrolet
18	Ricky Rudd	Ford
19	Dave Marcis	Pontiac
20	Jimmy Hensley	Ford
21	Clark Dwyer	Pontiac
22	Trevor Boys	Chevrolet
23	Tim Richmond	Pontiac
24	Terry Labonte	Chevrolet

FINISH	DRIVER	CAR
25	Buddy Arrington	Chrysler
26	Morgan Shepherd	Buick
27	Dean Combs	Oldsmobile
28	Doug Heveron	Chevrolet
29	Tommy Ellis	Chevrolet
30	Ronnie Thomas	Chevrolet
31	Mike Alexander	Oldsmobile

WINSTON 500

Time of Race: 2 hours, 53 minutes, 27 seconds
Average Speed: 172.988 mph
Margin of Victory: 1 car length

FINISH	DRIVER	CAR
1	Cale Yarborough	Chevrolet
2	Harry Gant	Chevrolet
3	Buddy Baker	Ford
4	Bobby Allison	Buick
5	Benny Parsons	Chevrolet
6	Richard Petty	Pontiac
7	Phil Parsons	Chevrolet
8	Dave Marcis	Pontiac
9	Bill Elliott	Ford
10	Ron Bouchard	Buick
11	Bobby Hillin	Chevrolet
12	Sterling Marlin	Chevrolet
13	Tommy Ellis	Chevrolet
14	Greg Sacks	Chevrolet
15	Kyle Petty	Ford
16	Jody Ridley	Chevrolet
17	Mike Alexander	Oldsmobile
18	Trevor Boys	Chevrolet
19	Tommy Gale	Chevrolet
20	Ronnie Thomas	Chevrolet
21	Joe Ruttman	Chevrolet
22	Ricky Rudd	Ford
23	Neil Bonnett	Chevrolet
24	Buddy Arrington	Chrysler
25	Terry Labonte	Chevrolet
26	Tim Richmond	Pontiac
27	Dale Earnhardt	Chevrolet
28	Dean Roper	Pontiac
29	Clark Dwyer	Chevrolet
30	Dick Brooks	Ford
31	Rusty Wallace	Pontiac
32	David Pearson	Chevrolet
33	Lake Speed	Chevrolet
34	Geoff Bodine	Chevrolet
35	Phil Barkdoll	Chevrolet
36	Doug Heveron	Chevrolet
37	Jim Sauter	Chevrolet
38	Darrell Waltrip	Chevrolet
39	Elliott Forbes-Robinson	Buick
40	Jimmy Means	Chevrolet

COORS 400

Time of Race: 2 hours, 55 minutes, 15 seconds
Average Speed: 85.702 mph
Margin of Victory: 1 car length

FINISH	DRIVER	CAR
1	Darrell Waltrip	Chevrolet
2	Neil Bonnett	Chevrolet
3	Geoff Bodine	Chevrolet
4	Ricky Rudd	Ford
5	Ron Bouchard	Buick
6	Rusty Wallace	Pontiac
7	Richard Petty	Pontiac
8	Terry Labonte	Chevrolet
9	Dick Brooks	Ford
10	Dave Marcis	Pontiac
11	Kyle Petty	Pontiac

FINISH	DRIVER	CAR
12	Bobby Allison	Buick
13	Mike Alexander	Oldsmobile
14	Tommy Ellis	Chevrolet
15	Joe Ruttman	Buick
16	Harry Gant	Chevrolet
17	Trevor Boys	Chevrolet
18	Sterling Marlin	Chevrolet
19	Dale Earnhardt	Chevrolet
20	Bill Elliott	Ford
21	Buddy Arrington	Dodge
22	Jimmy Means	Chevrolet
23	Ronnie Thomas	Chevrolet
24	D.K. Ulrich	Chevrolet
25	Clark Dwyer	Pontiac
26	J.D. McDuffie	Pontiac
27	Tommy Gale	Ford
28	Tim Richmond	Pontiac
29	Greg Sacks	Chevrolet
30	Maurice Randall	Chrysler

BUDWEISER 500

Time of Race: 4 hours, 12 minutes, 42 seconds
Average Speed: 118.717 mph
Margin of Victory: 4 seconds

FINISH	DRIVER	CAR
1	Richard Petty	Pontiac
2	Tim Richmond	Pontiac
3	Terry Labonte	Chevrolet
4	Bill Elliott	Ford
5	Dale Earnhardt	Chevrolet
6	Buddy Baker	Ford
7	Ricky Rudd	Ford
8	Ron Bouchard	Buick
9	Geoff Bodine	Chevrolet
10	Rusty Wallace	Pontiac
11	Bobby Allison	Buick
12	Kyle Petty	Ford
13	Joe Ruttman	Pontiac
14	Neil Bonnett	Chevrolet
15	Jimmy Means	Pontiac
16	D.K. Ulrich	Buick
17	Jerry Bowman	Ford
18	Trevor Boys	Chevrolet
19	Dave Marcis	Pontiac
20	Lake Speed	Chevrolet
21	Clark Dwyer	Chevrolet
22	Tommy Gale	Ford
23	Greg Sacks	Chevrolet
24	Bobby Hillin	Buick
25	Joe Fields	Buick
26	Harry Gant	Chevrolet
27	Dick May	Ford
28	Dean Combs	Oldsmobile
29	Ronnie Thomas	Chevrolet
30	Jim Southard	Buick
31	Buddy Arrington	Chrysler
32	J.D. McDuffie	Pontiac
33	Jerry Churchill	Chevrolet
34	Dick Brooks	Ford
35	Morgan Shepherd	Chevrolet

WORLD 600

Time of Race: 4 hours, 38 minutes, 34 seconds
Average Speed: 129.233 mph
Margin of Victory: 17 seconds

FINISH	DRIVER	CAR
1	Bobby Allison	Buick
2	Dale Earnhardt	Chevrolet
3	Ron Bouchard	Buick
4	Harry Gant	Chevrolet

5	Geoff Bodine	Chevrolet
6	Lake Speed	Chevrolet
7	Buddy Baker	Ford
8	Jody Ridley	Chevrolet
9	David Pearson	Chevrolet
10	Tim Richmond	Pontiac
11	Ricky Rudd	Ford
12	Neil Bonnett	Chevrolet
13	Dick Brooks	Ford
14	Tommy Ellis	Chevrolet
15	Rusty Wallace	Pontiac
16	Mike Alexander	Oldsmobile
17	Morgan Shepherd	Chevrolet
18	Dean Combs	Oldsmobile
19	Ken Ragan	Chevrolet
20	Jim Sauter	Chevrolet
21	Cale Yarborough	Chevrolet
22	Delma Cowart	Buick
23	Clark Dwyer	Chevrolet
24	Randy Baker	Buick
25	Tommy Gale	Ford
26	Darrell Waltrip	Chevrolet
27	Jimmy Means	Pontiac
28	Bill Elliott	Ford
29	Sterling Marlin	Chevrolet
30	Terry Labonte	Chevrolet
31	Phil Parsons	Chevrolet
32	Buddy Arrington	Dodge
33	Bobby Hillin	Chevrolet
34	Richard Petty	Pontiac
35	Trevor Boys	Chevrolet
36	Dave Marcis	Pontiac
37	Kyle Petty	Ford
38	Greg Sacks	Chevrolet
39	Connie Saylor	Pontiac
40	Doug Heveron	Chevrolet
41	Joe Ruttman	Chevrolet
42	Benny Parsons	Chevrolet

BUDWEISER 400

Time of Race: 2 hours, 25 minutes, 7 seconds
Average Speed: 102.910 mph
Margin of Victory: 9 seconds

FINISH	DRIVER	CAR
1	Terry Labonte	Chevrolet
2	Neil Bonnett	Chevrolet
3	Bobby Allison	Buick
4	Geoff Bodine	Chevrolet
5	Dale Earnhardt	Chevrolet
6	Tim Richmond	Pontiac
7	Joe Ruttman	Chevrolet
8	Kyle Petty	Ford
9	Ricky Rudd	Ford
10	Bill Elliott	Ford
11	Darrell Waltrip	Chevrolet
12	Dick Brooks	Ford
13	Trevor Boys	Chevrolet
14	Jim Robinson	Oldsmobile
15	Derrike Cope	Ford
16	Glen Francis	Pontiac
17	Clark Dwyer	Pontiac
18	D.K. Ulrich	Buick
19	Ron Rouchard	Buick
20	Rusty Wallace	Pontiac
21	Buddy Arrington	Chrysler
22	Harry Goularte	Buick
23	Richard Petty	Pontiac
24	Kevin Terris	Buick
25	Sumner McKnight	Chevrolet
26	Roy Smith	Pontiac
27	Ron Esau	Buick
28	Jim Bown	Buick
29	Harry Gant	Chevrolet
30	Rick McCray	Pontiac
31	Mike Alexander	Oldsmobile
32	Greg Sacks	Chevrolet
33	Ruben Garcia	Buick

34	Dave Marcis	Pontiac
35	Hershel McGriff	Pontiac
36	Scott Miller	Pontiac
37	Gary Mayeda	Ford
38	Jerry Jolly	Chevrolet
39	Bill Schmitt	Chevrolet
40	John Krebs	Oldsmobile

VAN SCOY DIAMOND MINES 500

Time of Race: 3 hours, 37 minutes, 8 seconds
Average Speed: 138.164 mph
Margin of Victory: 3.75 seconds

FINISH	DRIVER	CAR
1	Cale Yarborough	Chevrolet
2	Harry Gant	Chevrolet
3	Terry Labonte	Chevrolet
4	Bill Elliott	Ford
5	Tim Richmond	Pontiac
6	Darrell Waltrip	Chevrolet
7	Bobby Allison	Buick
8	Dale Earnhardt	Chevrolet
9	Benny Parsons	Chevrolet
10	Lake Speed	Chevrolet
11	Joe Ruttman	Chevrolet
12	Kyle Petty	Ford
13	Richard Petty	Pontiac
14	Neil Bonnett	Chevrolet
15	Dave Marcis	Pontiac
16	Bobby Hillin	Buick
17	Rusty Wallace	Pontiac
18	Ricky Rudd	Ford
19	Ron Bouchard	Buick
20	Dick Brooks	Ford
21	Phil Parsons	Chevrolet
22	Greg Sacks	Chevrolet
23	Buddy Arrington	Chrysler
24	Ronnie Thomas	Chevrolet
25	Clark Dwyer	Pontiac
26	Doug Heveron	Chevrolet
27	Tommy Gale	Ford
28	Bobby Wawak	Pontiac
29	Bob Riley	Pontiac
30	Steve Gray	Chevrolet
31	Jim Southard	Chevrolet
32	Trevor Boys	Chevrolet
33	Sterling Marlin	Chevrolet
34	Bobby Gerhart	Chevrolet
35	Buddy Baker	Ford
36	Geoff Bodine	Chevrolet
37	D.K. Ulrich	Buick
38	Jerry Bowman	Ford
39	J.D. McDuffie	Pontiac

MILLER HIGH LIFE 400

Time of Race: 2 hours, 58 minutes, 10 seconds
Average Speed: 134.705 mph
Margin of Victory: 2 seconds

FINISH	DRIVER	CAR
1	Bill Elliott	Ford
2	Dale Earnhardt	Chevrolet
3	Darrell Waltrip	Chevrolet
4	Harry Gant	Chevrolet
5	Lake Speed	Chevrolet
6	Bobby Allison	Buick
7	Geoff Bodine	Buick
8	Joe Ruttman	Chevrolet
9	David Pearson	Chevrolet
10	Buddy Baker	Ford
11	Dick Brooks	Ford
12	Kyle Petty	Ford

13	Cale Yarborough	Chevrolet
14	Rusty Wallace	Pontiac
15	Phil Parsons	Chevrolet
16	Tim Richmond	Pontiac
17	Neil Bonnett	Chevrolet
18	Buddy Arrington	Chevrolet
19	Bobby Hillin	Buick
20	Ron Bouchard	Buick
21	Dave Marcis	Pontiac
22	Morgan Shepherd	Chevrolet
23	Mike Alexander	Oldsmobile
24	Elliott Forbes-Robinson	Buick
25	Ronnie Thomas	Chevrolet
26	Ken Ragan	Chevrolet
27	David Simko	Buick
28	Benny Parsons	Chevrolet
29	D.K. Ulrich	Buick
30	Doug Heveron	Chevrolet
31	Terry Labonte	Chevrolet
32	Greg Sacks	Chevrolet
33	Joe Ruttman	Buick
34	Tommy Gale	Ford
35	Richard Petty	Pontiac
36	Jody Ridley	Chevrolet
37	Trevor Boys	Chevrolet
38	Tommy Ellis	Chevrolet
39	Clark Dwyer	Chevrolet
40	Ricky Rudd	Ford

PEPSI FIRECRACKER 400

Time of Race: 2 hours, 19 minutes, 59 seconds
Average Speed: 171.204 mph
Margin of Victory: under caution

FINISH	DRIVER	CAR
1	Richard Petty	Pontiac
2	Harry Gant	Chevrolet
3	Cale Yarborough	Chevtrolet
4	Bobby Allison	Buick
5	Benny Parsons	Chevrolet
6	Bill Elliott	Ford
7	Terry Labonte	Chevrolet
8	Dale Earnhardt	Chevrolet
9	Neil Bonnett	Chevrolet
10	Joe Ruttman	Chevrolet
11	Tim Richmond	Pontiac
12	Geoff Bodine	Chevrolet
13	Phil Parsons	Chevrolet
14	Tommy Ellis	Chevrolet
15	Ricky Rudd	Ford
16	Trevor Boys	Chevrolet
17	David Pearson	Chevrolet
18	Dave Marcis	Pontiac
19	Jody Ridley	Chevrolet
20	Rusty Wallace	Pontiac
21	Dean Roper	Pontiac
22	Mike Alexander	Oldsmobile
23	Dale Jarrett	Pontiac
24	Tommy Gale	Ford
25	Clark Dwyer	Chevrolet
26	Ken Ragan	Chevrolet
27	Connie Saylor	Chevrolet
28	Doug Heveron	Chevrolet
29	Ronnie Thomas	Chevrolet
30	Kyle Petty	Ford
31	Darrell Waltrip	Chevrolet
32	Dean Combs	Chevrolet
33	Sterling Marlin	Chevrolet
34	Ron Bouchard	Buick
35	Steve Moore	Chevrolet
36	Buddy Arrington	Chrysler
37	Bobby Hillin	Chevrolet
38	Dick Brooks	Ford
39	Greg Sacks	Chevrolet
40	Morgan Shepherd	Chevrolet
41	Buddy Baker	Ford
42	Lake Speed	Chevrolet

PEPSI 420

Time of Race: 3 hours, 5 minutes, 38 seconds
Average Speed: 80.908 mph
Margin of Victory: 1 car length

FINISH	DRIVER	CAR
1	Geoff Bodine	Chevrolet
2	Darrell Waltrip	Chevrolet
3	Dale Earnhardt	Chevrolet
4	Ron Bouchard	Buick
5	Bobby Allison	Buick
6	Terry Labonte	Chevrolet
7	Bill Elliott	Ford
8	Joe Ruttman	Chevrolet
9	Harry Gant	Chevrolet
10	Neil Bonnett	Chevrolet
11	Tommy Ellis	Chevrolet
12	Mike Alexander	Oldsmobile
13	Phil Parsons	Chevrolet
14	Tim Richmond	Pontiac
15	Kyle Petty	Ford
16	Ricky Rudd	Ford
17	Buddy Arrington	Chrysler
18	Rusty Wallace	Pontiac
19	Ken Schrader	Ford
20	Jeff Hooker	Pontiac
21	Ronnie Thomas	Chevrolet
22	Trevor Boys	Chevrolet
23	Dave Marcis	Pontica
24	Clark Dwyer	Chevrolet
25	Richard Petty	Pontiac
26	Morgan Shepherd	Buick
27	Dick Brooks	Ford
28	Jody Ridley	Chevrolet
29	Greg Sacks	Chevrolet
30	Sterling Marlin	Pontiac

LIKE COLA 500

Time of Race: 4 hours, 7 minutes, 21 seconds
Average Speed: 121.351 mph
Margin of Victory: 2 car lengths

FINISH	DRIVER	CAR
1	Harry Gant	Chevrolet
2	Cale Yarborough	Chevrolet
3	Bill Elliott	Ford
4	Terry Labonte	Chevrolet
5	Benny Parsons	Chevrolet
6	Rusty Wallace	Pontiac
7	Ron Bouchard	Buick
8	Kyle Petty	Ford
9	Tim Richmond	Pontiac
10	Dale Earnhardt	Chevrolet
11	Dick Brooks	Ford
12	Geoff Bodine	Chevrolet
13	Trevor Boys	Chevrolet
14	Joe Ruttman	Chevrolet
15	Clark Dwyer	Pontiac
16	Buddy Arrington	Chrysler
17	Phil Parsons	Chevrolet
18	Gene Coyle	Chevrolet
19	Neil Bonnett	Chevrolet
20	Jim Southard	Buick
21	Doug Heveron	Chevrolet
22	Darrell Waltrip	Chevrolet
23	Charles Poalillo	Chevrolet
24	Greg Sacks	Chevrolet
25	Jimmy Means	Pontiac
26	Dave Marcis	Pontiac
27	Richard Petty	Pontiac
28	Bobby Allison	Buick
29	Connie Saylor	Pontiac
30	Jerry Bowman	Ford
31	J.D. McDuffie	Pontiac
32	Bobby Wawak	Buick

33	Bobby Hillin	Chevrolet
34	Tommy Ellis	Chevrolet
35	Ken Ragan	Chevrolet
36	Tommy Gale	Ford
37	Jim Ingalls	Buick
38	Bobby Gerhart	Chevrolet
39	Ricky Rudd	Ford
40	Ronnie Thomas	Chevrolet

TALLADEGA 500

Time of Race: 3 hours, 12 minutes, 4 seconds
Average Speed: 155.485 mph
Margin of Victory: 1.66 seconds

FINISH	DRIVER	CAR
1	Dale Earnhardt	Chevrolet
2	Buddy Baker	Ford
3	Terry Labonte	Chevrolet
4	Bobby Allison	Buick
5	Cale Yarborough	Chevrolet
6	Darrell Waltrip	Chevrolet
7	Harry Gant	Chevrolet
8	Lake Speed	Chevrolet
9	Tommy Ellis	Chevrolet
10	Bill Elliott	Ford
11	Ken Ragan	Chevrolet
12	Rusty Wallace	Pontiac
13	Dave Marcis	Pontiac
14	Ricky Rudd	Ford
15	Bobby Hillin	Chevrolet
16	Ron Bouchard	Buick
17	Mike Alexander	Oldsmobile
18	Steve Moore	Chevrolet
19	Neil Bonnett	Chevrolet
20	Phil Parsons	Chevrolet
21	Buddy Arrington	Chrysler
22	Kyle Petty	Ford
23	Richard Petty	Pontiac
24	Trevor Boys	Chevrolet
25	Phil Barkdoll	Chevrolet
26	Geoff Bodine	Chevrolet
27	Ronnie Thomas	Chevrolet
28	Clark Dwyer	Chevrolet
29	Greg Sacks	Chevrolet
30	Morgan Shepard	Chevrolet
31	Eddie Bierschwale	Chevrolet
32	Sterling Marlin	Chevrolet
33	Tim Richmond	Pontiac
34	Jody Ridley	Chevrolet
35	Dick Brooks	Ford
36	A.J. Foyt	Oldsmobile
37	Joe Ruttman	Chevrolet
38	Elliott Forbes-Robinson	Chevrolet
39	Randy Baker	Buick
40	Grant Adcox	Chevrolet

CHAMPION SPARK PLUG 400

Time of Race: 2 hours, 35 minutes, 59 seconds
Average Speed: 153.863 mph - New Record
Margin of Victory: 1 second

FINISH	DRIVER	CAR
1	Darrell Waltrip	Chevrolet
2	Terry Labonte	Chevrolet
3	Bill Elliott	Ford
4	Harry Gant	Chevrolet
5	Cale Yarborough	Chevrolet
6	Benny Parsons	Chevrolet
7	Dale Earnhardt	Chevrolet
8	Buddy Baker	Ford
9	Richard Petty	Pontiac
10	Bobby Allison	Buick
11	Ron Bouchard	Buick

12	Ricky Ridd	Ford
13	Neil Bonnett	Chevrolet
14	Jody Ridley	Chevrolet
15	Tim Richmond	Pontiac
16	Lake Speed	Chevrolet
17	Kyle Petty	Ford
18	Dick Brooks	Ford
19	Dave Marcis	Pontiac
20	Joe Ruttman	Chevrolet
21	Bobby Hillin	Chevrolet
24	Mike Alexander	Oldsmobile
25	Rodney Combs	Buick
26	Jimmy Means	Chevrolet
27	Trevor Boys	Chevrolet
28	Morgan Shepard	Chevrolet
29	Phil Parsons	Chevrolet
30	Jeff Hooker	Pontiac
31	Buddy Arrington	Chrysler
32	Sterling Marlin	Chevrolet
33	Ken Shrader	Ford
34	Geoff Bodine	Chevrolet
35	Rusty Wallace	Pontiac
36	Tommy Ellis	Chevrolet
37	Doug Heveron	Chevrolet
38	Dean Combs	Chevrolet
39	David Pearson	Chevrolet
40	Clark Dwyer	Chevrolet

BUSCH 500

Time of Race: 3 hours, 7 minutes, 19 seconds
Average Speed: 85.365 mph
Margin of Victory: 1.44 seconds

FINISH	DRIVER	CAR
1	Terry Labonte	Chevrolet
2	Bobby Allison	Buick
3	Dick Brooks	Ford
4	Dave Marcis	Pontiac
5	Harry Gant	Chevrolet
6	Bill Elliott	Ford
7	Mike Alexander	Oldsmobile
8	Sterling Marlin	Oldsmobile
9	Greg Sacks	Chevrolet
10	Dale Earnhardt	Chevrolet
11	Tommy Gale	Ford
12	J.D. McDuffie	Pontiac
13	Buddy Arrington	Chrysler
14	Ron Bouchard	Buick
15	Clark Dwyer	Buick
16	Ricky Rudd	Ford
17	Richard Petty	Pontiac
18	Trevor Boys	Chevrolet
19	Morgan Shepherd	Chevrolet
20	Rusty Wallace	Pontiac
21	Darrell Waltrip	Chevrolet
22	Geoff Bodine	Chevrolet
23	Neil Bonnett	Chevrolet
24	Kyle Petty	Ford
25	Tim Richmond	Pontiac
26	Phil Parsons	Chevrolet
27	Ronnie Thomas	Chevrolet
28	Tommy Ellis	Chevrolet
29	Joe Ruttman	Chevrolet
30	Jimmy Means	Pontiac

SOUTHERN 500

Time of Race: 3 hours, 54 minutes, 2 seconds
Average Speed: 128.270 mph
Margin of Victory: 2 seconds

FINISH	DRIVER	CAR
1	Harry Gant	Chevrolet
2	Tim Richmond	Pontiac
3	Buddy Baker	Ford

Action from Daytona in 1997

FINISH	DRIVER	CAR
1	Darrell Waltrip	Chevrolet
2	Ricky Rudd	Ford
3	Dale Earnhardt	Chevrolet
4	Geoff Bodine	Chevrolet
5	Richard Petty	Pontiac
6	Kyle Petty	Ford
7	Neil Bonnett	Chevrolet
8	Terry Labonte	Chevrolet
9	Harry Gant	Chevrolet
10	Dick Brooks	Ford
11	Rusty Wallace	Pontiac
12	Morgan Shepherd	Pontiac
13	Ron Bouchard	Buick
14	Cale Yarborough	Chevrolet
15	Tommy Ellis	Chevrolet
16	Dave Marcis	Pontiac
17	Lennie Pond	Oldsmobile
18	Jimmy Means	Chevrolet
19	Buddy Baker	Ford
20	Tim Richmond	Pontiac
21	Greg Sacks	Pontiac
22	Jimmy Hensley	Ford
23	Buddy Arrington	Chrysler
24	Bill Elliott	Ford
25	Bobby Allison	Buick
26	Clark Dwyer	Chevrolet
27	Trevor Boys	Chevrolet
28	J.D. McDuffie	Pontiac
29	Derrike Cope	Ford
30	Joe Ruttman	Chevrolet

4	Rusty Wallace	Pontiac
5	Ricky Rudd	Ford
6	Dick Brooks	Ford
7	Phil Parsons	Chevrolet
8	Terry Labonte	Chevrolet
9	Benny Parsons	Chevrolet
10	Bobby Allison	Buick
11	Trevor Boys	Chevrolet
12	Geoff Bodine	Chevrolet
13	Joe Ruttman	Chevrolet
14	Lake Speed	Chevrolet
15	Bill Elliott	Ford
16	Jody Ridley	Chevrolet
17	Cale Yarborough	Chevrolet
18	Jimmy Means	Pontiac
19	Tommy Ellis	Chevrolet
20	Clark Dwyer	Chevrolet
21	Dave Marcis	Pontiac
22	Tommy Gale	Ford
23	Bobby Hillin	Chevrolet
24	J.D. McDuffie	Pontiac
25	H.B Bailey	Pontiac
26	Ken Ragan	Chevrolet
27	Randy Baker	Buick
28	Buddy Arrington	Chrysler
29	Richard Petty	Pontiac
30	Neil Bonnett	Chevrolet
31	Connie Saylor	Chevrolet
32	Kyle Petty	Ford
33	Ron Bouchard	Buick
34	Mike Alexander	Oldsmobile
35	Morgan Shepherd	Chevrolet
36	Slick Johnson	Chevrolet
37	Greg Sacks	Chevrolet
38	Dale Earnhardt	Chevrolet
39	Sterling Marlin	Chevrolet
40	Darrell Waltrip	Chevrolet
41	David Pearson	Chevrolet

WRANGLER SANFORSET 400

Time of Race: 2 hours, 53 minutes, 57 seconds
Average Speed: 74.780 mph
Margin of Victory: 3 seconds

DELAWARE 500

Time of Race: 4 hours, 28 minutes, 12 seconds
Average Speed: 111.856 mph
Margin of Victory: under caution

FINISH	DRIVER	CAR
1	Harry Gant	Chevrolet
2	Terry Labonte	Chevrolet
3	Ricky Rudd	Ford
4	Dave Marcis	Pontiac
5	Dale Earnhardt	Chevrolet
6	Neil Bonnett	Chevrolet
7	Dick Brooks	Ford
8	Ron Bouchard	Buick
9	Geoff Bodine	Chevrolet
10	Trevor Boys	Chevrolet
11	Darrell Waltrip	Chevrolet
12	Lennie Pond	Oldsmobile
13	Doug Heveron	Chevrolet
14	Kyle Petty	Ford
15	Jimmy Means	Chevrolet
16	J.D. McDuffie	Pontiac
17	Buddy Arrington	Chrysler
18	Clark Dwyer	Ford
19	Dick May	Ford
20	Jim Southard	Buick
21	Gene Coyle	Chevrolet
22	Morgan Shepherd	Chevrolet
23	Johnny Coy	Buick
24	Phil Good	Chrysler
25	Greg Sacks	Chevrolet
26	Buddy Baker	Ford
27	Tommie Crozier	Pontiac
28	Tim Richmond	Pontiac
29	Jody Ridley	Chevrolet
30	Rusty Wallace	Pontiac
31	Joe Fields	Buick
32	Bill Elliott	Ford
33	Joe Ruttman	Chevrolet
34	Tommy Ellis	Chevrolet
35	Ronnie Thomas	Chevrolet
36	Bobby Allison	Buick
37	Richard Petty	Pontiac
38	Jerry Bowman	Ford
39	Bobby Gerhart	Chevrolet
40	Jim Ingalls	Chevrolet

GOODY'S 500

Time of Race: 3 hours, 28 minutes, 55 seconds
Average Speed: 75.532 mph
Margin of Victory: 1 lap & 3 seconds

FINISH	DRIVER	CAR
1	Darrell Waltrip	Chevrolet
2	Terry Labonte	Chevrolet
3	Bill Elliott	Ford
4	Harry Gant	Chevrolet
5	Neil Bonnett	Chevrolet
6	Buddy Baker	Ford
7	Dave Marcis	Pontiac
8	Richard Petty	Pontiac
9	Lennie Pond	Oldsmobile
10	Kyle Petty	Ford
11	Dick Brooks	Ford
12	Dale Earnhardt	Chevrolet
13	Rusty Wallace	Pontiac
14	Doug Heveron	Buick
15	Jimmy Means	Pontiac
16	Ronnie Thomas	Chevrolet
17	Tommy Ellis	Chevrolet
18	Buddy Arrington	Dodge
19	Ron Bouchard	Buick
20	Phil Parsons	Chevrolet
21	Tim Richmond	Pontiac
22	Jimmy Hensley	Ford
23	Bobby Allison	Buick
24	Morgan Shepherd	Pontiac
25	J.D. McDuffie	Pontiac
26	Trevor Boys	Chevrolet
27	Ricky Rudd	Ford
28	Geoff Bodine	Chevrolet
29	Joe Ruttman	Chevrolet
30	Greg Sacks	Chevrolet
31	Sam Ard	Chevrolet

MILLER HIGH LIFE 500

Time of Race: 3 hours, 24 minutes, 41 seconds
Average Speed: 146.861 mph
Margin of Victory: 14.5 seconds

FINISH	DRIVER	CAR
1	Bill Elliott	Ford
2	Benny Parsons	Chevrolet
3	Cale Yarborough	Chevrolet
4	Harry Gant	Chevrolet
5	Terry Labonte	Chevrolet
6	Geoff Bodine	Chevrolet
7	Jody Ridley	Chevrolet
8	Ricky Rudd	Ford
9	Richard Petty	Pontiac
10	Bobby Allison	Buick
11	Ron Bouchard	Buick
12	Trevor Boys	Chevrolet
13	Dick Brooks	Ford
14	Rusty Wallace	Pontiac
15	Bobby Hillin	Chevrolet
16	Neil Bonnett	Chevrolet
17	Kyle Petty	Ford
18	Greg Sacks	Chevrolet
19	Jimmy Means	Pontiac
20	Elliott Forbes-Robinson	Buick
21	L.D. Ottinger	Chevrolet
22	Bobby Wawak	Buick
23	Morgan Shepherd	Chevrolet
24	Dave Marcis	Pontiac
25	Lennie Pond	Oldsmobile
26	Ken Schrader	Ford
27	Darrell Waltrip	Chevrolet
28	Dean Combs	Chevrolet
29	Buddy Baker	Ford
30	Tim Richmond	Pontiac
31	Phil Parsons	Chevrolet
32	Lake Speed	Chevrolet
33	Tommy Ellis	Chevrolet

FINISH	DRIVER	CAR
34	Connie Saylor	Chevrolet
35	Sterling Marlin	Chevrolet
36	Ken Ragan	Chevrolet
37	Doug Heveron	Chevrolet
38	David Pearson	Chevrolet
39	Dale Earnhardt	Chevrolet
40	Joe Ruttman	Chevrolet
41	Don Paul	Chevrolet

HOLLY FARMS 400

Time of Race: 2 hours, 45 minutes, 42 seconds
Average Speed: 90.525 mph
Margin of Victory: second

FINISH	DRIVER	CAR
1	Darrell Waltrip	Chevrolet
2	Harry Gant	Chevrolet
3	Bobby Allison	Buick
4	Neil Bonnett	Chevrolet
5	Rusty Wallace	Pontiac
6	Ricky Rudd	Ford
7	Dale Earnhardt	Chevrolet
8	Bill Elliott	Ford
9	Terry Labonte	Chevrolet
10	Buddy Baker	Ford
11	Dick Brooks	Ford
12	Lennie Pond	Oldsmobile
13	Tim Richmond	Pontiac
14	Tommy Ellis	Chevrolet
15	Phil Parsons	Chevrolet
16	Jimmy Means	Pontiac
17	Ken Schrader	Ford
18	Richard Petty	Pontiac
19	Bobby Gerhart	Chevrolet
20	Kyle Petty	Ford
21	Jeff Hooker	Pontiac
22	L.D. Ottinger	Chevrolet
23	Geoff Bodine	Chevrolet
24	Greg Sacks	Chevrolet
25	Lake Speed	Pontiac
26	Dave Marcis	Pontiac
27	Trevor Boys	Chevrolet
28	Ron Bouchard	Buick
29	Buddy Arrington	Chevrolet
30	J.D. McDuffie	Pontiac

WARNER W. HODGDON AMERICAN 500

Time of Race: 4 hours, 26 minutes, 35 seconds
Average Speed: 112.617 mph
Margin of Victory: 1 foot

FINISH	DRIVER	CAR
1	Bill Elliott	Ford
2	Harry Gant	Chevrolet
3	Terry Labonte	Chevrolet
4	Darrell Waltrip	Chevrolet
5	Bobby Allison	Buick
6	Morgan Shepherd	Chevrolet
7	Buddy Baker	Ford
8	Tim Richmond	Pontiac
9	Dave Marcis	Pontiac
10	Lennie Pond	Oldsmobile
11	Trevor Boys	Chevrolet
12	Bobby Hillin	Buick
13	Dale Earnhardt	Chevrolet
14	Ron Bouchard	Buick
15	Richard Petty	Pontiac
16	Dick May	Ford
17	Joe Millikan	Ford
18	Jimmy Means	Pontiac
19	Geoff Bodine	Chevrolet
20	Buddy Arrington	Dodge
21	Terry Schoonover	Chrysler
22	Jim Ingalls	Chevrolet
23	Ricky Rudd	Ford

FINISH	DRIVER	CAR
24	Kyle Petty	Ford
25	Bobby Fox	Chevrolet
26	Rusty Wallace	Pontiac
27	Mark Stahl	Ford
28	Bobby Wawak	Buick
29	Lake Speed	Chevrolet
30	Dick Brooks	Ford
31	Buddie Boys	Buick
32	Jerry Bowman	Ford
33	Neil Bonnett	Chevrolet
34	Joe Ruttman	Chevrolet
35	Greg Sacks	Chevrolet
36	J.D. McDuffie	Pontiac
37	Dale Jarrett	Chevrolet
38	Clark Dwyer	Pontiac
39	Jeff Hooker	Pontiac
40	Mike Potter	Ford

ATLANTA JOURNAL 500

Time of Race: 3 hours, 42 minutes, 31 seconds
Average Speed: 134.610 mph
Margin of Victory: .56 seconds

FINISH	DRIVER	CAR
1	Dale Earnhardt	Chevrolet
2	Bill Elliott	Ford
3	Ricky Rudd	Ford
4	Benny Parsons	Chevrolet
5	Bobby Allison	Buick
6	Darrell Waltrip	Chevrolet
7	Lake Speed	Chevrolet
8	Richard Petty	Pontiac
9	Sterling Marlin	Chevrolet
10	Dave Marcis	Pontiac
11	Cale Yarborough	Chevrolet
12	Ron Bouchard	Buick
13	Tim Richmond	Pontiac
14	Morgan Shepherd	Chevrolet
15	Rusty Wallace	Pontiac
16	Jimmy Means	Pontiac
17	Dick Brooks	Ford
18	Doug Heveron	Chevrolet
19	E. Forbes-Robinson	Buick
20	Buddy Baker	Ford
21	Neil Bonnett	Chevrolet
22	Kyle Petty	Ford
23	Trevor Boys	Chevrolet
24	Geoff Bodine	Chevrolet
25	David Pearson	Chevrolet
26	Harry Gant	Chevrolet
27	Ken Schrader	Ford
28	Phil Parsons	Chevrolet
29	Eddie Bierschwale	Buick
30	Terry Labonte	Chevrolet
31	Greg Sacks	Chevrolet
32	Jody Ridley	Chevrolet
33	Bobby Hillin	Chevrolet
34	Terry Schoonover	Chevrolet
35	Joe Ruttman	Chevrolet
36	Dean Combs	Chevrolet
37	Lennie Pond	Oldsmobile
38	Mark Stahl	Ford
39	Bob Penrod	Chevrolet
40	Ken Ragan	Chevrolet

WINSTON WESTERN 500

Time of Race: 3 hours, 10 minutes, 1 second
Average Speed: 98.448 mph
Margin of Victory: 5 seconds

FINISH	DRIVER	CAR
1	Geoff Bodine	Chevrolet
2	Tim Richmond	Pontiac

FINISH	DRIVER	CAR
3	Terry Labonte	Chevrolet
4	Bill Elliott	Ford
5	Benny Parsons	Chevrolet
6	Neil Bonnett	Chevrolet
7	Bobby Allison	Buick
8	Harry Gant	Chevrolet
9	Hershel McGriff	Pontiac
10	Joe Ruttman	Chevrolet
11	Dale Earnhardt	Chevrolet
12	Trevor Boys	Chevrolet
13	Bill Schmitt	Buick
14	Richard Petty	Pontiac
15	Ricky Rudd	Ford
16	Greg Sacks	Chevrolet
17	Lake Speed	Chevrolet
18	Derrike Cope	Ford
19	Sumner McKnight	Chevrolet
20	Dave Marcis	Pontiac
21	Jimmy Means	Pontiac
22	Morgan Shepherd	Chevrolet
23	Doug Heveron	Chevrolet
24	Dick Brooks	Ford
25	Clark Dwyer	Pontiac
26	Rusty Wallace	Pontiac
27	Ron Esau	Buick
28	Kyle Petty	Ford
29	Jim Robinson	Oldsmobile
30	J.D. McDuffie	Pontiac
31	Harry Goularte	Buick
32	Ruben Garcia	Buick
33	Scott Miller	Pontiac
34	Darrell Waltrip	Chevrolet
35	Ron Bouchard	Buick
36	Jim Bown	Buick
37	Rick McCray	Buick
38	Joe Millikan	Chevrolet
39	John Krebs	Oldsmobile
40	Bobby Rahal	Ford
41	Phil Parsons	Chevrolet

1985

DAYTONA 500

Time of Race: 2 hours, 54 minutes, 9 seconds
Average Speed: 172.265 mph
Margin of Victory: .94 seconds

FINISH	DRIVER	CAR
1	Bill Elliott	Ford
2	Lake Speed	Pontiac
3	Darrell Waltrip	Chevrolet
4	Buddy Baker	Oldsmobile
5	Ricky Rudd	Ford
6	Greg Sacks	Chevrolet
7	Geoff Bodine	Chevrolet
8	Rusty Wallace	Pontiac
9	Bobby Hillin	Chevrolet
10	Neil Bonnett	Chevrolet
11	Ken Schrader	Ford
12	Mike Alexander	Chevrolet
13	Bobby Wawak	Chevrolet
14	Jimmy Means	Chevrolet
15	Morgan Shepherd	Chrysler
16	Sterling Marlin	Chevrolet
17	Joe Ruttman	Chevrolet
18	Clark Dwyer	Ford
19	Lennie Pond	Chevrolet
20	Slick Johnson	Chevrolet
21	Ken Ragan	Chevrolet
22	Dick Brooks	Ford
23	Jim Sauter	Pontiac
24	Dave Marcis	Chevrolet

FINISH	DRIVER	CAR
25	Terry Labonte	Chevrolet
26	Harry Gant	Chevrolet
27	Trevor Boys	Chevrolet
28	David Pearson	Chevrolet
29	Phil Parsons	Chevrolet
30	A.J. Foyt	Oldsmobile
31	Benny Parsons	Chevrolet
32	Dale Earnhardt	Chevrolet
33	Bobby Allison	Buick
34	Richard Petty	Pontiac
35	Tim Richmond	Pontiac
36	Cale Yarborough	Ford
37	Kyle Petty	Ford
38	Ron Bouchard	Buick
39	Doug Heveron	Chevrolet
40	Delma Cowart	Chevrolet

MILLER HIGH LIFE 400

Time of Race: 3 hours, 11 minutes, 27 seconds
Average Speed: 67.945 mph
Margin of Victory: .3 seconds

FINISH	DRIVER	CAR
1	Dale Earnhardt	Chevrolet
2	Geoff Bodine	Chevrolet
3	Darrell Waltrip	Chevrolet
4	Ron Bouchard	Buick
5	Harry Gant	Chevrolet
6	Terry Labonte	Chevrolet
7	Kyle Petty	Ford
8	Dave Marcis	Oldsmobile
9	Tim Richmond	Pontiac
10	Lake Speed	Pontiac
11	Bobby Hillin	Chevrolet
12	Ronnie Thomas	Chevrolet
13	Lennie Pond	Chevrolet
14	Ken Schrader	Ford
15	Phil Parsons	Chevrolet
16	Bobby Allison	Buick
17	Phil Good	Dodge
18	Clark Dwyer	Ford
19	Butch Lindley	Chevrolet
20	J.D. McDuffie	Pontiac
21	Jimmy Means	Chevrolet
22	Bill Elliott	Ford
23	Neil Bonnett	Chevrolet
24	Trevor Boys	Chevrolet
25	Ricky Rudd	Ford
26	Richard Petty	Pontiac
27	Rusty Wallace	Pontiac
28	Rick Newsom	Chevrolet
29	Buddy Baker	Oldsmobile
30	Cecil Gordon	Chevrolet

CAROLINA 500

Time of Race: 4 hours, 21 minutes, 10 seconds
Average Speed: 114.953 mph
Margin of Victory: 8 inches

FINISH	DRIVER	CAR
1	Neil Bonnett	Chevrolet
2	Harry Gant	Chevrolet
3	Terry Labonte	Chevrolet
4	Lake Speed	Pontiac
5	Kyle Petty	Ford
6	Joe Ruttman	Chevrolet
7	Cale Yarborough	Ford
8	Richard Petty	Pontiac
9	Rusty Wallace	Pontiac
10	Dale Earnhardt	Chevrolet
11	Tim Richmond	Pontiac

FINISH	DRIVER	CAR
12	Geoff Bodine	Chevrolet
13	Greg Sacks	Chevrolet
14	Lennie Pond	Chevrolet
15	Slick Johnson	Ford
16	Buddy Arrington	Dodge
18	Darrell Waltrip	Chevrolet
19	Phil Parsons	Chevrolet
20	Dick Brooks	Ford
21	Jonathan Edwards	Buick
22	Jim Southard	Buick
23	Eddie Bierschwale	Chevrolet
24	Bobby Hillin	Chevrolet
25	Buddy Baker	Oldsmobile
26	Dave Marcis	Oldsmobile
27	Bobby Wawak	Buick
28	J.D. McDuffie	Pontiac
29	Bill Elliott	Ford
30	Jimmy Means	Pontiac
31	Bobby Allison	Buick
32	Ricky Rudd	Ford
33	Ron Bouchard	Buick
34	Ronnie Thomas	Chevrolet
35	Maurice Randall	Chrysler
36	Rick Newsom	Buick
37	Clark Dwyer	Ford
38	Morgan Shepherd	Chevrolet
39	Trevor Boys	Chevrolet
40	Ken Schrader	Ford

COCA-COLA 500

Time of Race: 3 hours, 33 minutes, 32 seconds
Average Speed: 140.273 mph
Margin of Victory: 2.64 seconds

FINISH	DRIVER	CAR
1	Bill Elliott	Ford
2	Geoff Bodine	Chevrolet
3	Neil Bonnett	Chevrolet
4	Ricky Rudd	Ford
5	Bobby Allison	Buick
6	Terry Labonte	Chevrolet
7	Ron Bouchard	Buick
8	Benny Parsons	Chevrolet
9	Dale Earnhardt	Chevrolet
10	Greg Sacks	Chevrolet
11	Kyle Petty	Ford
12	Bobby Hillin	Chevrolet
13	Richard Petty	Pontiac
14	Randy LaJoie	Chevrolet
15	Eddie Bierschwale	Chevrolet
16	Ken Schrader	Ford
17	Darrell Waltrip	Chevrolet
18	Buddy Arrington	Chrysler
19	Don Hume	Chevrolet
20	Clark Dwyer	Ford
21	Slick Johnson	Ford
22	Cale Yarborough	Ford
23	J.D. McDuffie	Chevrolet
24	Harry Gant	Chevrolet
25	Sterling Marlin	Chevrolet
26	Joe Ruttman	Chevrolet
27	Rusty Wallace	Pontiac
28	Jimmy Means	Chevrolet
29	David Pearson	Chevrolet
30	Tim Richmond	Pontiac
31	Lennie Pond	Chevrolet
32	Tom Sneva	Pontiac
33	Ken Ragan	Chevrolet
34	Mike Alexander	Chevrolet
35	H.B. Bailey	Pontiac
36	A.J. Foyt	Oldsmobile
37	Dave Marcis	Chevrolet
38	Dick Brooks	Ford
39	Buddy Baker	Oldsmobile
40	Lake Speed	Pontiac
41	Phil Parsons	Chevrolet

VALLEYDALE 500

Time of Race: 3 hours, 15 minutes, 42 seconds
Average Speed: 81.790 mph
Margin of Victory: 1 second

FINISH	DRIVER	CAR
1	Dale Earnhardt	Chevrolet
2	Ricky Rudd	Ford
3	Terry Labonte	Chevrolet
4	Buddy Baker	Oldsmobile
5	Rusty Wallace	Pontiac
6	Kyle Petty	Ford
7	Lake Speed	Pontiac
8	Richard Petty	Pontiac
9	Bobby Hillin	Chevrolet
10	Ken Schrader	Ford
11	Bill Elliott	Ford
12	Jimmy Means	Chevrolet
13	Bobby Allison	Buick
14	Clark Dwyer	Ford
15	Eddie Bierschwale	Chevrolet
16	Don Hume	Chevrolet
17	Ron Bouchard	Buick
18	Geoff Bodine	Chevrolet
19	Neil Bonnett	Chevrolet
20	Harry Gant	Chevrolet
21	Ronnie Thomas	Chevrolet
22	Sterling Marlin	Chevrolet
23	Darrell Waltrip	Chevrolet
24	Dave Marcis	Oldsmobile
25	Buddy Arrington	Chrysler
26	Mike Potter	Ford
27	J.D. McDuffie	Pontiac
28	Phil Parsons	Chevrolet
29	Joe Ruttman	Chevrolet
30	Tim Richmond	Pontiac

TRANSOUTH 500

Time of Race: 3 hours, 58 minutes, 8 seconds
Average Speed: 126.295 mph
Margin of Victory: 2.5 seconds

FINISH	DRIVER	CAR
1	Bill Elliott	Ford
2	Darrell Waltrip	Chevrolet
3	Tim Richmond	Pontiac
4	Terry Labonte	Chevrolet
5	Rusty Wallace	Pontiac
6	Neil Bonnett	Chevrolet
7	Geoff Bodine	Chevrolet
8	Phil Parsons	Chevrolet
9	Lake Speed	Pontiac
10	Bobby Allison	Buick
11	Joe Ruttman	Chevrolet
12	Kyle Petty	Ford
13	Ken Schrader	Ford
14	Harry Gant	Chevrolet
15	Jimmy Means	Pontiac
16	Ron Bouchard	Buick
17	Buddy Arrington	Ford
18	Morgan Shepherd	Ford
19	Eddie Bierschwale	Chevrolet
20	Bobby Hillin	Chevrolet
21	Don Hume	Chevrolet
22	Dick May	Ford
23	Mike Alexander	Chevrolet
24	Dale Earnhardt	Chevrolet
25	Ricky Rudd	Ford
26	Clark Dwyer	Ford
27	Buddy Baker	Oldsmobile
28	David Pearson	Chevrolet
29	Trevor Boys	Chevrolet
30	Cale Yarborough	Ford
31	Dave Marcis	Oldsmobile
32	Benny Parsons	Chevrolet
33	Richard Petty	Pontiac

34	Bobby Wawak	Chevrolet
35	Connie Saylor	Chevrolet
36	Slick Johnson	Ford
37	Ken Ragan	Chevrolet
38	Elton Dotson	Chevrolet
39	J.D. McDuffie	Pontiac
40	Jeff Hooker	Oldsmobile

NORTHWESTERN BANK 400

Time of Race: 2 hours, 39 minutes, 53 seconds
Average Speed: 93.818 mph
Margin of Victory: 1 car length

FINISH	DRIVER	CAR
1	Neil Bonnett	Chevrolet
2	Darrell Waltrip	Chevrolet
3	Bobby Allison	Buick
4	Ricky Rudd	Ford
5	Geoff Bodine	Chevrolet
6	Bill Elliott	Ford
7	Terry Labonte	Chevrolet
8	Dale Earnhardt	Chevrolet
9	Lake Speed	Pontiac
10	Harry Gant	Chevrolet
11	Tim Richmond	Pontiac
12	Kyle Petty	Ford
13	Ron Bouchard	Buick
14	Ken Schrader	Ford
15	Phil Parsons	Chevrolet
16	Dave Marcis	Oldsmobile
17	Jimmy Means	Pontiac
18	Clark Dwyer	Ford
19	Bobby Hillin	Chevrolet
20	Buddy Arrington	Ford
21	Richard Petty	Pontiac
22	Rusty Wallace	Pontiac
23	Don Hume	Chevrolet
24	J.D. McDuffie	Pontiac
25	Dick May	Buick
26	Ed Sanger	Chevrolet
27	Bobby Gerhart	Chevrolet
28	Brent Elliott	Buick
29	Eddie Bierschwale	Chevrolet
30	Buddy Baker	Oldsmobile

SOVRAN BANK 500

Time of Race: 3 hours, 36 minutes, 6 seconds
Average Speed: 73.022 mph
Margin of Victory: 3 seconds

FINISH	DRIVER	CAR
1	Harry Gant	Chevrolet
2	Ricky Rudd	Ford
3	Geoff Bodine	Chevrolet
4	Bobby Allison	Buick
5	Neil Bonnett	Chevrolet
6	Terry Labonte	Chevrolet
7	Richard Petty	Pontiac
8	Lake Speed	Pontiac
9	Phil Parsons	Chevrolet
10	Rusty Wallace	Pontiac
11	Kyle Petty	Ford
12	Buddy Baker	Oldsmobile
13	Bill Elliott	Ford
14	Jimmy Means	Pontiac
15	Buddy Arrington	Ford
16	Ken Schrader	Ford
17	Clark Dwyer	Ford
18	Bobby Hillin	Chevrolet
19	Don Hume	Chevrolet
20	Eddie Bierschwale	Chevrolet
21	Tim Richmond	Pontiac
22	Brent Elliott	Buick
23	Darrell Waltrip	Chevrolet
24	J.D. McDuffie	Pontiac

25	Dale Earnhardt	Chevrolet
26	Dave Marcis	Oldsmobile
27	Morgan Shepherd	Chevrolet
28	Ron Bouchard	Buick
29	Mike Alexander	Chevrolet
30	Ronnie Thomas	Chevrolet

WINSTON 500

Time of Race: 2 hours, 41 minutes, 4 seconds
Average Speed: 186.288 mph
Margin of Victory: 2 seconds

FINISH	DRIVER	CAR
1	Bill Elliott	Ford
2	Kyle Petty	Ford
3	Cale Yarborough	Ford
4	Bobby Allison	Buick
5	Ricky Rudd	Ford
6	Buddy Baker	Oldsmobile
7	Terry Labonte	Chevrolet
8	Dave Marcis	Chevrolet
9	Bobby Hillin	Chevrolet
10	Lake Speed	Pontiac
11	Geoff Bodine	Chevrolet
12	Jimmy Means	Chevrolet
13	Morgan Shepherd	Chevrolet
14	Buddy Arrington	Ford
15	J.D. McDuffie	Pontiac
16	Tim Richmond	Pontiac
17	Bosco Lowe	Chevrolet
18	Dick Skillen	Chevrolet
19	Eddie Bierschwale	Chevrolet
20	Ken Schrader	Ford
21	Dale Earnhardt	Chevrolet
22	Connie Saylor	Chevrolet
23	Clark Dwyer	Ford
24	Darrell Waltrip	Chevrolet
25	Sterling Marlin	Chevrolet
26	Neil Bonnett	Chevrolet
27	Richard Petty	Pontiac
28	Ron Bouchard	Buick
29	Benny Parsons	Chevrolet
30	Joe Ruttman	Chevrolet
31	Mike Alexander	Chevrolet
32	Bobby Wawak	Chevrolet
33	Don Hume	Chevrolet
34	Phil Parsons	Chevrolet
35	Phil Barkdoll	Chevrolet
36	David Pearson	Chevrolet
37	Rusty Wallace	Pontiac
38	Harry Gant	Chevrolet
39	Trevor Boys	Chevrolet

BUDWEISER 500

Time of Race: 4 hours, 3 minutes, 43 seconds
Average Speed: 123.094 mph
Margin of Victory: 29 seconds

FINISH	DRIVER	CAR
1	Bill Elliott	Ford
2	Harry Gant	Chevrolet
3	Kyle Petty	Ford
4	Ricky Rudd	Ford
5	Darrell Waltrip	Chevrolet
6	Tim Richmond	Pontiac
7	Richard Petty	Pontiac
8	Neil Bonnett	Chevrolet
9	Dave Marcis	Oldsmobile
10	Ken Schrader	Ford
11	Geoff Bodine	Chevrolet
12	Bobby Hillin	Chevrolet
13	Bobby Allison	Buick
14	Bob Riley	Pontiac
15	Tommie Crozier	Pontiac
16	Terry Labonte	Chevrolet

17	Phil Good	Chrysler
18	Rusty Wallace	Pontiac
19	Jerry Bowman	Ford
20	Ron Bouchard	Buick
21	Rick Newsom	Chevrolet
22	Buddy Baker	Oldsmobile
23	Buddy Arrington	Ford
24	Lake Speed	Pontiac
25	Dale Earnhardt	Chevrolet
26	James Hylton	Chevrolet
27	Jimmy Walker	Ford
28	Clark Dwyer	Ford
29	Phil Parsons	Chevrolet
30	Jimmy Means	Pontiac
31	J.D. McDuffie	Ford
32	Eddie Bierschwale	Chevrolet

COCA-COLA WORLD 600

Time of Race: 4 hours, 13 minutes, 52 seconds
Average Speed: 141.807 mph
Margin of Victory: 14 seconds

FINISH	DRIVER	CAR
1	Darrell Waltrip	Chevrolet
2	Harry Gant	Chevrolet
3	Bobby Allison	Buick
4	Dale Earnhardt	Chevrolet
5	Terry Labonte	Chevrolet
6	Lake Speed	Pontiac
7	Joe Ruttman	Chevrolet
8	Rusty Wallace	Pontiac
9	Tim Richmond	Pontiac
10	Dick Brooks	Chevrolet
11	Dave Marcis	Oldsmobile
12	Bobby Hillin	Chevrolet
13	Ricky Rudd	Ford
14	Kyle Petty	Ford
15	Neil Bonnett	Chevrolet
16	Geoff Bodine	Chevrolet
17	Slick Johnson	Ford
18	Bill Elliott	Ford
19	Eddie Bierschwale	Chevrolet
20	Tommy Ellis	Chevrolet
21	Mark Stahl	Ford
22	Buddy Arrington	Ford
23	Clark Dwyer	Ford
24	Mike Alexander	Chevrolet
25	Morgan Shepherd	Chevrolet
26	Richard Petty	Pontiac
27	David Pearson	Chevrolet
28	Michael Waltrip	Chevrolet
29	Ron Bouchard	Buick
30	Lennie Pond	Chevrolet
31	Jim Sauter	Pontiac
32	Jimmy Means	Pontiac
33	Phil Parsons	Chevrolet
34	Sterling Marlin	Chevrolet
35	Greg Sacks	Chevrolet
36	Dick Trickle	Chevrolet
37	Buddy Baker	Oldsmobile
38	Ken Schrader	Ford
39	J.D. McDuffie	Pontiac
40	Cale Yarborough	Ford
41	Trevor Boys	Chevrolet
42	Benny Parsons	Chevrolet

BUDWEISER 400

Time of Race: 2 hours, 23 minutes, 13 seconds
Average Speed: 104.276 mph
Margin of Victory: 5 seconds

FINISH	DRIVER	CAR
1	Terry Labonte	Chevrolet
2	Harry Gant	Chevrolet

3	Bobby Allison	Buick
4	Ricky Rudd	Ford
5	Kyle Petty	Chevrolet
6	Bill Elliott	Ford
7	Richard Petty	Pontiac
8	Darrell Waltrip	Chevrolet
9	Tim Richmond	Pontiac
10	Ken Schrader	Ford
11	Glen Steurer	Chevrolet
12	Dave Marcis	Oldsmobile
13	Jim Robinson	Oldsmobile
14	Sumner McKnight	Ford
15	Derrike Cope	Ford
16	Clark Dwyer	Ford
17	Bobby Hillin	Chevrolet
18	Eddie Bierschwale	Chevrolet
19	John Soares	Pontiac
20	Glen Francis	Pontiac
21	Bill Osborne	Buick
22	Geoff Bodine	Chevrolet
23	Ruben Garcia	Chevrolet
24	Rusty Wallace	Pontiac
25	Lake Speed	Pontiac
26	John Krebs	Oldsmobile
27	Neil Bonnett	Chevrolet
28	Jim Bown	Buick
29	Hershel McGriff	Pontiac
30	Dale Perry	Buick
31	Buddy Arrington	Chrysler
32	Ron Bouchard	Buick
33	Phil Parsons	Chevrolet
34	Bill Schmitt	Chevrolet
35	Buddy Baker	Oldsmobile
36	Greg Sacks	Chevrolet
37	Jimmy Means	Chevrolet
38	Blair Aiken	Chevrolet
39	Norm Palmer	Chevrolet
40	Dale Earnhardt	Chevrolet
41	Rick McCray	Chevrolet
42	J.D. McDuffie	Pontiac

VAN SCOY DIAMOND MINE 500

Time of Race: 3 hours, 35 minutes, 48 seconds
Average Speed: 138.974 mph
Margin of Victory: .02 seconds

FINISH	DRIVER	CAR
1	Bill Elliott	Ford
2	Harry Gant	Chevrolet
3	Darrell Waltrip	Chevrolet
4	Geoff Bodine	Chevrolet
5	Neil Bonnett	Chevrolet
6	Benny Parsons	Chevrolet
7	Ricky Rudd	Ford
8	Buddy Baker	Oldsmobile
9	Bobby Allison	Buick
10	Tim Richmond	Pontiac
11	Phil Parsons	Chevrolet
12	Lake Speed	Pontiac
13	Rusty Wallace	Pontiac
14	Kyle Petty	Chevrolet
15	Ken Schrader	Ford
16	Greg Sacks	Chevrolet
17	Lennie Pond	Chevrolet
18	Bobby Hillin	Chevrolet
19	Buddy Arrington	Ford
20	Clark Dwyer	Ford
21	Mike Potter	Ford
22	Jimmy Means	Pontiac
23	Bobby Wawak	Chevrolet
24	Cale Yarborough	Ford
25	J.D. McDuffie	Pontiac
26	Steve Gray	Chevrolet
27	Dave Marcis	Chevrolet
28	Terry Labonte	Chevrolet
29	Ron Bouchard	Buick
30	Phil Good	Dodge
31	Bobby Gerhart	Chevrolet
32	Bill Scott	Chevrolet
33	Richard Petty	Pontiac

34	Eddie Bierschwale	Chevrolet
35	Joe Ruttman	Chevrolet
36	Charlie Poalillo	Chevrolet
37	Jerry Bowman	Ford
38	Rick Newsom	Buick
39	Dale Earnhardt	Chevrolet
40	Ronnie Thomas	Chevrolet

MILLER 400

Time of Race: 2 hours, 45 minutes, 48 seconds
Average Speed: 144.724 mph
Margin of Victory: 13 seconds

FINISH	DRIVER	CAR
1	Bill Elliott	Ford
2	Darrell Waltrip	Chevrolet
3	Cale Yarborough	Ford
4	Tim Richmond	Pontiac
5	Dale Earnhardt	Chevrolet
6	Bobby Allison	Buick
7	Ricky Rudd	Ford
8	Neil Bonnett	Chevrolet
9	Dave Marcis	Chevrolet
10	Benny Parsons	Chevrolet
11	Geoff Bodine	Chevrolet
12	Kyle Petty	Chevrolet
13	Ron Bouchard	Buick
14	Lake Speed	Pontiac
15	Buddy Baker	Oldsmobile
16	Harry Gant	Chevrolet
17	David Pearson	Chew Chevrolet
18	Lennie Pond	Chevrolet
19	Phil Parsons	Chevrolet
20	Jim Sauter	Pontiac
21	Tommy Ellis	Chevrolet
22	Terry Labonte	Chevrolet
23	Buddy Arrington	Ford
24	Trevor Boys	Chevrolet
25	Clark Dwyer	Ford
26	Rusty Wallace	Pontiac
27	Bobby Wawak	Buick
28	Bobby Hillin	Chevrolet
29	Eddie Bierschwale	Chevrolet
30	Richard Petty	Pontiac
31	J.D. McDuffie	Pontiac
32	Jim Hull	Chevrolet
33	Tommie Crozier	Pontiac
34	Ken Schrader	Ford
35	Jimmy Means	Pontiac
36	Edward Cooper	Buick
37	Maurice Randall	Chrysler

PEPSI FIRECRACKER 400

Time of Race: 2 hours, 31 minutes, 12 seconds
Average Speed: 158.730 mph
Margin of Victory: 23.5 seconds

FINISH	DRIVER	CAR
1	Greg Sacks	Chevrolet
2	Bill Elliott	Ford
3	Darrell Waltrip	Chevrolet
4	Ron Bouchard	Buick
5	Kyle Petty	Chevrolet
6	Buddy Baker	Oldsmobile
7	Ricky Rudd	Ford
8	Terry Labonte	Chevrolet
9	Dale Earnhardt	Chevrolet
10	David Pearson	Chevrolet
11	Benny Parsons	Chevrolet
12	Neil Bonnett	Chevrolet
13	Mike Alexander	Chevrolet
14	Geoff Bodine	Chevrolet
15	Bobby Hillin	Chevrolet
16	Buddy Arrington	Ford
17	Tommy Ellis	Chevrolet

FINISH	DRIVER	CAR
18	Bobby Allison	Buick
19	Lennie Pond	Chevrolet
20	J.D. McDuffie	Chevrolet
21	Ken Schrader	Ford
22	Grant Adcox	Chevrolet
23	Dave Marcis	Chevrolet
24	Harry Gant	Chevrolet
25	Clark Dwyer	Ford
26	Trevor Boys	Chevrolet
27	Phil Parsons	Chevrolet
28	Tim Richmond	Pontiac
29	Richard Petty	Pontiac
30	A.J. Foyt	Oldsmobile
31	Eddie Bierschwale	Chevrolet
32	Jimmy Means	Chevrolet
33	Sterling Marlin	Chevrolet
34	Lake Speed	Pontiac
35	Joe Ruttman	Chevrolet
36	Cale Yarborough	Ford
37	Bobby Wawak	Chevrolet
38	Eldon Dotson	Chevrolet
39	Morgan Shepherd	Chevrolet
40	Connie Saylor	Chevrolet
41	Rusty Wallace	Pontiac

SUMMER 500

Time of Race: 3 hours, 43 minutes, 52 seconds
Average Speed: 134.008 mph
Margin of Victory: 5 seconds

FINISH	DRIVER	CAR
1	Bill Elliott	Ford
2	Neil Bonnett	Chevrolet
3	Darrell Waltrip	Chevrolet
4	Geoff Bodine	Chevrolet
5	Harry Gant	Chevrolet
6	Benny Parsons	Chevrolet
7	Kyle Petty	Chevrolet
8	Phil Parsons	Chevrolet
9	Ron Bouchard	Buick
10	Buddy Baker	Oldsmobile
11	Lake Speed	Pontiac
12	Bobby Allison	Buick
13	Lennie Pond	Chevrolet
14	Ricky Rudd	Ford
15	Ken Schrader	Ford
16	Clark Dwyer	Ford
17	Eddie Bierschwale	Chevrolet
18	Buddy Arrington	Ford
19	Doug Heveron	Ford
20	Trevor Boys	Chevrolet
21	Rick Newsom	Buick
22	Jerry Bowman	Ford
23	Jimmy Means	Pontiac
24	Bobby Gerhart	Chevrolet
25	Bobby Wawak	Buick
26	Terry Labonte	Chevrolet
27	Richard Petty	Pontiac
28	Joe Booher	Buick
29	Bobby Hillin	Chevrolet
30	Tim Richmond	Pontiac
31	Cale Yarborough	Ford
32	Mike Stolarcyk	Buick
33	Rusty Wallace	Pontiac
34	Greg Sacks	Buick
35	David Pearson	Chevrolet
36	Tommy Ellis	Chevrolet
37	Don Hume	Chevrolet
38	Dave Marcis	Chevrolet
39	Dale Earnhardt	Chevrolet
40	J.D. McDuffie	Ford

TALLADEGA 500

Time of Race: 3 hours, 21 minutes, 41 seconds
Average Speed: 148.772 mph
Margin of Victory: 1 second

FINISH	DRIVER	CAR
1	Cale Yarborough	Ford
2	Neil Bonnett	Chevrolet
3	Ron Bouchard	Buick
4	Bill Elliott	Ford
5	A.J. Foyt	Oldsmobile
6	Richard Petty	Pontiac
7	Harry Gant	Chevrolet
8	Lake Speed	Pontiac
9	Darrell Waltrip	Chevrolet
10	Davey Allison	Chevrolet
11	Ken Schrader	Ford
12	Sterling Marlin	Chevrolet
13	Tim Richmond	Pontiac
14	Buddy Baker	Oldsmobile
15	Greg Sacks	Buick
16	Buddy Arrington	Ford
17	Rusty Wallace	Pontiac
18	Ricky Rudd	Ford
19	Lennie Pond	Ford
20	Clark Dwyer	Ford
21	Bobby Wawak	Chevrolet
22	Phil Barkdoll	Chevrolet
23	Geoff Bodine	Chevrolet
24	Dale Earnhardt	Chevrolet
25	Kyle Petty	Chevrolet
26	Dave Marcis	Chevrolet
27	Bobby Allison	Chevrolet
28	J.D. McDuffie	Chevrolet
29	Rick Wilson	Chevrolet
30	Tommy Ellis	Chevrolet
31	Phil Parsons	Chevrolet
32	Trevor Boys	Chevrolet
33	Joe Ruttman	Chevrolet
34	Eddie Bierschwale	Chevrolet
35	David Pearson	Ford
36	Benny Parsons	Chevrolet
37	Delma Cowart	Chevrolet
38	Bobby Hilling, Jr.	Chevrolet
39	Terry Labonte	Chevrolet
40	Grant Adcox	Chevrolet
41	Connie Saylor	Chevrolet
42	Jimmy Means	Pontiac

CHAMPION SPARK PLUG 400

Time of Race: 2 hours, 54 minutes, 38 seconds
Average Speed: 137.430 mph
Margin of Victory: 4 seconds

FINISH	DRIVER	CAR
1	Bill Elliott	Ford
2	Darrell Waltrip	Chevrolet
3	Harry Gant	Chevrolet
4	Kyle Petty	Chevrolet
5	Benny Parsons	Chevrolet
6	Phil Parsons	Chevrolet
7	Rusty Wallace	Pontiac
8	Dick Trickle	Pontiac
9	Terry Labonte	Chevrolet
10	Buddy Arrington	Ford
11	Neil Bonnett	Chevrolet
12	Dave Marcis	Chevrolet
13	Mike Alexander	Chevrolet
14	Buddy Baker	Oldsmobile
15	Jimmy Means	Pontiac
16	Lake Speed	Pontiac
17	Ken Ragan	Chevrolet
18	Michael Waltrip	Chevrolet
19	Ronnie Thomas	Chevrolet
20	Ken Schrader	Ford
21	Eddie Bierschwale	Chevrolet
22	Dale Earnhardt	Chevrolet
23	Geoff Bodine	Chevrolet
24	Joe Booher	Chevrolet
25	Bobby Gerhart	Chevrolet
26	Bobby Hillin	Chevrolet
27	Bobby Wawak	Buick
28	Rick Baldwin	Chrysler

Fans flock to the track on race day.

29	J.D. McDuffie	Pontiac
30	Trevor Boys	Chevrolet
31	Ricky Rudd	Ford
32	Cale Yarborough	Ford
33	Greg Sacks	Buick
34	Clark Dwyer	Ford
35	Morgan Shepherd	Chevrolet
36	Bobby Allison	Ford
37	Richard Petty	Pontiac
38	Ron Bouchard	Buick
39	David Pearson	Ford
40	Tim Richmond	Pontiac

BUSCH 500

Time of Race: 3 hours, 27 minutes, 44 seconds
Average Speed: 81.388 mph
Margin of Victory: 3 car lengths

FINISH	DRIVER	CAR
1	Dale Earnhardt	Chevrolet
2	Tim Richmond	Pontiac
3	Neil Bonnett	Chevrolet
4	Darrell Waltrip	Chevrolet
5	Bill Elliott	Ford
6	Harry Gant	Chevrolet
7	Ron Bouchard	Buick
8	Richard Petty	Pontiac
9	Ricky Rudd	Ford
10	Lake Speed	Pontiac
11	Buddy Baker	Oldsmobile
12	Rusty Wallace	Pontiac
13	Joe Ruttman	Chevrolet
14	Ronnie Thomas	Chevrolet
15	Buddy Arrington	Ford
16	Kyle Petty	Chevrolet
17	Trevor Boys	Chevrolet
18	Clark Dwyer	Ford
19	Ken Schrader	Ford
20	Eddie Bierschwale	Chevrolet
21	Phil Parsons	Chevrolet
22	Bobby Allison	Buick
23	Dave Marcis	Oldsmobile
24	Bobby Hillin	Chevrolet

25	Geoff Bodine	Chevrolet
26	Mike Alexander	Chevrolet
27	Jimmy Means	Chevrolet
28	Greg Sacks	Buick
29	Terry Labonte	Chevrolet
30	Tommy Ellis	Chevrolet
31	Mike Potter	Ford

SOUTHERN 500

Time of Race: 4 hours, 8 minutes, 2 seconds
Average Speed: 121.254 mph
Margin of Victory: 2 seconds

FINISH	DRIVER	CAR
1	Bill Elliott	Ford
2	Cale Yarborough	Ford
3	Geoff Bodine	Chevrolet
4	Neil Bonnett	Chevrolet
5	Ron Bouchard	Buick
6	Ricky Rudd	Ford
7	Terry Labonte	Chevrolet
8	Benny Parsons	Chevrolet
9	Joe Ruttman	Chevrolet
10	Kyle Petty	Chevrolet
11	Tim Richmond	Pontiac
12	Richard Petty	Pontiac
13	Bobby Hillin	Chevrolet
14	Ken Schrader	Ford
15	Buddy Baker	Oldsmobile
16	Lake Speed	Pontiac
17	Darrell Waltrip	Chevrolet
18	Buddy Arrington	Ford
19	Dale Earnhardt	Chevrolet
20	Ken Ragan	Chevrolet
21	Harry Gant	Chevrolet
22	Pancho Carter	Chevrolet
23	Dave Marcis	Chevrolet
24	Michael Waltrip	Chevrolet
25	A.J. Foyt	Oldsmobile
26	Clark Dwyer	Ford
27	Jimmy Means	Chevrolet
28	Mike Potter	Buick
29	Slick Johnson	Ford
30	Bobby Allison	Ford
31	Trevor Boys	Chevrolet
32	Eddie Bierschwale	Chevrolet
33	Tommy Ellis	Chevrolet
34	H.B. Bailey	Pontiac
35	Greg Sacks	Buick
36	Tommy Houston	Chevrolet
37	Morgan Shepherd	Chevrolet
38	Rusty Wallace	Pontiac
39	Phil Parsons	Chevrolet
40	David Pearson	Ford

WRANGLER SANFORSET 400

Time of Race: 2 hours, 58 minutes, 54 seconds
Average Speed: 72.508 mph
Margin of Victory: 1 car length

FINISH	DRIVER	CAR
1	Darrell Waltrip	Chevrolet
2	Terry Labonte	Chevrolet
3	Richard Petty	Pontiac
4	Dale Earnhardt	Chevrolet
5	Ricky Rudd	Ford
6	Harry Gant	Chevrolet
7	Geoff Bodine	Chevrolet
8	Kyle Petty	Chevrolet
9	Neil Bonnett	Chevrolet
10	Tommy Ellis	Chevrolet
11	Lake Speed	Pontiac
12	Bill Elliott	Ford
13	Rusty Wallace	Pontiac

FINISH	DRIVER	CAR
14	Tim Richmond	Pontiac
15	Ken Schrader	Ford
16	Buddy Baker	Oldsmobile
17	Dave Marcis	Chevrolet
18	Ron Bouchard	Buick
19	Alan Kulwicki	Ford
20	Greg Sacks	Buick
21	Bobby Hillin	Chevrolet
22	Buddy Arrington	Ford
23	Jimmy Means	Pontiac
24	Clark Dwyer	Ford
25	Lennie Pond	Chevrolet
26	J.D. McDuffie	Pontiac
27	Phil Parsons	Chevrolet
28	Bobby Allison	Buick
29	Eddie Bierschwale	Chevrolet
30	Morgan Shepherd	Chevrolet

DELAWARE 500

Time of Race: 4 hours, 8 minutes, 52 seconds
Average Speed: 120.538 mph
Margin of Victory: 28 seconds

FINISH	DRIVER	CAR
1	Harry Gant	Chevrolet
2	Darrell Waltrip	Chevrolet
3	Ricky Rudd	Ford
4	Bobby Allison	Ford
5	Neil Bonnett	Chevrolet
6	Tim Richmond	Pontiac
7	Dale Earnhardt	Chevrolet
8	Ron Bouchard	Buick
9	Richard Petty	Pontiac
10	Lake Speed	Pontiac
11	Buddy Arrington	Ford
12	Phil Parsons	Chevrolet
13	Jimmy Means	Pontiac
14	Jerry Bowman	Ford
15	Kyle Petty	Ford
16	Ken Schrader	Ford
17	Bobby Wawak	Buick
18	Phil Good	Chrysler
19	Dave Marcis	Chevrolet
20	Bill Elliott	Ford
21	Alan Kulwicki	Ford
22	Morgan Shepherd	Chevrolet
23	Bobby Hillin	Chevrolet
24	Terry Labonte	Chevrolet
25	Geoff Bodine	Chevrolet
26	Tommy Ellis	Chevrolet
27	Eddie Bierschwale	Chevrolet
28	J.D. McDuffie	Ford
29	Greg Sacks	Buick
30	Clark Dwyer	Ford
31	Rusty Wallace	Pontiac
32	Rick Newsom	Buick
33	Joe Ruttman	Chevrolet
34	Trevor Boys	Chevrolet
35	Buddy Baker	Oldsmobile
36	Earle Canavan	Oldsmobile
37	Tommie Crozier	Pontiac
38	Chuck Walton	Chevrolet
39	Maurice Randall	Chrysler

GOODY'S 500

Time of Race: 3 hours, 43 minutes, 13 seconds
Average Speed: 70.694 mph
Margin of Victory: 2 car lengths

FINISH	DRIVER	CAR
1	Dale Earnhardt	Chevrolet
2	Darrell Waltrip	Chevrolet
3	Harry Gant	Chevrolet
4	Ricky Rudd	Ford
5	Kyle Petty	Ford

FINISH	DRIVER	CAR
6	Ron Bouchard	Buick
7	Tim Richmond	Pontiac
8	Bobby Hillin	Chevrolet
9	Neil Bonnett	Chevrolet
10	Bobby Allison	Buick
11	Lake Speed	Pontiac
12	Trevor Boys	Chevrolet
13	Jimmy Means	Pontiac
14	Greg Sacks	Buick
15	J.D. McDuffie	Pontiac
16	Bobby Wawak	Buick
17	Bill Elliott	Ford
18	Eddie Bierschwale	Chevrolet
19	Clark Dwyer	Ford
20	Phil Parsons	Chevrolet
21	Buddy Arrington	Ford
22	Richard Petty	Pontiac
23	Dave Marcis	Chevrolet
24	Geoff Bodine	Chevrolet
25	Rusty Wallace	Pontiac
26	Ken Schrader	Ford
27	Terry Labonte	Chevrolet
28	Brent Elliott	Buick
29	Morgan Shepherd	Chevrolet
30	Tommy Ellis	Chevrolet
31	Buddy Baker	Oldsmobile

HOLLY FARMS 400

Time of Race: 2 hours, 37 minutes, 44 seconds
Average Speed: 95.077 mph
Margin of Victory: 14 seconds

FINISH	DRIVER	CAR
1	Harry Gant	Chevrolet
2	Geoff Bodine	Chevrolet
3	Terry Labonte	Chevrolet
4	Dale Earnhardt	Chevrolet
5	Ricky Rudd	Ford
6	Ron Bouchard	Buick
7	Tim Richmond	Pontiac
8	Richard Petty	Pontiac
9	Dave Marcis	Chevrolet
10	Neil Bonnett	Chevrolet
11	Tommy Ellis	Chevrolet
12	Lake Speed	Pontiac
13	Phil Parsons	Chevrolet
14	Darrell Waltrip	Chevrolet
15	Ken Schrader	Ford
16	Greg Sacks	Buick
17	Bobby Hillin	Chevrolet
18	Clark Dwyer	Ford
19	Eddie Bierschwale	Chevrolet
20	Bobby Wawak	Buick
21	Jimmy Means	Pontiac
22	Trevor Boys	Chevrolet
23	Buddy Arrington	Ford
24	Bobby Gerhart	Chevrolet
25	Rusty Wallace	Pontiac
26	Mike Alexander	Chevrolet
27	Morgan Shepherd	Chevrolet
28	Kyle Petty	Ford
29	Buddy Baker	Oldsmobile
30	Bill Elliott	Ford
31	Bobby Allison	Buick

MILLER 500

Time of Race: 3 hours, 39 minutes, 48 seconds
Average Speed: 136.761 mph
Margin of Victory: 1 second

FINISH	DRIVER	CAR
1	Cale Yarborough	Ford
2	Bill Elliott	Ford

3	Geoff Bodine	Chevrolet
4	Darrell Waltrip	Chevrolet
5	Joe Ruttman	Folger's Chevrolet
6	Tim Richmond	Pontiac
7	Morgan Shepherd	Chevrolet
8	Buddy Baker	Oldsmobile
9	Bobby Hillin	Chevrolet
10	Richard Petty	Pontiac
11	Greg Sacks	Buick
12	Lake Speed	Pontiac
13	Alan Kulwicki	Ford
14	Bobby Allison	Ford
15	Ricky Rudd	Ford
16	Clark Dwyer	Ford
17	Buddy Arrington	Ford
18	Mike Alexander	Chevrolet
19	Davey Allison	Chevrolet
20	Dale Earnhardt	Chevrolet
21	Eddie Bierschwale	Chevrolet
22	Kyle Petty	Ford
23	Trevor Boys	Chevrolet
24	Harry Gant	Chevrolet
25	Ken Schrader	Ford
26	Ron Bouchard	Buick
27	Phil Parsons	Chevrolet
28	Ken Ragan	Ford
29	Sterling Marlin	Chevrolet
30	Rusty Wallace	Pontiac
31	Michael Waltrip	Chevrolet
32	A.J. Foyt	Oldsmobile
33	Terry Labonte	Chevrolet
34	Dave Marcis	Chevrolet
35	Don Paul	Chevrolet
36	Dick Trickle	Chevrolet
37	David Pearson	Ford
38	Jimmy Means	Pontiac
39	Lennie Pond	Chevrolet
40	Tommy Ellis	Chevrolet
41	Benny Parsons	Chevrolet
42	Neil Bonnett	Chevrolet

NATIONWISE 500

Time of Race: 4 hours, 13 minutes, 40 seconds
Average Speed: 118.344 mph
Margin of Victory: 1 second

FINISH	DRIVER	CAR
1	Darrell Waltrip	Chevrolet
2	Ron Bouchard	Buick
3	Harry Gant	Chevrolet
4	Bill Elliott	Ford
5	Geoff Bodine	Chevrolet
6	Tim Richmond	Pontiac
7	Ricky Rudd	Ford
8	Dale Earnhardt	Chevrolet
9	Rusty Wallace	Pontiac
10	Greg Sacks	Buick
11	Buddy Baker	Oldsmobile
12	Terry Labonte	Chevrolet
13	Phil Parsons	Chevrolet
14	Dave Marcis	Chevrolet
15	Neil Bonnett	Chevrolet
16	Buddy Arrington	Ford
17	Eddie Bierschwale	Chevrolet
18	Jimmy Means	Pontiac
19	Ken Schrader	Ford
20	Trevor Boys	Chevrolet
21	Randy Baker	Buick
22	Mike Potter	Ford
23	Jeff McDuffie	Chevrolet
24	Clark Dwyer	Ford
25	Bobby Hillin	Chevrolet
26	J.D. McDuffie	Pontiac
27	Alan Kulwicki	Ford
28	Cale Yarborough	Ford
29	Lake Speed	
30	Tommy Ellis	Chevrolet
31	Kyle Petty	Ford
32	D.K. Ulrich	Buick
33	Richard Petty	Pontiac

34	Bobby Wawak	Buick
35	Jerry Bowman	Ford
36	Jonathan Edwards	Buick
37	Craig Spetman	Chevrolet
38	Bobby Allison	Buick
39	Morgan Shepherd	Ford
40	Joe Ruttman	Chevrolet

ATLANTA JOURNAL 500

Time of Race: 3 hours, 34 minutes, 34 seconds
Average Speed: 139.597 mph
Margin of Victory: 4.25 seconds

FINISH	DRIVER	CAR
1	Bill Elliott	Ford
2	Cale Yarborough	Ford
3	Darrell Waltrip	Chevrolet
4	Dale Earnhardt	Chevrolet
5	Morgan Shepherd	Chevrolet
6	Terry Labonte	Chevrolet
7	Lake Speed	Pontiac
8	Harry Gant	Chevrolet
9	Greg Sacks	Buick
10	Richard Petty	Pontiac
11	Geoff Bodine	Chevrolet
12	Neil Bonnett	Chevrolet
13	Buddy Baker	Oldsmobile
14	Phil Parsons	Chevrolet
15	Ken Schrader	Ford
16	Ron Bouchard	Buick
17	Tim Richmond	Pontiac
18	Rick Wilson	Chevrolet
19	Bobby Hillin	Chevrolet
20	Buddy Arrington	Ford
21	Rusty Wallace	Pontiac
22	Alan Kulwicki	Ford
23	Rick Baldwin	Pontiac
24	Eddie Bierschwale	Chevrolet
25	Chet Fillip	Ford
26	Bobby Allison	Buick
27	J.D. McDuffie	Pontiac
28	Dave Marcis	Chevrolet
29	Kyle Petty	Chevrolet
30	Sammy Swindell	Chevrolet
31	Ricky Rudd	Ford
32	Joe Ruttman	Chevrolet
33	Benny Parsons	Chevrolet
34	Ken Ragan	Chevrolet
35	Connie Saylor	Chevrolet
36	Tommy Ellis	Chevrolet
37	Trevor Boys	Chevrolet
38	A.J. Foyt	Oldsmobile
39	Michael Waltrip	Chevrolet
40	Clark Dwyer	Ford
41	Jimmy Means	Pontiac
42	Davey Allison	Chevrolet

WINSTON WESTERN 500

Time of Race: 2 hours, 58 minutes, 3 seconds
Average Speed: 105.065 mph
Margin of Victory: 2 car lengths

FINISH	DRIVER	CAR
1	Ricky Rudd	Ford
2	Terry Labonte	Chevrolet
3	Neil Bonnett	Chevrolet
4	Harry Gant	Chevrolet
5	Dale Earnhardt	Chevrolet
6	Geoff Bodine	Chevrolet
7	Darrell Waltrip	Chevrolet
8	Richard Petty	Pontiac
9	Lake Speed	Pontiac
10	Ron Bouchard	Buick
11	Glen Steurer	Chevrolet

12	Jim Robinson	Oldsmobile
13	Bobby Hillin	Chevrolet
14	Ruben Garcia	Chevrolet
15	Bill Schmitt	Chevrolet
16	Jim Bown	Chevrolet
17	Bobby Allison	Buick
18	Dave Marcis	Chevrolet
19	Derrike Cope	Ford
20	Jimmy Means	Pontiac
21	Greg Sacks	Buick
22	Buddy Arrington	Ford
23	Ken Schrader	Ford
24	Bill Osborne	Buick
25	J.D. McDuffie	Pontiac
26	Hershel McGriff	Pontiac
27	Kyle Petty	Ford
28	Clark Dwyer	Ford
29	Blair Aiken	Chevrolet
30	John Soares	Pontiac
31	Bill Elliott	Ford
32	Eddie Bierschwale	Chevrolet
33	Phil Parsons	Chevrolet
34	Scott Autrey	Oldsmobile
35	Buddy Baker	Oldsmobile
36	Rusty Wallace	Pontiac
37	Tim Richmond	Pontiac
38	Bud Hickey	Chevrolet
39	Rick McCray	Chevrolet
40	Trevor Boys	Chevrolet
41	Ron Esau	Chevrolet

1986

DAYTONA 500

Time of Race: 3 hours, 22 minutes, 32 seconds
Average Speed of Race: 148.124 mph
Margin of Victory: 11.26 seconds

FINISH	DRIVER	CAR
1	Geoff Bodine	Chevrolet
2	Terry Labonte	Oldsmobile
3	Darrell Waltrip	Chevrolet
4	Bobby Hillin	Chevrolet
5	Benny Parsons	Oldsmobile
6	Ron Bouchard	Pontiac
7	Rick Wilson	Oldsmobile
8	Rusty Wallace	Pontiac
9	Sterling Marlin	Chevrolet
10	Lake Speed	Pontiac
11	Ricky Rudd	Ford
12	Jody Ridley	Ford
13	Bill Elliott	Ford
14	Dale Earnhardt	Chevrolet
15	Doug Heveron	Chevrolet
16	Kyle Petty	Ford
17	Dick Trickle	Chevrolet
18	Trevor Boys	Chevrolet
19	Tommy Ellis	Chevrolet
20	Tim Richmond	Chevrolet
21	Ken Ragan	Chevrolet
22	Morgan Shepherd	Chevrolet
23	Buddy Arrington	Ford
24	Phil Parsons	Oldsmobile
25	Jim Sauter	Pontiac
26	Buddy Baker	Oldsmobile
27	Cale Yarborough	Ford
28	Joe Ruttman	Buick
29	A.J. Foyt	Oldsmobile
30	Harry Gant	Chevrolet
31	Eddie Bierschwale	Chevrolet
32	Neil Bonnett	Chevrolet
33	Ken Schrader	Ford
34	Pancho Carter	Ford
35	Greg Sacks	Pontiac
36	Richard Petty	Pontiac
37	Mark Martin	Ford

38	Dave Marcis	Pontiac
39	Jimmy Means	Pontiac
40	Larry Pearson	Chevrolet
41	Kirk Bryant	Pontiac
42	Bobby Allison	Buick

MILLER HIGH LIFE 400

Time of Race: 3 hours, 2 minutes, 54 seconds
Average Speed: 71.078 mph
Margin of Victory: 4 seconds

FINISH	DRIVER	CAR
1	Kyle Petty	Ford
2	Joe Ruttman	Buick
3	Dale Earnhardt	Chevrolet
4	Bobby Allison	Buick
5	Darrell Waltrip	Chevrolet
6	Bobby Hillin	Buick
7	Neil Bonnett	Chevrolet
8	Geoff Bodine	Chevrolet
9	Dave Marcis	Chevrolet
10	Rusty Wallace	Pontiac
11	Jimmy Means	Pontiac
12	Davey Allison	Chevrolet
13	Doug Heveron	Ford
14	Buddy Arrington	Ford
15	Terry Labonte	Oldsmobile
16	J.D. McDuffie	Pontiac
17	Lake Speed	Pontiac
18	Ron Bouchard	Pontiac
19	Greg Sacks	Pontiac
20	Richard Petty	Pontiac
21	Bill Elliott	Chevrolet
22	Tim Richmond	Chevrolet
23	Ken Schrader	Ford
24	Tommy Ellis	Chevrolet
25	Micheal Waltrip	Pontiac
26	Trevor Boys	Chevrolet
27	Kirk Bryant	Pontiac
28	Harry Gant	Chevrolet
29	Phil Parsons	Oldsmobile
30	Ricky Rudd	Ford
31	Eddie Bierschwale	Chevrolet

GOODWRENCH 500

Time of Race: 4 hours, 9 minutes, 10 seconds
Average Speed: 120.488 mph
Margin of Victory: 1 second

FINISH	DRIVER	CAR
1	Terry Labonte	Oldsmobile
2	Harry Gant	Chevrolet
3	Richard Petty	Pontiac
4	Morgan Shepherd	Buick
5	Darrell Waltrip	Chevrolet
6	Cale Yarborough	Ford
7	Bill Elliott	Ford
8	Dale Earnhardt	Chevrolet
9	Neil Bonnett	Chevrolet
10	Lake Speed	Pontiac
11	Kyle Petty	Ford
12	Rusty Wallace	Pontiac
13	Ron Bouchard	Buick
14	Tommy Ellis	Chevrolet
15	Alan Kulwicki	Ford
16	Tim Richmond	Chevrolet
17	Buddy Arrington	Ford
18	Kirk Bryant	Pontiac
19	Jimmy Means	Pontiac
20	Geoff Bodine	Chevrolet
21	Michael Waltrip	Pontiac
22	Ken Schrader	Ford
23	Pancho Carter	Ford
24	Jonathan Edwards	Chevrolet
25	Davey Allison	Chevrolet

26	Ronnie Thomas	Chevrolet
27	Dave Marcis	Chevrolet
28	Ricky Rudd	Ford
29	Eddie Bierschwale	Pontiac
30	Phil Parsons	Oldsmobile
31	J.D. McDuffie	Pontiac
32	Earle Canavan	Pontiac
33	Joe Ruttman	Buick
34	Bobby Allison	Buick
35	Trevor Boys	Chevrolet
36	Wayne Slark	Chevrolet
37	Greg Sacks	Pontiac
38	Bobby Wawak	Chevrolet
39	Bobby Hillin	Buick
40	Rick Newsom	Buick

MOTORCRAFT 500

Time of Race: 3 hours, 46 minutes, 41 seconds
Average Speed: 132.126 mph
Margin of Victory: 1 second

FINISH	DRIVER	CAR
1	Morgan Shepherd	Buick
2	Dale Earnhardt	Chevrolet
3	Terry Labonte	Oldsmobile
4	Darrell Waltrip	Chevrolet
5	Bill Elliott	Ford
6	Benny Parsons	Oldsmobile
7	Tim Richmond	Chevrolet
8	Rusty Wallace	Pontiac
9	Bobby Allison	Buick
10	Geoff Bodine	Chevrolet
11	Richard Petty	Pontiac
12	Harry Gant	Chevrolet
13	Tommy Ellis	Chevrolet
14	Alan Kulwicki	Ford
15	Buddy Baker	Oldsmobile
16	Bobby Hillin	Buick
17	A.J. Foyt	Oldsmobile
18	Phil Parsons	Oldsmobile
19	Michael Waltrip	Pontiac
20	Buddy Arrington	Ford
21	Ken Schrader	Ford
22	Lake Speed	Pontiac
23	Bobby Wawak	Chevrolet
24	Trevor Boys	Chevrolet
25	Greg Sacks	Chevrolet
26	Ricky Rudd	Ford
27	Cale Yarborough	Ford
28	Kyle Petty	Ford
29	Jody Ridley	Ford
30	Eddie Bierschwale	Chevrolet
31	Kirk Bryant	Pontiac
32	Sterling Marlin	Chevrolet
33	Dave Marcis	Pontiac
34	Neil Bonnett	Chevrolet
35	Doug Heveron	Chevrolet
36	Chet Fillip	Ford
37	H.B. Bailey	Pontiac
38	Pancho Carter	Ford
39	Rick Wilson	Oldsmobile
40	Ron Bouchard	Pontiac
41	Jimmy Means	Pontiac
42	Joe Ruttman	Buick

VALLEYDALE MEATS 500

Time of Race: 2 hours, 58 minutes, 14 seconds
Average Speed: 89.747 mph
Margin of Victory: 10.69 seconds

FINISH	DRIVER	CAR
1	Rusty Wallace	Pontiac
2	Ricky Rudd	Ford
3	Darrell Waltrip	Chevrolet
4	Harry Gant	Chevrolet
5	Bill Elliott	Ford
6	Bobby Allison	Buick
7	Terry Labonte	Oldsmobile
8	Tim Richmond	Chevrolet
9	Kyle Petty	Ford
10	Dale Earnhardt	Chevrolet
11	Tommy Ellis	Chevrolet
12	Rick Wilson	Olds
13	Ken Schrader	Ford
14	Richard Petty	Pontiac
15	Alan Kulwicki	Ford
16	Butch Miller	Buick
17	Buddy Arrington	Ford
18	Trevor Boys	Chevrolet
19	Joe Ruttman	Buick
20	Davey Allison	Chevrolet
21	Doug Heveron	Chevrolet
22	Chet Fillip	Ford
23	Jody Ridley	Pontiac
24	Geoff Bodine	Chevrolet
25	Ron Bouchard	Pontiac
26	Ronnie Thomas	Chevrolet
27	Dave Marcis	Chevrolet
28	Bobby Hillin	Buick
29	Eddie Bierschwale	Pontiac
30	Neil Bonnett	Chevrolet
31	Morgan Shepherd	Ford
32	Michael Waltrip	Buick

TRANSOUTH 500

Time of Race: 3 hours, 53 minutes, 11 seconds
Average Speed: 128.994 mph
Margin of Victory: 3 car lengths

FINISH	DRIVER	CAR
1	Dale Earnhardt	Chevrolet
2	Darrell Waltrip	Chevrolet
3	Bobby Allison	Buick
4	Neil Bonnett	Chevrolet
5	Tim Richmond	Chevrolet
6	Rusty Wallace	Pontiac
7	Richard Petty	Pontiac
8	Bill Elliott	Ford
9	Kyle Petty	Ford
10	Ken Schrader	Ford
11	Alan Kulwicki	Ford
12	H.B. Bailey	Pontiac
13	Michael Waltrip	Pontiac
14	Harry Gant	Chevrolet
15	Rick Wilson	Oldsmobile
16	Mark Stahl	Ford
17	J.D. McDuffie	Pontiac
18	Connie Saylor	Ford
19	Bobby Wawak	Buick
20	Jody Ridley	Pontiac
21	Joe Ruttman	Buick
22	Cale Yarborough	Ford
23	Morgan Shepherd	Buick
24	Trevor Boys	Chevrolet
25	Jimmy Means	Pontiac
26	Ricky Rudd	Ford
27	Dave Marcis	Chevrolet
28	Benny Parsons	Oldsmobile
29	Tommy Ellis	Chevrolet
30	Buddy Baker	Oldsmobile
31	Phil Parsons	Oldsmobile
32	Terry Labonte	Oldsmobile
33	Sterling Marlin	Chevrolet
34	Eddie Bierschwale	Pontiac
35	Doug Heveron	Oldsmobile
36	Ronnie Thomas	Chevrolet
37	Ron Bouchard	Pontiac
38	Bobby Hillin	Buick
39	Davey Allison	Chevrolet
40	Geoff Bodine	Chevrolet

FIRST UNION 400

Time of Race: 2 hours, 49 minutes, 40 seconds
Average Speed: 88.408 mph
Margin of Victory: 1 second

FINISH	DRIVER	CAR
1	Dale Earnhardt	Chevrolet
2	Ricky Rudd	Ford
3	Geoff Bodine	Chevrolet
4	Darrell Waltrip	Chevrolet
5	Joe Ruttman	Buick
6	Bobby Allison	Buick
7	Harry Gant	Chevrolet
8	Kyle Petty	Ford
9	Bill Elliott	Ford
10	Rusty Wallace	Pontiac
11	Neil Bonnett	Chevrolet
12	Tim Richmond	Chevrolet
13	Bobby Hillin	Buick
14	Ken Schrader	Ford
15	Jody Ridley	Pontiac
16	Doug Heveron	Oldsmobile
17	Ron Bouchard	Pontiac
18	Alan Kulwicki	Ford
19	Morgan Shepherd	Chevrolet
20	Jimmy Means	Pontiac
21	Buddy Arrington	Ford
22	Willy T. Ribbs	Pontiac
23	Chet Fillip	Ford
24	Rick Baldwin	Ford
25	Dave Marcis	Chevrolet
26	Michael Waltrip	Pontiac
27	Terry Labonte	Oldsmobile
28	J.D. McDuffie	Pontiac
29	Richard Petty	Pontiac
30	Trevor Boys	Chevrolet

SOVRAN BANK 500

Time of Race: 3 hours, 25 minutes, 15 secods
Average Speed: 76.882 mph
Margin of Victory: 24 seconds

FINISH	DRIVER	CAR
1	Ricky Rudd	Ford
2	Joe Ruttman	Buick
3	Terry Labonte	Oldsmobile
4	Alan Kulwicki	Ford
5	Kyle Petty	Ford
6	Bobby Hillin	Buick
7	Ken Schrader	Ford
8	Bobby Allison	Buick
9	Derrike Cope	Ford
10	Jody Ridley	Pontiac
11	Michael Waltrip	Pontiac
12	Jimmy Means	Pontiac
13	Jerry Cranmer	Chevrolet
14	Trevor Boys	Chevrolet
15	Buddy Arrington	Ford
16	Dave Marcis	Chevrolet
17	Geoff Bodine	Chevrolet
18	J.D. McDuffie	Pontiac
19	Morgan Shepherd	Pontiac
20	Tim Richmond	Chevrolet
21	Dale Earnhardt	Chevrolet
22	Mike Skinner	Pontiac
23	Jimmy Hensley	Ford
24	Tommy Ellis	Chevrolet
25	Harry Gant	Chevrolet
26	Neil Bonnett	Chevrolet
27	Darrell Waltrip	Chevrolet
28	Richard Petty	Pontiac
29	Doug Heveron	Chevrolet
30	Rusty Wallace	Pontiac
31	Bill Elliott	Ford

WINSTON 500

Time of Race: 3 hours, 10 minutes, 16 seconds
Average Speed: 157.698 mph
Margin of Victory: 1 car length

FINISH	DRIVER	CAR
1	Bobby Allison	Buick
2	Dale Earnhardt	Chevrolet
3	Buddy Baker	Oldsmobile
4	Bobby Hillin	Buick
5	Phil Parsons	Oldsmobile
6	Morgan Shepherd	Buick
7	Richard Petty	Pontiac
8	Rick Wilson	Chevrolet
9	Ron Bouchard	Pontiac
10	Greg Sacks	Pontiac
11	Dave Marcis	Pontiac
12	Tim Richmond	Chevrolet
13	Rusty Wallace	Pontiac
14	Ronnie Thomas	Chevrolet
15	Doug Heveron	Pontiac
16	Jimmy Means	Chevrolet
17	Joe Ruttman	Buick
18	Pancho Carter	Chevrolet
19	Delma Cowart	Chevrolet
20	Benny Parsons	Oldsmobile
21	Harry Gant	Chevrolet
22	Buddy Arrington	Ford
23	Chet Fillip	Ford
24	Bill Elliott	Ford
25	Tommy Gale	Ford
26	Ken Schrader	Ford
27	Geoff Bodine	Chevrolet
28	Phil Barkdoll	Ford
29	Terry Labonte	Oldsmobile
30	Eddie Bierschwale	Chevrolet
31	Kyle Petty	Ford
32	Tommy Ellis	Chevrolet
33	Connie Saylor	Chevrolet
34	Darrell Waltrip	Chevrolet
35	Michael Waltrip	Pontiac
36	Ricky Rudd	Ford
37	Cale Yarborough	Ford
38	Trevor Boys	Chevrolet
39	Sterling Marlin	Chevrolet
40	Neil Bonnett	Chevrolet
41	Jim Sauter	Chevrolet
42	Jody Ridley	Pontiac

BUDWEISER 500

Time of Race: 4 hours, 20 minutes, 51 seconds
Average Speed: 115.009 mph
Margin of Victory: 3 seconds

FINISH	DRIVER	CAR
1	Geoff Bodine	Chevrolet
2	Bobby Allison	Buick
3	Dale Earnhardt	Chevrolet
4	Ricky Rudd	Ford
5	Darrell Waltrip	Chevrolet
6	Richard Petty	Pontiac
7	Bill Elliott	Ford
8	Bobby Hillin	Buick
9	Tommy Ellis	Chevrolet
10	Ken Schrader	Ford
11	Joe Ruttman	Buick
12	Michael Waltrip	Pontiac
13	Trevor Boys	Pontiac
14	Harry Gant	Chevrolet
15	Buddy Arrington	Ford
16	Jerry Cranmer	Chevrolet
17	Terry Labonte	Oldsmobile
18	Jody Ridley	Pontiac
19	Kyle Petty	Ford
20	J.D. McDuffie	Pontiac
21	Dave Marcis	Chevrolet

22	Gary Fedewa	Chevrolet
23	Alan Kulwicki	Ford
24	Jimmy Means	Pontiac
25	Rick Newsom	Buick
26	Rusty Wallace	Pontiac
27	Ron Bouchard	Pontiac
28	Neil Bonnett	Chevrolet
29	Jerry Bowman	Ford
30	Jerry Holden	Ford
31	Joe Booher	Chevrolet
32	Tim Richmond	Chevrolet
33	Mike Porter	Ford
34	Rick Baldwin	Ford
35	Doug Heveron	Chevrolet
36	Howard Mark	Chevrolet
37	Joe Fields	Ford

COCA-COLA 600

Time of Race: 4 hours, 16 minutes, 24 seconds
Average Speed: 140.406 mph
Margin of Victory: 5 seconds

FINISH	DRIVER	CAR
1	Dale Earnhardt	Chevrolet
2	Tim Richmond	Chevrolet
3	Cale Yarborough	Ford
4	Harry Gant	Chevrolet
5	Darrell Waltrip	Chevrolet
6	Bill Elliott	Ford
7	Sterling Marlin	Chevrolet
8	Ricky Rudd	Ford
9	Morgan Shepherd	Buick
10	Rusty Wallace	Pontiac
11	Terry Labonte	Oldsmobile
12	Bobby Allison	Buick
13	Neil Bonnett	Chevrolet
14	Lake Speed	Oldsmobile
15	Bobby Hillin	Buick
16	Dave Marcis	Ford
17	Buddy Baker	Oldsmobile
18	Brett Bodine	Chevrolet
19	Ron Bouchard	Pontiac
20	Kyle Petty	Ford
21	Jody Ridley	Pontiac
22	Mark Martin	Ford
23	Ken Schrader	Ford
24	Phil Parsons	Oldsmobile
25	Trevor Boys	Pontiac
26	Michael Waltrip	Pontiac
27	Alan Kulwicki	Ford
28	Connie Saylor	Ford
29	Eddie Bierschwale	Chevrolet
30	Derrike Cope	Ford
31	Geoff Bodine	Chevrolet
32	Joe Ruttman	Buick
33	Doug Heveron	Chevrolet
34	Benny Parsons	Oldsmobile
35	Tommy Ellis	Chevrolet
36	David Pearson	Chevrolet
37	Chet Fillip	Ford
38	Richard Petty	Chevrolet
39	Greg Sacks	Chevrolet
40	Brad Teague	Chevrolet
41	Ken Ragan	Pontiac

BUDWEISER 400

Time of Race: 2 hours, 22 minutes, 07 seconds
Average Speed: 105.083 mph
Margin of Victory: 4 feet

FINISH	DRIVER	CAR
1	Darrell Waltrip	Chevrolet
2	Tim Richmond	Chevrolet

3	Ricky Rudd	Ford
4	Rusty Wallace	Pontiac
5	Dale Earnhardt	Chevrolet
6	Richard Petty	Pontiac
7	Bobby Allison	Buick
8	Neil Bonnett	Chevrolet
9	Harry Gant	Chevrolet
10	Glen Steurer	Chevrolet
11	Bill Elliott	Ford
12	Terry Labonte	Oldsmobile
13	Chad Little	Ford
14	J.D. McDuffie	Pontiac
15	Jim Robinson	Oldsmobile
16	Ron Esau	Chevrolet
17	Ken Schrader	Ford
18	Bill Schmitt	Chevrolet
19	Buddy Arrington	Ford
20	Doug Heveron	Chevrolet
21	Clay Young	Buick
22	Jimmy Means	Pontiac
23	Ted Kennedy	Chevrolet
24	Terrry Petris	Chevrolet
25	Michael Waltrip	Pontiac
26	John Krebs	Oldsmobile
27	Morgan Shepherd	Pontiac
28	Hershel McGriff	Pontiac
29	Willy T. Ribbs	Chevrolet
30	Ruben Garcia	Chevrolet
31	Derrike Cope	Ford
32	Bobby Hillin	Buick
33	D.K. Ulrich	Chevrolet
34	Trevor Boys	Pontiac
35	Bill Osborn	Buick
36	Ray Kelly	Pontiac
37	Rick McCray	Buick
38	Dave Marcis	Pontiac
39	Geoff Bodine	Chevrolet
40	Rick Lach	Buick
41	Kyle Petty	Ford
42	Joe Ruttman	Buick

MILLER HIGH LIFE 500

Time of Race: 4 hours, 24 minutes, 50 seconds
Average Speed: 113.279 mph
Margin of Victory: under caution

FINISH	DRIVER	CAR
1	Tim Richmond	Chevrolet
2	Dale Earnhardt	Chevrolet
3	Cale Yarborough	Ford
4	Ricky Rudd	Ford
5	Bill Elliott	Ford
6	Rusty Wallace	Pontiac
7	Joe Ruttman	Buick
8	Kyle Petty	Ford
9	Geoff Bodine	Chevrolet
10	Bobby Hillin	Buick
11	Jody Ridley	Pontiac
12	Ron Bouchard	Pontiac
13	Bobby Allison	Buick
14	Dave Marcis	Pontiac
15	Tommy Ellis	Chevrolet
16	J.D. McDuffie	
17	D.K. Ulrich	Chevrolet
18	Morgan Shepherd	Buick
19	Richard Petty	Pontiac
20	Chet Fillip	Ford
21	Buddy Arrington	Ford
22	Jimmy Means	Pontiac
23	Neil Bonnett	Chevrolet
24	Jerry Cranmer	Chevrolet
25	Jack Ely	Chevrolet
26	Harry Gant	Chevrolet
27	Ken Schrader	Ford
28	Pancho Carter	Chevrolet
29	Randy LaJoie	Chevrolet
30	Jonathan Edwards	Buick
31	Phil Parsons	Oldsmobile
32	Eddie Bierschwale	Ford

33	Benny Parsons	Oldsmobile
34	Bobby Gerhart	Chevrolet
35	Terry Labonte	Oldsmobile
36	Buddy Baker	Oldsmobile
37	Rick Newsom	Buick
38	Buddie Boys	Pontiac
39	Michael Waltrip	Pontiac
40	Darrell Waltrip	Chevrolet

MILLER AMERICAN 400

Time of Race: 2 hours, 53 minutes, 21 seconds
Average Speed: 138.851 mph
Margin of Victory: 2 car lengths

FINISH	DRIVER	CAR
1	Bill Elliott	Ford
2	Harry Gant	Chevrolet
3	Geoff Bodine	Chevrolet
4	Buddy Baker	Oldsmobile
5	Darrell Waltrip	Chevrolet
6	Dale Earnhardt	Chevrolet
7	Bobby Hillin	Buick
8	Rick Wilson	Oldsmobile
9	Joe Ruttman	Buick
10	Ricky Rudd	Ford
11	Bobby Allison	Buick
12	Terry Labonte	Oldsmobile
13	Richard Petty	Pontiac
14	Tommy Ellis	Chevrolet
15	Tim Richmond	Chevrolet
16	Alan Kulwicki	Ford
17	Pancho Carter	Chevrolet
18	Jim Sauter	Pontiac
19	Rusty Wallace	Pontiac
20	Ken Schrader	Ford
21	Butch Miller	Chevrolet
22	Michael Waltrip	Pontiac
23	Gary Fedewa	Chevrolet
24	Bobby Wawak	Chevrolet
25	Neil Bonnett	Chevrolet
26	Chet Fillip	Ford
27	Eddie Bierschwale	Ford
28	Derrike Cope	Ford
29	Morgan Shepherd	Buick
30	Cale Yarborough	Ford
31	Mike Laws	Chevrolet
32	Kyle Petty	Ford
33	Phil Parsons	Oldsmobile
34	Jody Ridley	Pontiac
35	J.D. McDuffie	Pontiac
36	Ron Bouchard	Pontiac
37	Dave Marcis	Pontiac
38	James Hylton	Chevrolet
39	Willy T. Ribbs	Chevrolet
40	D.K. Ulrich	Chevrolet
41	Benny Parsons	Oldsmobile

PEPSI FIRECRACKER 400

Time of Race: 3 hours, 1 minute 56 seconds
Average Speed: 131.916 mph
Margin of Victory: 1.35 seconds

FINISH	DRIVER	CAR
1	Tim Richmond	Chevrolet
2	Sterling Marlin	Chevrolet
3	Bobby Hillin	Buick
4	Darrell Waltrip	Chevrolet
5	Kyle Petty	Ford
6	Ricky Rudd	Ford
7	Joe Ruttman	Buick
8	Rusty Wallace	Pontiac
9	Phil Parsons	Oldsmobile
10	Alan Kulwicki	Ford

11	Neil Bonnett	Chevrolet
12	Ken Schrader	Ford
13	Jody Ridley	Pontiac
14	Buddy Baker	Oldsmobile
15	Bobby Allison	Buick
16	Bill Elliott	Ford
17	Cale Yarborough	Ford
18	Michael Waltrip	Pontiac
19	Terry Labonte	Oldsmobile
20	Dave Marcis	Pontiac
21	Rick Wilson	Oldsmobile
22	Richard Petty	Pontiac
23	Jim Sauter	Chevrolet
24	Jimmy Means	Pontiac
25	Buddy Arrington	Ford
26	Grant Adcox	Chevrolet
27	Dale Earnhardt	Chevrolet
28	Pancho Carter	Chevrolet
29	Geoff Bodine	Chevrolet
30	Connie Saylor	Ford
31	Harry Gant	Chevrolet
32	Rodney Combs	Chevrolet
33	Doug Heveron	Chevrolet
34	Ken Ragan	Chevrolet
35	Eddie Bierschwale	Chevrolet
36	Benny Parsons	Oldsmobile
37	Morgan Shepherd	Buick
38	Tommy Ellis	Chevrolet
39	Greg Sacks	Chevrolet
40	Chet Fillip	Ford
41	Ron Bouchard	Pontiac
42	A.J. Foyt	Oldsmobile

SUMMER 500

Time of Race: 2 hours, 41 minutes, 08 seconds
Average Speed: 124,218 mph
Margin of Victory: .05 seconds

FINISH	DRIVER	CAR
1	Tim Richmond	Chevrolet
2	Ricky Rudd	Ford
3	Geoff Bodine	Chevrolet
4	Darrell Waltrip	Chevrolet
5	Bobby Allison	Buick
6	Terry Labonte	Oldsmobile
7	Dale Earnhardt	Chevrolet
8	Kyle Petty	Ford
9	Tommy Ellis	Chevrolet
10	Rick Wilson	Oldsmobile
11	Michael Waltrip	Pontiac
12	Chet Filip	Ford
13	Jimmy Means	Pontiac
14	Jim Sauter	Pontiac
15	Eddie Bierschwale	Ford
16	Doug Heveron	Chevrolet
17	Buddy Arrington	Ford
18	D.K. Ulrich	Chevrolet
19	J.D. McDuffie	Pontiac
20	Jack Ely	Chevrolet
21	Gary Fedewa	Chevrolet
22	Alan Kulwicki	Ford
23	Ken Schrader	Ford
24	Dave Marcis	Pontiac
25	Cale Yarborough	Ford
26	Jerry Cranmer	Chevrolet
27	Rusty Wallace	Pontiac
28	Bobby Gerhart	Chevrolet
29	Benny Parsons	Oldsmobile
30	Harry Gant	Chevrolet
31	Neil Bonnett	Chevrolet
32	Morgan Shepherd	Buick
33	Bobby Hillin	Buick
34	Richard Petty	Pontiac
35	Bill Elliott	Ford
36	Buddy Baker	Oldsmobile
37	Phil Parsons	Oldsmobile
38	Joe Ruttman	Buick
39	Jocko Maggiacomo	Oldsmobile
40	Cliff Hucul	Pontiac

TALLADEGA 500

Time of Race: 3 hours, 17 minutes, 59 seconds
Average Speed: 151.552 mph
Margin of Victory: 3 car lengths

FINISH	DRIVER	CAR
1	Bobby Hillin	Buick
2	Tim Richmond	Chevrolet
3	Ricky Rudd	Ford
4	Sterling Marlin	Chevrolet
5	Benny Parsons	Oldsmobile
6	Morgan Shepherd	Buick
7	Davey Allison	Chevrolet
8	Joe Ruttman	Buick
9	Kyle Petty	Ford
10	Bobby Allison	Buick
11	Rick Wilson	Oldsmobile
12	Jim Sauter	Pontiac
13	Phil Parsons	Oldsmobile
14	Michael Waltrip	Pontiac
15	Jimmy Means	Pontiac
16	Ronnie Thomas	Chevrolet
17	Ron Bouchard	Pontiac
18	Ken Ragan	Chevrolet
19	Rodney Combs	Chevrolet
20	Buddy Baker	Oldsmobile
21	Buddy Arrington	Ford
22	Harry Gant	Chevrolet
23	Geoff Bodine	Chevrolet
24	Cale Yarborough	Ford
25	Darrell Waltrip	Chevrolet
26	Dale Earnhardt	Chevrolet
27	Bill Elliott	Ford
28	Chet Fillip	Ford
29	Delma Cowart	Chevrolet
30	A.J. Foyt	Oldsmobile
31	Ken Schrader	Ford
32	Alan Kulwicki	Ford
33	Phil Barkdoll	Ford
34	Tommy Ellis	Chevrolet
35	Rusty Wallace	Pontiac
36	Dave Marcis	Pontiac
37	Richard Petty	Pontiac
38	Terry Labonte	Oldsmobile
39	Eddie Bierschwale	Chevrolet
40	Pancho Carter	Chevrolet

THE BUDWEISER AT THE GLEN

Time of Race: 2 hours, 12 minutes, 56 seconds
Average Speed: 90.463 mph
Margin of Victory: 1.45 seconds

FINISH	DRIVER	CAR
1	Tim Richmond	Chevrolet
2	Darrell Waltrip	Chevrolet
3	Dale Earnhardt	Chevrolet
4	Bill Elliott	Ford
5	Neil Bonnett	Chevrolet
6	Rusty Wallace	Pontiac
7	Ricky Rudd	Ford
8	Benny Parsons	Oldsmobile
9	Kyle Petty	Ford
10	Richard Petty	Pontiac
11	Morgan Shepherd	Pontiac
12	Bobby Allison	Buick
13	Dave Marcis	Chevrolet
14	Phil Parsons	Oldsmobile
15	Tommy Riggins	Pontiac
16	Ken Schrader	Ford
17	Michael Waltrip	Pontiac
18	George Follmer	Chevrolet
19	Geoff Bodine	Chevrolet
20	Rick Knoop	Chevrolet
21	Jimmy Means	Pontiac
22	Chet Fillip	Ford

FINISH	DRIVER	CAR
23	Rick Wilson	Oldsmobile
24	Buddy Arrington	Ford
25	J.D. McDuffie	Pontiac
26	Tom Rotsell	Ford
27	James Hylton	Chevrolet
28	Bobby Hillin	Buick
29	Al Unser, Sr.	Oldsmobile
30	Eddie Bierschwale	Ford
31	Pancho Carter	Chevrolet
32	Terry Labonte	Oldsmobile
33	Joe Ruttman	Buick
34	Harry Gant	Chevrolet
35	Phil Good	Ford
36	Jocko Maggiacomo	Buick

CHAMPION SPARK PLUG 400

Time of Race: 2 hours, 57 minutes, 28 seconds
Average Speed: 135.376 mph
Margin of Victory: 1.45 seconds

FINISH	DRIVER	CAR
1	Bill Elliott	Ford
2	Tim Richmond	Chevrolet
3	Darrell Waltrip	Chevrolet
4	Geoff Bodine	Chevrolet
5	Dale Earnhardt	Chevrolet
6	Rusty Wallace	Pontiac
7	Cale Yarborough	Ford
8	Harry Gant	Chevrolet
9	Phil Parsons	Oldsmobile
10	David Pearson	Chevrolet
11	Ken Schrader	Ford
12	Terry Labonte	Oldsmobile
13	Bobby Hillin	Buick
14	Alan Kulwicki	Ford
15	Chet Fillip	Ford
16	Eddie Bierschwale	Ford
17	Ken Ragan	Chevrolet
18	Richard Petty	Pontiac
19	Buddy Arrington	Ford
20	D.K. Ulrich	Chevrolet
21	Ricky Rudd	Ford
22	Bobby Gerhart	Chevrolet
23	Jim Hull	Oldsmobile
24	Bobby Allison	Buick
25	Jimmy Means	Pontiac
26	Benny Parsons	Oldsmobile
27	David Simko	Chevrolet
28	Kyle Petty	Ford
29	Rodney Combs	Pontiac
30	Joe Ruttman	Buick
31	J.D. McDuffie	Pontiac
32	Michael Waltrip	Pontiac
33	Butch Miller	Chevrolet
34	Neil Bonnett	Chevrolet
35	Dave Marcis	Chevrolet
36	Morgan Shepherd	Buick
37	Jim Sauter	Pontiac
38	Greg Sacks	Chevrolet
39	Tommy Ellis	Chevrolet
40	Rick Wilson	Oldsmobile
41	Buddy Baker	Oldsmobile

BUSCH 500

Time of Race: 3 hours, 3 minutes, 55 seconds
Average Speed: 86.934 mph
Margin of Victory: 8.55 seconds

FINISH	DRIVER	CAR
1	Darrell Waltrip	Chevrolet
2	Terry Labonte	Chevrolet
3	Geoff Bodine	Chevrolet

4	Dale Earnhardt	Chevrolet
5	Harry Gant	Chevrolet
6	Tim Richmond	Chevrolet
7	Richard Petty	Pontiac
8	Bobby Allison	Buick
9	Bobby Hillin	Buick
10	Alan Kulwicki	Ford
11	Neil Bonnett	Chevrolet
12	Tommy Ellis	Chevrolet
13	Michael Waltrip	Pontiac
14	Rusty Wallace	Pontiac
15	Dave Marcis	Chevrolet
16	Buddy Arrington	Ford
17	Joe Ruttman	Buick
18	Eddie Bierschwale	Oldsmobile
19	Bill Elliott	Ford
20	D.K. Ulrich	Chevrolet
21	Brad Teague	Chevrolet
22	Morgan Shepherd	Pontiac
23	Ricky Rudd	Ford
24	J.D. McDuffie	Pontiac
25	Chet Fillip	Ford
26	Rick Wilson	Oldsmobile
27	Jimmy Means	
28	Ken Schrader	Ford
29	Dale Jarrett	Pontiac
30	Kyle Petty	Ford

SOUTHERN 500

Time of Race: 4 hours, 8 minutes, 45 seconds
Average Speed: 121.068 mph
Margin of Victory: 2 seconds

FINISH	DRIVER	CAR
1	Tim Richmond	Chevrolet
2	Bobby Allison	Buick
3	Bill Elliott	Ford
4	Morgan Shepherd	Buick
5	Darrell Waltrip	Chevrolet
6	Ricky Rudd	Ford
7	Bobby Hillion, Jr.	Buick
8	Geoff Bodine	Chevrolet
9	Dale Earnhardt	Chevrolet
10	Cale Yarborough	Ford
11	Dave Marcis	Chevrolet
12	Alan Kulwicki	Ford
13	Jim Sauter	Pontiac
14	Kyle Petty	Ford
15	Jimmy Means	Pontiac
16	Michael Waltrip	Pontiac
17	H.B. Bailey	Pontiac
18	D.K. Ulrich	Chevrolet
19	Buddy Baker	Oldsmobile
20	Buddy Arrington	Ford
21	Terry Labonte	Chevrolet
22	Phil Parsons	Oldsmobile
23	Rusty Wallace	Pontiac
24	Neil Bonnett	Chevrolet
25	Eddie Bierschwale	Chevrolet
26	Connie Saylor	Ford
27	Harry Gant	Chevrolet
28	Rick Wilson	Oldsmobile
29	Jonathan Edwards	Chevrolet
30	Ron Bouchard	Pontiac
31	Benny Parsons	Oldsmobile
32	Mark Stahl	Ford
33	Donnie Allison	Chevrolet
34	J.D. McDuffie	Pontiac
35	Chet Fillip	Ford
36	Ken Schrader	Ford
37	Sterling Marlin	Chevrolet
38	Joe Ruttman	Buick
39	James Hylton	Chevrolet
40	Richard Petty	Pontiac

WRANGLER JEANS INDIGO 400

Time of Race: 3 hours, 5 minutes, 24 seconds
Average Speed: 70.161 mph
Margin of Victory: 2 car lengths

FINISH	DRIVER	CAR
1	Tim Richmond	Chevrolet
2	Dale Earnhardt	Chevrolet
3	Morgan Shepherd	Pontiac
4	Richard Petty	Pontiac
5	Neil Bonnett	Chevrolet
6	Joe Ruttman	Buick
7	Harry Gant	Chevrolet
8	Bobby Allison	Buick
9	Bill Elliott	Ford
10	Bobby Hillin	Buick
11	Eddie Bierschwale	Chevrolet
12	Buddy Arrington	Ford
13	Geoff Bodine	Chevrolet
14	Michael Waltrip	Pontiac
15	Alan Kulwicki	Ford
16	Jimmy Hensley	Ford
17	D.K. Ulrich	Chevrolet
18	Terry Labonte	Oldsmobile
19	Rusty Wallace	Pontiac
20	Kyle Petty	Ford
21	Tommy Ellis	Chevrolet
22	James Hylton	Chevrolet
23	Dave Marcis	Chevrolet
24	Ricky Rudd	Ford
25	Ken Schrader	Ford
26	Jimmy Means	Pontiac
27	Ron Shepherd	Oldsmobile
28	J.D. McDuffie	Pontiac
29	Darrell Waltrip	Chevrolet

DELAWARE 500

Average Speed: 4 hours, 22 minutes, 24 seconds
Average Speed: 114.329 mph
Margin of Victory: 6 seconds

FINISH	DRIVER	CAR
1	Ricky Rudd	Ford
2	Neil Bonnett	Chevrolet
3	Kyle Petty	Ford
4	Buddy Baker	Oldsmobile
5	Dave Marcis	Chevrolet
6	Joe Ruttman	Buick
7	Alan Kulwicki	Ford
8	Tommy Ellis	Chevrolet
9	Bobby Hillin	Buick
10	Morgan Shepherd	Pontiac
11	Mark Martin	Ford
12	Richard Petty	Pontiac
13	Rusty Wallace	Pontiac
14	Darrell Waltrip	Chevrolet
15	Buddy Arrington	Ford
16	Michael Waltrip	Pontiac
17	Johnny Coy, Jr.	Chevrolet
18	Joe Booher	Chevrolet
19	Terry Labonte	Oldsmobile
20	Bobby Allison	Buick
21	Dale Earnhardt	Chevrolet
22	Ken Schrader	Ford
23	Chet Fillip	Ford
24	Jimmy Means	Pontiac
25	Eddie Bierschwale	Chevrolet
26	Tim Richmond	Chevrolet
27	Bill Elliott	Ford
28	Geoff Boldine	Chevrolet
29	Brian Baker	Ford
30	Howard Rose	Pontiac
31	Cliff Hucul	Pontiac
32	Rick Wilson	Oldsmobile
33	Bobby Wawak	Chevrolet

34	Gary Fedewa	Chevrolet
35	Harry Gant	Chevrolet
36	Jerry Bowman	Ford
37	J.D. McDuffie	Pontiac
38	Roy Lee Hendrick	Ford
39	Tommie Crozier	Pontiac
40	Mike Potter	Ford

23	Michael Waltrip	Pontiac
24	Brent Elliott	Buick
25	Morgan Shepherd	Pontiac
26	J.D. McDuffie	Pontiac
27	Jimmy Means	Pontiac
28	D.K. Ulrich	Chevrolet
29	Trevor Boys	Chevrolet
30	Joe Millikan	Ford

GOODY'S 500

Time of Race: 3 hours, 35 minutes, 32 seconds
Average Speed: 73.191 mph
Margin of Victory: 2 car lengths

FINISH	DRIVER	CAR
1	Rusty Wallace	Pontiac
2	Geoff Bodine	Chevrolet
3	Harry Gant	Chevrolet
4	Darrell Waltrip	Chevrolet
5	Joe Ruttman	Chevrolet
6	Kyle Petty	Ford
7	Ken Schrader	Ford
8	Neil Bonnett	Chevrolet
9	Dave Marcis	Chevrolet
10	Tim Richmond	Chevrolet
11	Bill Elliott	Ford
12	Dale Earnhardt	Chevrolet
13	Alan Kulwicki	Ford
14	Michael Waltrip	Pontiac
15	Terry Labonte	Oldsmobile
16	Richard Petty	Pontiac
17	Bobby Hillin	Buick
18	Jimmy Hensley	Ford
19	Buddy Arrington	Ford
20	J.D. McDuffie	Pontiac
21	Bobby Allison	Buick
22	Jimmy Means	Pontiac
23	Jerry Cranmer	Chevrolet
24	Eddie Bierschwale	Chevrolet
25	Phil Good	Ford
26	Tommy Ellis	Chevrolet
27	D.K. Ulrich	Chevrolet
28	Ricky Rudd	Ford
29	Morgan Shepherd	Pontiac
30	Mike Skinner	Pontiac

HOLLY FARMS 400

Time of Race: 2 hours, 36 minutes, 53 seconds
Average Speed: 95.612 mph
Magin of Victory: 1.21 second

FINISH	DRIVER	CAR
1	Darrell Waltrip	Chevrolet
2	Geoff Bodine	Chevrolet
3	Richard Petty	Pontiac
4	Rusty Wallace	Pontiac
5	Harry Gant	Chevrolet
6	Joe Ruttman	Buick
7	Ricky Rudd	Ford
8	Dave Marcis	Chevrolet
9	Dale Earnhardt	Chevrolet
10	Terry Labonte	Oldsmobile
11	Tim Richmond	Chevrolet
12	Neil Bonnett	Chevrolet
13	Tommy Ellis	Chevrolet
14	Kyle Petty	Ford
15	Bobby Hillin	Buick
16	Bill Elliott	Ford
17	Alan Kulwicki	Ford
18	Ken Schrader	Ford
19	Buddy Arrington	Ford
20	Eddie Bierschwale	Chevrolet
21	Chet Fillip	Ford
22	Bobby Allison	Buick

OAKWOOD HOMES 500

Time of Race: 3 hours, 47 minutes, 2 seconds
Average Speed: 132.403 mph
Margin of Victory: 1.9 seconds

FINISH	DRIVER	CAR
1	Dale Earnhardt	Chevrolet
2	Harry Gant	Chevrolet
3	Neil Bonnett	Chevrolet
4	Ricky Rudd	Ford
5	Buddy Baker	Oldsmobile
6	Geoff Bodine	Chevrolet
7	Bill Elliott	Ford
8	Rusty Wallace	Pontiac
9	Darrell Waltrip	Chevrolet
10	Phil Parsons	Oldsmobile
11	Dave Marcis	Chevrolet
12	Larry Pearson	Chevrolet
13	Kyle Petty	Ford
14	Alan Kulwicki	Ford
15	Terry Labonte	Oldsmobile
16	Rodney Combs	Pontiac
17	Connie Saylor	Ford
18	Jimmy Means	Pontiac
19	Michael Waltrip	Pontiac
20	J.D. McDuffie	Pontiac
21	Ron Bouchard	Pontiac
22	Buddy Arrington	Ford
23	Ken Ragan	Chevrolet
24	Eddie Bierschwale	Oldsmobile
25	Joe Ruttman	Buick
26	Bobby Hillin	Buick
27	Tim Richmond	Chevrolet
28	Ken Schrader	Ford
29	Rick Wilson	Oldsmobile
30	Benny Parsons	Oldsmobile
31	Tommy Ellis	Chevrolet
32	Morgan Shepherd	Pontiac
33	Sterling Marlin	Chevrolet
34	David Sosobee	Chevrolet
35	Richard Petty	Pontiac
36	Cale Yarborough	Ford
37	A.J. Foyt	Oldsmobile
38	Chet Fillip	Ford
39	Delma Cowart	Chevrolet
40	Brad Teague	Chevrolet
41	Bobby Allison	Buick
42	Randy Baker	Chevrolet

NATIONWIDE 500

Time of Race: 3 hours, 57 minutes, 33 seconds
Average Speed: 126.381 mph
Margin of Victory: 2.53 seconds

FINISH	DRIVER	CAR
1	Neil Bonnett	Chevrolet
2	Ricky Rudd	Ford
3	Darrell Waltrip	Chevrolet
4	Harry Gant	Chevrolet
5	Buddy Baker	Oldsmobile
6	Dale Earnhardt	Chevrolet
7	Bill Elliott	Ford
8	Richard Petty	Pontiac
9	Joe Ruttman	Buick

10	Kyle Petty	Ford
11	Bobby Hillin	Buick
12	Alan Kulwicki	Ford
13	Michael Waltrip	Pontiac
14	Ken Schrader	Ford
15	Dick Trickle	Chevrolet
16	Eddie Bierschwale	Oldsmobile
17	Buddy Arrington	Ford
18	Charlie Baker	Chevrolet
19	Rusty Wallace	Pontiac
20	Tim Richmond	Chevrolet
21	J.D. McDuffie	Pontiac
22	Jimmy Means	Pontiac
23	Mike Skinner	Pontiac
24	Morgan Shepherd	Pontiac
25	Bobby Allison	Buick
26	Mike Potter	Ford
27	Jonathan Edwards	Buick
28	Tommie Crozier	Pontiac
29	Bobby Wawak	Chevrolet
30	Mark Stahl	Ford
31	Terry Labonte	Oldsmobile
32	Geoff Bodine	Chevrolet
33	Cale Yarborough	Ford
34	Dave Marcis	Chevrolet
35	Tommy Ellis	Chevrolet
36	Johnny Coy, Jr.	Chevrolet
37	Trevor Boys	Chevrolet
38	Joe Milliken	Ford
39	Buddie Boys	Chevrolet
40	Ronnie Thomas	Pontiac

ATLANTA JOURNAL 500

Time of Race: 3 hours, 15 minutes, 22 seconds
Average Speed: 152.523 mph
Margin of Victory: 1 lap, 3 seconds

FINISH	DRIVER	CAR
1	Dale Earnhardt	Chevrolet
2	Richard Petty	Pontiac
3	Bill Elliott	Ford
4	Tim Richmond	Chevrolet
5	Buddy Baker	Oldsmobile
6	Neil Bonnett	Chevrolet
7	Kyle Petty	Ford
8	Terry Labonte	Oldsmobile
9	Joe Ruttman	Buick
10	Phil Parsons	Oldsmobile
11	Benny Parsons	Oldsmobile
12	Tommy Ellis	Chevrolet
13	Rusty Wallace	Pontiac
14	Rick Wilson	Oldsmobile
15	Bobby Hillin	Buick
16	Bobby Allison	Buick
17	Ken Schrader	Ford
18	Alan Kulwicki	Ford
19	Ken Ragan	Chevrolet
20	Michael Waltrip	Pontiac
21	Buddy Arrington	Ford
22	Randy Baker	Chevrolet
23	Eddie Bierschwale	Oldsmobile
24	Mike Laws	Chevrolet
25	Ricky Rudd	Ford
26	Mark Martin	Ford
27	Morgan Shepherd	Pontiac
28	Harry Gant	Chevrolet
29	Jimmy Means	Pontiac
30	Connie Saylor	Ford
31	Jeff Swindell	Chevrolet
32	Sterling Marlin	Chevrolet
33	Dave Marcis	Chevrolet
34	Cale Yarborough	Ford
35	Bobby Gerhart	Chevrolet
36	David Sosebee	Chevrolet
37	Rodney Combs	Chevrolet
38	Geoff Bodine	Chevrolet
39	Darrell Waltrip	Chevrolet
40	Tom Bigelow	Chevrolet
41	H.B. Bailey	Chevrolet
42	Ron Bouchard	Pontiac

WINSTON WESTERN 500

Time of Race: 3 hours, 4 minutes, 46 seconds
Average Speed: 101.246 mph
Margin of Victory: 1 second

FINISH	DRIVER	CAR
1	Tim Richmond	Chevrolet
2	Dale Earnhardt	Chevrolet
3	Geoff Bodine	Chevrolet
4	Darrell Waltrip	Chevrolet
5	Joe Ruttman	Buick
6	Bobby Hillin	Buick
7	Bobby Allison	Buick
8	Rusty Wallace	Pontiac
9	Neil Bonnett	Chevrolet
10	Terry Labonte	Oldsmobile
11	Ken Schrader	Ford
12	Dave Marcis	Chevrolet
13	Mark Martin	Ford
14	Bill Schmitt	Chevrolet
15	Kyle Petty	Ford
16	Glen Steurer	Chevrolet
17	Jimmy Means	Pontiac
18	Buddy Arrington	Ford
19	Ricky Rudd	Ford
20	Al Unser, Sr.	Pontiac
21	Richard Petty	Pontiac
22	Ruben Garcia	Chevrolet
23	Bill Elliott	Ford
24	Alan Kulwicki	Ford
25	Jim Robinson	Oldsmobile
26	Hershel McGriff	Pontiac
27	Benny Parsons	Oldsmobile
28	Rick McCray	Ford
29	Buddy Baker	Oldsmobile
30	Ted Kennedy	Chevrolet
31	Michael Waltrip	Pontiac
32	Jim Bown	Chevrolet
33	Ron Esau	Oldsmobile
34	Terry Petris	Chevrolet
35	Chad Little	Ford
36	George Follmer	Chevrolet
37	Harry Gant	Chevrolet
38	Morgan Shepherd	Pontiac
39	Jim Fitzgerald	Chevrolet
40	Rick Wilson	Oldsmobile
41	Derrike Cope	Ford
42	John Krebs	Oldsmobile

1987

DAYTONA 500

Time of Race: 2 hours, 50 minutes, 12 seconds
Average Speed: 176.263 mph
Margin of Victory: 3 Car lengths

FINISH	DRIVER	CAR
1	Bill Elliott	Ford
2	Benny Parsons	Chevrolet
3	Richard Petty	Pontiac
4	Buddy Baker	Oldsmobile
5	Dale Earnhardt	Chevrolet
6	Bobby Allison	Buick
7	Ken Schrader	Ford
8	Darrell Waltrip	Chevrolet
9	Ricky Rudd	Ford
10	Cale Yarborough	Oldsmobile
11	Phil Parsons	Oldsmobile

12	Neil Bonnett	Pontiac
13	Bobby Hillin	Buick
14	Geoff Bodine	Chevrolet
15	Alan Kulwicki	Ford
16	Morgan Shepherd	Buick
17	Ken Ragan	Ford
18	Terry Labonte	Chevrolet
19	Rodney Combs	Oldsmobile
20	Greg Sacks	Pontiac
21	Ronnie Sanders	Ford
22	Michael Waltrip	Chevrolet
23	Trevor Boys	Chevrolet
24	Jimmy Means	Pontiac
25	J. D. McDuffie	Pontiac
26	Lake Speed	Oldsmobilre
27	Davey Allison	Ford
28	David Sosebee	Chevrolet
29	Tom Sneva	Oldsmobile
30	Sterling Marlin	Oldsmobile
31	Harry Gant	Chevrolet
32	Ron Bouchard	Chevrolet
33	Derrike Cope	Ford
34	Dave Marcis	Chevrolet
35	Kyle Petty	Ford
36	Eddie Bierschwale	Ford
37	Rick Wilson	Oldsmobile
38	Mark Stahl	Ford
39	Chet Fillip	Ford
40	Connie Saylor	Ford
41	Rusty Wallace	Pontiac
42	A. J. Foyt	Oldsmobile

GOODWRENCH 500

Time of Race: 4 hours, 15 minutes, 23 seconds
Average Speed: 117.556 mph
Margin of Victory: 11 seconds

FINISH	DRIVER	CAR
1	Dale Earnhardt	Chevrolet
2	Ricky Rudd	Ford
3	Neil Bonnett	Pontiac
4	Bill Elliott	Ford
5	Morgan Shepherd	Buick
6	Rusty Wallace	Pontiac
7	Darrell Waltrip	Chevrolet
8	Terry Labonte	Chevrolet
9	Davey Allison	Ford
10	Ken Schrader	Ford
11	Phil Parsons	Oldsmobile
12	Lake Speed	Oldsmobile
13	Bobby Allison	Buick
14	Bobby Hillin	Buick
15	Richard Petty	Pontiac
16	Kyle Petty	Ford
17	Michael Waltrip	Chevrolet
18	Eddie Bierschwale	Ford
19	Sterling Marlin	Oldsmobile
20	J. D. McDuffie	Pontiac
21	Charlie Baker	Chevrolet
22	Jimmy Means	Pontiac
23	Jerry Cranmer	Ford
24	Chet Fillip	Ford
25	Alan Kulwicki	Ford
26	D. K. Ulrich	Chevrolet
27	Bobby Wawak	Chevrolet
28	Cale Yarborough	Oldsmobile
29	Harry Gant	Chevrolet
30	Greg Sacks	Pontiac
31	Buddy Baker	Oldsmobile
32	Geoff Bodine	Chevrolet
33	Mark Stahl	Ford
34	Benny Parsons	Chevrolet
35	Dave Marcis	Chevrolet
36	Ron Bouchard	Chevrolet
37	James Hylton	Chevrolet
38	Tommy Ellis	Chevrolet
39	David Sosebee	Chevrolet
40	Patrick Latimer	Chevrolet
41	Jesse Samples, Jr.	Chevrolet
42	Jerry Holden	Chevrolet

MILLER HIGH LIFE 400

Time of Race: 2 hours, 39 minutes, 34 seconds
Average Speed: 81.520 mph
Margin of Victory: 46 seconds

FINISH	DRIVER	CAR
1	Dale Earnhardt	Chevrolet
2	Geoff Bodine	Chevrolet
3	Rusty Wallace	Pontiac
4	Bill Elliott	Ford
5	Terrry Labonte	Chevrolet
6	Alan Kulwicki	Ford
7	Kyle Petty	Ford
8	Dave Marcis	Chevrolet
9	Bobby Allison	Buick
10	Benny Parsons	Chevrolet
11	Bobby Hillin	Buick
12	Michael Waltrip	Chevrolet
13	Ken Schrader	Ford
14	Jimmy Means	Pontiac
15	Phil Parsons	Oldsmobile
16	J. D. McDuffie	Pontiac
17	Buddy Arrington	Ford
18	Eddie Bierschwale	Ford
19	Slick Johnson	Oldsmobile
20	Darrell Waltrip	Chevrolet
21	Sterling Marlin	Oldsmobile
22	Neil Bonnett	Pontiac
23	Richard Petty	Pontiac
24	Jerry Cranmer	Ford
25	Harry Gant	Chevrolet
26	Davey Allison	Ford
27	Tommy Ellis	Chevrolet
28	Ricky Rudd	Ford
29	Steve Christman	Pontiac
30	D. K. Ulrich	Chevrolet
31	Morgan Shepherd	Buick
32	Bobby Wawak	Chevrolet

MOTORCRAFT QUALITY PARTS 500

Time of Race: 3 hours, 44 minutes, 2 seconds
Average Speed: 133.689 mph
Margin of Victory: 41 seconds

FINISH	DRIVER	CAR
1	Ricky Rudd	Ford
2	Benny Parsons	Chevrolet
3	Rusty Wallace	Pontiac
4	Terry Labonte	Chevrolet
5	Davey Allison	Ford
6	Darrell Waltrip	Chevrolet
7	Neil Bonnett	Pontiac
8	Cale Yarborough	Oldsmobile
9	Kyle Petty	Ford
10	Morgan Shepherd	Buick
11	Rick Wilson	Oldsmobile
12	Ron Bouchard	Chevrolet
13	Sterling Marlin	Oldsmobile
14	Richard Petty	Pontiac
15	Geoff Bodine	Chevrolet
16	Dale Earnhardt	Chevrolet
17	Tommy Ellis	Chevrolet
18	H. B. Bailey	Pontiac
19	Bobby Allison	Buick
20	A. J. Foyt	Oldsmobile
21	David Sosebee	Oldsmobile
22	Steve Christman	Pontiac
23	D. K. Ulrich	Chevrolet
24	Bobby Hillin	Buick
25	Mike Potter	Chevrolet
26	Ken Ragan	Ford
27	Phil Parsons	Oldsmobile
28	Bill Elliott	Ford
29	Ken Schrader	Ford
30	Mark Stahl	Ford

31	Dave Marcis	Chevrolet
32	Jimmy Means	Pontiac
33	Alan Kulwicki	Ford
34	Harry Gant	Chevrolet
35	Lake Speed	Oldsmobile
36	Derrike Cope	Ford
37	Greg Sacks	Pontiac
38	Buddy Baker	Oldsmobile
39	Michael Waltrip	Chevrolet
40	J. D. McDuffie	Pontiac
41	Connie Saylor	Ford

VALLEYDALE MEATS 500

Time of Race: 3 hours, 31 minutes, 27 seconds
Average Speed: 75.621 mph
Margin of Victory: .78 seconds

FINISH	DRIVER	CAR
1	Dale Earnhardt	Chevrolet
2	Richard Petty	Pontiac
3	Ricky Rudd	Ford
4	Bill Elliott	Ford
5	Alan Kulwicki	Ford
6	Harry Gant	Chevrolet
7	Kyle Petty	Ford
8	Morgan Shepherd	Buick
9	Terry Labonte	Chevrolet
10	Dale Jarrett	Chevrolet
11	Neil Bonnett	Pontiac
12	Darrell Waltrip	Chevrolet
13	Michael Waltrip	Pontiac
14	Slick Johnson	Chevrolet
15	D. K. Ulrich	Chevrolet
16	Rusty Wallace	Pontiac
17	Ken Schrader	Ford
18	Mike Potter	Ford
19	Geoff Bodine	Chevrolet
20	Phil Parsons	Oldsmobile
21	J. D. McDuffie	Pontiac
22	Jerry Cranmer	Ford
23	Bobby Allison	Buick
24	Sterling Marlin	Oldsmobile
25	Eddie Bierschwale	Ford
26	Bobby Hillin	Buick
27	Dave Marcis	Chevrolet
28	Benny Parsons	Chevrolet
29	Jimmy Means	Pontiac
30	Ronnie Thomas	Chevrolet

SOVRAN BANK 500

Time of Race: 3 hours, 36 minutes, 44 seconds
Average Speed: 72.808 mph
Margin of Victory: 2.73 seconds

FINISH	DRIVER	CAR
1	Dale Earnhardt	Chevrolet
2	Rusty Wallace	Pontiac
3	Geoff Bodine	Chevrolet
4	Phil Parsons	Oldsmobile
5	Terry Labonte	Chevrolet
6	Bill Elliott	Ford
7	Ken Schrader	Ford
8	Bobby Allison	Buick
9	Neil Bonnett	Pontiac
10	Michael Waltrip	Chevrolet
11	Buddy Arrington	Ford
12	Kyle Petty	Ford
13	Derrike Cope	Chevrolet
14	Jimmy Means	Pontiac
15	Bobby Hillin	Buick
16	Ricky Rudd	Ford
17	Morgan Shepherd	Buick
18	Tony Spanos	Chevrolet
19	Sterling Marlin	Oldsmobile
20	Jerry Cranmer	Ford

21	Darrell Waltrip	Chevrolet
22	Richard Petty	Pontiac
23	Dave Marcis	Chevrolet
24	Eddie Bierschwale	Ford
25	Steve Christman	Pontiac
26	Benny Parsons	Chevrolet
27	Harry Gant	Chevrolet
28	Alan Kulwicki	Ford
29	Dale Jarrett	Chevrolet
30	Slick Johnson	Oldsmobile
31	J. D. McDuffie	Pontiac

TRANSOUTH 500

Time of Race: 4 hours, 5 minutes, 28 seconds
Average Speed: 122.540 mph
Margin of Victory: 3 seconds

FINISH	DRIVER	CAR
1	Dale Earnhardt	Chevrolet
2	Bill Elliott	Ford
3	Richard Petty	Pontiac
4	Sterling Marlin	Oldsmobile
5	Ken Schrader	Ford
6	Neil Bonnett	Pontiac
7	Harry Gant	Chevrolet
8	Ron Bouchard	Chevrolet
9	Phil Parsons	Oldsmobile
10	Darrell Waltrip	Chevrolet
11	Geoff Bodine	Chevrolet
12	Slick Johnson	Chevrolet
13	Kyle Petty	Ford
14	Alan Kulwicki	Ford
15	Cale Yarborough	Oldsmobile
16	Eddie Bierschwale	Ford
17	H. B. Bailey	Pontiac
18	D. K. Ulrich	Chevrolet
19	Michael Waltrip	Chevrolet
20	Rusty Wallace	Pontiac
21	Benny Parsons	Chevrolet
22	Morgan Shepherd	Buick
23	Bobby Hillin	Buick
24	Connie Saylor	Ford
25	Buddy Baker	Oldsmobile
26	Greg Sacks	Pontiac
27	Davey Allison	Ford
28	Bobby Allison	Buick
29	Bobby Wawak	Chevrolet
30	Ricky Rudd	Ford
31	Lake Speed	Oldsmobile
32	Terry Labonte	Chevrolet
33	Dave Marcis	Chevrolet
34	Rick Wilson	Oldsmobile
35	Jonathan Edwards	Chevrolet
36	Jimmy Means	Pontiac
37	Rodney Combs	Chevrolet
38	James Hylton	Chevrolet
39	Steve Christman	Pontiac
40	Tommy Ellis	Chevrolet
41	J. D. McDuffie	Pontiac

FIRST UNION 400

Time of Race: 2 hours, 39 minutes, 24 seconds
Average Speed: 94.103 mph
Margin of Victory: 1.2 seconds

FINISH	DRIVER	CAR
1	Dale Earnhardt	Chevrolet
2	Kyle Petty	Ford
3	Neil Bonnett	Pontiac
4	Alan Kulwicki	Ford
5	Ricky Rudd	Ford
6	Richard Petty	Pontiac
7	Phil Parsons	Oldsmobile
8	Terry Labonte	Chevrolet
9	Rusty Wallace	Pontiac

10	Bill Elliott	Ford
11	Harry Gant	Chevrolet
12	Dale Jarrett	Chevrolet
13	Bobby Hillin	Buick
14	Bobby Allison	Buick
15	Benny Parsons	Chevrolet
16	Ken Schrader	Ford
17	Sterling Marlin	Oldsmobile
18	Eddie Bierschwale	Ford
19	Slick Johnson	Oldsmobile
20	Rodney Combs	Chevrolet
21	Darrell Waltrip	Chevrolet
22	Jerry Cranmer	Ford
23	Bobby Baker	Chevrolet
24	Michael Waltrip	Chevrolet
25	Larry Pearson	Chevrolet
26	Dave Marcis	Chevrolet
27	Morgan Shepherd	Buick
28	Geoff Bodine	Chevrolet
29	Jesse Samples, Jr.	Chevrolet
30	Jimmy Means	Pontiac
31	Steve Christman	Pontiac
32	J. D. McDuffie	Pontiac

WINSTON 500

Time of Race: 3 hours, 4 minutes, 12 seconds
Average Speed: 154.228 mph
Margin of Victory: .78 seconds

FINISH	DRIVER	CAR
1	Davey Allison	Ford
2	Terry Labonte	Chevrolet
3	Kyle Petty	Ford
4	Dale Earnhardt	Chevrolet
5	Bobby Hillin	Buick
6	Rusty Wallace	Pontiac
7	Neil Bonnett	Pontiac
8	Ken Schrader	Ford
9	Lake Speed	Oldsmobile
10	Morgan Shepherd	Buick
11	Darrell Waltrip	Chevrolet
12	Benny Parsons	Chevrolet
13	Dave Marcis	Chevrolet
14	Sterling Marlin	Oldsmobile
15	Slick Johnson	Chevrolet
16	Richard Petty	Pontiac
17	Mark Stahl	Ford
18	Eddie Bierschwale	Ford
19	Steve Christman	Pontiac
20	Rick Wilson	Oldsmobile
21	Ken Ragan	Ford
22	Bill Elliott	Ford
23	Connie Saylor	Ford
24	Rick Knoop	Chevrolet
25	Michael Waltrip	Chevrolet
26	Greg Sacks	Pontiac
27	Ed Pimm	Buick
28	Dale Jarrett	Chevrolet
29	Harry Gant	Chevrolet
30	Ricky Rudd	Ford
31	Phil Parsons	Oldsmobile
32	Buddy Baker	Oldsmobile
33	Jimmy Means	Pontiac
34	Alan Kulwicki	Ford
35	Phil Barkdoll	Chevrolet
36	Joe Ruttman	Chevrolet
37	Cale Yarborough	Oldsmobile
38	Ron Bouchard	Buick
39	Bobby Allison	Buick
40	Geoff Bodine	Chevrolet
41	Chet Fillip	Ford

COCA-COLA 600

Time of Race: 4 hours, 33 minutes, 48 seconds
Average Speed: 131.483 mph
Margin of Victory: 33.53 seconds

FINISH	DRIVER	CAR
1	Kyle Petty	Ford
2	Morgan Shepherd	Buick
3	Lake Speed	Oldsmobile
4	Richard Petty	Pontiac
5	Darrell Waltrip	Chevrolet
6	Terry Labonte	Chevrolet
7	Buddy Baker	Oldsmobile
8	Phil Parsons	Oldsmobile
9	Jim Sauter	Pontiac
10	Rusty Wallace	Pontiac
11	Michael Waltrip	Chevrolet
12	Buddy Arrington	Ford
13	Neil Bonnett	Pontiac
14	Dave Marcis	Chevrolet
15	Jimmy Means	Pontiac
16	Davey Allison	Ford
17	Randy Baker	Chevrolet
18	Geoff Bodine	Chevrolet
19	Bobby Wawak	Chevrolet
20	Dale Earnhardt	Chevrolet
21	Brett Bodine	Chevrolet
22	Bobby Allison	Buick
23	Bill Elliott	Ford
24	Harry Gant	Chevrolet
25	Ricky Rudd	Ford
26	Benny Parsons	Chevrolet
27	Alan Kulwicki	Ford
28	Eddie Bierschwale	Ford
29	Ken Schrader	Ford
30	Rick Wilson	Oldsmobile
31	Larry Pearson	Chevrolet
32	Sterling Marlin	Oldsmobile
33	Connie Saylor	Chevrolet
34	Bobby Hillin	Buick
35	Allan Grice	Oldsmobile
36	Greg Sacks	Pontiac
37	Derrike Cope	Ford
38	Dale Jarrett	Chevrolet
39	Mark Martin	Oldsmobile
40	Brad Teague	Chevrolet
41	Steve Christman	Pontiac
42	Cale Yarborough	Oldsmobile

BUDWEISER 500

Time of Race: 4 hours, 25 minutes, 35 seconds
Average Speed: 112.958 mph
Margin of Victory: 7 seconds

FINISH	DRIVER	CAR
1	Davey Allison	Ford
2	Bill Elliott	Ford
3	Terry Labonte	Chevrolet
4	Dale Earnhardt	Chevrolet
5	Benny Parsons	Chevrolet
6	Ken Schrader	Ford
7	Darrell Waltrip	Chevrolet
8	Dave Marcis	Chevrolet
9	Neil Bonnett	Pontiac
10	Sterling Marlin	Oldsmobile
11	Buddy Baker	Oldsmobile
12	Ricky Rudd	Ford
13	Jimmy Means	Pontiac
14	Brett Bodine	Chevrolet
15	Alan Kulwicki	Ford
16	Larry Pollard	Chevrolet
17	Rusty Wallace	Pontiac
18	Buddy Arrington	Ford
19	Charles Rudolph	Chevrolet
20	Rodney Combs	Ford
21	Michael Waltrip	Chevrolet
22	Phil Parsons	Oldsmobile
23	J. D. McDuffie	Pontiac
24	Kyle Petty	Ford
25	Bobby Allison	Buick
26	Bobby Hillin	Buick
27	Gary Fedewa	Chevrolet

28	Geoff Bodine	Chevrolet
29	Rick Wilson	Oldsmobile
30	Harry Gant	Chevrolet
31	Jerry Bowman	Ford
32	Morgan Shepherd	Buick
33	Mike Potter	Ford
34	D. K. Ulrich	Chevrolet
35	Dale Jarrett	Chevrolet
36	Richard Petty	Pontiac
37	Steve Christman	Pontiac
38	Curtis Markham	Ford
39	Ron Shephard	Chevrolet

MILLER HIGH LIFE 500

Time of Race: 4 hours, 5 minutes, 57 seconds
Average Speed: 122.166 mph
Margin of Victory: 1 second

FINISH	DRIVER	CAR
1	Tim Richmond	Chevrolet
2	Bill Elliott	Ford
3	Kyle Petty	Ford
4	Cale Yarborough	Oldsmobile
5	Dale Earnhardt	Chevrolet
6	Bobby Allison	Buick
7	Ricky Rudd	Ford
8	Neil Bonnett	Pontiac
9	Geoff Bodine	Chevrolet
10	Buddy Baker	Oldsmobile
11	Phil Parsons	Oldsmobile
12	Davey Allison	Ford
13	Darrell Waltrip	Chevrolet
14	Bobby Hillin	Buick
15	Sterling Marlin	Oldsmobile
16	Michael Waltrip	Chevrolet
17	Ken Schrader	Ford
18	Trevor Boys	Chevrolet
19	Jimmy Means	Pontiac
20	Rodney Combs	Ford
21	Jimmy Horton	Ford
22	Charles Rudolph	Chevrolet
23	Jim Bown	Chevrolet
24	Bobby Wawak	Chevrolet
25	Buddy Arrington	Ford
26	Steve Christman	Pontiac
27	Dave Marcis	Chevrolet
28	J. D. McDuffie	Pontiac
29	Richard Petty	Pontiac
30	Alan Kulwicki	Ford
31	Morgan Shepherd	Buick
32	Harry Gant	Chevrolet
33	Benny Parsons	Chevrolet
34	Brett Bodine	Chevrolet
35	Dale Jarrett	Chevrolet
36	Greg Sacks	Pontiac
37	Terry Labonte	Chevrolet
38	Derrike Cope	Chevrolet
39	Bobby Gerhart	Chevrolet
40	Rusty Wallace	Pontiac

BUDWEISER 400

Time of Race: 2 hours, 26 minutes, 9 seconds
Average Speed: 102.183 mph
Margin of Victory: 1.5 seconds

FINISH	DRIVER	CAR
1	Tim Richmond	Chevrolet
2	Ricky Rudd	Ford
3	Neil Bonnett	Pontiac
4	Terry Labonte	Chevrolet
5	Bill Elliott	Ford
6	Richard Petty	Pontiac
7	Dale Earnhardt	Chevrolet
8	Bobby Allison	Buick

9	Sterling Marlin	Oldsmobile
10	Ken Schrader	Ford
11	Phil Parsons	Oldsmobile
12	Hershel McGriff	Pontiac
13	Bobby Hillin	Buick
14	Rick Wilson	Oldsmobile
15	Chad Little	Ford
16	Dave Marcis	Chevrolet
17	Jim Fitzgerald	Chevrolet
18	Dale Jarrett	Chevrolet
19	Ruben Garcia	Chevrolet
20	Harry Goularte	Chevrolet
21	Chet Fillip	Ford
22	Ron Esau	Chevrolet
23	Jimmy Means	Pontiac
24	Kyle Petty	Ford
25	Harry Gant	Chevrolet
26	Rick McCray	Ford
27	Geoff Bodine	Chevrolet
28	Alan Kulwicki	Ford
29	John Krebs	Oldsmobile
30	Darrell Waltrip	Chevrolet
31	Jim Bown	Oldsmobile
32	Michael Waltrip	Chevrolet
33	Bill Schmitt	Chevrolet
34	Benny Parsons	Chevrolet
35	Morgan Shepherd	Buick
36	Jim Robinson	Oldsmobile
37	J. D. McDuffie	Pontiac
38	Brett Bodine	Chevrolet
39	Roy Smith	Ford
40	George Follmer	Chevrolet
41	Rusty Wallace	Pontiac

MILLER AMERICAN 400

Time of Race: 2 hours, 41 minutes, 40 seconds
Average Speed: 148.454 mph
Margin of Victory: 1 second

FINISH	DRIVER	CAR
1	Dale Earnhardt	Chevrolet
2	Davey Allison	Ford
3	Kyle Petty	Ford
4	Tim Richmond	Chevrolet
5	Rusty Wallace	Pontiac
6	Bobby Hillin	Buick
7	Darrell Waltrip	Chevrolet
8	Ken Schrader	Ford
9	Benny Parsons	Chevrolet
10	Lake Speed	Oldsmobile
11	Geoff Bodine	Chevrolet
12	Richard Petty	Pontiac
13	Harry Gant	Chevrolet
14	Ricky Rudd	Ford
15	Dave Marcis	Chevrolet
16	Buddy Baker	Oldsmobile
17	Neil Bonnett	Chevrolet
18	Sterling Marlin	Chevrolet
19	Eddie Bierschwale	Ford
20	Dale Jarrett	Chevrolet
21	Phil Parsons	Oldsmobile
22	Brett Bodine	Chevrolet
23	Rodney Combs	Ford
24	Jim Sauter	Pontiac
25	Morgan Shepherd	Buick
26	Dave Simko	Chevrolet
27	Bobby Allison	Buick
28	Terry Labonte	Chevrolet
29	Greg Sacks	Pontiac
30	Rick Wilson	Oldsmobile
31	Alan Kulwicki	Ford
32	Ken Bouchard	Chevrolet
33	Cale Yarborough	Oldsmobile
34	Bill Elliott	Ford
35	Don Paul	Chevrolet
36	Butch Miller	Chevrolet
37	Buddy Arrington	Ford
38	Connie Saylor	Chevrolet
39	Michael Waltrip	Chevrolet
40	H. B. Bailey	Pontiac

PEPSI FIRECRACKER 400

Time of Race: 2 hours, 29 minutes, 0 seconds
Average Speed: 161.074 mph
Margin of Victory: 4 seconds

FINISH	DRIVER	CAR
1	Bobby Allison	Buick
2	Buddy Baker	Oldsmobile
3	Dave Marcis	Chevrolet
4	Darrell Waltrip	Chevrolet
5	Morgan Shepherd	Buick
6	Dale Earnhardt	Chevrolet
7	Ken Schrader	Ford
8	Rusty Wallace	Pontiac
9	Harry Gant	Chevrolet
10	Terry Labonte	Chevrolet
11	Brett Bodine	Buick
12	Bill Elliott	Ford
13	Bobby Hillin	Buick
14	Ricky Rudd	Ford
15	Phil Parsons	Oldsmobile
16	Sterling Marlin	Oldsmobile
17	Kyle Petty	Ford
18	Neil Bonnett	Pontiac
19	Michael Waltrip	Chevrolet
20	Davey Allison	Ford
21	Chet Fillip	Ford
22	Tim Richmond	Chevrolet
23	Dale Jarrett	Chevrolet
24	Cale Yarborough	Oldsmobile
25	Greg Sacks	Pontiac
26	Richard Petty	Pontiac
27	Larry Pollard	Chevrolet
28	Buddy Arrington	Ford
29	Jimmy Means	Chevrolet
30	Rick Wilson	Oldsmobile
31	Rodney Combs	Ford
32	Alan Kulwicki	Ford
33	Eddie Bierschwale	Ford
34	Ed Pimm	Buick
35	Benny Parsons	Chevrolet
36	Dave Pletcher	Ford
37	Mark Stahl	Ford
38	A. J. Foyt	Oldsmobile
39	Geoff Bodine	Chevrolet
40	Lake Speed	Oldsmobile
41	Brad Teague	Chevrolet

SUMMER 500

Time of Race: 4 hours, 6 minutes, 25 seconds
Average Speed: 121.745 mph
Margin of Victory: 1 second

FINISH	DRIVER	CAR
1	Dale Earnhardt	Chevrolet
2	Alan Kulwicki	Ford
3	Buddy Baker	Oldsmobile
4	Benny Parsons	Chevrolet
5	Davey Allison	Ford
6	Terry Labonte	Chevrolet
7	Neil Bonnett	Pontiac
8	Richard Petty	Pontiac
9	Dave Marcis	Chevrolet
10	Ken Schrader	Ford
11	Trevor Boys	Chevrolet
12	Dale Jarrett	Chevrolet
13	Charles Rudolph	Chevrolet
14	Rusty Wallace	Pontiac
15	Bobby Hillin	Buick
16	Rodney Combs	Ford
17	Buddy Arrington	Ford
18	Connie Saylor	Chevrolet
19	Darrell Waltrip	Chevrolet
20	Kyle Petty	Ford
21	Ronnie Shephard	Chevrolet
22	Brett Bodine	Chevrolet

FINISH	DRIVER	CAR
23	Steve Christman	Pontiac
24	Jocko Maggiacomo	Chevrolet
25	Sterling Marlin	Oldsmobile
26	Ricky Rudd	Ford
27	Bobby Allison	Buick
28	Bobby Gerhart	Chevrolet
29	Tim Richmond	Chevrolet
30	Harry Gant	Chevrolet
31	Derrike Cope	Chevrolet
32	Bill Elliott	Ford
33	Jimmy Horton	Ford
34	Geoff Bodine	Chevrolet
35	Greg Sacks	Pontiac
36	Morgan Shepherd	Buick
37	Michael Waltrip	Chevrolet
38	Jimmy Means	Chevrolet
39	Phil Parsons	Oldsmobile
40	Rick Wilson	Oldsmobile

TALLADEGA 500

Time of Race: 2 hours, 55 minutes, 10 seconds
Average Speed: 171.293 mph
Margin of Victory: 15 seconds

FINISH	DRIVER	CAR
1	Bill Elliott	Ford
2	Davey Allison	Ford
3	Dale Earnhardt	Chevrolet
4	Darrell Waltrip	Chevrolet
5	Cale Yarborough	Oldsmobile
6	Terry Labonte	Chevrolet
7	Lake Speed	Oldsmobile
8	Rusty Wallace	Pontiac
9	Kyle Petty	Ford
10	Buddy Baker	Oldsmobile
11	Tim Richmond	Chevrolet
12	Bobby Allison	Buick
13	Geoff Bodine	Chevrolet
14	Sterling Marlin	Oldsmobile
15	Ricky Rudd	Ford
16	Rick Wilson	Oldsmobile
17	Michael Waltrip	Chevrolet
18	Ken Schrader	Ford
19	Rodney Combs	Ford
20	Chet Fillip	Ford
21	Dale Jarrett	Chevrolet
22	Dave Marcis	Chevrolet
23	Alan Kulwicki	Ford
24	Delma Cowart	Chevrolet
25	J. D. McDuffie	Pontiac
26	Steve Christman	Pontiac
27	Dave Pletcher	Ford
28	Jerry Holden	Chevrolet
29	Phil Parsons	Oldsmobile
30	Benny Parsons	Oldsmobile
31	Harry Gant	Chevrolet
32	Neil Bonnett	Pontiac
33	Mark Stahl	Ford
34	Jeff Swindell	Chevrolet
35	A. J. Foyt	Oldsmobile
36	Jimmy Means	Chevrolet
37	Richard Petty	Pontiac
38	Brett Bodine	Chevrolet
39	Morgan Shepherd	Buick
40	Bobby Hillin	Buick

THE BUDWEISER AT THE GLEN

Time of Race: 2 hours, 24 minutes, 36 seconds
Average Speed: 90.682 mph
Margin of Victory: 12 seconds

FINISH	DRIVER	CAR
1	Rusty Wallace	Pontiac
2	Terry Labonte	Chevrolet
3	Dave Marcis	Chevrolet

4	Ricky Rudd	Ford
5	Benny Parsons	Chevrolet
6	Alan Kulwicki	Ford
7	Phil Parsons	Oldsmobile
8	Dale Earnhardt	Chevrolet
9	Bobby Allison	Buick
10	Tim Richmond	Chevrolet
11	Darrell Waltrip	Chevrolet
12	Kyle Petty	Ford
13	Buddy Baker	Oldsmobile
14	Richard Petty	Pontiac
15	Geoff Bodine	Chevrolet
16	Michael Waltrip	Chevrolet
17	Davey Allison	Ford
18	Harry Gant	Chevrolet
19	Jimmy Means	Pontiac
20	Buddy Arrington	Ford
21	Rick Wilson	Oldsmobile
22	Morgan Shepherd	Buick
23	Rodney Combs	Ford
24	J. D. McDuffie	Pontiac
25	Rick Knoop	Chevrolet
26	Tom Rotsell	Ford
27	Ken Schrader	Ford
28	Bill Elliott	Ford
29	Bobby Hillin	Buick
30	Mike Potter	Ford
31	Derrike Cope	Chevrolet
32	Sterling Marlin	Oldsmobile
33	Patty Moise	Chevrolet
34	Steve Christman	Pontiac
35	Jocko Maggiacomo	Chevrolet
36	Dale Jarrett	Chevrolet
37	Neil Bonnett	Pontiac
38	Trevor Boys	Chevrolet
39	Phil Good	Ford
40	Chuck Schroedel	Pontiac

CHAMPION SPARK PLUG 400

Time of Race: 2 hours, 53 minutes, 6 seconds
Average Speed: 138.648 mph
Margin of Victory: 76 seconds

FINISH	DRIVER	CAR
1	Bill Elliott	Ford
2	Dale Earnhardt	Chevrolet
3	Morgan Shepherd	Buick
4	Rusty Wallace	Pontiac
5	Davey Allison	Ford
6	Alan Kulwicki	Ford
7	Bobby Allison	Buick
8	Buddy Baker	Oldsmobile
9	Neil Bonnett	Pontiac
10	Geoff Bodine	Chevrolet
11	Richard Petty	Pontiac
12	Rick Wilson	Oldsmobile
13	Bobby Hillin	Buick
14	Phil Parsons	Oldsmobile
15	Sterling Marlin	Oldsmobile
16	Lake Speed	Oldsmobile
17	Darrell Waltrip	Chevrolet
18	Benny Parsons	Chevrolet
19	Greg Sacks	Pontiac
20	Michael Waltrip	Chevrolet
21	Brett Bodine	Chevrolet
22	J. D. McDuffie	Pontiac
23	Buddy Arrington	Ford
24	Jim Sauter	Pontiac
25	Ricky Rudd	Ford
26	Harry Gant	Chevrolet
27	Kyle Petty	Ford
28	Dave Simko	Chevrolet
29	Tim Richmond	Chevrolet
30	Ken Ragan	Ford
31	Rodney Combs	Ford
32	Bobby Wawak	Chevrolet
33	Terry Labonte	Chevrolet
34	Ken Schrader	Ford
35	Dave Marcis	Chevrolet
36	Charlie Rudolph	Chevrolet

37	Jimmy Means	Chevrolet
38	Derrike Cope	Ford
39	Dale Jarrett	Chevrolet
40	Cale Yarborough	Oldsmobile

BUSCH 500

Time of Race: 2 hours, 56 minutes, 56 seconds
Average Speed: 90.373 mph
Margin of Victory: 5.50 seconds

FINISH	DRIVER	CAR
1	Dale Earnhardt	Chevrolet
2	Rusty Wallace	Pontiac
3	Ricky Rudd	Ford
4	Terry Labonte	Chevrolet
5	Richard Petty	Pontiac
6	Geoff Bodine	Chevrolet
7	Rick Wilson	Oldsmobile
8	Harry Gant	Chevrolet
9	Bill Elliott	Ford
10	Neil Bonnett	Pontiac
11	Alan Kulwicki	Ford
12	Dale Jarrett	Chevrolet
13	Jimmy Means	Pontiac
14	Michael Waltrip	Chevrolet
15	Steve Christman	Pontiac
16	Derrike Cope	Ford
17	Buddy Arrington	Ford
18	Dave Marcis	Chevrolet
19	Phil Parsons	Oldsmobile
20	Sterling Marlin	Oldsmobile
21	Darrell Waltrip	Chevrolet
22	Bobby Allison	Buick
23	Rodney Combs	Ford
24	Morgan Shepherd	Buick
25	Brad Teague	Oldsmobile
26	Benny Parsons	Chevrolet
27	Ken Schrader	Ford
28	Kyle Petty	Ford
29	Bobby Hillin	Buick
30	Ronnie Thomas	Chevrolet

SOUTHERN 500

Time of Race: 2 hours, 23 minutes, 19 seconds
Average Speed: 115.520 mph
Margin of Victory: 5 seconds

FINISH	DRIVER	CAR
1	Dale Earnhardt	Chevrolet
2	Rusty Wallace	Pontiac
3	Richard Petty	Pontiac
4	Sterling Marlin	Oldsmobile
5	Terry Labonte	Chevrolet
6	Bobby Hillin	Buick
7	Ricky Rudd	Ford
8	Bill Elliott	Ford
9	Morgan Shepherd	Buick
10	Darrell Waltrip	Chevrolet
11	Ken Schrader	Ford
12	Phil Parsons	Oldsmobile
13	Cale Yarborough	Oldsmobile
14	Kyle Petty	Ford
15	Dale Jarrett	Chevrolet
16	Dave Marcis	Chevrolet
17	Buddy Baker	Oldsmobile
18	Geoff Bodine	Chevrolet
19	Michale Waltrip	Chevrolet
20	Brett Bodine	Chevrolet
21	Steve Christman	Pontiac
22	Jimmy Means	Chevrolet
23	Bobby Wawak	Chevrolet
24	Buddy Arrington	Ford
25	Eddie Bierschwale	Chevrolet
26	Bobby Allison	Buick

27	Rodney Combs	Ford
28	Rick Wilson	Oldsmobile
29	Davey Allison	Ford
30	Lake Speed	Oldsmobile
31	Benny Parsons	Chevrolet
32	Neil Bonnett	Pontiac
33	Mike Potter	Ford
34	Connie Saylor	Oldsmobile
35	H. B. Bailey	Pontiac
36	Trevor Boys	Oldsmobile
37	Jonathan Edwards	Chevrolet
38	Greg Sacks	Pontiac
39	Harry Gant	Chevrolet
40	Alan Kulwicki	Ford

WRANGLER JEANS INDIGO 400

Time of Race: 3 hours, 3 minutes, 56 seconds
Average Speed: 67.074 mph
Margin of Victory: 2.5 seconds

FINISH	DRIVER	CAR
1	Dale Earnhardt	Chevrolet
2	Darrell Waltrip	Chevrolet
3	Ricky Rudd	Ford
4	Bill Elliott	Ford
5	Richard Petty	Pontiac
6	Geoff Bodine	Chevrolet
7	Dave Marcis	Chevrolet
8	Terry Labonte	Chevrolet
9	Jimmy Means	Pontiac
10	Neil Bonnett	Pontiac
11	Steve Christman	Pontiac
12	Bobby Allison	Buick
13	Larry Pollard	Oldsmobile
14	Buddy Arrington	Ford
15	Bobby Hillin	Buick
16	Benny Parsons	Chevrolet
17	Rusty Wallace	Pontiac
18	Kyle Petty	Ford
19	Michael Waltrip	Chevrolet
20	Phil Parsons	Oldsmobile
21	Ken Schrader	Ford
22	Sterling Marlin	Oldsmobile
23	Alan Kulwicki	Ford
24	Trevor Boys	Ford
25	Harry Gant	Chevrolet
26	D. K. Ulrich	Chevrolet
27	Dale Jarrett	Chevrolet
28	Doug French	Buick
29	Ernie Irvan	Chevrolet
30	Morgan Shepherd	Buick

DELAWARE 500

Time of Race: 4 hours, 0 minutes, 34 seconds
Average Speed: 124.706 mph
Margin of Victory: 2 seconds

FINISH	DRIVER	CAR
1	Ricky Rudd	Ford
2	Davey Allison	Ford
3	Neil Bonnett	Pontiac
4	Bill Elliott	Ford
5	Sterling Marlin	Oldsmobile
6	Geoff Bodine	Chevrolet
7	Bobby Allison	Buick
8	Buddy Baker	Oldsmobile
9	Richard Petty	Pontiac
10	Darrell Waltrip	Chevrolet
11	Ken Schrader	Ford
12	Rusty Wallace	Pontiac
13	Brett Bodine	Chevrolet
14	Alan Kulwicki	Ford
15	Dave Marcis	Chevrolet

16	Benny Parsons	Chevrolet
17	Steve Christman	Pontiac
18	Michael Waltrip	Chevrolet
19	Buddy Arrington	Ford
20	Rick Knoop	Chevrolet
21	Larry Caudill	Oldsmobile
22	Jimmy Means	Pontiac
23	Kyle Petty	Ford
24	Rick Jeffrey	Chevrolet
25	Harry Gant	Chevrolet
26	Wayne Strout	Oldsmobile
27	Rick Wilson	Oldsmobile
28	J. D. McDuffie	Pontiac
29	Phil Parsons	Oldsmobile
30	David Simko	Chevrolet
31	Dale Earnhardt	Chevrolet
32	Terry Labonte	Chevrolet
33	Trevor Boys	Ford
34	Mark Gibson	Pontiac
35	Mike Potter	Ford
36	Cale Yarborough	Oldsmobile
37	Eddie Bierschwale	Chevrolet
38	Dale Jarrett	Chevrolet
39	Bobby Hillin	Buick
40	Morgan Shepherd	Buick

GOODY'S 500

Time of Race: 3 hours, 26 minutes, 31 seconds
Average Speed: 76.410 mph
Margin of Victory: 1 second

FINISH	DRIVER	CAR
1	Darrell Waltrip	Chevrolet
2	Dale Earnhardt	Chevrolet
3	Terrry Labonte	Chevrolet
4	Neil Bonnett	Pontiac
5	Morgan Shepherd	Buick
6	Alan Kulwicki	Ford
7	Sterling Marlin	Oldsmobile
8	Bobby Allison	Buick
9	Kyle Petty	Ford
10	Dale Jarrett	Chevrolet
11	Bill Elliott	Ford
12	Ken Schrader	Ford
13	Richard Petty	Pontiac
14	Harry Gant	Chevrolet
15	Ernie Irvan	Chevrolet
16	Phil Parsons	Oldsmobile
17	J. D. McDuffie	Pontiac
18	Michael Waltrip	Chevrolet
19	Steve Christman	Pontiac
20	Geoff Bodine	Chevrolet
21	Ricky Rudd	Ford
22	Bobby Hillin	Buick
23	Benny Parsons	Chevrolet
24	Greg Sacks	Pontiac
25	Slick Johnson	Oldsmobile
26	Curtis Markham	Ford
27	Dave Marcis	Chevrolet
28	Rusty Wallace	Pontiac
29	Buddy Arrington	Ford
30	Jimmy Means	Pontiac
31	Buddy Baker	Oldsmobile

HOLLY FARMS 400

Time of Race: 2 hours, 36 minutes, 9 seconds
Average Speed: 96.051 mph
Margin of Victory: 5.31 seconds

FINISH	DRIVER	CAR
1	Terry Labonte	Chevrolet
2	Dale Earnhardt	Chevrolet

3	Bill Elliott	Ford
4	Morgan Shepherd	Buick
5	Geoff Bodine	Chevrolet
6	Kyle Petty	Ford
7	Alan Kulwicki	Ford
8	Bobby Hillin	Buick
9	Richard Petty	Pontiac
10	Rusty Wallace	Pontiac
11	Neil Bonnett	Pontiac
12	Darrell Waltrip	Chevrolet
13	Ricky Rudd	Ford
14	Phil Parsons	Oldsmobile
15	Ken Schrader	Ford
16	Michael Waltrip	Chevrolet
17	Bobby Allison	Buick
18	Dale Jarrett	Chevrolet
19	Benny Parsons	Chevrolet
20	Sterling Marlin	Oldsmobile
21	Jimmy Means	Pontiac
22	Ernie Irvan	Chevrolet
23	Larry Pollard	Chevrolet
24	Trevor Boys	Ford
25	Ronnie Thomas	Chevrolet
26	Davey Allison	Ford
27	Buddy Arrington	Ford
28	Hut Stricklin	Oldsmobile
29	Steve Christman	Pontiac
30	Dave Marcis	Chevrolet
31	Harry Gant	Chevrolet
32	Slick Johnson	Ford

OAKWOOD HOMES 500

Time of Race: 3 hours, 54 minutes, 2 seconds
Average Speed: 128.443 mph
Margin of Victory: 1.5 seconds

FINISH	DRIVER	CAR
1	Bill Elliott	Ford
2	Bobby Allison	Buick
3	Sterling Marlin	Oldsmobile
4	Terry Labonte	Chevrolet
5	Richard Petty	Pontiac
6	Larry Pearson	Chevrolet
7	Lake Speed	Oldsmobile
8	Ernie Irvan	Chevrolet
9	Darrell Waltrip	Chevrolet
10	Kyle Petty	Ford
11	Ricky Rudd	Ford
12	Dale Earnhardt	Chevrolet
13	Brad Teague	Oldsmobile
14	Buddy Arrington	Ford
15	Steve Christman	Pontiac
16	Connie Saylor	Chevrolet
17	Ken Schrader	Ford
18	Dave Marcis	Chevrolet
19	Davey Allison	Ford
20	Morgan Shepherd	Buick
21	A. J. Foyt	Oldsmobile
22	Rusty Wallace	Pontiac
23	Mark Stahl	Ford
24	Cale Yarborough	Oldsmobile
25	Trevor Boys	Ford
26	Ken Ragan	Ford
27	Phil Parsons	Oldsmobile
28	Bobby Hillin	Buick
29	Alan Kulwicki	Ford
30	Rick Wilson	Oldsmobile
31	Geoff Bodine	Chevrolet
32	Brett Bodine	Chevrolet
33	Harry Gant	Chevrolet
34	Dale Jarrett	Chevrolet
35	Michael Waltrip	Chevrolet
36	Neil Bonnett	Pontiac
37	Rodney Combs	Chevrolet
38	Benny Parsons	Chevrolet
39	Derrike Cope	Ford
40	Jimmy Means	Chevrolet
41	Buddy Baker	Oldsmobile
42	Greg Sacks	Pontiac

AC DELCO 500

Time of Race: 4 hours, 13 minutes, 52 seconds
Average Speed: 118.258 mph
Margin of Victory: 2 seconds

FINISH	DRIVER	CAR
1	Bill Elliott	Ford
2	Dale Earnhardt	Chevrolet
3	Darrell Waltrip	Chevrolet
4	Terry Labonte	Chevrolet
5	Morgan Shepherd	Buick
6	Kyle Petty	Ford
7	Buddy Baker	Oldsmobile
8	Geoff Bodine	Chevrolet
9	Phil Parsons	Oldsmobile
10	Joe Ruttman	Pontiac
11	Sterling Marlin	Oldsmobile
12	Rusty Wallace	Pontiac
13	Harry Gant	Chevrolet
14	Ken Schrader	Ford
15	Benny Parsons	Chevrolet
16	Dale Jarrett	Chevrolet
17	Richard Petty	Pontiac
18	Alan Kulwicki	Ford
19	Michael Waltrip	Chevrolet
20	Jimmy Means	Pontiac
21	Trevor Boys	Oldsmobile
22	Dave Marcis	Chevrolet
23	Eddie Bierschwale	Chevrolet
24	Buddy Arrington	Ford
25	Connie Saylor	Chevrolet
26	Ronnie Thomas	Chevrolet
27	Greg Sacks	Pontiac
28	Mark Stahl	Ford
29	Hut Stricklin	Oldsmobile
30	Curtis Markham	Ford
31	Ricky Rudd	Ford
32	Steve Christman	Pontiac
33	Bobby Hillin	Buick
34	Kirk Bryant	Pontiac
35	Dave Simko	Chevrolet
36	Bobby Wawak	Chevrolet
37	Cale Yarborough	Oldsmobile
38	Bobby Allison	Buick
39	Butch Miller	Chevrolet
40	J. D. McDuffie	Pontiac
41	Brett Bodine	Chevrolet
42	Davey Allison	Ford

WINSTON WESTERN 500

Time of Race: 3 hours, 10 minutes, 49 seconds
Average Speed: 98.035 mph
Margin of Victory: 1 second

FINISH	DRIVER	CAR
1	Rusty Wallace	Pontiac
2	Benny Parsons	Chevrolet
3	Kyle Petty	Ford
4	Richard Petty	Pontiac
5	Bobby Allison	Buick
6	Darrell Waltrip	Chevrolet
7	Joe Ruttman	Pontiac
8	Terry Labonte	Chevrolet
9	Dave Marcis	Chevrolet
10	Geoff Bodine	Chevrolet
11	Alan Kulwicki	Ford
12	Jim Robinson	Oldsmobile
13	Phil Parsons	Oldsmobile
14	Davey Allison	Ford
15	Chad Little	Ford
16	George Follmer	Chevrolet
17	Dale Jarrett	Chevrolet
18	Rick Wilson	Oldsmobile

19	Ernie Irvan	Chevrolet
20	Derrike Cope	Chevrolet
21	Buddy Arrington	Ford
22	Irv Hoerr	Oldsmobile
23	Bill Elliott	Ford
24	Sterling Marlin	Oldsmobile
25	Morgan Shepherd	Buick
26	Michael Waltrip	Chevrolet
27	Jimmy Means	Pontiac
28	Harry Gant	Chevrolet
29	Ken Schrader	Ford
30	Dale Earnhardt	Chevrolet
31	Ricky Rudd	Ford
32	Harry Goularte	Chevrolet
33	Rick Hendrick	Chevrolet
34	Bobby Hillin	Buick
35	Rick McCray	Chevrolet
36	Bill Schmitt	Chevrolet
37	Jocko Maggiacomo	Chevrolet
38	Tom Kendall	Buick
39	Ruben Garcia	Chevrolet
40	Roy Smith	Ford
41	Glen Steurer	Chevrolet
42	Hershel McGriff	Pontiac

ATLANTA JOURNAL 500

Time of Race: 3 hours, 35 minutes, 25 seconds
Average Speed: 139.047 mph
Margin of Victory: 12.94 seconds

FINISH	DRIVER	CAR
1	Bill Elliott	Ford
2	Dale Earnhardt	Chevrolet
3	Ricky Rudd	Ford
4	Bobby Allison	Buick
5	Davey Allison	Ford
6	Alan Kulwicki	Ford
7	Benny Parsons	Chevrolet
8	Phil Parsons	Oldsmobile
9	Sterling Marlin	Oldsmobile
10	Buddy Baker	Oldsmobile
11	Joe Ruttman	Pontiac
12	Rusty Wallace	Pontiac
13	Kyle Petty	Ford
14	Bobby Hillin	Buick
15	Brett Bodine	Chevrolet
16	Hut Stricklin	Oldsmobile
17	Brad Teague	Oldsmobile
18	Darrell Waltrip	Chevrolet
19	H. B. Bailey	Pontiac
20	Randy Baker	Chevrolet
21	Mark Stahl	Ford
22	Buddy Arrington	Ford
23	Ken Ragan	Ford
24	Harry Gant	Chevrolet
25	Larry Pearson	Chevrolet
26	Greg Sacks	Pontiac
27	Rick Wilson	Oldsmobile
28	Terry Labonte	Chevrolet
29	Jimmy Means	Pontiac
30	Richard Petty	Pontiac
31	Geoff Bodine	Chevrolet
32	Dave Marcis	Chevrolet
33	Charlie Baker	Chevrolet
34	Curtis Markham	Ford
35	Ken Schrader	Ford
36	Dale Jarrett	Chevrolet
37	A. J. Foyt	Oldsmobile
38	Michael Waltrip	Chevrolet
39	Morgan Shepherd	Buick
40	Cale Yarborough	Oldsmobile
41	Lake Speed	Oldsmobile
42	Ed Pimm	Buick

1988

DAYTONA 500

Time of Race: 3 hours, 38 minutes, 08 seconds
Average Speed: 137.531 mph
Margin of Victory: 2 car lengths

FINISH	DRIVER	CAR
1	Bobby Allison	Buick
2	Davey Allison	Ford
3	Phil Parsons	Oldsmobile
4	Neil Bonnett	Pontiac
5	Terry Labonte	Chevrolet
6	Ken Schrader	Chevrolet
7	Rusty Wallace	Pontiac
8	Sterling Marlin	Oldsmobile
9	Buddy Baker	Oldsmobile
10	Dale Earnhardt	Chevrolet
11	Darrell Waltrip	Chevrolet
12	Bill Elliott	Ford
13	Bobby Hillin	Buick
14	Geoff Bodine	Chevrolet
15	Rick Wilson	Oldsmobile
16	Dale Jarrett	Buick
17	Ricky Rudd	Buick
18	Kyle Petty	Ford
19	Trevor Boys	Chevrolet
20	Dave Marcis	Chevrolet
21	Brad Teague	Oldsmobile
22	Michael Waltrip	Pontiac
23	Steve Moore	Chevrolet
24	Ed Pimm	Buick
25	Jimmy Means	Ford
26	Ralph Jones	Ford
27	Derrike Cope	Ford
28	Eddie Bierschwale	Oldsmobile
29	Harry Gant	Chevrolet
30	Rick Jeffrey	Chevrolet
31	Benny Parsons	Ford
32	Alan Kulwicki	Ford
33	A.J. Foyt	Oldsmobile
34	Richard Petty	Pontiac
35	Brett Bodine	Ford
36	Phil Barkdoll	Ford
37	Lake Speedy	Oldsmobile
38	Cale Yarborough	Oldsmobile
39	Connie Saylor	Chevrolet
40	Greg Sacks	Pontiac
41	Mark Martin	Ford
42	Morgan Shepherd	Buick

PONTIAC EXCITEMENT 400

Time of Race: 3 hours, 15 minutes, 54 seconds
Average Speed: 66.401 mph
Margin of Victory: 1 second

FINISH	DRIVER	CAR
1	Neil Bonnett	Pontiac
2	Ricky Rudd	Buick
3	Richard Petty	Pontiac
4	Darrell Waltrip	Chevrolet
5	Sterling Marlin	Oldsmobile
6	Lake Speed	Oldsmobile
7	Rusty Wallace	Pontiac
8	Bobby Hillin	Buick
9	Terry Labonte	Chevrolet
10	Dale Earnhardt	Chevrolet
11	Bobby Allison	Buick
12	Bill Elliott	Ford
13	Geoff Bodine	Chevrolet
14	Benny Parsons	Ford
15	Buddy Baker	Oldsmobile

16	Morgan Shepherd	Buick
17	Dave Marcis	Chevrolet
18	Kyle Petty	Ford
19	Brad Teague	Oldsmobile
20	Ken Schrader	Ford
21	Alan Kulwicki	Ford
22	Lennie Pond	Chevrolet
23	Ken Bouchard	Ford
24	Jimmy Means	Chevrolet
25	Mark Martin	Ford
26	Dale Jarrett	Oldsmobile
27	Brett Bodine	Ford
28	Harry Gant	Chevolet
29	Davey Allison	Ford
30	Phil Parsons	Oldsmobile
31	Michael Waltrip	Pontiac
32	Derrike Cope	Ford

GOODWRENCH 500

Time of Race: 4 hours, 9 minutes, 51 seconds
Average Speed: 120.159 mph
Margin of Victory: 3 car lengths

FINISH	DIVER	CAR
1	Neil Bonnett	Pontiac
2	Lake Speed	Oldsmobile
3	Sterling Marlin	Oldsmobile
4	Alan Kulwicki	Ford
5	Dale Earnhardt	Chevolet
6	Bill Elliott	Ford
7	Morgan Shepherd	Buick
8	Ken Bouchard	Ford
9	Davey Allison	Ford
10	Ken Schrader	Chevolet
11	Buddy Baker	Oldsmobile
12	Mark Martin	Ford
13	Michael Waltrip	Chevrolet
14	Rusty Wallace	Pontiac
15	Phil Parsons	Oldsmobile
16	Dale Jarrett	Oldsmobile
17	Ricky Rudd	Buick
18	Geoff Bodine	Chevrolet
19	Kyle Petty	Ford
20	Derrike Cope	Ford
21	Bobby Hillin	Buick
22	Bobby Allison	Buick
23	Dave Marcis	Chevrolet
24	Darrell Waltrip	Chevrolet
25	Ernie Irvan	Chevrolet
26	Rick Jeffrey	Ford
27	Brett Bodine	Ford
28	Harry Gant	Chevrolet
29	Dave Pletcher	Ford
30	Steve Moore	Chevrolet
31	Terry Labonte	Chevrolet
32	Eddie Bierschwale	Chevrolet
33	Benny Parsons	Ford
34	Ed Pimm	Buick
35	Mickey Gibbs	Ford
36	Rick Wilson	Oldsmobile
37	Mark Stahl	Ford
38	Charlie Baker	Chevolet
39	Brad Teague	Oldsmobile
40	Jimmy Means	Pontiac
41	Richard Petty	Pontiac

MOTORCRAFT QUALITY PARIS 500

Time of Race: 3 hours, 37 minutes, 42 seconds
Average Speed: 137.588 mph
Margin of Victory: 1.5 seconds

FINISH	DRIVER	CAR
1	Dale Earnhardt	Chevrolet
2	Rusty Wallace	Pontiac

3	Darrell Waltrip	Chevrolet
4	Terry Labonte	Chevrolet
5	Kyle Petty	Ford
6	Bobby Hillin	Buick
7	Buddy Baker	Oldsmobile
8	Ken Schrader	Chevrolet
9	Brett Bodine	Ford
10	Rick Wilson	Oldsmobile
11	Bobby Allison	Buick
12	Michael Waltrip	Chevrolet
13	Benny Parsons	Ford
14	Brad Noffsinger	Buick
15	Dave Marcis	Chevrolet
16	Ken Bouchard	Ford
17	Eddie Bierschwale	Chevrolet
18	Ernie Irvan	Chevroelt
19	Bill Elliott	Ford
20	Sterling Marlin	Oldsmobile
21	Harry Gant	Chevrolet
22	Neil Bonnett	Pontiac
23	Richard Petty	Pontiac
24	Ricky Rudd	Buick
25	Jim Sauter	Pontiac
26	Derrike Cope	Ford
27	Rodney Combs	Buick
28	David Sosebee	Ford
29	Dale Jarrett	Chevrolet
30	Morgan Shepherd	Bujick
31	Mark Martin	Ford
32	Cale Yarborough	Oldsmobile
33	Geoff Bodine	Chevrolet
34	A.J. Foyt	Oldsmobile
35	Ken Ragan	Ford
36	Brad Teague	Oldsmobile
37	Phil Parsons	Oldsmobile
38	Lake Speed	Oldsmobile
39	Alan Kulwicki	Ford
40	Davey Allison	Ford
41	H.B. Bailey	Pontiac
42	Jimmy Means	Pontiac

TRANSOUTH 500

Time of Race: 3 hours, 49 minutes, 07 seconds
Average Speed: 131.284 mph
Margin of Victory: 18.80 seconds

FINISH	DRIVER	CAR
1	Lake Speed	Oldsmobile
2	Alan Kulwicki	Ford
3	Davey Allison	Ford
4	Bill Elliott	Ford
5	Sterling Marlin	Oldsmobile
6	Mark Martin	Ford
7	Geoff Bodine	Chevrolet
8	Phil Parsons	Oldsmobile
9	Bobby Allison	Buick
10	Buddy Baker	Oldsmobile
11	Dale Earnhardt	Chevrolet
12	Dale Jarrett	Oldsmobile
13	Ken Bouchard	Ford
14	Eddie Bierschwale	Oldsmobile
15	Brett Bodine	Ford
16	H.B. Bailey	Pontiac
17	Bobby Hillin	Buick
18	Jimmy Horton	Ford
19	Neil Bonnett	Pontiac
20	Brad Teague	Chevrolet
21	Michael Waltrip	Pontiac
22	Ernie Irvan	Chevrolet
23	Terry Labonte	Chevrolet
24	Darrell Waltrip	Chevrolet
25	Rusty Wallace	Pontiac
26	Derrike Cope	Ford
27	Rick Wilson	Oldsmobile
28	Buddy Arrington	Ford
29	Ken Schrader	Chevrolet
30	Ricky Rudd	Buick
31	Greg Sacks	Pontiac
32	Rodney Combs	Buick

33	Steve Moore	Chevrolet
34	Benny Parsons	Ford
35	Jimmy Means	Pontiac
36	Brad Noffsinger	Buick
37	Dave Marcis	Chevrolet
38	Harry Gant	Chevrolet
39	Morgan Shepherd	Buick
40	Kyle Petty	Ford
41	Richard Petty	Pontiac

VALLEYDALE MEATS 500

Time of Race: 3 hours, 12 minutes, 23 seconds
Average Speed: 83.115 mph
Margin of Victory: 2 car lengths

FINISH	DRIVER	CAR
1	Bill Elliott	Ford
2	Mark Martin	Ford
3	Geoff Bodine	Chevrolet
4	Rusty Wallace	Pontiac
5	Bobby Allison	Buick
6	Richard Petty	Pontiac
7	Kyle Petty	Ford
8	Sterling Marlin	Oldsmobile
9	Dave Marcis	Chevrolet
10	Ken Schrader	Chevrolet
11	Neil Bonnett	Pontiac
12	Michael Waltrip	Pontiac
13	Benny Parsons	Ford
14	Dale Earnhardt	Chevrolet
15	Bobby Hillin	Buick
16	Terry Labonte	Chevrolet
17	Brett Bodine	Ford
18	Harry Gant	Chevrolet
19	Alan Kulwicki	Ford
20	Ricky Rudd	Buick
21	Ken Bouchard	Ford
22	Phil Parsons	Oldsmobile
23	Darrell Waltrip	Chevrolet
24	Derrike Cope	Ford
25	Rick Wilson	Oldsmobile
26	Ernie Irvan	Chevrolet
27	Brad Teague	Oldsmobile
28	Dale Jarrett	Oldsmobile
29	Davey Allison	Ford
30	Lake Speed	Oldsmobile
31	Buddy Baker	Oldsmobile
32	Jimmy Means	Pontiac

FIRST UNION 400

Time of Race: 2 hours, 31 minutes, 24 seconds
Average Speed: 99.075 mph
Margin of Victory: 1.51 seconds

FINISH	DRIVER	CAR
1	Terry Labonte	Chevrolet
2	Ricky Rudd	Buick
3	Dale Earnhardt	Chevrolet
4	Rusty Wallace	Pontiac
5	Kyle Petty	Ford
6	Richard Petty	Pontiac
7	Phil Parsons	Oldsmobile
8	Davey Allison	Ford
9	Geoff Bodine	Chevrolet
10	Bill Elliott	Ford
11	Ken Schrader	Chevrolet
12	Harry Gant	Chevrolet
13	Brett Bodine	Ford
14	Darrell Waltrip	Chevrolet
15	Alan Kulwicki	Ford
16	Sterling Marlin	Oldsmobile
17	Benny Parsons	Ford
18	Bobby Hillin	Buick

19	Neil Bonnett	Pontiac
20	Bobby Allison	Buick
21	Dale Jarrett	Oldsmobile
22	Derrike Cope	Ford
23	Rodney Combs	Buick
24	Ernie Irvan	Pontiac
25	Dave Marcis	Chervolet
26	Lake Speed	Oldsmobile
27	Ken Bouchard	Chevrolet
28	Rick Wilson	Oldsmobile
29	Mark Martin	Ford
30	Jimmy Means	Pontiac
31	Buddy Baker	Oldsmobile
32	Michael Waltrip	Pontiac

PANNILL SWEATSHIRTS 500

Time of Race: 3 hours, 31 minutes, 08 seconds
Average Speed: 74.740 mph
Margin of Victory: 1.99 seconds

FINISH	DRIVER	CAR
1	Dale Earnhardt	Chevrolet
2	Sterling Marlin	Oldsmobile
3	Bobby Hillin	Buick
4	Terry Labonte	Chevrolet
5	Darrell Waltrip	Chevrolet
6	Davey Allison	Ford
7	Buddy Baker	Oldsmobile
8	Bobby Allison	Buick
9	Phil Parsons	Oldsmobile
10	Ken Schrader	Chevrolet
11	Bill Elliott	Ford
12	Dave Marcis	Chevrolet
13	Dale Jarrett	Oldsmobile
14	Benny Parsons	Ford
15	Geoff Bodine	Chevrolet
16	Rusty Wallace	Pontiac
17	Kyle Petty	Ford
18	Ricky Rudd	Buick
19	Brad Teague	Oldsmobile
20	Alan Kulwicki	Ford
21	Brad Noffsinger	Buick
22	Michael Waltrip	Pontiac
23	Mark Martin	Ford
24	Jimmy Hensley	Ford
25	Rick Wilson	Oldsmobile
26	Harry Gant	Chevrolet
27	Brett Bodine	Ford
28	Lake Speed	Oldsmobile
29	Derrike Cope	Ford
30	Neil Bonnett	Pontiac
31	Ken Bouchard	Buick
32	Richard Petty	Pontiac

WINSTON 500

Time of Race: 3 hours, 11 minutes, 40 seconds
Average Speed: 156.547 mph
Margin of Victory: .21 seconds

FINISH	DRIVER	CAR
1	Phil Parsons	Oldsmobile
2	Bobby Allison	Buick
3	Geoff Bodine	Chevrolet
4	Terry Labonte	Chevrolet
5	Ken Schrader	Chevrolet
6	Sterling Marlin	Oldsmobile
7	Bill Elliott	Ford
8	Kyle Petty	Ford
9	Dale Earnhardt	Chevrolet
10	Rusty Wallace	Pontiac
11	Dale Jarrett	Buick
12	Mark Martin	Ford

13	Bobby Hillin	Buick
14	Neil Bonnett	Pontiac
15	Lake Speed	Oldsmobile
16	Buddy Baker	Oldsmobile
17	Greg Sacks	Pontiac
18	Cale Yarborough	Oldsmobile
19	Brett Bodine	Ford
20	Richard Petty	Pontiac
21	Brad Teague	Oldsmobile
22	Alan Kulwicki	Ford
23	Jimmy Means	Pontiac
24	Benny Parsons	Ford
25	Brad Noffsinger	Buick
26	Derrike Cope	Ford
27	Dave Marcis	Chevrolet
28	A.J. Foyt	Oldsmobile
29	Ricky Rudd	Buick
30	Rick Jeffrey	Chevrolet
31	Phil Barkdoll	Chevrolet
32	Ernie Irvan	Chevrolet
33	Michael Waltrip	Pontiac
34	Davey Allison	Ford
35	Rick Wilson	Oldsmobile
36	Harry Gant	Chevrolet
37	Darrell Waltrip	Chevrolet
38	Rodney Combs	Buick
39	Eddie Bierschwale	Oldsmobile
40	Mickey Gibbs	Chevrolet
41	Ken Ragan	Ford

COCA COLA 600

Time of Race: 4 hours, 49 minutes, 15 seconds
Average Speed: 124.460 mph
Margin of Victory: .24 seconds

FINISH	DRIVER	CAR
1	Darrell Waltrip	Chevrolet
2	Rusty Wallace	Pontiac
3	Alan Kulwicki	Ford
4	Brett Bodine	Ford
5	Davey Allison	Ford
6	Ken Schrader	Chevrolet
7	Ricky Rudd	Buick
8	Phil Parsons	Oldsmobile
9	Terry Labonte	Chevrolet
10	Greg Sacks	Pontiac
11	Ken Bouchard	Ford
12	Jimmy Means	Pontiac
13	Dale Earnhardt	Chevrolet
14	Bobby Hillin	Buick
15	Richard Petty	Pontiac
16	Kyle Petty	Ford
17	Bobby Allison	Buick
18	Rick Wilson	Oldsmobile
19	Bill Elliott	Ford
20	Joe Ruttman	Oldsmobile
21	Lake Speed	Oldsmobile
22	Ernie Irvan	Chevrolet
23	Michael Waltrip	Pontiac
24	Geoff Bodine	Chevrolet
25	Benny Parsons	Ford
26	Morgan Shepherd	Buick
27	Sterling Marlin	Oldsmobile
28	Eddie Bierschwale	Oldsmobile
29	Buddy Baker	Oldsmobile
30	Harry Gant	Chevrolet
31	Jimmy Horton	Ford
32	Rodney Combs	Buick
33	Brad Noffsinger	Buick
34	Dave Marcis	Chevrolet
35	H.B. Bailey	Pontiac
36	Neil Bonnett	Pontiac
37	Mark Martin	Ford
38	Cale Yarborough	Oldsmobile
39	Jim Sauter	Pontiac
40	Derrike Cope	Ford
41	Dale Jarrett	Chevrolet

BUDWEISER 500

Time of Race: 4 hours, 12 minutes, 41 seconds
Average Speed: 118.726 mph
Margin of Victory: 21 seconds

FINISH	DRIVER	CAR
1	Bill Elliott	Ford
2	Morgan Shepherd	Chevrolet
3	Rusty Wallace	Pontiac
4	Lake Speedy	Oldsmobile
5	Davey Allison	Ford
6	Alan Kulwicki	Ford
7	Rick Wilson	Oldsmobile
8	Geoff Bodine	Chevrolet
9	Mark Martin	Ford
10	Bobby Allison	Buick
11	Sterling Marlin	Oldsmobile
12	Terry Labonte	Chevrolet
13	Buddy Baker	Oldsmobile
14	Ken Bouchard	Ford
15	Richard Petty	Pontiac
16	Dale Earnhardt	Chevrolet
17	Bobby Hillin	Buick
18	Derrike Cope	Ford
19	Ricky Rudd	Buick
20	Dale Jarrett	Oldsmobile
21	Ken Schrader	Chevrolet
22	Benny Parsons	Ford
23	Darrell Waltrip	Chevrolet
24	Brad Noffsinger	Buick
25	J.D. McDuffie	Pontiac
26	Ernie Irvan	Chevrolet
27	Jimmy Means	Pontiac
28	Dana Patten	Buick
29	Rodney Combs	Buick
30	Joe Ruttman	Oldsmobile
31	Brett Bodine	Ford
32	Dave Marcis	Chevrolet
33	Kyle Petty	Ford
34	Jimmy Horton	Ford
35	Neil Bonnett	Pontiac
36	Michael Waltrip	Pontiac
37	Jay Sommers	Chevrolet
38	Joe Booher	Chevrolet
39	Phil Parsons	Oldsmobile
40	Eddie Bierschwale	Oldsmobile

BUDWEISER 400

Time of Race: 2 hours, 43 minutes, 03 seconds
Average Speed: 88.341 mph
Margin of Victory: .34 seconds

FINISH	DRIVER	CAR
1	Rusty Wallace	Pontiac
2	Terry Labonte	Chevrolet
3	Ricky Rudd	Buick
4	Dale Earnhardt	Chevrolet
5	Phil Parsons	Oldsmobile
6	Richard Petty	Pontiac
7	Mark Martin	Ford
8	Dale Jarrett	Oldsmobile
9	Sterling Marlin	Oldsmobile
10	Neil Bonnett	Pontiac
11	Michael Waltrip	Pontiac
12	Bill Schmitt	Chevrolet
13	Benny Parsons	Ford
14	Kyle Petty	Ford
15	Rick Hendrick	Chevrolet
16	Bill Elliott	Ford
17	Derrike Cope	Chevrolet
18	Tom Kendall	Buick
19	Buddy Baker	Oldsmobile
20	Ken Schrader	Chevrolet
21	Dave Marcis	Chevrolet
22	Bobby Allison	Buick
23	Chad Little	Ford

24	Bobby Hillin	Buick
25	John Krebs	Oldsmobile
26	Lake Speed	Oldsmobile
27	Roy Smith	Ford
28	Darrell Waltrip	Chevrolet
29	Joe Ruttman	Oldsmobile
30	Jocko Maggiacomo	Chevrolet
31	Ernie Irvan	Chevrolet
32	Davey Allison	Ford
33	Rick Wilson	Oldsmobile
34	Geoff Bodine	Chevrolet
35	Terry Petris	Chevrolet
36	Hershel McGriff	Pontiac
37	Rich McCray	Pontiac
38	Alan Kulwicki	Ford
39	Ruben Garcia	Chevrolet
40	Brett Bodine	Ford
41	Jim Bown	Chevrolet
42	Morgan Shepherd	Chevrolet
43	Jimmy Means	Pontiac

MILLER HIGH LIFE 500

Time of Race: 3 hours, 58 minutes, 21 seconds
Average Speed: 126.147 mph
Margin of Victory: 8.18 seconds

FINISH	DRIVER	CAR
1	Geoff Bodine	Chevrolet
2	Michael Waltrip	Pontiac
3	Rusty Wallace	Pontiac
4	Mark Martin	Ford
5	Davey Allison	Ford
6	Darrell Waltrip	Chevrolet
7	Buddy Baker	Oldsmobile
8	Phil Parsons	Oldsmobile
9	Ken Schrader	Chevrolet
10	Bill Elliott	Ford
11	Neil Bonnett	Pontiac
12	Kyle Petty	Ford
13	Dale Jarrett	Oldsmobile
14	Ken Bouchard	Ford
15	Bobby Hillin	Buick
16	Morgan Shepherd	Chevrolet
17	Joe Ruttman	Oldsmobile
18	Jimmy Horton	Ford
19	Brad Noffsinger	Buick
20	Jimmy Means	Pontiac
21	Buddy Arrington	Ford
22	Bobby Gerhart	Chevrolet
23	Lake Speed	Oldsmobile
24	Derrike Cope	Ford
25	Rick Wilson	Oldsmobile
26	Richard Petty	Pontiac
27	Alan Kulwicki	Ford
28	Sterling Marlin	Oldsmobile
29	Eddie Bierschwale	Oldsmobile
30	Ricky Rudd	Buick
31	Benny Parsons	Ford
32	Terry Labonte	Chevrolet
33	Dale Earnhardt	Chevrolet
34	Rodney Combs	Buick
35	Brett Bodine	Ford
36	Bob Schacht	Ford
37	Ernie Irvan	Chevrolet
38	Dave Marcis	Chevrolet
39	Bobby Allison	Buick
40	Jocko Maggiacomo	Chevrolet

MILLER HIGH LIFE 400

Time of Race: 2 hours, 36 minutes, 18 seconds
Average Speed: 153.551 mph
Margin of Victory: .28 seconds

FINISH	DRIVER	CAR
1	Rusty Wallace	Pontiac
2	Bill Elliott	Ford

3	Terry Labonte	Chevrolet
4	Dale Earnhardt	Chevrolet
5	Geoff Bodine	Chevrolet
6	Ken Schrader	Chevrolet
7	Phil Parsons	Oldsmobile
8	Darrell Waltrip	Chevrolet
9	Cale Yarborough	Oldsmobile
10	Mike Alexander	Buick
11	Ricky Rudd	Buick
12	Bobby Hillin	Buick
13	Buddy Baker	Oldsmobile
14	Mark Martin	Ford
15	Ernie Irvan	Chevrolet
16	Joe Ruttman	Oldsmobile
17	Ken Bouchard	Ford
18	Dave Marcis	Chevrolet
19	Neil Bonnett	Pontiac
20	Brad Noffsinger	Buick
21	Alan Kulwicki	Ford
22	Dana Patten	Buick
23	Buddy Arrington	Ford
24	Richard Petty	Pontiac
25	Dale Jarrett	Buick
26	Eddie Bierschwale	Oldsmobile
27	Brett Bodine	Ford
28	Michael Waltrip	Pontiac
29	Lake Speed	Oldsmobile
30	Rodney Combs	Buick
31	David Sosebee	Ford
32	Derrike Cope	Ford
33	Kyle Petty	Ford
34	Morgan Shepherd	Chevrolet
35	Davey Allison	Ford
36	Jimmy Means	Pontiac
37	Sterling Marlin	Oldsmobile
38	Benny Parsons	Ford
39	H.B. Bailey	Pontiac
40	Dave Simko	Pontiac
41	Rick Wilson	Oldsmobile

PEPSI FIRECRACKER 400

Time of Race: 2 hours, 36 minutes, 18 seconds
Average Speed: 163.302 mph
Margin of Victory: 18 inches

FINISH	DRIVER	CAR
1	Bill Elliott	Ford
2	Rick Wilson	Oldsmobile
3	Phil Parsons	Oldsmobile
4	Dale Earnhardt	Chevrolet
5	Darrell Waltrip	Chevrolet
6	Buddy Baker	Oldsmobile
7	Morgan Shepherd	Chevrolet
8	Ken Schrader	Chevrolet
9	Lake Speed	Oldsmobile
10	Greg Sacks	Pontiac
11	Joe Ruttman	Oldsmobile
12	Rusty Wallace	Pontiac
13	Bobby Hillin	Buick
14	Dale Jarrett	Buick
15	Mike Alexander	Buick
16	Geoff Bodine	Chevrolet
17	Mark Martin	Ford
18	Neil Bonnett	Pontiac
19	Terry Labonte	Chevrolet
20	Richard Petty	Pontiac
21	Michael Wlatrip	Pontiac
22	Ricky Rudd	Buick
23	Dave Marcis	Chevrolet
24	Kyle Petty	Ford
25	Ernie Irvan	Chevrolet
26	Patty Moise	Buick
27	Jimmy Means	Pontiac
28	Buddy Arrington	Chevrolet
29	Rick Jeffrey	Chevrolet
30	Ken Ragan	Ford
31	Eddie Bierschwale	Oldsmobile
32	Larry Moyer	Pontiac
33	Rodney Combs	Buick

BUILDING A BETTER RACETRACK

It doesn't rank among the world's most impressive construction projects, but in its own way the conversion of the -mile State Fairgrounds Raceway at Richmond, Virginia, into the 3/4-mile Richmond International Raceway is a tribute to what can be done when it absolutely, positively has to get done.

In this case, the demolition of the antiquated half-miler with its steel guardrailing, scaffolding and board bleachers, and primitive amenities and the construction of a state of-the-art, fan-friendly track on the same site was scheduled for late-February to early-September of 1988.

The people who made it happen were Paul Sawyer and his sons, Billy and Wayne. The family had been involved with NASCAR racing in Richmond for more than 40 years and had always wanted to build or operate something bigger and better than the fairgrounds track. After several failed attempts to buy land for a superspeedway in Virginia, the Sawyers decided in 1986 to tear down what they had and start from scratch.

Time was of the essence. They went into the 1988 season with Winston Cup races scheduled for February and September, giving them precious little "fat" time if things went bad. No sooner had the checkered flag fallen on the Pontiac 400 in February (which Neil Bonnett won) that Richard Petty

climbed upon a bulldozer and began digging up the frontstretch in a photo op that heralded the Sawyer's commitment to upgrade their facility.

Within weeks, the place looked like a war zone. Gone was the asphalt track, gone were the rough-hewn bleachers, gone were the dangerous and inadequate steel railings, gone were the catchfences, and gone were the outbuildings that had seen better decades. With weather playing into their hands, construction crews made great progress throughout the spring and summer.

Teams that showed up for the Miller High Life 400 the second weekend in September were amazed at the transformation. The old, flat, slow half-miler was a distant memory when compared to the 3/4-mile, D-shaped, moderately banked track that seated 70,000, more than twice as many as the old track. Today, RIR had almost 100,000 seats, a vast array of VIP and corporate luxury boxes, pedestrian and vehicular tunnels, clean and modern fan and competitior amenities, and one of the best lighting systems in all of NASCAR.

Granted, turning an old speedway into a new one doesn't rank up there with the building of the pyramids. On the other hand, it didn't take half-a-century, either.

34	Sterling Marlin	Oldsmobile
35	Benny Parsons	Ford
36	Ken Bouchard	Ford
37	A.J. Foyt	Oldsmobile
38	Davey Allison	Ford
39	Derrike Cope	Ford
40	Alan Kulwicki	Ford
41	Cale Yarborough	Oldsmobile
42	Brett Bodine	Ford

AC SPARK PLUG 500

Time of Race: 4 hours, 4 minutes, 10 seconds
Average Speed: 122.866 mph
Margin of Victory: 8.27 seconds

FINISH	DRIVER	CAR
1	Bill Elliott	Ford
2	Ken Schrader	Chevrolet
3	Davey Allison	Ford
4	Geoff Bodine	Chevrolet
5	Darrell Waltrip	Chevrolet
6	Morgan Shepherd	Pontiac
7	Mark Martin	Ford
8	Alan Kulwicki	Ford
9	Terry Labonte	Chevrolet
10	Harry Gant	Chevrolet
11	Dale Earnhardt	Chevrolet
12	Ricky Rudd	Buick
13	Rick Wilson	Oldsmobile
14	Sterling Marlin	Oldsmobile
15	Mike Alexander	Buick
16	Ken Bouchard	Ford
17	Michael Waltrip	Pontiac
18	Kyle Petty	Ford
19	Brad Noffsinger	Buick
20	Brett Bodine	Ford
21	Bobby Hillin	Buick
22	Ernie Irvan	Chevrolet
23	Buddy Baker	Oldsmobile
24	Rusty Wallace	Pontiac
25	Dale Jarrett	Oldsmobile
26	Bobby Gerhart	Chevrolet
27	Joe Ruttman	Oldsmobile
28	Richard Petty	Pontiac
29	Jimmy Horton	Ford
30	Dave Marcis	Chevrolet
31	Phil Parsons	Oldsmobile
32	Lake Speed	Oldsmobile
33	Derrike Cope	Ford
34	Greg Sacks	Pontiac
35	Benny Parsons	Ford
36	Rodney Combs	Buick

37	Mike Potter	Chevrolet
38	Eddie Bierschwale	Oldsmobile
39	Jimmy Means	Pontiac
40	Bob Schact	Ford

TALLEDEGA DIEHARD 500

Time of Race: 3 hours, 14 minutes, 12 seconds
Average Speed: 154.505 mph
Margin of Victory: 1 car length

FINISH	DRIVE	CAR
1	Ken Schrader	Chevrolet
2	Geoff Bodine	Chevrolet
3	Dale Earnhardt	Chevrolet
4	Rick Wilson	Oldsmobile
5	Rusty Wallace	Pontiac
6	Sterling Marlin	Oldsmobile
7	Mark Martin	Ford
8	Bill Elliott	Ford
9	Cale Yarborough	Oldsmobile
10	Buddy Baker	Oldsmobile
11	Phil Parsons	Oldsmobile
12	A.J. Foyt	Oldsmobile
13	Lake Speed	Oldsmobile
14	Terry Labonte	Chevrolet
15	Kyle Petty	Ford
16	Harry Gant	Chevrolet
17	Bobby Hillin	Buick
18	Dave Marcis	Chevrolet
19	Alan Kulwicki	Ford
20	Michael Waltrip	Pontiac
21	Richard Petty	Pontiac
22	Brad Noffsinger	Buick
23	Jimmy Means	Pontiac
24	Derrike Cope	Ford
25	Mike Alexander	Buick
26	Phil Barkdoll	Chevrolet
27	Benny Parsons	Ford
28	Brett Bodine	Ford
29	Rodney Combs	Buick
30	Ken Ragan	Ford
31	Eddie Bierschwale	Oldsmobile
32	Ernie Irvan	Chevrolet
33	Darrell Waltrip	Chevrolet
34	Mickey Gibbs	Ford
35	Ken Bouchard	Ford
36	Ron Esau	Chevrolet
37	Dale Jarrett	Buick
38	Greg Sacks	Pontiac
39	Davey Allison	Ford
40	Morgan Stephard	Pontiac
41	Ricky Rudd	Buick
42	Joe Ruttman	Oldsmobile

THE BUDWEISER AT THE GLEN

Time of Race: 2 hours, 56 minutes, 58 seconds
Average Speed: 74.096 mph
Margin of Victory: 1.5 car lengths

FINISH	DRIVER	CAR
1	Ricky Rudd	Buick
2	Rusty Wallace	Pontiac
3	Bill Elliott	Ford
4	Phil Parsons	Oldsmobile
5	Mike Alexander	Buick
6	Dale Earnhardt	Chevrolet
7	Morgan Shepherd	Ford
8	Sterling Marlin	Oldsmobile
9	Joe Ruttman	Oldsmobile
10	Ken Schrader	Chevrolet
11	Dale Jarrett	Oldsmobile
12	Rick Wilson	Oldsmobile

13	Bobby Hillin	Buick
14	Jimmy Means	Pontiac
15	Brad Noffsinger	Buick
16	Davey Allison	Ford
17	Richard Petty	Pontiac
18	Terry Labonte	Chevrolet
19	Alan Kulwicki	Ford
20	Darrell Waltrip	Chevrolet
21	Ron Esau	Oldsmobile
22	Tom Rotsell	Ford
23	Brett Bodine	Ford
24	Rodney Combs	Buick
25	Hershel McGriff	Pontiac
26	Dave Marcis	Chevrolet
27	Ken Bouchard	Ford
28	Mark Martin	Ford
29	Ernie Irvan	Pontiac
30	Patty Moise	Buick
31	Harry Gant	Chevrolet
32	Geoff Bodine	Chevrolet
33	Michael Waltrip	Pontiac
34	Kyle Petty	Ford
35	Jocko Maggiacomo	Chevrolet
36	J.D. McDuffie	Pontiac
37	Lake Speed	Oldsmobile
38	Neil Bonnett	Pontiac
39	Benny Parsons	Ford
40	Derrike Cope	Ford

CHAMPION SPARK PLUG 400

Time of Race: 2 hours, 33 minutes, 00 seconds
Average Speed: 156.863 mph
Margin of Victory: 4 seconds

FINISH	DRIVER	CAR
1	Davey Allison	Ford
2	Rusty Wallace	Pontiac
3	Bill Elliott	Ford
4	Morgan Shepherd	Oldsmobile
5	Lake Speed	Oldsmobile
6	Brett Bodine	Ford
7	Michael Waltrip	Pontiac
8	Kyle Petty	Ford
9	Rick Wilson	Oldsmobile
10	Geoff Bodine	Chevrolet
11	Sterling Marlin	Oldsmobile
12	Ken Schrader	Chevrolet
13	Terry Labonte	Chevrolet
14	Rodney Combs	Buick
15	Benny Parsons	Ford
16	Ricky Rudd	Buick
17	Darrell Waltrip	Chevrolet
18	Cale Yarborough	Oldsmobile
19	Jim Sauter	Pontiac
20	Phil Parsons	Oldsmobile
21	Harry Gant	Chevrolet
22	Dave Marcis	Chevrolet
23	Mike Alexander	Buick
24	Eddie Bierschwale	Oldsmobile
25	Ken Bouchard	Ford
26	Brad Noffsinger	Buick
27	Chad Little	Ford
28	H.B. Bailey	Pontiac
29	Dale Earnhardt	Chevrolet
30	Dana Patten	Buick
31	Mickey Gibbs	Ford
32	Mark Martin	Ford
33	Ernie Irvan	Pontiac
34	Derrike Cope	Ford
35	Donnie Allison	Oldsmobile
36	Alan Kulwicki	Ford
37	Bobby Hillin	Buick
38	Jimmy Means	Pontiac
39	Richard Petty	Pontiac
40	Neil Bonnett	Pontiac
41	Dale Jarrett	Buick
42	Greg Sacks	Pontiac

BUSCH 500

Time of Race: 3 hours, 22 minutes, 59 seconds
Average Speed: 78.775 mph
Margin of Victory: 1 car length

FINISH	DRIVER	CAR
1	Dale Earnhardt	Chevrolet
2	Bill Elliott	Ford
3	Geoff Bodine	Chevrolet
4	Davey Allison	Ford
5	Alan Kulwicki	Ford
6	Harry Gant	Chevrolet
7	Darrell Waltrip	Chevrolet
8	Richard Petty	Pontiac
9	Rusty Wallace	Pontiac
10	Bobby Hillin	Buick
11	Rodney Combs	Buick
12	Sterling Marlin	Oldsmobile
13	Kyle Petty	Ford
14	Neil Bonnett	Pontiac
15	Ernie Irvan	Pontiac
16	Ricky Rudd	Buick
17	Butch Miller	Oldsmobile
18	Mike Alexander	Buick
19	Phil Parsons	Oldsmobile
20	Lake Speed	Oldsmobile
21	Ken Schrader	Chevrolet
22	Terry Labonte	Chevrolet
23	Rick Wilson	Oldsmobile
24	Dave Mader	Pontiac
25	Brett Bodine	Ford
26	Dale Jarrett	Oldsmobile
27	Mark Martin	Ford
28	Rick Mast	Oldsmobile
29	Dave Marcis	Chevrolet
30	Derrike Cope	Ford
31	Michael Waltrip	Pontiac
32	Brad Noffsinger	Buick

SOUTHERN 500

Time of Race: 3 hours, 54 minutes, 27 seconds
Average Speed: 128.297 mph
Margin of Victory: .24 seconds

FINISH	DRIVER	CAR
1	Bill Elliott	Ford
2	Rusty Wallace	Pontiac
3	Dale Earnhardt	Chevrolet
4	Darrell Waltrip	Chevrolet
5	Sterling Marlin	Oldsmobile
6	Phil Parsons	Oldsmobile
7	Geoff Bodine	Chevrolet
8	Terry Labonte	Chevrolet
9	Davey Allison	Ford
10	Ricky Rudd	Buick
11	Ken Schrader	Chevrolet
12	Lake Speed	Oldsmobile
13	Benny Parsons	Ford
14	Mike Alexander	Buick
15	Alan Kulwicki	Ford
16	Neil Bonnett	Pontiac
17	Brett Bodine	Ford
18	Ken Bouchard	Ford
19	Mark Martin	Ford
20	Ernie Irvan	Chevrolet
21	Rodney Combs	Buick
22	Dave Marcis	Chevrolet
23	Jim Sauter	Oldsmobile
24	Jimmy Means	Pontiac
25	Michael Waltrip	Pontiac
26	Eddie Bierschwale	Oldsmobile
27	H.B. Bailey	Pontiac
28	Kyle Petty	Ford
29	Phillip Duffie	Buick

30	Bobby Hillin	Buick
31	Ken Ragan	Ford
32	Rick Mast	Oldsmobile
33	Richard Petty	Pontiac
34	Dale Jarrett	Oldsmobile
35	Derrike Cope	Ford
36	Randy Baker	Oldsmobile
37	Jimmy Horton	Ford
38	Rick Wilson	Oldsmobile
39	Morgan Shepherd	Buick
40	Harry Gant	Chevrolet

MILLER HIGH LIFE 400

Time of Race: 3 hours, 07 minutes, 57 seconds
Average Speed: 95.770 mph - Track Record
Margin of Victory: 3.37 seconds

FINISH	DRIVER	CAR
1	Davey Allison	Ford
2	Dale Earnhardt	Chevrolet
3	Terry Labonte	Chevrolet
4	Mark Martin	Ford
5	Alan Kulwicki	Ford
6	Kyle Petty	Ford
7	Bill Elliott	Ford
8	Darrell Waltrip	Chevrolet
9	Neil Bonnett	Pontiac
10	Dave Marcis	Chevrolet
11	Brett Bodine	Ford
12	Michael Waltrip	Pontiac
13	Greg Sacks	Oldsmobile
14	Bobby Hillin	Buick
15	Dale Jarrett	Oldsmobile
16	Sterling Marlin	Oldsmobile
17	Mike Alexander	Buick
18	Ken Schrader	Chevrolet
19	Ken Bouchard	Ford
20	Benny Parsons	Ford
21	Rodney Combs	Buick
22	Geoff Bodine	Chevrolet
23	Lee Faulk	Oldsmobile
24	Phil Parsons	Oldsmobile
25	Butch Miller	Oldsmobile
26	Ricky Rudd	Buick
27	Eddie Bierschwale	Oldsmobile
28	Ernie Irvan	Pontiac
29	Jimmy Means	Pontiac
30	Bob Schacht	Buick
31	Morgan Shepherd	Buick
32	Harry Gant	Chevrolet
33	Rick Wilson	Oldsmobile
34	Richard Petty	Pontiac
35	Rusty Wallace	Pontiac
36	Lake Speed	Oldsmobile

DELAWARE 500

Time of Race: 4 hours, 34 minutes, 21 seconds
Average Speed: 109.349 mph
Margin of Victory: 1.48 seconds

FINISH	DRIVER	CAR
1	Bill Elliott	Ford
2	Dale Earnhardt	Chevrolet
3	Rusty Wallace	Pontiac
4	Davey Allison	Ford
5	Geoff Bodine	Chevrolet
6	Kyle Petty	Ford
7	Mike Alexander	Buick
8	Neil Bonnett	Pontiac
9	Lake Speed	Oldsmobile
10	Ricky Rudd	Buick

11	Harry Gant	Chevrolet
12	Michael Waltrip	Pontiac
13	Ernie Irvan	Chevrolet
14	Phil Parsons	Oldsmobile
15	Chad Little	Ford
16	Dave Marcis	Chevrolet
17	Darrell Waltrip	Chevrolet
18	Terry Labonte	Chevrolet
19	Jimmy Means	Pontiac
20	Jimmy Horton	Ford
21	Bobby Hillin	Buick
22	Brett Bodine	Ford
23	Sterling Marlin	Oldsmobile
24	Rick Wilson	Oldsmobile
25	Ken Bouchard	Ford
26	Eddie Bierschwale	Oldsmobile
27	Benny Parsons	Ford
28	Dale Jarrett	Oldsmobile
29	Morgan Shepherd	Oldsmobile
30	Brad Teague	Ford
31	Alan Kulwicki	Ford
32	Jim Sauter	Oldsmobile
33	Dana Patten	Buick
34	Brad Noffsinger	Buick
35	Ken Schrader	Chevrolet
36	Derrike Cope	Ford
37	Randy LaJoie	Chevrolet
38	Richard Petty	Pontiac
39	Mark Martin	Ford
40	Rodney Combs	Buick

GOODY'S 500

Time of Race: 3 hours, 30 minutes, 26 seconds
Average Speed: 74.988 mph
Margin of Victory: 5.27 seconds

FINISH	DRIVER	CAR
1	Darrell Waltrip	Chevrolet
2	Alan Kulwicki	Ford
3	Rusty Wallace	Pontiac
4	Ken Schrader	Chevrolet
5	Geoff Bodine	Chevrolet
6	Bill Elliott	Ford
7	Terry Labonte	Chevrolet
8	Dale Earnhardt	Chevrolet
9	Mark Martin	Ford
10	Brett Bodine	Ford
11	Ernie Irvan	Pontiac
12	Greg Sacks	Oldsmobile
13	Dave Marcis	Chevrolet
14	Bobby Hillin	Buick
15	Brad Teague	Ford
16	Rick Wilson	Oldsmobile
17	Ken Bouchard	Ford
18	Davey Allison	Ford
19	Neil Bonnett	Pontiac
20	Benny Parsons	Ford
21	Phil Parsons	Oldsmobile
22	Kyle Petty	Ford
23	Jimmy Means	Pontiac
24	Ricky Rudd	Buick
25	Michael Waltrip	Pontiac
26	Sterling Marlin	Oldsmobile
27	Richard Petty	Pontiac
28	Lake Speed	Oldsmobile
29	Mike Alexander	Buick
30	Harry Gant	Chevrolet
31	Morgan Shepherd	Buick
32	Dale Jarrett	Oldsmobile

OAKWOOD HOMES 500

Time of Race: 3 hours, 50 minutes, 02 seconds
Average Speed: 130.677 mph
Margin of Victory: 1 car length

FINISH	DRIVER	CAR
1	Rusty Wallace	Pontiac
2	Darrell Waltrip	Chevrolet
3	Brett Bodine	Ford
4	Bill Elliott	Ford
5	Sterling Marlin	Oldsmobile
6	Bobby Hillin	Buick
7	Ken Schrader	Chevrolet
8	Ricky Rudd	Buick
9	Mark Martin	Ford
10	Terry Labonte	Chevrolet
11	Kyle Petty	Ford
12	Benny Parsons	Ford
13	Jim Sauter	Pontiac
14	Rob Moroso	Chevrolet
15	Brad Teague	Chevrolet
16	Morgan Shepherd	Buick
17	Dale Earnhardt	Chevrolet
18	Neil Bonnett	Pontiac
19	Davey Allison	Ford
20	Lee Faulk	Oldsmobile
21	Mike Alexander	Buick
22	Cale Yarborough	Oldsmobile
23	Michael Waltrip	Pontiac
24	Harry Gant	Chevrolet
25	Rick Wilson	Oldsmobile
26	Dave Marcis	Chevrolet
27	Phil Parsons	Oldsmobile
28	Alan Kulwicki	Ford
29	Greg Sacks	Oldsmobile
30	Tommy Ellis	Buick
31	Geoff Bodine	Chevrolet
32	Derrike Cope	Ford
33	Ken Bouchard	Ford
34	Lake Speed	Oldsmobile
35	Joe Ruttman	Chevrolet
36	A.J. Foyt	Oldsmobile
37	Dale Jarrett	Buick
38	Richard Petty	Pontiac
39	Mickey Gibbs	Ford
40	Eddie Bierschwale	Oldsmobile
41	Larry Pearson	Chevrolet
42	Jimmy Means	Pontiac

HOLLY FARMS 400

Time of Race: 2 hours, 39 minutes, 15 seconds
Average Speed: 94.192 mph
Margin of Victory: 1 car length

FINISH	DRIVER	CAR
1	Rusty Wallace	Pontiac
2	Phil Parsons	Oldsmobile
3	Geoff Bodine	Chevrolet
4	Terry Labonte	Chevrolet
5	Bill Elliott	Ford
6	Dale Earnhardt	Chevrolet
7	Ricky Rudd	Buick
8	Ken Schrader	Chevrolet
9	Mike Alexander	Buick
10	Greg Sacks	Oldsmobile
11	Davey Allison	Ford
12	Darrell Waltrip	Chevrolet
13	Bobby Hillin	Buick
14	Sterling Marlin	Oldsmobile
15	Lake Speed	Oldsmobile
16	Kyle Petty	Ford
17	Brett Bodine	Ford
18	Richard Petty	Pontiac
19	Mark Martin	Ford
20	Rick Wilson	Oldsmobile
21	Dave Marcis	Chevrolet
22	Morgan Shepherd	Buick
23	Dale Jarrett	Oldsmobile
24	Jimmy Means	Ford
25	Michael Waltrip	Pontiac
26	Ernie Irvan	Pontiac
27	Ken Bouchard	Ford

28	Neil Bonnett	Pontiac
29	Alan Kulwicki	Ford
30	Harry Gant	Chevrolet
31	Rob Moroso	Oldsmobile
32	Lee Faulk	Oldsmobile

AC DELCO 500

Time of Race: 4 hours, 29 minutes, 07 seconds
Average Speed: 111.557 mph
Margin of Victory: 13.50 seconds

FINISH	DRIVER	CAR
1	Rusty Wallace	Pontiac
2	Ricky Rudd	Buick
3	Terry Labonte	Chevrolet
4	Bill Elliott	Ford
5	Dale Earnhardt	Chevrolet
6	Mike Alexander	Buick
7	Harry Gant	Chevrolet
8	Phil Parsons	Oldsmobile
9	Kyle Petty	Ford
10	Neil Bonnett	Pontiac
11	Ken Schrader	Chevrolet
12	Greg Sacks	Oldsmobile
13	Benny Parsons	Ford
14	Morgan Shepherd	Buick
15	Ernie Irvan	Pontiac
16	Dave Marcis	Chevrolet
17	Jim Sauter	Oldsmobile
18	Ken Bouchard	Pontiac
19	Michael Waltrip	Pontiac
20	Ben Hess	Oldsmobile
21	Connie Saylor	Buick
22	Rick Wilson	Oldsmobile
23	Bobby Hillin	Buick
24	Lake Speed	Oldsmobile
25	Richard Petty	Pontiac
26	Alan Kulwicki	Ford
27	Davey Allison	Ford
28	Mark Martin	Ford
29	Brett Bodine	Ford
30	Geoff Bodine	Chevrolet
31	Darrell Waltrip	Chevrolet
32	Dale Jarrett	Oldsmobile
33	Eddie Bierschwale	Oldsmobile
34	Sterling Marlin	Oldsmobile
35	Brad Teague	Ford
36	Derrike Cope	Ford
37	Brad Noffsinger	Buick
38	Joe Ruttman	Buick
39	Jimmy Means	Pontiac
40	Rodney Combs	Chevrolet

CHECKER 500

Time of Race: 3 hours, 26 minutes, 57 seconds
Average Speed: 90.457 mph
Margin of Victory: 18.5 seconds

FINISH	DRIVER	CAR
1	Alan Kulwicki	Ford
2	Terry Labonte	Chevrolet
3	Davey Allison	Ford
4	Bill Elliott	Ford
5	Rusty Wallace	Pontiac
6	Geoff Bodine	Chevrolet
7	Bobby Hillin	Buick
8	Benny Parsons	Ford
9	Phil Parsons	Oldsmobile
10	Sterling Marlin	Oldsmobile
11	Dale Earnhardt	Chevrolet
12	Harry Gant	Chevrolet
13	Darrell Waltrip	Chevrolet

14	Ken Schrader	Chevrolet
15	Lake Speed	Oldsmobile
16	Derrike Cope	Ford
17	Kyle Petty	Ford
18	Dave Marcis	Chevrolet
19	Chad Little	Ford
20	Trevor Boys	Oldsmobile
21	Neil Bonnett	Pontiac
22	Ernie Irvan	Pontiac
23	Ken Bouchard	Pontiac
24	Jimmy Means	Pontiac
25	Brad Noffsinger	Buick
26	Ricky Rudd	Buick
27	Mike Alexander	Buick
28	Michael Waltrip	Pontiac
29	Rick Wilson	Oldsmobile
30	Roy Smith	Ford
31	Dale Jarrett	Oldsmobile
32	Jim Sauter	Pontiac
33	Gary Collins	Oldsmobile
34	Hershel McGriff	Pontiac
35	Richard Petty	Pontiac
36	Mark Martin	Ford
37	Bill Schmitt	Chevrolet
38	Greg Sacks	Oldsmobile
39	Johnny Rutherford	Oldsmobile
40	Eddie Bierschwale	Oldsmobile
41	Joe Ruttman	Ford
42	Jim Bown	Chevrolet
43	Brett Bodine	Ford

ATLANTA JOURNAL 500

Time of Race: 3 hours, 52 minutes, 09 seconds
Average Speed: 129.024 mph
Margin of Victory: 4.25 seconds

FINISH	DRIVER	CAR
1	Rusty Wallace	Pontiac
2	Davey Allison	Ford
3	Mike Alexander	Buick
4	Ricky Rudd	Buick
5	Darrell Waltrip	Chevrolet
6	Ken Schrader	Chevrolet
7	Michael Waltrip	Pontiac
8	Terry Labonte	Chevrolet
9	Bobby Hillin	Buick
10	Cale Yarborough	Oldsmobile
11	Bill Elliott	Ford
12	Sterling Marlin	Oldsmobile
13	Neil Bonnett	Pontiac
14	Dale Earnhardt	Chevrolet
15	Geoff Bodine	Chevrolet
16	Phil Parsons	Oldsmobile
17	Rick Wilson	Oldsmobile
18	Ernie Irvan	Pontiac
19	Dave Marcis	Chevrolet
20	Mark Martin	Ford
21	Larry Pearson	Chevrolet
22	Kyle Petty	Ford
23	Jim Sauter	Oldsmobile
24	Eddie Bierschwale	Oldsmobile
25	Alan Kulwicki	Ford
26	Brad Noffsinger	Buick
27	Brett Bodine	Ford
28	Greg Sacks	Oldsmobile
29	Rodney Combs	Buick
30	Harry Gant	Chevrolet
31	A.J. Foyt	Oldsmobile
32	Jimmy Horton	Ford
33	Derrike Cope	Ford
34	Benny Parsons	Ford
35	H.B. Bailey	Pontiac
36	Richard Petty	Pontiac
37	Lake Speed	Oldsmobile
38	Jimmy Means	Pontiac
39	Brad Teague	Chevrolet
40	Morgan Shepherd	Pontiac
41	Dale Jarrett	Buick
42	Tommy Ellis	Buick

1989

DAYTONA 500

Time of Race: 3 hours, , 22 minutes,, 04 seconds
Average Speed: 148.466 mph
Margin of Victory: 6 seconds

FINISH	DRIVER	CAR
1	Darrell Waltrip	Chevrolet
2	Ken Schrader	Chevrolet
3	Dale Earnhardt	Chevrolet
4	Geoff Bodine	Chevrolet
5	Phil Parsons	Oldsmobile
6	Rick Mast	Chevrolet
7	Alan Kulwicki	Ford
8	Rick Wilson	Oldsmobile
9	Terry Labonte	Ford
10	Eddie Bierschwale	Oldsmobile
11	Sterling Marlin	Oldsmobile
12	Harry Gant	Oldsmobile
13	Joe Ruttman	Pontiac
14	Larry Pearson	Buick
15	Morgan Shepherd	Pontiac
16	Ken Bouchard	Pontiac
17	Richard Petty	Pontiac
18	Rusty Wallace	Pontiac
19	Ricky Rudd	Buick
20	Dave Marcis	Chevrolet
21	Michael Waltrip	Pontiac
22	Ben Hess	Oldsmobile
23	Greg Sacks	Pontiac
24	J.D. McDuffie	Pontiac
25	Davey Allison	Ford
26	Lee Raymond	Ford
27	Mike Alexander	Buick
28	Ronnie Sanders	Chevrolet
29	Brett Bodine	Ford
30	Lake Speed	Oldsmobile
31	Phil Barkdoll	Oldsmobile
32	Dale Jarrett	Pontiac
33	Mark Martin	Ford
34	Mickey Gibbs	Pontiac
35	Bill Elliott	Ford
36	Chad Little	Ford
37	Rodney Combs	Pontiac
38	A.J. Foyt	Oldsmobile
39	Bobby Hillin	Buick
40	Charlie Baker	Chevrolet
41	Ernie Irvan	Pontiac
42	Neil Bonnett	Ford

GOODWRENCH 500

Time of Race: 4 hours, 20 minutes, 47 seconds
Average Speed: 115.122 mph
Margin of Victory: 1.6 seconds

FINISH	DRIVER	CAR
1	Rusty Wallace	Pontiac
2	Alan Kulwicki	Ford
3	Dale Earnhardt	Chevrolet
4	Geoff Bodine	Chevrolet
5	Mark Martin	Ford
6	Davey Allison	Ford
7	Sterling Marlin	Oldsmobile
8	Lake Speed	Oldsmobile
9	Greg Sacks	Pontiac
10	Jim Sauter	Pontiac
11	Dale Jarrett	Pontiac
12	Michael Waltrip	Pontiac
13	Dick Trickle	Buick
14	Neil Bonnett	Ford

15	Bobby Hillin	Buick
16	Richard Petty	Pontiac
17	Rick Wilson	Oldsmobile
18	Terry Labonte	Ford
19	Bill Elliott	Ford
20	Mickey Gibbs	Pontiac
21	Rick Mast	Chevrolet
22	Ben Hess	Oldsmobile
23	Ernie Irvan	Pontiac
24	Dave Mader	Pontiac
25	Ken Schrader	Chevrolet
26	Eddie Bierschwale	Oldsmobile
27	Morgan Shepherd	Pontiac
28	Jerry O'Neil	Chevrolet
29	Darrell Waltrip	Chevrolet
30	Larry Pearson	Buick
31	Harry Gant	Oldsmobile
32	Ricky Rudd	Buick
33	Jimmy Means	Pontiac
34	Brett Bodine	Ford
35	Dave Marcis	Chevrolet
36	Jim Bown	Chevrolet
37	J.D. McDuffie	Pontiac
38	Ken Bouchard	Pontiac
39	Phil Parsons	Oldsmobile
40	Rodney Combs	Buick
41	Hut Stricklin	Pontiac
42	Butch Miller	Chevrolet

MOTORCRAFT QUALITY PARTS 500

Time of Race: 3 hours, 34 minutes, 26 seconds
Average Speed: 139.684 mph
Margin of Victory: .65 second

FINISH	DRIVER	CAR
1	Darrell Waltrip	Chevrolet
2	Dale Earnhardt	Chevrolet
3	Dick Trickle	Buick
4	Kyle Petty	Pontiac
5	Sterling Marlin	Oldsmobile
6	Rick Wilson	Oldsmobile
7	Neil Bonnett	Ford
8	Hut Stricklin	Pontiac
9	Dale Jarrett	Pontiac
10	Morgan Shepherd	Pontiac
11	Bill Elliott	Ford
12	Ernie Irvan	Pontiac
13	Jimmy Horton	Pontiac
14	Phil Parsons	Oldsmobile
15	Ken Schrader	Chevrolet
16	Alan Kulwicki	Ford
17	Ben Hess	Oldsmobile
18	Jimmy Means	Pontiac
19	Geoff Bodine	Chevrolet
20	Michael Waltrip	Pontiac
21	Lake Speed	Oldsmobile
22	Larry Pearson	Buick
23	Eddie Bierschwale	Oldsmobile
24	Ricky Rudd	Buick
25	Rick Mast	Chevrolet
26	Greg Sacks	Pontiac
27	Richard Petty	Pontiac
28	A.J. Foyt	Oldsmobile
29	Harry Gant	Oldsmobile
30	Bobby Hillin	Buick
31	Rusty Wallace	Pontiac
32	Jim Sauter	Pontiac
33	Brett Bodine	Ford
34	Derrike Cope	Pontiac
35	Chad Little	Ford
36	Terry Labonte	Ford
37	Ken Bouchard	Pontiac
38	Mark Martin	Ford
39	Mickey Gibbs	Pontiac
40	Davey Allison	Ford
41	Jim Bown	Chevrolet
42	Dave Marcis	Chevrolet

PONTIAC EXCITEMENT 400

Time of Race: 3 hours, 20 minutes, 51 seconds
Average Speed: 89.619 mph
Margin of Victory: 2.8 seconds

FINISH	DRIVER	CAR
1	Rusty Wallace	Pontiac
2	Alan Kulwicki	Ford
3	Dale Earnhardt	Chevrolet
4	Ricky Rudd	Buick
5	Davey Allison	Ford
6	Larry Pearson	Buick
7	Darrell Waltrip	Chevrolet
8	Sterling Marlin	Oldsmobile
9	Ernie Irvan	Pontiac
10	Bill Elliott	Ford
11	Mark Martin	Ford
12	Lake Speed	Ford
13	Michael Waltrip	Pontiac
14	Harry Gant	Oldsmobile
15	Bobby Hillin	Buick
16	Rick Mast	Chevrolet
17	Rick Wilson	Oldsmobile
18	Geoff Bodine	Chevrolet
19	Ken Schrader	Chevrolet
20	Dave Marcis	Chevrolet
21	Neil Bonnett	Ford
22	Chad Little	Ford
23	Dale Jarrett	Pontiac
24	Ben Hess	Oldsmobile
25	Dick Trickle	Buick
26	Butch Miller	Chevrolet
27	Phil Parsons	Oldsmobile
28	Brett Bodine	Ford
29	Mickey Gibbs	Pontiac
30	Terry Labonte	Chevrolet
31	Eddie Bierschwale	Oldsmobile
32	Rodney Combs	Buick
33	Morgan Shepherd	Pontiac
34	Greg Sacks	Pontiac
35	Derrike Cope	Pontiac
36	Jim Sauter	Oldsmobile

TRANSOUTH 500

Time of Race: 4 hours, 20 minutes, 29 seconds
Average Speed: 115.475 mph
Margin of Victory: 1.05 second

FINISH	DRIVER	CAR
1	Harry Gant	Oldsmobile
2	Davey Allison	Ford
3	Geoff Bodine	Chevrolet
4	Mark Martin	Ford
5	Sterling Marlin	Oldsmobile
6	Bill Elliott	Ford
7	Alan Kulwicki	Ford
8	Rusty Wallace	Pontiac
9	Michael Waltrip	Pontiac
10	Lake Speed	Oldsmobile
11	Rick Wilson	Oldsmobile
12	Ricky Rudd	Buick
13	Dick Trickle	Buick
14	Brett Bodine	Ford
15	Richard Petty	Pontiac
16	Morgan Shepherd	Pontiac
17	Dave Marcis	Chevrolet
18	Terry Labonte	Ford
19	Jim Sauter	Pontiac
20	Larry Pearson	Buick
21	Eddie Bierschwale	Oldsmobile
22	Ken Bouchard	Pontiac
23	Ben Hess	Oldsmobile
24	Ernie Irvan	Pontiac
25	Greg Sacks	Pontiac
26	Bobby Hillin	Buick

FINISH	DRIVER	CAR
27	Ken Schrader	Chevrolet
28	Kyle Petty	Pontiac
29	Rodney Combs	Pontiac
30	Hut Stricklin	Pontiac
31	J.D. McDuffie	Pontiac
32	Jimmy Horton	Pontiac
33	Dale Earnhardt	Chevrolet
34	Rick Mast	Chevrolet
35	Derrike Cope	Pontiac
36	Darrell Waltrip	Chevrolet
37	Chad Little	Ford
38	Jimmy Means	Pontiac
39	Neil Bonnett	Ford
40	Dale Jarrett	Pontiac
41	Phil Parsons	Oldsmobile

VALLEYDALE MEATS 500

Time of Race: 3 hours, 30 minutes, 18 seconds
Average Speed: 76.034 mph
Margin of Victory: .26 second

FINISH	DRIVER	CAR
1	Rusty Wallace	Pontiac
2	Darrell Waltrip	Chevrolet
3	Geoff Bodine	Chevrolet
4	Davey Allison	Ford
5	Dick Trickle	Buick
6	Mark Martin	Ford
7	Greg Sacks	Pontiac
8	Ricky Rudd	Buick
9	Bill Elliott	Ford
10	Harry Gant	Oldsmobile
11	Michael Waltrip	Pontiac
12	Neil Bonnett	Ford
13	Jim Sauter	Pontiac
14	Rick Mast	Chevrolet
15	Sterling Marlin	Oldsmobile
16	Dale Earnhardt	Chevrolet
17	Brad Teague	Pontiac
18	Larry Pearson	Buick
19	Eddie Bierschwale	Oldsmobile
20	Alan Kulwicki	Ford
21	Rick Wilson	Oldsmobile
22	Dale Jarrett	Pontiac
23	Phil Parsons	Oldsmobile
24	Terry Labonte	Ford
25	Lake Speed	Oldsmobile
26	Morgan Shepherd	Pontiac
27	Bobby Hillin	Buick
28	Hut Stricklin	Pontiac
29	Ernie Irvan	Pontiac
30	Brett Bodine	Ford
31	Butch Miller	Chevrolet
32	Ken Schrader	Chevrolet

FIRST UNION 400

Time of Race: 2 hours, 46 minutes, 47 seconds
Average Speed: 89.937 mph
Margin of Victory: 3 seconds

FINISH	DRIVER	CAR
1	Dale Earnhardt	Chevrolet
2	Alan Kulwicki	Ford
3	Mark Martin	Ford
4	Dick Trickle	Buick
5	Terry Labonte	Ford
6	Ricky Rudd	Buick
7	Geoff Bodine	Chevrolet
8	Darrell Waltrip	Chevrolet
9	Rusty Wallace	Pontiac
10	Ernie Irvan	Pontiac
11	Davey Allison	Ford
12	Phil Parsons	Chevrolet

13	Neil Bonnett	Ford
14	Ken Schrader	Chevrolet
15	Ben Hess	Oldsmobile
16	Hut Stricklin	Pontiac
17	Morgan Shepherd	Pontiac
18	Eddie Bierschwale	Oldsmobile
19	Dale Jarrett	Pontiac
20	Dave Marcis	Chevrolet
21	Greg Sacks	Pontiac
22	Bill Elliott	Ford
23	Harry Gant	Oldsmobile
24	Larry Pearson	Buick
25	Rick Mast	Chevrolet
26	Sterling Marlin	Oldsmobile
27	Lake Speed	Oldsmobile
28	Brett Bodine	Ford
29	Michael Waltrip	Pontiac
30	Rick Wilson	Oldsmobile
31	Jim Sauter	Oldsmobile
32	Jimmy Means	Pontiac

PANNILL SWEATSHIRTS 500

Time of Race: 3 hours, 19 minutes, 41 seconds
Average Speed: 79.025 mph
Margin of Victory: 6.79 seconds

FINISH	DRIVER	CAR
1	Darrell Waltrip	Chevrolet
2	Dale Earnhardt	Chevrolet
3	Dick Trickle	Buick
4	Rick Wilson	Oldsmobile
5	Terry Labonte	Ford
6	Mark Martin	Ford
7	Ken Schrader	Chevrolet
8	Sterling Marlin	Oldsmobile
9	Dave Marcis	Chevrolet
10	Neil Bonnett	Ford
11	Lake Speed	Oldsmobile
12	Harry Gant	Oldsmobile
13	Phil Parsons	Oldsmobile
14	Davey Allison	Ford
15	Dale Jarrett	Pontiac
16	Geoff Bodine	Chevrolet
17	Ben Hess	Oldsmobile
18	Morgan Shepherd	Pontiac
19	Ernie Irvan	Pontiac
20	Bill Elliott	Ford
21	Bobby Hillin	Buick
22	Alan Kulwicki	Ford
23	Ricky Rudd	Buick
24	Richard Petty	Pontiac
25	Michael Waltrip	Pontiac
26	Chad Little	Ford
27	Brett Bodine	Motorcraft
28	Greg Sacks	Pontiac
29	Larry Pearson	Buick
30	Hut Stricklin	Pontiac
31	Rusty Wallace	Pontiac
32	Rick Mast	Chevrolet

WINSTON 500

Time of Race: 3 hours, 12 minutes, 30 seconds
Average Speed: 155.869 mph
Margin of Victory: 1 car length

FINISH	DRIVER	CAR
1	Davey Allison	Ford
2	Terry Labonte	Ford
3	Mark Martin	Ford
4	Morgan Shepherd	Pontiac
5	Darrell Waltrip	Chevrolet
6	Ken Schrader	Chevrolet
7	Harry Gant	Oldsmobile
8	Dale Earnhardt	Chevrolet
9	Neil Bonnett	Ford

10	Rusty Wallace	Pontiac
11	Bill Elliott	Ford
12	Geoff Bodine	Chevrolet
13	Alan Kulwicki	Ford
14	Sterling Marlin	Oldsmobile
15	Rick Wilson	Oldsmobile
16	A.J. Foyt	Oldsmobile
17	Phil Parsons	Oldsmobile
18	Lake Speed	Oldsmobile
19	Brett Bodine	Ford
20	Dave Marcis	Chevrolet
21	Michael Waltrip	Pontiac
22	Ben Hess	Oldsmobile
23	Richard Petty	Pontiac
24	Grant Adcox	Chevrolet
25	Ernie Irvan	Pontiac
26	Charlie Baker	Buick
27	Dick Trickle	Buick
28	Kyle Petty	Pontiac
29	Larry Pearson	Buick
30	Derrike Cope	Pontiac
31	Ricky Rudd	Buick
32	Phil Barkdoll	Oldsmobile
33	Hut Stricklin	Poantiac
34	Chad Little	Ford
35	Bobby Hillin	Buick
36	Jim Sauter	Pontiac
37	Greg Sacks	Pontiac
38	Ron Esau	Pontiac
39	Eddie Bierschwale	Oldsmobile
40	Dale Jarrett	Pontiac
41	Jimmy Means	Pontiac

COCA COLA 600

Time of Race: 4 hours, 9 minutes, 52 seconds
Average Speed: 144.077 mph
Margin of Victory: .99 second

FINISH	DRIVER	CAR
1	Darrell Waltrip	Chevrolet
2	Sterling Marlin	Oldsmobile
3	Ken Schrader	Chevrolet
4	Geoff Bodine	Chevrolet
5	Bill Elliott	Ford
6	Mark Martin	Ford
7	Neil Bonnett	Ford
8	Brett Bodine	Ford
9	Bobby Hillin	Buick
10	Ricky Rudd	Buick
11	Rick Mast	Chevrolet
12	Derrike Cope	Pontiac
13	Phil Parsons	Oldsmobile
14	Hut Stricklin	Pontiac
15	Ernie Irvan	Pontiac
16	Dave Marcis	Chevrolet
17	Kyle Petty	Chevrolet
18	Chad Little	Ford
19	Richard Petty	Pontiac
20	Ben Hess	Oldsmobile
21	Terry Byers	Chevrolet
22	Larry Pearson	Buick
23	Alan Kulwicki	Ford
24	Lake Speed	Oldsmobile
25	Tracy Leslie	Oldsmobile
26	Jerry O'Neil	Chevrolet
27	Michael Waltrip	Pontiac
28	Dale Jarrett	Pontiac
29	Dick Trickle	Buick
30	Greg Sacks	Pontiac
31	Rusty Wallace	Pontiac
32	Morgan Shepherd	Pontiac
33	Davey Allison	Ford
34	Allan Grice	Pontiac
35	Rick Wilson	Oldsmobile
36	Eddie Bierschwale	Oldsmobile
37	Jim Sauter	Pontiac
38	Dale Earnhardt	Chevrolet
39	Terry Labonte	Ford
40	Harry Gant	Oldsmobile
41	Jimmy Means	Pontiac
42	Butch Miller	Chevrolet

BUDWEISER 500

Time of Race: 4 hours, 6 minutes, 34 seconds
Average Speed: 121.670 mph
Margin of Victory: .51 second

FINISH	DRIVER	CAR
1	Dale Earnhardt	Chevrolet
2	Mark Martin	Ford
3	Ken Schrader	Chevrolet
4	Terry Labonte	Ford
5	Rusty Wallace	Pontiac
6	Ricky Rudd	Buick
7	Neil Bonnett	Ford
8	Bill Elliott	Ford
9	Darrell Waltrip	Chevrolet
10	Phil Parsons	Oldsmobile
11	Dale Jarrett	Pontiac
12	Hut Stricklin	Pontiac
13	Bobby Hillin	Buick
14	Rick Wilson	Oldsmobile
15	Brett Bodine	Ford
16	Dave Marcis	Chevrolet
17	Ernie Irvan	Pontiac
18	Lake Speed	Oldsmobile
19	Larry Pearson	Buick
20	Richard Petty	Pontiac
21	Dick Trickle	Buick
22	Michael Waltrip	Pontiac
23	Harry Gant	Oldsmobile
24	Jimmy Means	Pontiac
25	Alan Kulwicki	Ford
26	Sterling Marlin	Oldsmobile
27	Eddie Bierschwale	Oldsmobile
28	Derrike Cope	Pontiac
29	Geoff Bodine	Chevrolet
30	Norm Benning	Chevrolet
31	Jimmy Horton	Pontiac
32	Davey Allison	Ford
33	Morgan Shepherd	Pontiac
34	Jimmy Spencer	Pontiac
35	Bill Flowers	Buick

BANQUET FROZEN FOODS 300

Time of Race: 2 hours, 27 minutes, 03 seconds
Average Speed: 76.088 mph
Margin of Victory: .05 second

FINISH	DRIVER	CAR
1	Ricky Rudd	Buick
2	Rusty Wallace	Pontiac
3	Bill Elliott	Ford
4	Dale Earnhardt	Chevrolet
5	Lake Speed	Oldsmobile
6	Joe Ruttman	Pontiac
7	Morgan Shepherd	Pontiac
8	Rick Wilson	Oldsmobile
9	Davey Allison	Ford
10	Michael Waltrip	Pontiac
11	Neil Bonnett	Ford
12	Harry Gant	Oldsmobile
13	Bobby Hillin	Buick
14	Hershel McGriff	Pontiac
15	Terry Labonte	Ford
16	Dave Marcis	Chevrolet
17	Bill Schmitt	Chevrolet
18	Phil Parsons	Oldsmobile
19	Larry Pearson	Buick
20	Geoff Bodine	Chevrolet
21	Hut Stricklin	Pontiac
22	Darin Brassfield	Chevrolet
23	Ernie Irvan	Pontiac
24	Troy Beebe	Buick
25	Terry Fisher	Chevrolet
26	Richard Petty	Pontiac
27	Brett Bodine	Ford
28	Rick McCray	Pontiac

FINISH	DRIVER	CAR
29	Jim Bown	Chevrolet
30	Dick Trickle	Buick
31	Mark Martin	Ford
32	Dick Johnson	Ford
33	John Krebs	Pontiac
34	Eddie Bierschwale	Oldsmobile
35	Bill Cooper	Ford
36	Alan Kulwicki	Ford
37	Ken Schrader	Chevrolet
38	Darrell Waltrip	Chevrolet
39	Roy Smith	Ford
40	Sterling Marlin	Oldsmobile
41	Ron Esau	Oldsmobile
42	Dale Jarrett	Pontiac

MILLER HIGH LIFE 500

Time of Race: 3 hours, 48 minutes, 27 seconds
Average Speed: 131.320 mph
Margin of Victory: 2 seconds

FINISH	DRIVER	CAR
1	Terry Labonte	Ford
2	Harry Gant	Oldsmobile
3	Dale Earnhardt	Chevrolet
4	Ken Schrader	Chevrolet
5	Morgan Shepherd	Pontiac
6	Sterling Marlin	Oldsmobile
7	Dale Jarrett	Pontiac
8	Neil Bonnett	Ford
9	Larry Pearson	Buick
10	Brett Bodine	Ford
11	Lake Speed	Oldsmobile
12	Phil Parsons	Oldsmobile
13	Bobby Hillin	Buick
14	Michael Waltrip	Pontiac
15	Mark Martin	Ford
16	Davey Allison	Ford
17	Hut Stricklin	Pontiac
18	Dave Marcis	Chevrolet
19	Terry Byers	Chevrolet
20	Ricky Rudd	Buick
21	Bill Elliott	Ford
22	Rusty Wallace	Pontiac
23	Bobby Gerhart	Oldsmobile
24	Dick Trickle	Buick
25	Richard Petty	Pontiac
26	Ernie Irvan	Pontiac
27	Rick Wilson	Oldsmobile
28	Randy LaJoie	Chevrolet
29	Jimmy Means	Pontiac
30	Norm Benning	Chevrolet
31	Trevor Boys	Buick
32	Darrell Waltrip	Chevrolet
33	Jimmy Spencer	Pontiac
34	Alan Kulwicki	Ford
35	Geoff Bodine	Chevrolet
36	Derrike Cope	Pontiac
37	Jimmy Horton	Pontiac
38	Tommie Crozier	Chevrolet

MILLER HIGH LIFE 400

Time of Race: 2 hours, 52 minutes, 38 seconds
Average Speed: 139.023 mph
Margin of Victory: 2.09 seconds

FINISH	DRIVER	CAR
1	Bill Elliott	Ford
2	Rusty Wallace	Pontiac
3	Darrell Waltrip	Chevrolet
4	Ricky Rudd	Buick
5	Brett Bodine	Ford
6	Rick Wilson	Oldsmobile
7	Lake Speed	Oldsmobile
8	Sterling Marlin	Oldsmobile

9	Derrike Cope	Pontiac
10	Kyle Petty	Pontiac
11	Ken Schrader	Chevrolet
12	Mark Martin	Ford
13	Jimmy Spencer	Pontiac
14	Terry Labonte	Ford
15	Phil Parsons	Oldsmobile
16	Michael Waltrip	Pontiac
17	Dale Earnhardt	Chevrolet
18	Ernie Irvan	Pontiac
19	Larry Pearson	Buick
20	Bobby Hillin	Buick
21	Dave Marcis	Chevrolet
22	Dale Jarrett	Pontiac
23	Ronnie Thomas	Ford
24	Neil Bonnett	Ford
25	Dick Trickle	Buick
26	H.B. Bailey	Pontiac
27	Geoff Bodine	Chevrolet
28	Jimmy Means	Pontiac
29	Eddie Bierschwale	Oldsmobile
30	Richard Petty	Pontiac
31	Davey Allison	Ford
32	Harry Gant	Oldsmobile
33	Hut Stricklin	Pontiac
34	Mike Miller	Chevrolet
35	Morgan Shepherd	Pontiac
36	Alan Kulwicki	Ford
37	Bill Venturini	Chevrolet
38	Butch Miller	Chevrolet
39	Greg Sacks	Pontiac
40	Rodney Combs	Pontiac

PEPSI 400

Time of Race: 3 hours, 1 minute, 32 seconds
Average Speed: 132.207 mph
Margin of Victory: .18 second

FINISH	DRIVER	CAR
1	Davey Allison	Ford
2	Morgan Shepherd	Pontiac
3	Phil Parsons	Oldsmobile
4	Bill Elliott	Ford
5	Alan Kulwicki	Ford
6	Terry Labonte	Ford
7	Sterling Marlin	Oldsmobile
8	Dick Trickle	Buick
9	Ricky Rudd	Buick
10	Hut Stricklin	Pontiac
11	Brett Bodine	Ford
12	Jimmy Means	Pontiac
13	Grant Adcox	Chevrolet
14	Kyle Petty	Pontiac
15	Phil Barkdoll	Oldsmobile
16	Mark Martin	Ford
17	Rusty Wallace	Pontiac
18	Dale Earnhardt	Chevrolet
19	Darrell Waltrip	Chevrolet
20	Richard Petty	Pontiac
21	Neil Bonnett	Ford
22	Geoff Bodine	Chevrolet
23	Ernie Irvan	Pontiac
24	Lake Speed	Oldsmobile
25	Dave Marcis	Chevrolet
26	Derrike Cope	Pontiac
27	Jimmy Spencer	Pontiac
28	Bobby Hillin	Buick
29	Rick Wilson	Oldsmobile
30	Larry Pearson	Buick
31	Dale Jarrett	Pontiac
32	Harry Gant	Oldsmoible
33	Mark Gibson	Pontiac
34	Michael Waltrip	Pontiac
35	A.J. Foyt	Oldsmobile
36	Ken Schrader	Chevrolet
37	Stan Barrett	Ford
38	Jim Sauter	Pontiac
39	Patty Moise	Buick
40	Johnny McFadden	Pontiac

AC SPARK PLUG 500

Time of Race: 4 hours, 14 minutes, 34 seconds
Average Speed: 117.847 mph
Margin of Victory: 2.21 seconds

FINISH	DRIVER	CAR
1	Bill Elliott	Ford
2	Rusty Wallace	Pontiac
3	Mark Martin	Ford
4	Darrell Waltrip	Chevrolet
5	Harry Gant	Oldsmobile
6	Davey Allison	Ford
7	Ken Schrader	Chevrolet
8	Morgan Shepherd	Pontiac
9	Dale Earnhardt	Chevrolet
10	Brett Bodine	Ford
11	Bobby Hillin	Buick
12	Phil Parsons	Oldsmobile
13	Terry Labonte	Ford
14	Kyle Petty	Pontiac
15	Jimmy Spencer	Pontiac
16	Jim Sauter	Pontiac
17	Geoff Bodine	Chevrolet
18	Dale Jarrett	Pontiac
19	Dave Marcis	Chevrolet
20	Dick Trickle	Buick
21	Terry Byers	Chevrolet
22	Dick Johnson	Ford
23	Neil Bonnett	Ford
24	Jimmy Means	Pontiac
25	Rick Wilson	Oldsmobile
26	Ernie Irvan	Pontiac
27	Bob Schacht	Ford
28	Michael Waltrip	Pontiac
29	Lake Speed	Oldsmobile
30	Greg Sacks	Pontiac
31	Ricky Rudd	Buick
32	Eddie Bierschwale	Chevrolet
33	Jimmy Horton	Pontiac
34	Joe Ruttman	Oldsmobile
35	Derrike Cope	Pontiac
36	Sterling Marlin	Oldsmobile
37	Hut Stricklin	Pontiac
38	Richard Petty	Pontiac
39	Alan Kulwicki	Ford
40	Larry Pearson	Buick

TALLADEGA DIEHARD 500

Time of Race: 3 hours, 10 minutes, 441 seconds
Average Speed: 157.354 mph
Margin of Victory: .2 second

FINISH	DRIVER	CAR
1	Terry Labonte	Ford
2	Darrell Waltrip	Chevrolet
3	Mark Martin	Ford
4	Ken Schrader	Chevrolet
5	Rick Wilson	Oldsmobile
6	Morgan Shepherd	Pontiac
7	Kyle Petty	Pontiac
8	Harry Gant	Oldsmobile
9	Davey Allison	Fokrd
10	Neil Bonnett	Ford
11	Dale Earnhardt	Chevrolet
12	Bill Elliott	Ford
13	Hut Stricklin	Pontiac
14	Brett Bodine	Ford
15	Phil Barkdoll	Oldsmobile
16	Dick Trickle	Buick
17	Ricky Rudd	Buick
18	A.J. Foyt	Oldsmobile
19	Dave Marcis	Chevrolet
20	Ernie Irvan	Pontiac
21	Richard Petty	Pontiac

22	Larry Pearson	Buick
23	Dale Jarrett	Pontiac
24	Dick Johnson	Ford
25	Mickey Gibbs	Pontiac
26	Bill Ingram	Oldsmobile
27	Mark Stahl	Ford
28	Sterling Marlin	Oldsmobile
29	Bobby Hillin	Buick
30	Alan Kulwicki	Ford
31	Joe Ruttman	Oldsmobile
32	Rick Mast	Chevrolet
33	Patty Moise	Buick
34	Stan Barrett	Ford
35	Geoff Bodine	Chevrolet
36	Michael Waltrip	Pontiac
37	Rusty Wallace	Pontiac
38	Derrike Cope	Pontiac
39	Jimmy Means	Pontiac
40	Jimmy Spencer	Pontiac
41	Phil Parsons	Oldsmobile

BUDWEISER AT THE GLEN

Time of Race: 2 hours, 26 minutes, 55 seconds
Average Speed: 87.242 mph
Margin of Victory: 1.06 seconds

FINISH	DRIVER	CAR
1	Rusty Wallace	Pontiac
2	Mark Martin	Ford
3	Dale Earnhardt	Chevrolet
4	Davey Allison	Ford
5	Bobby Hillin	Buick
6	Morgan Shepherd	Pontiac
7	Sterling Marlin	Oldsmobile
8	Rick Wilson	Oldsmobile
9	Jim Sauter	Pontiac
10	Michael Waltrip	Pontiac
11	Larry Pearson	Buick
12	Darin Brassfield	Chevrolet
13	Richard Petty	Pontiac
14	Terry Labonte	Ford
15	Brett Bodine	Ford
16	Darrell Waltrip	Chevrolet
17	Phil Parsons	Oldsmobile
18	Bill Elliott	Ford
19	Harry Gant	Oldsmobile
20	Ken Schrader	Chevrolet
21	Geoff Bodine	Chevrolet
22	Hut Stricklin	Pontiac
23	Dale Jarrett	Pontiac
24	Ernie Irvan	Pontiac
25	Dave Marcis	Chevrolet
26	Stan Barrett	Ford
27	Tom Kendall	Chevrolet
28	Jimmy Spencer	Pontiac
29	Ricky Rudd	Buick
30	Oma Kimbrough	Chevrolet
31	Ted Thomas	Ford
32	Dick Johnson	Ford
33	Jimmy Means	Pontiac
34	Dick Trickle	Buick
35	J.D. McDuffie	Pontiac
36	Neil Bonnett	Ford
37	A.J. Foyt	Oldsmobile
38	Eddie Bierschwale	Oldsmobile
39	Alan Kulwicki	Ford
40	Derrike Cope	Pontiac

CHAMPION SPARK PLUG 400

Time of Race: 2 hours, 32 minutes, 11 seconds
Average Speed: 157.704 mph - Track Record
Margin of Victory: 15.71 seconds

FINISH	DRIVER	CAR
1	Rusty Wallace	Pontiac
2	Morgan Shepherd	Pontiac
3	Harry Gant	Oldsmobile
4	Hut Stricklin	Pontiac
5	Geoff Bodine	Chevrolet
6	Derrike Cope	Pontiac
7	Davey Allison	Ford
8	Ricky Rudd	Buick
9	Mark Martin	Ford
10	Alan Kulwicki	Ford
11	Ken Schrader	Chevrolet
12	Jimmy Spencer	Pontiac
13	Kyle Petty	Pontiac
14	Bobby Hillin	Buick
15	Neil Bonnett	Ford
16	Larry Pearson	Buick
17	Dale Earnhardt	Chevrolet
18	Richard Petty	Pontiac
19	Dick Trickle	Buick
20	Tracy Leslie	Oldsmobile
21	Joe Ruttman	Olds
22	Butch Miller	Chevrolet
23	Jim Sauter	Pontiac
24	Dave Marcis	Chevrolet
25	Ernie Irvan	Pontiac
26	Chad Little	Ford
27	Jimmy Means	Poantiac
28	Eddie Bierschwale	Oldsmobile
29	Ken Ragan	Ford
30	Rick Jeffrey	Pontiac
31	Michael Waltrip	Pontiac
32	Rick Wilson	Oldsmobile
33	Phil Parsons	Oldsmobile
34	Sterling Marlin	Oldsmobile
35	Greg Sacks	Pontiac
36	Brett Bodine	Ford
37	Darrell Waltrip	Chevrolet
38	Dale Jarrett	Pontiac
39	Bill Elliott	Ford
40	Terry Labonte	Ford

BUSCH 500

Time of Race: 3 hours, 04 minutes, 14 seconds
Average Speed: 85.554 mph
Margin of Victory: 5.04 seconds

FINISH	DRIVER	CAR
1	Darrell Waltrip	Chevrolet
2	Alan Kulwicki	Ford
3	Ricky Rudd	Buick
4	Harry Gant	Oldsmobile
5	Terry Labonte	Ford
6	Rusty Wallace	Pontiac
7	Bobby Hillin	Buick
8	Jimmy Spencer	Pontiac
9	Neil Bonnett	Ford
10	Dale Jarrett	Pontiac
11	Phil Parsons	Oldsmobile
12	Dave Marcis	Chevrolet
13	Rick Mast	Chevrolet
14	Dale Earnhardt	Chevrolet
15	Ernie Irvan	Pontiac
16	Geoff Bodine	Chevrolet
17	Brett Bodine	Ford
18	Sterling Marlin	Oldsmobile
19	Hut Stricklin	Pontiac
20	Mark Martin	Ford
21	Larry Pearson	Buick
22	Kyle Petty	Pontiac
23	Ken Schrader	Chevrolet
24	Bill Elliott	Ford
25	Davey Allison	Ford
26	Morgan Shepherd	Pontiac
27	Rick Wilson	Oldsmobile
28	Dick Trickle	Buick
29	Derrike Cope	Pontiac

30	Greg Sacks	Pontiac
31	Joe Ruttman	Olds
32	Michael Waltrip	Pontiac

HEINZ SOUTHERN 500

Time of Race: 3 hours, 42 minutes, 03 seconds
Average Speed: 135.462 mph - Track Record
Margin of Victory: 1.5 seconds

FINISH	DRIVER	CAR
1	Dale Earnhardt	Chevrolet
2	Mark Marin	Ford
3	Ricky Rudd	Buick
4	Rusty Wallace	Pontiac
5	Ken Schrader	Chevrolet
6	Harry Gant	Chevrolet
7	Bill Elliott	Ford
8	Bobby Hillin	Buick
9	Morgan Shepherd	Pontiac
10	Sterling Marlin	Oldsmobile
11	Rick Wilson	Oldsmobile
12	Geoff Bodine	Chevrolet
13	Michael Waltrip	Pontiac
14	Kyle Petty	Pontiac
15	Neil Bonnett	Ford
16	Brett Bodine	Ford
17	Dick Trickle	Buick
18	Davey Allison	Ford
19	Hut Stricklin	Pontiac
20	Dale Jarrett	Pontiac
21	Phil Parsons	Oldsmobile
22	Darrell Waltrip	Chevrolet
23	Rodney Combs	Oldsmobile
24	Ernie Irvan	Pontiac
25	Derrike Cope	Pontiac
26	Jimmy Means	Pontiac
27	H.B. Bailey	Pontiac
28	Dave Marcis	Chevrolet
29	Larry Pearson	Buick
30	Joe Ruttman	Oldsmobile
31	Johnny McFadden	Chevrolet
32	Alan Kulwicki	Ford
33	Terry Labonte	Ford
34	Mike Potter	Ford
35	Richard Petty	Pontiac
36	J.D. McDuffie	Pontiac
37	Jimmy Spencer	Oldsmobile
38	Greg Sacks	Pontiac
39	James Hylton	Buick

MILLER HIGH LIFE 400

Time of Race: 3 hours, 23 minutes, 40 seconds
Average Speed: 88.380 mph
Margin of Victory: 7.41 seconds

FINISH	DRIVER	CAR
1	Rusty Wallace	Pontiac
2	Dale Earnhardt	Chevrolet
3	Geoff Bodine	Chevrolet
4	Ricky Rudd	Buick
5	Harry Gant	Oldsmobile
6	Darrell Waltrip	Chevrolet
7	Neil Bonnett	Ford
8	Dick Trickle	Buick
9	Hut Stricklin	Pontiac
10	Davey Allison	Ford
11	Lennie Pond	Ford
12	Terry Labonte	Ford
13	Bobby Hillin	Buick
14	Lake Speed	Oldsmobile
15	Alan Kulwicki	Ford
16	Dave Marcis	Chevrolet
17	Mark Martin	Ford
18	Bill Elliott	Ford

19	Jimmy Means	Pontiac
20	Larry Pearson	Buick
21	Butch Miller	Chevrolet
22	Rick Wilson	Oldsmobile
23	Michael Waltrip	Pontiac
24	Ken Schrader	Chevrolet
25	Derrike Cope	Pontiac
26	Ernie Irvan	Pontiac
27	Morgan Shepherd	Pontiac
28	Sterling Marlin	Oldsmobile
29	Jimmy Spencer	Pontiac
30	Darin Brassfield	Chevrolet
31	J.D. McDuffie	Pontiac
32	Kyle Petty	Pontiac
33	Richard Petty	Pontiac
34	Brett Bodine	Ford
35	Dale Jarrett	Pontiac
36	Phil Parsons	Oldsmobile

PEAK PERFORMANCE 500

Time of Race: 4 hours, 4 minutes, 5 seconds
Average Speed: 122.909 mph
Margin of Victory: .28 second

FINISH	DRIVER	CAR
1	Dale Earnhardt	Chevrolet
2	Mark Martin	Ford
3	Ken Schrader	Chevrolet
4	Bill Elliott	Ford
5	Ricky Rudd	Buick
6	Michael Waltrip	Pontiac
7	Rusty Wallace	Pontiac
8	Derrike Cope	Pontiac
9	Brett Bodine	Ford
10	Jimmy Spencer	Pontiac
11	Kyle Petty	Pontiac
12	Jim Sauter	Pontiac
13	Phil Parsons	Oldsmobile
14	Terry Labonte	Ford
15	Bobby Hillin	Buick
16	Morgan Shepherd	Pontiac
17	Sterling Marlin	Oldsmobile
18	Darrell Waltrip	Chevrolet
19	Rick Wilson	Oldsmobile
20	Hut Striklin	Pontiac
21	Jimmy Means	Pontiac
22	Dave Marcis	Chevrolet
23	Dale Jarrett	Pontiac
24	Davey Allison	Ford
25	Dick Trickle	Buick
26	Neil Bonnett	Ford
27	Geoff Bodine	Chevrolet
28	Rob Moroso	Oldsmobile
29	Andy Belmont	Ford
30	Richard Petty	Pontiac
31	Norm Benning	Chevrolet
32	Alan Kulwicki	Ford
33	Ernie Irvan	Pontiac
34	J.D. McDuffie	Pontiac
35	Jack Ely	Buick
36	Lake Speed	Olds
37	Tommie Crozier	Chevrolet
38	Harry Gant	Oldsmobile
39	James Hylton	Buick
40	Larry Pearson	Buick

GOODY'S 500

Time of Race: 3 hours, 26 minutes, 15 seconds
Average Speed: 76.571 mph
Margin of Victory: Under Caution

FINISH	DRIVER	CAR
1	Darrell Waltrip	Chavrolet
2	Harry Gant	Oldsmobile

3	Dick Trickle	Buick
4	Rusty Wallace	Pontiac
5	Dale Jarrett	Pontiac
6	Ernie Irvan	Pontiac
7	Brett Bodine	Ford
8	Ricky Rudd	Buick
9	Dale Earnhardt	Chevrolet
10	Ken Schrader	Chevrolet
11	Terry Labonte	Ford
12	Michael Waltrip	Pontiac
13	Derrike Cope	Pontiac
14	Phil Parsons	Oldsmobile
15	Bill Elliott	Ford
16	Geoff Bodine	Chevrolet
17	Hut Stricklin	Pontiac
18	Rick Wilson	Oldsmobile
19	Greg Sacks	Pontiac
20	Sterling Marlin	Oldsmobile
21	Davey Allison	Ford
22	Lake Speed	Olds
23	Mark Martin	Ford
24	Richard Petty	Pontiac
25	Larry Pearson	Buick
26	Alan Kulwicki	Ford
27	Bobby Hillin	Buick
28	Morgan Shepherd	Pontiac
29	Tommy Ellis	Ford
30	Kyle Petty	Pontiac
31	Jimmy Means	Pontiac
32	Butch Miller	Chevrolet

ALL PRO AUTO PARTS 500

Time of Race: 3 hours, 20 minutes, 35 seconds
Average Speed: 149.863 mph
Margin of Victory: 4 seconds

FINISH	DRIVER	CAR
1	Ken Schrader	Chervolet
2	Harry Gant	Oldsmobile
3	Mark Martin	Ford
4	Bill Elliott	Ford
5	Davey Allison	Ford
6	Derrike Cope	Pontiac
7	Sterling Marlin	Oldsmobile
8	Rusty Wallace	Pontiac
9	Bobby Hillin	Buick
10	Morgan Shepherd	Pontiac
11	Terry Labonte	Ford
12	Brett Bodine	Ford
13	Rick Mast	Chevrolet
14	Darrell Waltrip	Chevrolet
15	Larry Pearson	Buick
16	Jimmy Spencer	Pontiac
17	Michael Waltrip	Pontiac
18	Tommy Ellis	Ford
19	Dave Marcis	Chevrolet
20	Phil Parsons	Oldsmobile
21	Ricky Rudd	Buick
22	Geoff Bodine	Chevrolet
23	Hut Stricklin	Pontiac
24	Dale Jarrett	Pontiac
25	Eddie Bierschwale	Oldsmobile
26	Mickey Gibbs	Pontiac
27	Ken Ragan	Ford
28	Alan Kulwicki	Ford
29	Kyle Petty	Pontiac
30	Dick Trickle	Buick
31	Brad Teague	Pontiac
32	Rodney Combs	Pontiac
33	Ernie Irvan	Pontiac
34	Richard Petty	Pontiac
35	Greg Sacks	Pontiac
36	Jerry O'Neil	Oldsmobile
37	Jimmy Means	Pontiac
38	Lake Speed	Oldsmobile
39	Rich Bickle	Buick
40	Jim Sauter	Pontiac
41	Rick Wilson	Oldsmobile
42	Dale Earnhardt	Chevrolet

Gary DeHart, crew chief for the No. 5 Terry Labonte/ Kellogg's team.

HOLLY FARMS 400

Time of Race: 2 hours, 46 minutes, 08 seconds
Average Speed: 90.289 mph
Margin of Victory: 3 seconds

FINISH	DRIVER	CAR
1	Geoff Bodine	Chevrolet
2	Mark Martin	Ford
3	Terry Labonte	Ford
4	Harry Gant	Oldsmobile
5	Morgan Shepherd	Pontiac
6	Bill Elliott	Ford
7	Rusty Wallace	Pontiac
8	Ernie Irvan	Pontiac
9	Ricky Rudd	Buick
10	Dale Earnhardt	Chevrolet
11	Alan Kulwicki	Ford
12	Dick Trickle	Buick
13	Ken Schrader	Chevrolet
14	Dave Marcis	Chevrolet
15	Bobby Hillin	Buick
16	Tommy Ellis	Ford
17	Brett Bodine	Ford
18	Jimmy Spencer	Pontiac
19	Sterling Marlin	Oldsmobile
20	Darrell Waltrip	Chevrolet
21	Davey Allison	Ford
22	Jimmy Means	Pontiac
23	Michael Waltrip	Pontiac
24	Larry Pearson	Buick
25	Lake Speed	Oldsmobile
26	Derrike Cope	Ford

27	Dale Jarrett	Pontiac
28	Phil Parsons	Oldsmobile
29	Rick Wilson	Oldsmobile
30	Hut Stricklin	Pontiac
31	Kyle Petty	Pontiac
32	Richard Petty	Pontiac

AC DELCO 500

Time of Race: 4 hours, 23 minutes, 10 seconds
Average Speed: 114.079 mph
Margin of Victory: 2.98 seconds

FINISH	DRIVER	CAR
1	Mark Martin	Ford
2	Rusty Wallace	Pontiac
3	Darrell Waltrip	Chevrolet
4	Ken Schrader	Chevrolet
5	Dick Trickle	Buick
6	Neil Bonnett	Ford
7	Geoff Bodine	Chevrolet
8	Bobby Hillin	Buick
9	Alan Kulwicki	Ford
10	Kyle Petty	Pontiac
11	Derrike Cope	Pontiac
12	Larry Pearson	Chevrolet
13	Rick Wilson	Oldsmobile
14	Terry Labonte	Ford
15	Bill Elliott	Ford
16	Ernie Irvan	Pontiac
17	Michael Waltrip	Pontiac
18	Greg Sacks	Pontiac
19	Lake Speed	Oldsmobile
20	Dale Earnhardt	Chevrolet
21	Brett Bodine	Ford
22	Hut Stricklin	Pontiac
23	Sterling Marlin	Oldsmobile
24	Phil Parsons	Oldsmobile
25	Bob Schact	Buick
26	Davey Allison	Ford
27	Joe Ruttman	Oldsmobile
28	Ricky Rudd	Buick
29	Harry Gant	Oldsmobile
30	Dave Marcis	Chevrolet
31	Jimmy Means	Pontiac
32	Jack Pennington	Chevrolet
33	Jim Sauter	Pontiac
34	Richard Petty	Pontiac
35	Jimmy Spencer	Oldsmobile
36	Morgan Shepherd	Pontiac
37	Jim Bown	Buick
38	Jerry O'Neil	Oldsmobile
39	Dale Jarrett	Pontiac
40	Charlie Baker	Buick

AUTOWORKS 500

Time of Race: 2 hours, 57 minutes, 08 seconds
Average Speed: 105.683 mph - Track Record
Margin of Victory: 2 car lenths

FINISH	DRIVER	CAR
1	Bill Elliott	Ford
2	Terry Labonte	Ford
3	Mark Martin	Ford
4	Darrell Waltrip	Chevrolet
5	Dale Jarrett	Pontiac
6	Dale Earnhardt	Chevrolet
7	Dick Trickle	Buick
8	Harry Gant	Oldsmobile
9	Michael Waltrip	Pontiac
10	Jimmy Spencer	Pontiac
11	Alan Kulwicki	Ford
12	Morgan Shepherd	Pontiac
13	Ken Schrader	Chevrolet
14	Derrike Cope	Pontiac
15	Dave Marcis	Chevrolet
16	Rusty Wallace	Pontiac

17	Jim Sauter	Pontiac
18	Bobby Hillin	Buick
19	Brett Bodine	Ford
20	Joe Ruttman	Chevrolet
21	Kyle Petty	Pontiac
22	Lake Speed	Oldsmobile
23	Hut Stricklin	Pontiac
24	Larry Pearson	Buick
25	Jimmy Means	Pontiac
26	Bill Schmitt	Chevrolet
27	Rodney Combs	Pontiac
28	Geoff Bodine	Chevrolet
29	Ricky Rudd	Buick
30	Sterling Marlin	Oldsmobile
31	Stan Barrett	Ford
32	Bobby Hamilton	Chevrolet
33	Ernie Irvan	Pontiac
34	Neil Bonnett	Ford
35	Ron Esau	Oldsmobile
36	Bill Sedgwick	Buick
37	Phil Parsons	Oldsmobile
38	Greg Sacks	Chevrolet
39	Davey Allison	Ford
40	Rick Wilson	Oldsmobile
41	Roy Smith	Pontiac
42	Richard Petty	Pontiac
43	Butch Miller	Chevrolet

ATLANTA JOURNAL 500

Time of Race: 3 hours, 33 minutes, 36 seconds
Average Speed: 140.229 mph
Margin of Victory: 25.71 seconds

FINISH	DRIVER	CAR
1	Dale Earnhardt	Chevrolet
2	Geoff Bodine	Chevrolet
3	Sterling Marlin	Oldsmobile
4	Ken Schrader	Chevrolet
5	Darrell Waltrip	Chevrolet
6	Kyle Petty	Pontiac
7	Bobby Hillin	Buick
8	Morgan Shepherd	Pontiac
9	Neil Bonnett	Ford
10	Lake Speed	Olds
11	Ernie Irvan	Pontiac
12	Derrike Cope	Pontiac
13	Alan Kulwicki	Ford
14	Ricky Rudd	Buick
15	Rusty Wallace	Pontiac
16	Dale Jarrett	Pontiac
17	Harry Gant	Oldsmobile
18	Rick Wilson	Oldsmobile
19	Larry Pearson	Buick
20	Hut Stricklin	Pontiac
21	Jim Sauter	Pontiac
22	Rich Bickle	Buick
23	Brett Bodine	Ford
24	Jack Pennington	Oldsmobile
25	Davey Allison	Ford
26	Michael Waltrip	Pontiac
27	Bill Elliott	Ford
28	Richard Petty	Pontiac
29	Greg Sacks	Pontiac
30	Mark Martin	Ford
31	Rick Mast	Chevrolet
32	Grant Adcox	Oldsmobile
33	Dave Marcis	Chevrolet
34	Rob Moroso	Oldsmobile
35	Dick Trickle	Buick
36	A.J. Foyt	Oldsmobile
37	Jimmy Spencer	Pontiac
38	Mickey Gibbs	Ford
39	Ken Ragan	Ford
40	Terry Labonte	Ford
41	Rodney Combs	Pontiac
42	Phil Parsons	Oldsmobile

1990

DAYTONA 500

Time of Race: 3 hours, 0 minutes, 59 seconds
Average Speed: 165.761 mph
Margin of Victory: 1 Car lengths

FINISH	DRIVER	CAR
1	Derrike Cope	Chevrolet
2	Terry Labonte	Oldsmobile
3	Bill Elliott	Ford
4	Levi Garrett	Chevrolet
5	Dale Earnhardt	Chevrolet
6	Bobby Hillin	Buick
7	Rusty Wallace	Pontiac
8	Michael Waltrip	Pontiac
9	Geoff Bodine	Ford
10	Morgan Shepherd	Ford
11	Neil Bonnett	Ford
12	Dick Trickle	Pontiac
13	Ernie Irvan	Ford
14	Darrell Waltrip	Chevrolet
15	Jimmy Spencer	Pontiac
16	Lake Speed	Oldsmobile
17	Brett Bodine	Buick
18	Harry Gant	Oldsmobile
19	Sterling Marlin	Oldsmobile
20	Davey Allison	Ford
21	Mark Martin	Ford
22	Butch Miller	Chevrolet
23	Dave Marcis	Chevrolet
24	Kyle Petty	Pontiac
25	Jack Pennington	Oldsmobile
26	Joe Ruttman	Pontiac
27	Larry Pearson	Buick
28	Rich Bickle	Oldsmobile
29	Jimmy Means	Pontiac
30	Rick Wilson	Oldsmobile
31	Jerry O'Neil	Oldsmobile
32	Eddie Bierschwale	Oldsmobile
33	Hut Stricklin	Chevrolet
34	Richard Petty	Pontiac
35	Alan Kulwicki	Ford
36	A. J. Foyt	Oldsmoible
37	Jimmy Horton	Oldsmobile
38	Rob Moroso	Oldsmobile
39	Phil Barkdoll	Oldsmobile
40	Ken Schrader	Chevrolet
41	Mike Alexander	Buick
42	Phil Parsons	Oldsmobile

PONTIAC EXCITEMENT 400

Time of Race: 3 hours, 15 minutes, 18 seconds
Average Speed: 92.158 mph
Margin of Victory: 3 seconds

FINISH	DRIVER	CAR
1	Mark Martin	Ford
2	Dale Earnhardt	Chevrolet
3	Ricky Rudd	Chevrolet
4	Bill Elliott	Ford
5	Dick Trickle	Pontiac
6	Rusty Wallace	Pontiac
7	Morgan Shepherd	Ford
8	Brett Bodine	Buick
9	Jimmy Spencer	Pontiac
10	Ken Schrader	Chevrolet
11	Kyle Petty	Pontiac
12	Darrell Waltrip	Chevrolet
13	Sterling Marlin	Oldsmobile
14	Mike Alexander	Buick
15	Rob Moroso	Oldsmobile
16	Chad Little	Ford

FINISH	DRIVER	CAR
17	Dave Marcis	Chevrolet
18	Jimmy Means	Pontiac
19	Mickey Gibbs	Ford
20	Davey Allison	Ford
21	Rick Mast	Pontiac
22	Ernie Irvan	Ford
23	Larry Pearson	Buick
24	Alan Kulwicki	Ford
25	Neil Bonnett	Ford
26	Phil Parsons	Oldsmobile
27	Michael Waltrip	Pontiac
28	Butch Miller	Chevrolet
29	Derrike Cope	Chevrolet
30	Rick Wilson	Oldsmobile
31	Bobby Hillin	Buick
32	Terry Labonte	Oldsmobile
33	Geoff Bodine	Ford
34	Bill Meacham	Oldsmobile
35	Richard Petty	Pontiac
36	Harry Gant	Oldsmobile

GOODWRENCH 500

Time of Race: 4 hours, 4 minutes, 21 seconds
Average Speed: 122.864 mph
Margin of Victory: 26 seconds

FINISH	DRIVER	CAR
1	Kyle Petty	Pontiac
2	Geoff Bodine	Ford
3	Ken Schrader	Chevrolet
4	Sterling Marlin	Oldsmobile
5	Rusty Wallace	Pontiac
6	Darrell Waltrip	Chevrolet
7	Morgan Shepherd	Ford
8	Jimmy Spencer	Pontiac
9	Terry Labonte	Oldsmobile
10	Dale Earnhardt	Chevrolet
11	Harry Gant	Oldsmobile
12	Derrike Cope	Chevrolet
13	Butch Miller	Chevrolet
14	Phil Parsons	Oldsmobile
15	Mickey Gibbs	Ford
16	Mike Alexander	Buick
17	Bobby Hillin	Buick
18	Rick Wilson	Oldsmobile
19	Rick Mast	Pontiac
20	Larry Pearson	Buick
21	Jimmy Means	Pontiac
22	Dave Marcis	Chevrolet
23	Dick Trickle	Pontiac
24	Mark Stahl	Ford
25	Brett Bodine	Buick
26	Mark Martin	Ford
27	Alan Kulwicki	Ford
28	Michael Waltrip	Pontiac
29	Ernie Irvan	Ford
30	Rob Moroso	Oldsmobile
31	Ricky Rudd	Chevrolet
32	Richard Petty	Pontiac
33	Bill Elliott	Ford
34	Davey Allison	Ford
35	J. D. McDuffie	Pontiac
36	Neil Bonnett	Ford
37	Charlie Baker	Buick
38	J. T. Hayes	Ford

MOTORCRAFT QUALITY PARTS 500

Time of Race: 3 hours, 10 minutes, 58 seconds
Average Speed: 156.849 mph
Margin of Victory: 32 seconds

FINISH	DRIVER	CAR
1	Dale Earnhardt	Chevrolet
2	Morgan Shepherd	Ford

3	Ernie Irvan	Oldsmobile
4	Ken Schrader	Chevrolet
5	Mark Martin	Ford
6	Kyle Petty	Pontiac
7	Geoff Bodine	Ford
8	Alan Kulwicki	Ford
9	Harry Gant	Oldsmobile
10	Sterling Marlin	Oldsmobile
11	Brett Bodine	Buick
12	Bill Elliott	Ford
13	Davey Allison	Ford
14	Dick Trickle	Pontiac
15	Jimmy Spencer	Pontiac
16	Bobby Hillin	Buick
17	Rick Wilson	Oldsmobile
18	Neil Bonnett	Ford
19	Chad Little	Ford
20	Butch Miller	Chevrolet
21	Buddy Baker	Ford
22	Dave Marcis	Chevrolet
23	Mike Alexander	Buick
24	Rusty Wallace	Pontiac
25	Richard Petty	Pontiac
26	Darrell Waltrip	Chevrolet
27	Ricky Rudd	Chevrolet
28	Mark Stahl	Ford
29	Derrike Cope	Chevrolet
30	Jack Pennington	Oldsmobile
31	Jimmy Means	Pontiac
32	H. B. Bailey	Pontiac
33	Rob Moroso	Oldsmobile
34	Larry Pearson	Buick
35	Rick Mast	Pontiac
36	Ken Ragan	Ford
37	Hut Stricklin	Pontiac
38	Michael Waltrip	Pontiac
39	Mickey Gibbs	Ford
40	Terry Labonte	Oldsmobile

TRANSOUTH 500

Time of Race: 4 hours, 20 minutes, 26 seconds
Average Speed: 124.073 mph
Margin of Victory: 25 seconds

FINISH	DRIVER	CAR
1	Dale Earnhardt	Chevrolet
2	Mark Martin	Ford
3	Davey Allison	Ford
4	Geoff Bodine	Ford
5	Morgan Shepherd	Ford
6	Harry Gant	Oldsmobile
7	Bill Elliott	Ford
8	Brett Bodine	Buick
9	Michael Waltrip	Pontiac
10	Ken Schrader	Chevrolet
11	Darrell Waltrip	Chevrolet
12	Bobby Hillin	Buick
13	Kyle Petty	Pontiac
14	Terry Labonte	Oldsmobile
15	Dave Marcis	Chevrolet
16	Chad Little	Ford
17	Butch Miller	Chevrolet
18	Rusty Wallace	Pontiac
19	Mike Alexander	Buick
20	Jack Pennington	Oldsmobile
21	Richard Petty	Pontiac
22	Dick Trickle	Pontiac
23	Alan Kulwicki	Ford
24	Ricky Rudd	Chevrolet
25	Jimmy Spencer	Pontiac
26	Ron Moroso	Oldsmobile
27	Derrike Cope	Chevrolet
28	Sterling Marlin	Oldsmobile
29	Rick Wilson	Oldsmobile
30	Neil Bonnett	Ford
31	Jimmy Means	Pontiac
32	Ernie Irvan	Oldsmobile
33	H. B. Bailey	Pontiac
34	Dick Johnson	Ford
35	J. D. McDuffie	Pontiac

36	Hut Stricklin	Chevrolet
37	Greg Sacks	Chevrolet
38	Mickey Gibbs	Chevrolet
39	Rick Mast	Pontiac
40	Buddy Baker	Ford

VALLEYDALE MEATS 500

Time of Race: 3 hours, 3 minutes, 15 seconds
Average Speed: 87.258 mph
Margin of Victory: 8 Inches

FINISH	DRIVER	CAR
1	Davey Allison	Ford
2	Mark Martin	Ford
3	Ricky Rudd	Chevrolet
4	Terry Labonte	Oldsmobile
5	Rick Wilson	Oldsmobile
6	Ken Schrader	Chevrolet
7	Sterling Marlin	Oldsmobile
8	Morgan Shepherd	Ford
9	Darrell Waltrip	Chevrolet
10	Kyle Petty	Pontiac
11	Dale Jarrett	Ford
12	Rick Mast	Pontiac
13	Dick Trickle	Pontiac
14	Butch Miller	Chevrolet
15	Dave Marcis	Chevrolet
16	Ernie Irvan	Oldsmobile
17	Bill Elliott	Ford
18	Jimmy Spencer	Pontiac
19	Dale Earnhardt	Chevrolet
20	Michael Waltrip	Pontiac
21	Bobby Hillin	Buick
22	Brett Bodine	Buick
23	Mike Alexander	Buick
24	Geoff Bodine	Ford
25	Phil Parsons	Oldsmobile
26	Richard Petty	Pontiac
27	J. D. McDuffie	Pontiac
28	Rusty Wallace	Pontiac
29	Jimmy Means	Pontiac
30	Rob Moroso	Oldsmobile
31	Alan Kulwicki	Ford
32	Derrike Cope	Chevrolet

FIRST UNION 400

Time of Race: 2 hours, 58 minutes, 46 seconds
Average Speed: 83.908 mph
Margin of Victory: 95 seconds

FINISH	DRIVER	CAR
1	Brett Bodine	Buick
2	Darrell Waltrip	Chevrolet
3	Dale Earnhardt	Chevrolet
4	Ricky Rudd	Chevrolet
5	Morgan Shepherd	Ford
6	Mark Martin	Ford
7	Rusty Wallace	Pontiac
8	Geoff Bodine	Ford
9	Davey Allison	Ford
10	Kyle Petty	Pontiac
11	Alan Kulwicki	Ford
12	Dave Marcis	Chevrolet
13	Harry Gant	Oldsmobile
14	Dale Jarrett	Ford
15	Terry Labonte	Oldsmobile
16	Ernie Irvan	Oldsmobile
17	Mike Alexander	Buick
18	Bill Elliott	Ford
19	Ken Schrader	Chevrolet
20	Jimmy Spencer	Pontiac
21	Derrike Cope	Chevrolet
22	Rick Wilson	Oldsmobile
23	Rick Mast	Chevrolet
24	Dick Trickle	Pontiac

25	Butch Miller	Chevrolet
26	Kenny Wallace	Pontiac
27	Michael Waltrip	Pontiac
28	Jimmy Means	Pontiac
29	Richard Petty	Pontiac
30	Bobby Hillin	Buick
31	Sterling Marlin	Oldsmobile
32	Rob Moroso	Oldsmobile

HANES ACTIVEWEAR 500

Time of Race: 3 hours, 23 minutes, 49 seconds
Average Speed: 77.423 mph
Margin of Victory: 4.50 seconds

FINISH	DRIVER	CAR
1	Geoff Bodine	Ford
2	Rusty Wallace	Pontiac
3	Morgan Shepherd	Ford
4	Darrell Waltrip	Chevrolet
5	Dale Earnhardt	Chevrolet
6	Ken Schrader	Chevrolet
7	Mark Martin	Chevrolet
8	Michael Waltrip	Pontiac
9	Dick Trickle	Pontiac
10	Bill Elliott	Ford
11	Jimmy Spencer	Pontiac
12	Brett Bodine	Buick
13	Rob Moroso	Oldsmobile
14	Dave Marcis	Chevrolet
15	Ernie Irvan	Oldsmobile
16	Kyle Petty	Pontiac
17	Derrike Cope	Chevrolet
18	Butch Miller	Chevrolet
19	Jimmy Means	Pontiac
20	Richard Petty	Pontiac
21	Bobby Hillin	Buick
22	Davey Allison	Ford
23	Ricky Rudd	Chevrolet
24	Bill Sedgwick	Chevrolet
25	Alan Kulwicki	Ford
26	Harry Gant	Oldsmobile
27	Rick Wilson	Oldsmobile
28	Jeff Purvis	Buick
29	Rick Mast	Pontiac
30	Dale Jarrett	Ford
31	Terry Labonte	Oldsmobile
32	Sterling Marlin	Oldsmobile

WINSTON 500

Time of Race: 3 hours, 8 minutes, 2 seconds
Average Speed: 159.571 mph
Margin of Victory: 2 Car Lengths

FINISH	DRIVER	CAR
1	Dale Earnhardt	Chevrolet
2	Greg Sacks	Chevrolet
3	Mark Martin	Ford
4	Ernie Irvan	Oldsmobile
5	Michael Waltrip	Pontiac
6	Terry Labonte	Oldsmobile
7	Kyle Petty	Pontiac
8	Morgan Shepherd	Ford
9	Hut Stricklin	Buick
10	Darrell Waltrip	Chevrolet
11	Jack Pennington	Oldsmobile
12	Brett Bodine	Buick
13	Alan Kulwicki	Ford
14	Dave Marcis	Chevrolet
15	Chad Little	Ford
16	Butch Miller	Chevrolet
17	Rick Mast	Pontiac
18	Bill Venturini	Chevrolet
19	Mickey Gibbs	Ford
20	Rusty Wallace	Pontiac
21	Jimmy Means	Pontiac
22	Bill Elliott	Ford

23	Bobby Hillin	Buick
24	Geoff Bodine	Ford
25	Davey Allison	Ford
26	Sterling Marlin	Oldsmobile
27	Dick Trickle	Pontiac
28	Ken Schrader	Chevrolet
29	Richard Petty	Pontiac
30	Phil Barkdoll	Oldsmobile
31	Buddy Baker	Ford
32	Jimmy Spencer	Pontiac
33	Ricky Rudd	Chevrolet
34	Dale Jarrett	Ford
35	Phil Parsons	Oldsmobile
36	Harry Gant	Oldsmobile
37	Rob Moroso	Oldsmobile
38	Lake Speed	Oldsmobile
39	Rick Wilson	Oldsmobile
40	Derrike Cope	Chevrolet

COCA-COLA 600

Time of Race: 4 hours, 21 minutes, 32 seconds
Average Speed: 137.650 mph
Margin of Victory: 2 Car Lengths

FINISH	DRIVER	CAR
1	Rusty Wallace	Pontiac
2	Bill Elliott	Ford
3	Mark Martin	Ford
4	Michael Waltrip	Pontiac
5	Ernie Irvan	Oldsmobile
6	Alan Kulwicki	Ford
7	Davey Allison	Ford
8	Morgan Shepherd	Ford
9	Derrike Cope	Chevrolet
10	Geoff Bodine	Ford
11	Ken Schrader	Chevrolet
12	Dick Trickle	Pontiac
13	Terry Labonte	Oldsmobile
14	Greg Sacks	Chevrolet
15	Buddy Baker	Ford
16	Dave Marcis	Chevrolet
17	Kyle Petty	Pontiac
18	Butch Miller	Chevrolet
19	Rick Wilson	Oldsmobile
20	Jack Pennington	Oldsmobile
21	Jimmy Spencer	Pontiac
22	Darrell Waltrip	Chevrolet
23	Jimmy Horton	Ford
24	Chad Little	Ford
25	Harry Gant	Oldsmobile
26	Rob Moroso	Oldsmobile
27	Richard Petty	Pontiac
28	Ricky Rudd	Chevrolet
29	Brett Bodine	Buick
30	Dale Earnhardt	Chevrolet
31	Rick Mast	Pontiac
32	Dale Jarrett	Ford
33	Rodney Combs	Pontiac
34	Bobby Hillin	Buick
35	Sterling Marlin	Oldsmobile
36	Tracy Leslie	Oldsmobile
37	Hut Stricklin	Buick
38	Lake Speed	Oldsmobile
39	Bobby Hamilton	Pontiac
40	Terry Byers	Pontiac
41	Ken Ragan	Ford
42	Larry Pearson	Pontiac

BUDWEISER 500

Time of Race: 4 hours, 2 minutes, 1 second
Average Speed: 123.960 mph
Margin of Victory: 1.24 seconds

FINISH	DRIVER	CAR
1	Derrike Cope	Chevrolet
2	Ken Schrader	Chevrolet

3	Dick Trickle	Pontiac
4	Mark Martin	Ford
5	Sterling Marlin	Oldsmobile
6	Morgan Shepherd	Ford
7	Ernie Irvan	Oldsmobile
8	Bill Elliott	Ford
9	Kyle Petty	Pontiac
10	Rusty Wallace	Pontiac
11	Ricky Rudd	Chevrolet
12	Dale Jarrett	Ford
13	Terry Labonte	Oldsmobile
14	Butch Miller	Chevrolet
15	Geoff Bodine	Ford
16	Bobby Hillin	Buick
17	Davey Allison	Ford
18	Brett Bodine	Buick
19	Darrell Waltrip	Chevrolet
20	Jimmy Horton	Ford
21	Richard Petty	Pontiac
22	Jimmy Means	Pontiac
23	Rick Wilson	Pontiac
24	Alan Kulwicki	Ford
25	J. D. McDuffie	Pontiac
26	Michael Waltrip	Pontiac
27	Hut Stricklin	Buick
28	Rick Mast	Chevrolet
29	Rob Moroso	Oldsmobile
30	Mike Potter	Pontiac
31	Dale Earnhardt	Chevrolet
32	Jimmy Spencer	Pontiac
33	Bobby Gerhart, Jr.	Chevrolet
34	Harry Gant	Oldsmobile
35	Dave Marcis	Chevrolet
36	Freddie Crawford	Chevrolet

BANQUET FROZEN FOODS 300

Time of Race: 2 hours, 41 minutes, 35 seconds
Average Speed: 69.245 mph
Margin of Victory: Under caution

FINISH	DRIVER	CAR
1	Rusty Wallace	Pontiac
2	Mark Martin	Ford
3	Ricky Rudd	Chevrolet
4	Geoff Bodine	Ford
5	Bobby Hillin	Buick
6	Sterling Marlin	Oldsmobile
7	Ernie Irvan	Oldsmobile
8	Irv Hoerr	Oldsmobile
9	Michael Waltrip	Pontiac
10	Rick Wilson	Oldsmobile
11	Alan Kulwicki	Ford
12	Hut Stricklin	Buick
13	Derrike Cope	Chevrolet
14	Dale Jarrett	Ford
15	Terry Fisher	Pontiac
16	Kyle Petty	Pontiac
17	Stan Barrett	Chevrolet
18	Ken Schrader	Chevrolet
19	Harry Gant	Oldsmobile
20	Bill Schmitt	Chevrolet
21	Bill Elliott	Ford
22	Jim Bowm	Chevrolet
23	John Krebs	Pontiac
24	Davey Allison	Ford
25	Mike Chase	Buick
26	Richard Petty	Pontiac
27	Jimmy Spencer	Pontiac
28	Butch Gilliland	Chevrolet
29	Morgan Shepherd	Ford
30	Troy Beebe	Buick
31	Butch Miller	Chevrolet
32	Dave Marcis	Chevrolet
33	Darrell Waltrip	Chevrolet
34	Dale Earnhardt	Chevrolet
35	Terry Labonte	Oldsmobile
36	Bill Sedgwick	Chevrolet
37	Chad Little	Ford
38	Tom Kendall	Chevrolet

39	Dick Trickle	Pontiac
40	Jack Sellers	Buick
41	Brett Bodine	Buick
42	Rob Moroso	Oldsmobile
43	Ted Kennedy	Oldsmobile
44	Hershel McGriff	Pontiac

MILLER GENUINE DRAFT 500

Time of Race: 4 hours, 8 minutes, 25 seconds
Average Speed: 120.60 mph
Margin of Victory: 2 seconds

FINISH	DRIVER	CAR
1	Harry Gant	Oldsmobile
2	Rusty Wallace	Pontiac
3	Geoff Bodine	Ford
4	Brett Bodine	Buick
5	Davey Allison	Ford
6	Hut Stricklin	Buick
7	Greg Sacks	Chevrolet
8	Darrell Waltrip	Chevrolet
9	Sterling Marlin	Oldsmobile
10	Kyle Petty	Pontiac
11	Morgan Shepherd	Ford
12	Derrike Cope	Chevrolet
13	Dale Earnhardt	Chevrolet
14	Mark Martin	Ford
15	Ken Schrader	Chevrolet
16	Bill Elliott	Ford
17	Ernie Irvan	Oldsmobile
18	Chad Little	Ford
19	Michael Waltrip	Pontiac
20	Terry Labonte	Oldsmobile
21	Jack Pennington	Oldsmobile
22	Dave Marcis	Chevrolet
23	Butch Miller	Chevrolet
24	Jim Sauter	Ford
25	Dick Trickle	Pontiac
26	Tommy Riggins	Oldsmobile
27	Jimmy Means	Pontiac
28	J. D. McDuffie	Pontiac
29	Bobby Hillin	Buick
30	Jimmy Spencer	Pontiac
31	Dale Jarrett	Ford
32	Ricky Rudd	Chevrolet
33	Randy LaJoie	Buick
34	Alan Kulwicki	Ford
35	Rick Wilson	Oldsmobile
36	Rob Moroso	Oldsmobile
37	Troy Beebe	Pontiac
38	Richard Petty	Pontiac
39	Jimmy Horton	Ford
40	Jerry O'Neil	Oldsmobile

MILLER GENUINE DRAFT 400

Time of Race: 2 hours, 39 minutes, 46 seconds
Average Speed: 150.219 mph
Margin of Victory: 22 seconds

FINISH	DRIVER	CAR
1	Dale Earnhardt	Chevrolet
2	Ernie Irvan	Oldsmobile
3	Geoff Bodine	Ford
4	Mark Martin	Ford
5	Harry Gant	Oldsmobile
6	Alan Kulwicki	Ford
7	Terry Labonte	Oldsmobile
8	Kyle Petty	Pontiac
9	Ricky Rudd	Chevrolet
10	Rick Wilson	Oldsmobile
11	Richard Petty	Pontiac
12	Derrike Cope	Chevrolet
13	Morgan Shepherd	Ford
14	Brett Bodine	Buick

15	Darrell Waltrip	Chevrolet
16	Rob Moroso	Oldsmobile
17	Rusty Wallace	Pontiac
18	Sterling Marlin	Oldsmobile
19	Dave Marcis	Chevrolet
20	Jimmy Spencer	Pontiac
21	Michael Waltrip	Pontiac
22	Phil Parsons	Pontiac
23	Butch Miller	Chevrolet
24	Dick Trickle	Pontiac
25	Bill Elliott	Ford
26	Greg Sacks	Chevrolet
27	Ken Schrader	Chevrolet
28	Bobby Hillin	Buick
29	Eddie Bierschwale	Oldsmobile
30	Bill Venturini	Chevrolet
31	Troy Beebe	Pontiac
32	Hut Stricklin	Buick
33	Lake Speed	Oldsmobile
34	Dale Jarrett	Ford
35	Ed Cooper	Oldsmobile
36	Davey Allison	Ford
37	J. D. McDuffie	Pontiac
38	Jack Pennington	Oldsmobile
39	Jimmy Means	Pontiac
40	Rodney Combs	Pontiac

PEPSI 400

Time of Race: 2 hours, 29 minutes, 10 seconds
Average Speed: 160.894 mph
Margin of Victory: 1.47 seconds

FINISH	DRIVER	CAR
1	Dale Earnhardt	Chevrolet
2	Alan Kulwicki	Ford
3	Ken Schrader	Chevrolet
4	Terry Labonte	Oldsmobile
5	Sterling Marlin	Oldsmobile
6	Bobby Hillin	Buick
7	Harry Gant	Oldsmobile
8	Dale Jarrett	Ford
9	Rob Moroso	Oldsmobile
10	Kyle Petty	Pontiac
11	Mark Martin	Ford
12	Jimmy Means	Pontiac
13	Ricky Rudd	Chevrolet
14	Rusty Wallace	Pontiac
15	Jimmy Spencer	Pontiac
16	Michael Waltrip	Pontiac
17	Jimmy Horton	Chevrolet
18	Jack Pennington	Oldsmobile
19	Dick Trickle	Pontiac
20	Dave Marcis	Chevrolet
21	Philip Duffie	Buick
22	Brett Bodine	Buick
23	Butch Miller	Chevrolet
24	Davey Allison	Ford
25	Geoff Bodine	Ford
26	Hut Stricklin	Buick
27	Chad Little	Ford
28	Derrike Cope	Chevrolet
29	Bill Elliott	Ford
30	Buddy Baker	Ford
31	Phil Barkdoll	Oldsmobile
32	Mickey Gibbs	Ford
33	Ernie Irvan	Oldsmobile
34	Morgan Shepherd	Ford
35	Charlie Glotzbach	Pontiac
36	Richard Petty	Pontiac
37	Greg Sacks	Chevrolet
38	A. J. Foyt	Oldsmobile
39	Rick Wilson	Oldsmobile
40	Terry Byers	Pontiac

AC SPARK PLUG 500

Time of Race: 4 hours, 1 minute, 48 seconds
Average Speed: 124.07 mph
Margin of Victory: 1.22 seconds

FINISH	DRIVER	CAR
1	Geoff Bodine	Ford
2	Bill Elliott	Ford
3	Rusty Wallace	Pontiac
4	Dale Earnhardt	Chevrolet
5	Davey Allison	Ford
6	Mark Martin	Ford
7	Ricky Rudd	Chevrolet
8	Butch Miller	Chevrolet
9	Richard Petty	Pontiac
10	Terry Labonte	Oldsmobile
11	Ken Schrader	Chevrolet
12	Bobby Hillin	Buick
13	Derrike Cope	Chevrolet
14	Harry Gant	Oldsmobile
15	Dick Trickle	Pontiac
16	Brett Bodine	Buick
17	Alan Kulwicki	Ford
18	Dale Jarrett	Ford
19	Jimmy Spencer	Pontiac
20	Darrell Waltrip	Chevrolet
21	Jimmy Means	Pontiac
22	Rick Mast	Pontiac
23	Michael Waltrip	Pontiac
24	Ken Ragan	Ford
25	Mike Potter	Pontiac
26	Ernie Irvan	Oldsmobile
27	Brian Ross	Pontiac
28	Dave Marcis	Chevrolet
29	Hut Stricklin	Buick
30	Sterling Marlin	Oldsmobile
31	Rick Wilson	Oldsmobile
32	Rob Moroso	Oldsmobile
33	Greg Sacks	Chevrolet
34	Jerry O'Neil	Oldsmobile
35	Kyle Petty	Pontiac
36	Morgan Shepherd	Ford
37	Tommy Riggins	Oldsmobile
38	Randy LaJoie	Buick
39	Dick Johnson	Ford

TALLADEGA DIEHARD 500

Time of Race: 2 hours, 52 minutes, 1 second
Average Speed: 174.430 mph
Margin of Victory: 26 seconds

FINISH	DRIVER	CAR
1	Dale Earnhardt	Chevrolet
2	Bill Elliott	Ford
3	Sterling Marlin	Oldsmobile
4	Alan Kulwicki	Ford
5	Ricky Rudd	Chevrolet
6	Ernie Irvan	Chevrolet
7	Derrike Cope	Chevrolet
8	Kyle Petty	Pontiac
9	Mark Martin	Ford
10	Bobby Hillin	Buick
11	Lake Speed	Oldsmobile
12	Rob Moroso	Oldsmobile
13	Jimmy Horton	Chevrolet
14	Hut Stricklin	Buick
15	Harry Gant	Oldsmobile
16	Ken Schrader	Chevrolet
17	Geoff Bodine	Ford
18	Greg Sacks	Chevrolet
19	Chad Little	Ford
20	Davey Allison	Ford
21	Michael Waltrip	Pontiac
22	Mickey Gibbs	Ford
23	Jack Pennington	Oldsmobile
24	Jimmy Spencer	Pontiac
25	Bill Venturini	Chevrolet
26	Morgan Shepherd	Ford
27	A. J. Foyt	Oldsmobile
28	Dave Marcis	Chevrolet
29	Richard Petty	Pontiac
30	Jimmy Means	Pontiac

NASCAR VISITS FRANCE

At first, the thought of NASCAR stock car entering the 24 hours, of LeMans endurance race in France seemed preposterous. They wouldn't stand a chance against the powerful and exotic purpose-built cars designed exclusively for twice-around-the-clock road racing at one of the world's best-known courses.

But there they were in June of 1976, a NASCAR-legal Dodge Daytona and a Ford Torino going through the tuning, testing, and scrutinizing that led to the 24 hours, of LeMans.

The cars and their crews were there because NASCAR founder Bill France, Sr. (retired at the time, but still very powerful behind the scenes) was trying to lure more European sports cars to the 24 hours, of Daytona sports car race at the Daytona International Speedway. France and the organizers of the LeMans race had created a special trophy to honor the team that had the best combined showing in the '76 LeMans race and '77 race in Daytona Beach.

Predictably, the American stock cars didn't fare very well. The Olympia Beer-sponsored Dodge of Hershel McGriff made only one lap before blowing its engine. Unwittingly, they had tuned their race engine for the octane they had been promised. Alas, it was a higher and thus terribly destructive within the combustion chambers.

The Ford that Junie Donlavey had brought for Dick Brooks and Dick Hutcherson did better, but didn't come close to finishing. It ran for better than 17 hours before the transmission went bad on the far end of the course, too far for Brooks to nurse it back to the garage.

Stock cars never went back to LeMans, but the memory of the Dodge and Ford lumbering around the famous circuit remained with the French for years. They called them "Les Grande Monsters," and compared to the rest of the field, they surely were.

31	Mark Stahl	Ford
32	Rusty Wallace	Pontiac
33	Brett Bodine	Buick
34	Butch Miller	Chevrolet
35	Rick Wilson	Oldsmobile
36	Dick Trickle	Pontiac
37	Stan Smith	Pontiac
38	Tracy Leslie	Oldsmobile
39	Dale Jarrett	Ford
40	Buddy Baker	Ford
41	Phil Parsons	Pontiac
42	Terry Labonte	Oldsmobile

BUDWEISER AT THE GLEN

Time of Race: 2 hours, 21 minutes, 49 seconds
Average Speed: 92.452 mph
Margin of Victory: 6 seconds

FINISH	DRIVER	CAR
1	Ricky Rudd	Chevrolet
2	Geoff Bodine	Ford
3	Brett Bodine	Buick
4	Michael Waltrip	Pontiac
5	Mark Martin	Ford
6	Morgan Shepherd	Ford
7	Dale Earnhardt	Chevrolet
8	Tom Kendall	Chevrolet
9	Ken Schrader	Chevrolet
10	Irv Hoerr	Oldsmobile
11	Alan Kulwicki	Ford
12	Bill Elliott	Ford
13	Rob Moroso	Oldsmobile
14	Terry Labonte	Oldsmobile
15	Sterling Marlin	Oldsmobile
16	Bobby Hillin	Buick
17	Kyle Petty	Pontiac
18	Richard Petty	Pontiac
19	Davey Allison	Ford

20	Dale Jarrett	Ford
21	Harry Gant	Oldsmobile
22	J. D. McDuffie	Pontiac
23	Hut Stricklin	Buick
24	Sarel van der Merwe	Chevrolet
25	Butch Miller	Chevrolet
26	Jerry O'Neil	Pontiac
27	Dick Johnson	Ford
28	Ernie Irvan	Chevrolet
29	Jimmy Spencer	Pontiac
30	Dick Trickle	Pontiac
31	Dave Marcis	Chevrolet
32	Rick Wilson	Oldsmobile
33	Tommy Riggins	Oldsmobile
34	Rusty Wallace	Pontiac
35	Derrike Cope	Chevrolet
36	Rick Ware	Pontiac
37	Oma Kimbrough	Buick
38	John Alexander	Ford
39	Jimmy Means	Pontiac
40	Greg Sacks	Chevrolet

CHAMPION SPARK PLUG 400

Time of Race: 2 hours, 52 minutes, 53 seconds
Average Speed: 138.822 mph
Margin of Victory: 1.70 seconds

FINISH	DRIVER	CAR
1	Mark Martin	Ford
2	Greg Sacks	Chevrolet
3	Rusty Wallace	Pontiac
4	Bill Elliott	Ford
5	Ricky Rudd	Chevrolet
6	Davey Allison	Ford
7	Geoff Bodine	Ford
8	Dale Earnhardt	Chevrolet
9	Morgan Shepherd	Ford
10	Dale Jarrett	Ford

11	Alan Kulwicki	Ford
12	Butch Miller	Chevrolet
13	Harry Gant	Oldsmobile
14	Terry Labonte	Oldsmobile
15	Hut Stricklin	Buick
16	Kyle Petty	Pontiac
17	Brett Bodine	Buick
18	Dave Marcis	Chevrolet
19	Derrike Cope	Chevrolet
20	Sterling Marlin	Oldsmobile
21	Bobby Hillin	Buick
22	Chad Little	Ford
23	Buddy Baker	Ford
24	Mike Chase	Pontiac
25	Jimmy Spencer	Pontiac
26	Rob Moroso	Oldsmobile
27	Jimmy Means	Pontiac
28	Bill Venturini	Chevrolet
29	Rick Wilson	Oldsmobile
30	Michael Waltrip	Pontiac
31	Ben Hess	Pontiac
32	Dick Trickle	Pontiac
33	Richard Petty	Pontiac
34	Rodney Combs	Pontiac
35	Ernie Irvan	Chevrolet
36	Rick Mast	Pontiac
37	Ken Ragan	Ford
38	Jack Pennington	Pontiac
39	Ted Musgrave	Chevrolet
40	Ken Schrader	Chevrolet
41	Ed Cooper	Oldsmobile

BUSCH 500

Time of Race: 2 hours, 54 minutes, 13 seconds
Average Speed: 91.782 mph
Margin of Victory: 21 seconds

FINISH	DRIVER	CAR
1	Ernie Iran	Chevrolet
2	Rusty Wallace	Pontiac
3	Mark Martin	Ford
4	Terry Labonte	Oldsmobile
5	Sterling Marlin	Oldsmobile
6	Alan Kulwicki	Ford
7	Dale Jarrett	Ford
8	Dale Earnhardt	Chevrolet
9	Michael Waltrip	Pontiac
10	Ricky Rudd	Chevrolet
11	Geoff Bodine	Ford
12	Ken Schrader	Chevrolet
13	Bill Elliott	Ford
14	Larry Pearson	Chevrolet
15	Bobby Hillin	Buick
16	Butch Miller	Chevrolet
17	Dick Trickle	Pontiac
18	Jimmy Spencer	Pontiac
19	Dave Marcis	Chevrolet
20	Greg Sacks	Chevrolet
21	Hut Stricklin	Buick
22	Jimmy Means	Pontiac
23	Davey Allison	Ford
24	Rick Mast	Pontiac
25	Brett Bodine	Buick
26	Harry Gant	Oldsmobile
27	Derrike Cope	Chevrolet
28	Kyle Petty	Pontiac
29	Richard Petty	Pontiac
30	Rob Moroso	Oldsmobile
31	Morgan Shepherd	Ford
32	Rick Wilson	Oldsmobile

HEINZ SOUTHERN 500

Time of Race: 4 hours, 4 minutes, 16 seconds
Average Speed: 122.141 mph
Margin of Victory: 4.19 seconds

FINISH	DRIVER	CAR
1	Dale Earnhardt	Chevrolet
2	Ernie Irvan	Chevrolet
3	Alan Kulwicki	Ford
4	Bill Elliott	Ford
5	Harry Gant	Oldsmobile
6	Mark Martin	Ford
7	Ricky Rudd	Chevrolet
8	Geoff Bodine	Ford
9	Derrike Cope	Chevrolet
10	Brett Bodine	Buick
11	Dick Trickle	Pontiac
12	Rick Wilson	Oldsmobile
13	Rob Moroso	Oldsmobile
14	Terry Labonte	Oldsmobile
15	Davey Allison	Ford
16	Dave Marcis	Chevrolet
17	Larry Pearson	Chevrolet
18	Sterling Marlin	Oldsmobile
19	Phil Parsons	Pontiac
20	Hut Stricklin	Buick
21	Morgan Shepherd	Ford
22	Jack Pennington	Oldsmobile
23	Jimmy Spencer	Pontiac
24	Rick Mast	Pontiac
25	Kyle Petty	Pontiac
26	Michael Waltrip	Pontiac
27	Charlie Glotzbach	Pontiac
28	Dale Jarrett	Ford
29	Butch Miller	Chevrolet
30	Greg Sacks	Chevrolet
31	Bobby Hillin	Buick
32	Lake Speed	Oldsmobile
33	Mark Stahl	Ford
34	Richard Petty	Pontiac
35	Chad Little	Ford
36	Jimmy Means	Pontiac
37	Philip Duffie	Buick
38	H. B. Bailey	Pontiac
39	Ken Schrader	Chevrolet
40	Rusty Wallace	Pontiac

MILLER GENUINE DRAFT 400

Time of Race: 3 hours, 8 minutes, 21 seconds
Average Speed: 95.567 mph
Margin of Victory: 1 second

FINISH	DRIVER	CAR
1	Dale Earnhardt	Chevrolet
2	Mark Martin	Ford
3	Darrell Waltrip	Chevrolet
4	Bill Elliott	Ford
5	Rusty Wallace	Pontiac
6	Kyle Petty	Pontiac
7	Dick Trickle	Pontiac
8	Ricky Rudd	Chevrolet
9	Geoff Bodine	Ford
10	Ken Schrader	Chevrolet
11	Bobby Hillin	Buick
12	Ernie Irvan	Chevrolet
13	Hut Stricklin	Buick
14	Michael Waltrip	Pontiac
15	Dave Marcis	Chevrolet
16	Davey Allison	Ford
17	Terry Labonte	Oldsmobile
18	Jimmy Means	Pontiac
19	Butch Miller	Chevrolet
20	Rick Wilson	Oldsmobile
21	Richard Petty	Pontiac
22	Charlie Glotzbach	Ford
23	Greg Sacks	Chevrolet
24	Sterling Marlin	Oldsmobile
25	Ron Esau	Chevrolet
26	Alan Kulwicki	Ford
27	Jimmy Spencer	Pontiac
28	Rob Moroso	Oldsmobile
29	Dale Jarrett	Ford
30	Morgan Shepherd	Ford

31	Brett Bodine	Buick
32	Chad Little	Ford
33	D. K. Ulrich	Pontiac
34	Mickey Gibbs	Ford
35	Derrike Cope	Chevrolet
36	Harry Gant	Oldsmobile

PEAK ANTIFREEZE 500

Time of Race: 3 hours, 58 minutes, 0 seconds
Average Speed: 125.945 mph
Margin of Victory: 1.38 seconds

FINISH	DRIVER	CAR
1	Bill Elliott	Ford
2	Mark Martin	Ford
3	Dale Earnhardt	Chevrolet
4	Harry Gant	Oldsmobile
5	Michael Waltrip	Pontiac
6	Dale Jarrett	Ford
7	Rusty Wallace	Pontiac
8	Kyle Petty	Pontiac
9	Davey Allison	Ford
10	Ken Schrader	Chevrolet
11	Hut Stricklin	Buick
12	Sterling Marlin	Oldsmobile
13	Derrike Cope	Chevrolet
14	Bobby Hillin	Buick
15	Terry Labonte	Oldsmobile
16	Richard Petty	Pontiac
17	Butch Miller	Chevrolet
18	Jimmy Spencer	Pontiac
19	Darrell Waltrip	Chevrolet
20	Brett Bodine	Buick
21	Greg Sacks	Chevrolet
22	Dave Marcis	Chevrolet
23	Dick Trickle	Pontiac
24	Jimmy Means	Pontiac
25	Morgan Shepherd	Ford
26	Ernie Irvan	Chevrolet
27	Rick Wilson	Oldsmobile
28	Rob Moroso	Oldsmobile
29	Alan Kulwicki	Ford
30	Jimmy Horton	Pontiac
31	Tommy Ellis	Oldsmobile
32	Ricky Rudd	Chevrolet
33	Jeff Purvis	Chevrolet
34	Jim Sauter	Pontiac
35	James Hylton	Buick
36	Geoff Bodine	Ford
37	Jerry Hufflin	Pontiac
38	Mike Potter	Pontiac
39	Tommy Riggins	Oldsmobile
40	J. D. McDuffie	Pontiac

GOODY'S 500

Time of Race: 3 hours, 26 minutes, 35 seconds
Average Speed: 76.386 mph
Margin of Victory: 2.16 seconds

FINISH	DRIVER	CAR
1	Geoff Bodine	Ford
2	Dale Earnhardt	Chevrolet
3	Mark Martin	Ford
4	Brett Bodine	Buick
5	Harry Gant	Oldsmobile
6	Alan Kulwicki	Ford
7	Davey Allison	Ford
8	Bill Elliott	Ford
9	Terry Labonte	Oldsmobile
10	Dale Jarrett	Ford
11	Ernie Irvan	Oldsmobile
12	Sterling Marlin	Oldsmobile
13	Hut Stricklin	Buick

14	Dave Marcis	Chevrolet
15	Rusty Wallace	Pontiac
16	Jimmy Means	Pontiac
17	Chad Little	Ford
18	Jimmy Spencer	Pontiac
19	Darrell Waltrip	Chevrolet
20	Rick Wilson	Oldsmobile
21	Rob Moroso	Oldsmobile
22	Dick Trickle	Pontiac
23	Kyle Petty	Pontiac
24	Derrike Cope	Chevrolet
25	Morgan Shepherd	Ford
26	Bobby Hillin	Buick
27	Ken Schrader	Chevrolet
28	Ricky Rudd	Chevrolet
29	Richard Petty	Pontiac
30	Michael Waltrip	Pontiac
31	Rick Mast	Chevrolet

TYSON HOLLY FARMS 400

Time of Race: 2 hours, 39 minutes, 53 seconds
Average Speed: 93.818 mph
Margin of Victory: 3.63 seconds

FINISH	DRIVER	CAR
1	Mark Martin	Ford
2	Dale Earnhardt	Chevrolet
3	Brett Bodine	Buick
4	Bill Elliott	Ford
5	Ken Schrader	Chevrolet
6	Ernie Irvan	Oldsmobile
7	Darrell Waltrip	Chevrolet
8	Rusty Wallace	Pontiac
9	Alan Kulwicki	Ford
10	Kyle Petty	Pontiac
11	Ricky Rudd	Chevrolet
12	Morgan Shepherd	Ford
13	Sterling Marlin	Oldsmobile
14	Bobby Hillin	Buick
15	Michael Waltrip	Pontiac
16	Geoff Bodine	Ford
17	Richard Petty	Pontiac
18	Rick Wilson	Pontiac
19	Dale Jarrrett	Ford
20	Hut Stricklin	Buick
21	Rob Moroso	Oldsmobile
22	Derrike Cope	Chevrolet
23	Jimmy Spencer	Pontiac
24	Chad Little	Ford
25	Dave Marcis	Chevrolet
26	Davey Allison	Ford
27	Terry Labonte	Oldsmobile
28	Harry Gant	Oldsmobile
29	Dick Trickle	Pontiac
30	Jimmy Means	Pontiac
31	Jeff Purvis	Chevrolet
32	Rick Mast	Chevrolet

MELLO YELLO 500

Time of Race: 3 hours, 38 minutes, 44 seconds
Average Speed: 137.428 mph
Margin of Victory: 2.59 seconds

FINISH	DRIVER	CAR
1	Davey Allison	Ford
2	Morgan Shepherd	Ford
3	Michael Waltrip	Pontiac
4	Kyle Petty	Pontiac
5	Alan Kulwicki	Ford
6	Ricky Rudd	Chevrolet
7	Derrike Cope	Chevrolet
8	Brett Bodine	Buick
9	Darrell Waltrip	Chevrolet

10	Dale Jarrett	Ford
11	Rick Wilson	Pontiac
12	Jack Pennington	
13	Dave Marcis	Chevrolet
14	Mark Martin	Ford
15	Bill Elliott	Ford
16	Sterling Marlin	Oldsmobile
17	Terry Labonte	Oldsmobile
18	Phil Parsons	Oldsmobile
19	Larrry Pearson	Chevrolet
20	Richard Petty	Pontiac
21	Mickey Gibbs	Ford
22	Eddie Bierschwale	Oldsmobile
23	Jimmy Horton	Pontiac
24	Chuck Bown	Chevrolet
25	Dale Earnhardt	Chevrolet
26	Harry Gant	Oldsmobile
27	Ernie Irvan	Chevrolet
28	Bobby Hamilton	Pontiac
29	Hut Stricklin	Buick
30	Dick Trickle	Pontiac
31	Bobby Hillin	Buick
32	Mark Stahl	Ford
33	Jimmy Hensley	Oldsmobile
34	Rick Mast	Chevrolet
35	Ken Schrader	Chevrolet
36	Geoff Bodine	Ford
37	Buddy Baker	Ford
38	Rusty Wallace	Pontiac
39	Jimmy Means	Pontiac
40	Chad Little	Ford
41	Jimmy Spencer	Pontiac

AC DELCO 500

Time of Race: 3 hours, 57 minutes, 25 seconds
Average Speed: 126.452 mph
Margin of Victory: Under caution

FINISH	DRIVER	CAR
1	Alan Kulwicki	Ford
2	Bill Elliott	Ford
3	Harry Gant	Oldsmobile
4	Geoff Bodine	Ford
5	Ken Schrader	Chevrolet
6	Sterling Marrlin	Oldsmobile
7	Ricky Rudd	Chevrolet
8	Darrell Waltrip	Chevrolet
9	Ernie Irvan	Chevrolet
10	Dale Earnhardt	Chevrolet
11	Mark Marlin	Ford
12	Morgan Shepherd	Ford
13	Terry Labonte	Oldsmobile
14	Bobby Hillin	Buick
15	Michael Waltrip	Pontiac
16	Dale Jarrett	Ford
17	Brett Bodine	Buick
18	Rick Wilson	Pontiac
19	Larry Pearson	Chevrolet
20	Kyle Petty	Pontiac
21	Richard Petty	Pontiac
22	Rick Mast	Chevrolet
23	Dave Marcis	Chevrolet
24	Jack Pennington	Oldsmobile
25	Chad Little	Ford
26	Tom Kendall	Chevrolet
27	Jim Bown	Pontiac
28	Jimmy Means	Pontiac
29	Davey Allison	Ford
30	Rick Jeffrey	Chevrolet
31	Jimmy Hensley	Oldsmobile
32	Rusty Wallace	Pontiac
33	Derrike Cope	Chevrolet
34	Hut Stricklin	Buick
35	Mike Skinner	Buick
36	Dick Trickle	Pontiac
37	Ted Musgrave	Chevrolet
38	Jeff Purvis	Chevrolet
39	Tracy Leslie	Oldsmobile
40	Charlie Baker	Buick

CHECKER 500

Time of Race: 3 hours, 13 minutes, 25 seconds
Average Speed: 96.786 mph
Margin of Victory: 53 seconds

FINISH	DRIVER	CAR
1	Dale Earnhardt	Chevrolet
2	Ken Schrader	Chevrolet
3	Morgan Shepherd	Ford
4	Darrell Waltrip	Chevrolet
5	Bill Elliott	Ford
6	Alan Kulwicki	Ford
7	Rick Mast	Chevrolet
8	Geoff Bodine	Ford
9	Ernie Irvan	Chevrolet
10	Mark Martin	Ford
11	Davey Allison	Ford
12	Gret Sacks	Chevrolet
13	Terry Labonte	Oldsmobile
14	Derrike Cope	Chevrolet
15	Brett Bodine	Buick
16	Sterling Marlin	Oldsmobile
17	Dave Marcis	Chevrolet
18	Bill Schmitt	Chevrolet
19	Rick Wilson	Oldsmobile
20	Bill Sedgwick	Chevrolet
21	Chad Little	Oldsmobile
22	Ted Musgrave	Pontiac
23	Richard Petty	Pontiac
24	Chuck Bown	Oldsmobile
25	Jimmy Means	Pontiac
26	Hut Stricklin	Buick
27	Rodney Combs	Pontiac
28	Jim Bown	Pontiac
29	Brent Kaeding	Chevrolet
30	Dale Jarrett	Ford
31	John Krebs	Pontiac
32	Ricky Rudd	Chevrolet
33	Gary Collins	Oldsmobile
34	Mark Reed	Chevrolet
35	Troy Beebe	Buick
36	Jeff Purvis	Chevrolet
37	Harry Gant	Oldsmobile
38	Rusty Wallace	Pontiac
39	Mike Chase	Buick
40	Dick Trickle	Pontiac
41	Kyle Petty	Pontiac
42	Bobby Hillin	Buick
43	Michael Waltrip	Pontiac

ATLANTA JOURNAL 500

Time of Race: 3 hours, 32 minutes, 34 seconds
Average Speed: 140.911 mph
Margin of Victory: 2.47 seconds

FINISH	DRIVER	CAR
1	Morgan Shepherd	Ford
2	Geoff Bodine	Ford
3	Dale Earnhardt	Chevrolet
4	Dale Jarrett	Ford
5	Darrell Waltrip	Chevrolet
6	Mark Marrtin	Ford
7	Ernie Irvan	Chevrolet
8	Alan Kulwicki	Ford
9	Rusty Wallace	Pontiac
10	Greg Sacks	Chevrolet
11	Ken Schrader	Chevrolet
12	Derrike Cope	Chevrolet
13	Hut Stricklin	Buick
14	—	Pontiac
15	Bill Elliott	Ford
16	Ricky Rudd	Chevrolet
17	Richard Petty	Pontiac
18	Brett Bodine	Buick
19	Harry Gant	Oldsmobile

20	Dave Mader	Pontiac
21	Terry Labonte	Oldsmobile
22	Bobby Hillin	Buick
23	Chuck Bown	Chevrolet
24	Steve Grissom	Oldsmobile
25	Davey Allison	Ford
26	Ted Musgrave	Pontiac
27	Chad Little	Ford
28	Jimmy Means	Pontiac
29	Rick Mast	Chevrolet
30	Rodney Combs	Pontiac
31	Jim Sauter	Ford
32	Pancho Carter	Ford
33	Rick Wilson	Oldsmobile
34	Dave Marcis	Chevrolet
35	Jimmy Horton	Chevrolet
36	Jack Pennington	Oldsmobile
37	Dick Trickle	Pontiac
38	Sterling Marlin	Oldsmobile
39	Jim Bown	Pontiac
40	Bobby Hamilton	Pontiac
41	Kyle Petty	Pontiac

1991

DAYTONA 500

Time of Race: 3 hours, 22 minutes, 30 seconds
Average Speed: 148.148 mph
Margin of Victory: Under Caution

FINISH	DRIVER	CAR
1	Ernie Irvan	Chevrolet
2	Sterling Marlin	Ford
3	Joe Ruttman	Oldsmobile
4	Rick Mast	Oldsmobile
5	Dale Earnhardt	Chevrolet
6	Dale Jarrett	Ford
7	Bobby Hillin	Oldsmobile
8	Alan Kulwicki	Ford
9	Ricky Rudd	Chevrolet
10	Bobby Hamilton	Oldsmobile
11	Dick Trickle	Pontiac
12	Eddie Bierschwale	Oldsmobile
13	Terry Labonte	Oldsmobile
14	Chad Little	Ford
15	Davey Allison	Ford
16	Kyle Petty	Pontiac
17	Mickey Gibbs	Pontiac
18	Robby Gordon	Ford
19	Richard Petty	Pontiac
20	Phil Barkdoll	Oldsmobile
21	Mark Martin	Ford
22	Brett Bodine	Buick
23	Jim Sauter	Pontiac
24	Darrell Waltrip	Chevrolet
25	Harry Gant	Oldsmobile
26	Derrike Cope	Chevrolet
27	Rusty Wallace	Pontiac
28	Bill Elliott	Ford
29	Hut Stricklin	Buick
30	Ted Musgrave	Pontiac
31	Ken Schrader	Chevrolet
32	Geoff Bodine	Ford
33	Rick Wilson	Buick
34	Morgan Shepherd	Ford
35	Dave Marcis	Chevrolet
36	Jeff Purvis	Oldsmobile
37	Buddy Baker	Pontiac
38	Michael Waltrip	Pontiac
39	Jimmy Means	Pontiac
40	Jimmy Spencer	Chevrolet
41	Sammy Swindell	Oldsmobile
42	Greg Sacks	Chevrolet

PONTIAC EXCITEMENT 400

Time of Race: 2 hours, 50 minutes, 47 seconds
Average Speed: 105.397 mph
Margin of Victory: 1.5 car lengths

FINISH	DRIVER	CAR
1	Dale Earnhardt	Chevrolet
2	Ricky Rudd	Chevrolet
3	Harry Gant	Oldsmobile
4	Rusty Wallace	Pontiac
5	Alan Kulwicki	Ford
6	Mark Martin	Ford
7	Darrell Waltrip	Chevrolet
8	Morgan Shepherd	Ford
9	Sterling Marlin	Ford
10	Ken Schrader	Chevrolet
11	Richard Petty	Pontiac
12	Davey Allison	Ford
13	Geoff Bodine	Ford
14	Terry Labonte	Oldsmobile
15	Dick Trickle	Pontiac
16	Chad Little	Ford
17	Michael Waltrip	Pontiac
18	Rick Wilson	Buick
19	Ted Musgrave	Pontiac
20	Bobby Hillin	Oldsmobile
21	Dale Jarrett	Ford
22	Hut Stricklin	Buick
23	Mickey Gibbs	Pontiac
24	Brett Bodine	Buick
25	Kyle Petty	Pontiac
26	Robby Gordon	Ford
27	Ernie Irvan	Chevrolet
28	Bobby Hamilton	Oldsmobile
29	Joe Ruttman	Oldsmobile
30	Bill Elliott	Ford
31	Jimmy Means	Pontiac
32	Derrike Cope	Chevrolet
33	Dave Marcis	Chevrolet
34	Jimmy Spencer	Chevrolet
35	Rick Mast	Oldsmobile

GOODWRENCH 500

Time of Race: 4 hours, 01 minutes, 57 seconds
Average Speed: 124.083 mph
Margin of Victory: 1.1 seconds

FINISH	DRIVER	CAR
1	Kyle Petty	Pontiac
2	Ken Schrader	Chevrolet
3	Harry Gant	Oldsmobile
4	Ricky Rudd	Chevrolet
5	Bill Elliott	Ford
6	Ernie Irvan	Chevrolet
7	Michael Waltrip	Pontiac
8	Dale Earnhardt	Chevrolet
9	Darrell Waltrip	Chevrolet
10	Morgan Shepherd	Ford
11	Dale Jarrett	Ford
12	Geoff Bodine	Ford
13	Brett Bodine	Buick
14	Mark Martin	Ford
15	Richard Petty	Pontiac
16	Davey Allison	Ford
17	Alan Kulwicki	Ford
18	Bobby Hillin	Oldsmobile
19	Rick Wilson	Buick
20	Mickey Gibbs	Pontiac
21	Bobby Hamilton	Oldsmobile
22	Chad Little	Ford
23	Dave Marcis	Chevrolet
24	Joe Ruttrman	Oldsmobile
25	Ted Musgrave	Pontiac
26	Rich Bickle	Oldsmobile

27	Jimmy Means	Pontiac
28	Rusty Wallace	Pontiac
29	Dick Trickle	Pontiac
30	Rick Mast	Oldsmobile
31	Hut Stricklin	Buick
32	Mike Skinner	Chevrolet
33	Sterling Marlin	Ford
34	Derrike Cope	Chevrolet
35	Jeff Purvis	Oldsmobile
36	Bill Meacham	Oldsmobile
37	Stanley Smith	Buick
38	Jimmy Spencer	Chevrolet
39	Terry Labonte	Oldsmobile
40	Andy Hillenburg	Buick

MOTORCRAFT QUALITY PARTS 500

Time of Race: 3 hours, 33 minutes, 14 seconds
Average Speed: 140.470 mph
Margin of Victory: 3.02 seconds

FINISH	DRIVER	CAR
1	Ken Schrader	Chevrolet
2	Bill Elliott	Ford
3	Dale Earnhardt	Chevrolet
4	Morgan Shepherd	Ford
5	Michael Waltrip	Pontiac
6	Ricky Rudd	Chevrolet
7	Sterling Marlin	Ford
8	Alan Kulwicki	Ford
9	Darrell Waltrip	Chevrolet
10	Rusty Wallace	Pontiac
11	Derrike Cope	Chevrolet
12	Rick Wilson	Buick
13	Hut Stricklin	Buick
14	Ernie Irvan	Chevrolet
15	Brett Bodine	Buick
16	Jimmy Spencer	Chevrolet
17	Mark Martin	Ford
18	Chad Little	Ford
19	Harry Gant	Oldsmobile
20	Dale Jarrett	Ford
21	Bobby Hillin	Oldsmobile
22	Jimmy Sauter	Pontiac
23	Geoff Bodine	Ford
24	Jeff Purvis	Oldsmobile
25	Mickey Gibbs	Pontiac
26	Wally Dallenbach	Ford
27	Joe Ruttman	Oldsmobile
28	Dick Trickle	Pontiac
29	Rick Mast	Oldsmobile
30	Dave Mader	Pontiac
31	Jimmy Means	Pontiac
32	Andy Hillenburg	Buick
33	Bobby Hamilton	Oldsmobile
34	Rich Bickle	Oldsmobile
35	Terry Labonte	Oldsmobile
36	Dave Marcis	Chevrolet
37	Ted Musgrave	Pontiac
38	Richard Petty	Pontiac
39	Kyle Petty	Pontiac
40	Davey Allison	Ford

TRANSOUTH 500

Time of Race: 3 hours, 41 minutes, 50 seconds
Average Speed: 135.594 mph - Track Record
Margin of Victory: 11.32 seconds

FINISH	DRIVER	CAR
1	Ricky Rudd	Chevrolet
2	Davey Allison	Ford
3	Michael Waltrip	Pontiac

4	Mark Martin	Ford
5	Rusty Wallace	Pontiac
6	Kyle Petty	Pontiac
7	Ernie Irvan	Chevrolet
8	Morgan Shepherd	Ford
9	Geoff Bodine	Ford
10	Sterling Marlin	Ford
11	Jimmy Spencer	Chevrolet
12	Bill Elliott	Ford
13	Rick Mast	Oldsmobile
14	Rick Wilson	Buick
15	Terry Labonte	Oldsmobile
16	Brett Bodine	Buick
17	Bobby Hillin	Oldsmobile
18	Dave Marcis	Chevrolet
19	Ken Schrader	Chevrolet
20	Bobby Hamilton	Oldsmobile
21	Ted Musgrave	Pontiac
22	Mickey Gibbs	Pontiac
23	Jimmy Means	Pontiac
24	Rich Bickle	Oldsmobile
25	Darrell Waltrip	Chevrolet
26	Joe Ruttman	Oldsmobile
27	Harry Gant	Oldsmobile
28	Randy Baker	Chevrolet
29	Dale Earnhardt	Chevrolet
30	J.D. McDuffie	Pontiac
31	Derrike Cope	Chevrolet
32	Hut Stricklin	Buick
33	Dave Mader	Pontiac
34	Alan Kulwicki	Ford
35	H.B. Bailey	Pontiac
36	Chad Little	Ford
37	Richard Petty	Pontiac
38	Bill Meacham	Oldsmobile
39	Dale Jarrett	Ford
40	Lake Speed	Pontiac

VALLEYDALE MEATS 500

Time of Race: 3 hours, 39 minutes, 37 seconds
Average Speed: 72.809 mph
Margin of Victory: 1/2 car length

FINISH	DRIVER	CAR
1	Rusty Wallace	Pontiac
2	Ernie Irvan	Chevrolet
3	Davey Allison	Ford
4	Mark Martin	Ford
5	Ricky Rudd	Chevrolet
6	Darrell Waltrip	Chevrolet
7	Dale Jarrett	Ford
8	Jimmy Spencer	Chevrolet
9	Terry Labonte	Oldsmobile
10	Morgan Shepherd	Ford
11	Harry Gant	Oldsmobile
12	Ted Musgrave	Pontiac
13	Joe Ruttman	Oldsmobile
14	Chad Little	Ford
15	Bobby Hillin	Oldsmobile
16	Hut Stricklin	Buick
17	Richard Petty	Pontiac
18	Rick Mast	Oldsmobile
19	Mickey Gibbs	Pontiac
20	Dale Earnhardt	Chevrolet
21	Kyle Petty	Pontiac
22	Brett Bodine	Buick
23	Michael Waltrip	Pontiac
24	Geoff Bodine	Ford
25	Lake Speed	Pontiac
26	Alan Kulwicki	Ford
27	Sterling Marlin	Ford
28	Bill Elliott	Ford
29	Ken Schrader	Chevrolet
30	Dick Trickle	Buick
31	Bobby Hamilton	Oldsmobile
32	Derrike Cope	Chevrolet
33	Rick Wilson	Buick

FIRST UNION 400

Time of Race: 3 hours, 8 minutes, 26 seconds
Average Speed: 79.604 mph
Margin of Victory: .81 second

FINISH	DRIVER	CAR
1	Darrell Waltrip	Chevrolet
2	Dale Earnhardt	Chevrolet
3	Jimmy Spencer	Chevrolet
4	Morgan Shepherd	Ford
5	Ken Schrader	Chevrolet
6	Davey Allison	Ford
7	Michael Waltrip	Pontiac
8	Bill Elliott	Ford
9	Mark Martin	Ford
10	Ernie Irvan	Chevrolet
11	Ricky Rudd	Chevrolet
12	Rick Mast	Oldsmobile
13	Lake Speed	Pontiac
14	Hut Stricklin	Buick
15	Derrike Cope	Chevrolet
16	Richard Petty	Pontiac
17	Ted Musgrave	Pontiac
18	Kyle Petty	Pontiac
19	Dave Marcis	Chevrolet
20	Bobby Hillin	Oldsmobile
21	Bobby Hamilton	Pontiac
22	Sterling Marlin	Ford
23	Harry Gant	Oldsmobile
24	Joe Ruttman	Oldsmobile
25	Dale Jarrett	Ford
26	Dick Trickle	Buick
27	Rick Wilson	Buick
28	Geoff Bodine	Ford
29	Alan Kulwicki	Ford
30	Brett Bodine	Buick
31	Terry Labonte	Oldsmobile
32	Rusty Wallace	Pontiac
33	Mickey Gibbs	Pontiac

HANES 500

Time of Race: 3 hours, 26 minutes, 41 seconds
Average Speed: 75.139 mph
Margin of Victory: 3.34 seconds

FINISH	DRIVER	CAR
1	Dale Earnhardt	Chevrolet
2	Kyle Petty	Pontiac
3	Darrell Waltrip	Chevrolet
4	Brett Bodine	Buick
5	Harry Gant	Oldsmobile
6	Jimmy Spencer	Chevrolet
7	Michael Waltrip	Pontiac
8	Davey Allison	Ford
9	Alan Kulwicki	Ford
10	Hut Stricklin	Buick
11	Ricky Rudd	Chevrolet
12	Dale Jarrett	Ford
13	Rick Mast	Oldsmobile
14	Richard Petty	Pontiac
15	Ernie Irvan	Chevrolet
16	Joe Ruttman	Oldsmobile
17	Bobby Hillin	Oldsmobile
18	Lake Speed	Pontiac
19	Bill Sedgwick	Chevrolet
20	Geoff Bodine	Ford
21	Rusty Wallace	Pontiac
22	Rick Wilson	Buick
23	Ken Schrader	Chevrolet
24	Ted Musgrave	Pontiac
25	Mickey Gibbs	Pontiac
26	Bill Elliott	Ford
27	Chad Little	Ford
28	Sterling Marlin	Ford
29	Mark Martin	Ford

30	Morgan Shepherd	Ford
31	Terry Labonte	Oldsmobile
32	Dick Trickle	Buick

WINSTON 500

Time of Race: 3 hours, 1 minute, 10 seconds
Average Speed: 165.620 mph
Margin of Victory: 11 seconds

FINISH	DRIVER	CAR
1	Harry Gant	Oldsmobile
2	Darrell Waltrip	Chevrolet
3	Dale Earnhardt	Chevrolet
4	Sterling Marlin	Ford
5	Michael Waltrip	Pontiac
6	Geoff Bodine	Ford
7	Ken Schrader	Chevrolet
8	Bill Elliott	Ford
9	Jimmy Spencer	Chevrolet
10	Rick Mast	Oldsmobile
11	Brett Bodine	Buick
12	Bobby Hamilton	Oldsmobile
13	Ricky Rudd	Chevrolet
14	Morgan Shepherd	Ford
15	Mickey Gibbs	Pontiac
16	Ted Musgrave	Pontiac
17	Bobby Hillin	Oldsmobile
18	Dave Marcis	Chevrolet
19	Phil Barkdoll	Oldsmobile
20	Jimmy Means	Pontiac
21	Stanley Smith	Buick
22	Davey Allison	Ford
23	Hut Stricklin	Buick
24	Mark Martin	Ford
25	Rick Wilson	Buick
26	Rusty Wallace	Pontiac
27	Alan Kulwicki	Ford
28	Derrike Cope	Chevrolet
29	Joe Ruttman	Oldsmobile
30	Jeff Purvis	Oldsmobile
31	Lake Speed	Pontiac
32	Ernie Irvan	Chevrolet
33	Kyle Petty	Pontiac
34	Wally Dallenbach	Ford
35	Dale Jarrett	Ford
36	Buddy Baker	Oldsmobile
37	Terry Labonte	Oldsmobile
38	Child Little	Ford
39	Greg Sacks	Oldsmobile
40	Richard Petty	Pontiac
41	Larry Pearson	Chevrolet

COCA COLA 600

Time of Race: 4 hours, 19 minutes, 5 seconds
Average Speed: 138.951 mph
Margin of Victory: 1.28 seconds

FINISH	DRIVER	CAR
1	Davey Allison	Ford
2	Ken Schrader	Chevrolet
3	Dale Earnhardt	Chevrolet
4	Harry Gant	Oldsmobile
5	Dale Jarrett	Ford
6	Hut Stricklin	Buick
7	Ernie Irvan	Chevrolet
8	Darrell Waltrip	Chevrolet
9	Ricky Rudd	Chevrolet
10	Terry Labonte	Oldsmobile
11	Sterling Marlin	Ford
12	Derrike Cope	Chevrolet
13	Kenny Wallace	Pontiac
14	Morgan Shepherd	Ford
15	Michael Waltrip	Pontiac

FINISH	DRIVER	CAR
16	Tommy Ellis	Ford
17	Ted Musgrave	Pontiac
18	Rick Wilson	Buick
19	Bobby Hillin	Oldsmobile
20	Richard Petty	Pontiac
21	Joe Ruttman	Oldsmobile
22	Rusty Wallace	Pontiac
23	Mark Martin	Ford
24	Eddie Bierschwale	Oldsmobile
25	Chad Little	Ford
26	Bill Elliott	Ford
27	Bobby Hamilton	Oldsmobile
28	Brett Bodine	Buick
29	Lake Speed	Pontiac
30	Rick Mast	Oldsmobile
31	Jimmy Spencer	Chevrolet
32	Dave Marcis	Chevrolet
33	Wally Dallenbach	Ford
34	Mickey Gibbs	Pontiac
35	Alan Kulwicki	Ford
36	Stanley Smith	Buick
37	Jim Sauter	Pontiac
38	Jimmy Means	Pontiac
39	Greg Sacks	Oldsmobile
40	Dick Trickle	Buick
41	Larry Pearson	Chevrolet

BUDWEISER 500

Time of Race: 4 hours, 9 minutes, 41 seconds
Average Speed: 120.152 mph
Margin of Victory: 1.18 seconds

FINISH	DRIVER	CAR
1	Ken Schrader	Chevrolet
2	Dale Earnhardt	Chevrolet
3	Harry Gant	Chevrolet
4	Ernie Irvan	Chevrolet
5	Mark Martin	Ford
6	Hut Stricklin	Buick
7	Darrell Waltrip	Chevrolet
8	Morgan Shepherd	Ford
9	Rusty Wallace	Pontiac
10	Ricky Rudd	Chevrolet
11	Bobby Hamilton	Oldsmobile
12	Joe Ruttman	Oldsmobile
13	Bill Elliott	Ford
14	Alan Kulwicki	Ford
15	Sterling Marlin	Ford
16	Davey Allison	Ford
17	Richard Petty	Pontiac
18	Ted Musgrave	Pontiac
19	Bobby Hillin	Pontiac
20	Rick Mast	Oldsmobile
21	Tommy Ellis	Ford
22	Lake Speed	Pontiac
23	Dave Marcis	Chevrolet
24	Terry Labonte	Oldsmobile
25	Rick Wilson	Buick
26	Kenny Wallace	Pontiac
27	Derrike Cope	Chevrolet
28	Jimmy Spencer	Chevrolet
29	Chad Little	Ford
30	Mickey Gibbs	Pontiac
31	J.D. McDuffie	Pontiac
32	Michael Waltrip	Pontiac
33	Brett Bodine	Buick
34	Bobby Labonte	Oldsmobile
35	Dale Jarrett	Ford

BANQUET FROZEN FOODS 300

Time of Race: 2 hours, 33 minutes, 20 seconds
Average Speed: 72.970 mph
Margin of Victory: 1 second

FINISH	DRIVER	CAR
1	Davey Allison	Ford
2	Ricky Rudd	Chevrolet
3	Rusty Wallace	Pontiac
4	Ernie Irvan	Chevrolet
5	Ken Schrader	Chevrolet
6	Terry Labonte	Oldsmobile
7	Dale Earnhardt	Chevrolet
8	Geoff Bodine	Ford
9	Mark Martin	Ford
10	Michael Waltrip	Pontiac
11	Brett Bodine	Buick
12	Lake Speed	Pontiac
13	Bill Schmitt	Ford
14	Mickey Gibbs	Pontiac
15	Bill Sedgwick	Chevrolet
16	Rick Wilson	Buick
17	Alan Kulwicki	Ford
18	Tom Kendall	Pontiac
19	Rick Mast	Oldsmobile
20	Bill Elliott	Ford
21	Bobby Hillin	Pontiac
22	Bobby Hamilton	Oldsmobile
23	Stanley Smith	Buick
24	Dave Marcis	Chevrolet
25	Darrell Waltrip	Chevrolet
26	Sterling Marlin	Ford
27	Harry Gant	Oldsmobile
28	Chad Little	Ford
29	Jimmy Spencer	Chevrolet
30	Derrike Cope	Chevrolet
31	Joe Ruttman	Oldsmobile
32	Hershel McGriff	Pontiac
33	Scott Gaylord	Oldsmobile
34	Richard Petty	Pontiac
35	Hut Stricklin	Buick
36	Irv Hoerr	Oldsmobile
37	Ted Musgrave	Pontiac
38	John Krebs	Pontiac
39	Robert Sprague	Ford
40	Mike Chase	Ford
41	Dale Jarrett	Ford
42	Morgan Shepherd	Ford
43	R.K. Smith	Pontiac

CHAMPION SPARK PLUG 500

Time of Race: 4 hours, 4 minutes, 34 seconds
Average Speed: 122.666 mph
Margin of Victory: 1.8 seconds

FINISH	DRIVER	CAR
1	Darrell Waltrip	Chevrolet
2	Dale Earnhardt	Chevrolet
3	Mark Martin	Ford
4	Harry Gant	Oldsmobile
5	Geoff Bodine	Ford
6	Ernie Irvan	Chevrolet
7	Ken Schrader	Chevrolet
8	Sterling Marlin	Ford
9	Morgan Shepherd	Ford
10	Derrike Cope	Chevrolet
11	Richard Petty	Pontiac
12	Davey Allison	Ford
13	Rick Wilson	Buick
14	Jimmy Spencer	Chevrolet
15	Bobby Hillin	Pontiac
16	Alan Kulwicki	Ford
17	Lake Speed	Pontiac
18	Michael Waltrip	Pontiac
19	Dale Jarrett	Ford
20	Ricky Rudd	Chevrolet
21	Terry Labonte	Oldsmobile
22	Joe Ruttman	Oldsmobile
23	Chad Little	Ford
24	Dave Marcis	Chevrolet
25	Rick Mast	Oldsmobile
26	Jimmy Means	Pontiac

27	Ted Musgrave	Pontiac
28	Hut Stricklin	Buick
29	Randy LaJoie	Buick
30	Mickey Gibbs	Pontiac
31	Rusty Wallace	Pontiac
32	Larry Pearson	Chevrolet
33	Brett Bodine	Buick
34	J.D. McDuffie	Pontiac
35	Bobby Hamilton	Oldsmobile
36	Bill Elliott	Ford
37	James Hylton	Chevrolet

MILLER GENUINE DRAFT 400

Time of Race: 2 hours, 29 minutes, 9 seconds
Average Speed: 160.912 mph - Track Record
Margin of Victory: 11.72 seconds

FINISH	DRIVER	CAR
1	Davey Allison	Ford
2	Hut Stricklin	Buick
3	Mark Martin	Ford
4	Dale Earnhardt	Chevrolet
5	Ernie Irvan	Chevrolet
6	Ken Schrader	Chevrolet
7	Darrell Waltrip	Chevrolet
8	Ricky Rudd	Chevrolet
9	Morgan Shepherd	Ford
10	Harry Gant	Oldsmobile
11	Bill Elliott	Ford
12	Dale Jarrett	Ford
13	Sterling Marlin	Ford
14	Mickey Gibbs	Pontiac
15	Bobby Hillin	Pontiac
16	Dave Marcis	Pontiac
17	Rusty Wallace	Pontiac
18	Lake Speed	Pontiac
19	Joe Ruttman	Oldsmobile
20	Larry Pearson	Chevrolet
21	Ted Musgrave	Pontiac
22	Bobby Hamilton	Chevrolet
23	Stanley Smith	Buick
24	Alan Kulwicki	Ford
25	Terry Labonte	Oldsmobile
26	Chad Little	Ford
27	Jimmy Means	Pontiac
28	Wally Dallenbach	Ford
29	Rick Mast	Oldsmobile
30	Buddy Baker	Oldsmobile
31	Rick Wilson	Buick
32	Jimmy Spencer	Chevrolet
33	H.B. Bailey	Pontiac
34	Michael Waltrip	Pontiac
35	Richard Petty	Pontiac
36	Brett Bodine	Buick
37	Jim Sauter	Pontiac
38	Eddie Bierschwale	Oldsmobile
39	Geoff Bodine	Ford
40	Bill Venturini	Chevrolet
41	Derrike Cope	Chevrolet

PEPSI 400

Time of Race: 2 hours, 30 minutes, 50 seconds
Average Speed: 159.116 mph
Margin of Victory: .18 second

FINISH	DRIVER	CAR
1	Bill Elliott	Ford
2	Geoff Bodine	Ford
3	Davey Allison	Ford
4	Ken Schrader	Chevrolet
5	Ernie Irvan	Chevrolet
6	Michael Waltrip	Pontiac
7	Dale Earnhardt	Chevrolet
8	Sterling Marlin	Ford
9	Ricky Rudd	Chevrolet

10	Jimmy Spencer	Chevrolet
11	Mark Martin	Ford
12	Rusty Wallace	Pontiac
13	Buddy Baker	Oldsmobile
14	Alan Kulwicki	Ford
15	Bobby Hillin	Pontiac
16	Hut Stricklin	Buick
17	Derrike Cope	Chevrolet
18	Dale Jarrett	Ford
19	Rick Mast	Oldsmobile
20	Morgan Shepherd	Ford
21	Larry Pearson	Chevrolet
22	Richard Petty	Pontiac
23	Harry Gant	Oldsmobile
24	Rick Wilson	Buick
25	Dave Marcis	Chevrolet
26	Jimmy Means	Pontiac
27	Mickey Gibbs	Pontiac
28	Bobby Hamilton	Oldsmobile
29	Chad Little	Ford
30	Jeff Purvis	Oldsmobile
31	Joe Ruttman	Oldsmobile
32	Darrell Waltrip	Chevrolet
33	Mike Chase	Oldsmobile
34	Wally Dallenbech, Jr.	Ford
35	Phil Barkdoll	Oldsmobile
36	Brett Bodine	Buick
37	Ted Musgrave	Pontiac
38	Lake Speed	Pontiac
39	Greg Sacks	Oldsmobile
40	Stanley Smith	Buick
41	Terry Labonte	Oldsmobile

MILLER GENUINE DRAFT 500

Time of Race: 3 hours, 52 minutes, 33 seconds
Average Speed: 115.459 mph
Margin of Victory: Under caution

FINISH	DRIVER	CAR
1	Rusty Wallace	Pontiac
2	Mark Martin	Ford
3	Geoff Bodine	Ford
4	Hut Stricklin	Buick
5	Sterling Marlin	Ford
6	Dale Jarrett	Ford
7	Ernie Irvan	Chevrolet
8	Brett Bodine	Buick
9	Bill Elliott	Ford
10	Joe Ruttman	Oldsmobile
11	Bobby Hamilton	Oldsmobile
12	Chad Little	Ford
13	Ted Musgrave	Pontiac
14	Davey Allison	Ford
15	Terry Labonte	Oldsmobile
16	Alan Kulwicki	Ford
17	Greg Sacks	Oldsmobile
18	Dave Marcis	Chevrolet
19	Irv Hoerr	Oldsmobile
20	Ricky Rudd	Chevrolet
21	Jimmy Means	Pontiac
22	Dale Earnhardt	Chevrolet
23	Ken Schrader	Chevrolet
24	Rick Wilson	Buick
25	J.D. McDuffie	Pontiac
26	Harry Gant	Oldsmobile
27	Rick Mast	Oldsmobile
28	Bobby Hillin	Pontiac
29	Darrell Waltrip	Chevrolet
30	Lake Speed	Pontiac
31	Richard Petty	Pontiac
32	John Paul, Jr.	Chevrolet
33	Gary Wright	Chevrolet
34	Morgan Shepherd	Ford
35	Dick Trickle	Pontiac
36	Derrike Cope	Chevrolet
37	Jimmy Spencer	Chevrolet
38	Michael Waltrip	Pontiac
39	Bill Venturini	Chevrolet
40	Gary Balough	Buick

DIEHARD 500

Time of Race: 3 hours, 23 minutes, 35 seconds
Average Speed: 147.3836 mph
Margin of Victory: 1½ car length

FINISH	DRIVER	CAR
1	Dale Earnhardt	Chevrolet
2	Bill Elliott	Ford
3	Mark Martin	Ford
4	Ricky Rudd	Chevrolet
5	Sterling Marlin	Ford
6	Rusty Wallace	Pontiac
7	Michael Waltrip	Pontiac
8	Dale Jarrett	Ford
9	Davey Allison	Ford
10	Joe Ruttman	Oldsmobile
11	Bobby Hillin	Pontiac
12	Chad Little	Ford
13	Buddy Baker	Oldsmobile
14	Morgan Shepherd	Ford
15	Darrell Waltrip	Chevrolet
16	Alan Kulwicki	Ford
17	Larry Pearson	Chevrolet
18	Richard Petty	Pontiac
19	Greg Sacks	Oldsmobile
20	Dick Trickle	Pontiac
21	Dave Marcis	Chevrolet
22	Phil Barkdoll	Oldsmobile
23	Jimmy Means	Pontiac
24	Terry Labonte	Oldsmobile
25	Mikes Chase	Oldsmobile
26	Ted Musgrave	Pontiac
27	Eddie Bierschwale	Chevrolet
28	Rick Mast	Oldsmobile
29	Hut Stricklin	Buick
30	Geoff Bodine	Ford
31	Stanley Smith	Buick
32	Brett Bodine	Buick
33	Ernie Irvan	Chevrolet
34	Bobby Hamilton	Oldsmobile
35	Derrike Cope	Chevrolet
36	Lake Speed	Pontiac
37	Jimmy Spencer	Chevrolet
38	Rick Wilson	Buick
39	Harry Gant	Oldsmobile
40	Ken Schrader	Chevrolet
41	Wally Dallenbach	Ford

BUDWEISER AT THE GLEN

Time of Race: 2 hours, 12 minutes, 28 seconds
Average Speed: 98.977 mph - Track Record
Margin of Victory: 7 seconds

FINISH	DRIVER	CAR
1	Ernie Irvan	Chevrolet
2	Ricky Rudd	Chevrolet
3	Mark Martin	Ford
4	Rusty Wallace	Pontiac
5	Dale Jarrett	Ford
6	Darrell Waltrip	Chevrolet
7	Bill Elliott	Ford
8	Hut Stricklin	Buick
9	Richard Petty	Pontiac
10	Davey Allison	Ford
11	Chad Little	Ford
12	Sterling Marlin	Ford
13	Derrike Cope	Chevrolet
14	Joe Ruttman	Oldsmobile
15	Dale Earnhardt	Chevrolet
16	John Paul, Jr.	Chevrolet
17	Dorsey Schroeder	Pontiac
18	Bobby Hillin	Pontiac
19	Rick Wilson	Buick
20	Jim Derhaag	Oldsmobile
21	Michael Waltrip	Pontiac
22	Geoff Bodine	Ford

CHAMPION SPARK PLUG 400

Time of Race: 2 hours, 51 minutes, 34 seconds
Average Speed: 142.972 mph
Margin of Victory: 10 inches

FINISH	DRIVER	CAR
23	Alan Kulwicki	Ford
24	Oma Kimbrough	Buick
25	Brett Bodine	Buick
26	Ted Musgrave	Pontiac
27	Jimmy Spencer	Chevrolet
28	Harry Gant	Oldsmobile
29	Bobby Hamilton	Oldsmobile
30	Ken Schrader	Chevrolet
31	Kim Campbell	Oldsmobile
32	Wally Dallenbach	Ford
33	Lake Speed	Pontiac
34	Terry Labonte	Oldsmobile
35	Rick Mast	Oldsmobile
36	Morgan Shepherd	Ford
37	Dave Marcis	Chevrolet
38	Irv Hoerr	Oldsmobile
39	Jimmy Means	Pontiac
40	J.D. McDuffie	Pontiac

FINISH	DRIVER	CAR
1	Dale Jarrett	Ford
2	Davey Allison	Ford
3	Rusty Wallace	Pontiac
4	Mark Martin	Ford
5	Bill Elliott	Ford
6	Harry Gant	Oldsmobile
7	Ernie Irvan	Chevrolet
8	Alan Kulwicki	Ford
9	Michael Waltrip	Pontiac
10	Ken Schrader	Chevrolet
11	Ricky Rudd	Chevrolet
12	Sterling Marlin	Ford
13	Buddy Baker	Oldsmobile
14	Hut Stricklin	Buick
15	Lake Speed	Pontiac
16	Terry Labonte	Oldsmobile
17	Ted Musgrave	Pontiac
18	Rick Mast	Oldsmobile
19	Bobby Hamilton	Oldsmobile
20	Dave Marcis	Chevrolet
21	Dick Trickle	Pontiac
22	Wally Dallenbach	Ford
23	Richard Petty	Pontiac
24	Dale Earnhardt	Chevrolet
25	Chad Little	Ford
26	Morgan Shepherd	Ford
27	Jimmy Means	Pontiac
28	H.B. Bailey	Pontiac
29	Mike Chase	Oldsmobile
30	Joe Ruttman	Chevrolet
31	Jim Sauter	Pontiac
32	Darrell Waltrip	Chevrolet
33	Bobby Hillin	Pontiac
34	Derrike Cope	Chevrolet
35	Geoff Bodine	Ford
36	Jimmy Spencer	Chevrolet
37	Brett Bodine	Buick
38	Bobby Labonte	Oldsmobile
39	Rick Wilson	Buick
40	Stanley Smith	Buick

BUD 500

Time of Race: 3 hours, 14 minutes, 56 seconds
Average Speed: 82.028 mph
Margin of Victory: 9 seconds

FINISH	DRIVER	CAR
1	Alan Kulwicki	Ford
2	Sterling Marlin	Ford

Hut Stricklin, who drives the No. 8 Circuit City Chevrolet

FINISH	DRIVER	CAR
1	Harry Gant	Oldsmobile
2	Ernie Irvan	Chevrolet
3	Ken Schrader	Chevrolet
4	Derrike Cope	Chevrolet
5	Terry Labonte	Oldsmobile
6	Sterling Marlin	Ford
7	Geoff Bodine	Ford
8	Dale Earnhardt	Chevrolet
9	Joe Ruttman	Chevrolet
10	Bobby Hamilton	Oldsmobile
11	Rick Mast	Oldsmobile
12	Davey Allison	Ford
13	Rick Wilson	Buick
14	Brett Bodine	Buick
15	Ricky Rudd	Chevrolet
16	Richard Petty	Pontiac
17	Hut Stricklin	Buick
18	Bill Elliott	Ford
19	Morgan Shepherd	Ford
20	Ted Musgrave	Pontiac
21	Greg Sacks	Oldsmobile
22	Kyle Petty	Pontiac
23	Dick Trickle	Pontiac
24	Darrell Waltrip	Chevrolet
25	Dale Jarrett	Ford
26	Randy Baker	Chevrolet
27	Michael Waltrip	Pontiac
28	Jimmy Means	Pontiac
29	Mark Martin	Ford
30	Larry Pearson	Chevrolet
31	Jimmy Spencer	Chevrolet
32	Rusty Wallace	Pontiac
33	Dave Marcis	Chevrolet
34	Lake Speed	Pontiac
35	Alan Kulwicki	Ford
36	Chad Little	Ford
37	Mark Stahl	Ford
38	James Hylton	Buick

MILLER GENUINE DRAFT 400

Time of Race: 2 hours, 57 minutes, 35 seconds
Average Speed: 101.361 mph
Margin of Victory: 4 car lengths

FINISH	DRIVER	CAR
1	Harry Gant	Oldsmobile
2	Davey Allison	Ford
3	Rusty Wallace	Pontiac
4	Ernie Irvan	Chevrolet
5	Ricky Rudd	Chevrolet
6	Alan Kulwicki	Ford
7	Darrell Waltrip	Chevrolet
8	Ken Schrader	Chevrolet
9	Bill Elliott	Ford
10	Sterling Marlin	Ford
11	Dale Earnhardt	Chevrolet
12	Bobby Hamilton	Oldsmobile
13	Rick Wilson	Buick
14	Geoff Bodine	Ford
15	Jimmy Spencer	Chevrolet
16	Derrike Cope	Chevrolet
17	Lake Speed	Pontiac
18	Brett Bodine	Buick
19	Terry Labonte	Oldsmobile
20	Dale Jarrett	Ford
21	Hut Stricklin	Buick
22	Ted Musgrave	Pontiac
23	Morgan Shepherd	Ford
24	Richard Petty	Pontiac
25	Wally Dallenbach	Ford
26	Kyle Petty	Pontiac
27	Rick Mast	Oldsmobile
28	Joe Ruttman	Oldsmobile
29	Dave Marcis	Chevrolet
30	Michael Waltrip	Pontiac
31	Kenny Wallace	Pontiac
32	Greg Sacks	Oldsmobile

3	Ken Schrader	Chevrolet
4	Mark Martin	Ford
5	Ricky Rudd	Chevrolet
6	Morgan Shepherd	Ford
7	Dale Earnhardt	Chevrolet
8	Darrell Waltrip	Chevrolet
9	Terry Labonte	Oldsmobile
10	Brett Bodine	Buick
11	Lake Speed	Pontiac
12	Richard Petty	Pontiac
13	Bobby Hamilton	Oldsmobile
14	Chad Little	Ford
15	Jimmy Spencer	Chevrolet
16	Ted Musgrave	Pontiac
17	Joe Ruttman	Oldsmobile
18	Ernie Irvan	Chevrolet
19	Harry Gant	Oldsmobile
20	Rick Wilson	Buick
21	Bill Elliott	Ford
22	Hut Stricklin	Buick
23	Dave Marcis	Chevrolet
24	Davey Allison	Ford
25	Michael Waltrip	Pontiac
26	Rick Mast	Oldsmobile
27	Dick Trickle	Pontiac
28	Dale Jarrett	Ford
29	Derrike Cope	Chevrolet
30	Bobby Hillin	Pontiac
31	Geoff Bodine	Ford
32	Rusty Wallace	Pontiac

HEINZ SOUTHERN 500

Time of Race: 3 hours, 45 minutes, 18 seconds
Average Speed: 133.508 mph
Margin of Victory: 10.97 seconds

33	Mark Martin	Ford
34	Chad Little	Ford
35	Jimmy Means	Pontiac
36	Larry Pearson	Chevrolet

PEAK ANTIFREEZE 500

Time of Race: 4 hours, 32 minutes, 17 seconds
Average Speed: 110.179 mph
Margin of Victory: 1 lap and 2.75 seconds

FINISH	DRIVER	CAR
1	Harry Gant	Oldsmobile
2	Geoff Bodine	Ford
3	Morgan Shepherd	Ford
4	Hut Stricklin	Buick
5	Michael Waltrip	Pontiac
6	Dick Trickle	Pontiac
7	Ricky Rudd	Chevrolet
8	Bobby Hamilton	Oldsmobile
9	Rick Mast	Oldsmboile
10	Dave Marcis	Chevrolet
11	Bill Elliott	Ford
12	Kyle Petty	Pontiac
13	Joe Ruttman	Oldsmobile
14	Ted Musgrave	Pontiac
15	Dale Earnhardt	Chevrolet
16	Chad Little	Ford
17	Sterling Marlin	Ford
18	Jimmy Spencer	Chevrolet
19	Darrell Waltrip	Chevrolet
20	Richard Petty	Pontiac
21	Mark Martin	Ford
22	Stanley Smith	Buick
23	Jimmy Means	Pontiac
24	Alan Kulwicki	Ford
25	Rusty Wallace	Pontiac
26	Terry Labonte	Oldsmobile
27	Steve Perry	Ford
28	Ernie Irvan	Chevrolet
29	Rick Wilson	Buick
30	Larry Pearson	Chevrolet
31	Davey Allison	Ford
32	Brett Bodine	Buick
33	Ken Schrader	Chevrolet
34	Dale Jarrett	Ford
35	Lake Speed	Pontiac
36	Derrike Cope	Chevrolet
37	James Hylton	Buick
38	Jerry Hill	Pontiac
39	Brian Ross	Chevrolet
40	Andy Belmont	Ford

GOODY'S 500

Time of Race: 3 hours, 31 minutes, 42 seconds
Average Speed: 74.535 mph
Margin of Victory: 1 second

FINISH	DRIVER	CAR
1	Harry Gant	Oldsmobile
2	Brett Bodine	Buick
3	Dale Earnhardt	Chevrolet
4	Ernie Irvan	Chevrolet
5	Mark Martin	Ford
6	Terry Labonte	Oldsmobile
7	Rusty Wallace	Pontiac
8	Ricky Rudd	Chevrolet
9	Ken Schrader	Chevrolet
10	Jimmy Hensley	Pontiac
11	Morgan Shepherd	Ford
12	Kyle Petty	Pontiac
13	Rick Mast	Oldsmobile
14	Sterling Marlin	Ford
15	Darrell Waltrip	Chevrolet

16	Hut Stricklin	Buick
17	Bobby Hamilton	Oldsmobile
18	Dale Jarrett	Ford
19	Derrike Cope	Chevrolet
20	Ted Musgrave	Pontiac
21	Dave Marcis	Chevrolet
22	Alan Kulwicki	Ford
23	Geoff Bodine	Ford
24	Chad Little	Ford
25	Michael Waltrip	Pontiac
26	Rick Wilson	Buick
27	Bill Elliott	Ford
28	Jimmy Spencer	Chevrolet
29	Davey Allison	Ford
30	Richard Petty	Pontiac
31	Joe Ruttman	Oldsmobile
32	Lake Speed	Pontiac

TYSON HOLLY FARMS 400

Time of Race: 2 hours, 39 minutes, 23 seconds
Average Speed: 94.113 mph
Margin of Victory: 1.47 seconds

FINISH	DRIVER	CAR
1	Dale Earnhardt	Chevrolet
2	Harry Gant	Oldsmobile
3	Morgan Shepherd	Ford
4	Davey Allison	Ford
5	Mark Martin	Ford
6	Rusty Wallace	Pontiac
7	Brett Bodine	Buick
8	Ken Schrader	Chevrolet
9	Dale Jarrett	Ford
10	Alan Kulwicki	Ford
11	Jimmy Hensley	Pontiac
12	Ricky Rudd	Chevrolet
13	Sterling Marlin	Ford
14	Terry Labonte	Oldsmobile
15	Geoff Bodine	Ford
16	Kyle Petty	Pontiac
17	Hut Stricklin	Buick
18	Bobby Hamilton	Oldsmobile
19	Richard Petty	Pontiac
20	Darrell Waltrip	Chevrolet
21	Chad Little	Ford
22	Ted Musgrave	Pontiac
23	Jimmy Spencer	Chevrolet
24	Bill Elliott	Ford
25	Rick Mast	Oldsmobile
26	Chuck Bown	Pontiac
27	Michael Waltrip	Pontiac
28	Jimmy Means	Oldsmobile
29	Joe Ruttman	Chevrolet
30	Derrike Cope	Chevrolet
31	Dave Marcis	Chevrolet
32	Rick Wilson	Buick
33	Ernie Irvan	Chevrolet

MELLO YELLO 500

Time of Race: 3 hours, 36 minutes, 17 seconds
Average Speed: 138.984 mph
Margin of Victory: 11.28 seconds

FINISH	DRIVER	CAR
1	Geoff Bodine	Ford
2	Davey Allison	Ford
3	Alan Kulwicki	Ford
4	Harry Gant	Oldsmobile
5	Sterling Marlin	Ford
6	Terry Labonte	Oldsmobile
7	Michael Waltrip	Pontiac
8	Brett Bodine	Buick

9	Darrell Waltrip	Chevrolet
10	Chad Little	Ford
11	Bill Elliott	Ford
12	Richard Petty	Pontiac
13	Rick Mast	Oldsmobile
14	Ted Musgrave	Pontiac
15	Kyle Petty	Pontiac
16	Joe Ruttman	Oldsmobile
17	Rick Wilson	Buick
18	Bobby Hillin	Chevrolet
19	Wally Dallenbach	Ford
20	Jimmy Hensley	Pontiac
21	Brad Teague	Chevrolet
22	Stanley Smith	Chevrolet
23	Jimmy Spencer	Chevrolet
24	Jimmy Means	Pontiac
25	Dale Earnhardt	Chevrolet
26	Dale Jarrett	Ford
27	Rusty Wallace	Pontiac
28	Morgan Shepherd	Ford
29	Bobby Hamilton	Oldsmobile
30	Ernie Irvan	Chevrolet
31	Greg Sacks	Oldsmobile
32	Ricky Rudd	Chevrolet
33	Derrike Cope	Chevrolet
34	Dave Marcis	Chevrolet
35	Mark Martin	Ford
36	Hut Stricklin	Buick
37	Kerry Teague	Chevrolet
38	Ken Schrader	Chevrolet
39	Gary Balough	Pontiac
40	Mike Skinner	Chevrolet
41	Dorsey Schroeder	Pontiac

AC DELCO 500

Time of Race: 3 hours, 55 minutes, 51 seconds
Average Speed: 127.292 mph - Track Record
Margin of Victory: .91 second

FINISH	DRIVER	CAR
1	Davey Allison	Ford
2	Harry Gant	Oldsmobile
3	Mark Martin	Ford
4	Geoff Bodine	Ford
5	Ken Schrader	Chevrolet
6	Bobby Hamilton	Oldsmobile
7	Dale Earnhardt	Chevrolet
8	Sterling Marlin	Ford
9	Kyle Petty	Pontiac
10	Bill Elliott	Ford
11	Rusty Wallace	Pontiac
12	Ricky Rudd	Chevrolet
13	Hut Stricklin	Buick
14	Jimmy Hensley	Pontiac
15	Derrike Cope	Chevrolet
16	Richard Petty	Pontiac
17	Morgan Shepherd	Ford
18	Rick Mast	Oldsmobile
19	Michael Waltrip	Pontiac
20	Rick Wilson	Buick
21	Ted Musgrave	Pontiac
22	Jimmy Spencer	Chevrolet
23	Chad Little	Ford
24	Randy LaJoie	Pontiac
25	Dale Jarrett	Ford
26	Dave Marcis	Chevrolet
27	Joe Ruttman	Chevrolet
28	Terry Labonte	Oldsmobile
29	Greg Sacks	Oldsmobile
30	Brett Bodine	Buick
31	Ernie Irvan	Chevrolet
32	Darrell Waltrip	Chevrolet
33	Alan Kulwicki	Ford
34	Ricky Craven	Oldsmobile
35	Jimmy Means	Pontiac
36	Mark Stahl	Ford
37	Keith VanHouten	Pontiac
38	Jerry Hill	Pontiac
39	Gary Brooks	Oldsmobile
40	James Hylton	Buick

PYROIL 500

Time of Race: 3 hours, 15 minutes, 31 seconds
Average Speed: 95.746 mph
Margin of Victory: 11.44 seconds

FINISH	DRIVER	CAR
1	Davey Allison	Ford
2	Darrell Waltrip	Chevrolet
3	Sterling Marlin	Ford
4	Alan Kulwicki	Ford
5	Rusty Wallace	Pontiac
6	Ernie Irvan	Chevrolet
7	Jimmy Spencer	Chevrolet
8	Geoff Bodine	Ford
9	Dale Earnhardt	Chevrolet
10	Morgan Shepherd	Ford
11	Ricky Rudd	Chevrolet
12	Terry Labonte	Oldsmobile
13	Bobby Hamilton	Oldsmobile
14	Brett Bodine	Buick
15	Rick Wilson	Buick
16	Derrike Cope	Chevrolet
17	Ken Schrader	Chevrolet
18	Ted Musgrave	Pontiac
19	Mark Martin	Ford
20	Kyle Petty	Pontiac
21	Bill Sedgwick	Chevrolet
22	Joe Ruttman	Oldsmobile
23	Harry Gant	Oldsmobile
24	Michael Waltrip	Pontiac
25	Bill Elliott	Ford
26	Mike Chase	Chevrolet
27	Hershel McGriff	Pontiac
28	Rick Mast	Oldsmobile
29	Butch Gilliland	Pontiac
30	Chad Little	Ford
31	Mike Wallace	Pontiac
32	Randy LaJoie	Pontiac
33	Larry Pearson	Chevrolet
34	Mark Reed	Chevrolet
35	Dale Jarrett	Ford
36	Stanley Smith	Buick
37	Bill Schmitt	Ford
38	Jeff Purvis	Chevrolet
39	Hut Stricklin	Buick
40	Dave Marcis	Chevrolet
41	Richard Petty	Pontiac
42	Gary Collins	Oldsmobile
43	Kenny Wallace	Pontiac

HARDEES 500

Time of Race: 3 hours, 37 minutes, 6 seconds
Average Speed: 137.968 mph
Margin of Victory: 10.44 seconds

FINISH	DRIVER	CAR
1	Mark Martin	Ford
2	Ernie Irvan	Chevrolet
3	Bill Elliott	Ford
4	Harry Gant	Oldsmobile
5	Dale Earnhardt	Chevrolet
6	Morgan Shepherd	Ford
7	Sterling Marlin	Ford
8	Geoff Bodine	Ford
9	Alan Kulwicki	Ford
10	Darrell Waltrip	Chevrolet
11	Ricky Rudd	Chevrolet
12	Dave Marcis	Chevrolet
13	Hut Stricklin	Buick
14	Larry Pearson	Chevrolet
15	Terry Labonte	Oldsmobile
16	Dale Jarrett	Ford
17	Davey Allison	Ford
18	Bobby Hamilton	Oldsmobile
19	Kyle Petty	Pontiac

20	Joe Ruttman	Chevrolet
21	Chad Little	Ford
22	Richard Petty	Pontiac
23	Kenny Wallace	Pontiac
24	Derrike Cope	Chevrolet
25	Stanley Smith	Buick
26	Greg Sacks	Oldsmobile
27	Eddie Bierschwale	Chevrolet
28	Rick Mast	Oldsmobile
29	Brett Bodine	Buick
30	Ted Musgrave	Pontiac
31	Randy LaJoie	Pontiac
32	Bobby Hillin	Chevrolet
33	Rick Wilson	Buick
34	Rusty Wallace	Pontiac
35	Jim Sauter	Pontiac
36	Wally Dallenbach	Ford
37	Ken Schrader	Chevrolet
38	Jimmy Spencer	Chevrolet
39	Mike Wallace	Oldsmobile
40	Michael Waltrip	Pontiac

1992

DAYTONA 500

Time of Race: 3 hours, 7 minutes, 12 seconds
Average Speed: 160.256 mph
Margin of Victory: 2 Car Lengths

FINISH	DRIVER	CAR
1	Davey Allison	Ford
2	Morgan Shepherd	Ford
3	Geoff Bodine	Ford
4	Alan Kulwicki	Ford
5	Dick Trickle	Oldsmobile
6	Kyle Petty	Pontiac
7	Terry Labonte	Chevrolet
8	Ted Musgrave	Chevrolet
9	Dale Earnhardt	Chevrolet
10.	Phil Parsons	Ford
11	Buddy Baker	Oldsmobile
12	Harry Gant	Oldsmobile
13	Rick Mast	Oldsmobile
14	Greg Sacks	Chevrolet
15	Wally Dallenbach	Ford
16	Richard Petty	Pontiac
17	Phil Barkdoll	Oldsmobile
18	Michael Waltrip	Pontiac
19	Dorsey Schroeder	Ford
20	Dave Marcis	Chevrolet
21	A.J. Foyt	Oldsmobile
22	Stanley Smith	Chevrolet
23	Rick Wilson	Ford
24	Hut Stricklin	Chevrolet
25	Delma Cowart	Ford
26	Darrell Waltrip	Chevrolet
27	Bill Elliott	Ford
28	Ernie Irvan	Chevrolet
29	Mark Martin	Ford
30	Mike Potter	Chevrolet
31	Rusty Wallace	Pontiac
32	Bobby Hamilton	Oldsmobile
33	Kerry Teague	Oldsmobile
34	Derrike Cope	Chevrolet
35	Sterling Marlin	Ford
36	Dale Jarrett	Chevrolet
37	Ken Schrader	Chevrolet
38	Bobby Hillin	Chevrolet
39	Chad Little	Ford
40	Ricky Rudd	Chevrolet
41	Brett Bodine	Ford
42	Bob Schacht	Oldsmobile

GOODWRENCH 500

Time of Race: 3 hours, 58 minutes, 2 seconds
Average Speed: 126.125 mph
Margin of Victory: 14 seconds

FINISH	DRIVER	CAR
1	Bill Elliott	Ford
2	Davey Allison	Ford
3	Harry Gant	Oldsmobile
4	Michael Waltrip	Pontiac
5	Ken Schrader	Chevrolet
6	Mark Martin	Ford
7	Terry Labonte	Oldsmobile
8	Brett Bodine	Ford
9	Hut Stricklin	Chevrolet
10	Darrell Waltrip	Chevrolet
11	Ernie Irvan	Chevrolet
12	Rick Mast	Oldsmobile
13	Morgan Shepherd	Ford
14	Geoff Bodine	Ford
15	Sterling Marlin	Ford
16	Richard Petty	Pontiac
17	Ted Musgrave	Oldsmobile
18	Bobby Hamilton	Oldsmobile
19	Derrike Cope	Chevrolet
20	Jimmy Spencer	Gold Chevrolet
21	Wally Dallenbach	Ford
22	Chad Little	Ford
23	Mike Skinner	Chevrolet
24	Dale Earnhardt	Chevrolet
25	Randy Baker	Chevrolet
26	Rusty Wallace	Pontiac
27	Jerry Hill	Pontiac
28	Ricky Rudd	Chevrolet
29	Kyle Petty	Pontiac
30	Phil Parsons	Ford
31	Alan Kulwicki	Ford
32	Stanley Smith	Chevrolet
33	Jimmy Means	Pontiac
34	Greg Sacks	Chevrolet
35	Delma Cowart	Ford
36	Dick Trickle	Ford
37	Dale Jarrett	Chevrolet
38	Andy Belmont	Ford
39	Dave Marcis	Chevrolet
40	Johnny McFadden	Chevrolet

PONTIAC EXCITEMENT 400

Time of Race: 2 hours, 52 minutes, 27 seconds
Average Speed: 104.378 mph
Margin of Victory: 18 inches

FINISH	DRIVER	CAR
1	Bill Elliott	Ford
2	Alan Kulwicki	Ford
3	Harry Gant	Oldsmobile
4	Davey Allison	Ford
5	Darrell Waltrip	Chevrolet
6	Ricky Rudd	Chevrolet
7	Sterling Marlin	Ford
8	Terry Labonte	Chevrolet
9	Hut Stricklin	Chevrolet
10	Morgan Shepherd	Ford
11	Dale Earnhardt	Chevrolet
12	Jimmy Spencer	Chevrolet
13	Dale Jarrett	Chevrolet
14	Ken Schrader	Chevrolet
15	Ernie Irvan	Chevrolet
16	Geoff Bodine	Ford
17	Rusty Wallace	Pontiac
18	Rick Mast	Oldsmobile
19	Derrike Cope	Chevrolet
20	Kyle Petty	Pontiac
21	Richard Petty	Pontiac
22	Dick Trickle	Ford

23	Chad Little	Ford
24	Wally Dallenbach	Ford
25	Ted Musgrave	Oldsmobile
26	Charlie Glotzbach	Ford
27	Stanley Smith	Chevrolet
28	Dave Marcis	Chevrolet
29	Jeff Fuller	Pontiac
30	Mark Martin	Ford
31	Bobby Hamilton	Oldsmobile
32	Greg Sacks	Chevrolet
33	Brett Bodine	Ford
34	Michael Waltrip	Pontiac
35	Jimmy Means	Pontiac

MOTORCRAFT QUALITY PARTS 500

Time of Race: 3 hours, 22 minutes, 44 seconds
Average Speed: 147,746 mph
Margin of Victory: 18.25 seconds

FINISH	DRIVER	CAR
1	Bill Elliott	Ford
2	Harry Gant	Oldsmobile
3	Dale Earnhardt	Chevrolet
4	Davey Allison	Ford
5	Dick Trickle	Ford
6	Geoff Bodine	Ford
7	Alan Kulwicki	Ford
8	Kyle Petty	Pontiac
9	Terry Labonte	Oldsmobile
10	Morgan Shepherd	Ford
11	Dale Jarrett	Chevrolet
12	Ricky Rudd	Chevrolet
13	Mark Martin	Ford
14	Derrike Cope	Chevrolet
15	Rusty Wallace	Pontiac
16	Richard Petty	Pontiac
17	Sterling Marlin	Ford
18	Charlie Glotzbach	Ford
19	Ted Musgrave	Chevrolet
20	Brett Bodine	Ford
21	Bobby Hillin	Chevrolet
22	Rick Mast	Oldsmobile
23	Chad Little	Ford
24	Bobby Hamilton	Oldsmobile
25	Ernie Irvan	Chevrolet
26	Jimmy Horton	Chevrolet
27	Wally Dallenbach	Ford
28	Michael Waltrip	Pontiac
29	Hut Stricklin	Chevrolet
30	Dave Marcis	Chevrolet
31	Greg Sacks	Chevrolet
32	Stanley Smith	Chevrolet
33	Mike Wallace	Oldsmobile
34	Lake Speed	Chevrolet
35	Dorsey Schroeder	Ford
36	Buddy Baker	Oldsmobile
37	Jimmy Spencer	Chevrolet
38	Jimmy Means	Pontiac
39	Darrell Waltrip	Chevrolet
40	Eddie Bierschwale	Oldsmobile
41	Ken Schrader	Chevrolet
42	Bob Schacht	Chevrolet

TRANSOUTH 500

Time of Race: 3 hours, 35 minutes, 50 seconds
Average Speed: 139.364 mph - Track Record
Margin of Victory: 8.8 seconds

FINISH	DRIVER	CAR
1	Bill Elliott	Ford
2	Harry Gant	Oldsmobile

3	Mark Martin	Ford
4	Davey Allison	Ford
5	Ricky Rudd	Chevrolet
6	Brett Bodine	Ford
7	Dick Trickle	Ford
8	Geoff Bodine	Ford
9	Terry Labonte	Oldsmobile
10	Dale Earnhardt	Chevrolet
11	Rusty Wallace	Pontiac
12	Ken Schrader	Chevrolet
13	Morgan Shepherd	Ford
14	Michael Waltrip	Pontiac
15	Ted Musgrave	Pontiac
16	Derrike Cope	Chevrolet
17	Rick Mast	Oldsmobile
18	Alan Kulwicki	Ford
19	Bob Schacht	Oldsmobile
20	Jimmy Means	Pontiac
21	Dale Jarrett	Chevrolet
22	Sterling Marlin	Ford
23	Bobby Hamilton	Oldsmobile
24	Darrell Waltrip	Chevrolet
25	Dave Marcis	Chevrolet
26	Ernie Irvan	Chevrolet
27	Kyle Petty	Pontiac
28	Greg Sacks	Chevrolet
29	Hut Stricklin	Chevrolet
30	Wally Dallenbach	Ford
31	Mike Potter	Chevrolet
32	Richard Petty	Pontiac
33	Chad Little	Ford
34	Dave Mader	Ford
35	Jerry Hill	Pontiac
36	Jimmy Spencer	Chevrolet
37	Johnny McFadden	Pontiac
38	Kerry Teague	Ford
39	James Hylton	Pontiac

FOOD CITY 500

Time of Race: 3 hours, 5 minutes, 15 seconds
Average Speed: 86.316 mph
Margin of Victory: .72 second

FINISH	DRIVER	CAR
1	Alan Kulwicki	Ford
2	Dale Jarrett	Chevrolet
3	Ken Schrader	Chevrolet
4	Terry Labonte	Oldsmobile
5	Dick Trickle	Ford
6	Ricky Rudd	Chevrolet
7	Morgan Shepherd	Ford
8	Hut Stricklin	Chevrolet
9	Rusty Wallace	Pontiac
10	Derrike Cope	Chevrolet
11	Brett Bodine	Ford
12	Geoff Bodine	Ford
13	Greg Sacks	Chevrolet
14	Ted Musgrave	Oldsmobile
15	Mark Martin	Ford
16	Dave Mader	Ford
17	Michael Waltrip	Pontiac
18	Dale Earnhardt	Chevrolet
19	Kyle Petty	Pontiac
20	Bill Elliott	Ford
21	Brad Teague	Pontiac
22	Wally Dallenbach	Ford
23	Chad Little	Ford
24	Ernie Irvan	Chevrolet
25	Darrell Waltrip	Chevrolet
26	Bobby Hamilton	Oldsmobile
27	Richard Petty	Pontiac
28	Davey Allison	Ford
29	Harry Gant	Oldsmobile
30	Rick Mast	Oldsmobile
31	Dave Marcis	Chevrolet
32	Sterling Marlin	Ford

FIRST UNION 400

Time of Race: 2 hours, 45 minutes, 28 seconds
Average Speed: 90.653 mph.
Margin of Victory: .15 second

FINISH	DRIVER	CAR
1	Davey Allison	Ford
2	Rusty Wallace	Pontiac
3	Ricky Rudd	Chevrolet
4	Geoff Bodine	Ford
5	Harry Gant	Oldsmobile
6	Dale Earnhardt	Chevrolet
7	Alan Kulwicki	Ford
8	Sterling Marlin	Ford
9	Terry Labonte	Oldsmobile
10	Brett Bodine	Ford
11	Dick Trickle	Ford
12	Morgan Shepherd	Ford
13	Ernie Irvan	Chevrolet
14	Derrike Cope	Chevrolet
15	Darrell Waltrip	Chevrolet
16	Mark Martin	Ford
17	Dale Jarrett	Chevrolet
18	Hut Stricklin	Chevrolet
19	Ted Musgrave	Oldsmobile
20	Bill Elliott	Ford
21	Greg Sacks	Chevrolet
22	Ken Schrader	Chevrolet
23	Rick Mast	Oldsmobile
24	Dave Marcis	Chevrolet
25	Bobby Hillin	Ford
26	Jimmy Spencer	Chevrolet
27	Bobby Hamilton	Oldsmobile
28	Kyle Petty	Pontiac
29	Michael Waltrip	Pontiac
30	Wally Dallenbach	Ford
31	Richard Petty	Pontiac
32	Jimmy Means	Pontiac

HANES 500

Time of Race: 3 hours, 22 minutes, 5 seconds
Average Speed: 78.086 mph
Margin of Victory: 12.125 seconds

FINISH	DRIVER	CAR
1	Mark Martin	Ford
2	Sterling Marlin	Ford
3	Darrell Waltrip	Chevrolet
4	Terry Labonte	Oldsmobile
5	Harry Gant	Oldsmobile
6	Morgan Shepherd	Ford
7	Ken Schrader	Chevrolet
8	Brett Bodine	Ford
9	Dale Earnhardt	Chevrolet
10	Bill Elliott	Ford
11	Hut Stricklin	Chevrolet
12	Greg Sacks	Chevrolet
13	Bobby Hamilton	Oldsmobile
14	Rick Mast	Oldsmobile
15	Jimmy Hensley	Ford
16	Alan Kulwicki	Ford
17	Dick Trickle	Ford
18	Kyle Petty	Pontiac
19	Wally Dallenbach	Ford
20	Ted Musgrave	Oldsmobile
21	Dave Mader	Ford
22	Derrike Cope	Chevrolet
23	Ricky Rudd	Chevrolet
24	Dave Marcis	Chevrolet
25	Ernie Irvan	Chevrolet
26	Davey Allison	Ford
27	Michael Waltrip	Pontiac
28	Dale Jarrett	Chevrolet
29	Richard Petty	Pontiac
30	Jimmy Means	Pontiac
31	Rusty Wallace	Pontiac
32	Geoff Bodine	Ford

WINSTON 500

Time of Race: 2 hours, 59 minutes, 1 second
Average Speed: 167.609 mph
Margin of Victory: 2 car lengths

FINISH	DRIVER	CAR
1	Davey Allison	Ford
2	Bill Elliott	Ford
3	Dale Earnhardt	Chevrolet
4	Sterling Marlin	Ford
5	Ernie Irvan	Chevrolet
6	Alan Kulwicki	Ford
7	Dale Jarrett	Chevrolet
8	Mark Martin	Ford
9	Morgan Shepherd	Ford
10	Kyle Petty	Pontiac
11	Rusty Wallace	Pontiac
12	Derrike Cope	Chevrolet
13	Geoff Bodine	Ford
14	Wally Dallenbach	Ford
15	Richard Petty	Pontiac
16	Brett Bodine	Ford
17	Rick Mast	Oldsmobile
18	Dave Mader	Ford
19	Dick Trickle	Ford
20	Bobby Hamilton	Oldsmobile
21	Ted Musgrave	Chevrolet
22	Hut Stricklin	Chevrolet
23	Ken Schrader	Chevrolet
24	Harry Gant	Oldsmobile
25	Jimmy Hensley	Ford
26	Ricky Rudd	Chevrolet
27	Dave Marcis	Chevrolet
28	Bobby Hallin, Jr.	Chevrolet
29	Darrell Waltrip	Chevrolet
30	Bob Schacht	Oldsmobile
31	Buddy Baker	Chevrolet
32	Jimmy Spencer	Chevrolet
33	Stanley Smith	Chevrolet
34	Jimmy Means	Pontiac
35	Greg Sacks	Chevrolet
36	Terry Labonte	Ford
37	Charlie Glotzbach	Ford
38	Michael Waltrip	Pontiac
39	Clay Young	Pontiac
40	Johnny McFadden	Pontiac

COCA COLA 600

Time of Race: 4 hours, 30 minutes, 43 seconds
Average Speed: 132.980 mph
Margin of Victory: .41 seconds

FINISH	DRIVER	CAR
1	Dale Earnhardt	Chevrolet
2	Ernie Irvan	Chevrolet
3	Kyle Petty	Pontiac
4	Davey Allison	Ford
5	Harry Gant	Oldsmobile
6	Terry Labonte	Oldsmobile
7	Alan Kulwicki	Ford
8	Ted Musgrave	Ford
9	Ricky Rudd	Chevrolet
10	Dick Trickle	Ford
11	Jimmy Hensley	Ford
12	Dale Jarrett	Chevrolet
13	Bobby Hillin	Chevrolet
14	Bill Elliott	Ford
15	Dave Marcis	Chevrolet
16	Greg Sacks	Chevrolet
17	Derrike Cope	Chevrolet
18	Rusty Wallace	Pontiac
19	Lake Speed	Ford
20	Brett Bodine	Ford
21	Bobby Hamilton	Oldsmobile
22	Sterling Marlin	Ford
23	Rick Mast	Oldsmobile
24	Randy Porter	Pontiac

FINISH	DRIVER	CAR
25	Michael Waltrip	Pontiac
26	Ken Schrader	Chevrolet
27	Jimmy Spencer	Chevrolet
28	Wally Dallenbach	Ford
29	Morgan Shepherd	Ford
30	Stanley Smith	Chevrolet
31	Bob Schacht	Chevrolet
32	Geoff Bodine	Ford
33	Mark Martin	Ford
34	Hut Stricklin	Chevrolet
35	Joe Ruttman	Oldsmobile
36	Charlie Glotzbach	Ford
37	Jim Sauter	Pontiac
38	Darrell Waltrip	Chevrolet
39	Dave Mader	Ford
40	Gary Balough	Chevrolet
41	Richard Petty	Pontiac
42	Jimmy Means	Pontiac

BUDWEISER 500

Time of Race: 4 hours, 34 minutes, 5 seconds
Average Speed: 109.456 mph
Margin of Victory: 26 seconds

FINISH	DRIVER	CAR
1	Harry Gant	Oldsmobile
2	Dale Earnhardt	Chevrolet
3	Rusty Wallace	Pontiac
4	Ernie Irvan	Chevrolet
5	Darrell Waltrip	Chevrolet
6	Ricky Rudd	Chevrolet
7	Hut Stricklin	Chevrolet
8	Jimmy Hensley	Ford
9	Dick Trickle	Ford
10	Morgan Shepherd	Ford
11	Davey Allison	Ford
12	Alan Kulwicki	Ford
13	Bill Elliott	Ford
14	Sterling Marlin	Ford
15	Michael Waltrip	Pontiac
16	Ted Musgrave	Ford
17	Geoff Bodine	Ford
18	Bobby Hamilton	Oldsmobile
19	Greg Sacks	Chevrolet
20	Richard Petty	Pontiac
21	Terry Labonte	Oldsmobile
22	Jimmy Horton	Chevrolet
23	Ken Schrader	Chevrolet
24	Mark Martin	Ford
25	David Marcis	Chevrolet
26	Chad Little	Ford
27	Dale Jarrett	Chevrolet
28	Mike Potter	Chevrolet
29	Kyle Petty	Pontiac
30	Brett Bodine	Ford
31	Jimmy Means	Pontiac
32	Rick Mast	Oldsmobile
33	Derrrike Cope	Chevrolet
34	Wally Dallenbach	For
35	James Hylton	Pontiac
36	Jerry O'Neil	Oldsmobile
37	Andy Belmont	Ford
38	Jerry Hill	Pontiac
39	D.K. Ulrich	Oldsmobile
40	Graham Taylor	Pontiac

SAVE MART 300

Time of Race: 2 hours, 17 minutes, 26 seconds
Average Speed: 81.4126 mph
Margin of Victory: 3.60 seconds

FINISH	DRIVER	CAR
1	Ernie Irvan	Chevrolet
2	Terry Labonte	Oldsmobile

FINISH	DRIVER	CAR
3	Mark Martin	Ford
4	Ricky Rudd	Chevrolet
5	Bill Elliott	Ford
6	Dale Earnhardt	Chevrolet
7	Rusty Wallace	Pontiac
8	Darrell Waltrip	Chevrolet
9	Ken Schrader	Chevrolet
10	Geoff Bodine	Ford
11	Rick Mast	Oldsmobile
12	Kyle Petty	Pontiac
13	Tommy Kendall	Pontiac
14	Alan Kulwicki	Ford
15	Brett Bodine	Ford
16	Sterling Marlin	Ford
17	Harry Gant	Oldsmobile
18	Derrike Cope	Chevrolet
19	Bill Sedgwick	Chevrolet
20	Michael Waltrip	Pontiac
21	Richard Petty	Pontiac
22	Ted Musgrave	Oldsmobile
23	Dave Marcis	Chevrolet
24	Bill Schmitt	Ford
25	Wally Dallenbach	Ford
26	Dick Trickle	Ford
27	Hut Stricklin	Chevrolet
28	Davey Allison	Ford
29	Morgan Shepherd	Ford
30	Jimmy Hensley	Ford
31	John Krebs	Pontiac
32	Ron Hornaday	Chevrolet
33	R.K. Smith	Pontiac
34	Bobby Hamilton	Oldsmobile
35	Mike Chase	Pontiac
36	Rick Scribner	Chevrolet
37	Rick Carelli	Chevrolet
38	Butch Gilliland	Pontiac
39	Dale Jarrett	Chevrolet
40	Jack Sellers	Buick
41	Irv Hoerr	Oldsmobile
42	Hershel McGriff	Chevrolet
43	Greg Sacks	Chevrolet

CHAMPION SPARK PLUG 500

Time of Race: 3 hours, 3 minutes, 18 seconds
Average Speed: 144.023 mph
Margin of Victory: 2.34 seconds

FINISH	DRIVER	CAR
1	Alan Kulwicki	Ford
2	Mark Martin	Ford
3	Bill Elliott	Ford
4	Ken Schrader	Chevrolet
5	Davey Allison	Ford
6	Kyle Petty	Pontiac
7	Sterling Marlin	Ford
8	Brett Bodine	Ford
9	Jimmy Hensley	Ford
10	Terry Labonte	Oldsmobile
11	Greg Sacks	Chevrolet
12	Derrike Cope	Chevrolet
13	Darrell Waltrip	Chevrolet
14	Geoff Bodine	Ford
15	Michael Waltrip	Pontiac
16	Richard Petty	Pontiac
17	Bobby Hamilton	Oldsmobile
18	Dave Marcis	Chevrolet
19	Ernie Irvan	Chevrolet
20	Mike Potter	Buick
21	Jerry O'Neil	Buick
22	Dale Jarrett	Chevrolet
23	Harry Gant	Oldsmobile
24	Rusty Wallace	Pontiac
25	Morgan Shepherd	Ford
26	James Hylton	Pontiac
27	Wally Dallenbach	Ford
28	Dale Earnhardt	Chevrolet
29	Dick Trickle	Ford
30	Rick Mast	Oldsmobile
31	Hut Stricklin	Chevrolet

FINISH	DRIVER	CAR
32	Bobby Gerhart	Chevrolet
33	Ted Musgrave	Ford
34	Jimmy Horton	Chevrolet
35	Jimmy Means	Pontiac
36	Ricky Rudd	Chevrolet
37	Chad Little	Ford
38	Jerry Hill	Pontiac
39	Mark Thompson	Ford
40	Andy Belmont	Ford

MILLER GENUINE DRAFT 400

Time of Race: 2 hours, 37 minutes, 12 seconds
Average Speed: 152.672 mph
Margin of Victory: 3.31 seconds

FINISH	DRIVER	CAR
1	Davey Allison	Ford
2	Darrell Waltrip	Chevrolet
3	Alan Kulwicki	Ford
4	Kyle Petty	Pontiac
5	Ricky Rudd	Chevrolet
6	Mark Martin	Ford
7	Harry Gant	Oldsmobile
8	Ted Musgrave	Ford
9	Dale Earnhardt	Chevrolet
10	Bill Elliott	Ford
11	Geoff Bodine	Ford
12	Morgan Shepherd	Ford
13	Ken Schrader	Chevrolet
14	Greg Sacks	Chevrolet
15	Richard Petty	Pontiac
16	Charlie Glotzbach	Ford
17	Bobby Hillin	Chevrolet
18	Wally Dallenbach	Ford
19	Brett Bodine	Ford
20	Dick Trickle	Ford
21	Chad Little	Ford
22	Derrike Cope	Chevrolet
23	Jimmy Means	Pontiac
24	Dale Jarrett	Chevrolet
25	James Hylton	Chevrolet
26	Jimmy Horton	Chevrolet
27	Michael Waltrip	Pontiac
28	Rick Mast	Oldsmobile
29	Jimmy Hensley	Ford
30	Ernie Irvan	Chevrolet
31	Bobby Hamilton	Oldsmobile
32	Sterling Marlin	Ford
33	Mike Potter	Chevrolet
34	Andy Belmont	Ford
35	Hut Stricklin	Chevrolet
36	Dave Marcis	Chevrolet
37	Rusty Wallace	Pontiac
38	Terry Labonte	Oldsmobile
39	Jim Sauter	Pontiac
40	Stanley Smith	Chevrolet
41	H.B. Bailey	Pontiac

PEPSI 400

Time of Race: 2 hours, 20 minutes, 47 seconds
Average Speed: 170.457 mph
Margin of Victory: 2 Car Lengths

FINISH	DRIVER	CAR
1	Ernie Irvan	Chevrolet
2	Sterling Marlin	Ford
3	Dale Jarrett	Chevrolet
4	Geoff Bodine	Ford
5	Bill Elliott	Ford
6	Ken Schrader	Chevrolet
7	Ricky Rudd	Chevrolet
8	Mark Martin	Ford
9	Rusty Wallace	Pontiac

FINISH	DRIVER	CAR
10	Davey Allison	Ford
11	Wally Dallenbach	Ford
12	Brett Bodine	Ford
13	Darrell Waltrip	Chevrolet
14	Kyle Petty	Pontaic
15	Jimmy Hensley	Ford
16	Ted Musgrave	Chevrolet
17	Rick Mast	Oldsmobile
18	Hut Stricklin	Chevrolet
19	Morgan Shepherd	Ford
20	Charlie Glotzbach	Ford
21	Terry Labonte	Ford
22	Stanley Smith	Chevrolet
23	Harry Gant	Oldsmobile
24	Chad Little	Ford
25	Bobby Hillin	Chevrolet
26	Greg Sacks	Chevrolet
27	Michael Waltrip	Pontiac
28	Phil Barkdoll	Oldsmobile
29	Brad Teague	Chevrolet
30	Alan Kulwicki	Ford
31	Andy Belmont	Ford
32	Dave Marcis	Chevrolet
33	Bobby Hamilton	Chevrolet
34	Derrike Cope	Chevrolet
35	Dick Trickle	Ford
36	Richard Petty	Pontiac
37	Bobby Gerhart	Chevrolet
38	Eddie Bierschwale	Oldsmobile
39	Jimmy Means	Pontiac
40	Dale Earnhardt	Chevrolet

MILLER GENUINE DRAFT 500

Time of Race: 3 hours, 43 minutes, 47 seconds
Average Speed: 134.058 mph
Margin of Victory: 1.31 seconds

FINISH	DRIVER	CAR
1	Darrell Waltrip	Chevrolet
2	Harry Gant	Oldsmobile
3	Alan Kulwicki	Ford
4	Ricky Rudd	Chevrolet
5	Ted Musgrave	Ford
6	Mark Martin	Ford
7	Kyle Petty	Pontiac
8	Brett Bodine	Ford
9	Dick Trickle	Ford
10	Dale Jarrett	Chevrolet
11	Sterling Marlin	Ford
12	Ken Schrader	Chevrolet
13	Bill Elliott	Ford
14	Jimmy Hensley	Ford
15	Morgan Shepherd	Ford
16	Terry Labonte	Oldsmobile
17	Chad Little	Ford
18	Rusty Wallace	Pontiac
19	Derrike Cope	Chevrolet
20	Richard Petty	Pontiac
21	Hut Stricklin	Chevrolet
22	Bobby Hamilton	Oldsmobile
23	Dale Earnhardt	Chevrolet
24	Rick Mast	Oldsmobile
25	Bobby Hillin	Chevrolet
26	Michael Waltrip	Pontiac
27	Mike Potter	Chevrolet
28	Andy Belmont	Ford
29	Greg Sacks	Chevrolet
30	Geoff Bodine	Ford
31	Dave Marcis	Chevrolet
32	Wally Dallenbach	Ford
33	Davey Allison	Ford
34	Jimmy Horton	Chevrolet
35	Jerry O'Neil	Oldsmobile
36	Lake Speed	Ford
37	Ernie Irvan	Chevrolet
38	Bob Schacht	Chevrolet
39	Jimmy Means	Pontiac
40	James Hylton	Pontiac

KULWICKI'S SHINING MOMENT

The closest Winston Cup championship margin in history was the 10-points by which Alan Kulwicki beat Bill Elliott in 1992. It took a magical set of circumstances and precise planning in the season-ending race near Atlanta for the Wisconsin native to beat Elliott, the homestate hero from nearby Dawsonville.

Kulwicki went into the 328-lap, 500-mile race at the Atlanta Motor Speedway 30 points behind points-leader Davey Allison and 10 points ahead of third-place Elliott. There were dozens of finish-position combinations by which any of the three drivers could win the title, and each driver knew every one of them.

Allison seemed headed for his first NASCAR championship until crashing with Ernie Irvan on the frontstretch and falling from contention with 125 miles remaining. That left the title up for grabs between Elliott and Kulwicki, and each man did what he had to do: Elliott won the race (his fifth victory of the season) and scored 180 points. Kulwicki, a two-time race winner, finished second by more than eight seconds, but led the most laps and also scored 180 points. The final accounting after 29 races: Kulwicki with 4,078 points, Elliott with 4,068 and Allison with 4,015

Tragically, Kulwicki didn't get to enjoy his hard-earned success nearly long enough. On April 1, 1993, less than five months after winning the Winston Cup and the admiration of millions, Kulwicki and three other men where killed when the team's private plane stalled, crashed, and burned on final approach to Tri-Cities Regional Airport at Bristol, Tennessee.

DIEHARD 500

Time of Race: 2 hours, 5 minutes, 11 seconds
Average Speed: 176.309 mph
Margin of Victory: .19 second

FINISH	DRIVER	CAR
1	Ernie Irvan	Chevrolet
2	Sterling Marlin	Ford
3	Davey Allison	Ford
4	Ricky Rudd	Chevrolet
5	Bill Elliott	Ford
6	Kyle Petty	Pontiac
7	Michael Waltrip	Pontiac
8	Chad Little	Ford
9	Ken Schrader	Chevrolet
10	Brett Bodine	Ford
11	Rusty Wallace	Pontiac
12	Ted Musgrave	Chevrolet
13	Morgan Shepherd	Ford
14	Wally Dallenbach	Ford
15	Richard Petty	Pontiac
16	Hut Stricklin	Chevrolet
17	Harry Gant	Oldsmobile
18	Terry Labonte	Ford
19	Greg Sacks	Chevrolet
20	Mark Martin	Ford
21	Dale Jarrett	Chevrolet
22	Derrike Cope	Chevrolet
23	Darrell Waltrip	Chevrolet
24	Bobby Hamilton	Chevrolet
25	Alan Kulwicki	Ford
26	Rick Mast	Oldsmobile
27	Stanley Smith	Chevrolet
28	Dick Trickle	Ford
29	Dave Marcis	Chevrolet
30	Charlie Glotzbach	Ford
31	Jimmy Hensley	Ford
32	Jimmy Means	Pontiac
33	Randy Porter	Pontiac
34	Robby Gerhart	Chevrolet
35	T.W. Taylor	Pontiac
36	Stan Fox	Chevrolet
37	Delma Cowart	Ford
38	Geoff Bodine	Ford
39	Andy Belmont	Ford
40	Dale Earnhardt	Chevrolet

BUDWEISER AT THE GLEN

Time of Race: 1 hour, 27 minutes, 21 seconds
Average Speed: 88.980 mph
Margin of Victory: Under Caution

FINISH	DRIVER	CAR
1	Kyle Petty	Pontiac
2	Morgan Shepherd	Ford
3	Ernie Irvan	Chevrolet
4	Mark Martin	Ford
5	Wally Dallenbach	Ford
6	Rusty Wallace	Pontiac
7	Alan Kulwicki	Ford
8	Terry Labonte	Oldsmobile
9	Dale Earnhardt	Chevrolet
10	Brett Bodine	Ford
11	Ted Musgrave	Ford
12	Darrell Waltrip	Chevrolet
13	Ricky Rudd	Chevrolet
14	Bill Elliott	Ford
15	Dale Jarrett	Chevrolet
16	Sterling Marlin	Ford
17	Dave Marcis	Chevrolet
18	Harry Gant	Oldsmobile
19	Scott Sharp	Chevrolet
20	Davey Allison	Ford
21	Ken Schrader	Chevrolet
22	Bobby Hamilton	Oldsmobile
23	Bobby Hillin	Chevrolet
24	Dick Trickle	Ford
25	Jerry O'Neil	Oldsmobile
26	Jimmy Hensley	Ford
27	Geoff Bodine	Ford
28	Richard Petty	Pontiac
29	Ed Ferree	Chevrolet
30	Bob Schacht	Oldsmobile
31	Greg Sacks	Chevrolet
32	Rick Mast	Oldsmobile
33	Mike Potter	Buick
34	Derrike Cope	Chevrolet
35	Michael Waltrip	Pontiac
36	Hut Stricklin	Chevrolet
37	Todd Bodine	Ford
38	Denny Wilson	Pontiac
39	James Hylton	Pontiac

CHAMPION SPARK PLUG 400

Time of Race: 2 hours, 47 minutes, 46 seconds
Average Speed: 146.056 mph
Margin of Victory: 4.94 seconds

FINISH	DRIVER	CAR
1	Harry Gant	Oldsmobile
2	Darrell Waltrip	Chevrolet
3	Bill Elliott	Ford
4	Ernie Irvan	Chevrolet
5	Davey Allison	Ford
6	Kyle Petty	Pontiac
7	Sterling Marlin	Ford
8	Dale Jarrett	Chevrolet
9	Mark Martin	Ford
10	Morgan Shepherd	Ford
11	Ken Schrader	Chevrolet
12	Brett Bodine	Ford
13	Rick Mast	Olds
14	Alan Kulwicki	Ford
15	Bobby Hamilton	Ford
16	Dale Earnhardt	Chevrolet
17	Chad Little	Ford
18	Richard Petty	Pontiac
19	Dick Trickle	Ford
20	Wally Dallenbach	Ford
21	Rusty Wallace	Pontiac
22	Michael Waltrip	Pontiac
23	Terry Labonte	Oldsmobile
24	Hut Stricklin	Ford
25	Ted Musgrave	Ford
26	Bobby Hillin	Chevrolet
27	Jeff Purvis	Chevrolet
28	Eddie Bierschwale	Oldsmobile
29	Jimmy Hensley	Ford
30	Mike Potter	Chevrolet
31	Jeff McClure	Chevrolet
32	Dave Marcis	Chevrolet
33	Derrike Cope	Chevrolet
34	Lake Speed	Ford
35	Stanley Smith	Chevrolet
36	Ricky Rudd	Chevrolet
37	Stan Fox	Chevrolet
38	Jimmy Horton	Chevrolet
39	Jimmy Means	Chevrolet
40	Geoff Bodine	Ford
41	Greg Sacks	Chevrolet

BUD 500

Time of Race: 2 hours, 55 minutes, 20 seconds
Average Speed: 91.198 mph
Margin of Victory: 9.28 seconds

FINISH	DRIVER	CAR
1	Darrell Waltrip	Chevrolet
2	Dale Earnhardt	Chevrolet
3	Ken Schrader	Chevrolet
4	Kyle Petty	Pontiac
5	Alan Kulwicki	Ford
6	Bill Elliott	Ford
7	Jimmy Hensley	Ford
8	Ricky Rudd	Chevrolet
9	Brett Bodine	Ford
10	Rusty Wallace	Pontiac
11	Geoff Bodine	Ford
12	Derrike Cope	Chevrolet
13	Morgan Shepherd	Ford
14	Michael Waltrip	Pontiac
15	Sterling Marlin	Ford
16	Richard Petty	Pontiac
17	Dale Jarrett	Chevrolet
18	Jim Sauter	Chevrolet
19	Wally Dallenbach	Ford
20	Jimmy Spencer	Ford
21	Bobby Hamilton	Oldsmobile
22	Ted Musgrave	Ford

FINISH	DRIVER	CAR
23	Dick Trickle	Ford
24	Jimmy Means	Pontiac
25	Mark Martin	Ford
26	Harry Gant	Oldsmobile
27	Hut Stricklin	Chevrolet
28	Ernie Irvan	Chevrolet
29	Rick Mast	Oldsmobile
30	Davey Allison	Ford
31	Terry Labonte	Oldsmobile
32	Dave Marcis	Chevrolet

MOUNTAIN DEW SOUTHERN 500

Time of Race: 3 hours, 9 minutes, 10 seconds
Average Speed: 129.114 mph
Margin of Victory: Under Caution

FINISH	DRIVER	CAR
1	Darrell Waltrip	Chevrolet
2	Mark Martin	Ford
3	Bill Elliott	Ford
4	Brett Bodine	Ford
5	Davey Allison	Ford
6	Dale Jarrett	Chevrolet
7	Kyle Petty	Pontiac
8	Alan Kulwicki	Ford
9	Rusty Wallace	Pontiac
10	Ricky Rudd	Chevrolet
11	Hut Stricklin	Ford
12	Derrike Cope	Chevrolet
13	Ken Schrader	Chevrolet
14	Terry Labonte	Oldsmobile
15	Jimmy Hensley	Ford
16	Harry Gant	Oldsmobile
17	Bobby Hillin	Chevrolet
18	Dave Marcis	Chevrolet
19	Geoff Bodine	Ford
20	Richard Petty	Pontiac
21	Bobby Hamilton	Ford
22	Jimmy Means	Pontiac
23	Rick Mast	Oldsmobile
24	Wally Dallenbach	Ford
25	Ernie Irvan	Chevrolet
26	Lake Speed	Ford
27	Dick Trickle	Ford
28	Sterling Marlin	Ford
29	Dale Earnhardt	Chevrolet
30	Ted Musgrave	Ford
31	Morgan Shepherd	Ford
32	Andy Belmont	Ford
33	Mike Potter	Buick
34	Chad Little	Ford
35	Michael Waltrip	Pontiac
36	Jim Sauter	Chevrolet
37	James Hylton	Pontiac
38	Johnny McFadden	Pontiac

MILLER GENUINE DRAFT 400

Time of Race: 2 hours, 31 minutes, 59 seconds
Average Speed: 104.6613 mph
Margin of Victory: 3.59 seconds

FINISH	DRIVER	CAR
1	Rusty Wallace	Pontiac
2	Mark Martin	Ford
3	Darrell Waltrip	Chevrolet
4	Dale Earnhardt	Chevrolet
5	Geoff Bodine	Ford
6	Ricky Rudd	Chevrolet
7	Morgan Shepherd	Ford
8	Harry Gant	Oldsmobile
9	Ken Schrader	Chevrolet
10	Ted Musgrave	Ford
11	Ernie Irvan	Chevrolet
12	Kyle Petty	Pontiac
13	Terry Labonte	Oldsmobile

14	Bill Elliott	Ford
15	Alan Kulwicki	Ford
16	Richard Petty	Pontiac
17	Jimmy Hensley	Ford
18	Brett Bodine	Buick1
19	Davey Allison	Ford
20	Dick Trickle	Ford
21	Sterling Marlin	Ford
22	Jeff Purvis	Chevrolet
23	Wally Dallenbach	Ford
24	Dave Marcis	Chevrolet
25	Dale Jarrett	Chevrolet
26	Jim Sauter	Chevrolet
27	Chad Little	Ford
28	Rick Mast	Oldsmobile
29	Jimmy Means	Pontiac
30	Hut Stricklin	Ford
31	Jimmy Horton	Chevrolet
32	Bobby Hamilton	Ford
33	Michael Waltrip	Pontiac
34	Stanley Smith	Chevrolet
35	Derrike Cope	Chevrolet

PEAK ANTIFREEZE 500

Time of Race: 4 hours, 20 minutes, 13 seconds
Average Speed: 115.289 mph
Margin of Victory: .47 second

FINISH	DRIVER	CAR
1	Ricky Rudd	Chevrolet
2	Bill Elliott	Ford
3	Kyle Petty	Pontiac
4	Davey Allison	Ford
5	Morgan Shepherd	Ford
6	Harry Gant	Oldsmobile
7	Terry Labonte	Oldsmobile
8	Ted Musgrave	Ford
9	Derrike Cope	Chevrolet
10	Bobby Hamilton	Ford
11	Ernie Irvan	Chevrolet
12	Dale Jarrett	Chevrolet
13	Jimmy Hensley	Ford
14	Geoff Bodine	Ford
15	Hut Stricklin	Ford
16	Rusty Wallace	Pontiac
17	Michael Waltrip	Pontiac
18	Jim Sauter	Chevrolet
19	Mark Martin	Ford
20	Darrell Waltrip	Chevrolet
21	Dale Earnhardt	Chevrolet
22	Brett Bodine	Ford
23	Jimmy Means	Pontiac
24	Rick Mast	Oldsmobile
25	Mike Potter	Buick
26	Dave Marcis	Chevrolet
27	Dick Trickle	Ford
28	Richard Petty	Pontiac
29	Chad Little	Ford
30	Ken Schrader	Chevrolet
31	Wally Dallenbach	Ford
32	Jeff Purvis	Chevrolet
33	Sterling Marlin	Ford
34	Alan Kulwicki	Ford
35	James Hylton	Pontiac
36	Graham Taylor	Chevrolet

GOODY'S 500

Time of Race: 3 hours, 29 minutes, 13 seconds
Average Speed: 75.424 mph
Margin of Victory: .19 second

FINISH	DRIVER	CAR
1	Geoff Bodine	Ford
2	Rusty Wallace	Pontiac
3	Brett Bodine	Ford

4	Kyle Petty	Pontiac
5	Alan Kulwicki	Ford
6	Dick Trickle	Ford
7	Sterling Marlin	Ford
8	Mark Martin	Ford
9	Rick Mast	Oldsmobile
10	Ricky Rudd	Chevrolet
11	Terry Labonte	Oldsmobile
12	Ted Musgrave	Ford
13	Ken Schrader	Chevrolet
14	Wally Dallenbach	Ford
15	Darrell Waltrip	Chevrolet
16	Davey Allison	Ford
17	Jimmy Hensley	Ford
18	Richard Petty	Pontiac
19	Harry Gant	Oldsmobile
20	Derrike Cope	Chevrolet
21	Morgan Shepherd	Ford
22	Jim Sauter	Chevrolet
23	Dale Jarrett	Chevrolet
24	Hut Stricklin	Ford
25	Dave Marcis	Chevrolet
26	Jeff Purvis	Chevrolet
27	Ernie Irvan	Chevrolet
28	Bobby Hamilton	Ford
29	Michael Waltrip	Pontiac
30	Bill Elliott	Ford
31	Dale Earnhardt	Chevrolet

TYSON HOLLY FARMS 400

Time of Race: 2 hours, 19 minutes, 43 seconds
Average Speed: 107.360 mph - Track Record
Margin of Victory: 5.34 seconds

FINISH	DRIVER	CAR
1	Geoff Bodine	Ford
2	Mark Martin	Ford
3	Kyle Petty	Pontiac
4	Rusty Wallace	Pontiac
5	Sterling Marlin	Ford
6	Ernie Irvan	Chevrolet
7	Brett Bodine	Ford
8	Terry Labonte	Oldsmobile
9	Darrell Waltrip	Chevrolet
10	Dale Jarrett	Chevrolet
11	Davey Allison	Ford
12	Alan Kulwicki	Ford
13	Harry Gant	Oldsmobile
14	Ted Musgrave	Ford
15	Ricky Rudd	Chevrolet
16	Michael Waltrip	Pontiac
17	Morgan Shepherd	Ford
18	Dick Trickle	Ford
19	Dale Earnhardt	Chevrolet
20	Rich Bickle	Ford
21	Rick Mast	Oldsmobile
22	Derrike Cope	Chevrolet
23	Ken Schrader	Chevrolet
24	Wally Dallenbach	Ford
25	Jimmy Hensley	Ford
26	Bill Elliott	Ford
27	Richard Petty	Pontiac
28	Dave Marcis	Chevrolet
29	Jim Sauter	Chevrolet
30	Hut Stricklin	Ford
31	Bobby Hamilton	Ford
32	Jeff Purvis	Chevrolet

MELLO YELLO 500

Time of Race: 3 hours, 15 minutes, 47 seconds
Average Speed: 153.537 mph - Track 500 Mile Record
Margin of Victory: 1.88 seconds

FINISH	DRIVER	CAR
1	Mark Martin	Ford
2	Alan Kulwicki	Ford

3	Kyle Petty	Pontiac
4	Jimmy Spencer	Ford
5	Ricky Rudd	Chevrolet
6	Ernie Irvan	Chevrolet
7	Ken Schrader	Chevrolet
8	Harry Gant	Oldsmobile
9	Dick Trickle	Ford
10	Geoff Bodine	Ford
11	Ted Musgrave	Ford
12	Terry Labonte	Chevrolet
13	Morgan Shepherd	Ford
14	Dale Earnhardt	Chevrolet
15	Bobby Hamilton	Ford
16	Sterling Marlin	Ford
17	Derrike Cope	Chevrolet
18	Jimmy Hensley	Ford
19	Davey Allison	Ford
20	Wally Dallenbach	Ford
21	Jim Sauter	Chevrolet
22	Bob Schacht	Oldsmobile
23	Michael Waltrip	Pontiac
24	Dale Jarrett	Chevrolet
25	Rich Bickle	Ford
26	Lake Speed	Ford
27	Richard Petty	Pontiac
28	Brett Bodine	Ford
29	Jerry O'Neil	Oldsmobile
30	Bill Elliott	Ford
31	Hut Stricklin	Ford
32	Poncho Carter	Ford
33	Chad Little	Ford
34	Darrell Waltrip	Chevrolet
35	Rick Mast	Oldsmobile
36	Stanley Smith	Chevrolet
37	Rusty Wallace	Pontiac
38	Jimmy Means	Pontiac
39	Dave Marcis	Chevrolet
40	Bobby Hillin	Chevrolet

AC DELCO 500

Time of Race: 3 hours, 49 minutes, 37 seconds
Average Speed: 130.748 mph - Track Record
Margin of Victory:.91 second

FINISH	DRIVER	CAR
1	Kyle Petty	Pontiac
2	Ernie Irvan	Chevrolet
3	Ricky Rudd	Chevrolet
4	Bill Eilliott	Ford
5	Sterling Marlin	Ford
6	Harry Gant	Oldsmobile
7	Brett Bodine	Ford
8	Dale Earnhardt	Chevrolet
9	Terry Labonte	Oldsmobile
10	Davey Allison	Ford
11	Jimmy Spencer	Chevrolet
12	Alan Kulwicki	Ford
13	Morgan Shepherd	Ford
14	Derrike Cope	Chevrolet
15	Dale Jarrett	Chevrolet
16	Dick Trickle	Ford
17	Rick Mast	Oldsmobile
18	Jimmy Hensley	Ford
19	Bobby Hamilton	Ford
20	Michael Waltrip	Pontiac
21	Rusty Wallace	Pontiac
22	Darrell Waltrip	Chevrolet
23	Wally Dallenbach	Ford
24	Chad Little	Ford
25	Richard Petty	Pontiac
26	Jimmy Means	Pontiac
27	Mike Wallace	Ford
28	Mike Skinner	Chevrolet
29	Ted Musgrave	Ford
30	Mark Martin	Ford
31	Dave Blaney	Pontiac
32	Ken Schrader	Chevrolet
33	Greg Sacks	Chevrolet
34	Jimmy Horton	Chevrolet
35	Geoff Bodine	Ford

36	Lake Speed	Ford
37	Jerry O'Neil	Oldsmobile
38	Dave Marcis	Chevrolet
39	Mike Potter	Pontiac
40	Johnny McFadden	Chevrolet

PYROIL 500

Time of Race: 3 hours, 0 minutes, 12 seconds
Average Speed: 103.885 mph
Margin of Victory: 3.22 seconds

FINISH	DRIVER	CAR
1	Davey Allison	Ford
2	Mark Martin	Ford
3	Darrell Waltrip	Chevrolet
4	Alan Kulwicki	Ford
5	Jimmy Spencer	Ford
6	Ken Schrader	Chevrolet
7	Derrike Cope	Chevrolet
8	Bobby Hamilton	Ford
9	Sterling Marlin	Ford
10	Dale Earnhardt	Chevrolet
11	Michael Waltrip	Pontiac
12	Brett Bodine	Ford
13	Wally Dallenbach	Ford
14	Harry Gant	Oldsmobile
15	Hut Stricklin	Chevrolet
16	Terry Labonte	Oldsmobile
17	Rick Mast	Oldsmobile
18	Lake Speed	Ford
19	Kyle Petty	Pontiac
20	Dale Jarrett	Chevrolet
21	Jimmy Hensley	Ford
22	Richard Petty	Pontiac
23	John Krebs	Chevrolet
24	Ted Musgrave	Ford
25	Ron Hornaday	Chevrolet
26	Jeff Davis	Ford
27	Bill Sedgwick	Chevrolet
28	Rusty Wallace	Pontiac
29	Butch Gilliland	Pontiac
30	Ricky Rudd	Chevrolet
31	Bill Elliott	Ford
32	Stanley Smith	Chevrolet
33	Bill Schmitt	Ford
34	Ernie Irvan	Chevrolet
35	Dave Marcis	Chevrolet
36	Jeff Purvis	Chevrolet
37	Scott Gaylord	Pontiac
38	Morgan Shepherd	Ford
39	Geoff Bodine	Ford
40	Dick Trickle	Ford
41	Rick Scribner	Chevrolet
42	Rick Carelli	Chevrolet

HOOTERS 500

Time of Race: 3 hours, 44 minutes, 20 seconds
Average Speed: 133.322 mph
Margin of Victory: 8.06 seconds

FINISH	DRIVER	CAR
1	Bill Elliott	Ford
2	Alan Kulwicki	Ford
3	Geoff Bodine	Ford
4	Jimmy Spencer	Ford
5	Terry Labonte	Chevrolet
6	Rusty Wallace	Pontiac
7	Sterling Marlin	Ford
8	Jimmy Hensley	Ford
9	Ted Musgrave	Ford
10	Dale Jarrett	Chevrolet
11	Morgan Shepherd	Ford
12	Bobby Hamilton	Ford
13	Harry Gant	Oldsmobile
14	Michael Waltrip	Pontiac

FINISH	DRIVER	CAR
15	Derrike Cope	Chevrolet
16	Kyle Petty	Pontiac
17	Chad Little	Ford
18	Lake Speed	Ford
19	Eddie Bierschwale	Oldsmobile
20	Mike Wallace	Pontiac
21	Jimmy Means	Ford
22	Dave Marcis	Chevrolet
23	Darrell Waltrip	Chevrolet
24	Jimmy Horton	Chevrolet
25	Ricky Rudd	Chevrolet
26	Dale Earnhardt	Chevrolet
27	Davey Allison	Ford
28	Rick Mast	Oldsmobile
29	Ernie Irvan	Chevrolet
30	Bobby Hillin	Ford
31	Jeff Gordon	Chevrolet
32	Mark Martin	Ford
33	Bob Schacht	Oldsmobile
34	Rich Bickle	Ford
35	Richard Petty	Pontiac
36	Ken Schrader	Chevrolet
37	Dick Trickle	Ford
38	Wally Dallenbach	Ford
39	Stanley Smith	Chevrolet
40	Brett Bodine	Ford

1993

DAYTONA 500

Time of Race: 3 hours, 13 minutes, 35 seconds
Average Speed: 154.972 mph
Margin of Victory: .16 second

FINISH	DRIVER	CAR
1	Dale Jarrett	Chevrolet
2	Dale Earnhardt	Chevrolet
3	Geoff Bodine	Ford
4	Hut Stricklin	Ford
5	Jeff Gordon	Chevrolet
6	Mark Martin	Ford
7	Morgan Shepherd	Ford
8	Ken Schrader	Chevrolet
9	Sterling Marlin	Ford
10	Wally Dallenbach	Ford
11	Terry Labonte	Chevrolet
12	Rick Mast	Ford
13	Jimmy Spencer	Ford
14	Lake Speed	Ford
15	Ted Musgrave	Ford
16	Michael Waltrip	Pontiac
17	Brett Bodine	Ford
18	Darrell Waltrip	Chevrolet
19	Jim Sauter	Ford
20	Bobby Labonte	Ford
21	Harry Gant	Chevrolet
22	Phil Parsons	Chevrolet
23	Kenny Wallace	Pontiac
24	Chad Little	Ford
25	Jimmy Horton	Chevrolet
26	Alan Kulwicki	Ford
27	Bobby Hamilton	Ford
28	Davey Allison	Ford
29	Derrike Cope	Ford
30	Ricky Rudd	Chevrolet
31	Kyle Petty	Pontiac
32	Rusty Wallace	Pontiac
33	Dave Marcis	Chevrolet
34	Rick Wilson	Pontiac
35	Bobby Hillin	Ford
36	Al Unser, Jr.	Chevrolet
37	Ernie Irvan	Chevrolet
38	Joe Ruttman	Ford

FINISH	DRIVER	CAR
39	Bill Elliott	Ford
40	Jimmy Hensley	Ford
41	Dick Trickle	Ford

GOODWRENCH 500

Time of Race: 4 hours, 1 minute, 10 seconds
Average Speed: 124.486 mph
Margin of Victory: .5 second

FINISH	DRIVER	CAR
1	Rusty Wallace	Pontiac
2	Dale Earnhardt	Chevrolet
3	Ernie Irvan	Chevrolet
4	Alan Kulwicki	Ford
5	Mark Martin	Ford
6	Dale Jarrett	Chevrolet
7	Ted Musgrave	Ford
8	Phil Parsons	Chevrolet
9	Geoff Bodine	Ford
10	Terry Labonte	Chevrolet
11	Bill Elliott	Ford
12	Ricky Rudd	Chevrolet
13	Hut Stricklin	Ford
14	Davey Allison	Ford
15	Bobby Hamilton	Ford
16	Jimmy Spencer	Ford
17	Rick Wilson	Pontiac
18	Derrike Cope	Ford
19	Bobby Hillin	Ford
20	Wally Dallenbach	Ford
21	Dave Marcis	Chevrolet
22	Brett Bodine	Ford
23	Kenny Wallace	Pontiac
24	Ken Schrader	Chevrolet
25	Jimmy Hensley	Ford
26	Michael Waltrip	Pontiac
27	Ed Ferree	Chevrolet
28	Sterling Marlin	Ford
29	Dick Trickle	Ford
30	Darrell Waltrip	Chevrolet
31	Harry Gant	Chevrolet
32	Kyle Petty	Pontiac
33	Bobby Labonte	Ford
34	Jeff Gordon	Chevrolet
35	Morgan Shepherd	Ford
36	John Chapman	Pontiac
37	Mike Potter	Ford
38	Jerry Hill	Chevrolet
39	Rick Mast	Ford
40	James Hylton	Pontiac

PONTIAC EXCITEMENT 400

Time of Race: 2 hours, 47 minutes, 7 seconds
Average Speed: 107.709 mph
Margin of Victory: 4.38 seconds

FINISH	DRIVER	CAR
1	Davey Allison	Ford
2	Rusty Wallace	Pontiac
3	Alan Kulwicki	Ford
4	Dale Jarrett	Chevrolet
5	Kyle Petty	Pontiac
6	Jeff Gordon	Chevrolet
7	Mark Martin	Ford
8	Darrell Waltrip	Chevrolet
9	Harry Gant	Chevrolet
10	Dale Earnhardt	Chevrolet
11	Ernie Irvan	Chevrolet
12	Geoff Bodine	Ford
13	Jimmy Spencer	Ford
14	Morgan Shepherd	Ford
15	Ricky Rudd	Chevrolet
16	Phil Parsons	Chevrolet
17	Ted Musgrave	Ford
18	Hut Stricklin	Ford

19	Derrike Cope	Ford
20	Ken Schrader	Chevrolet
21	Dick Trickle	Ford
22	Bobby Hamilton	Ford
23	Michael Waltrip	Pontiac
24	Terry Labonte	Chevrolet
25	Rick Wilson	Pontiac
26	Kenny Wallace	Pontiac
27	Wally Dallenbach	Ford
28	Bobby Hillin	Ford
29	Bobby Labonte	Ford
30	Lake Speed	Ford
31	Sterling Marlin	Ford
32	Brett Bodine	Ford
33	Bill Elliott	Ford
34	Jimmy Hensley	Ford
35	Rick Mast	Ford
36	Dave Marcis	Chevrolet

MOTORCRAFT 500

Time of Race: 3 hours, 17 minutes, 26 seconds
Average Speed: 150.442 mph
Margin of Victory: 18 seconds

FINISH	DRIVER	CAR
1	Morgan Shepherd	Ford
2	Ernie Irvan	Chevrolet
3	Rusty Wallace	Pontiac
4	Jeff Gordon	Chevrolet
5	Ricky Rudd	Chevrolet
6	Geoff Bodine	Ford
7	Kyle Petty	Pontiac
8	Brett Bodine	Ford
9	Bill Elliott	Ford
10	Jimmy Spencer	Ford
11	Dale Earnhardt	Chevrolet
12	Sterling Marlin	Ford
13	Davey Allison	Ford
14	Michael Waltrip	Pontiac
15	Bobby Hillin	Ford
16	Kenney Wallace	Pontiac
17	Derrike Cope	Ford
18	Bobby Labonte	Ford
19	Ted Musgrave	Ford
20	Hut Stricklin	Ford
21	Harry Gant	Chevrolet
22	Jimmy Means	Ford
23	Greg Sacks	Ford
24	Rick Wilson	Pontiac
25	Wally Dallenbach	Ford
26	Bobby Hamilton	Ford
27	Jimmy Horton	Chevrolet
28	Lake Speed	Ford
29	Ken Schrader	Chevrolet
30	Rick Mast	Ford
31	Dale Jarrett	Chevrolet
32	Mark Martin	Ford
33	Terry Labonte	Chevrolet
34	Dave Marcis	Chevrolet
35	Darrell Waltrip	Chevrolet
36	Alan Kulwicki	Ford
37	Dick Trickle	Ford
38	Joe Ruttman	Ford
39	Phil Parsons	Chevrolet
40	Bob Schacht	Oldsmobile

TRANSOUTH 500

Time of Race: 3 hours, 33 minutes, 29 seconds
Average Speed: 139.958 mph
Margin of Victory: 1.63 seconds

FINISH	DRIVER	CAR
1	Dale Earnhardt	Chevrolet
2	Mark Martin	Ford

3	Dale Jarrett	Chevrolet
4	Ken Schrader	Chevrolet
5	Rusty Wallace	Pontiac
6	Alan Kulwicki	Ford
7	Kyle Petty	Pontiac
8	Geoff Bodine	Ford
9	Terry Labonte	Chevrolet
10	Morgan Shepherd	Ford
11	Davey Allison	Ford
12	Brett Bodine	Ford
13	Wally Dallenbach	Ford
14	Bill Elliott	Ford
15	Rick Mast	Ford
16	Darrell Waltrip	Chevrolet
17	Derrike Cope	Ford
18	Bobby Labonte	Ford
19	Ricky Rudd	Chevrolet
20	Dick Trickle	Ford
21	Sterling Marlin	Ford
22	Ernie Irvan	Chevrolet
23	Bobby Hamilton	Ford
24	Jeff Gordon	Chevrolet
25	Dave Marcis	Chevrolet
26	Rick Wilson	Oldsmobile
27	Bob Schacht	Oldsmobile
28	Hut Stricklin	Ford
29	Jimmy Spencer	Ford
30	Ted Musgrave	Ford
31	Jimmy Means	Ford
32	Kenny Wallace	Pontiac
33	Michael Waltrip	Pontiac
34	James Hylton	Pontiac
35	Bobby Hillin	Ford
36	Phil Parsons	Chevrolet
37	Harry Gant	Chevrolet
38	Mike Potter	Ford
39	Norm Benning	Oldsmobile

FOOD CITY 500

Time of Race: 3 hours, 8 minutes, 43 seconds
Average Speed: 84.730 mph
Margin of Victory: .82 seconds

FINISH	DRIVER	CAR
1	Rusty Wallace	Pontiac
2	Dale Earnhardt	Chevrolet
3	Kyle Petty	Pontiac
4	Jimmy Spencer	Ford
5	Davey Allison	Ford
6	Darrell Waltrip	Chevrolet
7	Morgan Shepherd	Ford
8	Mark Martin	Ford
9	Brett Bodine	Ford
10	Rick Mast	Ford
11	Wally Dallenbach	Ford
12	Derrike Cope	Ford
13	Kenny Wallace	Pontiac
14	Michael Waltrip	Pontiac
15	Ted Musgrave	Ford
16	Jimmy Means	Ford
17	Jeff Gordon	Chevrolet
18	Geoff Bodine	Ford
19	Joe Ruttman	Ford
20	Sterling Marlin	Ford
21	Terry Labonte	Chevrolet
22	Dick Trickle	Ford
23	Ernie Irvan	Chevrolet
24	Bobby Labonte	Ford
25	Rick Wilson	Pontiac
26	Ricky Rudd	Chevrolet
27	Hut Stricklin	Ford
28	Harry Gant	Chevrolet
29	Lake Speed	Ford
30	Bill Elliott	Ford
31	Phil Parsons	Chevrolet
32	Dale Jarrett	Chevrolet
33	Bobby Hillin	Ford
34	Ken Schrader	Chevrolet
35	Bobby Hamilton	Ford

FIRST UNION 400

Time of Race: 2 hours, 41 minutes, 59 seconds
Average Speed: 92.602 mph
Margin of Victory: 1.66 seconds

FINISH	DRIVER	CAR
1	Rusty Wallace	Pontiac
2	Kyle Petty	Pontiac
3	Ken Schrader	Chevrolet
4	Davey Allison	Ford
5	Darrell Waltrip	Chevrolet
6	Terry Labonte	Chevrolet
7	Ricky Rudd	Chevrolet
8	Morgan Shepherd	Ford
9	Sterling Marlin	Ford
10	Bill Elliott	Ford
11	Ernie Irvan	Chevrolet
12	Jimmy Hensley	Ford
13	Harry Gant	Chevrolet
14	Jimmy Spencer	Ford
15	Kenny Wallace	Pontiac
16	Dale Earnhardt	Chevrolet
17	Brett Bodine	Ford
18	Phil Parsons	Chevrolet
19	Rick Mast	Ford
20	Michael Waltrip	Pontiac
21	Wally Dallenbach	Ford
22	Hut Stricklin	Ford
23	Rick Wilson	Pontiac
24	Ted Musgrave	Ford
25	Bobby Labonte	Ford
26	Bobby Hillin	Ford
27	Jimmy Means	Ford
28	Geoff Bodine	Ford
29	Bobby Hamilton	Ford
30	Derrike Cope	Ford
31	Mark Martin	Ford
32	Dale Jarrett	Chevrolet
33	Dick Trickle	Ford
34	Jeff Gordon	Chevrolet

HANES 500

Time of Race: 3 hours, 18 minutes, 33 seconds
Average Speed: 79.078 mph
Margin of Victory: Under Caution

FINISH	DRIVER	CAR
1	Rusty Wallace	Pontiac
2	Davey Allison	Ford
3	Dale Jarrett	Chevrolet
4	Darrell Waltrip	Chevrolet
5	Kyle Petty	Pontiac
6	Geoff Bodine	Ford
7	Brett Bodine	Ford
8	Jeff Gordon	Chevrolet
9	Terry Labonte	Chevrolet
10	Mark Martin	Ford
11	Rick Mast	Ford
12	Bobby Labonte	Ford
13	Jimmy Hensley	Ford
14	Dick Trickle	Ford
15	Dave Marcis	Chevrolet
16	Michael Waltrip	Pontiac
17	Rick Wilson	Ford
18	Ken Schrader	Chevrolet
19	Morgan Shepherd	Ford
20	Phil Parsons	Chevrolet
21	Sterling Marlin	Ford
22	Dale Earnhardt	Chevrolet
23	Bobby Hillin	Ford
24	Kenny Wallace	Pontiac
25	Derrike Cope	Ford
26	Hut Stricklin	Ford
27	Bill Elliott	Ford
28	Ted Musgrave	Ford

29	Ricky Rudd	Chevrolet
30	Jimmy Spencer	Ford
31	Harry Gant	Chevrolet
32	Ernie Irvan	Chevrolet
33	Bobby Hamilton	Ford
34	Wally Dallenbach	Ford

WINSTON 500

Time of Race: 3 hours, 13 minutes, 4 seconds
Average Speed: 155.412 mph
Margin of Victory: 1 Car Length

FINISH	DRIVER	CAR
1	Ernie Irvan	Chevrolet
2	Jimmy Spencer	Ford
3	Dale Jarrett	Chevrolet
4	Dale Earnhardt	Chevrolet
5	Joe Ruttman	Ford
6	Rusty Wallace	Pontiac
7	Davey Allison	Ford
8	Derrike Cope	Ford
9	Jimmy Hensley	Ford
10	Michael Waltrip	Pontiac
11	Jeff Gordon	Chevrolet
12	Mark Martin	Ford
13	Rick Mast	Ford
14	Kenny Wallace	Pontiac
15	Morgan Shepherd	Ford
16	Rick Wilson	Pontiac
17	Bobby Hillin	Ford
18	Kyle Petty	Pontiac
19	Phil Parsons	Chevrolet
20	Hut Stricklin	Ford
21	Ken Schrader	Chevrolet
22	Bill Elliott	Ford
23	Harry Gant	Chevrolet
24	Sterling Marlin	Ford
25	Ritchie Petty	Ford
26	Darrell Waltrip	Chevrolet
27	Geoff Bodine	Ford
28	Ted Musgrave	Ford
29	Wally Dallenbach	Ford
30	Brett Bodine	Ford
31	Dick Trickle	Ford
32	Jimmy Means	Ford
33	Greg Sacks	Ford
34	Lake Speed	Ford
35	Bobby Labonte	Ford
36	Jimmy Horton	Chevrolet
37	Terry Labonte	Chevrolet
38	Rich Bickle	Ford
39	Jeff Purvis	Chevrolet
40	Ken Bouchard	Ford
41	Ricky Rudd	Chevrolet

SAVE MART SUPERMARKETS 300

Time of Race: 2 hours, 25 minutes, 17 seconds
Average Speed: 77.013 mph
Margin of Victory: .53 second

FINISH	DRIVER	CAR
1	Geoff Bodine	Ford
2	Ernie Irvan	Chevrolet
3	Ricky Rudd	Chevrolet
4	Ken Schrader	Chevrolet
5	Kyle Petty	Pontiac
6	Dale Earnhardt	Chevrolet
7	Wally Dallenbach	Ford
8	Rick Wilson	Pontiac
9	Terry Labonte	Chevrolet
10	Hut Stricklin	Ford
11	Jeff Gordon	Chevrolet

12	Sterling Marlin	Ford
13	Dale Jarrett	Chevrolet
14	Morgan Shepherd	Ford
15	Davey Allison	Ford
16	Bobby Labonte	Ford
17	Bill Elliott	Ford
18	Derrike Cope	Ford
19	Harry Gant	Chevrolet
20	Dick Trickle	Ford
21	Rick Carelli	Chevrolet
22	Tommy Kendall	Ford
23	Michael Waltrip	Pontiac
24	Brett Bodine	Ford
25	P. J. Jones	Ford
26	Bill Sedgwick	Chevrolet
27	Jimmy Spencer	Ford
28	Dave Marcis	Chevrolet
29	Rick Mast	Ford
30	Dirk Stephens	Ford
31	Bill Schmitt	Ford
32	Butch Gilliland	Chevrolet
33	Dorsey Schroeder	Ford
34	John Krebs	Chevrolet
35	Darrell Waltrip	Chevrolet
36	Kenny Wallace	Pontiac
37	Phil Parsons	Chevrolet
38	Rusty Wallace	Pontiac
39	Ted Musgrave	Ford
40	Mark Martin	Ford
41	Bobby Hillin	Ford
42	Jeff Davis	Ford
43	Hershel McGriff	Chevrolet

COCA COLA 600

Time of Race: 4 hours, 7 minutes, 25 seconds
Average Speed: 145.504 mph
Margin of Victory: 3.73 seconds

FINISH	DRIVER	CAR
1	Dale Earnhardt	Chevrolet
2	Jeff Gordon	Chevrolet
3	Dale Jarrett	Chevrolet
4	Ken Schrader	Chevrolet
5	Ernie Irvan	Chevrolet
6	Bill Elliott	Ford
7	Jimmy Spencer	Ford
8	Bobby Labonte	Ford
9	Morgan Shepherd	Ford
10	Geoff Bodine	Ford
11	Darrell Waltrip	Chevrolet
12	Phil Parsons	Chevrolet
13	Michael Waltrip	Pontiac
14	Kyle Petty	Pontiac
15	Jimmy Hensley	Ford
16	Bobby Hillin	Ford
17	Greg Sacks	Ford
18	Harry Gant	Chevrolet
19	Dick Trickle	Ford
20	Hut Stricklin	Ford
21	Rich Bickle	Ford
22	Mike Wallace	Pontiac
23	Kenny Wallace	Pontiac
24	Sterling Marlin	Ford
25	Jimmy Horton	Chevrolet
26	Ted Musgrave	Ford
27	Lake Speed	Ford
28	Mark Martin	Ford
29	Rusty Wallace	Pontiac
30	Davey Allison	Ford
31	Rick Mast	Ford
32	Rick Wilson	Pontiac
33	Terry Labonte	Chevrolet
34	Chad Little	Ford
35	Joe Ruttman	Ford
36	Derrike Cope	Ford
37	Ricky Rudd	Chevrolet
38	Jimmy Means	Ford
39	Dave Marcis	Chevrolet
40	Wally Dallenbach	Ford
41	Brett Bodine	Ford

BUDWEISER 500

Time of Race: 4 hours, 44 minutes, 6 seconds
Average Speed: 105.600 mph
Margin of Victory: .38 second

FINISH	DRIVER	CAR
1	Dale Earnhardt	Chevrolet
2	Dale Jarrett	Chevrolet
3	Davey Allison	Ford
4	Mark Martin	Ford
5	Ken Schrader	Chevrolet
6	Rick Mast	Ford
7	Harry Gant	Chevrolet
8	Jimmy Spencer	Ford
9	Morgan Shepherd	Ford
10	Bobby Hamilton	Ford
11	Rick Wilson	Pontiac
12	Wally Dallenbach	Ford
13	Kenny Wallace	Pontiac
14	Ted Musgrave	Ford
15	Hut Stricklin	Ford
16	Brett Bodine	Ford
17	Bill Elliott	Ford
18	Jeff Gordon	Chevrolet
19	Bobby Labonte	Ford
20	Terry Labonte	Chevrolet
21	Rusty Wallace	Pontiac
22	Jimmy Hensley	Ford
23	Geoff Bodine	Ford
24	Darrell Waltrip	Chevrolet
25	Bobby Hillin	Ford
26	Jimmy Means	Ford
27	Michael Waltrip	Pontiac
28	Dick Trickle	Ford
29	Kyle Petty	Pontiac
30	Lake Speed	Ford
31	Derrike Cope	Ford
32	Ernie Irvan	Chevrolet
33	Sterling Marlin	Ford
34	P. J. Jones	Ford
35	Ricky Rudd	Chevrolet
36	Dave Marcis	Chevrolet
37	Phil Parsons	Chevrolet
38	Greg Sacks	Ford

CHAMPION SPARK PLUG 500

Time of Race: 3 hours, 37 minutes, 23 seconds
Average Speed: 138.005 mph
Margin of Victory: 5.08 seconds

FINISH	DRIVER	CAR
1	Kyle Petty	Pontiac
2	Ken Schrader	Chevrolet
3	Harry Gant	Chevrolet
4	Jimmy Spencer	Ford
5	Ted Musgrave	Ford
6	Davey Allison	Ford
7	Morgan Shepherd	Ford
8	Sterling Marlin	Ford
9	Ricky Rudd	Chevrolet
10	Bill Elliott	Ford
11	Dale Earnhardt	Chevrolet
12	Rick Wilson	Pontiac
13	Hut Stricklin	Ford
14	Phil Parsons	Chevrolet
15	Kenny Wallace	Pontiac
16	Rick Mast	Ford
17	Jimmy Hensley	Ford
18	Greg Sacks	Ford
19	Dale Jarrett	Chevrolet
20	Bobby Labonte	Ford
21	Michael Waltrip	Pontiac
22	Jimmy Means	Ford
23	Dave Marcis	Chevrolet
24	Geoff Bodine	Ford

FINISH	DRIVER	CAR
25	Wally Dallenbach	Ford
26	Kerry Teague	Chevrolet
27	Lake Speed	Ford
28	Jeff Gordon	Chevrolet
29	Brett Bodine	Ford
30	Darrell Waltrip	Chevrolet
31	Mark Martin	Ford
32	Terry Labonte	Chevrolet
33	Derrike Cope	Ford
34	Ernie Irvan	Chevrolet
35	Trevor Boys	Pontiac
36	Dick Trickle	Ford
37	Jimmy Horton	Chevrolet
38	Bobby Hillin	Ford
39	Rusty Wallace	Pontiac
40	Graham Taylor	Ford

MILLER GENUINE DRAFT 400

Time of Race: 2 hours, 41 minutes, 38 seconds
Average Speed: 148.484 mph
Margin of Victory: 1.74 seconds

FINISH	DRIVER	CAR
1	Ricky Rudd	Chevrolet
2	Jeff Gordon	Chevrolet
3	Ernie Irvan	Chevrolet
4	Dale Jarrett	Chevrolet
5	Rusty Wallace	Pontiac
6	Mark Martin	Ford
7	Morgan Shepherd	Ford
8	Sterling Marlin	Ford
9	Bill Elliott	Ford
10	Harry Gant	Chevrolet
11	Rick Mast	Ford
12	Kyle Petty	Pontiac
13	Phil Parsons	Chevrolet
14	Dale Earnhardt	Chevrolet
15	Ted Musgrave	Ford
16	Ken Schrader	Chevrolet
17	Geoff Bodine	Ford
18	Jimmy Spencer	Ford
19	Darrell Waltrip	Chevrolet
20	Terry Labonte	Chevrolet
21	Hut Stricklin	Ford
22	Greg Sacks	Ford
23	Jimmy Hensley	Ford
24	Dave Marcis	Chevrolet
25	Wally Dallenbach	Ford
26	Jim Sauter	Chevrolet
27	Derrike Cope	Ford
28	Jimmy Means	Ford
29	Kenny Wallace	Pontiac
30	Lake Speed	Ford
31	Dick Trickle	Ford
32	H. B. Bailey	Pontiac
33	Bobby Hillin	Ford
34	Rick Wilson	Pontiac
35	Davey Allison	Ford
36	Bobby Labonte	Ford
37	Michael Waltrip	Pontiac
38	P. J. Jones	Ford
39	Brett Bodine	Ford
40	Clay Young	Ford
41	Jimmy Horton	Chevrolet

PEPSI 400

Time of Race: 2 hours, 38 minutes, 9 seconds
Average Speed: 151.755
Margin of Victory: .16 seconds

FINISH	DRIVER	CAR
1	Dale Earnhardt	Chevrolet
2	Sterling Marlin	Ford
3	Ken Schrader	Chevrolet
4	Ricky Rudd	Chevrolet

5	Jeff Gordon	Chevrolet
6	Mark Martin	Ford
7	Ernie Irvan	Chevrolet
8	Dale Jarrett	Chevrolet
9	Terry Labonte	Chevrolet
10	Ted Musgrave	Ford
11	Rick Wilson	Pontiac
12	Bobby Hillin	Ford
13	Darrell Waltrip	Chevrolet
14	Morgan Shepherd	Ford
15	Greg Sacks	Ford
16	Rick Mast	Ford
17	Bobby Hamilton	Ford
18	Rusty Wallace	Pontiac
19	Brett Bodine	Ford
20	Bill Elliott	Ford
21	Harry Gant	Chevrolet
22	Michael Waltrip	Pontiac
23	Jeff Purvis	Chevrolet
24	Derrike Cope	Ford
25	Phil Parsons	Chevrolet
26	Dick Trickle	Ford
27	Dave Marcis	Chevrolet
28	Kenny Wallace	Pontiac
29	Loy Allen	Ford
30	P. J. Jones	Ford
31	Davey Allison	Ford
32	Ritchie Petty	Ford
33	Kyle Petty	Pontiac
34	Jimmy Hensley	Ford
35	Wally Dallenbach	Ford
36	Jimmy Means	Ford
37	Geoff Bodine	Ford
38	Jimmy Horton	Chevrolet
39	Jimmy Spencer	Ford
40	Hut Stricklin	Ford
41	Bobby Labonte	Ford

SLICK 50 300

Time of Race: 2 hours, 59 minutes, 45 seconds
Average Speed: 105.947 mph
Margin of Victory: 1.31 seconds

FINISH	DRIVER	CAR
1	Rusty Wallace	Pontiac
2	Mark Martin	Ford
3	Davey Allison	Ford
4	Dale Jarrett	Chevrolet
5	Ricky Rudd	Chevrolet
6	Sterling Marlin	Ford
7	Jeff Gordon	Chevrolet
8	Kyle Petty	Pontiac
9	Bill Elliott	Ford
10	Bobby Labonte	Ford
11	Jimmy Hensley	Ford
12	Geoff Bodine	Ford
13	Brett Bodine	Ford
14	Morgan Shepherd	Ford
15	Ernie Irvan	Chevrolet
16	Rick Mast	Ford
17	Harry Gant	Chevrolet
18	Jimmy Spencer	Ford
19	Darrell Waltrip	Chevrolet
20	Bobby Hillin	Ford
21	Kenny Wallace	Pontiac
22	Derrike Cope	Ford
23	Michael Waltrip	Pontiac
24	Ted Musgrave	Ford
25	Hut Stricklin	Ford
26	Dale Earnhardt	Chevrolet
27	Wally Dallenbach	Ford
28	Rick Wilson	Pontiac
29	Ken Bouchard	Ford
30	Dave Marcis	Chevrolet
31	Terry Labonte	Chevrolet
32	Greg Sacks	Ford
33	Dick Trickle	Ford
34	Jimmy Means	Ford
35	Lake Speed	Ford
36	Joe Nemechek	Chevrolet
37	Jeff Burton	Ford
38	Ken Schrader	Chevrolet

| 39 | Phil Parsons | Chevrolet |
| 40 | Jerry O'Neil | Chevrolet |

MILLER GENUINE DRAFT 500

Time of Race: 3 hours, 44 minutes, 59 seconds
Average Speed: 133.343 mph
Margin of Victory: .78 second

FINISH	DRIVER	CAR
1	Dale Earnhardt	Chevrolet
2	Rusty Wallace	Pontiac
3	Bill Elliott	Ford
4	Morgan Shepherd	Ford
5	Brett Bodine	Ford
6	Ken Schrader	Chevrolet
7	Sterling Marlin	Ford
8	Dale Jarrett	Chevrolet
9	Harry Gant	Chevrolet
10	Darrell Waltrip	Chevrolet
11	Ricky Rudd	Chevrolet
12	Geoff Bodine	Ford
13	Mark Martin	Ford
14	Michael Waltrip	Pontiac
15	Bobby Labonte	Ford
16	Terry Labonte	Chevrolet
17	Wally Dallenbach	Ford
18	Phil Parsons	Chevrolet
19	Bobby Hamiltion	Ford
20	Bobby Hillin	Ford
21	Rick Wilson	Pontiac
22	Dave Marcis	Chevrolet
23	Kenny Wallace	Pontiac
24	Jimmy Spencer	Ford
25	Ken Bouchard	Ford
26	Jimmy Horton	Chevrolet
27	Kyle Petty	Pontiac
28	Hut Stricklin	Ford
29	Derrike Cope	Ford
30	Dick Trickle	Ford
31	Ernie Irvan	Chevrolet
32	Greg Sacks	Ford
33	Ted Musgrave	Ford
34	Kerry Teague	Chevrolet
35	John Krebs	Chevrolet
36	Rick Mast	Ford
37	Jeff Gordon	Chevrolet
38	Clay Young	Ford
39	Jimmy Hensley	Ford
40	T. W. Taylor	Ford

DIEHARD 500

Time of Race: 3 hours, 15 minutes, 1 second
Average Speed: 153.858 mph
Margin of Victory: .005 second

FINISH	DRIVER	CAR
1	Dale Earnhardt	Chevrolet
2	Ernie Irvan	Chevrolet
3	Mark Martin	Ford
4	Kyle Petty	Pontiac
5	Dale Jarrett	Chevrolet
6	Greg Sacks	Ford
7	Morgan Shepherd	Ford
8	Harry Gant	Chevrolet
9	Brett Bodine	Ford
10	Wally Dallenbach	Ford
11	Bill Elliott	Ford
12	Hut Stricklin	Ford
13	Bobby Hillin	Ford
14	Terry Labonte	Chevrolet
15	Bobby Labonte	Ford
16	Geoff Bodine	Ford
17	Rusty Wallace	Pontiac
18	Lake Speed	Ford
19	Dick Trickle	Ford
20	Michael Waltrip	Pontiac

21	Jeff Purvis	Chevrolet
22	Phil Parsons	Chevrolet
23	Rick Wilson	Pontiac
24	Ricky Rudd	Chevrolet
25	Jimmy Means	Ford
26	Loy Allen	Ford
27	Sterling Marlin	Ford
28	Jimmy Hensley	Ford
29	Dave Marcis	Chevrolet
30	Jimmy Spencer	Ford
31	Jeff Gordon	Chevrolet
32	Ken Schrader	Chevrolet
33	Ted Musgrave	Ford
34	Neil Bonnett	Chevrolet
35	Kenny Wallace	Pontiac
36	Derrike Cope	Ford
37	Darrell Waltrip	Chevrolet
38	Rick Mast	Ford
39	Jimmy Horton	Chevrolet
40	Stanley Smith	Chevrolet
41	Ritchie Petty	Ford
42	Robby Gordon	Ford

BUDWEISER AT THE GLEN

Time of Race: 2 hours, 36 minutes, 4 seconds
Average Speed: 84.771 mph
Margin of Victory: 3.84 seconds

FINISH	DRIVER	CAR
1	Mark Martin	Ford
2	Wally Dallenbach	Ford
3	Jimmy Spencer	Ford
4	Bill Elliott	Ford
5	Ken Schrader	Chevrolet
6	Sterling Marlin	Ford
7	Bobby Labonte	Ford
8	P. J. Jones	Ford
9	Kenny Wallace	Pontiac
10	Harry Gant	Chevrolet
11	Derrike Cope	Ford
12	Michael Waltrip	Pontiac
13	Scott Lagasse	Chevrolet
14	Darrell Waltrip	Chevrolet
15	Ernie Irvan	Chevrolet
16	Geoff Bodine	Ford
17	Hut Stricklin	Ford
18	Dale Earnhardt	Chevrolet
19	Rusty Wallace	Pontiac
20	Brett Bodine	Ford
21	Joe Nemechek	Chevrolet
22	Rick Wilson	Pontiac
23	Terry Labonte	Chevrolet
24	Ricky Rudd	Chevrolet
25	Tommy Kendall	Ford
26	Kyle Petty	Pontiac
27	Lake Speed	Ford
28	Morgan Shepherd	Ford
29	Scott Gaylord	Oldsmobile
30	Todd Bodine	Ford
31	Jeff Gordon	Chevrolet
32	Dale Jarrett	Chevrolet
33	Phil Parsons	Chevrolet
34	Ted Musgrave	Ford
35	Bobby Hillin	Ford
36	Ed Ferree	Chevrolet
37	Rick Mast	Ford
38	Dorsey Schroeder	Ford

CHAMPION SPARK PLUG 400

Time of Race: 2 hours, 46 minutes, 1 second
Average Speed: 144.564 mph
Margin of Victory: 1.28 seconds

FINISH	DRIVER	CAR
1	Mark Martin	Ford
2	Morgan Shepherd	Ford

38	Jimmy Horton	Chevrolet
39	Dick Trickle	Chevrolet
40	Todd Bodine	Ford
41	Rich Bickle	Ford

BUD 500

Time of Race: 3 hours, 1 minute, 21 seconds
Average Speed: 88.172 mph
Margin of Victory: .14 second

FINISH	DRIVER	CAR
1	Mark Martin	Ford
2	Rusty Wallace	Pontiac
3	Dale Earnhardt	Chevrolet
4	Harry Gant	Chevrolet
5	Rick Mast	Ford
6	Jimmy Hensley	Ford
7	Brett Bodine	Ford
8	Geoff Bodine	Ford
9	Kenny Wallace	Pontiac
10	Michael Waltrip	Pontiac
11	Bill Elliott	Ford
12	Bobby Hillin	Ford
13	Morgan Shepherd	Ford
14	Phil Parsons	Chevrolet
15	Bobby Labonte	Ford
16	Lake Speed	Ford
17	Dave Marcis	Chevrolet
18	Jimmy Means	Ford
19	Greg Sacks	Ford
20	Jeff Gordon	Chevrolet
21	Wally Dallenbach	Ford
22	Ricky Rudd	Chevrolet
23	Sterling Marlin	Ford
24	Ken Schrader	Chevrolet
25	Jimmy Spencer	Ford
26	Ernie Irvan	Chevrolet
27	Derrike Cope	Ford
28	Rick Wilson	Pontiac
29	Dale Jarrett	Chevrolet
30	Kyle Petty	Pontiac
31	Dale Jarrett	Chevrolet
32	Hut Stricklin	Ford
33	Bobby Hamilton	Ford
34	Terry Labonte	Chevrolet

MOUNTAIN DEW SOUTHERN 500

Time of Race: 3 hours, 28 minutes, 34 seconds
Average Speed: 137.932 mph
Margin of Victory: 1.51 seconds

FINISH	DRIVER	CAR
1	Mark Martin	Ford
2	Brett Bodine	Ford
3	Rusty Wallace	Pontiac
4	Dale Earnhardt	Chevrolet
5	Ernie Irvan	Ford
6	Ricky Rudd	Chevrolet
7	Harry Gant	Chevrolet
8	Morgan Shepherd	Ford
9	Ken Schrader	Chevrolet
10	Kenny Wallace	Pontiac
11	Wally Dallenbach	Ford
12	Dale Jarrett	Chevrolet
13	Michael Waltrip	Pontiac
14	Bobby Labonte	Ford
15	Jimmy Spencer	Ford
16	Kyle Petty	Pontiac
17	Derrike Cope	Ford
18	Bill Elliott	Ford
19	Bobby Hamilton	Ford
20	Geoff Bodine	Ford
21	Phil Parsons	Chevrolet
22	Jeff Gordon	Chevrolet
23	Jimmy Hensley	Ford
24	Bobby Hillin	Ford

Eddie Wood, part of the famous Wood Brothers Racing team and co-crew chief of the No. 21 car driven by Michael Waltrip.

3	Jeff Gordon	Chevrolet
4	Dale Jarrett	Chevrolet
5	Ted Musgrave	Ford
6	Rusty Wallace	Pontiac
7	Lake Speed	Ford
8	Bobby Labonte	Ford
9	Dale Earnhardt	Chevrolet
10	Bill Elliott	Ford
11	Bobby Hillin	Ford
12	Greg Sacks	Ford
13	Darrell Waltrip	Chevrolet
14	Brett Bodine	Ford
15	Jimmy Hensley	Ford
16	Michael Waltrip	Pontiac
17	Sterling Marlin	Ford
18	Kyle Petty	Pontiac
19	Phil Parsons	Chevrolet
20	Jimmy Spencer	Ford
21	Derrike Cope	Ford
22	Dave Marcis	Chevrolet
23	Kenny Wallace	Pontiac
24	Geoff Bodine	Ford
25	Jimmy Means	Ford
26	P. J. Jones	Ford
27	Ken Schrader	Chevrolet
28	Rick Wilson	Pontiac
29	Terry Labonte	Chevrolet
30	Harry Gant	Chevrolet
31	Wally Dallenbach	Ford
32	Ernie Irvan	Chevrolet
33	Rick Mast	Ford
34	Hut Stricklin	Ford
35	Ricky Rudd	Chevrolet
36	Jim Sauter	Ford
37	Joe Nemechek	Chevrolet

25	Greg Sacks	Ford
26	Jeff Purvis	Chevrolet
27	Todd Bodines	Ford
28	Darrell Waltrip	Chevrolet
29	Dave Marcis	Chevrolet
30	Rick Wilson	Pontiac
31	Sterling Marlin	Ford
32	Rick Mast	Ford
33	Terry Labonte	Chevrolet
34	Ted Musgrave	Ford
35	Mike Skinner	Ford
36	Hut Stricklin	Ford
37	H. B. Bailey	Pontiac
38	Brad Teague	Chevrolet
39	Jimmy Means	Ford

MILLER GENUINE DRAFT 400

Time of Race: 3 hours, 9 seconds
Average Speed: 99.917 mph
Margin of Victory: .57 second

FINISH	DRIVER	CAR
1	Rusty Wallace	Pontiac
2	Bill Elliott	Ford
3	Dale Earnhardt	Chevrolet
4	Ricky Rudd	Chevrolet
5	Brett Bodine	Ford
6	Mark Martin	Ford
7	Darrell Waltrip	Chevrolet
8	Terry Labonte	Chevrolet
9	Kyle Petty	Pontiac
10	Jeff Gordon	Chevrolet
11	Harry Gant	Chevrolet
12	Ken Schrader	Chevrolet
13	Bobby Labonte	Ford
14	Dale Jarrett	Chevrolet
15	Wally Dallenbach	Ford
16	Jeff Purvis	Chevrolet
17	Hut Stricklin	Ford
18	Rick Mast	Ford
19	Michael Waltrip	Pontiac
20	Phil Parsons	Chevrolet
21	Jimmy Hensley	Ford
22	Ted Musgrave	Ford
23	Dave Marcis	Chevrolet
24	Sterling Marlin	Ford
25	Dick Trickle	Chevrolet
26	Jimmy Means	Ford
27	Bobby Hillin	Ford
28	Derrike Cope	Ford
29	Rick Wilson	Pontiac
30	Morgan Shepherd	Ford
31	Greg Sacks	Ford
32	Kenny Wallace	Pontiac
33	Todd Bodine	Ford
34	Geoff Bodine	Ford
35	Jimmy Spencer	Ford
36	Ernie Irvan	Ford

SPLITFIRE SPARK PLUG 500

Time of Race: 4 hours, 59 minutes
Average Speed: 100.334 mph
Margin of Victory: .41 second

FINISH	DRIVER	CAR
1	Rusty Wallace	Pontiac
2	Ken Schrader	Chevrolet
3	Darrell Waltrip	Chevrolet
4	Dale Jarrett	Chevrolet
5	Harry Gant	Chevrolet
6	Jimmy Spencer	Ford
7	Bobby Labonte	Ford
8	Terry Labonte	Chevrolet
9	Morgan Shepherd	Ford
10	Bill Elliott	Ford
11	Sterling Marlin	Ford

12	Bobby Hillin	Ford
13	Jeff Purvis	Chevrolet
14	Kyle Petty	Pontiac
15	Wally Dallenbach	Ford
16	Kenny Wallace	Pontiac
17	Jimmy Means	Ford
18	Rick Mast	Ford
19	Dave Marcis	Chevrolet
20	Greg Sacks	Ford
21	Ricky Rudd	Chevrolet
22	Jimmy Horton	Chevrolet
23	Michael Waltrip	Pontiac
24	Jeff Gordon	Chevrolet
25	Dick Trickle	Ford
26	Ernie Irvan	Ford
27	Dale Earnhardt	Chevrolet
28	Ted Musgrave	Ford
29	Hut Stricklin	Ford
30	Geoff Bodine	Ford
31	Mark Martin	Ford
32	Derrike Cope	Ford
33	Lake Speed	Ford
34	Rick Wilson	Pontiac
35	Todd Bodine	Ford
36	Bob Schacht	Chevrolet
37	Phil Parsons	Chevrolet

GOODY'S 500

Time of Race: 3 hours, 32 minutes, 57 seconds
Average Speed: 74.101 mph
Margin of Victory: 2.77 seconds

FINISH	DRIVER	CAR
1	Ernie Irvan	Ford
2	Rusty Wallace	Pontiac
3	Jimmy Spencer	Ford
4	Ricky Rudd	Chevrolet
5	Dale Jarrett	Chevrolet
6	Brett Bodine	Ford
7	Terry Labonte	Chevrolet
8	Michael Waltrip	Pontiac
9	Morgan Shepherd	Ford
10	Kyle Petty	Pontiac
11	Jeff Gordon	Chevrolet
12	Bill Elliott	Ford
13	Ken Schrader	Chevrolet
14	Geoff Bodine	Ford
15	Kenny Wallace	Pontiac
16	Mark Martin	Ford
17	Jeff Purvis	Chevrolet
18	Darrell Waltrip	Chevrolet
19	Phil Parsons	Chevrolet
20	Derrike Cope	Ford
21	Dave Marcis	Chevrolet
22	Bobby Hillin	Ford
23	Hut Stricklin	Ford
24	Lake Speed	Ford
25	Todd Bodine	Ford
26	Rick Mast	Ford
27	Wally Dallenbach	Ford
28	Greg Sacks	Ford
29	Dale Earnhardt	Chevrolet
30	Sterling Marlin	Ford
31	Ted Musgrave	Ford
32	Bobby Labonte	Ford
33	Harry Gant	Chevrolet
34	Jimmy Hensley	Pontiac

TYSON HOLLY FARMS 400

Time of Race: 2 hours, 34 minutes, 46 seconds
Average Speed: 96.920 mph
Margin of Victory: 1.64 seconds

FINISH	DRIVER	CAR
1	Rusty Wallace	Pontiac
2	Dale Earnhardt	Chevrolet

3	Ernie Irvan	Ford
4	Kyle Petty	Pontiac
5	Ricky Rudd	Chevrolet
6	Harry Gant	Chevrolet
7	Terry Labonte	Chevrolet
8	Rick Mast	Ford
9	Dale Jarrett	Chevrolet
10	Ken Schrader	Chevrolet
11	Darrell Waltrip	Chevrolet
12	Bobby Labonte	Ford
13	Jimmy Spencer	Ford
14	Michael Waltrip	Pontiac
15	Wally Dallenbach	Ford
16	Mark Martin	Ford
17	Lake Speed	Ford
18	Bill Elliott	Ford
19	Sterling Marlin	Ford
20	Derrike Cope	Ford
21	Brett Bodine	Ford
22	Bobby Hillin	Ford
23	Todd Bodine	Ford
24	John Andretti	Chevrolet
25	Jeff Purvis	Chevrolet
26	Jay Hedgecock	Ford
27	Kenny Wallace	Pontiac
28	Hut Stricklin	Ford
29	Ted Musgrave	Ford
30	Dick Trickle	Chevrolet
31	Geoff Bodine	Ford
32	Morgan Shepherd	Ford
33	Rick Wilson	Pontiac
34	Jeff Gordon	Chevrolet

MELLO YELLO 500

Time of Race: 3 hours, 14 minutes, 31 seconds
Average Speed: 154.357 mph — Track Record (500 Miles)
Margin of Victory: 1.83 seconds

FINISH	DRIVER	CAR
1	Ernie Irvan	Ford
2	Mark Martin	Ford
3	Dale Earnhardt	Chevrolet
4	Rusty Wallace	Pontiac
5	Jeff Gordon	Chevrolet
6	Jimmy Spencer	Ford
7	Kyle Petty	Pontiac
8	Ricky Rudd	Chevrolet
9	Ken Schrader	Chevrolet
10	Bill Elliott	Ford
11	Lake Speed	Ford
12	Harry Gant	Chevrolet
13	Geoff Bodine	Ford
14	Morgan Shepherd	Ford
15	Brett Bodine	Ford
16	Terry Labonte	Chevrolet
17	Sterling Marlin	Ford
18	Rick Mast	Ford
19	Darrell Waltrip	Chevrolet
20	Bobby Hillin	Ford
21	Ted Musgrave	Ford
22	Dick Trickle	Chevrolet
23	Hut Stricklin	Ford
24	Wally Dallenbach	Ford
25	Joe Nemechek	Chevrolet
26	Dale Jarrett	Chevrolet
27	Michael Waltrip	Pontiac
28	Bobby Labonte	Ford
29	Jeremy Mayfield	Ford
30	Mike Wallace	Ford
31	John Andretti	Chevrolet
32	Greg Sacks	Ford
33	Chad Little	Ford
34	Jerry O'Neil	Chevrolet
35	Kenny Wallace	Pontiac
36	Rick Wilson	Pontiac
37	Bobby Hamilton	Ford
38	Jim Sauter	Ford
39	Derrike Cope	Ford
40	Rich Bickle	Ford
41	Andy Hillenburg	Chevrolet
42	Todd Bodine	Ford

AC-DELCO 500

Time of Race: 4 hours, 23 minutes, 16 seconds
Average Speed: 114.036 mph
Margin of Victory: 3.23 seconds

FINISH	DRIVER	CAR
1	Rusty Wallace	Pontiac
2	Dale Earnhardt	Chevrolet
3	Bill Elliott	Ford
4	Harry Gant	Chevrolet
5	Mark Martin	Ford
6	Ernie Irvan	Ford
7	Darrell Waltrip	Chevrolet
8	Ken Schrader	Chevrolet
9	Dick Trickle	Chevrolet
10	Geoff Bodine	Ford
11	Morgan Shepherd	Ford
12	Sterling Marlin	Ford
13	Kyle Petty	Pontiac
14	Ricky Rudd	Chevrolet
15	Terry Labonte	Chevrolet
16	Lake Speed	Ford
17	Rick Mast	Ford
18	Michael Waltrip	Pontiac
19	Derrike Cope	Ford
20	Jimmy Spencer	Ford
21	Jeff Gordon	Chevrolet
22	Bobby Labonte	Ford
23	Joe Nemechek	Chevrolet
24	Hut Stricklin	Ford
25	Todd Bodine	Ford
26	Rick Wilson	Pontiac
27	Dave Marcis	Chevrolet
28	Ted Musgrave	Ford
29	Jimmy Means	Ford
30	Dale Jarrett	Chevrolet
31	Wally Dallenbach	Ford
32	Greg Sacks	Ford
33	Bobby Hillin	Ford
34	Jimmy Horton	Chevrolet
35	Brett Bodine	Ford
36	Mike Wallace	Ford
37	Kenny Wallace	Pontiac
38	Jerry Hill	Chevrolet
39	John Andretti	Chevrolet
40	T. W. Taylor	Ford
41	Loy Allen	Ford

SLICK 50 500

Time of Race: 3 hours, 6 minutes, 30 seconds
Average Speed: 100.375 mph
Margin of Victory: .17 second

FINISH	DRIVER	CAR
1	Mark Martin	Ford
2	Ernie Irvan	Ford
3	Kyle Petty	Pontiac
4	Dale Earnhardt	Chevrolet
5	Bill Elliott	Ford
6	Ricky Rudd	Chevrolet
7	Darrell Waltrip	Chevrolet
8	Bobby Labonte	Ford
9	Michael Waltrip	Pontiac
10	Rick Mast	Ford
11	Morgan Shepherd	Ford
12	Harry Gant	Chevrolet
13	Lake Speed	Ford
14	Terry Labonte	Chevrolet
15	Ted Musgrave	Ford
16	Dale Jarrett	Chevrolet
17	Kenny Wallace	Pontiac
18	Bobby Hillin	Ford
19	Rusty Wallace	Pontiac

20	Rick Wilson	Pontiac
21	Rick Carelli	Chevrolet
22	Ron Hornaday	Chevrolet
23	Derrike Cope	Ford
24	Chuck Bown	Chevrolet
25	Todd Bodine	Ford
26	Loy Allen	Ford
27	Jimmy Spencer	Ford
28	Brett Bodine	Ford
29	Steve Grissom	Chevrolet
30	Sterling Marlin	Ford
31	Dick Trickle	Chevrolet
32	Jimmy Hensley	Chevrolet
33	Ken Schrader	Chevrolet
34	Wally Dallenbach	Ford
35	Jeff Gordon	Chevrolet
36	Hut Stricklin	Ford
37	Terry Fisher	Pontiac
38	Rich Woodland	Oldsmobile
39	Mike Chase	Chevrolet
40	John Andretti	Chevrolet
41	Wayne Jacks	Pontiac
42	Dirk Stephens	Ford
43	Geoff Bodine	Ford

HOOTERS 500

Time of Race: 3 hours, 59 minutes, 12 seconds
Average Speed: 125.221 mph
Margin of Victory: 5.66 seconds

FINISH	DRIVER	CAR
1	Rusty Wallace	Pontiac
2	Ricky Rudd	Chevrolet
3	Darrell Waltrip	Chevrolet
4	Bill Elliott	Ford
5	Dick Trickle	Chevrolet
6	Michael Waltrip	Pontiac
7	Dale Jarrett	Chevrolet
8	Ted Musgrave	Ford
9	Phil Parsons	Ford
10	Dale Earnhardt	Chevrolet
11	Kyle Petty	Pontiac
12	Ernie Irvan	Ford
13	Terry Labonte	Chevrolet
14	Bobby Labonte	Ford
15	Mike Wallace	Pontiac
16	Jimmy Spencer	Ford
17	Sterling Marlin	Ford
18	Dave Marcis	Chevrolet
19	Derrike Cope	Ford
20	Mark Martin	Ford
21	Bobby Hamilton	Ford
22	Hut Stricklin	Ford
23	Rick Wilson	Pontiac
24	Greg Sacks	Ford
25	Jimmy Hensley	Chevrolet
26	Lake Speed	Ford
27	Ken Schrader	Chevrolet
28	Harry Gant	Chevrolet
29	Loy Allen	Ford
30	Kenny Wallace	Pontiac
31	Jeff Gordon	Chevrolet
32	Morgan Shepherd	Ford
33	Wally Dallenbach	Ford
34	T. W. Taylor	Ford
35	Rick Carelli	Chevrolet
36	Rich Bickle	Ford
37	Rick Mast	Ford
38	Jimmy Horton	Chevrolet
39	Geoff Bodine	Ford
40	Brett Bodine	Ford
41	Bobby Hillin	Ford
42	Neil Bonnett	Chevrolet

1994

DAYTONA 500

Time of Race: 3 hours, 11 minutes, 10 seconds
Average Speed: 156.931 mph

FINISH	DRIVER	CAR
1	Sterling Marlin	Chevrolet
2	Ernie Irvan	Ford
3	Terry Labonte	Chevrolet
4	Jeff Gordon	Chevrolet
5	Morgan Shepherd	Ford
6	Greg Sacks	Ford
7	Dale Earnhardt	Chevrolet
8	Ricky Rudd	Ford
9	Bill Elliott	Ford
10	Ken Schrader	Chevrolet
11	Geoff Bodine	Ford
12	Bobby Hamilton	Pontiac
13	Mark Martin	Ford
14	Lake Speed	Ford
15	Jimmy Hensley	Ford
16	Bobby Labonte	Pontiac
17	Wally Dallenbach	Pontiac
18	Joe Ruttman	Ford
19	Jimmy Horton	Ford
20	Dick Trickle	Chevrolet
21	Derrike Cope	Ford
22	Loy Allen	Ford
23	Chuck Bown	Ford
24	Bobby Hillin	Ford
25	Dave Marcis	Chevrolet
26	Jeff Burton	Ford
27	Rick Mast	Ford
28	Darrell Waltrip	Chevrolet
29	Chad Little	Ford
30	Jeremy Mayfield	Ford
31	Michael Waltrip	Pontiac
32	Brett Bodine	Ford
33	Hut Stricklin	Ford
34	Harry Gant	Chevrolet
35	Dale Jarrett	Chevrolet
36	Todd Bodine	Ford
37	Jimmy Spencer	Ford
38	Ted Musgrave	Ford
39	Kyle Petty	Pontiac
40	Robert Pressley	Chevrolet
41	Rusty Wallace	Ford
42	John Andretti	Chevrolet

GOODWRENCH 500

Time of Race: 3 hours, 59 minutes, 43 seconds
Average Speed: 125.239 mph

FINISH	DRIVER	CAR
1	Rusty Wallace	Ford
2	Sterling Marlin	Chevrolet
3	Rick Mast	Ford
4	Mark Martin	Ford
5	Ernie Irvan	Ford
6	Brett Bodine	Ford
7	Dale Earnhardt	Chevrolet
8	Kyle Petty	Pontiac
9	Ken Schrader	Chevrolet
10	Michael Waltrip	Pontiac
11	Ricky Rudd	Ford
12	Jimmy Spencer	Ford
13	Ted Musgrave	Ford
14	Dick Trickle	Chevrolet
15	Geoff Bodine	Ford
16	Morgan Shepherd	Ford
17	Terry Labonte	Chevrolet
18	Dale Jarrett	Chevrolet

FINISH	DRIVER	CAR
19	Bobby Labonte	Pontiac
20	Jeff Burton	Ford
21	Lake Speed	Ford
22	Jimmy Hensley	Ford
23	Darrell Waltrip	Chevrolet
24	John Andretti	Chevrolet
25	Chuck Bown	Ford
26	Hut Stricklin	Ford
27	Wally Dallenbach	Pontiac
28	Greg Sacks	Ford
29	Derrike Cope	Ford
30	Steve Grissom	Chevrolet
31	Mike Skinner	Ford
32	Jeff Gordon	Chevrolet
33	Bobby Hillin	Ford
34	Todd Bodine	Ford
35	Dave Marcis	Chevrolet
36	Joe Nemechek	Chevrolet
37	Harry Gant	Chevrolet
38	Bobby Hamilton	Pontiac
39	Bill Elliott	Ford
40	Loy Allen	Ford
41	Rich Bickle	Ford
42	Billy Standridge	Ford

PONTIAC EXCITEMENT 400

Time of Race: 3 hours, 3 minutes, 3 seconds
Average Speed: 98.334 mph

FINISH	DRIVER	CAR
1	Ernie Irvan	Ford
2	Rusty Wallace	Ford
3	Jeff Gordon	Chevrolet
4	Dale Earnhardt	Chevrolet
5	Kyle Petty	Pontiac
6	Mark Martin	Ford
7	Rick Mast	Ford
8	Brett Bodine	Ford
9	Terry Labonte	Chevrolet
10	Dale Jarrett	Chevrolet
11	Ken Schrader	Chevrolet
12	Bill Elliott	Ford
13	Ted Musgrave	Ford
14	Lake Speed	Ford
15	Morgan Shepherd	Ford
16	Darrell Waltrip	Chevrolet
17	Chuck Bown	Ford
18	Ricky Rudd	Ford
19	Sterling Marlin	Chevrolet
20	Jeff Burton	Ford
21	Joe Nemechek	Chevrolet
22	Jimmy Spencer	Ford
23	Steve Grissom	Chevrolet
24	Bobby Labonte	Pontiac
25	Todd Bodine	Ford
26	Bobby Hillin	Ford
27	Jeremy Mayfield	Ford
28	Greg Sacks	Ford
29	Derrike Cope	Ford
30	John Andretti	Chevrolet
31	Michael Waltrip	Pontiac
32	Geoff Bodine	Ford
33	Bobby Hamilton	Pontiac
34	Harry Gant	Chevrolet
35	Ward Burton	Chevrolet
36	Jimmy Hensley	Ford
37	Dick Trickle	Chevrolet

PUROLATOR 500

Time of Race: 3 hours, 24 minutes, 58 seconds
Average Speed: 146.136 mph

FINISH	DRIVER	CAR
1	Ernie Irvan	Ford
2	Morgan Shepherd	Ford

FINISH	DRIVER	CAR
3	Darrell Waltrip	Chevrolet
4	Jeff Burton	Ford
5	Mark Martin	Ford
6	Lake Speed	Ford
7	Greg Sacks	Ford
8	Jeff Gordon	Chevrolet
9	Ricky Rudd	Ford
10	Jimmy Spencer	Ford
11	Ted Musgrave	Ford
12	Dale Earnhardt	Chevrolet
13	Kyle Petty	Pontiac
14	Terry Labonte	Chevrolet
15	Bobby Labonte	Pontiac
16	Ken Schrader	Chevrolet
17	Hut Stricklin	Ford
18	Joe Nemechek	Chevrolet
19	Bobby Hamilton	Pontiac
20	Steve Grissom	Chevrolet
21	Jeff Purvis	Chevrolet
22	Loy Allen	Ford
23	Michael Waltrip	Pontiac
24	Rusty Wallace	Ford
25	Sterling Marlin	Chevrolet
26	Rick Mast	Ford
27	Mike Wallace	Ford
28	Dick Trickle	Chevrolet
29	Jimmy Hensley	Ford
30	Harry Gant	Chevrolet
31	Brett Bodine	Ford
32	Bill Elliott	Ford
33	Todd Bodine	Ford
34	Derrike Cope	Ford
35	Dale Jarrett	Chevrolet
36	Dave Marcis	Chevrolet
37	Rich Bickle	Ford
38	Geoff Bodine	Ford
39	Curtis Markham	Ford
40	Ward Burton	Chevrolet
41	Chuck Bown	Ford
42	John Andretti	Chevrolet

TRANSOUTH FINANCIAL 400

Time of Race: 3 hours, 1 minutes, 20 seconds
Average Speed: 132.432 mph

FINISH	DRIVER	CAR
1	Dale Earnhardt	Chevrolet
2	Mark Martin	Ford
3	Bill Elliott	Ford
4	Dale Jarrett	Chevrolet
5	Lake Speed	Ford
6	Ernie Irvan	Ford
7	Ken Schrader	Chevrolet
8	Harry Gant	Chevrolet
9	Ricky Rudd	Ford
10	Ted Musgrave	Ford
11	Kyle Petty	Pontiac
12	Chuck Bown	Ford
13	Jimmy Hensley	Ford
14	Steve Grissom	Chevrolet
15	Michael Waltrip	Pontiac
16	Derrike Cope	Ford
17	Hut Stricklin	Ford
18	Mike Wallace	Ford
19	Joe Nemechek	Chevrolet
20	Jeff Burton	Ford
21	Ward Burton	Chevrolet
22	Todd Bodine	Ford
23	Rich Bickle	Ford
24	Brad Teague	Ford
25	Bobby Hamilton	Pontiac
26	Darrell Waltrip	Chevrolet
27	Jimmy Spencer	Ford
28	Dave Marcis	Chevrolet
29	Dick Trickle	Chevrolet
30	Greg Sacks	Ford
31	Jeff Gordon	Chevrolet
32	Morgan Shepherd	Ford
33	Rusty Wallace	Ford
34	Sterling Marlin	Chevrolet

35	Terry Labonte	Chevrolet
36	Brett Bodine	Ford
37	Rick Mast	Ford
38	John Andretti	Chevrolet
39	Bobby Labonte	Pontiac
40	Geoff Bodine	Ford
41	Wally Dallenbach	Pontiac

FOOD CITY 500

Time of Race: 2 hours, 58 minutes, 22 seconds
Average Speed: 89.647

FINISH	DRIVER	CAR
1	Dale Earnhardt	Chevrolet
2	Ken Schrader	Chevrolet
3	Lake Speed	Ford
4	Geoff Bodine	Ford
5	Michael Waltrip	Pontiac
6	Bobby Labonte	Pontiac
7	Rusty Wallace	Ford
8	Sterling Marlin	Chevrolet
9	Bobby Hamilton	Pontiac
10	Dave Marcis	Chevrolet
11	Greg Sacks	Ford
12	Steve Grissom	Chevrolet
13	Brett Bodine	Ford
14	Hut Stricklin	Ford
15	Darrell Waltrip	Chevrolet
16	Joe Nemechek	Chevrolet
17	Wally Dallenbach	Pontiac
18	Morgan Shepherd	Ford
19	Ted Musgrave	Ford
20	Kyle Petty	Pontiac
21	Mark Martin	Ford
22	Jeff Gordon	Chevrolet
23	Chuck Bown	Ford
24	Terry Labonte	Chevrolet
25	Ward Burton	Chevrolet
26	Todd Bodine	Ford
27	Derrike Cope	Ford
28	Mike Wallace	Ford
29	Rick Mast	Ford
30	Bill Elliott	Ford
31	Jeff Burton	Ford
32	Ricky Rudd	Ford
33	Ernie Irvan	Ford
34	Dick Trickle	Chevrolet
35	Jimmy Spencer	Ford
36	Dale Jarrett	Chevrolet
37	Harry Gant	Chevrolet

FIRST UNION 400

Time of Race: 2 hours, 36 minutes, 33 seconds
Average Speed: 95.816 mph

FINISH	DRIVER	CAR
1	Terry Labonte	Chevrolet
2	Rusty Wallace	Ford
3	Ernie Irvan	Ford
4	Kyle Petty	Pontiac
5	Dale Earnhardt	Chevrolet
6	Ricky Rudd	Ford
7	Geoff Bodine	Ford
8	Harry Gant	Chevrolet
9	Ken Schrader	Chevrolet
10	Rick Mast	Ford
11	Michael Waltrip	Pontiac
12	Lake Speed	Ford
13	Mark Martin	Ford
14	Bobby Hamilton	Pontiac
15	Jeff Gordon	Chevrolet
16	Wally Dallenbach	Pontiac
17	Sterling Marlin	Chevrolet

18	Bill Elliott	Ford
19	Todd Bodine	Ford
20	Hut Stricklin	Ford
21	Ted Musgrave	Ford
22	Morgan Shepherd	Ford
23	Brett Bodine	Ford
24	Dick Trickle	Chevrolet
25	Dale Jarrett	Chevrolet
26	Bobby Labonte	Pontiac
27	Derrike Cope	Ford
28	Darrell Waltrip	Chevrolet
29	Dave Marcis	Chevrolet
30	Jeremy Mayfield	Ford
31	John Andretti	Chevrolet
32	Jimmy Spencer	Ford
33	Jeff Burton	Ford
34	Greg Sacks	Ford
35	Chuck Bown	Ford
36	Jay Hedgecock	Ford

HANES 500

Time of Race: 3 hours, 25 minutes, 43 seconds
Average Speed: 76.700 mph

FINISH	DRIVER	CAR
1	Rusty Wallace	Ford
2	Ernie Irvan	Ford
3	Mark Martin	Ford
4	Darrell Waltrip	Chevrolet
5	Morgan Shepherd	Ford
6	Todd Bodine	Ford
7	Chuck Bown	Ford
8	Rick Mast	Ford
9	Bill Elliott	Ford
10	Ted Musgrave	Ford
11	Dale Earnhardt	Chevrolet
12	Ricky Rudd	Ford
13	Bobby Hamilton	Pontiac
14	Steve Grissom	Chevrolet
15	Terry Labonte	Chevrolet
16	Ward Burton	Chevrolet
17	Michael Waltrip	Pontiac
18	Jimmy Spencer	Ford
19	Bobby Labonte	Pontiac
20	Hut Stricklin	Ford
21	Dale Jarrett	Chevrolet
22	Joe Nemechek	Chevrolet
23	Jimmy Hensley	Ford
24	Brett Bodine	Ford
25	Jay Hedgecock	Ford
26	Kyle Petty	Pontiac
27	Sterling Marlin	Chevrolet
28	Derrike Cope	Ford
29	Greg Sacks	Ford
30	Lake Speed	Ford
31	Ken Schrader	Chevrolet
32	Dick Trickle	Chevrolet
33	Jeff Gordon	Chevrolet
34	Geoff Bodine	Ford
35	John Andretti	Chevrolet
36	Jeff Burton	Ford

WINSTON SELECT 500

Time of Race: 3 hours, 10 minutes, 32 seconds
Average Speed: 157.478 mph

FINISH	DRIVER	CAR
1	Dale Earnhardt	Chevrolet
2	Ernie Irvan	Ford

3	Michael Waltrip	Pontiac
4	Jimmy Spencer	Ford
5	Ken Schrader	Chevrolet
6	Greg Sacks	Ford
7	Lake Speed	Ford
8	Sterling Marlin	Chevrolet
9	Sterling Marlin	Chevrolet
10	Morgan Shepherd	Ford
11	Steve Grissom	Chevrolet
12	Ted Musgrave	Ford
13	Bobby Hamilton	Pontiac
14	Kyle Petty	Pontiac
15	Darrell Waltrip	Chevrolet
16	Dave Marcis	Chevrolet
17	Brett Bodine	Ford
18	Hut Stricklin	Ford
19	Bill Elliott	Ford
20	Rick Mast	Ford
21	Dale Jarrett	Chevrolet
22	Bobby Labonte	Pontiac
23	Harry Gant	Chevrolet
24	Jeff Gordon	Chevrolet
25	Ricky Rudd	Ford
26	Kirk Shelmerdine	Ford
27	Chuck Bown	Ford
28	Todd Bodine	Ford
29	John Andretti	Chevrolet
30	Jimmy Hensley	Ford
31	Derrike Cope	Ford
32	Terry Labonte	Chevrolet
33	Rusty Wallace	Ford
34	Wally Dallenbach	Pontiac
35	Jeff Purvis	Chevrolet
36	Dick Trickle	Chevrolet
37	Jeremy Mayfield	Inn Ford
38	Mark Martin	Ford
39	Jeff Burton	Ford
40	Loy Allen	Ford
41	Geoff Bodine	Ford
42	Joe Nemechek	Chevrolet

SAVE MART SUPERMARKETS 300

Time of Race: 2 hours, 24 minutes, 27 seconds
Average Speed: 77.458 mph

FINISH	DRIVER	CAR
1	Ernie Irvan	Ford
2	Geoff Bodine	Ford
3	Dale Earnhardt	Chevrolet
4	Wally Dallenbach	Pontiac
5	Rusty Wallace	Ford
6	Ted Musgrave	Ford
7	Morgan Shepherd	Ford
8	Mark Martin	Ford
9	Ken Schrader	Chevrolet
10	Harry Gant	Chevrolet
11	Kyle Petty	Pontiac
12	Dale Jarrett	Chevrolet
13	Brett Bodine	Ford
14	Ricky Rudd	Ford
15	Jeff Burton	Ford
16	Michael Waltrip	Pontiac
17	Bobby Labonte	Pontiac
18	Darrell Waltrip	Chevrolet
19	John Andretti	Chevrolet
20	Hut Stricklin	Ford
21	Chuck Bown	Ford
22	Joe Nemechek	Chevrolet
23	Mike Wallace	Ford
24	Greg Sacks	Ford
25	Dave Marcis	Chevrolet
26	Jimmy Spencer	Ford
27	Butch Gilliland	Chevrolet
28	Terry Labonte	Chevrolet
29	Sterling Marlin	Chevrolet
30	Bill Elliott	Ford
31	Mike Chase	Chevrolet
32	Lake Speed	Ford
33	Bobby Hamilton	Pontiac
34	Rick Mast	Ford

35	Steve Grissom	Chevrolet
36	Ward Burton	Chevrolet
37	Jeff Gordon	Chevrolet
38	Todd Bodine	Ford
39	Ron Hornaday	Chevrolet
40	Gary Collins	Ford
41	Rick Carelli	Chevrolet
42	John Krebs	Chevrolet
43	Derrike Cope	Ford

COCA-COLA 600

Time of Race: 4 hours, 18 minutes, 10 seconds
Average Speed: 139.445 mph

FINISH	DRIVER	CAR
1	Jeff Gordon	Chevrolet
2	Rusty Wallace	Ford
3	Geoff Bodine	Ford
4	Dale Jarrett	Chevrolet
5	Ernie Irvan	Ford
6	Ricky Rudd	Ford
7	Harry Gant	Chevrolet
8	Todd Bodine	Ford
9	Dale Earnhardt	Chevrolet
10	Michael Waltrip	Pontiac
11	Loy Allen	Ford
12	Hut Stricklin	Ford
13	Chuck Bown	Ford
14	Lake Speed	Ford
15	Sterling Marlin	Chevrolet
16	Ted Musgrave	Ford
17	Bobby Hamilton	Pontiac
18	Derrike Cope	Ford
19	Jimmy Spencer	Ford
20	Randy LaJoie	Ford
21	Jeremy Mayfield	. Ford
22	Bill Elliott	Ford
23	Mike Wallace	Ford
24	Ken Schrader	Chevrolet
25	Wally Dallenbach	Pontiac
26	Kyle Petty	Pontiac
27	Greg Sacks	Ford
28	Morgan Shepherd	Ford
29	Jeff Burton	Ford
30	Darrell Waltrip	Chevrolet
31	Rick Mast	Ford
32	Mark Martin	Ford
33	Joe Nemechek	Chevrolet
34	Rich Bickle	Ford
35	Terry Labonte	Chevrolet
36	John Andretti	Chevrolet
37	Ward Burton	Chevrolet
38	Dick Trickle	Chevrolet
39	Steve Grissom	Chevrolet
40	Bobby Labonte	Pontiac
41	Brad Teague	Ford
42	Brett Bodine	Ford
43	Billy Standridge	Ford

BUDWEISER 500

Time of Race: 4 hours, 52 minutes, 36 seconds
Average Speed: 102.529 mph

FINISH	DRIVER	CAR
1	Rusty Wallace	Ford
2	Ernie Irvan	Ford
3	Ken Schrader	Chevrolet
4	Mark Martin	Ford
5	Jeff Gordon	Chevrolet
6	Darrell Waltrip	Chevrolet

7	Michael Waltrip	Pontiac
8	Sterling Marlin	Chevrolet
9	Hut Stricklin	Ford
10	Wally Dallenbach	Pontiac
11	Kyle Petty	Pontiac
12	Lake Speed	Ford
13	Mike Wallace	Ford
14	Joe Nemechek	Chevrolet
15	Loy Allen	Ford
16	Todd Bodine	Ford
17	Jimmy Hensley	Ford
18	Dave Marcis	Chevrolet
19	Ricky Rudd	Ford
20	Bobby Labonte	Pontiac
21	Chuck Bown	Ford
22	John Andretti	Chevrolet
23	Derrike Cope	Ford
24	Greg Sacks	Ford
25	Morgan Shepherd	Ford
26	Terry Labonte	Chevrolet
27	Steve Grissom	Chevrolet
28	Dale Earnhardt	Chevrolet
29	Dale Jarrett	Chevrolet
30	Rick Mast	Ford
31	Bill Elliott	Ford
32	Brett Bodine	Ford
33	Jeff Burton	Ford
34	Bobby Hamilton	Pontiac
35	Ted Musgrave	Ford
36	Billy Standridge	Ford
37	Ward Burton	Chevrolet
38	Dick Trickle	Chevrolet
39	Jimmy Spencer	Ford
40	Brad Teague	Ford
41	Geoff Bodine	Ford
42	Harry Gant	Chevrolet

UAW-GM TEAMWORK 500

Time of Race: 3 hours, 52 minutes, 55 seconds
Average Speed: 128.801 mph

FINISH	DRIVER	CAR
1	Rusty Wallace	Ford
2	Dale Earnhardt	Chevrolet
3	Ken Schrader	Chevrolet
4	Morgan Shepherd	Ford
5	Mark Martin	Ford
6	Jeff Gordon	Chevrolet
7	Ernie Irvan	Ford
8	Brett Bodine	Ford
9	Rick Mast	Ford
10	Bill Elliott	Ford
11	Michael Waltrip	Pontiac
12	Kyle Petty	Pontiac
13	Hut Stricklin	Ford
14	Todd Bodine	Ford
15	Ted Musgrave	Ford
16	Harry Gant	Chevrolet
17	Wally Dallenbach	Pontiac
18	Terry Labonte	Chevrolet
19	Geoff Bodine	Ford
20	Dale Jarrett	Chevrolet
21	Ricky Rudd	Ford
22	Jeff Burton	Ford
23	Lake Speed	Ford
24	Greg Sacks	Ford
25	Bobby Labonte	Pontiac
26	Steve Grissom	Chevrolet
27	Bobby Hamilton	Pontiac
28	Rich Bickle	Ford
29	Jimmy Hensley	Ford
30	Darrell Waltrip	Chevrolet
31	Loy Allen	Ford
32	Joe Nemechek	Chevrolet
33	Dave Marcis	Chevrolet
34	Dick Trickle	Chevrolet
35	John Andretti	Chevrolet
36	Mike Wallace	Ford
37	Jimmy Spencer	Ford

38	Sterling Marlin	Chevrolet
39	Chuck Bown	Precision Rest. Serv. Ford
40	Derrike Cope	Ford
41	Bob Keselowski	Ford
42	Ward Burton	Chevrolet

MILLER GENUINE DRAFT 400

Time of Race: 3 hours, 11 minutes, 58 seconds
Average Speed: 125.022 mph

FINISH	DRIVER	CAR
1	Rusty Wallace	Ford
2	Dale Earnhardt	Chevrolet
3	Mark Martin	Ford
4	Ricky Rudd	Ford
5	Morgan Shepherd	Ford
6	Ken Schrader	Chevrolet
7	Joe Nemechek	Chevrolet
8	Michael Waltrip	Pontiac
9	Ted Musgrave	Ford
10	Darrell Waltrip	Chevrolet
11	Bill Elliott	Ford
12	Jeff Gordon	Chevrolet
13	Rick Mast	Ford
14	Dale Jarrett	Chevrolet
15	Bobby Labonte	Pontiac
16	Bobby Hillin	Ford
17	Kyle Petty	Pontiac
18	Ernie Irvan	Ford
19	Kenny Wallace	Ford
20	Terry Labonte	Chevrolet
21	Jeff Burton	Ford
22	Hut Stricklin	Ford
23	Jimmy Spencer	Ford
24	Loy Allen	Ford
25	Jeremy Mayfield	Ford
26	Steve Grissom	Chevrolet
27	Jeff Purvis	Chevrolet
28	Geoff Bodine	Ford
29	Ward Burton	Chevrolet
30	Rich Bickle	Ford
31	Todd Bodine	Ford
32	Brett Bodine	Ford
33	Greg Sacks Ford	
34	Sterling Marlin	Chevrolet
35	Harry Gant	Chevrolet
36	John Andretti	Chevrolet
37	Derrike Cope	Ford
38	Robby Gordon	Ford
39	Tim Steele	Ford
40	Lake Speed	Ford
41	Bobby Hamilton	Pontiac
42	Jimmy Hensley	Ford

PEPSI 400

Time of Race: 2 hours, 34 minutes, 17 seconds
Average Speed: 155.558 mph

FINISH	DRIVER	CAR
1	Jimmy Spencer	Ford
2	Ernie Irvan	Ford
3	Dale Earnhardt	Chevrolet
4	Mark Martin	Ford
5	Ken Schrader	Chevrolet
6	Geoff Bodine	Ford
7	Todd Bodine	Ford
8	Jeff Gordon	Chevrolet
9	Morgan Shepherd	Ford
10	Lake Speed	Ford
11	Dale Jarrett	Chevrolet
12	Mike Wallace	Ford
13	Michael Waltrip	Pontiac

14	Ted Musgrave	Ford
15	Terry Labonte	Chevrolet
16	Brett Bodine	Ford
17	Ricky Rudd	Ford
18	Jeff Burton	Ford
19	Bill Elliott	Ford
20	Rich Bickle	Ford
21	Dick Trickle	Chevrolet
22	Bobby Labonte	Pontiac
23	Derrike Cope	Ford
24	Bobby Hamilton	Pontiac
25	Darrell Waltrip	Chevrolet
26	Rusty Wallace	Ford
27	Dave Marcis	Chevrolet
28	Sterling Marlin	Chevrolet
29	Rick Mast	Ford
30	Jeremy Mayfield	Ford
31	Harry Gant	Chevrolet
32	Jimmy Hensley	Ford
33	Steve Grissom	Chevrolet
34	Kyle Petty	Pontiac
35	John Andretti	Chevrolet
36	Ward Burton	Chevrolet
37	Greg Sacks	Ford
38	Jeff Purvis	Chevrolet
39	Joe Nemechek	Chevrolet
40	Loy Allen	Ford
41	Ritchie Petty	Ford
42	Hut Stricklin	Ford
43	Tim Steele	Ford

SLICK 50 300

Time of Race: 3 hours, 37 minutes, 24 seconds
Average Speed: 87.599 mph

FINISH	DRIVER	CAR
1	Ricky Rudd	Ford
2	Dale Earnhardt	Chevrolet
3	Rusty Wallace	Ford
4	Mark Martin	Ford
5	Todd Bodine	Ford
6	Morgan Shepherd	Ford
7	Ted Musgrave	Ford
8	Kyle Petty	Pontiac
9	Rick Mast	Ford
10	Sterling Marlin	Chevrolet
11	Terry Labonte	Chevrolet
12	Brett Bodine	Ford
13	Bobby Labonte	Pontiac
14	Dale Jarrett	Chevrolet
15	Lake Speed	Ford
16	Bill Elliott	Ford
17	Harry Gant	Chevrolet
18	Dave Marcis	Chevrolet
19	Joe Nemechek	Chevrolet
20	Randy LaJoie	Ford
21	Rich Bickle	Ford
22	Mike McLaughlin	Chevrolet
23	Darrell Waltrip	Chevrolet
24	Ken Schrader	Chevrolet
25	Greg Sacks	Ford
26	Jeremy Mayfield	Ford
27	John Andretti	Chevrolet
28	Mike Wallace	Ford
29	Jimmy Hensley	Ford
30	Ernie Irvan	Ford
31	Geoff Bodine	Ford
32	Jimmy Spencer	Ford
33	Steve Grissom	Chevrolet
34	Dick Trickle	Chevrolet
35	Derrike Cope	Ford
36	Hut Stricklin	Ford
37	Michael Waltrip	Pontiac
38	Jeff Burton	Ford
39	Jeff Gordon	Chevrolet
40	Bobby Hamilton	Pontiac
41	Tim Steele	Ford
42	Ward Burton	Chevrolet

MILLER GENUINE DRAFT 500

Time of Race: 3 hours, 40 minutes, 28 seconds
Average Speed: 136.075 mph

FINISH	DRIVER	CAR
1	Geoff Bodine	Ford
2	Ward Burton	Chevrolet
3	Joe Nemechek	Chevrolet
4	Jeff Burton	Ford
5	Morgan Shepherd	Ford
6	Ricky Rudd	Ford
7	Dale Earnhardt	Chevrolet
8	Jeff Gordon	Chevrolet
9	Rusty Wallace	Ford
10	Dale Jarrett	Chevrolet
11	Todd Bodine	Ford
12	Sterling Marlin	Chevrolet
13	Bobby Labonte	Pontiac
14	Michael Waltrip	Pontiac
15	Terry Labonte	Chevrolet
16	Wally Dallenbach	Pontiac
17	Bill Elliott	Ford
18	Loy Allen	Ford
19	Derrike Cope	Ford
20	Lake Speed	Ford
21	Jeremy Mayfield	Ford
22	Hut Stricklin	Ford
23	Bobby Hamilton	Pontiac
24	Jimmy Spencer	Ford
25	John Andretti	Chevrolet
26	Dave Marcis	Chevrolet
27	Kyle Petty	Pontiac
28	Darrell Waltrip	Chevrolet
29	Steve Grissom	Chevrolet
30	Mike Wallace	Ford
31	Mark Martin	Ford
32	Ted Musgrave	Ford
33	Tim Steele	Ford
34	Rich Bickle	Ford
35	Brett Bodine	Ford
36	Greg Sacks	Ford
37	Ernie Irvan	Ford
38	Harry Gant	Chevrolet
39	Ken Schrader	Chevrolet
40	Rick Mast	Ford
41	Billy Standridge	Ford
42	Bob Schacht	Ford

DIEHARD 500

Time of Race: 3 hours, 3 minutes, 50 seconds
Average Speed: 163.217 mph

FINISH	DRIVER	CAR
1	Jimmy Spencer	Ford
2	Bill Elliott	Ford
3	Ernie Irvan	Ford
4	Ken Schrader	Chevrolet
5	Sterling Marlin	Chevrolet
6	Mark Martin	Ford
7	Ricky Rudd	Ford
8	Wally Dallenbach	Pontiac
9	Kenny Wallace	Ford
10	Terry Labonte	Chevrolet
11	Michael Waltrip	Pontiac
12	Bobby Labonte	Pontiac
13	Mike Wallace	Ford
14	Lake Speed	Ford
15	Morgan Shepherd	Ford
16	Todd Bodine	Ford
17	Brett Bodine	Ford
18	Steve Grissom	Chevrolet
19	Kyle Petty	Pontiac
20	Rick Mast	Ford
21	Harry Gant	Chevrolet
22	Bobby Hamilton	Pontiac
23	Bobby Hillin	Ford

THE END OF AN ERA

Richard Petty (who else, right?) made history when he won a 200-lap race at the half-mile State Fairgrounds Raceway in Raleigh on Sept. 30, 1970. It was the 42nd race of that season, the 989th major event in NASCAR history and the last dirt-track Cup race in NASCAR ever sanctioned.

Petty, driving his familiar No. 43 Plymouth, started sixth, and led one time for 112 laps to post the victory. It was the 15th win of the season and the 117th of his career.

As he was in most areas of NASCAR racing, Petty was one of the tour's best dirt-track racers. But the Petty listed No. 1 in the NASCAR record book under "most dirt-track wins" is Lee Petty, who got 43 of his 54 career victories on dirt tracks in the '50s and early '60s.

Today, Dave Marcis stands alone as the only active driver to run a Winston Cup dirt-track race. He's the only Cup driver to appreciate the irony of the popular bumper sticker that proclaims: "Dirt's For Racing, Asphalt's For Getting There."

24	Darrell Waltrip	Chevrolet
25	Hut Stricklin	Ford
26	Jeff Burton	Ford
27	Dave Marcis	Chevrolet
28	Brad Teague	Ford
29	Greg Sacks	Ford
30	Jimmy Hensley	Ford
31	Jeff Gordon	Chevrolet
32	Jeremy Mayfield	Ford
33	Geoff Bodine	Ford
34	Dale Earnhardt	Chevrolet
35	Joe Nemechek	Chevrolet
36	Jeff Purvis	Chevrolet
37	Loy Allen	Ford
38	Tim Steele	Ford
39	Dale Jarrett	Chevrolet
40	John Andretti	Chevrolet
41	Ted Musgrave	Ford
42	Rusty Wallace	Ford

BRICKYARD 400

Time of Race: 3 hours, 1 minute, 51 seconds
Average Speed: 131.977 mph

FINISH	DRIVER	CAR
1	Jeff Gordon	Chevrolet
2	Brett Bodine	Ford
3	Bill Elliott	Ford
4	Rusty Wallace	Ford
5	Dale Earnhardt	Chevrolet
6	Darrell Waltrip	Chevrolet
7	Ken Schrader	Chevrolet
8	Michael Waltrip	Pontiac
9	Todd Bodine	Ford
10	Morgan Shepherd	Ford
11	Ricky Rudd	Ford
12	Terry Labonte	Chevrolet
13	Ted Musgrave	Ford
14	Sterling Marlin	Chevrolet
15	Lake Speed	Ford
16	Bobby Labonte	Pontiac
17	Ernie Irvan	Ford
18	Greg Sacks	Ford
19	Jeff Burton	Ford
20	Joe Nemechek	Chevrolet
21	Bobby Hillin	Ford
22	Rick Mast	Ford
23	Wally Dallenbach	Pontiac
24	Bobby Hamilton	Pontiac
25	Kyle Petty	Pontiac
26	Jeremy Mayfield	Ford
27	Derrike Cope	Ford
28	John Andretti	Chevrolet
29	Rich Bickle	Ford

30	A.J. Foyt	Ford
31	Ward Burton	Chevrolet
32	Jimmy Hensley	Ford
33	Danny Sullivan	Chevrolet
34	Jeff Purvis	Chevrolet
35	Mark Martin	Ford
36	Hut Stricklin	Ford
37	Harry Gant	Chevrolet
38	Geoff Brabham	Ford
39	Geoff Bodine	Ford
40	Dale Jarrett	Chevrolet
41	Dave Marcis	Chevrolet
42	Mike Chase	Chevrolet
43	Jimmy Spencer	Ford

THE BUD AT THE GLEN

Time of Race: 2 hours, 21 minutes, 7 seconds
Average Speed: 93.752 mph

FINISH	DRIVER	CAR
1	Mark Martin	Ford
2	Ernie Irvan	Ford
3	Dale Earnhardt	Chevrolet
4	Ken Schrader	Chevrolet
5	Ricky Rudd	Ford
6	Terry Labonte	Chevrolet
7	Darrell Waltrip	Chevrolet
8	Joe Nemechek	Chevrolet
9	Jeff Gordon	Chevrolet
10	Harry Gant	Chevrolet
11	Dale Jarrett	Chevrolet
12	Bill Elliott	Ford
13	Lake Speed	Ford
14	Wally Dallenbach	Pontiac
15	Todd Bodine	Ford
16	Morgan Shepherd	Ford
17	Rusty Wallace	Ford
18	Bobby Labonte	Pontiac
19	Ted Musgrave	Ford
20	Michael Waltrip	Pontiac
21	Dave Marcis	Chevrolet
22	Tom Kendall	Ford
23	Steve Grissom	Chevrolet
24	Ward Burton	Chevrolet
25	Jeff Burton	Ford
26	Sterling Marlin	Chevrolet
27	Mike McLaughlin	Chevrolet
28	Brett Bodine	Ford
29	Geoff Bodine	Ford
30	Hut Stricklin	Ford
31	Butch Leitzinger	Chevrolet
32	Dick Trickle	Chevrolet
33	Jimmy Hensley	Ford
34	Bobby Hamilton	Pontiac

FINISH	DRIVER	CAR
35	P.J. Jones	Ford
36	Scott Lagasse	Chevrolet
37	Kyle Petty	Pontiac
38	Rick Mast	Ford
39	Greg Sacks	Ford
40	Derrike Cope	Ford

GM GOODWRENCH DEALER 400

Time of Race: 2 hours, 51 minutes, 32 seconds
Average Speed: 139.914 mph

FINISH	DRIVER	CAR
1	Geoff Bodine	Ford
2	Mark Martin	Ford
3	Rick Mast	Ford
4	Rusty Wallace	Ford
5	Bobby Labonte	Pontiac
6	Kyle Petty	Pontiac
7	Bill Elliott	Ford
8	Terry Labonte	Chevrolet
9	Darrell Waltrip	Chevrolet
10	Ricky Rudd	Ford
11	Ken Schrader	Chevrolet
12	Brett Bodine	Ford
13	Lake Speed	Ford
14	Michael Waltrip	Pontiac
15	Jeff Gordon	Chevrolet
16	Mike Wallace	Ford
17	John Andretti	Pontiac
18	Derrike Cope	Ford
19	Steve Grissom	Chevrolet
20	Jimmy Spencer	Ford
21	Joe Nemechek	Chevrolet
22	Loy Allen	Ford
23	Jeremy Mayfield	Ford
24	Ted Musgrave	Ford
25	Harry Gant	Chevrolet
26	Morgan Shepherd	Ford
27	Rick Carelli	Chevrolet
28	Jeff Purvis	Ford
29	Ward Burton	Chevrolet
30	Dale Jarrett	Chevrolet
31	Phil Parsons	Ford
32	Greg Sacks	Ford
33	Jeff Burton	Ford
34	Sterling Marlin	Chevrolet
35	Rich Bickle	Ford
36	Dave Marcis	Chevrolet
37	Dale Earnhardt	Chevrolet
38	Todd Bodine	Ford
39	Billy Standridge	Ford
40	Bobby Hillin	Ford
41	Dick Trickle	Chevrolet

GOODY'S 500

Time of Race: 2 hours, 55 minutes, 1 seconds
Average Speed: 91.363 mph

FINISH	DRIVER	CAR
1	Rusty Wallace	Ford
2	Mark Martin	Ford
3	Dale Earnhardt	Chevrolet
4	Darrell Waltrip	Chevrolet
5	Bill Elliott	Ford
6	Sterling Marlin	Chevrolet
7	Michael Waltrip	Pontiac
8	Todd Bodine	Ford
9	Harry Gant	Chevrolet
10	Rick Mast	Ford
11	Ted Musgrave	Ford
12	Ricky Rudd	Ford
13	Kenny Wallace	Ford
14	Brett Bodine	Ford
15	Kyle Petty	Pontiac
16	Derrike Cope	Ford
17	Dick Trickle	Chevrolet

FINISH	DRIVER	CAR
18	Morgan Shepherd	Ford
19	Ken Schrader	Chevrolet
20	Jeff Burton	Ford
21	Jeremy Mayfield	Ford
22	Brad Teague	Ford
23	Geoff Bodine	Ford
24	Mike Wallace	Ford
25	Lake Speed	Ford
26	Dale Jarrett	Chevrolet
27	Greg Sacks	Ford
28	Bobby Hamilton	Pontiac
29	Joe Nemechek	Chevrolet
30	John Andretti	Pontiac
31	Bobby Labonte	Pontiac
32	Jeff Gordon	Chevrolet
33	Terry Labonte	Chevrolet
34	Steve Grissom	Chevrolet
35	Hut Stricklin	Ford
36	Ward Burton	Chevrolet

MOUNTAIN DEW SOUTHERN 500

Time of Race: 3 hours, 55 minutes, 5 seconds
Average Speed: 127.952 mph

FINISH	DRIVER	CAR
1	Bill Elliott	Ford
2	Dale Earnhardt	Chevrolet
3	Morgan Shepherd	Ford
4	Ricky Rudd	Ford
5	Sterling Marlin	Chevrolet
6	Jeff Gordon	Chevrolet
7	Rusty Wallace	Ford
8	Jeff Burton	Ford
9	Dale Jarrett	Chevrolet
10	Terry Labonte	Chevrolet
11	Kenny Wallace	Ford
12	Kyle Petty	Pontiac
13	Darrell Waltrip	Chevrolet
14	Hut Stricklin	Ford
15	Phil Parsons	Ford
16	John Andretti	Pontiac
17	Mike Wallace	Ford
18	Butch Miller	Ford
19	Greg Sacks	Ford
20	Rick Mast	Ford
21	Loy Allen	Ford
22	Bobby Hamilton	Pontiac
23	Steve Grissom	Chevrolet
24	Billy Standridge	Ford
25	Mark Martin	Ford
26	Todd Bodine	Ford
27	Geoff Bodine	Ford
28	Dave Marcis	Chevrolet
29	Brett Bodine	Ford
30	Brad Teague	Ford
31	Michael Waltrip	Pontiac
32	Ken Schrader	Chevrolet
33	Jeremy Mayfield	Ford
34	Ward Burton	Chevrolet
35	Derrike Cope	Ford
36	Bobby Labonte	Pontiac
37	Jimmy Spencer	Ford
38	Dick Trickle	Chevrolet
39	Ted Musgrave	Ford
40	Lake Speed	Ford
41	Harry Gant	Chevrolet
42	Joe Nemechek	Chevrolet

MILLER GENUINE DRAFT 400

Time of Race: 2 hours, 52 minutes, 59 seconds
Average Speed: 104.156 mph

FINISH	DRIVER	CAR
1	Terry Labonte	Chevrolet
2	Jeff Gordon	Chevrolet
3	Dale Earnhardt	Chevrolet

FINISH	DRIVER	CAR
4	Rusty Wallace	Ford
5	Ricky Rudd	Ford
6	Mark Martin	Ford
7	Steve Grissom	Chevrolet
8	Brett Bodine	Ford
9	Ken Schrader	Chevrolet
10	Darrell Waltrip	Chevrolet
11	John Andretti	Pontiac
12	Dick Trickle	Chevrolet
13	Sterling Marlin	Chevrolet
14	Morgan Shepherd	Chevrolet
15	Bill Elliott	Ford
16	Dale Jarrett	Chevrolet
17	Ted Musgrave	Ford
18	Geoff Bodine	Ford
19	Derrike Cope	Ford
20	Todd Bodine	Ford
21	Lake Speed	Ford
22	Harry Gant	Chevrolet
23	Mike Wallace	Ford
24	Bobby Labonte	Pontiac
25	Ward Burton	Chevrolet
26	Michael Waltrip	Pontiac
27	Greg Sacks	Ford
28	Joe Nemechek	Chevrolet
29	Dave Marcis	Chevrolet
30	Hut Stricklin	Ford
31	Loy Allen	Ford
32	Kenny Wallace	Ford
33	Rick Mast	Ford
34	Bobby Hamilton	Pontiac
35	Jimmy Spencer	Ford
36	Jeff Green	Ford
37	Jeremy Mayfield	Ford
38	Kyle Petty	Pontiac

SPLITFIRE SPARK PLUG 500

Time of Race: 4 hours, 26 minutes, 32 seconds
Average Speed: 112.556 mph

FINISH	DRIVER	CAR
1	Rusty Wallace	Ford
2	Dale Earnhardt	Chevrolet
3	Darrell Waltrip	Chevrolet
4	Ken Schrader	Chevrolet
5	Geoff Bodine	Ford
6	Kyle Petty	Pontiac
7	Terry Labonte	Chevrolet
8	Steve Grissom	Chevrolet
9	Lake Speed	Ford
10	Morgan Shepherd	Ford
11	Jeff Gordon	Chevrolet
12	Derrike Cope	Ford
13	Harry Gant	Chevrolet
14	Ted Musgrave	Ford
15	Rick Mast	Ford
16	Todd Bodine	Ford
17	Bobby Labonte	Pontiac
18	Ricky Rudd	Ford
19	Mark Martin	Ford
20	Kenny Wallace	Ford
21	Dick Trickle	Chevrolet
22	Loy Allen	Ford
23	Tim Fedewa	Ford
24	Jeremy Mayfield	Ford
25	John Andretti	Pontiac
26	Brett Bodine	Ford
27	Ward Burton	Chevrolet
28	Bill Elliott	Ford
29	Mike Wallace	Ford
30	Sterling Marlin	Chevrolet
31	Bobby Hamilton	Pontiac
32	Hut Stricklin	Ford
33	Michael Waltrip	Pontiac
34	Dale Jarrett	Chevrolet
35	Dave Marcis	Chevrolet
36	Joe Nemechek	Chevrolet
37	Jeff Burton	Ford
38	Greg Sacks	Ford
39	Jimmy Spencer	Ford
40	Brad Teague	Ford

GOODY'S 500

Time of Race: 3 hours, 24 minutes, 34 seconds
Average Speed: 77.139 mph

FINISH	DRIVER	CAR
1	Rusty Wallace	Ford
2	Dale Earnhardt	Chevrolet
3	Bill Elliott	Ford
4	Kenny Wallace	Ford
5	Dale Jarrett	Chevrolet
6	Ken Schrader	Chevrolet
7	Sterling Marlin	Chevrolet
8	Harry Gant	Chevrolet
9	Ted Musgrave	Ford
10	Darrell Waltrip	Chevrolet
11	Jeff Gordon	Chevrolet
12	Steve Grissom	Chevrolet
13	Bobby Hamilton	Pontiac
14	Terry Labonte	Chevrolet
15	Morgan Shepherd	Ford
16	Mark Martin	Ford
17	Derrike Cope	Ford
18	Geoff Bodine	Ford
19	Michael Waltrip	Pontiac
20	Jimmy Spencer	Ford
21	John Andretti	Pontiac
22	Joe Nemechek	Chevrolet
23	Hut Stricklin	Ford
24	Kyle Petty	Pontiac
25	Ricky Rudd	Ford
26	Greg Sacks	Ford
27	Brad Teague	Ford
28	Mike Wallace	Ford
29	Rick Mast	Ford
30	Brett Bodine	Ford
31	Bobby Labonte	Pontiac
32	Dick Trickle	Ford
33	Todd Bodine	Ford
34	Lake Speed	Ford
35	Ward Burton	Chevrolet
36	Jeff Burton	Ford

TYSON HOLLY FARMS 400

Time of Race: 2 hours, 32 minutes, 15 seconds
Average Speed: 98.522 mph

FINISH	DRIVER	CAR
1	Geoff Bodine	Ford
2	Terry Labonte	Chevrolet
3	Rick Mast	Ford
4	Rusty Wallace	Ford
5	Mark Martin	Ford
6	Bill Elliott	Ford
7	Dale Earnhardt	Chevrolet
8	Jeff Gordon	Chevrolet
9	Ted Musgrave	Ford
10	Kenny Wallace	Ford
11	Ricky Rudd	Ford
12	Bobby Hamilton	Pontiac
13	Darrell Waltrip	Chevrolet
14	Ken Schrader	Chevrolet
15	Bobby Labonte	Pontiac
16	Dick Trickle	Chevrolet
17	John Andretti	Pontiac
18	Ward Burton	Chevrolet
19	Derrike Cope	Ford
20	Steve Grissom	Chevrolet
21	Michael Waltrip	Pontiac
22	Hut Stricklin	Ford
23	Jimmy Spencer	Ford
24	Dave Marcis	Chevrolet
25	Lake Speed	Ford
26	Kyle Petty	Pontiac
27	Jeremy Mayfield	Ford
28	Jeff Burton	Ford
29	Jeff Green	Ford

FINISH	DRIVER	CAR
30	Morgan Shepherd	Ford
31	Sterling Marlin	Chevrolet
32	Harry Gant	Chevrolet
33	Brett Bodine	Ford
34	Joe Nemechek	Chevrolet
35	Greg Sacks	Ford
36	Phil Parsons	Ford

MELLO YELLO 500

Time of Race: 3 hours, 26 minutes, 0 seconds
Average Speed: 145.922 mph

FINISH	DRIVER	CAR
1	Dale Jarrett	Chevrolet
2	Morgan Shepherd	Ford
3	Dale Earnhardt	Chevrolet
4	Ken Schrader	Chevrolet
5	Lake Speed	Ford
6	Brett Bodine	Ford
7	Terry Labonte	Chevrolet
8	Derrike Cope	Ford
9	Darrell Waltrip	Chevrolet
10	Michael Waltrip	Pontiac
11	Joe Nemechek	Chevrolet
12	Rick Mast	Ford
13	Dick Trickle	Chevrolet
14	Kenny Wallace	Ford
15	Bobby Hillin	Ford
16	Jimmy Spencer	Ford
17	Mike Wallace	Ford
18	Ted Musgrave	Ford
19	Bobby Hamilton	Pontiac
20	Jeremy Mayfield	Ford
21	Hut Stricklin	Ford
22	Harry Gant	Chevrolet
23	Joe Ruttman	Ford
24	John Andretti	Pontiac
25	Jeff Burton	Ford
26	Steve Grissom	Chevrolet
27	Loy Allen	Ford
28	Jeff Gordon	Chevrolet
29	Ricky Rudd	Ford
30	Kyle Petty	Pontiac
31	Robert Pressley	Chevrolet
32	Geoff Bodine	Ford
33	Bill Elliott	Ford
34	Billy Standridge	Ford
35	Greg Sacks	Ford
36	Sterling Marlin	Chevrolet
37	Rusty Wallace	Ford
38	Todd Bodine	Ford
39	Mark Martin	Ford
40	Jimmy Hensley	Ford
41	Ward Burton	Chevrolet
42	Bobby Labonte	Pontiac

AC DELCO 500

Time of Race: 3 hours, 57 minutes, 30 seconds
Average Speed: 126.408 mph

FINISH	DRIVER	CAR
1	Dale Earnhardt	Chevrolet
2	Rick Mast	Ford
3	Morgan Shepherd	Ford
4	Ricky Rudd	Ford
5	Terry Labonte	Chevrolet
6	Bill Elliott	Ford
7	Mark Martin	Ford
8	Dick Trickle	Chevrolet
9	Ward Burton	Chevrolet
10	Lake Speed	Ford
11	Jeff Burton	Ford
12	Dale Jarrett	Chevrolet

FINISH	DRIVER	CAR
13	Ted Musgrave	Ford
14	Sterling Marlin	Chevrolet
15	Kenny Wallace	Ford
16	Mike Wallace	Ford
17	Joe Nemechek	Chevrolet
18	Brett Bodine	Ford
19	Jeremy Mayfield	Ford
20	Butch Miller	Ford
21	Todd Bodine	Ford
22	Rick Carelli	Chevrolet
23	Darrell Waltrip	Chevrolet
24	Randy McDonald	Chevrolet
25	John Andretti	Pontiac
26	Michael Waltrip	Pontiac
27	Hut Stricklin	Ford
28	Bobby Labonte	Pontiac
29	Jeff Gordon	Chevrolet
30	Steve Grissom	Chevrolet
31	Harry Gant	Chevrolet
32	Ken Schrader	Chevrolet
33	Bobby Hamilton	Pontiac
34	Dave Marcis	Chevrolet
35	Rusty Wallace	Ford
36	Kyle Petty	Pontiac
37	Derrike Cope	Ford
38	Jimmy Spencer	Ford
39	Greg Sacks	Ford
40	Geoff Bodine	Ford
41	Billy Standridge	Ford
42	Loy Allen	Ford

SLICK 50 500

Time of Race: 2 hours, 54 minutes, 12 seconds
Average Speed: 107.463 mph

FINISH	DRIVER	CAR
1	Terry Labonte	Chevrolet
2	Mark Martin	Ford
3	Sterling Marlin	Chevrolet
4	Jeff Gordon	Chevrolet
5	Ted Musgrave	Ford
6	Kyle Petty	Pontiac
7	Ricky Rudd	Ford
8	Geoff Bodine	Ford
9	Dale Jarrett	Chevrolet
10	Darrell Waltrip	Chevrolet
11	Bobby Hamilton	Pontiac
12	Morgan Shepherd	Ford
13	Brett Bodine	Ford
14	Lake Speed	Ford
15	Ken Schrader	Chevrolet
16	Bobby Labonte	Pontiac
17	Rusty Wallace	Ford
18	Kenny Wallace	Ford
19	Dave Marcis	Chevrolet
20	Jeremy Mayfield	Ford
21	Ward Burton	Chevrolet
22	Steve Grissom	Chevrolet
23	Harry Gant	Chevrolet
24	Hut Stricklin	Ford
25	Joe Nemechek	Chevrolet
26	Greg Sacks	Ford
27	Jeff Burton	Ford
28	Mike Wallace	Ford
29	PontiacJ. Jones	Ford
30	Derrike Cope	Ford
31	Mike Chase	Chevrolet
32	Todd Bodine	Ford
33	Rick Carelli	Chevrolet
34	Ron Hornaday, Jr.	Chevrolet
35	Bill Elliott	Ford
36	Michael Waltrip	Pontiac
37	Rich Bickle	Chevrolet
38	Jimmy Spencer	Ford
39	Dick Trickle	Chevrolet
40	Dale Earnhardt	Chevrolet
41	Loy Allen	Ford
42	Rick Mast	Ford
43	John Andretti	Pontiac

HOOTERS 500

Time of Race: 3 hours, 21 minutes, 3 seconds
Average Speed: 148.982 mph

FINISH	DRIVER	CAR
1	Mark Martin	Ford
2	Dale Earnhardt	Chevrolet
3	Todd Bodine	Ford
4	Lake Speed	Ford
5	Mike Wallace	Ford
6	Morgan Shepherd	Ford
7	Derrike Cope	Ford
8	Terry Labonte	Chevrolet
9	Dale Jarrett	Chevrolet
10	Michael Waltrip	Pontiac
11	Ken Schrader	Chevrolet
12	Jimmy Hensley	Ford
13	John Andretti	Pontiac
14	Ricky Rudd	Ford
15	Jeff Gordon	Chevrolet
16	Hut Stricklin	Ford
17	Pancho Carter	Ford
18	Jeff Green	Ford
19	Randy LaJoie	Ford
20	Jimmy Spencer	Ford
21	Darrell Waltrip	Chevrolet
22	Kyle Petty	Pontiac
23	Joe Nemechek	Chevrolet
24	Bobby Hamilton	Pontiac
25	Kenny Wallace	Ford
26	Steve Grissom	Chevrolet
27	Rick Mast	Ford
28	Ted Musgrave	Ford
29	Ken Bouchard	Ford
30	Gary Bradberry	Ford
31	Jeff Burton	Ford
32	Rusty Wallace	Ford
33	Harry Gant	Chevrolet
34	Geoff Bodine	Ford
35	Robert Pressley	Chevrolet
36	Brett Bodine	Ford
37	Bobby Labonte	Pontiac
38	Bill Elliott	Ford
39	Greg Sacks	Ford
40	Sterling Marlin	Chevrolet
41	Ward Burton	Chevrolet
42	Loy Allen	Ford
43	Bobby Hillin	Ford

1995

DAYTONA 500

Time of Race: 3 hours, 31 minutes, 42 seconds
Average Speed: 141.710 mph
Margin of Victory: .61 second

FINISH	DRIVER	CAR
1	Sterling Marlin	Chevrolet
2	Dale Earnhart	Chevrolet
3	Mark Martin	Ford
4	Ted Musgrave	Ford
5	Dale Jarrett	Ford
6	Michael Waltrip	Pontiac
7	Steve Grissom	Chevrolet
8	Terry Labonte	Chevrolet
9	Ken Schrader	Chevrolet
10	Morgan Shepherd	Ford
11	Dick Trickle	Ford
12	Kyle Petty	Pontiac

FINISH	DRIVER	CAR
13	Ricky Rudd	Ford
14	Lake Speed	Ford
15	Ward Burton	Chevrolet
16	Ricky Craven	Chevrolet
17	Loy Allen	Ford
18	Bobby Hamilton	Pontiac
19	Joe Ruttman	Ford
20	Geoff Bodine	Ford
21	Rick Mast	Ford
22	Jeff Gordon	Chevrolet
23	Bill Elliott	Ford
24	Jeff Burton	Ford
25	Brett Bodine	Ford
26	Robert Pressley	Chevrolet
27	John Andretti	Ford
28	Ben Hess	Ford
29	Randy LaJoie	Pontiac
30	Bobby Labonte	Chevrolet
31	Derrike Cope	Ford
32	Darrell Waltrip	Chevrolet
33	Davy Jones	Ford
34	Rusty Wallace	Ford
35	Jeremy Mayfield	Ford
36	Dave Marcis	Chevrolet
37	Todd Bodine	Ford
38	Jeff Purvis	Chevrolet
39	Mike Wallace	Ford
40	Steve Kinser	Ford
41	Phil Parsons	Ford
42	Joe Nemechek	Chevrolet

GOODWRENCH 500

Time of Race: 3 hours, 59 minutes, 15 seconds
Average Speed: 125.305 mph
Margin of Victory: 1.19 seconds

FINISH	DRIVER	CAR
1	Jeff Gordon	Chevrolet
2	Bobby Labonte	Chevrolet
3	Dale Earnhardt	Chevrolet
4	Ricky Rudd	Ford
5	Dale Jarrett	Ford
6	Steve Grissom	Chevrolet
7	Mark Martin	Ford
8	Derrike Cope	Ford
9	Ward Burton	Chevrolet
10	Kyle Petty	Pontiac
11	Bill Elliott	Ford
12	Sterling Marlin	Chevrolet
13	John Andretti	Ford
14	Brett Bodine	Ford
15	Mike Wallace	Ford
16	Ricky Craven	Chevrolet
17	Michael Waltrip	Pontiac
18	Jeremy Mayfield	Ford
19	Jeff Burton	Ford
20	Kenny Wallace	Ford
21	Geoff Bodine	Ford
22	Dick Trickle	Ford
23	Dave Marcis	Chevrolet
24	Rusty Wallace	Ford
25	Randy LaJoie	Pontiac
26	Terry Labonte	Chevrolet
27	Steve Kinser	Ford
28	Loy Allen	Ford
29	Joe Nemechek	Chevrolet
30	Jimmy Spencer	Ford
31	Todd Bodine	Ford
32	Lake Speed	Ford
33	Ted Musgrave	Ford
34	Morgan Shepherd	Ford
35	Rick Mast	Ford
36	Bobby Hamilton	Pontiac
37	Davy Jones	Ford
38	Darrell Waltrip	Chevrolet
39	Ken Schrader	Chevrolet
40	Jimmy Hensley	Chevrolet
41	Greg Sacks	Pontiac
42	Robert Pressley	Chevrolet

PONTIAC EXCITEMENT 400

Time of Race: 2 hours, 49 minutes, 8 seconds
Average Speed: 106.425 mph
Margin of Victory: 1.25 seconds

FINISH	DRIVER	CAR
1	Terry Labonte	Chevrolet
2	Dale Earnhardt	Chevrolet
3	Rusty Wallace	Ford
4	Ken Schrader	Chevrolet
5	Sterling Marlin	Chevrolet
6	Derrike Cope	Ford
7	Darrell Waltrip	Chevrolet
8	Mark Martin	Ford
9	Bobby Hamilton	Pontiac
10	John Andretti	Ford
11	Geoff Bodine	Ford
12	Dick Trickle	Ford
13	Ted Musgrave	Ford
14	Lake Speed	Ford
15	Morgan Shepherd	Ford
16	Bill Elliott	Ford
17	Jeremy Mayfield	Ford
18	Brett Bodine	Ford
19	Greg Sacks	Pontiac
20	Dave Marcis	Chevrolet
21	Ricky Rudd	Ford
22	Ward Burton	Chevrolet
23	Michael Waltrip	Pontiac
24	Jimmy Spencer	Ford
25	Dale Jarrett	Ford
26	Mike Wallace	Ford
27	Randy LaJoie	Pontiac
28	Steve Kinser	Ford
29	Loy Allen	Ford
30	Bobby Labonte	Chevrolet
31	Jeff Burton	Ford
32	Joe Nemechek	Chevrolet
33	Kyle Petty	Pontiac
34	Rick Mast	Ford
35	Robert Pressley	Chevrolet
36	Jeff Gordon	Chevrolet
37	Todd Bodine	Ford
38	Ricky Craven	Chevrolet

PUROLATOR 500

Time of Race: 3 hours, 19 minutes, 32 seconds
Average Speed: 150.115 mph
Margin of Victory: .19 second

FINISH	DRIVER	CAR
1	Jeff Gordon	Chevrolet
2	Bobby Labonte	Chevrolet
3	Terry Labonte	Chevrolet
4	Dale Earnhardt	Chevrolet
5	Dale Jarrett	Ford
6	Morgan Shepherd	Ford
7	Sterling Marlin	Chevrolet
8	Ricky Rudd	Ford
9	Mark Martin	Ford
10	Rusty Wallace	Ford
11	Rick Mast	Ford
12	Ricky Craven	Chevrolet
13	Derrike Cope	Ford
14	Kyle Petty	Pontiac
15	Lake Speed	Ford
16	Joe Nemechek	Chevrolet
17	Bobby Hamilton	Pontiac
18	Steve Grissom	Chevrolet
19	Ted Musgrave	Ford
20	John Andretti	Ford
21	Todd Bodine	Ford
22	Dick Trickle	Ford
23	Brett Bodine	Ford
24	Davy Jones	Ford
25	Billy Standridge	Ford

FINISH	DRIVER	CAR
26	Bill Elliott	Ford
27	Ken Schrader	Chevrolet
28	Dave Marcis	Chevrolet
29	Greg Sacks	Pontiac
30	Geoff Bodine	Ford
31	Robert Pressley	Chevrolet
32	Jimmy Spencer	Ford
33	Jeff Burton	Ford
34	Darrell Waltrip	Chevrolet
35	Michael Waltrip	Pontiac
36	Jeremy Mayfield	Ford
37	Jeff Purvis	Chevrolet
38	Jimmy Hensley	Chevrolet
39	Randy LaJoie	Pontiac
40	Mike Wallace	Ford
41	Steve Kinser	Ford
42	Phil Parsons	Ford

TRANSOUTH FINANCIAL 400

Time of Race: 3 hours, 35 minutes, 35 seconds
Average Speed: 111.392 mph
Margin of Victory: 1.05 seconds

FINISH	DRIVER	CAR
1	Sterling Marlin	Chevrolet
2	Dale Earnhardt	Chevrolet
3	Ted Musgrave	Ford
4	Todd Bodine	Ford
5	Derrike Cope	Ford
6	Steve Grissom	Chevrolet
7	Michael Waltrip	Pontiac
8	Morgan Shepherd	Ford
9	Bobby Hamilton	Pontiac
10	John Andretti	Ford
11	Ken Schrader	Chevrolet
12	Brett Bodine	Ford
13	Geoff Bodine	Ford
14	Billy Standridge	Ford
15	Mike Wallace	Ford
16	Randy LaJoie	Pontiac
17	Bill Elliott	Ford
18	Loy Allen	Ford
19	Jeff Burton	Ford
20	Davy Jones	Ford
21	Darrell Waltrip	Chevrolet
22	Greg Sacks	Pontiac
23	Rusty Wallace	Ford
24	Dave Marcis	Chevrolet
25	Ward Burton	Chevrolet
26	Rick Mast	Ford
27	Bobby Labonte	Chevrolet
28	Dick Trickle	Ford
29	Lake Speed	Ford
30	Robert Pressley	Chevrolet
31	Jeremy Mayfield	Ford
32	Jeff Gordon	Chevrolet
33	Joe Nemechek	Chevrolet
34	Terry Labonte	Chevrolet
35	Kyle Petty	Pontiac
36	Jimmy Spencer	Ford
37	Mark Martin	Ford
38	Dale Jarrett	Ford
39	Chuck Bown	Chevrolet
40	Steve Kinser	Ford
41	Ricky Rudd	Ford
42	Ricky Craven	Chevrolet

FOOD CITY 500

Time of Race: 2 hours, 53 minutes, 47 seconds
Average Speed: 92.011 mph
Margin of Victory: 5.74 seconds

FINISH	DRIVER	CAR
1	Jeff Gordon	Chevrolet
2	Rusty Wallace	Ford

3	Darrell Waltrip	Chevrolet
4	Bobby Hamilton	Pontiac
5	Ricky Rudd	Ford
6	Dale Jarrett	Ford
7	Terry Labonte	Chevrolet
8	Mark Martin	Ford
9	Sterling Marlin	Chevrolet
10	Robert Pressley	Chevrolet
11	Steve Grissom	Chevrolet
12	Randy LaJoie	Pontiac
13	Derrike Cope	Ford
14	Bill Elliott	Ford
15	Rick Mast	Ford
16	Jimmy Spencer	Ford
17	Lake Speed	Ford
18	Ted Musgrave	Ford
19	John Andretti	Ford
20	Morgan Shepherd	Ford
21	Ward Burton	Chevrolet
22	Michael Waltrip	Pontiac
23	Geoff Bodine	Ford
24	Davy Jones	Ford
25	Dale Earnhardt	Chevrolet
26	Ken Schrader	Chevrolet
27	Brett Bodine	Ford
28	Jeff Burton	Ford
29	Ricky Craven	Chevrolet
30	Dick Trickle	Ford
31	Chuck Bown	Chevrolet
32	Bobby Labonte	Chevrolet
33	Todd Bodine	Ford
34	Dave Marcis	Chevrolet
35	Kyle Petty	Pontiac
36	Greg Sacks	Pontiac

FIRST UNION 400

Time of Race: 2 hours, 26 minutes, 27 seconds
Average Speed: 102.424 mph (Race Record)
Margin of Victory: 13.48 seconds

FINISH	DRIVER	CAR
1	Dale Earnhardt	Chevrolet
2	Jeff Gordon	Chevrolet
3	Mark Martin	Ford
4	Rusty Wallace	Ford
5	Steve Grissom	Chevrolet
6	Ted Musgrave	Ford
7	Sterling Marlin	Chevrolet
8	Rick Mast	Ford
9	Brett Bodine	Ford
10	Darrell Waltrip	Chevrolet
11	Dale Jarrett	Ford
12	Ken Schrader	Chevrolet
13	Bobby Hamilton	Pontiac
14	Geoff Bodine	Ford
15	Bobby Labonte	Chevrolet
16	Terry Labonte	Chevrolet
17	John Andretti	Ford
18	Robert Pressley	Chevrolet
19	Morgan Shepherd	Ford
20	Joe Nemechek	Chevrolet
21	Todd Bodine	Ford
22	Michael Waltrip	Pontiac
23	Randy LeJoie	Pontiac
24	Ward Burton	Chevrolet
25	Lake Speed	Ford
26	Jeff Burton	Ford
27	Jimmy Spencer	Ford
28	Bill Elliott	Ford
29	Ricky Rudd	Ford
30	Derrike Cope	Ford
31	Kyle Petty	Pontiac
32	Dick Trickle	Ford
33	Ricky Craven	Chevrolet
34	Dave Marcis	Chevrolet
35	Greg Sacks	Pontiac
36	Mike Wallace	Ford

HANES 500

Time of Race: 2 hours, 35 minutes, 44 seconds
Average Speed: 72.145 mph
Margin of Victory: 81 second

FINISH	DRIVER	CAR
1	Rusty Wallace	Ford
2	Ted Musgrave	Ford
3	Jeff Gordon	Chevrolet
4	Darrell Waltrip	Chevrolet
5	Mark Martin	Ford
6	Ken Schrader	Chevrolet
7	Dale Jarrett	Ford
8	Bobby Hamilton	Pontiac
9	Kyle Petty	Pontiac
10	Bobby Labonte	Chevrolet
11	Brett Bodine	Ford
12	Bill Elliott	Ford
13	Sterling Marlin	Chevrolet
14	Joe Nemechek	Chevrolet
15	Michael Waltrip	Pontiaca
16	Jeremy Mayfield	Ford
17	Robert Pressley	Chevrolet
18	Ricky Craven	Chevrolet
19	Steve Grissom	Chevrolet
20	Elton Sawyer	Ford
21	Kenny Wallace	Ford
22	Greg Sacks	Pontiac
23	Dave Marcis	Chevrolet
24	Dick Trickle	Ford
25	Ward Burton	Chevrolet
26	Lake Speed	Ford
27	Mike Wallace	Ford
28	Derrike Cope	Ford
29	Dale Earnhardt	Chevrolet
30	Ricky Rudd	Ford
31	Morgan Shepherd	Ford
32	John Andretti	Ford
33	Hut Stricklin	Ford
34	Rick Mast	Ford
35	Geoff Bodine	Ford
36	Terry Labonte	Chevrolet

WINSTON SELECT 500

Time of Race: 2 hours, 47 minutes, 43 seconds
Average Speed: 178.902 mph
Margin of Victory: .18 second

FINISH	DRIVER	CAR
1	Mark Martin	Ford
2	Jeff Gordon	Chevrolet
3	Morgan Shepherd	Ford
4	Darrell Waltrip	Chevrolet
5	Bobby Labonte	Chevrolet
6	Bill Elliott	Ford
7	Geoff Bodine	Ford
8	Todd Bodine	Ford
9	Jimmy Spencer	Ford
10	Loy Allen	Ford
11	Ted Musgrave	Ford
12	Michael Waltrip	Pontiac
13	Randy LaJoie	Pontiac
14	Jeremy Mayfield	Ford
15	Bobby Hamilton	Pontiac
16	Lake Speed	Ford
17	Ricky Craven	Chevrolet
18	Robert Pressley	Chevrolet
19	Dale Jarrett	Ford
20	Rusty Wallace	Ford
21	Dale Earnhardt	Chevrolet
22	Ricky Rudd	Ford
23	Mike Wallace	Ford
24	Hut Stricklin	Ford
25	Jeff Burton	Ford
26	Terry Labonte	Chevrolet

FINISH	DRIVER	CAR
27	Elton Sawyer	Ford
28	Rick Mast	Ford
29	Jeff Purvis	Chevrolet
30	Brett Bodine	Ford
31	Kyle Petty	Pontiac
32	Ward Burton	Chevrolet
33	Davy Jones	Ford
34	Dave Marcis	Chevrolet
35	Greg Sacks	Pontiac
36	Kenny Wallace	Ford
37	Steve Grissom	Chevrolet
38	Dick Trickle	Ford
39	Sterling Marlin	Chevrolet
40	Ken Schrader	Chevrolet
41	John Andretti	Ford
42	Derrike Cope	Ford

SAVEMART SUPERMARKETS 300

Time of Race: 2 hours, 38 minutes, 18 seconds
Average Speed: 70.681mph
Margin of Victory: .32 seconds

FINISH	DRIVER	CAR
1	Dale Earnhardt	Chevrolet
2	Mark Martin	Ford
3	Jeff Gordon	Chevrolet
4	Ricky Rudd	Ford
5	Terry Labonte	Chevrolet
6	Ted Musgrave	Ford
7	Sterling Marlin	Chevrolet
8	Todd Bodine	Ford
9	Ken Schrader	Chevrolet
10	Michael Waltrip	Pontiac
11	John Andretti	Ford
12	Derrike Cope	Ford
13	Bobby Labonte	Chevrolet
14	Bobby Hamilton	Pontiac
15	Morgan Shepherd	Ford
16	Rick Mast	Ford
17	Jimmy Spencer	Ford
18	Jeff Burton	Ford
19	Bill Elliott	Ford
20	Rusty Wallace	Ford
21	Ward Burton	Chevrolet
22	Geoff Bodine	Ford
23	Dale Jarrett	Ford
24	Dick Trickle	Ford
25	Ricky Craven	Chevrolet
26	Steve Grissom	Chevrolet
27	Dave Marcis	Chevrolet
28	Kyle Petty	Pontiac
29	Brett Bodine	Ford
30	Robert Pressley	Chevrolet
31	Doug George	Ford
32	Randy LaJoie	Pontiac
33	Hut Stricklin	Ford
34	Mike Wallace	Ford
35	Darrell Waltrip	Chevrolet
36	Davy Jones	Ford
37	Joe Nemechek	Chevrolet
38	Terry Fisher	Pontiac
39	Wally Dallenbach	Chevrolet
40	Lake Speed	Ford
41	Ken Pedersen	Ford
42	Butch Gilliand	Ford
43	Dan Obrist	Chevrolet

COCA-COLA 600

Time of Race: 3 hours, 56 minutes, 55 seconds
Average Speed: 151.952 mph
Margin of Victory: 6.28 seconds

FINISH	DRIVER	CAR
1	Bobby Labonte	Chevrolet
2	Terry Labonte	Chevrolet
3	Michael Waltrip	Pontiac
4	Sterling Marlin	Chevrolet
5	Ricky Rudd	Ford
6	Dale Earnhardt	Chevrolet
7	Hut Stricklin	Ford
8	Lake Speed	Ford
9	Bobby Hamilton	Pontiac
10	Ricky Craven	Chevrolet
11	Morgan Shepherd	Ford
12	Mike Wallace	Ford
13	Steve Grissom	Chevrolet
14	Rick Mast	Ford
15	Ted Musgrave	Ford
16	Dick Trickle	Ford
17	John Andretti	Ford
18	Darrell Waltrip	Chevrolet
19	Derrike Cope	Ford
20	Joe Nemechek	Chevrolet
21	Chuck Bown	Chevrolet
22	Jeremy Mayfield	Ford
23	Randy LaJoie	Pontiac
24	Robert Pressley	Chevrolet
25	Elton Sawyer	Ford
26	Geoff Bodine	Ford
27	Jimmy Spencer	Ford
28	Mark Martin	Ford
29	Kyle Petty	Pontiac
30	Ken Schrader	Chevrolet
31	Kenny Wallace	Ford
32	Dale Jarrett	Ford
33	Jeff Gordon	Chevrolet
34	Rusty Wallace	Ford
35	Brett Bodine	Ford
36	Loy Allen	Ford
37	Dave Marcis	Chevrolet
38	Todd Bodine	Ford
39	Bill Elliott	Ford
40	Jeff Burton	Ford
41	Ward Burton	Chevrolet
42	Chad Little	Ford

MILLER GENUINE DRAFT 500

Time of Race: 4 hours, 10 minutes, 15 seconds
Average Speed: 119.880 mph
Margin of Victory: 22 second

FINISH	DRIVER	CAR
1	Kyle Petty	Pontiac
2	Bobby Labonte	Chevrolet
3	Ted Musgrave	Ford
4	Hut Stricklin	Ford
5	Dale Earnhardt	Chevrolet
6	Jeff Gordon	Chevrolet
7	Sterling Marlin	Chevrolet
8	Michael Waltrip	Pontiac
9	Rusty Wallace	Ford
10	Joe Nemechek	Chevrolet
11	Ken Schrader	Chevrolet
12	Derrike Cope	Ford
13	Rick Mast	Ford
14	Mike Wallace	Ford
15	Bill Elliott	Ford
16	Steve Grissom	Chevrolet
17	Jeremy Mayfield	Ford
18	Kenny Wallace	Ford
19	Robert Pressley	Chevrolet
20	Darrell Waltrip	Chevrolet
21	Brett Bodine	Ford
22	Ricky Craven	Chevrolet
23	Randy LaJoie	Pontiac
24	Bobby Hamilton	Pontiac
25	Jeff Burton	Ford
26	Morgan Shepherd	Ford
27	Geoff Bodine	Ford
28	Greg Sacks	Pontiac
29	Jimmy Spencer	Ford
30	Todd Bodine	Ford
31	Ricky Rudd	Ford
32	Dick Trickle	Ford
33	Chuck Bown	Chevrolet

34	Lake Speed	Ford
35	Mark Martin	Ford
36	Dave Marcis	Chevrolet
37	Terry Labonte	Chevrolet
38	Ward Burton	Chevrolet
39	John Andretti	Ford
40	Dale Jarrett	Ford
41	Elton Sawyer	Ford
42	Bobbly Hillin	Ford

UAW-GM TEAMWORK 500

Time of Race: 3 hours, 37 minutes, 50 seconds
Average Speed: 137.720 mph
Margin of Victory: 1.64 seconds

FINISH	DRIVER	CAR
1	Terry Labonte	Chevrolet
2	Ted Musgrave	Ford
3	Ken Schrader	Chevrolet
4	Sterling Marlin	Chevrolet
5	Hut Stricklin	Ford
6	Bill Elliott	Ford
7	Morgan Shepherd	Ford
8	Dale Earnhardt	Chevrolet
9	Michael Waltrip	Pontiac
10	Brett Bodine	Ford
11	Mark Martin	Ford
12	Joe Nemechek	Chevrolet
13	Ricky Rudd	Ford
14	Geoff Bodine	Ford
15	Bobby Hamilton	Pontiac
16	Jeff Gordon	Chevrolet
17	Rusty Wallace	Ford
18	Steve Grissom	Chevrolet
19	Ward Burton	Chevrolet
20	Derrike Cope	Ford
21	Rick Mast	Ford
22	Dick Trickle	Ford
23	Bobby Hillin	Ford
24	Todd Bodine	Ford
25	Jeremy Mayfield	Ford
26	Ricky Craven	Chevrolet
27	Bobby Labonte	Chevrolet
28	Lake Speed	Ford
29	Chuck Bown	Chevrolet
30	John Andretti	Ford
31	Dave Marcis	Chevrolet
32	Mike Wallace	Ford
33	Greg Sacks	Pontiac
34	Jimmy Horton	Ford
35	Pancho Carter	Ford
36	Jeff Burton	Ford
37	Robert Pressley	Chevrolet
38	Dale Jarrett	Ford
39	Kyle Petty	Pontiac
40	Randy LaJoie	Pontiac
41	Jimmy Spencer	Ford
42	Darrell Waltrip	Chevrolet

MILLER GENUINE DRAFT 400

Time of Race: 2 hours, 58 minutes, 58 seconds
Average Speed: 134.141 mph
Margin of Victory: 27 second

FINISH	DRIVER	CAR
1	Bobby Labonte	Chevrolet
2	Jeff Gordon	Chevrolet
3	Rusty Wallace	Ford
4	John Andretti	Ford
5	Morgan Shepherd	Ford
6	Dale Jarrett	Ford
7	Sterling Marlin	Chevrolet
8	Mark Martin	Ford
9	Terry Labonte	Chevrolet
10	Ted Musgrave	Ford
11	Lake Speed	Ford

12	Michael Waltrip	Pontiac
13	Bobby Hillin	Ford
14	Bill Elliott	Ford
15	Dave Marcis	Chevrolet
16	Dick Trickle	Ford
17	Robert Pressley	Chevrolet
18	Ward Burton	Chevrolet
19	Derrike Cope	Ford
20	Steve Grissom	Chevrolet
21	Geoff Bodine	Ford
22	Jeremy Mayfield	Ford
23	Elton Sawyer	Ford
24	Chuck Bown	Chevrolet
25	Bobby Hamilton	Pontiac
26	Darrell Waltrip	Chevrolet
27	Ken Schrader	Chevrolet
28	Joe Nemechek	Chevrolet
29	Todd Bodine	Ford
30	Jimmy Spencer	Ford
31	Jeff Burton	Ford
32	Mike Wallace	Ford
33	Ricky Craven	Chevrolet
34	Rick Mast	Ford
35	Dale Earnhardt	Chevrolet
36	Kenny Wallace	Ford
37	Hut Stricklin	Ford
38	Ricky Rudd	Ford
39	Jeff Purvis	Chevrolet
40	Brett Bodine	Ford
41	Randy LaJoie	Pontiac
42	Kyle Petty	Pontiac

PEPSI 400

Time of Race: 2 hours, 23 minutes, 44 seconds
Average Speed: 166.976 mph
Margin of Victory: .21 second

FINISH	DRIVER	CAR
1	Jeff Gordon	Chevrolet
2	Sterling Marlin	Chevrolet
3	Dale Earnhardt	Chevrolet
4	Mark Martin	Ford
5	Ted Musgrave	Ford
6	Ken Schrader	Chevrolet
7	Kyle Petty	Pontiac
8	Ricky Rudd	Ford
9	Jimmy Spencer	Ford
10	Bill Elliott	Ford
11	Robert Pressley	Chevrolet
12	Dick Trickle	Ford
13	Derrike Cope	Ford
14	Geoff Bodine	Ford
15	Michael Waltrip	Pontiac
16	Hut Stricklin	Ford
17	Greg Sacks	Ford
18	Jeff Burton	Ford
19	Terry Labonte	Chevrolet
20	Brett Bodine	Ford
21	Lake Speed	Ford
22	Ricky Craven	Chevrolet
23	Todd Bodine	Ford
24	Morgan Shepherd	Ford
25	Dave Marcis	Chevrolet
26	Rick Mast	Ford
27	Rusty Wallace	Ford
28	Bobby Hillin	Ford
29	Chuck Bown	Chevrolet
30	Jimmy Hensley	Pontiac
31	Loy Allen	Ford
32	Jeremy Mayfield	Ford
33	John Andretti	Ford
34	Darrell Waltrip	Chevrolet
35	Ward Burton	Chevrolet
36	Andy Hillenburg	Pontiac
37	Mike Wallace	Ford
38	Joe Nemechek	Chevrolet
39	Jeff Purvis	Chevrolet
40	Bobby Hamilton	Pontiac
41	Bobby Labonte	Chevrolet
42	Dale Jarrett	Ford
43	Steve Grissom	Chevrolet

Ray Evernham, crew chief for 1997 Winston Cup champion, No. 24 Jeff Gordon

SLICK 50 300

Time of Race: 2 hours, 57 minutes, 56 seconds
Average Speed: 107.029 mph
Margin of Victory: 1.23 seconds

FINISH	DRIVER	CAR
1	Jeff Gordon	Chevrolet
2	Morgan Shepherd	Ford
3	Mark Martin	Ford
4	Terry Labonte	Chevrolet
5	Ricky Rudd	Ford
6	Rusty Wallace	Ford
7	Derrike Cope	Ford
8	Ted Musgrave	Ford
9	Sterling Marlin	Chevrolet
10	Ken Schrader	Chevrolet
11	Rick Mast	Ford
12	Jimmy Spencer	Ford
13	Robert Pressley	Chevrolet
14	Michael Waltrip	Pontiac
15	Bobby Labonte	Chevrolet
16	Bobby Hamilton	Pontiac
17	Darrell Waltrip	Chevrolet
18	Bill Elliott	Ford
19	Joe Nemechek	Chevrolet
20	Bobby Hillin	Ford
21	Brett Bodine	Ford
22	Dale Earnhardt	Chevrolet
23	Elton Sawyer	Ford
24	Lake Speed	Ford
25	Jeff Burton	Ford
26	Jeremy Mayfield	Ford
27	Hut Stricklin	Ford
28	Steve Grissom	Chevrolet
29	Dave Marcis	Chevrolet
30	Dale Jarrett	Ford
31	Ricky Craven	Chevrolet
32	Mike Wallace	Ford
33	John Andretti	Ford
34	Dick Trickle	Ford
35	Geoff Bodine	Ford
36	Todd Bodine	Ford
37	Kyle Petty	Pontiac
38	Rick Bickle	Pontiac
39	Ward Burton	Chevrolet
40	Chuck Bown	Chevrolet
41	Jimmy Hensley	Pontiac

MILLER GENUINE DRAFT 500

Time of Race: 3 hours, 43 minutes, 49 seconds
Average Speed: 134.038 mph
Margin of Victory: .19 second

FINISH	DRIVER	CAR
1	Dale Jarrett	Ford
2	Jeff Gordon	Chevrolet
3	Ricky Rudd	Ford
4	Ted Musgrave	Ford
5	Bill Elliott	Ford
6	Geoff Bodine	Ford
7	Mark Martin	Ford
8	Jeremy Mayfield	Ford
9	Joe Nemechek	Chevrolet
10	Dick Trickle	Ford
11	Ward Burton	Chevrolet
12	Bobby Hillin	Ford
13	Rick Mast	Ford
14	Terry Labonte	Chevrolet
15	Brett Bodine	Ford
16	Rusty Wallace	Ford
17	Jimmy Spencer	Ford
18	Sterling Marlin	Chevrolet
19	Bobby Hamilton	Pontiac
20	Dale Earnhardt	Chevrolet
21	Michael Waltrip	Pontiac
22	Lake Speed	Ford
23	Todd Bodine	Ford
24	Morgan Shepherd	Ford
25	Ricky Craven	Chevrolet
26	Mike Wallace	Ford
27	Jeff Burton	Ford
28	Kyle Petty	Pontiac
29	Elton Sawyer	Ford
30	Rich Bickle	Pontiac
31	Steve Grissom	Chevrolet
32	Jimmy Hensley	Pontiac
33	Dave Marcis	Chevrolet
34	Robert Pressley	Chevrolet
35	Bobby Labonte	Chevrolet
36	Darrell Waltrip	Chevrolet
37	Kenny Wallace	Ford
38	John Andretti	Ford
39	Derrike Cope	Ford
40	Ken Schrader	Chevrolet
41	Hut Stricklin	Ford

DIEHARD 500

Time of Race: 2 hours, 53 minutes, 15 seconds
Average Speed: 173.188 mph
Margin of Victory: .05 second

FINISH	DRIVER	CAR
1	Sterling Marlin	Chevrolet
2	Dale Jarrett	Ford
3	Dale Earnhardt	Chevrolet
4	Morgan Shepherd	Ford
5	Bill Elliott	Ford
6	Kyle Petty	Pontiac

7	Mark Martin	Ford
8	Jeff Gordon	Chevrolet
9	Michael Waltrip	Pontiac
10	Jimmy Spencer	Ford
11	Ted Musgrave	Ford
12	Mike Wallace	Ford
13	Jeremy Mayfield	Ford
14	Elton Sawyer	Ford
15	Derrike Cope	Ford
16	Bobby Hillin	Ford
17	Rick Mast	Ford
18	Chad Little	Ford
19	Dave Marcis	Chevrolet
20	Ward Burton	Chevrolet
21	Bobby Hamilton	Pontiac
22	Jeff Burton	Ford
23	Joe Nemechek	Chevrolet
24	Geoff Bodine	Ford
25	Steve Grissom	Chevrolet
26	Ricky Craven	Chevrolet
27	Robert Pressley	Chevrolet
28	Brett Bodine	Ford
29	Todd Bodine	Ford
30	Rusty Wallace	Ford
31	Bobby Labonte	Chevrolet
32	Ken Schrader	Chevrolet
33	Terry Labonte	Chevrolet
34	John Andretti	Ford
35	Lake Speed	Ford
36	Hut Stricklin	Ford
37	Chuck Bown	Chevrolet
38	Dick Trickle	Ford
39	Loy Allen	Ford
40	Randy LaJoie	Pontiac
41	Ricky Rudd	Ford
42	Jeff Purvis	Chevrolet
43	Darrell Waltrip	Chevrolet

BRICKYARD 400

Time of Race: 2 hours, 34 minutes, 38 seconds
Average Speed: 155.206 mph - Race Record
Margin of Victory: .37 second

FINISH	DRIVER	CAR
1	Dale Earnhardt	Chevrolet
2	Rusty Wallace	Ford
3	Dale Jarrett	Ford
4	Bill Elliott	Ford
5	Mark Martin	Ford
6	Jeff Gordon	Chevrolet
7	Sterling Marlin	Chevrolet
8	Rick Mast	Ford
9	Bobby Labonte	Chevrolet
10	Morgan Shepherd	Ford
11	Bobby Hamilton	Pontiac
12	John Andretti	Ford
13	Terry Labonte	Chevrolet
14	Michael Waltrip	Pontiac
15	Geoff Bodine	Ford
16	Ted Musgrave	Ford
17	Darrell Waltrip	Chevroletg
18	Dick Trickle	Ford
19	Ken Schrader	Chevrolet
20	Ricky Rudd	Ford
21	Todd Bodine	Ford
22	Hut Stricklin	Ford
23	Jimmy Spencer	Ford
24	Brett Bodine	Ford
25	Kyle Petty	Pontiac
26	Mike Wallace	Ford
27	Joe Nemechek	Chevrolet
28	Robert Pressley	Chevrolet
29	Jeremy Mayfield	Ford
30	Steve Grissom	Chevrolet
31	Ricky Craven	Chevrolet
32	Jimmy Hensley	Pontiac
33	Greg Sacks	Chevrolet
34	Lake Speed	Ford
35	Ward Burton	Chevrolet
36	Kenny Wallace	Ford
37	Rich Bickle	Pontiac
38	Jeff Burton	Ford

39	Bobby Hillin	Ford
40	Derrike Cope	Ford
41	Elton Sawyer	Ford

THE BUD AT THE GLEN

Time of Race: 2 hours, 11 minutes, 54 seconds
Average Speed: 103.030 mph - Race Record
Margin of Victory: 1.01 seconds

FINISH	DRIVER	CAR
1	Mark Martin	Ford
2	Wallay Dallenbach	Pontiac
3	Jeff Gordon	Chevrolet
4	Ricky Rudd	Ford
5	Terry Labonte	Chevrolet
6	Bobby Labonte	Chevrolet
7	John Andretti	Ford
8	Darrell Waltrip	Chevrolet
9	Geoff Bodine	Ford
10	Ricky Craven	Chevrolet
11	Bill Elliott	Ford
12	Butch Leitzinger	Pontiac
13	Ted Musgrave	Ford
14	Michael Waltrip	Pontiac
15	Derrike Cope	Ford
16	Brett Bodine	Ford
17	Dale Jarrett	Ford
18	Jimmy Spencer	Ford
19	Ward Burton	Chevrolet
20	Lake Speed	Ford
21	Sterling Marlin	Chevrolet
22	Steve Grissom	Chevrolet
23	Dale Earnhardt	Chevrolet
24	Dave Marcis	Chevrolet
25	Jeremy Mayfield	Ford
26	Rusty Wallace	Ford
27	Bobby Hillin	Ford
28	Dick Trickle	Ford
29	Elton Sawyer	Ford
30	Morgan Shepherd	Ford
31	Joe Nemechek	Chevrolet
32	Todd Bodine	Ford
33	Bobby Hamilton	Pontiac
34	Robert Pressley	Chevrolet
35	Ron Fellows	Chevrolet
36	Ken Schrader	Chevrolet
37	Rick Mast	Ford
38	Jeff Burton	Ford
39	Kyle Petty	Pontiac
40	Hut Stricklin	Ford

GM GOODWRENCH DEALER 400

Time of Race: 2 hours, 32 minutes, 9 seconds
Average Speed: 157.739 mph
Margin of Victory: 6.80 seconds

FINISH	DRIVER	CAR
1	Bobby Labonte	Chevrolet
2	Terry Labonte	Chevrolet
3	Jeff Gordon	Chevrolet
4	Sterling Marlin	Chevrolet
5	Rusty Wallace	Ford
6	Ward Burton	Chevrolet
7	Ricky Craven	Chevrolet
8	Bobby Hamilton	Pontiac
9	Bill Elliott	Ford
10	Hut Stricklin	Ford
11	Michael Waltrip	Pontiac
12	Jeremy Mayfield	Ford
13	Dick Trickle	Ford
14	Jimmy Spencer	Ford
15	Darrell Waltrip	Chevrolet
16	Morgan Shepherd	Ford
17	Lake Speed	Ford
18	Robert Pressley	Chevrolet
19	Todd Bodine	Ford

20	Mike Wallace	Ford
21	Elton Sawyer	Ford
22	Jimmy Hensley	Pontiac
23	Jeff Burton	Ford
24	Kenny Wallace	Ford
25	Dave Marcis	Chevrolet
26	Ken Schrader	Chevrolet
27	Geoff Bodine	Ford
28	Ted Musgrave	Ford
29	Steve Grissom	Chevrolet
30	Ricky Rudd	Ford
31	Rick Mast	Ford
32	Joe Nemechek	Chevrolet
33	Dale Jarrett	Ford
34	Derrike Cope	Ford
35	Dale Earnhardt	Chevrolet
36	Brett Bodine	Ford
37	John Andretti	Ford
38	Mark Martin	Ford
39	Bobby Hillin	Ford
40	Greg Sacks	Chevrolet
41	Gary Bradberry	Chevrolet
42	Kyle Petty	Pontiac

GOODY'S 500

Time of Race: 3 hours, 15 minutes .03 second
Average Speed: 81.979 mph
Margin of Victory: 10 seconds

FINISH	DRIVER	CAR
1	Terry Labonte	Chevrolet
2	Dale Earnhardt	Chevrolet
3	Dale Jarrett	Ford
4	Darrell Waltrip	Chevrolet
5	Mark Martin	Ford
6	Jeff Gordon	Chevrolet
7	Sterling Marlin	Chevrolet
8	Mike Wallace	Ford
9	Jeff Burton	Ford
10	Derrike Cope	Ford
11	Bobby Labonte	Chevrolet
12	Geoff Bodine	Ford
13	Ted Musgrave	Ford
14	Ken Schrader	Chevrolet
15	Michael Waltrip	Pontiac
16	Joe Nemechek	Chevrolet
17	Morgan Shepherd	Ford
18	Jimmy Spencer	Ford
19	John Andretti	Ford
20	Bobby Hamilton	Pontiac
21	Rusty Wallace	Ford
22	Steve Grissom	Chevrolet
23	Bill Elliott	Ford
24	Robert Pressley	Chevrolet
25	Greg Sacks	Chevrolet
26	Rick Mast	Ford
27	Dave Marcis	Chevrolet
28	Brett Bodine	Ford
29	Lake Speed	Ford
30	Jeremy Mayfield	Ford
31	Rich Bickle	Pontiac
32	Ricky Craven	Chevrolet
33	Hut Stricklin	Ford
34	Ward Burton	Pontiac
35	Dick Trickle	Ford
36	Ricky Rudd	Ford

MOUNTAIN DEW SOUTHERN 500

Time of Race: 4 hours, 8 minutes, 7 seconds
Average Speed: 121.231 mph
Margin of Victory: .66 second

FINISH	DRIVER	CAR
1	Jeff Gordon	Chevrolet
2	Dale Earnhardt	Cehvrolet

3	Rusty Wallace	Ford
4	Ward Burton	Pontiac
5	Michael Waltrip	Pontiac
6	Ricky Rudd	Ford
7	Hut Stricklin	Ford
8	Bobby Labonte	Chevrolet
9	Lake Speed	Ford
10	Sterling Marlin	Chevrolet
11	Morgan Shepherd	Ford
12	John Andretti	Ford
13	Bobby Hillin	Ford
14	Bobby Hamilton	Pontiac
15	Derrike Cope	Ford
16	Jeff Burton	Ford
17	Robert Pressley	Chevrolet
18	Ricky Craven	Chevrolet
19	Terry Labonte	Chevrolet
20	Ed Berrier	Chevrolet
21	Rich Bickle	Pontiac
22	Ted Musgrave	Ford
23	Ken Schrader	Chevrolet
24	Kyle Petty	Pontiac
25	Joe Nemechek	Chevrolet
26	Rick Mast	Ford
27	Steve Grissom	Chevrolet
28	Dale Jarrett	Ford
29	Jimmy Spencer	Ford
30	Jeremy Mayfield	Ford
31	Brett Bodine	Ford
32	Elton Sawyer	Ford
33	Mark Martin	Ford
34	Loy Allen	Ford
35	Geoff Bodine	Ford
36	Dick Trickle	Ford
37	Dave Marcis	Chevrolet
38	Greg Sacks	Chevrolet
39	Mike Wallace	Ford
40	Darrell Waltrip	Chevrolet
41	Bill Elliott	Ford
42	Todd Bodine	Ford

MILLER GENUINE DRAFT 400

Time of Race: 2 hours, 52 minutes, 19 seconds
Average Speed: 104.459 mph
Margin of Victory: 5.6 seconds

FINISH	DRIVER	CAR
1	Rusty Wallace	Ford
2	Terry Labonte	Chevrolet
3	Dale Earnhardt	Chevrolet
4	Dale Jarrett	Ford
5	Bobby Hamilton	Pontiac
6	Jeff Gordon	Chevrolet
7	John Andretti	Ford
8	Ricky Rudd	Ford
9	Ken Schrader	Chevrolet
10	Ted Musgrave	Ford
11	Ward Burton	Pontiac
12	Rick Mast	Ford
13	Jeff Burton	Ford
14	Bill Elliott	Ford
15	Mark Martin	Ford
16	Brett Bodine	Ford
17	Bobby Labonte	Chevrolet
18	Dick Trickle	Ford
19	Geoff Bodine	Ford
20	Kenny Wallace	Ford
21	Lake Speed	Ford
22	Darrell Waltrip	Chevrolet
23	Jeremy Mayfield	Ford
24	Todd Bodine	Ford
25	Kyle Petty	Pontiac
26	Joe Nemechek	Chevrolet
27	Morgan Shepherd	Ford
28	Michael Waltrip	Pontiac
29	Ricky Craven	Chevrolet
30	Robert Pressley	Chevrolet
31	Jimmy Spencer	Ford
32	Hut Stricklin	Ford
33	Sterling Marlin	Chevrolet

34	Derrike Cope	Ford
35	Dave Marcis	Chevrolet
36	Bobby Hillin	Ford
37	Greg Sacks	Chevrolet
38	Elton Sawyer	Ford

MBNA 500

Time of Race: 4 hours, 0 minutes, 30 seconds
Average Speed: 124.740 mph
Margin of Victory: 2.34 seconds

FINISH	DRIVER	CAR
1	Jeff Gordon	Chevrolet
2	Bobby Hamilton	Pontiac
3	Rusty Wallace	Ford
4	Joe Nemechek	Chevrolet
5	Dale Earnhardt	Chevrolet
6	Sterling Marlin	Chevrolet
7	Derrike Cope	Ford
8	Mark Martin	Ford
9	Bobby Labonte	Chevrolet
10	Ricky Rudd	Ford
11	Ted Musgrave	Ford
12	Ken Schrader	Chevrolet
13	Bobby Hillin	Ford
14	Robert Pressley	Chevrolet
15	Terry Labonte	Chevrolet
16	Jimmy Spencer	Ford
17	Brett Bodine	Ford
18	Bill Elliott	Ford
19	Jeremy Mayfield	Ford
20	Jeff Burton	Ford
21	Ward Burton	Pontiac
22	Ricky Craven	Chevrolet
23	Dick Trickle	Ford
24	Geoff Bodine	Ford
25	Steve Grissom	Chevrolet
26	Kyle Petty	Pontiac
27	Dave Marcis	Chevrolet
28	Rick Mast	Ford
29	Michael Waltrip	Pontiac
30	Dale Jarrett	Ford
31	Mike Wallace	Ford
32	Lake Speed	Ford
33	Morgan Shepherd	Ford
34	Michael Ritch	Chevrolet
35	Rich Bickle	Pontiac
36	Darrell Waltrip	Chevrolet
37	Todd Bodine	Ford
38	Hut Stricklin	Ford
39	John Andretti	Ford
40	Elton Sawyer	Ford

GOODY'S 500

Time of Race: 3 hours, 33 minutes, 24 seconds
Average Speed: 73.946 mph
Margin of Victory: 1.3 seconds

FINISH	DRIVER	CAR
1	Dale Earnhardt	Chevrolet
2	Terry Labonte	Chevrolet
3	Rusty Wallace	Ford
4	Bobby Hamilton	Pontiac
5	Geoff Bodine	Ford
6	Bill Elliott	Ford
7	Jeff Gordon	Chevrolet
8	Darrell Waltrip	Chevrolet
9	Derrike Cope	Ford
10	Dale Jarrett	Ford
11	Kyle Petty	Pontiac
12	Mark Martin	Ford
13	John Andretti	Ford
14	Bobby Labonte	Chevrolet

15	Dick Trickle	Ford
16	Jeremy Field	Ford
17	Mike Wallace	Ford
18	Jimmy Spencer	Ford
19	Morgan Shepherd	Ford
20	Lake Speed	Ford
21	Ward Burton	Pontiac
22	Brett Bodine	Ford
23	Sterling Marlin	Chevrolet
24	Todd Bodine	Ford
25	Michael Waltrip	Pontiac
26	Steve Grissom	Chevrolet
27	Ricky Rudd	Ford
28	Rick Mast	Ford
29	Ted Musgrave	Ford
30	Joe Nemechek	Chevrolet
31	Jeff Burton	Ford
32	Ken Schrader	Chevrolet
33	Elton Sawyer	Ford
34	Robert Pressley	Chevrolet
35	Ricky Craven	Chevrolet
36	Hut Stricklin	Ford

TYSON HOLLY FARMS 400

Time of Race: 2 hours, 25 minutes, 38 seconds
Average Speed: 102.998 mph
Margin of Victory: 86 seconds

FINISH	DRIVER	CAR
1	Mark Martin	Ford
2	Rusty Wallace	Ford
3	Jeff Gordon	Chevrolet
4	Terry Labonte	Chevrolet
5	Ricky Rudd	Ford
6	Ernie Irvan	Ford
7	Dale Jarrett	Ford
8	Ken Schrader	Chevrolet
9	Dale Earnhardt	Chevrolet
10	Bill Elliott	Ford
11	Geoff Bodine	Ford
12	Michael Waltrip	Pontiac
13	Derrike Cope	Ford
14	Darrell Waltrip	Chevrolet
15	Sterling Marlin	Chevrolet
16	Bobby Hamilton	Pontiac
17	John Andretti	Ford
18	Bobby Labonte	Chevrolet
19	Dick Trickle	Ford
20	Ted Musgrave	Ford
21	Ricky Craven	Chevrolet
22	Brett Bodine	Ford
23	Morgan Shepherd	Ford
24	Bobby Hillin	Ford
25	Hut Stricklin	Ford
26	Rick Mast	Ford
27	Rich Bickle	Pontiac
28	Dave Marcis	Chevrolet
29	Jimmy Hensley	Cheveolet
30	Kyle Petty	Pontiac
31	Steve Grissom	Chevrolet
32	Joe Nemechek	Chevrolet
33	Robert Pressley	Chevrolet
34	Elton Sawyer	Ford
35	Lake Speed	Ford
36	Jimmy Spencer	Ford

UAW-GM QUALITY 500

Time of Race: 3 hours, 26 minutes, 48 seconds
Average Speed: 145.358 mph
Margin of Victory: .97 second

FINISH	DRIVER	CAR
1	Mark Martin	Ford
2	Dale Earnhardt	Chevrolet

3	Terry Labonte	Chevrolet
4	Ricky Rudd	Ford
5	Dale Jarrett	Ford
6	Sterling Marlin	Chevrolet
7	Ward Burton	Pontiac
8	Bobby Labonte	Chevrolet
9	Rusty Wallace	Ford
10	Bobby Hamilton	Pontiac
11	Derrike Cope	Ford
12	Jimmy Spencer	Ford
13	John Andretti	Ford
14	Morgan Shepherd	Ford
15	Kyle Petty	Pontiac
16	Geoff Bodine	Ford
17	Michael Waltrip	Pontiac
18	Hut Stricklin	Ford
19	Ted Musgrave	Ford
20	Bill Elliott	Ford
21	Lake Speed	Ford
22	Joe Nemechek	Chevrolet
23	Mike Wallace	Ford
24	Bobby Hillin	Ford
25	Ricky Craven	Chevrolet
26	Todd Bodine	Ford
27	Brett Bodine	Ford
28	Elton Sawyer	Ford
29	Jeremy Mayfield	Ford
30	Jeff Gordon	Chevrolet
31	Jeff Burton	Ford
32	Dick Trickle	Ford
33	Greg Sacks	Chevrolet
34	Darrell Waltrip	Chevrolet
35	Ken Schrader	Chevrolet
36	Rick Mast	Ford
37	Loy Allen	Ford
38	Rich Bickle	Pontiac
39	Jimmy Hensley	Chevrolet
40	Dave Marcis	Chevrolet
41	Steve Grissom	Chevrolet
42	Robert Pressley	Chevrolet
43	Gary Bradberry	Chevrolet

AC-DELCO 400

Time of Race: 3 hours, 28 minutes, 56 seconds
Average Speed: 114.778 mph
Margin of Victory: 1.9 second

FINISH	DRIVER	CAR
1	Ward Burton	Pontiac
2	Rusty Wallace	Ford
3	Mark Martin	Ford
4	Terry Labonte	Chevrolet
5	Jeff Burton	Ford
6	Sterling Marlin	Chevrolet
7	Dale Earnhardt	Chevrolet
8	Ricky Craven	Chevrolet
9	Joe Nemechek	Chevrolet
10	Bill Elliott	Ford
11	Jeremy Mayfield	Ford
12	Darrell Waltrip	Chevrolet
13	Ricky Rudd	Ford
14	Steve Grissom	Chevrolet
15	Geoff Bodine	Ford
16	Dick Trickle	Ford
17	Todd Bodine	Ford
18	Morgan Shepherd	Ford
19	Derrike Cope	Ford
20	Jeff Gordon	Chevrolet
21	Bobby Hillin	Ford
22	Ted Musgrave	Ford
23	Dale Jarrett	Ford
24	Lake Speed	Ford
25	John Andretti	Ford
26	Jimmy Spencer	Ford
27	Brett Bodine	Ford
28	Hut Stricklin	Ford
29	Robert Pressley	Chevrolet
30	Bobby Hamilton	Pontiac
31	Elton Sawyer	Ford
32	Kyle Petty	Pontiac

33	Ken Schrader	Chevrolet
34	Rick Mast	Ford
35	Gary Bradberry	Chevrolet
36	Shane Hall	Pontiac
37	Greg Sacks	Chevrolet
38	Michael Waltrip	Pontiac
39	Mike Wallace	Ford
40	Bobby Labonte	Chevrolet

DURA-LUBE 500

Time of Race: 3 hours, 3 minutes, 15 seconds
Average Speed: 102.128 mph
Margin of Victory: .53 seconds

FINISH	DRIVER	CAR
1	Ricky Rudd	Ford
2	Derrike Cope	Ford
3	Dale Earnhardt	Chevrolet
4	Rusty Wallace	Ford
5	Jeff Gordon	Chevrolet
6	Ted Musgrave	Ford
7	Morgan Shepherd	Ford
8	Mark Martin	Ford
9	Rick Mast	Ford
10	Ken Schrader	Chevrolet
11	Dale Jarrett	Ford
12	Sterling Marlin	Chevrolet
13	Terry Labonte	Chevrolet
14	Bill Elliott	Ford
15	John Andretti	Ford
16	Geoff Bodine	Ford
17	Brett Bodine	Ford
18	Joe Nemechek	Chevrolet
19	Robert Pressley	Chevrolet
20	Jeremy Mayfield	Ford
21	Bobby Hillin	Ford
22	Lake Speed	Ford
23	Jeff Burton	Ford
24	Ricky Craven	Chevrolet
25	Todd Bodine	Ford
26	Kenny Wallace	Ford
27	Ron Hornaday	Chevrolet
28	Dave Marcis	Chevrolet
29	Dick Trickle	Ford
30	Elton Sawyer	Ford
31	Bobby Hamilton	Pontiac
32	Steve Grissom	Chevrolet
33	Jimmy Spencer	Ford
34	Michael Waltrip	Pontiac
35	Hut Stricklin	Ford
36	Mike Wallace	Ford
37	Bobby Labonte	Chevrolet
38	Darrell Waltrip	Chevrolet
39	Kyle Petty	Pontiac
40	Ernie Irvan	Ford
41	Doug George	Ford
42	Ward Burton	Pontiac
43	Greg Sacks	Chevrolet
44	Ernie Cope	Chevrolet

NAPA 500

Time of Race: 3 hours, 3 minutes, 3 seconds
Average Speed: 163.633 mph - Track Record
Margin of Victory: 3.74 seconds

FINISH	DRIVER	CAR
1	Dale Earnhardt	Chevrolet
2	Sterling Marlin	Chevrolet
3	Rusty Wallace	Ford
4	Bill Elliott	Ford
5	Ward Burton	Pontiac
6	Jimmy Spencer	Ford
7	Ernie Irvan	Ford
8	Bobby Labonte	Chevrolet
9	Bobby Hillin	Ford

10	Ricky Rudd	Ford
11	Geoff Bodine	Ford
12	Michael Waltrip	Pontiac
13	Terry Labonte	Chevrolet
14	Joe Nemechek	Chevrolet
15	John Andretti	Ford
16	Darrell Waltrip	Chevrolet
17	Mark Martin	Ford
18	Jeremy Mayfield	Ford
19	Lake Speed	Ford
20	Brett Bodine	Ford
21	Rick Mast	Ford
22	Morgan Shepherd	Ford
23	Dick Trickle	Ford
24	Loy Allen	Ford
25	Bobby Hamilton	Pontiac
26	Jeff Purvis	Chevrolet
27	Ted Musgrave	Ford
28	Elton Sawyer	Ford
29	Gary Bradberry	Chevrolet
30	Ricky Craven	Chevrolet
31	Dale Jarrett	Ford
32	Jeff Gordon	Chevrolet
33	Kyle Petty	Pontiac
34	Greg Sacks	Chevrolet
35	Derrike Cope	Ford
36	Jeff Burton	Ford
37	Dave Marcis	Chevrolet
38	Hut Stricklin	Ford
39	Steve Grissom	Chevrolet
40	Todd Bodine	Ford
41	Robert Pressley	Chevrolet
42	Ken Schrader	Chevrolet

1996

DAYTONA 500

Time of Race: 3 hours, 14 minutes, 25 seconds
Average Speed: 154.308 mph
Margin of Victory: .12 second

FINISH	DRIVER	CAR
1	Dale Jarrett	Ford
2	Dale Earnhardt	Chevrolet
3	Ken Schrader	Chevrolet
4	Mark Martin	Ford
5	Jeff Burton	Ford
6	Wally Dallenbach	Ford
7	Ted Musgrave	Ford
8	Bill Elliott	Ford
9	Ricky Rudd	Ford
10	Michael Waltrip	Ford
11	Jimmy Spencer	Ford
12	Jeff Purvis	Chevrolet
13	Ricky Craven	Chevrolet
14	Lake Speed	Ford
15	Dave Marcis	Chevrolet
16	Rusty Wallace	Ford
17	Bobby Labonte	Chevrolet
18	Kyle Petty	Pontiac
19	Jeremy Mayfield	Ford
20	Bobby Hamilton	Pontiac
21	Kenny Wallace	Ford
22	Hut Stricklin	Ford
23	Johnny Benson	Pontiac
24	Terry Labonte	Chevrolet
25	Elton Sawyer	Ford
26	Ward Burton	Pontiac
27	Steve Grissom	Chevrolet
28	Rick Mast	Pontiac
29	Darrell Waltrip	Chevrolet
30	Robert Pressley	Chevrolet
31	Morgan Shepherd	Ford
32	Brett Bodine	Ford
33	Chad Little	Pontiac

34	Geoff Bodine	Ford
35	Ernie Irvan	Ford
36	Loy Allen	Ford
37	Mike Wallace	Ford
38	John Andretti	Ford
39	Joe Nemechek	Chevrolet
40	Sterling Matlin	Chevrolet
41	Derrike Cope	Ford
42	Jeff Gordon	Chevrolet
43	Dick Trickle	Ford

GOODWRENCH 400

Time of Race: 3 hours, 30 minutes, 26 seconds
Average Speed: 113.959 mph

FINISH	DRIVER	CAR
1	Dale Earnhardt	Chevrolet
2	Dale Jarrett	Ford
3	Ricky Craven	Chevrolet
4	Ricky Rudd	Ford
5	Steve Grissom	Chevrolet
6	Sterling Marlin	Chevrolet
7	Kenny Wallace	Ford
8	Derrike Cope	Ford
9	Joe Nemechek	Chevrolet
10	Rick Mast	Pontiac
11	Kyle Petty	Pontiac
12	Mike Skinner	Chevrolet
13	Jeff Burton	Ford
14	Ernie Irvan	Ford
15	Bill Elliott	Ford
16	Darrell Waltrip	Chevrolet
17	Mike Wallace	Ford
18	Bobby Hillin	Ford
19	Jeremy Mayfield	Ford
20	Johnny Benson	Pontiac
21	Dave Marcis	Chevrolet
22	Rusty Wallace	Ford
23	Wally Dallenbach	Ford
24	Bobby Hamilton	Pontiac
25	Lake Speed	Ford
26	Robert Pressley	Chevrolet
27	Jimmy Spencer	Ford
28	Brett Bodine	Ford
29	Ken Schrader	Chevrolet
30	Hut Stricklin	Ford
31	Ted Musgrave	Ford
32	Mark Martin	Ford
33	Bobby Labonte	Chevrolet
34	Terry Labonte	Chevrolet
35	Michael Waltrip	Ford
36	Loy Allen	Ford
37	Morgan Shepherd	Ford
38	John Andretti	Ford
39	Geoff Bodine	Ford
40	Jeff Gordon	Chevrolet
41	Ward Burton	Pontiac

PONTIAC EXCITEMENT 400

Time of Race: 2 hours, 55 minutes, 11 seconds
Average Speed: 102.750 mph
Margin of Victory: .56 seconds

FINISH	DRIVER	CAR
1	Jeff Gordon	Chevrolet
2	Dale Jarrett	Ford
3	Ted Musgrave	Ford
4	Jeff Burton	Ford
5	Mark Martin	Ford
6	Bobby Hamilton	Pontiac
7	Rusty Wallace	Ford
8	Terry Labonte	Chevrolet
9	Ricky Rudd	Ford
10	Bill Elliott	Ford

11	Sterling Marlin	Chevrolet
12	John Andretti	Ford
13	Ward Burton	Pontiac
14	Ken Schrader	Chevrolet
15	Kenny Wallace	Ford
16	Robert Pressley	Chevrolet
17	Ricky Craven	Chevrolet
18	Lake Speed	Ford
19	Rick Mast	Pontiac
20	Kyle Petty	Pontiac
21	Steve Grissom	Chevrolet
22	Derrike Cope	Ford
23	Bobby Labonte	Chevrolet
24	Mike Wallace	Ford
25	Brett Bodine	Ford
26	Bobby Hillin	Ford
27	Darrell Waltrip	Chevrolet
28	Jeremy Mayfield	Ford
29	Jimmy Spencer	Ford
30	Elton Sawyer	Ford
31	Dale Earnhardt	Chevrolet
32	Morgan Shepherd	Ford
33	Geoff Bodine	Ford
34	Joe Nemechek	Checrolet
35	Dave Marcis	Chevrolet
36	Michael Waltrip	Ford
37	Johnny Benson	Pontiac
38	Ernie Irvan	Ford
39	Hut Stricklin	Ford
40	Wally Dallenbach	Ford

PUROLATOR 500

Time of Race: 3 hours, 5 minutes, 42 seconds
Average Speed: 161.298 mph
Margin of Victory: 4.28 seconds

FINISH	DRIVER	CAR
1	Dale Earnhardt	Chevrolet
2	Terry Labonte	Chevrolet
3	Jeff Gordon	Chevrolet
4	Ernie Irvan	Ford
5	Jeremy Mayfield	Ford
6	Ken Schrader	Chevrolet
7	Jimmy Spencer	Ford
8	Ricky Rudd	Ford
9	Michael Waltrip	Ford
10	Bill Elliott	Ford
11	Dale Jarrett	Ford
12	Ricky Craven	Chevrolet
13	Sterling Marlin	Chevrolet
14	Dick Trickle	Ford
15	Ward Burton	Pontiac
16	Bobby Hamilton	Pontiac
17	Joe Nemechek	Chevrolet
18	Ted Musgrave	Ford
19	Elton Sawyer	Ford
20	Wally Dallenbach	Ford
21	John Andretti	Ford
22	Kyle Petty	Pontiac
23	Geoff Bodine	Ford
24	Brett Bodine	Ford
25	Hut Stricklin	Ford
26	Mark Martin	Ford
27	Robert Pressley	Chevrolet
28	Bobby Hillin	Ford
29	Dave Marcis	Chevrolet
30	Morgan Shepherd	Ford
31	Bobby Labonte	Chevrolet
32	Darrell Waltrip	Chevrolet
33	Mike Wallace	Ford
34	Rick Mast	Pontiac
35	Derrike Cope	Ford
36	Rusty Wallace	Ford
37	Kenny Walkace	Ford
38	Johnny Benson	Pontiac
39	Steve Grissom	Chevrolet
40	Chuck Bown	Ford
41	Lake Speed	Ford

TRANSOUTH FINANCIAL 400

Time of Race: 3 hours, 12 minutes, 26 seconds
Average Speed: 124.792 mph
Margin of Victory: 1.4 seconds

FINISH	DRIVER	CAR
1	Jeff Gordon	Chevrolet
2	Bobby Labonte	Chevroet
3	Ricky Craven	Chevrolet
4	Rusty Wallace	Ford
5	Terry Labonte	Chevrolet
6	Mark Martin	Ford
7	Ted Musgrave	Ford
8	Morgan Shepherd	Ford
9	Ricky Rudd	Ford
10	Jeff Burton	Ford
11	Sterling Marlin	Chevrolet
12	Kyle Petty	Pontiac
13	Bill Elliott	Ford
14	Dale Earnhardt	Ford
15	Dale Jarrett	Ford
16	Bobby Hamilton	Pontiac
17	Kenny Wallace	Ford
18	Jeremy Mayfield	Ford
19	Rick Mast	Pontiac
20	Hut Stricklin	Ford
21	Mike Wallace	Ford
22	Geoff Bodine	Ford
23	Dave Marcis	Chevrolet
24	Johnny Benson	Pontiac
25	Lake Speed	Ford
26	Steve Grissom	Chevrolet
27	Brett Bodine	Ford
28	Ken Schrader	Chevrolet
29	Michael Waltrip	Ford
30	Elton Sawyer	Ford
31	Joe Nemechek	Ford
32	Jimmy Spencer	Ford
33	Ernie Irvan	Ford
34	Darrell Waltrip	Chevrolet
35	Dick Trickle	Ford
36	Robert Pressley	Chevrolet
37	Wally Dallenbach	Ford
38	Ward Burton	Pontiac
39	Derrike Cope	Ford
40	John Andretti	Ford
41	Bobby Hillin	Ford

FOOD CITY 500

Time of Race: 1 hour, 59 minutes, 47 seconds
Average Speed: 91.308 mph
Margin of Victory: Under Caution

FINISH	DRIVER	CAR
1	Jeff Gordon	Chevrolet
2	Terry Labonte	Chevrolet
3	Mark Martin	Chevrolet
4	Dale Earnhardt	Chevrolet
5	Rusty Wallace	Ford
6	Dale Jarrett	Ford
7	Bobby Labonte	Chevrolet
8	Dick Trickle	Ford
9	Ricky Craven	Chevrolet
10	Michael Waltrip	Ford
11	Hut Stricklin	Ford
12	Rick Mast	Pontiac
13	Jimmy Spencer	Ford
14	Ricky Rudd	Ford
15	Kyle Petty	Pontiac
16	Ernie Irvan	Ford
17	Robert Pressley	Chevrolet
18	Sterling Marlin	Chevrolet
19	Geoff Bodine	Ford
20	Brett Bodine	Ford

21	Jeremy Mayfield	Ford
22	Derrike Cope	Ford
23	Jeff Burton	Ford
24	Wally Dallenbach	Ford
25	Ted Musgrave	Ford
26	Darrell Waltrip	Chevrolet
27	Steve Grissom	Chevrolet
28	Bill Elliott	Ford
29	Ken Schrader	Chevrolet
30	Morgan Shepherd	Ford
31	Joe Nemechek	Chevrolet
32	Bobby Hamilton	Pontiac
33	Ward Burton	Pontiac
34	Kenny Wallace	Ford
35	Lake Speed	Ford
36	Mike Skinner	Chevrolet
37	Elton Sawyer	Ford

FIRST UNION 400

Time of Race: 2 hours, 35 minutes, 39 seconds
Average Speed: 96.370 mph
Margin of Victory: .239 second

FINISH	DRIVER	CAR
1	Terry Labonte	Chevrolet
2	Jeff Gordon	Chevrolet
3	Dale Earnhardt	Chevrolet
4	Robert Pressley	Chevrolet
5	Sterling Marlin	Chevrolet
6	Ernie Irvan	Ford
7	Ricky Craven	Chevrolet
8	Bobby Hamilton	Pontiac
9	Ken Schrader	Chevrolet
10	Bobby Labonte	Chevrolet
11	Dale Jarrett	Ford
12	Ted Musgrave	Ford
13	Derrike Cope	Ford
14	Rick Mast	Pontiac
15	Ricky Rudd	Ford
16	Hut Stricklin	Ford
17	Michael Waltrip	Ford
18	Kenny Wallace	Ford
19	Geoff Bodine	Ford
20	Jeremy Mayfield	Ford
21	Bill Elliott	Ford
22	Dick Trickle	Ford
23	Brett Bodine	Ford
24	Johnny Benson	Pontiac
25	Darrell Waltrip	Chevrolet
26	Steve Grissom	Chevrolet
27	Morgan Shepherd	Ford
28	Wally Dallenbach	Ford
29	Jeff Burton	Ford
30	Kyle Petty	Pontiac
31	Jimmy Spencer	Ford
32	Elton Sawyer	Ford
33	Rusty Wallace	Ford
34	John Andretti	Ford
35	Lake Speed	Ford
36	Joe Nemechek	Chevrolet
37	Mark Martin	Ford

GOODY'S HEADACHE POWDER 500

Time of Race: 3 hours, 13 minutes, 50 secinds
Average Speed: 81.410 mph-Race Record
Margin of Victory: 2.526 seconds

FINISH	DRIVER	CAR
1	Rusty Wallace	Ford
2	Ernie Irvan	Ford
3	Jeff Gordon	Chevrolet
4	Jeremy Mayfield	Ford
5	Dale Earnhardt	Chevrolet
6	Bobby Hamilton	Pontiac

7	Ken Schrader	Chevrolet
8	Bobby Labonte	Chevrolet
9	Ted Musgrave	Ford
10	Sterling Marlin	Chevrolet
11	Lake Speed	Ford
12	Ricky Craven	Chevrolet
13	Bill Elliott	Ford
14	Kenny Wallace	Ford
15	Rick Mast	Pontiac
16	Darrell Waltrip	Chevrolet
17	Michael Waltrip	Ford
18	Brett Bodine	Ford
19	Jimmy Spencer	Ford
20	Morgan Shepherd	Ford
21	Mark Martin	Ford
22	Jeff Burton	Ford
23	Ricky Rudd	Ford
24	Terry Labonte	Chevrolet
25	Johnny Benson	Pontiac
26	Joe Nemechek	Chevrolet
27	Geoff Bodine	Ford
28	Derrike Cope	Ford
29	Dale Jarrett	Ford
30	Kyle Petty	Pontiac
31	Hut Stricklin	Ford
32	Mike Wallace	Ford
33	Stacy Compton	Cehvrolet
34	Robert Pressley	Chevrolet
35	Dave Marcis	Chevrolet
36	John Andretti	Ford

WINSTON SELECT 500

Time of Race: 3 hours, 20 minutes, 2 seconds
Average Speed: 149.999 mph
Margin of Victory: .22 second

FINISH	DRIVER	CAR
1	Sterling Marlin	Chevrolet
2	Dale Jarrett	Ford
3	Dale Earnhardt	Chevrolet
4	Terry Labonte	Chevrolet
5	Michael Waltrip	Ford
6	Steve Grissom	Chevrolet
7	Robert Pressley	Chevrolet
8	Ted Musgrave	Ford
9	John Andretti	Ford
10	Johnny Benson	Pontiac
11	Bobby Hamilton	Pontiac
12	Wally Dallenbach	Ford
13	Joe Nemechek	Chevrolet
14	Kenny Wallace	Ford
15	Rick Masters	Pontiac
16	Jeff Burton	Ford
17	Mike Skinner	Chevrolet
18	Kyle Petty	Pontiac
19	Dick Trickle	Ford
20	Ken Schrader	Chevrolet
21	Darrell Waltrip	Chevrolet
22	Hut Stricklin	Ford
23	Brett Bodine	Ford
24	Bobby Labonte	Chevrolet
25	Chuck Bown	Ford
26	Geoff Bodine	Ford
27	Ward Burton	Pontiac
28	Ricky Rudd	Ford
29	Derrike Cope	Ford
30	Rusty Wallace	Ford
31	Ernie Irvan	Ford
32	Jeremy Mayfield	Ford
33	Jeff Gordon	Chevrolet
34	Mark Martin	Ford
35	Jeff Purvis	Chevrolet
36	Ricky Craven	Chevrolet
37	Elton Sawyer	Ford
38	Mike Wallace	Ford
39	Dave Marcis	Chevrolet
40	Jimmy Spencer	Ford
41	Bill Elliott	Ford
42	Lake Speed	Ford
43	Morgan Shepherd	Ford

SAVE MART SUPERMARKETS 300

Time of Race: 2 hours, 24 minutes, 3 seconds
Average Speed: 77.673 mph
Margin of Victory: .46 second

FINISH	DRIVER	CAR
1	Rusty Wallace	Ford
2	Mark Martin	Ford
3	Wally Dallenbach	Ford
4	Dale Earnhardt	Chevrolet
5	Terry Labonte	Chevrolet
6	Jeff Gordon	Chevrolet
7	Ricky Rudd	Ford
8	Ken Schrader	Chevrolet
9	Bobby Labonte	Chevrolet
10	Ward Burton	Pontiac
11	John Andretti	Ford
12	Dale Jarrett	Ford
13	Hut Stricklin	Ford
14	Darrell Waltrip	Chevrolet
15	Sterling Marlin	Chevrolet
16	Lake Speed	Ford
17	Bobby Hamilton	Pontiac
18	Johnny Benson	Pontiac
19	Rick Masters	Pontiac
20	Brett Bodine	Ford
21	Jimmy Spencer	Ford
22	Michael Waltrip	Ford
23	Ted Musgrave	Ford
24	Morgan Shepherd	Ford
25	Steve Grissom	Chevrolet
26	Jeff Burton	Ford
27	Kenny Wallace	Ford
28	Tommy Kendall	Ford
29	Dick Trickle	Ford
30	Kyle Petty	Pontiac
31	Ricky Craven	Chevrolet
32	Jeremy Mayfield	Ford
33	Dave Marcis	Chevrolet
34	Robert Pressley	Chevrolet
35	Jeffrey Krogh	Chevrolet
36	Larry Gunselman	Ford
37	Rich Woodland	Chevrolet
38	Scott Gaylord	Chevrolet
39	Derrike Cope	Ford
40	Goeff Bodine	Ford
41	Joe Nemechek	Chevrolet
42	Ernie Irvan	Ford
43	Bobby Hillin	Ford
44	Mike Wallace	Ford

COCA-COLA 600

Time of Race: 4 hours, 03 minutes, 56 seconds
Average Speed: 147.581 mph
Margin of Victory: 11.982 seconds

FINISH	DRIVER	CAR
1	Dale Jarrett	Ford
2	Dale Earnhardt	Chevrolet
3	Terry Labonte	Chevrolet
4	Jeff Gordon	Chevrolet
5	Ken Schrader	Chevrolet
6	Sterling Marlin	Chevrolet
7	Mark Martin	Ford
8	Michael Waltrip	Ford
9	Ernie Irvan	Ford
10	Geoff Bodine	Ford
11	Ward Burton	Pontiac
12	Rick Masters	Pontiac
13	Darrell Waltrip	Chevrolet
14	Derrike Cope	Ford
15	Ricky Rudd	Ford
16	Steve Grissom	Chevrolet

FINISH	DRIVER	CAR
17	Jimmy Spencer	Ford
18	Jeff Burton	Ford
19	Wally Dallenbach	Ford
20	Dick Trickle	Ford
21	Elton Sawyer	Ford
22	Bobby Labonte	Chevrolet
23	Kyle Petty	Pontiac
24	Brett Bodine	Ford
25	Joe Nemechek	Chevrolet
26	Bobby Hillin	Ford
27	John Andretti	Ford
28	Hut Stricklin	Ford
29	Morgan Shepherd	Ford
30	Ted Musgrave	Ford
31	Bobby Hamilton	Pontiac
32	Kenny Wallace	Ford
33	Robert Pressley	Chevrolet
34	Rusty Wallace	Ford
35	Lake Speed	Ford
36	Todd Bodine	Ford
37	Ricky Craven	Chevrolet
38	Johnny Benson	Pontiac
39	Mike Wallace	Ford
40	Dave Marcis	Chevrolet
41	Jeremy Mayfield	Ford
42	Chuck Bown	Ford
43	Chad Little	Pontiac

MILLER GENUINE DRAFT 500

Time of Race: 4 hours, 04 minutes, 25 seconds
Average Speed: 122.741 mph
Margin of Victory: 3.90 seconds

FINISH	DRIVER	CAR
1	Jeff Gordon	Chevrolet
2	Terry Labonte	Chevrolet
3	Dale Earnhardt	Chevrolet
4	Ernie Irvan	Ford
5	Bobby Labonte	Chevrolet
6	Jimmy Spencer	Ford
7	Rusty Wallace	Ford
8	Ricky Rudd	Ford
9	Jeff Burton	Ford
10	Ken Schrader	Chevrolet
11	Michael Waltrip	Ford
12	Jeremy Mayfield	Ford
13	Ted Musgrave	Ford
14	Ricky Craven	Chevrolet
15	Todd Bodine	Ford
16	Ward Burton	Pontiac
17	Johnny Benson	Pontiac
18	Kyle Petty	Pontiac
19	Mike Wallace	Ford
20	Kenny Wallace	Ford
21	Bobby Hamilton	Pontiac
22	Wally Dallenbach	Ford
23	Derrike Cope	Ford
24	Brett Bodine	Ford
25	Joe Nemechek	Chevrolet
26	Lake Speed	Ford
27	Greg Sacks	Chevrolet
28	Dick Trickle	Ford
29	Bobby Hillin	Ford
30	Geoff Bodine	Ford
31	Dave Marcis	Chevrolet
32	Morgan Shepherd	Ford
33	John Andretti	Ford
34	Hut Stricklin	Ford
35	Rick Masters	Pontiac
36	Dale Jarrett	Ford
37	Hermie Sadler	Chevrolet
38	Gary Bradberry	Ford
39	Darrell Waltrip	Chevrolet
40	Mark Martin	Ford
41	Sterling Marlin	Chevrolet
42	Steve Grissom	Chevrolet

UAW-GM TEAMWORK 500

Time of Race: 3 hours, 35 minutes, 40 seconds
Average Speed: 139.104 mph
Margin of Victory: 3.688 seconds

FINISH	DRIVER	CAR
1	Jeff Gordon	Chevrolet
2	Ricky Rudd	Ford
3	Geoff Bodine	Ford
4	Mark Martin	Ford
5	Bobby Hamilton	Pontiac
6	Morgan Shepherd	Ford
7	Terry Labonte	Chevrolet
8	Jimmy Spencer	Ford
9	Jeff Burton	Ford
10	Todd Bodine	Ford
11	Sterling Marlin	Chevrolet
12	Wally Dallenbach	Ford
13	Bobby Hillin	Ford
14	Michael Waltrip	Ford
15	Jeremy Mayfield	Ford
16	John Andretti	Ford
17	Ricky Craven	Chevrolet
18	Ken Schrader	Chevrolet
19	Ted Musgrave	Ford
20	Kyle Petty	Pontiac
21	Joe Nemechek	Chevrolet
22	Steve Grissom	Chevrolet
23	Loy Allen	Ford
24	Randy MacDonald	Ford
25	Johnny Benson	Pontiac
26	Dick Trickle	Ford
27	Derrike Cope	Ford
28	Rick Masters	Pontiac
29	Hut Stricklin	Ford
30	Darrell Waltrip	Chevrolet
31	Rusty Wallace	Ford
32	Dale Earnhardt	Chevrolet
33	Robert Pressley	Chevrolet
34	Lake Speed	Ford
35	Ward Burton	Pontiac
36	Jeff Green	Chevrolet
37	Kenny Wallace	Ford
38	Dale Jarrett	Ford
39	Ernie Irvan	Ford
40	Brett Bodine	Ford
41	Bobby Labonte	Chevrolet

MILLER GENINE DRAFT 400

Time of Race: 2 hours, 24 minutes, 23 seconds
Average Speed: 166.033 mph
Margin of Victory: 1.10 seconds

FINISH	DRIVER	CAR
1	Rusty Wallace	Ford
2	Terry Labonte	Chevrolet
3	Sterling Marlin	Chevrolet
4	Jimmy Spencer	Ford
5	Ernie Irvan	Ford
6	Jeff Gordon	Chevrolet
7	Mark Martin	Ford
8	Ted Musgrave	Ford
9	Dale Earnhardt	Chevrolet
10	Dale Jarrett	Ford
11	Morgan Shepherd	Ford
12	Bobby Labonte	Chevrolet
13	Wally Dallenbach	Ford
14	Bobby Hillin	Ford
15	Bobby Hamilton	Pontiac
16	Ken Schrader	Chevrolet
17	Jeff Burton	Ford
18	Rick Masters	Pontiac
19	Lake Speed	Ford
20	Todd Bodine	Ford
21	Geoff Bodine	Ford
22	Brett Bodine	Ford

FINISH	DRIVER	CAR
23	Robert Pressley	Chevrolet
24	John Andretti	Ford
25	Darrell Waltrip	Chevrolet
26	Dave Marcis	Chevrolet
27	Hut Stricklin	Ford
28	Loy Allen	Ford
29	Ricky Craven	Chevrolet
30	Jeremy Mayfield	Ford
31	Ricky Rudd	Ford
32	Michael Waltrip	Ford
33	Kenny Wallace	Ford
34	Steve Grissom	Chevrolet
35	Ward Burton	Pontiac
36	Joe Nemechek	Chevrolet
37	Johnny Benson	Pontiac
38	Kyle Petty	Pontiac
39	Dick Trickle	Ford
40	Derrike Cope	Ford

PEPSI 400

Time of Race: 1 hour, 48 minutes, 36 seconds
Average Speed: 161.602 mph
Margin of Victory: .104 second

FINISH	DRIVER	CAR
1	Sterling Marlin	Chevrolet
2	Terry Labonte	Chevrolet
3	Jeff Gordon	Chevrolet
4	Dale Earnhardt	Chevrolet
5	Ernie Irvan	Chevrolet
6	Dale Jarrett	Ford
7	Michael Waltrip	Ford
8	Ken Schrader	Chevrolet
9	Brett Bodine	Ford
10	Jimmy Spencer	Ford
11	Mark Martin	Ford
12	Wally@error?:Dallenbach	Ford
13	Ted Musgrave	Ford
14	Jeff Burton	Ford
15	Morgan Shepherd	Ford
16	Bobby Hamilton	Pontiac
17	Robert Pressley	Chevrolet
18	Joe Nemechek	Chevrolet
19	Hut Stricklin	Ford
20	Rick Masters	Pontiac
21	Jeff Purvis	Chevrolet
22	Ricky Craven	Chevrolet
23	John Andretti	Ford
24	Kyle Petty	Pontiac
25	Johnny Benson	Pontiac
26	Darrell Waltrip	Chevrolet
27	Jeremy Mayfield	Ford
28	Dick Trickle	Ford
29	Lake Speed	Ford
30	Loy Allen	Ford
31	Rusty Wallace	Ford
32	Bobby Hillin	Ford
33	Ricky Rudd	Ford
34	Geoff Bodine	Ford
35	Gary Bradberry	Ford
36	Dave Marcis	Chevrolet
37	Bill Elliott	Ford
38	Kenny Wallace	Ford
39	Greg Sacks	Chevrolet
40	Bobby Labonte	Chevrolet
41	Ward Burton	Pontiac
42	Derrike Cope	Ford

JIFFY LUBE 300

Time of Race: 3 hours, 12 minutes, 30 seconds
Average Speed: 98.930 mph
Margin of Victory: 5.470 seconds

FINISH	DRIVER	CAR
1	Ernie Irvan	Ford
2	Dale Jarrett	Ford

3	Ricky Rudd	Ford
4	Jeff Burton	Ford
5	Robert Pressley	Chevrolet
6	Terry Labonte	Chevrolet
7	Rusty Wallace	Ford
8	Ken Schrader	Chevrolet
9	Johnny Benson	Pontiac
10	Michael Waltrip	Ford
11	Ted Musgrave	Ford
12	Dale Earnhardt	Chevrolet
13	Rick Masters	Pontiac
14	Bill Elliott	Ford
15	Geoff Bodine	Ford
16	Brett Bodine	Ford
17	Jimmy Spencer	Ford
18	Wally Dallenbach	Ford
19	Kenny Wallace	Ford
20	Bobby Hamilton	Pontiac
21	Bobby Hillin	Ford
22	Morgan Shepherd	Ford
23	Hut Stricklin	Ford
24	Lake Speed	Ford
25	Ward Burton	Pontiac
26	Ricky Craven	Chevrolet
27	Dick Trickle	Ford
28	Kyle Petty	Pontiac
29	Sterling Marlin	Chevrolet
30	Greg Sacks	Chevrolet
31	Bobby Labonte	Chevrolet
32	Randy MacDonald	Ford
33	Mark Martin	Ford
34	Jeff Gordon	Chevrolet
35	Joe Nemechek	Chevrolet
36	Jeremy Mayfield	Ford
37	Darrell Waltrip	Chevrolet
38	Derrike Cope	Ford
39	Dave Marcis	Chevrolet
40	John Andretti	Ford

MILLER GENUINE DRAFT 500

Time of Race: 3 hours, 27 minutes, 03 seconds
Aversge Speed: 144.892 mph
Margin of Victory: .300 second

FINISH	DRIVER	CAR
1	Rusty Wallace	Ford
2	Ricky Rudd	Ford
3	Dale Jarrett	Ford
4	Ernie Irvan	Ford
5	Johnny Benson	Pontiac
6	Sterling Marlin	Chevrolet
7	Jeff Gordon	Chevrolet
8	Lake Speed	Ford
9	Mark Martin	Ford
10	Derrike Cope	Ford
11	Goeff Bodine	Ford
12	Jeremy Mayfield	Ford
13	Michael Waltrip	Ford
14	Dale Earnhardt	Chevrolet
15	Ken Schrader	Chevrolet
16	Terry Labonte	Chevrolet
17	Morgan Shepherd	Ford
18	Dick Trickle	Ford
19	Ted Musgrave	Ford
20	Ricky Craven	Chevrolet
21	Bill Elliott	Ford
22	Ward Burton	Pontiac
23	John Andretti	Ford
24	Jimmy Spencer	Ford
25	Robert Pressley	Chevrolet
26	Kyle Petty	Pontiac
27	Brett Bodine	Ford
28	Dave Marcis	Chevrolet
29	Greg Sacks	Chevrolet
30	Rick Masters	Pontiac
31	Randy McDonald	Ford
32	Hut Stricklin	Ford
33	Wally Dallenbach	Ford

34	Joe Nemechek	Chevrolet
35	Jeff Burton	Ford
36	Kenny Wallace	Ford
37	Bobby Hamilton	Ford
38	Bobby Hillin	Ford
39	Bobby Hamilton	Pontiac
40	Darrell Waltrip	Chevrolet
41	Jeff Green	Chevrolet

DIEHARD 500

Time of Race: 2 hours, 34 minutes, 21 seconds
Average Speed: 133.387 mph
Margin of Victory: .146 second

FINISH	DRIVER	CAR
1	Jeff Gordon	Chevrolet
2	Dale Jarrett	Ford
3	Mark Martin	Ford
4	Ernie Irvan	Ford
5	Jimmy Spencer	Ford
6	Geoff Bodine	Ford
7	Jeff Burton	Ford
8	Bobby Labonte	Chevrolet
9	Darrell Waltrip	Chevrolet
10	Rusty Wallace	Ford
11	Dave Marcis	Chevrolet
12	Kyle Petty	Pontiac
13	Bill Elliott	Ford
14	Morgan Shepherd	Ford
15	Joe Nemechek	Chevrolet
16	Jeremy Mayfield	Ford
17	Bobby Hamilton	Pontiac
18	Johnny Benson	Pontiac
19	Ricky Craven	Chevrolet
20	Kenny Wallace	Ford
21	Loy Allen	Ford
22	Brett Bodine	Ford
23	Gary Bradberry	Ford
24	Terry Labonte	Chevrolet
25	Greg Sacks	Chevrolet
26	Ken Schrader	Chevrolet
27	Derrike Cope	Ford
28	Dale Earnhardt	Chevrolet
29	Sterling Marlin	Chevrolet
30	Lake Speed	Ford
31	Robert Pressley	Chevrolet
32	Wally Dallenbach	Ford
33	Ward Burton	Pontiac
34	Hut Stricklin	Ford
35	Bobby Hillin	Ford
36	Ted Musgrave	Ford
37	Ricky Rudd	Ford
38	Dick Trickle	Ford
39	John Andretti	Ford
40	Jeff Purvis	Chevrolet
41	Rick Masters	Pontiac
42	Michael Waltrip	Ford

BRICKYARD 400

Time of Race: 2 hours, 52 minutes, 2 seconds
Average Speed: 139.508 mph
Margin of Victory: Under Caution

FINISH	DRIVER	CAR
1	Dale Jarrett	Ford
2	Ernie Irvan	Ford
3	Terry Labonte	Chevrolet
4	Mark Martin	Ford
5	Morgan Shepherd	Ford
6	Ricky Rudd	Ford
7	Rusty Wallace	Ford
8	Johnny Benson	Pontiac

9	Rick Masters	Pontiac
10	Bill Elliott	Ford
11	Jeff Burton	Ford
12	Jimmy Spencer	Ford
13	Lake Speed	Ford
14	Derrike Cope	Ford
15	Dale Earnhardt	Chevrolet
16	Ken Schrader	Chevrolet
17	Wally Dallenbach	Ford
18	Hut Stricklin	Ford
19	John Andretti	Ford
20	Geoff Bodine	Ford
21	Ted Musgrave	Ford
22	Brett Bodine	Ford
23	Dick Trickle	Ford
24	Bobby Labonte	Chevrolet
25	Jeremy Mayfield	Ford
26	Bobby Hillin	Ford
27	Joe Nemechek	Chevrolet
28	Michael Waltrip	Ford
29	Gary Bradberry	Ford
30	Robert Pressley	Chevrolet
31	Bobby Hamilton	Pontiac
32	Greg Sacks	Chevrolet
33	Kenny Wallace	Ford
34	Ricky Craven	Chevrolet
35	Dave Marcis	Chevrolet
36	Ward Burton	Pontiac
37	Jeff Gordon	Chevrolet
38	Kyle Petty	Pontiac
39	Sterling Marlin	Chevrolet
40	Darrell Waltrip	Chevrolet

THE BUD AT THE GLEN

Time of Race: 2 hours, 23 minutes, 17 seconds
Average Speed: 92.334 mph
Margin of Victory: .440 seconds

FINISH	DRIVER	CAR
1	Geoff Bodine	Ford
2	Terry Labonte	Chevrolet
3	Mark Martin	Ford
4	Jeff Gordon	Chevrolet
5	Bobby Labonte	Chevrolet
6	Dale Earnhardt	Chevrolet
7	Michael Waltrip	Ford
8	Joe Nemechek	Chevrolet
9	Morgan Shepherd	Ford
10	Wally Dallenbach	Ford
11	Sterling Marlin	Chevrolet
12	Ted Musgrave	Ford
13	Dorsey Schroeder	Ford
14	Brett Bodine	Ford
15	Johnny Benson	Pontiac
16	Derrike Cope	Ford
17	Lake Speed	Ford
18	Darrell Waltrip	Chevrolet
19	Jimmy Spencer	Ford
20	Butch Leitzinger	Chevrolet
21	Jeff Burton	Ford
22	Jeremy Mayfield	Ford
23	Kyle Petty	Pontiac
24	Dale Jarrett	Ford
25	Ken Schrader	Chevrolet
26	John Andretti	Ford
27	Rick Masters	Pontiac
28	Dave Marcis	Chevrolet
29	Bobby Hillin	Ford
30	Robert Pressley	Chevrolet
31	Kenny Wallace	Ford
32	Ward Burton	Pontiac
33	Rusty Wallace	Ford
34	Ricky Rudd	Ford
35	Ernie Irvan	Ford
36	Ricky Craven	Chevrolet
37	Hut Stricklin	Ford
38	Bobby Hamilton	Pontiac
39	Dick Trickle	Ford

GM GOODWRENCH DEALER 400

Time of Race: 2 hours, 51 minutes, 41 seconds
Average Speed: 139.792 mph
Margin of Victory: .168 second

FINISH	DRIVER	CAR
1	Dale Jarrett	Ford
2	Mark Martin	Ford
3	Terry Labonte	Chevrolet
4	Ernie Irvan	Ford
5	Jeff Gordon	Chevrolet
6	Bobby Labonte	Chevrolet
7	Johnny Benson	Pontiac
8	Ricky Rudd	Ford
9	Jeff Burton	Ford
10	Jimmy Spencer	Ford
11	Morgan Shepherd	Ford
12	Geoff Bodine	Ford
13	Bobby Hamilton	Pontiac
14	Bill Elliott	Ford
15	Ken Schrader	Chevrolet
16	Rick Masters	Pontiac
17	Dale Earnhardt	Chevrolet
18	Ricky Craven	Chevrolet
19	Bobby Hillin	Ford
20	Jeremy Mayfield	Ford
21	Jim Sauter	Pontiac
22	Darrell Waltrip	Chevroley
23	Ted Musgrave	Ford
24	Derrike Cope	Ford
25	Michael Waltrip	Ford
26	Hut Stricklin	Ford
27	Joe Nemechek	Chevrolet
28	Brett Bodine	Ford
29	Mike Wallace	Ford
30	Greg Sacks	Chervolet
31	John Andretti	Ford
32	Lake Speed	Ford
33	Sterling Marlin	Chevrolet
34	Wally Dallenbach	Ford
35	Ward Burton	Pontiac
36	Chad Little	Pontiac
37	Kenny Wallace	Ford
38	Dick Trickle	Ford
39	Rusty Wallace	Ford
40	Dave Marcis	Chevrolet
41	Robert Pressley	Chevrolet

GOODY'S HEADACHE POWDER 500

Time of Race: 2 hours, 55 minutes, 12 seconds
Average Speed: 91.267 mph
Margin of Victory: .630 second

FINISH	DRIVER	CAR
1	Rusty Wallace	Ford
2	Jeff Gordon	Chevrolet
3	Mark Martin	Ford
4	Dale Jarrett	Ford
5	Terry Labonte	Chevrolet
6	Michael Waltrip	Ford
7	Jimmy Spencer	Ford
8	Ward Burton	Pontiac
9	Ricky Rudd	Ford
10	Bobby Hamilton	Pontiac
11	Darrell Waltrip	Chevrolet
12	Ted Musgrave	Ford
13	Ken Schrader	Chevrolet
14	Brett Bodine	Ford
15	Kenny Wallace	Ford
16	Lake Speed	Ford
17	Jeremy Mayfield	Ford
18	Sterling Marlin	Ford
19	Morgan Shepherd	Ford
20	Hut Stricklin	Ford
21	Ricky Craven	Chevrolet

THE UNBREAKABLE RECORDS

It's probably safe to say that three Winston Cup records are out of reach: Richard Petty's 200 career victories, his 27-win season of 1967, and his 10 consecutive wins during that 27-win streak.

Petty won 27 of the 49 races contested in 1967, races on tracks ranging from 2.7 miles at Riverside, California, to one-fifth mile at Islip, New York. The '67 season opened at Augusta, Georgia, in November of 1966 and ended at Weaverville, North Carolina, exactly 51 weeks later.

His unprecedented winning streak began August 12 at Winston-Salem and went through the Oct. 1 race at North Wilkesboro, about 50 miles to the west of where it had started. In between, Petty and his No. 43 Plymouth won at Columbia, South Carolina; Savannah, Georgia.; Darlington; Hickory, North Carolina; Richmond, Virginia; Beltsville,

Maryland; Hillsborough, North Carolina; and Martinsville, Virginia.

Columbia, Savannah, Richmond, and Hillsborough were dirt, the rest asphalt. Except for the 500-mile Labor Day weekend race at Darlington, every race during the streak was on a short track. Petty was the pole-sitter in six of the 10 en route to 19 poles that season.

"It was one of them times when nothing went wrong for us," Petty said years later. "We weren't always the fastest car during that streak, but we were always close to the fastest and always found a way to win. The other cats just had bad luck a lot of those nights."

Yeah, right. Their only bad luck was having to face The King every weekend.

22	Bobby Hillin	Ford
23	Chad Little	Chevrolet
24	Dale Earnhardt	Chevrolet
25	Wally Dallenbach	Ford
26	Dick Trickle	Ford
27	Dave Marcis	Chevrolet
28	Johnny Benson	Pontiac
29	Derrike Cope	Ford
30	Gary Bradberry	Ford
31	Jim Sauter	Pontiac
32	Bobby Labonte	Chevrolet
33	Robert Pressley	Chevrolet
34	Joe Nemechek	Chevrolet
35	Rick Masters	Pontiac
36	Ernie Irvan	Ford
37	Jeff Burton	Ford
38	John Andretti	Ford
39	Geoff Bodine	Ford

MOUNTAIN DEW SOUTHERN 500

Time of Race: 3 hours, 41 minutes, 34 seconds
Average Speed: 135.757 mph
Margin of Victory: 5.230 seconds

FINISH	DRIVER	CAR
1	Jeff Gordon	Chevrolet
2	Hut Stricklin	Ford
3	Mark Martin	Ford
4	Ken Schrader	Chevrolet
5	John Andretti	Ford
6	Bobby Labonte	Chevrolet
7	Ernie Irvan	Ford
8	Sterling Marlin	Chevrolet
9	Bill Elliott	Ford
10	Lake Speed	Ford
11	Johnny Benson	Pontiac
12	Dale Earnhardt	Chevrolet
13	Kenny Wallace	Ford
14	Dale Jarrett	Ford
15	Todd Bodine	Ford
16	Ricky Rudd	Ford

17	Kyle Petty	Pontiac
18	Bobby Hillin	Ford
19	Bobby Hamilton	Pontiac
20	Chad Little	Chevrolet
21	Geoff Bodine	Ford
22	Rick Mast	Pontiac
23	Jimmy Spencer	Ford
24	Morgan Shepherd	Ford
25	Wally Dallenbach	Ford
26	Terry Labonte	Chevrolet
27	Robert Pressley	Chevrolet
28	Brett Bodine	Ford
29	Ted Musgrave	Ford
30	Dave Marcis	Chevrolet
31	Jeff Burton	Ford
32	Darrell Waltrip	Chevrolet
33	Michael Waltrip	Ford
34	Derrike Cope	Ford
35	Gary Bradberry	Ford
36	Dick Trickle	Ford
37	Jeremy Mayfield	Ford
38	Rusty Wallace	Ford
39	Ed Berrier	Ford
40	Ward Burton	Pontiac
41	Loy Allen	Ford
42	Ricky Craven	Chevrolet

MILLER 400

Time of Race: 2 hours, 50 minutes, 40 seconds
Average Speed: 105.469 mph
Margin of Victory: 10 second

FINISH	DRIVER	CAR
1	Ernie Irvan	Ford
2	Jeff Gordon	Chevrolet
3	Jeff Burton	Ford
4	Dale Jarrett	Ford
5	Terry Labonte	Chevrolet
6	Rusty Wallace	Ford
7	Bobby Hamilton	Pontiac
8	Derrike Cope	Ford

9	Mark Martin	Ford
10	Johnny Benson	Pontiac
11	Bobby Labonte	Chevrolet
12	Ricky Rudd	Ford
13	Ken Schrader	Chevrolet
14	Michael Waltrip	Ford
15	Ted Musgrave	Ford
16	Bill Elliott	Ford
17	Geoff Bodine	Ford
18	Kyle Petty	Pontiac
19	Rick Masters	Pontiac
20	Dale Earnhardt	Chevrolet
21	Sterling Marlin	Chevrolet
22	Darrell Waltrip	Chevrolet
23	Morgan Shepherd	Ford
24	Hut Stricklin	Ford
25	Brett Bodine	Ford
26	Robert Pressley	Chevrolet
27	Dick Trickle	Ford
28	Ricky Craven	Chevrolet
29	Jeremy Mayfield	Ford
30	Jimmy Spencer	Ford
31	Lake Speed	Ford
32	Bobby Hillin	Ford
33	Wally Dallenbach	Ford
34	Dave Marcis	Chevrolet
35	Todd Bodine	Ford
36	John Andretti	Ford
37	Ward Burton	Pontiac
38	Kenny Wallace	Ford
39	Joe Nemechek	Chevrolet
40	Chad Little	Chevrolet

MBNA 500

Time of Race: 4 hours, 43 minutes, 58 seconds
Average Speed: 105.646 mph
Margin of Victory: .441 second

FINISH	DRIVER	CAR
1	Jeff Gordon	Chevrolet
2	Rusty Wallace	Ford
3	Dale Jarrett	Ford
4	Bobby Labonte	Chevrolet
5	Mark Martin	Ford
6	Rick Mast	Pontiac
7	Ward Burton	Pontiac
8	Kyle Petty	Pontiac
9	Michael Waltrip	Ford
10	Bobby Hamilton	Pontiac
11	Geoff Bodine	Ford
12	Bobby Hillin	Ford
13	Lake Speed	Ford
14	John Andretti	Ford
15	Jeremy Mayfield	Ford
16	Dale Earnhardt	Chevrolet
17	Sterling Marlin	Chevrolet
18	Morgan Shepherd	Ford
19	Mike Skinner	Chevrolet
20	Kenny Wallace	Ford
21	Terry Labonte	Chevrolet
22	Ken Schrader	Chevrolet
23	Dick Trickle	Ford
24	Johnny Benson	Pontiac
25	Joe Nemechek	Chevrolet
26	Dave Marcis	Chevrolet
27	Brett Bodine	Ford
28	Bill Elliott	Ford
29	Wally Dallenbach	Ford
30	Jimmy Spencer	Ford
31	Derrike Cope	Ford
32	Robert Pressley	Chevrolet
33	Ted Musgrave	Ford
34	Ricky Rudd	Ford
35	Ricky Craven	Ford
36	Ernie Irvan	Ford
37	Gary Bradberry	Ford
38	Hut Stricklin	Ford
39	Darrell Waltrip	Chevrolet
40	Jeff Burton	Ford
41	Chad Little	Chevrolet

HANES 500

Time of Race: 3 hours, 11 minutes, 54 seconds
Average Speed: 82.223 mph - Race Record
Margin of Victory: .490 seconds

FINISH	DRIVER	CAR
1	Jeff Gordon	Chevrolet
2	Terry Labonte	Chevrolet
3	Bobby Hamilton	Pontiac
4	Rick Mast	Pontiac
5	John Andretti	Ford
6	Morgan Shepherd	Ford
7	Geoff Bodine	Ford
8	Kyle Petty	Pontiac
9	Mark Martin	Ford
10	Kenny Wallace	Ford
11	Jeff Burton	Ford
12	Ernie Irvan	Ford
13	Dick Trickle	Ford
14	Michael Waltrip	Ford
15	Dale Earnhardt	Chevrolet
16	Dale Jarrett	Ford
17	Johnny Benson	Pontiac
18	Bill Elliott	Ford
19	Jimmy Spencer	Ford
20	Ted Musgrave	Ford
21	Bobby Labonte	Chevrolet
22	Wally Dallenbach	Ford
23	Darrell Waltrip	Chevrolet
24	Bobby Hillin	Ford
25	Hut Stricklin	Ford
26	Ricky Craven	Chevrolet
27	Joe Nemechek	Chevrolet
28	Lake Speed	Ford
29	Dave Marcis	Chevrolet
30	Ken Schrader	Chevrolet
31	Sterling Marlin	Chevrolet
32	Robert Pressley	Chevrolet
33	Stacy Compton	Chevrolet
34	Jeremy Mayfield	Ford
35	Ricky Rudd	Ford
36	Rusty Wallace	Ford

TYSON HOLLY FARMS 400

Time of Race: 2 hours, 34 minutes, 54 seconds
Average Speed: 96.837 mph
Margin of Victory: 1.73 seconds

FINISH	DRIVER	CAR
1	Jeff Gordon	Chevrolet
2	Dale Earnhardt	Chevrolet
3	Dale Jarrett	Ford
4	Jeff Burton	Ford
5	Terry Labonte	Chevrolet
6	Rick Mast	Pontiac
7	Ricky Rudd	Ford
8	Bobby Hamilton	Pontiac
9	Mark Martin	Ford
10	Rusty Wallace	Ford
11	Sterling Marlin	Chevrolet
12	Michael Waltrip	Ford
13	Bobby Labonte	Chevrolet
14	Morgan Shepherd	Ford
15	Kenny Wallace	Ford
16	Hut Stricklin	Ford
17	Johnny Benson	Pontiac
18	Ken Schrader	Chevrolet
19	Ted Musgrave	Ford
20	Jimmy Spencer	Ford
21	Bill Elliott	Ford
22	Ricky Craven	Chevrolet
23	Brett Bodine	Ford
24	John Andretti	Ford
25	Lake Speed	Ford
26	Joe Nemechek	Chevrolet
27	Darrell Waltrip	Chevrolet

FINISH	DRIVER	CAR
28	Jeremy Mayfield	Ford
29	Dave Marcis	Chevrolet
30	Geoff Bodine	Ford
31	Kyle Petty	Pontiac
32	Jeff Green	Chevrolet
33	Robert Pressley	Chevrolet
34	Wally Dallenbach	Ford
35	Bobby Hillin	Ford
36	Ernie Irvan	Ford
37	Derrike Cope	Ford

UAW-GM QUALITY 500

Time of Race: 3 hours, 30 minutes, 00 seconds
Average Speed: 143.143 mph
Margin of Victory: 3.84 seconds

FINISH	DRIVER	CAR
1	Terry Labonte	Chevrolet
2	Mark Martin	Ford
3	Dale Jarrett	Ford
4	Sterling Marlin	Chevrolet
5	Ricky Craven	Chevrolet
6	Dale Earnhardt	Chevrolet
7	Ward Burton	Pontiac
8	Rusty Wallace	Ford
9	Michael Waltrip	Ford
10	Bill Elliott	Ford
11	Jeff Burton	Ford
12	Lake Speed	Ford
13	Ricky Rudd	Ford
14	Johnny Benson	Pontiac
15	Rick Mast	Pontiac
16	Jimmy Spencer	Ford
17	Ted Musgrave	Ford
18	Derrike Cope	Ford
19	Bobby Hamilton	Pontiac
20	Geoff Bodine	Ford
21	Todd Bodine	Ford
22	Chad Little	Pontiac
23	Morgan Shepherd	Ford
24	Greg Sacks	Chevrolet
25	Hut Stricklin	Ford
26	Jeff Green	Chevrolet
27	Billy Standridge	Ford
28	Brett Bodine	Ford
29	Ken Schrader	Chevrolet
30	Kenny Wallace	Ford
31	Jeff Gordon	Chevrolet
32	Robert Pressley	Chevrolet
33	Wally Dallenbach	Ford
34	Loy Allen	Ford
35	Dick Trickle	Ford
36	Bobby Hillin	Ford
37	Ernie Irvan	Ford
38	Robby Gordon	Chevrolet
39	John Andretti	Ford
40	Bobby Labonte	Chevrolet
41	Kyle Petty	Pontiac
42	Darrell Waltrip	Chevrolet
43	Jeremy Mayfield	Ford

AC-DELCO 400

Time of Race: 3 hours, 16 minutes, 3 seconds
Average Speed: 122.320 mph - Race Record
Margin of Victory: 3.397 seconds

FINISH	DRIVER	CAR
1	Ricky Rudd	Ford
2	Dale Jarrett	Ford
3	Terry Labonte	Chevrolet
4	Ernie Irvan	Ford
5	Jeff Burton	Ford
6	Bobby Labonte	Chevrolet
7	Mark Martin	Ford
8	Rusty Wallace	Ford
9	Dale Earnhardt	Chevrolet
10	Jimmy Spencer	Ford
11	Hut Stricklin	Ford
12	Jeff Gordon	Chevrolet
13	Sterling Marlin	Chevrolet
14	Michael Waltrip	Ford
15	Geoff Bodine	Ford
16	Brett Bodine	Ford
17	Ward Burton	Pontiac
18	Ted Musgrave	Ford
19	Kenny Wallace	Ford
20	Todd Bodine	Chevrolet
21	Darrell Waltrip	Chevrolet
22	Ricky Craven	Chevrolet
23	Ken Schrader	Chevrolet
24	Joe Nemechek	Chevrolet
25	Kyle Petty	Pontiac
26	John Andretti	Ford
27	Gary Bradberry	Ford
28	Bobby Hamilton	Pontiac
29	Morgan Shepherd	Ford
30	Dave Marcis	Chevrolet
31	Dick Trickle	Ford
32	Bill Elliott	Ford
33	Bobby Hillin	Ford
34	Jeremy Mayfield	Ford
35	Lake Speed	Ford
36	Wally Dallenbach	Ford
37	Robert Pressley	Chevrolet
38	Rick Mast	Pontiac
39	Derrike Cope	Ford
40	Johnny Benson	Pontiac
41	Billy Standridge	Ford
42	Robby Gordon	Chevrolet

DURA-LUBE 500

Time of Race: 2 hours, 50 minutes, 38 seconds
Average Speed: 109.709 mph - Race Record
Margin of Victory: 1.23 seconds

FINISH	DRIVER	CAR
1	Bobby Hamilton	Pontiac
2	Mark Martin	Ford
3	Terry Labonte	Chevrolet
4	Ted Musgrave	Ford
5	Jeff Gordon	Chevrolet
6	Geoff Bodine	Ford
7	Ernie Irvan	Ford
8	Dale Jarrett	Ford
9	Bobby Labonte	Chevrolet
10	Darrell Waltrip	Chevrolet
11	Todd Bodine	Chevrolet
12	Dale Earnhardt	Chevrolet
13	Mike Skinner	Chevrolet
14	Ricky Rudd	Ford
15	Wally Dallenbach	Ford
16	Michael Waltrip	Ford
17	Morgan Shepherd	Ford
18	Jimmy Spencer	Ford
19	John Andretti	Ford
20	Dick Trickle	Ford
21	Bill Elliott	Ford
22	Ward Burton	Pontiac
23	Jack Sprague	Pontiac
24	Dave Marcis	Chevrolet
25	Joe Nemechek	Chevrolet
26	Brett Bodine	Ford
27	Sterling Marlin	Chevrolet
28	Lake Speed	Ford
29	Kyle Petty	Pontiac
30	Hut Stricklin	Ford
31	Jeff Burton	Ford
32	Johnny Benson	Pontiac
33	Lance Hooper	Pontiac
34	Ricky Craven	Chevrolet
35	Ken Schrader	Chevrolet
36	Robert Pressley	Chevrolet

37	Kenny Wallace	Ford
38	Rick Mast	Pontiac
39	Bobby Hillin	Ford
40	Rusty Wallace	Ford
41	Jeffrey Krogh	
42	Robby Gordon	Chevrolet
43	Derrike Cope	Ford
44	Jeremy Mayfield	Ford

NAPA 500

Time of Race: 3 hours, 39 minutes, 13 seconds
Average Speed: 134.661 mph
Margin of Victory: .41 seconds

FINISH	DRIVER	CAR
1	Bobby Labonte	Chevrolet
2	Dale Jarrett	Ford
3	Jeff Gordon	Chevrolet
4	Dale Earnhardt	Chevrolet
5	Terry Labonte	Chevrolet
6	Bobby Hamilton	Pontiac
7	Mark Martin	Ford
8	Ricky Rudd	Ford
9	Jeff Burton	Ford
10	Rusty Wallace	Ford
11	Michael Waltrip	Ford
12	Ward Burton	Pontiac
13	Rick Mast	Pontiac
14	Jimmy Spencer	Ford
15	Sterling Marlin	Chevrolet
16	Bobby Hillin	Ford
17	Hut Stricklin	Ford
18	Greg Sacks	Pontiac
19	Lake Speed	Ford
20	Bill Elliott	Ford
21	Brett Bodine	Ford
22	Chad Little	Pontiac
23	Elton Sawyer	Ford
24	John Andretti	Ford
25	Dave Marcis	Chevrolet
26	Geoff Bodine	Ford
27	Johnny Benson	Pontiac
28	Morgan Shepherd	Ford
29	Billy Standridge	Ford
30	Ken Schrader	Chevrolet
31	Ted Musgrave	Ford
32	Todd Bodine	Chevrolet
33	Robert Pressley	Chevrolet
34	Joe Nemechek	Chevrolet
35	Ricky Craven	Chevrolet
36	Ernie Irvan	Ford
37	Darrell Waltrip	Chevrolet
38	Gary Bradberry	Ford
39	Loy Allen	Ford
40	Wally Dallenbach	Ford
41	Randy Baker	Chevrolet
42	Jack Sprague	Pontiac

APPENDIX: 1998 SCHEDULES

1998 NASCAR WINSTON CUP SERIES SCHEDULE

DATE	EVENT	TRACK
Sunday, February 8	Bud Shootout	Daytona International Speedway**
Thursday, February 12	Gatorade 125s	Daytona International Speedway**
Sunday, February 15	Daytona 500	Daytona International Speedway
Sunday, February 22	GM Goodwrench Service Plus 400	North Carolina Motor Speedway
Sunday, March 1	Las Vegas 400	Las Vegas Motor Speedway
Sunday, March 8	PRIMESTAR 500	Atlanta Motor Speedway
Sunday, March 22	Transouth Financial 400	Darlington Raceway
Sunday, March 29	Food City 500	Bristol Motor Speedway
Sunday, April 6	Texas 500	Texas Motor Speedway
Sunday, April 19	Goody's Headache Powder 500	Martinsville Speedway
Sunday, April 26	Diehard 500	Talladega Superspeedway
Sunday, May 3	California 500	California Speedway
Saturday, May 16	The Winston	Charlotte Motor Speedway**
Sunday, May 24	Coca-Cola 600	Charlotte Motor Speedway
Sunday, May 31	MBNA Platinum 400	Dover Downs International Speedway
Saturday, June 6	Pontiac Excitement 400	Richmond International Raceway
Sunday, June 14	Miller Lite 300	Michigan Speedway

Sunday, June 21	Pocono 500	Pocono Raceway
Sunday, June 28	Save Mart/Kragen 300	Sears Point Raceway
Saturday, July 4	Pepsi 400	Daytona International Speedway
Sunday, July 12	Jiffy Lube 300	New Hampshire International Speedway
Sunday, July 26	Pennsylvania 500	Pocono Raceway
Saturday, August 1	Brickyard 400	Indianapolis Motor Speedway
Sunday, August 9	The Bud at the Glen	Watkins Glen International
Sunday, August 16	DeVilbiss 500	Michigan Speedway
Saturday, August 22	Goody's Headache Powder 500	Bristol Motor Speedway
Sunday, August 30	New Hampshire 300	New Hampshire International Speedway
Sunday, September 6	Southern 500	Darlington Raceway
Saturday, September 12	Exide NASCAR Select Batteries 400	Richmond International Raceway
Sunday, September 20	MBNA Gold 400	Dover Downs International Speedway
Sunday, September 27	NAPA Autocare 500	Martinsville Speedway
Sunday, October 4	UAW-GM Quality 500	Charlotte Motor Speedway
Sunday, October 11	Winston 500	Talladega Superspeedway
Sunday, October 25	Dura-Lube 500	Phoenix International Raceway
Sunday, November 1	AC Delco 500	North Carolina Motor Speedway
Sunday, November 8	NAPA 500	Atlanta Motor Speedway

**Non-championship point events

1998 NASCAR BUSCH SERIES SCHEDULE

DATE	TRACK
Saturday, February 14	Daytona International Speedway
Saturday, February 21	North Carolina Motor Speedway
Saturday, February 28	Las Vegas Motor Speedway
Saturday, March 7	Atlanta Motor Speedway
Sunday, March 15	Nashville Speedway
Saturday, March 21	Darlington Raceway
Saturday, March 28	Bristol Motor Speedway
Saturday, April 4	Texas Motor Speedway
Saturday, April 11	Hickory Motor Speedway
Saturday, April 25	Talladega Superspeedway

Saturday, May 9	New Hampshire International Speedway
Sunday, May 17	Nazareth Speedway
Saturday, May 23	Charlotte Motor Speedway
Saturday, May 30	Dover Downs International Speedway
Friday, June 5	Richmond International Speedway
Sunday, June 14	Pikes Peak International Raceway
Sunday, June 26	Watkins Glen International
Sunday, July 5	Milwaukee Mile
Saturday, July 11	Myrtle Beach Speedway
Sunday, July 19	California Speedway
Saturday, July 25	South Boston Speedway
Friday, July 31	Indianapolis Raceway Park
Saturday, August 15	Michigan Speedway
Friday, August 21	Bristol Motor Speedway
Saturday, September 5	Darlington Raceway
Friday, September 11	Richmond International Raceway
Saturday, September 19	Dover Downs International Speedway
Saturday, October 3	Charlotte Motor Speedway
Saturday, October 17	Gateway International Raceway
Saturday, October 31	North Carolina Motor Speedway
Sunday, November 15	Metro-Dade Motorsports Complex

1998 NASCAR CRAFTSMAN TRUCK SERIES SCHEDULE

DATE	**TRACK**
Sunday, January 18	Walt Disney World Speedway
Saturday, April 4	Metro-Dade Homestead Motorsports Complex
Sunday, April 19	Phoenix International Raceway
Saturday, April 25	Portland Speedway
Saturday, May 9	Evergreen Speedway
Saturday, May 23	I-70 Speedway
Saturday, May 30	Watkins Glen International
Friday, June 5	Texas Motor Speedway
Saturday, June 20	Bristol Motor Speedway
Saturday, June 27	Colorado National Speedway
Saturday, July 4	Milwaukee Mile
Sunday, July 12	Nazareth Speedway
Saturday, July 18	California Speedway

Thursday, July 30	Indianapolis Raceway Park
Sunday, August 2	New Hampshire International Speedway
Saturday, August 8	Flemington Speedway
Saturday, August 15	Nashville Speedway USA
Sunday, August 23	Heartland Park Topeka
Saturday, August 29	Louisville Motor Speedway
Thursday, September 10	Richmond International Raceway
Sunday, September 13	Memphis Motorsports Park
Saturday, September 19	Gateway International Raceway
Saturday, September 26	Martinsville Speedway
Sunday, October 11	Sears Point Raceway
Sunday, October 18	Mesa Marin Raceway
Saturday, October 24	Phoenix International Raceway
Sunday, November 8	Las Vegas Motor Speedway

**Non-championship point events

INDEX

Morris, Buckshot 14
Morton, Read 215
Mosley, Mike 68
Mountain Dew 500 78, 132–3
Murphy, Danny 4
Musgrave, Ted 112, 125, 173, 232
Myers, Billy 237

N

NAPA 500 139
NASCAR CD-ROM
  Racing Pod 95
NASCAR Cafe 95, 152
NASCAR on film 283–9
NASCAR organizations 292–3
NASCAR Silicon Motor
  Speedway 152
NASCAR SpeedPark 152
NASCAR Thunder 95, 152, 254
NASCAR web sites 295–300
National 500 55–6
Needham, Hal 78
Nelson, Gary 78–9, 85, 154
Nemechek, Joe 110, 158, 181
Nemechek, John 181
New Hampshire International
  Speedway 27–8, 101, 108, 265
Newman, Paul 216
Newton, Bob 89
NHRA Historical Service Center 256
NMPA Stock Car Hall of Fame/Joe
  Weatherly Museum 258
North Carolina Motor Speedway
  26, 266

O

Olds, Ransom 3
Ontario Motor Speedway 28, 45
Orr, Rodney 110
Osterlund, Rod 52, 72, 75, 77, 206
Owens, Cotton 29, 206
Owens, Randy 231

P

Panch, Marvin 33, 196
Pardue, Jimmy 34, 238
Parks, Raymond 206
Parrott, Buddy 75–6, 107, 131

Parsons, Benny 50, 56, 59, 75–6, 80,
  83, 87, 91–2, 196, 211, 230
Parsons, Phil 90–1
Paschal, Jim 37, 196–7
PE-2 217
Pearson, David 31, 34–6, 38–9,
  46–7, 51, 54–6, 59–61, 63–5,
  191, 197, 307
Pearson, Larry 158
Pennsylvania 500 129
Penske Racing South 207–8
Penske, Roger 26, 28, 61, 99, 101,
  207–8
Pepsi 400 128
Periodicals about NASCAR 291–2
Petersen Automotive Museum 256
Petree, Andy 215
Petty Enterprises 217
  See also PE-2
Petty, Kyle 64, 80–1, 84–5, 88, 103,
  105, 107, 112, 147, 181, 217, 231
Petty, Lee 9, 12–5, 18–9, 24–5, 29,
  32–3, 197, 238–9
Petty, Maurice 55, 81
Petty, Richard 18, 29, 31–41, 44–51,
  53–65, 70–2, 76–8, 80–2, 86–7,
  90–1, 97, 107–8, 114, 142–3,
  145, 147–8, 198–9, 217, 226,
  236–8, 246, 251, 284, 287–8, 307
Phoenix International Raceway 267
Pit crew duties 229–33
Pittman, Runt 172
Pocono 500 125–6
Pocono International Raceway 27,
  45–6, 58, 268, 277, 279
Pond, Lennie 51, 54, 63, 206
Pontiac Excitement 400 119
Precision Products Racing 211
Pressley, Robert 112, 183
Priddy, Thomas 237
Primestar 500 119–20
Prince, Tab 237

Q

QVC Shopping Network 97, 251

R

R. E. Olds Transportation
  Museum 264
R. J. Reynolds Tobacco Co. 43–4,
  53, 70, 84, 101–2, 144

Rahilly, Bob 218
Rathmann, Dick 12, 13, 199
Reagan, Ronald 82, 145
Records 301–17
Reed, Jim 206
Reese, Charlie 4–5, 23
Restrictor plate racing 242–4
Rexford, Bill 10, 11, 199
Reynolds, Burt 78, 284
Ribbs, Willy T. 63
Rich, Mike 231
Richard Childress Racing 208,
  214, 241
  See also Childress, Richard
Richert, Doug 76
Richmond International
  Raceway 269
Richmond, Tim 79–81, 83, 85, 87–8,
  199–200
Rider, Chuck 214
Ridley, Jody 75, 78, 206, 220
Robbins, Marty 80
Robert Yates Racing 213–4, 219
Roberts, Fireball 10, 18, 33, 34, 200,
  237–8
Robertson, T. Wayne 70
Rogers, Craig 101
Rogers, Kenny 284
Rollcages 240
Rollins, Shorty 24
Roper, Jim 7, 9
Ross, Earl 57–8, 206
Roush, Jack 134, 209, 241
Roush Racing 209, 211, 213, 221
"RPM 2Night" 98
Rubinstein, Rich 73
Rudd Performance Motorsports
  210–1
Rudd, Ricky 61, 64, 70–1, 81–3,
  85–7, 89, 93, 103, 105, 110,
  113, 115, 124, 129, 156, 172,
  249–50, 307
Ruttman, Joe 79, 81, 163–4
Ryan, Terry 60

S

Sabates, Felix 103, 216
Sacks, Greg 84–5

Safety measures 235–44

Salvino, Ralph 72

Sauter, Jim 79

Save Mart Supermarkets 300 122–3

Sawyer, Paul 25

Scars Point Raceway 27

Schiffman, Steve 151–2

Schoonover, Terry 83, 237

Schrader, Ken 84, 91, 105, 178

Scott, Wendell 24, 201, 283

Sears Point Raceway 270

Shaw, Ben 4

Shepherd, Morgan 77, 86, 104, 108, 173

Single-season records, drivers 307–11

Single-season records, owners 314–7

Skinner, Mike 114, 128, 163–5, 177–8

Smith, Bruton 26, 101, 146

Smith, Jack 24, 201

Smith, Jimmy 161

Smith, Larry 56, 237

Southern 500 7–8, 10, 23, 25, 68, 84

Speakman, Tom 98

Speed, Lake 84, 90–1, 120, 171–2

Spencer, Jimmy 109–11, 176, 281

Sponsorship 67–73, 97–102, 245–52

Sportsman Division 155

Sprague, Jack 164

Stacy, J. D. 77, 79–80

Stacy, Nelson 33, 206

State Fairgrounds Raceway, Richmond 25

Stavola Brothers Racing 209–10

Stott, Ramo 60

STP Company 71–2, 246

Stricklin, Hut 114, 120, 134, 138, 171

Strictly Stock 6–7, 141, 155

Sullivan, Danny 69

T

Talladega Superspeedway 26, 39–40, 271

TBS 98

Teague, Marshall 6, 201

Team Sabco 216–7

Team Winston 213

Texaco Inc. 246–8

Texas International Raceway 272, 276

Texas Motor Speedway 28, 98–9

Thomas, Herb 11–3 15–6, 18, 201–2, 239

Thomas, Ronnie 62

Thompson, Kathy 96

Thompson, Speedy 16, 18–9, 29, 202, 239

Tide detergent 70–1

TranSouth Financial 252

TranSouth Financial 400 120–1

Trickle, Dick 103, 184, 281

Turner, Curtis 9, 31, 35, 202

Tuthill, Bill 6

U

Ulrich, D. K. 62

Union 400 110

V

Valvoline, Inc. 246–8, 252

Venable, Jim 161

Vessels, Scoop 161

Videos about NASCAR See Films about NASCAR

Viewer tips 223–7

W

Wade, Billy 33–4, 206, 238

Wallace, Kenny 108, 111, 183–4

Wallace, Mark 218–9

Wallace, Rusty 69, 75, 82, 86, 88–93, 99, 105, 107–12, 114, 119, 121–3, 135, 167, 281, 288, 307

Waltrip, Darrell 48, 51, 57, 59–65, 71, 75–81, 84–5, 87, 91–3, 105, 107, 123, 136, 145, 173, 175, 211–2, 249, 281, 307

Waltrip, Michael 105, 111, 175

Washington, Joe 96–7

Watkins Glen International 27, 273

Weatherly, Joe 25, 32–4, 202–3, 235–8, 258

Web sites for NASCAR 295–300

Welborn, Bob 24, 203

Welsh, Mike 69

Western Carolina 500 22

Westmoreland, Hubert 7, 9

Wheeler, H.A. "Humpy" 26, 60–1, 63, 145–6

White, Jack 9

White, Rex 29, 30–1, 203

Whiteman, Paul 5

Wilson, Woody 31

Winston All-Star Race 145

Winston Cup Series 7, 9, 10, 45, 85, 141, 144, 151, 165

Winston 500 84

Winston Million 145–6

Winton, Alexander 3

Wood Brothers Racing Museum 263

Wood Brothers Racing Team 212, 229, 239

Wood, Glen 203–4, 212, 239

World 600 75

Wrangler Jeans 72

Y

Yarborough, Cale 33, 35, 37–8, 47–8, 50, 54, 56, 58, 61–4, 75–81, 83–5, 91–2, 128, 144–5, 204–5, 221, 235, 249, 307

Yarbrough, LeeRoy 33, 205

Yates, Richard 214

Yates, Robert 213–4, 248, 251

Z

Zervakis, Emanuel 31

PHOTO CREDITS

Photographs used in *Inside Sports NASCAR Racing* were received from the following sources:

Craftsman Truck Series: 162

Inside Sports Magazine: 27, 44, 47, 48, 50, 55, 57, 60, 65, 76, 79, 86, 88, 90, 92, 146, 188, 191, 198, 200, 204, 230, 236, 239, 240

Al Pearce: 3, 5, 11, 14, 18, 30, 36, 38, 111, 113, 143, 147

RJ Reynolds Co.: 158, 167, 168, 169, 171, 172, 173, 175, 176, 177, 178, 179, 180 (Steve Grissom), 181-185

Stanley Publishing: 254-273

W. Dennis Winn: 46, 70, 71, 82, 96, 97, 100, 104, 106, 109, 115, 118, 120, 125, 130, 134, 138, 148, 152, 153, 154, 163, 166, 168, 170, 174, 180 (Ernie Irvan), 232, 233, 243, 247, 250, 277, 278, 279, 287, 290, 304, 323, 365, 373, 420, 438, 446, 483, 500, 518, 536.

All photos used in the 16-page color insert were taken by W. Dennis Winn.